DICTIONARY OF INDIAN BIOGRAPHY

DICTIONARY OF
INDIAN BIOGRAPHY

By

C. E. BUCKLAND, C.I.E.
(Indian Civil Service, retired).

*HENRY WHITTEMORE
LIBRARY*

*STATE COLLEGE
FRAMINGHAM, MASS.*

HASKELL HOUSE PUBLISHERS Lᴛᴅ.
Publishers of Scarce Scholarly Books
NEW YORK. N. Y. 10012
1968

First Published 1906

HASKELL HOUSE PUBLISHERS LTD.
Publishers of Scarce Scholarly Books
280 LAFAYETTE STREET
NEW YORK, N. Y. 10012

Library of Congress Catalog Card Number: 68-26350

Haskell House Catalogue Item # 277

Printed in the United States of America

PREFACE

THERE are Biographical Dictionaries which contain lives of Indian celebrities, and there are many biographies of individuals who have distinguished themselves in India. But the Dictionaries are large, expensive works, and the separate " Lives " or " Memoirs " are often lengthy or inaccessible. There is no single volume of moderate size, containing such information as is sufficient for the ordinary reader, regarding the careers and doings of the large number of persons connected with India, in history, by their exploits, services, and writings. The object of this " Dictionary of Indian Biography " is to supply this want. It purports to be a handy Work of Reference, giving the main facts of the lives of about 2,600 persons— English, Indian, Foreign, men or women, living or dead—who have been conspicuous in the history of India, or distinguished in the administration of the country, in one or other of its branches, or have contributed to its welfare, service, and advancement by their studies and literary productions, or have gained some special notoriety. Such a work must be limited by considerations of time, space, and cost. It has been thought desirable to commence the present volume from about 1750 A.D., a date which admits of the inclusion of Lord Clive and his contemporaries in Southern India, when the English power in India was being established. It has been found necessary to treat the lives in an indicative rather than in an exhaustive manner. It is impossible to include everybody who has been in India, and nothing has been harder than the attempt to fix a standard of merit to entitle its possessor to inclusion. No one consulted has been able to suggest a criterion of " distinction." The titles and decorations of the various Orders of Knighthood afford no certain ground. A complete and full Biographical Dictionary for India could only be undertaken, and might well be undertaken, by Government Agency, or under a financial guarantee of the cost of production. In all the difficulties of the problem, it is only possible to decide, for inclusion or exclusion, upon general principles, general reputation, or notoriety : and the many persons omitted for want of space are likely to challenge the conclusions of the Editor. Again, in such a work, unintentional omissions are sure to occur, in spite of all precautions, but they can be supplied in future editions. In many cases, even of prominent names, sufficient biographical information is not available, or, at any rate, has not come to hand. It is equally impossible to avoid, entirely, mistakes of dates or facts : the sources of information consulted often disclose discrepancies, which personal knowledge has sometimes been able to determine. Accuracy has been a main object in the compilation, but the short lives cannot be made more accurate than the sources of information permit. In the *Addenda* will be found a few notices which were accidentally omitted from the body of the work, or were obtained too late to be included in their proper places.

A copious Bibliography has been appended. It contains the names of a number of works which may advantageously be consulted by those who are desirous of acquiring a greater knowledge of the individuals treated in the Dictionary of Indian Biography, or of the history of India, than can be conveyed in the brief notices in the Dictionary itself. It will also be useful to the general reader of Indian literature. A separate list of the chief Works of Reference consulted is subjoined to this Preface.

The Indian names of places have been spelt, for the most part, according to the Jonesian (or Hunterian) system of transliteration adopted by the Government of India. But that system allows, by way of compromise, a number of names, which have in times past been spelt phonetically, to retain their popular, though irregular, forms. Opinions differ as to the extent to which such disregard of strict transliteration may be permitted. In this work, some of the familiar words have been retained, and, in all cases, the attempt has been made to adapt the spelling to the plain and simple sound of a word : no dots or accents have been used. The Indian names of persons have been arranged on a system by which they can be most easily found. In many cases, the territory with which the person is connected supplies the keyword. In the case of Hindus, not designated territorially, the family name should be first sought. In some cases (e.g. among the Parsis), where the family name has been dropped, the name which is used as a surname is put first. In the case of some Hindus, and of Muhammadans, who have no name common to all the members of a family, the arrangement is according to the first names in their alphabetical order. Some common names have been spelt in the different ways which their owners have adopted for themselves.

The greater portion of the compilation, as well as the editing, has fallen on the Editor. At the same time, his acknowledgments are due to all who have afforded him assistance and information. He has specially to thank Mr. H. Wigram, of the Madras Civil Service (retired), now of Messrs. Swan, Sonnenschein & Co., for his co-operation and ready counsel ; the Editor of the *Athenæum* for kindly permitting the publication of lists of names in his Journal : the officers in charge of the India Office Library, for their unfailing courtesy and stores of knowledge put at his disposal : and certain officers in India for their welcome help : their names are not mentioned, lest it should be supposed that any portion of the Dictionary has any official authority.

Corrections and suggestions will be thankfully received.

THE EDITOR.

61, Cornwall Gardens, London, S.W.,
    November 1st, 1905.

WORKS OF REFERENCE CONSULTED

Account of the Mutinies in Oudh, An, M. R. Gubbins : 1858.
Addiscombe : its Heroes and Men of Note, Col. H. M. Vibart : 1894.
Allgemeine Deutsche Biographie : 1875.
American, European and Oriental Literary Record, Trübner's : 1865-89.
Annual Register, The.
Asiatic Annual Register for the years 1800-1811, The : 1801-12.
Asiatic Quarterly Review, The : 1886-1905.
Asiatic Society, Journals of the Royal.
Assam, A Statistical Account of, W. W. Hunter : 1879.

Bengal Army, History of the Rise and Progress of the, Capt. A. Broome : 1850.
Bengal Artillery, List of Officers who have served in the Regiment of the, by Maj.-
        General F. W. Stubbs : 1892.
———————— Memoir of the Services of the, Capt. E. Buckle : edited by J. W. Kaye :
    1852.
Bengal, A Statistical Account of, W. W. Hunter : 1875-7.
Bengal Civil Servants, 1780-1838, Dodwell and Miles : 1839.
Bengal Establishment, A General Register of the Honourable E. I. Company's
    Civil Servants of the, from 1790 to 1842, by Ram Chandra Das and H. T.
        Prinsep : 1844.
Bengal Obituary, The, Holmes & Co. : 1848.
Bengal under the Lieutenant-Governors, 1854-98, C. E. Buckland : 1901.
Biographical Treasury, A, Maunder.
Biographie Universelle, Ancienne et Moderne : 1811-53.
Bombay and Western India, J. Douglas : 1893.
Bombay Civil Servants, 1793-1839, Dodwell and Miles : 1839.
Book of Dignities, The, H. Ockerby : 1890.
British India and its Rulers, H. S. Cunningham : 1881.
British Indian Military Depositary, The, S. Parlby : 1822-7.

Calcutta Review, The : 1844-1905.
Celebrities of the Century, L. C. Saunders : 1887.
Centenary Review of the Asiatic Society of Bengal, 1784-1883 : 1885.
Chambers's Biographical Dictionary, G. D. Patrick and F. H. Groome : 1897.
Collection of Treaties, Engagements, and Sunnuds relating to India, etc., A, C. U.
        Aitchison, continued by others : 1892.
Comprehensive History of India, A, H. Beveridge : 1858-62.
Conversations Lexikon, Brockhaus : 1882.
———————— Meyer : 1893.
Cyclopædia of India, E. Balfour : 1885.

Decisive Battles of India, The, G. B. Malleson : 1883.
Dictionary of Biography, Lippincott : 1881.
Dictionary of General Biography, A, W. L. R. Cates : 1881.
Dictionary of National Biography : 1885-1903.
Dictionary of Universal Biography, Beeton : 1869-70.
Dictionnaire Universel des Contemporains, G. Vapereau : 1893.
Dizionario Biografico degli Scrittori Contemporanei, A. de Gubernatis : 1879.

Early Annals of the English in Bengal, The, C. R. Wilson: 1895, 1900.
Early Records of British India, J. T. Wheeler: 1878.
East India Military Calendar, The, J. Philippart: 1823-4.
East Indian Gazetteer, The, W. Hamilton: 1815.
Echoes from Old Calcutta, H. E. Busteed: 1897.
Eminent Persons, Biographies reprinted from the " Times," 1870-94: 1892-7.
Encyclopædia Britannica, The.
Encyclopædia of Missions, The, Dwight, Tupper, and Bliss: 1904.

Forty-one Years in India, Earl Roberts: 1898.

Gazetteer of the Territories under the Government of the E. I. Co., A, E. Thornton : 1857.
General Biographical Dictionary, The, A. Chalmers: 1812-7.
Gentleman's Magazine, The.
Glimpses of Old Bombay and Western India, J. Douglas. 1900.
Golden Book of India, The, R. Lethbridge: 1893.
Government of India, The, Sir C. P. Ilbert: 1898.

Heroines of Ind, M. Dutt: 1897.
Historical Sketches of the South of India, M. Wilks: 1810-7.
History of India, H. G. Keene: 1893.
——————— Roper Lethbridge: 1881-93.
——————— J. C. Marshman: 1867-93.
——————— James Mill, 1817 : ed. by H. H. Wilson: 1858.
History of India from the Earliest Ages, The, J. T. Wheeler: 1867-81.
History of India : Hindoo and Mohammedan Periods, M. Elphinstone : 1841, 1889.
History of the British Empire in India, E. Thornton: 1841-5: L. J. Trotter : 1866-99.
History of the Indian Mutiny, A, G. W. Forrest: 1904.
——————————————— T. R. E. Holmes: 1891.
——————————————— G. B. Malleson: 1878-80.
History of the Indian Navy, 1613-1863, C. R. Low: 1877.
History of the Madras Army, W. J. Wilson: 1882-8.
History of the Military Transactions of the British Nation in Indostan from the year 1745, A, R. Orme: 1775-8.
History of the Sepoy War, J. W. Kaye: 1864-76.
History of the War in Afghanistan, J. W. Kaye: 1857.
Homeward Mail, The, 1857-1905.

Imperial Dictionary of Universal Biography, The.
Imperial Gazetteer of India, The, W. W. Hunter, 14 vols.: 1885-7.
India and its Native Princes, L. Rousselet: 1878.
India : its Administration and Progress, J. Strachey: 1903.
India Lists, The.
Indian Civil Service List, The, 1880, A. C. Tupp: 1880.
Indian Directory : Thacker & Co.
Indian Empire : its People, History and Products, The, W. W. Hunter: 1893.
Indian Polity, G. T. Chesney: 1868: 1894.
India Office Lists, The.
India on the Eve of the British Conquest : a Historical Sketch, S. Owen: 1872.
India's Princes, M. Griffiths: 1894.

Kabul Insurrection of 1841-2, The, V. Eyre: 1879.

Last Century of Universal History, 1767-1867, The, A. C. Ewald: 1868.
List of Inscriptions on Tombs and Monuments in Bengal, C. R. Wilson: 1896.
Lives of Indian Officers, J. W. Kaye: 1867.

Madras Civil Servants, 1780-1839, Dodwell and Miles: 1839.
Medical Officers of the E. I. Co.'s Service, 1764-1837, Dodwell and Miles: 1839.
Memorials of Old Haileybury College, F. C. Danvers and others: 1894.
Men and Events of my Time in India, R. Temple: 1882.
Men and Women of the Time, V. G. Plarr: 1897.
Men of the Reign, T. H. Ward: 1885.
Men of the Time, T. Cooper: 1875.
Men whom India has Known, J. J. Higginbotham: 1874.
Military History of the Madras Engineers and Pioneers, The, H. M. Vibart: 1881-3.
Modern History of the Indian Chiefs, Rajas, Zemindars, The, L. Ghose: 1879-81.
Mogul Empire, The, H. G. Keene: 1866.
Monumental Register, The, De Rozario: 1815.

Narrative of the War in Afghanistan in 1838-9, H. Havelock: 1840.
New Biographical Dictionary, A, T. Cooper: 1883.
New General Biographical Dictionary, A, H. J. Rose: 1857.
Nouveau Dictionnaire, Larousse.
Nouvelle Biographie Generale: 1860.

Obituary Notices in the " Times."
Officers of the Indian Army, 1760-1837, Dodwell and Miles: 1838.
Official Lists.
Oriental Biographical Dictionary, An, T. W. Beale: 1881 ; edited by H. G. Keene:
    1894.
Oriental Christian Biography, W. H. Carey: 1852.
Our Indian Empire, C. Macfarlane: 1844.

Panjab and Delhi in 1857, The, J. Cave-Browne: 1861.
Particular Account of the European Military Adventurers of Hindustan, A, 1734-
    1803, H. Compton.
Peerage, Baronetcy and Knightage, Burke: 1904.
Pillars of the Empire, T. H. S. Escott: 1879.

Rajas and Nawabs of the N.W.P. : 1877.
Rajas of the Panjab, The, L. H. Griffin: 1873.
Report on the Old Records of the India Office, G. M. C. Birdwood: 1891.
Representative Indians, G. Paramaswaran Pillai: 1902.
Representative Men of India, S. Jehangir: 1889.
Royal Military Calendar, The, J. Philippart: 1815-6.
Rulers of India Series, The, W. W. Hunter.

Selections from Calcutta Gazettes, W. S. Seton-Karr and H. Sandeman: 1864-9.
Sepoy Generals, G. W. Forrest: 1901.
Sepoy Revolt, The, J. J. McLeod Innes: 1897.
Short Account of the Lives of the Bishops of Calcutta, A, W. C. Bromehead: 1876.
Short History of India, A, J. T. Wheeler · 1889.
Sketches of some Distinguished Anglo-Indians, W. F. B. Laurie: 1887-8.
———————————————— **Indian Women,** Mrs. E. F. Chapman: 1891.
Story of the Nations, The : the volumes of the Series relating to India.

The First Afghan War and its Causes, H. M. Durand: 1879.
Twelve Indian Statesmen, G. Smith: 1898.
Twelve Pioneer Missionaries, G. Smith: 1900.

Who's Who : 1904, 1905.

ABBREVIATIONS

A.D.C.=Aide de Camp.
A.G.=Adjutant-General.
A.A.G.=Assistant Adjutant-General.
D.A.G.=Deputy Adjutant-General.
D.A.A.G.=Deputy Assistant Adjutant-General.
A.G.G.=Agent to the Governor-General.
A.M.D.=Army Medical Department.
B.A.=Bachelor of Arts.
B.C.S.=Bengal Civil Service.
B.L.=Bachelor of Law, or of Letters.
Bo.C.S.=Bombay Civil Service.
C.B.=Companion of the Bath.
C.I.E.=Companion of the Indian Empire.
C. in C.=Commander in Chief.
C.I.=Crown of India.
C.J.=Chief Justice.
C.M.G.=Companion of St. Michael and St. George.
C.M.S.=Church Missionary Society.
C.O.=Commanding Officer.
C.S.I.=Companion of the Star of India.
C.V.O.=Commander of the Royal Victorian Order.
D.C.L.=Doctor of Civil Law.
D.D.=Doctor of Divinity.
D.I.G.=Deputy Inspector-General.
D.L.=Deputy Lieutenant.
 „   Doctor of Laws.
D.N.B.=Dictionary of National Biography.
D.S.O.=Distinguished Service Order.
E.I.Co.=East India Company.
F.G.S.=Fellow of the Geological Society.
F.I.C.=Fellow of Institute of Chemistry.
F.I.I.=Fellow of Institute of Journalists.
F.L.S.=Fellow of the Linnæan Society.
F.M.=Field Marshal

F.R.A.S.=Fellow of the Royal Asiatic Society.
F.R.C.I.=Fellow of the Royal Colonial Institute.
F.R.C.P.=Fellow of the Royal College of Physicians.
F.R.C.S.=Fellow of the Royal College of Surgeons.
F.R.C.V.S.=Fellow of the Royal College of Veterinary Surgeons.
F.R.G.S.=Fellow of the Royal Geographical Society.
F.R.S.=Fellow of the Royal Society.
F.R.S.E.=Fellow of the Royal Society of Edinburgh.
F.S.A.=Fellow of the Society of Antiquaries.
F.S.A.S.=Fellow of the Society of Antiquaries of Scotland
F.S.S.=Fellow of the Statistical Society.
F.S.S.A.=Fellow of the Society of Science and Art.
F.Z.S.=Fellow of the Zoological Society.
G.C.B.=Knight Grand Cross of the Bath.
G.C.H.=Knight Grand Cross of the Order of the Guelphs.
G.C.I.E.=Knight Grand Commander of the Indian Empire.
G.C.M.G.=Knight Grand Cross of St. Michael and St. George.
G.C.S.I.=Knight Grand Commander of the Star of India.
G.C.V.O.=Knight Grand Cross of the Royal Victorian Order.
G.M.I.E.=Grand Master of the Indian Empire.
G.M.S.I.=Grand Master of the Star of India.
H.B.M.=His (or Her) Britannic Majesty.
H.E.I.C.S.=Honourable East India Company's Service.

H.H.=His Highness, or His Honour.

H.M.=His (or Her) Majesty.

H.R.H.=His (or Her) Royal Highness.

I.C.S.=Indian Civil Service.

I.M.S.=Indian Medical Service.

J.A.S.B.=Journal of the Asiatic Society of Bengal.

J.P.=Justice of the Peace.

J.R.A.S.=Journal of the Royal Asiatic Society.

K.B.=Knight Bachelor or Knight Companion of the Bath.

K.C.=King's Counsel.

K.C.B.=Knight Commander of the Bath.

K.C.H.=Knight Commander of the Order of the Guelphs.

K.C.I.E.=Knight Commander of the Indian Empire.

K.C.M.G.=Knight Commander of St. Michael and St. George.

K.C.S.I.=Knight Commander of the Star of India.

K.C.V.O.=Knight Commander of the Royal Victorian Order.

K.G.=Knight of the Garter.

K.P.=Knight of St. Patrick.

K.T.=Knight of the Thistle.

LL.B.=Bachelor of Laws.

LL.D.=Doctor of Laws.

L.M.=Licentiate in Midwifery.

L.R.C.P.=Licentiate of the College of Physicians.

L.S.A.=Licentiate of the College of Apothecaries.

M.A.=Master of Arts.

M.A.O.=Muhammadan Anglo-Oriental.

M.D.=Doctor of Medicine.

M.I.=Madras Infantry.

M.P.=Member of Parliament.

M.R.A.S.B.=Member of the Royal Asiatic Society of Bengal.

N.B.=North Britain.

N.I.=Native Infantry.

N.W.P.=North-West Provinces.

O.U.B.C.=Oxford University Boat Club.

P.C.=Privy Councillor.

Ph.D.=Doctor of Philosophy.

P.M.O.=Principal Medical Officer.

P.W.D.=Public Works Department.

Q.C.=Queen's Counsel.

Q.M.G.=Quarter-Master-General.

A.Q.M.G.=Assistant Quarter-Master-General.

D.A.Q.M.G.=Deputy-Assistant Quarter-Master-General.

D.Q.M.G.=Deputy Quarter-Master-General.

q.v.=quod vide=which see.

R.A.=Royal Academy.

,, =Royal Artillery.

R.A.S.J.=Royal Asiatic Society's Journal

R.E.=Royal Engineer.

R.M.A.=Royal Military Academy.

R.M.C.=Royal Military College.

R.N.=Royal Navy.

R.N.R.=Royal Naval Reserve.

S.P.C.K.=Society for Promoting Christian Knowledge.

S.P.G.=Society for the Propagation of the Gospel.

T.C.D.=Trinity College, Dublin.

U.P.=United Provinces.

V.C.=Victoria Cross.

V.D.=Volunteer Decoration.

Y.M.C.A.=Young Men's Christian Association.

Z.D.M.G.=Zeitschrift der Deutschen Morgenlandischen Gesellschaft.

DICTIONARY

OF

INDIAN BIOGRAPHY

ABADIE, HENRY RICHARD (1841-)

Entered the Army, 1858 : served in the Abyssinian campaign, 1868, and the Afghan War, 1879–80, including the capture of Kandahar : commanded the Eastern District, 1899–1900 : Maj-General : C.B. : Lieutenant-Governor of Jersey, 1900-4.

ABBOTT, AUGUSTUS (1804–1867)

Born Jan. 7, 1804 : son of H. A. Abbott : brother of Sir Frederick, and Sir James A.: educated at Warfield, Winchester, Addiscombe : entered the Bengal Artillery, 1819 : served at Bhartpur in 1825–6 : in 1838–9 was in the Army of the Indus, in the march to Kandahar, and the pursuit to Girishk, at the siege of Ghazni, and the occupation of Kabul : was in the Kohistan fighting with Sale, and under him, on his return to Jalalabad ; commanded the Artillery during the siege of Jalalabad and the defeat of Akbar Khan on April 7, 1842 : commanded the Artillery in Pollock's relieving Army, at Tezin on Sep. 12, 1842, and the re-occupation of Kabul : C. B. : Hony. A. D. C. to Governor - Generals : Inspr - General of Ordnance, 1855 : retired, 1859 : Maj-General, 1860 : died Feb. 25, 1867.

ABBOTT, SIR FREDERICK (1805–1892)

Brother of Sir James Abbott, and son of Henry Alexius Abbott, a Calcutta merchant : born June 13, 1805 : educated at Warfield and Addiscombe : entered Bengal Engineers, 1823 : Maj-General, 1858 : arrived in India, 1823 : in the Burmese war of 1824–26 : employed in the P. W. D. and garrison-engineer at Calcutta in 1841 : Chief Engineer in Pollock's relieving force in 1842, and at the e-occupation of Kabul : in the first

Sikh war and at Sobraon in 1846 : directed the bridge and pontoon operations : C. B. : retired in 1847 : Lieutenant-Governor of the Addiscombe Military College, 1851–61 : knighted, 1854 : Member of Council of Military Education, and Commissioner of National Defence : died Nov. 4, 1892.

ABBOTT, H. EDWARD STACEY (1855–)

Son of General Abbott, Bengal Infantry : educated at St. Elizabeth College, Guernsey, and R.M.A. Woolwich : entered the Army, 1874 : served in India, in the Afghan War, 1878–80 : P.W.D. Panjab ; Hazara expedition 1888 : Under Secretary P.W.D. Panjab : Chitral Relief force, 1895 : Superintending Engineer, P. W. D.: Lt.-Colonel R.E. : D.S.O.

ABBOTT, SIR JAMES (1807–1896)

Brother of Sir F. Abbott : born March 12, 1807 : educated at Blackheath and Addiscombe : entered the Royal Artillery in 1823 : arrived in India, 1823 : served at Bhartpur, 1825–6 : in the Revenue Survey : with the Army of the Indus in 1838–9, to Kandahar : in 1839, with D' Arcy Todd to Herat, and sent by him to Khiva to negotiate with the Khan for the release of Russian captives held by him : on the Khan's behalf crossed the Caspian, and went to St. Petersburg and on to England, 1840 : after some political employ, he was Commissioner of Hazara from 1845 to 1853, and held the country against the Sikhs in the second Sikh War, 1848–9 : his name is preserved in the town of Abbottabad ; commanded a column in the Black Mountain expedition, 1852 : C. B., 1873 : K. C. B., 1894 : General, 1877 : retired from the Army, 1879 : died Oct. 6, 1896. He was also

B

"a poet, antiquarian, and man of letters;" wrote a *Narrative of a Journey from Herat to Khiva, Moscow and St. Petersburg, etc.*, and about Alexander the Great in the Panjab, etc.

ABBOTT, SAUNDERS ALEXIUS (1811–1894)

Maj-General: born July 9, 1811: son of Henry Alexius Abbott, merchant, Calcutta; educated privately and at Addiscombe; joined the Bengal Infantry in 1828: appointed, in 1836, Assistant in the Revenue Survey under Sir H Lawrence (*q.v.*): held Survey charges, 1838–42: present at Mudki, Dec. 18, 1845, bringing the reserves from Kasauli and Sabathu by forced marches: also as A.D.C. to Lord Hardinge at Firozshahr; dangerously wounded: Deputy Commissioner of Umbala, 1847: of Hoshiarpur, 1849: in charge there during the mutiny; Commissioner of Lucknow, 1858–63; Brevet-Major, 1846; Hon. A.D.C. to Governor-Generals, until he retired Sep. 1864: after retirement was Agent of the Sind, Panjab, and Delhi railway at Lahore for years, and afterwards on the Home Board of Direction: died at Brighton, Feb. 7, 1894.

ABDUL HAK, SIRDAR DILER JUNG UL MULK (1853–96)

Son of a small hereditary chieftain in the Dekkan: joined the Bombay Government service before he was 20: in the police, captured a dangerous *dakait*: made C. I. E.: joined the Hyderabad service: Sir Salar Jung sent him to England to obtain an alteration in the guarantee which the Nizam had given on his State railway: for effecting this, he was handsomely rewarded: was given a mining monopoly in the Nizam's state, from which he made a personal profit of nearly a quarter of a million: but, after the publication of the facts in 1888, he suffered political downfall at Hyderabad: and strove in vain to regain his position in the Nizam's service: died May, 1896.

ABDUL LATIF, NAWAB BAHADUR (1828-1893)

Son of a leading pleader in the *Sadr Diwani* Court at Calcutta: born, March, 1828: educated at the Calcutta Madrasa: entered Government service in 1846:

appointed a Deputy Magistrate in 1849: acted sometimes as Presidency Magistrate: Member of the Bengal Legislative Council for several years, and of the Calcutta Corporation: J. P.: on the Central Board of Examiners; Fellow of the Calcutta University: on the Income Tax Commission for Calcutta, 1861–5: founder and secretary, from 1863, of the Muhammadan Literary and Scientific Society, and several other public bodies: Nawab, 1880: C. I. E. 1883: Nawab Bahadur, 1887: often consulted by Government, as the most progressive and enlightened among the Muhammadans of Bengal, whose interests and aspirations he never ceased to urge: died 1893.

ABDUL MUSSEAH, REV. (? –1827)

Born at Delhi; his original name was Sheikh Salih: son of a learned man, a teacher: became a Munshi at Lucknow to Englishmen: served at the Oudh Court, and was a trooper under the Mahrattas: he turned to Christianity on hearing preaching at Cawnpur, and was baptized at Calcutta by Rev. D. Brown (*q.v.*) in 1811, receiving his name Abdul Musseah; became in 1812 a catechist of the C.M.S., a teacher and preacher and writer of commentaries on Scripture, making converts: about 1820 he received Lutheran ordination, and undertook Missionary work, remaining at Agra till 1825: ordained by Bishop Heber as minister of the Established Church at Calcutta, 1825: died March 4, 1827.

ABEL, CLARKE (1780–1826)

Physician to Lord Macartney on the mission to China, and, as naturalist, made extensive collections, which were lost: also physician to Lord Amherst, when Governor-General: died in India, Nov. 24, 1826.

ABERCROMBY, SIR JOHN (1772–1817)

Son of Sir Ralph Abercromby: born 1772: entered the Army, 1786: served in Flanders, W. Indies, and as Military Secretary to his father in Egypt: seized in 1803 and imprisoned by Napoleon, to 1808: C. in C., Bombay, 1809: in command of the expedition for the capture Mauritius, 1810: C. in C., and temporary Governor at Madras, May 21, 1813, until Sep. 16, 1814: Lt-General, 1812:

K.C.B., 1814 : M.P. for Clackmannan, 1815 : G.C.B., 1816 : died Feb. 14, 1817.

ABERCROMBY, SIR ROBERT (1740–1827)

Younger brother of Sir Ralph : entered the Army in 1758 : served in North America till the peace in 1763 : and again, from 1776 to 1783, throughout the war to the capitulation of Yorktown : went to India 1788, and, in 1790, was Governor of Bombay and C. in C. there : Maj-General, 1790. After operations on the Malabar coast, he joined Lord Cornwallis in attacking and defeating Tippoo at Seringapatam in 1792 : K. B. : succeeded Lord Cornwallis as C. in C. in India, Oct. 1793, being at the same time Member of the Supreme Council till Feb. 1797 : he defeated the Rohillas at Batina in Rohilkund in 1794 : Lt-General in 1797 : M.P. for Clackmannan County in 1798 : Governor of Edinburgh Castle, 1801 : General, 1802 : died Nov. 1827.

ABERIGH - MACKAY, GEORGE ROBERT (1848–1881)

Born July 25, 1848 : son of Rev. Dr. James Aberigh-Mackay, Chaplain in Bengal : educated privately in Scotland, at Magdalen College School, Oxford, and St. Catherine's College, Cambridge : entered the Education Department at Bareli in the N. W. P., 1870 : Professor of English Literature at the Delhi College, 1873 : Tutor to the Raja of Ratlam, Central India, and Principal of the College there, 1876 : Principal of the Rajkumar College at Indore, 1877 : Fellow, Calcutta University, 1880 : wrote a number of educational works : also Notes on Western Turkistan, a Hand-book of Hindustan, a Manual of Indian Sport, Native Chiefs and their States, The sovereign Princes and Chiefs of Central India : at one time wrote largely for the Pioneer, and constantly for other English and Indian papers, including letters in the Bombay Gazette under the nom de plume " The Political Orphan " : but his best work was his Twenty-one Days in India, being the Tour of Sir Ali Baba, a series of sketches of Indian life and society which appeared in Vanity Fair in 1878-9, and were afterwards published together. For brilliant wit, his work has not been approached in modern days in India. His bright and

sympathetic humour, his " suspicion of cynicism which is the soul of modern pathos," his freedom from malice, his command of style and language, the keen edge and truth of his criticisms, his grasp and range, took the public by storm : a distinguished literary career lay before him, when he died, Jan. 12, 1881, from tetanus, caused by a chill caught at lawn-tennis : he was also an ardent sportsman, and lover of birds and animals.

ABRAHAMS, LIONEL (1869–)

Educated at City of London School : scholar of Balliol College, Oxford : Arnold Prize : entered the India Office 1893 : Assistant Financial Secretary, 1901 : Financial Secretary, 1902 : contributed to the Dictionary of Political Economy.

ADAM, SIR FREDERICK (? –1853)

Governor : son of Right Hon. William Adam : entered the Army, 1795 : in the Guards, 1799 : in Egypt, 1800-1 : in Sicily and Spain : A.D.C. to the Prince Regent : Maj-General : commanded a Brigade at Waterloo : K. C. B. : Lord High Commissioner of the Ionian Islands, 1824–6 : G.C.M.G. : P.C., 1831 : Governor of Madras, 1832–7 : G.C.B., 1840 : Colonel of the 57th and 21st regts. : General, 1846 : died Aug. 17, 1853.

ADAM, JOHN (1779–1825)

Son of Right Hon. W. Adam : born May 4, 1779, educated at Charterhouse and Edinburgh University : writer in the E. I. Co.'s service, reached Calcutta, Feb. 1796 : three years at Patna : head assistant in the judicial-revenue Secretariat : in May, 1802, was Head of the " Governor-General's office " : in 1804, Deputy Secretary in the Secret and Political Departments : in 1809, Secretary in the Military Department : in 1812, Secretary in the Secret, Foreign and Political Departments : Private Secretary in 1817 and Political Secretary to the Marquis of Hastings, whom he accompanied during the Mahratta-Pindari war, greatly influencing his policy of establishing the British supremacy : was " the very able and very conservative " Member of the Supreme Council, 1819-25 : opposed the liberty of the Press as unsuited to India, and the financial transactions of Palmer & Co with the Nizam :

acted as Governor General from Lord
Hastings' departure in Jan. until Lord
Amherst's arrival in Aug., 1823 :
adopted a strong and active policy : a
Regulation was passed, in April, 1823,
to curb the public Press : under it, John
Silk Buckingham, who had established
the *Calcutta Journal* and criticised Government, satirically commenting upon an
appointment made by Government, was
deprived of his licence and deported to
England. The Court of Directors approved Adam's policy, and the Privy
Council concurred. Adam was the first
to grant public money, a lakh of rupees a
year, in support of native education :
devoted town duties to public works :
increased civil judicial establishments :
added four regiments to the Bengal
Army : was given a renewed term as
Member of Council : he died at sea, off
Madagascar, June 4, 1825. His picture,
by Chinnery, is in the Town Hall, Calcutta, and a tablet to his memory is in
St. John's Church there, testifying to his
merits.

ADAM, WILLIAM PATRICK (1823–1881)

Governor : son of Admiral Sir Charles
Adam, K.C.B. : born 1823 : educated at
Rugby and Trinity College, Cambridge :
B.A. : called to the bar by the Inner
Temple, 1849 : Private Secretary to Lord
Elphinstone, Governor of Bombay, 1853–
58 : M.P. for Clackmannan and Kinross,
1859–80 : Lord of the Treasury, 1865–6,
and 1868–73 : First Commissioner of
Works in 1873, and Privy Councillor :
' Whip ' of the Liberal party, 1874–80,
and Governor of Madras, Dec. 20, 1880 :
died at Ootacamund May 24, 1881 : his
eldest son was created a Baronet in recognition of his father's public services :
his widow was given the rank of a
Baronet's widow and made a member of
the Order of the Crown of India.

ADAMS, ANDREW LEITH (? –1882)

Naturalist, Army-Surgeon and Surgeon-Major from 1848 to 1873 : Professor
of Zoology at Dublin, and of Natural
History at Cork : wrote *Wanderings of
a Naturalist in India*, and *The Western
Himalayas and Cashmere :* F. G. S. :
F. R. S. : and LL.D. of Aberdeen : died
in Aug. 1882.

ADAMS, REV. JAMES WILLIAMS (1840–1903)

Educated at Trinity College, Dublin :
ordained, 1863 : on the Bengal Ecclesiastical Establishment, 1868–1887 : chosen,
1879, to be Chaplain to the Kabul Field
Force : was at Charasia and other engagements, and in Lord Roberts' march from
Kabul to Kandahar : won the Victoria
Cross—the only clergyman who ever
gained it—in the Chardeh valley, near
Kabul, in Dec. 1879 : first saved a
wounded man of the 9th Lancers, by
dismounting and supporting him until
relieved ; he then, up to his waist in water,
and under a heavy fire from the Afghans
within a few yards, by sheer strength
dragged out two more men of the same
regiment from under their horses in a
ditch. He also saw service as Chaplain
in Burma. On his retirement, in 1887,
he was appointed Rector of Postwick,
Norfolk ; died at Ashwell Rectory near
Ockham, on Oct. 20, 1903. " Padre "
Adams, as he was called, had immense
influence with the British soldier, who
adored him. He was Chaplain in Ordinary
to H.M., 1901.

ADAMS, SIR JOHN WORTHINGTON (1764–1837)

Entered the Army 1780 : fought
under Sir R. Abercromby (*q. v.*) against
the Rohillas : was at the capture of
Seringapatam, 1799 : commanded his
regt. in 1809, on active service in Central
India : C. B., 1815 : held commands in
Kumaon, Nagpur, the Dekkan : took
Chanda in 1818, was at Bhartpur in 1826 :
commanded the Sirhind Division, May,
1828 : Maj-General 1830 : Colonel of the
16th Bengal, N.I. : K. C. B. : died March 9,
1837, at Sabathu.

ADAMS, THOMAS (? –1764)

Major : an officer of the school of
Clive : in 1763 succeeded to a command
in Bengal : defeated Mir Kasim, Nawab
of Bengal, performing splendid exploits
during the campaign : he started, just
after a British reverse, with a few English
veterans and a handful of sepoys : defeated one of the Nawab's Generals at
Katwa : marched on Murshidabad and
occupied it : won a brilliant victory at
Gheria : dislodged the enemy from their
position of great strength at the pass of

Udwanala : took Monghyr : marched on Patna, and took it by assault, though he was so broken down by illness that he could scarcely retain his command. Mir Kasim had fled from Patna on the approach of the English : Adams pursued him as far as the boundary of Oudh : he then handed over the command to Knox and died, worn out, Jan. 16, 1764.

ADYE, SIR JOHN MILLER (1891–1900)

Born Nov. 1, 1819, son of Major J.P. Adye, R.A. : entered the Royal Artillery in Dec. 1836 : in the Crimea as Brig-Major to the Artillery ; Brevet-Lt-Colonel, 1854, and C. B. : through the mutiny as A.A.G. for Royal Artillery : with General Windham at Cawnpur and at the defeat of the Gwalior contingent, Dec. 6, 1857 : commanded the R.A. in Madras in 1859 : D.A.G. of Artillery in India, 1863 ; in the Sitana' (Umbeyla) campaign : Director of Artillery at the War Office, 1870 : to the Crimea in 1872, to report on the British cemeteries and monuments : Governor of R.M.A. Woolwich, 1875 : wrote largely on the question of the Russians in Central Asia and on Afghanistan, opposing a forward policy : Surveyor-General of Ordnance, 1880 : Chief of the Staff to Lord Wolseley in the Egyptian campaign, 1882 : Governor of Gibraltar, 1883–1886 : K.C.B. in 1873 : Commander of the Legion of Honour, 1874 : G.C.B. in 1882, and the Order of the Medjidie : General, Nov. 20, 1884 : died Aug. 26, 1900. He wrote on India, viz., *The Defence of Cawnpur, Sitana, a Mountain Campaign, Indian Frontier History*, and an autobiography.

AFGHANISTAN, ABDUR RAHMAN, AMIR OF (1844–1901)

Son of Afzal Khan, and grandson of the Amir Dost Muhammad : confirmed by Shir Ali, in 1863, in a government in Turkistan : took part in the civil war between his father and his uncle Shir Ali (*q.v.*) : escaped to Bokhara when his father was imprisoned in 1864 : collected a force and defeated Shir Ali at Shekhabad in May, 1866, and recovered Kabul for his father : on the latter's death, in 1867, became C. in C. to his uncle Muhammad Azim : retired to Balkh : he was defeated at Tinak Khan, by Yakub on behalf of Shir Ali, on Jan. 3, 1869, and made for Bokhara, receiving an allowance from Russia : remained for 10 years at Samarkand. In 1880 he watched events from Balkh, and, when Yakub Khan abdicated and was sent to India, negotiations were opened with Abdur Rahman, who proceeded to Charikar, was recognised as Amir of Kabul by the British Government in July, 1880, and finally nominated Amir on Aug. 10 : he subsequently occupied Kandahar when evacuated by the British forces, lost it to his uncle Ayub Khan (*q.v.*) in 1881, but personally recovered it from Ayub in Sep. 1881 : established his power throughout Afghanistan, and had frontier disputes with Russia : visited the Viceroy, Lord Dufferin, at Rawul Pindi, March, 1885, to discuss Afghan affairs, and was then made G.C.S.I. At the time of the Penjdeh incident with Russia, in April, 1885, he showed great forbearance. He had to repress risings in various parts of the kingdom : defeated his cousin Ishak, Governor of Turkistan. In 1893 he received Sir M. Durand's mission to settle a number of frontier questions, which at times had nearly led to hostilities with the British. He ruled with a rod of iron. G C.B., 1895 : disappointed at not being allowed to have a diplomatic agent resident in London, for which he asked through his son Nasrulla, in 1895. During his reign he employed English firms and experts to work for him at Kabul, and greatly strengthened his kingdom and military power, but maintained the traditional Afghan policy of keeping foreigners in general out of his country : in an autobiography he showed his confidence in the British alliance : he died Oct. 3, 1901.

AFGHANISTAN, DOST MUHAMMAD KHAN, AMIR OF (1791–1863)

Twentieth son of Payinda Khan (executed 1799), who was chief of the Barakzais, and brother of Fateh Khan, the Barakzai " Mayor of the Palace " of Mahmud Shah, of the Abdalis, or Duranis. As the result of the fighting among the members of the Durani and Barakzai families from the time of Payinda Khan, Dost Muhammad established himself in 1822–3 in Kabul, Kashmir having been lost to the Sikhs in 1819, Herat and Peshawar not being in his power. He defeated Shah Shuja, the Sadazai or, Durani, late Amir, at Kandahar in 1833 :

but lost Peshawar to the Sikhs in 1834 : styled himself Amir in 1833. In 1837 Burnes was sent on an embassy to Kabul, to oppose Persian designs on Herat : Dost Muhammad was found to be intriguing with Russia, and a Russian Envoy appeared at Kabul : Lord Auckland's Government decided to depose Dost Muhammad and reinstate Shah Shuja as Amir : on the approach of the British force in 1839 Dost Muhammad fled to Bokhara, but escaped, advanced on Kabul, made a stand at Bajgah, but was defeated and fled again : after a success against the English at Parwandarra, he surrendered, Nov. 3, 1840, to the English envoy and was sent down to Calcutta : at the end of the first Afghan war, in 1842, he returned to Kabul and resumed his reign : in the Panjab campaign of 1848-9, he sent assistance to the Sikhs : he concluded the treaty of Peshawar with the Governor-General in March, 1855, by which the independence of Afghanistan was recognised : and a subsidy was given to him, under an agreement made in Jan. 1857 : he regained Kandahar in Jan. 1856 : remained quiet and staunch to the British during the mutiny : established his power throughout Afghanistan, capturing Herat, May 27, 1863 : died at Herat, June 9, 1863 : was a strong ruler, and leader of men, but cruel and unscrupulous.

AFGHANISTAN, SHIR ALI, AMIR OF (1820-1879)

Fifth son of Dost Muhammad (q.v.), whom he accompanied in exile to India : succeeded him on his death, at Herat, in 1863, being recognised by the Government of India : civil war ensued between him and his brothers. He lost his eldest son, Muhammad Ali, in the battle of Kajhbaz, in 1865, when he defeated his brother Muhammad Amir and took Kandahar : lost Kabul to his nephew, Abdur Rahman : imprisoned, 1864, his brother Afzal, who regained his freedom after the battle of Shekhabad in May, 1866, was proclaimed Amir, but died 1867. Shir Ali at one time had lost Kabul and Kandahar, but, having recovered Kabul from his brother Muhammad Azam, defeated Abdur Rahman (q. v.), son of Afzal, on Jan. 3, 1869, drove him out and was recognised as Amir by the Government of India. Lord Mayo received him in darbar at Umbala

in 1869. Shir Ali returned disappointed from the darbar, and showed resentment at the failure of his requests and his subsequent treatment by the British Government : in 1873 he sent an envoy, Saiyad Nur Muhammad, to India, to make certain proposals, which were not accepted : negotiations took place in 1877 between the envoy and Sir L. Pelly, on behalf of the Governor-General, Lord Lytton, but were fruitless. Abdullah Jan, named in 1873 as his heir, died in 1877. In 1878 Shir Ali was found to have received, at Kabul, a Russian mission under General Stolietoff : he stopped Sir Neville Chamberlain's mission at Ali Masjid, and the second Afghan war ensued. On the approach of the British forces, Shir Ali fled from Kabul and died at Mazar-i-Sharif, in Afghan Turkistan, on Feb. 21, 1879.

AGA ALI SHAH (? -1885)

Like his father, Aga Khan, the spiritual head of the Khoja community, from whom he received tribute in Asia and Africa : best known to Englishmen as a keen sportsman, a strong supporter of the turf : Member of the Bombay Legislative Council : succeeded by his son, Aga Sultan Muhammad Shah : died in 1885.

AGA KHAN (1800-1881)

The venerable spiritual head of the Khoja community, of Shia Muhammadans : descendant of the mysterious and dreaded " old man of the mountains " : claimed to be descended from Ali and Fatima : fled from Persia 40 years before his death, after an attempt to gain the Persian throne, at which his family aimed : assisted the British with his light horse in the Afghan war, 1842 : received Rs. 1,000 a month as pension : resided a short time in Calcutta, and then 30 years in Bombay, holding his court in grand style, and taking a leading part in turf and sporting matters : the keenest racing man in India : exercised almost absolute control over his subjects, " a king without a territory," the annual tribute from his followers amounting to a lakh of rupees : died April 12, 1881.

AGA SULTAN MUHAMMAD SHAH (1875-)

Born 1875 : Aga Khan : succeeded his

father, Aga Ali Shah, as head of Ismaili Muhammadans : has many religious followers in East Africa, Central Asia and India : attended the Coronation (1902) as guest of the English nation : K.C.I.E. 1898 : G.C.I.E. 1902 : Member of the Governor General's Legislative Council : has the Zanzibar and Prussian Orders.

AGNEW, PATRICK ALEXANDER VANS (1822-1848)

I.C.S. : son of Lt.-Colonel P. Vans Agnew, a Director of the E.I.Co : educated at Haileybury : arrived in India in 1841 : Assistant to the Superintendent of the Cis-Satlaj States, and at Sobraon in 1846 : after political work connected with Kashmir was assistant to the British Resident at Lahore : was sent in 1848 with Lt. Anderson to Multan, to introduce both a change in the *personnel* of the native Government and new fiscal arrangements : they were treacherously attacked on April 20, 1848, wounded and subsequently murdered by Mulraj's retainers, with his knowledge : this outrage led to the second Sikh War of 1848-9, after which the Panjab was annexed.

AGNEW, SIR WILLIAM FISCHER (1847-1903)

Son of General Agnew, of the Indian Staff Corps : called to the bar at Lincoln's Inn, 1870 : joined the bar of the Calcutta High Court : edited, from 1877, the Indian Law Reports, Calcutta : was Law Lecturer, Presidency College, 1879 : Recorder of Rangoon, 1884-1900, officiating in 1885-6 as a Judge of the Calcutta High Court : knighted, 1899 : retired in 1900 : edited several books on Indian Law : died Dec. 26, 1903.

AHLIA BAI (? -1795)

Wife of Khandi Rao Holkar, (who died 1754),son of Malhar Rao Holkar, of Indore. On the latter's death, in 1765, Mali Rao, son of Khandi and Ahlia, succeeded to the throne, but died in 9 months. Then Ahlia assumed the government, chose Takaji Holkar as her minister, and ruled till her death in 1795. She transacted business daily, unveiled, in open *darbar* from 2 p.m : had great ability and character, was deeply religious, and governed admirably.

AHMAD KHAN, SIR SYAD, KHAN BAHADUR (1817-1898)

Educational reformer : born Oct. 17, 1817, at Delhi, of a noble family : his ancestors came into India from Central Asia, and held high office under the Mogul Emperors : he entered Government service in 1837 and rose to be a subordinate Judge in the N.W.P. In the mutiny he rendered faithful service to the British at Bijnur, saving their lives : he wrote a pamphlet in Urdu on the causes of the mutiny. He was devoted to antiquarian research and was a Member of the Royal Asiatic Society : in 1864 he formed a Translation Society at Ghazipur (afterwards moved to Alighar) and had several valuable English works translated into Urdu. He visited England in 1869, and left his son (afterwards Mr. Justice Mahmud of the Allahabad High Court), to be educated at Cambridge. He wrote a reply to Sir W. W. Hunter's work on *The Indian Musalmans—are they bound in Conscience to rebel against the Queen ?* In 1876 he retired from Government service, and in 1877 commenced the Anglo-Oriental College at Alighar. He was a Member of the Legislative Council, N.W.P. and an Additional Member of the Governor General's Legislative Council, 1878-1882 : was made a K.C.S.I. in 1888 : a man of extreme courtesy combined with personal dignity : to his College he devoted his whole energy and means : died March 27, 1898 : wrote *Archæological History of Delhi* 1847 : F.R.A.S. 1864.

AHMAD SHAH ABDALI, or DURANI (? -1772)

Son of an Afghan chief of the tribe of Abdal, near Herat : held a command under Nadir Shah : after whose death, in 1747, he attacked the Persians, seized Kandahar, Kabul and Lahore : in 1748 he attacked the Moguls in Hindustan : returned to Kabul, but, in 1757, came down on Delhi and Agra, plundered Mathura and returned to Kandahar : about 1758, in response to an invitation from India, he advanced against the Mahrattas, then in great power, and defeated them at Panipat, Jan. 1761 : returned to Kabul : again invaded India in 1767 : returned to Afghanistan with little success, but some plunder : died 1772, succeeded by his second son, Timur Shah.

AHMAD, SYAD (? – ?)

Of Bareli : a horseman under Amir Khan (*q.v.*): went to Delhi, became a disciple of Shah Abdul Aziz, a famous devotee there : became a religious teacher and reformer, aiming at the restoration of pure Muhammadanism : went to Calcutta in 1821 : to Mecca, 1822 : to Bombay, 1823 : wrote the *Incitement to Religious War*, and opened a *jihad* against the Sikhs in 1826 : was killed in battle, and the movement terminated.

AINSLIE, WHITELAW (1766–1836)

Joined the E. I. Co's medical service in 1788, and served in Madras : in 1810 he was made Superintending Surgeon, and retired in 1815 : he wrote on cholera, fever, the *Materia Medica of Hindostan, Materia Indica*, and similar subjects : died April 29, 1836.

AIREY, SIR JAMES TALBOT (1812–1898)

Son of Lt-General Sir George Airey, and brother of Lord Airey : born Sep. 6, 1812 : entered the Army in 1830 : in 1841 he accompanied General Elphinstone (*q.v.*) to Kabul as his A. D. C. : in Dec. he was one of the hostages given up to Akbar Khan : they were released in Sep. 1842 : was present under McCaskill (*q.v.*) at Istalif : in the Gwalior campaign in 1843 : at Punniar : served in the Guards in the Crimea : C.B. : Colonel, 1859 : Lt-General and K.C.B. in 1877 : retired as General in 1881 : died Jan. 1, 1898.

AITCHISON, SIR CHARLES UMPHERSTON (1832–1896)

I.C.S. : born May 20, 1832, son of Hugh Aitchison, of Edinburgh : educated at the High School and University there : and at the University of Halle : passed in the first competitive examination, while Haileybury was being abolished : arrived in India in 1856 : he narrowly escaped the massacre of Europeans at Hissar in 1857 : was Under Secretary in the Foreign Department of the Government of India, 1859–65, and, after some executive work, was Foreign Secretary, 1868–78. Sharing, as he did, the views of Lord Lawrence on questions of Central Asian and Afghan policy, he was strongly opposed to the measures which led to the second Afghan

War of 1878–80. He was Chief Commissioner of British Burma from March, 1878, to July, 1880 ; Lieutenant-Governor of the Panjab, 1882–87 ; Member of the Supreme Council from April, 1887, to Nov. 1888 : also President of the important Public Service Commission in 1887–88 : K.C.S.I. in 1881, C.I.E. in 1882 : also LL.D. of Edinburgh and honorary M.A. of Oxford. He compiled the first edition of the *Treaties, Engagements and Sunnuds*, an authoritative work of reference, always quoted under his name : wrote also *The Native States of India*, and *Lord Lawrence* in the Rulers of India series : he died at Oxford Feb. 18, 1896.

AITKEN, EDWARD HAMILTON (1851-

Son of the Rev. James Aitken, missionary, Free Church of Scotland : passed the B.A. and M.A. examinations of the Bombay University at the head of the list : Latin reader in the Dekkan College, 1880–6 : entered the Customs and Salt Department : writes under the name of E. H. A. : author of *Tribes on my Frontier, Behind the Bungalow, The Naturalist on the Prowl, Five Windows of the Soul, Common Birds of Bombay* : Chief Collector of Customs, Karachi.

AITKEN, ROBERT HOPE MONCRIEFF (? –1887)

Of the 13th Bengal N.I. : served in the Panjab campaign, 1848–9 : in the mutiny, at Lucknow, in the operations before Cawnpur, and in the Oudh campaign, 1858 : gained the V.C. for acts of gallantry during the defence of the Lucknow Residency : Inspr-General of Police in Oudh : Colonel 1876 : died Sep. 18, 1887.

AITKEN, WILLIAM (1846–)

Son of James Aitken, of Falkirk, N.B., educated at Edinburgh Academy and Heidelberg : entered the Royal Artillery, 1867, Captain in 1878 : in Afghan war, 1878–80 : in the Mahsud Waziri expedition, 1881 : Major, 1884 : served in the Burma expedition, 1885–87 : Brevet Lt-Colonel : in the Chitral Relief Force, 1895 : C.B. : Brevet Colonel, 1897 : served with the Malakand Field Force, and in the Mohmand and Buner expeditions, 1897–8 : commanded the Mountain Artillery, Rawul Pindi, Panjab, till 1899 :

A.D.C. to his Majesty : and Colonel on the Staff, commanding R.A., Scottish District since 1899.

AIYAR, SIR SHESHADRI (1845-1901)

Son of a Brahman of Palghat in the District of Malabar : educated at the Provincial School at Calicut and the Presidency College in Madras : entered the Government service as translator in the Collector's office at Calicut : transferred in 1868 to Mysore under Ranga Charlu (*q.v.*). In 13 years he filled various subordinate offices until the rendition of the State to its ruler in 1881 : then he became Personal Assistant to Runga Charlu, whom he succeeded as Diwan in 1883. For 17 years he laboured assiduously to promote the economic and industrial development of the State. He began with a debt of 30 lakhs and left with a surplus of 175 lakhs. In railway, irrigation, and mining works immense progress was made during his administration : his unpopularity was due to his showing preference in his appointments to " outsiders " over natives of the State : a high-principled and accomplished statesman : received a handsome bonus of 4 lakhs on his retirement in 1900 : made C.S.I. in 1887, K.C.S.I. in 1893 : Fellow of the Madras University : died Sep. 13, 1901.

AIYAR, SIR TIRUVARUR MUTU-SAWMY (1832-1895)

Born Jan. 28, 1832 : of a poor but respectable family in the Tanjore District : his father died when he was young, and his mother had not the means to educate him : began life as assistant to a village accountant : in 1846, Tahsildar Mutusawmy Naik was struck with his intelligence, and sent him to the Madras High School. He was a favourite pupil of E. B. Powell (*q.v.*) : after serving for a time in the Tanjore District, was appointed a Deputy Inspector of Schools in 1856 : and, later, District Munsif of Tranquebar : in 1859, Deputy Collector of Tanjore : in 1865, Sub-Judge of S. Canara : in 1868, Police Magistrate at Madras : passed the B.L. degree at the University, and became a Judge of the Small Cause Court : in 1878, C.I.E. and Judge of the High Court, where he remained for 15 years ; acting as Chief Justice for 3 months

in 1893 : K.C.I.E. : was very learned in Hindu Law and a sound English lawyer, somewhat timid in coming to a decision : died Jan. 25, 1895.

AJUDHIA NATH PANDIT (1840-1892)

A Kashmiri Brahman : born April 8, 1840 : his father, Kedar Nath, was a merchant at Agra and for some time Diwan to the Nawab of Jaffhar : educated at the Agra College : in 1862 joined the bar. When the seat of Government was moved from Agra to Allahabad he migrated there : in 1869 Professor of Law at Agra : very successful as a pleader, and amassed a fortune : continued his studies in Persian and Arabic : became a member of the N.W.P. Legislative Council ; Fellow of the Calcutta and Allahabad Universities ; a prominent member of the National Congress in 1888, and afterwards became Joint General Secretary : a man of strong individuality : died Jan. 11, 1892.

AKBAR KHAN (? -1849)

Eldest son of Dost Mahammad (*q.v.*), the Amir of Afghanistan : distinguished himself against the Sikhs, and took an active part in the insurrection in Kabul in 1841 against Shah Shuja, the Amir and the British forces : at the conference to which the envoy, Sir W. H. Macnaghten, was invited on Dec. 23, 1841, outside Kabul, he treacherously murdered Macnaghten : the British hostages, including women and children, were given over to him, when the British army retreated from Kabul and was destroyed, in Jan., 1842, by the Afghans and the climate : he treated them chivalrously : he attacked Sale's garrison near Jalalabad, but was beaten off on April 7, 1842, by a force under Havelock : he was again routed, in Aug., 1842, at Tezin by the relieving force under General Pollock : he died 1849, in Kabul, after the restoration of Dost Muhammad.

ALCOCK, ALFRED WILLIAM (1859-)

Educated at Mill Hill, Blackheath, Westminster, and Aberdeen University : Assistant Professor of Zoology, Aberdeen University, 1883-85 : joined the Indian Medical Service, 1885 : served in the Panjab Frontier Force : Surgeon Naturalist to the Marine Survey of India on board the *Investigator*, 1888–1892 : Superintendent of the Indian Museum and Professor of Zoology in the Medical College, Calcutta, since 1893 : C.I.E.: author of *A Naturalist in Indian Seas* and numerous zoological monographs : Major.

ALEXANDER, SIR JAMES (? – ?)

Entered the Bengal Artillery, 1820 : at capture of Bhartpur, 1825–6 : commanded the Artillery under Pollock in Afghanistan, 1842 : forced the Khyber Pass, at Tezin and Kabul : in the Gwalior campaign, at Maharajpur, 1843 : in the Satlaj campaign, 1845–6, at Badiwal, Aliwal, Sobraon: C.B. : K.C.B., 1871 General, ˙872 : retired, 1887.

ALEXANDER, SIR JAMES FDWARD (1803–1885)

Born Oct. 16, 1803 : son of Edward Alexander, of Powis : educated at Edinburgh, Glasgow and the R.M.C., Sandhurst : to Madras as a cadet in 1820 : Adjutant of the bodyguard to Sir Thomas Munro, and served in the Burmese war of 1824 : left the E. I. Co.'s army in 1825, but saw much active service, with the Persian army, in the Balkans, Portugal, S. Africa, Canada, the Crimea, New Zealand : employed on Government expeditions in exploring and surveying in Central Africa and New Brunswick, for which he was knighted : took a leading part in the removal of 'Cleopatra's Needle' to England, 1867–77 : made C.B. in 1873, retired as Lt-General, and became General in 1881 : died April 2, 1885 : wrote *Travels from India to England by way of Burma, Persia, Turkey, etc.*, 1827, and other works : was Knight Commander of the Lion and Sun : F.R.S. Edinburgh : F.R.G.S. : F.R.A.S. : F.S.S.A.

ALI IBRAHIM KHAN, NAWAB (? -1793 ?)

Of Patna : " Daroga " of the Court at Ben .res, that is, President of the tribunal there, in the time of Warren Hastings' Governorship : besides a number of compositions, he compiled the *Gulzar-i Ibrahim*, described as an anthological biography of Hindustani poets, written 1772–1784 : he had a poetical name, Khatil : died 1793 or 1794.

ALISON, SIR ARCHIBALD, BARONET (1826–   )

General : son of Sir. A. A., the historian : born Jan. 21, 1826 : educated at Glasgow and Edinburgh Universities : entered the Army in 1846 : served in the Crimea ; in the Indian mutiny he was Military Secretary to Sir Colin Campbell, then C. in C. in India ; lost his arm at the relief of Lucknow in Nov., 1857 : made C.B. : served in the Ashanti expedition in 1873–4 : made K.C.B. and later G.C.B. : Commandant of the Staff College, 1877 : Head of the Intelligence Department, 1878–8 : in the Egyptian campaign of 1882, commanded at Alexandria, and the Highland Brigade at Tel-el-Kebir : C. in C. in Egypt, 1882–3 : commanded the Aldershot Division from 1883 : Adjutant-General, 1888 : retired from the Army, 1893 : member of the Council of India, 1889–1899 : wrote a number of articles in *Blackwood's Magazine*.

ALIVERDI KHAN (1676 ?–1756)

Nawab Nazim of Bengal, Bihar and Orissa : son of Mirza Muhammad, a Turkoman employed at Delhi : entered the service of Nawab Shujauddin, governor of Orissa (son-in-law of Nawab Murshid Kali Jafar Khan) as a commander of troops : in 1726, Jafar Khan died, Shujauddin succeeded him as Nawab Nazim, and Aliverdi Khan became General of the Imperial troops : in 1729 he was appointed Governor of Bihar by Nawab Shujauddin, and, later, became free from any dependence on the Nizam of Bengal : in 1739 Shujauddin died, and was succeeded by his son, Sarfaraz Khan, Aliverdi continuing to be governor of Bihar : in 1740 Aliverdi quarrelled with the Nawab Sarfaraz, defeated and killed him in battle and seized the Nizamat : he was known in Bengal as Muhabat Jang. From 1741 the Mahrattas invaded Bengal, and their leader, Bhashkar Pandit, was inveigled by Aliverdi to a conference, and treacherously killed : the Mahratta raids spread consternation throughout Bengal, and, after fighting with them up to 1751, Aliverdi made peace by ceding Orissa to them and agreeing to an annual payment of 12 lakhs of rupees. Aliverdi allowed the English to protect themselves in 1742, by digging the Mahratta ditch round the Company's territory to stop the

Mahratta raids. In 1753 he adopted his grandson, Surajuddaula, and declared him his successor. On April 9, 1756, Aliverdi died at the age of 80, at Murshidabad.

ALLARD, JEAN FRANCOIS (1785–1839)

General : born in France, March 8, 1785 : served in the French Cavalry from 1803 : in Italy : A.D.C. to Marshal Brune : after Waterloo, went to Persia ; thence through Kandahar and Kabul to Lahore : entered Ranjit Singh's service in March, 1822, and drilled Sikh cavalry for him on the European model : engaged in numerous campaigns : of high character and much liked and respected by Europeans : was General in the French Army, and Political Agent of the French Government at Lahore : died at Peshawar, Jan. 23, 1839, and buried at Lahore.

ALLARDYCE, ALEXANDER (1841–1896)

Educated at Aberdeen University : for years connected with Blackwood, and his chief adviser in the management of the magazine : went to India as a journalist on the staff of the Indian *Statesman :* declined a civil appointment offered him : went to Ceylon : was special correspondent there in connexion with H.R.H. the Prince of Wales' visit to the East : on returning to England, wrote for Reviews and Magazines : wrote novels with success, such as *The City of Sunshine, Earl's Court,* a biography of Admiral Keith, and other similar works : died April 22, 1896.

ALLEN, CHARLES (1808–1884)

I.C.S. : born July 29, 1808 : son of Rev. David Bird Allen : educated at Westminster and Haileybury : went to India 1827 : served chiefly in the N.W.P. : Magte. Collr. of Moradabad, 1837 : Hamirpur, 1841 : Settlement Officer in Bundelkund : Judge at Agra, 1843–9 : and at Fatehghar : acted as Foreign Secretary to the Government of India, 1852 : Financial Secretary, 1854 : and Member of the Legislative Council of India, 1854 : retired, 1857 : died, Nov. 5, 1884 : was J.P. and Alderman and Mayor of Tenby, and High Sheriff of Pembrokeshire, 1876 : wrote in support of Lord Dalhousie *The Yellow Pamphlet* in answer to Colonel G. B.

Malleson's *Red Pamphlet* at the time of the mutiny.

ALLEN, SIR GEORGE WILLIAM (1831–1900)

Son of James Allen : founder of the *Pioneer* and *Civil and Military Gazette,* the first daily newspapers published elsewhere than in the Presidency towns in India : promoted private enterprise : C.I.E., 1879 : K.C.I.E., 1897 : died Nov. 4, 1900.

ALMS, JAMES (1728–1791)

Naval officer : born July 15, 1728, of humble origin, entered the Navy early : served in the East Indies : narrowly escaped when his ship sank in a storm in April, 1749, near Fort St. David : commanded an East Indiaman in the Bombay-China trade : was present at the capture of Gheria, the stronghold of the pirate Angria in 1756. After service in other stations, he, in 1780, commanded the *Monmouth,* 60 guns, joining Sir Edward Hughes in the Indian seas : was present in the engagements of 1782 off Sadras, Providien, Negapatam, Trincomalee, in which his ship suffered severely and his losses were heavy : his health gave way : retired in 1784, and died June 8, 1791.

AMEER ALI, SYAD (1849–)

Born April 6, 1849 : son of Syad Saadat Ali, of Unao, Oudh, of a family originally from Persia : descendant of Muhammad through the Imam Ali-ar-Raza, of Mashad: educated at Hughli College : M.A. and B.L., Calcutta : called to the bar at the Inner Temple, 1873, practised in the High Court, Calcutta : Fellow of the Calcutta University, 1874 : Magistrate and Chief Magistrate, Calcutta, 1878–81 : Lecturer on Muhammadan Law, 1875–9 : Member of the Bengal Legislative Council, 1878–83 : and of the Governor General's Legislative Council, 1883–5 : Tagore Law Professor, 1884 : C.I.E.: Puisne Judge of the Calcutta High Court, 1890–1904 : President of the Committee of the Hughli Imambara, 1876–1904 : founder of the Central National Muhammadan Association, and its Secretary, 1876–90 : a strong advocate of English education and of the education of Indian ladies : very influential among the Muhammadans in Bengal : wrote *A Critical Examination of*

the *Life and Teachings of Muhammad,
The Spirit of Islam, The Ethics of Islam,
A Short History of the Saracens, Personal
Law of the Muhammadans, Students'
Handbook of Muhammadan Law, Muham-
madan Law*: was joint author of *A
Commentary on the Indian Evidence Act,*
and of *A Commentary on the Bengal Tenancy
Act :* has frequently written articles in
The Nineteenth Century, and is engaged
on a *History of Muhammadan Civilization
in India.*

AMHERST OF ARAKAN, WILLIAM PITT, FIRST EARL (1773–1857)

Governor-General : born in Jan. 1773 :
sent on an embassy to China in 1816 :
arrived in Calcutta as Governor-General,
Aug. 1, 1823 : it devolved on him to
allay the excitement caused by the action
of the Government towards the Press
and Mr. J. S. Buckingham (*q.v.*) In
Feb., 1824, the Burmese having occupied
countries near Bengal and attacked British
territory, Amherst declared war and
despatched an expedition, which captured Rangoon, Martaban and Prome :
peace was made by the treaty of Yandaboo, 1826, by which Assam and Tenasserim
were ceded to the British. In Jan., 1826,
the capture of Bhartpur by Lord Combermere took place, when the British Government restored the youthful Raja Balwant
Singh, whom Government had recognized,
to the throne, which had been seized by a
cousin, Durjan Sal. Lord Amherst was
made an Earl. He was the first Governor-
General to spend, in 1827, the summer in
Simla : left India March 10, 1828 : died
March 13, 1857.

AMIR ALI KHAN, NAWAB BAHADUR (1810–1879)

Born at Barh, March 10, 1810 : appointed, 1829, Assistant to the Ambassador
of Nasiruddin Hyder, King of Oudh : in
1838 Deputy Assistant Superintendent
in the Presidency Special Commissioner's
Court at Calcutta : in 1845, Government
Pleader in the *Sadr Diwani Adalat* : in
1857, Personal Assistant to the Commissioner of Patna : in 1864 Khan
Bahadur and Member of the Bengal
Legislative Council : entered the service
of the late ex-King of Oudh, and appointed
a Commissioner to settle the debts of the
late Nawab Nazim of Bengal : in 1875

made Nawab : in 1878 the Sultan of
Turkey made him a Companion of the
Order of the Osmanli : died Nov., 1879.

AMIR KHAN (1790 ?–after 1877)

A wealthy banker and money-lender of
Patna : was arrested and tried as a
member of a Wahabi conspirary, at Patna,
in 1871, on various charges of attempting
to wage war against the Queen : convicted and sentenced to transportation
for life, with forfeiture of property, and
released on the proclamation of the Queen
as Empress of India, Jan. 1, 1877.

AMIR KHAN (? –1834)

Born in Rohilkund, of Afghan parents :
at 20 went with followers to Malwa :
took service under Bhopal : next under
the Mahrattas : from 1799 to 1806 commanded the army of Jaswant Rao Holkar :
next under the Raja of Jaipur : always
committing plunder and depredations :
attacked the Mahrattas, in Nagpur, but
returned to his own capital, Sironj, to
defend it against the British : he was
essentially a Pindari : when the British
entered Malwa in 1817, negotiations passed
between them and Amir Khan, which
resulted in his abandoning the predatory
system, dismissing his army, and being
allowed to keep the lands he held under
grants from Holkar : he received territory
and a gift of money from the British :
and, by the Treaty of Nov. 15, 1817, was
confirmed in his possessions. The Principality of Tonk was thus established, and
Amir Khan's descendants are still Nawabs
there : he died 1834.

AMOS, ANDREW (1791–1860)

Lawyer : born in India, 1791 : son of
James Amos, merchant : educated at
Eton, and Trinity College, Cambridge :
Fellow, 1813 : called to the bar by the
Middle Temple : had a large practice :
Recorder of Oxford, Nottingham, and
Banbury : a member of the Criminal Law
Commission for some years : Professor
of English Law at University College,
London, 1829–37 : Legal Member (suc-
ceeding Macaulay) of the Supreme Coun-
cil of the Governor-General, 1838–42 :
had much to do with the abolition of
slavery in India, and the framing of the
Penal Code. On return to England he

became a County Court Judge, and Downing Professor of Laws at Cambridge : wrote on a number of legal and literary subjects : died April 18, 1860.

AMPTHILL, OLIVER ARTHUR VILLIERS RUSSELL, BARON
(1869-)

Born Feb. 19, 1869 : son of the first Baron (better known as Lord Odo Russell) educated at Eton, and New College, Oxford : rowed in the Oxford University Eight, 1889–91 : President of the O.U.B.C. 1891 : President of the Oxford Union Society, 1891 : won the Pair Oars at Henley Regatta with Guy Nickalls, 1890–91 : Private Secretary to Rt. Hon. J. Chamberlain : Governor of Madras, from Dec., 1900 : Viceroy and Governor-General from April 30 to Dec., 1904.

AMYATT (? –1763)

A Bengal Civilian : chief of the English factory at Patna in 1759 : a member of the Calcutta Council when Vansittart (q.v.) was Governor in Bengal. Amyatt had been superseded by Clive's appointment of Vansittart, and therefore constantly opposed all his measures : sent on a mission to Mir Kasim, Nawab of Bengal : it was unsuccessful, and war was imminent, but Amyatt was given leave to return to Calcutta : meanwhile, however, the disaster took place at Patna : Amyatt was attacked and murdered by Mir Kasim's troops before he had reached his destination, 1763.

ANDERSON, DAVID (? – ?)

Employed by Warren Hastings on important negotiations ; sent on an embassy to Madhava Rao Sindia, at the close of the first Mahratta war, to conclude peace, 1782 : accompanied by his brother, Lieut. James Anderson, as his assistant : he remained with Sindia as Political Resident until Warren Hastings left India, 1785, when James succeeded as Resident. The conciliatory attitude of the Mahratta Government at a critical period was due to the exertions of the brothers Anderson. David was examined as a witness at Hastings' trial, 1790, being then President of the Committee of Revenue.

ANDERSON, SIR GEORGE WILLIAM
(1791–1857)

I.C.S. : entered the Bombay Civil Service in 1806 : drew up the " Bombay Code of 1827 ": was a Judge of the *Sadr* Court, and, in 1835, was appointed to the Indian Law Commission : in 1838 he became Member of Council, Bombay : from April, 1841, to June, 1842, acted as Governor of Bombay, between Sir J. Rivett-Carnac and Sir G. Arthur : retired in 1844 : in 1849 was knighted and appointed Governor of the Mauritius, but after 16 months was transferred to Ceylon as Governor, and made K.C.B. : resigned in 1855 : died March 12, 1857.

ANDERSON, SIR HENRY LACON
(1807–1879)

I.C.S. : eldest son of Sir George William Anderson, K.C.B. (q.v.) : educated at Haileybury : went to Bombay in the Civil Service, 1820 : Secretary to Government, Bombay, in the Secret, Political and Judical Departments, 1855 : Chief Secretary, 1861 : member of the Legislative Council, Bombay : resigned, 1865 : Secretary in the Judicial Department at the India Office, 1866 : K.C.S.I., 1867 : died April 7, 1879.

ANDERSON, JAMES (? –1809)

In the medical service of the E. I. Co. : served in Madras : appointed Assistant Surgeon, 1765 : Surgeon, 1786 : Member of the Madras Medical Board, 1800 : a distinguished botanist : worked at developing the cochineal dye, and introducing the cultivation of silk : wrote for some years on sugar-cane, the coffee-plant, cotton, and the apple : died Aug. 5, 1809.

ANDERSON, JOHN (1795–1845)

Of the E.I.Co.'s service : went out to Pulo Penang, or Prince of Wales' Island, in 1813, as a writer : after the usual succession of minor appointments he became, in 1827, senior merchant, Secretary to Government, and Malay translator : was employed in negotiations with the neighbouring potentates of Sumatra, etc. : died Dec. 2, 1845 : wrote several works about the Malayan Peninsula, the British settlements, and the adjacent countries and their commerce.

ANDERSON, REV. JOHN (1805–1855)

Missionary: born in 1805, son of a Scotch farmer: educated at Edinburgh University: ordained in 1836 a minister of the Church of Scotland, and was sent as missionary to Madras: founded the Madras Christian College, which, after 1843, was continued in connexion with the Scotch Free Church: the education there afforded was greatly appreciated, and with Mrs. Anderson's help the education of native girls of all castes and creeds was successfully undertaken: he died at Madras in 1855.

ANDERSON, JOHN (1833–1900)

Son of Thomas Anderson: born Oct. 4, 1833, at Edinburgh: M.D. at Edinburgh University, 1862, obtaining the gold medal for zoology: President of the Royal Physical Society, Edinburgh, which he helped to found: Professor of Natural History in the Free Church College, Edinburgh: in 1865 appointed Curator, and, later, Superintendent of the Indian Museum, Calcutta, an office which he held till he retired in 1886. He was a member, as naturalist, of scientific expeditions to Upper Burma and Yunnan in 1867: in the same direction, as far as the Burmese frontier, in 1875–6: and to the Mergui Archipelago in 1881–2: wrote full accounts of his travels, adding largely to the science of marine and general zoology, and anatomy: also on the reptiles and fauna of Egypt: and contributed to the proceedings of learned societies: F.R.S. in 1879: LL.D. of Edinburgh, 1885: Fellow of the Linnæan Society and of the Society of Antiquaries, and Vice-President of the Zoological Society of London: died Aug. 15, 1900. ·

ANDERSON, THOMAS (1832–1870)

Botanist: born Feb. 26, 1832, and took his M.D. degree at Edinburgh University in 1853: joined the Medical Service, Bengal, in 1854, at Calcutta: was at Delhi during the mutiny: was, in 1860, Superintendent of the Botanic Garden at Sibpur, opposite Calcutta, introduced many improvements, and laboured specially for the cultivation of cinchona in India, which afterwards was effected: in 1864 he organised the Forest Department in Bengal: died Oct. 26, 1870, at Edinburgh: published an account of the flora of Aden, and worked at the flora of India generally.

ANDREW, JAMES (1774?–1833)

A Scotchman, educated at Aberdeen: had a school at Addiscombe, which the E. I. Co. took over for the education of their engineer and artillery officers: on its purchase in 1809 he was appointed Headmaster and Professor of Mathematics: retired about 1823 and died June 13, 1833.

ANDREW, SIR WILLIAM PATRICK (1807–1887)

Born 1807: son of Patrick Andrew: educated at Edinburgh and Oxford: was for a short time in India in his younger days: published a work on *Indian Railways*, 1846: devoted much attention to the promotion of railway and telegraphic communication between England and India: specially advocating the scheme for an Euphrates Valley Railway: submitted to the Home .Government his schemes for the defence of India: published, during 40 years, a number of works, letters and papers, and delivered lectures on the subject of Indian railways, the Euphrates Valley route, and the importance of the Indus and its provinces: was founder and Chairman of the Sind, Panjab and Delhi Railway: in 1856 he arranged with Government for the establishment of telegraphic communication with India: lectured and wrote on the Central Asian question, 1872–86: wrote to the *Times* on the *Advance of Russia*: wrote *India and her Neighbours*, 1878: advocated the construction of railway lines to the Bolan and the Khyber: advocated the 5'6" gauge for Indian railways: Chairman in 1879 of a meeting to promote the construction of a railway from the Persian Gulf to Constantinople and the Mediterranean: was called " an apostle of railways," " the railway statesman," " the pioneer of railway enterprise ": continued to urge the advantage of the Euphrates Valley line as alternative to that of the Red Sea : knighted, 1882: C.I.E.: Fellow of many scientific societies: died March 11, 1887.

ANQUETIL, THOMAS JOHN (1781–1842)

Native of Jersey: entered the Army, 1803: served in the Mahratta campaign, attached to the Light Brigade, commanded the Pioneer Corps, the 57th N.I., and the 44th N.I. successively : Adjutant-General of General Stevenson's force in the Shekhawati campaign : D.A.G. : commanded the Oudh Contingent as Brigadier : Inspecting Officer of all the Contingents : as a Lt-Colonel and Brigadier commanded Shah Shuja's army : in the retreat from Kabul was killed at Jagdalak on Jan. 12, 1842.

ANQUETIL DU PERRON, ABRAHAM HYACINTHE (1731–1805)

Brother of L. P. Hyacinthe, the French historian : born at Paris in 1731 : being bent on studying Oriental languages, he went to India as a private soldier in 1754, and acquired considerable knowledge of Sanskrit, translating a dictionary in that language : on the taking of Pondicherry by the English he returned to Europe and conveyed his MSS. to Paris, where he was appointed Oriental interpreter to the King's Library : was Member of the Academy of Inscriptions and Belles Lettres, and the National Institute, and one of the most celebrated of the literati of Europe : he died Jan. 17, 1805.

ANSON, HON. AUGUSTUS HENRY ARCHIBALD (1835–77)

Younger brother of the Earl of Lichfield : born 1835 : entered the Army 1853, in the Rifle Brigade : in the Crimea : joined the 84th regt. : in the mutiny, was A.D.C. to Sir J. Hope Grant : wounded at the siege of Delhi : at Bulandshahr deserved his V.C., and gained it as a Captain at the capture of the Sikandarbagh on Sir Colin Campbell's relief of Lucknow, Nov. 16, 1857 : died Nov. 17, 1877.

ANSON, HON. GEORGE (1797–1857)

General : second son of the first Viscount Anson : served at Waterloo in the Guards : was M.P. from 1818 for many years : in 1853, appointed to command a Division in India : C. in C. Madras, 1854, and C. in C. in India, 1856 : was at Simla when the mutiny broke out in May, 1857, and hastened down to the plains : while on the march from Umbala to Delhi with a force, he died of cholera at Karnal, May 27, 1857.

ANSTEY, THOMAS CHISHOLM (1816–1873)

Barrister and political writer : born in London, 1816 : educated at Wellington and University College, London : called to the bar at the Middle Temple, 1839 : became, in the Oxford movement, a Roman Catholic, and Professor of Law at the Roman Catholic College near Bath : wrote on legal and political subjects : was M.P. for Youghal 1847–52, when his excessive speaking in Parliament was much resented : appointed Attorney General at Hongkong, 1854, but was suspended by the Governor, Sir John Bowring, in 1858 : after a short time at Calcutta, he was very successful at the Bombay bar, and in 1865 acted for a few months as a Judge of the High Court : failing to obtain work at the English bar, he returned to Bombay and died there, Aug 17, 1873 : his violent temper stood in his way through life, leading him into constant quarrels with his profession and society

ANSTRUTHER, SIR ALEXANDER (1769–1819)

Judge : son of Sir R. Anstruther, *Bart* : born Sep. 10, 1769 : called to the bar at Lincoln's Inn, and published legal reports : was Advocate-General, Madras, 1803 : Recorder of Bombay, 1812 : knighted : died July 16, 1819.

ANSTRUTHER, SIR JOHN (1753–1811)

Chief Justice : born March 27, 1753 : son of Sir John Anstruther, *Bart.* : educated at Glasgow : called to the bar at Lincoln's Inn, 1779 : was M.P. for Cockermouth, 1790–96 : supported C. J. Fox, and was one of the managers of the impeachment of Warren Hastings, having to speak on certain of the charges : in 1797, appointed Chief Justice of Bengal, made a Baronet, and retired to England, 1806 : Privy Councillor : re-entered Parliament : died in London, Jan. 26, 1811.

APPA SAHIB (? –1840)

Raja of Nagpur : when Regent, in 1816, he put to death his cousin, Parsoram, or Parsoji, Bhonsla, an idiot Raja of Nagpur, and succeeded the late Raja's uncle, Raghoji Bhonsla II (*q.v.*) as Raja : Baji Rao appointed him nominal C. in C. of the

Peshwa's army: Appa treacherously attacked the British under Mr. Jenkins, Resident of Nagpur, and was defeated at Sitabaldi, Nov., 26–7, 1817: taken prisoner, he escaped from custody and sought refuge, in 1818, at Jodhpur, where he is said to have died in 1840.

APPLEYARD, FREDERICK ERNEST
(1829–)

Son of F. N. Appleyard, a Cursitor of the High Court of Chancery: educated at Elizabeth College, Guernsey: entered the 80th regt., 1850: served in the second Burmese war: present at Martaban, the storming of Rangoon and taking of Prome: exchanged to the 7th R. Fusiliers: in the Crimea: wounded at Alma, 1854, and the Redan, 1855: present at Inkerman, in the trenches at Sebastopol: commanded a Brigade in the Afghan campaign, 1878–80: Maj-General, and C.B.

ARBUTHNOT, SIR ALEXANDER
JOHN (1822–)

I.C.S.: son of the Bishop of Killaloe: born Oct. 11, 1822: educated at Rugby and Haileybury: entered the Madras Civil Service, 1842: Director of Public Instruction, 1855: Chief Secretary to Government, Madras, 1862: Additional Member of the Legislative Council, Madras, 1862: Member of Council, Madras, 1867–72: Acting Governor of Madras, Feb. to May, 1872: K.C.S.I.: 1873: Member of the Supreme Council, 1875–80: C.I.E.: President of the Council, 1878 and 1879: Vice-Chancellor of Madras and Calcutta Universities: Member of the Council of India, 1887–97: author of *Selections from Minutes of Maj-General Sir Thomas Munro*, *Life of Lord Clive*, and a number of articles in the *Dictionary of National Biography*.

ARBUTHNOT, SIR CHARLES GEORGE
(1824–1899)

Son of the Bishop of Killaloe, and brother of Sir A. J. Arbuthnot (*q.v.*): born May 19, 1824: educated at Rugby and the R.M.A., Woolwich: entered the Royal Artillery 1843: served in the Crimea: became Lt-Colonel 1864: went to India in 1868: C.B., 1871: D.A.G. of Artillery, 1873–7: Inspr-General of Artillery in India, 1877–80: in the

second Afghan War was employed as Brig-General, first in the Kandahar Field force and later in the Khyber: K.C.B. in 1881: D.A.G. of Artillery in England, 1880–3: Inspr-General of Artillery, 1883: and President of the Ordnance Committee, 1885: in 1886 was made C. in C. Bombay, and transferred to Madras in the same year: succeeded Lord Roberts in the command in Burma in 1887: retired from Madras in 1891: General, 1890: G.C.B., 1894: died April 14, 1899.

ARBUTHNOT, GEORGE (1772–1843)

Went, with his brother Robert, who was Chief Secretary in Ceylon, to Colombo, in 1800: thence to Madras and joined a Mr. Lautour in business: on the latter's death the firm was reconstituted, under the name of Arbuthnot & Co., which it still bears: retired from India in 1823, and settled in England.

ARBUTHNOT, SIR GEORGE GOUGH
(1848–)

Born Aug. 28, 1848: educated at Eton: partner in the firm of Arbuthnot & Co., Madras: Member of the Legislative Council, Madras: Chairman of the Chamber of Commerce, Madras: Fellow of the Madras University: Chairman of the Famine Relief Fund: Knight Bachelor.

ARBUTHNOT, WILLIAM URQU-
HART (1807–1874)

I.C.S.: fifth son of Sir William Arbuthnot, *Bart*: born 1807: educated at the Edinburgh High School and Haileybury: went to Madras, 1826: became Agent to the Governor at Vizagapatam: resigned the service, 1846: joined the firm of Arbuthnot & Co. at Madras: retired to England in 1858: was one of the original members, chosen by the Crown, of the new Council of India, from Sep. 21, 1858, under the Statute of 1858: more than once he declined the appointment of Finance Minister in India: died Dec. 11, 1874

ARCOT, AZIM JAH, PRINCE OF
(1800–1874)

Uncle of Muhammad Ghaus (*q.v.*), the Nawab of the Carnatic, whom he succeeded, but only as the first Prince of Arcot, the title granted to him in 1867, with a pension and various concessions, a personal salute of 15 guns, etc. : died Jan. 14, 1874.

ARCOT, GHULAM MUHAMMAD ALI, KHAN BAHADUR, PRINCE OF
(1882–)

Born 1882 : succeeded his father, Muhammad Munawwar Ali, 1903 : Premier Muhammadan nobleman of the Carnatic and acknowledged head of the Muhammadan community of the Madras Presidency : was given the title of Khan Bahadur in 1897.

ARCOT, SIR MUHAMMAD MUNAW-WAR ALI KHAN BAHADUR, PRINCE OF (1856–1903)

Son of Muazzaz-ud-daula, and nephew of Intizam-ul-mulk, whom he succeeded as Prince of Arcot, 1889 : leader of the Muhammadan community in the Madras Presidency, and held in high esteem by it and the British authorities : Khan Bahadur, 1876 : K.C.I.E., 1897 : died at the Delhi Imperial Assemblage, Jan. 4, 1903.

ARDAGH, SIR JOHN CHARLES
(1840–)

Maj-General, R.E. : educated at Trinity College, Dublin : entered the Royal Engineers in April, 1859 : passed the Staff College : his services in Europe, on frontier commissions, and in Africa on military campaigns, have been distinguished : in India he was Private Secretary to the Marquis of Lansdowne, Governor-General and Viceroy, from Dec., 1888, to Jan., 1894, and also to the Earl of Elgin, in the same appointment, Jan. to April, 1894 : is C.B. (Civil 1878, Military 1884): C.I.E. (1892): K.C.I.E. (1894): K.C.M.G. (1902): also Hon. LL.D. of Trinity College, Dublin.

ARGYLL, GEORGE DOUGLAS CAMP-BELL, EIGHTH DUKE OF
(1823–1900)

Statesman : K.G., K.T., P.C. : born April 30, 1823 : his connection with India began when he was Secretary of State for India in Mr. Gladstone's administration, 1868–1874 : when in opposition, he wrote and spoke strongly against the forward Afghan policy of the Conservative Government. In 1865 he wrote *India under Dalhousie and Canning*, and in 1899 *The*

Eastern Question : he always showed great interest in, and knowledge of, Indian questions : he died April 24, 1900.

ARMSTRONG, SIR GEORGE CARLYON HUGHES, BARONET (1836–)

Educated privately : entered the Indian Army, 1855 : served throughout the Indian mutiny : severely wounded, 1857 : retired as Captain on pension, and became orderly officer of the R.M.C., Addiscombe, until it was broken up : subsequently became proprietor and editor of the *Globe* newspaper, and received a Baronetcy in 1892.

ARNOLD, SIR EDWIN (1832–1904)

Poet : born June 10, 1832 : educated at Rochester, King's College, London, and University College, Oxford, (Scholar) : gained the Newdigate Verse Prize, 1853 : Principal of the Government Dekkan College, in Poona, 1856–1861 : Fellow of the Bombay University : joined the *Daily Telegraph* newspaper in London, and became its editor : visited and admired Japan, and married a Japanese lady in 1897 : made a C.S.I. : and K.C.I.E. in 1888 : held Orders from the rulers of Siam, Japan, Turkey and Persia : distinguished as a poet, scholar, teacher, journalist and man of letters : wrote *The Light of Asia, Indian Idylls*, Indian poetry, etc. : died March 24, 1904.

ARNOLD, THOMAS WALKER
(1864–)

Born April 19, 1864 : educated at the City of London School and Magdalen College, Cambridge : Professor at the M.A.O. College, Alighar : Professor of Philosophy at the Government College, Lahore : Dean of the Oriental Faculty, Panjab University : Assistant Librarian at the India Office, 1904 : Professor of Arabic at University College, London, since 1904 : published *The Preaching of Islam*, 1896 : *Al Mutazilah*, 1902.

ARNOLD, WILLIAM DELAFIELD
(1828–1859)

Son of Dr. Arnold, of Rugby : born April 7, 1828 : educated at Rugby : student of Christ Church, Oxford : went to India in 1848, into the Native Infantry : was an Assistant Commissioner in the Panjab, and, in 1856, Director of Public

c

Instruction : did good service in organising the Department : died at Gibraltar on April 9, 1859, on his way to England : wrote essays on social and Indian subjects, and *Oakfield, or Fellowship in the East :* his brother, Matthew Arnold, wrote *A Southern Night* in memory of him, and alluded to him in *Stanzas from Carnac.*

ARNOULD, SIR JOSEPH (1814–1886)

Judge : son of Joseph Arnould : born Nov. 12, 1814 : educated at Charterhouse and Wadham College, Oxford : Newdigate Verse Prize, 1834 : Fellow of his College : called to the bar by the Middle Temple, contributed to journalism and wrote legal works : in 1859 was made a Judge of the Bombay Supreme (afterwards the High) Court, and knighted : retired in 1869 : died Feb. 16, 1886.

ARTHUR, SIR GEORGE, BARONET (1784–1854)

Son of John Arthur of Plymouth : entered the Army in 1804 : served in Italy, 1806, Egypt, 1807, Sicily, 1808, Walcheren, 1809 : D.A.A.G. : Military Secretary to the Governor of Jersey : Major in a regiment in Jamaica, 1812 : Lieutenant-Governor of British Honduras and Colonel, 1814–22 : Lieutenant-Governor of Van Diemen's Land, 1824–37 : received the Hanoverian Order : Lieutenant-Governor of Upper Canada, 1837–41 : made Baronet in 1841 : Governor of Bombay from June 9, 1842 to Aug. 5, 1846, during the difficult time of the latter portion of the first Afghan War, and of Lord Ellenborough's tenure of office as Governor-General : appointed provisional Governor-General : after retirement he was made a Privy Councillor and D.C.L., Oxford : Lt-General, and Colonel of the 50th regt. : died Sep. 19, 1854.

ASHBURNER, LIONEL ROBERT (1827)

I.C.S.: born 1827: educated at Haileybury: entered the Bombay Civil Service in 1848, and retired in 1883 : in the mutiny, 1857, raised and organized a body of horse and foot to protect the E. frontier of Gujarat : was Special Commissioner to try offences against the State : tried and convicted certain chiefs : C.S.I. : Member of Council in Bombay, 1877–83 : acted as Governor of Bombay from March 13 to April 28, 1880.

ASHBURNHAM, HON. THOMAS (? – 1872)

General : son of George, third Earl of Ashburnham, K.G. : entered the Army, 1823 : Lt-Colonel, 1835 : commanded a Brigade in the Satlaj campaign, 1845–6, at Firozshahr and Sobraon : C.B. : A.D.C. to the Queen : appointed to the command of the forces in China, 1857 : transferred to a military command in India : returned to England, 1858 : Colonel of the 82nd regt., 1859 : General, 1868 : died March 3, 1872.

ASMAN JAH, BAHADUR, NAWAB SIR (1839–1898)

Great-grandson of the second Nizam of Hyderabad : born 1839 : Minister of Justice in 1869, and acted as Prime Minister and Regent during Sir Salar Jang's absence in Europe : on the latter's death, in 1883, he became a member of the Council of Regency : represented the Nizam at Queen Victoria's Jubilee, 1887 : was for 7 years Prime Minister of Hyderabad, 1887 : made K.C.I.E., 1887 : died 1898.

ASTELL, HENRY GODFREY (1816–1903)

I.C.S. : son of William Astell, (*q.v.*), Chairman of the Directors of the E.I. Co. : educated at Eton and Haileybury : in the mutiny was Judge of Azimghar, N.W.P. : was supported by two companies of sepoys and some cavalry of doubtful loyalty, when he was attacked by about 2,000 rebels : after an engagement, in which his cavalry deserted, he was forced to retire to his entrenchments and Ghazipur : was later besieged at Jaunpur, until relieved by General Lugard with a force from Lucknow : died July 6, 1903.

ASTELL, WILLIAM (1774–1847)

Son of Godfrey Thornton, Bank of England Director : changed his name to Astell, 1807 : was Director of the E.I. Co., 1807–46, and M.P. for Bridgewater 1807–32, afterwards for Bedfordshire : Chairman of the Directors in 1810, 1824, 1830, 1838 : much opposed to Lord Ellenborough's administration of India : Colonel of the Royal East India Volunteers : died March 7, 1847.

ATKINSON, EDWIN FELIX THOMAS (? –1890)

I.C.S. : educated at Trinity College, Dublin : went out to the N.W.P., 1862 :

Census officer in the N.W.P., 1881 : compiled the Gazetteer of the N.W.P. :. Accountant-General of the N.W.P., and of Bengal : President of the Asiatic Society of Bengal : took a keen interest in intellectual pursuits : died Sep. 18, 1890.

ATKINSON, JAMES (1780-1852)

Born March 9, 1780 : studied medicine at Edinburgh and London : joined the Bengal Medical service, 1805 : Civil Surgeon at Backerganj, to 1813 : studied Persian : Assay Master of the Mint, 1813-28 : officiating Deputy Professor of Persian at Fort William College, 1818, Superintendent of the Government Gazette, 1817, and of the Press from 1823 : commenced the *Calcutta Annual Register*, 1823 : in 1833, became Surgeon to the 55th N.I. : in 1838-41, went to Kabul with the Army of the Indus, as Superintending Surgeon : returned to Bengal in 1841 : member of the Medical Board, 1845 : retired, 1847 : died Aug. 7, 1852 : published a number of translations from the Persian classics, many of them in verse, including a portion, and an epitome, of the *Shah Nameh* : edited the Persian *Hatim Tai* : contributed publications to the Oriental Translation Fund : e.g. *On the Loves of Laili and Majnun* : wrote, 1842, an illustrated narrative of the expedition into Afghanistan : was also an artist of considerable merit : brought out lithographed *Sketches in Afghanistan*.

AUBER, PETER (1770-1866)

Entered the India House at 16 : rose to be Assistant Secretary, and afterwards Secretary to the E. I. Co., 1829-36 : after 50 years' service, retired in 1836, on a pension of £2000 a year, thus drawing £60,000 as pension. His name stands as the author of two important works, viz., an *Analysis of the Constitution of the E.I. Co. with supplement*, 1826-8 : and *Rise and Progress of British Power in India*, 1837 : but his claim to have written the firstnamed has been disputed : died 1866.

AUCHMUTY, SIR SAMUEL (1756-1822)

General : born in New York, 1756, the grandson of a Scotch settler in Boston : saw service, first as a volunteer, from 1777 in the Army, in N. America : went to India in 1783 in the 52nd regt. : became Adjutant : promoted to Captain in the 75th, in 1788 : was in the campaigns of 1790-1 against Tippoo, and at the first siege of Seringapatam under Lord Cornwallis in 1792 : D.Q.M.G. at Calcutta : Military Secretary to Sir Robert Abercromby (*q.v.*) when C. in C., 1795-7 : in his campaign against the Rohillas : returned to England in 1797 : commanded a force from the Cape to Egypt to co-operate with Sir D. Baird and Sir Ralph Abercromby against the French : Adjutant-General in Egypt : K.C.B. in 1803 : in 1806-7, Brig-General in S. America at Monte Video and Buenos Ayres : Maj-General in 1808 : went out to Madras as C. in C., May, 1810 : in 1811 took Java and Batavia, and defeated the Dutch at Cornelis and Samarang : left Madras for England in March, 1813 : Lt-General : G.C.B., 1815 : C. in C., and Privy Councillor in Ireland, 1821 : died Aug. 11, 1822.

AUCKLAND, GEORGE EDEN, EARL OF (1784-1849)

Governor General : second son of the first Lord Auckland : born Aug. 25, 1784 : educated at Christ Church, Oxford : called to the bar, 1809 : President of the Board of Trade and Master of the Mint, 1833 : First Lord of the Admiralty, 1834-35 : G.C.B. : appointed Governor-General of India, April 4, 1836. In 1836-7 he sent Burnes (*q.v.*) on a mission to Kabul : in distrust of the Amir, Dost Muhammad, who received in 1837 the Russian officer, Vitkievitch, at Kabul, and with a view to counteract Russian influence there, Auckland, under pressure of the English Government, decided to dethrone Dost Muhammad (*q.v.*) and reinstate Shah Shuja (*q.v.*) as Amir : his declaration of war was issued on Oct. 1, 1838 : the facts of the first Afghan War are well known : Dost Muhammad fled in Aug., 1839 : Shah Shuja, though set up in 1839, and supported till 1841, was unpopular as a ruler : the British force was reduced : the subsidies were diminished : the Afghans rose in 1841 : Sir A. Burnes was murdered on Nov. 2, 1841, and the envoy, Sir W. Macnaghten on Dec. 23, : the British army was destroyed in its retreat from Kabul to the Khyber. Lord Auckland was made an Earl in 1839, on the capture of Kabul : he had left India on March 12, 1842, before Pollock's avenging Army had advanced beyond Jalalabad. Afghan affairs chiefly engaged Auckland's attention. In 1840 the British Resident at Ava was expelled by the King of Burma and not re-established. Auckland was again First Lord of the Admiralty in 1846 : died Jan. 1, 1849.

AUFRECHT, THEODOR (1822-   )

Born Jan. 7, 1822, at Leschnitz in Silesia : educated at the College of Oppeln : studied Sanskrit and Philology at Berlin, and later the ancient languages of Northern Europe : Privat-docent at Berlin University, 1850 : went to England, 1852, to study Sanskrit : Professor of Sanskrit and Philology at Edinburgh University, 1862 : Professor of Philology at Bonn, 1875-89 : now Professor of the Comparative Study of Languages at Bonn : Lèvi calls him the " illustrious veteran of Indian studies " : he is especially noted for his catalogues of Sanskrit MSS. : among his works may be mentioned : *De accentu compositorum Sanskriticorum,* 1847 : *Halayudha's Abhidhanaratnamata,* 1861 : *Die Hymnen des Rigweda,* 1877 : *Blüten aus Hindostan,* 1873 : *Das Aitareya Brahmana,* 1879 : his catalogues of Sanskrit MSS., at the Bodleian Library (1859-64), and at Cambridge (1869) : *Catalogus catalogorum,* a register of Sanskrit works and authors, 1891-3 : and *Katalog der Sanskrit Handschriften der Universitäts-Bibliothek zu Leipzig,* 1901.

AUSTEN, CHARLES JOHN (1779-1852)

Son of Rev. George Austen, and brother of Miss Austen : entered the Navy early : served against the Dutch and French, and on a number of stations : at the bombardment of Acre, 1840, for which he was made C.B. : Rear Admiral, 1846 : Naval C. in C. of the E. India station, 1850 : in the second Burmese war, died of cholera at Prome, Sep. 29, 1852.

AUSTEN, SIR FRANCIS WILLIAM (1774-1865)

Brother of Jane Austen, the novelist : born April 23, 1774 : educated at the Royal Naval Academy : entered the Navy in 1788 : was on the East India station, in the *Perseverance,* from 1788 to 1801, and again from 1807 to 1809 in the *St. Albans,* 64 guns : his services were rewarded by the E. I. Co : served also in the North Sea, Baltic and West Indies : Admiral of the Fleet, 1863 : K.C.B., 1837 : G.C.B., 1860 : died Aug. 10, 1865.

AUSTIN, CHARLES SUMNER (1837-1903)

Educated at Merchant Taylors' school, and St. John's College, Oxford : Senior Fellow : edited the *Madras Times* and afterwards the *Athenæum* and *Daily News* of Madras : Correspondent of the London *Times* during the siege of Paris and the Commune, 1870 : also in the Ashanti war, and at Simla, and in the S. States of America : a brilliant and very vivid writer : Dr. : died May 2, 1903.

AVITABILE, PAOLO DI BARTO-LOMEO (1791-after 1845)

General : a Neapolitan : born Oct. 25 1791 : served in the Neapolitan forces, 1807-9 : and in the Artillery under King Joseph Buonaparte and Murat in the Imperial Army : left Italy, and went, *via* Constantinople, to Persia, 1820 : after 6 years there, joined Ranjit Singh in the Panjab : made Governor of Wazirabad, and of Peshawar in 1834 : ruled by fear and severity and with success : gave great assistance to General Pollock and the Army of Retribution, 1842 : left Peshawar, 1843, took refuge at Jalalabad and in India and returned to Europe : received a sword from the Court of Directors : a General in the French Army : died in a few years near Naples.

AWDRY, SIR JOHN WITHER (1795-1878)

Born 1795 : educated at Winchester and Christ Church, Oxford : Fellow of Oriel : called to the bar from the Middle Temple in 1822 : after being Puisne Judge of the Bombay Supreme Court, from 1830, was Chief Justice, 1839-42 : knighted 1830 : D.C.L. of Oxford, 1844 : one of the Commissioners of Oxford University : died June, 1878.

AYLMER, FENTON JOHN (1862-   )

Born April 5, 1862 : son of Captain F. J. Aylmer, 97th regt. : educated privately and at R.M.A., Woolwich : entered the Royal Engineers, 1880 : served in India since 1883 : in the Burma war, 1886-87 : the Hazara expedition

1891 : in the Hunza expedition, 1891-2 : Isazai expedition, 1892 : Chitral expedition, 1895 : at the storming of the Nilt Fort in 1891-2 : he obtained his V.C., and Brevet Majority : Colonel R.E.

AYLMER, HON. ROSE WHITWORTH
(1779–1800)

Born Oct., 1779 : only daughter of Henry, fourth Baron Aylmer, and his wife Catherine, who was sister to Lord Whitworth, Ambassador to Buonaparte in 1803. Walter Savage Landor wrote verses to her at Swansea about 1796-7, and she lent him the book which suggested the subject of his poem " Gebir." She went to India in 1878 with her aunt (*née* Whitworth) wife of Sir Henry Russell (*q.v.*), Puisne judge, afterwards Chief Justice of Bengal, and became engaged to Sir Henry's son, afterwards second Baronet, but died of cholera on March 2, 1800, at her uncle's house in Calcutta. Landor's elegy on her death was published in 1806. She was buried in the cemetery in South Park Street, Calcutta, the inscription on her tomb being taken from Young's *Night Thoughts*, iii. 70.

AYRTON, ACTON SMEE (1816-1886)

Born 1816 : son of Frederick Ayrton, barrister at Bombay : practised as a solicitor at Bombay, 1836-50, when he returned to England : Chairman of the Board of Directors of the Great Indian Peninsular Railway : called to the bar from the Middle Temple, 1853 : M.P. for the Tower Hamlets, 1857-74 : Parliamentary Secretary to the Treasury in Gladstone's Administration, 1868-9 : Privy Councillor : First Commissioner of Works, 1869-73 : Judge Advocate General, 1873-4 : defeated in his candidatures for the Tower Hamlets, 1874, and for the Mile End Division, 1885 : died Nov. 30, 1886.

AYUB KHAN, (1849–   )

Fourth son of Shir Ali, Amir of Afghanistan, brother of Yakub Khan (*q.v.*) : was long a fugitive in Persia, but was appointed Governor of Herat by Yakub in 1879 : he advanced thence upon Kandahar in July, 1880, and at Maiwand, on the 27th, defeated General Burrows and his force : besieged Kandahar : on Sep. 1. he fought the battle of Kandahar against Sir F. Roberts (*q.v.*), who had marched

thither from Kabul, and was routed, fleeing towards Herat : in July, 1881, he defeated Amir Abdur Rahman's troops and captured Kandahar, but, being defeated there by the Amir, fled to Persia, where he was made a prisoner of state : he escaped and tried to cross the Afghan frontier in 1887, but was repulsed, and surrendered to the British Agent at Mashad : eventually he was made over to the Government of India and interned in India, being kept at Rawul Pindi.

BABA, SIR KHEM SINGH BEDA
(1830–   )

Fourteenth in direct descent from Sikh Guru, the great reformer : Member of Legislative Council of the Panjab for two years : K.C.I.E.

BADCOCK, SIR ALEXANDER ROBERT (1844–   )

Born Jan. 11, 1844 : educated at Elstree and Harrow : entered the Indian Army, 1861 : served in the Bhutan Campaign, 1864-5 : Hazara, 1868 : Perak, 1875-6 : Afghanistan, 1878–80, in the Commissariat Department : at the Peiwar Kotal, and in the engagements at Kabul : Chief Commissariat officer of Sir F. Roberts' force on the Kabul-Kandahar march in Aug. 1880, and in the battle of Kandahar : made C.B. : was Q.M.G. in India, 1900 : C.S.I. : K.C.B. in 1902 : Member of the Council of India in 1901.

BADEN POWELL, BADEN HENRY
(1841-1901)

I.C.S. : born 1841 : son of Professor Baden Powell of Oxford : educated at St. Paul's School : in the Civil Service in the Panjab, 1861-89 : served in the Indian Forest Department : was an authority on Indian land tenures : for some years a Judge of the Chief Court of the Panjab : wrote *Land Systems of British India, The Indian Village Community* : helped to establish the Lahore University : M.A. Oxford, 1894 : C.I.E. : died Jan. 2, 1901.

BADGER, REV. GEORGE PERCY
(1815-1888)

Born in April, 1815 : spent his youth at Malta, and 1835-36 at Bairut to learn Arabic : ordained in 1841 : for his knowledge of the East and of Arabic was sent as a delegate to the Eastern Churches, including the Nestorians, in Kurdistan, 1842-5 and 1850 : appointed a Chaplain under the Bombay Government, 1845 : his knowledge of Arabic was utilised at Aden and under Outram in the Persian expedition of 1856-7 : in 1860 he helped to settle the troubles in Oman : was Secretary to Sir Bartle Frere's mission to Zanzibar, 1872 : D.C.L. in 1873 : died Feb. 21, 1888 : wrote *The Nestorians and their Rituals, A History of the Imaums and Sayyids of Oman*, 1871 : on *Muhammad and Muhammadanism* : and an *English-Arabic Lexicon*, besides other works : F.Z.S. : F.S.A.

BAIGRIE, ROBERT (? -1877)

Colonel : son of John Baigrie : joined the E. I. Co.'s Bombay Infantry, 1848 : served in the Panjab campaign, 1848-9 : at Multan, Gujarat, the pursuit and surrender of the Sikhs, the occupation of Peshawar : at the siege of Sebastopol, 1855 : in the Persian war, 1856-7 : at the Khushab, Muhamra, Ahwaz : in Sir H. Rose's force in the mutiny : Bombay Staff Corps, 1861 : A.Q.M.G. at Mhow, 1865 : and in Abyssinia, 1867-8 : Brevet Lt-Colonel : Q.M.G. of the Bombay Army : C.B., 1873 : died at Poona, Sep. 25, 1877 : an accomplished artist.

BAILEY, REV. BENJAMIN (1791-1871)

Missionary for 40 years in Travancore : distinguished as a linguist and botanist, and author of a Malayalam dictionary : died, 1871.

BAILLIE, JOHN (1772-1833)

Lt-Colonel : younger son of George Baillie, of Leys Castle, Inverness : entered the service of the E.I. Co. in 1791 : took part in the military operations of the Mahratta war, 1803 : but his principal services in India were political : as Political Agent, 1803-7, he succeeded, under great difficulties, in establishing British authority in Bundelkund, and in transferring to the Company a large and valuable territory : for his services, he was appointed Resident at Lucknow, 1807-15, he established the celebrated " Guard " or " Gate," which still bears his name at Lucknow : after leaving India, he was appointed, 1823, a Director of the E.I. Co. : M.P. for Hendon in 1820 : and in 1830 for the Burghs of Inverness,

in which town is his portrait by Raeburn : died in London, April 20, 1833. From the commencement of his career, Baillie was a devoted student of Oriental languages, and was the first Professor of Arabic and Persian, when the College of Fort William was instituted in 1801 : published several important works, and made a large and choice collection of oriental works, at his house in Inverness, which was presented by his heirs to the University of Edinburgh. A *Digest of Mohummudan Law*, which he left unfinished, was completed and greatly enlarged by his son, Neil B. E. Baillie, (1799-1883), an Indian Jurist of some eminence : it is still a standard work of reference.

BAILLIE, WILLIAM (? -1782)

Entered the E.I. Co.'s service in the Madras N. I., 1759 : Lt-Colonel, 1775 : served against Hyder Ali, 1767-8 : held a command at Pondicherry, 1779, against the French : and in the Guntur Sircars in 1780 : defeated, in 1780, a portion of Hyder Ali's invading army under Tippoo near Perambakam : was unable to join Sir Hector Munro's army, but, on receipt of small reinforcements, advanced from Polilore to do so : was attacked by Hyder's force and overwhelmed, Sep. 10, 1780 : severely wounded and captured : with the few survivors was kept prisoner at Seringapatam, generally in chains : died in captivity, Nov. 13, 1782.

BAIRD, SIR DAVID, BARONET (1757-1829)

General : son of William Baird, of Newbyth : born Dec., 1757 : entered the Army in the 2nd foot, in 1772 : came to England from Gibraltar in 1776 : went to India in the 73rd in 1779-80 : was in Colonel Baillie's force which was overwhelmed by Hyder Ali at Perambakam, Sep. 10, 1780 : was imprisoned by Hyder Ali at Seringapatam for 3½ years, and released at the Treaty of Mangalore in 1784. His mother, knowing his intractable temper, remarked, on hearing of his imprisonment, that " she pitied the man who was chained to our Davie." He commanded a Brigade, and served under Lord Cornwallis at the capture of Savandrug in 1791, and at Seringapatam in 1792 : in 1793 he took Pondicherry : commanded a Brigade at the Cape of Good Hope in 1797, and, returning to India in 1798, as Maj-General, led the storming party at the siege of Seringapatam on May 4, 1799, after which he considered himself slighted at Colonel Arthur Wellesley (afterwards Duke of Wellington, (*q.v.*) being placed in command at Seringapatam : commanded the Dinapur Brigade, 1800 : led an expedition to Egypt down the Nile in 1801, to co-operate with the British army, and was at the capture of Alexandria : led back the Egyptian Indian army, 1802 : in 1802 he commanded a Division of the Madras Army, but, when again placed under General A. Wellesley for the Mahratta war, resigned and returned to, England, being captured on the voyage by the French : was knighted and became Lt-General : in 1805–6 was sent to retake the Cape of Good Hope from the Dutch : served at Copenhagen, and in Spain, in 1808, losing an arm at Corunna : was made K.B., 1809, and a Baronet, and General in 1814 : G.C.B., 1815 : C. in C. in Ireland, in 1820 : Governor of Fort George, 1829 : died in Perthshire, Aug. 18, 1829.

BAKER, EDWARD NORMAN
(1857–   )

I.C.S. : educated at Christ's College, Finchley : went out to Bengal in the Civil Service, 1878 : Under Secretary to the Governor of Bengal, and to the Government of India, Finance Department, 1885 : Deputy Secretary, 1892–5 : Secretary, 1902–5 : Financial Secretary to the Government of Bengal and Member of Bengal Legislative Council, 1898–1902 : Financial Member of the Supreme Council, 1905 : C.S.I., 1900.

BAKER, SIR THOMAS DURAND (1837–1893

Son of Rev. John Durand Baker, Vicar of Bishop's Pawton, Devon : born March 23, 1837 : educated at Cheltenham : entered the 18th Royal Irish regt., 1854 : served in the Crimea, 1854–6 : in the Indian mutiny was with the Central India Field Force : passed the Staff College, 1862 : in the New Zealand war, 1863–67 : was Assistant Adjutant and Q.M.G. in Ashanti Expedition, 1873–4, and Chief of the Staff : C.B. : A.D.C. to the Queen : attached to the Russian Army during the Russo-Turkish war, 1877 : Military Secretary to Lord Lytton, Viceroy of India, 1878 : in 1879, commanded a Brigade

under Lord Roberts, through the Kuram to Kabul, commanded at Charasia Oct. 6, 1879, and was engaged in many of the fights near Kabul : was in Lord Roberts' Kabul-Kandahar march, Aug., 1880, and the battle of Kandahar : K.C.B. 1881 : in the Boer War 1881 as Brig-General : in 1884 was Adjutant-General in India : in the Burmese expedition, 1886–7 : commanded a Division in Bengal, 1887–90 : Q.M.G. of the Army, 1890 : Lt-General, 1891 : died at Pau, Feb. 9 1893.

BAKER, SIR WILLIAM ERSKINE
(1808–1881)

Son of Capt. Joseph Baker, R.N. : born Nov. 29, 1808 : educated at Ludlow and Addiscombe : joined the Bengal Engineers 1826 : to India, 1828 : employed in canal work : led an attacking column in the battle of Sobraon, in the Sikh war of 1845–6 : rendered excellent service in the P.W.D., as Superintending Engineer of the Delhi canals, and of the Sind canals and forests, Director of the Ganges canal, and Consulting Engineer for Railways : Secretary to the Government of India in the P.W.D., 1854–5 : Colonel, 1857 : in 1858 was made Military Secretary at the India Office : Member of the Council of India, 1861–1875 : K.C.B., 1870 : General, 1877 : died at Barnwell, Somersetshire, Dec. 16, 1881.

BALFOUR, EDWARD GREEN (1813–1889)

Doctor and author : son of Capt. George Balfour, and nephew of Joseph Hume, M.P. : born Sep. 6, 1813 : educated at Montrose, and Edinburgh University : in 1839 went to India in the Medical Department, serving in both the Bombay and Madras Armies : became full Surgeon in 1852 : wrote medical papers on subjects relating to the health of the troops, and besides his profession did much useful work : studied Oriental languages, and founded the Muhammadan public library at Madras : established, in 1850, a Government Central Museum, and was Superintendent for 9 years : published an Encyclopædia of India, which went through several editions : and commenced the Mysore Museum, 1866 : was Political Agent with the Nawab of the Carnatic for years : as Deputy Inspr-General of Hospitals, 1862–1870, he served in the stations under the Madras command, and as Surgeon-General, Madras, 1871–76, paid much attention to female medical education, for which the Madras Medical College was thrown open : Fellow of the Madras University : retired in 1876, and died Dec. 8, 1889.

BALFOUR, FRANCIS (before 1769– after 1807)

M.D. at Edinburgh : entered the E.I. Co.'s medical service in Bengal, 1769 : and retired, 1807, to Edinburgh : was an intimate friend of Warren Hastings, dedicated a book to him, and corresponded with him from Benares : he wrote *The Forms of Herkern, a Persian Letter-writer* and contributed papers on Oriental subjects to the Asiatic Society of Bengal, besides writing medical works.

BALFOUR, SIR GEORGE (1809–1894)

Born 1809 : son of Capt. George Balfour : brother of E. G. Balfour (*q.v.*) : educated at Eddiscombe : joined the Madras Artillery, 1825, the Royal Artillery, 1826 : served in the Malacca campaign, 1832–33 : in China with the Madras force, 1840–2 : and was Colonel at Shanghai from 1843 for some years : on the Madras Military Board 1849–57, and Inspr-General of Ordnance : C.B., 1854 : on the Military Finance Commission of 1859–60, and Head of the Military Finance Department, 1860–62, doing valuable work in these appointments : in England, employed on the Recruiting Commission, 1866 and 1868–70 : as Assistant to the Controller in Chief at the War Office, 1868–71 : K.C.B., 1871 : M.P. Kincardineshire, 1872–1892 : became a General in 1877 : died, March 12, 1894 : his wife was a daughter of Joseph Hume, M.P.

BALL, GEORGE (1761–1811)

Colonel : served in Lord Lake's campaign, and described as a very meritorious and distinguished officer : died when Adjutant-General of the Bengal Army, Dec. 8, 1811 : buried at Calcutta.

BALL, VALENTINE (? –1895)

Doctor : in the Geological Survey of India for 17 years : Treasurer of the Asiatic Society of Bengal, 1881 : contributed papers on the Geology of the Nicobar Islands and of the vicinity of Port Blair : Professor of Geology at Dublin : F.R.S. :

Director of the National Museum, Dublin, 1883 : died June 15, 1895 : wrote valuable works on geology and jungle life in India : edited, in 1889, *J. B. Tavernier's Travels in India*, 1676 : C.B.

BALLANTYNE, JAMES ROBERT (1813–1864)

Born Dec. 13, 1813 : educated at Kelso, Edinburgh New Academy and College : studied Oriental languages : taught them at the Naval and Military Academy, Edinburgh, 1839 : in India was Principal of the College at Benares, 1845–61 : became Librarian of the India Office : while in India studied the highest Sanskrit ethical and philosophical literature : published Sanskrit works and lectures on systems of Indian philosophy, also papers on Hindu philosophy and logic : wrote a Hindustani grammar and selections : and a Mahratti grammar : LL.D. : died Feb. 16, 1864.

BALLARD, JOHN ARCHIBALD (1830–1880)

Born June 20, 1830 : son of a Calcutta merchant : educated at Addiscombe : joined the Bombay Engineers in 1850 : on his way to England in 1854, he went to Constantinople, and joined the Turkish Army, as Lt-Colonel, at the siege of Silistria by the Russians, and in the attack on the Russians at Giurgevo : in the Crimean campaign, including the siege of Sebastopol, the operations at Eupatoria and the occupation of Kertch : he also commanded a Turkish Brigade in Omar Pasha's campaign in Mingrelia : was conspicuous for his cool bravery in action : C.B., 1856 : served as A.Q.M.G. in the Persian war of 1856–7, and in the same capacity in the Indian mutiny in the Rajputana Field Force : was Mint-master at Bombay, 1861, and Chairman of the Bombay Port Trust : retired at end of 1878 as Lt-General : wrote articles for *Blackwood's Magazine*, on Indian subjects : LL.D. of Edinburgh : he died near the battlefield of Thermopylæ April 2, 1880.

BALRAMPUR, MAHARAJA, SIR DRIGBIJAI SINGH, of (1818–1882)

Son of Raja Arjun Singh : descendant of a long line of chieftains of the Janwar clan of Rajputs : succeeded his brother Raja Jai Narain Singh, in 1836 : spent his early years fighting with his neighbours, the Pathans of Utraula and the Chauhan Rajas of Tulsipur, also with the Oudh revenue officials : driven out of Balrampur by Raja Darshan Singh, who pursued him into Nipal territory : restored to his Raj : distinguished himself in the mutiny as one of the five loyal talukdars : received the fugitives from Sikraura and Gonda, 19 persons, and several children : sheltered and escorted them to Gorakhpur : remained faithful, and was proscribed by the rebels : joined the advancing British forces and remained in the field till the restoration of order : rewarded with the title of Maharaja Bahadur and vast landed estates confiscated from rebels, with a reduced land revenue assessed in perpetuity : in 1866, K.C.S.I. : salute of 9 guns, in 1877 :} Member of the Governor-General's Legislative Council : a great patron of education, instituting schools on his estates before their general introduction elsewhere : founded one of the first hospitals in Oudh outside Lucknow, and a medical school : a noted sportsman : a fall from an elephant hastened his death, which occurred on May 27, 1882.

BANAJI, FRAMJI COWASJI (1767–1851)

Born in Bombay April 3, 1767 : son of Cowasji Byramji (1744–1834) merchant, and of a family which settled in Bombay from near Surat,1690, and traded with England, China and Burma. He was a scientific agriculturist, and improved agriculture in W. India : took a leading part in establishing the Agri-Horticultural Society of Bombay, 1830 : was a Vice-President : the Bombay Government gave him, 1829, some villages in Salsette, where he settled cultivators, and successfully managed the Pawai estate : instituted many charities for the native community : some for the Parsis : made wells and tombs : a large Tower of Silence, 1832 : a Fire Temple, 1845 : a school for Parsi children, for instruction in the Avesta : was a leading member of the Parsi *panchayat*, 1817–51, and an original Trustee of their communal funds from 1823 : was a prominent member of the Native Education Society from 1827, of the Elphinstone College committee from 1835 : Director of the Board of Education from 1841 : was nominated, 1834, one of the first 12 native J.P.s : a Government Director of the Savings' Bank : helped to establish

the old Bombay Bank, 1840 : Director of the G.I.P. Railway, 1844 : suffered pecuniary losses in his business, which curtailed his means, but not his zeal, for philanthropic charity : died Feb. 12, 1851 : after a public meeting of all classes, the Framji Institute was erected in his memory, where public meetings are generally held, and an extensive Library is located.

BANDULA, MENGYEE MAHA (? – 1825)

Burmese Statesman and General : in Oct., 1819, he led a successful expedition against the chief of Manipur : in 1821 he attacked Assam : in 1823, the Burmese invaded British possessions near Chittagong, occupying the island of Shapuri on Sep. 24, 1823 : in March, 1824, Bandula marched to Arakan, attacked an English force at Ramu, near Chittagong, and defeated it : Lord Amherst declared war against the Burmese. On May 11, 1824, the British.Army took Rangoon, but were unable to advance. Bandula was recalled from Arakan and ordered to proceed against the English forces. As C. in C., he approached Rangoon and stockaded his 60,000 men : but was attacked and defeated, Dec., 1824. He retired to Donabew, a strongly defended position, which the British Army under General Campbell reached on April 1, 1825. The siege of the place by the English had just begun when Bandula was killed by a shell from the British.Artillery,and the Burmese army fled.

BANERJEA, DURGAGATI, RAI BAHADUR (1838–1903)

Born Jan. 19, 1838 : member of the Subordinate, and Provincial Executive Service, Bengal : Deputy Magistrate, 1856 : Personal Assistant to the Commissioner of Patna for 15 years : Member of the Salaries Commission, 1885 : Member of the Bengal Legislative Council, 1895 : and of the Calcutta Corporation : Deputy Collector of Calcutta, Superintendent of Excise Revenue and Collector of Stamp Revenue, 1889–1901 : retired, 1901 : C.I.E., 1895 : died March 26, 1903.

BANERJEA, REV. KRISHNA MOHAN (1813–1885)

Born 1813 : son of Jiban Krishna Banerjea, a member of a high caste

Brahman family in Calcutta : educated at the Hindu College : in 1829, became a teacher in the Hare School, Calcutta : came under the influence of Derozio and Dr. Duff, and was converted to Christianity in 1833 : became a teacher in the C.M.S. School in Calcutta, and in 1837 was ordained a clergyman in the Church of England : from 1852 to 1868, was a Professor in Bishop's College, Calcutta : Fellow, 1858, of the Calcutta University : Doctor of Law, 1876 : Examining Chaplain to the Bishop of Calcutta : Examiner in Sanskrit, Hindi, Tamil, and Uriya : M.R.A.S.B., also of the British Indian Association, Calcutta Corporation, and Board of Examiners : was made a C.I.E. : was in his later years regarded by Government as a Head and Leader of the Indian Community : wrote many books and pamphlets, chief among which are *Dialogues on Hindu Philosophy* and *Aryan Witness :* he knew eleven languages well : his name will pass to posterity as a great scholar and linguist : died May 11, 1885.

BANERJI, SIR GURU DAS (1844–   )

Born near Calcutta, Jan. 26, 1844 : educated at the Hare School, Presidency College and Calcutta University : B.A. (1863), M.A. (1864) in Mathematics, gold medal : B.L. (1865) : Law Lecturer at the Berhampur College : began to practise in the High Court in 1872 : Doctor of Law in 1876 : Tagore Law Professor, 1878 : lectured on " Hindu Law of Marriage and Stridhan " : Fellow of the Calcutta University, 1879 : member of the Bengal Legislative Council, 1887 : acted as Judge of the High Court, 1888, confirmed in Jan. 1889 : Vice-Chancellor of the Calcutta University, 1890–3 : member, 1902, of the Indian Universities' Commission : retired in Jan., 1904 : knighted the same year : wrote *A Few Thoughts on Education.*

BANERJI, HEM CHANDRA (1838–1902)

Educated in his village and at the Hindu College, Calcutta : Scholar : entered Government service in the Military Auditor General's office : B.A. : munsif at Howrah and Serampur : practised as a High Court Vakil from 1862, and became Senior Government Pleader : as a Bengali poet he had perhaps no rival in modern Bengal : died 1902.

BANERJI, KALI CHURN (? –   )

Educated at the Calcutta University : M.A. : B.L. : a leading pleader in the Calcutta High Court : member of the Bengal Legislative Council : Registrar of the Calcutta University : President Y.M.C.A., Calcutta : a Brahman convert to Christianity : has taken a prominent part in all social, religious and educational movements of the day.

BANERJI, SURENDRANATH (1848–   )

Second son of Durga Charan Banerji, medical practitioner, Calcutta : born Nov., 1848 : educated at the Doveton College, Calcutta : B.A., 1868 : passed in England the competitive examination for the Indian Civil Service, 1869 : went out to Bengal, 1871 : Assistant Magistrate at Sylhet : ceased to be a member of the Civil Service in March, 1874 : became a Professor of English Literature in the Metropolitan Institution, 1876 : joined the Free Church Institution and Duff College, 1881 : founded the Ripon College, 1882 : proprietor of the weekly *Bengalee* in 1878 : imprisoned for one month in the civil side of the Presidency Jail, 1883, for contempt of court : established the Indian Association, 1876 : represented the Calcutta Corporation in the Bengal Legislative Council, 1893 : President of the 11th meeting of the Indian National Congress at Poona, 1895, of the 18th at Ahmadabad, 1902 : elected a Fellow of the Calcutta University by the Graduates, 1904.

BANKS, JOHN SHERBROOKE (1811–1857)

Major : joined the Indian Army in 1829 : was employed on civil duties for a time, but in 1842 served in Pollock's Kabul force : was in the Military Secretariat : accompanied Lord Dalhousie to Burma, and was on his personal Staff : joined the Oudh Commission and became Commissioner of Lucknow : was in the Residency during the siege, and succeeded Sir Henry Lawrence as Chief Commissioner from the latter's death until his own on July 21, 1857.

BARBOUR, SIR DAVID MILLER (1841–   )

I.C.S. : born 1841 : educated at Queen's College, Belfast : went to India, 1863 : served in Lower Bengal, until he became Under Secretary, Financial Department of the Government of India, 1872 : Accountant General, Bengal : Secretary to Government of Bengal, Revenue Department, 1882 : member of the Bengal Legislative Council, 1882 : Secretary to the Government of India, Financial Department, 1882 : C.S.I., 1887 : Member of the Royal Commission in England on gold and silver, 1886 : Financial Member of the Supreme Council of the Governor General, 1888–1893 : K.C.S.I., 1889 : Member of the Indian Currency Commission, 1898 : K.C.M.G., 1899 : Member and Chairman of several important Royal Commissions and Committees on the currency and finance of other countries, and on questions involving great financial considerations : wrote *The Theory of Bimetallism.*

BARCLAY, GEORGE WALTER WOODFALL (1847–   )

Son of Charles Barclay, Surgeon-General Madras Army : born Aug. 25, 1847: educated at St. Andrews, in Germany, and at Edinburgh University : M.A., 1867 : in the Indian Government Telegraph Department, 1868–71 : editor of the Calcutta *Englishman*, 1872–77 : Fellow of the Calcutta University : left India, 1877 : F.R.S.E., 1883 : J.P. : sometime acting Editor of the *Calcutta Review*, and of *Vanity Fair* : has held various local appointments at Edinburgh.

BARKER, SIR GEORGE ROBERT (1817–1861)

Educated at the R.M.A., Woolwich : entered the Royal Artillery in 1834 : served in the Crimea : became a Colonel : in the Indian mutiny served under Sir Colin Campbell, commanding as Brigadier the siege Artillery at the capture of Lucknow, March, 1858 : commanded a Brigade in subsequent operations : captured Birwa : K.C.B. : died at Simla, July 27, 1861.

BARKER, SIR ROBERT, BARONET (1729 ?–1789)

Served in the Carnatic and Bengal from 1754 : as a Captain accompanied Clive to Calcutta in 1757, commanding the Artillery at Chandernagore and Plassy : returned to Madras, 1758 : served in 1792 in Colonel Draper's expedition from Madras to the Phillippine Islands : knighted in 1763 : raised the 24th N.I. 1876 : Brig-General, 1770, and provincial C. in C., Bengal, in 1773 : in July, 1772, a treaty was signed in his presence between the Nawab Wazir of Oudh and the Rohillas against the Mahrattas : after a quarrel with Warren Hastings he left India : became M.P. for Wallingford : Baronet, 1781 : died Sep. 14, 1789.

BARLOW, SIR GEORGE HILARO, BARONET (1762–1847)

Governor : son of William Barlow, of Bath : joined the Bengal Civil Service in 1778 : when employed, 1788–96, in the Revenue Secretariat, he had to carry out the Permanent Settlement of 1793 in Bengal : was Chief Secretary in 1796 : became Member of the Supreme Council from Oct., 1801, and Vice-President in Council until, on Lord Cornwallis' death on Oct. 5, 1805, he, as provisional Governor-General, acted in that capacity until Lord Minto's arrival on July 31, 1807 : Baronet, 1803 : and K.C.B. : though he had supported Wellesley's policy of extending British power, he continued Cornwallis' policy of neutrality and conciliation towards the Native States, making concessions to Sindia and Holkar, and annulling protective treaties with Chiefs in Rajputana. In 1807 he went to Madras as Governor from Dec. 24 : there he quarrelled with the principal officers of both services : the military combined in a general mutiny, which Barlow suppressed vigorously : he was recalled and made over charge at Madras on May 21, 1813 : G.C.B., 1815 : died in England, Dec. 18, 1846.

BARNARD, SIR HENRY WILLIAM (1799–1857)

Son of the Rev. William Barnard : born in 1799 : was educated at Westminster and Sandhurst : joined the Guards in 1814 : was at the occupation of Paris : served in Jamaica and Canada : in the Crimea : Maj-General : commanded, first a Brigade, and later a Division, and was Chief of the Staff to General Simpson : K.C.B., 1856 : in 1857, went to India as General of the Sirhind Division. Upon General Anson's death at Karnal, Barnard succeeded to the command, and, moving towards Delhi, defeated the rebels at Badli-ka-sarai on June 8 : died of cholera on the ridge at Delhi, July 5, 1857.

BARNES, SIR EDWARD (1776-1838)

Commander-in-Chief : entered the Army in 1792 : Colonel, 1810 : served in the Peninsula, from 1812, commanding a Brigade, and was in several battles : Adjutant - General at Waterloo : severely wounded : K.C.B. : went to Ceylon, 1819 : Governor there from 1824 to 1831 : put down the last outbreaks of the Kandy chiefs there : Lt-General, 1825 : General, 1831, and C. in C. in India, 1831-33 : Colonel, 31st foot : and G.C.B. : became M.P. for Sudbury in 1837 : died March 19, 1838.

BARNES, SIR HUGH SHAKSPEAR (1853-)

I.C.S. : son of James Ralph Barnes, I.C.S. : born 1853 : educated at Malvern : joined the Civil Service, at Allahabad, 1874 : Private Secretary to the Financial Member of Council, 1876 : Political Officer, Kandahar, 1880 : Political Agent, Quetta, 1883 : Under Secretary, Foreign Department, 1889 : Deputy Secretary, 1890 : Revenue Commissioner,' Quetta, 1891 : Resident in Kashmir, 1894 : A.G.G. and Chief Commissioner, Beluchistan, 1896 : Foreign Secretary to the Government of India, 1900-3 : President of Central Committee for the Delhi *Darbar*, 1902-3 : Lieutenant-Governor of Burma, 1903-5 : Member of the Council of India, 1905 : K.C.S.I., 1903 : K.C.V.O., 1903.

BARODA, MALHAR RAO, MAHARAJA GAEKWAR OF (? -1882)

Succeeded his brother, Khandi Rao, in Nov., 1870, as ruler of Baroda : complaints of his misrule having reached Government an inquiry was held in 1873, and time to reform was allowed him : before the time elapsed an attempt was made in 1874 to poison the Resident, Colonel R. Phayre (*q.v.*) : in 1875, the Gaekwar was tried by a mixed Commission : the three British officers found him guilty : the three native members declared the charge not proven : he was then deposed for gross misgovernment, and deported to Madras, where he died in 1882.

BARODA, SIR SAYAJI RAO III MAHARAJA GAEKWAR SHAMSHIR BAHADUR OF (1863-)

Maharaja : born March 10, 1863 : descended from the founders of the Baroda dynasty : adopted on May 27, 1875, by Jamnabai, widow of the Gaekwar Khandi Rao : educated at the Maharaja's School at Baroda : was installed, 1875 : during his minority, there was a Council of Regency under a British officer and Raja Sir Tanjore Madhava Rao K.C.S.I. (*q.v.*) : on Dec. 28, 1881, he was given the administration of the State : made G.C.S.I. in 1887 : an enlightened ruler, and holds advanced views on social questions : he has several times visited Europe.

BARR, SIR DAVID WILLIAM KEITH (1846-)

Born Nov. 29, 1846 : entered . the Army, 1864 : served in the Abyssinian expedition : boundary settlement officer in the Malwa Bhil country : Assistant to the A.G.G. for Central India, 1870 : Political agent at Jodhpur, 1878-9 : in Baghelkund and Rewa : Resident at Gwalior, 1887 : in Kashmir, 1892 : A.G.G. for Central India, 1895 : Resident at Hyderabad, Feb. 24, 1900-March, 1905 : C.S.I. : K.C.S.I, 1903 : Member of the Council of India, 1905.

BARRAS, PAUL FRANCOIS JEAN NICOLAS, COMTE DE (1755-1829)

Chasseur of the French regiment of Pondicherry : taken prisoner at the capture of Pondicherry in 1778 by Sir Hector Munro : at the request of the French Governor, Barras' regiment was permitted to retain its colours : he became a prisoner on parole in Madras and Poonamali : returning to France, he rose to prominence as a Director during the Revolution : he was under orders to return to India, with other commissaires, but they never started : he became Commandant-General of the armies of Paris.

BARROW, SIR EDMUND GEORGE (1852-)

Maj-General : born Jan. 28, 1852 : son of Maj-General Joseph Lyon Barrow, C.B., R.A. : joined the Army, Dec. 1781 : D.A.Q.M.G. : with the Indian Contingent in Egypt, 1882, and in the Intelligence Branch, Bengal, 1885-7 : Assistant Secretary to the Government of India, Military Department, 1887-91 : Deputy Secretary, 1897-1900 : Secretary, 1901-3 : D.A.G. Bengal, 1900 : served in the Afghan War, 1879, Egyptian expedition, 1882,

Tirah campaign, 1897-8 : Chief Staff Officer, China expedition, 1900 : Commanding First Division, Northern Army Corps, 1904.

BARROW, LOUSADA (? -1877)

Joined the Madras cavalry in 1836, and saw constant service, being engaged in the S. Mahratta country in 1844-5, and under Havelock in many actions in the mutiny : in the Alambagh under Outram : present at the siege and capture of Lucknow : Brevets of Major and Lt-Colonel : C.B. in 1858 : Commissioner of Lucknow, 1864 : Maj-General, 1870 : Chief Commissioner of Oudh, Jan.–April, 1871 : died Oct. 1, 1877.

BARTH, MARIE ETIENNE AUGUSTE (1834-)

Born March 22, 1834, at Strasburg : son of Etienne Barth, of the Rhone au Rhin Canal Company : educated at the Collège Royal (now Lycée Impérial) at Strasburg : Professor of Rhetoric and Philosophy at the College at Bouxwiller, 1857-61 : then retired from the public service to devote himself to Indian study : lived first at Strasburg, then at Geneva, (1871-76), and lastly removed to Paris : member of many learned societies : Sociètè Asiatique, 1857 : Academy of Inscriptions, 1893 : Royal Asiatic Society, 1894, etc.: Collaborator in the *Journal Asiatique*, *Revue Critique*, etc. His chief works are: *Les Religions de l'Inde*, 1880 (also translated into English) *Inscriptions Sanskrites du Cambodge*, 1885 : *L'Inde ; Buddhisme, Jainisme, Hindouisme*, 1894, etc. : has published a yearly bulletin of the religions of India in the *Revue de l'Histoire des Religions*, 1885, etc.

BARTHELEMY SAINT-) HILAIRE, JULES (1805-1895)

Born Aug. 19, 1805, in Paris : studied Sanskrit under Eugène Burnouf : early entered public life : attached to the Ministry of Finance, 1825-38 : an editor of the *Globe*, 1825-30 : as a journalist, signed the protest against the July ordinances of Charles X. : became famous as a politician and ardent Republican, and lived through several revolutions : held office several times, as colleague of Victor Cousin in the Ministry of Public Instruction : in 1848, as Secretary of the provisional Government : from 1871, took an active part in public affairs, as member of the National Assembly : Minister of Foreign Affairs in 1880, etc. : yet he was greatest as a scholar, and student of Philosophy : was Professor of Greek and Latin Philosophy at the Collège de France, 1838-52, Member of the Institute, 1839 : in this year, began his study of Sanskrit Philosophy : administrator of the Collège de France, 1849 : accompanied Lesseps on his journey to Egypt, 1855, to explore the Isthmus of Suez. After the death of Eugène Burnouf, Barthelèmy took his place as a writer on Indian matters in the *Journal des Savants :* died Nov. 24, 1895 : best known as a Greek scholar : the great achievement of his life was his translation of Aristotle : also did valuable work as an Indianist : among his publications are *Des Vedas*, 1854 : *Du Bouddhisme*, 1855 : *Le Bouddha et sa religion*, 1866 : *L'Inde Anglaise*, 1887, etc.

BARTOLOMEO, FRA PAOLINO DE SAN, or JOHN PHILIP WERDIN, (1748-1806)

Studied at Prague : joined the Carmelites at Rome and learned Oriental languages : went to the Malabar coast in 1774 : stayed there 14 years, and was appointed Vicar-general and Apostolic visitor : returned to Rome in 1790, to superintend the printing of religious works for the use of Indian missionaries : studied Sanskrit, published a Sanskrit grammar in Tamil in 1790, and wrote largely of his Indian travels and experiences : he died in 1806.

BARWELL, RICHARD (1741-1804)

Son of William Barwell (who was Governor of Bengal in 1748) : born in Calcutta, Oct. 8, 1741, and joined as a " writer " in Bengal under the E.I. Co. in 1758 : made a Member of the Supreme Council under the Regulating Act of 1773, which made Warren Hastings Governor-General, and steadily supported him in Council against Francis, Clavering, and Monson : fought a duel with Clavering in April, 1775 : resigned his seat in Council on Oct. 1, 1781, retiring with a large fortune, reported to have been irregularly acquired : he appears to have had two houses in Calcutta, one at the present

"Writers' Buildings," the other "Kidder-pur House" in Alipur: M.P. for St. Ives and Winchester, and died Sep. 2, 1804. The story is told of him, as illustrative of the luxurious living of those days, that he said "bring more curricles." The *Echoes from Old Calcutta* by Dr. Busteed contains a picture of Barwell and some account of his life and character.

BASEVI, JAMES PALLADIS (? – 1871)

Son of the architect, George Basevi: was educated at Rugby, Cheltenham and Addiscombe: went to India in the E.I. Co.'s Engineers, 1851: joined the P.W.D. in Bengal: was transferred in 1856 to the Great Trigonometrical Survey, and did valuable work, especially in the principal triangulation: he also did good service in reconnaissances in the Mahsud-Waziri expedition, 1860, and in the wild tracts of Jaipur and Bustar on the east coast, 1862: Captain, R.E.: in 1864, he was selected specially to conduct some highly scientific investigations proposed by the Royal Society, for the determination of gravity at certain stations of the great meridional arc of triangles extending from Cape Comorin to the Himalayas, by pendulum observations, which lasted some years, and necessitated exposure at high altitudes. He crossed Kashmir and Ladak and travelled through the Chanch-enmo valley to the Chinese frontier to make observations at above 16,000 feet: he burst a blood-vessel, and died July 17, 1871, "a martyr to his love of science," an officer "of sterling worth and excellent abilities."

BATEMAN-CHAMPAIN, SIR JOHN UNDERWOOD (1835–1887)

Son of Colonel Agnew Champain: born July 22, 1835: educated at Cheltenham, the Edinburgh Military Academy, and Addiscombe: went to India in the Bengal Engineers, 1854: in the mutiny was in the action of Badli-ka-sarai on June 8, 1857, and at the siege and capture of Delhi: was in several other engagements: at the capture of Lucknow in March, 1858, by Sir Colin Campbell: at the taking of Jagdishpur: in 1862 he went to Persia in connection with the Government telegraph system: in 1865, became Assistant to the Director of the Indo-European Telegraph Department, and in 1870 be-

came himself the Director : took the additional name of Bateman : to complete and maintain the through telegraphic communication, he had to travel constantly to Persia, the Persian Gulf, Turkey, Russia and India : in 1869 he narrowly escaped drowning in the wreck of the P. and O. S.S. *Carnatic:* he was made K.C.M.G. Dec. 31, 1885 : was on the Councils of the Royal Geographical Society and of the Society of Telegraph Engineers : died Feb. 1, 1887.

BATH, THOMAS HENRY THYNNE FIFTH MARQUIS OF (1862–)

Born July 16, 1862 : son of the 4th Marquis : educated at Eton and Balliol College, Oxford : Private Secretary to the Earl of Iddesleigh, First Lord of the Treasury, 1886–7 : Assistant Private Secretary to the Chancellor of the Exchequer, Lord Goschen : M.P. for Frome, 1886–92, and 1895–6 : succeeded his father in the peerage, 1896 : Lord Lieutenant of Somerset : Under Secretary of State for India, 1905.

BAYLEY, CHARLES STUART (1854–)

I.C.S. : son of Capt. Daniel Bayley, Bengal Cavalry : and grandson of W. B Bayley (*q.v.*) : educated at Harrow and Heidelberg : entered the Indian Civil Service, 1877 : Political Agent in Bikanir : General Superintendent for suppressing of Thagi and Dakaiti : Agent to the Governor-General, Central India : C.S.I. Resident at Hyderabad, 1905.

BAYLEY, SIR EDWARD CLIVE (1821– 1884)

I.C.S. : son of E. Clive Bayley : born Oct., 1821 : educated at Haileybury : went to India in 1842 : served in the N.W.P., and the Panjab : Under Secretary in the Foreign Department in 1849 : called to the bar at the Middle Temple in 1857 : in the mutiny, was Under Secretary to Sir J. P. Grant when temporary Lieutenant-Governor of the "Central" Provinces : Magte. of Allahabad : was for a short time Foreign Secretary in 1861 : Home Secretary to the Government of India, 1862–72, and Member of the Supreme Council, 1873–78 : K.C.S.I. in 1877 : and C.I.E. : Vice-Chancellor of the Calcutta University, 1869–74, five times President of the

Asiatic Society of Bengal, and Vice-President of the Royal Asiatic Society for 3 years : died April 30, 1884 : made considerable contributions to Indian history, numismatics, antiquities, and archæology by his papers for the Asiatic Societies and other writings.

BAYLEY, SIR STEUART COLVIN
(1836-   )

I.C.S. : born Aug. 26, 1836 : the youngest son of W. Butterworth B. (*q.v.*): educated at Eton and Haileybury : arrived in India, March, 1856 : held minor appointments in Bengal : was Commissioner of Patna during the Bihar famine of 1874 : C.S.I., 1875 : Secretary to the Government of Bengal, 1877 : Additional Secretary to the Government of India, 1877 : Personal Assistant to the Viceroy (Lord Lytton) for famine affairs, 1877 : K.C.S.I., 1878 : Home Secretary, 1878 : Chief Commissioner of Assam, 1878-80 : Resident at Hyderabad, 1881-2 : C.I.E., 1881 : Member of the Supreme Council, 1882-7 : Lieutenant-Governor of Bengal from July to Dec., 1879,and from 1887-90 ; on leaving India he became Secretary in the Political Department at the India Office, 1890-95 : Member of the Council of India, 1895.

BAYLEY, WILLIAM BUTTERWORTH
(1782-1860)

I.C.S. : son of Thomas Butterworth Bayley : educated at Eton and Cambridge : went to India in 1799 : served in 1803 in the " Governor-General's Office," in the brilliant circle under Lord Wellesley : Registrar of the *Sadr* Court, 1807 : Judge of Burdwan and other places : in 1814 Secretary in the Judicial and Revenue Department, and in 1819 Chief Secretary to the Government : temporary Member of the Supreme Council from July to Dec., 1822, and substantively from 1825 to 1830 : then he retired : he officiated as Governor-General from March to July, 1828, between Lord Amherst and Lord W. Bentinck : President of the Board of Trade, 1830 : Vice-President and Depy. Governor of Bengal : in 1833 he became a Director of the E. I. Co., and Chairman of the Court in 1840 : retired 1858 : he died May 29, 1860. Kaye writes of his high official reputation, adding that " his unfailing kindness of heart and suavity of manner

endeared him to all who had the privilege of coming within the reach of their genial influences."

BAYLY, ALFRED WILLIAM LAMBART
(1856-   )

Educated at Wellington : joined 108th regt., 1874 : Bombay Staff Corps, 1879 : Staff College, 1893 : D.A.A. and Q.M.G : Burma expedition, 1886-87 : Afghan war, 1880-81 : Soudan, 1885 : Burma, 1886-87: South Africa, 1899-1900 : Colonel, C.B. D.S.O.

BEADON, SIR CECIL (1816-1880)

I.C.S. : son of Richard Beadon, grandson of Dr. Beadon, Bishop of Bath and Wells : born in 1816 : educated at Eton and Haileybury : went out to Bengal in 1836 : Under Secretary to the Bengal Government in 1843 : Secretary to the Board of Revenue, 1847 : Member of the Commission on the Indian postal system : Secretary to the Government of Bengal, 1852 : Home Secretary to the Government of India, 1854 : Foreign Secretary, 1859 : Member of the Supreme Council 1860-2, and Lieutenant Governor of Bengal,April, 1862, to April, 1867. During this period the mission, which met with insults, was sent to Bhutan in 1864 : and the Orissa famine of 1866-7 occurred : for the latter, Beadon was much blamed and, on an official inquiry, his famine administration was severely censured : always sanguine, he had failed to estimate adequately the signs of distress and the local conditions : and he suffered from ill-health : his general administration showed marked ability : K.C.S.I. in May, 1866 : died July 18, 1880.

BEALE, THOMAS WILLIAM (? - 1875)

A clerk in the office of the Board of Revenue, N.W.P. : a learned scholar, who assisted Sir H. M. Elliot in his work on the Muhammadans in India : he wrote the *Miftah-ul-Tawarikh*, and an Oriental Biographical Dictionary : died at a great age, at Agra, 1875.

BEAMES, JOHN (1837-1902)

I.C.S : born June 21, 1837 : son of Rev. Thomas Beames : educated at Merchant Taylors' School and at Haileybury, 1856-7 : went to India, 1858 : served in the Panjab, 1859-61 : afterwards, in Lower Bengal, Commissioner of various Divisions and Member of the Board of Revenue : retired, 1893 : an Oriental scholar : wrote in the *J.A.S.B* : and in the *Indian Antiquary* : also *Outlines of Indian Philology*, 1867 : edited Sir H. Elliot's *Supplemental Glossary of Indian Terms*, 1869 : his chief work was *A Comparative Grammar of the Aryan Languages*, 1872-9 : and a Bengali Grammar, 1891 : wrote in the Imperial, and Asiatic Quarterly Reviews : died May 42, 1902.

BEATSON, GEORGE STEWARD (? - 1874)

M.D. Glasgow, 1836 : entered the Army Medical Department, 1838 ; served in Ceylon, 1839-51 : in the Burmese war of 1852 : the Crimea, Ionian Islands, Madras : Surgeon-General in India and P.M.O. of European troops, 1863-8, and again, 1871-4 : was in charge of Netley Hospital 1868-71 : Honorary Physician to the Queen : C.B. 1869 : died at Simla, June 7, 1874.

BEATSON, STUART BROWNLOW (1854-   )

Born July 11, 1854 : son of Capt. W. S. Beatson, of the H.E.I.C.S : educated at Wellington : joined the Indian Army, 1873 : served on N.W. Frontier, 1878, in Afghanistan, 1878-80 : Egypt, 1882 : N.W. Frontier, 1897-98 : South Africa, 1901 : Inspr-General of Imperial Service Troops : Colonel and C.B.

BEATSON, WILLIAM FERGUSON (1804-1872)

General : son of Captain Robert Beatson, R.E : entered the Bengal Army in 1820 : served, while on furlough, with the British Legion in Spain, 1835-6 : at the capture of Jigni in Bundelkund, 1840 : Chirgong, 1841 : in the Sind compaign, 1844 : served under Sir C. Napier, 1845, in the Bugti hills : commanded the Nizam's cavalry : took Rymow from the Rohillas in 1848 : organised the Bashi-bazouks in the Crimean campaign, 1854-5 : in the mutiny, raised two regiments of cavalry, named, "Beatson's Horse" : commanded the Allahabad Division, 1866, and the Umbala Division, 1869 : died Feb. 4, 1872.

BECHER, SIR ARTHUR MITFORD (1816-1887)

General : son of Colonel G. Becher :

educated at Addiscombe : was in the Afghan war, 1839 : at Ghazni : in the Satlaj campaign, 1845-6 : at Mudki, Firozshahr, Sobraon : Brevet - Major : A.D.C. to the Governor-General : in the Panjab campaign, 1848-9 : at the siege and capture of Multan, and at Gujarat : Q.M.G. in India, 1852-63 : severely wounded at the siege of Delhi, 1857 : C.B., 1858 : Bengal Staff Corps : commanded the Sirhind Division, 1865-9 : Maj-General, 1861 : died Oct, 5. 1887.

BECHER, JOHN REID (1819-1884)

General : son of Colonel John Becher, of the Bengal Cavalry : born 1819 : educated at Bruce Castle, Tunbridge Wells, and Addiscombe : went to India in the Bengal Engineers in 1839 : from Firozpur with Wild's Brigade, to relieve Ali Masjid in Jan. 1842, and on with General Pollock's advance to Kabul : in Satlaj campaign, at Sobraon, Feb. 10, 1846, severely wounded : engaged in Rajputana boundary settlements, 1847, and on land inquiries in the Panjab : Deputy Secretary to the Panjab Board of Administration : Deputy Commissioner of Hazara, 1853-9 : C.B : in Sydney Cotton's expedition of 1858 against the Sitana fanatics : Commissioner of the Derajat, 1862 : and of Peshawar, 1864 : retired in 1866 : died July 9, 1884 : one of the distinguished group of officers employed in the Panjab under the Lawrences in the early days after its annexation in 1849 : " of all prominent Panjab officials there was certainly none more loved and respected than Becher."

BECHER, RICHARD (? -1782)

Related to Anne Becher, mother of W. M. Thackeray the novelist : went out to Calcutta as a writer in the E. I. Co.'s service, 1743 : in 1756 was Fourth in the Bengal Council and Chief of Dacca : when Calcutta was taken by Suraj-ud-daula, Becher with his family escaped from the city, with others : returning, 1757, when Calcutta was retaken by the English. In 1761 Becher was dismissed from the Company's service for having signed Clive's independent letter of remonstrance to the Directors two years before. Six years later, 1767, when Clive was Governor of Bengal, Becher was re-appointed to the Bengal Council, and in 1769 was made Resident at Murshidabad, with local control of the revenue administration of Bengal. He deserves to be remembered for his heroic efforts, in the face of misrepresentation and slander, to alleviate the horrors of the great famine of 1770 in Bengal : noted for his honesty, during his 13 years of service under the Company : took no private gifts or bribes. In 1774, he retired to England with a modest fortune, which he soon after risked and lost in trying to help a friend : returned to India : was given a subordinate post as head of the Calcutta Mint, 1781 ; died Nov. 17, 1782, at Calcutta.

BECK, THEODORE (1859–1899)

Of a Quaker family : educated at a Quaker school, at London University, Scholar of Trinity College, Cambridge : President of the Union Debating Society : appointed Principal of the M.A.O. College, Alighar, when he was only 24 : he reorganized the College, establishing order out of chaos, reformed the discipline, introduced improvements, adjusted the finances, was devoted to his work and in warm sympathy with the Muhammadans : working with Sir Syad Ahmad (*q.v.*) until his death, in 1898, and afterwards with the trustees of the institution : died at Simla, Sep. 2, 1899.

BECKWITH, SIR THOMAS SYDNEY
(1772–1831)

Son of Maj-General J. Beckwith : joined the 71st regt. in India in 1791, then under Col. D. Baird (*q.v.*) : was at the siege of Seringapatam by Lord Cornwallis in 1792 and the taking of Pondicherry by Baird in 1793 : served also in Ceylon, at Copenhagen, at Hanover, in Denmark, the Peninsula, Canada : Maj-General and K.C.B., 1814 : Lt-General, 1830 : was appointed C. in C. at Bombay in 1829: died of fever at Mahableshwar, Jan. 19, 1831.

BEDDOME, RICHARD HENRY
(1830–)

Born May 11, 1830 : son of R. B. Beddome: educated at Charterhouse : joined the Madras Army : was Quartermaster and Interpreter of his regiment, 42nd Infantry, 1856 : Assistant Conservator of Forests, Madras, 1857 : Head of the Madras Forest Department, 1860 to 1882, when he retired as Colonel : Fellow of the Madras University, 1880 : author of *The Flora Sylvatica of the Madras Presi-*

dency, (400 trees), *The Ferns of Southern India*, (345 plates), *Hand-book to the Ferns of India*, besides pamphlets on new reptiles and land shells discovered by him in India.

BEIDERLINDEN, RIGHT REV. BERNARD, D.D. (1842–)

German : born at Münster, Aug. 18, 1842 : entered the Society of Jesus, Aug. 23, 1865 : arrived in India, Nov. 6, 1879 : occupied various posts in colleges, etc., became Superior of the Jesuit Mission, Oct. 4, 1882 : nominated first Catholic Bishop of Poona, Suffragan of Bombay, Dec. 22, 1886, consecrated, Feb. 27, 1887, at Allahabad : still in occupation of the See.

BELL, REV. DR. ANDREW, D.D.
(1753–1832)

" The eminent founder of the Madras system of education " : son of a barber at St. Andrew's : born March 27, 1753 : educated at St. Andrew's School and University : ordained, 1784 : M.D. : tutor in Virginia, 1774–9 : went to India, 1787 : in 2 years he had obtained and held simultaneously eight Army chaplaincies : in 1789 he was Chaplain of St. Mary's, Madras, and Superintendent of the Madras Male Orphan Asylum, and there introduced a system of mutual instruction by the boys, who were thus alternately learners and teachers, one half of the class teaching the other half : accompanied Genl. Braithwaite to capture of Pondicherry, 1793 : with a pension from the E.I.Co.,he returned to England in 1797, and laboured hard to spread his system at home and abroad : it was adopted in places : Rector of Swanage, 1801, Master of Sherburn Hospital, 1809 : as Superintendent, in 1811, of the National Society for promoting the education of the poor in the principles of the Established Church, he could advance his Madras system, but it could not be an entire system of education : he was made LL.D : also a Prebendary of Westminister : gave £120,000 to found a College at St. Andrew's : died Jan. 27, 1832, and was buried in Westminster Abbey : a tablet erected to his memory.

BELL, THOMAS EVANS (1825–1887)

Major : born Nov. 11,1825 : son of William Bell : educated at Wandsworth : went

D

to Madras in the E. I. Co's military service, 1841 : joined the 2nd Madras Europeans : appointed Assistant Commissioner at Nagpur, 1855, lost his appointment, 1860, for insubordination to the Chief Commissioner in advocating the claims of the dispossessed ruling family : all the measures recommended by Major Bell were, however, approved and carried out by Lord Canning, and he was appointed Deputy Commissioner of Police at Madras, 1861 : retired 1863 : devoted the remainder of his life to advocating measures for the benefit of India and its people : wrote *The Task of To-day*, 1852 : *The English in India*, 1859 : *The Empire in India*, 1864 : *Remarks on the Mysore Blue Book*, 1866 : *The Mysore Reversion*, 1865 : *Retrospects and Prospects of Indian Policy*, 1868 : *The Oxus and the Indus*, 1869 : 1874 : *The Great Parliamentary Bore*, 1869 : *Our Great Vassal Empire*, 1870, *The Bengal Reversion*, 1872 : *Last Counsels of an Unknown Counsellor*, 1877 : *Memoirs of General John Briggs*, 1886 : died Sep. 12, 1887.

BELLEW, HENRY WALTER (1834–1892)

Son of Capt. H. W. Bellew, of the Bengal Army : born Aug. 30, 1834 : educated at St. George's Hospital, London M.D. : in the Crimean war : went to India in the Bengal Medical service, 1856 : with Sir H. B. Lumsden's (*q.v.*) mission to Kandahar in 1857–8 : in the Umbeyla campaign : Civil Surgeon of Peshawar : interpreter at the Umbala *darbar* of 1869 with the Amir Shir Ali : was on Sir R. Pollock's mission to Seistan, 1871, and Sir T. D. Forsyth's mission to Kashgar and Yarkand, 1873–4 : C.S.I. in 1873 : Chief Political officer at Kabul in the second Afghan war : retired as Surgeon-General, 1886 : died July 26, 1892 : he had a faculty for learning Oriental languages, and wrote about them as well as about medical subjects and the countries which he had visited and their inhabitants.

BELLEW, REV. JOHN CHIPPENDALL MONTESQUIEU (1823–1874)

Son of Capt. R. Higgins : born Aug. 3, 1823 : educated at Lancaster, and St. Mary's Hall, Oxford : took his mother's family name in 1844 : ordained in 1848 : went to Calcutta in 1851 and became Chaplain of St. John's Church for 4 years : edited there the *Bengal Hurkaru* : returning to England in 1855, he became a popular preacher in London, but in 1868 was a convert to Roman Catholicism, and supported himself by public readings and literary work : he had great success as a master of elocution and from his handsome appearance : he died June 19, 1874.

BELLI, JOHN (? – ?)

Born in England, of a noble Italian family, probably of Viterbo, his mother being a lady of Spanish origin named Bivar : entered the E. I. Co's. service and became Private Secretary to Warren Hastings, about 1770-5 : he married a sister of Sir Charles Cockerell; his daughters married Dr. Howley, Archbishop of Canterbury; E. Horsley Palmer, M.P. and Sir C. E. Carrington (*q.v.*)

BENARES, BALWANT SINGH, RAJA OF (1717–? 1770)

Son of Mansa Ram : and father of Chait Singh (*q.v.*) : all of the Dhuinhar caste : succeeded his father, 1740 : died Aug. 19 1770, being succeeded by Chait Singh : Balwant was the real founder and consolidator of the Benares Raj.

BENARES, CHAIT SINGH, RAJA OF (? –1810)

Son of Balwant Singh, the Raja of Benares, who died in 1770, when Chait Singh became Raja : in 1775 was declared independent of Oudh (of which he had been a vassal) and made tributary to the English Govermnent on a fixed annual payment : in 1778, Warren Hastings demanded from him, besides the annual tribute, five lakhs of rupees, which were recovered from him with the help of troops. Similar demands were made from him in 1779 and 1780 : in the latter year, a contingent of men was demanded, according to his tenure as Raja, for the public service : he evaded, and did not furnish a single man : a fine of 50 lakhs was imposed, and Warren Hastings personally went to Benares, to levy the fine on Chait Singh, who received him submissively. Chait Singh was made, Aug. 16, 1781, a prisoner in his own palace at Benares, but his people rose, attacked and killed the guards. In the confusion, Chait Singh escaped. Hastings withdrew to Chunar :

Major Popham advanced in force, and defeated Chait Singh's forces at Benares, Latifpur and Bijaighar : the tribute was doubled, when a nephew of Chait Singh was made Raja. Chait Singh, with a few followers, took refuge in Gwalior and lived there until his death on March 29, 1810.

BENARES, SIR ISRI PRASAD NARA-YAN SINGH, MAHARAJA BAHA-DUR of (1822–1889)

Born 1822 : nephew and adopted son of Raja Udit Singh of Benares, whom he succeeded in 1835 : belonged to the Bhuinhar family, from which came Balwant Singh and Chait Singh : he rendered conspicuous service during the mutiny and largely assisted in maintaining order in the city and neighbouring country : made Maharaja Bahadur in 1859 : G.C.S.I. in 1877 : received the title of " His Highness " in 1889 as a personal distinction : and a salute of 15 guns : had no son, and was succeeded in his immense estates by his nephew, the present Maharaja : was a great patron of literature, several poets resided at his court and wrote works under the Maharaja's name : died June 13, 1889.

BENARES, MAHARAJA SIR PRABHU NARAIN SINGH, BARADUR OF (1855–)

Born Nov. 26, 1855 : succeeded as nephew and adopted son of Maharaja Isri Prasad (*q.v.*), on June 13, 1889 : received the title of His Highness as a personal distinction in Sep. 1889 : G.C.I.E., Jan. 1898 : has a salute of 13 guns.

BENDALL, CECIL (1856–)

Born July 1, 1856 : educated at City of London School, Trinity and Caius Colleges, Cambridge : first class, Classical Tripos, and first class Indian Languages Tripos : Fellow, Caius College, 1879–85 : at the British Museum, in the Department of Oriental MSS. and printed books, 1882–98 : Curator of Oriental Literature in the Cambridge University Library,1892 : Professor of Sanskrit at University College, London, 1885–1903, and at Cambridge since 1903 (previously Sanskrit lecturer there): travelled in India and Nipal, 1884–5 and 1898–9 : on the Council of the R. A .S., 1901 : published *A Journey of Literary and Archæological Research in Nipal and Northern India,* 1886 : and Catalogues of Buddhist Sanskrit MSS at Cambridge, and of ,Sanskrit Pali books, and MSS, in the British Museum, besides other works on Sanskrit.

BENFEY, THEODOR (1809–1881)

Born Jan. 28, 1809 : studied from 1824 at Gottingen : Doctor of Philosophy, 1828 : also studied at Munich : taught at Frankfort, 1830–4 : made Privat Docent, 1834 : ordinary Professor of the philosophical faculty, 1862 : laboured at classical philology, Sanskrit language and literature, and the science of language : left his mark on Oriental research : in the front rank as a Vedic scholar and Sanskrit grammarian : studied the early fable literature of India and other countries : edited the *Sama Veda,* 1848 : wrote a Sanskrit-English Dictionary, 1866, and a Grammar of the Vedic language : Fellow of the Society of Letters, Göttingen : F.R.A.S. of Great Britain, and of other learned societies : wrote *Vedica und Linguistica,* 1880 : *Vedica und Verwandtes,* 1880 : died June 30, 1881.

BENFIELD, PAUL (? –1810)

In the E. I. Co.'s Civil Service : went to India in 1764 : in Madras he made money by trade, lending, and contracts, and had large money dealings with the Nawab of the Carnatic : one of these being unfavourably regarded by the Court of Directors in 1777, he resigned the service and retired to England, 1779 : but, having demanded an inquiry and explained, he was reinstated and returned to Madras, finally retiring in 1793 : lost his fortune in speculations and died in want, 1810 : M.P. for Cricklade in 1780.

BENGALI, SORABJI SHAPURJI (1831 –1893)

Born Feb. 15, 1831 : son of a Calcutta merchant : educated at the Education Society's school (now Elphinstone High School) in Bombay : employed in the Bombay branch of the Bank of Ceylon and subsequently in the Commercial Bank of India : went, in 1853, to the Mercantile Bank and, in 1858, became Assistant to Muncherji Framji Cama : was well read in Gujarati and English and brought out several Gujarati periodicals. In 1868, he visited Europe. He assisted Naoroji

Furdunji (*q.v.*) in advocating social and political reforms : they were joint Honorary Secretaries to the Parsi Law Association from 1855, which obtained certain legislative measures for the Parsis : in 1871 he was consulted by the Governor of Bombay on the new Municipal Act, became a Member of the Bombay Corporation, and, in 1876, a Member of the Bombay Legislative Council ; was a Fellow of the Bombay University : owing to his exertions, the Indian Factory Act of 1881 became law : in 1881 he was made C.I.E. and Sheriff of Bombay : in 1885, was a member of the Abkari Commission : died April 4, 1893.

BENTINCK, LORD WILLIAM CAVEN-DISH (1774–1839)

Governor-General : son of the 3rd Duke of Portland, born Sep. 14, 1774 : entered the Army 1791, saw service in the Netherlands, in Italy, with the Austrian forces : Governor of Madras, from Aug., 1803, to Sep., 1807, when on account of the mutiny of sepoys against their officers at Vellore, for which he was held responsible, the Court of Directors recalled him: changes affecting the sepoys had been introduced by the C. in C., with the support of the Governor. He was employed in Portugal and commanded a Brigade at Corunna : as Lt-General he was C. in C. in Sicily, 1811, served in Spain, and led an expedition against Genoa, 1814. After 13 years without employment, he was Governor of Bengal from July, 1828, was C. in C. from May, 1833, and the first Governor-General of India from Nov., 1834, to March, 1835 : it devolved on him to insist on economies to restore financial equilibrium, to reform the land revenue settlement in the N.W.P., to establish a Board of Revenue in the N.W.P. and reorganize the judicial courts, to devote funds to education through the medium of English, and to increase the employment of educated natives in higher offices. He also by Regulation abolished the practice of suttee, and suppressed the Thags. He took over the administration of Mysore. He met Ranjit Singh, ruler of the Panjab, on the Satlaj. In general he reformed the administration in a liberal spirit, and established the principle that, in the Government of India, the interests of the people should have the first claim. His memory is still cherished by the natives.

The eloquent inscription on his statue in Calcutta was written by Macaulay (*q.v.*) (Legal Member of Council from Nov., 1834.) Bentinck was greatly regretted on his retirement. He became M.P. for Glasgow in 1837 : refused a peerage, and died June 17, 1839.

BENTLEY, JOHN (? – ?)

Member of the Asiatic Society of Bengal : wrote *Historical View of Hindu Astronomy*, 1823 : his earlier treatise, on the *Antiquity of the Suryasiddhanta*, 1799, threw doubts on the antiquity of Indian astronomy, and called forth a severe critique in the *Edinburgh Review*, to which Bentley replied in the *Asiatic Researches* : one of the greatest mathematicians of his time in India : he also wrote, on the *Principal Eras and Dates of the Ancient Hindus*.

BENWELL, JOSEPH AUSTIN (?– ?)

Artist : resided for some time, prior to 1856, in India : conspicuous for original and pleasing delineations of native life, landscape and buildings in India, evidently drawn on the spot : chiefly known as a draughtsman on wood of Eastern subjects, principally Indian and Chinese : exhibited at the Royal Academy up to 1883 : illustrated Capt. M. Rafter's *Our Indian Army*, and Capper's *Three Presidencies of India :* nearly all his drawings on wood are in the periodicals and journals of the 'sixties, such as the *Illustrated London News*, and, to about 1876, the publications of the Religious Tract Society: he illustrated also *The Indian Nabob of 100 years ago*, by G. E. Sargent in *The Leisure Hour* for 1858, a story of considerable merit of the British conquest and settlement of Bengal: he painted a series of dissolving views of Indian life, exhibited in London before 1862 : his signature on drawings is usually J.B. but occasionally J.A.B.

BERAR, RAGHOJI BHONSLA II, RAJA OF (? –1816)

Raja of Nagpur, or Berar : succeeded his father, Madhoji Bhonsla, as Raja in 1788, took part in the victory of the Mahrattas over Nizam Ali of Hyderabad at Kurdla in March, 1795. After the treaty of Bassein (Dec. 1802), he joined in the Mahratta war against the British, and was beaten at Assaye on Sep. 23, 1803, and again at Argaum on Nov. 28, 1803 : he had then to cede Cuttack and Berar to the English, so that only Nagpur remained to him : his demand for their restoration was refused : he died in 1816.

BERAR, RAGHOJI BHONSLA III, RAJA OF (1808 ?–1853)

Raja of Nagpur : grandson of Raghoji Bhonsla II (*q.v.*), adopted by his widow and made Raja as a child of 9, after the flight of Appa Sahib (*q.v.*). When he died in 1853, leaving no heir or relation with any claim, Nagpur was incorporated into British territory.

BERESFORD, GEORGE READ EDWARD (1815–1857)

Born Aug. 3, 1815 : son of Thomas Beresford : went to India, 1834–5 : appointed first manager of the Cawnpur Bank, about 1843 : transferred, 1849, to be the head manager of the Delhi Bank : massacred with his wife and five daughters, on May 11, 1857, at the Bank-house at Delhi, by the mutineers from Meerut : Beresford had declined the offer of escaping with his family, refusing to abandon his charge of the Bank : he and his family defended themselves on the roof of an out-house, but were overpowered : a tablet was placed to their memory in the Church at Delhi : he was a learned Oriental scholar, keen archæologist and photographer : author of *The Handbook of Delhi.*

BERESFORD, LORD WILLIAM LES-LIE DE LA POER (1847–1900)

Third son of the fourth Marquis of Waterford : born July 20, 1847 : educated at Eton : entered the 9th Lancers in 1867 : A.D.C. to Viceroys of India, 1875 to 1881, and Military Secretary to the Viceroys from 1881 to 1894. He saw service in the Jowaki expedition, 1877–8 ; in the Zulu war, 1879, where he gained the Victoria Cross ; in the Afghan war, 1880, and was in Burma, 1886 : Lt-Colonel in 1890 : K.C.I.E., 1894. On Dec. 30, 1893, he was entertained at a fare-well dinner at the Town Hall, Calcutta, by 180 friends : it was then said of him that he " had raised the office [of Military Sec-retary] to a science, and himself from an

official into an institution, and acquired a reputation absolutely unique " : retired from India in 1894 : died in England, Dec. 28, 1900. He was invaluable as A.D.C. and Military Secretary to successive Viceroys : popular and active : a keen sportsman and successful rider of steeple-chases : and polo-player : and for years kept a stud of racehorses with which he won the Viceroy's Cup six times and the other principal races at race-meetings in India. In England, also, he had a racing stable, and was one of the first to have American horses and jockeys.

BERNADOTTE, JOHN BAPTISTE JULIUS (1764–1844)

King of Sweden and Norway, as Charles XIV : born of humble parents at Pau in Bearne, 1764 : he enlisted in the French army in 1780, and was, when a serjeant, taken prisoner at the siege of Cuddalore in 1783 : became General in 1793, served in Napoleon's campaigns : and became, as Charles XIV, King of Sweden and Norway in 1818 : died March 8, 1844.

BERNARD, SIR CHARLES EDWARD (1837–1901)

I.C.S. : son of Dr. J. F. Bernard, of Clifton, and nephew of the first Lord Lawrence : born in 1837 : educated at Rugby, Addiscombe and Haileybury : be-gan his service in the Panjab in 1858 : in the Central Provinces till 1871 : from 1871 to 1875 was Secretary to the Bengal Government, member of the Bengal Legislative Council, famine Secretary dur-ing the Bihar famine of 1874 : C.S.I., 1875 : Secretary to Sir R. Temple on his famine mission to Madras and Bombay in 1877 : Home Secretary to the Government of India, 1878–80 : Chief Commissioner of Burma, 1880–1888 : K.C.S.I., 1886 : on retirement from India was appointed Secretary in the Revenue and Statistics Department, India Office : retired in 1901. He died at Chamouni Sep. 19, 1901. In 1893 he edited the autobio-graphical Memoirs of Sir George Campbell. (*q.v.*) Bernard was remarkable for his personal activity and indefatigable energy. No one has worked harder throughout an arduous career. An officer of the highest principles in public and private life, he gained universal esteem and affection, even from those who differed from his views.

BERNOULLI, JEAN (1744–1807)

Born at Basle, Nov. 4, 1744 : son of the elder Jean Bernoulli : belonged to a family celebrated as mathematicians : Jean the younger was a great astronomer : from 1763 was in this capacity a member of the Academy of Sciences at Berlin : became Director of the Mathematical Class at the Academy : wrote also on geographical subjects : notably his *Description historique et géographique de l'Inde*, 1786, consisting of his French translation of Père Joseph Tieffenthaler's *Géographie de l'Indoustan* (originally in Latin), *Recherches historiques et chronologiques sur l'Inde*, by Anquetil du Perron, with the addition of maps by James Rennell : died at Berlin, July 13, 1807.

BESANT, ANNIE (1847–   )

Born Oct. 1, 1847 : daughter of William Page Wood : educated privately in England, Germany and France : married Rev. Frank Besant, 1867, but legally separated from him, 1872 : joined the National Secular Society, 1874 : worked with Charles Bradlaugh M.P. in Labour and Socialist movements : co-editor of the *National Reformer*, member of the Fabian Society, and Social Democratic Federation : was a member of the London School Board, 1887–90 : joined the Theosophical Society, 1880 : and became a devoted pupil of Madame Blavatsky : founded the Central Hindu College at Benares, 1898 : author of many books and pamphlets, including *Karma, Four Great Religions, Dharma, Esoteric Christianity, The Religious Problem in India*, etc : joint-editor of the *Theosophical Review*.

BEST, SAMUEL (1808 ?–1851)

Captain, Madras Engineers : entered the service in 1826 : Secretary to the Board of Revenue in the P.W.D., 1842 : planned the Singapore fortifications, and was made Superintendent of roads in Madras, 1845 : under him road-making was very well managed under fixed rules : he executed many important works in the Madras Presidency : such as the Southern Trunk Road and the Goolcheroo Pass : and made valuable contributions to the Madras Literary Transactions and the Madras Engineering papers : died of jungle fever at Chitore on his return from the hills, Oct. 5, 1851.

BETHUNE, SIR HENRY LINDESAY, BARONET (1787–1851)

Son of Major M. E. Lindesay : joined the Madras Artillery in 1810 : was six feet eight in height : was in Sir John Malcolm's mission to Persia in 1810, stayed there some years to drill the Persian Army, fighting with it against the Russians : returned to England in 1821 and left the E.I. Co.'s service : assumed the name of Bethune : again; out to Persia in 1834, helped to quell a rebellion, was made a Baronet at the Shah's request : in 1836–9 was again in Persia, and died at Tabriz in 1851.

BETHUNE, JOHN ELLIOT DRINKWATER (1801–1851)

Son of Lt-Colonel J. Drinkwater Bethune : educated at Trinity College, Cambridge : called to the bar, 1827 : was Counsel to the Home Office for many years : became Legal Member of the Supreme Council of the Government of India in April, 1848. Besides his ordinary work in charge of legislation and as Member of Council, Bethune was President of the Council of Education : he established the Bethune School, which still exists, for the Education of native girls; died at Calcutta Aug. 12, 1851.

BHANDARKAR, RAMKRISHNA GOPAL (1837–   )

Orientalist and social reformer : born July 6, 1837 : educated at Ratnagiri and Elphinstone College, Bombay : M.A., 1866 : Dakhshina Fellow there 1859, and later in the Dekkan College, Poona, till 1864 : in the Bombay Education Department, 1864–93 : Head-master of Hyderabad (Sind) and Ratnagiri High Schools, 1864–9 : acting Professor of Sanskrit and Oriental Languages in Elphinstone College, Assistant Professor many years, till 1881 : Professor of Sanskrit at Dekkan College, Poona, 1882–93 : Fellow of Bombay University from 1866; Syndic, 1873–81 ; Vice-Chancellor, 1893–5 : Hon. LL.D., 1904 : Member of the Governor-General's Legislative Council, 1903–4, when the Universities Act was passed : Member of Bombay Legislative Council, 1904–5 : Fellow of Calcutta University, 1887 : Member of learned Societies, e.g. R.A.S. London, 1874 ; R.A.S. Bombay, 1865 ; German Oriental Society, 1887 ; American

Oriental Society, 1887; Asiatic Society of Italy, 1887; of Imperial Academy of Science, St. Petersburg, 1888 : Foreign member of the French Institute, 1895 : also of the International Congress of Orientalists, London, 1874; and of Vienna, 1886, which he attended : C.I.E., 1887 : retired from service, 1893 : Hon. Phil. Dr. Gottingen University : has contributed largely to the Journals and Transactions of learned Societies, especially in Bombay, on philological and antiquarian subjects : also to the *Indian Antiquary :* first lecturer on the Wilson Lectureship, Bombay University : reported on his searches for Sanskrit MSS. in the Bombay Presidency : edited the text of the Sanskrit *Malati-Madhava :* and has written Sanskrit educational works : is a leader of the enlightened religious movement of the Prathna Samaj in W. India : as a social reformer has practically supported the re-marriage of widows, and in politics is a moderate progressive.

BHASKARANANDA, SWAMI (1833–1899)

Motiram (his early name) was born in the village of Maithilalpur in Cawnpur, about 6 miles from the residence of Nana Sahib (*q.v.*) : at 8, he learnt the elements of Sanskrit, and completed his study on Panini (grammar) at 17 : renounced the world, went on pilgrimage, and wandered in search of knowledge : studied Vedanta philosophy at Ujain, became a Sanyasi (devotee) at 27, assuming the name of Bhaskarananda, (the sun-enchanted). For mental discipline, he kept silence for several months, and often roamed about the banks of the Ganges with head uncovered in the sun for hours together : lived for several years at Hardwar absorbed in the study of *Bhagavat Gita* and the *Upanishads :* migrated to Benares and lived a life of great austerity, devotion, contemplation and study, till he died in July, 1899 : was a bright-looking ascetic, always cheerful and of intense spiritual energy : European savants and Princes, going to Benares, used to visit him : three marble statues have been raised in his honour.

BHATAWADEKAR, SIR BHATCHAN-DRA KRISHNA (1852–)

Educated at Elphinstone High School and Grant Medical College, Bombay :

Chief Medical Officer in the Baroda State, 1875–85 : President of the Bombay Municipal Corporation : author of several treatises : made a Knight Bachelor, Feb. 7, 1900.

BHAU DAJI, OR RAMKRISHNA VITAL (1821–1874)

A Sarasvat Gond Brahman, and son of a small farmer of Mandra, in Goa : educated in the Native Education Society's School in Bombay, and became a teacher in the Elphinstone School : joined, 1845, the Grant Medical College as a student, and graduated in 1850 : as a practitioner, achieved great popularity and success : made original researches in the use of Indian drugs, with a special view to discovering a cure for leprosy in its earlier stages, and contributed some valuable papers to the *Antiquary :* was a member of the chief educational and learned Societies in Bombay : a Fellow of the University, a Justice of the Peace, the first native Sheriff of Bombay in 1869 and 1871 : was also Dr. : died of paralysis in 1874.

BHIDE, GOPALRAO HARI (1843–1896)

A native of Mahapada in the Presidency of Bombay : son of a learned Brahman of the old type, who, too poor to maintain his family, migrated to Kalyan : educated at Poona : entered the railway service as a signaller, employed in the Berars and afterwards at Nagpur : became a clerk in the Magistrate's office and read law : in 1869 became a Pleader and obtained a lucrative practice : devoted himself to social reforms, particularly female education, the re-marriage of widows, and improvement of modes of agriculture : through his advice the first proprietary cotton mill was established at Nagpur : died Jan. 4, 1896.

BHOPAL, NAWAB SHAH JEHAN, BEGAM OF (1838–1901)

Born July 3, 1838 : proclaimed ruler of Bhopal, Jan. 10, 1847, her mother, Sikandar Begam (*q.v.*) being Regent : abdicated May 1, 1860, in favour of her mother, on whose death, Oct. 30, 1868, she succeeded to the government of the State : she married, first Bakshi Bahi Muhammad Khan, (who died 1867), and had one daughter, the present Nawab

Sultan Jehan Begam : and second in 1871, her Prime Minister, Nawab Maulvi Muhammad Sadik Hussein, of a noble Bokhara family : she was made G.C.S.I, in 1872, and administered her State with ability, benevolence, and loyalty to the Government of India : Member of the Order of the Crown of India : died June 16, 1901.

BHOPAL, NAWAB SIKANDAR BEGAM OF (1816-1868)

Daughter of Nuzzur Mahomed Khan, the Nawab of Bhopal and the Kudsia Begam : born in 1816 : married, April 18, 1835, her cousin the Nawab Jehangir Muhammad Khan : after his death, on Dec. 9, 1844, she was appointed Regent, in Feb. 1847, and behaved with great loyalty to the British Government in the mutiny. In 1859 she was proclaimed Ruler, her daughter, Shah Jehan, resigning her rights during the mother's life. Sikandar Begam ruled with great vigour, ability and loyalty to the British Government : she received rewards after the mutiny, was made K.C.S.I. in 1861 : G.C.S.I. in 1866 : made the pilgrimage to Mecca in 1863 : died Oct. 30, 1868.

BHOWNAGRI, SIR MANCHERJI MERWANJI (1851-   )

Son of a distinguished Parsi merchant : educated at the Elphinstone College and Bombay University : began life as a journalist : State agent in Bombay for the Bhaunagar Raja, 1873 : M.P. for Bethnal Green since 1895 : author of *History of the Constitution of the East India Company*, a Gujarati translation of *H.M.'s Life in the Highlands*. K.C.I.E.

BICKERTON, SIR RICHARD, BARONET (1727-1792)

Entered the Navy, 1739 : served in the W. Indies, the Mediterranean, the Channel, again the W. Indies and Channel : knighted, 1773 : Baronet, May, 1778 : in the battle of Ushant, July, 1778 : to the E. Indies as Commodore, 1782-4 : at the action off Cuddalore, June, 1783 : C. in C. at the Leeward Islands : Vice-Admiral, 1790 : Port Admiral at Plymouth till his death, Feb. 25, 1792 : M.P. for Rochester.

BICKNELL, HERMAN (1830-1875)

Son of E. Bicknell : born April 2, 1830 : educated at Paris, Hanover, University College, St. Bartholomew's : took his medical degree in 1855 : gazetted Assistant Surgeon : first to Hongkong, then to Mianmir near Lahore in 1856 : was Staff Assistant Surgeon : served through the mutiny and travelled widely, exploring in Tibet and the Himalayas : in 1861, resigned his commission. In 1862, as an English Muhammadan gentleman he resided in Cairo, and, undisguised, performed a pilgrimage to Mecca : he travelled also in Persia, to perfect his translation of Hafiz : visited the Kum mosque in Persia, 1869 : eminent as a linguist and traveller : died March 14, 1875.

BIDDULPH, JOHN (1840-   )

Colonel : born July 25, 1840 : son of Robert Biddulph, of Ledbury : educated at Westminster : entered the Bengal Cavalry and arrived in India, 1858 : served in the mutiny : joined the Indian Staff Corps : A.D.C. to Lord Northbrook when Viceroy, 1872-6 : member of the mission to Yarkand, 1873-4 : employed on a secret mission to countries beyond Gilgit, 1877 : acting A.G.G. Beluchistan, May–Nov., 1882 : Political Agent, Bhopawar, 1882 : Haraoti and Tonk, 1886 : Resident and Commissioner, Ajmir, 1890 : Officiating Agent, Beluchistan, 1891 : acting Resident at Gwalior, 1892 : Resident at Baroda, 1893 : reverted to military duty, 1895 : author of *Tribes of the Hindu Kush*, 1880 : *The Nineteenth and their Times*, 1899 : *Stringer Lawrence*, 1901.

BIDDULPH, SIR MICHAEL ANTHONY SHRAPNEL (1823-1904)

Son of the Rev. Thomas Shrapnel Biddulph, of Amroth Castle, Pembrokeshire : born in 1823 : educated at Woolwich : entered the Royal Artillery in 1843 : Captain, 1850 : Brevet-Major, 1854 : Maj-General, 1877 : General, 1886 : he served throughout the Crimean campaign : in India he was Deputy Adjutant General of Artillery, 1868-73, and commanded the Rohilkund District in 1876 : in the Afghan war of 1878-80, he commanded the Quetta Field Force, and a Division of the Kandahar Field Force : was present at the occupation of Kandahar, and the engagement at Khushk-i-Nakhand, and, later, commanded the Thal-Chotiali Field Force : C.B., 1873 : K.C.B. in 1879 : President of the Ordnance Committee, 1886–9 : retired in 1900 : G.C.B. : from 1879 till his death he held appointments about the Court, and was Gentleman Usher of the Black Rod from 1896 : died July 23, 1904.

BIDIE, GEORGE (1830–)

Educated at Aberdeen Grammar School and University : entered the Madras Medical Service, 1856 : served in the mutiny : Professor of Botany, Madras Medical College : Superintendent of Lunatic Asylum, 1866–70 : Secretary of head office of Medical Department, 1870–3 : in charge of the Government Central Museum, 1872–85 : Surgeon - General of Madras, 1886–90 : discovered a preventive for insect pest in coffee plantations : author of several works, including *Handbook of Practical Pharmacy*, *Nilgiri Parasitical Plants*, etc. : C.I.E., 1883.

BIGANDET, RIGHT REV. PAUL AMBROSE (1813–1894)

Born 1813 at Besancon : educated there, and studied for two years at the Seminary of Foreign Missions, Paris : in 1837, sent by the Roman Church as missionary to Malacca : removed to Burma, and in 1856 was consecrated Bishop of Ramatha and Administrator of Pegu and Ava (soon after the annexation of Lower Burma) : from 1870 was Vicar-Apostolic of Southern Burma : his residence for 50 years in that country was marked by many labours, not only that of organizing the Roman Catholic mission there, but also by his work in the promotion of native education, and the service he rendered to Buddhistic literature : he died at Rangoon, March 16, 1894 : a noted Pali scholar, and the great authority on Burmese Buddhism : his most important work, the *Life of Gautama*, first published in 1858, went through three editions : it is based entirely on native Burmese MSS., and is one of the standard works of the 19th century : wrote also a *Memoir on the Phoongis, or Religious Buddhists*, 1865.

BIGNOLD, THOMAS FRANCIS (? – 1888)

I.C.S. : educated at Canis College, Cambridge : Scholar : entered the Bengal Civil Service by competition : went to India, 1859 : served in Lower Bengal :

District Judge at several places : wrote *Leviora : being the rhymes of a successful competitor*, 1888 : died in Melbourne while his book was still in the Press in Calcutta.

BILGRAMI, SAYYID ALI (1851–)

Son of Sayyid Zainuddin Husain Khan Bahadur, of the Bengal Provincial Service, a member of the well-known [family of Sayyids of Bilgram who emigrated to India from Wasit in Mesopotamia : born Nov. 10, 1851 : educated at Canning College, Lucknow ; Patna College, Bankipur, and Thomason Civil Engineering College, Rurki : M.A., and B.L. : in 1876, visited Europe and England in the suite of Sir Salar Jang I. (*q.v.*) : joined the Royal School of Mines, passed the Examination for the Associateship in two years, and obtained the Murchison Medal in Geology. On return to India, in 1879, he entered the service of the Nizam of Hyderabad : became Secretary in the Departments of Public Works, Railways and Mines for nearly ten years : retired in 1901 to settle in England : was Examiner in Sanskrit to the University of Madras from 1890–2 : received the title of Shams-al-ulama for Arabic learning in 1891 : Gold Medallist, Calcutta University : in 1902 was appointed Lecturer in Mahratti to the University of Cambridge : has published *Civilization of the Arabs*, translated from the French of Dr. Gustav Le Bon : *Manual of Medical Jurisprudence, Monograph on the Book of Kalila and Damna, Notes on the Educational Value of Persian as compared with Sanskrit, A Guide to the Cave Temples of Ellora, The Geology and Economic Minerals of Hyderabad*, etc : appointed, 1902, by the India Office, to catalogue the collections of Arabic and Persian MSS., known as the Delhi MSS., a work of some magnitude.

BIRCH, SIR RICHARD JAMES HOLWELL (1803–1875)

Son of the R. C. Birch of the Indian Civil Service, who was a grandson of J. Z. Holwell (*q.v.*) : born in 1803 : entered the Indian Army, 1821 : held several Staff appointments : was Judge-Advocate General in Bengal, 1841 : in the Sikh wars of 1845–6, and 1848–9 : had a Brigade after Chilianwala : distinguished himself at Gujarat : C.B., 1849 : under Sir Colin Campbell on the frontier in 1850 : Secretary to the Govt. of India in the Military Dept., from 1852 for several years, including the mutiny : K.C.B. in 1860 : retired 1861 : Lt-General : died Feb. 25, 1875.

BIRD, SIR GEORGE CORRIE
(1838–   )

Born, 1838 : entered the Indian Army, 1856 :   Maj-General, 1895 :   General, 1899 : served in the mutiny : in Afghan war, 1878–80 : at Ahmad Kheyl : Brevet Lt-Colonel : in Burma, 1892–3 : in the N.W. Frontier campaign, 1897–8 : commanded the Oudh district, 1895–6 : the Panjab Frontier Force, 1897–8 : C.B., 1890 : K.C.I.E., 1899.

BIRD, JAMES (? – ?)

Belonged to the Bombay Medical Establishment : member of the Medical Board : Secretary to the Bombay Asiatic Society, 1844–7 : wrote on various subjects, historical and archæological, connected with India : author of an Analysis of the *Mirat-i-Ahmadi, A History of the Province of Gujarat,* translated from the Persian.

BIRD, LOUIS SAUNDERS (1792–1874)

Lt-General :   entered the E. I. Co.'s Bengal Army in 1808 : at the capture of the Mauritius, 1810 : under Ochterlony in the Nipal war, 1816 : in Oudh in 1816–7 : in the Pindari war, 1817–9 : in Bundelkund, 1821 : in Hariana, 1824–5 : against the Kols, 1832–3 : in the Satlaj campaign of 1845–6 : in the battles of Mudki, Firozshahr, Badiwal, Aliwal : Brevet Lt-Colonel : commanded a Brigade in the suppression of the Sonthal insurrection in 1855–6 : died April 14, 1874.

BIRD, MARY (1789–1834)

Born, May 29, 1789, daughter of Robert Bird, of Taplow : went to India, 1823, to her brother R.M. Bird (*q.v.*) at Gorakhpur : helped the Mission there, and learnt Hindustani : removed to Calcutta, 1830, and carried on mission and education work there, in the native zenanas, and by opening Bible classes, Sunday and Girls' Schools : published works translated into Hindustani :   died of cholera on her birthday, May 29, 1834.

BIRD, ROBERT MERTTINS (1788–1853)

I.C.S. : arrived in India Nov. 1808 : at first held subordinate judicial appoint-

ments, but in 1829 became Commissioner of Revenue in the Gorakhpur Division of the N.W.P. : in 1832 was made Member of the new Board of Revenue, N.W.P., and from 1833–41 was in charge of the settlement of the land revenue of that Province : the work was most thoroughly done and established Bird's reputation for all time as a revenue officer : his report was elaborate, embracing other topics besides the assessment of the revenue : retired in 1842, and gave much attention to the Church Missionary Society : died Aug. 22, 1853.

BIRD, WILLIAM WILBERFORCE
(? –1857)

I.C.S. : arrived in India, 1803 : Judge and Magistrate of Benares, 1814 : Commissioner there, 1826 : Member of the Board of Revenue, 1829 : Provisional Member of Council, 1837, and Extra Member of the Board of Customs, Salt and Opium, 1837 : Member of the Supreme Council, 1838 : President of the Council of Education, 1842 : President of the Council, 1842, and Deputy-Governor of Bengal, 1840, and 1842 ; as Senior Member of Council officiated as Governor-General, June 15 to July 23, 1844 : retired, 1844 : died June 1, 1857.

BIRDWOOD, CHRISTOPHER (1807–1882)

General: born March 12, 1807 : son and grandson of E. I. Co's agents at Plymouth : entered the E. I. Co.'s Military service as Ensign 1825 : Capt. 1837 : Maj-General, 1868 : Lt-General, 1876 : Adjutant and Interpreter of the 3rd Bombay N.I. at Bombay, and Fort-Adjutant at Asirghar : commissariat officer at Mhow, 1839, other stations, and Aden, 1847 : Assistant Commissary General at Bombay and Executive Commissariat officer there during the Persian war, 1856–7 : rendered also invaluable service during the mutiny, organizing the bullock train between Bombay, Wassind and Mhow, on which Sir H. Rose's operations depended : consulted constantly by Lord Elphinstone, Governor of Bombay, and highly esteemed by the native community, who called him Birdwood Maharaja : he always accompanied the Commissioner of Police, C. Forjett, (*q.v.*) in interviews with their leaders : was Commissary-General, Bombay Army : recommended for the C.B. by Lord Elphinstone, who constantly testified to his merits as a first-class commissariat officer : he became General in 1877 and retired after 52 years' service, 45 actually spent in India : died July 4, 1882.

BIRDWOOD, SIR GEORGE CHRISTOPHER MOLESWORTH (1834-)

Born at Belgaum, Dec. 8, 1832, son of General Christopher Birdwood, of the Indian Army (*q.v.*) : educated at Plymouth Grammar School, Dollar Academy and Edinburgh University (M.D.) : entered Bombay Medical Service 1854 : served in Persian war, 1856–7, and on return to Bombay took a prominent part in the life of the city, influencing, by his great popularity with the leaders of native thought, the endowments which were made to the newly established University : the construction of some of the public buildings : and the carrying out of improvements which have earned for the town and island the title of "Bombay the Beautiful." He was for a time Professor of Anatomy and Physiology, and of Materia Medica and Botany at Grant Medical College : also Curator of the Government Central Museum : Hony. Secy. Bombay Branch of the Royal Asiatic Society and of the Agri-Horticultural Society : Registrar of the University : one of the founders of the Victoria and Albert Museum and the designer of the Victoria gardens at Byculla : Sheriff of Bombay, 1846 : returning to England on account of ill-health, he joined the staff of the India Office, and was Special Assistant there in the Revenue and Statistical Department from 1878 to 1899, when he retired after two extensions of service beyond the ordinary age limit. He held a leading position in all the principal International Exhibitions from 1857 to 1901 : founded Primrose Day : author of *Economic Vegetable Products of the Bombay Presidency*, 1888 ; *The Industrial Arts of India*, 1888 ; *Report on the Old Records of the India Office*, 1891 : *First Letter Book of the East India Company*, 1895 : of papers on *The Genus Boswellia* (Frankincense Trees) : on *Incense*, and other articles in *Encyc. Brit* : and of erudite prefaces and introductions to various well-known works, such as Count d' Alviella's *Migrations des Symboles*, besides many

official reports on economic products, etc. : a prolific contributor to leading journals and reviews, including the *Times*, the *Athenæum*, the *Quarterly Review*, and the *Journal* of the Society of Arts, the latter containing a great number of his speeches and essays in connexion with the work of the Society. C.S.I., 1877 ; K.C.I.E., 1877 : LL.D. (Cambridge) 1886 : Knight of Grace of St. John of Jerusalem.

BIRDWOOD, HERBERT MILLS (1837-)

I.C.S : born May 29, 1837 : son of General Christopher Birdwood : educated at Exeter, Edinburgh University, and Peterhouse, Cambridge : wrangler in 1858 : Fellow : went to Bombay in the Civil Service, 1859 : Under Secretary to the Bombay Government, Judicial and Political Departments, 1863 : Registrar of the High Court, Bombay : District Judge ; Judicial Commissioner in Sind, 1881 : Judge of the Bombay High Court, officiating, and permanently from 1885 : Member of Council, Bombay, 1892–7 : C.S.I., 1893 : edited legal works.

BIRRELL, JAVRIL (1800–1878)

General : born Sep. 15, 1800 : entered the E. I. Co's service in 1816 : in the first Burmese war, 1825–6 : in the Afghan war of 1839–40 : at Ghazni, and in the Waziri valley : in the Satlaj campaign of 1845–6, at Firozshahr and Sobraon : General. 1876 : died Oct. 27, 1878.

BISSET, SIR WILLIAM SINCLAIR SMITH (1843-)

Colonel : born Nov. 13, 1843 : son of Rev. James Bisset,D.D. : educated at Woolwich : joined the Royal Engineers : to India, 1866 : entered the Railway Branch, held a number of subordinate appointments connected with railway construction and management : served in the Afghan war, 1878–80 : Manager of the Rajputana-Malwa Railway, 1875–84 : Agent of the Bombay, Baroda and Central India Railway, 1884–93 : C.I.E., 1888 : Secretary to the Government of India, P.W.D., 1893–7, and Director-General of Railways : K.C.I.E., 1897 : Government Director of Indian Railway Companies at the India Office, 1897–01 : retired from the India Office, 1901 : Chairman of the S. Mahratta Railway Co.

BISUDHWANANDA, SWAMI (1820–1899)

Bansidhar (his original name) was a son of a Kanauj Brahman of Cawnpur, born near Hyderabad, (in the Dekkan): learnt some Persian and Urdu under a Maulvi : entered the Nizam's service, was an excellent horseman, and a great favourite, but, failing to obtain justice in a quarrel over a horse, he set fire to all his earthly possessions, besmeared his body with the ashes, and left Hyderabad, visited places of pilgrimage and sacred shrines, observed the strictest discipline of a monk, took to studying Sanskrit, and in a few years became an accomplished grammarian (Panini School) : spent three years at Hardwar in study and meditation : removed to Benares, and took up his abode at a *ghat*; read all the Darsans (Hindu philosophy) ; became a Sanyasi (devotee) ; assumed a new name, Bisudhwananda, ("unalloyed peace "), and occupied the seat of Gaurswami at Ahlia Bai's Brahmapuri, till his death in April, 1899 : of high stature, strong will, great piety, and profound learning, he commanded great respect among all classes : princes and people sought his advice : he was a great admirer of British rule in India.

BITTLESTON, SIR ADAM (1817–1892)

Educated at Merchant Taylors' school : called to the bar from the Inner Temple, 1841 : Puisne Judge of the Supreme Court, Madras, 1858–62 : knighted : and of the High Court, Madras, 1862–70, when he retired : died Jan. 18, 1892.

BLACKBURNE, SIR WILLIAM (1764–1839)

Political : joined the Madras Army in 1782 : served against the Poligars in 1784, and in the defeat of Tippoo, 1892 : was Interpreter of Mahratti at Tanjore in 1787 under the Resident, and was himself Resident, 1801–23 : remodelled the administration there and in Pudukota : was sent on missions to Travancore : Maj-General : knighted 1838 : died Oct. 16, 1839.

BLACKER, VALENTINE (1778–1823)

Soldier, historian : born Oct. 19, 1778 : entered the Madras Army, 1798 : in the Mysore campaign : at Malavilli : in the Nizam's country : was Q.M.G. 1810 : was under Sir Thomas Hislop at Mahidpur in 1817 and in the Dekkan : Lt-Colonel and Surveyor-General of India : C.B. in 1818 : died at Calcutta, 1823 : wrote a military memoir of the Mahratta war of 1817–19.

BLACKLOCK, AMBROSE (1816–1873)

Doctor : son of a medical officer of the Navy ; born in 1816 : educated at Edinburgh : joined the medical service in Madras in 1840 : Professor of Surgery, and Surgeon, General Hospital, Madras, 1851 : in 1858 Professor of Medicine, and Physician there : in 1870 Deputy Inspector-General : died at Chitore Feb. 11, 1873

BLACKWOOD, GEORGE FREDERICK (1838–1880)

Major : son of Major William Blackwood of the Bengal Army : born 1838 : educated at the Edinburgh Academy, and Addiscombe : joined the Bengal Artillery : Lieut., 1857 : in the mutiny served with the Rohilkund movable column : commanded the Artillery in the Lushai expedition of 1871–2 under General Bourchier (*q.v.*) : at Tipai Mukh and other actions : Brevet Major : commanded the Artillery under General Burrows at Maiwand on July 27, 1880 : fell in battle : his little band of men was the last which made any stand against Ayub Khan's forces.

BLACKWOOD, SIR HENRY, BARONET (1770–1832)

Son of Sir John Blackwood, *Bart.* : born Dec. 28, 1770 : entered the Navy, 1781 : was employed on various stations in several ships : continually engaged : was at Trafalgar, 1805, and at the blockade of Toulon, 1810 : Baronet, 1814 : K.C.B. 1819 : was C. in C. on the East Indian station, 1819–22 : Vice-Admiral, 1821, and commanded at the Nore, 1827-30 : died Dec. 17, 1832.

BLAIR, JAMES (1828–1905)

Born Jan. 27, 1828 : son of Captain E. M. Blair of the Bengal Cavalry : entered the Army in 1844 : in the mutiny of 1857–9 : fought at Nimbhara and Ziran : was at the sieges of Neemuch and Kotah, and in the pursuit of Tantia Topi : gained the V.C. for gallant and daring conduct on two occasions, on Aug. 12, 1857 at Neemuch and Oct. 23, 1857, at Jeerum : Political Resident and Brig-General at Aden,

1882-5 : Lt-General, 1889 : C.B., 1889 : General, 1894 : died Jan. 1905.

BLAIR, SIR ROBERT (? - ?)

Joined the E. I. Co's 1st European Infantry in Bengal, 1773 : with General Goddard's force from Bengal to Bombay, 1778-81: A.D.C. to Col. W. Blair commanding in the Doab, 1786-8 : took the fortress of Sasni, 1802 : in the Mahratta war, under Lake, at Alighar, Delhi, Agra, 1803 : commanded at Cuttack, 1808 : Maj-General, 1810 : commanded Fort William and neighbouring districts, 1812 : retired, 1817 : K.C.B., 1815 : Lt-General, 1817.

BLAKISTON, JOHN (1788-1867)

Son of Sir Mathew Blakiston, *Bart.* : born 1788 : educated at Winchester : joined the Madras Engineers and the 27th regt. : as Major, present at Assaye, Bourbon, the Mauritius, and in the Peninsula campaign : the sole survivor of the regiment massacred in the mutiny of Vellore, 1806 : and returned with (Sir R.R.) Gillespie, who came to the rescue : wrote *Twelve Years Military Adventures*, 1829 : and *Twenty Years in Retirement*, 1836 : died 1867.

BLAND, NATHANIEL (1803-1865)

Born Feb. 3, 1803 : son of Nathaniel Bland (formerly called Crumpe) who took his mother's name : educated at Eton, 1818, and Christ Church, Oxford, 1821-5 : was a distinguished Persian scholar : sent contributions to the *R.A.S.J.*, 1843-53 : on Persian chess : on the Pote collection of Oriental MSS. in the Eton College Library, etc : took to gambling, had to sell his estate, and took his own life, Aug. 10, 1865.

BLANEY, THOMAS (1823-1903)

Doctor : born in Ireland ; went to India, 1836, as apprentice in the subordinate medical service of the E. I. Co. at Bombay : studied at the Grant Medical College : in Government service until 1860 : took up private practice at Bombay : made a large fortune, which he spent chiefly in charity : became J.P., Town Councillor : Member of the Municipal Corporation : was connected with civil administration for 30 years : twice

President of the Municipal body : carried schemes for abundant water-supply from Vihar and Tansa lakes : twice Sheriff of Bombay : for many years Chairman of joint Government and Municipal Committee for education : Coroner of Bombay, 1876-93 : C.I.E. : a fine statue of him erected in Bombay by his fellow citizens : died there April 1, 1903 : Member of the Royal Asiatic Society, Bombay, and a frequent contributor to the columns of the *Bombay Gazette*.

BLANFORD, HENRY FRANCIS (1834-1893)

Son of W. Blanford : born June 3, 1834 : educated at Brighton, Brussels, and the Royal School of Mines : entered the Geological Survey of India in 1855 : transferred to the Education Department in Bengal, 1862 : Professor at the Presidency College, 1872 : became Meteorological Reporter, first to the Government of Bengal and later to the Government of India : Hony. Secretary of the Asiatic Society of Bengal, 1863-8 : F.G.S. 1862 : F.R.S. 1880 : retired in 1880 : died Jan. 23, 1893. The excellence of his work in geology and meteorology, as displayed in his official duties, and his contributions to scientific publications, is acknowledged.

BLANFORD, WILLIAM THOMAS (1832-1905)

Born Oct. 7, 1832 : son of William Blanford : educated at the Royal School of Mines (Scholar,) and Mining Academy, Freiburg : in the Geological Survey of India, 1855-82 : Geologist of the Abyssinian Expedition up to Magdala, 1868 : on the Persian Boundary Commission, 1872 : President of the Asiatic Society of Bengal, 1878-9 : of the Geological Society, 1888-90 : received its Wollaston medal, 1883 : Treasurer of the Society : Vice-President of the Royal Society, 1892-3, 1901-3 : published works on the Geology and Zoology of Abyssinia and Persia ; a manual of Geology on India, 1879 : President of the Geological section of the British Association meeting in Canada, 1884: edited *The Fauna of British India* : was author of the *Mammalia*, 1888-91, and of the *Birds*, 1895, 1898 : C.I.E., 1904 : LL.D. Montreal, and F.R.S., 1874 : on its Council and Vice-President : died June 23, 1905.

BLAVATSKY, HELENA PETROVNA
(1831–1891)

Born at Ekaterinoslav : daughter of Colonel Peter Hahn, of a noble family of Mechlenburg, settled in Russia : married at 17 a husband of 60, but they soon separated : she travelled widely, in Europe, America and Asia, round the Cape to Bombay : after an unsuccessful attempt to enter Tibet, *viâ* Nipal, she entered it in disguise in 1855, *viâ* Kashmir, was lost in the desert and brought back to the frontier : after numerous adventures and further travels in India, she was in the United States in 1873 and for 6 years in N. York, becoming a naturalized American : she studied spiritualism, and in 1875 founded, with Colonel Olcott, the Theosophical Society : wrote books and pamphlets in support of her theories : settled in London, 1887 : brought out a magazine, *Lucifer, the Light-bringer* : wrote *The Secret Doctrine, the Synthesis of Science, Religion and Philosophy*, 1888, and *The Key of Philosophy*, 1889 : died in London, May 8, 1891.

BLISS, SIR HENRY WILLIAM
(1840–)

I.C.S. : son of Rev. James Bliss : born 1840 : educated at Merton, Oxford, B.A. joined the Madras Civil Service, 1863 : after holding subordinate appointments, was Commissioner of Salt Revenue and Abkari Revenue, 1878 : on special duty on these subjects : Fellow of the Madras University, 1882 : Member of the Finance Committee, 1886 : Member of the Board of Revenue, 1887 : first Member, 1889 : C.I.E., 1889 : Member of the Governor-General's Legislative Council, 1890–2 : Member of Council, Madras, 1893–8 : K.C.I.E., 1897 : retired, 1898 : Member of the London County Council for the Holborn Division, 1901.

BLOCHMANN, HENRY FERDINAND
(1838–1878)

Linguistic scholar : born at Dresden Jan. 8, 1838, the son of a printer : educated there, at Leipzig, and Paris : entered the English Army in 1858 to get out to India, left the Army, and joined the P. and O. Co.'s service as interpreter : in 1860 was made Assistant Professor of Urdu and Persian at the Calcutta Madrasa : graduated at the Calcutta University, 1861 : after 3 years at the Doveton College, removed to the Madrasa, 1865, and became its President until his death : he was philological Secretary to the Asiatic Society of Bengal, and contributed many learned papers : translated Abul-Fazl's *A in-i-Akbari*, the first volume, and wrote *The Prosody of the Persians* : he had a profound knowledge of Persian and Arabic : died July 13, 1878.

BLOSSET, SIR ROBERT HENRY (1776 –1823)

Son of the Rev. Dr. Henry Peckwell, an eminent preacher : he took his mother's name of Blosset : educated at Oxford : was Recorder of Cambridge : was appointed Chief Justice of Bengal in 1821 :· died Feb. 1, 1823. There are a monument and hatchmênt to his memory at St. John's Church, Calcutta.

BLUNT, CHARLES HARRIS (1824– 1900)

Maj-General : entered the Army, 1842 : was in the Bengal Horse Artillery : was in the Satlaj campaign, 1846, at Sobraon : also in the Panjab campaign : in the mutiny, raised " Blunt's Horse," was at the siege of Delhi, battle of Najafghar, action at Agra, (Lord Clyde's) relief of Lucknow, where he was the hero of a very dashing performance with the guns at the Sikandarbagh, at the action of Shamsabad, the capture of the fort and town of Kalpi : Brevets of Major and Colonel : C.B : Lord Roberts refers to his splendid courage in leading his guns in the advance on Lucknow : his troops suffered severely at Delhi and Agra, " seldom, if ever, has a battery and its commander had a grander record to show " : died. Aug 15, 1900.

BLUNT, SIR CHARLES WILLIAM, BARONET (1731–1802)

Of Cleery, Hants : born 1731 : son of Sir Henry Blunt, second Baronet, whom he succeeded in 1759 : lived in Great Ormonde St. till about 1767 : at Odiham, Hants, till about 1775 : at Blunt House, Croydon, to about 1780 : went out as a writer in the E. I. Co.'s service to India, 20 years before his death : obtained a lucrative appointment in the bullock contract, besides a share in the Post-office : formed honourable and advantageous connexions : died Sep, 27, 1802, at Pulta, near Calcutta, leaving £100,000, three-fourths of it to his eldest son,

C. R. Blunt, fourth Baronet (born 1778 : M.P. for Lewes, 1832) : his portrait by Barclay is in the possession of his grandson, the present Baronet : letters from him are among the Hastings papers in the British Museum : one of his daughters married Sir C. Imhoff, stepson of Warren Hastings : he built a mausoleum for the sepulture of his race-horses, which was still to be seen in India about 1845 : many pictures of his horses are preserved.

BLYTH, EDWARD (1810-1873)

Born Dec. 23, 1810 : was a druggist at Tooting, but Natural History was the absorbing study of his life : in 1841 he was appointed Curator of the Museum of the Asiatic Society of Bengal : retired in 1862 : wrote a great number of reports and papers on Zoology, especially on birds and mammals, in the Society's journals and in newspapers : he was said to have been the founder of the science of Zoology in India : his work was highly estimated by Darwin and Gould : died Dec. 27, 1873.

BODEN, JOSEPH (? -1811)

Entered the E. I. Co.'s Bombay Native Army in 1781 : Lt-Colonel 1806 : held appointments on the Staff in Bombay : was Member of the Military Board : retired in 1807 and died Nov. 21, 1811. Though not a Sanskrit scholar, and not a writer, he left a large sum of money to found, after his daughter's death, a professorship of Sanskrit at Oxford. H. H. Wilson (q.v.) was the first professor appointed, in 1832.

BOGLE, SIR ARCHIBALD (1805-1870)

Entered the E. I. Co.'s military service, 1823 : was D.A.G. at Dinapur, 1827 : commanded the Arakan battalion and police corps, 1828 : Commissioner in Arakan, 1837 : afterwards in Tenasserim and Martaban : knighted, 1853 : Maj-General, 1862 : died June 12, 1870.

BOGLE, GEORGE (1746-1781)

Son of George Bogle : born Nov. 26, 1746 : educated at Haddington, Glasgow, Edinburgh University, Enfield : entered the E. I. Co.'s service in 1769 : was appointed by Warren Hastings on May 13, 1774, to lead an embassy to the Teshu Lama of Tibet, for the purpose of opening up trade and friendly relations with that country : he proceeded by Tassisudon in Bhutan, through Phari, to Desherigpay (north of the Tsanpu River), saw the Teshu Lama, accompanied him to Teshu Lumbo, and returned thence to India, 1775 : in 1779 he was appointed Collector of Rangpur and established a fair, to encourage trade with Bhutan and Tibet. A second embassy of Bogle to Tibet was contemplated, but was postponed, the Teshu Lama going to Pekin : Bogle proposed meeting him at Pekin, but died at Calcutta on April 3, 1781 : the journal of his embassy has been published.

BÖHTLINGK, OTTO VON (1815-1904)

Born May 30, 1815, at St. Petersburg : studied there and at Dorpat, Berlin, Bonn : returned to St. Petersburg, 1842. At first, his scholarship was directed to the study of Arabic and Persian, but he became celebrated as a worker in Sanskrit. In 1840, he published *Grammaire Sanskrite* (Panini's), 1843 : *Dissertation sur l'accent Sanskrit* : edition and German translation of *Sakuntala de Kalidasa : Chrestomathie Sanskrite*, 1877. The great work of his life was his *Sanskrit Dictionary*, 7 vols. brought out with the collaboration of Professors Röth and Weber, 1852-75 : died at Leipzig in 1904.

BOLES, THOMAS (? - ?)

Lt.-Colonel : was a volunteer in the 36th regt., 1783 : acting Ensign, 1784-5 : a conductor of Stores : attached to Artillery, 1786-7 : Ensign in the Madras Army, 1788 : A.A.G., Madras Army for 5 years : D.A.G., 1807 : when Lt.-General H. Macdowall, C. in C., Madras, signed an order, Jan. 28, 1809, censuring his Q.M.G., Capt. Munro, Boles, as Depy. A.G., was ordered by Col. Capper, the Adjt-General, to circulate the order to the Army. For circulating, under his signature, this censure of Capt. Munro, Boles was suspended from the service of the E. I. Co., by the Government of Madras (Sir G. Barlow), Jan. 31, 1809 : and declined to apologize for his conduct. The Madras Government prevented his going home, sent him to Bengal in June, 1809, whence he went to England. The Court of Directors, to whom he appealed in 1810, recorded in Feb. 1811, their opinion that Boles would not have been justified in refusing to obey General Macdowall's order. Boles' suspension was continued to Oct. 1811, when he was restored to the service.

BOLTON, CHARLES WALTER
(1850-   )

I.C.S. : son of Dr. J. Bolton : educated at University College School, the Royal College, Mauritius, and King's College, London : went out to Lower Bengal, 1872 : Under Secretary to the Bengal Government, 1879 : Secretary to the Board of Revenue, 1897 : Chief Secretary to the Bengal Government, 1896 : Member of the Board, 1900 : Additional Member of the Governor-General's Legislative Council, 1900–1902 : C.S.I., 1897.

BOLTS, WILLIAM (1740 ?-1808)

Born about 1740 : was a merchant of Dutch extraction : being in Calcutta in 1759, he was taken into the E. I. Co.'s service : engaged in private trade, like other civil servants : was Second in Council at Benares, 1764 : being censured by the Court of Directors for his private trading under the Company's authority and re-called, he resigned in 1766, quarrelled with the Bengal authorities, was arrested in 1768, and deported to England as an interloper. In his *Considerations on Indian Affairs*, 1772, he attacked the Bengal Government : Verelst replied, and Bolts published another work in 1775. He made a large fortune in India, but could not take it away : he spent what he had in England in defending the lawsuits brought against him by the E. I. Co. for some years. He entered the Austrian service, became a Colonel, and founded stations in India for an Austrian Company : these came to nothing : he died in Paris in 1808.

BONARJEE, REV. SHIB CHUNDER
(1830-1897)

A Brahman, of good family : educated at the Duff College, and baptized by the Rev. Dr. Duff in 1847 : held various missionary charges : celebrated both for his eloquent preaching and his philan-thropy : was the author of a *Life of Christ* in Bengali, and a large number of tracts : universally regarded as one of the leading ministers of the Bengali Church.

BONNERJEE, WOMESH CHUNDER
(1844-   )

Second son of Grees Chunder Bonnerjee, attorney of the High Court, Calcutta :

born Dec. 29, 1844 : educated at the Oriental Seminary and Hindu School : in 1864, in receipt of a scholarship from Mr. R. J. Jijibhai of Bombay, went to England to study law : called to the bar from the Middle Temple : joined the Calcutta High Court Bar, 1868 : acted as the Standing Counsel to Government in 1882, 1884, 1886-7 : presided over the First Indian National Congress at Bombay, 1885 : Fellow of the Calcutta University : President of the Faculty of Law, 1880 : represented the Calcutta University in the Bengal Legislative Council, 1893 : retired from the Calcutta Bar, 1901, to practise before the Judicial Committee of the Privy Council in England.

BOPP, FRANCIS (1791-1867)

Born at Mentz, Sep. 14, 1791 : educated at Aschaffenburg, under Windischmann, the celebrated Oriental scholar : went to Paris, 1812, for 5 years : chiefly studied Sanskrit : settled in Gottingen : became in 1821 Extraordinary, and in 1825 Ordinary Professor of Oriental Literature and General Philology at Berlin University, till his death : a prominent Member of the Royal Society at Berlin : wrote his *Analytical Comparison of the Sanskrit, Greek, Latin and Teutonic Languages* in the Annals of Oriental Literature, 1820 : greatly encouraged and facilitated the study of Sanskrit : his Sanskrit Grammar passed through several editions, 1827-63 : an original foreign member of the R.A.S. from June 7, 1823 : his *Comparative Grammar* was translated into English, 1845-50 : he died Oct. 23, 1867.

BORTON, SIR ARTHUR (1814-1893)

Son of the Rev. J. D. Borton : born Jan. 20, 1814 : educated at Eton : entered the Army, 1832, rose to be General, 1877 : went to India in 1835, served in the Afghanistan campaign of 1842 under General Pollock : was at Tezin, in the Kohistan, and at Istalif on Sep. 29 : in the battles of the Satlaj campaign of 1845-6 : in the Crimea : C.B. : in Canada : commanded the Mysore Division of Madras Army, 1870-5 : K.C.B. : Governor and C. in C. of Malta in 1877 : G.C.M.G., 1880 : G.C.B., 1884 : died Sep. 7, 1893.

BOSCAWEN, HON. EDWARD (1711-1761)

Son of first Viscount Falmouth : born 'Aug. 19, 1711 : joined the Navy, 1726 :

served on a number of stations, the Mediterranean, the West Indies, the Home station, the Channel, at the Nore, at Cape Finisterre, 1747 : and in that year was appointed C. in C. of the sea and land forces in the E. Indies : passed the Mauritius without taking it from the French : reached Fort St. David, July, 1748: failed, after a repulse at Ariancopang, which he captured later, in taking Pondicherry by both sea and land : lost ships in stormy weather : at the peace of Aix-la-Chapelle, took possession of Madras on its restoration by the French, Aug. 21, 1749 : and returned to England : held more commands in N. America : a Lord of the Admiralty : at the siege of Louisberg against the French in Europe : was made P.C. : died Jan. 10, 1761.

BOULGER, DEMETRIUS CHARLES (1853–)

Born July 14, 1853 : educated at Kensington Grammar School and privately : has contributed to all the leading journals on questions relating to India, China, Egypt and Turkey since 1876 : founded, in conjunction with Sir Lepel Griffin, the *Asiatic Quarterly Review* in 1885, and edited it for some years : author of *Life of Yakub Beg of Kashgar, England and Russia in Central Asia, Central Asian Portraits, Armies of the Native States of India, Central Asian Questions, Lord William Bentinck, Story of India, India in the Nineteenth Century, History of China*, of which several editions have been published, *Life of Gordon, Life of Sir Stamford Raffles*, etc.

BOURCHIER, SIR GEORGE (1821–1898)

Son of Rev. Edward Bourchier : educated at Addiscombe : entered the Bengal Artillery, 1838 : in the Gwalior campaign, 1843–4 : at Punniar : in the mutiny commanded a battery at Trimmu Ghat : at the siege and capture of Delhi : at Bulandshahr, Alighar, Agra, Sir Colin Campbell's relief of Lucknow, at Cawnpur : Brevet Colonel and C.B. : commanded the R.A. in Bhutan, 1864–6 : commanded the E. frontier district, 1871, and the Cachar column in the Lushai expedition, 1871–2 : K.C.B., 1852 : Maj-General : died March 15, 1898.

BOURDILLON, SIR JAMES AUSTIN (1848–)

I.C.S. : born at Madras, March, 1848 : son of J. D. Bourdillon (*q.v.*) : educated at Marlborough : Captain of the Cricket XI : went out to India, 1870 : Superintendent of the Census of Bengal, 1880–3 : acting Secretary to the Bengal Government, Financial Department, 1893–5 : Commissioner of Patna, in the famine, 1897 : C.S.I., 1898 : Chief Secretary to the Government of Bengal, 1900 : Member of the Famine Commission in India, 1901 : Member of the Board of Revenue, 1902 : for some years Member of the Bengal Legislative Council : acted as Lieutenant-Governor of Bengal, Nov. 1902–Nov. 1903 : Resident in Mysore, 1903 : K.C.S.I., Jan. 1904 : V.D., 1896, for long service as a volunteer in the Calcutta Light Horse and Bihar Light Horse.

BOURDILLON, JAMES DEWAR (1811–1883)

I.C.S : son of the Rev. T. Bourdillon: educated at Ramsgate and Haileybury : joined the Civil Service at Madras in 1828 : was Secretary to the Board of Revenue and Secretary to Government in the Revenue and P.W.D. : advocated irrigation and the improvement of communications : was an authority on land revenue and the despatch of public business : retired in 1861 : died May 21, 1883.

BOURGUIEN, LOUIS (? – ?)

Louis Bernard : a Frenchman : went to India with Admiral Suffrein : from Pondicherry went to Calcutta and enlisted in the E.I. Co.'s service : was a cook and pyrotechnist : employed by Begam Samru : in 1794 by De Boigne : under Perron in 1800, in Sindia's service : fought against George Thomas (*q.v.*) : and was defeated by him at Georgeghar : later, made Thomas surrender at Hansi : captured Rohtak, 1803 : after the defeat of Colonel Pedron by Lake at Alighar, Bourguien revolted against Perron : the latter surrendered to the British, and Bourguien, as General, held command of Sindia's troops for a fortnight, until he himself was defeated by Lake at the battle of Delhi, Sep. 11, 1803 : three days afterwards he surrendered to Lake : was sent to Calcutta : returned to France, with great wealth, and was heard of no more.

E

BOWRING, LEWIN BENTHAM
(1824–   )

I.C.S.: born July 15, 1824 : third son of Sir George Bowring : educated at Exeter, Leipzig and Haileybury, 1841–3 : went out to India, 1843 : Deputy Commissioner in the Panjab, 1849–54 : Private Secretary to Lord Canning, when Viceroy, April, 1858 to 1862 : Chief Commissioner of Mysore and Coorg, 1862–70 : retired, 1870 : C.S.I., 1867 : author of *Eastern Experiences, Hyder Ali and Tippoo Sultan*, and contributions to the Asiatic Society of Bengal.

BOWSER, SIR THOMAS (1748–1833)

Born 1748, at Kirkby Thore, Westmorland : educated at Appleby Grammar School : entered the E.I. Co.'s Army at 24 : at the taking of Tanjore in 1773 : for 3 years engaged in the capture of forts in the N. Sircars : at the siege of Pondicherry, 1778 : in the Guntur Sircar campaign, 1779 : as a Lieutenant, in Sir Hector Munro's army in 1780, sent to help Col. Baillie and, with him, taken prisoner by Hyder Ali in the Perambakam disaster, Sept. 1780 : confined at Seringapatam 3 years and 8 months : loaded with irons for 3 years and 4 months : liberated, 1784 : to England for 3 years : published in 1788 his *Memoirs of The Late War in Asia* : served under Medows in 1792, at the storming of Dindigul : given by Cornwallis the command of a sepoy battalion : served under General Braithwaite at the siege of Pondicherry, 1798 : employed against the Raja of Ramnad : effected the reduction of Ceylon, 1796 : took fort Calpentein and Colombo : sent to reduce the French force under Perron at Hyderabad : at Seringapatam, May 4, 1799 : stormed the fortress of Gooty : commanded from Hyderabad a mixed force, joining Colonel A. Wellesley, against Doondia Waugh : to England, 1803 : again to India in 1820 : commanded the Mysore Division : was temporarily C. in C. of Madras Army, 1824–6, on the death of Sir Alexander Campbell : retired, May, 1826 : was a Lt-General and K.C.B. : died June, 1833.

BOYD, HUGH (1746–1794)

Son of Alexander Macaulay : took his mother's name, Boyd : born in Oct. 1746 : educated at Dublin, and graduated at Trinity College, 1765 : studied law, and contributed to journals and literature : in 1781 became Secretary to Lord Macartney, Governor of Madras : sent on a mission to Ceylon, captured by the French and kept a prisoner at Bourbon for some months : became Master Attendant at Madras, and conducted the *Madras Courier :* wrote the *Indian Observer* papers, and the *Hircarrah :* it was said that he was the author of the *Letters of Junius*, a supposition which he never positively contradicted : his works were collected and published : died Oct. 15, 1764.

BRACKENBURY, SIR HENRY
(1837–   )

Born Sept. 1, 1837 : educated at Eton and R.M.C., Woolwich : joined the Royal Artillery, 1856 : in the Indian mutiny : served in Central India, 1857–8 : Ashanti war, 1873–4 : Zulu war, 1879–80 : Private Secretary to Lord Lytton, the Viceroy of India, 1880 : Military Attaché at Paris, 1881–2 : commanded River Column, Egypt, 1884–5 : promoted Maj-General for distinguished service in the field : Director of Military Intelligence, 1886–91 : Military Member of the Supreme Council of India, 1891–6 : Director-General of Ordnance at the War Office, 1899 : K.C.B., 1894 : K.C.S.I., 1896 : G.C.B., 1900 : General R.A., 1901 : P.C.

BRADDON, SIR EDWARD NICHOLAS COVENTRY (1829–1904)

Son of Henry Braddon, and brother of Miss Braddon the novelist : went out to India in 1847 to join the mercantile house of Bagshaw and Co., in Calcutta, but preferred work in the Mofussil : while he was employed on the E.I. Railway, the Sonthal rebellion of 1855 broke out, in which he rendered such excellent service that he was appointed an Assistant Commissioner in the Sonthal *Parganas :* during the mutiny he served in the Volunteer force under Sir George Yule, Commissioner of Bhagalpur, and, after the mutiny, on that officer's invitation, joined the Oudh Commission, where he remained until Oudh was amalgamated with the N.W.P. in 1877 : resigned the Service and went to Tasmania, where he rose to be Premier and Agent-General for Tasmania in London : K.C.M.G., 1891 : published *Life in India*, and *Thirty Years of Shikar*, in 1895 : died Feb. 3, 1904.

BRADFORD, SIR EDWARD RIDLEY COLBORNE, BARONET (1836–)

Born July 27, 1836 : son of Rev. W. M. K. Bradford : educated at Marlborough : entered the Madras Army, 1854 : Colonel in 1884 : served in the Persian campaign, 1856–7 : in the Indian mutiny, in the N.W. Provinces, 1858–9 : commanded a regt. of the Central India Horse, 1860 : entered the Political Department : General Superintendent for suppressing Thagi and Dakaiti, 1874 : attended H.R.H. the Prince of Wales on his tour in India, 1875–6 : Agent to the Governor-General for Rajputana : Secretary in the Political and Secret Department, India Office, 1887 : accompanied H.R.H. Prince Edward, Duke of Clarence, on his tour in India, 1889–90 : A.D.C. to the Queen, 1889–93 : Chief Commissioner of Police in the Metropolis, 1890–1903 : K.C.S.I., 1885 : G.C.B. : G.C.V.O., 1902 : Extra Equerry to the King, 1902 : Baronet, 1902.

BRADFORD, SIR THOMAS (1777–1853)

Son of Thomas Bradford : born Dec. 1, 1777 : entered the Army, 1793 : served in Ireland, Scotland, S. America, the Peninsula : commanded the Portuguese Division at Vittoria in 1813 as Maj-General : K.C.B., 1814 : held commands in France and Scotland : was C. in C. in Bombay, 1825–9 : G.C.B., 1838 : General, 1841 : died Nov. 28, 1853.

BRADSHAW, JOHN (1845–1894)

Born June 4, 1845 : son of Rev. William Hanna Bradshaw, A.M., Rector of Kilsheery : educated at Enniskillen Royal School, at Portora, and Trinity College, Dublin : Senior Moderator in History, Literature, and Law, T.C.D. : appointed Head-master of Bishop Corrie's Grammar School, Madras, 1868 : and of the Provincial School, Mangalore, 1870 : Inspector of Schools, 1872 : Fellow, Madras University, 1875 : he was essentially an educationalist : his knowledge and experience were exceptional : his life work was an endeavour to place native education on a sound basis : edited many works for Middle and High Schools : besides *An English Anthology*, 1885, *Milton* and *Gray* for the Aldine Poets, *Chesterfield's Letters*, etc. : and the *Life of Sir Thomas Munro*, for the Rulers of India series : died at Madras, Jan. 5, 1894.

BRANDIS, SIR DIETRICH (1824–)

Born 1824 : educated at the Universities of Copenhagen, Gottingen and Bonn : lecturer on Botany at Bonn, 1849 : joined the Indian Forest Department in 1856 : Inspr-General of Forests, 1864 : C.I.E., 1878 : retired, 1883 : Member of the Board of Visitors of Cooper's Hill College, 1886 : K.C.I.E., 1887 : author of the *Forest Flora of N.W. and Central India* 1874 : Director of the practical course of forestry on the Continent in connexion with Cooper's Hill College, 1887–96.

BRANFOOT, ARTHUR MUDGE (1848–)

Born Feb. 29, 1848 : son of Jonathan Haigh Branfoot, M.D. : educated at Epsom College, and Guy's Hospital : entered the I.M.S., 1872 : held various civil appointments connected with the Madras Medical College, 1872–9 : Professor of Midwifery there, and Superintendent Madras Government Maternity Hospital, 1879–98 : C.I.E., 1898 : P.M.O., Rangoon and Bangalore, 1898–1903 : retired, 1903 : President, Medical Board, India Office, 1904 : contributed to medical journals and societies.

BRASYER, JEREMIAH (1812–1897)

Colonel : brought up as a gardener in Kent : enlisted in the Bengal Artillery, 1833 : Sergt-Major, 26th regt., Bengal N.I. Sept., 1839 : served in the Afghan war, 1842 : at the forcing of the Khyber : at Mamu Kheyl, Jagdalak, Haft Kotal, Tezin, with the Artillery : in the Sikh campaigns : at Mudki, Firozshahr and Sobraon, with the 26th N.I. : Ensign, 1846 : interpreter to the Firozpur regt. of Sikhs, and commanded them, "Brasyer's Sikhs," in the mutiny, 1857–8 : with his regt. as the sole garrison, he held the fortress of Allahabad, the key of Upper India, at the most critical moment : through his energy and resolute attitude, his Sikhs remained loyal : " no man risen from the ranks has ever done a deed evincing such force of character and desperate resolution, and securing such invaluable results " : at the capture of Lucknow, March, 1858 : Lt-Colonel and C.B., 1858 : retired Oct. 1861 : died March 15, 1897.

BRATHWAITE, SIR JOHN (? – ?)

A noted officer in the Indian wars during the latter part of the 18th century :

as Major, 1772, he marched against the Poligars of Madura and Tinnevelly : Lt-Colonel : captured, 1779, the French settlement of Mahé : took an active part in the war with Hyder Ali : in 1780, Colonel, and in command of the troops in Tanjore : his defeat by Tippoo near Annagudi in 1782 was a serious blow to the Southern Army : he himself was wounded and taken prisoner, but released on the conclusion of peace in 1784 : held high command in the Madras Army, 1792 : when war broke out with the French Republic, Brathwaite took Pondicherry, 1793 : Maj-General in 1800.

BREEKS, JAMES WILKINSON (1830–1872)

I.C.S. : born March 5, 1830 : arrived at Madras in 1849 : was Private Secretary to the Governor of Madras, Sir W. Denison, 1861–64, accompanying him to Calcutta when he acted as Governor-General, between Lord Elgin and Sir John Lawrence. In 1867 Breeks was appointed Commissioner of the Nilgiris : in 1871 he was called upon to make collections of objects among the aboriginal tribes for the Indian Museum, Calcutta : he fell ill and died June 7, 1872 : he wrote a valuable report on the tribes and sepulchral monuments of the Nilgiris, published under the editorship of his widow in 1873.

BRIGGS, HENRY GEORGE (1824–1872)

Born in Bombay, Oct. 20, 1824 : son of Henry Briggs : travelled in S. Africa, 1843 : in China, 1845 : settled in Bombay, 1846, in the office of Briggs & Co. : served in the Bombay Secretariat : went to Karachi : edited, 1854, the *Sindian*, and, 1855, the Sind *Kossid*, both long since defunct : became, 1856, Assistant Secretary at Bombay to the G.I.P. Railway: Secretary to the Bombay Municipality, 1860–2 : was a merchant and agent at Bombay and Hingolee, 1863 : he wrote, 1849, *Cities of Gujārashtra*, a book of travel in Gujarat, containing curious information gleaned from travellers in India : of whose rare works he made an extensive collection: published *The Parsis or Modern Zardushtians*, 1852, which has now been superseded : wrote an historical account of the Nizam, 1861, a valuable work containing special information. His firm failed in the share mania of 1865 ; he travelled in Gujarat, and

settled in Calcutta, entering the P.W.D. there : in May, 1872, he went again to Bombay ; died there July 4, 1872.

BRIGGS, JOHN (1785–1875)

Entered the E. I. Co.'s Madras Army in 1801 : served in the Mahratta wars : accompanied Sir J. Malcolm on his mission to Persia, 1810 : became Resident at Satara, and in 1831 was Senior Member of the Board of Administration of Mysore : resigned in 1832, and was Resident at Nagpur, 1832–5, when he retired : Maj-General, 1838. As Member of the Court of Proprietors of the E.I. Co., he opposed Lord Dalhousie's policy : he translated Ferishta's *Muhammadan Power in India* and the *Siyar-ul-muta' akhkhirin* from Persian into English : was F.R.S. : died April 27, 1875.

BRIGHT, JOHN (1811–1889)

Born Nov. 16, 1811 : son of Jacob Bright, of Rochdale : educated there and at Ackworth, York, Newton : joined his father in managing mills, travelled, and entered politics : co-operated with Cobden against the Corn Laws : M.P. for Durham, 1843 ; for Manchester, 1847, 1852 ; for Birmingham, 1857–85 : in his political life he paid special attention to India : in 1848, was Chairman of the Committee, for which he moved, to inquire into the obstacles to the cultivation of cotton in India : helped to raise a fund for a private Commission of inquiry : opposed the renewal of the Charter of the E. I. Co. in 1853 : spoke, 1853, strongly in favour of making the Government of India a Department of the Government, with a Minister of State and a Council : in the discussions on the transfer of the Government of India to the Crown, in 1858, and again in 1879, he advocated a policy of decentralization, by the substitution of federated Provincial Governments for a Central Government : urged, in 1859, the reduction of military expenditure in India : declined to be Secretary of State for India, 1868, being unwilling, as a Quaker, to be mixed up with military matters : advocated developments of India by public works and canals, 1878–9 : spoke against the Afghan war of 1878–80 : D.C.L., 1886 : died March 27, 1889 : his general career in Parliament, his share in English politics, and his eloquent speeches, need not be dwelt upon here.

BRIGHT, SIR ROBERT ONESIPHO-RUS (1823-1896)

Born July 7, 1823 : son of Robert Bright, merchant, educated at Rugby and Winchester : joined the 19th regt. in 1843, and served continuously with it until, in 1871, he obtained a Brigade command : served in the Bulgarian campaign, 1854 : in the Crimea, present at all the battles : in 1868 commanded the first Brigade Hazara Field Force, and against the Black Mountain tribes : commanded the Meerut Division, 1878-83 : in the Afghan war, 1879-80, commanded the Khyber Line Field Force : constantly mentioned in despatches during his career : Brevet Lt-Colonel : Knight of the Legion of Honour : C.B. in 1868 : K.C.B. and the thanks of Parliament after the Afghan war : Colonel of his regt., 1886 : Lt-General : G.C.B., 1894 : died Nov. 15, 1896.

BRIND, SIR JAMES (1808-1888)

Son of Walter Brind : born July 10, 1808 : educated at Addiscombe : joined the Bengal Artillery in 1827 : in 1854 he commanded the Artillery in Sir Sydney Cotton's force against the Mohmands : at the siege of Delhi in the mutiny he commanded a battery, called after him : showed great bravery and activity : it was said that he never slept, and that he should be covered with Victoria Crosses from head to foot : commanded the Artillery in a number of engagements in 1858 : in Oudh, Rohilkund and the pursuit of Firozshah : Brevet Colonel and C.B. : was Inspr-General of Artillery, 1865 : K.C.B., 1869 : commanded the Sirhind Division, 1873-8 : General, 1877 : G.C.B., 1884 : died Aug. 3, 1888 : he was married five times.

BRISTOW, JOHN (? - ?)

Appointed Resident of Lucknow, by direct order of the Court of Directors, on Nathaniel Middleton's recall in 1774, after the Rohilla war, by a majority in Council against Warren Hastings : Bristow was not friendly with Hastings : was a constant attendant of P. Francis' levées : he was superseded at Lucknow in 1781, by Hastings' order, replaced by Middleton, but re-established in 1782, when Middleton was recalled : Bristow assumed the powers of Government at Lucknow, aiming at the annihilation of the Nawab's authority, on which the Nawab complained against Bristow's administration : Bristow's defence was discussed by the parties in the Supreme Council : he was recalled by a decision of Dec. 31, 1783, Hastings being authorized to have separate charge of the E.I. Co's concerns in Oudh, for which he repaired to Lucknow in March-Aug. 1784.

BROADFOOT, GEORGE (1807-1845)

Born 1807 : son of Rev. W. Broadfoot : entered the Madras Native Infantry in 1826 : in 1841 was sent to Kabul commanding the escort with the families of Shah Shuja and Zaman Shah : in Oct. 1841 he accompanied Sir R. Sale's force from Kabul to Jalalabad : which he fortified, and became garrison engineer there during the siege by the Afghans : he animated the whole defence and prevented a surrender : was with General Pollock's Army in the campaign of 1842, and distinguished himself in the actions in the Khyber, at Tezin and Mamu Kheyl : C.B. : made Commissioner of Tenasserim and, later, Agent to the Governor-General on the N.W. frontier : he was a Major in the Sikh war of 1845-6 : was mortally wounded at Firozshahr, Dec. 21, 1845.

BROADFOOT, WILLIAM (1841-   )

Born Oct. 15, 1841 : son of Alexander Broadfoot : educated privately and at Addiscombe : joined the Royal Engineers, 1860 : Major, 1881, on retirement : served with the Hazara Field Force, 1868 : in the Irrigation Department in the Panjab, 1864-8 : Assistant Secretary to the Panjab Government, 1868-78 : has written *The Career of Major George Broadfoot, C.B.*, 1888 : *Billiards* in the Badminton Library : numerous articles in the principal Reviews, Magazines, the *Athenæum*, the *Times Encyclopædia Britannica*, Biographies in the *D.N.B.*, and the *R.E. Journal* : F.R.G.S : is the Referee of the R. Geographical Society on Afghanistan, Beluchistan, India.

BROCKHAUS, HERMAN (1806-1877)

Born at Amsterdam, Jan. 28, 1806 : son of Friedrich Arnold Brockhaus, founder of the Leipzig publishing house : studied Oriental literature at Leipzig, Gottingen, Bonn, and frequented Oriental libraries at Copenhagen, Paris, London, Oxford :

Professor Extraordinarius of Oriental Languages at Jena, 1839 : and Professor Ordinarius of Indian Lanugages and Literature, at Leipzig, 1848 : lectured chiefly on Sanskrit, which was his speciality, though he had studied Hebrew, Arabic, Persian, and lectured on Pali, Zend and Chinese : edited the *Katha-sarit-sagara* of Sanskrit stories, 1839–66, which first led to the scientific study of the origin of Popular Tales : also edited the *Prabodha-Chandrodaya*, a comedy, 1834–45 : the Zend *Vendidad Sade* : *Hafiz* and the *Seven Wise Masters* : was a founder of the Zeitschrift der Deutschen Morgenland-ischen Gesellschaft : wrote for scientific journals : died Jan. 5, 1877.

BRODRICK, HON. WILLIAM ST. JOHN FREMANTLE (1856–   )

Born Dec. 14, 1856 : eldest son of third Viscount Middleton : educated at Eton and Balliol College, Oxford : President of the Oxford Union Society : M.P. for West Surrey, 1880–5; for Guildford Division of Surrey, since 1885 : Financial Secretary to the War Office, 1886–92 : Under Secretary of State for War, 1895–8 : Under Secretary of State for Foreign Affairs, 1898–1900 : Secretary of State for War, 1900–3, during part of the S. African War : Secretary of State for India since 1903 : P.C. 1897 : J.P. : D.L.

BROOKE, SIR GEORGE (1793–1882)

Born 1793 : son of Henry Brooke : educated at the R.M.A., Woolwich : entered the Royal Artillery, 1808 : saw service in Bundelkund, 1809–10 : in the Nipal war, 1815–6 : and in the Mahratta war, 1817 : present at the sieges of Hatras and Bhartpur ; in the battles of the Satlaj campaign, 1845–6 : Brigadier in the Panjab in 1848 : commanded Horse Artillery at Chilianwala and Gujarat : C.B., 1849 : K.C.B., 1867 : General, 1870 : retired, 1877 : died Dec. 31, 1882.

BROOKE, HENRY (1725?–1786)

Son of Rev. Henry Brooke, Rector of Kinawley and Kilina, Ireland : born about 1725 : joined the E.I. Co'.s Civil Service, and rose to be a Member of the Madras Council : took, with George Stratton, a prominent part in the arrest and deposition of Lord Pigot, the Governor of Madras, in 1776 : and was one of the four sentenced on Feb. 10, 1780, in the King's Bench to pay a fine of £1,000 each for their action : died in Dublin, March 26, 1786.

BROOKE, SIR JAMES (1803–1868)

Raja of Sarawak : son of Thomas Brooke of the India Civil Service : born at Benares in 1803 : educated at Norwich : ran away from school and entered the Bengal Native Infantry in 1819 : served in the Burmese war of 1824 : was wounded and sent home : resigned the E. I. Co.'s service in 1830 : in 1838 he sailed in a private vessel to Borneo, to Sarawak : and became its Raja in 1841 by invitation : there he passed the remainder of his career, suppressing rebellion, piracy, cruelty, and establishing civilized govern-ment : retired in 1860 : was made K.C.B : D.C.L. Oxford : died in 1868.

BROOKE, JOHN CHEAPE (1818–1899)

General : son of Colonel C. W. Brooke : joined the 63rd Bengal N.I., 1836 : raised and disciplined the Mewar Bhils, and gained great influence over them and the neigh-bouring chiefs : during the mutiny, kept a large tract of country quiet : Political Agent at Jodhpur and Jaipur, 1860–70 : A.G.G. for Rajputana, 1870–3 : died Jan. 23, 1899.

BROOKE, ROBERT (1746?–1802?)

Son of Robert Brooke : entered the E. I. Co.'s Bengal Army in 1764 : engaged at the battle of Baxar and under Lord Clive against Kasim Ali and Shuja-ud-daula and against Hyder Ali of Mysore in 1768–9 : put down a revolt in Kora, and was made Collector : served in the Raj-mahal hills against the Mahrattas, and in the Rohilla war : his services terminated in 1775 : lost his money in attempting to establish cotton manufacture in Ireland : Governor of St. Helena, 1787–1801 : died soon after his retirement.

BROUGHTON, THOMAS DUER (1778–1835)

Son of Rev. T. Broughton : educated at Eton : went to India in 1795 in the Bengal Army : was at the siege of Serin-gapatam in 1799, and military Resident with the Mahrattas in 1802 : commanded the island of Java : Colonel, 1829 : died Nov. 16, 1835 : wrote *Letters from a Mahratta Camp*, and *Selections from the*

Popular Poetry of the Hindus, 1814 : Hony. Secy. R.A.S.

RROUGHTON DE GYFFORD, JOHN CAM HOBHOUSE, BARON (1786–1869)

Son of Sir Benjamin Hobhouse, *Bart.* born June 27, 1786 : educated at Bristol, Westminister and Trinity College, Cambridge : friend of Byron and travelled with him on the Continent : committed to Newgate from Dec. 14, 1819, to Feb. 29, 1820, for breach of privilege of the House of Commons : M.P. for Westminster, 1820 : succeeded as Baronet in 1831 : Secretary at War, 1832–3 : Chief Secretary for Ireland, 1833, resigned : M.P. for Nottingham, 1834 : Commissioner of Woods and Forests : President of the Board of Control, April 23, 1835, to Sep. 4, 1841 : again from July 8, 1846, to Feb. 3, 1852 : on his advice the appointment of Lord Heytesbury in 1835–6 to succeed Lord W. Bentinck as Governor-General was cancelled : he supported Lord Auckland's Afghan policy : M.P. for Harwich in 1848 : made a peer in 1851 : K.C.B. in 1852 : died June 3, 1869 : wrote his *Recollections of a Long Life*, and a number of papers on literary, classical, political and historical subjects.

BROWN, CHARLES PHILIP (1798–1884)

I.C.S. : born in India, 1798 : son of the Rev. David Brown (*q.v.*) : educated by his father in India : and at Haileybury : went to Madras in the Civil Service, 1817 : Judge of Masulipatam ; Persian and Telugu Translator to Government : Post Master General, Madras : Member of the Council of Education : early made a special study of Telugu and became a great scholar : compiled a Telugu-English and English-Telugu Dictionary, 1845–53, and Grammar, 1840, and translated the Bible into Telugu : published *Chronological Tables* : and various works in Telugu : wrote on´that language and other subjects in the *Madras Journal of Literature* : retired, 1855 : Honorary Professor of Telugu in London University : on the Council of the R.A.S : died 1884.

BROWN, REV. DAVID (1763–1812)

Born in 1763 : educated at Scarborough, Hull, and Magdalen College,

Cambridge : ordained and went to Calcutta as a Chaplain in Bengal in 1786 : held several clerical charges, including the ministry of the Old Church, 21 years, and 10 years the senior Presidency chaplaincy, and laboured greatly in the cause of missions and aid to native Christians : was held in great esteem by the English residents : founded the Auxiliary Bible Society : Provost of the College of Fort William, Aug. 18, 1800 : in 1812 he embarked on a ship which was wrecked in the Bay of Bengal : was rescued, and returned to Calcutta, but died there directly, June 14, 1812.

BROWN, FRANCIS CARNAC (1792–1868)

Born at Mahé, Nov. 10, 1792 : son of Murdoch Brown (*q.v.*) : educated in England and France (where he was detained at the rupture of the peace of Amiens) : joined the 80th foot : Lieutenant and A.D.C. : retired on half pay to help his father manage the Anjrakandy estate : J.P. : returned to Europe, 1838 : was an active member of the committee of the " British India Society," the first organization established to promote reform in India, and afterwards of the " India Reform Society " : died at Tellicherry, Sep. 23, 1868 : author of pamphlets on Indian subjects, *Letters to and from the Government of Madras relating to the Disturbances in Canara in April*, 1837–8 : *Free Trade and the Cotton Question with reference to India, being a Memorial from the British merchants of Cochin*, 1847 : *Obstructions to Trade in India*, 1862 : *The Supply of Cotton from India*, 1863 : his knowledge of native customs and native matters generally on his side of India was probably unrivalled among Englishmen : he was able to explain many things relating to the natives which others had not been able to understand.

BROWN, SIR JOHN CAMPBELL (1812–1890)

Entered the Medical Service of the Bengal Army, 1836 : in the first Afghan war : became Surgeon-General, 1870 : C.B., 1858 : K.C.B., 1875 : died July 27, 1890.

BROWN, MURDOCH (1750–1828)

Born at Edinburgh, 1750, left Scotland for Lisbon merely for the voyage, but never returned : found work at Lisbon, made his way through Europe : in 1775 went out as Consul to Calicut for the Empress Maria Theresa of Austria : engaged in trade, of which Jonathan Duncan, Governor of Bombay, wrote, 1792, as the most considerable of any British subject on that side of India : he lost eleven ships, East Indiamen, of 1,000 tons or more in the war with France : in 1798 he took over from Government as a plantation " Five Tarras of Randaterra " (The Anjrakandy estate) in Malabar : was granted, in 1802, a 99 years' lease, being the earliest English landholder in India : the natives regarded him as their Raja : none but the lowest caste would work on the estate, which was wasted by war : he educated his tenants and Christianized them by native catechists and German missionaries, raising them in the scale of civilization : he spoke seven European and five or six Oriental languages : died at Tellicherry, 1828.

BROWNE, CHARLES ALFRED (1802–1866)

Son of William Loder Browne : born Dec., 1802 : was a Midshipman, R.N : educated at Addiscombe : joined the Madras Army, 1820 : in 15th and 12th regts. : examiner in Hindustani and Persian : Military Secretary to Government, Madras, 1857 : Adjutant-General : commanded at Nagpur, 1862 : commanded the N. Division, Madras Army, 1863 : retired, 1864 : wrote a Persian grammar : established, 1833, Sunday schools at Madras and the Black Town, the first in the Madras Presidency: died Feb. 14, 1866.

BROWNE, JAMES (? – ?)

Major : in the E. I. Co.'s service, *temp.* Warren Hastings : Collector of the Jungleterry districts, 1773 : had difficult work in administering the country and settling disturbances : sent by the Council on an embassy to Shah Alam at Delhi to negotiate with him for assistance against the Sikhs : Resident at Delhi, 1782 : recalled, when Warren Hastings left for England, 1785 : published, in 1787, his *Indian Tracts*, which, he says, were written by order of Hastings, describing the Jungleterry districts, and giving an account of the Sikhs.

BROWNE, SIR JAMES (1839–1896)

Born Sep. 16, 1839 : son of Robert Browne : educated at Cheltenham and Addiscombe : appointed to the Bengal Engineers, 1857 : served in the N.W. Frontier campaign against the Mahsud-Waziris, 1860, in the Umbeyla campaign, 1863 : Executive Engineer in the Panjab : in 1876 surveyed for a railway from Sukkur to Quetta : Political Officer at Quetta : in the Afghan war, 1878–9, Political with Sir D. Stewart's advance to Kandahar : C.S.I. 1879 : in Egypt, in 1882, commanded the Royal Engineers of the Indian Contingent : at Tel-el-Kebir : C.B. 1882 : superintended the construction of the Indus bridge, 1875 : Engineer in Chief of the Sind-Peshin railway, 1883–7 : Q.M.G. in India, 1889–90 : Chief Commissioner of British Beluchistan, March, 1892 : died there, June 13, 1896 : K.C.S.I : General.

BROWNE, SIR SAMUEL (1824–1901)

Son of James Browne, M.D : born Oct. 13, 1824 : entered the Bengal Army, 1840 : in the Panjab campaign of 1848–49 : at Chilianwala and Gujarat : in the mutiny, with the 2nd Panjab cavalry, in the movable column of the Panjab : under Sir Colin Campbell in Oudh, lost an arm : gained the V.C : for his action at Nuria, near Philibhit, when he attacked the rebels, and was severely wounded in hand-to-hand fight : commanded the Guides in 1864 : accompanied H.R.H. the Prince of Wales on his Indian tour,1875–6 : K.C.S.I. : Military Member of the Supreme Council, Aug. 9 to Nov. 5, 1878 : commanded the first Division of the Peshawar Field Force, in the Afghan war, 1878–9 : captured Ali Masjid, occupied Jalalabad : K.C.B : retired, 1879 : General : G.C.B., 1901 : died March 14, 1901 : he invented the military sword belt, called after him.

BROWNE, SIR THOMAS GORE (1807–1887)

Son of Robert Browne : born July 3, 1807 : entered the Army 1824 : in the campaign, in 1842, of the first Afghan war commanded his regiment as Major : was in the repulse of Haikalzai, at Kandahar, Kabul and Istalif, and through the Khyber to India : C.B., 1843 : was Governor of St. Helena, New Zealand,

Tasmania, Bermuda: K.C.M.G., 1869: died April 17, 1887.

BROWNLOW, SIR CHARLES HENRY
(1831-)

Born 1831 : son of Colonel George A. Brownlow : entered the Indian Army : served in the Panjab campaign, 1848 : Hazara, 1852-3 : Mohmand expedition, 1854 (severely wounded) : Yusafzai expedition, 1858 : China war, 1860 : Umbeyla campaign, 1863 : C.B. : Hazara, 1868 : commanded the Southern column, Lushai expedition, 1871-2 : K.C.B. : A.D.C. to the Queen, 1869- 81 : Assistant Military Secretary at Horse Guards, 1879-80 : G.C.B. 1887 : retired.

BRUCE, CHARLES ALEXANDER
(1793-1871)

Born Jan. 11, 1793 : at Jorehat, Assam : was the first explorer of tea tracts in Assam, and discoverer of the indigenous tea plant in Assam : was appointed Superintendent of Tea cultivation under the Government of India until the tea industry was adopted by private enterprise, as stated on a memorial tablet to him in the Church at Tezpur : wrote a report on the manufacture of tea, and on the export and produce of the tea plantations in Assam, 1839 : died April 23, 1871.

BRUCE, JOHN (1745-1826)

Historian : educated at Edinburgh University, and Professor of Logic there : appointed Keeper of the State Paper Office, and Historiographer of the E. I. Co.: M.P. for a borough in Cornwall, 1809-14 : and for a short time Secretary of the Board of Commissioners for the affairs of India, i.e. the Board of Control : F.R.S : died April 16, 1826. He wrote on philosophy as well as history : his chief works relating to India were *Historical View of Plans for the Government of British India*, 1793 : *Annals of the E. I. Co. from their establishment by the Charter of Queen Elizabeth*, 1600, *to the Union of the London and English E. I. Companies*, 1707-8, 1810 : *Report on the Renewal of the E. I. Co.'s exclusive Privileges of Trade for 20 years from March* 1794-1811.

BRUCE, SIR HENRY LE GEYT (1824-1899)

Entered the Army 1842, in the Bengal Artillery : in the Gwalior campaign, at Maharajpur : in the Satlaj campaign, 1845-6 : at Badiwal, Aliwal, Sobraon : in the Panjab campaign, 1848-9 ; at Sadulapur, Chilianwala, Gujarat : in the mutiny at the second relief of Lucknow, at Cawnpur and many engagements : C.B. 1875 : retired as Lt-General, 1878 : K.C.B. : 1898 : died April 15, 1899.

BRUCE, RICHARD ISAAC (1840-)

Born 1840 : son of Jonathan Bruce : served in the Afghan war, 1878-9 : on the N.W. Frontier of India : at Daulatzai, 1884 : in the Zhob Valley expedition, 1890 : co-operated in the opening of the Gomal Pass, 1890 : British Commissioner of the Afghan-Waziristan Delimitation Commission, 1894 : at Wano, 1894 : in Waziristan, 1894-5 : a Commissioner in the Panjab : author of a Gazetteer of Dera Ghazi Khan, and a manual of Beluchi : a History of the Marri-Beluch tribe : of *The Forward Policy and its Results*.

BRUTTON, NICHOLAS (1780-1843)

Entered the Army,1795 : went to India : at Seedaseer, 1799, and at the siege of Seringapatam, May 4, 1799 : in the Canara campaign ; under Lord Lake, 1804-5 : at the siege of Bhartpur, 1805 : under General St. Leger on the Satlaj, 1809 : in the Pindari campaigns of 1812 and 1817 : in the Nipal war of 1815 : at the siege of Hatras : retired in 1837 from the 11th Hussars, as Lt-Colonel : died March 26, 1843.

BRYANT, SIR JEREMIAH (? -1845)

Maj-General : appointed to E. I. Co.'s Army, 1798 : served in Oudh : in the Mahratta war : in Bundelkund : at Deeg, 1804 : Town and Fort Major, Fort William, 1815 : Judge Advocate General, 1817, 1824 : in the Dekkan war : at Bhartpur, 1826 : knighted, 1829 : C.B. : commanded the 14th N.I., 1835 : Director E. I. Co., 1841 : died June 10, 1845.

BRYDGES, SIR HARFORD JONES, BARONET (1764-1847)

In the E. I. Co.'s Civil Service : son of Harford Jones of Presteign : born Jan. 12, 1764 : assumed the name of Brydges from his mother's family : Envoy to Persia, 1807-1811 : Baronet in 1807 : resigned in 1811 : D.C.L., 1831 : Privy Councillor : died March 17, 1847 : wrote on Persian affairs and his mission.

BRYDON, WILLIAM (1811–1873)

Born Oct. 9, 1811 : entered the E. I. Co.'s medical service in 1835 : served with Sir H. Fane and Lord Auckland : sent in 1839 with a regiment to the first Afghan war. When the Army retreated from Kabul in Jan. 1842, Brydon was attached to the 6th regt. of Shah Shuja's Hindustani Infantry and, alone, of 13,000 persons, reached Jalalabad alive on January 13, 1842 : he was in the garrison of Jalalabad under Sir R. Sale, and with General Pollock's army to Kabul and back in 1842 : in the mutiny of 1857 he was, by a curious fate, again besieged, being in the Lucknow garrison, and was uninjured throughout the siege : C.B., 1858 : retired, 1859, as Surgeon-Major of the Bombay Army : died March 20, 1873.

BUCHAN, GEORGE (? – ?)

I.C.S. : appointed a writer on the Madras Establishment, Aug. 1792 : Assistant under the Secretary in the Military, Political and Scout Department, and French Translator, 1794 ? also for supplying "beetle," tobacco, and "gangee" in 1795 : Paymaster to the Malacca expedition, 1796 : sub-Secretary in the above Department, 1799 : Secretary in the Public and Commercial Department, 1801 ; in the Military Department, 1801 : Chief Secretary, 1803 : Private Secretary to Government, 1809 : went home, 1810 : "out of the service," 1814.

BUCHANAN, REV. DR. CLAUDIUS (1766–1815)

Born March 12, 1766 : son of Alexander Buchanan : educated at Inverary and Glasgow University ; Queen's College,Cambridge, 1791–5 : ordained, 1795 : went to Calcutta as a Chaplain on the Establishment, 1797 : at Barrackpur and Calcutta : was Professor and Vice-Provost of the College of Fort William, 1799–1807, when the latter appointment was abolished : he devoted himself to the promotion of Christianity and to native education : he made two prolonged tours in Southern and Western India, 1806–7, to ascertain the circumstances and facts of the various religions of the country and suggest measures : he returned to England in 1808, and advocated the appointment of Bishops in India and the cause of missions, besides publishing translations of the Scriptures in Malayalam, Syriac, etc. : he wrote *Christian Researches in Asia*, 1810 : *Colonial Ecclesiastical Establishment*, and papers about Christianity and Christian Missions in India : he was D.D. of Glasgow and Cambridge : died Feb. 9, 1815.

BUCHANAN, LEWIS MANSERGH (1836–)

Son of John Buchanan, of Co. Tyrone, Ireland : volunteered for the Crimea : served in the Indian mutiny in the 88th Connaught Rangers : author of *Through the Himalayas and Chinese Tibet* : Colonel : C.B.

BUCHANAN-HAMILTON, FRANCIS (1762–1829)

Doctor : born Feb. 15, 1762, son of Thomas Buchanan, doctor : took his degree of M.D. at Edinburgh in 1783 : after serving on a man-of-war, joined the E.I. Co.'s service in 1794 : employed on a mission to the Court of Ava, and on various botanical, zoological and statistical inquiries in Chittagong and Tippera, and, in 1800–1, through Mysore, Canara and Malabar, on which he wrote a full report : went to Nipal in 1802 : he was Surgeon to Lord Wellesley, and accompanied him to England in 1805. The records of his subsequent inquiries in several Bengal districts and Assam were deposited at the India House in 1816 and not utilized for 22 years. He was Superintendent of the Botanic Garden, Calcutta, 1814–5, when he returned to Scotland and took the additional name of Hamilton on succeeding to his mother's property : F.R.S. and F.R.A.S., and contributed largely to the literary and scientific societies to which he belonged : wrote on the History of Nipal, the Genealogy of the Hindu gods, the Fishes of the Ganges, etc : died June 15, 1829.

BUCK, SIR EDWARD CHARLES (1838–)

I.C.S. : educated at Norwich and Oakham School, and Clare College, Cambridge : entered the Bengal Civil Service in 1862 and retired in 1897 : represented the Indian Government at the Colonial Exhibition, 1886 : Secretary to the Government of India, 1882–97 : Knight Bachelor and K.C.S.I.

BUCKINGHAM, JAMES SILK (1786–1855)

Son of Christopher Buckingham : born Aug. 25, 1786 : was at sea from 1796 : went to India, 1815 : in 1818, at Calcutta, he brought out the *Calcutta Journal*, attacked Government so vigorously that, in 1823, his licence was taken away by Mr. J. Adam (*q.v.*), and he was deported from the country : years afterwards, the E.I. Co. gave him a pension of £200 a year : went to India again when the restrictions on the Press had been removed : M.P. for Sheffield, 1832–7 : conducted the *Oriental Herald* and *Colonial Review*, 1824–9, and was connected with other journals, besides writing largely on social and political subjects : travelled extensively to and from India : wrote *Arabia*, 1825 : *Mesopotamia and Adjacent Countries*, 1827 : *Assyria and Media*, 1830 : travelled also in Europe and N. America : and gave lectures in England : died June 30, 1855.

BUCKINGHAM AND CHANDOS, RICHARD PLANTAGENET CAMP-BELL-TEMPLE-NUGENT-BRYDGES-CHANDOS-GRENVILLE, THIRD DUKE OF (1823–1889)

Governor : born Sep. 10, 1823, only son of the second Duke : educated at Eton and Christ Church, Oxford : M.P. for Buckingham, 1846–57 : Junior Lord of the Treasury, 1852 : as Marquis of Chandos was Chairman of the London and N.W. Railway, 1853–61 : succeeded as Duke, 1861 : Lord President of the Council, 1866–7 : Secretary for the Colonies, 1867–8 : Governor of Madras from Nov. 1875 to Dec. 1880 : had to deal with the severe famine of 1877, when immense numbers of the population came on relief works and gratuitous relief, and there was great mortality : built Government House at Ootacamund : Chairman of Committees in the House of Lords, 1886–9 : P.C. : G.C.S.I. : C.I.E. : D.C.L. : died March 26, 1889 : when the Dukedom became extinct.

BUCKINGHAMSHIRE, ROBERT HO-BART, FOURTH EARL OF (1760–1816)

Son of third Earl : born May 6, 1760 : educated at Westminster : joined 7th regt., 1776 : served in the American war : Major : M.P. in both the English and Irish Parliaments : Secretary to the Lord Lieutenant of Ireland, 1789–93 : Privy Councillor, 1793 : was, as Lord Hobart, Governor of Madras from Sep. 1794 to Feb. 1798 : led an expedition to Malacca and destroyed the Dutch settlements : by his independence he came into antagonism with the Governor-General, Sir John Shore, over the affairs of the Nawab of the Carnatic, when Hobart desired to make financial reforms : the Court of Directors recalled him, but supported his action in Tanjore affairs : Hobart co-operated with the Governor-General against Tippoo : called up to the House of Lords, 1798 : helped to arrange the union with Ireland, 1799 : Secretary for War and the Colonies, 1801–4 : became Earl, 1804 : appointed President of the Board of Control, April 4, 1812 : and spoke on the renewal of the E.I. Co.'s charter, 1813 : died Feb. 4, 1816.

BUCKLAND, CHARLES EDWARD (1847–)

I.C.S. : son of Charles Thomas Buckland, I.C.S. : born Sep. 19, 1847 : educated at Laleham, Eton, and Balliol College, Oxford : joined the Civil Service in Bengal, 1870 : Private Secretary to Sir Richard Temple, when Lieutenant-Governor of Bengal, 1874–7, and Governor of Bombay, 1877–8 : Revenue, and Chief Secretary to Government of Bengal, and Member of the Bengal Legislative Council : Senior Member of the Board of Revenue : retired in 1904 : C.I.E., 1895 : author of *Bengal under the Lieutenant Governors* : editor of *The Dictionary of Indian Biography*.

BUCKLAND, CHARLES THOMAS (1824–1894)

I.C.S. : son of the Rev. John Buckland : born Feb. 27, 1824 : educated at Laleham, Eton, and Haileybury : gained his appointment to the Indian Civil Service by competition at Eton : went to India in 1844 : served throughout his career in Bengal, making a reputation for ability and independence as an administrator : Junior Secretary to the Governor of Bengal : Member of the Bengal Legislative Council, and Member of the Board of Revenue, Calcutta : retired in 1881 : died March 21, 1894.

BÜHLER, JOHANN GEORG (1837-1898)

Born July 19, 1837, at Borstel, in Hanover: son of a pastor: educated at Hanover and Gottingen: graduated in Oriental languages and Archæology, 1858: studied Sanskrit at Paris, London, Oxford: became an eminent Orientalist: Professor of Oriental Languages at the Elphinstone College, Bombay, 1863: Superintendent of Sanskrit Studies, Poona, 1866: Educational Inspector, N. Division, Bombay Presidency, 1868, 1872: edited Sanskrit texts: several times deputed to collect Sanskrit texts: discovered over 5,000 MSS., which the Indian Government distributed among British Universities and Collections, and Indian Societies and Institutions: left India, 1880: gave much attention to ancient inscriptions, doing important work as an epigraphist: wrote on Indian inscriptions: brought out, with Sir R. West (q.v.), a digest of Hindu Law: wrote a Sanskrit Primer, editions of Sanskrit works: published a Glossary of the oldest Prakrit dictionary: collaborated in the series of Sacred Books of the East: translated the Laws of Manu: became Professor of Indian Philology and Archæology at the University of Vienna: edited an Encyclopædia of Indo-Aryan Philology: contributed his Indische Paläographie, 1896: was member of the Royal Asiatic and other learned Societies: drowned in Lake Constance, April 8, 1898.

BUIST, GEORGE (1805-1860)

Doctor: born Aug. 22, 1805: son of the Rev. J. Buist: educated at St. Andrews and Edinburgh: became a preacher and lecturer, and editor of newspapers in Scotland from 1832 to 1839, when he became editor of the Bombay Times till 1857: he opposed the Government policy in Kabul in 1842: from Jan. 1858 he brought out the Bombay Standard, which was amalgamated with the Bombay Times in 1860. He was Inspector of Observatories in Bombay for many years, and wrote on scientific subjects, meteorology, geology, antiquities, for the Bombay Asiatic Society's Journal: he was instrumental in the establishment of a number of observatories, and founded the Bombay Reformatory School of Industry: a Municipal Commissioner in Bombay:

appointed, in 1859, Superintendent of the Government Press, Allahabad, and Curator of Government books: died at Calcutta, Oct. 1, 1860: described as "India's foremost man of letters," "not only famous as the most successful of Indian journalists, but as the thoughtful and enterprising man of science": he devoted himself to scientific philanthropy.

BULANDSHAHR, LACHHMAN SINGH, RAJA OF (1826-1896)

A Rajput of the Jadon clan: his grandfather held a high post in Sindia's Army, and died at Alighar in 1801: his sons resided in Agra, and held lands near the city: Lachhman Singh entered Government service in 1847: employed as a translator in the Secretariat at Agra: rendered good service during the mutiny: rewarded with a Khilat, and a small parcel of revenue-free land in the Agra district: employed in the Educational Department, and promoted to a Deputy Collectorship: wrote a Statistical Memoir of the Bulandshahr District, and translated various official works, besides the Sakuntala, in Hindi: in 1877, was made Raja as a personal distinction: after his retirement, resided at Bulandshahr, and died there in July, 1896.

BURDWAN, MAHARAJA DHIRAJ BIJAY CHAND MAHTAB BAHADUR OF (1881-)

Born Oct. 19, 1881: son of Raja Ban Bihari Kapur (q.v.): succeeded in 1885: was installed as Maharaja in Feb., 1903.

BURDWAN, MAHTAB CHAND RAI, MAHARAJA ADHIRAJ BAHADUR OF (1820-1879)

Son of Maharaja Tej Chand Rai: born Nov. 17, 1820: succeeded to the Burdwan Raj (which pays over 40 lakhs annually of Government Revenue), on April 16, 1832: made Maharaja Adhiraj Bahadur, Aug. 30, 1833: on Jan. 1, 1877, was granted a salute of 13 guns as a personal distinction, and the title of "His Highness": appointed to the Governor-General's Legislative Council in 1864: during the Sonthal rebellion of 1855, and in the mutiny, he helped Government greatly with transport, and by maintaining communications: established a college, schools, hospitals and dispensaries on his estates; widely supported charities, and gave munificent contributions on occasions of epidemic fever, famines and calamities : encouraged literature and learning : though not always a strict observer of Hinduism, he maintained his numerous religious endowments and temples : while he did not seek popularity, he was highly respected by both Europeans and his countrymen, for his independence, high character and public spirit : died at Bhagalpur, Oct. 26, 1879.

BURGESS, JAMES (1832-)

Born Aug. 14, 1832 : educated at Dumfries, Glasgow, Edinburgh : went to India, 1855 : engaged in educational work in Calcutta and Bombay : Archæological Surveyor and Reporter for W. India, 1874 : and for S. India, 188ᵣ : Director-General of the Archæological Survey of India, 1886 : Fellow of the Bombay University : retired, 1889 : attended the Geneva Oriental Congress, 1894, as representative of India : edited the *Indian Antiquary*, 1872–84 : published scientific papers in the *Philosophical Magazine*, *Archæological Survey Reports*, *Epigraphica Indica*, 1889–94 : published various archæological works, as *The Rock Temples of Elephanta*, 1871 : *Temples of Somnath, Junaghar and Girnar, The Rock Temples of Ajanta, The Rock Temples of India* (with J. Fergusson), 1880 : *Buddhist Art in India*, 1901.

BURGOYNE, JOHN (1722–1792)

General : son of Captain John Burgoyne : educated at Westminster : entered the Army in the 13th Light Dragoons, 1740 : M.P. for Midhurst, 1761 : for Preston, 1768 : spoke, moving for a Select Committee, on the Government of India, 1772, urging the principle (afterwards adopted by Fox and Pitt in their India Bills) of Government control over the E. I. Co. : in the attack in Parliament on Lord Clive, May 3, 1773, Burgoyne, Chairman of the Committee, was the accuser, and carried condemnatory resolutions against Clive : commanded in America in 1774, and surrendered at Saratoga, Oct. 17, 1777 : C. in C. in Ireland, 1782 : was a manager of the impeachment of Warren Hastings, 1787 : died June 4, 1792.

BURGOYNE, SIR JOHN, BARONET (1739–1785)

General : born 1739 : entered the Army young : served in the 7th and other regts. : Lt-Colonel of 58th regt., 1764 : and of 14th Light Dragoons : raised, in 1781, the first regt. of European cavalry sent to India, called the 23rd Light Dragoons, afterwards the 19th Dragoons and the 19th Hussars, which he took to Madras : Maj-General, 1783 : he and Sir Robert Fletcher were the champions of what they considered the rights and privileges of the King's service as against the authority of the E.I. Co.'s Governor and Council : both were recalled, but Burgoyne died at Madras, Sep. 23, 1785 : buried in the Fort Church there.

BURKE, EDMUND (1729–1797)

Son of Richard Burke : born Jan. 12, 1729 : educated at Ballitore and Trinity College, Dublin, 1743–8 : entered at the Middle Temple, but not called to the bar : took to literature : founded the *Annual Register*, 1759 : Private Secretary to Lord Rockingham, Prime Minister, 1765 : M.P. for Wendover, 1765–74 : for Bristol, 177ᵢ–80 : for Malton, 1781–94 : Paymaster of the Forces, 1782–3 : his connexion with India extended over many years : he attacked the E. I. Co., 1766 : refused, in 1772, an offer by the E. I. Co.'s Directors, of an appointment to reform their adminstration : opposed Lord North's " Regulating Act," 1773 : was member of the Committee on the affairs of the E.I. Co., 1783, wrote both the *Ninth Report* on the trade of Bengal and the system pursued by Warren Hastings, and the *Eleventh Report* on the system of presents : drafted Fox's East India Bill, 1783 : attacked Hastings in a speech on the debts of the Nawab of Arcot, 1785, and again on the Rohilla war, 1786 : impeached Hastings before the House of Lords, May, 1787 : led the impeachment at the trial of Hastings in Westminster Hall, Feb., 1788 : secured its continuation in a new Parliament, 1790 : spoke for nine days in May–June, 1794, in reply to Hastings' defence : Hastings was acquitted in April, 1795 : Burke died July 9, 1797 : no further allusion need be made here to his writings, speeches in Parliament and political career, which are well known apart from his relations to India.

BURKE, WILLIAM AUGUSTUS (1769–1837)

Entered the Army as a Hospital Mate on Sep. 13, 1795, and rose, through the grades of Regimental Surgeon, Apothecary, Surgeon, etc. to be, on Oct. 5, 1825, Inspr-General of Hospitals of the Forces in the East Indies, until his death. In 1817, he was Physician-General in the Mauritius, was present at the capture of nearly all the French and Dutch colonies in the West Indies and South America : served in Europe, including the Mediterranean and Gibraltar : and was at the capture of Bhartpur by Lord Combermere in 1826 : died at Calcutta, May 22, 1837.

BURLTON, PHILIP BOWLES (1803–1829)

Son of William Burlton : joined the Bengal Artillery at Dumdum in 1821 : was transferred to Africa : was actively employed in the Burmese war of 1824 : devoted himself zealously to discovering the sources of the Brahmaputra and Irawadi, and solving geographical questions : he also wrote about the Assamese : was murdered, with Lt. Bedingfield of the Artillery, by the Khasias at Nunklow, in Assam : died April 4, 1829.

BURNE, SIR OWEN TUDOR (1837–   )

Maj-General : son of the Rev. Henry Thomas Burne : entered the Army, 1855 : served in the Crimea and in the Indian mutiny : present in 15 actions, including the siege and capture of Lucknow : promoted for gallantry in the field : Military Secretary to Lord Strathnairn, when C.-in-C. in India, 1861 : Private Secretary to Lord Mayo, Viceroy of India, 1869–72 : Political A.D.C. to the Secretary of State for India, 1872 : Assistant Secretary, 1873, and later, Secretary, Political and Secret Department, India Office, 1874 : Private Secretary to Lord Lytton, Viceroy of India, 1876–7 : Member of the Council of India, 1887–97 : author of Clyde and Strathnairn, in the " Rulers of India " series ; Lord Strathnairn, Imperial Assemblage at Delhi, etc. : C.I.E., 1877 : K.C.S.I., 1879.

BURNELL, ARTHUR COKE (1840–1882)

I.C.S. : born 1840 : son of Arthur Burnell, of the E.I. Co.'s Marine Service : educated at Bedford and King's College : after passing the open competitive examination, went to Madras, 1860 : held minor appointments and, from 1870, district judgeships in various districts, longest at Tanjore, until 1880, when his health, always indifferent, gave way. On his retirement, the Madras Government recorded their regret for being " prematurely deprived of the services of so distinguished a scholar " : died Oct. 12, 1882. He began early to collect Sanskrit MSS., and made an extensive collection, which he presented to the India Office Library : was an excellent Sanskrit scholar : published translations from Sanskrit, and catalogues : also knew some Tibetan, Arabic, Kawi, Japanese, Coptic and Pali : travelled in Arabia, Egypt, Nubia : wrote a Handbook of South Indian Palæography, on The Portuguese in India, The Aindra School of Sanskrit Grammarians, 1875 : made a catalogue of the Tanjore Library, and, with Sir H. Yule, compiled the Hobson-Jobson, a Glossary of Anglo-Indian colloquial words and phrases : besides many papers on law, languages, ethnography and inscriptions : C.I.E. : and Ph.D. of the University, Strasburg.

BURNES, SIR ALEXANDER (1805–1841)

Political : son of James Burnes : born May 16, 1805, connected with the family of the poet Burns : educated at Montrose Academy : entered the E. I. Co.'s military service at 16 : Interpreter at Surat in 1823 : transferred to Cutch in 1825 : sent, in 1830, on a mission, with a gift of horses, to Ranjit Singh at Lahore, and to explore the country : in 1832, travelled, under the orders of Government, in N. India, Afghanistan, Bokhara and Persia : in England in 1833–5, was lionized as a traveller : received the medal of the Royal Geographical Society, and elected member of learned Societies : on return to India, he succeeded, by negotiation at Hyderabad (Sind), in warding off war with the Amirs, who agreed to a survey of the Indus : in 1836, Burnes was sent on a mission, nominally commercial, but really political, to Dost Muhammad, Amir of

Kabul : his discovery of Russia's intrigues, and the arrival of a Russian agent at Kabul, led to his advice, that Dost Muhammad, the reigning Amir, should be supported : but this advice was not accepted, the Amir's requests were rejected, and, by the second Afghan war, Shah Shuja was to be reinstated. Burnes was sent to Sind and Beluchistan, to prepare the way of the British Army : he was made, later, Political Agent at Kabul under the Envoy Sir W. H. Macnaghten : Shah Shuja was re-made Amir : Burnes was knighted, made Lt-Colonel : 'and C.B. : for 2 years, at Kabul, he had a subordinate position : the Afghan mob rose, not without warning, on Nov. 2, 1841, and Burnes was assassinated. It came to light, in 1861, that some of Burnes' despatches from Kabul, in 1839, had been altered, so as to convey opinions opposite to his. The matter was brought before Parliament, on an application for an inquiry : but Lord Palmerston's Government resisted the motion, which was defeated on the ground of the interval of time that had passed since the occurrence.

BURNES, JAMES (1801–1862)

Elder brother of Sir Alexander Burnes, (q.v.) : born Feb. 12, 1801 : educated at Edinburgh University and London hospitals : went out to Bombay with his brother, 1821 : was Residency Surgeon at Cutch : in the expedition of 1825 against Sind : invited, in 1827, by the Amirs to Sind : from 1837, he held medical and other scientific appointments at Bombay, and was Secretary and Member of the Medical Board and, finally, Physician-General, retiring in 1849 : President of the Medical and Physical Society : Vice-President of the Bombay Asiatic Society : was LL.D. of Glasgow, 1834 : F.R.C.P. of Edinburgh : F.R.S. and a Knight of the Guelphic Order : wrote a Narrative of a Visit to Sind, and a History of Cutch : died Sep. 19, 1862.

BURNEY, HENRY (? –1845?)

Captain : attached to the 20th (Marine) N.I. : on duty at Prince of Wales' Island : learnt Malay : acquired knowledge of the Archipelago and Malacca : appointed Military Secretary of the Penang Government : employed to negotiate with Malay and Siamese Chiefs : Political Agent to Siamese States, 1825 : Envoy to Siam :

obtained the release of 1,400 Burmans and Peguese : Deputy Commissioner of Tenasserim, 1827–9 : Resident at the Court of Ava, 1829–38 : contributed papers to the J.A.S.B., about Ava : wrote a Historical Review of the Political Relations between British India and Ava : had a Dictionary of Pali compiled : returned to India, 1842 : died there in 1845–6.

BURNOUF, EMILE LOUIS (1821–   )

Born at Valognes, Aug. 25, 1821 : cousin of the Orientalist, Eugene Burnouf (q.v.) : studied at Paris : appointed Professor of Oriental studies at Nancy, 1854 : in 1867, Director of the École Française at Athens : returned to France in 1875, and settled at Paris : as an Indian scholar, his chief works are :—his Sanskrit Grammar, brought out in collaboration with Leupol, 1859 : a Sanskrit and French Dictionary, 1863–5 : Essai sur le Vèda, 1863 : Bhagavad-Gita, translation, 1861, 1895.

BURNOUF, EUGENE (1801–1852)

Born at Paris, Aug. 12, 1801 : son of Jean Louis Burnouf, grammarian : a pupil of Chezy : studied at the College of Louis-le-Grand : scholar : gave up his profession, the law, and took to Oriental languages : gave instruction in Sanskrit, 1824 : published in 1826, with Lassen of Bonn, the Essai sur le Pali : appointed Professor of General and Comparative Grammar in the Normal School at Paris, 1829–33 : and of Indian Languages and Literature at the Coliège de France, 1832 : a founder of the Société Asiatique in Paris : published, 1833, a commentary on the Yacna, dealing with the language, literature, and history of the Parsis : brought out his Études sur la langue et les textes Zendes, 1840–50 : the earliest to study Zend MSS. at first hand, giving a great impulse to the study of that language, and assistance in the decipherment of the old Persian cuneiform inscriptions : wrote 3 vols. of his work on the text and translation of the Bhagavat Purana, 1840–4 : and began an introduction to the History of Indian Buddhism, 1844 : translated a Sanskrit work on Le Lotus de la Bonne Loi, 1852, and the Vendidad Sade, 1829 : and wrote on the Buddhist inscriptions on pillars and rocks : left other Zend works and a Pali grammar and dictionary nearly complete : Permanent

64   DICTIONARY OF INDIAN BIOGRAPHY

Secretary of the Academy of Inscriptions :
Member of the Institute of France since
1832 : a great European Orientalist :
died May 28, 1852.

BURRELL, LITTELLUS (1753-1827)

Maj-General : born in 1753 : entered
the E. I. Co.'s Bengal Army as a volunteer
in 1770 : Corporal, 1771 ; Serjeant, 1772 ;
Serjeant-Major, 1775 ; Ensign, 1779 ; Maj-
General, 1821 : was at the battle of
Cutra, April 23, 1774 : in the capture of
Gwalior under Popham in 1780 : fought
under Col. John Gardiner at Malavilli :
and Seringapatam, 1799 : engaged in
Mysore, in Lord Lake's campaigns of 1803,
and 1804-5 : commanded a Brigade in
1817 against the Pindaris, and, later, the
British forces in Oudh, and at Cuttack :
after 1821 he retired, and died Sep. 13,
1827.

BURROW, REUBEN (1747-1792)

A distinguished mathematician and
astronomer : born Dec. 30, 1747, son of a
farmer : educated at Leeds : became a
clerk, usher, schoolmaster, assistant astronomer and schoolmaster at Greenwich,
arithmetical teacher at the Tower, edited
the Royal Almanack, went to India in 1782,
learnt Sanskrit : wrote to Warren Hastings,
then Governor-General : appointed to
teach mathematics to the Engineers, and
on the Survey of Bengal : an early member
of the Asiatic Society of Bengal, for whom,
and the Asiatic Researches, he contributed
eleven papers about the mathematics and
astronomy of the Hindus : died at Baxar,
June 7, 1792.

BURTON, SIR RICHARD FRANCIS (1821-1890)

Traveller, author and linguist : son of
Colonel J. Netterville Burton : born
March 19, 1821 : educated on the continent, without system, and was at Trinity
College, Oxford, for 5 terms from 1840 :
to India, 1842, in the Bombay Native
Army : made himself proficient in Oriental
languages and studied Muhammadan life
and customs thoroughly, at Baroda and
in the Sind Survey : wrote on Pushto and
Beluchi : while in England, from 1849 to
1853, he published works on languages
and his Indian experiences. In 1853 he
made the pilgrimage to Mecca in disguise,
without being detected, and wrote a full

account of it. In 1854 he visited Somaliland with the leave of the Bombay Government : wrote Footsteps in E. Africa : in
1855, served in the Crimean war in the
Bashibazouks : on leave from India, led
an expedition with Speke to discover the
sources of the Nile, 1856-9 : gained the
gold medal of the Royal Geographical
Society, 1859 : left the Indian service,
only visiting that country again in 1876,
to Aden, Sind and Goa. The rest of his
life was spent in the Consular service at
Fernando Po, in Brazil, Damascus, Trieste
(1872-90), and in extensive travels in
North and South America, on the Gold
Coast, and in other countries adjacent to
his consular appointments. His literary
work was very considerable. He wrote
on Camoens and translated the Lusiad :
planned a great Book of the Sword : and
translated the Arabian Nights, with a
fulness of text and notes which laid bare
his minute knowledge of Oriental nature :
his works exceeded 50 volumes. His wife
accompanied him wherever possible in
his appointments and travels : and wrote
a life of him, which was corrected by
another account : made K.C.M.G. in 1885 :
died at Trieste, Oct. 20, 1890.

BUSSY-CASTELNAU, CHARLES JOSEPH PATISSIER, MARQUIS DE (1718-1785)

French officer : was in La Bourdonnais'
expedition to India in 1746 : through his
influence, Salabat Jang was made Nizam
of Hyderabad in 1751, on the death of
Muzaffar Jang : Bussy secured French
ascendency at Hyderabad and the grant
of the Northern Sircars : fighting for the
Nizam, he defeated the Nawab of Savanore,
but was, through jealousy, ordered in 1756
to leave the Nizam's territory : soon
regained his supremacy : refused assistance to Surajuddaula, Nawab Nazim of
Murshidabad in 1757 : he seized Vizagapatam and other English fortresses, and
secured Daulatabad for Salabat Jang. In
June, 1758, when at the zenith of his
power, he was recalled by Lally, the new
French Governor-General at Pondicherry :
in the battle of Wandiwash, in which Sir
Eyre Coote defeated Lally, in Jan., 1760,
Bussy was taken prisoner by the English,
but released. After the capture of
Pondicherry on Jan. 16, 1761, no mention
is made of Bussy in India until 1783, when

he was landed with French troops, by Admiral Suffrein, to reinforce Cuddalore, then besieged by the English. On the declaration of peace between France and England, Bussy withdrew the French troops from the support of Tippoo. He is said to have gained a large fortune in India and to have been highly regarded by Dupleix. He died at Pondicherry, Jan. 1785.

BUSTEED, HENRY ELMSLEY
(1833–)

Brig-Surgeon : entered the Madras Medical service, 1856 : served in the Indian mutiny : at the relief of Lucknow, 1857 : was in the Assay Department of the Mints at Madras, Bombay, and Calcutta, successively : confirmed as Assay-master, Calcutta, 1872 : acted as Mint-master, 1873 and 1875 : retired, June, 1886 : C.I.E., 1887 : author of *Echoes from Old Calcutta*.

BUTLER, THOMAS ADAIR (1835–1901)

Major : son of Rev. Stephen Butler : educated privately : joined the 1st Bengal Fusiliers : in the mutiny, at the assault of Delhi, displayed great bravery : wounded : at the attack on Lucknow, March 9, 1858, twice swam the River Gumti and gained the V.C. : in the attack on Ruiya, April 15, 1858 : in the N.W. frontier campaign, 1863 : died May 17, 1901.

BYTHESEA, JOHN (1827–)

Born June 15, 1827 : son of Rev. G. Bythesea : educated at Grosvenor College, Bath : entered the Navy, 1841 : Rear-Admiral, 1877 : gained the V.C. in the Russian war, 1854–5 : saw service in China and elsewhere, in command of various vessels : Naval Attaché at Washington, 1865–7 : Consulting Naval Officer to the Government of India, 1874–80 : C.B. : C.I.E.

CADELL, ALAN (1841–)

I.C.S. : born July 28, 1841 : son of John Cadell : educated at Edinburgh Academy and University and in Germany : entered the Bengal Civil Service, 1862 : was Commissioner of Agra and Rohilkund : Member of the Board of Revenue, and Member of the Legislative Council, United Provinces : acted as Lieutenant-Governor of the United Provinces, Jan. to Nov., 1895, and as temporary Member of the Governor-General's Supreme Council, Feb. to May, 1896 : C.S.I. in 1895 · retired in 1897.

CADELL, JESSIE ELLEN (1844–1884)

Born Aug. 23, 1844 : daughter of William Nash, merchant, London : was an excellent French scholar : was in India, 1858–64 : went with her husband, Capt. Henry Mowbray Cadell (died 1867), to Peshawar : wrote a novel, *Ida Craven*, on frontier life, 1876 : and *Worthy* : learnt Hindustani, Persian and some Arabic, studied *Omar Khayyam*, and prepared a superior edition and translation, published, 1899 : wrote an article on it in *Fraser's Magazine* : was closely connected with the Anglo-Indian Association, 1873–81 : her health gave way, and she died June 17, 1884.

CADELL, SIR ROBERT (1825–1897)

General : son of H. F. Cadell : educated at Edinburgh Academy and Addiscombe : entered the Madras Artillery, 1843 : on the Turkish Staff in the Crimea, 1854–5 : served in the Indian mutiny : Inspr-General of Ordnance at Madras, 1876–81 : C.B., 1873 : General, 1883, and Colonel Commandant, R.A., 1885 : K.C.B., 1894 : died June 30, 1897.

CADELL, THOMAS (1835–)

Colonel : born Sep. 5, 1835 : son of H. F. Cadell, of Cockenzie, Haddington-shire : educated at Edinburgh University, Grange, Sunderland and abroad : served with the 2nd European Bengal Fusiliers (now the Munsters), at the siege of Delhi and subsequent operations, and with the 3rd Bengal Cavalry in the Oudh campaign : commanded a flying column in Bundelkund. After the mutiny, Cadell entered the Political Department and served in Central India and Rajputana : was Chief Commissioner of the Andamans from 1879 to 1892 : received his V.C. for saving life on two occasions at the Flagstaff Picket, Delhi, on June 12, 1857, bringing in wounded men under severe fire.

CAILLAUD, JOHN (1724–1812)

Born 1724 : joined Onslow's regt., afterwards the 8th King's, in 1743 : fought at Fontenoy and Culloden : petitioned the E.I. Co. for a Commission in 1752 :

F

joined Stringer Lawrence at Trichinopoly with troops in 1753 : was repulsed before Madura in April, 1757 : defended Trichinopoly : defeated the Mysoreans near Madura : in Nov. 1759, he arrived at Calcutta, appointed to the chief military command in Bengal : took command of the British force co-operating with the Nawab of Bengal to protect Bihar against the Shahzada : defeated the Emperor at Sirsi, Feb. 22, 1760 : took a prominent part in deposing Mir Jafar, and setting up Mir Kasim : Lt-Colonel in the E. Indies, Jan. 1760 : reverted to Madras, 1761 : Brig-General, 1763 : appointed C. in C., Madras, in succession to Lawrence, 1766 : took possession of the Northern Sircars for the E. I. Co. in 1766 : concluded a treaty with Nizam Ali of Hyderabad to pay a yearly tribute of 7 lakhs for the Sircars : resigned, Jan. 1767, and went to England : D.C.L., Oxford, 1773 : he died in England, at Aston Rowant, Dec. 26, 1812.

CAINE, WILLIAM SPROSTON (1842–1903)

Born March 26, 1842, son of Nathaniel Caine, wine merchant : educated at Birkenhead Park School : entered his father's business : preached : was M.P. for Scarborough, 1880 : Civil Lord of the Admiralty, 1884 : M.P. for Barrow-in-Furness, 1886 : resigned his seat, 1886 : M.P. for E. Bradford, 1892–5, for Camborne from 1900 : Temperance and India were his two chief subjects : was a strong teetotaler, and advocate of advanced temperance : President of the National Temperance Federation, and of similar Associations : a severe critic of the Government of India, and great friend of the natives of India : paid much attention to the Indian Excise (liquor) question : was strongly opposed to the Opium trade : paid visits to India : criticized missionary work in India : was a Member of the Royal Commission on Indian Expenditure : died March 17, 1903 : wrote *Picturesque India*, and *Young India*.

CAIRD, SIR JAMES (1816–1892)

One of the greatest authorities of his time on all agricultural subjects : son of James Caird, born June, 1816 : educated at Edinburgh High School and University :

farmed for 20 years : engaged in the Free Trade controversy : reported on Ireland in 1850, and for the *Times* on agricultural depression : was M.P. for Dartmouth and the Stirling Burghs : 1857–65 : toured in America, and served on various Commissions : F.R.S., C.B. and K.C.B. in 1882 : visited India for six months in 1878–9, as a Member of Sir R. Strachey's Indian Famine Commission : published an account of his experiences, first in the *Nineteenth Century*, and afterwards in a volume, *India, the Land and the People :* was afterwards a Member of other Commissions on land questions : Ll..D. of Edinburgh : on the Board of Agriculture in 1889, and Privy Councillor : died Feb. 9, 1892.

CALDWELL, SIR ALEXANDER (1763–1839)

Son of William Caldwell : born Feb. 1, 1763 : educated at Woolwich, and joined the Bengal Artillery in 1783 : commanded at Midnapur in 1792 : was at Pondicherry in 1793 : in 1798 led the Artillery which defeated the Nizam's Army : he was at the battle of Malavilli, and the sieges of Seringapatam in 1799, and Gooty : in 1800 to Calcutta as A.D.C. to Maj-General G. Green. In 1811, he commanded the Artillery in Sir A. Auchmuty's expedition to Java, being present at the Batavia and Cornelis engagements : commanded the Artillery at Agra in 1812 against Zaman Shah : C.B. in 1817 : retired, 1821 : Maj-General and K.C.B. in 1839 : G.C.B. in 1838 : died Dec. 6, 1839.

CALDWELL, SIR JAMES LILLYMAN (1770–1863)

Son of Major Arthur Caldwell, and nephew of General Sir Alexander Caldwell (*q.v.*) : born Nov. 22, 1770 : joined the Madras Engineers of the E. I. Co. in 1789 : became General, 1854 : was in the Mysore campaign of 1791–2 under Lord Cornwallis against Tippoo and in all the fighting up to the siege of Seringapatam in Feb.–March, 1792 : led a party in the final assault on Seringapatam on May 4, 1799. After 10 years on civil public works, he was, in 1810–11, Chief Engineer on the expedition to Mauritius : defeated the French by sea and took the island. In Madras, from 1811, he had more engineering work, and was special Surveyor of fortresses : C.B. in 1815 : was Commissioner for the restoration of French settlements on the Coromandel and Malabar coasts, and Chief Engineer of Madras in 1816 : retired in 1837 and was made K.C.B. : and G.C.B., 1848 : died June 28, 1863. He painted in water-colours with great skill.

CALDWELL, RIGHT REV. ROBERT (1814–1891)

Missionary and linguist : born May 7, 1814 : at first he studied art in Dublin : went to Glasgow University : B.A., 1837 : sent by the London Missionary Society to Madras, 1838 : ordained, 1841 : joined the English Church, 1841, and the Society for the Propagation of the Gospel : also in 1841 made his residence at Idaiyangudi, "the shepherds' abode," in Tinnevelly, and entered on his 50 years' missionary work, during which the Christians of Tinnevelly increased from 6,000 to 100,000. He was, in 1877, consecrated Bishop of Tinnevelly as coadjutor to the Bishop of Madras : resigned his Bishopric on Jan. 31, and died at Kodaikanal on the Pulny Hills on Aug. 28, 1891. He studied comparative philology, and his linguistic attainments were great : helped to revise the Tamil Prayer Book and Bible, collected Sanskrit MSS : published a *Comparative Grammar of the Dravidian or South Indian Family of Languages* in 1856 : wrote on the "Tinnevelly Shanars," the general, political and mission history of Tinnevelly, besides other works on religion : LL.D. of Glasgow, 1857, and D.D. of Durham, 1874.

CALL, SIR JOHN, BARONET (1732–1801)

Son of John Call : born in 1732 : went to India in 1749, with Benjamin Robins, Chief Engineer and Captain-General of Artillery : arrived at Fort William, 1750 : deputed to fortify St. David near Madras, 1751 : accompanied Clive, 1752, against the French : Engineer-in-Chief at Fort St. David, 1752–7 : Chief Engineer at Madras and the Coromandel Coast, 1758 : at the siege of Pondicherry and Vellore : was in the war of 1767–8 against Hyder Ali : Member of Council, Madras, in 1768 : retired, 1770, to England : was High Sheriff of Cornwall, 1771 : Commissioner on Crown Lands, Woods, and Forests, 1782 :

M.P. for Callington from 1784 : Baronet in 1791 : F.R.S. : became blind in 1795 : died March 1, 1801.

CALLCOTT, MARIA, LADY (1785–1842)

Daughter of Rear-Admiral George Dundas, whom she accompanied to India early in 1808 : she married Capt. Thomas Graham, R.N., 1809 : and travelled in India : returned to England, 1811 : sailed with her husband for S. America in 1821 : he died off Cape Horn in 1822 : she married, in 1827, Augustus Wall Callcott, R.A., who was knighted on the Queen's Accession, 1837 : she died Nov. 28, 1842 : she wrote, as Maria Graham, *Journal of a Residence in India*, 1812 *Letters on India*, 1814, besides other works on travels, etc. : including *Little Arthur's History of England*, 1835.

CAMA, PESTONJI HORMUSJI (1805–1893)

Son of Hormusji Cama : of a Gujarat Parsi family : in commercial partnership with his brothers, 1828 to 1871 : the Cama family established the first Indian house of business in London, in 1855 : Pestonji Cama led a retired life : made a large trust for charitable purposes : and gave Rs. 164,000 for the Cama Hospital for Females and Children in Bombay : a staunch supporter of native female education : warmly interested in the cause of reform and progress in native movements : promoted the Victoria Gardens, and various associations for the advancement of natives : an early Freemason : C.I.E., 1887 : died about Jan. 21, 1893.

CAMAC, JACOB (? – ?)

In the 84th regt. till 1763 : Lieutenant, Oct., 1763 : commanded the 24th Bengal Infantry from 1766 for many years at Ramghar : served in 1779 under Popham against Sindia, whom he defeated at Durdah : Lt-Colonel, Jan., 1781 : retired, Dec. 2, 1782 : died of fever in Ireland.

CAMERON, AYLMER (1833–)

Son of Lt-Colonel W. G. Cameron, Grenadier Guards : served in the Seaforth Highlanders (72nd), in the Crimea, and in the Indian mutiny : severely wounded at the storming of Kotah, where he gained his V.C. : commanded the King's Own Borderers, 1881-1883 : Chief of the Intelligence Department, 1883-6 : Commandant of Royal Military College, Sandhurst, 1886-8 : General.

CAMERON, CHARLES HAY (1795-1880)

Barrister : son of Charles Cameron : born on Feb. 11, 1795 : called to the bar from Lincoln's Inn, 1820 : was a Commissioner on judicial affairs in Ceylon, and the poor-laws, in 1831-3 : after the statute of 1833, he was appointed Member of the Law Commission and went to India in 1835 : co-operated in law-making and codification with Macaulay, the Legal Member : was in 1843 himself Legal Member of the Supreme Council till 1848 : and President of the Council of Education : retired in 1848 : went to Ceylon in 1875, and died there, May 8, 1880.

CAMERON, GEORGE POWLETT (1806-1882)

Son of Captain Robert Cameron, R.N. : entered the E. I. Co.'s military service, 1821 : served in the S. Mahratta country, 1824-5 : served in Portugal, 1832-3 : sent to Constantinople and Persia : served in the Persian Army, 1836-8 : commanding at Tabriz : visited Circassia : C.B. : Political Agent with the Nawab of Arcot, in Madras, 1842 : in command in the Nilgiri Hills, 1855 : retired, 1858 : wrote an account of his travels, 1845, and *The Romance of Military Life*, 1853 : died Feb. 12, 1882.

CAMERON, JOHN ALEXANDER (? -1885)

Went out to India in a merchant's house : acted as Editor of the *Bombay Gazette* : was a special war-correspondent in the Afghan war, 1878, on the Kandahar side : went out to the battle-field of Maiwand, July 27, 1880 : was similarly employed as correspondent in Egypt, Madagascar, Tonquin, the Nile expedition, from 1880-5 : killed in the fighting after Abuklea on Jan. 18, 1885 : a tablet put up to his memory in St. Paul's Cathedral.

CAMPBELL, SIR ARCHIBALD (? -1791)

Maj-General and K.B. : Captain in 1758, wounded at Quebec ; as Colonel, captured Savannah in 1778 : made Governor of Jamaica : appointed Governor of Madras, April 6, 1786 : and in the same year C. in C. During his period of rule he attempted a settlement of the vexed question concerning the revenues of the Carnatic : the treaty of 1787 was his work. Ill-health caused him to resign in 1789 : he died 1791, and was buried in Westminster Abbey. ,

CAMPBELL, SIR ARCHIBALD, BARONET (1769-1843)

Son of Captain A. Campbell : born March 12, 1769 : entered the Army, 1787 : went to Bombay, 1788, and served under Sir Robert Abercromby, 1790-2 : was at Seringapatam, 1792 : at Cochin, 1795, and the defeat of the Dutch in Ceylon, 1796 : was at Seedaseer and the final siege of Seringapatam, 1799 : served in Portugal and under Sir John Moore, 1808 : commanded a Portuguese regt., 1810 : was Brig-General with the Portuguese, 1811 : knighted, 1814 : K.C.B. 1815 : was Portuguese Maj-General, 1816, in command at Lisbon : went to India again with his regiment, 1821 : commanded in the first Burmese war, 1824-6, and took Rangoon and Prome, and, marching on Ava, made the Treaty of Yandaboo in Feb., 1826 : G.C.B. : governed the ceded Provinces still 1829, when he returned to England : Baronet, 1831 : Lieutenant-Governor of New Brunswick, 1831-7 : Lt-General, 1838 : was unable through ill-health to accept the appointment of C. in C. Bombay in 1839 : Colonel of the 62nd regt., 1840 : died Oct. 6, 1843.

CAMPBELL, CHARLES HAY (? -1832)

Major, son of William Campbell : entered the Bengal Artillery in 1805 : served under Lord Lake : was, in 1801, Adjutant and Quarter-master of Artillery : held other appointments on the General Staff of the Army : Deputy Secretary in the Military Department and in charge of the Cossipur Gun Factory : wrote, in the *British Indian Military Repository*, papers on professional subjects, including the History of Sieges in Bengal : he died May 19, 1832.

CAMPBELL, SIR COLIN (1776-1847)

Son of John Campbell : was born in 1776 : from the Perth Academy he ran away to sea, 1792 : brought home from

Jamaica : Midshipman on an East India-man, 1793 : joined the militia, 1795 ; the Army, 1799 : went to India in 1801–2 : was under Arthur Wellesley at Ahmadna-gar, Assaye and Argaum : A.D.C. to Lord Wellesley, and returned with him to England, 1805 : served in Hanover, Denmark, in Portugal, the Peninsula : was at a number of engagements, and was A.Q.M.G : K.C.B., in 1814 : was at Waterloo : Maj - General, 1825 : Lt-Governor of Nova Scotia, 1833 : Governor of Ceylon, 1839–47 : died in England, June 13, 1847

CAMPBELL, DONALD (1751–1804)

Captain of a Cavalry regt. in the service of the Nawab of the Carnatic : at the age of 30 he made a journey to India and published an account of it, 1795 : travelled *viâ* Venice, Trieste, Zante, Alexandria, Cyprus, Aleppo, Badgad, Russia and Bushire : by sea to Bombay and Goa : shipwrecked on the coast on his way to Madras : captured by Hyder Ali's soldiers and imprisoned at Hydernagar, in com-pany with one Hall, to whom he was chained. Hall died in prison, and his gaoler refused to remove the corpse for several days : eventually, on General Matthew's approach, he was released in order to negotiate with him on behalf of Hyat Singh, Hyder's General : with despatches for the Governments of Bom-bay and Madras, he proceeded by sea to Anjengo, travelled by land through Travancore, Tinnevelly, Madura, Trichi-nopoly, Tanjore to Negapatam, and Madras : with Lord Macartney's permis-sion, went on to Calcutta and, on behalf of Hyat Singh, negotiated with Warren Hastings : returned overland to Madras and Anjengo : thence by sea to Bombay : again visited Madras and China, and re-turned to England in 1785, after four years' absence : died June 5, 1804.

CAMPBELL, SIR EDWARD FITZ-GERALD, BARONET (1822–1882)

Son of Maj-General Sir Guy Campbell, *Bart.* C.B., born Oct. 25, 1822 : educated at Sandhurst : entered the Army in the 60th Rifles, 1841 : Lt-Colonel, 1870 : retired 1872 : served with distinction in the Panjab campaign of 1848–9, was at the siege of Multan and at Gujarat : in 1849 was A.D.C., to the C. in C., Sir C. Napier : was at the siege of Delhi in 1857 :

Military Secretary to Lord Canning when Governor-General, 1857–61 : was Assistant Inspector of Volunteers, 1864 : died Nov. 23, 1882.

CAMPBELL, SIR GEORGE (1824–1892)

I.C.S. : son of Sir G. Campbell of Eden-wood, of the E.I. Co.'s Medical service : born in 1824 : educated at the Edinburgh New Academy, St. Andrew's, Madras College, and the University, Haileybury : went to India, 1842 : served in the N.W.P. and Cis-Satlaj States : and in 1849 in the Panjab after the annexation, which he had advocated in the *Mofussilite* newspaper. While on furlough he was called to the bar from the Inner Temple, 1854, and wrote *Modern India*, 1852 : in 1855, he assisted J. R. Golvin in the government of the N.W.P., and became Commissioner of the Cis-Satlaj States : was engaged in the mutiny of 1857,about Delhi, Agra, Cawpur, Lucknow : was provisional Civil Commissioner : accidentally cap-tured three guns : wrote letters on the mutiny to the *Times*,and an official account of it for Lord Canning : was second Civil Commissioner for Oudh : appointed Judge of the High Court, Calcutta, 1862 : was head of the Commission on the Orissa famine of 1866-7 : Chief Commissioner of the Central Provinces in Nov., 1867 : Lieutenant-Governor of Bengal from March, 1871, to April, 1874, when, on account of ill-health, he retired, having commenced the relief operations against the Bengal famine of 1873-4. His rule in Bengal was very energetic, being intended to rouse the Province from its alleged lethargy. He passed the District Road Cess Act, and gave a great impetus to Education, especially primary : K.C.S.I. in 1873 : M.P. for Kirkcaldy 1875–92, but was not successful as a politician : died at Cairo, Feb. 18, 1892 : wrote several works : the chief being *The Ethnology of India, The Capital of India, Tenure of Land in India, The Eastern Question*, besides papers on Ethnology and languages and land questions : he was D.C.L. of Oxford, 1870. His auto-biography was, after his death, edited by Sir C. E. Bernard (*q.v.*)

CAMPBELL, SIR JAMES MACNABB (1847–1903)

I.C.S. : born 1847 : son of Rev. J. M. Campbell, D.D. : educated at Glasgow :

70   DICTIONARY OF INDIAN BIOGRAPHY

D.C.L. Glasgow : went out to Bombay,
1869 : Under Secretary to Government
in Political, Judicial Departments, 1880 :
acted as Commissioner of Customs, Salt,
Opium and Abkari, 1897 : Chairman of
the Bombay Plague Committee, 1897 :
Commissioner, 1900 : retired, 1900 : C.I.E.,
1885 : K.C.I.E. 1897 : compiled the
Bombay Gazetteer, 1873–84, in 26 volumes :
wrote a history of Mandoghar, the capital
of the Muhammadan kingdom of Malwa,
and " Notes on the Spirit Basis of Belief
and Custom," in the *Indian Antiquary*,
1894–1901 : died May 26, 1903.

CAMPBELL, JOHN (1753–1784)

Son of John Campbell, Lord Stonefield :
born Dec. 7, 1753 : entered the Army
in 1771 : served in America : went as
Lt-Colonel to India in 1782 : was engaged
against Hyder Ali : was at Bednore and
Anantapur : the British force being
driven into Mangalore by Tippoo, Campbell was left in command and made the
famous defence of that town from May,
1783, to Jan., 1784, when he was compelled
to surrender : he died, from his exertions,
Feb. 23, 1784.

CAMPBELL, SIR JOHN (1802–1878)

Son of John Campbell of Lochead : born
in 1802 : entered the E. I. Co's service,
1820 : served in Madras : in 1834 was in
command in subduing the hill tribes in
Orissa : in the Gumsur war, 1836–7 : was
deputed, 1837–42, to the civil duty of
stopping the practices of human sacrifice
and female infanticide among the Khonds
of Orissa : went to China, 1842 : C.B. :
was again sent to his former duty among
the Khonds, 1847–9 : returned to Scotland, 1855 : Maj-General, 1872 : died
April 22, 1878 : published a personal
narrative of his 13 years' (not uninterrupted) work among the Khonds, which
led to controversy with the family of the
officer who had, in his absence, favoured
a different policy with that native race.

CAMPBELL, JOHN (1817–   )

Surgeon-major : born April 27, 1817 :
son of Capt. Thomas Campbell R.N. :
educated at St. George's,London, Aberdeen
University, and King's College : entered
the Bengal Medical Service in 1840 :
served in the Afghan war, 1842, on the
line of the Khyber, and with Pollock's

force : with Sir Charles Napier in Sind :
in the Indian mutiny was at Chinhut and
the siege of Lucknow, for which he received
his C.B.

**CAMPBELL, LORN ROBERT HENRY
DICK** (1846–   )

Entered the Army, 1863 : served in the
Hazara expedition, 1868 ; Dour Valley
expedition, 1872 ; Afghanistan, 1878–9 ;
Mahsud-Waziri expedition, 1881 ; China,
1900–01, where he commanded the lines
of communication : commands the
Bundelkund District, India, since 1901 :
Maj-General.

CAMBPELL, WALTER, MAJOR
(1864–   )

Joined the Gordon Highlanders, 1887 :
served in the Waziristan Field Force,
1894–5 ; Chitral Relief Force, 1895 ;
Tirah expedition,1897–8, including Dargai,
Sampagha, and Arhanga ; South Africa,
1899–1902, with 1st Batt. Gordon Highlanders : Brig-Major, Highland Brigade,
and D.A.A.G., Army Head Quarters :
D.A.Q.M.G., Head Quarters Staff : D.S.O.

CANARAN, CHURIA (1812–1876)

Born at Mahé, 1812 : son of a jailor
at Tellicherry, whom he succeeded, 1829–
32 : learnt several languages besides his
own vernacular Malayalam, and rose, from
his first appointment in 1832, through a
succession of posts in the judicial and
revenue offices, to be a Deputy Magistrate-Collector in 1859, retiring as a first-
class officer at the end of 1869, after 39
years' service, having performed such excellent work in respect to the Moplah disturbances in Malabar, 1852–5, his coura-
geous conduct exposing him to great
danger, that for his "conspicuous and
most valuable " services therein and in
revenue matters, he was granted a pension
equal to his full pay : died Oct. 18, 1876.

CANDY, SIR EDWARD TOWNSHEND
(1845–   )

I.C.S. : born April 15, 1845 : son of Major
Thomas Candy : educated at Cheltenham :
entered the Bombay Civil Service, 1865 :
was Judicial Assistant to the Political
Agent, Kattiawar, 1872–82 : officiating
Judicial Commissioner in Sind, 1886–7 :
Vice-Chancellor of the Bombay University,
1897–1902 : Judge of the Bombay High
Court, 1889–1902 : Member of the Police

Commission, 1902–3 : retired in 1903 : C.S.I. in 1903 : Knight Bachelor in 1904.

CANNING, CHARLES JOHN, EARL (1812–1862)

Governor-General and first Viceroy : third son of George Canning the statesman': born Dec. 14, 1812 : educated at Putney, Eton, privately, and at Christ Church, Oxford : first class in classics and second class in mathematics : M.P. for Warwick in 1836 : succeeded to his mother's peerage in 1837 : Under-Secretary for Foreign Affairs, 1841–6, and Chief Commissioner for Woods and Forests : was a follower of Sir Robert Peel : Postmaster-General in Lord Aberdeen's and Lord Palmerston's Governments in 1853–5 : Governor-General of India, Feb. 29, 1856 : Viceroy from Nov. 1, 1858. In his first year of office he had to arrange for the war with Persia, in which Sir James Outram (q.v.) had the command. The events of the mutiny of 1857–8 constitute the history of India rather than the biography of Canning. Its causes orginated before his time. He was not alone in failing at first to appreciate adequately the symptoms and the extent of the out-. break : but, on grasping its character, he rose to the occasion. He detained troops on their way to China, and expedited the dispatch of reinforcements to the affected districts of Upper India. He showed calmness, courage, judgment, firmness, foresight, and acquired the name of " Clemency Canning " for his moderation in punishment, and his repression of vindictiveness. He became unpopular on account of this policy. He trusted his chief officers, Sir Henry, and Sir John, Lawrence, his commanders in the field, his immediate advisers and others : but preserved his own right to decide, when he disagreed with them. For a time he assumed personally the government of the N.W.P. By his Oudh proclamation he confiscated, with exceptions, the land of that province. This led to the controversy which ended in the resignation of Lord Ellenborough, the President of the Board of Control. He carried out the transfer on Nov. 1, 1858, of the Government of India from the E. I. Co. to the Crown : and was made an Earl. In 1859–60 and 1860–1 he made prolonged tours in Upper India. He had to deal with all the troubles resulting from the mutiny, the

reorganization of the finances and of the Army required for India : the reforms in the Indian Councils, the development of education, the question of the income-tax, the grant of adoption sunnuds to native chiefs, with the famine of 1860–1 in the N.W.P. The death of Lady Canning from fever, in Nov. 1861, was universally deplored. He left India on March 18, 1862, in bad health : died June 17, 1862, and was buried in Westminster Abbey. He had been made K.G. for his services in India.

CANNING, CHARLOTTE ELIZABETH, COUNTESS (1817–1861)

Daughter of Lord Stuart de Rothesay ; born March 31, 1817, married, Sep. 5, 1835, in London to the Hon. Charles John Canning, afterwards Earl Canning, (q.v.), first Viceroy of India. She was constantly at Court as Lady-in-Waiting in attendance on Queen Victoria. Her death at Calcutta, Nov. 18, 1861, was deeply lamented. She returned to Calcutta on Nov. 8, after a month's visit to Darjeeling. She had caught jungle fever on her way down, when passing through the malarious country at the foot of the hills and in the Purnea district. She was buried in Barrackpur Park, on the banks of the Ganges. All accounts testify to her noble, simple and beautiful character, her talents and mental gifts, her personal appearance,her graciousness and dignity : in the trying time of the mutiny she rendered great help to her husband by her devotion, loyalty and self-sacrifice, by her calm and steady courage, her patience and self-possession, " no one was ever more admired and looked up to by every class of her Majesty's subjects." Lord Canning wrote this inscription for the monument over her grave : " Honours and praises written on a tomb are at best but vain-glory : but that her charity, humility, meekness and watchful faith in her Saviour will, for that Saviour's sake, be accepted of God and be to her a glory everlasting, is the firm trust of those who knew her best and most dearly loved her in life, and who cherish the memory of her, departed."

CANNING, GEORGE (1770–1827)

Son of George Canning : born April 11, 1770 : educated at Eton and Christ Church, Oxford : M.P. for Newport, 1794 : for

Wendover, 1797 : Under Secretary for Foreign Affairs, 1796–9 : Commissioner of the Board of Control (commonly called the India Board) 1799–1800 : Foreign Secretary, 1807 : fought a duel with Lord Castlereagh, Sep. 22, 1809 : M.P. for Liverpool, 1812 : President of the Board of Control, June 4, 1816, to Jan. 12, 1821 : nominated Governor - General of India March, 1822, but, on Lord Castlereagh's death, Canning resigned that appointment and again became Foreign Secretary, 1822 : M.P. for Harwich, 1822 : Prime Minister, April, 1827, and Chancellor of the Exchequer : died Aug. 8, 1827 : father of Earl Canning (q.v.), Viceroy and Governor-General, 1856–62.

CAPEL, HON. SIR THOMAS BLADEN
(1776–1853)

Son of fourth Earl of Essex : born Aug. 25, 1776 : was in the Navy, 1791-1847, rising to be Admiral : served on various stations, and under Nelson at the Nile and Trafalgar : at the forcing of the Dardanelles, 1807 : off N. America : K.C.B., 1832 : and from 1834 to 1837 was Naval C. in C. in the E. Indies, in the *Winchester*, 50 guns: G.C.B., 1852 : died March 4, 1853.

CAPON, SIR DAVID (1793–1869)

Born in Bombay, 1793: educated in England : entered the E. I. Co.'s military service, 1809 : joined the Bombay N.I., 1810 : in the Palampur expedition, 1813 : in the Konkan, 1817 : commanded troops at Aden, 1838 : twice attacked by large bodies of Arabs : commanded a Brigade of the Bombay Army at the siege of Multan, 1848–9 : in the subsequent pursuit of the Sikhs : K.C.B., 1862 : General, 1868 : died Dec. 17, 1869.

CAPPEL, SIR ALBERT JAMES LEPPOC
(1836–   )

Born 1836 : served in the Crimea 1855–6 : entered the Indian Telegraph Department, 1857, and was Director of Indian Telegraphs, 1883–9 : K.C.I.E. in 1887.

CAPPER (? –1809)

Colonel in the Madras Army : influential in the affairs of Fort St. George in the latter part of the 18th century : on more than one occasion was employed by the Governors in civil and ecclesiastical negotia-

tions : as, e.g. in 1787, in the time of Sir Archibald Campbell, when the Council had to settle important matters with regard to the Roman Catholic population of Madras, and French influence had to be excluded : saw active service and fought " with spirit and gallantry " at Arikera, under Colonel Montresor, 1800 : distinguished himself under Wellesley : became Lt-Colonel and Adjutant-General. When Sir George Barlow was Governor of Madras, Capper became implicated in the disputes between General Hay Macdowall, C. in C. of the Madras Army, and the Civil Authorities, 1809 : Macdowall had resigned in Jan. and left for England : the responsibility of publishing his Army Order against Munro (which gave further offence to the Madras Government) rested with Colonel Capper, and his suspension was the result : he, too, started for England, but was lost at sea on the voyage, March, 1809.

CAREY, ARTHUR DOUGLAS (? –   )

I.C.S. : educated at the City of London School : went out to Bombay, 1865 : Collector of Salt Revenue, 1881 : acting Commissioner of Inland Customs, 1881 : in 1885 travelled, *viâ* Ladak to Northern Tibet, to Lake Mungtsa, Khotan, Kuchar, Lake Lob, Tsaidam, Urumtsi, Yarkand, to Ladak : Commissioner of Customs, Salt, Opium and Abkari, 1891 : on special duty to Lisbon, in connexion with Goa Treaty negotiations, 1891–2 : retired 1893.

CAREY, EUSTACE (1791–1855)

Missionary : son of Thomas Carey, a non-commissioned officer: nephew of the Rev. Dr. W. Carey (q.v.) : born March 22, 1791 : educated at Bristol College : arrived at Serampur as a missionary in 1814 ; founded a missionary establishment at Calcutta, 1817 : left India, 1825 : urged the cause of missions in England : wrote about missions and a memoir of W. Carey : died July 19, 1855.

CAREY, FELIX (1782–1822)

Missionary : son of the Rev. Dr. W. Carey (q.v.) : went with his parents to India : assisted his father in his Biblical translations : besides many translations in Bengali, he published a Burmese grammar, and began a Burmese dictionary and Pali grammar : he died at Serampur, Nov. 10, 1822.

CAREY, MARY (1741–1801)

Of Indian birth : wife of Peter Carey, a seafaring man : the last of the 23 survivors of the 146 persons imprisoned in the Black Hole of Calcutta on June 20, 1756 :· her husband died there, or afterwards in the fighting at Fulta : her subsequent fate is uncertain, but the tradition of her being carried off by the Nawab's people is not authentic. She married again, her second husband being a military officer. She confirmed, at an interview on Aug. 13, 1799, Holwell's account of the Black Hole tragedy : she died March 28, 1801, at Calcutta.

CAREY, REV. DR. WILLIAM (1761–1834)

Missionary: born Aug. 17, 1761, in Northamptonshire : son of Edmund Carey, a village schoolmaster : apprenticed to a shoemaker at Hackleton : joined the congregation of Baptists in 1783, and at 22 was publicly baptized : studied Greek, Latin and Hebrew under great privations ; had charge of a congregation at Leicester in 1789, and joined in forming a Baptist missionary society at Kettering, 1792 : sent out as their first missionary to Bengal in 1794, lost all his property in the Hughli and was destitute in Calcutta. After cultivating in the Sundarbans, he became Superintendent of an indigo factory in the Malda district for 5 years, built a church there, and preached in the villages. Being prevented by the E. I. Co. from establishing a mission in British territory, he formed with others, in 1799, a missionary settlement at Serampur under the protection of the Danish Governor, Colonel Bie : there he first translated the Bible into Bengali and printed it, and it was afterwards translated into 26 languages. Carey also published dictionaries and many grammars of languages and other Indian works : edited the *Ramayana* and Roxburgh's *Flora Medica*. In 1801 he was appointed to be a Professor of Sanskrit, Bengali and Mahratti at the new College of Fort William, and in 1805 he founded the Bow Bazar Mission Chapel in Calcutta : in 1807 he was made D.D. by the Brown University in the United States. Notwithstanding official warnings against over-zeal his mission prospered, and many out-stations were established : he died at Serampur, June 9, 1834.

CARMICHAEL, DAVID FREMANTLE (1830–1903)

I.C.S.: son of D. D. Carmichael Smyth : he resumed the family name of Carmichael : educated at Harrow and Haileybury, 1849–50 : went to Madras in the Civil Service, 1851 : Private Secretary to Sir C. Trevelyan when Governor, 1859 : Revenue Secretary to Government, 1875 : Chief Secretary, 1877 : Member of Council, 1878–83 : died Sep. 30, 1903.

CARNAC, JOHN (1716–1800)

Entered the E. I. Co.'s service in 1758, as Captain, from H.M.'s 39th regt. : in 1760 commanded at Patna, and in 1761 defeated the Delhi Emperor near Bihar, and took prisoner M. Law with his men : beat off Shuja-ud-daula's attack on Patna, April, 1764 : was Brig-General in 1764, and defeated the Mahrattas in the Doab in 1765 : received the Emperor Shah Alam and the Wazir Shuja-ud-daula, and closed the war : M.P. for Leominster, 1767 : in 1776–9, was Member of Council, Bombay : Member of the Superintending Committee on the expedition against Poona, 1778 : and was dismissed the E. I. Co.'s service for his share in the convention of Wargaum, Jan. 14, 1779 : died at Mangalore on a sea voyage, Nov. 9, 1800.

CARNATIC, AZIM-UD-DAULA, NAWAB OF THE (1775–1819)

Son of Amir-ul-umra : nephew of Umdat-ul-umra (*q.v.*), and grandson of Muhammad Ali (*q.v.*) : born 1775 : on the death of his uncle, Azim-ud-daula, accepted the British terms, which Ali Husain, the reputed son of Umdat, had refused, and was given the succession. An engagement was made with him on July 31, 1801, by which he gave up the government of the Carnatic to the E. I. Co., and allowances were assigned for his personal expenses and for his family : he lived quietly, and died Aug. 3, 1819.

CARNATIC, GHULAM MUHAMMAD GHAUS, LAST NAWAB OF THE (1824–1855)

Succeeded as a child to his father Nawab Azim Jah, Nov. 12, 1825 : instituted as Nawab in 1842 by Lord Elphinstone, Governor of Madras : on his death without issue, Oct. 7, 1855, Government declared the title, privileges, and immunities of the Nawab's family to be at an end.

CARNATIC, MUHAMMAD ALI KHAN WALAJAH, NAWAB OF THE (1717–1795)

Second son of Anwar-ud-din Khan, Nawab of the Carnatic : present at the battle of Ambur, escaped to Trichinopoly : he was appointed Nawab by Nasir Ali, the Nizam of the Dekkan, in 1749 : was besieged at Trichinopoly by Chanda Sahib and the French, until relieved by the English : on his behalf Clive took Arcot, 1751, and he was successfully supported as Nawab by the English, both against Chanda Sahib, the candidate assisted by the French, and against the rebellious Poligars : recognized as Nawab by the Treaty of Paris of 1763, and acknowledged as independent of the Nizam by the Mogul Emperor in 1765 : entitled Walajah : he contracted large debts to the E. I. Company and the English adventurers who crowded his court and preyed upon him : he assigned districts for their payment : by Treaties of 1763, 1781, 1785, 1787, 1792, arrangements were made for their liquidation, by the English managing the Carnatic, etc. : he died Oct. 16, 1795 : his intrigues with Tippoo were discovered after the fall of Seringapatam in 1799, whereupon the English assumed the government of the Carnatic, making provision for the family of the Nawab.

CARNATIC, UMDAT-UL-UMRA, NAWAB OF THE (1748–1801)

Son of Muhammad Ali (q.v.), whom he succeeded in Oct. 1795. After the fall of Seringapatam in May, 1799, treasonable correspondence between Tippoo and Umdat-ul-umra and his father came to light : the British Government thereupon repudiated the existing treaty of 1792 with the Nawab of the Carnatic, and resolved to assume the government of the Carnatic, making a provision for the family of the Nawab. Umdat-ul-umra died July 15, 1801, before the proposed arrangements could be concluded.

CARPENTER, ALFRED (1847–)

Son of Charles Carpenter, R.N. : born Aug. 2, 1847 : educated at Brighton College : entered the Royal Navy, 1861,

and retired as Captain in 1895 : served in the Challenger scientific expedition : Soudan expedition 1884 : and while in charge of the Marine Survey of India, piloted the war flotilla under fire to Mandalay and Bhamo in 1885, for which he received his D.S.O.

CARPENTER, MARY (1807–1877)

Daughter of Dr. Lant Carpenter : born April 3, 1807 : devoted her life to philanthropy : opened schools at Bristol, for girls, for the reformation of juvenile criminals : also ragged and industrial schools : and worked for the passing of the Industrial Schools Act. Her attention had been attracted to India by the presence of Raja Rammohan Roy (q.v.) at Bristol in 1833, and by the visits of native gentlemen. She visited India in 1866–7, 1868–9, 1869–70, 1875–6, with a view to improve female education, reformatory schools, and the management of the jails. She was in communication with the authorities in India, and at the India Office, and with the leading native gentlemen, such as Keshab Chandra Sen (q.v.), with whom she founded a " National Indian Association " at Bristol in 1870, to bring Indian visitors and English inquirers into closer relations. Many of her suggestions for reforms and improvements were adopted. She paid visits to Germany and America. Among her publications were Last Days in England of the Raja Rammohan Roy, 1866 : and Six Months in India, 1868. She died on June 14, 1877.

CARR, RIGHT REV. THOMAS (1788–1859)

Educated at St. John's College, Cambridge : B.A., 1813 : Senior Optime : Bishop of Bombay, 1837–51, when he resigned from ill-health : appointed Rector of Bath, 1854 : universally esteemed there : a member of the Evangelical section of the Establishment : died at Bath, Sep. 5, 1859.

CARRINGTON, SIR CODRINGTON EDMUND (1769–1849)

Born Oct. 22, 1769 : son of Codrington Carrington : educated at Winchester : called to the bar by the Middle Temple, 1792 : Bencher, 1832 : practised as an advocate at the Calcutta bar, 1792–9, being junior Counsel to the E.I. Co. : was an intimate friend of Sir William Jones (*q.v.*) : when in England, he made a code of law for Ceylon : was appointed Chief Justice there and knighted, 1801 : retired in 1806 from ill-health. M.P. for St. Mawes, 1826–31 : was D.C.L. 1810 : F.R.S., J.P. and F.S.A. : died Nov. 28, 1849.

CARTIER, JOHN (1733–1802)

Governor : arrived in India as a writer in E. I. Co.'s service : was a factor and assistant at Dacca, whence he was expelled in 1756 : joined other fugitives at Fulta : served as a volunteer under Clive in re-taking Bengal, and was praised by Court of Directors : Chief of Dacca factory, 1761 : Second in Council at Calcutta, 1767 : succeeded H. Verelst as Governor of Bengal, Dec. 26, 1769 : followed, as Governor, by Warren Hastings, April 13, 1772 : eulogized by Edmund Burke for his government of Bengal : died in Kent, Jan. 25, 1802.

CASEMENT, SIR WILLIAM (1780–1844)

Maj-General : appointed to Bengal, 1795 : served in India 47 years and 6 months : in Lord Lake's campaigns, at Alighar, 1803, Deeg, 1804 : D.Q.M.G. in the Nipal war, 1815 : Secretary to the Government of India in the Military Department for 20 years from June, 1818 : Colonel, 23rd N.I., 1824 : K.C.B., 1837 : was Member of the Supreme Council from June 17, 1839 : died of cholera at Cossipur, April 16, 1844 : his bust is in the Town Hall, Calcutta.

CASSELS, ANDREW (1812–1886)

Of an old Scotch family, resident at Manchester : he opened in 1843 in Bombay the firm of Peel, Cassels & Co. : returned to England, 1851 : Director of the Manchester Chamber of Commerce, 1861 : Member of the Council of India, 1874–84 : Vice-President, 1875, of the Society of Arts : a great authority on Indian cotton : died Aug. 2, 1886.

CASSELS, WALTER RICHARD (1826–   )

Son of Robert Cassels : educated privately and abroad : spent some years in Italy, and in 1856 joined the mercantile firm of Peel, Cassels & Co. in Bombay : was a Fellow of the Bombay University : a Member of the Legislative Council, Bombay, 1863 : left India in 1865 and devoted himself to literature : wrote poems, 1850 and 1856, *Cotton in the Bombay Presidency*, 1869 ; *Supernatural Religion*, 1874–6, and 1879 : *The Gospel according to Peter*, 1894, etc. etc.

CASTLEREAGH, ROBERT STEWART, VISCOUNT (1769–1822)

Second Marquis of Londonderry (April, 1821–Aug. 1822), better known as Lord Castlereagh : son of the first Marquis : born June 18, 1769 : M.P. for Tregony, 1794–6 : for Oxford, 1796–7, and other places : his career lay in English and European politics, and his only connexion with India was as President of the Board of Control (the India Board), Sep. 9, 1802— Feb. 14, 1806, in the Addington and W. Pitt Administrations : while holding this office, he supported the Governor-General, Lord Wellesley, whom he admired, against the Court of Directors : fought a duel with George Canning, Sep. 22, 1809 : Foreign Secretary, 1812–33 : died by his own hand, Aug. 12, 1822.

CAUTLEY, SIR PROBY THOMAS (1802–1871)

Colonel : son of the Rev. Thomas Cautley : born Jan. 3, 1802 : educated at Charterhouse and Addiscombe : entered the Bengal Artillery, 1819 : was assistant to Colonel Robert Smith in reconstructing the old irrigation channel of the Doab Canal from 1824–30, but was at the siege of Bhartpur in 1826 : held charge of the above canal, 1831–43 : framed the project of the Ganges Canal, sanctioned by the Court of Directors in 1841, and constructed between 1843 and 1854. He left India in 1854, Lord Dalhousie ordering a salute to be fired in his honour : and his bust was placed in the Calcutta Town Hall : K.C.B. : from 1858–68, Member of the Council of India. He had a controversy with Sir Arthur Cotton (*q.v.*) on the engineering of the Ganges Canal, in which further work and improvement were found to be required. He explored largely in the Sivalik range of hills in India, and acquired many fossils of scientific value, which he presented to the British Museum : contributed many papers to the Asiatic Society of Bengal and to the Geological Society, chiefly on fossils : died Jan. 25, 1871.

CAVAGNARI, SIR PIERRE LOUIS NAPOLEON (1841-1879)

Lt-Colonel : son of General Adolphe Cavagnari : born July 4, 1841, educated at Christ's Hospital and Addiscombe : was naturalized in 1857 : entered the E. I. Co.'s Army, 1858 : in the Oudh campaign in the mutiny : joined the Staff Corps, 1861, and the Panjab Commission as an Assistant Commissioner : had charge of the Kohat district, 1866 to 1877, and, as Deputy Commissioner of Peshawar, accompanied several frontier expeditions, 1868-78 : C.S.I. in 1877 : he was a member of Sir N. Chamberlain's mission to Shir Ali, in the autumn of 1878, when it was stopped at Ali Masjid by the Amir's officer. When Yakub Khan had become Amir, on the death of Shir Ali, Major Cavagnari negotiated the treaty of Gandamak with him, May 26, 1879 : K.C.B. He was appointed Resident at Kabul and was residing, from July, 1879, at the Bala Hissar in Kabul, when the Afghan troops rose, attacked his residence, and he and his staff were all killed, Sep. 3, 1879.

CAVAYE, WILLIAM FREDERICK (1845-)

Colonel : son of General Cavaye : born 1845 : educated at Edinburgh Academy and Sandhurst : commanded the 2nd Royal Sussex regt. : Military Secretary to H.R.H. the Duke of Connaught, when C. in C. in Bombay : has since held several Staff appointments : served in the Zulu war, 1879, and in the S. African war, 1900-2.

CAVE-BROWNE, EDWARD RABAN- (1835-)

Born May 29, 1835 : son of Lt-Colonel Edward Cave-Browne : educated at the College School, Taunton : clerk in the East India House, 1854 : rose to be Accountant-General in the India Office from 1893 : retired in 1900 : C.S.I. in 1898.

CAVENAGH, SIR ORFEUR (1821-1891)

General : son of James Gordon Cavenagh : educated at Addiscombe : entered the Army : was through the Gwalior campaign : lost a leg at Maharajupr, 1843 : in the Satlaj campaign at Badiwal : in charge of the Mysore Princes and ex-Amirs of Sind : had political charge of Sir Jang Bahadur and the Nipalese embassy to England, 1850 : was Town Major of Fort William, Calcutta, during the mutiny : frustrated the plot of the mutineers to seize the Fort : recommended the formation of the Volunteer Guards : Governor of the Straits Settlements, 1859-67 : Lt-General, 1874 : K.C.S.I., 1881 : died July 7, 1891 : wrote *Reminiscences of an Indian Official.*

CHALMERS, SIR JOHN M. (1756-1818)

Son of Patrick Chalmers : joined the Madras Infantry in 1775 : made a gallant defence of Coimbatore, June-Nov. 1791, with only a small force, against Tippoo's troops : obliged to capitulate : taken prisoner to Seringapatam, his release effected by Cornwallis in Feb. 1792 : commanded the force at Travancore, 1803-9, and the N. Division of the Madras Army, 1812-7 : Maj-General, 1812 : K.C.B., 1815. After 42 years' service in Madras, he died on the voyage home, March 31, 1818.

CHALMERS, MACKENZIE DALZELL (1847-)

Born Feb. 7, 1847 : son of Rev. F. Chalmers, D.D., educated at King's College, London, and Trinity College, Oxford : served in the Indian Civil Service, 1869-72 : held several legal appointments as Judge of County Courts and Acting Chief Justice of Gibraltar : Legal Member of the Viceroy's Council, 1896, retired, 1899 : Parliamentary Counsel to the Treasury, 1902-3 : Permanent Under Secretary in the Home Department, 1903 : contributed Articles to the *Dictionary of Political Economy,* and the *Encyclopædia Britannica :* author of *Digest of the Law of Sale, Digest of the Law of Bills of Exchange :* C.S.I. : C.B.

CHALMERS, ROBERT (? -1878)

Lt-Colonel : joined the Indian Army, 1849 : in the mutiny his regt., the 1st Oudh Irregular Infantry, mutinied : he narrowly escaped to Allahabad : joined a regt. proceeding to relieve Cawnpur : carried back news of the massacre at Cawnpur, 44 miles, to Allahabad, through country teeming with a hostile population : was in Havelock's engagements about Cawnpur, in the relief of Lucknow, in its subsequent defence, the fighting at Alambagh, and the final capture of Lucknow, in March, 1858 : died, which commanding the 14th Bengal Lancers, Aug. 11, 1878.

CHAMBERLAIN, SIR CRAWFORD TROTTER (1821–1902)

Third son of Sir Henry O. Chamberlain, *Bart.*, younger brother of Sir Neville Bowles Chamberlain (*q.v.*) : born May, 1821 : entered the Army in 1837, was in the Afghan war of 1839–42, at the siege and capture of Ghazni, and in various actions near Kandahar : in the Panjab campaign in 1848–9 : at Chilianwala and Gujarat, in the pursuit of the Sikh Army and its final surrender : wounded : Brevet-Major : commanded the 1st Irregular Cavalry, Skinner's Horse, over whom he had extraordinary influence : in the mutiny in 1857 distinguished himself by disarming, with " undaunted courage and coolness," the 62nd and 69th Bengal N.I., at Multan : engaged against the rebels, and was besieged in a *sarai* for some days : Lt-Colonel after the mutiny : C.S.I. in 1866 : General in 1880 : G.C.I.E. in 1897 : died Dec. 13, 1902.

CHAMBERLAIN, REV. JOHN (1777–1821)

Son of John Chamberlain : born July 24, 1777 : accepted as a probationer for missionary work, 1798 : preached at Olney : studied under Dr. Ryland at the Academy at Bristol : sent to India by the Baptist Missionary Society in 1802, *via* America : arrived at Serampur, Jan. 1803 : visited Dinajpur, 1804 : established himself at Katwa, May, 1804 : carried on a cloth business, and built a school : visited Berhampur : removed to Agra, 1811 : sent down to Calcutta by order of Government : appointed, 1812, tutor at Sardhana to David Dyce Sombre, great-grandson of Begam Samru : established schools and preached frequently : also at Hardwar, for which he was ordered to Calcutta, 1815 : went to India by and up the river to Ghazipur : settled at Monghyr, 1816 : made missionary tours to Benares, Mirzapur, etc. : ordered home for ill-health, Sep.. 1821 : died at sea, Dec. 6, 1821.

CHAMBERLAIN, SIR NEVILLE BOWLES (1820–1902)

Field Marshal : second son of Sir Henry Orlando Chamberlain, first Baronet : born 1820 : educated for a short time at

Woolwich : at 17 entered the Bengal Army: in the first Afghan war was with Nott's force : at the occupation of Kandahar, at Ghazni, Kabul and Istalif : constantly wounded : was in the Governor-General's bodyguard : in the Gwalior campaign, D.A.Q.M.G. : at Maharajpur : in the second Sikh war, at Chilianwala and Gujarat : complimented by the C. in C. for personal gallantry : Commandant of Panjab Military Police : Military Secretary to the Panjab Government : Commandant of the Panjab Frontier Force : commanded several expeditions against the frontier tribes : in the mutiny of 1857 was in charge of the movable column of the Panjab until he became Adjutant-General of the Army at Delhi, and Brig-General : severely wounded there and disabled : C.B. and A.D.C. to Queen Victoria : commanded operations against the Waziris : K.C.B. : commanded in the Umbeyla campaign in 1863, until severely wounded when personally leading an assault of a difficult position : Maj-General : G.C.S.I., 1873 : G.C.B., 1875 : commanded the Madras Army, 1876–81 : in 1878 selected, by Lord Lytton, to lead a special mission to the Amir Shir Ali : the stopping of the mission at Ali Masjid was the immediate ground of the second Afghan war : he was personally in harmony with Lord Lawrence's frontier policy : Military Member of Supreme Council, Nov. 1878–Jan. 1879 : retired, 1881 : severely criticised the policy of part of the Boer war, 1899–1902 : Field Marshal in 1900 : died Feb. 17, 1902.

CHAMBERLAIN, SIR NEVILLE FRANCIS FITZGERALD (1856–)

Born Jan. 13, 1856 : son of Lt-Colonel Charles Chamberlain, C.B. : educated abroad and at Brentwood School, Essex : joined the Army, 1873 : Central India Horse, 1876 : on the staff of Sir F. Roberts through the Afghan war, 1878–80 : A.D.C. to Sir F. Roberts when C. in C., Madras, 1881–5 : Persian Interpreter, 1885–90 : served in the Burma campaign, 1886–7 : re-organized the Kashmir Army, 1890–7 : commanded the Khyber Force, 1899 : Private Secretary to Lord Roberts in S. African war : Inspr-General Royal Irish Constabulary since 1900 : C.B. in 1900 : K.C.B., 1903 : retired as Colonel from the Indian Staff Corps.

CHAMBERS, SIR CHARLES HARCOURT (1789-1828)

Born Aug. 31, 1789 : nephew of Sir Robert Chambers, (1737-1803), C.J. Bengal (1789-99) : educated at Cambridge, Fellow of Trinity College : B.A., 1809 : M.A., 1814 : practised at the bar at the Mayor's Court, Chester, and elsewhere : in 1823 appointed a Puisne Judge of the new Supreme Court, Bombay, opened May 8, 1824 : knighted by Geo. III : the Supreme Court, while he was judge, passed severe strictures on the arbitrary proceedings of the executive officers of the E. I. Co., including the magistracy and the police : the Civil Government defied the Court's authority and instructed the Company's officers not to assist the Court's officials : the Court refused to register a stringent Regulation of the Bombay Government against the liberty of the Press : on the death of the Chief Justice, Sir E. West, on Aug. 13, 1828, Chambers acted as C.J., and continued opposing the Government : Lord Ellenborough, as President of the Board of Control, supported the Executive : Chambers, still in opposition, died Oct. 13, 1828, leaving Sir J. P. Grant (q.v.) alone : buried in the Cathedral, Bombay : he wrote, in England, on legal subjects.

CHAMBERS, SIR ROBERT (1737-1803)

Son of Robert Chambers, of Newcastle : born 1737, educated there and at Lincoln College, Oxford (Exhibitioner) : Fellow of University College, 1761 ; M.A., 1761; B.C.L., 1765 ; Vinerian Professor of Law, 1762-77 : Principal of New Inn Hall, Oxford, in 1766. In 1744 he joined the Calcutta Supreme Court as second Judge, Sir Elijah Impey being Chief : knighted in 1778 : lived for several years in a garden-house at Bhawanipur : he became Chief Justice in 1791 : retired in 1799 : declined a peerage : died in Paris, May 9, 1803 : a monument by Nollekens is in the Temple Church, where he was buried. He was a friend of Dr. Johnson from 1766, and of Sir Philip Francis in Calcutta. He was one of the Judges on the trial of Nuncomar for forgery, when the latter was convicted, and hanged on Aug. 5, 1775. Chambers left some legal writings, and a collection of Sanskrit MSS.

CHAMIER, FRANCIS EDWARD ARCHIBALD (1833-)

Maj-General : son of Henry Chamier of the Madras Civil Service : born May 13, 1833 : educated at Cheltenham : joined the Indian Army : Adjutant of the Calcutta Volunteers, 1857 : Persian Interpreter to Sir James Outram in first relief, defence, siege and capture of Lucknow : commanded the Raja of Kapurthala's troops in the Oudh campaign, 1858 : C.I.E.

CHAMIER, HENRY (1795-1867)

I.C.S. : educated at Haileybury, 1811-12 : went out to Madras, 1813 : entered the Secretariat, 1827 : became Chief Secretary, 1837-42 : Member of Council, Madras, Jan. 1843 – Jan. 1848 : when he retired : died Feb. 4, 1867.

CHAMIER, JOHN (? – ?)

I.C.S. : appointed a writer, 1772 : Factor, 1778 : Junior Merchant, 1780 : absent in England for 7 years : Senior Merchant, 1787 : Secretary, 1790, in the Military, Political, and Secret Departments, and Judge Advocate General : " Chief " of Vizagapatam, for 6 years : Chief Secretary to Madras Government, 1801 : Provisional Member of Council, Madras, 1802 : confirmed as Member, 1803 : resigned, 1805 : returned to England.

CHAMIER, STEPHEN (1834-)

Born Aug. 17, 1834 : son of Henry Chamier of the Madras Civil Service : educated at Cheltenham and Addiscombe : entered the Madras Artillery, 1853 : transferred to Royal Artillery, 1861 : commanded mountain battery in Burma against the Karens, 1856 : served in the Indian mutiny, 1857-8, and was present at Cawnpur under Sir Charles Windham, at the siege of Lucknow under Sir Colin Campbell, and in the Oudh campaign : Brevet-Major, and C.B. : Inspr-General of Ordnance, Madras, 1881-6 : Lt-General, R.A.

CHAMPION, ALEXANDER (? – ?)

Second in command to (Sir Hector) Munro, 1764, when opposed to Shuja-ud-daula : in the battle of Baxar, Oct. 23, 1764 : Colonel : succeeded Sir Robert Barker, as C. in C. of the Bengal Army, June 18, 1774, to Oct. 29, 1774 : commanded a Brigade in 1774, asked for by the Nawab Wazir of Oudh,against the Rohillas: defeated them near Tassunih, April 23, 1774: retired 1774: resided at Bath many years.

CHANDA, SAHIB (? -1752)

Another name of Husain Dost Khan, son-in-law of Dost Ali Khan, Nawab of Arcot, 1732–40, and his Diwan : regarded as a great soldier of his time : he obtained possession of the Hindu kingdom of Trichinopoly by cajoling the Rani, 1736. The Mahrattas invaded the Carnatic, 1740, besieged Chanda in Trichinopoly, and took him prisoner in 1741 to Satara : Dupleix in 1748 procured his release for a large ransom. On the death of Anwaruddin, the Nawab of the Carnatic, in 1749, at the battle of Ambur against Chanda Sahib and Muzaffar Jang (the claimant to succeed as Nizam), Chanda was proclaimed as Nawab : the British supported Muhammad Ali, son of Anwaruddin, as their candidate for the Nawabship, while the French supported Chanda's aspirations. Muhammad Ali fled from Ambur to Trichinopoly, where he was besieged by Chanda : in the fighting that ensued Chanda surrendered to the Raja of Tanjore, in May, 1752, who barbarously put him to death and sent his head to Muhammad Ali.

CHANDRA, BHOLANATH (1822–)

Born 1822: educated at the Hindu College : in 1843 became a clerk in the Union Bank, Calcutta ; afterwards apprenticed to Messrs Haworth, Hardman & Co. : appointed, in 1845, their agent for their Cossipur Sugar Refinery: served for 30 years : began to publish his " Travels " serially in the *Englishman's Saturday Journal* in 1866–7 : issued together in 2 vols. in 1869, in England, with an introduction by J. T. Wheeler (*q.v.*) : published, in 1894, a life of Raja Digambar Mitra, C.S.I. : an auther of undoubted literary ability and powers of observation.

CHANDRAVARKAR, NARAYAN GANESH (1855–)

Educated at Elphinstone College, Bombay : pleader of the Bombay High Court and Judge of that Court since 1901 : succeeded Mr. Justice Ranade as leader of the Indian Social reform movement.

CHANDU LAL, MAHARAJA (1766– 1845)

Born 1766 : at first a subordinate in the Customs Department at Hyderabad under his uncle, Rai Nanak Ram : in 1806 Peshkar, and, after Mir Alam's death, became the real Minister of the Nizam's Government, though Munir-ul-mulk was Diwan : was highly regarded by Henry Russell, the Resident at Hyderabad from 1811–20. Chandu Lal ruled Hyderabad for about 35 years : retired Sep. 1843, from the Peshkarship, on a monthly pension of Rs. 30,000 : died April 15, 1845.

CHAPMAN, EDWARD FRANCIS (1840–)

General : born 1840 : son of Henry Chapman : entered the Bengal Artillery, 1858 : served in the Abyssinian war, 1867– 8 : accompanied Sir Douglas Forsyth as Secretary to Yarkand in 1873–4 : in the Afghan war, of 1878–80, was Chief of the Staff in Sir F. Roberts' march from Kabul to Kandahar : C.B : and Brevet Lt-Colonel : in Burma campaign, 1885–6 : Military Secretary to Sir Donald Stewart, when C. in C. in India : Q.M.G. in India : Director of Military Intelligence, 1891–6 : commanded the Scottish District, 1896– 1901 : Colonel Commanding Royal Artillery : F.R.G.S : A.D.C. to Queen Victoria, 1881.

CHAPMAN, ROBERT BARCLAY (1829–)

I.C.S. : born Nov. 21, 1829 : son of Jonathan Chapman : educated at Haileybury : entered the Bengal Civil Service, 1849 : and rose to be Secretary to the Government of India in the Finance Department, 1869–81, when he retired : C.S.I.

CHASTENAY, HENRY (1794–1822)

B.C.S. : arrived in India as a writer in Bengal, Nov. 1811 : served always at the headquarters of the Government : Private Secretary to the Marquess of Hastings, when Governor - General : died May 2, 1822 : buried at Calcutta.

CHATTERJI, BANKIM CHANDRA (1838–1894)

Bengali novelist and prose writer : son of Jadab Chandra Chatterji, a Deputy

Magistrate : born June 27, 1838 : educated at the Midnapur School, Hughli and Presidency Colleges : in 1858 he was the first native of India to take the B.A. degree, Calcutta : at once appointed to be a Deputy Magistrate, and became a prominent member of the Provincial service, acting for a time as Assistant Secretary to the Bengal Government. His reputation was made in literature, as the Bengali novelist of his time : his novels were numerous, and are said to be still popular : he brought out a literary magazine, 1872, and wrote the first Bengali historical novel, under the title of *Durges Nandini*. This was followed by *Kapala Kandala, Mrinalini,* and *Bisha Brikka*, which was translated into English and very favourably criticised by Professor Darmesteter : *Debi Chandurani, Ananda Matha,* and *Krishna Kanter Will :* wrote also on Hindu religion, Kirshna, the Vedas, and Hindu literature : made Rai Bahadur and C.I.E : retired from Government service in 1891: died April 8, 1894.

CHATTERTON, THE RIGHT REV. EYRE (1863–   )

Born July 22, 1863 : son of A. T. Chatterton : educated at Haileybury and Dublin University : ordained 1887 : Head of the Dublin University Mission to Chota-Nagpur, 1891–1900 : Bishop of Nagpur, Central Provinces, 1903 : D.D : author of *The Story of Fifty Years' Mission in Chota-Nagpur :* F.R.G.S.

CHAVANNES, EDOUARD (1865–   )

Born Oct. 5, 1865, at Lyons : son of Emile Chavannes, engineer : educated at l'Ecole normale supérieure : his work as a scholar has dealt principally with Chinese subjects, often in relation to India : entrusted with a scientific mission to China, 1889–93 : appointed Professor of the Chinese Language and Literature at the Collège de France, 1893 : Secretary of the Société Asiatique, 1895 : Member of the Institute, 1903 : The following works by him treat of the travels of Chinese Buddhist pilgrims in India : *I-tsing, Les religieux éminents,* 1894 : *Voyage de Song Yun dans l'Udyana et le Gandhara,* (a translation) in the *Bulletin de l'Ecole francaise d'Extreme Orient,* 1903, etc. : *Documents sur les Tou-kine (Turks) occidentaux,* 1903, treats of several questions relating to India. He has also written largely in the *Journal Asiatique,* on the Chinese inscriptions of Bodh Gaya in the *Revue de l'Histoire des Religions,* and in other periodicals.

CHAVASSE, WILLIAM (1785–1814)

An officer of the E. I. Co.'s service, who tried, with a companion, to explore the route of the 10,000 Greeks, as described in Xenophon's *Anabasis.* They were taken prisoners by a local chief near Bagdad, but released on payment of ransom. Chavasse died of fever there.

CHEAPE, SIR JOHN (1792–1875)

Son of John Cheape : born in 1792 : educated at Woolwich and Addiscombe : joined the Bengal Engineers in 1809, rose to be Maj-General in 1854: was under Lord Hastings in the Pindari war, in the Nerbudda Field Force, 1817 : at the siege of Asirghar and in the Burmese war, 1824–6 : was Chief Engineer at the siege of Multan, 1848, and at Gujarat in the Panjab campaign : C.B. : in the second Burmese war of 1852–3, was second in command under General Godwin at first, and later, in 1853, commanded, and took Pegu : the provinces of Pegu and Tenasserim were annexed : K.C.B : A.D.C. to Queen Victoria : retired, 1857 : Colonel Commandant of Engineers, 1862 : G.C.B., 1865 : General, 1866 : died March 30, 1875.

CHELMSFORD, FREDERICK AUGUSTUS THESIGER, SECOND BARON (1827–1905)

Born May 31, 1827 : son of first Baron (Lord Chancellor, 1858–9) : educated at Eton : succeeded to title, 1879 : entered the Army in the Grenadier Guards, 1844 : served in the Crimea : Lt.-Colonel in the 95th regt. in the mutiny, in Central India : Adjutant-General in the Abyssinian campaign, 1867–8 : C.B. and A.D.C. to Queen Victoria : Adjutant-General in India : commanded the forces in the Kafir war, 1878 : succeeded his father, Oct. 1878 : at Isandhwala, Gingilhovo, Ulundi : Lieutenant of the Tower, 1884–9 : General, 1888 : G.C.B. : G.C.V.O : died April 9, 1905.

CHERRY, GEORGE FREDERICK (1761–1799)

B.C.S. : son of George Cherry : born 1761 : entered the Bengal Civil Service, 1778 :

accompanied Lord Cornwallis as his Persian Secretary to Madras, where, in 1792, peace was made with Tippoo at Seringapatam : Cherry's picture of Tippoo is at the India Office : appointed Resident at Benares, 1793 : there murdered by Wazir˙ Ali, the reputed son of the late Nawab Asaf-ud-daula of Oudh, on Jan. 14, 1799.

CHESNAYE, GEORGE COCHET
(1837-1904)

Born Sep. 1837 : entered the Bengal Medical Service, 1859 : Deputy Surgeon-General, 1889 : did excellent service at Mian Mir and Umritsar in the cholera epidemic of 1861 : in the Hazara Field Force, 1868 : Black Mountain expedition : Lushai expedition, 1871-2 : Afghan war, 1878-80 : from Ali Masjid to Gandamak, 1878, to Kabul 1879 : in the Kabul-Kandahar march : in the battle of Mazra, near Kandahar : in the expedition against the Marris : Deputy Surgeon - General, Lahore, 1889-94 : when he retired : died April 12, 1904.

CHESNEY, SIR GEORGE TOMKYNS
(1830-1895)

Son of Capt. Charles Cornwallis Chesney of the Bengal Artillery : born April 30, 1830 : educated at Blundell's school, Tiverton, and Addiscombe : entered the Bengal Engineers, 1848, and became General in 1882 : went to India in 1850 : in the P.W.D. until the mutiny : in the Badli-ka-sarai action, June, 8, 1857 : at the capture of the ridge at Delhi : Brig-Major, R.E. at Delhi : in the assault on Sep. 14 : was President of the Engineering College at Calcutta, and head of the P.W.D. Account Department in 1860 : President of the Royal Indian Civil Engineering College at Cooper's Hill, 1871-80, of which he had prepared the constitution, etc. : Secretary to the Government of India in the Military Department, 1880-6 : Military Member of the Supreme Council, July, 1886-April, 1891 : M.P. for Oxford, 1892 : C.S.I. 1883 : C.I.E. 1886 : C.B. 1887 : K.C.B. 1890 : died March 31, 1895. He wrote a number of books : the principal were *Indian Polity* : *The Battle of Dorking*, a military-political Magazine article which made a great sensation : *The True Reformer*, *The Dilemma*, *The Private Secretary*, besides other articles in Magazines and Reviews.

CHETTY, GAZULU LAKSHMINARASU
(1806-1868)

Son of an indigo merchant : joined his father in trade and amassed a large fortune at the time of the American war : founded the Madras Native Association, of which he was President : opposed the proselytizing tendencies of the missionaries and successfully resisted the attempt made to introduce the Bible as a text-book in Government Schools in 1843 : was forward in the agitation carried on in 1853-5 regarding the grievances of the natives, which led to the Torture Commission : after incurring much odium as a seditious person, in 1861 he was made a C.S.I. : he next directed his attention to the affairs of Mysore and the Tanjore widows : lost most of his fortune and died a poor man, leaving a name for patriotism and self-sacrifice.

CHIBU, LAMA (? -1866)

Was sprung from an old and respectable Sikhim family of Tibetan origin : dwelt at Tumlong near the Raja of Sikhim : was early a man of influence and mark, learnt Hindustani, a qualification which gave him much political importance. When Sir Joseph Hooker and Dr. Campbell were imprisoned by the Sikhim Court, he befriended them throughout, and as a reward obtained a very large estate of about 75,000 acres near Darjeeling, on the annexation of Sikhim territory. In 1864 he accompanied Sir Ashley Eden through out his mission to Bhutan and, with con-siderable personal danger, exerted himself to bring the negotiations to a successful issue : died in 1866.

CHINNERY, GEORGE (1766-1852)

Artist : exhibited in the Royal Academy, 1790-1846 : painted in Dublin and London and went to China, from which country he visited India : he " made spirited sketches of scenes in India" : was at Madras, 1802-7 or 8, and afterwards painted many pictures at Calcutta : was at Canton in 1830 and died at Maçao in 1852 : references to his works in India occur in Indian literature : his name and his skill are remembered there to this day.

CHITNAVIS, GUNGADHAR MADHO
(1863-)

Born 1863 : Hony. Magistrate : Presi-dent of the Nagpur District Council since

G

1888: and of the Nagpur Municipality since 1894 : represented the Central Provinces as Member of the Governor-General's Legislative Council, 1893–5 : leader of the Prabhu community : guest of the nation, representing the Central Provinces, at H.M. the King's Coronation, 1902 : C.I.E., 1895.

CHRISTIE, JOHN (1805–1869)

Entered the Indian Army, 1822, and the 3rd Light Cavalry, 1823 : at the capture of Bhartpur, 1826 : was selected by the C. in C., Sir Henry Fane, to raise, for Shah Shuja's force, the 1st Irregular Cavalry, later known as Christie's Horse, which he commanded to the end of the first Afghan war, 1839–42 : was at the occupation of Kandahar and pursuit of the Sirdars to the Helmund under Sir Robert Sale : at Ghazni, and Kabul in 1839 : accompanied Outram in pursuit of the Amir Dost Muhammad across the Hindu Kush : in the Kandahar Division under Sir W. Nott in 1842 : at the occupation of Ghazni and Kabul, the taking of Istalif, and the final march through the Khyber to India : was at the battle of Punniar, 1843 : in the Satlaj campaign of 1845–6, at Mudki, Firozshahr and Sobraon : Brevet-Major : throughout the Panjab campaign, including Chilianwala and Gujarat, and the pursuit of the Sikhs and Afghans, always in command of his regiment : Brevet-Lt-Colonel : returned from England to India on the outbreak of the mutiny, commanded the Dinapur Brigade, and kept Patna perfectly quiet : afterwards in command at Barrackpur and Berhampur : commanded the 3rd Bengal Cavalry : Maj-General, 1861 : joined the Bengal Staff Corps, 1866 : C.B., 1867 : and A.D.C. to Queen Victoria : received many medals and the Order of the Durani for his services in Afghanistan : died at San Remo, May 7, 1869 : buried there.

CHRISTIE, S. T. (? –1876)

Lt-General : entered the Army, 1836 : served with the 80th regt. in the Burmese war, 1852-3 : commanded the storming party at Martaban : at the operations at Rangoon : at the capture of Prome : in the Indian mutiny commanded a movable column : at Fatehpur : at the siege of Lucknow : commanded a Field Force in the Oudh campaign, wounded : C.B. : Lt-General 1876 : died Oct. 5, 1876.

CHURCHILL, LORD RANDOLPH HENRY SPENCER (1849–1894)

Son of the sixth Duke of Marlborough : born Feb. 13, 1849 : educated at Eton, and Merton College, Oxford : M.P. for Woodstock, 1874–1885; for South Paddington, 1885 to his death. The greater portion of his career in politics and the House of Commons had no connexion with India. He made a tour in that country in the cold weather of 1884–5, in which he studied its administration, and gained experience which was valuable to him when he was Secretary of State for India from June 24, 1885, to Feb. 5, 1886. In that post he made a reputation for his administrative capacity, his industry, knowledge of details, and despatch of business. He sanctioned the Burmese war of 1885–6 and the annexation of Upper Burma, and concluded the Russo-Afghan Frontier negotiations. He also sanctioned Mr. Colman Macaulay's visit to Pekin, with a view to a subsequent mission to Lhasa, which was afterwards stopped. He was on a sea voyage round the world for his health, when he had to leave Madras and return to England, and died there, Jan. 24, 1894.

CLAPPERTON, ANDREW BALFOUR (1794–1847)

Captain : Master-attendant at Calcutta : went to sea in 1808 in the E. I. Co.'s mercantile service : served in the expeditions against the Isle of France and Java : commanded merchant-ships to and from Calcutta for years; " no man in the country's service ever bore a higher character." He safely rounded Cape Horn, with a lascar crew, in 1822–3 : having served as second and first Assistant, he became Master-attendant, 1840–2, and was confirmed in 1847, but died, Sep. 20. He was at various times Judge Advocate of the Marine Committee of Enquiry : regarded as a tried and valuable officer of the Company, and much esteemed in society.

CLARE, JOHN FITZGIBBON, SECOND EARL OF (1792–1851)

Governor : born June 10, 1792 : son of the first Earl, Lord Chancellor of Ireland :

succeeded his father in 1902 : educated at Christ Church, Oxford : Governor of Bombay, March 21, 1831, till March 17, 1835 : Privy Councillor, 1830 : G.C.H., 1835 : K.P., 1845 : died Aug. 18, 1851.

CLARKE, SIR ALURED (1745 ?–1832)

Field-Marshal: born about 1745 : entered the Army, 1759: served in Germany, Ireland, America: was Lieutenant-Governor of Jamaica, 1782–90 : on the way to India, in 1795, he co-operated with Lord Keith in the capture of Cape Town from the Dutch E. I. Co. : in India was C. in C. in Madras, Jan., 1796 till March, 1797 : Member of the Supreme Council and provisional C. in C. Bengal from April,1797, and confirmed in the Chief Command in India in May, 1798, retaining it till July, 1801. He was in command of the force with Sir John Shore when the latter, as Governor-General, went to Lucknow to depose Wazir Ali and set up Saadat Ali as Nawab of Oudh in Jan. 1798. He acted as Governor-General from the resignation of Sir John Shore in March, 1798, till the arrival of Lord Mornington in May, 1798. He was K.B. in 1797 : General in 1802 : G.C.B., 1815 : Field-Marshal in 1830, and died Sep. 16, 1832.

CLARKE, SIR ANDREW (1824–1902)

Son of Col. Andrew Clarke : born 1824 : educated at King's School, Canterbury, and Woolwich : entered the Royal Engineers, 1844 : was A.D.C. to Sir W. Denison, Governor of Tasmania, 1849–53 : in the Maori war, New Zealand : on the staff of Sir George Grey : Surveyor-General of Victoria : Minister for Public Lands in the Legislative Assembly at Melbourne : nine years Director of Works for the Navy : Governor and C. in C. of the Straits Settlements, 1873–5 : P.W.D. Member of the Supreme Council of the Governor-General, 1875–80 : Commandant of the School of Military Engineering at Chatham, 1880–2 : Inspr-General of Fortifications, 1882–6 : retired in 1886 as Lt-General : K.C.M.G., 1873 : G.C.M.G., 1885 : Col. Commandant R.E. : unsuccessfully contested Chatham in 1886 and 1893 : Agent-General to the Colony of Victoria for many years : died March 29, 1902 : also C.B. and C.I.E.

CLARKE, CHARLES BARRON (1832–)

Born June 17, 1832 : son of Turner Poulter Clarke : educated at King's College, London, Trinity and Queen's Colleges, Cambridge : third wrangler, 1856 : Mathematical Lecturer at Queen's College, 1857–65 : joined the Education Department in Bengal : Inspector of Schools, 1866–87: retired 1887: F.R.S. : an ardent Botanist : has written numerous papers on Botany, also on Anthropology, Geography, and Music : and *Speculations from Political Economy*, 1886.

CLARKE, SIR CHARLES MANSFIELD, BARONET (1839–)

General : son of Sir Charles Clarke, second *Bart.* : born Dec. 13, 1839 : entered the Army in 1856 : served in New Zealand, South Africa, War Office, Ireland and at Aldershot : commanded the Colonial Forces at the Cape, 1880–2 : C. in C. in Madras, 1893–8 : Q.M.G., 1899–1903 : Governor of Malta since 1903 : G.C.B. in 1901.

CLARKE, LONGUEVILLE (? –1860 ?)

For many years a prominent barrister of the Supreme Court, Calcutta : where, it is stated, he founded the Ice House, the Bar Library, and the Metcalfe Hall.

CLARKE, TREDWAY (1764–1858)

General : entered the E. I. Co.'s military service in 1780 : on arriving in Madras was engaged in the war against Hyder Ali : wounded at the storming of Chillumbram : in command of the Artillery at Fort St. George from 1783 : under General Medows and Lord Cornwallis in the fighting with Tippoo in 1790–2, including Bangalore, Seringapatam, Pondicherry and the hill-forts : from 1798, Head Commissary of Ordnance at Fort St. George : returned to England in 1811 : offered the command of the Artillery at Madras in 1820 : prevented by ill-health from accepting it : died in 1858.

CLARK-KENNEDY, JOHN (1817–1867)

Son of Lt-General Sir A. K. Clark-Kennedy : born in 1817 : entered the Army in 1833 : served in China : at the sieges of Multan in 1848, and the battle of Gujarat : at the pursuit and surrender of the Sikhs, and defeat of the Afghans :

with Colin Campbell (Lord Clyde) at the occupation of Peshawar, March 21, 1849 : served in the Crimea : Maj-General : died at Cairo on Dec. 18, 1867.

CLAVERING, SIR JOHN (1722–1777)

Son of Sir James Clavering : born in 1722 : entered the Guards, was Brig-General in the attack on Guadaloupe in 1759 : Horace Walpole wrote " Clavering was the real hero of Guadaloupe. He has come home covered with more laurels than a boar's head " : he was sent to Hesse-Cassel in 1760 : became Lt-General in 1770 : in 1774 went to India : C. in C. in India and one of the four Members of the Supreme Council under the Regulating Act of 1773 : lived at Calcutta in Mission Row : he, Francis, and Monson opposed Warren Hastings and Barwell in the Supreme Council. He was made K.B. on Nov. 9, 1776 : he fought, in April, 1775, a duel with Barwell : he supported Nuncomar in his charges against Warren Hastings. When Warren Hastings' resignation was tendered by his agent in England —but repudiated in India by Hastings— Clavering claimed to be Governor-General, but his claim was rejected by the Supreme Court.   Clavering died Aug. 30, 1777.

CLEGHORN, HUGH FRANCIS CLARKE (1820–1895)

Born 1820 : his father was Administrator-General in the Supreme Court, Madras : educated at Edinburgh and St. Andrew's : went to Madras in the medical service, 1842 : Professor of Botany in the Madras University, 1852 : entrusted by the Governor of Madras, Lord Harris, to form a Government Forest Department : became Inspr-General of Forests and established an excellent system of conservancy and management : retired, 1869 : for many years he selected the candidates for the Indian Forest Service : died May 16, 1895 : LL.D. : F.R.S.E.

CLEGHORN, JAMES (1841–   )

Son of John Cleghorn : born 1841 : educated at Edinburgh University and Royal College of Surgeons, Edinburgh : M.D. St. Andrew's : entered Indian Medical Service, 1865 : served in the Bhutan campaign, 1864–5 : and rose to be Director-General of the I.M.S. and Sanitary Commissioner, 1895 : Fellow of

the Allahabad University : retired, 1898 : published various medical papers : Hony. Surgeon to H.M. the King : C.S.I.

CLERK, SIR GEORGE RUSSELL (1800–1889)

I.C.S. : son of John Clerk : educated at Haileybury: entered the Service as " writer " in 1817 : after holding some unimportant appointments in Bengal, he entered the Political Department : was in the Secretariat, in Rajputana, at Delhi, Political Agent at Umbala and Ludiana : Envoy at Lahore, 1842 : Agent to the Governor-General on the North-Western Frontier during the first Afghan war, in which capacity he pushed forward reinforcements with energy, and, after the massacre of the Army, urged a policy of retribution.   He was Lieutenant-Governor of the N.W.P., June to Dec. 1843 : Provisional Member of the Supreme Council, 1844 : twice Governor of Bombay, from 1847 to 1848 : K.C.B. : and from 1860–2. He refused the government of the Cape, but served there on boundary and political work, 1853–4 : was Under Secretary and Secretary to the Board of Control in 1856–8, and permanent Under Secretary of State for India, 1858–60. He was a Member of the Council of India, 1863–76 : K.C.S.I., 1861 : G.C.S.I., 1866 : died July 25, 1889.

CLERK, SIR GODFREY (1835–   )

General : son of Sir George Russell Clerk (q.v.), the Governor of Bombay : born Oct. 25, 1835 : entered the Army, 1851 : served with the Rifle Brigade in the Indian mutiny and N.W. Frontier campaign : Adjutant-General of the Madras Army, 1880–5 : Assistant Military Secretary at Headquarters,'1886–7 : D.A.G. to the Forces, 1887–92: commanding Belfast District, 1892–3 : Lieutenant of the Tower of London, 1897–1900 : Groom in Waiting to Queen Victoria, and to H.M the King : C.B. : K.C.V.O. in 1902.

CLEVELAND, AUGUSTUS (1755–1784)

Of the Bengal Civil Service : said to have been a cousin of Lord Teignmouth (q.v.) : was Collector and Judge of the Diwani Adalat (Civil Court) of the districts of Bhagalpur, Monghyr and Rajmahal : proceeding in the Atlas Indiaman, to the Cape for his health, he died at sea,

Jan. 12 or 13, 1784 : his remains were brought back to Calcutta, and interred in the South Park Street Cemetery. Warren Hastings had a monument erected to him with a lengthy inscription : another monument was put up by his native subordinates and others at Bhagalpur. The inscription on the latter runs : " Who, without bloodshed or terrors of authority, employing only the means of conciliation, confidence and benevolence, attempted and accomplished the entire subjection of the lawless ánd savage inhabitants of the jungle-territory of Rajmahal, who had long infested the neighbouring lands by their predatory incursions, inspired them with a taste for the arts of civilized life, and attached them to the British Government by a conquest over their minds, the most permanent as the most rational mode of dominion." He has been called " the *dulce decus* of the early Civil Service." This was the voyage of the *Atlas* in which Mrs. Warren Hastings returned to England.

CLINTON, CHARLES HENRY ROLLE TREFUSIS, TWENTIETH BARON
(1834–1904)

Son of the 19th Baron : born 1834 : educated at Eton, and Christ Church, Oxford · M.P. 1857–66, when he succeeded to the peerage : Under Secretary of State for India, 1867–8 : Charity Commissioner : died March 29, 1904.

CLIVE, ROBERT, BARON (1725–1774)

Governor of Bengal : son of Richard Clive : born Sep. 29, 1725 : educated at Lostock, Market Drayton. Merchant Taylors' and Hemel Hempstead : his youth marked by energy, courage, and adventure : reached Madras as a " writer " in the E. I. Co.'s Civil Service in 1744 : in the capitulation of Madras, 1746 : escaped to Fort St. David : obtained military employ in 1848 : at Boscawen's siege of Pondicherry : fought at Devikota, 1749, on behalf of the Tanjore ruler : at the flight at Valkonda : seized Arcot on Aug. 31, 1751, to divert Chanda Sahib from besieging Muhammad Ali at Trichinopoly : was himself besieged with his small party in the fort of Arcot for 50 days by Chanda Sahib's superior force, which he beat off successfully : one of the most brilliant feats in history : defeated Raja Sahib and the French at Caveripak, 1752 : destroyed the town of Dupleix Fatehabad : defeated French Army near Trichinopoly : took Covelong and Chingleput : in England, 1753–6 : returned to India as Lt-Colonel : on his way out through Bombay captured, on Feb. 13, 1756, Gheria, the stronghold of the pirate Angria : became Lieutenant-Governor of Fort St. David, June 20, 1756 : after the Black Hole tragedy, Clive was sent up to Bengal in Oct.–Dec. 1756 : took Calcutta and Hughli from the Nawab Suraj-ud-daula : again defeated him and took Chandernagore : through Omichund, whom he deceived by the fraud of two copies, one of them being fictitious, of the treaty, made a treaty with Mir Jafar to desert the Nawab : fought the battle of Plassey, June 23, 1757 ; routed the Nawab, who fled and was killed : installed Mir Jafar as Nawab, and received large sums from him : made Governor of Bengal : asserted himself against his colleagues in the Government : defeated the Dutch near Chinsura : sent Colonel Forde to the N. districts of Madras : to England again, 1760–5 : made Baron Clive of Plassey in 1762 : K.C.B. in 1764 : M.P. for Shrewsbury : described as a " heaven-born General " : quarrelled with Sullivan, Chairman of the E. I. Co.'s Directors, and defeated him : reappointed Governor of Bengal and C. in C. to reform the abuses prevailing there in his absence : held office May 3, 1765, till Jan. 1767 : obtained from the Emperor of Delhi, Shah Alam, the " *diwani*," i.e. authority to administer the Civil Government and collect the revenue, of Bengal, Bihar and Orissa, Aug. 12, 1765 : restored Oudh to Shuja-ud-daula : reformed the administration, checking malpractices and giving adequate salaries : measures of retrenchment provoked mutiny, which he promptly repressed : finally retired in 1767, poorer than in 1765 : a £70,000 legacy from Mir Jafar he devoted to " the Clive Fund " for military men : attacked in England by numerous enemies, his administration subjected to Parliamentary inquiry : partly condemned,but it was finally decided that Clive had rendered great and meritorious services to his country : worn out by ill-health and persecution, he took his own life, Nov. 22, 1774. His character much discussed : his bravery, ability, masterfulness, power of leading and governing are generally admitted : but his deceit of

Omichund cannot be justified, and his acceptance of large presents from Mir Jafar can only be excused by special considerations of contemporary custom, and their openness.

CLOSE, SIR BARRY, BARONET (1756–1813)

Appointed to the Madras Army in 1771 : besieged at Tellicherry in 1780 by Hyder Ali's troops : conducted boundary negotiations with Tippoo's Commissioners : was present at the sieges of Seringapatam in 1792 and 1799, as Deputy, and Assistant Adjutant-General : his services warmly acknowledged by the C. in C., General Harris : appointed Resident of Mysore in 1799, and Resident of Poona in 1801, remaining there for ten years. He, there, as Resident, negotiated the Treaty of Bassein of Dec. 31, 1802, with the Peshwa, Baji Rao : retired to England in 1811 : created a Baronet : died April 20, 1813.

CLYDE, COLIN CAMPBELL, BARON (1792–1863)

Field-Marshal, son of Colin Macliver, a carpenter : took his mother's name of Campbell : born Oct. 20, 1792 : entered the Army in 1808 : served in Portugal under Sir Arthur Wellesley and Sir John Moore : was in the expedition to Walcheren, 1809 : served in the Peninsular from 1810 to 1813, distinguishing himself by his gallantry : Captain, 1813 : was in Nova Scotia, at Gibraltar, in the W. Indies : Major, 1825 : Lt-Colonel, 1832 : in the China war of 1842 : C.B. : to India in 1846 : Brigadier at Lahore : was engaged in the second Sikh war, at Ramnagar, Chilianwala and Gujarat :. commanded the Peshawar Division : K.C.B. in 1849 : commanded the Highland Brigade in the Crimea, at Alma, Balaclava : G.C.B. in 1855 : Lt-General, 1856 : D.C.L. of Oxford : went out at a day's notice in July, 1857, to be C. in C. in. India during the mutiny, hurried up reinforcements to Cawnpur, and thence, in Nov. 1857, relieved Lucknow, carrying off the garrison, defeated the rebels at Cawnpur, and, in March, 1858, besieged and took Lucknow on the 19th : subsequently he reduced the rebels of Northern India to submission : General, and made Lord Clyde of Clydesdale, in 1858 : and received a pension from the E.I. Co. :

returned to England in 1860 : was one of the first Knight Commanders of the Star of India in 1861 : was made Field-Marshal in 1862 : died on Aug. 14, 1863, and was buried in Westminster Abbey. His military career was one of the greatest of the century : his victories in India and his modest and exemplary character made him a hero to the public.

COBB, JAMES (1756–1818)

Appointed a clerk in the Secretary's office at the India House, March 28, 1771 : became Assistant Secretary, June 2, 1802 : Secretary, Jan. 7, 1814 : between 1779 and 1809, he wrote a large number of pieces of various kinds for the stage : died 1818.

COCKBURN, THOMAS (1763– ?)

Appointed a writer at Fort St. George, 1779 : Member of the Board of Revenue in 1793 : in 1798 Lord Mornington strongly recommended him to the second Lord Clive, then Governor of Madras : in 1801 he was induced by the Court of Directors not to retire : was employed in settling the affairs of the Nawab of Arcot, and gave evidence before the House of Commons Committee on the affairs of the E. I. Co., in 1812. In 1813 he published a brochure in the form of an imaginary speech to be delivered by an M.P. on *Legislative Interference in the Conversion of the Indian Population to Christianity.*

COCKBURN, SIR WILLIAM, BARONET (1768–1835)

Son of Colonel James Cockburn : born in a camp in 1768 : entered the Army when only 10 years old : in the American war, and a captain at 15 : in India 1790–1802 : in the first Mysore war, and at Seringapatam in 1792, where he acted as Engineer : Lt-General, 1821 : died March 19, 1835.

COCKERELL, HORACE ABEL (1833–   )

I.C.S. : born Sep. 19, 1833 : educated at Eton and Haileybury, 1851–2 : went out to Lower Bengal, 1853 : officiating Chairman of the Calcutta Corporation and Commissioner of Police, 1869 and 1872 : Commissioner of several Divisions : Secretary to the Bengal Government, Judicial and Political Departments, 1877–82 :

Member of the Board of Revenue,˙ 1882–87 : acting Lieutenant-Governor of Bengal, Aug. 11 to Sep. 17, 1885 : C.S.I. : retired 1887.

COCKS, ARTHUR HERBERT (1819–1881)

I.C.S. : son of the Hon. Philip James Cocks : born April 18, 1819 : educated at Haileybury : went to India in 1837 : served in Sind under Sir C. Napier : in the Panjab campaign was Political Officer to Lord Gough at Ramnagar, Chilianwala, Gujarat : after the annexation in 1849 served in the Panjab : in the mutiny was Judge of Mainpuri : served in the volunteers at Agra, and in the Alighar district : C.B., 1860 : retired, 1863 : died Aug. 29, 1881.

CODRINGTON, OLIVER (1837–   )

Born May 5, 1837 : son of Rev. T. S. Codrington, Vicar of Wroughton, Wilts : educated at the Royal Free Grammar School, Marlborough, and the London Hospital : M.D. : F.S.A. : in the Army Medical Department, June, 1859–1885 : served in the N. Zealand war, 1864–6 : retired with honorary rank of Deputy Surgeon-General : formerly Secretary of the Bombay Asiatic Society, now Hony. Librarian of the Royal Asiatic and Royal Numismatic Societies : has written a Manual of Musulman Numismatics and various papers on Oriental Numismatic and Archæological subjects.

COFFIN, SIR ISAAC CAMPBELL (1800–1872)

Son of Capt. Coffin, R.N. : born 1800 : reached India in the E. I. Co.'s Army in 1819 : joined at Madras in 1821 : served in the first Burma war, 1824, and at stations held by the Madras Army : commanded, from 1855, the Hyderabad subsidiary force : and a Division of the Madras Army in 1859–64 : K.C.S.I., 1866 : Lt-General, 1869 : died Oct 1, 1872.

COGHILL, KENDAL (1832–   )

Colonel : son of Admiral Sir J. Coghill, *Bart.* : born Oct. 21, 1832 : educated at Cheltenham : joined the Indian Army, 1851 : served in Burma, 1853–5 : Adjutant of his regt. (2nd European Bengal Fusiliers) during the mutiny, 1857–8 : present at Badli-ka-sarai and siege of Delhi, and several subsequent actions : Brig-Major at Cawnpur and Barrackpur : Assistant A.G. at Lucknow and Calcutta : and of the Presidency Division, 1861–1870 : exchanged to 19th Hussars, which he commanded in Egyptian campaign, 1882 : C.B.

COGHLAN, SIR WILLIAM M. (1803–1885)

General : son of Captain J. Coghlan, C.B., R.N. : joined the Artillery in India, 1820 : in the Kolapur Field Force, 1826–7 : Brig-Major of Artillery in Sind and Afghanistan in 1838–40 : at Ghazni Kabul, Kandahar, capture of Kelat : Political Resident and Commandant at Aden, 1854–63 : he carried out, 1856–7, the occupation of Perim (previously taken possession of in 1799) as suggested by Lord Elphinstone (*q.v.*) : commanded against Arabs, 1858 : stormed the fort of Shekh Othmar : K.C.B., 1864 : died Nov. 25, 1885.

COKE, SIR JOHN (1806–1897)

Maj-General : son of the Rev. F. Coke : born 1806 : entered ¦E.I. Co.'s Service, 1823 : served in the 10th Bengal N.I. : raised the 1st Panjab Infantry at Peshawar, 1849 : commanded it till 1858 : in the Indian mutiny was in 14 engagements, including the siege of Delhi : Sheriff of Herefordshire, 1879 : died Dec. 18, 1897 : K.C.B.

COLE, SIR CHRISTOPHER (1770–1836)

Captain, R.N. : son of Humphrey Cole : born June 10, 1770 : entered the Navy, 1780 : went to India, 1789, under Commodore William Cornwallis, and again in 1804 in the *Culloden* under Sir Edward Pellew : C. in C. in the E. Indies : took Sir John Malcolm on his mission to Persia, *viâ* Bushire, 1808 : relieved the garrison of Amboyna, 1810 : captured Neira, the principal of the Banda islands : thanked by the Governor-General of India : served on the Malabar coast, 1811, and against Java : D.C.L. of Oxford : knighted, 1812 : K.C.B., 1815 : M.P. for Glamorganshire, 1817–30 : died Aug. 24, 1836.

COLEBROOKE, HENRY THOMAS (1765–1837)

Son of Sir George Colebrooke, *Bart.*, Chairman of the E.I. Co.'s Directors in

1769 : born June 15, 1765 : privately educated: went to India in 1782–3. In his early years, as Assistant Collector in Tirhut and Purnea, he took keenly to sport : his first literary work was on the Agriculture and Commerce of Bengal, in which he opposed the monopoly policy of the E. I. Co. At first he disliked Oriental literature, but feeling compelled, in the exercise of his duties, to learn law through the Sanskrit language, he published a translation of a *Digest of Hindu Law*, 1791, in which his appointment in 1795 to Mirzapur, near Benares, facilitated his Sanskrit studies : also wrote in the *Asiatic Researches*, his first paper, in 1794, being " On the Duties of a Faithful Hindu Widow " : also, on the " Origin of Caste " : was sent on a mission to the Raja of Berar at Nagpur in 1799–1801, without success : appointed in 1801 to be a Judge of the *Sadr Diwani Adalat*, and four years later became the Head of that Court : was also, unsalaried, Professor of Hindu Law and Sanskrit at the College of Fort William, Calcutta : was a Member of the Supreme Council from 1807 to 1812, retaining his seat in the *Sadr* Court : after his 5 years in Council, Colebrooke returned to the Court, and next became a Member of the Board of Revenue, till the close of 1814 : was President of the Asiatic Society of Bengal from 1807 to 1814, when he left India. He made a voyage to the Cape on business in 1821–2 : after his return thence, he became Director of the Royal Asiatic Society, which he helped to found in 1823 : became totally blind, and died March 10, 1837. His literary and scientific labours were immense. A great mathematician, a zealous astronomer and profound Sanskrit scholar, his writings always commanded the highest attention : he has been described as *facile princeps* among Sanskrit scholars. He wrote also on the Vedas, on Sanskrit grammar, and a lexicon, on the Sect of Jains, on Indian Jurisprudence and Roman law, besides other papers on Hindu Law, philosophy and customs, Indian algebra, on astronomy, the height of the Himalayas, botany, geology, comparative philology, etc., in contributions to the Transactions of the learned Societies—the Astronomical, Linnæan, Geological and Asiatic—to which he belonged, as well as to the Royal Societies of London and Edinburgh : he was a Member of several foreign Academies also : he gave, in 1818, his valuable collection of Sanskrit MSS. to the E. I. Co.'s Library.

COLEBROOKE, SIR THOMAS EDWARD, BARONET (1813–1890)

Son of Henry Thomas Colebrooke (*q.v.*) : born in Calcutta in 1813 : succeeded as Baronet in 1838 : was nearly 40 years M.P. for Taunton and Lanarkshire : was not a scholar, but was in sympathy with Oriental scholars and with research : was President of the Royal Asiatic Society, 1864–6, 1875–7, 1881 : published the *Life of Mountstuart Elphinstone, Essays by H. T. Colebrooke, The Creeds of India*, a pamphlet : edited and published a third volume of Elphinstone's *India* : died Jan. 11, 1890.

COLEMAN, JAMES GEORGE (1824–1883)

Born 1824 : was originally in the Marine Service : became partner with Mr. Macdowell, and later sole proprietor in a firm at Madras, which by great industry and application he made a flourishing and profitable business : did much for the social and public welfare of the community : joined the Volunteer movement at its commencement ; became its Lt-Colonel and commanded the Duke's Own Artillery Corps : was an active member of the Municipal Corporation : and a member of the Madras Legislative Council from 1879 : contributed largely to charitable institutions ; died at Royapuram, Madras, Dec. 14, 1883 : one of the foremost of the Eurasian Community of Madras.

COLGAN, MOST REV. DR. JOSEPH, D.D. (1824–   )

Born in Ireland, April 1, 1824 : educated at Navan and Maynooth College : arrived in India, 1844 : held various appointments in Madras until he became Vicar Apostolic, titular Bishop of Aureliopolis : and Archbishop in 1886 : Personal Assistant to the Pontifical Throne, 1894 : a Fellow of the Madras University : published works on Roman Catholicism.

COLLEN, SIR EDWIN HENRY HAYTER (1843–   )

Born June 17, 1843 : son of Henry Collen : Maj-General : educated at Royal Military Academy, Woolwich : entered the Royal Artillery, 1863 : served in the Abyssinian war, 1868 : Secy. to the Indian Army Commission, 1879 : Afghan war, 1880 : Soudan, 1885 : Secretary to the Government of India, Military Department, 1887–96 : Military Member of Governor-General's Supreme Council, 1896 –1901 : C.I.E., 1889 : C.B., 1897 : K.C.I.E., 1893 : G.C.I.E., 1901.

COLLETT, SIR HENRY (1836-1901)

Lt-General : born 1836 : son of the Rev. W. Collett : educated at Tonbridge : entered the Bengal Army in 1855 : saw much service : was in the Sitana campaign under Sydney Cotton, 1858 : in the Oudh campaign in 1858–9 : in the Khasia and Jaintia rebellion, 1862–3 : severely wounded at Oomkrong : in the Abyssinian campaign, 1868 : in the Afghan war, 1878–80 : at Peiwar Kotal, in the Khost valley, the Kabul-Kandahar march and the battle of Kandahar : C.B. : commanded a Brigade in the Burma expedition, 1886–8 : commanded the E. Frontier district with the Chin-Lushai expeditionary force, 1889–90 : commanded the Manipur Field Force, 1891 : K.C.B. : was a botanist with considerable knowledge, and wrote on the flora of Simla : died Dec. 21, 1901.

COLLEY, SIR GEORGE POMEROY (1835-1881

Maj-General : son of 'the Hon. George Francis Colley, who was originally Pomeroy : born Nov. 1835 : educated at the R.M.C. Sandhurst (highly distinguished), joined the 2nd Queen's in 1852 : served at the Cape, and held a Border Magistracy there, 1857–8 : served in China, was at the action of the Taku forts and the advance on Pekin : Brevet - Major, 1863 : entered the Staff College and passed with distinction : appointed Professor there, and wrote articles on the Army in the *Encyclopædia Britannica* : in the Ashanti campaign, 1873 : went to Natal on a special mission, to the Transvaal, and Swaziland : was Military Secretary to Lord Lytton when Viceroy and Governor-General of India, 1876–8 : Private Secretary, 1878–80, but during 1879 was Chief on the Staff to Sir Garnet Wolseley in Zululand and the Transvaal, until recalled late in that year to India. He was C.B., 1873 : C.M.G., 1878 : K.C.S.I., 1879. Early in 1880

he was appointed High Commissioner for South Eastern Africa, and Governor and C. in C., Natal : in the fighting with the Boers which ensued, Colley was defeated at Laing's Nek, and was killed in the Boers' attack on Majuba Hill, Feb. 26, 1881. Colley had studied deeply the questions of the Indian frontier and Central Asia, and exercised much influence on the military and political policy of Lord Lytton's administration.

COLLINS, SIR ARTHUR JOHN HAMMOND (1834–   )

Son of John Collins : born 1834 : called to the bar from Gray's Inn, 1860 : Q.C. and Bencher, 1877 : also a barrister of the Middle Temple : Recorder of Poole, 1873–9, and of Exeter, 1879–85 : Chief Justice of the High Court, Madras, 1885–99 : knighted, 1885 : Vice-Chancellor of the Madras University, 1889–99.

COLLINS, JOHN (? –1807)

Colonel : joined the E. I. Co.'s Bengal Infantry, 1770 : Major in 1794 : appointed Resident at the Court of Daulat Rao Sindia (*q.v.*), 1795–1803, but, though he'had much power over him, failed to dissuade him from fighting against the English : Collins, therefore, in 1803 left Sindia, who was defeated at Assaye and Argaum in that year. Collins was also sent on a mission to Jaipur in 1799. After the Mahratta war, Collins was Resident at Lucknow, at the Court of the Nawab Wazir, and died there June 11, 1807. He was called " King Collins," and is described as " cold, imperious, and overbearing," so that Metcalfe (*q.v.*) declined to remain under him.

COLQUHOUN, ARCHIBALD ROSS (1848–   )

Son of Dr. Archibald Colquhoun, H.E.I.C.S. : educated at Edinburgh University and abroad : entered the Indian Public Works Department, 1871 : explored from Canton to Bhamo for best railway route between Burma and China, 1881–2 : Deputy Commissioner Upper Burma, 1885–9 : Administrator in Mashonaland, 1890 : retired, 1894 : travelled extensively in Siberia, Mongolia and China, etc., 1900–3 : author of *Across Chryse*, 1883 ; *Amongst the Shans*, 1885 ; *The Key of the Pacific*, 1895 ; *Russia against*

India, 1900, etc. etc. : F.R.G.S. : *Times* Correspondent on several occasions : has written a number of geographical and political papers.

COLVILE, SIR JAMES WILLIAM (1810-1880)

Son of Andrew Wedderburn Colvile : born 1810 : educated at Eton, and Trinity College, Cambridge : called to the bar from the Inner Temple in 1835 : was appointed in 1845 to be Advocate-General, Bengal : made a Puisne Judge of the Supreme Court, Calcutta, 1848 : knighted : Chief Justice, 1855-9, when he retired : was President of the Council of Education, and of the Asiatic Society of Bengal, 1848-59 : also Vice-President of the Governor-General's Legislative Council : after his retirement, he was Privy Councillor, and first Assessor, and, later, Member of the Judicial Committee : F.R.S. : died Dec. 6, 1880.

COLVILLE, SIR CHARLES (1769-1843)

Entered the Army, 1781, in 28th regt. : Lt-Colonel in 13th foot in 1796 : served in the Irish rebellion, 1798 : in Egypt, 1801-2 : commanded his regiment to Bermuda, 1808 : Brigadier in the Peninsula, 1810-14 : commanded a Division at Waterloo : C. in C. at Bombay, Oct. 9, 1819 to 1826 : Colonel of 5th Fusiliers, 1835 : General, 1837 : G.C.B. : G.C.H. : died March 27, 1843.

COLVIN, SIR AUCKLAND (1838-   )

I.C.S. : son of John Russell Colvin (*q.v*) : born 1838 : educated at Eton and Haileybury, 1855-7 : served, chiefly in the N.W.P., 1858-79 : officiating Secretary to N.W.P. Government, 1873, 1875 : Comptroller-General, Egypt, 1880-2 : K.C.M.G., 1881 : Financial Adviser to the Khedive, 1882-3 : Financial Member of the Supreme Council, 1883-7 : Lieutenant Governor of the N.W.P. and Oudh, 1887-92 : retired, 1892 : K.C.S.I., 1892 : C.I.E. : Chairman of the Burma Railways Co. : and of the Egyptian Delta Light Railways Co. : wrote *John Russell Colvin*, in the " Rulers of India " series, 1895.

COLVIN, 'JAMES MORRIS COLQUHOUN (1870-   )ǀ

Major : son of J. C. Colvin, B.C.S : born Aug. 26, 1870 : educated at Charterhouse : joined the Royal Military Academy,

Woolwich : joined the Royal Engineers, 1888 : served in the Chitral Relief expedition, 1895, and in the Malakand Field Force, 1897, where he won the V.C, : in South Africa in 1901-2 : Intelligence Department, India : Staff Captain for Mobilisation, 1903.

COLVIN, JOHN RUSSELL (1807-1857)

Lieutenant-Governor : I.C.S. : son of James Colvin, Calcutta merchant : born in Calcutta, May 29, 1807 : educated at St. Andrews and at Haileybury : went to Bengal in 1826, to Hyderabad in 1827 : was Assistant and Deputy Secretary in the Judicial and Revenue Departments of the Government of India, 1831-5 : Secretary to the Board of Revenue, 1835 : Private Secretary to the Governor-General, Lord Auckland, 1836-42 ; and is said to have exercised considerable influence over the latter's Afghan policy. He was Resident in Nipal, 1845, Commissioner of Tenasserim, 1846 : Judge of the *Sadr* Court at Calcutta : Lieutenant-Governor of the N.W.P. from Nov. 7, 1853. It was said that Colvin " over-governed " : he worked with extraordinary industry, and greatly increased the business of the Government : his action in the mutiny has been the subject of controversy : he issued, in May, a proclamation which was not entirely approved: the violence of the outbreak fell upon him without warning, and the forces at his disposal were inadequate to meet it. He was " worn out by the unceasing anxieties and labours of his charge "—so ran Lord Canning's notification of his death : he fell ill, became worse, and died in cantonments on Sep. 9, 1857 : and was buried in the fort at Agra. Sir Auckland Colvin, in his life of his father, J. R. Colvin, in the " Rulers of India " series, has exhausted the subject.

COLVIN-SMITH, SIR COLVIN (1829-   )

Born Aug. 4, 1829 : son of Rev. Robert Smith, D.D. of Old Macker, Aberdeen : educated at Grammar School and King's College and University, Aberdeen : M.D. of Aberdeen : and L.R.C.S. Edinburgh : entered the Madras Army, 1851 : served in second Burma war, 1852-3, and in the Indian mutiny, 1857-9 : Principal medical officer with Indian Contingent in Egyptian campaign, 1882 : C.B., 1882 :

present at Tel-el-Kebir and Zagazig: retired in 1884 : Honorary Surgeon to the late Queen and to H.M. the present King : K.C.B. in 1903.

COMBERMERE, STAPLETON COTTON, FIRST VISCOUNT (1773–1865)

Field-Marshal: son of Sir R. S. Cotton, fifth Baronet: M.P.: born Nov. 1773 : educated at Westminster, and at a private Military Academy in Bayswater : entered the Army in 1790, in the 23rd Fusiliers ; served in Flanders : was Lt-Colonel of a Cavalry regt. at the Cape on his way to India, where he was engaged in 1799 against Tippoo, being at Malvailli and Seringapatam: returned to England, 1800 : was M.P. for Newark, 1806–14 : as Maj-General he commanded, first a Brigade in the Peninsula, from 1808, and later the whole cavalry Division : succeeded as Baronet in 1809 : was at Talavera and Salamanca : K.C.B. in 1812 : and at other engagements, including the Pyrenees campaign and Toulouse : was made Baron Combermere in May, 1814, and received a pension. He commanded the allied cavalry in France in 1815–6 : was Governor of Barbados 1817–20, and Commander-in-Chief in Ireland, 1822–5 : as C. in C. in India, 1825–1830, he besieged and took Bhartpur on Jan. 18, 1826, and was made Viscount in 1827 : Constable of the Tower, 1852 : Field-Marshal, 1855 : he was G.C.B. in 1815 : G.C.H. in 1817 : D.C.L. in 1830 : Privy Councillor, 1843 : K.C.S.I., 1861 : died Feb. 21, 1865.

COMPTON, SIR HERBERT ABINGDON DRAPER (1770–1846)

Son of Walter Abingdon Compton: entered the E.I. Co.'s Army as a private soldier : went to India : bought himself out of the Army : articled himself in an office in Madras : returned home, and wrote for newspapers in London : called to the bar at Lincoln's Inn in 1808 : joined the Madras bar, and became Advocate-General there, and at Calcutta : was knighted and made Chief Justice of the Bombay Supreme Court, April 11, 1831: retired in 1839, and died Jan. 14, 1846.

COMYN, SIR ROBERT BUCKLEY (1792–1853)

Son of the Rev. Thomas Comyn : born Oct. 26, 1792 : educated at Merchant Taylors' School and St. John's College, Oxford : called to the bar at Lincoln's Inn in 1814 : appointed a Puisne Judge of the Calcutta Supreme Court in 1825 : knighted : Chief Justice of Madras from July 1, 1835, until March 11, 1842 : D.C.L. Oxford : Bencher of the Middle Temple : died May 23, 1853. He wrote on legal and historical subjects.

CONNEMARA, ROBERT BOURKE, FIRST BARON (1827–1902)

Governor : born June 11, 1827: son of fifth Earl of Mayo, brother of sixth Earl of Mayo (q.v.), Viceroy and Governor-General : educated at Enniskillen and Trinity College, Dublin : called to the bar at the Inner Temple, 1852 : M.P. for King's Lynn, 1868, 1874 : Under Secretary for Foreign Affairs, 1874–80 : and again 1885–6 : P.C., 1880 : Governor of Madras, Dec. 8, 1886–Dec 1, 1890 : G.C.I.E. : made a Peer, May 12, 1887 : died Sep. 3, 1902.

CONOLLY, ARTHUR (1807–1842 ?)

Son of Valentine Conolly : born July 2, 1807 : educated at Rugby and Addiscombe : went to India in the same ship as Bishop Heber : joined the Bengal Cavalry, 1823 : at Bhartpur, 1826 : from leave in England he returned to India through Central Asia, viâ St. Petersburg, Tiflis, Teheran, Astrabad: nearly killed by the Turcomans on his way to Khiva : from Astrabad to Mashad, Herat, Kandahar, Sind : wrote an account of his journey : was in the Political Department in Rajputana, 1834–8 : Captain : made another journey viâ Vienna, Constantinople, Bagdad, Teheran and Herat : joined Macnaghten's Staff at Kabul, 1840 : in Sep. he was sent as Envoy to Khiva, viâ Merv, and to Khokand, and, on the invitation of the Amir Nasirulla of Bokhara, sent through Stoddart, went on there, but was treacherously imprisoned, in Oct. or Dec. 1841 : he and Stoddart were executed in captivity, probably on June 17, 1842. His few letters described their sufferings in their dungeon : his prayer-book, full of his writing, was delivered to his sister in London in 1862.

CONOLLY, EDWARD BARRY (1808–1840)

Brother of Arthur Conolly[7](q.v.) : was Captain in the Bengal Cavalry and Commandant of Sir W. Macnaghten's escort at Kabul, when he was killed, fighting in the Kohistan under Sir R. Sale, on Sep. 29, 1840 : he had written papers for the Journal of the Asiatic Society of Bengal.

CONOLLY, HENRY VALENTINE (1806-1855)

I.C.S.: brother of Arthur Conolly (q.v.) : educated at Rugby, went to Madras, 1824 : served in Bellary, and for many years as District Officer of the Malabar district : he was murdered in his own house by Moplah fanatics on Sep. 11, 1855 : he had been nominated to be provisional Member of Council, Madras.

CONRAN, HENRY (1738-1810)

Major : served in the American war, 1755-6 : under Wolfe, at Quebec, in 1759 : returned to England and retired as Major about 1780 : went to India by way of Aleppo and the desert with a packet from the Court of Directors to the Bengal Government : appointed to the Staff of Warren Hastings, on whose retirement, in 1785, Conran remained in Calcutta and died there, May 15, 1810.

CONWAY, THOMAS HENRY SOMER-SET (? -1837)

Brig-General : entered the E. I. Co.'s military service in 1793 : reached Madras, 1795 : in the expedition to Ceylon, 1796 : in that to Manilla, 1797 : in several campaigns : in Mysore, 1799 : in the Ceded Districts, 1801-2 : Mahratta war, 1803-6 : under Sir T. Hislop, 1815 : in the Pindari war, 1817-8 : Adjutant-General of the Madras Army, from 1809 : C.B., 1819 : employed on a military mission to Bengal, 1828-30 : appointed to command the Hyderabad Subsidiary Force : died of cholera, May 14, 1837.

COOCH BEHAR, MAHARAJA SIR NRIPENDRA BHUP BAHADUR OF (1862-)

Born Oct. 4, 1862 : succeeded his father in 1863, the State being under official management during his minority : educated at the Wards' Institute, Benares, and at Bankipur, Patna : Maharaja Bahadur, 1880 : installed in 1883 as a Ruling Chief : G.C.I.E., 1887 : Hony. Lt-Colonel of the 6th Bengal Cavalry : through the Tirah campaign on the Staff of General Yeatman-Briggs : present at Dargai and Samana : C.B., 1898 : Hony. A.D.C. to H.M. the King : married in 1878 the daughter of Keshab Chandra Sen (q.v.). The Maharaja has visited England several times : he is a keen sportsman and has excelled in polo, tennis, and other games. The Maharani Sunity Devi has been a Member of the Imperial Order of the Crown of India since 1887.

COOKE, EDWARD (1772-1799)

Son of Colonel Cooke : became a Captain in the Royal Navy : appointed to the Sybille in 1795, served in her at the Cape, and in the East Indies : off the Sandheads, in the Bay of Bengal, the Sybille fought between 9 p.m. on Feb. 28, 1799, and 2.30 a.m. on March 1, the French ship Forte, a much larger and better armed frigate, and captured her in the Balasore roads, 150 of the Forte's men being killed and wounded. Cooke received very severe wounds, of which he died at Calcutta, May 23, 1799. The E.I. Co. erected a monument to him in the South Park Street Cemetery, Calcutta.

COOKE, THEODORE (1836-)

Born 1836 : son of Rev. John Cooke, Rector of Ardinan, Co. Tipperary : educated at Dublin University, highly distinguished : went to India as Engineer of the Bombay-Baroda line, 1860 : erected the Bassein bridge, 1865 : Principal of Civil Engineering College at Poona, 1865 : acted as Director of Public Instruction in Bombay : Director of Botanical Survey of Western India, and Director of Agriculture : Fellow of the Bombay University : retired in 1893, and was Sub-Director of the Imperial Institute : author of Manual of Heat, Manual of Geology, Flora of Bombay Presidency : C.I.E. in 1891.

COOPER, MANACKJI BEJONJI (1845-1904)

Born Sep. 15, 1845 : educated at Sir Jamsetji Jijibhai's Institution and the Elphinstone College, Bombay : headmaster of the Fort High School, Bombay, for nearly 20 years : the pioneer of higher education by private non-missionary enterprise in Western India. Sir W. W. Hunter, President of the Education Commission of 1882, stated that had there been others like Cooper in the chief centres of India, the Commission would never have been appointed, because his work had solved the problem of the Commission : the first Parsi schoolmaster to visit England, 1875, to study the educational systems of the West and apply them to his work in India. He was a household word among Bombay students : was popularly known as Manackji Master : his High School officially bore the highest reputation : he edited Pope's Homer's *Iliad* : died Aug. 4, 1904.

COOPER, THOMAS THORNVILLE
(1839–1878)

Traveller : son of John J. Cooper : born Sep. 13, 1839 : educated at Bishopwearmouth. When he was on a voyage to Australia for his health, the crew mutinied : he went to India, 1859: joined the firm of Arbuthnot & Co. at Madras : travelled to Rangoon and on to Shanghai : fought against the Taiping rebels : in 1868, he tried to travel from Hankow, through Tibet, to India, was stopped at Batang and near Weisi and imprisoned, and, *viâ* the Yangtsze, reached Hankow in Nov. 1868: in 1869, trying to reach China from Sadiya in Assam was stopped at Prun. The India Office employed him with the Panthay mission to London : he was then made Political Agent at Bhamo : returned home for his health : attached to the India Office : reappointed in 1876 to Bhamo, and was murdered there by one of his own guards, April 24, 1878. He wrote *Travels of a Pioneer of Commerce in Pigtail and Petticoats*, 1871 : and *Mishmee Hills*, 1873.

COOTE, SIR EYRE (1726–1783)

Born in 1726: fourth son of the Rev. Dr. Chidley Coote : entered the Army in 1745 : went to India in 1754 with the 39th regt. and became Captain on June 18, 1755. Part of this regiment was included in the force dispatched from Madras to Bengal in 1756 against the Nawab Surajuddaula, after his capture of Calcutta. Coote was present at its recapture, at the taking of Chandernagore, and at the victory of Plassey, on June 23, 1757 : Clive, it is said, acted on his advice among others to give immediate battle. In Jan. 1759, he was gazetted Lt-Colonel of the 84th regt., and to command the troops in Madras. In the war with the French, under

Lally, he took Wandiwash, Nov. 30, 1759, and the fort of Carangooly, relieved Trichinopoly, defeated the French at Wandiwash, Jan. 22, 1760, and took Arcot. He besieged Lally in Pondicherry, while a naval force attacked it by sea. On its surrender in Jan., 1761, the French power in India completely collapsed : Coote returned to England in 1762, and was received with honour : became a Colonel on April 4, 1765, and M.P. for Leicester. In 1769 he was reappointed to command the troops in Madras, but resigned and returned to England in Oct. 1770, where he was made K.B. Aug. 31, 1771 : Maj-General Sep. 29, 1775 : Lt-General on Aug. 29, 1777 : and Commander-in-Chief in India, on April 17, 1777. He succeeded General Clavering as Member of the Supreme Council at Calcutta on March 24, 1779. When Hyder Ali of Mysore declared war, invaded the Carnatic in 1780 and defeated Colonel Baillie at Perambakam, Warren Hastings despatched Coote to Madras, which he reached on Nov. 5, 1780. Early in 1781 Coote took the field against Hyder, raised the siege of Wandiwash, marched on Cuddalore, attacked Chelambakam and won a decided victory at Porto Novo, July 1, 1781, besides defeating Hyder at Perambakam, Aug. 27, effecting the relief of Vellore and the capture of Chittore. His last encounter with Hyder was the indecisive skirmish at Arnee, June 2, 1782. Coote's failing health compelled him to resign the command in Madras and take a change to Calcutta. Only partially recovered, he returned to Madras early in 1783, but on the voyage was chased by the French. The anxiety and exposure produced a relapse, which proved fatal on April 28, 1783, two days after his arrival at Madras. His body was taken to England and interred at Rockburne, in Hampshire. A monument in Westminster Abbey was erected to him by the East India Company. His military capacity has been highly praised, as also his patience, temper, activity and energy, valour and coolness. His enforcement of discipline was tempered by kindness, which endeared him to his soldiers.

COPLESTON, RIGHT REV. REGINALD STEPHEN (1845–)

Son of Rev. R. E. Copleston : educated at Merton College, Oxford : married a daughter of the late Archbishop Trench : Fellow and Tutor of St. John's College, Oxford : was appointed Bishop of Colombo in 1875 : translated to Calcutta and became Metropolitan of India in 1902. Author of *Buddhism* : *Primitive and Present*.

CORBETT, SIR STUART (? –1865)

Commanded the 25th N.I. in the Panjab campaign of 1848–9, at Sadulapur, Chilianwala and Gujarat : C.B. : in the mutiny was Brig-General commanding at Mianmir : co-operated boldly and successfully with the civil authorities in totally disarming the native troops there on parade, May 13, 1857, seizing the Fort at Lahore, and sending English troops to secure Umritsar : K.C.B. : died at Naini Tal, Aug. 1, 1865.

CORDERY, JOHN GRAHAM (1833–1900)

I.C.S. : educated at Rugby and Balliol College, Oxford : went out to the Panjab in 1856 : while at Peshawar, he translated the *Iliad* into English verse : served in Berar : was D.P.I. in the Panjab in 1872 : Commissioner of Peshawar : Resident at Hyderabad, 1883 : C.S.I. : retired, 1888 : translated the *Odyssey* : died April 8, 1900.

CORNISH, HUBERT (1757–1823)

Son of James Cornish of Teignmouth : born 1757 : was Private Secretary (1793–8) to his brother-in-law, Sir John Shore (Lord Teignmouth), during the whole term of his Governor-Generalship (a younger brother, George Cornish, being at the same time A.D.C.) : they both returned to England with Sir J. Shore in 1798 : Hubert settled at Exeter : a lawyer by profession and an accomplished artist and musician : died 1823.

CORNISH, HUBERT (1776–1832)

Son of James Cornish, M.D. : born 1776 : a nephew of Sir John Shore (*q.v.*) : went to India in the Civil Service, 1797 : was stationed at Benares in 1797, when Cherry (*q.v.*) the A.G.G., and other officers and Europeans were murdered treacherously by the orders of Wazir Ali (*q.v.*) : he jumped upon a horse which Sir J. Shore had given him, and was one of the few civilians who escaped : became a Judge in Bengal : retired about 1830 to his estate near Totnes : died Aug. 25, 1832.

CORNISH, WILLIAM ROBERT (1828–1897)

Educated at St. George's Hospital : entered the Madras Army as Assistant Surgeon, 1854 : Secretary to the Director-General, Medical Department, 1860–70 : Sanitary Commissioner to Madras Government, 1870–80 : did good service during the famine of 1877 : C.I.E. : Surgeon-General in 1880 : retired, 1885 : Member of the Legislative Council, Madras, 1883 : Fellow of the Madras University, 1867 : wrote on medical subjects : died Oct. 19, 1897 : F.R.C.S.

CORNWALLIS, CHARLES, FIRST MARQUIS (1738–1805)

Governor-General : son of Charles, first Earl : born Dec. 31, 1738 : educated at Eton : entered the Guards, 1756 : studied at the Military Academy, Turin : served in Germany, 1758–62 : at Minden : M.P. for Eye : became Earl in June, 1762 : Lord of the Bedchamber : Constable of the Tower, 1770 : Maj-General, 1775 : served in the American war, 1776 : second in command in 1778 to Sir H. Clinton : forced to capitulate at Yorktown on Oct. 19, 1781, no blame attaching to him : in 1782, and 1785, he refused to go to India, but, against his will, accepted the Governor-Generalship in 1786 : held the appointment from Sep., 1786, being also C. in C. : and K.G. : he reformed both the civil and military services : in Dec. 1790, he took the command in Madras against Tippoo : captured Bangalore, March 21, 1791 : defeated Tippoo near Seringapatam : took Nandidrug, Oct. 19 : Savandrug, Dec. 21 : besieged Seringapatam, Feb. 1792, when Tippoo submitted, and signed peace, ceding territory and paying a large indemnity : Cornwallis created a Marquis, Aug., 1792. He then announced the permanent settlement of the land revenue to be paid by the *zamindars* in Bengal, 1793, acting against the advice of Sir John Shore : he reformed the Law Courts : he sailed for Madras to attack Pondicherry, but it had surrendered before his arrival : he left Madras, homewards, on Oct. 10, 1793. From England, he was sent to military service on the continent : was Master-General of the Ordnance from 1795 : when military questions caused anxiety in Bengal, Cornwallis was re-appointed Governor-General on Feb. 1, 1797 : did not proceed to India : his services were required as Viceroy and C. in C., Ireland, to crush the rebellion of 1798 : defeated the French there under General Humbert : supported the Act of Union, but resigned the Viceroyalty in 1801, when the King declined to agree to Catholic Emancipation : deputed to negotiate the Peace of Amiens, 1802. In 1805 he was re-appointed Governor-General and C. in C. in India, and assumed charge on July 30 : sent out to inaugurate a pacific régime instead of the expansive policy of Lord Wellesley. But it was too severe a tax on his age and health. On his way up-country, in pursuit of his pacific policy, he died at Ghazipur, Oct. 5, 1805. Statues were erected in his honour at Calcutta and Madras.

CORNWALLIS, SIR WILLIAM (1744–1819)

Son of Charles, first Earl Cornwallis : entered the Navy, 1755 : engaged constantly during his service, in N. America, the Mediterranean, W. Indies, etc., until, in 1789, he went out to India as naval C. in C. : in 1791, when there was war against Tippoo, he insisted on searching French ships for contraband of war, and, when war against France broke out, he seized French ships, Chandernagore and Pondicherry : returned to England, 1794, and saw further service in the Channel and the W. Indies : G.C.B. : died July 5, 1819.

CORRIE, THE RIGHT REV. DANIEL (1777–1837)

Bishop : son of John Corrie : born April, 1777 : educated privately, at Clare Hall, and Trinity Hall, Cambridge (Exhibitioner) : ordained, 1802 : went to Calcutta as a Bengal chaplain, 1806 : appointed to various chaplaincies up-country, and did mission work also : was Senior Chaplain in Calcutta, 1817 : Archdeacon in 1823 : thrice, as Commissary, carried on the administration of the diocese on the deaths of Bishops : was the first Bishop of Madras from 1835 to his death on Feb. 5, 1837 : was LL.D. : Bishop Corrie's Grammar School in Madras, and his statue in the Cathedral there perpetuate his memory. He was a friend of Charles Simeon and Henry Martyn at Cambridge.

COSBY, SIR HENRY AUGUSTUS MONTAGU (1743–1822)

Son of Captain Alexander Cosby : born in 1743 : was a volunteer at the capture of Gheria, the fort of the pirate Angria, in 1756 : was in Coote's attack on Pondicherry, 1760–1 : at the captures of Vellore and Madura, at Rajamundry, at the Chengama Pass, Errore, Arlier, and Vellore again : Adjutant-General : at the siege of Tanjore in 1773 : served against the Chitore Poligars, 1777 : commanded, in 1778, the Nawab of Arcot's cavalry, and led it against Hyder Ali with success : made prisoner at the Cape on his way to England, 1782, but soon released : knighted in 1782 : Brig-General in India, 1784–6 : held commands at Trichinopoly and Tinnivelly : to England, 1786 : Lt-General : died Jan. 17, 1822.

COTES, SARA JEANETTE (? –)

Born in Canada : daughter of Charles Duncan, merchant : married Everard Cotes, Press Correspondent with Government of India, Simla : was on the staff of *Washington Post*, *Toronto Globe*, and *Montreal Star*. Author of *A Social Departure* (Letters from Japan), *An American Girl in London*, *The Simple Adventures of a Mem-Sahib*, *The Story of Sonny Sahib*, *On the other Side of the Latch*, *Those Delightful Americans*, *His Honour and a Lady*, etc., etc.

COTTON, SIR ARTHUR THOMAS (1803–1899)

Irrigation Engineer : son of Henry Calverley Cotton : born May 15, 1803 : educated at Addiscombe : entered the Madras Engineers, arriving there 1821 : in the first Burmese war, 1825–6 : led storming parties : from 1828 employed upon irrigation works in Southern India, in the Cavery, Coleroon, Godavery and Krishna rivers, making anicuts (dams) on the Coleroon (1835–6), for the irrigation of the Tanjore, Trichinopoly, and South Arcot Districts : the anicut on the Godavery, below Rajamundry, for the irrigation of the Godavery district, 1847–52 : he projected the anicut on the Krishna, which other officers carried out. These works have been found invaluable in improving the condition of the people and the food supply, and averting famine, besides being very successful financially :

other smaller works have followed them. Chief Engineer, 1852 : Commandant of Engineers, 1856 : he was knighted in 1861, made K.C.S.I. in 1866 : retired in 1862, and continued to advocate irrigation and canals as preferable to railway communication. He had a controversy with Sir Proby Cautley (*q.v.*) about the latter's Ganges Canal. He was admittedly the greatest Indian authority of his age on the subject of irrigation : he founded, it has been said, a School of Indian Hydraulic Engineering in the officers trained under him : General in 1877 : died July 24, 1899 : wrote a book on *Public Works in India.*

COTTON, SIR GEORGE (1842-1905)

Born in Ireland, 1842 : educated in England : went to Bombay in 1863, as Manager of East Indian Cotton Agency. In partnership with Mr. James Greaves commenced the firm of Greaves, Cotton & Co., Bombay, and James Greaves & Co., Manchester : Fellow of the Bombay University, Chairman of the Municipal Corporation, and Sheriff of Bombay in 1897 : knighted in 1897 : died Feb. 5, 1905.

COTTON, RIGHT REV. DR. GEORGE EDWARD LYNCH (1813-1866)

Bishop of Calcutta and Metropolitan of India and Ceylon : son of Captain T. Cotton : born Oct. 29, 1813, his father dying about the same time : educated at Westminster, and Trinity College, Cambridge : took his degree in 1836 as a Senior Optime in mathematics, and eighth in the Classical Tripos : appointed in 1837 by Dr. Arnold to a mastership at Rugby : became Fellow of Trinity : left Rugby in 1852 to become Head Master of Marlborough College, where he effected numerous improvements : consecrated Bishop of Calcutta on May 13, 1858 : reached Calcutta that year. He acquired universal confidence and respect besides influence with the Government, so that he was able to do much for the Church of England and for Anglo-Indian education. He succeeded in establishing schools at the chief hill-stations for the education of Anglo-Indian and Eurasian children, whose parents could not afford to send them to England. He maintained his position and principles as Bishop of the Church of England, while

assisting missionary work and other Christian developments. His capacity as an administrator, organizer and educator was acknowledged. He made the long tours required by the size of his metropolitan charge and the paucity of Bishops. Returning from one of them, he was drowned at Kushtia on the Gorai River in Bengal, on Oct. 6, 1866, while re-embarking on a steamer. He lost his footing on a badly constructed platform, fell into the river and disappeared. His loss was regarded as a public calamity, which the Government officially announced.

COTTON, SIR HENRY JOHN STEDMAN (1845-   )

I.C.S. : son of J. J. Cotton, Madras Civil Service : born Sep. 13, 1845 : educated at Magdalen College School, Brighton College, and King's College, London : entered the Bengal Civil Service, 1867 : held numerous appointments until he became Secretary to the Bengal Government, Revenue Department, 1888 ; Secretary in the Financial Department, 1889 ; Chief Secretary, 1891-6 ; acting Home Secretary to the Government of India, 1896 : Chief Commissioner of Assam, 1896-1902, when he retired : K.C.S.I., 1902 : has since sought to influence the public mind by his letters to the *Times* in opposition to Lord Curzon's policy in Tibet : author of *New India, or India in Transition,* besides official publications.

COTTON, JAMES SUTHERLAND (1847-   )

Son of J. J. Cotton, Madras Civil Service : born July 17, 1847 : educated at Magdalen College School, Brighton College, Winchester, and Trinity College, Oxford (Scholar) First Class in Moderations and Final Classical School : was Editor of the *Academy* : is now employed as editor in England of the forthcoming revised edition of the *Imperial Gazetteer of India* : author of *India* (Citizen Series), *Mountstuart Elphinstone* (" Rulers of India " Series), *Decennial Report on the Moral and Material Progress of India,* 1885 : *Quinqennial Report on Education in India,* 1898.

COTTON, JOHN (1783-1860)

I.C.S. : went to Madras : many years Collector of Tanjore : after retirement from India he was Director of the E.I.

Co., 1833–53 : Chairman of the Court, 1843 : died 1860.

COTTON, JOSEPH (1745–1825)

Son of Dr. Nathaniel Cotton : born March 7, 1745 : entered the Royal Navy in 1760, which he left for the E.I. Co.'s mariné service : commanded an East Indiaman in two voyages : made his fortune and retired : was Deputy Master of the Trinity House for 20 years, and Director of the E. I. Co. from 1795 to 1823, and of the E.I. Docks Company : died Jan. 26, 1825.

COTTON, SIR SYDNEY (1792–1874)

Son of Henry Calverley Cotton, and brother of Sir Arthur T. Cotton (q.v.) : born Dec. 2, 1792 : arrived in India in a regiment of Dragoons, 1810 : served in the Madras, Bombay, and Bengal Presidencies for many years : in the Pindari war, 1817–8 : in Burma, 1828 : in Sind, under Sir C. Napier, 1842–3 : in the Carnatic and Mysore : on the Staff in Madras and Bangalore : commanded in various stations and was A.D.C. to Lord Combermere and Military Secretary : commanded on the N.W. frontier in 1853, in the Kohat Pass, against the Afridis and, later, the Mohmands : was, in the mutiny, Brig-General at Peshawar and, owing to his foresight and decision, there was no serious disturbance there—" the right man for the place " : commanded an expedition against the fanatical colony of Sitana : Maj-General and K.C.B., 1858 : commanded the N.W. district in England : Lt-General, 1866 : Governor of Chelsea Hospital, 1872 : G.C.B., 1873 : died Feb. 20, 1874 : he was " a thorough soldier, an officer of unusual energy and activity " : he wrote *Nine Years on the N.W. Frontier*, 1854–63, and on *The Central Asian Question*.

COTTON, SIR WILLOUGHBY (1783–1860)

Son of Admiral Rowland Cotton : cousin of Lord Combermere : born in 1783 : educated at Rugby (where he led a rebellion) : entered the Guards, 1798 : served in Hanover, 1805 : Copenhagen, 1807; in the Peninsula, 1809–14 : went to India in 1821 : commanded a Brigade in the first Burmese war, 1825–6 : Maj-General and K.C.H., 1830 : commanded in Jamaica, 1829–34 : commanded the Bengal Division of the Army of the Indus, 1838–

9 : K.C.B., 1838 : at Ghazni : left Kabul in 1839 for another command : G.C.B., 1840 : Lt-General, 1841 : C. in C. at Bombay, April, 1847, to Dec. 1850 : General, 1854 : Colonel of the 98th foot : and later of the 32nd foot : died May 4, 1860.

COUCH, SIR RICHARD (1817–   )

Son of Richard Couch : born July 11, 1817 : educated privately : called to the bar from the Middle Temple, 1841 : Recorder of Bedford, 1858–62 : Puisne Judge of the High Court, Bombay, 1862–6 : Chief Justice, 1866–70 : Chief Justice of Bengal, at Calcutta, 1870–5 : presided at the trial of the Gaekwar of Baroda, 1875 : Member of the Judicial Committee of the Privy Council, 1881–1901 : Privy Councillor, 1875.

COUGHLAN, CORNELIUS (1828–   )

Son of Edward Coughlan : born June, 1828 : educated at Eyrecourt, Co. Galway : served as Private, Corporal, Sergeant, Colour-Sergeant and Serg-Major in the 75th regt. for 21 years : and as Serg-Major in the Connaught Rangers for 21 years : was present at the siege of Delhi (when he won his V.C. for several acts of bravery), and relief of Lucknow.

COUPER, SIR GEORGE EBENEZER WILSON, BARONET (1824–   )

I.C.S. : son of Colonel Sir George Couper, *Bart.*, Comptroller of the Household of H.R.H. the Duchess of Kent : born 1824 : educated at Sandhurst and Haileybury : entered the Bengal Civil Service in 1846 : joined the Panjab Commission in 1849 : served in the Indian mutiny, through the siege of Lucknow under Sir ¡Henry Lawrence, and after his death under Brig-General Inglis and Sir James Outram : Chief Commissioner in Oudh, 1871–6 : Lieutenant-Governor of the N.W. Provinces, 1876 : retired 1882 : C.B. : K.C.S.I. : C.I.E.

COURT, CLAUDE AUGUSTE (1793– ?)

General : born Sep. 26, 1793 : educated at the Ecole Polytechnique, Paris, 1812–3 : entered the French Army, 1813 : saw active service, 1813–5 : left the Army, 1818 : served in Persia, and joined Ranjit Singh's forces, with Avitabile (q.v.) in

H

1827: improved Ranjit's Sikh Artillery greatly: paid much attention to archæology and coins: after Ranjit's death, the Sikh troops attacked Court, who was protected by Ventura (q.v.): retired from Lahore to France.

COURTIN, JACQUES IGNACE (? – ?)

Son of François Courtin, Chevalier: Chief of the French Factory at Dacca: received for two months the members of the English Factory at Dacca, when it was seized by the Nawab of Dacca, after the capture of Calcutta by the Nawab Surajuddaula, 1756: and sent them to the English at Fulta, 1756: he left Dacca, with 35 boats, on June 22, 1757, and wandered about the districts of Rangpur, Dinajpur, Jalpaiguri: received an Embassy from the King of Tibet: fought with the Faujdar of Rangpur: arrived at Murshidabad, March 10, 1758, to surrender to the English: allowed by Clive to go to Chandernagore and Pondicherry: Member of the Supreme Council there: in the capitulation there, Jan. 1761: went to France, and probably became the Conseiller au Conseil des Indes.

COWELL, EDWARD BYLES (1826–1903)

Born Jan. 23, 1826: son of Charles Cowell: educated at Ipswich: early attracted to Sir W. Jones' works: studied Persian: entered a merchant's office: went to Magdalen Hall, Oxford: first class, 1854: studied from 1853, under H. H. Wilson (q.v.): joined the Education Department and became Professor of History and Political Economy at the Presidency College, Calcutta, 1856: also Principal of the Sanskrit College, in 1858: left India, 1864: was the first Professor of Sanskrit at Cambridge, 1867: Fellow of Corpus Christi College, Cambridge: LL.D. of Edinburgh: D.C.L. of Oxford. After he was elected Professor of Sanskrit, the study of Oriental languages increased at Cambridge: the Semitic Languages Tripos was established, 1878: the Indian Languages Tripos, 1903: the Oriental Languages Tripos, 1895: a Board of Oriental studies was formed, and a Board of I.C.S. studies: he taught Sanskrit, Indian philosophy, comparative philology, Persian, Pali, Zend, etc.: his publications were numerous. From early days, he wrote on Persian poetry, the Hindu drama, etc., in the *Westminster Review*, also in the *Asiatic Journal, Journal of Philology, Gentleman's Magazine, J.A.S. Bengal, Calcutta Review*: on Prakrit Grammar: translated and edited many Sanskrit works, both at Calcutta and Cambridge: knew also modern languages, including Welsh, and the classics: D.C.L., 1896: received the Gold Medal of the Royal Asiatic Society, 1898: died Feb. 9, 1903.

COWLEY, HENRY WELLESLEY, FIRST BARON (1773–1847)

Born Jan. 20, 1773: youngest son of the first Earl of Mornington: brother of Marquess Wellesley (q.v.), and Duke of Wellington (q.v.): served in the Army, before going as Secretary of legation to Stockholm, 1792: Private Secretary to his brother, Marquess Wellesley, when Governor-General, 1798–1801: a Commissioner for the settlement of Mysore after its capture, 1799: sent to England to explain the war with Tippoo in 1799–1800: sent on a mission to Oudh, negotiated treaty for cession of certain districts by the Nawab: Lieutenant-Governor of the ceded districts of Oudh, 1801–3: left India, 1803: M.P. for Eye, 1807–9: Secretary to the Treasury, 1808–9: P.C., 1809: Secretary to Embassy to Spain, 1809, and Ambassador, 1811–22: knighted 1812: G.C.B., 1815: Ambassador to Vienna, 1823–31: to Paris, 1841–6: made Baron Cowley, 1828: died April 27, 1847.

COX, CHARLES VYVYAN (1819–   )

Maj-General: son of the Rev. John Cox, Rector of Cheddington and Vicar of Stockland: born Sep. 24, 1819: educated at King's School, Sherborne, and Military Academy, Addiscombe: entered the Bengal Artillery, 1838: served in the Gwalior campaign, 1843–4: Satlaj campaign, 1845–6: present at the battles of Mudki, Firozshahr and Sobraon: Panjab campaign, 1848–9: present at battles of the Chenab, Chilianwala and Gujarat: throughout the Indian mutiny, 1857: retired in 1872: C.B. in 1871.

COX, SIR EDMUND C., FIFTEENTH BARONET (1856–   )

Son of the 14th Baronet: born 1856: educated at Marlborough and Trinity

DICTIONARY OF INDIAN BIOGRAPHY 99

College, Cambridge : appointed Assistant Inspr-General of Police in Bombay, 1877 : author of *Short History of the Bombay Presidency, Tales of Ancient India.*

COX, PERCY ZACHARIAH (1864–)

Major : son of Arthur Cox : born Nov. 20, 1864 : educated at Harrow and Sandhurst : joined the Army in 1884, and the Indian Staff Corps in 1889 : employed in the Political Department at Zaila, Somali coast, 1893 : Berbera, 1894–5 : H.B.M.'s Consul and Political Agent, Muscat, since 1899 : C.I.E. in 1902 : F.R.G.S. : F.Z.S.

COXHEAD, JAMES ALFRED (1851–)

Colonel : born 1851 : son of John Coxhead : educated at Merchant Taylors, Henley, and R.M.A., Woolwich : entered the Royal Artillery, 1872 : was Private Secretary and A.D.C. to Sir Henry Norman when Governor of Jamaica, 1883–7 : served at the Malakand Pass, 1895, and relief of Chitral : commanded the R.A. Indian Contingent in S. Africa till relief of Ladysmith : C.B. in 1900.

CRAIG, SIR JAMES HENRY (1748–1812)

Son of Henry Craig : born 1748 : entered the 30th regt. at 15, completed his military education on the Continent : served in N. America, 1774–81, was at Bunker's Hill and other actions : Adjutant-General in the Netherlands, 1794 : Maj-General : commanded a force to capture the Cape of Good Hope : on the arrival of Sir Alured Clarke's force from India the Dutch surrendered : Craig commanded at the Cape, 1795–7 : K.C.B., 1797 : commanded the Division at Benares, 1797–1802, in a difficult time, during the massacre there : Lt-General, 1801 : commanded in Italy and Sicily, 1805–6 : Governor-General of Canada, 1807–11 : General, 1812 : died Jan. 12, 1812.

CRANBROOK, GATHORNE GATHORNE-HARDY, FIRST EARL OF (1814–)

Born Oct. 1, 1814 : son of John Hardy, M.P. : educated at Shrewsbury and Oriel College, Oxford : Hon. Fellow of Oriel : called to the bar at the Inner Temple, 1840 : M.P. for Leominster, 1856–65 : for Oxford University, 1865–78 : made a Viscount, 1878 : an Earl, 1892 : Under Secretary for the Home Department, 1858–9, Secretary, 1867–8 : Secretary for War, 1874–8 : Secretary of State for India, March 30, 1878, to April 28, 1880 : President of the Council, 1885 and 1886–92 : G.C.S.I. : P.C. : D.C.L. : LL.D. : D.L. : J.P.

CRAWFORD, SIR THOMAS (1824–1895)

Son of George Crawford : educated at Edinburgh : M.D. : entered the Army Medical Service, 1848 : in the Burmese war, 1852–3, at the capture of Rangoon and Bassein, and other actions : served in the Crimea : P.M.O. in the N. Mahratta country and the Dekkan in 1857–8 : Superintending Surgeon of the Sirhind circle : head of the A.M.D. in Ireland : Surgeon-General in India, in the second Afghan war : Director-General of the Army Medical Service, 1882–9 : K.C.B., 1885 : LL.D., Edinburgh : died Oct. 12, 1895.

CRAWFURD, JOHN (1783–1868)

Son of Samuel Crawfurd : born Aug. 13, 1783 : educated at Bowmore, and in medicine at Edinburgh : from 1803, served as an Army medical officer, for 5 years, chiefly in Upper India : transferred to Penang : studied the Malays : was with Lord Minto in the expedition to Java, 1811 : employed in diplomatic offices there, 1811–7 : wrote a *History of the Indian Archipelago*, 1820 : sent, in 1821, as Envoy to Siam and Cochin China : administered the Government of Singapore, 1823–6 : Commissioner of Pegu, 1826 : Envoy to the Court of Ava : retired to England, 1827 : wrote narratives of his missions, *A Grammar and Dictionary of the Malay Language*, 1852 : *A Descriptive Dictionary of the Indian Islands and adjacent Countries*, 1856 : also, papers on ethnology for scientific journals : took an active part in Geographical and Ethnological Societies : was an unrivalled authority on the Eastern Archipelago : died May 11, 1868.

CREALOCK, HENRY HOPE (1831–1891)

Son of William Arthur Crealock : born March 31, 1831 : educated at Rugby : entered the Army in the 90th regt., 1848 : served in the Crimea, 1854–5 : D.A.Q.M.G.: and in China, 1857–8 : was in the Indian mutiny campaigns of 1858-9, on the staff of Sir W. R. Mansfield : present at Bareli and Shahjahanpur : served again in China, Military Secretary to the Earl of Elgin, 1860 : at St. Petersburg and Vienna : and commanded a Division in Zululand, 1879 : C.M.G. : was a Lt-General in 1884 : died May 31, 1891 : he was an excellent artist and made many drawings of Indian and Chinese warfare and scenery.

CROFT, SIR ALFRED WOODLEY (1841-)

Son of C. H. Croft : born Feb. 7, 1841 : educated at Mannamead School, Plymouth, and Exeter College, Oxford : entered the Bengal Educational Department, 1866 : Director of Public Instruction in Bengal, 1877-97 : Member of the Education Commission, 1882-3 : Member of the Bengal Legislative Council, 1887-92 : President of the Asiatic Society of Bengal, 1892-3 : Vice-Chancellor of the Calcutta University, 1894-6 : Hon. LL.D., 1897 : K.C.I.E., 1887.

CROMER, EVELYN BARING, FIRST EARL (1841-)

Son of Henry Baring, M.P. : born Feb. 26, 1841 : educated at Ordnance School, Carshalton, and R.M.A., Woolwich : entered the Royal Artillery, 1858 : Major in 1876 : Private Secretary to Lord Northbrook, Viceroy of India, 1872-6 : Financial Member of the Supreme Council of the Governor-General, 1880-3 : has since been employed in Egypt, and is now Minister Plenipotentiary in the Diplomatic Service : Agent and Consul General in Egypt since 1883 : P.C. : G.C.B. : G.C.M.G. : K.C.S.I. : C.I.E. : Baron, 1892 : Viscount, 1898 : Earl, 1901.

CROMMELIN, CHARLES (? - ?)

Governor : son of Marc Antoine Cromelin, of a Huguenot family : joined the E. I. Co.'s service in Bombay, 1732 : Governor of Bombay, 1760-7 : returned to England, had great losses in trade, returned to India, 1772, as a free merchant : was residing at Canton, 1777 : was British Consul at Goa, 1784 : it has been suggested that this was the Charles Cromelin (*sic*) who died Dec. 25, 1788, aged 81, and was buried at the old English Cemetery, Kalkapur, Murshidabad.

CROOKE, WILLIAM (1848-)

I.C.S. : born Aug. 6, 1848 : educated at the Grammar School, Tipperary, and at Trinity College, Dublin : arrived in India, 1871 : served in the N.W.P. and Oudh : Magistrate and Collector : retired, 1896 : author of *Rural and Agricultural Glossary, N.W.P. and Oudh*, 1888 : an Ethnographical Handbook for the N.W.P. and Oudh, 1890 : *The N.W.P. of India, their History*, etc., 1897 : *The Popular Religion and Folklore of Northern India*, 1896 : and a Gazetteer of Jalesar : *The Tribes and Castes of the N.W.P. and Oudh*, 1896 : also of a revised edition of Burnell's and Yule's *Hobson-Jobson*, and numerous papers in the *Journal of the Anthropological Institute and Folklore Society*.

CROSS, JOHN KYNASTON (1832-1887)

Son of Thomas Cross : head of the Firm of Crosses, Winkworth & Co. : Under Secretary of State for India, Jan., 1883 to June, 1885 : died March 20, 1887.

CROSS, RICHARD ASSHETON, FIRST VISCOUNT (1823-)

Born May 30, 1823 : son of William Cross : educated at Rugby and Trinity College, Cambridge : called to the bar at the Inner Temple, 1849 : M.P. for Preston, 1857-62, and S. Lancashire, 1868-86 : Home Secretary, 1874-80 and 1885-6 : Secretary of State for India, Aug. 4, 1886, to Aug. 19, 1892 : Lord Privy Seal, 1895-1900 : made a Viscount, 1886 : P.C. : G.C.S.I., 1892 : D.C. L. : LL.D., Cambridge, 1878 : G.C.B., 1880 : F.R.S. : author of legal works.

CROSTHWAITE, SIR CHARLES HAWKES TODD (1835-)

I.C.S. : son of Rev. John Clarke Crosthwaite : born Dec. 25, 1835 : educated at Merchant Taylors' and St. John's College, Oxford : entered the Bengal Civil Service, 1857 : served chiefly in the N.W.P. : Chief Commissioner of British Burma, 1883-4 : Chief Commissioner of Central Provinces, 1885-6 : Chief Commissioner of Burma, 1887-90 : Member of the Governor - General's Supreme Council, 1890-1, and in 1892 : Lieutenant-Governor of N.W.P. and Oudh, 1892-5 : Member of the Council of India, 1895-1905 : author of *Notes on the N.W. Provinces of India*, 1870 : K.C.S.I., in 1888.

CROSTHWAITE, SIR ROBERT JOSEPH
(1841-   )

I.C.S. : son of Rev. John C. Crosthwaite : born Jan. 17, 1841 : educated at Merchant Taylors and Brasenose College, Oxford : entered the Bengal Civil Service, 1863 : served chiefly in the N.W.P. : was Judicial Commissioner of Burma and Central Provinces : Agent to the Governor-General in Central India and in Rajputana: called to the bar from the Middle Temple, 1868 : K.C.S.I. in 1897.

CROWE, SIR JOSEPH ARCHER (1825-1896)

Journalist, art-critic, and diplomatist : son of Eyre Evans Crowe: born Oct. 20, 1825 : artist of *Illustrated London News* in the Crimea : present at the engagements : appointed Superintendent of the " Sir Jamsetji Jijihbai's School of Design " at Bombay, 1857 : Editor, successively, of the *Bombay Gazette* and *Bombay Standard*, and correspondent of the *Daily News* and *Times* during the mutiny : Secretary of the Bombay Chamber of Commerce : left India owing to ill-health, 1859 : *Times'* correspondent in Italian war of 1859 : present at Solferino : appointed Consul-General for Saxony, 1860 : entered diplomatic service, 1880 : Commercial Attaché for Europe, 1882-1895 : joint author with Cavalcasella of Histories of Flemish and Italian Painters, Lives of Titian and Raphael : published a volume of *Reminiscences* : died Sep. 6, 1896.

CSOMA, DE KÖROS, ALEXANDER
(1784-1842)

Traveller and student of philology : son of Andrew Csoma : born April 4, 1784, at Koros in Transylvania : educated, 1815-8, at the College of Novo Enyed : Doctor of Medicine at Gottingen. To ascertain the origin of his countrymen, the Hungarians, whose primitive seat he expected to discover in the heart of Central Asia, he left Bucharest, Jan. 1, 1820 : travelled to Constantinople, Alexandria, Syria, Bagdad, Teheran, Mashad, Bokhara, Kabul, Lahore, Kashmir, Leh : studied Tibetan thoroughly in monasteries in Ladak, chiefly at Yangla, in Zanskar, 1823-6 : was at Sabathu, 1824-5 : allowed Rs. 50 a month by the Government of India : made a third journey to Kanum in Kunawar, studying Tibetan at a

Buddhist monastery till 1830 : reached Calcutta, April, 1831 : published a Tibetan grammar and dictionary, vocabulary, etc. : made Honorary Member of the Asiatic Society of Bengal, 1834 : studied Sanskrit, and was appointed Librarian of the Society : travelled, 1836-7, to study Oriental languages, to Jalpaiguri and Titalya : at Calcutta 1837-42 : started for Lhasa in 1842 : reached Darjeeling, March 24 : died April 11 : and was buried there : " an indefatigable and unpresuming student". a scholar of extreme modesty : knew 17 languages, ancient and modern.

CUBBON, SIR MARK (1785-1861)

Born Sep. 8, 1785 : went to India in the Madras Infantry in 1800 : Captain in 1816 : in the Commissariat Department in the Pindari war, 1817-8, and in Madras. When the people of Mysore rebelled, in 1831, against the oppression and bad government of their Hindu Raja, Lt-Colonel Cubbon was a member of the Commission of Enquiry : after which the Government of India assumed the administration of the province and Cubbon was made Commissioner, first joint, and in 1834 sole, of Mysore : and soon afterwards of Coorg also : this post he held for 27 years, governing the province despotically but successfully, through native agency, and exercising a profuse hospitality : Lt-General, 1852 : C.B., 1856 : K.C.B., 1859. He never married or left India until he retired in 1861, after 60 years' service in India, when he died at Suez, on April 23. His equestrian statue is in the Cubbon Park at Bangalore : when unveiled, it had been daubed with the three Brahmanical marks on the forehead.

CUBITT, WILLIAM GEORGE (1835-1903)

Colonel : son of Major W. Cubitt of the Bengal Army : educated at Laleham : joined the 13th Bengal N.I., 1853 : served in the Sonthal campaign, 1855 : in the Dafla expedition, 1874-5 : Afghan war, 1878-80 : Akha expedition, 1883-4 : Burmese expedition, 1886-7 : in the mutiny won the Victoria Cross at Chinhut on June 30, 1857, for saving the lives of three men at the risk of his own : in the defence of the Residency at Lucknow :

wounded : D.S.O. for his services in Burma : retired 1892 : died Jan. 25, 1903.

CUNINGHAM, SIR WILLIAM JOHN
(1848–   )

I.C.S. : born Nov. 20, 1848 : son of Alexander Cuningham : educated at Edinburgh Academy and privately : went out to Bombay, 1870 : served as Assistant to the Chief Commissioner of Mysore : Under Secretary to the Government of India, Foreign Department, 1885, : Secretary in the Foreign Department, 1894–1901 : C.S.I., 1894 : K.C.S.I., 1897.

CUNNINGHAM, SIR ALEXANDER FREDERICK DOUGLAS (1852–)

I.C.S. : son of Sir Alexander Cunningham, K.C.I.E., C.S.I. (q.v.) : educated at Kensington Grammar School and King's College, London : went to the Panjab in 1872 : Political officer in the Khyber, 1879 : Under Secretary to the Panjab Government, 1884 : Commissioner and Superintendent of the Peshawar Division, 1892, and from 1894 : K.C.I.E., 1901 : retired.

CUNNINGHAM, SIR ALEXANDER
(1814–1893)

Son of Allan Cunningham : born Jan. 23, 1814 : educated at Christ's Hospital and Addiscombe : obtained an Indian cadetship, through Sir Walter Scott : reached India in June, 1833 : A.D.C. to Lord Auckland, 1836 : Executive Engineer to the King of Oudh, 1840 : engaged in suppressing the rebellion in Bundelkund : was at Punniar, Dec. 19, 1843 : Executive Engineer at Gwalior, 1844–5 : was in the first Sikh war, 1846, as field engineer : occupied Kangra and Kulu : demarcated boundaries : was at Chilianwala and Gujarat in the second Sikh war, 1848–9 : Chief Engineer in Burma, 1856–8 : and in the N.W.P., 1858–61 : retired from the Army as Maj-General in 1861 : he was then made the first Archæological Surveyor to the Government of India, 1861–5 : the department was abolished in 1865, but revived in 1870, with Cunningham as Director : he held the post until he retired in 1885 : C.S.I. : C.I.E. : and K.C.I.E. in 1887. Apart from his official reports of his annual tours and his occasional contributions to the Asiatic Society of Bengal's journals, he wrote, inter alia,

on Ladak, The Bhilsa Topes, The Ancient Geography of India, The Buddhist Period, Corpus Inscriptionum Indicarum, The Stupa of Bharhat, The Book of Indian Eras, Mahabodhi. After retirement, he paid much attention to numismatics, on which he was an eminent authority : parted with his coins at cost price to the British Museum : died Nov. 28, 1893.

CUNNINGHAM, FRANCIS (1820–1875)

Son of Allan Cunningham, and brother of Sir Alexander (q.v.) : born 1820 : educated at Addiscombe : joined the Madras Army, 1838 : was distinguished as an engineer in the defence of Jalalabad, 1842 : served in the Civil Commission in Mysore under Sir Mark Cubbon, and retired in 1861. He edited Marlowe, Massinger and Ben Jonson, by which he is best known : also wrote for the Saturday Review : he died Dec. 3, 1875.

CUNNINGHAM, SIR HENRY STEWART (1832–)

Born 1832 : son of Rev. J. W. Cunningham, Vicar of Harrow : educated at Harrow and Trinity College, Oxford : called to the bar, 1859 : Advocate-General in Madras, 1872 : Judge of the Calcutta High Court, 1877–87 : Member of the Indian Famine Commission, 1878–9 : author of The Chronicles of Dustypore, The Heriots, The Cæruleans, Sybilla, and other novels : also Earl Canning (" Rulers of India " series). He married in 1877 a daughter of Lord Lawrence : K.C.I.E. in 1889.

CUNNINGHAM, JAMES MACNABB
(1829–1905)

Educated at Edinburgh University : M.D. : entered the Bengal Medical Service, 1851 : Secretary to the Sanitary Commissioner, 1866 : Professor of Hygiene, Calcutta Medical College, 1866 : Sanitary Commissioner, Bengal, 1869 : Sanitary Commissioner with the Government of India, 1875–85, and Surgeon-General, 1880–5 : retired, 1885 : Member of the Army Sanitary Committee, 1891–96 : author of Cholera—what can the State do to Prevent it ? represented the Government of India at the Paris International Sanitary Congress, 1894 : C.S.I.,

1885 : Honorary Surgeon to the Queen, 1888 : died June 26, 1905.

CUNNINGHAM, JOSEPH DAVEY (1812–1851)

Son of Allan Cunningham and brother of Sir Alexander (*q.v.*) : born June 9, 1812 : educated at private schools and at Addiscombe, where his career was very distinguished : Sir Walter Scott obtained a cadetship for him : he went to Chatham and to India in the Bengal Engineers in 1834 : appointed assistant to Colonel Claud Wade (*q.v.*), the Agent on the Sikh frontier : fortified Firozpur, 1837 : was for 8 years in political employ : at the interview with Ranjit Singh, in the Khyber, at Ludiana, at Peshawar, with the Amir Dost Muhammad at Jammu, agent at Bahawalpur : Captain, etc. 1845 : in the first Sikh war was at Badiwal, Aliwal, and Sobraon : was Political Agent at Bhopal, 1846 : published the *History of the Sikhs.* This work, though favourably received in general, gave offence to some of Cunningham's superiors, as he stated that in the Sikh war two of the Sikh generals were bought : this was strenuously denied by high officers : the result to Cunningham was the loss of his political appointment and relegation to ordinary duty, on the ground of having used in his History information confidentially known to him in his official capacity. He died at Umbala, Feb. 28, 1851.

CURETON, SIR CHARLES (1826–1891)

Son of Charles Robert Cureton : born Nov. 25, 1826 : joined the E.I. Co.'s Army, 1843 : eventually became General in 1888 : served in the first Sikh war, was at Aliwal, Jan. 28, 1846 : in the Panjab campaign, 1848–9, was A.D.C. to his father : and in the N.W. frontier operations of 1849–52 and 1860 : helped to subdue the Sonthal rebellion, 1856 : in the Indian mutiny he raised and commanded Cureton's regiment of Multani native cavalry, was present at an action against Sealkot rebels at Trimmu Ghat, and a number of actions in 1858–9, showing great personal bravery : in charge of Intelligence Department in Rohilkund and Oudh, 1858–9 : commanded the Oudh Division of the Bengal Army, 1879–84 : C.B., 1869 : K.C.B., 1891 : died July 11, 1891.

CURETON, CHARLES ROBERT (1789–1848)

Brig-General : born in 1789 : entered the Shropshire Militia, 1806 : disguised as a sailor, he fled from creditors, and enlisted in a dragoon regiment in 1808 : served in the Peninsula, was in many actions, Talavera, Badajos, Salamanca, Madrid, Vittoria, etc. : gazetted as Ensign, 1814 : worked up to Lt-Colonel in 1846 : went to India in 1822 : was at the siege of Bhartpur, Jan. 19, 1826 : was in the Afghan war, 1839, under Sir J. Keane, at Ghazni, July 23, 1839, and the occupation of Kabul : was at Maharajpur on Dec. 29, 1843 : C.B., 1844 : in the Satlaj campaign was under Sir Harry Smith : commanded the cavalry at Aliwal, and a Brigade of cavalry at Sobraon, gaining the highest praise as a cavalry commander : made A.D.C. to the Queen : and Adjutant-General to the Queen's forces in India, 1846 : in the second Sikh war he was killed at Ramnagar, Nov. 22, 1848.

CURETON, EDWARD BURGOYNE (1822–1894)

Born May, 1822 : son of Brig-General C. R. Cureton (*q.v.*) : Ensign, 13th foot, 1839 : in the 16th Lancers in the battle of Maharajpur, Dec. 29, 1843 : at Mudki, Dec. 18, 1845 : at Sobraon, Feb. 10, 1846 : in the Kafir war, 1851–3 : in the Crimea from July, 1855 : Lt-General : retired, 1881 : died Feb. 9, 1894.

CURRIE, BERTRAM WODEHOUSE (1827–1896)

Born 1827 : son of Raikes Currie educated at Eton : entered his father's banking business, which, in 1864, was amalgamated and became Glyn, Mills, Currie & Co.: in Dec. 1880, was appointed a Member of the Council of India, re-appointed 1890, served till 1895 : in 1892, represented England at the International monetary conference at Brussels : in 1893 was member of Lord Herschell's Committee, which decided on closing the Indian Mints to the free coinage of silver : was on other financial Commissions : initiated in 1895 the Gold Standard Defence Association : died Dec. 29, 1896.

CURRIE, SIR FREDERICK, BARONET (1799-1875)

I.C.S.: son of Mark Currie : born Feb. 3, 1799 : educated at Charterhouse and Haileybury : reached India, 1820 : was a Judge of the *Sadr Adalat* (court) in the N.W.P., 1840 : Foreign Secretary to the Government of India, 1842 : with Sir Henry Hardinge in the first Sikh war, 1845–6, and, after Sobraon, drew up the treaty with the Sikhs : made Baronet in Jan. 1847 : officiated as Member of the Supreme Council, April, 1847 to Jan. 1848 : resigned his seat, and succeeded Sir Henry Lawrence as Resident at Lahore in 1848 : accepted the resignation of Mulraj, the Governor of Multan : confirmed as Member of Supreme Council, resuming his seat, March, 1849 : retired in 1853 : was elected a Director of the E.I. Co. in 1854, Chairman, 1857 : Member of the Council of India from 1858 : D.C.L., Oxford in 1866 : died Sep. 11, 1875.

CURWEN, HENRY (1845-1892)

Journalist and writer : born in 1845 : son of Henry Curwen : educated at Rossall : followed a literary career in London until he went to India in 1876, as Assistant-Editor of the *Times of India*, Bombay, of which he became Editor in 1880 and joint-proprietor in 1889 : died on board ship, Feb. 22, 1892, on his way homewards : wrote several novels, and translations of French poetry, and contributed articles to periodical literature : described his tour in the famine districts of 1876–7 : under his editorship the *Times of India* was well conducted and favourably regarded.

CURZON OF KEDLESTON, GEORGE NATHANIEL, FIRST BARON (1859-   )

Viceroy and Governor-General : born Jan. 11, 1859, son of Rev. fourth Baron Scarsdale : educated at Eton and Balliol College, Oxford : President of the Union Society, 1880 : Fellow of All Souls' College, 1883 : gained the Arnold Essay Prize, 1884 : Assistant Private Secretary to the Marquis of Salisbury, 1885 : Under Secretary of State for India, 1891–2 : for Foreign Affairs, 1895–8 : travelled in Central Asia, Persia, Afghanistan, the Pamirs, Siam, Indo-China, the Korea :

M.P. for Southport Division, 1886–98 : published *Russia in Central Asia*, 1889 : *Persia and the Persian Question*, 1892 : *Problems of the Far East*, 1894 : Viceroy and Governor-General of India from Jan. 6, 1899, to April, 1904 : paid much attention to the control and defence of the frontiers of India, changing the policy on the N.W. frontier : created a Chief Commissionership of the Trans-Indus districts : enforced the blockade of Waziristan : showed distrust of Russian objects and Russian methods : visited the Persian gulf, with a view to prevention of any enroachment on British interest, to increase trade and maintain sphere of influence in Persia : despatched Tibet mission to carry out Anglo-Chinese convention of 1890 and trade regulations of 1893, and check Russian influence in Tibet : the mission leading to war with Tibet and the treaty of Lhasa, Sep. 1904 : examined into every branch of the administration, to introduce improvements : " it has not always been a popular policy " : appointed several Commissions, on the Universities, to reform Higher Education, on Irrigation, on the Police : had to deal with a famine in Bombay : aimed at improving relations with the native Chiefs, and the character of their rule : reformed the four Chiefs' colleges : founded the Imperial Cadet Corps : settled the question of the Berars : set on foot the Victoria Memorial Hall, obtaining large subscriptions from wealthy natives : held the Delhi Coronation Darbar of Dec. 1902–Jan. 1903 : reduced Lower Bengal by three Divisions, adding them to Assam to make a new Lieutenant-Governorship : had large financial surpluses, twice reduced the Salt Tax, and removed the Income Tax on the lowest incomes : passed some important legislative measures, such as the Universities Act, the Official Secrets Act, the Indian Mines Act, the Ancient Monuments Preservation Act, the Co-operative Credit Societies' Act : G.M.S.I., G.M.I.E., P.C., F.R.S., J.P., D.C.L. : re-appointed Viceroy and Governor-General in 1904 : returned to India, Dec. 1904 : Lord Warden of the Cinque Ports, 1903–4 : in Aug., 1905, resigned the Viceroyalty on a point arising out of an adverse decision of the Cabinet on a difference of opinion between the C. in C. (Lord Kitchener) and the rest of the Government of India regarding military affairs in India.

CUST, ROBERT NEEDHAM (1821-·)

I.C.S. : son of Hon. and Rev. H. C. Cust, brother of Earl Brownlow : born Feb. 24, 1821 : educated at Eton and Haileybury : entered the Bengal Civil Service, 1843, and retired in 1867 : served in the N.W.P. and Panjab : present at the battles of Mudki and Firozshahr, 1845, and Sobraon, 1846 : called to the bar from Lincoln's Inn, 1855 : took part in the settlement of the Panjab after the mutiny, 1858 : Home Secretary to the Government of India, 1864-5 : is now Hon. Secretary of the Royal Asiatic Society, and has published many books on the religions and languages of the world, the two last being *Five Essays on Religious Conceptions*, 1897, and *Life Memoir*, 1899 : LL.D. of Edinburgh, 1885.

D'ACHE, COMTE (1700 ? or 1716 ?– 1775)

Vice-Admiral : served with distinction, but without important command, up to 1757, when he was made Commander of the French Naval forces in Indian seas : reached the Coromandel coast, April, 1758, commanding the squadron which took Lally's expedition to India : beaten, off Negapatam, by the English Fleet under Admiral Pocock : declined to co-operate with Lally against Madras : again defeated off Tranquebar, Aug. 1, 1758 : sailed for the Isle of France : took for his fleet a million francs, intended for Pondicherry : returned after a year from Isle of France : defeated off Fort St. David, Sep. 10, 1759, by Pocock : went to Pondicherry, but abandoned it Sep. 17, and never returned, staying at the Isle of France : thus, inefficient and constantly defeated, he lost in a few months the French cause in South India : the commerce of the Compagnie des Indes was irretrievably destroyed : on his return to France, he received promotion in the Navy and honours, without restoring his reputation by any distinguished action : became an accuser of Lally : died, 1775.

DA CUNHA, J. GERSON (1842-1900)

Doctor : born in Arpora, Goa : claimed to belong to a family of Brahman converts to Christianity : educated at Goa, Bombay, and in Europe : returned to Bombay as a medical practitioner : a

man of letters and antiquarian research : Vice-President of the R.A.S., Bombay, 1892 : Knight of several foreign orders : read many valuable papers on history, archæology, languages, numismatics before the R.A.S. : also wrote largely : a history of Chaul and Bassein, and the *Origin of Bombay*, 1900 : on the subject of Buddha's Tooth : a man of great culture and a keen numismatist : his collection of Indian coins, said to number 15,000, was considered one of the finest in the world, and was valued at several lakhs of rupees : he died July 3, 1900.

D'AGUILAR, SIR CHARLES LAWRENCE (1821-)

Born 1821 : son of Lt-General Sir George D'Aguilar, K.C.B. : educated at R.M.A., Woolwich : entered the Royal Artillery, 1838 : Military Secretary to the Commander of the China Forces, 1843-8 : served in the Crimea and in the Indian mutiny : General commanding Woolwich District, 1874-9 : Lt-General, 1877 : Col. Commandant R.H.A. : G.C.B., 1887.

D'AGUILAR, SIR GEORGE CHARLES (1784-1855)

Son of Capt. Joseph D'Aguilar : born Jan. 1784 : joined the 86th regt. in India, 1799 : served in the Mahratta war of 1803-5 : at Bhartpur in 1806 under Lord Lake : to England in 1809 : in the Walcheren expedition : in Sicily : on a special mission to Constantinople : in Spain : in Flanders : C.B. in 1834 : commanded in China, and in 1847 Canton submitted to him : K.C.B. in 1851 : Lt-General : died May 21, 1855 : wrote military manuals and treatises.

DALGLEISH, ANDREW (? –1888)

An energetic pioneer of trade : for years he journeyed for commercial purposes between Kashmir and Yarkand : joined a Central Asian Trading Company : went with a party to Yarkand, and afterwards made frequent journeys to Kashgar : in 1883 he had a free passport from the Chinese to enter Chinese Turkistan : went as Turkish interpreter with A. D. Carey (*q.v.*) in 1885 from Kashmir round Chinese Turkistan and along the frontier of Tibet : was killed near the Karakoram, en route to Yarkand, by a Kakar Pathan in 1888 : his map specially acknowledged by the Geographical Society.

DALHOFF, RIGHT REV. THEODORE, D.D. (1837-   )

Second Catholic Archbishop of Bombay : a German, born in Westphalia, April 20, 1837 : entered the Society of Jesus, April 14, 1859 : arrived in India, Jan. 28, 1866 : ordained priest, Dec. 25, 1868 : held several posts of Superiorship at Bandora, St. Xavier's College, Bombay, and St. Vincent's High School, Poona : as Vicar-General, on the death of Archbishop Porter, administered the diocese : Archbishop of Bombay, Dec. 6, 1891 : consecrated in Bombay Cathedral, Jan. 31, 1892 : in 1891 visited Europe, and again in 1895 ; built the Church of the Holy Name, Bombay (opened Jan. 15, 1905), with Archiepiscopal Residence and Convent School attached : is proprietor of the *Bombay Catholic Examiner* (now called the *Examiner*), a weekly religious paper of wide circulation, now in its fifty-fifth year : still at work in his 69th year.

DALHOUSIE, GEORGE RAMSAY, NINTH EARL OF (1770-1838)

General : son of the eighth Earl : born in 1770, entered the Army in the Dragoon Guards in 1789, was in several regiments : became Maj-General in 1805, Lt-General, 1813 : G.C.B. : General, 1830 : served at Martinique, 1792 : in the Irish rebellion of 1798 : in Holland, Egypt, the Peninsula and France : created Baron Dalhousie in the Peerage of the United Kingdom in Aug. 1815 : Lt-Governor of Nova Scotia, 1816 : Captain-General and Governor of Canada, Nova Scotia, etc., 1819-28 : and commanded the forces from 1819 : was C. in C. in the East Indies, 1829-32 : father of the first Marquis of Dalhousie (*q.v.*) : died March 21, 1838.

DALHOUSIE, JAMES ANDREW BROWN-RAMSAY, FIRST MARQUIS OF (1812-1860)

Governor-General : third son of the ninth Earl, C. in C. in India (*q.v.*) : born April 22, 1812 : educated at Harrow and Christ Church, Oxford : M.P. for Haddingtonshire, 1837 : succeeded his father, March, 1838 : Vice-President of the Board of Trade in Peel's administration, 1843 : Privy Councillor, 1843 : President of the Board and in the Cabinet, 1845 : declined a seat in the Cabinet offered him in July,

1846, by Lord John Russell, who appointed him Governor-General of India in 1847 : assumed office, Jan. 12, 1848. After the rebellion of Mulraj at Multan, the second Sikh war broke out : Dalhousie went up to the Panjab-Satlaj frontier and supervised the operations : annexed the Panjab in March, 1849 : was made a Marquis : made Sir Henry Lawrence President of the Board of Administration, and, in 1853, made Sir John Lawrence Chief Commissioner of the Panjab : his controversy with Sir C. J. Napier, the C. in C., regarding certain new regulations affecting the grant to the Sepoys of compensation for dearness of provisions, led to the latter's resignation. Dalhousie's internal administration of the country was thorough and comprehensive : he introduced and laid down a system for the construction of railways ; joined the provinces by telegraphs ; organized the imperial postal system ; created the Departments of Public works, Jails, Forests, Survey, and Education ; dealt with the strength and composition of the Army in India ; reorganized and expanded the Legislative Council ; created a separate Lieutenant-Governorship of Lower Bengal (to relieve the Governor-General of his direct personal charge of that Province) : he declared war on the King of Burma in 1852, and supervised it himself, visiting the country and annexing Pegu : made treaties with the Khan of Kelat and Amir of Afghanistan : the Berars were assigned for the payment of the Hyderabad debts. Dalhousie has been blamed for the annexation of Satara, Nagpur, Tanjore, Jhansi, Oudh, for reducing the title of the Nawab of the Carnatic to Prince of Arcot, for terminating the ex-Peshwa's pension the fact is, that where annexations were effected, according to the doctrine of lapse, i.e. on the failure of natural heirs, that policy was not Dalhousie's, but a policy which had been previously declared and acted upon and was, in each case, sanctioned by higher authority : in the case of Oudh, he personally was opposed to annexation, but his Council advocated it and the authorities in England ordered it, on account of the continued maladministration by the King, after repeated warnings : Dalhousie restricted the application of the doctrine of lapse to cases of Hindu dependent states. He was also blamed for weakening the European Army in India : in fact, he had protested against reduction of the English Army in India for the Crimean and Persian wars, and had given full attention to military affairs : he abolished numerous Boards and established responsible Departments in their places : his despatches were not attended to at the India House, and he was never able to defend himself and his administration. He suffered from ill-health, during the prolongation of his appointment in 'India, and was too ill after his retirement, on Feb. 29, 1856, to defend his policy : and the English Governments failed to support him. Thus the outbreak of the mutiny was unjustly attributed to his alleged policy in respect of annexation, neglect of military matters, and the reduced strength of the English Army in India. His assailants have been amply refuted by his later biographers, especially in Sir W. Lee Warner's *Life of the Marquis of Dalhousie*, 1904. The death, from exhaustion after sea-sickness, of Lady Dalhousie in 1853, in sight of England, affected him deeply. Always a very hard worker, he sought distraction in " work, work," and in his public duties. His final minute of Feb. 28, 1856, contains a summary of his administration. He was masterful in character and impatient of opposition. " In the three words, conquest, consolidation and development, his work may be summed up " (Sir W. W. Hunter). He stands out as " the great Proconsul " of modern times. After retirement he held no office but that of Lord Warden of the Cinque Ports, 1852–60. He died Dec. 19, 1860. His statue is in Calcutta, where the Dalhousie Institute was erected in his memory.

DALLAS, SIR GEORGE, BARONET
(1758–1833)

Son of Robert Dallas : born April 6, 1758 : educated at Geneva : entered the E. I. Co.'s civil service at eighteen, was noticed by Warren Hastings, appointed Collector of Rajshahi : returned to England for ill-health, 1788 : deputed by Calcutta residents to present a petition against Pitt's East India Bill : made a Baronet in 1798 : M.P., 1800–2, for Newport : wrote a poem *The India Guide* : a pamphlet in vindication of Warren Hastings, 1789 : a vindication of the Marquis Wellesley's wars in Hindustan and the Dekkan, 1806,

besides papers on Ireland and France, and on Trade between India and Europe, in which he advocated a greater freedom and liberality in trade between the countries : died Jan. 14, 1833.

DALLAS, SIR THOMAS (? –1839)

Was a cavalry officer in the Carnatic, and under Colonel Arthur Wellesley, and at the siege of Seringapatam : distinguished himself : K.C.B. : died Aug. 12, 1839.

DALRYMPLE, ALEXANDER
(1737–1808)

Son of Sir James Dalrymple, *Bart.*: born July 24, 1737 : went out to Madras in the E.I. Co.'s Civil service, in May, 1753 : Lord Pigot, to whom he had been recomended, put him into the Secretariat and taught him to write : the historian Orme also befriended him : he became Deputy Secretary : in 1759–62 he made a voyage to the Eastern Archipelago in the interest of commerce : after returning to Madras he sailed again to the islands and reached Canton in 1764. He returned to England in 1765 to push his schemes of extending commerce to the East, but received no encouragement : failed to obtain the command of an expedition to observe the transit of Venus in 1769 : then turned his attention to geography and hydrography, and published a Chart of the Bay of Bengal in 1772 : appointed Member of Council in Madras, 1775, but in 2 years was recalled on an unfounded charge of misconduct : in 1779 made hydrographer to the E.I. Co., and in 1795 also to the Admiralty : dismissed from this appointment in May, 1808 : died of vexation, June, 19, 1808 : published a number of works, chiefly on voyages, charts, historical and political papers, including the *Oriental Repertory*, 1791–4.

DALRYMPLE, JAMES (? –1800)

Commanded the 29th battalion in Madras, 1788 : at the storming of Gurrumcondah in Nov. 1791 : took Raichur for the Nizam from insurgents, March, 1796 : in the Nizam's contingent under General A. Wellesley, 1799 : in the assault of Seringapatam, May 4, 1799 : after the capture commanded the Hyderabad Subsidiary Force : took several forts from Dhoondia Waugh, the freebooter, and defeated him, Aug. 17, 1799, at Shikarpur, expelling him from Mysore : died, much regretted by General Wellesley, at Hyderabad, Dec., 1800.

DALRYMPLE, WILLIAM LISTON (1845-   )

Born June 29, 1845 : educated at High School, Edinburgh, Wimbledon and Sandhurst : joined 44th regt., 1863, and 88th Connaught Rangers, 1864 : passed Staff College, 1873 : served at Ashanti, Bermuda, D.A.A., and Q.M.G., Northern District : A.A.G., Colonial Forces, South Africa, 1878 : Brig-Major S. Africa Field Force, 1879 : Military Secretary to Lord Lytton when Viceroy of India, 1880 : A.Q.M.G. of India, 1883-4 : D.Q.M.G., India, 1891-3 : Brig-General, India, 1893-8 : C.B., 1893 : retired.

DALTON, EDWARD TUITE (1815-1880)

Entered the Army, 1835 : in expeditions against frontier tribes of Assam, 1839-40, and 1842 : commanded an expedition and captured the Mishmi chief who had murdered the French missionaries Kirk and Bourry on the Tibetan frontier : Commissioner of Chota Nagpur in 1858 : with the Field Force against the Palamau rebels, and in 1858-9 against the Singbhum insurgents : C.S.I. : Maj-General, 1877 : died Dec. 30, 1880 : wrote *The Descriptive Ethnology of Bengal*, 1872.

DALTON, JOHN (1725-1811)

Son of Capt. James Dalton of the 6th regt. : born 1725 : appointed to Hanmer's Marine regt., 1741 : 2nd Lt. of Marines on the *Preston*, 1743 : to Fort St. David, 1745 : the French took Madras, 1746 : the Marine regts. being reduced at the peace with France, Dalton joined the Independent Companies under Admiral Boscawen (*q.v.*) : became a Captain in the E.I. Co.'s service : in the expedition to Devikota, 1749 : Muhammad Ali, son of Anwaruddin, late Nawab of the Carnatic, fled on his father's death to Trichinopoly and applied to the English for help : Dalton was in the force sent to his aid : was in the retreat at Volkonda, June, 19, 1751 : at Wootatoor and at Kistnavaram : in the fighting on behalf of Muhammad Ali against Chanda Sahib (*q.v.*) near Trichinopoly : Dalton made Commandant there, June, 15, 1752, to keep it for Muhammad Ali against the Dalwai (the

Regent of Mysore), and Morari Rao the Mahratta : defended it with great skill and courage against famine, treachery, blockade and the French also : relieved by Major Stringer Lawrence, May, 6, 1753, and again Sep. 21 : resigned the E.I. Co.'s service March 1, 1754, and returned to England : died July 11, 1811.

D'ALVIELLA, COUNT GOBLET (1846-   )

Born Aug. 10, 1846 : educated at Brussels and Paris : LL.D. of the University of Glasgow : Hibbert Lecturer at Oxford, 1891 : accompanied H.M. King Edward VII, then H.R.H. the Prince of Wales, on his Indian tour in 1875-6 : Author of *Inde et Himalaye*, 1877 : *Contemporary Evolution of Religious Thought in England, America and India*, 1885 : *Ce que l'Inde doit à la Grèce*, 1897, etc.

DALY, SIR HENRY DERMOT (1821-1895)

Son of Lt-Colonel Francis Dermot Daly : born Oct. 25, 1821 : joined the first Bombay European regt. in 1840, became Adjutant, was present at the fighting at Multan in 1848, in the second Sikh war, at Gujarat on Feb. 22, 1849, and in the pursuit of the Sikhs : in 1849 he raised the first Panjab Cavalry and saw service on the frontier, against the Afridis, and under Sir Colin Campbell in 1852. In the mutiny he commanded the Guides' Cavalry in their march of 580 miles in 22 days from Mardan to Delhi : was at the siege of Delhi, at the capture of Lucknow in March, 1858, and in the Oudh campaign : in 1861 he commanded the Central India Horse, and in 1871 was made Agent to the Governor-General for Central India : K.C.B., 1875 : C.I.E., 1880 : General in 1888 : G.C.O., 1889 : retired in 1882 : died July 21, 1895.

DALY, HUGH (1860-   )

Born 1860 : son of Sir H.D. Daly (*q.v.*) : entered Gloucestershire regt. 1881 : joined the Indian Staff Corps : Captain, 1892 : served in Burmese expedition, 1886-7 : Superintendent of the Northern Shan States, 1888 : C.I.E. : Assistant, and, later, Deputy-Secretary to the Government of India, Foreign Department : Major and C.S.I., 1903 : Agent to the Governor-General for Central India, 1905.

DALYELL, SIR ROBERT ANSTRU-THER (1831-1890)

I.C.S. : born Oct. 7, 1831 : son of Colonel John Dalyell : educated at Cheltenham and Haileybury : went to Madras in Jan., 1851 : became Secretary to the Board of Revenue in 1867, Secretary to Government, Revenue Department, in 1868 : Chief Secretary, 1870 : Member of the Board of Revenue, 1873 : made a special report on the Excise administration in 1874 : Chief Commissioner of Mysore in 1875-6, and additional Member of the Governor-General's Legislative Council, 1873-7 : retired from India, 1877 : Member of the Council of India, 1877-87 : C.S.I., in 1879 : K.C.I.E., 1887 : LL.D. of St. Andrews, 1885 : died Jan. 18, 1890.

DAMANT, GUYBON HENRY (1846-1879)

I.C.S. : born May 9, 1846 : educated at St. Paul's School, London, and Christ's College, Cambridge : Scholar and Exhibitioner : went out to Bengal, 1869 : served in Cachar, Assam, and on special duty to Manipur, 1876 : was Deputy Commissioner of the Garo Hills, 1877, and Political Agent in the Naga Hills, Assam, 1878 : on his way to Khonoma, to seize some ammunition which the Nagas had stored, was killed by them, Oct. 14, 1879 : took keen interest in literature and philology : wrote on folk-lore, and the Manipuri language in the *J.A.S.B.*, *J.R.A.S.*, and the *Indian Antiquary*: most of the MSS. of his *Manipur Dictionary* were destroyed by the Nagas in the stockade at Kohima.

DAMPIER, HENRY LUCIUS (1828-   )

I.C.S. : born 1828 : son of W. Dampier, I.C.S.: educated at Eton : entered the B.C.S., 1848 : Member of the Orissa famine Commission,1867: Secretary to the Government of Bengal : officiating Home Secretary to the Government of India, 1872 : Member of Bengal Legislative Council, 1867-84 : Member of the Board of Revenue, 1877 : President of Rent Law Commission, 1881 : retired, 1884 : C.I.E.

DANCE, SIR NATHANIEL (1748-1827)

Son of James Dance : born June 20, 1748, entered the E. I. Co's naval service, 1759 : was in command of a ship in 1787. As Commodore of a fleet of 16 Indiamen and some country ships in 1804, homeward bound from Canton, he fell in with a French squadron off Pulo Aor, near the S. end of the straits of Malacca, and by his skill and boldness deceived them and put them to flight on Feb. 15, saving his own fleet and its valuable cargo. He was knighted and pensioned by the E. I. Co. : died March 25, 1827.

DANE, SIR LOUIS WILLIAM (1856-   )

I.C.S. : born March 21, 1856 : son of Richard Martin Dane, M.D., C.B. : arrived in India, 1876 : served in the Panjab : Private Secretary to the Lieutenant-Governor, 1879-82 : Officiating Registrar of the Chief Court, 1886 : Settlement Officer, Gurdaspur, 1887 : Deputy Commissioner, Peshawar, 1892 : Chief Secretary to the Panjab Government, 1898: Resident in Kashmir, 1901 : Foreign Secretary to the Government of India, 1903 : C.S.I., 1904 : Head of the Mission to Kabul, 1904-5, to negotiate a Treaty with the Amir of Afghanistan : made K.C.I.E. on his return.

DANIELL, THOMAS (1749-1840)

Painter : son of an innkeeper : born in 1749 : was in India painting for ten years, from 1784, with his nephew William (*q.v.*), and published his pictures : brought out their *Oriental Scenery* in 1808 : Royal Academician in 1799 : F.R.S., F.R.A.S., and F.S.A.: exhibited his pictures at the Academy and at the British Institute : published other collections of pictures : died March 19, 1840.

DANIELL, WILLIAM (? -1837)

Artist, R.A : at 14 accompanied his uncle, Thomas Daniell (*q.v.*), also an artist, to India : in 10 years they travelled many thousand miles, from Cape Comorin to Srinagar, and on their return published *Oriental Scenery*, in 6 volumes, completed in 1808. He exhibited largely at the Academy and the British Institute : published also *A Picturesque Voyage to India*, *Zoography*, *The Panorama of Madras*, 1832, the *City of Lucknow*, and the *Oriental Annual*, besides other pictures of British scenery. He was made a Royal Academician in 1822 : died Aug. 16, 1837.

DANVERS, FREDERICK CHARLES
(? -)

Educated at Merchant Taylors' School and King's College, London : joined the East India House as a writer, 1853 : and the India Office, 1858 : Registrar and Superintendent of Records, 1884 : deputed to Lisbon, 1891–2, to examine the Portuguese records relating to India, and to the Hague, 1893–4 : wrote extensively on Indian questions, including public works, famines, coal, statistics, agriculture, on *Chiefs, Agents, and Governors of Bengal*, 1888 : *The India Office Records*, 1889 : on the Portuguese records and *A History of the Portuguese in India*, 1894.

DANVERS, SIR JULAND (1826–1902)

Born March 19, 1826 : son of Frederick Dawes Danvers : educated at King's College, London : entered the E.I. Co.'s home service, 1842 : Private Secretary to two Chairmen of the Court, 1848–53 : on the transfer of India to the Crown, Danvers became, at the India Office, Secretary in the Railway and Telegraph Department, and Deputy Director of Indian Railways, 1858–61 : Government Director of Indian Railways, 1861–92 : Secretary in the Public Works, Railway and Telegraph Departments, 1880–92 : visited India, 1875–6 : wrote the annual official reports on Indian railways presented to Parliament, 1859–82 : was constantly examined before Parliamentary Committees on Railway and Finance questions : K.C.S.I., 1886 : retired 1892 : died Oct. 18, 1902.

DARBHANGA, MAHARAJA BAHADUR SIR LACHMESWAR SINGH, OF (1856–1898)

Elder son of Maharaja Maheswar Singh of Darbhanga : born 1856 : educated by an English tutor, Chester Macnaghten (*q.v.*) : occupied, as head of the Maithili Brahmins, a Hindu of Hindus, and the possessor of very large estates in Bihar, a very important position in Bihar and Bengal : sincerely devoted to religion : largely directed the management of his property and effected great improvements : made Maharaja Bahadur and K.C.I.E. : a Member of both the Legislative Councils of Bengal and the Governor-General : contributed handsomely to all objects of charity, medical aid, educational endowments and objects of general public utility : as President of the British Indian and other Landowners' Associations, his influence was chiefly felt in questions affecting landed property : died Dec. 17, 1898.

DARBHANGA, MAHARAJA BAHADUR SIR RAMESWAR SINGH OF
(1860 –)

Born Jan. 16, 1860 : younger son of Maharaja Maheswar Singh : educated at the Queen's College, Benares, and at home by Chester Macnaghten (*q.v.*) : in 1878 was appointed by Lord Lytton to the Statutory Civil Service : served as Assistant Magistrate of Darbhanga, Chapra and Bhagalpur : resigned in 1885 : was created Raja Bahadur, of Bachaur : in 1888 was appointed a Member of the Bengal Legislative Council, as representative of the landowners of Bengal and Bihar : succeeded to the Darbhanga Raj on the death of his elder brother, Maharaja Sir Lachmeswar Singh, on Dec. 17, 1898 : made Maharaja Bahadur : in 1899 and 1904 was elected by the non-official members of the Bengal Legislative Council as their representative in the Governor-General's Legislative Council : President of several Landowners' Associations : Kaisar-i-Hind Gold Medal, 1900 : in 1902 made K.C.I.E., and appointed a member of the Police Commission.

DARMESTETER, JAMES (1849–1894)

Born March 28, 1849, in Alsace, of a poor Jewish family : son of Cerf, and brother of Arsène, Darmesteter : delicate, puny, and almost deformed : educated at the Lycée Condorcet, Paris : Doctor in Letters, 1877 : devoted himself to Oriental scholarship and literature : became the greatest authority of his time on Zoroastrian literature : appointed Assistant-Professor of Zend at the Ecole des Hautes Études, 1877 : and in 1892, Director : was appointed Professor of Persian at the Collège de France, 1885, and Secretary of the Société Asiatique : wrote *Études Iraniennes*, 1883, and on the language and literature of ancient Persia : travelled in India, to study his subjects locally : residing there, Feb. 1886—Feb. 1887, chiefly at Bombay, Peshawar and Hazara : wrote *Letters sur l'Inde*, 1888, *The Popular Songs of the Afghans*, with an introduction on their language, history and literature, 1890 ; a complete translation, 1892–3, of the Zendavesta, published in the *Sacred Books of the East* : and *Selected*

Essays, published 1895 : was an Editor of the *Revue Critique*, and, later, of the *Revue de Paris* : wrote in them, and in the *Journal des Débats*, critical notices of books and Oriental essays : wrote on the mythology of the Avesta, 1875 : *Ormuzd et Ahriman*, 1877 : *Essais Orientaux*, 1883 : also on the *History of the Jewish People*, in the *Nouvelle Revue* : and the *Prophets of Israel*, 1892 : died at Maisons-Lafitte, Oct. 19, 1894.

DAS, SARAT CHANDRA, RAI BAHA-DUR (1849-)

Born July 18, 1849 : educated at Chittagong and the Calcutta Presidency College : and in that College's Engineering Department : in 1874 was appointed Head Master of the Bhutia boarding school at Darjeeling : began to study Tibetan from Lama Ugyen Gyatso, a teacher there : in 1878 the latter, on a visit to Tashi Lhumpo (Teshu Lumbo) in Tibet, obtained an invitation and passport for Sarat Chandra to visit Lhasa : in June, 1879, they started together to visit Lhasa with a servant : returned after six months from Tashi Lhumpo to Darjeeling : in Nov. 1881, they again went to Tashi Lhumpo, and on to Lhasa : wrote his *Narrative of a Journey to Lhasa*, and *Narrative of a Journey round Lake Palti (Yamdok), and in Lhokha, Yarlung and Sakya* : in 1884 Sarat accompanied Colman Macaulay (*q.v.*) to the Lachen Valley in Sikhim, and in 1885 went with him to Pekin : made C.I.E., Jan. 1886 : received a reward from the Royal Geographial Society, 1887 : founded the Buddhist Text Book Society, 1892 : made Rai Bahadur, 1896 : the Royal Geographical Society published *His Travels in Tibet*, in 1899 : completed his *Tibetan-English Dictionary* in 1902 : from Sep. 1881 served the Government of Bengal as Tibetan translator : retired from service July, 1904 : engaged in compiling a Sanskrit-English dictionary.

DAUD SHAH (? -1897)

Of the Lahkan Kheyl, a branch of a tribe of the Ghilzais : at the age of 20 he joined the Army of Amir Dost Muhammad Khan and became Akbar Khan's orderly officer. Shir Ali made him captain for services rendered at the battle of Kajhbaz on June 6, 1865, in which Sirdar Muhammad Ali Khan, eldest son of Shir Ali, was killed. Daud Shah showed great bravery during a campaign at Khost and was raised to the rank of General : he defeated Abdur Rahman's forces in Turkistan, and settled the country in Shir Ali's name, but, having quarrelled with General Muhammad Alam, he was recalled to Kabul and imprisoned by Shir Ali. Soon released, he acted as Commander-in-Chief when Yakub Khan rebelled against his father Shir Ali, and when General Faramurz Khan, commanding the Amir's forces, was killed by Aslam Khan, son of Amir Dost Muhammad. Upon Yakub's second rebellion, an army was sent to Herat in which Daud Shah was given a command, but Shir Ali, finding no General at Kabul, recalled him and entrusted him with all army affairs at the capital. In Jan. 1879, when Shir Ali fled to Turkistan, after the capture of Ali Masjid and the Peiwar Kotal by the British troops, Daud Shah was left at Kabul with Yakub Khan and accompanied him to meet Sir S. Browne at Gandamak. He was Yakub's Commander-in-Chief at the time of the massacre of Sir Louis Cavagnari in Sep. 1879, and Yakub's flight to the British camp. During Sir F. Roberts' tenure of Sherpur, at Kabul, Daud Shah was arrested about Dec. 18, 1879, and deported to India : died at Rawul Pindi, Dec. 25, 1897.

DAVIDS, T. W. RHYS (1843-)

LL.D., Ph.D. : born May 12, 1843 : son of Rev. T. W. Davids : educated at Brighton School and Breslau University : entered Ceylon Civil Service, 1866 : barrister, Middle Temple, 1877 : delivered Hibbert Lectures, 1881 : author of *Buddhism*, 1878 ; *Buddhism, its History and Literature*, 1896 : *Buddhist India*, 1902, and numerous other works connected with Buddhist Texts, etc. : Secretary and Librarian, Royal Asiatic Society : Professor of Pali and Buddhist Literature, University College, London.

DAVIDSON, ARTHUR (? -)

Colonel : son of W. Davidson : educated privately at Petersham : joined the 60th Rifles, 1876 : served in Afghan war, 1878–80 : at Kandahar and Ahmad Kheyl : A.D.C. to Sir Donald Stewart at Kabul : A.D.C. to Sir John Ross in Sir F.

Roberts' march from Kabul to Kandahar and the battle there: served in Marri expedition under General Macgregor : in Boer war with Natal Field Force, 1881, and in Egyptian war, 1882 : present at Tel-el-Kebir : served under Sir Charles Warren in Bechuanaland, 1884 : A.D.C. to H.R.H. The Duke of Cambridge, 1890–5 : Equerry in Waiting to Queen Victoria, 1896–1901, and to the King : C.B. in 1902 : C.V.O.

DAVIDSON, CUTHBERT (1810–1862)

Colonel : born May 24, 1810 : son of Sir David Davidson : educated privately and at Edinburgh : went to India as a military cadet, 1826 : joined the 16th N.I. : A.D.C. to Lord W. Bentinck in Madras : in 1836, joined Sir R. Grant's Staff, when Governor of Bombay : commanded a regiment of the Nizam's cavalry : first Assistant at Hyderabad under General Low and General Fraser : Resident at Baroda for 3 years : Resident at Hyderabad, 1857–62 : helped to bring Sir Salar Jang into office as Prime Minister : in the formidable attack on the Residency, July 17, 1857 : his life was attempted in the Nizam's Darbar, March 15, 1859 : C.B. after the mutiny : distinguished for his courage, composure and resolution : died Aug. 2, 1862.

DAVIDSON, JOHN (1845–   )

Colonel : son of Alexander Davidson, M.D. : born 1845 : educated at Winchester : entered the Army, 1863 : joined the Panjab Cavalry, 1866 : A.A.G. Panjab Frontier Force, 1875 : served in the Jowaki-Afridi expedition, 1877–8 : D.A.Q.M.G., Afghan campaign, 1878–9 : A.Q.M.G., Waziri expedition, 1880 : Military Secretary, Panjab Government, 1885–6 : Colonel on Staff, Chitral, 1896–8 : C.B. : Author of Notes on Bashgali-Kafir Language, 1902.

DAVIES, THOMAS ARTHUR HARK-NESS (1857–   )

Born Nov. 29, 1857 : son of Maj-General Horatio Nelson Davies : educated at Wellington College : joined the Devon Regt., 1876 : served as D.A.A.G. in Burma, 1894–7 : in the Afghan war, 1880 : the Wuntho expedition in Burma, 1892 : commanded the Kachen Hills expedition in Burma, 1893 : in the Tirah expedition, 1897, and in the South African war, 1899–

1902, including relief of Ladysmith : Brevet Lt-Colonel, and D.S.O.

DAVIES, SIR ROBERT HENRY (1824–1902)

I.C.S. : son of Sir David Davies, K.C.H., Physician to William IV : educated at Charterhouse and Haileybury, 1841-3 : went to the N.W.P. in the Civil Service, 1844 : in the mutiny, served with the troops in the Benares Division : was besieged at Azimghar, while Magistrate : was in the pursuit of Kooer Singh : Secretary to the Panjab Government, 1859: Financial Commissioner in Oudh, 1864 : Chief Commissioner of Oudh, 1865–71 : Lieutenant-Governor of the Panjab, Jan., 1871, to April, 1877 : K.C.S.I. 1874 : C.I.E. 1877 : Member of the Council of India, March, 1885–95 : died Aug. 23, 1902.

DAVIES, SIR WILLIAM GEORGE (1828–1898)

Maj-General : son of Dr. S. Davies : educated at London University College School : entered the Bengal Army, 1839 : served on the Peshawar frontier under Sir Colin Campbell : appointed Assistant Commissioner in the Panjab : Financial Commissioner, 1883 : Member of the Governor-General's Legislative Council : as Commissioner of Delhi was President of the Executive Committee of the Imperial Assemblage, 1877 : C.S.I. : retired, 1887 : K.C.S.I. : died June 12, 1898.

DAVIS, GEORGE M'BRIDE (1846–   )

Born March 29, 1846 : son of Dr. W. A. Davis : educated at Queen's College, Belfast : entered Bengal Medical Service, 1869, and became Surgeon-Colonel, 1897 : served in Mahsud-Waziri expedition, 1881 : Miranzai expedition, 1891 : Hazara expedition, 1891 : as P.M.O. in Waziristan expedition, 1894–5 : as P.M.O. in Tirah expedition, 1897–8 : was present at Dargai : in China expedition, 1901 : C.B. in 1898, and D.S.O., 1895 : is Principal Medical Officer, Panjab Frontier Force.

DAVIS, SAMUEL (1760–1819)

Went to Bengal as an officer of Engineers : was an excellent artist : accompanied Turner's Embassy to Tibet in 1783, but he himself did not advance beyond Bhutan : he was afterwards admitted to the E.I. Co.'s civil service : was District Judge and Agent to the Governor-General at Benares and had an observatory there : as a mathematician and astronomer, he identified astronomical references in Sanskrit works. When Wazir Ali, the deposed Nawab of Oudh, revolted in Jan., 1799, and murdered Mr. Cherry, then the Governor-General's Agent, he afterwards, with a crowd of followers, attacked Davis, who, on Jan. 14, 1799, successfully defended himself and his family, standing at the top of a staircase, pike in hand, until rescued by British troopers. Davis became a Director of the E. I. Co., from 1810 to 1819, and wrote the well-known *Fifth Report* on the Permanent Settlement : F.R.S. : died June 16, 1819.

DAVISON, SIR HENRY (? -1860)

Was a Puisne Judge of the Supreme Court, Madras, Dec. 1856 : succeeded Sir W. Yardley as Chief Justice, Bombay, in April, 1858 : transferred in April–May, 1859, to be Chief Justice, Madras, in succession to Sir C. Rawlinson : died at Ootacamund, Nov. 3 or 4, 1860.

DAWKINS, SIR CLINTON EDWARD (1859–)

Born 1859 : son of C. G. A. Dawkins of the Foreign Office: educated at Cheltenham and Balliol College, Oxford : entered the India Office, 1884 : Private Secretary to Lord Cross, Secretary of State, 1886, and to Mr. Goschen, Chancellor of Exchequer, 1889 : Under Secretary of State for Finance in Egypt, 1895 : Financial Member of the Supreme Council in India, 1899–1900 : Partner in Messrs. J. S. Morgan & Co. : author of *Appendix to Milner's England in Egypt* : C.B. in 1901, and K.C.B., 1902.

DAY, FRANCIS (1829–1889)

Son of William Day : born March 2, 1829 : educated at Shrewsbury and St. George's Hospital, London : joined the E.I. Co.'s Medical Service at Madras, 1852 : served in the Burmese war of 1852–54 : Surgeon-Major in 1872 : Deputy Surgeon-General in 1876, when he retired. An eminent naturalist : Ichthyology was the real work of his life : he investigated, for Government, the condition of Indian

fisheries : his last appointment was as Inspr-General of Fisheries in India, where he was recognized as the chief authority on Indian fishes and pisciculture. After his retirement, he pursued his studies in the same subject, gaining medals at several exhibitions between 1875 and 1883. He was made C.I.E. in 1885 : LL.D. of Edinburgh in 1889 : F.Z.S., and F.L.S. : was Indian Commissioner at the Fisheries Exhibition, 1883. Collections made by him are at Calcutta, Cambridge, London, etc. He wrote extensively on Fish and Fisheries, in separate works and in contributions to the Journals of learned Societies : wrote *The Fishes of India, The Fishes of Malabar, The British and Irish Salmonidæ, The Fishes of the Andaman and Nicobar Islands, The Fishes of the Nilgiri Hills and Wynaad, The Fishes of Great Britain and Ireland :* also, *The Land of the Perumals,* 1863 : *Tropical Fevers,* etc. : died July 10, 1889.

DE, REV. LAL BEHARI (1826–1894)

Educated at the General Assembly's Institution, under the Rev. Dr. Duff : at 17 was converted to Christianity : in 1851 authorized to preach, and ordained in 1855 : in 1857 he gave up preaching, and entered the Bengal Educational Department : spent most of his career at Hughli as Professor of History and English Literature : he retired in his 63rd year : died about Oct., 1894 : he wrote against Vedantism and the preaching of Keshab Chandra Sen (*q.v.*), and conducted a Journal to diffuse Christianity. His novel, *Gobinda Samanta,* a tale of peasant life in Bengal, and other writings, attracted considerable attention : wrote also *Reminiscences of Dr. Duff,* 1879.

DEALTRY, THE RIGHT REV. THOMAS, D.D. (1796–1861)

Bishop : born of poor parents in Yorkshire in 1796 : went up to St. Catherine's Hall, Cambridge, as a pensioner in 1825 : first class in the Law Class List, 1827–8 : LL.B. in 1829 : after being ordained, was a curate at Cambridge and came under the influence of the Rev. C. Simeon, who obtained for him a chaplaincy in the Bengal Establishment. Reaching Calcutta in 1829, he was appointed to the old Mission church, and remained in charge of it till 1835, when he was made Archdeacon

I

of Calcutta: held the post till his departure to England in 1848. He was there offered the Bishopric of Madras, was consecrated, became D.D., and returned to Madras as Bishop in Feb., 1850. In the latter years of Bishop Wilson, who died 1858, Dealtry did much of his touring and visitation work in Upper India : was an active and liberal supporter of Missions and Missionaries : died March 4, 1861.

DEANE, HAROLD ARTHUR (1854–)

Lt-Colonel : born April 1, 1854 : son of Rev. Henry Deane : educated at Ipswich Grammar School : entered the English Army, 1874, and the Indian Staff Corps, 1877 : served in the Afghan war, 1879–80 : District Superintendent of Police, Andamans, 1880–5 : entered the Panjab Commission and served as Assistant and Deputy Commissioner till 1895 : Chief Political Officer with Chitral Relief Force : Political Agent at Malakand : Political Resident in Kashmir, 1900–1 : Chief Commissioner and Agent to the Governor-General, N.W. Frontier Province, 1901 : C.S.I., 1896.

DEANE, THOMAS (1841–)

Colonel : born May 12, 1841 : son of Sir Thomas Deane : educated privately : joined the Indian Army, 1862, in Madras Cavalry : attached to 21st Hussars, 1863–9 : Viceroy's Bodyguard, 1869 : Military Secretariat, Government of India, 1877 : Staff Officer to the Controller General, Supply and Transport, Afghan war, 1879 : Director Army Remount Department, 1887–8 : and again 1889–98 : on special service in S. Africa, 1900–1 : Agent in England for Government of India Army Studs : C.B. in 1897.

DEASY, HENRY HUGH PETER (1866–)

Born 1866 : son of Right Hon. Richard Deasy, Lord Justice of Appeal (Ireland) : educated at Bournemouth and Dublin : joined the 16th Lancers, 1888, and resigned his commission, 1897 : explored Western Tibet, 1896 : received the Founders' Gold Medal from the Royal Geographical Society for exploring and survey work in Central Asia for nearly three years : created a record in motoring, by driving 450 miles in 21 hours : author of *In Tibet and Chinese Turkistan*, 1901.

DEB, RAJA BINAYA KRISHNA (1866–)

Of the Sovabazar Raj family (Kaisthya): great-grandson of Maharaja Naba Krishna Bahadur (of the time of Clive and Warren Hastings) : and son of Maharaja Komul Krishna Deb, landowner in the Tippera district : born Aug. 15, 1866 : educated privately : holds various honorary appointments in Calcutta, Municipal Commissioner, Member of the District Board, 24 Parganas, Governor of the Mayo Hospital, etc. : made a Raja in 1895 for loyal services : given the silver Kaisar-i-Hind medal, 1902 : has founded and maintains a number of schools, dispensaries and other charitable institutions : promoted philanthropic objects and sporting clubs : has written *Agra Reflections* and the *Early History and Growth of Calcutta*, and had a memoir written of Maharaja Naba Krishna : has initiated the Hindu sea-voyage movement, founded the Sovabazar Benevolent Society, and encouraged literary institutions and journalistic enterprises.

DEB, RAJA BAHADUR KALI KRISHNA (1808–1874)

Second son of Raja Raj Krishna of Sovabazar, and grandson of Raja Naba Krishna, the *Diwan* of Lord Clive: was made Raja Bahadur in 1833 : from 1867 was the leader of Hindu Society and in the van of all movements on behalf of the native community : Fellow of the Calcutta University : J.P. : and Vice-President of the British Indian Association : sincerely advocated female education : died at Benares on April 11, 1874.

DEB, MAHARAJA BAHADUR, SIR NARENDRA KRISHNA (1822–1903)

Born Oct. 10, 1822 : son of Raja Raj Krishna Bahadur, and grandson of Maharaja Naba Krishna Bahadur, of the Sovabazar family : educated at the Hindu College : was, for a short time, in Government service : was a Municipal Commissioner of Calcutta, and Justice of the Peace : Honorary Magistrate : several times President and Vice-President of the British Indian Association : Fellow of the Calcutta University : made Raja, 1875 : Member of the Governor-General's Legislative Council : Maharaja, 1877 : and K.C.I.E., in 1888 : Maharaja Bahadur,

1892 : held a number of minor honorary offices : died March 20, 1903.

DEB, SIR RADHA KANTA, RAJA BAHADUR (1784–1867)

Born in Calcutta, March 11, 1784, son of RajaGopi Mohan Deb,and great grandson of Munshi, afterwards Maharaja, Naba Krishna Deb, Persian Secretary and *Diwan* to Lord Clive : received his English education at Cumming's Calcutta Academy : studied Sanskrit, Arabic, Persian : his life was devoted to cultivating and disseminating knowledge : was the first modern Hindu to advocate home female education, zealously established native schools, and compiled in 36 years a comprehensive Sanskrit dictionary, which was acknowledged by learned European Societies, and by Queen Victoria with a medal. In religion he was rigidly conservative and strictly orthodox, while devoted to the cause of education : wrote a Bengali reader. He was a Director of the Hindu College : Secretary of the School-book Society, established in 1818 : prominently connected with the Government Sanskrit College, and the Bengal Asiatic Society: Honorary Magistrate and Justice of the Peace for Calcutta in 1855 : President of the British Indian Association from 1851 until his death at Brindaban on April 19, 1867 : Raja Bahadur on July 10, 1837, and K.C.S.I. in 1866 : was an active supporter of all public movements.

DE BOIGNE, BENOIT, COUNT (1751–1830)

A Savoyard: born at Chambery on March 8, 1751 : entered the French Army at 17: left it in 5 years for the Russian service, and was taken prisoner at Tenedos. Being released, he, travelling *viâ* Alexandria, Cairo, and Suez, joined the 6th Madras N.I. in the E.'I. Co.'s service in 1778, at Madras. Fancying himself neglected, he resigned, and, abandoning his intention of making a journey overland to Europe, joined Madhava Rao Sindia, who made great use of him to train his troops and loaded him with wealth. He left Sindia in 1789, and entered into trade, but rejoined Sindia in 1790 with greater powers, and on higher terms : won for him the battles of Patan, June 20, 1790, and Merta in Sep. 1790, defeating mixed forces of Pathans, Rajputs, Moguls, etc. He became C. in C. of Sindia's army, and, during Sindia's absence in the Dekkan, defeated Holkar at Lakhairi in Sep. 1793. On Sindia's death, in 1794, De Boigne continued to serve his successor, Daulat Rao Sindia. He resigned his command in Dec. 1795, on account of ill-health. He had a house at Alighar from 1783 until he left India in Sep. 1796. He lived at first near London, and then went to Paris. It was alleged that he advised and assisted Napoleon Bonaparte in his designs against the English in India. This has been completely contradicted by his grandson : De Boigne during his career in India maintained friendly relations with the E. I. Co. In 1803, he settled at Buisson, at Chambery, applying his wealth to benevolent and patriotic purposes, to which he gave 3,678,000 francs. Honours were heaped upon him : he was held in the greatest respect. He died June 21, 1830, leaving 20 millions of francs.

DE BRATH ERNEST, (1858–   )

Born Dec. 12, 1858 : son of Felix de Brath : educated privately : joined the Buffs, 1876, and the Indian Staff Corps, 1879 : served in the Afghan war, 1879–80 : Mahsud-Waziri expedition, 1881 : Hazara expedition, 1891 ; Dongola expedition, 1896, as Brig-Major at Suakin : Brevet-Lt-Colonel : Colonel, 1899 : in the Military Secretariat since 1892 : Secretary Military Department, Government of India, since 1902 : C.I.E. in 1903 : Maj-General : C.B.

DELAFOSSE, HENRY GEORGE (1835–1905)

Son of Major Henry Delafosse, C.B. : born 1835 : educated at Addiscombe : entered the Army, 1854, and became a Maj-General, 1887 : served in Indian mutiny : was at Cawnpur, as Lieutenant in the 53rd N.I. : and served with the Artillery in the siege there : on June 22, 1857,showed great bravery in extinguishing the flames of a burning ammunition wagon, which was under severe fire : and was one of the four men who escaped in a boat from the massacre of Europeans at the Sati Chaura Ghat on June 27, 1857 : in Havelock's relief of Lucknow, and the retaking of Cawnpur : in the Sikhim expedition, 1861 : in the Umbeyla campaign, 1863 : C.B., 1887 : retired, 1887 : died Feb. 10, 1905.

DE LAUNEY, EUSTACE BENEDICT
(1715-1777)

A Flemish soldier of fortune, in the service of Martanda Varma of Travancore : he built the Travancore lines which were captured by Tippoo in 1790 : also the fort of Udayagiri, 38 miles S.E. of Trivandrum : remembered among the natives as Istach (Eustache),the Valiya Kappithan, or great captain : died 1777, buried at Udayagiri.

DE MEURON, CHARLES DANIELL
(1738-1806)

Maj-General : son of Theodore de Meuron, justicier : born May 6, 1738 : at 17 fought in a body of Swiss Marines for the French, against the English at Rochefort : in 1757, on the *Florissant* nearly escaped capture by the English : joined the Swiss Guards, 1763 : Captain and Colonel, 1768 : as proprietary colonel raised in 1781 the Neuchatel regiment de Meuron, 1,020 strong, for the Dutch E.I. Co. : reached the Cape, Jan. 1782 : sent on to Ceylon to reinforce Suffrein : to Cuddalore, June 1783 : returned to Ceylon and the Cape, and again Ceylon, where he, then Colonel, left the regiment, of which the Commanding Officer was his brother Pierre Frederich (*q.v.*) : in 1795, C. D. de Meuron after prolonged negotiations ceded the regiment to England : the transfer was ratified at Madras, 1797 : de Meuron went to England, 1797, and was occupied in recruiting, and in the negotiations for completing the transfer, 1798 : was made a British Maj-General : retired : died at Neuchatel April 6, 1806.

DE MEURON, PIERRE FREDRICH
(1746-1813)

Brother of C. D. (*q.v.*) : born 1746 : commanded the regiment de Meuron under the Dutch in Ceylon : when the English invaded Ceylon in August, 1795, several detachments of the regiment were defeated : that under P. F. de Meuron held out : on its cession to England, in 1795, it embarked for Tuticorin : where de Meuron was made, by Lord Hobart, Military Governor of Ceylon, 1797-8 : commanded the troops there till 1799 : then commanded at Vellore, and Arnee, while the regiment was in the Mysore campaign of 1799 : took the regiment from Vellore to Madras, 1801, and left for London : he retired,

1807, settled at Neuchatel, died there, March 30, 1813 : the regiment was disbanded in 1816, after 14 years' service under the Dutch, 21 years' under the English.

DEMPSTER, FRANCIS ERSKINE
(1858-   )

Born July 9, 1858 : son of Capt. H. L. Dempster : educated at Edinburgh Academy, the Institution and University, and at Cooper's Hill College : joined the Indian Telegraph Department, 1878 : served in the Afghan war, 1879-80 : Chin-Lushai expedition, 1889 : Chitral expedition, 1895 : C.I.E. 1896 : Superintendent of the Indian Government Telegraphs.

DENING, LEWIS (1848-   )

Entered the Army, 1867, and became Lt-Colonel, 1893 : served in Afghan war, 1878-9 : Burmese expedition, 1886-88 : Dongola expedition, 1896, and N.W. Frontier, 1897 : D.S.O. 1887, and C.B. 1903 : Colonel on Staff, commanding 2nd Class District in India since 1903.

DENISON, SIR WILLIAM THOMAS
(1804-1871)

Governor, and Colonel : son of. John Denison : born May 3, 1804 : educated at Sunbury, Eton, and the R.M.A., Woolwich : joined the R.E. in 1826 : made the Rideau Canal in Canada, 1827-31 : employed at Woolwich, Chatham, on inspection at Bermuda till 1847, when, as Captain R.E. he went to Van Diemen's Land as Lieutenant-Governor, and was knighted. From 1854 to 1861 he was Governor of New South Wales and titular Governor-General of Australia : K.C.B., 1856 : Governor of Madras from Feb. 1861 : held strong views on military questions, and did not conceal his unfavourable estimate of the character of the natives of India : was opposed to their admission into the Legislative Councils and to the establishment of subordinate Legislative Councils at all : his previous experience made him an authority on public works, roads, railways, etc. While Governor of Madras he was summoned to Calcutta on Lord Elgin's death and acted as Viceroy and Governor-General from Dec. 2, 1863, until Sir John Lawrence assumed charge on Jan. 12, 1864. During this time, he arranged for the continuation of the Umbeyla campaign against the Sitana stronghold of Hindustani fanatics,considering that a retirement from the expedition would be unwise : went home from Madras in March, 1866 : died Jan. 19, 1871 : wrote *Varieties of Viceregal Life* and essays on social and educational subjects.

DENNEHY, SIR THOMAS (1829–)

Served in Sonthal campaign, 1855–6 ; Indian mutiny, 1857–8 : Political Agent, Dholpur, Rajputana, 1879–85 : extra Groom in Waiting to Queen Victoria, 1888, and to H.M. the King, 1901 : K.C.I.E., 1896.

DENNIE, WILLIAM HENRY (1785 ?– 1842)

Born about 1785 : son of Henry Dennie : joined the 22nd regt., 1802, in India : served in Lord Lake's campaigns, 1804–5 : at the taking of the Mauritius, 1810 : in the 13th regt. in the first Burmese war : Brevet-Lt-Colonel : C.B.: in the Afghan war, 1838–9 : commanded a Brigade : led the storming party at Ghazni : to Kabul : defeated part of Dost Muhammad's army at Bameean, Sep. 18, 1840 : after which the Dost surrendered : went with Sir R. Sale's force from Kabul to Jalalabad, 1841 : in the siege there, Nov. 1841–April 1842 : commanded after Sale was wounded : was fatally wounded in a sortie on April 6, 1842 : was A.D.C. to the Queen : his services inadequately recognized : wrote a *Narrative of Campaigns in Sind, Beluchistan, and Afghanistan*, published 1843.

DEPELCHIN, FATHER HENRY, S.J. (1822–1900)

Born at Russeignies, in Belgium, Jan. 28, 1822 : entered the Society of Jesus, 1842 : educated at Belgium Colleges for 5 years : ordained : took his last vows, Oct. 1859 : reached Calcutta, Nov. 1859, with a small pioneer Jesuit mission and reopened St. Xavier's College, Jan. 16, 1860 : was military chaplain at Fort William, 1860–4 : when he returned to St. Xavier's : as Superior, raised the number of pupils from 100 to 500 : resigned the Rectorship of St. Xavier's, Oct. 1871 : went to take charge of the Mission at Midnapur, but was transferred

to Bombay, managing for 6 years a new St. Xavier's there : to Belgium : thence led the "Zambesi" Jesuit Mission to S. Africa, 1879 : crushed in an accident, 1882 : to Belgium, 1883 : returned to India, Jan. 1888, to be the Rector of St. Joseph's Seminary at Darjeeling : erected the St. Joseph's College at North Point there, and was its Superior till his death, May 26, 1900.

DERBY, EDWARD HENRY STANLEY, FIFTEENTH EARL OF (1826–1893)

Son of fourteenth Earl of Derby, thrice Prime Minister : born July, 1826 : educated at Rugby and Trinity College, Cambridge : M.P. for King's Lynn, 1848 : travelled widely in N. and S. America : visited India, 1851–2 : Under Secy. for the Colonies, 1852 : Secretary for the Colonies, 1858 : was in charge of the Bill for transferring in 1858 the Government of India from the E. I. Company to the Queen : Secretary of State for India from Sep. 2, 1858, to June 18, 1859 : made Foreign Secretary : became Earl in 1869 : again Foreign Secretary : resigned, March, 1878 : Colonial Secretary in Mr. Gladstone's Government : presided over Royal Commissions : died April 21, 1893.

DE RENZY, SIR ANNESLEY CHARLES CASTRIOT (1829–)

Born May 6, 1829 : son of Thomas De Renzy : educated at Trinity College, Dublin : entered the Bengal Medical Service, 1851 : present at the capture of Rangoon, 1852 : served in the mutiny, 1857–8 : siege and capture of Lucknow, 1858 : Naga campaign and capture of Khonoma, 1879, as P.M.O. : First Sanitary Commissioner of the Panjab : Surgeon-General : retired, 1882 : was made a K.C.B. 1902 : author of several Sanitary Reports.

DEROZIO, HENRY LOUIS VIVIAN (1809–1831)

Eurasian poet and teacher : born in Calcutta, April 10, 1809 : son of Francis Derozio, a Calcutta merchant : educated at Drummond's Academy in Dharmtala : left school at 14 for commercial work, which he gave up, joining an uncle in indigo at Bhagalpur. At 18 he published a volume of poems and obtained a teachership at the Hindu College : was very successful as a teacher of philosophy, but lost his appointment, though the charges against him, of propagating atheism and encouraging disobedience, failed : still continued to exercise great influence over his former pupils, many of whom became distinguished men : contributed to journalism and established a newspaper, the *East Indian*. His name is still revered in his community as a great teacher. He died of cholera, Dec. 23, 1831 : he wrote the *Fakir of Jungheera* and other poems.

DE SALIS, RODOLPH (1811–1880)

Lt.-General : son of Jerome, Count de Salis : born May, 1811 : entered the Army in 1830 : Lt-Colonel, 1854 : served with the 8th Hussars in Turkey and the Crimea, in all the battles : commanded the regt. in the mutiny, in Rajputana and Central India, present at Kotah, Chandairi, Kotahkasarai, Gwalior, Powri, and several other engagements : C.B., 1861 : Lt-General, 1877 : died March 13, 1880.

DE SOUZA, SIR WALTER EUGENE (1846–1897)

Son of Laurence de Souza : educated at Downside College, Somerset : Consul for Portugal at Calcutta, 1870–8, Consul General, 1878–84 : Member for Westminster on the London County Council, 1895 : very philanthropic and munificent in his benefactions to charities, for which he was knighted, 1879 : Count of the Roman Empire, and held other foreign distinctions : died April 13, 1897.

DEUSSEN, PAUL (1845–   )

Born Jan. 7, 1845, at Oberdreis near Coblenz : son of Adam Deussen, pastor : educated at Schulpforta near Naumburg : studied at Bonn, Tübingen and Berlin : Sanskrit under Lassen and Gildemeister, classical philology, theology : Phil. Dr. at Marburg, 1869 : teacher at the Gymnasiums at Minden and Marburg, 1869–72, and tutor in Russian families at Geneva, Aix-la-Chapelle, and Terny in Russia, 1872–80 : taught philosophy (the subject to which he was chiefly devoted) and Sanskrit, as Privat-docent at the University of Geneva : and philosophy at the Polytechnic School at Aix-la-Chapelle, 1875–9. While at Geneva, his resolution was made to devote his life to the study

of Indian philosophy (1873). Since his return from Russia, and residence in Berlin, from 1881 to 1889, this has been his main work : taught philosophy at Berlin University, first as Privat-docent, then as Professor : since 1889, Ordinary Professor of Philosophy at the University of Kiel : has travelled much in various parts of the world : over the greater part of India, 1892–3. In 1904, the Order of the Red Eagle, 4th Class, was conferred upon him. Among his chief works may be mentioned : *Das System des Vedânta*, 1883 : *Die Sutras des Vedanta*, 1887 : *On the Philosophy of the Vedanta in its relations to Occidental Metaphysics*, Bombay, 1893 ; *Sechzig Upanishads des Veda*, 1897 : *Geschichte der Philosophie* (I and II on the Vedic Hymns and Upanishads : III–VI in preparation), 1894, 1899 : " Outlines of Indian Philosophy," in the *Indian Antiquary*, 1902 : *Erinnerungen an Indien*, 1904.

DEVIS, ARTHUR WILLIAM (1763–1822)

Son of an artist : born Aug. 10, 1763 : at the age of 20 appointed by the E. I. Co. draughtsman to an expedition : wrecked in the *Antelope* : went to Macao and Canton, and arrived in Calcutta about 1791 : returned to England, 1795 : painted a picture of " Cornwallis receiving the two sons of Tippoo Sahib as Hostages " for the treaty of 1792 : painted 30 pictures of Indian subjects : also the death of Nelson in the *Victory* : exhibited 65 pictures in the Academy, 1779–1821 : died Feb. 11, 1822.

DEVONSHIRE, SPENCER COMPTON CAVENDISH, EIGHTH DUKE OF (1833–   )

Born July 23, 1833 : succeeded his father in the title, 1891 : educated at Trinity College, Cambridge : M.P from 1857 : held a number of appointments in the Governments since 1862 : as Marquis of Hartington was Secretary of State for India from April, 1880, to Dec. 1882 : K.G. : P.C. : D.C.L. : LL.D.

DEY, RAJ KRISHNA (? –1840)

Doctor : was the first Hindu who used a dissecting knife, and was regarded, therefore, as the leader of a reformation in medical science among his countrymen :

educated at the Hindu College, 1833–7, and at the Medical College, Calcutta, where he took his degree, 1838 : accepted service in the N.W.P., and placed in charge of the Delhi Dispensary, Aug., 1839 : died 1840.

DEY, RAM DULAL (1759–1825)

Born near Dum Dum, 1759 : employed in a subordinate capacity in mercantile work, as a bill-collector, and a *Sarkar* of ships : one day, on behalf of his master, he bid at an auction for a lost ship, and bought it for Rs. 14,000 : he immediately was offered one lakh more for the same ship : his master gave one lakh to Ram Dulal, who, with this capital, started business, and acquired immense wealth : died in Calcutta, in 1825, leaving property of fabulous amount : remembered as the Bengali millionaire.

DICK, GEORGE (1739–1818)

Entered the E. I. Co.'s service in 1759 : was Accountant and Director of the Company's Bank : rose to be the Governor of Bombay, 1792–5 : never left Bombay but once for a trip to Bankot : died May 9, 1818.

DICK, SIR ROBERT HENRY (1785–1846)

Born about 1785, his father being in the E.I.¹Co.'s medical service : entered the 75th regt. in 1800 : served in Sicily, Egypt, the Peninsula, being present at several battles : C.B., 1814 : in Flanders : at Waterloo : K.C.H. in 1832 : Maj-General, 1837 : K.C.B. in 1838 : commanded a Division in Madras, 1838, and acting C. in C. there, 1841–2 : commanded a Division in Bengal, and an infantry Division in the first Sikh war : was killed at Sobraon, Feb. 10, 1846, by one of the last shots of the day.

DICK-CUNYNGHAM, WILLIAM HENRY (1851–1900)

Lt-Colonel : son of Sir William Hanmer Dick-Cunyngham, *Bart.* : entered the 92nd Highlanders, 1872 : Lt-Colonel, 1897, in the Gordon Highlanders : in the Afghan war, 1879–80, in Sir Donald Stewart's advance to Kandahar : in the Thal Chotiali force : in the Kuram Valley Field Force under Sir F. Roberts : at Ali Khel : at Charasia : in the operations round Kabul, 1879 : gained the V.C. for

gallantry in an attack on Dec. 13, 1879 : in the Kabul-Kandahar march and subsequent battle : with his regt. in theBoer war : killed at Ladysmith, Jan. 6, 1900, while commanding the 2nd battalion.

DICKENS, WILLIAM POPHAM (1834–)

Colonel : born March 19, 1834 : son of Stephen Dickens, M.D., D.I.G. of Hospitals, Bengal : educated at Blundell's, Twerton, Charterhouse and Addiscombe : entered the Madras Army, 1853 : joined the Madras Staff Corps : Lt-Colonel, 1879 : Brevet-Colonel, 1883 : Colonel-Commandant, 3rd Madras L.I., 1884 : served in the Burmese expedition in command of the Toungoo and Ningyan (Pyinmana) column, 1885–7 : D.S.O., 1887 : C.B., 1891 : on the unemployed Supernumerary List.

DICKINSON, JOHN (1815–1876)

Born Dec. 28, 1815 : educated at Eton : son of a papermaker : entered no profession, but took up an independent line as a reformer of India : wrote letters on the cotton and roads of Western India, 1851 : became Honorary Secretary of the "Indian Reform Society," formed in 1853, and was made its Chairman on John Bright's resignation of that office in 1861 : maintained a correspondence with the Maharaja Holkar of Indore : wrote *India, its Government under a Bureaucracy*, in 1852, and *Dhar not restored*, in 1864, besides other pamphlets and papers on Indian subjects : died Nov. 23, 1876.

DIGBY, WILLIAM (1849–1904)

Son of William Digby : born May 1, 1849 : educated privately : became a journalist in 1868 in England : in Ceylon, 1871–6 : Editor of *Madras Times*, 1877–9 : wrote some interesting articles on old Madrasis : returned to England : became Secretary of National Liberal Club in 1887 : connected with the Indian National Congress : Editor of *India*, 1890–2 : Secretary of Famine Fund for Southern India, for which £800,000 were subscribed : contested two Parliamentary seats without success : author of *The Famine Campaign in Southern India*, 1876–8 ; *Indian Problems for English Consideration* ; *India for the Indians* ; *Prosperous British India*, 1901 ; *Life of Sir Arthur Cotton*, etc. etc. :

became a partner in Hutchinson & Co., East India Merchants, 1888 : C.I.E. for his honorary services in India in connexion with the Famine Relief Funds, 1877–9 : died Sep. 24, 1904.

DIKSHIT, PANDIT SANKARA BAL-KRISHNA (? –1898)

A member of the Bombay Educational Department, and a well-known contributor to the *Indian Antiquary* ; considered by archæologists as an authority on the astronomical and chronological systems of the Hindus : the verification of the dates in ancient Hindu records was his principal subject : was the first to point out the right method of studying the question : collaborated with R. Sewell (*q.v.*) in the preparation of the *Indian Calendar,* published in 1896 : died of fever, 1898 : an enthusiastic and disinterested worker, and a winning personality.

DILLON, GEORGE FREDERICK HORACE (? –   )

Entered the Indian Army, 1882 : served in Burma, 1886–7 : Lushai expedition, 1889 : Waziristan Field Force, 1894–5 : N.W. Frontier, 1897 : in the Buner Field Force : Commandant 26th Bengal Infantry : C.B., 1903.

DILLON, SIR MARTIN ANDREW (1826–   )

General : born 1826 : entered the Army, 1843 : served in Panjab, 1848–9 : Kohat Pass, 1850 : Crimea, 1856 : Indian mutiny, 1857–9 : China, 1860 : Abyssinia, 1867–8 : Brig-Major,Nipal Frontier : A.A.G., China: Military Secretary, Bombay : Military Secretary, Abyssinia : Military Secretary to Lord Napier of Magdala when C. in C., India : commanded the Lucknow and Rawul Pindi Divisions, 1884–8 : K.C.B., 1887 : and G.C.B., 1902 : C.S.I. and A.D.C. to the Queen.

DIXON, SIR HENRY GREY (1850–   )

Born Aug. 14, 1850 : son of Colonel John Dixon : educated at Bridgeman's and Woolwich : joined 25th regt., 1868 : served in the Afghan war, 1878–80 : Chitral, 1895 : C.B. : Tirah, 1897–8 : S. Africa, 1901–2 : K.C.B. : Brig-General on Staff : A.D.C. to H.M. the King, 1901.

DOBSON, GEORGE EDWARD (1848–1895)

Doctor and Zoologist : born Sep. 4, 1848 : son of Parke Dobson : educated at Enniskillen and Trinity College, Dublin, where he graduated with distinction : entered the A.M.D. in 1868 : was F.L.S. : F.R.S. : F.Z.S. : conducted investigations and became the chief author on chiroptera and insectivora : studied Indian bats, and wrote papers about them in the Journal of the Asiatic Society of Bengal, and other scientific journals : wrote a catalogue of chiroptera for the British Museum, and was in charge of the Museum at Netley : wrote also in the *Encyclopædia Britannica,* and on zoology and anatomy : retired in 1888 : died Nov. 26, 1895.

DODGSON, SIR DAVID SCOTT (1822–1898)

Son of the Rev. J. Dodgson : entered the Army, 1838 : in the Bengal Infantry : became General, 1888 : in the Jodhpur campaign, 1839 : in the Afghan war under General Pollock, 1842, from the Khyber to Kabul : in the Satlaj campaign, 1846, at Badiwal and Aliwal : Brig-Major at Benares when the native troops mutinied, June, 4, 1857 : A.A.G. with Havelock's force, at the first relief of Lucknow and subsequent defence, until Sir Colin Campbell's relief : in the occupation of the Alambagh and at the capture of Lucknow, 1858 : C.B. : K.C.B. 1896 : died May 26, 1898.

DODSON, REV. THOMAS HATHA-WAY (1862–

Born May 11, 1862 : son of George Dodson : educated at Merchant Taylors and Exeter College, Oxford : graduated in 1885 : ordained Deacon, 1885, and Priest, 1888 : Fellow and Tutor of St. Augustine's College, Canterbury, 1887–8 : went out in 1889 to be Principal of S.P.G. College, Trichinopoly, where he rebuilt the greater part of the College : Fellow of the Madras University, 1892 : retired, 1896, from ill-health : author of several pamphlets on missionary work.

D'OLDENBURG, SERGE (1863–   )

Born Sep. 14, 1863 : son of Theodore d'Oldenburg, General in the Russian Army: educated at the Warsaw Gymnasium, and at the Faculty of Oriental Languages,

St. Petersburg; where he was Private Docent of Sanskrit from 1889, and afterwards Professor till 1899: Member of the Imperial Academy of Sciences, 1900: Perpetual Secretary of the Academy, 1904: Cand. Faculty Oriental Languages, 1885: Mag. Sanskrit Literature, 1894: since 1898 Hon. Secy. of the Oriental Section of the Russian Imperial Archæological Society: Member of Council of the R.I. Geographical Society: Member of the Russian Committee for the Exploration of Central Asia: has written on Buddhism, Indian Art, Comparative Literature: edits the *Bibliotheca Buddhica* for the Imperial Academy.

DONALD, DOUGLAS (1865–   )

Born Nov. 19, 1865: son of C. J. S. Donald, Panjab Provincial Civil Service: educated at Bishop Cotton's School, Simla: joined the Panjab Police Force, 1888: appointed Commandant B.M. Police, Kohat, 1890: served under Sir William Lockhart in the Miranzai expedition, 1891: with Colonel Haughton, 36th Sikhs, during the attack on Samana posts, and subsequently in the Tirah Field Force: went to the Khyber, 1898, and to Kohat, 1899. Author of *Note on Adan Kheyl Afridis*: C.I.E., 1903.

DONKIN, SIR RUFANE SHAW (1773–1841)

Son of General Robert Donkin: born 1773: educated at Westminster: entered the Army in 1778: Lieutenant, 1779: Captain, 1793: served in the West Indies, at Copenhagen, in Sicily and the Peninsula, and, as Maj-General in 1811, went out in 1815 to Madras and Bengal, where he commanded a Division in the Mahratta war of 1817–8, with skill: K.C.B., 1818: acted as Governor of the Cape: he became G.C.H., F.R.S., F.R.G.S.: was M.P. for Berwick and for Sandwich: was Surveyor of the Ordnance: General, 1838: died May 1, 1841: was a student, and contributed literary papers to Journals.

DORAN, SIR JOHN (1824–1903)

Born Oct. 1, 1824: entered the Bengal Army, 1842: served in Satlaj campaign, 1845–6: Hazara expedition, 1852–3: Oudh campaign, 1858–9: China war, 1860: Lushai expedition, 1871–2: Jowaki-Afridi expedition, 1877–8: Afghan war,

1878–80: C.B. in 1872, and K.C.B. in 1898: Lt-General, 1887: died Sep. 29, 1903.

DORIN, JOSEPH ALEXANDER (1802–1872)

I.C.S.: son of a merchant: born Sep. 15, 1802: educated at Henley and Haileybury: reached India in 1821, and joined the Financial Department, in which he continued throughout his career, never leaving Calcutta: was Secretary to the Bank of Bengal, 1829: Deputy Accountant-General: and reorganized the Indian finances: the first Financial Secretary in Jan. 1843: Member of the Supreme Council from May 10, 1853, to May 1, 1858: partly under Dalhousie, partly under Canning. Against Lord Dalhousie's views, he, as President in Council, advocated the annexation of Oudh, which was carried out. In the mutiny, he urged the adoption of severe military measures, being one of the first to realize the character of the revolt. His "hospitable establishment" was remembered for many years. After retirement, his name was more than once considered for a seat in the Council of India, but he never obtained it: died Dec. 22, 1872.

DORMER, HON. SIR JAMES CHARLEMAGNE (1834–1893)

Lt-General: son of 11th Baron Dormer: born 1834: entered the 13th regt., 1853: in the Crimea: in the mutiny, at the relief of Azimghar, in the campaign in Gorakhpur: A.D.C. to Sir Colin Campbell: in Oudh and Trans-Gogra campaign: Brevet-Major: went to China in 1860 as A.A.G.: at the Taku forts and entry to Pekin: served on the Staff: Colonel, 1875: in Egypt in 1882, as D.A.G.: at Alexandria, Tel-el-Kebir, etc.: Maj-General: Nile expedition, 1885: commanded the Nile Field Force: and the troops in Egypt, 1887–90: C. in C. Madras, March 6, 1891: C.B., 1881: K.C.B., 1889: mauled by a tiger, and died from the wounds, May 3, 1893.

DORWARD, SIR ARTHUR ROBERT FORD (?   )

Entered the Royal Engineers, 1868: served in the Afghan war, 1878–80: Burmese expedition, 1885–8, when he was made Brevet-Major and D.S.O.:

commanded R.E. in Jamaica, 1897-9: commanded British troops in Chinese expedition, 1900, until arrival of Indian contingent : was present at action of Tientsin : Commissioner at Wei-hai-wei, 1899-1901 : commanded troops at Shanghai, 1902 : commanding troops Straits Settlements since 1903 : K.C.B. in 1900.

DOUGLAS, RIGHT REV. HENRY ALEXANDER, D.D. (1821-1875)

Born Feb. 22, 1821 : son of Henry Alexander Douglas, who was brother of the sixth Marquis of Queensberry : educated at Glasgow University and Balliol College, Oxford : ordained, after taking his degree, in 1845 : Dean of Capetown in 1845 : appointed Bishop of Bombay, 1868 : died in London, Dec. 13, 1875.

DOUGLAS, JAMES (1826-1904)

Born June 4, 1826 : son of William Douglas : educated at Sorbie Parish School and privately in Edinburgh : went to Karachi in 1864 as Agent of the Chartered Bank of India, Australia and China : Agent in Bombay, 1865-72 : Exchange and bullion broker, 1873-1901 : Sheriff of Bombay, 1893 and 1902 : Fellow of the Bombay University, 1895 : devoted his leisure to researches : retired in 1902 : was author of *Bombay and Western India*, 1893 ; *Glimpses of Old Bombay*, 1900 : and wrote, in the local press, articles on the archæology and history of W. India : died Aug. 3, 1904.

DOUGLAS, SIR THOMAS MONTEATH (1787-1868)

Son of Thomas Monteath : born 1787 : entered the E. I. Co.'s Bengal Army in 1806: served in the Bundelkund campaigns, 1809-10 : in the Nipal war of 1815, the Pindari war of 1818, the Merwarra campaign of 1820, at the seige of Bhartpur, 1826 : Lt-Colonel, 1834 : commanded his regiment in the forcing of the Khyber and the capture of Kabul, 1838 : C.B. : in the Khurd Kabul and Jagdalak actions : was second in command at Sale's defence of Jalalabad until it was relieved by Pollock : was in the subsequent campaign to Kabul : A.D.C. to Queen Victoria : left India about 1845 : added the name of Douglas to his own in 1851 : K.C.B and General, 1865 : died Oct., 1868.

DOVETON, SIR JOHN (1768-1847)

Son of Frederick Doveton : born 1768 : entered the Madras Cavalry in 1785 : served against Tippoo, both in Cornwallis' campaign of 1791-2 and in Harris' of 1799, and in the pursuit of the bandit Dhoondia Waugh, under Colonel Wellesley : commanded the Hyderabad Contingent in 1814, which was utilized in the Pindari war of 1817. After the battle of Sitabaldi in Nov., 1817, Doveton marched to Nagpur to assist the Resident, Jenkins, against Appa Sahib, the Bhonsla Raja. Appa surrendered, and his troops, after a fight, abandoned Nagpur to Doveton, who was made C.B. in 1818 and K.C.B. in 1819 : retired, 1820 : Lt-General and G.C.B. 1837 : died at Madras, Nov. 7, 1847.

DOVETON, SIR JOHN (1783-1857)

Son of Sir William Webber Doveton : born 1783 : to Madras in the E.I. Co.'s military service, 1798 : A.D.C. to the Marquis Wellesley, while Governor-General : saw service in the campaign of 1799-1803, against the Mahrattas, and in 1817 : commanded a Division in the Nizam's Army : commanded a Division in Madras, 1833 : K.C.B., 1838 : General, 1854 : died Sep. 23, 1857.

DOVETON, JOHN (1800 ?-1853)

Educated as an orphan at a charity school in Madras : entered the Nizam of Hyderabad's Army in 1817 : rose to be Captain Commandant. On inheriting an uncle's fortune, he resigned his commission, and retired to London : died on Oct. 15, 1853. Being an Eurasian, he bequeathed nearly £50,000 to be divided between the Parental Academy at Calcutta, which was thereupon called the Doveton College, and the Doveton College at Madras.

DOW, ALEXANDER (? -1779)

Born in Perthshire : having reached Bencoolen as a sailor, he became Secretary to the Governor : entered the E. I. Co.'s military service in 1760 : Captain, 1764 : Lt-Colonel, 1769 : he published translations from the Persian in 1768 and produced, at Drury Lane, *Zingis*, a tragedy, 1769 ; *Sethona*, a tragedy, in 1774 : he also wrote historical works on India. Died at Bhaglapur, July 31, 1779.

DOWDESWELL, WILLIAM (1761–1828)

Son of the Right Honble. William Dowdeswell: born 1761: entered the Army, 1780: M.P. for Tewkesbury, 1792: was in the campaign of 1793, at Valenciennes, and at Dunkirk: Governor of the Bahamas, 1797–1802: Private Secretary to Lord W. Bentinck, Governor of Madras, 1803: commanded a Division under Lord Lake against Bhartpur, and later the Cawnpur Division: acted as C. in C. in India in 1807: soon left India: Lt-General, 1810: retired 1811: became a collector of valuable prints: died Dec. 1, 1828.

DOWDESWELL, GEORGE (1765–1852)

Son of George Dowdeswell, M.D.: in the E. I. Co's Civil Service: became Secretary to the Government of India: and Member of the Supreme Council, Dec. 1814, to Jan. 1820: Vice-President of the Council and Deputy-Governor of Bengal, Oct. 1817, to July 1818: died Feb. 6, 1852.

DOWSON, JOHN (1820–1881)

Born 1820: assistant to his uncle at the Royal Asiatic Society: tutor at Haileybury: Professor of Hindustani at University College, London, and Staff College, Sandhurst, 1855–77: wrote a Hindustani Grammar: edited Sir H. M. Elliot's *History of India as told by its own Historians*, 8 vols., 1867–77: and a *Classical Dictionary of Hindu Mythology and Religion, Geography, History and Literature*, 1879: wrote also for the *Encyclopædia Britannica*, and the Royal Asiatic Society, on Indian Inscriptions and the Indian Alphabet: died Aug. 23, 1881.

D'OYLY, SIR CHARLES, BARONET (1781–1845)

I.C.S.: son of Sir John Hadley D'Oyly, the sixth Baronet, Collector of Calcutta: born in India, Sep. 18, 1781: educated in England: entered the E. I. Co.'s service at 15: Assistant Registrar of the Court of Appeal, Calcutta, 1798: Collector of Dacca, 1808: Opium Agent in Bihar, 1821: Commercial Resident at Patna, 1831: Senior Member of the Board of Customs, Salt and Opium, 1833: retired 1839: died Sep. 24, 1845. He is best remembered for his pictures of Indian scenery and Indian life. He wrote *The European in India, Antiquities of Dacca, Tom Raw the Griffin*, and other works, with many illustrations.

DRAKE, ROGER (? – ?)

A noted official in the time of Lord Clive: arrived in Bengal, May 26, 1737: President of Council and Governor of Calcutta from Aug. 8, 1752 to 1758: he gave offence to Suraj-ud daula, the new Nawab of Bengal, by a letter with regard to the strengthening of the fortifications of Calcutta: the attack on the City followed: Drake escaped in the last boat that left the Fort, 1756: his desertion of his post brought reproach upon him, and J. Z. Holwell (*q.v.*), who had stayed behind, was chosen to the command: Drake was dismissed from his post by the Directors, 1757.

DRAPER, ELIZABETH (1744–1778)

Daughter of Major Sclater: born at Anjengo, April 5, 1744: educated in England: went to India, 1757: married in July, 1758, Daniel Draper, of the E.I. Co.'s Civil Service, Secretary to Government, 20 years her senior. When in England in 1766–7, she met Lawrence Sterne, the humourist, who became infatuated with her, addressing her as " Bramine " in amorous letters, and writing the *Journal to Eliza* for her. She returned to India in 1767, and saw Sterne no more: lived with her husband at Tellicherry, Surat and Bombay, but unhappily, and, on Jan. 12, 1773, fled from his house at Mazagon, Bombay, with a Naval officer, repairing to her uncle's at Rajamundry: returned to England in 1774. Sterne had died in 1768. She published as *Letters of Yorick to Eliza*, some of Sterne's letters to her, including her answers. She died Aug. 3, 1778, and was buried in the Cathedral cloisters at Bristol. Draper became a Member of Council, at Bombay, and died Oct. 10, 1782. Her name and story were recalled, by L'Abbè Raynal, who had seen her in India, and by James Forbes in his *Oriental Memoirs*, and some of her letters have been preserved.

DRAPER, SIR WILLIAM (1721–1787)

Son of Ingleby Draper: born 1721: educated at Eton and King's College,

Cambridge : Fellow : joined the Army, 1744 : at Culloden : in Flanders with the 1st Foot-Guards : in 1757 as Lt-Colonel, took the 79th to Madras : in the siege of Fort St. George, 1757–9 : too ill to take command of the troops at Madras in 1759, returned to England : in 1762 commanded, from Madras, the expedition against the Spaniards at Manilla : carried the place by assault : Lieut-Governor of Great Yarmouth : in 1765 Colonel of the 16th foot : knighted in 1766 : had a literary controversy with " Junius," defending the C. in C. the Marquis of Granby : Lt-General in 1777 : Lieutenant-Governor of Minorca in 1779 : in the surrender of Fort St. Philip in 1782 to the French and Spaniards : brought charges of misconduct against Lt-General the Hon. James Murray, the Governor, which he failed to substantiate, so that he was commanded to make an apology : he died Jan. 8, 1787.

DREW, FREDERICK (1836–1891)

Son of John Drew : born Aug. 11, 1836 : educated at the Royal School of Mines, and joined the Geological Survey in 1855. He was employed by the Maharaja of Kashmir, from 1862, to search for minerals and supervise his forest administration, and was Governor of Ladak : retired after 10 years. He was a science master at Eton, 1879–91, and died Oct. 28, 1891. He wrote *The Jammu and Kashmir Frontiers*, and *The Northern Barrier of India* : F.G.S. in 1858, and Member of its Council, 1874–6.

DRUMMOND, HON. SIR EDMUND (1813–1895)

I.C.S. : son of sixth Viscount Strathallan : born 1813 : educated at Eton and Haileybury, 1830–1 : went to Bengal in 1833 : Accountant-General, 1856 : Auditor-General, 1860 : Financial Secretary to the Government of India, 1862 : Lieutenant-Governor of the N.W.P. 1863 –8 : Member of the Council of India. 1875–85 : K.C.I.E., 1887 : died Jan. 10. 1895.

DRYSDALE, SIR WILLIAM (1819–1900)

Son of Major James Drysdale : educated at the Military Academy, Edinburgh : joined the 4th Dragoons, 1835 : served in the 9th Lancers, 1841–65 : in the Afghan war, 1839–40 : at Ghazni : in the

Gwalior campaign, at Punniar, 1843 : in the Satlaj and Panjab campaigns, 1845–6 and 1848–9 : at Sobraon, Ramnagar, Chilianwala, Gujarat : at the siege of Delhi in the mutiny : in the actions at Bulandshahr, Alighar, Agra : at the relief of Lucknow : Brevets of| Major and Lt-Colonel : C.B. : Lt-General, 1881 : K.C.B., 1893 : died Aug. 7, 1900.

DUBOIS, JEAN A. (1765–1848)

Abbè : ordained at 27 in the diocese of Viviers, in 1792 : escaped from the massacres of the French Revolution, and, the same year, leaving France for mission work under the Missions Etrangères, was first attached to the Pondicherry mission : after Seringapatam, 1799, he was invited to visit it, to reconvert the forced perverts to Islam. He was 31 years in India, living entirely among the people from 17 to 18 years, chiefly in Mysore, where he established, at Sathalli, an agricultural settlement of reconverted Christians. His *Description of the Character, Manners and Customs of the People of India, and of their Institutions, Religious and Civil*, was stated to be " the most correct, comprehensive and minute account extant in any European language of the Hindus " of S. India : the Madras Government bought the MSS. from him in 1806 for 2,000 pagodas : this was translated in London in 1816, and was for long the only published edition : meanwhile, in 1815, the Abbè had revised and amplified his work, but this was not published until 1897. On returning to France in June, 1823, with a pension from the E.I. Co., he published *Letters on the State of Christianity in India*, containing his conviction that the conversion of the Hindus was impossible. He became a Director, and, from 1836 to 1839, Superior of the Missions Etrangères at Paris, where he died Feb. 17, 1848.

DUFF, REV. DR. ALEXANDER (1806–1878)

Missionary : son of James Duff : born on April 25, 1806 : educated at Moulin, Kirkmichael, Perth, St. Andrew's University, under Dr. Chalmers : invited by the Committee of the General Assembly of the Church of Scotland on Foreign Missions to become their first missionary to India : he was ordained in 1829 and went out to Calcutta in 1829–30 :| he was twice shipwrecked on the voyage, near the Cape and off Sagar island : lost his library : at Calcutta he declared his policy, to afford, in the English language, education inseparably combined with the Christian faith as its animating spirit : the Duff College was soon founded, and,proving very successful, attracted a very large number of pupils, not without troubles on account of conversions. He received much help from Sir C. Trevelyan (*q.v.*) and from the decision of Government of March 7, 1835, in favour of the promotion of European science and literature through English rather than the Oriental languages. During his visit home, 1834–40, for his health, he made speeches, collected money, and laboured hard in organizing his mission : he was D.D. of Aberdeen in 1835. He was in India again from 1840 to 1850, and from 1856 to 1863 : made extensive tours in the cause of missions : was opposed to the Government policy in the mutiny : assisted greatly in the establishment of the Calcutta University in 1857, the shape it assumed, its educational measures and examinations. When away from India, he was made Moderator of the General Assembly of the Free Church in 1851 : he travelled in the United States in 1854, and made constant speeches, and was made LL.D., New York : he inspired the Government Education Despatch to India of 1854. On his finally leaving Calcutta, memorials were erected to him. He travelled in South Africa in 1864. In 1867 he became the first Professor of Evangelistic Theology at the Free Church College, Edinburgh. He was again Moderator of the General Assembly in 1873. He wrote on *India and Indian Missions*, and edited the *Calcutta Review*, 1845–9, writing articles in it, besides other publications chiefly connected with his mission work : died Feb. 12, 1878.

DUFFERIN AND AVA, FREDERICK TEMPLE HAMILTON-TEMPLE BLACKWOOD, FIRST MARQUESS OF (1826–1902)

Son of Price, first Baron Dufferin, of the Irish peerage, and of Helen Selina, grand-daughter of Richard Brinsley Sheridan : born June 21, 1826 : educated at Eton and Christ Church, Oxford : Lord in Waiting, 1849–50 : Peer of the United Kingdom, 1850 : on a special mission to

Vienna, 1855 : British Commissioner in Syria in 1860 to inquire into the massacres of Christians : K.C.B. : Under Secretary of State for India, 1864–6 : Under Secretary for War, 1866 : Chancellor of the Duchy of Lancaster, 1868 : Earl, 1871 : Governor General of Canada, 1872–8 : Ambassador to St. Petersburg, 1879 : Ambassador to Constantinople, 1881 : Special Commissioner to Egypt, 1882–3, after Arabi's rebellion : Viceroy and Governor-General of India, 1884–8. He did much, by his personal influence, to allay the excitement and race feeling which had arisen from the controversy over the " Ilbert Bill " in the time of his predecessor : he met the Amir Abdur Rahman in *darbar* at Rawal Pindi, 1885 : Upper Burma was annexed on his advice : his administration was marked by firmness and vigour underlying his tact and suavity : the Countess of Dufferin's Fund for the medical relief of native women was established : made Marquis in 1888, with the additional title of Ava : Ambassador to Rome, 1888–91 : to Paris, 1891–6 : his latter years were clouded by financial troubles in connexion with a business enterprise of which he had insufficient knowledge to exercise control : he retained the goodwill of the shareholders and public sympathy : he was K.P. : G.C.B. : G.C.S.I. : G.C.M.G. : G.C.I.E. : P.C. : D.C.L. : LL.D. : F.R.S. : President of the Geographical Society : Rector of Edinburgh and St. Andrew's : Doctor of Oriental Learning, Panjab University : Lord Warden of the Cinque Ports, 1891–5 : wrote *Letters from High Latitudes*, and on Irish questions : also *Speeches in India*, 1890 : died Feb. 12, 1902.

DUFFERIN AND AVA, HARRIET GEORGINA, DOWAGER MARCHIONESS OF (? –)

Eldest daughter of Archibald Rowan Hamilton of Killyleagh Castle, County Down : married Oct. 23, 1862, the (late) Marquis of Dufferin and Ava (*q.v.*), afterwards Governor-General and Viceroy of India : when in India, she established the National Association for supplying female medical aid to the women of India, with the object of bringing European medical science within the reach of native women of the higher castes, the money collected being credited to " The Countess of Dufferin's Fund " : V.A. : C.I. : Grand

Cross of the Turkish Order of the Lion and Sun : she has written *Our Viceregal Life in India*, 1890 : *My Canadian Journal*, 1891.

DUNCAN, DAVID (1839–   )

Born Nov. 5, 1839 : son of David Duncan : educated at Edinburgh, Aberdeen and Berlin Universities : Professor of Logic and Moral Philosophy in Madras Presidency College, 1870–84 : Principal of Presidency College, 1884–92 : Registrar, University of Madras : Director of Public Instruction, Madras, 1892–9 : Vice-Chancellor of Madras University, 1899 : retired, 1899 : author (with others) of *Herbert Spencer's Descriptive Sociology* : now engaged in writing *Biography of Herbert Spencer*.

DUNCAN, JONATHAN (1756–1811)

Governor : Indian Civilian : son of Alexander Duncan : born May 15, 1756 : arrived at Calcutta in the E.I. Co.'s service in 1772 : made Resident and Superintendent at Benares, 1788 : suppressed scandals in the administration and infanticide : was Governor of Bombay for the unprecedented time of 16 years from Dec. 27, 1795, to Aug. 11, 1811, dying at Bombay : he recognized a very large number of small chiefs as sovereign princes, a policy which was not elsewhere adopted : his time was synchronous with the later war against Tippoo, the Mahratta wars, and Baird's expedition to Egypt, the pacification of Gujarat and Kattiawar, in all of which he played a great part. He was buried at Bombay, and a monument was erected in his honour, with the inscription " He was a good man and a just," and a scroll bearing the words " Infanticide abolished in Benares and Kattiawar."

DUNDAS, JAMES (1842–1879)

Son of [George Dundas, Scotch judge : born Sep. 12, 1842 : educated at the Edinburgh Academy and Addiscombe : went to India in the Royal Engineers, March, 1862 : became a Captain : gained his V.C. in the Bhutan expedition of 1864–5 for personal bravery in storming, under very trying conditions, a blockhouse, defended by 200 desperate men : in the Afghan war of 1878–80, he and another officer were killed by an accident on the occasion of the blowing up of a fort

near Kabul on Dec. 23, 1879 : he was an officer of high professional merit and promise.

DUPLEIX, MARQUIS JOSEPH FRANCIS (1697–1764)

Son of a French farmer-general, Director of the Company of the Indies : born Jan. 1697 : sent to sea : made several voyages to America and India : made First Councillor and Military Commissioner of the Superior Council at Pondicherry in 1720 : accumulated a fortune : made Intendant, or Superintendent, of the factory at Chandernagore, 1730 : developed its coasting trade : Governor of Pondicherry, 1741, and Director-General of the French factories in India : declared himself Nawab of the Mogul Empire and Commander of 4,500 Horse : when war with England broke out, 1744, he sought help from Anwaruddin, the Nawab of the Carnatic : La Bourdonnais came to his aid, from the Isle of France, and took Madras, Sep. 21, 1746 : great jealousy between him and Dupleix, who refused to surrender Madras and defeated the Nawab's force at St. Thomé : Dupleix violated the treaty with the English, by retaining Madras, and by his treatment of them : his attack on Fort St. David failed, 1748 : the English attack under Boscawen by land and sea on Pondicherry was unsuccessful : Madras was restored to the English in 1749, after the peace of Aix-la-Chapelle. In the contests in Southern India, Dupleix, striving to found French ascendency there, took the side of Muzaffar Jang and Salabat Jang successively against Nasir Jang for the Subadarship of the Dekkan, and of Chanda Sahib against Anwaruddin and Muhammad Ali successively for the Nawabship of the Carnatic. By 1751, Dupleix's policy was, after a struggle, for a time successful. Muhammad Ali, at Trichinopoly, applied to the English for help. Stringer, Lawrence and Clive, going to his aid, defeated the French, Dupleix being badly served by his generals. He acquired the Northern Sircars from the Nizam and, after Chanda's death, claimed to be, and was nominated, Nawab of the Carnatic : was made a Marquis, 1752 : his forces met with further reverses from the English : the French Ministers and Company of the Indies objected to his schemes and fighting, as being obstructive to trade, and ruinously expensive : they insisted on peace, and recalled Dupleix, who was superseded by Godeheu, 1754, ruined by him and left India, Oct. 14, 1754 : his claims, for private money expended, disregarded and unsatisfied : his services ignored : he died in comparative poverty in France, Nov. 10, 1764 : the greatest Frenchman in India : the first to see how Europeans might rule in India and employ native troops : ambitious, prescient, full of resource, will, and genius : had great knowledge of native character : inferior in the field of action, and not a soldier : he failed for want of support from France : his statue was erected at Pondicherry in 1870.

DURAND, ALGERNON GEORGE ARNOLD (1854–)

Born March 31, 1854 : son of Maj-General Sir H. M. Durand, R.E. (q.v.) : entered the Army, 1872 : served in Afghanistan, 1878–80 : was A.D.C. to Lord Ripon, Viceroy of India, 1881–2 : British Agent at Gilgit, 1889–93 : commanded troops in Hanza-Nagar expedition, 1891 : Military Secretary to the Earl of Elgin, when Viceroy of India, 1894–9 : author of The Making of a Frontier, 1899 : C.B., 1892 : C.I.E., 1897.

DURAND, SIR EDWARD LAW, BARONET (1845–)

Born June 5, 1845 : son of Sir H. M. Durand, R.E. (q.v.): educated at Bath, Repton and Guildford : entered 96th regt., 1865 : B.S.C., 1868: Assistant Commissioner Afghan Boundary, 1884–6 : Resident in Nipal, 1888 : retired, 1893, as Lt-Colonel : created a Baronet, 1892 : C.B.

DURAND, SIR HENRY MARION (1812– 1871)

Son of a cavalry officer: born Nov. 6, 1812 : educated at Leicester and Addiscombe: entered the Bengal Engineers, 1828: went to India in 1829–30, in the same ship as Dr. A. Duff (q.v.) : appointed to irrigation work in the N.W.P. : it was proposed to make him Secretary of the Board of Revenue, N.W.P., but instead he went, in 1838, with the Army to Kabul viâ Kandahar, and headed the party that blew open the Kabul gate of Ghazni, July 23, 1839 : returned soon to India from Kabul : went out from England,

after leave, as Private Secretary to Lord Ellenborough (Governor-General, 1842–4) : was present at Maharajpur, became Captain in 1843 : was Commissioner of Tenasserim, 1844, until removed by Sir Herbert Maddock, the President in Council, in 1846 : he obtained no redress in England. In the Sikh war, 1848–9, Durand was at Chilianwala and Gujarat : Brevet-Major : became Political Agent at Gwalior and Bhopal successively : wrote there largely for the Calcutta Review : in 1856 was Inspecting-Engineer, Presidency Circle, until Lord Canning made him Agent to the Governor-General for Central India. In the mutiny he was compelled, by the strength of the insurrection of Holkar's native troops at Indore, to retire thence, fought several actions, and reconquered Western Malwa : C.B. and Brevet-Colonel : deputed to England to represent the views of the Government of India on the re-construction of the Army in India : Member of the Council of India, 1859–61 : Foreign Secretary to the Government of India, 1861–65 : Military Member of the Governor-General's Supreme Council, April 27, 1865, until he became Lieutenant-Governor of the Panjab, June 1, 1870 : Maj-General and K.C.S.I. in 1867 : he was accidentally killed at Tonk on Jan. 1, 1871, his howdah, on an elephant's back, being crushed under the arch of a gateway : Durand was thrown violently to the ground and picked up insensible : he recovered consciousness after several hours, but remained paralyzed—his spine had been injured—and passed away without pain. No officer in India at the time had a greater reputation for ability, experience, high principles, force of character : he held strong views and expressed them strongly. The Secretary of State wrote of him : " The life of such a man is an example to the Service, and her Majesty's Government deeply deplore his death."

DURAND, SIR HENRY MORTIMER (1850–)

I.C.S. : born Feb. 14, 1850 : son of Maj-General Sir H. M. Durand (q.v.) : educated at Blackheath School, and Eton House, Tunbridge : barrister of Lincoln's Inn, 1872 : entered the Bengal Civil Service, 1873 : Political Secretary to Sir F. Roberts in Kabul campaign, 1879 :

C.S.I., 1881 : Foreign Secretary in India, 1884–94 : conducted the mission to Amir of Afghanistan, 1893 : Minister at Teheran, 1894–1900 : Minister at Madrid, 1900–4 : Minister at Washington, 1904 : was made K.C.I.E., 1889 ; K.C.S.I. 1894 ; G.C.M.G., 1900 ; P.C., 1901 : wrote *The Life of Maj-General Sir H. M. Durand*, and *Helen Trevelyan*.

DUTT, AKHOY KUMAR (1821–1886)

Born in the Burdwan District : educated in his village school, and at the Oriental Seminary, Calcutta : contributed to the Bengali *Prabhakar* : editor of the *Tattwabodhini Patrika*, founded by Debendranath Tagore (*q.v.*) in connexion with the Adi Brahma Samaj : first headmaster of the Calcutta Normal School : was a pioneer of Bengali prose : wrote several works of considerable merit and erudition : his *Religious Sects of India*, in Bengali, is still a standard work : studied languages : the first to publish essays in Bengali on scientific subjects : has left a name as a thinker and author of Bengali literature : died 1886.

DUTT, CALICA DAS (1841–)

Born July 3, 1841 : son of Rai Goloke Nath Dutt : educated at Krishnagar Collegiate School and Calcutta Presidency College : B.A., 1861 : B.L., 1861 : served as a Munsif, Deputy Magistrate and Deputy Collector, under the Bengal Government, and in 1869 was made Diwan of the Cooch Behar State, where he has remained ever since : in 1883 became member of the Cooch Behar State Council : received the title of Rai Bahadur, 1891 : and was made C.I.E., 1900.

DUTT, MICHAEL MADHUSUDAN (1824–1873)

Son of Raj Narayan Dutt, a pleader in the *Sadr* Court : born Jan. 25, 1824 : educated in the Hindu College under Derozio. When his father wished to marry him, he ran away to the Missionaries, and on Feb. 9, 1843, was baptized as a Christian : remained at Bishop's College, Calcutta, for four years, 1843–7, and then went to Madras, where he lived in great poverty : returning to Calcutta, 1856, he became Interpreter in the Calcutta Police Court : enjoyed considerable reputation as a writer of Bengali blank verse, which he created and introduced

into the language. In 1862 he went to England, and was called to the bar : practised at the Calcutta bar from 1867, but without any marked success. In literary circles his memory is treasured : he helped to promote a national drama and theatre : produced some meritorious dramas, farces and poems : knew several Oriental and European languages, besides Greek and Latin : his improvidence and failings ruined a promising career : died in a charitable hospital, June 29, 1873.

DUTT, RAJENDRA (1818–1889)

Born in Calcutta, 1818 : educated at Drummond's School, and at the Hindu College : joined the Calcutta Medical College, to be trained in medical science : after leaving the College, he opened a dispensary at his own house and commenced allopathic treatment, helped by Dr. Durga Charan Banerji : in 1853, opened the Hindu Metropolitan College as a protest against the laxity displayed in the Hindu College, and began to study homœopathy : in 1857, started a business firm, Dutt, Linzu & Co., with Europeans as partners, which failed in 1861 : thereupon he established a homœopathic dispensary : in 1864, Dr. Berigny came to Calcutta, and with him began to spread homœopathic treatment : in 1867 he converted Dr. Mahendra Lal Sarkar (*q.v.*) to homœopathy : lost great wealth in business speculations : was very generous : died June, 1889.

DUTT, ROMESH CHUNDER (1848–)

I.C.S. : born Aug. 13, 1848 : son of Isan Chunder Dutt : educated at Hare's School, Presidency College, Calcutta, and University College, London : passed the Indian Civil Service Examination, 1869 : joined the Civil Service, 1871 : became a Divisional Commissioner, 1894–5 : retired in 1897 : C.I.E., 1892 : is a Fellow of the Calcutta University and Barrister of the Middle Temple : has been Lecturer on Indian History at University College, London : author of a series of historical and social novels, and a translation of the RigVeda and other Sanskrit religious works in Bengali, also of *Civilisation in Ancient India, Lays of Ancient India, Ramayana and Mahabharata in English Verse, Economic History of British India, 1757– 1900*, 2 vols., etc.

DUTT, SASI CHANDRA, RAI BAHA-DUR (1825-1886)

Born 1825 : educated at the Hindu College : entered the Government Treasury as a clerk : transferred to the Bengal Secretariat, and eventually became its Registrar : retired in 1873 : made Rai Bahadur : in 1884 he brought out in England his works in ten volumes, including a *History of Bengal, Essays on Miscellaneous Subjects, Great Wars of India, Half-Hours with Nature, Realities of Indian Life, The Times of Yore, The Wild Tribes of India*, as well as his verses in English : died in 1886.

DUTT, TORU (1856-1877)

Torulata Dutta, the youngest daughter of Govinda Chandra Dutt, a native Christian convert : born at Calcutta in 1856 : she and her elder sister, Aru, were taken to England by their father for education, 1869-73 : studied French at Nice, and English thoroughly : attended lectures at Cambridge and St. Leonards : on their return to Calcutta, Toru Dutt studied Sanskrit and French, and began to contribute poetical compositions and essays to local magazines, especially to the *Bengal Magazine*. In 1874 Aru died of consumption. In 1876 Toru published a collection of her lyrics translated from the French, *A Sheaf Gleaned in French Fields*, showing considerable acquaintance with French and English literature, very favourably reviewed in the English and French Press. She also died of consumption on Aug. 30, 1877 : the sisters were good musicians : neither of them married. Besides her ballads and legends of Hindustan, poems and translations, Toru left the MS. of a French novel entitled *Le Journal de Mdlle. D'Arvers*.

DYAS, JOSEPH HENRY (1824-1868)

Born April 7, 1824 : son of Capt. Joseph Dyas of the 51st K.O.L.I. : educated at Delgany, Dungannon, Addiscombe : entered the Bengal Engineers : went to India, 1845 : just too late for Sobraon : with the Army to Lahore : at the taking of the fort of Kangra, 1846 : Assistant Superintendent of the W. Jamna Canal : prepared and worked on the Bari Doab Canal project from 1850 : Director of Canals at Madhupur, 1856 : in the mutiny was at Trimmu Ghat, July

16, 1857 : Capt., 1857 : in 1864, Lt-Colonel and Chief Engineer, N.W.P. : died March 4, 1868, "a sacrifice to his devotion to his duty and his work" in the Canal Department : he had a faculty for mechanical invention.

DYCE, GEORGE HUGH COLES (1846-)

Born 1846 : entered the Indian Army, 1864, and became a Colonel in 1894 : Colonel on the Staff at Firozpur, 1897-8 : Multan, 1898 : Tochi Valley and Bannu, 1898-1900 : Brig-General, Allahabad, 1900 : D.A.G. Bengal, 1900-1 : served in Hazara campaign, 1868 : Afghan war, 1878-80 : Mahsud-Waziri expedition, 1881 : Burmese war, 1886-7 : Waziristan expedition, 1894-5 : and Chitral Relief, 1895 : C.B., 1896.

DYCE-SOMBRE, DAVID OCHTER-LONY (1808-1851)

Born at Sardhana in 1808 : great-grandson of Walter Reinhard, called Sombre (Samru) for his sombre appearance: his father, G. A. Dyce, commanded the Begam Sombre's, or Samru's, troops : D. O. Dyce inherited a great fortune from the Begam on her death in 1836 : he had become a Roman Catholic and been made Chevalier of the Order of Christ. He reached England in 1839, and made a figure in society : married the daughter of Lord St. Vincent : M.P. for Sunbury, 1841-2, but was unseated for bribery. He was treated as a lunatic and declared by a Commission to be of unsound mind : escaped from his keeper and went to France in 1843, where, in 1849, he wrote a contention against the allegations of his lunacy : tried to have the decision set aside, but died in London on July 1, 1851 : his will gave rise to much litigation.

EARDLEY-WILMOT, REVELL (1842-)

Born Aug. 29, 1842 : son of Sir J. E. Eardley-Wilmot, *Bart.* : educated at Winchester : entered the Army, 1860 : Brevet-Lt-Colonel, 1881 : Maj-General, 1895 : served in the Bhutan expedition, 1864-5 (wounded) : Jowaki expedition as A.D.C. : Kabul war, 1878-89 : attack of Ali Masjid, Charasia, and taking of Kabul : C.B.

K

EARLE, SIR HENRY, THIRD BARONET (1854-   )

Born Aug. 15, 1854 : educated at Eton and Trinity College, Oxford : entered the Army : served in Jowaki campaign, 1877 : Afghan war, 1878–80 : Egyptian war, 1882 : Burma war, 1886–7 : Tirah, 1897–8 (severely wounded) : South Africa, 1899–1900 (severely wounded) : D.S.O. for services in Burma.

EARLE, WILLIAM (1833–1885)

Son of Sir Hardman Earle, *Bart.*, born May 18, 1833 : educated at Winchester : entered the 49th regt., in 1851 : served with it through the Crimea, exchanged into the Grenadier Guards in 1857 : served at Gibraltar ; in Nova Scotia, as Military Secretary to the General in N. America : Colonel : was Military Secretary to Lord Northbrook when Viceroy and Governor-General, 1872–76 : C.S.I., 1876 : in Egypt in 1882 : in command at Alexandria : C.B. : and in 1884–85, as Maj-General, commanded the Nile column destined for Khartoum. In an attack on Arabs, entrenched at Kirbekan, he was shot in the forehead and killed, on Feb. 10, 1885.

EAST, SIR EDWARD HYDE BARONET (1764–1847)

Born in Jamaica, Sep. 9, 1764 : called to the bar from the Inner Temple, 1786 : M.P. for Great Malvern : published the *Term Reports* of cases in the King's Bench for many years, and a work on the Criminal Law : Chief Justice of Bengal from 1813 to 1821 : knighted on appointment : took a leading part in the establishment of the Hindu College at Calcutta : made a Baronet in 1823 : M.P. for Winchester, 1823–30 : member of the Judicial Committee of the Privy Council, 1833 : member of Council of the Royal Asiatic Society : F.R.S. : bencher of the Inner Temple : died Jan. 8, 1847.

EASTWICK, EDWARD BACKHOUSE (1814–1883)

Born 1814 : son of Capt. Robert William Eastwick : educated at Charterhouse and Merton College, Oxford : Postmaster : joined a Bombay N.I. regt., 1836 : early devoted himself to Oriental languages : served in the Political Department in Kattiawar and Sind : did literary work, on the History of the Parsis and a Sindi vocabulary : about 1842 he gave up India, through ill-health : studied at Frankfort and translated Bopp's *Comparative Grammar* : noticed by H. H. Wilson (*q.v.*), and appointed Professor of Hindustani at the E.I. College, Haileybury, 1845 : F.R.S., 1851 : Assistant Political Secretary at the India Office, 1859 : called to the bar, Middle Temple, 1860 : Secretary of Legation at Teheran to the Court of Persia, 1860–3 : published *The Journal of a Diplomatist* : Commissioner for arranging a Venezuelan loan, 1864 and 1867 : Private Secretary to Lord Cranborne (afterwards Marquis of Salisbury) when Secretary of State for India, July, 1866, to March, 1867 : C.B. : M.P. for Penrhyn and Falmouth, 1868–74 : M.A., Oxford, 1875 : translated the *Gulistan*, the *Anwar-i-Suhaili, Prem Sagar, Bagh-o-Bahar*, and other works in Oriental languages : made several journeys to India : wrote a Hindustani grammar, Murray's Handbooks for India, accounts of his experiences in Sind, Persia, and Venezuela, and the *Kaisarnama-i-Hind* (an account of the native states, etc.), and articles in the *Encyclopædia Britannica* · was F.S.A. : died July 16, 1883.

EASTWICK, ROBERT WILLIAM (1772–1865)

Captain : born June 25, 1772 : educated at Merchant Taylors' school : went to sea, 1784, in the merchant service : pressed into the Navy, 1790 : soon left it : entered the E.I. Co.'s marine service, 1792 : went to Bombay : joined the Indian Service : sailed everywhere in Eastern waters : commanded a ship in 1793 : owned and commanded the *Endeavour*, which was captured by a French frigate, *La Forte*, 1799, and rescued by the English man-of-war, *La Sybille*, on March 1, 1799 : his own ship lost to him : sailed to Bussora, Sumatra, New Holland, Sydney, Norfolk Island, China, Buenos Ayres, Monte Video, to England : several times shipwrecked, and went through numerous adventures : finished his active career in 1825 : lost his sight in 1832, and was blind for 33 years till his death on Dec. 31, 1865 : "a skilful and fearless sailor " : father of Captain W. J. E. (*q.v.*) and of E. B. E., (*q.v.*) : his life is recorded in *A Master Mariner*. by H. Compton, 1891.

EASTWICK, WILLIAM JOSEPH
(1808–1889)

Captain : born 1808 : son of Capt. Robert William Eastwick : educated at Winchester : went to India in the Bombay Army, 1826 : served in the Kolapur and S. Mahratta country : in the Political Department : Assistant to Sir H. Pottinger in Sind : negotiated a treaty with the Amirs of Hyderabad, 1839 : secured the freedom of the Indus to commercial enterprise : in the first Afghan war : obtained supplies for Nott at Kandahar, 1841 : to England, 1841, and did not return to India : Director of the E.I. Co., 1846 : Deputy Chairman, 1858 : Member of the Council of India, Sep. 21, 1858 : retired, 1868 : died Feb. 24, 1889.

EDEN, THE HON. SIR ASHLEY
(1831–1887)

Indian Civil Service : third son of the third Lord Auckland, Bishop of Bath and Wells, and nephew of the Governor-General Lord ʹAuckland : born on Nov. 13, 1831 : educated at Rugby, Winchester, and Haileybury : arrived in India in 1852 : distinguished himself in the Sonthal insurrection, 1855 : Secretary to the Bengal Government from 1862–71, and in the Bengal Legislative Council : employed to make a treaty with the Raja of Sikhim in 1861, and as envoy to Bhutan in 1863–4, where he was subjected to gross indignities, and compelled to sign a treaty which the British Government repudiated and declared war on Bhutan. Eden was Chief Commissioner of British Burma, 1871–7, acting, in 1875, as Member of the Supreme Council. He was Lieutenant-Governor of Bengal, 1877 to 1882, and President of the Army Commission for some months in 1879. In Bengal he exhibited such capacity, and attained such success : in his administration, that his retirement was universally deplored, and a statue erected in his honour in Calcutta. He was in the Council of India from 1882 till his death on July 8, 1887. He was made C.S.I. in 1874, and K.C.S.I. in 1878. Though last in his term at Haileybury, he was one of the ablest officers of modern times : his common sense and penetration were combined with fearlessness and force in the statement of his views.

EDEN, HON. EMILY (1797–1869)

Daughter of the first Baron Auckland, sister of the second Baron, first Earl (*q.v.*), whom she accompanied to India, while Governor-General, from 1836 to 1842 : born March 3, 1797 : she published *Portraits of the People and Princes of India*, 1844, and *Up the Country*, 1866, and two volumes of her *Letters from India* were published in 1872 by her niece, Eleanor Eden. She also wrote the novels *The Semi-detached House*, and *The Semi-attached Couple*. Her writings contain an interesting account of the social and domestic life of a Governor-General and his household. She died Aug. 5, 1869.

EDGAR, SIR JOHN WARE (1839–1902)

I.C.S. : born Sep. 16, 1839 : arrived in India, in the Indian Civil Service, in Feb. 1862 : did good service in Cachar in connexion with the raids of the Lushai tribes, and accompanied the Lushai expedition of 1871–2, as Political Officer to the Northern Column : as Deputy Commissioner of Darjeeling he paid much attention to Sikhim, Buddhism, and Tibet frontier questions : President of the Bengal Excise Commission, 1881–3 : Chief Secretary to the Government of Bengal, 1887–91 : Member of the Governor-General's Legislative Council, Jan., 1892 : retired in April, 1892 : C.S.I. in 1872, and K.C.I.E. in May, 1889 : died at Florence on June 4, 1902 : devoted himself in his later years to historical studies, chiefly on subjects connected with Northern Buddhism and modern Latin Christianity.

EDGE, SIR JOHN (1841–   )

Born July 28, 1841 : son of Benjamin Booker Edge, of Clonbrook : educated at Trinity College, Dublin : joined the Irish bar, 1864, and the English bar, from the Middle Temple, 1866 : Chief Justice of High Court, N.W.P., 1886–98 : Bencher of Middle Temple, 1898 : Member of the Council of India, 1898.

EDMONSTONE, SIR GEORGE FREDERICK (1813–1864)

I.C.S.: son of Neil Benjaminʹ Edmonstone (*q.v.*) : born April, 1813 : educated at Hailebyury, 1829–31 : went to the N.W.P. in 1831 : after the Satlaj campaign of

1845-6 was Commissioner of the Cis-Stalaj States : Financial Commissioner in the Panjab, 1853 : Foreign Secretary to the Government of India, 1855, and during the mutiny : Lieutenant-Governor of the N.W.P., Jan. 19, 1859, to Feb. 27, 1863 : K.C.B., Dec., 1863 : died Sep. 24, 1864.

EDMONSTONE, NEIL BENJAMIN
(1765-1841)

I.C.S. : born Dec. 6, 1765 : son of Sir Archibald Edmonstone, *Bart.*, M.P. : went to Calcutta in the Civil Service, 1783 : appointed early to the Secretariat, and became Persian translator to Government : Private Secretary to the acting Governor-General, Sir Alured Clarke (*q.v.*) in April, 1798 : and Sir G. H. Barlow (*q.v.*) in Feb. 1807 : with Lord Wellesley in Madras for the campaign against Tippoo : Secretary in 1801 to the Government of India in the Foreign Department : Chief Secretary to Government, 1809 : Member of the Supreme Council, Oct. 30, 1812, to Jan. 17, 1818 : became in 1820 a Director of the E.I. Co. : died May 4, 1841.

EDWARDES, SIR HERBERT BEN-JAMIN (1819-1868)

Maj-General : son of the Rev. B. Edwardes : born Nov. 12, 1819 : educated at Richmond and King's College, London, where he distinguished himself in the debating society : obtained an Indian cadetship from Sir R. Jenkins (*q.v.*) : reached India in 1841 : sent to the Panjab. Early in his career he published " Brahmini Bull's Letters in India to his cousin John Bull in England " in the *Delhi Gazette*, criticising the military and political system. He was A.D.C. to Sir Hugh Gough at Mudki and Sobraon in 1845-6 : after which Sir Henry Lawrence, Resident at Lahore, took him as an Assistant. Edwardes, in 1847, pacified the district of Bannu, levelled 400 forts, and initiated civilization. On the murder of Vans Agnew and Anderson at Multan and the rebellion of Mulraj in April, 1848, Edwardes collected a force of tribesmen and, with the aid of the Nawab of Bahawalpur, and Colonel Van Cortlandt of the Sikh service, attacked Mulraj and the rebels, defeating them at Kineyri and Sadusain, maintaining the war for months until General Whish arrived and took Multan. He was made Brevet-Major and C.B. : received the

thanks of Parliament and a special gold medal from the Court of Directors : D.C.L. of Oxford : after holding charge of the Jalandhar and Hazara districts, he was in 1853 made Commissioner of Peshawar. He proposed to Government to make a treaty with Dost Muhammad, the Amir of Afghanistan : with Lord Dalhousie's approval, but after some doubts on Sir John Lawrence's part, treaties were made with the Amir in March, 1855, and 1857, really the work of Edwardes. The Amir and the Afghans remained quiet during the mutiny of 1857. On its outbreak, Edwardes suggested the formation of a movable column for the Panjab : he was told by Lord Canning to " hold on to Peshawar." He zealously, at this time and after, advocated the adoption of a more Christianizing policy in the government of India. While on furlough he was made K.C.B. in 1860 : LL.D. of Cambridge : Commissioner of Umbala, 1862-5 : and then left India for his health : K.C.S.I. in 1866 : he took much interest in mission work in his retirement, and wrote part of the life of Sir Henry Lawrence : died Dec. 23, 1868 : a memorial was erected to him in Westminster Abbey. He wrote also *A Year on the Panjab Frontier in* 1848-9. He has been described as one of the most remarkable men that the Indian Army has ever produced. His bravery and brilliancy were universally recognized. Sir John Lawrence wrote of him as a " born ruler of men."

EDWARDES, SIR STANLEY DE BURG (1840-   )

Born March 29, 1840 : son of Capt. George Harris Edwardes, Bengal Army : educated at Mount Radford School, Exeter : entered the Bombay Army, 1857, and became Colonel, 1876 : Maj-General, 1885 : Lt-General, 1886, and General, 1896 : served during Indian mutiny in pursuit of Tantia Topi, 1858 : D.A.Q.M.G. Abyssinian expedition, 1868 : Chief Director of Transport, Afghan campaign, 1879-80 : commanded Quetta District, 1881-4 ; N. Division, Bombay Army, 1887-9 : K.C.B., 1898.

EDWARDS, SIR JAMES BEVAN
(1834-   )

Born 1834 : educated at R.M.A., Woolwich : entered the Royal Engineers, 1852, and became General, 1891 : served in Crimean war : Indian mutiny : China, 1864 : Suakim expedition, 1885 : Commandant of School of Military Engineering, 1885–8 : commanded the troops in China, 1889–90 : M.P. for Hythe, 1895–9 : C.B., 1877 : K.C.M.G., 1891.

EDWARDS, JOHN BURNARD
(1857-)

Born May 6, 1857 : son of R. M. Edwards, B.C.S.: edu̇cated at Haileybury and Sandhurst : entered the Army 1878, and became Major 1898 : served in Afghan war, 1878–80, Chitral Relief Force, 1895 : in charge of Gwalior Imperial Service Transport Corps : D.S.O. : Inspecting Officer of Imperial Service Cavalry in Central India, 1891–6 : second in command 1st regt. Central India Horse.

EGERTON, CHARLES CHANDLER
(1798–1885)

Born April, 1798 : his father was a clergyman : educated for the medical profession at St. Thomas' and Guy's hospitals : F.C.S., 1819: entered the E. I. Co.'s medical service in 1823 as an oculist to deal with a special epidemic: oculist at the Eye Hospital, and first Surgeon at the Medical College Hospital, Calcutta : left India 1847 : died May, 1885.

EGERTON, SIR CHARLES COMYN
(1848-)

Born 1848 : educated at Rossall : entered the Army, 1867, and became Colonel, 1895 : served in the Afghan war, 1879–80 : Hazara expedition, 1888 : Miranzai expedition : severely wounded : Brevet-Lt-Colonel, and D.S.O. : Waziristan Field Force, 1894–5 : C.B. : Dongola expedition : commanded Tochi Field Force, 1897–8: K.C.B., 1903: commanded the Somaliland Force from 1903.

EGERTON, PHILIP HENRY (1824–1893)

I.C.S. : son of William Egerton (of the B.C.S., 1792–1820) : born Aug. 9, 1824 : educated at the Naval ·and Military Academy, Edinburgh : R.M. College, Sandhurst, and Haileybury, 1840–2 : went to India, 1842 : served in the N.W.P. to 1850 : Magte-Collr. of Delhi, 1855–9, but was on leave during the siege in 1857 and could not rejoin till Oct., when he vigor-

ously restored order in the city and district. Commissioner of Umritsar, 1859, and of Rawul Pindi, 1868 : retired, 1872 : wrote *Journal of a Tour through Spiti*, 1864 : died Jan. 17, 1893.

EGERTON, SIR ROBERT EYLES
(1827-)

I.C.S. : son of William Egerton : born 1827 : educated at Exeter College, Oxford and Haileybury, 1847–9 : served in India, 1849–82 : Deputy Commissioner of Lahore in the mutiny : Commissioner of Nagpur, 1869 : Financial Commissioner of the Panjab, 1871 : Member of the Governor-General's Legislative Council, 1871–4 : Lieutenant Governor of the Panjab, 1778– 82 : K.C.S.I., 1879 : C.I.E. : J.P. : D.L.

ELERS, GEORGE (1777–1842)

Partly of German parentage : obtained a commission in the 12th regt. : arrived in Madras, 1797 : served against Tippoo, but was ill at Vellore during the siege of Seringapatam : accompanied Col. Wellesley to Coorg and stayed with him at Seringapatam as his guest for three months. His Memoirs were edited from the orginal MS. by Lord Monson and George Leveson-Gower and published in 1903.

ELGIN AND KINCARDINE, JAMES BRUCE, EIGHTH EARL OF
(1811–1863)

(Twelfth Earl of Kincardine) : born July 20, 1811 : educated at Eton and Christ Church, Oxford : Fellow of Merton College, 1832 : M.P. for Southampton, 1841 : succeeded his father in 1841 : was made Governor of Jamaica, 1842, and, in 1846, Governor-General of Canada—an appointment fraught with difficulties—which he retained till 1854 : for his services he was raised to the English peerage. In 1857 he was sent to China as special envoy : on his way there, he, at Lord Canning's request, diverted to India, troops intended for China, which were urgently required for the suppression of the Indian mutiny. He made the Tientsin Treaty with China, securing several important objects. In 1859 he became Postmater-General in Lord Palmerston's Government. In 1860 he was again sent to China to obtain the ratification of the Tientsin treaty, which had not been carried out. He destroyed the Summer Palace, as a punishment for

Chinese treachery and the murder of Englishmen. In Jan., 1862, he went to India as Viceroy, arriving at Calcutta in March. After spending the summer at Simla in 1863, he proceeded on tour in Upper India. He died of heart complaint, brought on by over-exertion, at Dharmsala on Nov. 20, 1863, and was there buried.

ELGIN AND KINCARDINE, VICTOR ALEXANDER BRUCE, NINTH EARL OF (1849-   )

Born May 16, 1849 : son of eighth Earl (q.v.), who was Plenipotentiary to China, and Viceroy of India, 1862-3 : educated at Eton and Balliol College, Oxford : First Commissioner of Works, 1886 : Viceroy and Governor-General of India, 1894-9 : Chairman of the Royal Commission to investigate the conduct of the S. African campaign : and of the inquiry into the disputes between the Scotch Churches : K.G. : G.C.S.I. : G.C.I.E. : P.C. : LL.D. of St. Andrew's.

ELIAS, NEY (1844-1897)

Son of Ney Elias : born Feb. 10, 1844 : educated at London, Paris, Dresden : F.R.G.S., 1865 : went to Shanghai in a merchant's firm in 1866 : led an expedition in 1868 to examine the channels of the Hoang-ho river : in 1872 crossed the Gobi desert, nearly 5,000 miles from the Great Wall to Nijni Novgorod : gold medal of the R.G.S., 1873 : joined the Indian Foreign Office, 1874 : served at Mandalay and in Ladak : travelled over the Karakorum to Yarkand, 1879 : and Kashgar, 1885 : from Yarkand to the Pamirs and the Oxus, 1885 : Badakshan, Balkh, Chitral, N. Afghanistan : was in Sikhim, 1888-9 : in the Shan States, 1889 -90 : Agent at Mashad and Consul-General : retired from the service, 1896. He had gained a great knowledge of the countries of Central Asia : and wrote several reports on his journeys : he died suddenly, May 31, 1897. He declined, in 1888, to receive the C.I.E. decoration.

ELIOT, SIR JOHN (1839-   )

Educated at St. John's College, Cambridge (2nd, Wrangler and 1st Smith's Prizeman) : Fellow of St. John's College, 1869-70 : Professor of Mathematics, Rurki Engineering College, 1869-72 : Muir Central College, Allahabad, 1872-4 : Pro-

fessor of Physics, Presidency College, Calcutta : Meteorological Reporter to Government of Bengal, 1874-86 : Meteorological Reporter to Government of India, 1886-1904 : Director-General of Indian Observations since 1899 : C.I.E., 1897 : K.C.I.E., 1903 : retired 1904.

ELIOTT, SIR DANIEL (1798-1872)

I.C.S. : son of Sir William Eliott : born March 3, 1798 : educated at the Edinburgh Academy and at Haileybury : went out to Madras in 1817 : Secretary to the Board of Revenue, 1827 : Member of the Board, 1836 : was the Madras Member of the Indian Law Commission in 1838 : Member of Council, Madras, 1848 to 1853 : President of various Boards in Madras, 1850 : Madras Member of the Legislative Council of India, 1854-9 : K.C.S.I. in May 1867 : died Oct. 30, 1872.

ELIOTT-LOCKHART, PERCY CLARE (1867-   )

Born Sep. 21, 1867 : son of Col. W. Eliott-Lockhart, R.A. : educated at Bath : joined 1st West India regt., 1887, and Indian Staff Corps, 1890 : served in Waziristan expedition, 1894-5 : Chitral, 1895 : N.W. frontier, 1897-8, defence of Malakand, operations in Bajaur, Mohmand and Buner : D.S.O : author of A Frontier Campaign : Captain in Queen's Own Corps of Guides.

ELLENBOROUGH, EDWARD LAW, FIRST EARL OF (1790-1871)

Governor-General : son of Edward, Baron Ellenborough, Lord Chief Justice of England : born Sep. 8, 1790 : educated at Eton and St. John's College, Cambridge : M.P. for St. Michael's, Cornwall, 1813 : was Lord Privy Seal, 1828 : President of the Board of Control, from 1828 to 1830, from Dec., 1834 to April, 1835, and for a third time in Sep.-Oct., 1841. He, in 1832, sent Alexander Burnes (q.v.) to Lahore, and on to Central Asia : was for a forward policy and for the transfer of the Government of India to the Crown. In Oct., 1841, he was nominated to be Governor-General, and held the appointment from Feb. 28, 1842, to June 15, 1844. He desired a peace policy, but was never free of war. He pushed on the Chinese war and brought it to a conclusion successfully. He desired to withdraw from interference with Afghanistan, after rescuing the Kabul captives and restoring British prestige, and eventually sanctioned Sir W. Nott's withdrawal from Kandahar *viâ* Ghazni, Kabul and Peshawar. Pollock's Army of retribution forced its way through the Khyber to Kabul, and Afghanistan was evacuated in Oct–Nov., 1842. Ellenborough's bombastic proclamation, on the recovery of the gates of Somnath from Ghazni, exposed him to ridicule. The troops retiring from Kabul were received at Firozpur with exaggerated pomp. He annexed Sind, by means of Sir Charles Napier's victories, in 1842, though the justification for this act has been seriously questioned. He interfered in the affairs of the Gwalior State, where the Army had rebelled and expelled the regent Mama Sahib : he was present at the battle of Maharajpur, Dec. 28, 1843 : a fresh treaty was made with the State. Being disrespectful and out of control, he was recalled by the Court of Directors in June, 1844, against the views of the Cabinet : was created an Earl : in 1846 he was made First Lord of the Admiralty, and in 1858, Feb. to June, was again President of the Board of Control. In this capacity, he addressed a despatch to Lord Canning regarding the latter's Oudh proclamation, which the Cabinet disavowed, and Ellenborough had to resign his office. During his Indian career, he preferred the military to political officers, and was unpopular with the civilians. His ability and eloquence were brilliant, but his other qualities detracted from his practical usefulness in high office. He died Dec. 22, 1871.

ELLES, SIR EDMUND ROCHE
(1848–   )

Born June 9, 1848 : son of Malcolm Jamieson Elles : educated privately and at Woolwich : entered the Royal Artillery, 1867 : Colonel, 1891 : Maj-General, 1900 : in the Lushai expedition, 1871–2 : D.A.Q.M.G. of the Indian contingent to Egypt, 1882 : A.Q.M.G. Hazara expedition, 1888 : in the Indian Frontier expedition, 1897 : commanded the Peshawar District, 1895–1900 : Adjutant-General, 1900–1 : second in command of Sir M. Durand's mission to Kabul, 1893 : Military Member of Supreme Council, April 11, 1901–5 : C.B., 1893 : K.C.B., 1898 : K.C.I.E., 1903.

ELLES, SIR WILLIAM KIDSTON
(1837–1896)

Son of Malcolm J. Elles : educated at Sandhurst : entered the 54th regt. : served in the Crimea, 1854–5 : in the mutiny, 1857–8, at battle of Cawnpur, defeat of Gwalior contingent, capture of Lucknow, Hazara campaign : Black Mountain expedition, 1868 : Burmese war, 1886–7 : C.B. : A.D.C. to Queen Victoria, 1881–90 : commanded in the Hazara expedition, 1891 : K.C.B. : commanded 1st class district, Bengal, 1890–5 : in command of the Bengal Army, 1895 : Lt-General, 1895 : died at Naini Tal, Aug. 5, 1896.

ELLIOT, EDWARD KING (1811–1865)

Lt-Colonel : entered the Army, 1829 : joined the 43rd N.I. : served in the first Afghan war : was Assistant to Sir H. C Rawlinson in a political capacity at Kandahar : was Deputy Commissioner of Sagar : Judicial Commissioner at Nagpur : Chief Commissioner of the Central Provinces : Agent of the Governor-General for Rajputana : died at Nasirabad, Oct. 11, 1865.

ELLIOT, SIR EDWARD LOCKE
(1850–   )

Born Jan. 28, 1850 : son of Colonel Edward King Elliot : entered the Army, 1868 : and the Indian Staff Corps : became Colonel, 1898 : served in the Afghan war, 1878–9 : Burmese expedition, 1886–7 : D.S.O. : Dongola expeditionary force, 1896 : C.B. : Inspr-General of Cavalry in India, 1898 : in South Africa, 1901–2 : K.C.B., 1902 : Maj-General.

ELLIOT, SIR HENRY MIERS (1808–1853)

I.C.S. : son of John Elliot : born March 1, 1808 : educated at Winchester : gained his appointment to the E.I. Co.'s Civil Service by open competition, 1826 : served in the N.W.P. : Secretary to the Board of Revenue : Foreign Secretary to the Government of India, 1847 : accompanied Lord Hardinge and Lord Dalhousie to the Panjab : negotiated the treaty with the Sikhs, 1849 : K.C.B : brought out the first volume of a *Bibliographical Index to the Historians of Muhammadan India*, his materials for *The History of India, as told by its own Historians*, were edited after his death by Professor John Dowson (*q.v.*) and Sir E. C. Bayley, (*q.v.*) : his *Memoirs* of the History, Folklore, and Distribution of the Races of the N.W.P. were edited by Mr. J. Beames (q.v.): he died at the Cape of Good Hope on his way home, Dec. 20, 1853. A mural tablet in St. Paul's Cathedral, at Calcutta, testifies to his remarkable abilities and attainments, his manly rectitude of conduct, his gentle disposition and noble qualities. He (like Augustus Cleveland) (q.v.) was called by Sir W. W. Hunter the dulce decus of the Bengal Civil Service.

ELLIOT, HUGH (1752–1830)

Governor: son of Sir Gilbert Elliot, M.P.: born April 6, 1752: educated privately, at Paris, and Christ Church, Oxford: at a military school abroad: served with the Russian Army against the Turks, 1772: Minister at Munich, 1773–6: Envoy and Minister to Prussia, 1777: at Copenhagen, 1782–91: on a secret mission to Paris, 1791: Minister at Dresden until 1803: at Naples, 1803: recalled thence: Governor of the Leeward Islands, 1809–13: P.C.: Governor of Madras, Sep. 16, 1814, to June 10, 1820: died Dec. 10, 1830: buried in Westminster Abbey.

ELLIOT, SIR WALTER (1803–1887)

I.C.S.: born Jan. 16, 1803: son of James Elliot: educated privately: at Doncaster and Haileybury: went to Madras in 1820: specially rewarded for remarkable proficiency in Tamil and Hindustani at 20: served in the S. Mahratta country, until 1833: was a keen sportsman and adventurous with big game: in the insurrection of Kittur, 1824, when several officers were killed, he and another officer, Stevenson, were prisoners of the rebels for six weeks: in 1843, made an adventurous journey to Mocha, Red Sea coast of Abyssinia, Egypt and Palestine: Private Secretary to Lord Elphinstone, Governor of Madras. 1837–42: Member of the Board of Revenue, but was sent in 1845 to inquire into the maladministration of Guntur: appointed Commissioner of the whole of the Northern Sircars till Dec. 1854, when he became a Member of Council, Madras, till Dec. 1859. As Senior Member of Council, he contributed greatly by his steadfast calmness, during the temporary absence of Lord Harris, to the preservation of peace and order in the Presidency: also, in 1858, carried on the Government during Lord Harris' ill-health: took much interest in education and supported Christian missions: acquired much knowledge of archæology, natural history, numismatics, and Indian history: wrote for scientific Journals on the above subjects: notably on coins and Hindu inscriptions: assisted Darwin and Owen in their researches: his collection of Buddhist marbles from Amravati is in the British Museum: a member of many learned Societies: K.C.S.I. in 1866: F.R.S., 1877: LL.D. of Edinburgh, 1878: became blind, and died March 1, 1887.

ELLIOTT, CHARLES (1776 ? –1856)

Voluntarily passed through the college of Fort William: judge of Fatehghar at 30: judge of Bareli: Court of Appeal: Judge of the Sadr Court at Calcutta, 1821: in 1822, to Delhi as Senior Member of the Board, N.W.P: and A.G.G. at the Court of the Great Mogul: returned to England, 1826: published a translation of the Life of the Great Mogul: F.R.S.: F.R.A.S.: died May 4, 1856.

ELLIOTT, SIR CHARLES ALFRED (1835–)

I.C.S.: son of the Rev. H. V. Elliott of Brighton: born Dec. 1835: educated at Harrow and Trinity College, Cambridge: after open competition, arrived in India in Nov. 1856: served in the N.W.P., Oudh and Central Provinces: was Secretary to the N.W.P. Government, 1870–7: Famine Commissioner, Mysore, 1877: C.S.I., 1878: Secretary to the Famine Commission (Sir Richard Strachey's), 1878: Census Commissioner, 1880: Chief Commissioner of Assam, 1881: President of the Committee for the retrenchment of public expenditure, 1886: Member of the Supreme Council, 1887–90: Lieutenant-Governor of Bengal, 1890–5. He wrote the Chronicles of Unao, the Reports of the Mysore famine, and of the Famine, and Finance Commissions. Since his retirement, in 1895, he has been Finance Member of the London School Board, and Member of the Educational Committee for London County Council. Throughout his career, Sir Charles Elliott has laboured with great energy and ability in his various charges, and made a reputation as an expert in Settlement, Famine, Finance, and Education.

ELLIOTT, SIR WILLIAM HENRY
(1792–1874)

Son of Capt. John Elliott, R.N.: born in 1792, entered the 51st regt. in 1809, remained in it until 1852 : served in the Peninsula, was at Waterloo, at Cambrai, in the Ionian Islands, Australia, Van Diemen's Land, New Zealand, Bangalore : in 1852, he commanded the Madras Brigade in the Burmese war, under General Godwin : was at the capture of Rangoon and the storming of the Shwe-Dagon pagoda in April, 1852 : in the capture of Donabew : C.B. and Commandant at Rangoon, where he detected and defeated a plot to kill all the English in that city : Maj-General in 1857 : K.C.B. in 1862 : G.C.B. in 1870 : General in 1871 : died on Feb. 27, 1874.

ELLIS, SIR BARROW HERBERT
(1823–1887)

I.C.S.: born Jan. 24, 1823 : son of S. Herbert Ellis, a leading member of the Jewish community : educated at University College School, London University, and Haileybury : went to Bombay in 1843 : served in Sind from 1851–58, acting for some time as Chief Commissioner during Sir Bartle Frere's absence : was Chief Secretary to the Bombay Government and Member of Council, Bombay, 1865–70 : Member of the Supreme Council of the Governor-General, 1869–75 : K.C.S.I. in Oct. 1875, and Member of the Council of India, 1875–85 : after his retirement he was an authority among his co-religionists, and a Member and Vice-President of the Royal Asiatic Society : died June 20, 1887.

ELLIS, FRANCIS WHYTE (? –1819)

I.C.S.: Oriental linguist : joined at Madras in 1796 : Secretary to the Board of Revenue, 1802 : Collector of Madras, 1810 : died of cholera at Ramnad, March 10, 1819. He was an excellent Tamil and Sanskrit scholar : published a commentary and translation of *The Sacred Kurral,* and exposed the forgery of Sanskrit MSS. at Pondicherry by Jesuit missionaries : he wrote papers on the Tamil, Telugu and Malayalam languages, and was an expert authority on " Mirasi right ": and on information regarding the Madras Presidency.

ELLIS, ROBERT STAUNTON (1825–1877)

I.C.S. : went out to Madras in 1844 : was Deputy Commissioner of Nagpur and Superintendent of Police in the mutiny : C.B. : was Chief Secretary to the Madras Government, 1870 : Member of Council at Madras, 1872–7 : retired : Member of the Council of India in 1877 : died Oct. 9, 1877.

ELPHINSTONE, JOHN, THIRTEENTH BARON (1807–1860)

Governor : and Lt-General : son of John, twelfth Lord Elphinstone : born June 23, 1807 : succeeded his father in 1813 : entered the Royal Horse Guards in 1826 : was a Lord-in-waiting, 1835–7 : G.C.H. in 1836 : Governor of Madras from March 1837, to Sep. 1842, during an uneventful period : encouraged the practice of resorting to the Nilgiri hills for the hot weather : travelled in Kashmir and Upper India : returned to England in 1845 : Lord-in-waiting again : Governor of Bombay, Dec. 1853, to May, 1860, during the mutiny, in which he showed his capacity for administration, suppressing all risings and annihilating a conspiracy in Bombay. He afforded great assistance to the Government of India by sparing troops from Bombay for the disaffected parts of the country : G.C.B. in 1858 : raised to the Peerage of the United Kingdom, 1859 : died July 19, 1860.

ELPHINSTONE, MOUNTSTUART
(1779–1859)

Governor : I.C.S. : son of John, eleventh Baron Elphinstone : born Oct. 6, 1779 : educated at the High School, Edinburgh, and at Kensington : went out to Bengal as a "writer" in the E.I. Co.'s service in 1795 : stationed at Benares, he had to ride for his life when European officers, including Cherry, the Agent to the Governor-General, were massacred there in Jan. 1799, by order of Wazir Ali, the Ex-Nawab of Oudh. In 1801 he was appointed Assistant to Sir Barry Close, the Resident at the court of Baji Rao, the Peshwa at Poona : at the battles of Assaye and Argaum, he was on the Staff of Colonel Arthur Wellesley, who told him that he ought to have been a soldier. He was Resident at Nagpur from 1804 to 1808 : was sent as Envoy to Kabul, with a view to establish English influence there against the supposed French designs on India: Shah Shuja received him at Peshawar on March 5, 1809 : the negotiations produced little result, as Shah Shuja was himself ejected from Afghanistan in 1809. Elphinstone was appointed Resident at Poona in 1811. In 1815 he insisted on the surrender of Trimbakji Danglia, the Peshwa's minister, for the murder of Gungadhar Sastri, the minister and envoy of the Gaekwar of Baroda, at Poona. In 1817 Elphinstone concluded the treaty dated June 13, of Poona, as dictated to the Peshwa, who, however, continued to intrigue. Elphinstone was, for a time, superseded by Sir T. Hislop, the General commanding the Army collected against the Pindaris : the Peshwa eventually attacked the British force at Kirki on Nov. 5, 1817, and was defeated : Elphinstone's residence at Poona, library, and papers were all burnt : he himself showed great skill and military courage : he annexed the Peshwa's territory, as ordered, and administered it, interfering as little as possible with native usages. He was Governor of Bombay from Nov. 1819, to Nov. 1827 : instituted legislative and judicial reforms, had a code of Regulations drawn up, and advanced popular education. The Elphinstone College was founded in his honour. He travelled in Europe, 1827–9, and led a retired life : twice refused the offer of the Governor-Generalship of India, and declined the Under Secretaryship of the Board of Control and a special mission to Canada. He wrote *An Account of the Kingdom of Caubul and its Dependencies in Persia, Tartary and India*, 1815 : his *History of India*, 1841, for which he was called the Tacitus of modern historians : and *The Rise of British Power in the East*, edited in 1887 by Sir E. Colebrooke. He was not ambitious, occupied his time with study, and maintained his interest in Indian affairs, being regarded as the Nestor of Indian statesmanship. He was a Vice-President of the Royal Asiatic Society. He combined through life a keenness for field sports with his love of books and the despatch of public business. Bishop Heber wrote of him, " Of Mr. Elphinstone everybody spoke highly " : no Indian civilian has gained a greater name as a statesman and a ruler. He died Nov. 20, 1859 : a statue was erected in St. Paul's Cathedral in his honour.

ELPHINSTONE, WILLIAM GEORGE KEITH (1782–1842)

Maj-General : son of Hon. William Fullerton Elphinstone, Director of the E.I. Co. : entered the Army, 1804, in the 24th foot : served with distinction in various parts of the world : Lt-Colonel of the 33rd foot in 1813, and served with it at Waterloo : made C.B. : A.D.C. to George IV. 1825 : became Maj-General, 1837 : commanded the Benares Division, 1839–41, when, in the first Afghan war, he succeeded Sir Willoughby Cotton as Commander in Chief at Kabul, towards the close of 1841, and, on the murder of Sir W. Macnaghten, on December 23, 1841, failed entirely, through old age and ill-health, to take measures for the safety of the force. During the disastrous retreat of the Army from Kabul, in Jan. 1842, he surrendered as a hostage of Akbar Khan : and died of dysentery at Tezin on April 23, 1842.

ELSMIE, GEORGE ROBERT (1838–)

I.C.S. : Born Oct. 31, 1838 : son of George Elsmie : educated at Marischal College and University, Aberdeen, and Haileybury : joined the Bengal Civil Service, 1858 : Judge, Chief Court, Panjab, 1878–85 : Financial Commissioner, Panjab, 1887–93 : Member of the Governor-General's Legislative Council, 1888–93 : Vice-Chancellor, Panjab University, 1885–7. Author of *Epitome of Kabul Correspondence*, 1864 ; *Notes on Peshawar Crime*, 1884 ; *Lumsden of the Guides*, 1899 ; *Field Marshal Sir Donald Stewart*, 1903 : C.S.I., 1893.

EMPSON, WILLIAM (1791–1852)

Born in 1791 : educated at Winchester and Trinity College, Cambridge : B.A., 1812 : between 1823 and 1849 wrote largely for the *Edinburgh Review*, " a valued contributor on political, legal, and literary subjects " : he edited the *Review* from 1849 to 1852. His friendship with Dr. Arnold, begun at Winchester, continued through life. He was appointed in 1824 Professor of Polity and the Laws of England at the E.I. Co.'s College, Haileybury. His lectures, especially those on general jurisprudence and Indian law, were much appreciated by the better students. He was much liked by his pupils, over whom he had considerable influence. " To form the mind of those young men, many of whom, as magistrates and judges, were to affect the interests of thousands and millions, was to him a duty of a solemn, or rather of a sacred, kind." He died Dec. 10, 1852.

ENGLAND, SIR RICHARD (1793–1883)

Son of Lt-General Richard England : born in 1793 : educated at Winchester and the Royal Military College, Marlow : entered the Army in 1808 : served in the Walcheren expedition, Sicily, Canada, at the Cape as Brig.-General, in the Kafir war, 1836–7 : went to Belgaum in 1839 : commanded a Bombay Division in 1841 : after a repulse at Haikalzai on March 28, 1842, he joined General Nott at Kandahar, and in the defeat of Akbar Khan at the Kojak : in the retirement in 1842 from Kandahar, he commanded the force through the Bolan into Sind : but his operations were generally wanting in success : K.C.B. in 1843 : commanded a Division in the Crimea in 1854–5, and was at Alma, Inkerman, the Redan, and distinguished himself : G.C.B., 1856 : General, 1863 : retired, 1877 : died Jan. 19, 1883.

ENGLISH, FREDERICK (1816–1878)

Maj-General : entered the Army in 1833 : in the mutiny, with a wing of the 53rd regt., defeated 1,000 mutineers, chiefly of the Ramghar battalion : C.B. : cleared Bihar and defeated mutineers at Gopalganj : in a number of other actions : commanded the 53rd at the siege and capture of Lucknow : at Faizabad and Tulsipur : Maj-General, 1864 : died Nov. 5, 1878.

ERSKINE, HENRY NAPIER BRUCE (1832–1893)

I.C.S. : son of William Erskine (q.v.) : born 1832 : arrived at Bombay, 1853 : Commissioner of the Northern Division, 1877–9 : Commissioner in Sind, 1879–87 : died Dec. 4, 1893.

ERSKINE, JAMES CLAUDIUS (1821–1893)

I. C.S. : son of William Erskine (q.v.) : born May 20, 1821 : educated at St. Andrew's and Haileybury : went to Bombay, 1840 : was Private Secretary,

1843–6, to Sir G. Arthur, Governor of Bombay : Secretary to Government of Bombay in the General and Judicial Department, 1854 : first Director of Public Instruction in W. India, 1855–9 : Additional Member of the Governor-General's Legislative Council, 1860 : Vice-Chancellor of the Calcutta University : Judge of the Bombay High Court, 1862–3 : Member of Council, Bombay, Oct. 1865, to May 1867 : retired, 1867 : died June 5, 1893.

ERSKINE, WILLIAM (1773–1852)

Son of David Erskine : born Nov. 8, 1773 : educated at the Royal High School and Edinburgh University : was a lawyer's apprentice, 1792–9 : went to India in 1803–4 with Sir James Mackintosh : at Bombay he became clerk to the Small Cause Court, a stipendiary magistrate, Secretary and Vice-President to the Literary Society—to which he contributed numerous articles on the Parsis, their language, religion and literature, and on the Buddhists, etc. : became Master in Equity in the Recorder's Court in 1820 : was a Member of Mountstuart Elphinstone's Committee for framing the Bombay code of Regulations : he left India in 1823, having lost his legal offices on a charge of defalcations : in 1826 he published his translation of Babar's autobiographical memoirs from a Persian version, with a full commentary, a standard work. He was Provost of St. Andrew's, 1836–9 : died at Edinburgh, May 20, 1852 : wrote History of India under Babar and Humayun, edited by his son, 1854.

ESDAILE, JAMES (1808–1859)

Son of Rev. Dr. Esdaile : born Feb. 6, 1808 : graduated as M.D. at Edinburgh in 1830 : reached Calcutta in the E.I. Co.'s medical service in 1831 : in charge of the Hughli hospital in 1838 : devoted himself to the study of mesmerism and performed some surgical operations by its aid as an anæsthetic with remarkable success : his experiments were scientifically investigated, and he was made Superintendent of a small hospital for mesmerism in 1846, and Presidency Surgeon. Disliking India, he retired in 1851 : wrote Mesmerism in India and its Practical Application in Surgery and Medicine, Natural and Mesmeric Clairvoyance and other medical works : died Jan. 10, 1859.

ETHE, C. HERMANN (1844-)

Born Feb. 13, 1844 : grandson of Karl Laphe : educated at Greifswald and Leipzig Universities : came to Oxford in 1872 to complete Catalogue of Persian, Turkish, Hindustani and Pashtu MSS., in Bodleian Library, and to compile Catalogue of Arabic MSS. : catalogued Persian MSS. in India Office Library : Public Examiner for Honours School of Oriental Languages, Oxford, 1887-9, and since 1893 : Professor of German and Oriental Languages, University College, Aberystwyth, since 1875.

EVANS, SIR GRIFFITH HUMPHREY PUGH (1840-1902)

Son of John Evans, of Lovesgrove : born Jan. 13, 1840 : educated at Bradfield and Lincoln College, Oxford (Scholar) : called to the bar from Lincoln's Inn, 1867 : joined the bar of the High Court, Calcutta : Member of the Governor-General's Legislative Council, 1877 to 1899 : K.C.I.E. in 1892 : acting Advocate-General and Member of the Bengal Legislative Council, 1895 : he took a prominent part, on behalf of the public, in the arrangements for composing the controversy over the "Ilbert Bill" in 1883 : died Feb. 6, 1902.

EVANS, SIR WILLIAM DAVID (1767-1821)

Son of John Evans : born May 25, 1767 : educated at Harrow : an attorney from 1789 to 1794, when he was called to the bar from Gray's Inn : wrote on legal and political questions : was a stipendiary magistrate at Manchester, 1813 : Vice-Chancellor of the County Palatine of Lancaster, 1815 : in 1819 he became Recorder of Bombay and was knighted : but died there Dec. 5, 1821.

EVEREST, SIR GEORGE (1790-1866)

Surveyor-General of India : born July 4, 1790 : son of Tristram Everest : educated at Great Marlow and Woolwich : went to India in 1806 to the Bengal Artillery : selected by Sir Stamford Raffles to survey Java, 1813-5 : Chief Assistant of the Great Trigonometrical Survey, 1817 : succeeded Colonel Lambton as Superintendent of the Great Trigonometrical Survey, 1823 : F.R.S., 1827 : studied the English ordnance survey : was appointed by the Court of Directors to be Surveyor General of India, 1830 : also engaged in measurements of the great Arc of Meridian of India, 21 degrees in length, from Cape Comorin to the Northern frontier, 1832-41 : Lt-Colonel, 1838 : retired in 1843 : published in 1847 an account of his work on the great Meridional Arc of India between two base lines : Member of the Council of the Royal and Geographical Societies : Fellow of the Astronomical and Royal Asiatic Societies : C.B. : and knighted in 1861 : died Dec. 1, 1866 : Mount Everest, 29,002 feet high, in the Himalayas on the borders of Nipal and Tibet, the highest known mountain in the world, was named after him.

EWALD, GEORGE HEINRICH AUGUST (1803-1875)

Born at Gottingen, Nov. 1803 : a celebrated Oriental scholar : educated at Gottingen University : at 20 was a Professor at the College of Wolfenbuttel : held the Chairs of Philosophy and Oriental languages and theology at Gottingen : when suspended, for political reasons, in 1837, he came to England, but returned to Gottingen : became a member of the German Parliament : author of many critical works, especially on the Hebrew language and Biblical history : died 1875.

EWART, SIR JOHN ALEXANDER (1821-1904)

Born June 11, 1821 : son of Lt-General John Frederick Ewart, C.B. : educated at Sandhurst : joined the 35th regt., 1838 : exchanged to 93rd Highlanders, 1848 : served in Crimea and Indian mutiny : at Alma, Balaclava, Inkerman and siege of Sebastopol : at relief of Lucknow : commanded the leading party of stormers at the assault of the Sikandarbagh : severely wounded : lost his left arm by a cannon-ball at Cawnpur in Dec. 1857 : C.B. : Lt-Colonel of 93rd Highlanders, 1858 : commanded 78th Highlanders, 1859-64 : A.D.C. to Queen Victoria : Maj-General, 1872 : Lt-General, 1877 : commanded the Allahabad Division in India, 1877-80 : General, 1884 : K.C.B., 1887 : recommended for the V.C. : died June 18, 1904 : author of *A few Remarks about the British Army*, and *The Story of a Soldier's Life*.

EWART, SIR JOSEPH (1831–)

Born 1831 : son of Andrew Ewart : educated privately : entered the E.I. Co.'s medical service, 1854 : served in the Mewar Bheel Corps in the Indian mutiny : Professor of Medicine, Calcutta : retired as Deputy Surgeon-General, 1879. Author of several works relating to Indian Sanitation, Pathology and Snake Poisoning : Mayor of Brighton, 1891–4 : Knight Bachelor, 1895.

EWER, WALTER (1784–1863)

I.C.S.: son of a Governor of the settlement at Bencoolen : privately educated : joined the Bengal Civil Service in 1803 : distinguished at the College of Fort William : employed at Rajshahi, at Amboyna, again at Rajshahi, 1816 : Superintendent of Police in Bengal, Bihar, and Orissa, and the conquered and ceded Provinces for 10 years : Judge of the *Sadr* Court, N.W.P., until he resigned in 1839–40 : well versed in music and astronomy : read the inscriptions on the Kutb at Delhi in 1822 through his telescope : F.R.G.S. : F.R.S. : died in London, Jan. 5, 1863.

EYRE, HENRY (1834–)

Born Feb. 4, 1834 : son of Rev. C. W. Eyre : educated at Harrow and Christ Church, Oxford : joined 2nd Battalion Rifle Brigade, 1855 : present at siege and fall of Sebastopol : A.D.C. to Lt-General, Sir W. Eyre, 1855 : served with Rifle Brigade through the Indian mutiny, 1857–8 : present at taking of Lucknow, siege of Kalpi, etc. : commanded 4th Notts R.V., 1865–92 : C.B., 1897.

EYRE, SIR VINCENT (1811–1881)

General : son of Capt. Henry Eyre : born Jan. 22, 1811 : educated at Norwich Grammar School, and at Addiscombe : joined the Bengal Artillery, 1828 : was, in 1839, Commissary of Ordnance to the Kabul Field Force : took ordnance stores to Kabul in 1840 : after the rising in Nov. 1841, Eyre and his family started, in Jan. 1842, for India, but were detained by Akbar Khan as hostages : he published a journal of his 9 months' captivity, which terminated on Sep. 21, 1842 : he returned to India with Pollock's force : commanded the Artillery of the Gwalior contingent, 1844 : was at Thayetmyo in Burma in 1857, but was recalled to India :

on his way up country in July, he heard at Baxar of the siege of Arrah, that is, of some Government officers being besieged there by mutineers : after severe fighting he effected their relief, and defeated Kooer Singh of Jagdishpur, all on his own responsibility : he was recommended for the Victoria Cross : was at the relief of Lucknow in Sep. 1857, commanded the Artillery at the Alambagh : at the capture of Lucknow in March, 1858 : C.B. and Lt-Colonel : Superintendent of the Ishapur Powder Factory : on the Army Amalgamation Commission, and Inspr-General of Ordnance, 1862 : retired, 1863 : K.C.S.I., 1867 : in the Franco-Prussian war he organized an ambulance service for the sick and wounded : died Sep. 22, 1881 : had great qualities as an officer, in literature, and in private life.

EXMOUTH, EDWARD PELLEW, FIRST VISCOUNT (1757–1833)

Son of Samuel Pellew : born April 19, 1757 : educated at Truro : entered the Navy, 1770 : served with great gallantry in various parts of the world : and was made a Baronet in 1796 : M.P. for Barnstaple, 1802 : Naval C. in C. in the East Indies in 1804, and Rear Admiral : destroyed the Dutch ships of war, 1807 : enforced strict discipline, and reduced the amount of punishment : Vice Admiral, 1808, returned to England : C. in C. in the North Sea, 1810 : in the Mediterranean, 1811 : at Plymouth, 1817–21 : made a Peer, 1814 : K.C.B. and G.C.B., 1815 : bombarded Algiers, 1816 : died Jan. 23, 1833.

FABRICIUS. REV. JOHN PHILIP (1714–1791)

Danish Missionary : native of Frankfort-on-the-Maine : graduate of Halle : a Lutheran : arrived in India, 1740 : went to Madras in service of S.P.C.K., 1742 : assisted at the English Church when required : when Fort St. George surrendered to the French, 1746, he took refuge at the Dutch settlement at Pulicat : and again, when Count Lally and his army appeared in Dec. 1758 : returned, on the raising of the siege, to Vepery : plundered by the Muhammadans : ministered at Vellore, 1772–3 : up to 1780, greatly trusted by Government and the people : mismanaged the funds : imprisoned for debt for 18 months, 1787–9 : relieved by Gericke (*q.v.*) in 1788, as head of the Vepery Mission and school : died there, 1791 : a Tamil scholar : partly translated the New Testament into Tamil : compiled a Tamil Dictionary, and wrote Lyrics in Tamil.

FAGAN, CHRISTOPHER GEORGE FORBES (? ,–)

Educated at Harrow : joined the Army, 1875 : Lt-Colonel, 1901 : served in the Afghan war, 1879–80 : Asst. Dist. Superintendent of Police, Panjab, 1885 : Assistant Resident, Hyderabad, 1892 : Assistant Political Agent, Bussora, 1897 : Political Agent, Muscat, 1898, Kotah, 1900 : Political Agent, Ulwar, Rajputana, since 1901.

FALCONER, FORBES (1805–1853)

Born Sep. 10, 1805 : son of Gilbert Falconer : educated at Marischal College, Aberdeen : early studied Oriental languages, Hebrew, Arabic, Persian at Aberdeen, at Paris for 5 years, and at German Universities : Professor of Oriental Languages at University College, London : translated from the *Bostan*, and two poems of Jami, and other poets : published a Persian Grammar : M.R.A.S., London and Paris : died Nov. 7, 1853.

FALCONER, HUGH (1808–1865)

Botanist : son of David Falconer : born Feb. 29, 1808 : educated at Forres and Aberdeen University : M.D. of Edinburgh in 1829 : studied geology and Indian fossils : joined the E.I. Co.'s medical service in Bengal, 1830 : succeeded Dr. Royle in 1832 as Superintendent of the Botanic Gardens, Saharanpur : made, with other officers, important discoveries of fossils, mammals and reptiles in the Sivalik hills : served on the Tea Commission of 1834, and superintended the manufacture of the first Indian tea : he travelled in 1837–8 to Kashmir and Beluchistan, and in the Astor Valley discovered assafœtida : contributed many plants and fruit trees from Kashmir to Saharanpur : while in England, 1843–7, he wrote on geology, fossils and botany, his botanical collections and work being subsequently utilized : was engaged on the arrangement and exhibition of Indian fossils in the British Museum : he commenced the publication of the *Fauna Antiqua Sivalensis*. From 1848 to 1855 he was, on Dr. Wallich's death, Superintendent of the Botanic Garden at Sibpur, Howrah, opposite to Calcutta : Professor of Botany in the Calcutta Medical College : and adviser of the Government of India on vegetable products : wrote on teak, cinchona, fossils, etc. : after retirement, he continued his studies in palæcatology, fossil mammals and pre-historic man : visited museums, served on a Royal Commission on the sanitary condition of India, writing papers on his own subjects : F.R.S. in 1845 : Vice-President of the Royal Society : he died Jan. 31, 1865. A selection of his palæontological papers was published under the editorship of Dr. Murchison.

FALKLAND, LUCIUS BENTINCK CARY, TENTH VISCOUNT
; (1803–1884)

Son of the ninth Viscount : Lord of the Bedchamber to King William IV, 1830, and to Queen Victoria, 1839 : representative Peer of Scotland, 1831–2 : made a Peer of the United Kingdom : Lord-in-Waiting, 1837–9 : Governor of Nova Scotia, 1840–6 · Captain of the Yeomen of the Guard, 1846–8 : Governor of Bombay, 1848–53 : G.C.H., 1831 : P.C., 1837 : died at Montpelier, France, March 12, 1884.

FALLON, S. W. (1817–1880)

Born at Calcutta, 1817 : entered the Bengal Education Department in his 20th year : was Inspector of Schools : in 1857, published a Hindustani-English Law and Commercial Dictionary : Phil. Dr. of Halle : published, 1875–9, his Hindustani-English Dictionary, illustrated from Hindustani literature and folklore : and part of an English-Hindustani Dictionary : retired, 1875 : resided at Delhi : to England, 1880 : died Oct. 3, 1880.

FANE, SIR HENRY (1778–1840)

General : born Nov. 26, 1778 : son of Hon. Henry Fane, and grandson of the eighth Earl of Westmoreland : entered the Dragoon Guards, 1792 : M.P. for Lyme Regis, then a family borough, 1796–1818 : Lt-Colonel, 1797 : A.D.C. to George III. : saw much service, chiefly in cavalry commands, through the Peninsular campaign :

K.C.B. : Lt-General, 1819 : G.C.B., 1825 : Master-General of the Ordnance and M.P. for Sandwich, 1829 : General, 1837 : C. in C. in India, 1835-9 : objected so strongly to the policy of the first Afghan war that he resigned his appointment, but his resignation was not accepted : his health failing, he resigned again in 1839, and died on the voyage home, off the Azores, on March 24, 1840.

FANE, WALTER (1828-1885)

Son of Rey. Edward Fane : born 1828 : entered the Army, 1845 : in the Panjab Irregular Cavalry, 1849-57 : in several N.W. frontier expeditions : in the pursuit and capture of Tantia Topi, 1859 : Captain, 1860 : in the Madras Staff Corps : Colonel, 1875 : raised a regiment of irregular cavalry for the China war, 1860 : at the Peiho forts : commanded " Fane's Horse " at Sinho, Chinkiawhaw, and the capture of Pekin : C.B. : Maj-General, 1879 : died June 16, 1885.

FANSHAWE, SIR ARTHUR UPTON (1848–)

I.C.S. : son of Rev. J. Fanshawe : educated at Repton : entered the Bengal Civil Service, 1871 : served in the Central Provinces : Postmaster General, Bombay, 1882 : Officiating Secretary in the Finance and Commerce Department to the Government of India, 1888 : Director-General of the Post Office, India, 1889 : C.S.I., 1896 : K.C.I.E., 1903.

FARRUKHABAD, AHMAD KHAN BANGASH, NAWAB OF (? –1771)

Son of Muhammad Khan Bangash, Nawab : collected a force of Afghans and defeated and slew the Deputy of the Wazir Safdar Jang, who had confiscated territories belonging to his family, 1750 : the Wazir called in the Mahrattas, which led to his ultimate ruin : reigned till his death in Nov. 1771.

FARQUHAR, JOHN (1751-1826)

Born in 1751 of poor parents in Scotland : went to Bombay in the E.I. Co.'s military service : incapacitated for active service by a wound : transferred to Bengal : became a free merchant and learnt chemistry. Lord Cornwallis employed him to inquire into the circumstances of the Government gunpowder factory at Pulta : made Superintendent of the factory, and, later, sole contractor : thus acquired a fortune : returned to England, and became partner in the agency house, Basset, Farquhar & Co., and in Whitbread's Brewery. He was a curious mixture of penuriousness and largeness in expenditure at his pleasure : bought Fonthill Abbey in 1822 for £330,000 : he was a good scholar, excellent in the sciences, and greatly admired the Brahmanical system : died July 6, 1826, leaving a million and a half.

FAUSBÖLL, MICHAEL VIGGO (1821–)

Son of Rev. Christian Nissen Fausböll : born Sep. 22, 1821, in Jutland : educated at a Latin Grammar School, Aarhus, 1834 –8 : and at Copenhagen University from 1838, studying Oriental languages under N. L. Westergaard (*q.v.*) : University Gold Medallist, 1843 : Assistant Librarian at the University Library, Copenhagen, 1861-78 : Professor of Indian Philology and Sanskrit at that University, 1878-1902 : Member of Royal Danish Society of Sciences, 1876 : Bopp's Prizeman, 1888 : Hon. M.R.A.S. 1890 : Commander of the Order of Dannebrog, and possessor of the Silver Cross of that Order : founded the study of Pali in Europe, and was called the "Father of Pali study " : has published the *Dhammapadani*, 1855 : the *Suttanipata*, 1-2, 1885-94 : the *Jataka*, 1-7, 1877-97 : an Indian Mythology according to the Mahabharata, 1902.

FAWCETT, HENRY (1833-1884)

Son of William Fawcett, J.P. : born Aug. 26, 1833 : educated at Alderbury, Queen-wood, King's College, London, Peterhouse and Trinity Hall, Cambridge : seventh Wrangler and Fellow, 1856 : totally lost his sight by an accident out shooting, Sep. 1858 : wrote a *Manual of Political Economy*, and frequently on political and economic subjects : elected Professor of Pol. Econy. at Cambridge, 1863 : M.P. for Brighton, 1865 and 1868 : for Hackney, 1874 and 1880 : adopted, as a Radical member, an independent line in public measures : for his marked interest in Indian affairs he was known as the " Member for India " : dwelling on the poverty of India, he strenuously advocated economy, justice to the Indian revenues, and the native interests. Thus, he opposed the charging of the Ball to the Sultan (1867) upon Indian revenues : by his persistence the Committees on Indian finance were appointed 1871–4 : he spoke fully and forcibly on Indian budgets : was a member of the Committee on Indian Public Works, 1878 : opposed the Malta expedition, 1878, and the debit of any of the charge to India : opposed the Afghan war, 1878–80 : wrote on Indian Finance in the *Nineteenth Century*, 1879 : his views, though contested at the time, since generally accepted : his knowledge and character gained him great respect and influence in Indian affairs : as Postmaster-General, from 1880, effected many administrative improvements : P.C. : F.R.S., 1882 : D.C.L. Oxford, 1881 : Doctor of Political Economy, Wurzburg, 1882 : a corresponding member of the Institute of France, 1884 : LL.D. and Lord Rector of Glasgow University, 1883 : died at Cambridge, Nov. 6, 1884 : a national monument to him placed in Westminster Abbey.

FAY, MRS. (? –1817)

Wife of Anthony Fay, a barrister of Lincoln's Inn, who went to India to practise in the courts of Calcutta : they travelled viâ Egypt and the Red Sea : their ship touched at Calicut, where they were seized by Hyder Ali's officers and imprisoned for 15 weeks, suffering hardships and privations : they escaped and reached Madras in 1779–80, and proceeded to Calcutta. She published an account of her travels from England to Calcutta, *Original Letters from India*, Calcutta, 1817, dying there during their publication.

FAYRER, SIR JOSEPH, BARONET (1824–)

Born Dec. 6, 1824 : son of Commander Robert J. Fayrer, R.N. : educated at King's College, London and Edinburgh : M.D., 1859 : entered the Bengal medical service, 1850 : served in the first Burmese war, throughout the Indian mutiny, and defence of Lucknow, where he was Residency Surgeon from Aug. 1853 : and Civil Surgeon : Professor, Medical College, Calcutta : Surgeon-General : Fellow of the Calcutta University : President of the Asiatic Society of Bengal, 1867 : C.S.I., 1867 : President, Medical Board, India Office, 1874–95 : accompanied H.R.H.

the Duke of Edinburgh on his Indian tour, 1869–70, and H.R.H. the Prince of Wales on his Indian tour, 1875–6 : author of *The Thanatophidia of India* : of many medical works on Tropical Diseases : *Life of Sir Ranald Martin, C.B.*, *Recollections of My Life*, etc. : K.C.S.I. : first Baronet, 1896 : Physician Extraordinary to H.M. the King since 1901 : F.R.C.P. : F.R.S. : LL.D., Edinburgh : Member of many foreign Medical Academies : and President and Member of Medical Societies in England.

FEER, HENRI LEON (1830–1902)

Born at Rouen, Nov. 22, 1830 : Professor of Tibetan, 1864, at the Bibliotheque Nationale, Paris, and at the École des Langues Orientales, 1865 : Lecturer in Tibetan and Mongol at the Collège de France, 1869 : Librarian of the MSS. Department of the National Library, Paris, 1872 : and, later, Conservateur-Adjoint : wrote in the learned French Reviews : knew Tibetan, Mongol, Sanskrit and Pali : translated from Tibetan : was learned in Buddhist literature : by his translations, made known the Buddhist literature of Nipal and Tibet : wrote for the *Grande Encyclopedie* and the *Journal Asiatique* : edited Pali texts : wrote *Textes tirès du Kandjour* : translated from the Tibetan : *Etudes Buddhiques*, 1871–85 : *Le Thibet, pays, peuple, et religion*, 1886 : edited the *Samyutta-Nikaya* for the Pali Text Society : Member of the Société Asiatique from 1856, of its Council, 1869 : died March, 10, 1902.

FENDALL, JOHN (1762 ? –1825)

I.C.S. : to India as a writer in 1777 became a Puisne Judge of the *Sadr* Court Sep. 9, 1817 : Chief Judge, 1819 : Member of the Supreme Council, May 20, 1820 : died Nov. 10. 1825.

FENWICK, GEORGE ROE (? – 1904)

Major : served in the Crimea : to India as a Captain with his regt., the 93rd Highlanders : contributed to the *Englishman* in Calcutta : joined its staff as Assistant Editor and Editor, on retiring from the Army : Major in the Calcutta Volunteer Corps, which he resuscitated : went to Simla, and founded the *Civil and Military Gazette* as a weekly paper : became its

Editor when it was issued as a daily paper at Lahore: left India and joined the *Broad Arrow* in England, becoming its Editor: died in 1904.

FERGUSSON, JAMES (1808–1886)

Son of Dr. William Fergusson: born Jan. 22, 1808: educated at the Edinburgh High School, and privately: went to India, at first into business at Calcutta: and in ten years at his indigo factory made sufficient to retire upon: lost some of his money afterwards: travelled largely in India to study styles of Architecture, 1835–42: finally left India in 1845: joined the Royal Asiatic Society, 1840, and became a Vice-President: was General Manager of the Crystal Palace Company, 1856–8: a member in 1857 of the Royal Commission on the defences of the United Kingdom: Secretary to the First Commissioner of Public Works in 1869, and was later designated "Inspector of Public Buildings and Monuments." He wrote "*Picturesque Illustrations of Ancient Architecture in Hindostan*; *The Rock-cut Temples of India*; a number of valuable papers in the *Transactions of the Royal Institute of British Architects*; *An Historical Enquiry into the True Principles of Beauty in Art*, on a new system of substituting earthworks for masonry in fortification, on the topography of Jerusalem; a *Handbook of Architecture*; *A History of the Modern Styles of Architecture*; *A History of Architecture in all Countries*; *History of Indian and Eastern Architecture, Tree and Serpent Worship, The Parthenon*, etc. etc., besides other works on Architecture and connected subjects. It was said of him that he invested the historical study of Architecture, particularly Indian Architecture, with a new interest. He received the gold medal for Architecture from the Institute of British Architects, and was often consulted on architectural questions. He was D.C.L.: F.R.S: F.G.S.: LL.D: died Jan. 9, 1886.

FERGUSSON, SIR JAMES, SIXTH BARONET (1832–   )

Born 1832: son of Sir James Fergusson, fifth Baronet: educated at Rugby and University College, Oxford: succeeded as Baronet, 1849: entered the Grenadier Guards, 1851: Lieut. and Captain, 1854: served in the Crimean war, Alma and Inkerman (wounded) and siege of Sebastopol: M.P. for Ayrshire, 1854, 1857, 1865: retired from the Army, 1856: Under Secretary of State for India, 1866–7: Under Secretary in the Home Department, 1867–8: Governor of S. Australia, 1868: of New Zealand, 1873–5: of Bombay, 1880–5: Under Secretary of State, Foreign Office, 1886–91: Postmaster-General, 1891–2: P.C.: G.C.S.I.: K.C.M.G.: C.I.E.: LL.D.

FIELD, SIR JOHN (1821–1899)

General: entered the Army, 1839: joined the 6th N.I. in 1840: served in the Afghan and Sind campaigns, 1841–4: on the Bolan, Quetta, Kandahar line, and at Haikalzai: in the mutiny of 1857 protected Poona with his native regt.: at the capture of Dwarka: in Abyssinia 1867–8 commanded the advance Brigade: at capture of Magdala: C.B.: A.D.C. to Queen Victoria: Maj-General, 1879: Judge Advocate-General of the Bombay Army: K.C.B., 1887: died April 16, 1899.

FILOSE, JEAN BAPTISTE (1775–1846)

Colonel: son of Michael Filose (*q.v.*): born at Faizabad, March, 1775: educated at Calcutta: served under the Mogul Emperor at Delhi: adopted by a Frenchman, La Fontaine: entitled Itmaduddaula by the Emperor: took service under Daulat Rao Sindia: kept under arrest by Perron (*q.v.*): defeated by the British in the Mahratta war of 1803: employed in reducing refractory chiefs in Bundelkund, Malwa, etc., for Sindia: again arrested for 18 months: constantly engaged in fighting with Rajputs and Bundelas for Sindia: his troops constantly mutinous for arrears of pay: again under arrest for 7 years, restored in 1824, deprived of his command in 1843: ordered by Tara Bai to take command of the Army at Chanda against the English: defeated: transferred his offices to his grandson, Peter: died May 2, 1864: his grandson, Sir Michael Filose, employed as architect, etc., at Gwalior.

FILOSE, MICHAEL ? –after 1797)

Colonel: a Neapolitan adventurer: in the French Army at Madras: reached Calcutta about 1770: served the Nawab

L

of Oudh, the Rana of Gohud, and commanded a regt. under Madhava Rao Sindia (*q.v.*) : in 1797, Nana Farnavis, when on a visit to Daulat Rao Sindia, was taken prisoner : whether by Filose's treachery or not, has been disputed : he decamped to Bombay, set out for Europe, and died.

FIRMINGER, REV. THOMAS AUGUSTUS (1812-1884)

Born in London in 1812 : son of Dr. Thomas Firminger, who prepared candidates for Haileybury : educated at Pembroke College, Cambridge : took his degree, 1837 : appointed Chaplain of the E.I. Co., 1846 : served at Sagar, at Firozpur, during the second Sikh war : toured in India from 1854, made many drawings : had two pictures in the Royal Academy : Chaplain at Howrah, 1857 : and at Chinsura, 1859 : published his *Manual of Gardening for India*, 1863 : in the Bhutan expedition, 1864-5 : retired, 1868 : died Jan. 18, 1884.

FIROZ SHAH (? - ?)

Son of Mirza Nazim (who was grandson of Shah Alam) and of Abadi Begam, cousin of Akbar Shah, King of Delhi : educated by Mirza Illahibaksh, who married his mother : went to Mecca with her in 1855 : returned to Bombay after the mutiny broke out : became leader of the rebels at Mandiswar : driven from there by Colonel (Sir H. M.) Durand in Nov. 1857 : went to Rohilkund with his force : beaten thence by Sir Colin Campbell : entered Oudh : tried to join Tantia Topi in Central India : defeated by General (Lord) Napier at Ranod, Dec. 17, 1858 : fled, and joined Tantia Topi : the rebels were broken up and dispersed : Firoz Shah hid in the Sironj jungles : he escaped in disguise as a pilgrim to Karbela and lived there many years : was one of the leading and irreconcilable insurgents in the mutiny.

FIRUZ MULLA BIN KAWOOS (1758-1830)

Native of Broach, born 1758 : son of Mulla Kawoos, a priest of the Parsis of Bombay : when 10 years old, accompanied his father on a journey to Persia ; they carried with them letters from the Indian Zoroastrians for the solving of religious questions : on their return, after an absence of twelve years, they settled at Bombay : Firuz Mulla, himself a Parsi priest, of the Kadmi sect from 1794, and great student of Oriental language, was induced by Jonathan Duncan (*q.v.*) to write the Persian poem *George Nama*, a history of India from its discovery by the Portuguese and of the English in India to 1819 : this was an epic poem, called after George III., and dedicated to Queen Victoria : he was a great collector of Persian and Arabic MSS. : published in 1818, the *Desatir*, a very ancient religious Persian work : assisted the foundation of the *Bombay Samachar* in 1822, and wrote largely in it : led a retired and ascetic life, devoted to his studies : much sought by scholars, English and Asiatic, and held in the highest respect ; he wrote also on the advantages of vaccination : on his death, on Oct. 8, 1830, his collection was left as a gift in the charge of the Elders of the Kadmi Zoroastrians : it now forms the Mulla Firuz Library in Bombay : the Madrasa bearing his name was founded in 1854, for the instruction of Zoroastrians in their sacred lore.

FISHER, THOMAS (1772-1836)

Son of Thomas Fisher : entered the E. India House, 1786, as a clerk : searcher of records there, 1816-34 : died July 20, 1836 : had considerable talent for drawing, and was a distinguished antiquary : made drawings of monumental remains, antiquities and collections : was F.S.A. of Perth and London : for nearly 50 years contributed to the *Gentleman's Magazine*, writing for it long biographical memoirs of eminent men who had distinguished themselves in India : also wrote for the *Asiatic Journal*, the *Congregational Magazine* : worked in the cause of anti-slavery, and was a Director of the London Missionary Society, in which his knowledge of the East was valuable : died 1836.

FITZ CLARENCE, LORD FREDERICK (1799-1854)

Born Dec. 9, 1799: son of William IV and Mrs. Jordan : entered the Army, 1814 : given the rank of a son of a Marquess, 1831 : G.C.H., 1831 : Military Governor of Portsmouth, 1840 : Lt-General, 1851 : Colonel of 36th regt., 1851 : C. in C., Bombay, Nov. 1852 : died Oct. 30, 1854.

FITZGERALD, CHARLES JOHN OSWALD (1840–)

Born June 6, 1840 : son of General James Fitzgerald : educated at Edinburgh Academy : joined the Indian Army, 1857 : served in the mutiny : Adjutant of Central India Horse, 1860 : Adjutant 3rd Cavalry Hyderabad Contingent, 1862 : commanded 3rd H.C. Cavalry in Afghan campaign, 1880 : Political A.D.C. to Secretary of State for India, 1882 : commanded his regiment in the Burma campaign, 1886–8 : C.B., 1887.

FITZGERALD, SIR GERALD (1833–)

Son of Francis Fitzgerald, Galway : educated at S. Mary's College, Galway, and in France : began life as a clerk in the War Office, 1856, and became Assistant Comptroller-General of India, 1869 : Accountant-General of Madras, 1871; Burma,1873 : served under the Egyptian Government, 1877–84 : Accountant-General of the Navy, 1885 : K.C.M.G., 1885.

FITZGERALD, SIR WILLIAM GERALD SEYMOUR VESEY (1841–)

Born 1841 : son of Right Hon. Sir William R. S. Vesey Fitzgerald, Governor of Bombay : educated at Harrow and Oriel College, Oxford : Political A.D.C. to the Secretary of State for India, 1874 : K.C.I.E., 1887 : C.S.I., 1887.

FITZGERALD, SIR WILLIAM ROBERT SEYMOUR VESEY (1818–1885)

Governor ; son of William, second Baron Fitzgerald and Vesey : born 1818 : educated at Oriel College, Oxford : Newdigate Prize, 1835 : B.A., 1837 : called to the bar, from Lincoln's Inn, 1839 : M.P. for Horsham, 1852–65 : Under Secretary for Foreign Affairs, 1858–9 : was Governor of Bombay from March 6, 1867, to May 6, 1872 : Privy Councillor, 1866 : K.C.S.I. in 1867 : G.C.S.I. in 1868 : again M.P. for Horsham, 1874–5 : Chief Charity Commissioner, 1875 : D.C.L. of Oxford : died June 28, 1885.

FITZGERALD AND VESEY, WILLIAM VESEY, LORD (1783–1843)

Born 1783 : son of Rt. Hon. James Fitzgerald : educated at Christ Church, Oxford : M.P. for Ennis, 1898 and 1831 :

for Clare County, 1818 : for boroughs in Cornwall, 1829–30 : Lord of the Treasury, and Privy Councillor in Ireland and England : EnvoyExtraordinary to Sweden, 1820–3 : President of the Board of Trade, 1828 : acceded to his mother's Irish Peerage, 1832 : made an English Peer, 1835 : President of the Board of Control, 1841–3 : F.S.A. and President of the Royal Asiatic Society : died May 11, 1843.

FITZPATRICK, SIR DENNIS (1837–)

I.C.S. : born 1837 : educated at Trinity College, Dublin : entered the Indian Civil Service : called to the bar from the Inner Temple : acted as Judge of the Panjab Chief Court, 1876–7 : was Secretary to the Government of India in the Legislative Department, 1877–85 : Secretary in the Home Department, 1885: acting Chief Commissioner of the Central Provinces. 1885– 87 : Acting Resident in Mysore : Chief Commissioner of Assam : Resident at Hyderabad : Lieutenant-Governor of the Panjab, 1892–7 : Member of the Council of India since 1897 : K.C.S.I., 1890.

FLEET, JOHN FAITHFULL (1847–)

I.C.S. : educated at Merchant Taylors and University College, London : went out to Bombay, 1867 : epigraphist to the Government of India, 1883 : Commissioner in Bombay, Central and Southern Divisions, and Commissioner of Customs : C.I.E., 1884 : retired, 1897 : Hon. Ph.D. of Gottingen, 1892 : author of *Gupta Inscriptions : Dynasties of the Kanarese Districts :* and numerous contributions to the *Indian Antiquary*, the *Archæological Reports of W. India*, the *Epigraphia Indica* : joint proprietor and Editor of the *Indian Antiquary*, 1885–91.

FLETCHER, SIR HENRY, BARONET (1727–1807)

Born 1727 : commanded two vessels of the E.I. Co.: after good service and retirement, he became Director of the E.I. Co. for 18 years, and Chairman of the Court in 1782 and 1783 : M.P. for Cumberland, 1768–1806 : Baronet, 1782 : in Fox's India Bill, which was not carried, he was nominated one of the 7 Commissioners for the affairs of Asia : stated his opinion in Parliament that it would have been better for England and Europe if the

East Indies had never been discovered ; but that India, having once been acquired, must never be given up : died March 25, 1807.

FLETCHER, SIR ROBERT (? -1776)

When a Lieutenant in the Madras Army, he was summarily dismissed for writing an insolent letter to Government, but apologized and was reinstated at Coote's intercession : served in the war, 1760-1 : sent to reconnoitre the French settlements at Bourbon and in the Mauritius : in the Manilla expedition, 1762 : transferred to Bengal as Major, 1763 : Brigadier, 1766 : fomented and encouraged the mutiny of officers against the withdrawal of extra *batta*, 1766 : cashiered : restored : to Madras as Colonel, 1771 : C. in C. Madras, 1772 : being obstructive, was sent to command at Trichinopoly, 1773 : pleaded privilege as M.P. and claimed to return to England, which was allowed : returned to Madras as C. in C. 1775 : was arrested by Lord Pigot's order, Aug. 23, 1776, for causing mutiny among the troops :' implicated in the arrest of Lord Pigot, Aug. 25, 1776 : died on his way to Mauritius, Dec. 1776.

FLOYD, SIR JOHN, BARONET
(1748-1818)

Son of Capt. John Floyd : born Feb. 22, 1748 : entered the Army as Cornet in Elliot's Light Dragoons in 1760 : was riding master in 1763 to his regt.,the 15th Hussars: went to India in 1781-2, as Lt-Colonel of the 19th Light Dragoons: greatly distinguished himself as a cavalry commander on the Coromandel coast in Cornwallis' campaign of 1791-2, especially at Sattimanga-lum, 1790, and afterwards against Tippoo : was at Bangalore, and Arikera, in 1791 : at Seringapatam, 1792 : at the capture of Bangalore, 1793 : Maj-General, 1794 : in the second war with Tippoo, commanded the cavalry under General Harris : was at Malavilli, and commanded the covering Army during the siege of Seringapatam, 1799 : returned to England in 1800 : held command in Ireland : General, 1812 : Governor of Gravesend and Tilbury : Baronet, 1816 : died Jan, 10. 1818.

FORBES, ARCHIBALD (1838-1900)

The famous war correspondent : son of the Rev. Lewis William Forbes : born

1838 : educated at Aberdeen and Edinburgh : enlisted in the Royal Dragoons, 1857 : left the Army in 1867 : wrote on military life in the public Press . after conducting a weekly journal, 1867-71, made his reputation as a war correspondent for the *Daily News*, in the Franco-Prussian war, 1870-1 : the Russo-Turkish war of 1877 : the Zulu war, 1879-80 : and other wars : in India as a special correspondent in the Bengal-Bihar famine of 1874, where—as Sir R. Temple wrote, " he pourtrayed with graphic force and absolute fidelity, for the information of the English public, the mortal peril to which the people were exposed, and from which they could be rescued only by the utmost exertion of the Government " :—during the visit of H.R.H. the Prince of Wales to India, 1875-6, during the Afghan War, 1878-9, and went to Mandalay, to have interviews with King Theebaw.   He visited the United States and Australia as a lecturer and correspondent.   Besides his works on wars in other countries, and on other distinguished soldiers, he wrote *The Afghan Wars of* 1839 *and* 1879 ; *Havelock*, and *Colin Campbell, Lord Clyde* ("Men of Action" series), and on certain distinguished officers in *The Soldiers I have Known* : died March 30, 1900.

FORBES, ARTHUR (1843-   )

I.C.S. : son of Rev. E. Forbes, D.D. : educated at Sedburgh and St. John's College,Cambridge : steered the Cambridge Eight against Oxford in 1866 and 1867 : went to Bengal in the Indian Civil Service, 1867 : Deputy Commissioner in Assam, 1875 : Officiating Commissioner of Excise, Bengal, 1890 : Commissioner of Dacca, 1891 : Patna, 1892-6 : Chota Nagpur, 1896-1902 : C.S.I., 1895.

FORBES, SIR CHARLES, BARONET
(1774-1849)

Son of the Rev. George Forbes : born in 1774 : educated at Aberdeen University (afterwards Lord Rector): went out to India and was for many years head of the firm of Forbes & Co., of Bombay : on returning to England he became M.P. for Beverley, 1812-18, and represented Malmesbury, 1818-32 : when he left India the natives gave him a service of plate : and, 27 years after he had left Bombay, his statue by Sir F. Chantrey was placed in the Bombay Town Hall : he had a high reputation in the commerical world, and had done much to develop the country, and raise the status of the natives : he steadily demanded justice for India in Parliament and the Court of Proprietors of the E.I. Co. : became Forbes of Newe : made Baronet in 1823 : died Nov. 20, 1849.

FORBES, DAVID (1777 ?–1849)

Son of a Scottish minister, joined the 78th Highlanders, 1790 : served in the Netherlands, at Quiberon and Belle Isle : went to India in 1796 : escorted Sir John Shore to Lucknow in 1798 to depose Wazir Ali (*q.v.*) : in the Mahratta campaign of 1803 : at Ahmadnagar, etc. : in the Java expedition of 1811–13 under Sir S. Auchmuty, led the assaults at Waltevreede and Cornelis : was at Probolingo (in Java) in 1813 : Lt-Colonel, 1814 : returned home in 1817, the only officer of forty-two who had gone out : C.B., 1838 : Maj-General, 1846 : died March 29, 1849.

FORBES, DUNCAN (1798–1868)

Born April 28, 1798, of poor parents : became a village schoolmaster : went to Perth Grammar School, 1818 : M.A. of St. Andrew's in 1823,and LL.D. in 1847: taught in Calcutta, at the Calcutta Academy, 1823–6 : became assistant teacher of Hindustani in London, 1826 : Professor of Oriental languages at King's College, London, taking pupils, 1837–61 : made a catalogue of the Persian MSS. at the British Museum, 1849–55 : wrote a *History of Chess*, including its invention in India : also a number of works, grammars, dictionaries, manuals in Oriental languages, Arabic, Persian, Hindustani, Bengali : so that his name, though he made no claim to profound scholarship, is well known to students : Member of the Royal Asiatic Society : died Aug. 17, 1868.

FORBES, SIR JOHN (1817–   )

Of Inverarnan, Aberdeenshire : born June 10, 1817 : entered 3rd Bombay Light Cavalry (now 33rd Queen's Own Light Cavalry), 1835 : became Colonel, 1864 : General, 1886 : served in the field Force in Sind : at the siege of the Kojak : in ʰAfghanistan, 1841–2, including the advance on Kandahar, Ghazni and Kabul, action at Guine, under Genl. Nott : in the Field Force in Sind in 1843 : at the battle of Hyderabad : in the Persian ¡expeditionary force, 1856–7, at the assault and capture of the fort of Reshire : of the surrender of Bushire : at Barazjan and in action of Khushab (severely wounded) : Brevet-Major : C.B. : with the Central Indian Field Force from capture of Jhansi and siege of Ratghar to the fall of Kalpi : Brevet-Colonel : present at the battle of Solferino with the staff of the King of Italy : commanded a Division of the Bombay Army, 1876–81 : K.C.B., 1881 : appointed Hon. Col. 33rd Queen's Own Light Cavalry, 1904 : G.C.B.

FORBES, GORDON SULLIVAN (1820–1893)

I.C.S. : born March 29, 1820 : son of Gordon Forbes, B.C.S. : educated at Cheam and Haileybury, 1836–8 : went to Madras, 1838 : was Collector of Ganjam, 1858–67, and did good work in the famine relief operations, 1866–7 : Member of the Board of Revenue, Madras, and Additional Member of the Governor-General's Legislative Council : retired, 1874 : died April 26, 1893 : wrote *Wild Life in Canara*, a work on Natural History and Sport : helped to found a charity in Madras for the relief of destitute Europeans in India.

FORBES, JAMES (1749–1819)

I.C.S. : born in 1749 : went out to Bombay in 1765 : was Private Secretary to Col. Keating in 1775 and Chaplain of the force in the expedition to assist Raghoba : held minor charges in India, but made a competency and left India in 1784, with 150 volumes of materials, including drawings, of Indian subjects : after the rupture of the Peace of Amiens he was detained in France till 1804, when he returned to England : published his *Oriental Memoirs*, in four volumes, 1813–5 : F.R.S. and F.S.A : Montalembert, the historian, was his grandson : died Aug. 1, 1819.

FORCHHAMMER, EMMANUEL (1851–1890)

Born March 12, 1851, in Switzrland : son of a Protestant pastor : educated at home and New Orleans : studied medicine, graduated, Doctor : Assistant Surgeon at a hospital : turned to languages : travelled among American Indian tribes : to Europe, 1875, to Leipzig : studied Sanskrit, Pali,

Tibetan, Chinese, Arabic : appointed, 1879,'Professor of Pali at the Government High School, Rangoon : investigated the sacred and vernacular literature of Burma : catalogued Pali MSS., and wrote on Burmese law : edited the *Tripitaka*, or Buddhist Canon : besides his educational work, studied other Burmese vernaculars, Shan, Karen, etc. : wrote on Indo-Chinese languages and Burmese dialects : employed on archæological investigations and decipherment of ancient inscriptions : made an archæological survey of Arakan : surveyed the temple ruins of Pagan, 1888 : collected a quantity of MSS., etc. : did good work as antiquarian and philologist in Burma : died April 26, 1890.

FORD, ARTHUR (1834-   )

Born Aug. 15, 1834 : son of Arthur Ford : educated at Grosvenor College, Bath, and St. John's College, Cambridge : entered R.A., 1855 : Lt-Colonel, 1881 : Colonel : retired, 1883 : served in the Indian mutiny, 1857-8 : relief, siege and capture of Lucknow : wounded : Assistant Director of Artillery studies at Woolwich, 1870-3 : Inspector of Explosives, Home Office, 1873-99 : C.B., 1895.

FORD, WILLIAM (1821-1905)

I.C.S. : born Nov. 29, 1821 : son of Sir Francis Ford, *Bart.* : educated at Haileybury : entered the Bengal Civil Service, 1843 : served in the Indian mutiny, in the Gurgaon district : saved a number of Christian fugitives : present at the siege of Delhi ; saw service with General Showers : Commissioner of Multan, 1862 : Agent at Bahawalpur, 1866, where he suppressed a mutiny : C.S.I., 1866 : author of several novels, of which the latest is *Prince Baber and his Wives :* wrote also *A Viceroy of India* (Lord Lawrence) ; died June 18, 1905.

FORDE, ARTHUR W. (?-1883-5 ?)

Was engaged on the construction of Irish railways : went to India, 1855, as Chief Engineer of the B.B. and C.I. Railways : advocated the light railway system for purely agricultural districts, with tramways and feeder lines : wrote a pamphlet " *10,000 miles against 5,000,*" and lectured in Bombay on " Railway Extension in India, with special reference to the export of wheat " : practised as

Consulting Engineer in Bombay and other parts of India : was for 7 years Consulting Engineer to the Bombay Municipality : constructed the first wet-dock, the Sassoon dock at Colaba, Bombay : engaged on the water-supply and drainage of Bombay : M.I.C.E. : retired, after about 30 years in India, soon after 1880 : died about 1883-5.

FORDE, FRANCIS (? -1770)

Colonel : son of Matthew Forde : Captain in the 39th regt., 1746 : Major, 1755 : was repulsed in an attack on Nellore, May, 1757 : joined the E.I. Co.'s Army in Bengal, 1758, as second to Clive : sent by Clive in Oct. 1758, with 500 Europeans and 2,000 sepoys to Vizagapatam, to create a diversion against the French in the Northern Sircars : defeated the Marquis de Conflans (who had replaced Bussy) at Condore, Dec. 1758 : took Rajamundry and Masulipatam in April, 1759 : thus gaining the N. Sircars and expelling the French : defeated the Dutch at Chinsura : went to England with Clive, who was his friend : and, on his recommendation,was one of the Commission of three (with Vansittart and Serafton) sent from England in 1769 to overhaul the Bengal administration : after touching at the Cape in Dec. 1769, their vessel was lost at sea.

FORDYCE, SIR JOHN (? -1877)

Lt-General : entered the Bengal Artillery in 1822 : was in the first Burmese war, at the capture of Arakan : in the Satlaj campaign of 1845-6 : at Firozshahr and Sobraon : in the advance on Lahore : in the Panjab campaign of 1848-9, at Chilianwala and Gujarat, in the pursuit of the Sikhs, and of the Afghans to the Khyber : commanded the Artillery in the Yusafzai country in 1849 and at the forcing of the Kohat Pass in 1850 by Sir C. Napier : Colonel Commandant, 1873 : K.C.B., 1877.

FORJETT, CHARLES (? -1890)

Deputy, and, later, the Commissioner of Police, Bombay, from 1855, and President of the Board, or Chief Municipal Commissioner of Bombay : his energetic action, in Sep. 1857, stopped a contemplated sepoy outbreak and saved Bombay : his high character, knowledge of the natives and fitness for his position generally admitted : much trusted by Lord Elphinstone, the Governor of Bombay : was presented with purses on retirement, and received an extra pension : regarded himself as slighted, being undecorated : died Jan. 27, 1890 : wrote *Our Real Danger in India*, 1877.

FORLONG, JAMES GEORGE RORKE
(1824–1904)

Maj-General : born Nov. 1824 : educated as an Engineer : joined the Indian Army, 1843 : in the S. Mahratta Company, 1845–6 : in the Madras Army, 1847 : in the second Burmese war, 1852 : after the annexation, was head of the P.W.D. there : travelled widely, 1858–9 : on special public works, inquiries and construction of prisons in the Andamans : Superintending Engineer in Bengal, N.W.P., Rajputana, 1861–71 : Secretary and Chief Engineer, Oudh, 1872–7 : retired : wrote largely in periodicals on religions, archæology, philology : wrote the *Rivers of Life, or the Faiths of Mankind in all Lands*, 1883 ; *Short Studies in the Science of Comparative Religions, embracing all the Religions of Asia* : a student of exploration, thought, and research in Oriental subjects : well versed in Indian religions and folklore of the East : died March 29, 1904.

FORREST, GEORGE WILLIAM
(1846–   )

Born Jan. 8, 1846 : son of Capt. George Forrest, V.C. : educated privately and at St. John's College, Cambridge : appointed to Bombay Educational Department, 1872 : Census Commissioner at Bombay, 1882 : on special duty in connexion with Bombay Records, 1884–8 : Professor of English History, Elphinstone College, 1887 : Director of Bombay Records, 1888 : Assistant Secretary to the Government of India : Director of Government of India Records, 1894–1900 : C.I.E., 1899 : wrote articles on "The Deforestation of India" in the *Bombay Gazette* : author of various *Selections from State Papers* : *The Administration of Warren Hastings*, *The Administration of Lord Lansdowne*, *Sepoy Generals, Cities of India, History of the Indian Mutiny*, etc. : F.R.G.S.

FORREST, THOMAS (1729 ?–1802 ?)

Midshipman, R.N., in 1745 : in the E.I. Co.'s service after 1748 : commanded a ship from 1762 : made fifteen voyages from India to the East, and four from England to India : he formed a settlement in 1770 at Balambangan, and in 1774–6 explored in New Guinea, the Sulu Archipelago, the Moluccas, etc., and wrote an account of his voyages : employed by Warren Hastings to obtain news of the French fleet which had escaped the English ships; he found it at Achin, and the information was very valuable. He made a voyage "from Bengal to Quedah " in 1783, and a voyage "from Calcutta to the Mergui Archipelago," 1790, discovering the Forrest Strait : besides other papers, he wrote a *Treatise on the Monsoons in East India*, 1782 : died about 1802.

FORSTER, GEORGE (? –1792)

In the E.I. Co.'s Civil Service, in 1782 : he travelled from India through Kashmir, Afghanistan, Herat, Persia, by the Caspian Sea to Russia : wrote *A Journey from Bengal to England, through the Northern Part of India, Kashmir, Afghanistan, and Persia, and into Russia by the Caspian Sea*, 1798 : also *Sketches of the Mythology and Customs of the Hindus :* in 1792, he died at Nagpur, on an embassy to the Mahrattas.

FORSTER, HENRY (1793–1862)

Son of Henry Pitts Forster (*q.v.*), of the E.I. Co.'s Civil Service : entered the Mahratta Army, but joined " Skinner's Horse " in 1816 : was second in command in 1822 : was in the Pindari campaign, and at Mahidpur : about 1834 he raised the Shekhawati Brigade and won several engagements against insurgents in Rajputana : was in the Satlaj campaign of 1845–6 with his Brigade : made C.B. and Colonel in the Queen's Army in 1854. In the mutiny his Shekhawati battalion was deputed to reduce the rebel 34th N.I., in Chota Nagpur : died in Calcutta, Oct. 9, 1862.

FORSTER, HENRY PITTS (1766 ?–1815)

In the E.I. Co.'s Bengal Civil Service, joined in 1783 : Registrar of the *Sadr Diwani Adalat* of the Twenty-four *Parganas*, 1794 : published the first English-Bengali vocabulary in 1799–1802, and, largely through his efforts, Bengali became the official as well as the literary language of

Bengal : studied Sanskrit, and laboriously translated a native grammar : became master of the Calcutta Mint : died in India, Sep. 10, 1815.

FORSYTH, JAMES (1838–1871)

Born in 1838 : took his M.A. degree : went to India as acting Conservator of Forests : served in the Central Provinces as Deputy Commissioner of Nimar : joined the Staff Corps : was a keen sportsman : wrote *The Sporting Rifle and its Projectiles*, 1863 : made a long tour in the Central Provinces, 1862–4, and wrote *The Highlands of Central India : Notes on their Forests and Wild Tribes, Natural History and Sports*, which appeared in 1871, after his death on May 1, 1871.

FORSYTH, SIR JOHN (1799–1883)

Principal Inspr-General in H.M.S. Indian Medical Department, Bengal : Honorary Physician to Queen Victoria : died Jan. 14, 1883 : C.B., 1862 : K.C.S.I., 1881.

FORSYTH, REV. NATHANIEL (1769–1816)

Born 1769 in Dumfriesshire : educated at Glasgow, and at the Divinity Hall, under the Rev. Professor G. Lawson, of the New Burgher Associate Synod : became a tutor at an academy, Islington, and a candidate for missionary work : arrived in Bengal, Dec. 1798, as the first missionary sent out by the London Missionary Society : allowed to preach in Dr. Dunwiddie's lecture-room in Cossitolla, Calcutta : also at the General Hospital and the Fort : held charge of the Settlement Church at Chinsura, and managed a large school there, 1805 : he and Dr. Carey opened the Lal Bazar Chapel, Jan. 1, 1809 : died at Chandernagore, Feb. 11, 1816.

FORSYTH, SIR THOMAS DOUGLAS (1827–1886)

I.C.S. : son of Thomas Forsyth, merchant : born Oct. 7, 1827 : educated at Sherborne, Rugby and Haileybury : arrived at Calcutta, 1848 : went to the Panjab, after the annexation of 1849 : at the outbreak of the mutiny was Deputy Commissioner of Umballa : reported on the disaffection, and controlled the Sikh States : was a Special Commissioner for punishing the rebels, after the fall of Delhi : Secretary to the Chief Commissioner of Oudh : C.B. : went to Leh in 1867 to promote trade with Turkistan : established the Palampur fair : sent to Russia on diplomatic mission : obtained from the Russian Government an acknowledgment that certain disputed territories belonged to the Amir of Afghanistan : went in 1870 to Yarkand : in 1872, lost his appointment as Commissioner of Umbala for supporting his subordinate's measures in putting down the Kooka outbreak at Malair Kotla : led a mission to Kashgar, 1873–4 : K.C.S.I. in 1874 : Additional Member of the Governor-General's Legislative Council, 1874 : Envoy to Burma in 1875 : obtained an agreement to the independence of the Karenni states : retired in 1877 : died Dec. 17, 1886.

FORTESCUE, THOMAS (1784–1872)

I.C.S. : born 1784 : son of Gerald Fortescue, Secretary to his cousin Henry Wellesley (1773–1847 : Baron Cowley, 1828), youngest brother of the Marquess Wellesley, who was Lieutenant-Governor of the ceded Province of Oudh from Nov. 1801 to 1803, when he quitted India : Fortescue was Commissioner at Delhi, 1803 : died Sep. 7, 1872.

FORTESCUE, ROBERT (1813–1880)

Born Sep. 16, 1813 : educated at the Edrom Parish School : became a Superintendent in the Royal Horticultural Society's garden at Chiswick : visited China, Java, Manilla, 1842–6, as collector : to China again in 1848, to collect tea plants and seeds for the E.I. Co. : in 1851 introduced many of them into the N.W.P. : wrote a *Report on the Tea Plantations in the N.W.P.*, and *Two Visits to the Tea Countries of China, and the British Plantations in the Himalayas*, 1853 : also visited Formosa, and wrote other accounts of his travels in the Far East : died April 13, 1880.

FOSTER, SIR CHARLES JOHN (1818–1896)

Son of Edward Foster : entered the Army, 1836 : served with the 16th Lancers in the Afghan war, 1841–2, under Sir J. Keane : at Ghazni : at Maharajpur, 1843 : and in the Satlaj campaign, 1846 :

at Badiwal, Aliwal and Sobraon : Captain, 1847 : General, 1885 : Member of the Council of India, 1878–88 : C.B., 1877 : Colonel of the 21st Hussars, 1872–6, and of the 16th Lancers, 1886 : K.C.B., 1893 : died Feb. 11, 1896.

FOSTER, WILLIAM (1863–)

Born Nov. 19, 1863 : son of William Foster : educated at Cooper's Grammar School and London University : joined the India Office, 1882 : edited India Office List, 1891–5 : Assistant to the Registrar and Superintendent of Records, 1901 : Hon. Secretary to the Hakluyt Society, 1893–1902 : has edited several old records, including *The Embassy of Sir Thomas Roe to the Court of the Great Mogul*, 1615–19, and, with Sir G. Bird-wood, *The First Letter-book of the East India Company*, 1600–19.

FOULIS, SIR EDWARD (1768–1843)

Arrived in India, 1789 : in the 3rd Cavalry in Mysore under Cornwallis, 1791–2 : at sieges of Bangalore, Savandrug, Seringapatam, Pondicherry : in the Mysore war under General Harris, 1788–91, at Malavilli and Seringapatam : under Col. A. Wellesley, against Dhoondia Waugh, saw much active service : Remount agent for Madras cavalry, 1807 : commanded Light Cavalry, 1815 : in Pindari war, 1817 : commanded at Arcot, 1819 : held various cavalry commands : Maj-General, 1837 : K.C.B. : died April 12, 1843.

FOWLER, SIR HENRY HARTLEY (1830–)

Born May 16, 1830 : educated at Woodhouse Grove School, and St. Saviour's Grammar School : Mayor of Wolverhampton, 1863 : M.P. for Wolverhampton since 1880 : Under Secretary, Home Department, 1884–5 : Financial Secretary to the Treasury, 1886 : President of the Local Government Board, 1892–4 : Secretary of State for India, March 10, 1894, to July 5, 1895 : G.C.S.I., 1895 : P.C. : D.L.

FOX, CHARLES JAMES (1749–1806)

Third son of Henry Fox, Lord Holland : born Jan. 24, 1749 : educated at Wandsworth, Eton and Hertford College, Oxford, 1764–6 : M.P. for Midhurst, 1768 : for Westminster, 1780 : held office in the Government, 1770–2 : 1772–4 : attacked Lord Clive in Parliament, 1773 ; Foreign Secretary, 1782–3, 1806 : Fox introduced into Parliament, Nov. 18, 1783, his Bills, prepared with Burke's aid, for the better Government of India : by the first Bill, he proposed to establish a Board of 7 Commissioners to hold office for 4 years and have absolute control over the patronage and Government of India : with a Board of 8 Assistant Councillors to administer the commercial affairs of the E.I. Co. : by the second Bill, restrictions were imposed upon the free action of the Governor-General. The first Bill passed the House of Commons, but was rejected by the House of Lords, by the King's influence, Dec. 17, 1783 : the second Bill made no progress. When his party attacked Warren Hastings, 1786, Fox spoke for the Rohilla charge, and June 13, brought forward the Benares charge, which he carried : spoke in favour of the charge relating to the Begams of Oudh, 1787 : took a leading part in settling the articles of impeachment of Hastings : was a manager of the trial : again led the Benares charge in the trial, 1788 : spoke against the abatement of the impeachment by the dissolution of Parliament, 1789 : died Sep. 13, 1806.

FOX, HENRY WATSON (1817–1848)

Missionary : son of George Townshend Fox : born 1817 : educated at Rugby and Wadham College, Oxford : ordained, 1840 : to Madras in 1841 as a missionary of the Church Missionary Society : worked at Masulipatam : visited the Nilgiris, Travancore, Tinnivelly : became Assistant Secretary to the Society : died at Durham, Oct. 14, 1848 : wrote *Chapters on Missions in South India.*

FRANCIS, SIR PHILIP (1740–1818)

Son of the Rev. Philip Francis : born Oct. 22, 1740 : educated at Dublin and St. Paul's School : became a junior clerk in the Secretary of State's office : Secretary to General E. Bligh and at the capture of Cherbourg in 1758 : Secretary to Lord Kinnoull's Embassy at Lisbon, 1760 : amanuensis to Pitt, 1761–2 : clerk at the War Office, 1762 : resigned in March, 1772, for some unexplained reason. During those years, " Junius' letters "

154   DICTIONARY OF INDIAN BIOGRAPHY

appeared, which for many grounds have been attributed to Francis. Their identity, first suggested by Taylor in 1813, 1816, may be considered to have been established. After the passing of the Regulating Act of 1773 for India, Francis was appointed a member of the new Supreme Council in India. He and his colleagues, Clavering and Monson, arrived at Calcutta on Oct. 19, 1774 : these three opposed Warren Hastings, the Governor-General, and Barwell (*q.v.*), the remaining Member of the Supreme Council : being a majority, they had great power. Francis took the side of Nuncomar (*q.v.*), after the latter had accused Hastings of corruption. Nuncomar was hanged for forgery on Aug. 5, 1775. The death of Monson, on Sep. 25, 1776, gave Hastings the casting vote. Barwell left India in March, 1780 : Francis resumed his opposition to Hastings, who wrote a minute accusing Francis of faithlessness and breach of trust and honour. Francis challenged him, and a duel took place on Aug. 17, 1780, in which Francis was badly wounded. He left India in Dec. 1780. In 1778 Francis was defendant in a *crim. con.* charge brought against him by G. F. Grand of the Indian Civil Service. Francis was sentenced by Impey to pay 50,000 rupees damages. He retired with a large fortune, but was very coldly received in England, except at Court. He became M.P. for Yarmouth, 1784 : assisted Burke in preparing the charges against Hastings, but was not accepted as a manager of the impeachment. M.P. for Bletchingley, 1790 ; for Appleby, 1802 : K.C.B. in Oct. 1806 : made an elaborate speech on India in April, 1805 : he hoped to be Governor-General of India, but failed to obtain it from Fox, with whom he quarrelled : he died Dec. 22, 1818. It is said that he made many anonymous contributions to the Press : his capacity, industry, courage, and certain good principles in his character have to be set against his malignity, vindictiveness, and unscrupulous conduct : his life and career have been minutely investigated.

FRANCKLIN, WILLIAM (1763-1839)

Son of Thomas Francklin : born 1763 : educated at Westminster and Trinity College, Cambridge : entered the E.I.

Co.'s Bengal N.I., 1783 : Lt-Colonel, 1814 : regulating officer, Bhagalpur, 1815 : retired in India, 1825 : travelled in Persia in 1786 : published his journal : wrote *The History of the Reign of Shah-Aulam, the present Emperor of Hindustan,* 1798 : *Inquiry concerning the Site of the Ancient Palibothra,* 1815-22 : besides translations, literary papers, contributions to Asiatic Researches, etc. : Member of the Asiatic Society of Bengal, and Member of Council and Librarian of the Royal Asiatic Society : died in India, April 12, 1839.

FRANKLIN, SIR BENJAMIN (1844-   )

Educated at University College, London, and Paris : entered the Indian Medical Service, 1869 : Civil Surgeon, Simla, 1881-6 : Inspr-General of Hospitals, N.W.P., 1899 : and Panjab, 1900-1 : Director-General, Indian Medical Service : C.I.E., 1898 : K.C.I.E., 1903.

FRANKS, SIR JOHN (1770-1852)

Son of Thomas Franks : born in 1770 : took his degree at Trinity College, Dublin : called to the Irish bar, 1792 : appointed in 1825 a Judge of the Supreme Court, Calcutta, and knighted : retired for his health in 1834 : died Jan. 11, 1852.

FRANKS, SIR THOMAS HARTE (1808-1862)

Son of William Franks : born 1808 : entered the 10th regt. in 1825 : Lt-Colonel, 1845 : to India in 1842 : in the first Sikh war, 1845-6 : was at Sobraon, wounded : C.B. : in the Panjab campaign of 1848-9, was at the siege of Multan, Surajkund, and at Gujarat : Colonel, 1854 : commanded the Jalandhar Brigade, 1855 : in the mutiny, as Brig-General, marched across the frontier of Oudh, and joined with Jang Bahadur of Nipal : defeated the rebels, Banda Husain, at Chanda, and Mehndi Husain Nazim at Hamirpur in Feb. 1858, but failed to take Daurara fort : joined Sir Colin Campbell at the capture of Lucknow, March, 1858 : Maj-General and K.C.B., 1858 : returned to England : died Feb. 5, 1862.

FRASER, ALEXANDER (1824-1898)

General : son of James Fraser : educated at Addiscombe : entered the Indian

Engineers, 1843 : in the Satlaj campaign, 1845–6 : and the Panjab campaign, 1848–9 : in the Burmese war, 1852–3 : employed on the construction of lighthouses on the coast of Burma : Chief Engineer in the N.W.P., 1873–9 : Member of the. Supreme Council, March–June, 1880 : C.B. : died June 11, 1898.

FRASER, SIR ANDREW HENDER-- SON LEITH (1848–)

I.C.S. : born Nov. 14, 1848 : son of Rev. A. G. Fraser, D.D. : educated at Edinburgh Academy and University : entered the Indian Civil Service, 1871 : served in the Central Provinces : Officiating Secretary to the Government of India, Home Department, 1898–9 : Chief Commissioner of Central Provinces, 1899 : President of the Indian Police Commission, 1902–3 : Lieutenant-Governor of Bengal since Nov. 1903 : C.S.I., 1897 : K.C.S.I., 1903.

FRASER, SIR CHARLES CRAWFURD (1829–1895)

Son of Lt-Colonel Sir James John Fraser, *Bart.* : joined the 11th Hussars : served with the 7th Hussars at the siege and capture of Delhi, 1857 : Brevet-Major : gained the V.C. on Dec. 31, 1858, for rescuing, while under sharp fire, an officer and some men from drowning in the river Rapti : in the Abyssinian expedition, 1867–8 : at capture of Magdala : C.B. : A.D.C. to the C. in C. 1873–80 : Inspr-General of Cavalry, 1879–84 : Maj-General : K.C.B. : M.P. for N. Lambeth, 1885–92 : died June 7, 1895.

FRASER, HUGH (? –1858)

Of the Bengal Engineers : Chief Engineer at Agra when the mutiny of 1857 broke out : C.B. : Colonel : made Chief Commissioner for Agra and its dependencies, Sep. 30, 1857, to Feb. 9, 1858 : acted with energy : died at Mussoorie, Aug. 12, 1858.

FRASER, JAMES (1713–1754)

Born 1713 : son of Alexander Fraser of Reelick : went to India, to Surat : resided there, 1730–40 : learnt Sanskrit and Zend : returning to England for about two years, he wrote a history of Nadir Shah, the King of Persia, who invaded India : Fraser returned to India

as a factor in the E.I. Co.'s service : rose to be a Member of Council at Surat, where he stayed six years : he brought to England some 200 Sanskrit and Zend MSS., the first " collection " brought to Europe, which are now in the Bodleian Library at Oxford : he had formed plans of working in Zend and Sanskrit, but died early, Jan. 21, 1754.

FRASER, JAMES BAILLIE (1783–1856)

Born June 11, 1783 : son of Edward Satchell Fraser : with his brother William (*q.v.*), and an escort, explored the Himalayas in 1815, to the sources of the Jamna and Ganges : in 1821, he accompanied Dr. Jukes to Persia, to Mashad, Kurdistan and Tabriz : in 1833–4, on a diplomatic mission to Persia, he rode from Semlin to Constantinople, and from Stamboul to Teheran : attended on the Persian Princes on their visit to England, 1835–6 : wrote narratives of his travels in Persia and connected countries, and some works of fiction : also the *Military Memoir of Lt-Colonel James Skinner* : C.B., 1851 : was also an amateur artist : died Jan. 1856.

FRASER, JAMES STUART (1783–1869)

Son of Colonel Charles Fraser : born July 1, 1783 : educated at Ham and Glasgow University : joined the Madras N.I., 1800 : escorted the Mysore Princes to Bengal, 1807 : A.D.C. to Sir G. Barlow, when Governor of Madras : Private Secretary, 1810 : Deputy Commissary in the Madras expedition to Mauritius, 1810 : Military Secretary to the Governor of Madras, 1813 : Commandant at Pondicherry, 1816 : Commissioner for the restitution of French and Dutch possessions, 1816–7, having great knowledge of the French language : Secretary to Government in the Military Department, 1834 : in several actions in Coorg : Resident in Mysore, and Chief Commissioner of Coorg : Resident at Travancore and Cochin, 1836 : Resident at Hyderabad from Sep. 1838, to Dec. 1852 : resigned his appointment because of strained relations with Lord Dalhousie : Lt-General, 1851 : General, 1862 : died Aug. 22, 1869.

FRASER, WILLIAM (1784–1835)

I.C.S. : son of Edward Satchell Fraser, brother of James Baillie Fraser (*q.v.*) :

went to Bengal in 1799 : Secretary to Sir D. Ochterlony at Delhi, 1805 : Secretary to Mountstuart Elphinstone (q.v.) on his mission to Kabul : Political Agent to General Martindell's Army, 1815 : travelled with his brother to the Himalayas : settled Garhwal, 1819 : Member of the Board of Revenue, N.W.P., 1826 : Resident at Delhi, 1830–5 : shot dead, on March 22, 1835, while riding at Delhi, by Kareem Khan, at the instigation of Shams-ud-din, Nawab of Firozpur : both of them were hanged.

FRASER-TYTLER, SIR JAMES MAC-LEOD BANNATYNE (1821–   )

Born 1821 : entered the Bengal Army 1841, and became General, 1877 : served in the Afghan campaign, 1842, (severely wounded, Khyber Pass), A.D.C. to Lord Gough, Satlaj campaign, 1845–6 : at the battles of Mudki, Firozshahr, Sobraon : in the Panjab campaign, 1848–9, at Chilianwala and Gujarat : Indian mutiny, 1857 : at the relief of Lucknow : severely wounded Bhutan campaign, 1864–5 : C.B., 1857 : K.C.B., 1867.

FRAZER, ROBERT WATSON (1854–   )

I.C.S. : born 1854 : educated at Rathmines school, Kingstown school and Trinity College, Dublin : entered the Madras Civil Service, 1877, but retired, 1886 ; invalided in consequence of fever contracted in the Rumpa rebellion. Lecturer, University Extension, on Indian Architecture : Principal Librarian and Secretary of London Institution : Lecturer in Tamil and Telegu, University College. Author of British India ("Story of the Nations" series), A Literary History of India, 1898.

FRENCH, RIGHT REV. THOMAS VALPY (1825–1891)

Bishop : son of the Rev. Peter French : born Jan. 1, 1825 : educated at Reading and Burton Grammar schools, Rugby, and University College, Oxford : Fellow, there, 1848 : ordained, 1848 : Principal of St. John's College, Agra, 1850 : founded Reynell Taylor's Derajat mission, 1861 : Vicar of Cheltenham, 1865–9 : founded the divinity school at Lahore, 1869 : first Bishop of Lahore, Dec. 1877 : D.D. of Oxford : resigned in 1887 : died at Muscat, as a missionary there, May 14, 1891 : was a good linguist, and distinguished as an evangelist.

FRERE, SIR HENRY BARTLE EDWARD, BARONET (1815–1884)

Governor : I.C.S. : sixth son of Edward Frere, and nephew of John Hookham Frere : born March 29, 1815, educated at Bath and Haileybury : went to India in 1834, by the overland route, making his way with difficulty viâ Cairo, Kosseir, Jeddah, Mocha, and a pilgrim vessel to Bombay : Assistant Revenue Commissioner for some years to H. E. Goldsmid (q.v.) in investigating land assessments : Private Secretary to Sir G. Arthur, Governor of Bombay, 1842 : Resident at Satara, 1846 : on the annexation of Satara in 1848–9 (to which he was opposed), Frere was appointed Commissioner : Chief Commissioner in Sind, 1850–9 : greatly advanced the Province in every way, conciliated the Amirs, improved Karachi harbour, developed institutions, controlled the frontier and the tribes : in the mutiny he nearly denuded Sind of troops to help the Panjab and South Mahratta country : repressed attempts at mutiny, and kept Sind quiet and loyal : his great services were highly valued in England and India : K.C.B. in 1859 : Member of the Governor-General's Supreme Council from Dec. 1859, to April, 1862 : helped greatly in the restoration of financial equilibrium and in the establishment of Legislative Councils : Governor of Bombay from April, 1862, to March, 1867 : advanced education, built colleges, pushed on railways, established the Bombay municipality, demolished the old ramparts of the town, initiated female education. Over-trading, speculation, and the restoration of peace in America (causing a fall in cotton) brought on a commercial crisis, in which the Bank of Bombay was involved : Frere's policy during this period was the subject of unfavourable criticism. He was Member of the Council of India, 1867–77 : G.C.S.I. : D.C.L. : President of the Geographical and Asiatic Societies : sent to Zanzibar, in 1872, to negotiate a treaty for the suppression of the slave-trade : P.C. : LL.D. : accompanied H.R.H. the Prince of Wales in his Indian tour, 1875–6 : Baronet and G.C.B. : appointed, in 1887, Governor of the Cape and High Commissioner in S. Africa : brought a war with the Kafirs to conclusion, 1878 : became engaged in the Zulu war, 1879 : and in troubles regarding the Transvaal with the Boers : the English Government recalled Frere in 1880 for his conduct in relation to the Zulu war and alleged disregard of orders : he defended himself on his return to England : he advocated a forward policy with regard to Afghanistan : died May 29, 1884 : buried in St. Paul's Cathedral : his statue erected on the Thames Embankment : he was an eminent public servant, combining strong character under a kindly and courteous demeanour : and was earnest in his religious views. He wrote a number of papers on the questions of the day, connected with India : also a memoir of his uncle above-named.

FRERE, WILLIAM EDWARD (1811–1880)

I.C.S. : born June 6, 1811 : third son of Edward Frere : and brother of Sir H. B .E. Frere (*q.v.*) : educated at Swansea and Haileybury : went to Bombay, 1830 : Judge of Dharwar, and of the *Sadr* Court : Member of Council, Bombay, 1860–5 : retired : travelled round the world : Commissioner to inquire into the health of the coolies in Demerara, 1870 ; in Mauritius, 1872 : C.M.G., 1875 : died March 23, 1880.

FREYER, P. JOHNSTON (? –)

Educated at Erasmus Smith's College, Galway ; Royal University of Ireland, Steeven's Hospital, Dublin, and Paris : entered the Indian medical service, 1875 : held civil and military appointments : Medical officer to the Lieutenant-Governor, N.W.P : and subsequently to H.H. the Nawab of Rampur, who gave him, on recovery from an illness, a very large fee for his services : practises since retirement in London : Surgeon to St. Peter's Hospital for Stone.

FRYER, SIR FREDERICK WILLIAM RICHARDS (1845–)

I.C.S. : son of F. W. Fryer : entered the Bengal Civil Service, 1864 : called to the bar from the Middle Temple, 1880 : Commissioner, Central Division, Upper Burma, 1886 : Financial Commissioner, Burma, 1888 : Acting Chief Commissioner of Burma, 1892–4 : Officiating Financial Commissioner, Panjab : Additional Member of the Governor-General's Legislative Council, 1894–5 : Lieutenant-Governor of Burma, 1897–1903 : K.C.S.I., 1895.

FULLARTON, WILLIAM (1754–1808)

Colonel : son of William Fullerton : born 1754 : educated at Edinburgh University : raised a Scotch regt. and gazetted Commandant of the 98th in 1780 : went to India : engaged near Madras, in the second Mysore war with Hyder Ali, 1780–2 : at the suppression of the Kollars of Madras, and capture of Dindigul : commanded the troops south of the Coleroon, 1783 : took Dharapuram, Palghat and Coimbatore : showed military ability : returned to England on the peace : wrote his *View of English Interests in India*, 1787 : F.R.S. of London and Edinburgh : raised the 23rd Dragoons : M.P., 1787–1803 : appointed first Commissioner for Trinidad : tried his colleague, Col. Thomas Picton, for torturing a Spanish girl : died Feb. 13, 1808.

FULLER, JOSEPH BAMFYLDE (1854 –)

I.C.S. : son of Rev. J. Fuller : educated at Marlborough : entered the Indian Civil Service, 1875 : Commissioner of Settlements C.P., 1885 : Secretary to Govt. of India, Revenue and Agriculture Department, 1901–2 : Chief Commissioner of Assam, from April, 1902 : C.I.E., 1892 : C.S.I., 1902 : Lieutenant-Governor of Eastern Bengal and Assam, 1905.

FURDUNJI, NAOROJI (1817–1885)

Born in March, 1817, at Broach : educated at the Native Education Society's school at Bombay, where he afterwards became a teacher : Assistant Professor of the Elphinstone Institution and leader of the " Young Bombay " Party : was chiefly instrumental in establishing the first girls' school, native library, literary society, debating club, political association, body for improving the condition of women, institution for religious and social reforms, law association and the first educational periodicals. In 1836, he was appointed Native Secretary and Translator to Sir Alexander Burnes (*q.v.*) at Kabul, but returned to Bombay before the Afghan war broke out. In 1845 he was appointed Interpreter of the High Court of Bombay, and retired in 1864, devoting the rest of his life to improving the condition of the people. He laboured to obtain the passing of the Parsi Matrimonial and Succession Act. He visited England on three occasions, lectured before the East India Association, and gained the high opinion of many prominent Englishmen : an influential member of the Municipality of Bombay : C.I.E. in 1884 : died Sep. 22, 1885.

FURSE, GEORGE ARMAND (1834–)

Colonel : born Aug. 21, 1834 : son of William Henry Furse : educated privately and abroad : joined 42nd Highlanders, 1855 : served in the Crimea and the Indian mutiny : present at siege of Lucknow : on special service : to Ashanti, 1873–4 : A.D.C. to C. in C. Bombay, 1874–8 : A.A.G., Soudan expedition, 1884–5 : C.B., 1887 : author of several works on military transport and administration.

FYERS, SIR WILLIAM AUGUSTUS (1816–1895)

General : joined the Army, 1834 : at the capture of Karachi : Captain in the 40th regt. in the Afghan war, 1841–2, under Nott at Kandahar and Kabul, and in the return to India : in the Crimea : in the mutiny, commanded a battalion at Cawnpur : at the capture of Lucknow : died Nov. 10, 1895 : K.C.B.

FYLER, LAWRENCE (1809–1873)

Maj-General : served in the 16th Lancers in the first Afghan war : was at Maharajpur, 1843 : in the Satlaj campaign of 1845–6 : at Badiwal and Aliwal (severely wounded) : with the 3rd Lancers in the Panjab campaign, 1848–9 : in the Crimea with the 12th Lancers : retired 1860 : C.B., 1869 : died Sep. 21, 1873.

FYTCHE, ALBERT (1820–1892)

Born 1820 : son of John Fytche : educated at Rugby and Addiscombe : joined the Bengal Army, 1839 : served in Arakan against the Wallengs, 1841 : entered the Arakan Commission, 1845 : in the Panjab campaign, 1848–9 : at Chilianwala and Gurajat : severely wounded : Deputy Commissioner of Bassein, 1853 : constantly engaged against the Burmese : Commissioner of Tenasserim, 1857 : Chief Commissioner of British Burma, March, 1867–March, 1871 : negotiated a Treaty with the King of Burma : Maj-General, 1868 :

C.S.I : died June 17, 1892 : wrote *Burma Past and Present*, 1878.

GALBRAITH, SIR WILLIAM (1837–)

Born 1837 : son of Rev. John Galbraith of Tuam : entered the 85th regt., 1855 : Lt-Colonel, 1879 : Colonel, 1883 : Maj-General, 1893 : served in Afghan war as A.A.G., 1878–80 : Hazara expedition, 1888 : A.A.G. and Q.M.G. Ireland, 1882–6 : commanded 2nd class District India, 1886–90 : Adjutant-General in India, 1890–5 : commanded Quetta District, 1895–9 : retired, 1899 : K.C.B., 1897.

GALLOWAY, SIR ARCHIBALD (1780 ?–1850)

Maj-General : son of James Galloway : joined the 14th Bengal N.I. in 1800 : served in several regiments : Colonel of the 58th N.I. in 1836 : was in the defence of Delhi and at the siege of Bhartpur : member of the Military Board : C.B., 1838 : K.C.B., 1848 : Chairman of the Court of Directors of the E. I. Co., 1849 : died April 6, 1850 : wrote several works on India, among them on Muhammadan Law : *Observations on the Law and Constitution of India*, 1825 ; *Notes on the Siege of Delhi in 1804*, etc. ; on *Sieges in India* and on the Government of India, 1832.

GALLWEY, SIR THOMAS JOSEPH (1852–)

Born April 14, 1852 : son of Henry Gallwey : educated at Stonyhurst and Royal University, Ireland : entered the Army Medical Department, 1874 : and became Colonel, 1898 : served in the Afghan war, 1878–80 : the Egyptian expedition, 1882 ; Kassassin and Tel-el-Kebir, the Soudan expedition, 1884–5 ; Dongola expedition, 1896 : C.B. : Nile expedition, 1897–8 : P.M.O., South Africa, 1899–1901 : K.C.M.G. : P.M.O., India, since 1902.

GAMBIER, SIR EDWARD JOHN (1794–1879)

Son of Samuel Gambier, nephew of Baron Gambier : born in 1794 : educated at Eton and Trinity College, Cambridge : Fellow : called to the bar at Lincoln's Inn, 1822 : a municipal corporation Commissioner, 1833 : Recorder of Prihce of Wales' Island, and knighted 1834 : Puisne Judge of the Madras Supreme Court, 1836 : Chief Justice, 1842 : retired in 1849 : died May 31, 1879.

GAMBLE, JAMES SYKES (1847–)

Born July 2, 1847, son of Harpur Gamble, M.D. : educated at Royal Naval School, New Cross; Magdalen College, Oxford ; and at Nancy, France : entered the Indian Forest Department, 1871, and rose to be Conservator of Forests, N.W.P., and Oudh, and Director of Imperial Forest School, Dehra Dun : author of *A Manual of Indian Timbers*, 1881 ; *The Bamboos of British India*, 1885 : C.I.E., 1899 : F.R.S. : F.L.S.

GARCIN DE TASSY, JOSEPH HELIO-DORE (1794–1878)

French Oriental scholar : born Jan. 25, 1794 : studied Oriental languages under Baron Silvestre de Sacy: published a work on Oriental literature, 1822, in which year he was Secretary of the Société Asiatique, then established : the first Professor of Hindustani at the special school of Oriental languages, 1828 : he wrote a *History of Hindi and Hindustani Literature*, and *Hindustani Authors and their Works*, the *Rudiments of Hindustani and Hindi*, *Allegories, Poetic Recitations and Popular Songs of Arabic, Persian, Hindustani and Turkish* : edited Sir W. Jones' Persian Grammar in 1845, and translated El-Attar's *Language of Birds* : wrote a number of annual progress reports on the whole field of Indian literature : on the Muhammadan religion, on *Islam d'après le Coran*, 1874: on the Rhetoric and Prosody of the Muslim Nations, and on the religious Poetry of the Persians : in 1854–5 he translated the poet Wali, and *The Adventures of Kamrup* : contributed largely to the *Journals of the Société Asiatique* : was a member of the Royal Asiatic Society and of the French Institute from 1838 : received the Cross of the Legion of Honour, 1837 : died at Paris, Sep. 3, 1878.

GARDNER, ALEXANDER HAUGH-TON (1785–1877)

Adventurer : Colonel : born 1785, in N. America, son of a Doctor, a Scotch emigrant : educated for 9 years at St. Xavier, Mexico : was 5 years in Ireland :

left America, 1812 : travelled to Lisbon, Madrid, Cairo, Trebizond, Astrakhan, Astrabad, Herat (1819), to near Khiva, Astrakhan, across the Caspian and Aral Seas, near Uratube, Kunduz, Anderab, to Afghanistan : took service under Habibulla Khan, nephew of the Amir Dost Muhammad (*q.v.*), engaged in the fights tween them : after Habibulla's flight in 1826, Gardner wandered, through Kafiristan, Badakshan, Shighnan, among the Kirghiz, to Yarkand, Leh, Srinagar, Gilgit, Chitral, Kabul, Kandahar (1830), Girishk (imprisoned for 9 months), to Kabul, to Dost Muhammad, to Bajour, Peshawar, Lahore (1832), where he joined Ranjit Singh's service, as Colonel of Artillery : engaged in campaigns, in Bannu, against the Afghans (1835), etc. : commanded the Jammu artillery : after Ranjit Singh's death (1839), Gardner shared in the fighting about the succession and was at Lahore when the first Sikh war against the British was declared : but was given no active part in either Sikh war : was exiled from Lahore : entered Golab Singh's service in Jammu-Kashmir (1846), and remained there till he died at Jammu, Jan. 22, 1877 : buried at Sealkot : in his old age was visited by high officers.

GARDNER, WILLIAM (1821–1897)

Quartermaster-Sergeant : entered the 42nd Royal Highlanders, 1841, served through the Crimea, and through the mutiny : present at the siege of Delhi, the capture of Lucknow and the action at Bareli, where he gained the V.C. for saving the life of Colonel Cameron when attacked by three Ghazis at once, of whom he killed two : retired 1862, and became a drill instructor of Volunteers : died Oct. 1897.

GARDNER, WILLIAM LINNÆUS (1770–1835)

Son of Major Valentine Gardner, and nephew of the first Lord Gardner : entered the British Army in the 89th foot in 1783, and, passing through several regiments, was Captain in the 30th foot in 1794, which he left, to join, in 1798, Maharaja Jaswant Rao Holkar of Indore, raising and commanding a Brigade of Infantry for him. He married a Princess of Cambay. Holkar accusing Gardner of treachery, the latter would have killed the Maharaja, but was prevented. He then entered the service of Amrit Rao at Poona. Leaving such adventurous employment, he joined Lord Lake in 1804, and raised and commanded a regiment of irregular horse under him and Sir David Ochterlony in Nipal and Rajputana : local Lt-Colonel, 1819 : his regiment, " Gardner's Horse," became the 2nd Bengal Cavalry. He settled at Khasganj, N.W.P. : died July 29, 1835.

GARNETT, ARTHUR WILLIAM (1829-1861)

Son of William Garnett : born June 1, 1829 : educated at Addiscombe : went to India in the Bengal Engineers, 1848 : in the siege of Multan in 1848 : held the Chenab fords at Gujarat, 1849 :| was in the pursuit of the Sikhs : served in Kohat in 1850 : reconstructed the fort there, and made " Fort Garnett " and other defensive positions and roads on the Afghan frontier : engaged in frontier expeditions, and kept the frontier quiet in the mutiny : in the P.W.D. Secretariat : died in 1861 in Calcutta : Colonel.

GARSTIN, JOHN (1756-1820)

Maj-General : born 1756 : educated for the Army : given a commission, by George III, in the Engineers : the first of his family to go out to India : rose to be Maj-General of his Corps : Surveyor-General of Bengal, and Chief Engineer : chiefly employed in the construction of civil works, especially the large " Golah " at Bankipur, intended as a granary in case of famine : was also the architect of Government House, Calcutta : " Garstin's Place " in that city still preserves his name : translated Paul Frisi's *Rivers and Torrents* from the Italian, 1818 : the work is dedicated to Warren Hastings, his friend and patron : died Feb. 16, 1820 : and was buried at Calcutta.

GARTH, SIR RICHARD (1820-1903)

Son of the Rev. Richard Garth : born March 11, 1820 : educated at Eton and Christ Church, Oxford : he was Captain of the Oxford cricket eleven in 1840 and 1841: called to the bar, at Lincoln's Inn, in 1847 : was Q.C. and a Bencher in 1866 : was Conservative M.P. for Guildford, 1866-8 : and Chief Justice of Bengal from 1875 to 1886 : knighted in 1875 : made a Privy Councillor, 1889 : after his retire-

ment retained his interest in Indian questions : wrote *A few Plain Truths about India* : died March 23, 1903.

GARVOCK, SIR JOHN (? - 1878)

General : entered the Army, 1835 : Brig-Major in Sir Harry Smith's Division in the Satlaj campaign, 1845-6 : at all the battles : on his Staff in the Boer war, 1848, and Kafir war, 1850-2 : Q.M.G. in Ceylon : Brigadier at Dover : commanded the Peshawar Division : succeeded Sir N. Chamberlain in command in the Umbeyla campaign, 1863 : K.C.B. : commanded the N. district in England, 1866-71 : the S. district, 1877-8 : G.C.B., 1875 : died Nov. 10, 1878.

GASELEE, SIR ALFRED (1843-)

Born June 3, 1843 : entered the Indian Army, 1863, and became Colonel, 1893 : Brig-General, N.W. Frontier, 1898 : served in Aybssinian expedition, 1868 : Bizoti expedition, 1869 : Jowaki-Afridi expedition, 1877-8 : Afghan war, 1878-80 : Kandahar : Brevet-Major : Zhob Valley, 1884 : Hazara, 1891 : C.B., 1891 : Isaza, 1892 : Waziristan, 1894-5 : Tirah expedition, commanding 2nd Brigade, 1897-8 : K.C.B., 1898 : Officiating Q.M.G. India, 1898 : commanding 2nd class District, 1898-1901 : commanded British Forces in China, 1900 : Maj-General : G.C.I.E., 1901.

GATACRE, JOHN (1841-)

Son of Edward Lloyd Gatacre : born 1841 : educated privately : joined the Bombay Army, 1857, and Bombay Staff Corps, 1866 : commanded his regt., 1884-91 : Brig-General at Nagpur, 1891-6 : Maj-General, 1897 : served in the Indian mutiny at Khandesh, 1858 : China war, 1860 : Afghan war, 1879-80 : Burmese expedition, 1886-8 : C.B. 1887.

GATACRE, SIR WILLIAM FORBES (1843-)

Born 1843 : entered the Army, 1862 : Staff College, 1874 : served in the Hazara expedition as D.A.G. and D.Q.M.G., 1888 : D.S.O. : Burma, 1889 : Chitral, 1895 : C.B. : Soudan, 1898 : K.C.B. : President of the Plague Committee, Bombay, 1897 : commanded 3rd Division in S. Africa, 1899-1900 : Maj-General commanding the 10th Division, 4th Army Corps, at Colchester till 1904.

GAURISHANKAR UDAYASHANKAR
(1805–1891)

Born Aug. 21, 1805 : entered the service of the Bhaunagar State in 1822 : was employed in various political and revenue duties : became Assistant Diwan in 1839, and Diwan in 1846 : introducing many judicial and revenue reforms, and asserted the State's rights against its neighbours : developed its port, commerce, roads, etc. : appointed Joint Administrator of the State during a minority : C.S.I. in 1877 : retired from the service of the State in 1879 : in 1886, became a Sanyasi, i.e. ascetic, renouncing the world : known as Swami Satchidanund Sarasvati : died Dec. 1, 1891.

GAWLER, JOHN COX (? –1882)

Colonel : served with the 73rd regt. in the Kafir war, 1850–3 : in the engagements : district adjutant of Natal at the end of the war : in the Indian mutiny, towards the end : in 1860–1 commanded as Brigadier a considerable Field Force against the Raja of Sikhim : took the Raja's residence, and forced him to accept the treaty dictated to him : penetrated to the Tibet frontier : Keeper of H.M.'s regalia at the Tower of London : died July 31, 1882.

GEARY, GRATTAN (? –1900)

Editor of the *Times of India* : and subsequently acquired the *Bombay Gazette* : took a prominent part in Bombay municipal affairs and was at one time Chairman of the Corporation : wrote *Through Asiatic Turkey : a Narrative of a Journey from Bombay to the Bosphorus*, 1878 : an able writer, and indefatigable worker : exerted no little influence on public events in India : died Sep. 1900.

GELL, RIGHT REV. FREDERICK
(1810–1902)

Son of Rev. Philip Gell : educated at Trinity College, Cambridge : Scholar : Bell University Scholar : Fellow of Christ's College, 1843 : ordained, 1843 : lecturer and tutor : Cambridge Preacher at Chapel Royal, Whitehall : Domestic Chaplain to Bishop of London (Dr. Tait) : Bishop of Madras, 1861–98, when he retired : died at Coonoor, March 25, 1902 : D.D.

GENTIL, JEAN BAPTISTE JOSEPH
(1726–1799)

Born at Bagnols, June 25, 1726 : of noble family : in 1752 went out to India as officer in an Infantry regt. : served with distinction under Dupleix, Law of Lauriston, Lally, etc. After the collapse of the French power in India and the surrender of Pondicherry to the English, in 1761, Gentil served for a time under Mir Kasim, Nawab of Bengal, then under Shuja-ud-daula, Nawab of Oudh, who loaded him with honours : was most generous in helping less fortunate fellow countrymen, and enrolled a body of them to serve under the Nawab : after the defeat of the Nawab at Baxar, Gentil helped to negotiate peace between him and the English : after Shuja-ud-daula's death in 1775, Gentil was compelled by the English to leave, and in 1778 returned to France : appointed Colonel of Infantry : was already Chevalier of St. Louis, 1771 : died in poverty, having lost his pension at the Revolution, at Bagnols, Feb. 15, 1799 : author of *Memoires sur l'Indoustan, Histoire des Radjahs de l'Hindoustan,* etc. : his collection of Persian MSS. is in the Bibliotheque Nationale, Paris.

GERARD, ALEXANDER (1792–1839)

Son of Gilbert Gerard, D.D. and brother of James Gilbert (*q.v.*) and Patrick (*q.v.*) : born Feb. 17, 1792 : joined the Bengal N.I. in 1808 : employed in survey work in 1812–7 and after, and 1825–7 : ascended great heights in the Himalayas and penetrated into Tibet : in 1821, he ascended the Charang Pass, over 17,000 ft.; the Keeobrang Pass, over 18,000 ft., and Mount Tahigung, over 22,000 ft.; travelled from Sabathu to Shipki in Chinese Tartary, and from Shipki to Chinese Tibet, and wrote an account of his attempt to penetrate to the lake Mansarowar : he retired early from ill-health, in 1836 : died Dec. 15, 1839.

GERARD, JAMES GILBERT (1795–1835)

Son of Gilbert Gerard, D.D. : born 1795 : entered the E.I. Co.'s Bengal medical service in 1814 : accompanied his brother Alexander in his Himalayan travels : in 1831 went with (Sir Alexander)

M

Burnes (*q.v.*) to Bokhara, though in bad health : detained by illness at Mashad and Herat, and died, worn out, at Sabathu, March 31, 1835. His scientific accuracy was valuable in connexion with the geographical information acquired by the expedition.

GERARD, SIR MONTAGU GILBERT
(1843-1905)

General : born 1843 : son of Colonel Archibald Gerard : educated at Stonyhurst : entered the R.A., 1864, and Bengal Staff Corps, 1870 : Central India Horse, 1870-95 : served in Abyssinia, 1868 : Brig-Major in the Afghan war, 1878-80 : in the advance to Kabul : in the Kabul-Kandahar march and battle of Kandahar : Brevets Major and Lt-Colonel : in the campaign in Egypt, 1882, as D.A.A. and Q.M.G. : at Tel-el-Kebir : C.B. : on Secret Service in Persia, 1881-2, and 1885 : Military Attaché, St. Petersburg, 1892-3 : Commissioner for Delimitation of Pamir Boundary, 1895 : General commanding Hyderabad Contingent, 1896-9 : commanding Oudh District, 1899 : C.S.I., 1896 : K.C.S.I., 1897 : K.C.B., 1902 : attached to the Russian Forces in Manchuria, 1904-5 : died of pneumonia at Irkutsk, July, 1905 : wrote *Leaves from the Diaries of a Soldier and Sportsman during Twenty Years' Service in India, Afghanistan, Egypt, and Other Countries*, 1865-85.

GERARD, PATRICK (1794-1848)

Son of Gilbert Gerard, D.D., and brother of Alexander and James Gilbert : born June 11, 1794 : entered the Bengal N.I., in 1812 : Captain, 1828 : invalided, 1832 : died Oct. 4, 1848 : recorded observations on the climate of Sabathu and Kotghar, and wrote on meteorology, and the Himalayas and their mineral products, in scientific journals.

GERICKE, REV. CHRISTIAN WILHELM (1742-1803)

A devoted Danish missionary and evangelist : native of Colberg in Pomerania : graduate of Halle : reached Tranquebar, 1767 : to Cuddalore, 1767, joining the S.P.C.K. and Hutteman there : assisted at Trichinopoly : during the attack by Mysoreans and French on Cuddalore, he interceded, to prevent destruction of British life and property : on its capture, in 1782, he removed to Negapatam till he took charge of the Vepery Mission, 1788, whence he visited other stations : appointed Dutch translator, 1792 : Naval Chaplain of H.M.S. *Victorious* and of the Naval Hospital at Vepery, 1796-1803 : Chaplain and Secretary of the Female Orphan Asylum, Madras, 1788-1803 : fortunate in his speculations with the Mission balances, and died rich, leaving a considerable sum to the Vepery Mission : in personal character stood high with the Government : died on a visit to Vellore, 1803.

GHOSE, CHUNDER MADHAB
(1838-   )

Son of Rai Bahadur Durga Persad Ghose, Deputy Collector : born Feb. 26, 1838 : educated at the Hindu and Presidency Colleges : passed the Pleadership examination, 1859 : was Government Pleader at Burdwan, 1860-2 : practised as pleader in the *Sadr* Court, 1862, and as Vakil of the High Court from 1862, attaining a prominent position : Member of the Bengal Legislative Council, 1883-5 : Fellow of the Calcutta University, 1885 : President of the Board of Examiners for Pleaders, 1892 : Puisne Judge of the Calcutta High Court, from Jan. 12, 1885 : Fellow of the Calcutta University and President of the Faculty of Law : has established charitable institutions in his native village : is President of the Bengal Kayastha Sabha.

GHOSE, GRISH CHANDRA,
(1829-1869)

Born 1829 : educated at the Oriental Seminary : established a weekly paper, *The Bengal Recorder*, in 1849 : in 1850 entered the Military Pay Examiners' office, of which he ultimately became the Registrar, drawing a salary of Rs. 350 a month. *The Bengal Recorder* was converted into the *Hindu Patriot* in 1853, and Haris Chandra Mukerji became its principal editor, but Grish Chandra continued his connexion with the paper as a contributor. In 1859, he and his brother were introduced into the Dalhousie Institute for their literary attainments : in 1861, the *Bengalee* newspaper was started, and Grish Chandra accepted the editorship in addition to his own official duties : in 1868 he published a Life of Ram Dulal Dey (*q.v.*) the Bengali millionaire : died suddenly in Sep. 1869.

GHOSE, HARA CHANDRA (1808-1868)

Educated at the Hindu College under David Hare (*q.v.*), and Derozio (*q.v.*) : was appointed a Munsif in 1832 and rose high in the native judicial service. In 1852 he was made junior Magistrate of Calcutta, and in 1854 a Judge of the Small Cause Court : held the post till his death in 1868. His bust, in marble, was placed in the main entrance of the Court.

GHOSE, KASI PRASAD (1809-1873)

Born Aug. 1809 : admitted as a free scholar in the Hindu College, Oct. 1821 : in Dec. 1828, reviewed *Mill's History of British India* at the request of Prof. H. H. Wilson for the *Government Gazette* and the *Asiatic Journal* : in 1829 left the Hindu College : in 1831, published his first volume, *Shair and other Poems* : in 1834 published, anonymously, his *Memoir of Native Indian Dynasties*, which had previously appeared in D. L. Richardson's *Literary Gazette* ; in 1840, Richardson included some of his poetical compositions in his *Selections from the British Poets* : in Nov. 1846, he established the weekly journal, *The Hindu Intelligencer*, which he discontinued in 1857 on the passing of " The Gagging Act " by Lord Canning : in 1838, the Dharma Sabha was founded : he opposed all social reforms : was a Justice of the Peace of the City of Calcutta, and Honorary Presidency Magistrate : died Nov. 11, 1873.

GHOSE, MAN MOHAN (1844-1896)

Lawyer : born March, 1844 : a member of an old Kayastha family in Bikrampur, in the district of Dacca : son of Ram Lochan Ghose, a Subordinate Judge and friend of Raja Rammohan Roy, with whose views he sympathized : educated at the Krishnagar Collegiate School and the Presidency College, Calcutta. In 1861, he founded the *Indian Mirror*, then issued fortnightly : in 1862, he went to England and stood for the Indian Civil Service Examination in 1864 and 1865, but without success : in 1866, he was called to the bar, and in 1867 joined the Calcutta High Court as the first Indian barrister : delivered a series of lectures against the open competitive examinations for the Indian Civil Service. In 1885, he was sent to England as delegate from Bengal, to speak on Indian questions : visited England again in 1887, 1890, 1895, sometimes with his family. As a barrister, he was engaged in several notable cases, and achieved great success. He became, in 1873, Secretary of the Bethune College, and, as a member of the National Congress, was a strong advocate for the separation of judicial and executive functions of District Officers : Fellow of the Calcutta University : died Oct. 17, 1896.

GHOSE, RAM GOPAL (1815-1868)

Son of a petty shopkeeper : born Oct. 1815 : educated at the Hindu College in Calcutta. He early entered on a mercantile career, and after gaining experience, first as banian and later as partner in a European firm, he, with his acquired capital, opened a firm under the name of R. G. Ghose & Co., with a branch at Akyab. He was a very active member of the Bengal Chamber of Commerce. In 1849 he was offered the post of Second Judge of the Calcutta Small Cause Court, but declined it. He was one of the earliest " politicians " in Bengal, taking part in all political movements, and was connected with several literary and self-improvement associations. He brought out one or two newspapers, and attempted to rouse the sympathy of the British public with Indian grievances : was a recognized leader of the Native community, as a reformer, a patriot, an eloquent speaker, and in force of character, and did much to advance native society : through his exertions a statue was erected to David Hare : took a leading part in defence of what were termed " The Black Acts " in 1849 : took great interest in education, and was one of the first to send his daughter to the Bethune School : was a Fellow of the University, and of various Societies : Hony. Magistrate and J.P. for Calcutta : appointed by Government a member of several committees : on the Council of Education, 1848-55 : Member of the Bengal Legislative Council, 1862-4 : died Jan. 25, 1868.

GHULAM HASSAN KHAN, NAWAB SIR (? -1881)

An Alizai Pathan : son of Ashik Muhammad Khan, ruler of the Tonk subdivision of Dera Ismail Khan under Ranjit Singh: offered his services to Government: distinguished himself by capturing Fort Laki when held by Sikh rebels in 1848, and frustrated the advance of the rebel garrison of Bannu to Multan: aided Reynell Taylor (*q.v.*) at Bannu, 1851–7: in 1857–8 as native commandant took to Lahore the Multan horse, 2,000 strong, which he had raised: under Colonel Cureton, C.B., led them in 15 general actions: for five years after the mutiny, 1859–64, was Envoy at Kabul and accompanied the Afghan army to Herat: Nawab, 1863: C.S.I., 1868: commanded the Bahawalpur Army, 1868: on the Staff of H.R.H. the Prince of Wales, 1875–6: was sent in advance to the Amir of Kabul in 1878: was a trusted and honoured counsellor during the campaigns of 1878–80 at Kandahar and Kabul: was made hereditary Nawab and K.C.S.I. and given *jagirs:* was officially declared to be " a gallant soldier, an able counsellor and a chivalrous gentleman " : died 1881.

GHULAM HUSSEIN KHAN TABA-TABA, SYAD (? – ?)

Muhammadan nobleman: his maternal ancestors were Syads: Zainul-abidin was his maternal grandfather: related, as a cousin, to Aliverdi of Bihar: son of Hidayat Ali Khan, a Deputy Governor of Bihar: born at Shahjahanabad: Mir Munshi, or Secretary, of the Mogul Emperor: resided at the Court of the Nawab of Bengal, Bihar and Orissa: representative of Mir Kasim (*q.v.*) at Calcutta, until removed: served under the British: befriended by General Goddard, Resident at Chunarghar: entered, with permission, the Nawab of Oudh's service for a time: left it: wrote the *Siyar-almuta' akhkhirin,* a " Review of Modern Times," i.e. " The Manners of the Moderns, the Chronicle of the Decay of the Mogul Empire and Muhammadan Domination of India, during the reigns of the seven last emperors of Hindustan, written in Persian, showing the progress of the English in Bengal up to 1780 A.D. " : translated by M. Raymond (*q.v.*), a French Creole, who assumed the name of Haji Mustapha: published in 1789: dedicated to Warren Hastings: it was lost at sea on the way to England: a subsequent edition of about one-sixth of the work was issued by General J. Briggs.

of the Madras Army: the *Sair,* or *Siyar-ul-mutakherin* (its usual name) has been highly regarded by great authorities.

GIB, SIR WILLIAM ANTHONY (1827–)

Born Jan. 9, 1827: son of Colin Gib, R.N.: educated privately: joined Madras Army, 1843: served in Khandesh, 1844, and Indian mutiny, 1857–9: commanded the 25th regt. M.I. in expeditionary force to Malta, 1878: commanded a Brigade in Afghan war, 1879–80, and troops in action of Mazina: C.B.: held various civil and military appointments in India, including the command of the 1st class District of Sikandarabad: General: K.C.B., 1897.

GIBBS, JAMES (1825–1886)

I.C.S.: born 1825: son of Right Hon. Michael Gibbs, Lord Mayor, 1845: educated at Merchant Taylors' and Haileybury, 1844–6: called to the bar at the Inner Temple, 1864: went to Bombay in the Civil Service, 1846: Judicial Assistant to the Commissioner in Sind: Special Commissioner for Income Tax, 1860: President of the Income Tax Commission: Judge of Poona, 1864: Puisne Judge of the High Court, Bombay: President of the Asiatic Society, Bombay: Member of Council, Bombay, April, 1874, to April, 1879: Member of the Supreme Council, May, 1880, to May, 1885: Vice-Chancellor of the Bombay University, 1870–9: died Oct. 30, 1886: C.S.I.: C.I.E.

GIBBS, SIR SAMUEL (? –1815)

Joined the 102nd foot in 1783: served in Canada, at Gibraltar, the Mediterranean, at Ostend, in the W. Indies, 1799: commanded the 59th at the Cape, 1805–6: and in the Travancore war, 1808–9: was in the expedition of 1811 under Sir S. Auchmuty to Java: distinguished himself: at Fort Cornelis, and led the final attack on the Dutch General Janssens: then left India: in Holland, in 1812: in the United States, in the attack on New Orleans: severely wounded, and died Jan. 9, 1815: K.C.B.: Maj-General.

GIBSON, ALEXANDER (1800–1867)

Born Oct. 24, 1800: M.D. of Edinburgh: went to India in the E.I. Co.'s medical service in 1825 : served in the. Indian navy : vaccinator for the Dekkan and Khandesh, 1836 : studied botany and agriculture : Superintendent of the Dapuri botanic garden near Poona, 1838–67 : aimed at introducing new trees and plants and drugs : Conservator of Forests, Bombay, 1847–60 : F.L.S., 1853 : wrote on Bombay Forests and Flora : died Jan. 16, 1867.

GIDHOUR, MAHARAJA SIR JAI MANGAL SINGH BAHADUR, OF (? –1889)

During the Sonthal rebellion, 1855, he rendered valuable service to the Government, for which he received rewards : during the Sepoy mutiny he helped the Government greatly in the protection of Bihar, and was made " Maharaja Bahadur," and K.C.S.I. : a *jagir* was granted to him in 1864 : during the Bengal famine of 1874 he gave great assistance, and the title of " Maharaja " was extended to his son : in 1877, at the Delhi Imperial Assemblage, this title was made hereditary in his family : he died in 1889 : grandfather of Maharaja Sir Ravaneshwar Singh (*q.v.*).

GIDHOUR, MAHARAJA SIR RAVANE-SHAR PRASAD SINGH BAHADUR, OF (1860–   )

Member of Bengal Legislative Council, 1893–5, and 1895–7 and 1901 : title of Maharaja made hereditary, 1877 : K.C.I.E. 1895.

GILBERT, SIR WALTER RALEIGH, BARONET (1785–1853)

Son of Rev. Edmund Gilbert : born 1785 : joined the 15th Bengal N.I. in 1801 : present at the actions at Alighar, Delhi, Agra, Laswari in 1803, at Deeg and Lake's unsuccessful attacks on Bhartpur : Commandant of the Calcutta native militia, 1815 : Superintendent of the Mysore Princes, 1816, and on Lord Hastings' Staff : A.G.G. on the S.W. frontier, 1822 : Colonel of the 1st European Fusiliers, 1832 : Maj-General, 1841 : Lt-General, 1851 : commanded a Division in the first Sikh war at Mudki, Firozshahr, and Sobraon : K.C.B., 1846 : and in the Panjab campaign : at Chilianwala and Gujarat : after the last-named battle he commanded in the pursuit of the Sikhs,

who surrendered to him at Hoormuck and Rawul Pindi, the Afghans flying to the Khyber : G.C.B. : Baronet in 1851 : Military Member of the Supreme Council, Dec. 1852, to Feb. 1853 : he was a famous sportsman, and paid much attention to horse-racing : died May 12, 1853.

GILCHRIST, JOHN BORTHWICK (1759–1841)

Born in 1759 : educated at Heriot's Hospital, Edinburgh : to Calcutta in the E.I. Co.'s medical service, 1794 : was the first to reduce to a system the language, then unsettled, called Hindustani : published a dictionary and grammar in it, and popularized its study : he was also well versed in Sanskrit and Persian : the Marquis Wellesley made him Principal of the College of Fort William at Calcutta in 1800 : he supervised the preparation of works in Hindu and Urdu by native scholars, and himself wrote chiefly on those languages : left India in 1804 : LL.D. of Edinburgh : acted as Oriental Professor at Haileybury, Feb. to May, 1806 : retired in 1809 : taught privately in Oriental languages, 1816–8 : Professor of Hindustani at the Oriental Institution, 1818–26 : his method of obtaining remuneration for his teaching, by the sale of his works, was irregular, and he turned to abusing his employers. After giving up his Professorship, he still taught Hindustani for a time : died in Paris, Jan. 9, 1841 : a scholarship in his name was founded in Calcutta.

GILDEMEISTER, JOHANNES GUSTAV (1812–1890)

Born July 20, 1812, at Klein Siemen in Mecklenburg : studied theology and Oriental languages at Gottingen and Boon : Sanskrit under Schlegel and Lassen : Privat-docent at Bonn, 1839, for Oriental languages and literature : Extraordinary Professor at Bonn, 1844 : Professor, in 1845, of theology and Oriental literature at the University of Marburg ; also Librarian there for ten years: Professor of Oriental languages and literature at Bonn, 1859, retaining this post till his death, on March 11, 1890. A controversialist as well as a scholar : of wide and varied interests and learning : thorough and conscientious in all his work : a great teacher and noted librarian : yet has left no great monument of his industry behind him. Among his works on Indian subjects are : *Die falsche Sanskrit-philologie,* 1840 ; *Bibliothecae Sanskritae specimen,* 1847 ; a new edition of Lassen's *Anthologia Sanskritica,* 1865 ; one of the founders of the Deutsche Morgenländische Gesellschaft.

GILL, ROBERT (? –1875)

Major : antiquary, artist and sportsman : entered the Indian Army in 1842 : his regimental service was apparently uneventful : he is remembered for his work, as follows. In 1844, the Court of Directors of the E.I. Co. ordered that copies should be made of the frescoes in the Buddhist excavations at Ajanta : Gill was appointed about 1844–6 to the work, and spent the remainder of his life, about thirty years, at Ajanta, doing it : living in the *sarai* in which Colonel (Sir) Arthur Wellesley (*q.v.*) had quarters after Assaye. With great labour, Gill, working in feverish jungle, and in dark recesses (haunted by wild animals), copied in full size and oils the principal frescoes, about thirty in number, and sent them to England, about 1855. Of these paintings, twenty-five, exhibited at the Crystal Palace, were burnt in 1866 : five at the India office escaped : some of those burnt had been copied by George Scharf to illustrate the works of Mrs. Manning. The Ajanta frescoes were again copied, under Government orders, in 1872–85 by Mr. John Griffiths, Principal of the Bombay School of Art : and the results were published, 1896. Other drawings by Gill, *i.e.,* of ground plans of the caves, and architectural details, are still known to exist : he was also an expert photographer, as shown in his two books, viz. *The Rock-cut Temples of India,* illustrated by his 74 photographs, 1864 : and *One Hundred Stereoscopic Illustrations of Architecture and Natural History in W. India,* 1864, both books with descriptions by J. Fergusson (*q.v.*). Gill, as a sportsman, killed above 150 tigers, mostly on foot, his name being well known for his prowess for nearly half a century : he died while being conveyed, very ill, from Ajanta to Bhosawal, where he was buried.

GILLESPIE, SIR ROBERT ROLLO
(1766–1814)

Of an old Scottish family : born Jan. 21, 1766 : educated at Kensington and near

Newmarket : joined the 3rd Irish Horse in 1783 : was acquitted on a verdict of " justifiable homicide," after shooting a man in a duel : went to Jamaica, 1792 : recovered from yellow fever : to St. Domingo : fired on while swimming with a flag of truce : Adjutant-General at St. Domingo, 1796 : personally killed six out of eight men attacking him : received a sword of honour from the Jamaica House of Assembly : tried by court martial at Colchester, 1804 : honourably acquitted : stationed at Arcot in Madras : from there, 14 miles off, rescued the survivors of the 69th foot from the mutineers at Vellore, July 10, 1806 : commanded the cavalry against Ranjit Singh in 1809 : commandant at Bangalore : commanded the Mysore Division : was Brig-General in 1811 : commanded the advance of Sir S. Auchmuty's expedition to Java : led the attack at Cornelis : left in command at Java : deposed the Sultan of Palimbang in Sumatra : defeated Javanese chiefs at Yodhyakarta : Maj-General, 1812 : left Java : commanded at Meerut : and a Division in the Nipal war : killed, leading an attack on Fort Kalanga, near Deyra Doon, Oct. 31, 1814 : but named as K.C.B. on Jan. 1, 1815 : a monument to him by Chantrey in St. Paul's Cathedral. His military actions were all distinguished by his reckless courage : he was also a keen sportsman.

GIRAUD, HERBERT JOHN (1817–1888)

Son of John Thomas Giraud : born April 14, 1817 : took his M.D. degree at Edinburgh University, 1840 : entered the E.I. Co.'s Bombay Medical Service, 1842 : Professor of Chemistry and Botany, and afterwards Principal of the Grant Medical College, Bombay : Principal of Sir Jamsetji Jijibhai's Hospital : Chemical Analyst to the Bombay Government : Deputy Inspr-General of the Army Medical Service : Fellow of the Bombay University : Surgeon on the Staff of several Governors of Bombay : stated to have been the first to introduce the study of chemistry and botany into W. India : wrote papers on chemical and botanical subjects, including toxicology, for scientific journals : retired, 1867 : died Jan. 12, 1888.

GLADWIN, FRANCIS (? –1813 ?)

Was in the Bengal Army : encouraged by Warren Hastings in his studies in

Oriental literature : translated a portion of Abul Fazl's *Ain-i-Akbari*, 1783–6 : member of the Asiatic Society of Bengal : published a *History of Hindustan*, 1788 : a number of translations of Persian writers, including the *Gulistan* : a Persian-Hindustani-English dictionary, 1809 : was first Professor of Persian at the College of Fort William, 1801 : Collector of Customs at Patna, 1802 : Commissary resident at Patna, 1808 : he died about 1813.

GLEIG, REV. GEORGE ROBERT
(1796–1888)

Born April 20, 1796 : son of Bishop George Gleig : educated at Glasgow and Balliol College, Oxford : entered the Army, 1812 : served in the Peninsula and America : took his degree, 1819 : ordained, 1820 : Chaplain of Chelsea Hospital, 1834 : Chaplain-General of the Forces, 1844–75 : died July 9, 1888 : wrote largely for Reviews and Magazines : also, among other works, *The Life of Sir Thomas Munro*, *The History of India*, *Sale's Brigade in Afghanistan*, Lives of "*Lord Clive*," and "*Warren Hastings*."

GLENELG, CHARLES GRANT, BARON
(1778–1866)

Son of Charles Grant (*q.v.*) : born Oct. 26, 1778, at Kidderpur, Bengal : came to England, 1790 : educated at Magdalen College, Cambridge : Fellow : won Claudius Buchanan's (*q.v.*) University Prize poem on "The Restoration of Learning in the East " : called to the bar at Lincoln's Inn, Jan. 30, 1807 : M.P. from 1811–35 for Inverness and the county : Lord of the Treasury, 1813 : Chief Secretary for Ireland, 1819–23 : and Privy Councillor : Vice-President of the Board of Trade, 1823–7 : President of the Board, and Treasurer of the Navy, 1827–8 : President of the Board of Control from Nov. 22, 1830, to Dec. 15, 1834. It devolved on him to carry the Bill, in 1833, for the renewal of the E.I. Co.'s charter : the Company retained its political status, but its property was vested in the Crown : the Bishopric in India was increased. He was Secretary for the Colonies, 1835–9 : made a peer in 1835 : abolished West Indian Slavery : his policy in Canada was attacked on all sides, and he resigned in 1839, receiving a pension and the office

of Commissioner of the Land-Tax : died April 23, 1866. and the title became extinct.

GOBLET D'ALVIELLA, COUNT EUGENE (1846–)

Born Aug. 10, 1846, at Brussels : son of Count Louis Goblet d'Alviella, member of the Belgian House of Representatives : educated at Brussels and Paris : took the degrees of D.Polit.Science, D.LL. and D.Phil., at Brussels : called to the bar : became a member of the Provincial Council of Brabant, 1872 : managed, 1874–92, the *Revue de Belgique :* in 1875, accompanied H.R.H. the Prince of Wales to India, as special correspondent of the *Indépendence Belge :* afterwards visited Sikhim and the Buddhist monasteries on the Tibet frontier : sat in the Belgian House of Representatives, 1878–84 : member of the Senate, 1892 : Secretary of the Senate since 1900 : appointed Professor of the History of Religions in 1884, and still occupies this post : Hibbert Lecturer at Oxford and London, 1891 : 1896–8, Rector of the University of Brussels : 1897, elected President of the Royal Academy of Belgium : Senator of Belgium, 1894 : Secretary of the Senate since 1900 : author of works dealing with both the ancient civilization and the modern development of India under British rule : *Inde et Himalaya ; Souvenirs de Voyage*, 1877, 1880 ; *L'Histoire religieuse chez les Anglais, les Americains, et les Hindous*, 1884 ; *La Migration des Symboles*, 1891 ; *Ce que l'Inde doit a la Grèce*, 1897 : and numerous articles on the people and religions of India in the *Revue de Belgique, Revue des Deux Mondes*, etc. : M.R.A.S. : LL.D. of the University of Glasgow, 1901.

GODDARD, THOMAS (1740 ?–1783)

Grandson of Thomas Goddard, Canon of Windsor : at Madras with his regiment under Coote, 1759–61 : at the capture of Pondicherry, Jan. 16, 1761 : in the 84th regt. in the Bengal campaign, 1763 : joined the Bengal Army : raised "Goddard's battalion " of sepoys at Murshidabad in 1764 : served in quelling the mutiny at Patna, 1766 : at capture of Burrareah, near Chapra, 1770 : and against the Mahrattas in Rohilkund, 1772 : in command at Berhampur. 1774 : and of the contingent at Lucknow, 1776 : commanded, in succession to Colonel Leslie, the Bengal contingent which marched across India to aid the Bombay Army against the Mahrattas, 1778–81 : took Mhow : Ahmadabad on Feb. 15, 1780 : defeated Sindia : captured Bassein, Dec. 11, 1780 : threatened Poona : Goddard was compelled to retreat : treaty with Sindia, Oct. 1781 : Brig-General : appointed C. in C. of the Bombay Army : retired for ill-health : died at sea, off the Land's End, July 7, 1783.

GODEHEU, M. (? – ?)

Member of Council at Chandernagore and befriended by Dupleix while the latter was the Intendant there, before 1741 : Director of the Company of the Indies in France : sent out by the French Ministry as Commissary of the French King, and Governor-General of the French Settlements, to supersede Dupleix, conclude peace with the English, and examine Dupleix's accounts : reached Pondicherry, Aug. 1, 1754 : ruined Dupleix by rejecting his claims for sums advanced from his private means, and by his reports : in negotiating with Saunders, the English Governor at Madras, Godeheu reversed Dupleix's policy, and gave up nearly all the points at issue, thus diminishing the French position in India : left Pondicherry for France in Feb. 1755.

GODLEY, SIR JOHN ARTHUR
(1847–   )

Born June 11, 1847, son of J. R. Godley : educated at Rugby and Balliol College, Oxford : Hertford, Ireland and Eldon Law Scholar : Fellow of Hertford College, 1874 : Private Secretary to Mr. Gladstone when Prime Minister, 1872–4 and 1880–2 : Commissioner of Inland Revenue, 1882–3 : Under Secretary of State for India since 1883 : K.C.B., 1893.

GODWIN, SIR HENRY THOMAS
(1784–1853)

Joined the 9th foot in 1799 : served in Hanover in 1805 : in the Peninsula, 1808 : Brevet-Major and C.B. : went to India as Lt-Colonel of the 41st, 1822 : throughout the first Burmese war, 1824–6, including capture of Rangoon and occupation of Martaban : Maj-General, 1846 : commanded a Division in Bengal, 1850 : and held the Command-in-Chief of the

Force in the second Burmese war, 1852–3 : captured Rangoon, April, 1852, Bassein in May, Pegu in June : commanded the Sirhind Division : died at Simla, Oct. 26, 1853, from the effects of the Burmese campaigns : made K.C.B., but died before the notification reached him.

GODWIN-AUSTEN, HENRY HAVER-SHAM (1834–   )

Born July 6, 1834 : son of Robert A. C. Godwin-Austen, a distinguished geologist : educated at Sandhurst : entered the Army, 1851 : went to India, 1852 : served in the second Burmese war and Panjab : entered the Trigonometrical Survey of India, 1857 : surveyed large tracts in the Himalayas : on special duty with Bhutan Field Force, 1864 : President of Section E (Geography) of British Association, 1883 : author of *On the Land and Freshwater Mollusca of British India*, 1882–99 : contributed to several scientific Journals on geology, ethnology and natural history : Lt-Colonel : retired, 1877.

GOETHALS, MOST REV. ARCH-BISHOP (1833–1901)

Born 1833, in Belgium : of a family of wealth and influence : had a distinguished career in Europe : was Count of the Roman Empire, and a Domestic Chaplain to the Pope, before he went to Calcutta in 1878, to be, at first, Bishop : like the other Vicariates and Prefects Apostolic in India, he was subject to the Archbishop at Goa : from 1886, under the *concordat* between the Portuguese authorities at Goa and the Vatican, he became Archbishop under the constitution issued by the Pope, which converted the 16 Vicariates into regular dioceses and appointed him Archbishop by special proclamation. He was thus, for 15 years, head of the Roman Catholic Church in India, under the direction of the Congregation of the Propaganda at Rome : he devoted his energies and his wealth to the interests of the See, especially in the development of churches, convents and schools : died at Calcutta, July 4, 1901 : described as a most distinguished prelate and true, devoted friend to India.

GOLDNEY, PHILIP (1802–1857)

Son of Thomas Goldney : born Nov. 21, 1802 : educated privately : entered the E.I. Co.'s Bengal Army, 1821 : served in Sind, from 1844 : became Collector-Magistrate there : in the expedition to the Trucki hills : had great influence over the Beluchis : increased the area of canal cultivation : commanded a Brigade sent to annex Oudh : in charge of the Faizabad Division, when the mutiny of 1857 broke out : fortified the town : compelled to leave in boats : killed at Begamji, on the Gogra, 30 miles from Faizabad, about June 9, 1857.

GOLDNEY, THOMAS HOLLROW
(1847-)

Born Oct. 10, 1847 : son of Colonel Philip Goldney, Bengal Army : educated privately : joined the English Army, and subsequently the Bengal Staff Corps : served in Sikhim expedition, 1888 : expedition to Dongola, 1896 : N.W. Frontier of India, 1897, relief of Chakdara : Mohmand expedition, 1897-8 : C.B. : Colonel.

GOLDSMID, SIR FREDERICK JOHN
(1818-)

Maj-General : son of Lionel P. Goldsmid : educated at Paris and King's College, London : entered the Madras Army, 1839 : served in China war, 1840-1 : in Eastern Crimea with Turkish troops, 1855-6 : on special missions and political employment under Bombay Government, 1862-4 : Director of Government Indo-European Telegraph, 1865-70 : Colonel, 1870 : Boundary Commissioner to settle Perso-Kelat frontier, and arbitrator in the Perso-Afghan Boundary settlement, Seistan, 1870-2 : Maj-General, 1875 : British Commissioner on International Commission for Indian immigrants in Reunion, 1877-80 : British Controller of Daira Sanieh, Egypt, 1880-3 : author of *Telegraph and Travel*, 1874 ; *James Outram, a Biography*, 1880, and contributor to *Encyclopædia Britannica* : C.B., 1866 : K.C.S.I., 1871 : F.R.G.S.

GOLDSMID, HENRY EDWARD
(1812-1855)

Of the Bombay Civil Service : born May 9, 1812 : son of Edward Goldsmid : educated privately and at Haileybury : went to the Bombay Presidency, 1832 : became assistant to the Revenue Commissioner, Mr. Williamson, in 1835 : devised the Revenue Survey and assessment system of Western India, and applied it, 1835-45 : Private Secretary to Sir G. R. Clerk, Governor of Bombay, 1847-8 : Secretary in the Revenue Department in 1848, and Chief Secretary, 1854. He was the founder of a school of revenue officers who gave effect to the *ryotwari* system of direct tenure of the cultivators from the Government as landlord : the system generally adopted in W. India : Goldsmid died at Cairo, Jan. 3, 1855.

GOLDSTÜCKER, THEODORE
(1821-1872)

Born Jan. 18, 1821, at Königsberg : educated at the University, Königsberg, 1836, and at Bonn, studying Sanskrit under Schlegel and Lassen, devoting himself chiefly to philosophy and Oriental languages : stayed in Paris and Berlin, but finally lived in England, 1850, when he was appointed Professor of Sanskrit, University College, London : held this post till his death : an authority on Sanskrit philology : he wrote on *Panini, his Place in Sanskrit Literature*, 1861 : an unfinished *Dictionary, Sanskrit and English* ; an edition de luxe of the *Mahabhashya*, an Indian Commentary on Panini's Grammar, published in 1874 by the Indian Government after Goldstücker's death. He also wrote for the English public, in various Encyclopædias, popular articles on Indian philosophy and mythology, published after his death as *Literary Remains*, 1879 : founded the Society for the Publication of Sanskrit Texts in London, 1866 : Member of the Royal Asiatic Society and of its Council : President of the Philological Society, before which he read papers, but would not publish them : respected as an authority on ancient Hindu literature and law, and consulted on the Hindu Law of Inheritance by the Government of India : referred to also by scholars and statesmen, in Europe and India. His last work was *On the Deficiencies in the Present Administration of Hindu Law* : he died March 6, 1872.

GOLIGHTLY, ROBERT EDMUND
(1856-)

Born Sep. 15, 1856 : son of Rev. Canon Golightly : educated at Eton and Sandhurst : joined the Army, 1875 : became Captain, 1886 : served at Kandahar and Ghazni, 1878, and in march from Kandahar to Kabul and battle of Ahmad Kheyl : marched with Sir F. Roberts from Kabul to Kandahar : with King's Royal Rifles in Boer campaign, 1880 : Adjutant, 1881–5 : commanded Mounted Infantry in Burma Field Force, 1886–7 : D.S.O : A.A.G., Meerut, 1889 : commanded 1st Battalion Imperial Yeomanry in S. Africa, 1900–1 : promoted Colonel in Reserve of Officers.

GOMM, SIR WILLIAM MAYNARD
(1784–1875).

Field-Marshal : born Nov. 10, 1784 : son of Lt-Colonel William Gomm : Ensign and Lieutenant in the 9th regt. in 1794 : studied at Woolwich until 1799 : served in Holland, 1799 : at Ferrol, 1800 : Hanover, 1805 : in the Copenhagen expedition, 1807 : at Corunna : on the Walcheren expedition, 1809 : in the Peninsula, 1810 : in many of the engagements : Lt-Colonel : K.C.B. : in the Coldstream Guards : at Waterloo, Q.M.G. to Picton's Division : Maj-General, 1837 : commanded the troops in, and Lieutenant-Governor of, Jamaica, 1839–42 : Governor and C. in C. of the Mauritius, 1842–9 : Lt-General, 1846 : disappointed of the Commandership in Chief in India in 1849, after being told of his appointment, but, on the resignation of Sir Charles Napier (who had been separately appointed), became C. in C. in India from Dec. 6, 1850 to 1855 : General in 1854 : G.C.B. in 1859 : Field-Marshal, 1868 : Constable of the Tower of London, 1872 : D.C.L. and LL.D. : died March 15, 1875.

GONDAL, THAKUR SAHIB OF
(1865–   )

Born Oct. 24, 1865 : educated at the. Rajkumar College, Rajkot, and Edinburgh University : Hon. LL.D. Edin., 1887 : M.B. and G.M. Edin. 1895 : D.C.L., Oxford, 1892 : M.D. Edin., 1895 : F.R.C.P. Edin., 1895 : Fellow of the. Bombay University : F.R.S.E., 1900 : K.C.I.E., 1887 : G.C.I.E., 1897 : author of *A Short History of Aryan Medical Science*, *Journal of a Visit to England*.

GOODFELLOW, CHARLES AUGUSTUS (? –   )

Entered Royal Bombay Engineers, 1855 : became Lt-General, 1892 : served in the Indian mutiny, 1857–8 : V.C. : Kattiawar Field Force, 1859 : Abyssinian

expedition : Brevet-Major : un-employed supernumerary, 1896.

GOPAL, MADAN, RAI BAHADUR
(? –1904)

Began his career as a pleader at Delhi : called to the bar in 1887 : practised at the Lahore Chief Court, obtained a leading position at the bar : Fellow of the Panjab University in 1888 : leading member of the Senate : Rai Bahadur in 1896 : member of the Panjab Legislative Council, in 1898, 1900, 1902 : died at Delhi, Aug. 11, 1904.

GORDON, SIR BENJAMIN LUMSDEN
(1833–   )

Born July 8, 1833 : educated at Edinburgh Academy and Addiscombe : joined the Madras Artillery, 1852 : served in the Horse Artillery in the Indian mutiny : present at the relief of Lucknow, battle of Cawnpur, etc. : Lt-Colonel, 1875 : commanded R.A. in Sir F. Roberts' advance on Kabul : at Charasia and Kabul : C.B. : commanded a Brigade in Madras, 1884–6 : Maj-General in command in Lower Burma : commanded Burma District, 1889–91, when he retired : K.C.B. 1899.

GORDON, CHARLES GEORGE
(1833–1885)

Maj-General, R.E. : son of General H.W. Gordon of the Royal Artillery : born Jan. 18, 1833 : educated at Taunton and the R.M.A., Woolwich : entered the Army in 1852 : served in the Crimea, China, Egypt. His connexion with India was curious and brief : in May, 1880, he, being then a Colonel, went to India as Private Secretary to Lord Ripon, who was going out as Viceroy of India. They arrived in Bombay on June 1 : on the 3rd Gordon resigned his appointment, explaining that the duties were distasteful, that he saw he could not hope to do anything really to the purpose in the face of vested interests, and that his views were diametrically opposed to those of the official classes. Some years later, he recommended the strengthening of the British naval force on the Indian station, and that our main communication with India should be by the Cape route. His services in Africa and elsewhere, and his death at Khartoum, on Jan. 26, 1885, are matters of national history.

GORDON, SIR JAMES DAVIDSON
(1835-1889)

I.C.S. : son of Evelyn Meadows Gordon : born 1835 : educated at Haileybury, 1852-4 : joined the Civil Service in Lower Bengal, 1854 : Private Secretary, Jan. 23, 1866, to Lord Lawrence, when Viceroy and Governor-General : Judicial Commissioner of Mysore, 1873 : Chief Commissioner of Mysore, 1878, Resident, 1881 : retired, 1883 : C.S.I., 1866 : K.C.S.I., 1881 : died June 27, 1889.

GORDON, SIR JOHN BURY, FIFTH BARONET (1779-1835)

Born in India, April 6, 1779 : son of Sir John James Gordon : entered the 22nd Light Dragoons, 1813 : Captain 13th Light Dragoons, 1821 : entered the Nizam's service, 1822 : commanded the force at capture of Fort Mohun : and the Elichpur Horse (5th Nizam's Cavalry), 1822 : the 4th Nizam's Cavalry, 1826 : raised Gordon's Horse (since 30th Lancers): died at Madras, July 23, 1835, when the Baronetcy became extinct.

GORDON, JOHN CHARLES FREDERICK (? -)

Entered the Army, 1869 : became Lt-Colonel, 1899 : served in the Mahsud-Waziri expedition and Egyptian war, 1882 : N.W. Frontier in command of 6th Bengal Cavalry : with the Kuran movable column : Tirah expedition, 1897-8 : C.I.E., 1897.

GORDON, SIR JOHN JAMES HOOD
(1832-)

Born Jan. 12, 1832 : son of Captain William Gordon : entered the Army, 1849, and became General, 1894 : joined the Indian Staff Corps, 1861 : served in the Indian mutiny, 1857-8 : Jowaki-Afridi expedition, 1877-8 : Afghan war, 1878-9 : in command of the 29th Panjab N.I., at Peiwar Kotal, etc. : in the Mahsud-Waziri expedition, 1881 : Burmese expedition, 1886-7 : Assistant Military Secretary at the War Office, 1890-7 : C.B., 1879 : K.C.B., 1898 : Member of the Council of India since 1897.

GORDON, PETER (? - ?)

Merchant, missionary, traveller : his father was domiciled in Calcutta as an owner and commander of the *Wellesley*

merchantman, and Commodore of the expedition to Egypt : Peter was captured by the French in 1809, but escaped : entered, 1810, into the country service in India : served the E.I. Co. occasionally to 1824 : obtained valuable contracts from the E.I. Co. : published, 1816, a book about his adventures : made two voyages from Calcutta to Okhotsk in a schooner of 65 tons, 1817-8 : travelled across Russia to Persia, 1820 : arrested in 1827 by orders of the Assistant Collector of Madura : imprisoned two months : wrote various works about his career, e.g. on his imprisonment and escape, 1816 : on his tour through Persia, 1820 : on India, on the E.I. Co. : *Christian Researches in Southern India*, 1834 : and about China.

GORDON, SIR THOMAS EDWARD
(1832-)

Born Jan. 12, 1832 : son of Captain William Gordon : educated at Edinburgh Military Academy : entered the 4th regt., 1849 : the Indian Staff Corps, 1861 : and became General, 1894 : served in India, N.W. Frontier campaign, 1851 : Indian mutiny, 1857-9 : to Kashgar, as second in command of the Mission, with Sir T. Douglas Forsyth, 1873 : C.S.I., 1874 : in the Afghan war, 1879-80 : D.A.G. Bengal, 1879-83 : Military Attaché in Persia, 1889-93 : K.C.I.E., 1893 : K.C.B., 1900.

GORDON, WILLIAM (1824-)

Born Feb. 10, 1824 : son of Adam Gordon of Cairnfield : educated at Addiscombe : joined the Bengal Army, 1842 : served at siege of Multan as Field Engineer, 1848-9 : at battle of Gujarat, in command of a Company of Pioneers : in the Indian mutiny as Brig-Major and D.A.Q.M.G. : District Inspector of Musketry, 1860-2 : Chief Inspector of Musketry, 1862-8 : Brig-General, 1878 : commanded three Districts : Maj-General, 1882 : retired, 1883 : C.I.E., 1878.

GORDON, WILLIAM EAGLESON
(1866-)

Born May 4, 1866 : son of W. E. Gordon, M.D. : educated at Edinburgh University : joined the Gordon Highlanders, 1888 : served in Chitral Relief expedition, 1895 : Tirah expedition, 1897-8 : adjutant of 1st Battalion Gordon Highlanders throughout the S. African campaign : dangerously wounded at Magersfontein : V.C.

GORE, ST. GEORGE CORBET
(1849–   ).

Colonel : born at Paramatta, N.S.W.' Feb. 24, 1849 : son of Rev. W. F. Gore : educated at Lancing and Woolwich : joined the Royal Engineers, 1870 : served in India, since 1872 : joined the Survey Department : in the Afghan war, 1879–80 : present at Ahmad Kheyl : Afghan Boundary Commission, 1884–6 : Brevet-Major : Surveyor-General of India, 1899–1904 : C.S.I. : retired.

GOREH, REV. NEHEMIAH GOREH
(1825–1895)

His original name was Nilkanta Sastri : born near Jhansi, Feb. 8, 1825 : of a Mahratta Brahman family of hereditary Prime Ministers of the Peshwas : educated at Benares in Sanskrit lore : baptized March 14, 1848, at Jaunpur : accompanied Dulip Singh (q.v.) to England as his Sanskrit tutor : attended theological lectures at the Islington College of the Church Missionary Society : returned to India, 1855 : entered Bishop's College, Calcutta : ordained, 1870 : wrote on religious subjects : wrote also the *Rational Refutation of the Hindu Philosophical Systems* : joined the mission of the Scottish Episcopal Church to Chanda, in the Central Provinces : and the Cowley Fathers at Bombay, Poona and Indore : died Oct. 29, 1895 : helped to revise the Hindi and Mahratti Prayer Book : had influence with the Brahmans, Muhammadans and Parsis, and with Pandita Ramabai.

GORRESIO, COMMENDATORE GASPARO (1808–1891)

Born 1808 : Professor of Sanskrit at Turin : made the first translation, into a European language, of the *Ramayana*, published at Paris, 1843–56 : Librarian of the University of Turin : the "father of Sanskrit philology" of his time : "Senatore di Regno" for his literary merits : appointed member of the French Academy : died May, 1891.

GORST, RIGHT HON. SIR JOHN ELDON (1835–   )

Born 1835 : son of Edward Chaddock Gorst (who took the name of Lowndes

in 1853) : educated at Preston Grammar School and St. John's College, Cambridge : Fellow : 3rd Wrangler, 1857 : called to the bar from the Inner Temple, 1865 : Solicitor General, 1885–6 : Under Secretary of State for India, 1886–91 : Financial Secretary to the Treasury, 1891–2 : Vice-President of the Council of Education, 1895–1902 : M.P. for Cambridge and Chatham between 1866 and 1892 : since then M.P. for Cambridge University : LL.D. : F.R.S. : K.C. : author of *The Maori King*.

GOUGH, SIR CHARLES JOHN STANLEY (1832–   )

Born Jan. 28, 1832 : entered the 5th Bengal European Cavalry, 1848 : General, 1894 : served in the Panjab campaign, 1848–9 : Indian mutiny, 1857–8 : Bhutan war, 1864–5 : Afghan war, 1878–80, in command of a Brigade, through the Khyber, to Kabul : K.C.B. 1881 : commanded Hyderabad Contingent, 1881 : and a Division of the Bengal Army, 1886–90 : author of *The Sikhs and the Sikhs War* : gained the V.C. for gallantry on four occasions in the mutiny : in the first of them, at Kharkowda, near Rohtak, on Aug. 15, 1857, saved his brother, who was wounded : killed two of the enemy : G.C.B., 1895.

GOUGH, HUGH, FIRST VISCOUNT
(1779–1869)

Field-Marshal : born Nov. 3, 1779 : fourth son of George Gough : entered the Militia, 1793, the Army in 1794 : Adjutant of the 119th at fifteen : with the 78th in 1895 at the capture of the Cape : served in the W. Indies until 1803 : in the Peninsula force, 1809, at Talavera, Barossa, Tarifa, Vittoria, Nivelle, twice severely wounded : knighted, 1815 : Maj-General, 1830 : K.C.B., 1831 : commanded the Mysore Division of the Madras Army, 1857 : sent to command at Canton, 1841 : captured the forts, penetrated 170 miles up the Yang-tze-kiang, won several actions, concluded the treaty of Nankin, 1842 : G.C.B. and Baronet : returned to Madras as C. in C. and became C. in C. in India, 1843 : defeated Sindia's troops at Maharajpur, Dec. 28, 1843 : took the command in person in the first Sikh war, 1845–6, and won the battles of Mudki, Dec. 18, 1845 ; Firozshahr, Dec. 21, and Sobraon, Feb. 10, 1846, Lord Hardinge, the Governor-

General, serving under his command: made Baron Gough, of Ching-keangfoo in China, Maharajpur and the Satlaj in the East Indies: commanded again in the second Sikh war, 1848-9, and won the battles of Ramnagar, Nov. 22, 1846; Chilianwala, Jan. 13, 1849. The result of Chilianwala was regarded as being so indecisive that Sir Charles Napier was sent out to supersede Gough, but, before his arrival, Gough had won Gujarat, Feb. 21, 1849, the Sikhs being thoroughly defeated. He retired in May, 1849; was made Viscount Gough of Gujarat and Limerick: received thanks of Parliament and a pension, and freedom of the City of London: General in 1854: sent in 1856 to Sebastopol to invest Pelissier and others with the Order of the Bath: K.P. in 1857: P.C. in 1859: K.C.S.I. in 1861: Field Marshal in 1862: he died March 2, 1869. He is said to have commanded in more general actions than any British officer in the century, the Duke of Wellington excepted. He was very popular with the soldiers.

GOUGH, SIR HUGH HENRY (1833-)

Born Nov. 14, 1833: son of George Gough: educated privately: entered the Bengal Army, 1853: in Hodson's Horse, served throughout the Indian mutiny: at siege of Delhi, relief and capture of Lucknow: V.C. on Nov. 12, 1857, on the advance to the relief of Lucknow: was in Abyssinia: C.B.: Afghan campaign, several times wounded: in command of the Cavalry Brigade on the Kabul-Kandahar march: General: Keeper of Crown Jewels, 1898-1904: Lieutenant-Governor of the Channel Islands, 1904: G.C.B., 1896: author of *Old Memories*, 1897.

GOUGH, HUGH SUTLEJ (1848-)

Born Feb. 4, 1848: son of General Sir J. B. Gough: educated at Royal Naval School, Gosport, and Emmanuel College, Cambridge: served in R.N. 1862-5: entered 10th Hussars, 1868: became Colonel, 1888, and Maj-General, 1900: A.D.C. to C. in C., India, 1876-81: served in Afghan war, 1878-9: Egyptian campaign, 1884: Bechuanaland expedition, 1884-5: commanded 18th Hussars, 1889-93: Assistant A.G. for Cavalry, 1893-8: C.M.G., 1886: C.B., 1899: Lieutenant-Governor of Jersey, 1904.

GOUGH, SIR JOHN BLOOMFIELD (1804-1891)

General: son of Very Rev. Thomas Bunbury Gough, and nephew of Lord Gough: born 1804: entered the Army through the R.M. College, 1820: Captain in the 3rd Light Dragoons: went to India with his uncle: on his Staff through all his battles in China, Gwalior, the Satlaj and Panjab compaigns: commanded the cavalry Brigade at Mudki and Firozshahr: severely wounded at Sobraon: Colonel: A.D.C. to Queen Victoria: C.B.: Q.M.G. of the Queen's Troops in India: Colonel of the Royal Scots Greys, 1864: K.C.B. 1867: G.C.B., 1876: died Sep. 22, 1891.

GOUR, HARI SINGH (1868-)

A Rajput: born Nov. 26, 1868, at Sagar, C.P. educated at the High School there, at the Jabalpur College, at Hislop College, Nagpur: to England, 1889: graduated at Cambridge in Moral Sciences and Law, 1892: called to the bar at the Inner Temple, 1892; returning to India, he first entered the Central Provinces Commission: resigned it for the bar: Secretary of the District Council at Raipur, 1897-1905: wrote on the Law of Transfer: M.A.: LL.D. Dublin: D.C.L: a social reformer and political speaker.

GOVER, CHARLES E. (? -1872)

Son of Thomas Gover: appointed Principal and Secretary of the Madras Military Orphan Male Asylum at Egmore in 1864: member of the Royal Asiatic Society, 1868-72: also of the Society of Arts: and Fellow of the Anthropological Society: wrote on *Indian Weights and Measures*, on Indian folk-lore, and a collection of Essays, *The Folk-songs of Southern India*, 1872: died at Madras, Sept. 20, 1872.

GOWER, SIR ERASMUS (1742-1814)

Son of Abel Gower: entered the Navy in 1755: served on various stations in N. America, Jamaica, etc.: in 1781 commanded the *Medea* frigate in the E. Indies: captured the *Vryheid*, a Dutch ship, at Cuddalore in 1783: and retook the *Chaser* with despatches: present in engagement between Suffrein and Sir E. Hughes (*q.v.*) off Cuddalore: in 1792-4, with Lord Macartney and his embassy to China:

commanded the *Triumph* and the *Neptune* : Admiral in 1809 : died June 21, 1814.

GRAHAM, JOHN (1805–1839)

Botanist : went to India in 1826 : appointed by Sir John Malcolm, then Governor of Bombay, to be Deputy Post-master-General of the Bombay Presidency : also Superintendent of the Bombay Botanic Garden : to which he added many plants, both exotic and indigenous : was printing a catalogue of Bombay plants when he died, May 28, 1839.

GRAHAM, THOMAS (? –)

Entered the Bengal Artillery, 1858 : became Maj-General, 1891 : served in the Hazara expedition : Afghan war, 1878–80 : Brevet-Lt-Colonel : Burma expedition : in Command of the Sikhim expedition, 1888–9 : C.B. : Manipur, 1891.

GRAND, CATHERINE NOEL JUDDE (1762–1835)

Born at Tranquebar, Nov. 21, 1762 : daughter of a Dane, M. Peter John Worlée, Chevalier de Saint Louis, Capitaine du Port, of Chandernagore : married July 10, 1777, George François Grand, of the Indian Civil Service (formerly in the E.I. Co.'s military service), then Secretary to the Salt Committee and Head Assistant and Examiner in the Secretary's office. In Feb. 1779, Grand brought an action against (Sir) Philip Francis, then Member of the Supreme Council, for criminal conversation on Dec. 8, 1778, with the wife of the plaintiff, and after trial before Impey, C.J., and Chambers and Hyde, JJ., obtained, on March 6, 1779, a judgment in his favour, and 50,000 *sicca* rupees as damages: and later a divorce from Mrs. Grand: she lived at Hughli under Francis' protection in 1779, and went to Europe in 1780–1. She resided partly in France, where she also obtained a divorce, and partly in England, and about 1797 came under the notice of Talleyrand, the liaison leading to their marriage on Sep. 10, 1802, which was forced on by the influence of Napoleon to allow the Foreign Ambassadresses to visit her. They lived at Neuilly, but were separated about 1815. After a sojourn in England, she returned to France, and lived at Auteuil : she died Dec. 10, 1835, and was buried at Mont Parnasse.

GRAND, GEORGE FRANCOIS (1748 ?–1821)

Native of Lausanne : educated there : in early life sent to England : obtained, in 1766, a cadetship in Bengal : Lieutenant, 1768 : Captain in 1773 : after furlough in Europe, he was nominated to a writership in 1776 : soon became Secretary to the Salt Committee at Calcutta. On July 10, 1777, he married C. N. J. Worlée (*q.v.*), and, 1779, obtained 50,000 *sicca* rupees damages in an action at Calcutta against (Sir) Philip Francis, for *crim. con.* with his wife : divorced her later : she went to Europe, eventually marrying Talleyrand and figuring as Princesse de Benevento : Grand, in 1782, was Collector of Tirhut and Hajipur, and promoted the indigo manufacture in Bihar to his own advantage. In 1788 he was appointed Judge and Magistrate at Patna, warned to give up his indigo concerns, and finally removed from the service. He returned to Europe, and in France, by the influence of his former wife with Talleyrand, obtained the post of Privy Councillor of the Government of the Cape of Good Hope, from the Batavian Republic in 1802 : later, became Inspector of H.M.'s woods and lands there under the British : married again, and died at the Cape in 1821.

GRANT, SIR ALEXANDER, BARONET (1826–1884)

Son of Sir Robert Innes Grant, seventh Baronet : born Sep. 13, 1826 : educated at Harrow and Balliol College, Oxford : Scholar : played twice in the Harrow Cricket Eleven against Eton and Winchester : Fellow of Oriel, 1849 : became private tutor : succeeded as Baronet in 1856 : published the *Ethics of Aristotle* in 1857 : went to Madras in 1859, as Inspector of Schools : became Professor of History, at the Elphinstone Institution, Madras, in 1860, and Principal in 1862 : in 1863 he became Vice-Chancellor of the Bombay University, till 1868 : in 1865, Director of Public Instruction in the Bombay Presidency : Member of the Legislative Council, Bombay, in 1868 : made his mark on education in India : became Principal of the Edinburgh University in 1868 : D.C.L. and LL.D. of Cambridge, Edinburgh and Glasgow : F.R.S. of Edinburgh : wrote on Aristotle and Xenophon and

The Story of the University of Edinburgh : on female education, endowed schools, and articles in Reviews, etc. : died suddenly Nov. 30, 1884.

GRANT, CHARLES (1746-1823)

Born April 16, 1746, the date of the battle of Culloden, at which his father, Alexander, was severely wounded : educated at Elgin : apprenticed at Cromarty, 1758, and a clerk in London, 1763-67 : went to India in 1767 : attended to the private trade of Richard Becher, the Resident at Murshidabad : worked hard in the terrible Bengal famine of 1770 : suffered from fever : returned to Scotland, 1771-2 : and went out again as a " writer " to Bengal, in 1772-3 : became a " factor," and then Secretary to the Board of Trade at Calcutta : in 1781 commercial resident at Malda, in charge of the silk filature : the post was very lucrative : Grant had his accounts examined by Cornwallis, who expressed a wish that all the Company's servants were equally scrupulous : in 1787 he was made Fourth Member of the Board of Trade, with the superintendence of all the Company's trade in Bengal. He supported mission work in Bengal. When the mission church (J. Z. Kiernander's) in Calcutta was attached by the Sheriff, Grant paid down 10,000 rupees to save it, and assigned it to the Church Missionary Society. He retired in 1790. He wrote, in 1792, his *Observations on the State of Society among the Asiatic Subjects of Great Britain*, advocating the cause of missions and education : it was printed for Parliament in 1813 : he wrote the despatch from England on the Permanent Settlement of 1793 : he became M.P. for Inverness in 1802, and for the county from 1804-18 : he was Chairman of the Court of Directors in 1805, 1809, and 1815, and in Parliament took a leading part in all discussions on the E.I. Co.'s affairs, such as the renewal of the Charter in 1813, the China trade, missions, the Press, etc. : he opposed the Marquess Wellesley's warlike policy, and supported in 1808 the motion for his impeachment. In the new Charter he obtained an annual grant for education in India, the appointment of Bishops in India, and greater freedom for missionary work. He promoted the establishment of the E.I. Co.'s College at Hertford Castle in 1806, moved to Haileybury in 1809. He was a prominent member of the Clapham sect and of the religious Societies, and had much influence in the selection of missionary chaplains for India. He was Chairman of the Commissioners for the issue of Exchequer Bills, and served on the Commission for the building of churches. He retired from Parliament in 1818, and died on Oct. 31, 1823 : the E.I. Co. placed a memorial of him in St. George's Church, Bloomsbury. No one, at the time of Charles Grant, laboured harder to raise the moral condition of India, its inhabitants and officials, or had greater influence in the settlement of Indian affairs than he had, as Director of the E.I. Co. and as M.P. : he had remarkable moral courage, a masterful hand, a determined will, and a hot temper under control.

GRANT, SIR CHARLES (1836-1903)

Son of Sir Robert Grant (*q.v.*) : born in 1836 : educated at Harrow, Trinity College, Cambridge, Haileybury : went to India, 1858 : served in the N.W.P. and Central Provinces : Secretary to the Chief Commissioner, 1861 : Commissioner, 1870 : compiled the *Central Provinces Gazetteer* : acted as Judicial Commissioner and as Chief Commissioner in 1879 : Member of the Governor-General's Legislative Council, 1879-80 : Acting Home Secretary, 1880 : Foreign Secretary to the Government of India, 1881-85 : when he retired : K.C.S.I., 1885 : died April 12, 1903.

GRANT, CHARLES JAMES WILLIAM (? -)

Son of Lt-General D. G. S. Grant : educated privately and at Sandhurst : joined the Army, 1882, and the Madras Staff Corps, 1884 : A.D.C. to Lt-General Dormer, C. in C. in Madras, 1891 : Officiating A.A.G., Madras District, 1897 : served in the Burma expedition, 1886-7 : in Manipur, where he proceeded to assistance of Chief Commissioner's defeated escort : stormed and held Thobal, till relieved, March 31-April 9, 1891 : severely wounded : Captain and Brevet-Major and V.C. : second in command 32nd Burma Infantry Frontier Force.

GRANT, HUGH GOUGH (1845-)

Born July 23, 1845 : son of Field Marshal Sir Patrick Grant : educated at

Eton and Sandhurst: served with the Seaforth Highlanders, 1863–95 : in the Madras famine, 1877–8 :   Brig-Major during Afghan war, 1879–80, and in Mahsud-Waziri expedition, 1881 : served in Black Mountain expedition, 1891 : A.A.G., Panjab command, 1895–7 : commanded Regimental Districts in Scotland : retired : C.B., 1900.

GRANT, JAMES (? – ?)

In the service of the E.I. Co. : was stationed in Bengal, 1784–9 : selected by the Government to superintend the native management of the revenues : found himself obliged to expose the abuses connected with the whole system of native agency : appointed Chief Sarishtadar, or general superintendent of native revenue accounts under the Board of Revenue, 1786 : his tract,—*An Inquiry into the Nature of Zemindary Tenures in the Landed Property of Bengal*, 1791—gives the best account of the native revenue system.

GRANT, JAMES AUGUSTUS (1827–1892)

The African traveller : born April 11, 1827 : son of James Grant : educated at Nairn and Aberdeen schools and at the Marischal College, Aberdeen : joined the 8th Bengal N.I. in 1846 : was present at Multan and Gujarat : Adjutant : was with the 78th Highlanders at the relief of Lucknow : accompanied J. H. Speke on his African expedition, 1861–4, including the discovery of the source of the Nile : received the Gold Medal of the Geographical Society, 1864 : C.B., 1866 : in the Intelligence Department in the Abyssinian expedition : C.S.I. : retired as Lt-Colonel, 1868 : died Feb. 11, 1892 : wrote *A Walk across Africa*, 1864 : and in scientific Journals about his travels.

GRANT, SIR JAMES HOPE (1808–1875)

Son of Francis Grant : born July 22, 1808 : educated at Edinburgh and Hofwyl, Switzerland : remained in the 9th Lancers from Colonel in 1826 to Maj-General in 1858 : Brig-Major to Lord Saltoun in the first Chinese war, 1840–2 : C.B. : in the first Sikh war, 1845–6, including Sobraon : in the Panjab campaign of 1848–9, at Ramnagar, Chilianwala and Gujarat :   Brevet-Lt-Colonel : was at Umbala when the mutiny broke out :

Brigadier of the cavalry : at Badli-ka-sarai : at the siege of Delhi : the relief of Lucknow : Cawnpur : commanded movable columns and the trans-Gogra force : K.C.B., 1858 : commanded in the second Chinese war, 1860–1 : captured the Taku forts and Pekin : G.C.B. : C. in C. at Madras, Dec. 1861–May, 1865 : Q.M.G. of the Army, 1865–70 : in command at Aldershot, 1870, where he initiated the autumn manœuvres, and introduced many improvements : he was strong in his religious views : died March 7, 1875.

GRANT, JAMES WILLIAM (1788–1865)

Born Aug. 12, 1788 : son of Robert Grant : was in the E.I. Co.'s Civil Service, 1805–49 : devoted himself to astronomy, the microscope and other scientific pursuits : he made a granite observatory on the Elchies estates, and there had the " Trophy Telescope " : he was F.R.A.S., 1864 : died Sep. 17, 1865.

GRANT, SIR JOHN PETER (1774–1848)

Son of William Grant, M.D. of London and Rothiemurchus : born Sep. 21, 1774 : succeeded his uncle in the Rothiemurchus estate in 1790 : educated at Cambridge : read law at Edinburgh : called to the bar from Lincoln's Inn, 1802 : M.P. for Great Grimsby and Tavistock : went to Bombay in 1827 as a Puisne Judge of the Supreme Court there : knighted : when the Bombay Government interfered to prevent the execution of decrees of the Court, a rupture took place, and Grant closed the Court in April, 1829 : Lord Ellenborough, at the Board of Control, appointed a new Chief Justice, Sir J. Dewar, and a new Judge, writing that Grant " will be like a wild elephant led between two tame ones." Grant resigned his appointment, left Bombay in Sep. 1830, and went over to Calcutta : practised there at the bar, and became a Puisne Judge, 1833–48, of the Calcutta Supreme Court. He died May 17, 1848, on his voyage homewards : he wrote on legal subjects.

GRANT, SIR JOHN PETER (1807–1893)

I.C.S. : son of Sir John Peter Grant (*q.v.*) : born Nov. 23, 1807 : educated at Eton, Edinburgh University, Haileybury : went to India in 1828 : served for four years in the N.W.P. : Secretary in 1832 to the Board of Revenue, Calcutta :

served in the Government of India Secretariat : was Superintendent of the Botanic Garden : Secretary to Lord Macaulay's Indian Law Commission, Private Secretary to the Governor-General : Commissioner for payment of the Maharaja of Mysore's debts : inquired into the proceedings for the suppression of *meriah*, or human sacrifices, in Ganjam : from 1848 to 1852 he was Secretary to the Government of Bengal under the Governor-General and, in his absence, under the Deputy Governor : was Secretary to the Government of India in the Home and Foreign Departments, 1852-4 : Member of the Governor-General's Supreme Council, 1854-9 : and, for a portion of that time, Lieutenant-Governor of the "Central" Provinces during the mutiny : Lieutenant-Governor of Bengal, 1859-62. As Member of Council he advocated annexation of Oudh, which was carried, instead of Lord Dalhousie's less thorough scheme : he passed an Act to legalize the marriage of Hindu widows. As Lieutenant-Governor, he had to deal with the indigo disturbances—incurring unpopularity with the planters in his determination to do justice to the cultivators—and with troubles from tribes on the frontier. In both these capacities he showed great ability, in writing, in speech, and in action : greatly trusted by Lords Dalhousie and Canning : K.C.B. in 1862. After the rebellion in Jamaica, in 1865, he was Governor of that island, 1866-73 : the whole administration was reformed by him, the finances re-organized, and sound political and fiscal principles applied by the light of his previous experience : died Jan. 6, 1893.

GRANT, MALCOLM (1762-1831)

Joined the E.I. Co.'s Bombay Army in 1777 : served against the Mahrattas, 1779, and with Goddard's (*q.v.*) force at Bassein, in 1780-1 : in Malabar, until 1788, and again from 1792 to 1798 : commanded against the Mahrattas, was in the capture of Mysore, under General James Stuart at Mangalore, in Canara, and Jamalghar : in the chief command in Malabar and Canara, 1804 : captured Savandrug : returned to England, 1807 : Maj-General, 1813 : Lt-General, 1815 : died Sep. 28, 1831.

GRANT, SIR PATRICK (1804-1895)

Field Marshal : son of Major John Grant, 97th foot : born Sep. 11, 1804 : Ensign, 1820 : joined the 11th Bengal N.I. in Jan. 1821 : rose to be General, 1870 : Field Marshal, June, 1883 : Goldstick in Waiting to Queen Victoria, 1885 : raised the Hariana Light Infantry, 1836 : organized the N.W. Frontier Force in 1841 : Deputy-Adjutant-General, 1843 : in the Gwalior campaign at Maharajpur : in the first Sikh war was at Mudki, acting there as Adjutant-General ; at Firozshahr, and Sobraon : C.B.: Adjutant-General of the Bengal Army, 1846 : at Chilianwala and Gujarat : Brevet-Colonel and A.D.C. to Queen Victoria : served against the N.W. frontier tribes : C. in C. of the Madras Army, 1856 : K.C.B. : C. in C. in India, temporarily, in the mutiny, between General Anson (*q.v.*) and Lord Clyde (*q.v.*) : retired in 1861 : G.C.B. : C. in C. at Malta, 1867-72 : G.C.M.G., 1868 : Governor of the Chelsea Hospital, 1874-95 : died March 28, 1895.

GRANT, SIR ROBERT (1779-1838)

Governor : second son of Charles Grant (*q.v.*) : born in Bengal in 1779 : went to England, 1790 : educated at Magdalen College, Cambridge, Craven Scholar, 1799 : third wrangler, Chancellor's Medallist and Fellow : called to the bar at Lincoln's Inn, 1807 : M.P. for various constituencies from 1818 to 1834 : advocated Jewish emancipation from civil disabilities : Judge Advocate General, 1832 : Governor of Bombay from March 17, 1835 : knighted in 1834 : and G.C.H. : died of apoplexy at Dapuri, July 9, 1838 : wrote *Sketch of the History of the E.I. Co., from its First Foundation to 1773* : a *View* of the *System and Merits of the East India College, Haileybury*, and a volume of sacred poems, which was edited by his brother, Lord Glenelg. The Grant Medical College at Bombay was erected as a memorial to him.

GRANT, SIR WILLIAM KEIR (1772-1852)

Son of Archibald Keir, I.C.S. : born in 1772 : joined the 15th King's Light Dragoons, 1792 : served in Flanders, 1794 : saved the German Emperor, Francis II, at Villiers-en-Couche : served in Germany : and in Italy with the Russian and Austrian armies, in several

N

battles: Adjutant-General of the King's troops in Bengal, 1806: commanded the advance on the Satlaj, 1810: against Amir Khan, the Pathan freebooter, in 1814: C. in C. in Java, 1815: commanded part of the Army of the Dekkan against the Pindaris, 1817: also against Sawantwari and Cutch, 1819: defeated the piratical Arabs in the Persian Gulf in 1819-20, and arranged for the complete suppression of piracy: assumed the name of Keir Grant, instead of Grant Keir: K.C.B., 1822: Lt-General, 1825: G.C.H., 1835: General, 1841: died May 7, 1852.

GRANT-DUFF, JAMES CUNNINGHAM
(1789-1858)

Son of John Grant and Margaret Duff: born July 8, 1789: educated at Marischal College, Aberdeen: joined the E.I. Co.'s military service at Bombay in 1805: was at the storming of Maliah, 1808: became Adjutant and Interpreter of his regiment: was Assistant to Mountstuart Elphinstone, then Resident of Poona, who had a high opinion of him: as Captain, he served against the Peshwa, Baji Rao, when the latter was dethroned in 1818, and was then made Resident of Satara, administering the State in the Raja's name till 1822, and making treaties with the Satara *jagirdars*. After five years he retired to Scotland and brought out the *History of the Mahrattas* in 1826. He took the additional names of Duff and Cunningham on succeeding to landed estates: died Sep. 23, 1858. Sir M. E. Grant-Duff (*q.v.*), formerly Governor of Madras, is his son.

GRANT-DUFF, SIR MOUNTSTUART ELPHINSTONE (1829-   )

Born Feb. 21, 1829: son of James Cunningham Grant-Duff (*q.v.*): educated at Edinburgh University, The Grange, Bishop Wearmouth, and Balliol College, Oxford: barrister of the Inner Temple: M.P. for the Elgin Burghs, 1857-81: Under Secretary of State for India, 1868-74: and for the Colonies, 1880-1: Privy Councillor, 1880: Governor of Madras, 1881-6: advanced education and science: constructed the Marina at Madras: President of the Royal Geographical Society, 1889-93: President of the Royal Historical Society, 1892-9: Author of *Studies in European Politics*, *Elgin Speeches*,

Notes of an Indian Journey, *Memoir of Sir H. S. Maine*, *Notes from a Diary*, etc., etc.: C.I.E., 1881: G.C.S.I., 1886: F.R.S.: D.L.

GRAVES, BENJAMIN CHAMNEY
(1845-   )

Born Feb. 2, 1845: son of Henry Graves: educated at Kingstown school and Woolwich: joined R.A., 1866, and Indian Staff Corps, 1871: Brevet-Colonel, 1897: served in Afghan war, 1879-80: commanded Garhwal Rifles, 1893-8: served with Malakand Field Force, 1897, and in the N.W. Frontier campaign, 1897-8: C.B.

GREATHED, SIR EDWARD HARRIS
(1812-1881)

Son of Edward Greathed: born 1812: educated at Westminster: entered the Army, 1832: in the mutiny was with the 8th regt. at the siege of Delhi and led the regt. to the assault: after its fall, was placed in command of the column to open up the country between the Jamna and the Ganges: in the fighting at Bulandshahr, Alighar and Agra: commanded a Brigade at Sir Colin Campbell's relief of Lucknow: at the engagement before Cawnpore on Dec. 6, 1857: at Khudaganj and the occupation of Fatehghar: Colonel and C.B.: D.C.L., 1859: K.C.B., 1865: commanded E. district in England, 1872-7: Brevet-General, 1880: died Nov. 19, 1881.

GREATHED, WILLIAM WILBERFORCE HARRIS (1826-1878)

Son of Edward Greathed: born Dec. 21, 1826: educated at Addiscombe: joined the Bengal Sappers and Miners at Meerut in 1846: was in the siege and capture, Jan. 2, 1849, of Multan: present at Gujarat: Consulting Engineer for Railways at Allahabad, 1855-7: in the mutiny, he twice conveyed despatches from Agra to Meerut through the mutineers: was at the siege of Delhi, directing the left attack: severely wounded: was at several engagements as Engineer of the Doab Field Force: directed as Engineer at the attack on Lucknow and its capture: C.B.: and Brevet-Major: was A.D.C. to Sir R. Napier in China: at the capture of Pekin: Brevet-Lt-Colonel: Assistant Military Secretary to the Horse Guards, 1861-5: Head of the Irrigation Department,

N.W.P., 1867-75 : made the Agra and Lower Ganges canals : retired from India, 1876 : died Dec. 29, 1878 : Maj-General.

GREAVES, SIR GEORGE RICHARDS
(1831-   )

Born Nov. 9, 1831 : son of Capt. George Greaves, 60th Rifles : educated at Sandhurst : joined the 70th regt. : served in the Indian mutiny : New Zealand war, 1860-6 : Ashanti campaign, 1874 : Soudan, 1885 : Chief Secretary and Commissioner, Cyprus, 1878 : Adjutant-General in India, 1879 : commanded a Division in India, 1886 : C. in C., Bombay, 1890 : resigned, 1893 : became General, 1896, and retired : K.C.M.G., 1881 : K.C.B., 1885 : G.C.B.

GREEN, SIR EDWARD (1810-1891)

Son of James Green : educated at Addiscombe : entered the Indian Army, 1827 : in the Afghan war, 1841-2 : saw active service at Hyderabad, Sind, with the 22nd regt., in defence of the Residency and at the battle of Hyderabad : also as A.A.G. against the Cutchi Hill Tribes, 1844-5 : at the capture of Multan, at Gujarat, and pursuit and surrender of the Sikhs : Adjutant-General, Bombay, 1856-60 : commanded a Division, 1862-5 : died May 9, 1891 : General : K.C.B.

GREEN, SIR GEORGE W. G.
(1825-1891)

General : son of the Rev. G. W. G. Green : educated at Bridgnorth : entered the Indian Army in 1841 : served in Sind and in the Panjab campaign of 1848-9 : at Gujarat : commanded the 2nd Panjab N.I., through the mutiny : at the siege of Delhi : at Sir Colin Campbell's relief of Lucknow, Nov. 1857 : C.B., 1858 : Lt-General, 1877 : died Nov. 27, 1891 : K.C.B., 1877.

GREEN, SIR WILLIAM HENRY RHODES (1823-   )

Born May 31, 1823 : son of Vice-Admiral Sir Andrew P. Green, K.C.B. : educated at King's College, and Brussels : entered the Indian Army, 1841, and joined the Sind Irregular Horse, 1846 : served throughout the mutiny, 1848-9 : present at siege of Multan and battle of Gujarat : employed on special duty during the Crimean war, as

Colonel in the Turkish Army : present at Balaclava and Inkerman and siege of Sebastopol : severely wounded : Adjt-General of Turkish Bashi-Bazouks in Asia Minor and Bulgaria : A.A.G., Persian war, 1856-7 : Indian mutiny, 1857-8 : Political Agent in Beluchistan, 1859 : Officiating Chief Commissioner of Sind : Political Superintendent of N.W. Frontier of Sind, 1866-8 : retired, 1874 : K.C.S.I., 1866 : C.B. : author of *Papers on Defence of N.W. Frontier of India.*

GREER, RICHARD TOWNSEND
(1854-   )

I.C.S. : born Oct. 14, 1854 : son of Rev. George Samuel Greer, Rector of Bullhalbert, co. Down, Ireland : educated at Kingstown school, co. Dublin : Member of the Irish International Football Team : went to Bengal, 1877 : employed in Assam : Deputy Commissioner of Sibsagar, and Sylhet : Assistant Secretary to the Chief Commissioner, 1884 : Magte-Collector of Tippera : Deputy Commissioner, Darjeeling, 1893-9 : Inspr-General of Police, Bengal, 1899-1900 : Chairman of the Calcutta Corporation since 1900 : C.S.I., 1904.

GREY, SIR CHARLES EDWARD
(1785-1865)

Son of R. W. Grey : born 1785 : educated at University College, Oxford : Fellow of Oriel College : called to the bar, 1811 : Commissioner in Bankruptcy, 1817 : Judge of the Supreme Court, Madras, 1820 : knighted : Chief Justice, Bengal, 1825-32 : Commissioner to Canada, 1835-6 : G.C.H. : M.P. for Tynemouth, 1838-41 : Governor of Barbados, 1841-6 : Governor of Jamaica, 1847-53 : died June 1, 1865.

GREY, SIR JOHN (1780 ?-1856)

Son of Charles Grey, and great-nephew of the first Earl Grey : joined the 75th foot in 1798 : served in the war against Tippoo : at Malavilli and Seringapatam : was in the Peninsula, at Ciudad Rodrigo : commanded a Division in Bengal, 1840-5 : commanded against 12,000 Mahrattas at Punniar and defeated them, Dec. 29, 1843 : K.C.B. : commanded a Division in the Satlaj campaign, 1845-6 : C. in C. and Member of Council, Bombay, 1850-2 : Lt-General, 1851 : died Feb. 19, 1856.

GREY, LEOPOLD JOHN HERBERT
(1840-)

Born July 1, 1840 : son of L. J. H. Grey : educated at Cheltenham : joined the Bengal Army, 1857 : served with Panjab Frontier Force on the N.W. Frontier, 1857–62 : Bhutan campaign, 1865–6, as Political Officer : Commissioner of Hissar Division, 1882 : retired, 1894 : re-employed as Superintendent of the Bahawalpur State, 1899–1902 : C.S.I., 1877.

GREY, SIR WILLIAM (1818–1878)

Born 1818 : son of Edward Grey, Bishop of Hereford, and grandson of first Earl Grey : was at Christ Church, Oxford, but left it to enter the War Office : educated at Haileybury : went to India in 1840 : Private Secretary to Sir Herbert Maddock, Deputy Governor of Bengal, 1845–7 : served in the Bengal Secretariat, and in the Secretariat of the Government of India, in the Home and Foreign Departments : Secretary to the Bank of Bengal, 1851–4 : Secretary to the Government of Bengal,1854–7: Director General of the Post Office : Secretary to the Home Department, 1859 : Member of the Governor-General's Supreme Council, from April, 1862, to April, 1867 : had considerable difference of opinion with Sir John Lawrence, the Governor-General. When discussions arose after the Orissa famine, he opposed the proposed abolition of the Bengal Legislative Council, and, instead of any reduction in the status of the Bengal Government, advocated its assimilation to the Governments of Madras and Bombay. He held strong opinions about taxation, and his views did not agree with those of Lord Mayo : K.C.S.I. in 1871 : retired on March 1, 1871 : Governor of Jamaica, 1874–7 : died May 15, 1878.

GRIERSON, GEORGE ABRAHAM
(1851-)

I.C.S. : born Jan. 7, 1851 : son of George Abraham Grierson, LL.D., Queen's Printer for Ireland : educated at St. Bee's School, Shrewsbury ; Trinity College, Dublin (Exhibitioner): went out to Bengal, 1873 : Inspector of Schools, Bihar, 1880 : Additional Commissioner of Patna, and Opium Agent, Bihar, 1896 : in charge of the Linguistic Survey with the Government of India, 1898–1902 : retired, 1902 :

C.I.E., 1894 : Ph.D. (Halle) 1894 : D. Litt. of Trin. Coll., Dublin, 1902 : Member of the Asiatic Society of Bengal and of the Royal Asiatic Society, the Folklore, and other Societies. His principal writings are *Introduction to the Maithili Language, A Handbook to the Kaithi Character, Seven Grammars of the Bihari Dialects, Bihar Peasant Life, The Modern Vernacular Literature of Hindustan, Notes on Tulsi Das, The Satsaiya of Bihari, Essays on Kashmiri Grammar, The Linguistic Survey of India, The Languages of India :* the Chapters on Vernacular Languages and Vernacular Literatures in the forthcoming edition of the *Imperial Gazetteer.*

GRIESBACH, CHARLES LUDOLF
(1847-)

Born Dec. 11, 1847 : son of G. L. Griesbach of Zobelsberg : educated at Vienna University : Member of ten Scientific Societies : joined the Royal Fusiliers, 1874 : and Geological Survey of India, 1878 : on special service during the Afghan war : present at Maiwand, July 27, 1880 : siege and battle of Kandahar, 1880 : Afghan Boundary Commission, 1884–6 : C.I.E. : on special duty with H.H. the Amir, in Afghanistan, 1888–9 : Miranzai expedition, 1890–1 : Burma, 1892 : S. Africa, 1896–7 : Director of the Geological Survey of India : retired.

GRIFFIES-WILLIAMS, SIR W. L., BARONET (1800–1877)

Son of Sir George Griffies-Williams, *Bart.* : born in 1800 : entered the Indian Army, 1819 : served in the first Burmese war, 1824–6 : at the siege and storming of Punnullah and capture of Munnohur, 1844–5 : in the second Burmese war, 1852 : became Baronet in 1870 : died May 23, 1877.

GRIFFIN, SIR LEPEL HENRY
(1840-)

I.C.S. : born 1840 : joined the Civil Service in the Panjab, 1860 : Chief Secretary to the Panjab Government, 1870 : Chief Political Officer in Afghanistan,1880 : negotiated with Abdur Rahman (*q.v.*), who became Amir of Afghanistan : Resident at Indore : Agent to the Governor-General for Central India, 1881–8 : retired, 1889 : Chairman of East India Association : author of *The Panjab Chiefs,* 1865 ; *The Law of Inheritance in Chiefships,*

1869; *The Rajas of the Panjab*, 1870; *The Great Republic*, 1884; *Famous Monuments of Central India*, 1888; *Ranjit Singh*, 1894 : founded the *Asiatic Quarterly Review* in conjunction with D. Boulger : K.C.S.I., 1881.

GRIFFITH, RALPH THOMAS HOTCHKIN (1826–   )

Born May 25, 1826 : son of Rev. R. C. Griffith : educated at Warminster, Uppingham and Queen's College, Oxford : University Boden Sanskrit Scholar : Assistant Master, Marlborough, 1849–53 : Professor of English Literature, Benares College, 1854–62 : Principal of Benares College, 1863–78 : Director of Public Instruction, N.W.P., and Oudh, 1878–85 : retired, 1885 : author of *Specimens of Old Indian Poetry*, 1852 ; *The Birth of the War-God*, 1853 ; *Idylls from the Sanskrit*, 1866 ; *Scenes from the Ramayan*, 1868 ; *The Ramayan of Valmiki*, 1870–5 ; *The Hymns of the Rig-veda*, 1889–92 ; *The Hymns of the Atharva-veda*, 1895–6 ; *The Texts of the White Yajur-veda*, 1899 : founder and editor of the *Pandit*, a Sanskrit journal, for eight years : C.I.E., 1885.

GRIFFITH, WILLIAM (1810–1845)

Son of Thomas Griffith : born March 4, 1810 : studied medicine : educated at the University of London : went to Madras in 1832, in the E.I. Co.'s medical service : botanical member of an expedition to Assam, 1835, in connexion with the search for, and discovery of, the tea plant : explored between Sadiya and Ava : and from Assam to Ava and Rangoon : attached in 1837 to Pemberton's embassy to Bhutan : in 1839, accompanied the Army of the Indus to Kabul, and went beyond the Hindu Kush to Khorasan : on medical duties to Malacca in 1841–2 : made enormous and valuable collections of dried plants on his journeys : they were distributed from Kew after his death : he also made researches in Natural History and valuable collections : acting Superintendent of the Botanic Garden, near Calcutta, and Professor of Botany at the Medical College, Calcutta : again to Malacca in 1844, and died there, Feb. 9, 1845 : his valuable notes and collected papers were published in nine volumes after his death, at the expense

of the E.I. Co. : the editorial work is said to have been badly done : he had the greatest reputation for his " achievements as ' one of the most brilliant of Indian botanists ' " : he published papers in scientific Journals.

GROSE, JOHN HENRY (before 1750—after 1783)

A writer in the E.I. Co's service, son of Francis Grose : went out to Bombay in 1750: in 1757 he published *A Voyage to the East Indies*, of which there were subsequent editions and a French translation. He was a Member of the Society of Arts.

GROTE, ARTHUR (1814–1886)

I.C.S. : son of George Grote, and brother of the historian, George Grote : born Nov. 29, 1814 : educated at Haileybury : went to Bengal in 1833 : rose to be Commissioner and Member of the Board of Revenue, Calcutta, 1861–8 : was President of the Asiatic Society of Bengal, 1859–62 and in 1865 : left India, 1868 : a prominent member and a Vice-President of the Royal Asiatic Society : wrote papers on Botany and Natural History : F.L.S. and F.Z.S : died Dec. 4, 1886.

GROVES, ANTHONY NORRIS (1795–1853)

Born 1795 : educated at Lymington and Fulham : learnt chemistry, dentistry and surgery : resided at Plymouth and became a founder of the sect of Plymouth brethren : devoted himself to missionary work from 1829 : went overland to Bagdad and taught Christianity there : from Bagdad to Bombay in 1833 : stayed in India till 1852, visiting England twice during that time. In India he visited the missionary stations, chiefly on the west coast and in the Madras Presidency : practised dentistry for a year in Madras : laboured steadily for years in his work of evangelization : his preaching was very successful : died at Bristol, May 20, 1853. He wrote journals of his journey to Bagdad and of his residence there.

GROWSE, FREDERIC SALMON (1837–1893)

I.C.S. : son of Robert Growse : born 1837 : educated at Oriel College, and Queen's College, Oxford (Scholar) : went to India to the N.W.P. in 1860 : served in Mathura and Bulandshahr: built a Catholic Church at Mathura: wrote *Mathura, a District Memoir,* 1880 : and an English translation of the *Ramayana* of Tulsi Das, 1883 (said to occupy the place almost of a Bible among the people of the N.W. Provinces) : also *Bulandshahr,* 1884 : he ardently defended the purity of the vernacular Hindi, as opposed to the official Hindustani : Member of the Asiatic Society of Bengal : a learned Oriental scholar and archæologist : C.I.E., 1879 : retired 1890 : died May 19, 1893.

GRÜNWEDEL, ALBERT (1856–   )

Born at Munich, July 31, 1856 : son of Karl Grünwedel, an artist : educated at the Max-Gymnasium at Munich, and later (1876–82) studied Archæology, classical Philology, Sanskrit, Pali, Tibetan, at the Munich University : Dr. : chiefly known as a Tibetan scholar, and leading authority in the history of Indian (especially Buddhist) art : has been, since 1882, Assistant Director of the Royal Museums at Berlin, and is Director of the Asiatic Section of the Berlin Ethnographical Museum (1904) : Corresponding Member of the Royal Bavarian Academy of Sciences at Munich (1900), and of the Oriental Division of the Archæological Society at St. Petersburg (1901) : his chief works are : *Buddhistische Kunst in Indien,* 1893, etc., translated into English in 1901 : his *Lepcha-English Dictionary,* compiled from General Mainwaring's MSS., 1898 : *Mythologie des Buddhismus in Tibet und der Mongolei,* 1900. His *Report* on his archæological labours in Idikutsari (Turfan), 1905, is the result of his travels (1902–3) in Chinese Turkistan (Turfan) in the company of Dr. Huth.

GUBBINS, MARTIN RICHARD
(1812–1863)

I.C.S. : educated at Haileybury, 1829–30 : went out to India in 1830 : served in the N.W.P. and in Oudh on its annexation in 1856, when he was made its Financial Commissioner. In the mutiny, he took a leading part in the operations at Lucknow : had charge of the Intelligence Department : advocated various measures, some of which were adopted, and some, such as the disarmament of the native troops, were not accepted by Sir H. Lawrence : served throughout the siege of Lucknow : " retrenched and completed

the post which bore his name, and was eminent among those who fought hard and laboured unceasingly." After the relief, he was with Sir Colin Campbell at Cawnpur: ill-health then compelled him to go to England. He was Judge of the Agra Chief Court, 1858–63 : died May 6, 1863 : wrote *The Mutinies in Oudh.*

GUBERNATIS, COUNT ANGELO DE
(1840–   )

Born April 7, 1840, at Turin : descended from ancient family of Provence : studied first at Turin : in 1862, sent by the Italian Government to continue his philological studies in Berlin under Weber and Bopp : appointed, 1863, Professor of Sanskrit and Comparative Literature at the Institut des Études Superieures in Florence : in 1881, King Humbert confirmed to him the title of Count, borne formerly by his ancestors : visited India in 1885 and 1886, and on his return founded an Indian Museum, and an Italian Asiatic Society at Florence : appointed, 1890, to his present position, Professor of Sanskrit and Italian Literature at the University of Rome : has travelled much, and is a prolific and many-sided writer, poet, dramatist, author of many works on Italian literature, and a Sanskritist : has written on the mythology of the Vedas : *Le fonti vediche dell' epopea,* 1867, etc. : other works are :—*Piccola enciclopedia Indiana,* 1867 ; *Letteratura Indiana,* 1883 : *Storia dei viaggiatori italiani nelle Indie,* 1875 ; *Il Dio Indra nel Rigveda* : *Primi Venti Inni del Rigveda* (translated with notes) : *Drammi indiani,* in verse : *Zoological Mythology,* etc. : elected an honorary member of the Royal Asiatic Society, and of its branch in Bombay, besides belonging to other learned Societies : delegate of the Italian Government at International Congresses of Orientalists.

GUISE, JOHN CHRISTOPHER
(1826–1895)

Lt- General : son of Sir J. Guise, *Bart.* : born 1826 : entered the Army, 1845 : served in the Crimea with the 90th Light Infantry : in the mutiny at siege and capture of Lucknow : led the attack on the Sikandrabagh : V.C. for gallantry in action on Nov. 16 and 17, 1857, at Lucknow : C.B. : died Feb. 5, 1895.

GUNDERT, REV. HERMAN (1814-1893)

Born at Stuttgart, 1814 : worked in the Basel Evangelical Mission in Malabar and Canara, 1839-63 : at Tellicherry : Inspector of Government Schools in Malabar and Canara, 1860 : a learned scholar : wrote Malayalam grammar and other books, including a dictionary and Bible translations : retired, 1865 : Editorial Secretary and Principal of the Calver Verlagsverein : died 1893.

GUY, SIR PHILIP M. N. (1804-1878)

Son of Melmoth Guy : educated privately and at the Military College,Brussels : entered the Army, 1824 : was in the 5th regt. for 37 years, commanding it for 10 : in the mutiny, commanded the Dinapur district in 1857 : in several engagements : commanded an Infantry Brigade under Sir Hope Grant : and at the Alambagh during and after the second relief of Lucknow, and at its capture : C.B. : held commands at Colchester, China and Jersey : K.C.B., 1873 : General, 1877 : died March 10, 1878.

GWALIOR, DAULAT RAO SINDIA, MAHARAJA OF (1780-1827)

Succeeded his great uncle and adoptive father Madhava (Madhoji) Sindia (q.v.), in 1794: he organized a formidable army under French officers, plundered Poona,seized Ahmadnagar : declined an alliance with the British against an Afghan invasion : was defeated at Poona in 1802 by Jaswant Rao Holkar. In 1803 he was allied with the Raja of Berar to defeat the objects of the Treaty of Bassein : they were routed by General Arthur Wellesley at Assaye on Sep. 23, 1803, and at Argaum on Nov. 28, 1803 : he was forced to sign the Treaty of Sirji Anjenguam, Dec. 30, 1803, and cede territory : Lord Lake also defeated his forces at Alighar on Aug. 29, 1803, at Delhi and Agra, and at Laswari on Nov. 1 : he submitted in 1805 : Lord Cornwallis in 1805 restored Gohad and Gwalior to him. Daulat Rao continued to give trouble by the support he gave to the Pindaris and their depredations, and was compelled by Lord Hastings to make another treaty in 1817 : as he failed in his engagements, the fort of Asirghar was taken from him : he died March 21, 1827.

GWALIOR, SIR JIAJI RAO SINDIA, MAHARAJA OF (1835-1886)

His real name was Bagirat Rao : was adopted by his predecessor's (Jankoji) widow, Tara Bai : grave disturbances broke out regarding the regency : the Regent, Mama Sahib, the Maharaja's father-in-law, was driven out. Lord Ellenborough sent an army to Gwalior, to whom the usurper, Dada Khasgeewala, surrendered. The State Army was defeated at Maharajpur and Punniar on Dec. 29, 1843, and a treaty made at Gwalior in Jan. 1844, when Jiaji was placed on the throne. He paid great attention to military affairs and the improvement of his army. During the mutiny, the Maharaja remained loyal to the British, though the contingent force at Gwalior rebelled : from Tantia Topi and the Rani of Jhansi, he fled to Agra, but was re-established by Sir Hugh Rose at Gwalior : he was handsomely rewarded for his loyalty in the mutiny. Another treaty was made with him in 1864. The Fort at Gwalior was restored to him in 1885 and the British cantonment at Morar abandoned. He sat in 1875 as a member of the Court to try the then Gaekwar of Baroda for attempting to poison Colonel R. Phayre. He entertained H.R.H. the Prince of Wales in 1876. He was a G.C.S.I : and a General : died June 20, 1886.

GWALIOR, MADHAVA (MADHOJI) RAO SINDIA, MAHARAJA OF (1730-1794)

Son of Ranoji Sindia, who, originally a slipper bearer of the Peshwa, rose to be an officer of rank : Madhava was illegitimate, the fourth of his five sons. He and his brother Dattaji were present in the war of 1751 against the French and at the battle of Panipat, where the Peshwa was completely defeated by the Afghans under Shuja, 1760-1 : after this battle, which virtually overthrew the Mahratta design to conquer the whole of India, Madhava became ruler of Ujain, in succession to his father. In the following years, he was an ally of the Poona Regent Raghunath, or Raghoba, fighting against the Jats of Bhartpur and against the Rohillas, annexing the fort of Gwalior and generally consolidating his power. Intrigues at the Courts of the Peshwa and of the Emperor of Delhi against the British ended in the treaty of Salbai between the Peshwa and the British in 1782, and led Warren Hastings to appreciate his talents so greatly that he left him virtually a free hand in the administration of Central India and Hindustan. He now came to be recognized as an independent Prince, though nominally the vassal of the Peshwa and the Delhi Emperor : with the aid of De Boigne, who entered his service about this time, he soon made himself feared by his neighbours, but in his attempt to attack the Raja of Jaipur was repulsed by a conspiracy of Rajput chiefs and Ismail Beg, who defeated him. In the revolt of Ghulam Kadir against the Emperor of Delhi, in 1788, Sindia took no part, but, after Delhi was retaken, he espoused the cause of the blind Emperor. One of his first acts was to re-engage De Boigne as Commander of his forces. He defeated Ismail Beg and the Rajputs in 1790, and entered the town of Ajmir. In 1791 he formed the famous alliance with Lord Cornwallis against Tippoo, which ended in the latter's defeat at Seringapatam. In 1794 he proceeded to Poona to invest the young Peshwa with the Vice-regency of the Empire, and received from him the title of Deputy Vice-Regent. In his absence, his territories were attacked by Ismail Beg and Holkar, who were both defeated by De Boigne. Madhava Rao died suddenly at Poona on Feb. 12, 1794, and it is not improbable that he was the victim of foul play on the part of Nana Farnavis, who was jealous of his influence. He early recognized the military power of the British, and did not oppose them for long. In his schemes of self-aggrandizement, he worked as the subordinate of the Peshwa and the Delhi Emperor.

GWALIOR, MAHARAJA SIR MADHO RAO SINDIA BAHADUR, OF (1876–   )

Born Oct. 20, 1876 : succeeded to the Raj, July 3, 1886 : Hon. Colonel British Army, 1898 : went to China as Orderly Officer to General Sir A. Gaselee, 1901, and provided the expedition with a hospital ship at his own expense : G.C.S.I., 1895 : went to England for the Coronation of H.M. King Edward VII in 1902 : Hon. LL.D., Cambridge : Hon. and Extra A.D.C. to the King.

GWATKIN, FREDERICK STAPLETON (1849–   )

Born Jan. 30, 1849 : son of F. Gwatkin : educated at Rugby and Trinity College, Cambridge : M.A. : entered the Army, 1872, and Indian Staff Corps, 1875 : served in Afghanistan, Egypt, Soudan, Lushai Hills, Chin-Lushai Hills, Manipur, Chitral and Tirah : Brevet-Major and Brevet-Lt-Colonel : D.A.A.G., Assam : Military Secretary to C. in C. in India : A.A.G., Peshawar District : Colonel on the Staff, commanding Sialkot : C.B., 1902.

HADLEY, GEORGE (? –1798)

Joined the E.I. Co.'s Bengal A'rmy, 1763 : retired, 1771 : wrote and published grammatical treatises on Hindustani in 1772 and 1796, and Persian, 1776, with vocabularies : died Sep. 10, 1798.

HADOW, REGINALD CAMPBELL (1851–   )

Son of Patrick Douglas Hadow : educated at Cheltenham : entered the Army, 1870, and the Bengal Staff Corps, 1876 : became Brevet-Colonel, 1892 : served during the Afghan war, 1878–80 : present at Ahmad Kheyl and Urzoo : in the march from Kabul to Kandahar, and battle of Kandahar : Soudan expedition, 1885, present at Tofrek and Tamai : second Miranzai expedition, 1891 : Chitral relief, 1895 : D.S.O. : Tirah expedition, 1897 : present at Dargai : severely wounded at Khangarbur : commanded 15th Sikhs : retired.

HAFFKINE, WALDEMAR MORDECAI WOLFF (1860–   )

Born March 15, 1860 : son of Aaron Haffkine, Odessa : educated at Berdiansk College (S. Russia) and Odessa University : engaged in research work at Zoological Museum, Odessa, 1883–8 : Assistant Professor of Physiology, Geneva, 1888–9 : assistant to Pasteur in Paris, 1889–93 : on bacteriological duty in India since 1893 : Director-in-Chief, Government Plague Research Laboratory, Bombay : C.I.E. : author of works of general Microbiology, Cholera, Plague, etc.

HAFIZ RAHMAT KHAN (1710 ?–1774)

A famous Rohilla chief : born about 1710 in Afghanistan : uncle of Ali Muhammad, chief of the Rohillas, who had settled on the N.W. frontier of Oudh : joined his people in 1739 and received large grants of land from his nephew : on the death of Ali Muhammad, he was made " Hafiz " or " guardian " of his sons : but betrayed the trust and made himself virtual ruler of the country : entered into alliance with the Nawab of Oudh, Shuja-ud-daula, against the Mahrattas, engaging to pay him 40 lakhs in return for his aid. Sir Robert Barker, the English general, attested the treaty. The Mahrattas were driven out, but Rahmat Khan failed to fulfil his part of the engagement. The destruction of the Rohillas was the result : they were defeated at Miranpur Katra by the united forces of the Nawab and the English : Hafiz Rahmat Khan was killed in the battle (1774) : a man of education, and of literary attainments : a strong ruler, and on the whole a beneficent one, both towards the Rohillas and as regards his Hindu subjects.

HAINES, SIR FREDERICK PAUL
(1819–   )

Field Marshal : son of Gregory Haines, C.B. : entered the Army, 1839 : Military Secretary to Sir Hugh Gough, C. in C., India, 1845–9 : served in the Satlaj campaign, 1845–6 : present at Mudki and Firozshahr : in the Panjab campaign of 1848–9, at Ramnagar, the Chenab, Chilianwala, Gujarat : Crimea, 1854–5 : C. in C. Madras, 1871–5 : C. in C. India, 1876–81, during the Afghan war, 1879–80 : thanked by Parliament : K.C.B., 1871 : General and G.C.B., 1877 : G.C.S.I.

HALDANE, JAMES AYLMER LOW-THORPE (1862–   )

Born Nov. 17, 1862 : son of D. Rutherford Haldane, M.D. : educated at Wimbledon school, Edinburgh Academy, and at the Staff College : joined the Gordon Highlanders, 1882 : served in Waziristan expedition, 1894–5 : Chitral, 1895 : Tirah expedition, 1897–8 : A.D.C. to Sir W. Lockhart : present at Dargai : D.S.O. : South Africa, 1899–1900 : taken prisoner and escaped from Pretoria : author of How we Escaped from Pretoria.

HALHED, NATHANIEL BRASSEY
(1751–1830)

I.C.S. : born May 25, 1751 : son of William Halhed, Director of the Bank of England : educated at Harrow, and Christ Church, Oxford : went to Bengal in the E.I. Co.'s service : published A Code of Gentoo Laws on Ordinations of the Pandits, from a Persian Translation, 1776 : and in 1778 a Bengali grammar, printed at Hughli, at the first printing-press in India : in its preface, he drew attention to the similarity between Sanskrit and European languages : returned to England, 1785 : M.P. for Lymington, 1790–5 : took the part of the lunatic prophet Richard Brothers, an act which was fatal to his career : in 1809 he was appointed to a post in the East India House : he imitated Martial's epigrams and translated Aristænetus : he wrote A Narrative of the Events in Bombay and Bengal relative to the Mahratta Empire, 1779 : his Oriental MSS. were purchased by the British Museum : died Feb. 18, 1830.

HALIFAX, CHARLES WOOD, VISCOUNT (1800–1885)

Born Dec. 20, 1800 : son of Sir Francis Lindley Wood, second Baronet : educated at Eton and Oriel College, Oxford : double first, 1821 : was M.P. for Grimsby and Wareham, and for Halifax, 1832–65 : joint Secretary to the Treasury, 1832 : Secretary to the Admiralty, 1835–9 : Chancellor of the Exchequer, 1846–52 : P.C. : and succeeded to the Baronetcy in 1846 : was President of the Board of Control, Dec. 1852, to Feb. 1855, and passed the India Charter Act of 1853 : First Lord of the Admiralty, 1855–8 : G.C.B., 1856 : Secretary of State for India, 1859–66 : during this time he passed several important measures for the reorganization of the Indian Army, the constitution of the Indian Legislative Councils, and the establishment of the High Courts, and by the end of this period the equilibrium of Indian finance had been practically restored : M.P. for Ripon, 1865 : created Viscount Halifax, 1866 : Lord Privy Seal, 1870–4 : made his reputation by his excellent discharge of his duties, his business qualities and judicious administration : died Aug. 8, 1885.

HALL, FITZ-EDWARD (1825–1901)

Born at Troy in New York State : graduated at Harvard University, 1846 :

Doctor: went to India, 1850: was Anglo-Sanskrit Professor at Benares, 1851: the first American to publish a text in Sanskrit: in the mutiny was Inspector of Schools in the Education Department in Central India: was beleaguered for 6 months in Sagar Fort: at Benares, in 1859, published a *Contribution towards an Index of the Philosophy of the Indian Philosophical Systems*, and essays in the *J.A.S.* Bengal, and other Oriental studies: in 1862 was Professor of Sanskrit and Indian Jurisprudence at King's College, London: Librarian at the India Office: retired, 1869: worked on Dr. Murray's Oxford English Dictionary: wrote *Modern English* in 1870: died Feb. 11, 1901.

HALL, HENRY (1789–1875)

General: son of the Ven. Archdeacon Hall: born 1789: entered the Bengal Army, 1805: was D.A.Q.M.G. under Ochterlony in the Pindari war, 1817–8: performed the duties of the Guide and Intelligence Department: appointed, in 1822, to civilize the turbulent race of Mhairs: raised a Mhair corps (which remained faithful in 1857, helped to save Ajmir and European lives). Through Hall's exertions, female infanticide, slavery, sale of women, murder and universal plunder, are said to have completely ceased: C.B. in 1838: died in Aug., 1875.

HALLETT, HOLT S. (? –)

Son of T. P. L. Hallett, LL.D: educated at Kensington school and Charterhouse: qualified for Engineer on L. and N.W. Railway: employed in construction work, 1860–8: entered Indian P.W.D., 1868, and served in Burma: retired in 1880: proposed connexion of Indian, Burmese and Chinese railways, and surveyed the country, 1881–5: author of *A Thousand Miles on an Elephant; Development of our Eastern Markets; Indian Taxation, Ancient and Modern; India and her Neighbours; Indian Factory Legislation; Extension of Railways*, etc.

HALLIDAY, SIR FREDERICK JAMES (1806–1901)

I.C.S.: born Dec. 26, 1806: son of Thomas Halliday of Ewell: educated at St. Paul's school, Rugby, and Haileybury: went out to Bengal in June, 1825: was Secretary to the *Sadr* Board of Revenue in 1836: Secretary to the Government of Bengal, 1838: Officiating Secretary to the Government of India in 1842: Secretary to the Home Department of the Government of India, 1849. While on furlough, in 1852–3, he was on 16 occasions examined before the Committees of the Lords and Commons on Indian subjects in connexion with the renewal of the E.I. Company's Charter: Member of the Governor-General's Supreme Council, Dec. 1853, to April, 1854: the first Lieutenant-Governor of Bengal, from May 1, 1854, to May 1, 1859. His term of office as Lieutenant-Governor was eventful: the Sonthal insurrection required the movement of troops and strong measures for its suppression: the Indian mutiny did not eventually assume such proportions in Lower Bengal as in Upper India, but the earliest indications appeared at Barrackpur and Berhampur: outbursts occurred in other parts of the Lower Provinces, and, during the whole two years, Halliday's vigilance and administrative capacity were severely tried and never failed. He was held in high estimation by Lord Dalhousie, and had great influence with Lord Canning, who said of him, after the mutiny, that for many months he had been the "right hand of the Government." Halliday recorded a Minute on "The Mutinies as they affected the Lower Provinces under the Government of Bengal." He had also to deal with the new conditions attending the creation of Bengal into a separate Lieutenant-Governorship, and arising from the great Education despatch of 1854 from England, important Rent and Revenue legislation, and the introduction of Railways. He received the thanks of Parliament for his mutiny services: was made K.C.B. in 1860: and was Member of the Council of India from 1868 to 1886: he died Oct. 22, 1901. Of lofty stature and splendid physique, Halliday appeared to be the embodiment of great power, an impression which was strengthened by whatever he said, or wrote.

HAMILTON, ALEXANDER (1762–1824)

Captain: in the military service of the E.I. Co.: M.A.S.B.: the date of his return to England is not recorded: prosecuted his study of Sanskrit at the British Museum and in Paris: when the war with France broke out again after the peace of Amiens, he was detained in Paris as a hostage : taught Sanskrit to French savants : made a Catalogue of the Sanskrit MSS. in the National Library at Paris, which was published by Langlès (*q.v.*) : was Professor of Sanskrit at Haileybury, May, 1806–18 : F.R.S.,1808 : published the *Hitopadesa* in Sanskrit, 1811 : a treatise on the terms of Sanskrit grammar, 1815 : a key to the Chronology of the Hindus, 1820 : wrote articles on Ancient Indian Geography, and contributed to the *Edinburgh Review* : died Dec. 30, 1824.

HAMILTON, CHARLES (1753 ?–1792)

Born about 1753 : son of Charles Hamilton, merchant : went to India in the E.I. Co.'s military service in 1776 : was one of the first members of the Asiatic Society of Bengal : served in the expedition against the Rohillas, and wrote an account of them in 1787 : translated the *Hedaya*, or guide to Muhammadan Law, from Persian, 1791. He died March 14, 1792, in England, before he could take up the post of Resident in Oudh, to which he had been appointed.

HAMILTON, EDWARD OWEN FISHER (1854–   )

Son of William James Hamilton : born Feb. 17, 1854 : joined the Army, 1873 : served in the Afghan war, 1878–80 : Burma war, 1886–7 : Hazara expedition, 1891 : Tochi valley, 1896 : Malakand Field Force, 1897 : D.A.A.G. : Tirah expedition, 1897–8 : Africa, 1899–1900 : Brig-General : commanding 2nd class District in India, since 1902 : C.B., 1902.

HAMILTON, LORD GEORGE FRANCIS (1845–   )

Born Dec. 17, 1845 : son of 1st Duke of Abercorn : educated at Harrow : M.P. for Middlesex County, 1868–85 : M.P. for Ealing Division, 1885 : Under Secretary of State for India, 1874–8 : Vice-President of Council, 1878–80 : First Lord of the Admiralty, 1885–92 : P.C. : Chairman of London School Board, 1894–5 : Secretary of State for India, 1895–1903 : resigned.

HAMILTON, SIR IAN STANDISH MONTEITH (1853–   )

Son of Colonel Christian Monteith Hamilton, born Jan. 16, 1853 : educated at Cheam and Wellington : entered the Army, 1873 : served in the Afghan war, 1878–80 : Boer war, 1881 : at Majuba Hill : Nile expedition, 1884–5 : Burma expedition, 1886–7 : Brevet-Lt-Colonel, 1891 : Chitral relief, 1895 : C.B. : Tirah campaign, 1897–8 : South Africa, 1899–1901 : Chief of the Staff to Lord Kitchener, 1901–2 : K.C.B. : D.S.O. : Quarter-Master-General of the Army, 1903 : attached to the Japanese Army, 1904–5.

HAMILTON, SIR JOHN, BARONET (1755–1835)

Son of James Hamilton : born Aug. 4, 1755 : joined the Bengal Native Infantry of the E.I. Co. in 1773 : present in the attacks on Cooch Behar, and at the capture of Gwalior, in the operations against the Mahrattas in 1778 : served also in the King's troops against Tippoo, in the campaign of 1790–1 : left India and was afterwards at San Domingo, at the Cape, in the Peninsula in 1809–13 : Lt-General, 1814 : Baronet, 1815 : K.C.B. and K.C.H. : died Dec. 24, 1835.

HAMILTON, SIR ROBERT NORTH COLLIE, BARONET (1802–1887)

Son of Sir Frederick Hamilton, fifth Baronet : born April 7, 1802 : educated at Haileybury : went to India in 1819 : served in the N.W.P. : Commissioner of Agra : Secretary to the N.W.P. Government in 1843 : Resident at Indore, with Holkar, from 1844 : succeeded as Baronet, in 1853 : was made Agent to the Governor-General for Central India in 1854 : returned from leave in England in the mutiny of 1857 : and rejoined at Indore : was ordered to prepare a plan for the pacification of Central India, which was accepted : he, as Political Officer, accompanied Sir Hugh Rose in his Central Indian campaign in 1858 : was at the capture of Jhansi and defeat of Tantia Topi : at the restoration of Gwalior to Sindia : K.C.B., and the thanks of Parliament for his mutiny services : provisional Member of the Supreme Council, 1859 : retired in 1859, from ill-health : died May 30, 1887.

HAMMOND, SIR ARTHUR GEORGE (1843–   )

Born 1843 : son of Major T. G. Hammond : educated at Sherborne and Addiscombe : entered the Indian Staff Corps, 1861 : Colonel, 1890 : served in the Jowaki-Afridi expedition, 1877-8 : in the Guides in the Afghan war, 1878-80 : gained the V.C. on the Asmai Heights, near Kabul, Dec. 14, 1879 : Hazara expedition, 1888 : D.S.O., Hazara expedition, 1891 : C.B. : Brevet-Colonel, Isazai expedition, 1892 : Chitral relief, 1895 : Tirah expedition, 1897-8 : commanded a Brigade : A.D.C. to Queen Victoria.

HAMPSON, SIR GEORGE FRANCIS, BARONET (1860-)

Born Jan. 14, 1860 : educated at Charterhouse and Exeter College, Oxford : author of various scientific works, including *The Moths of India*, published by the India Office, 1892-6.

HANBURY, SIR JAMES ARTHUR (1832-)

Born 1832 : educated at Trinity College, Dublin : entered the Army Medical Department, 1853 : served in China, India, and America : in the Afghan campaign, as P.M.O. of a Division, 1878-9 : in Sir F. Roberts' march from Kabul to Kandahar, Aug. 1880 : Egypt, 1882 : Surgeon-General, Madras Presidency, 1888-92 K.C.B., 1892.

HANDCOCK, ARTHUR GORE (1840-)

Born 1840 : son of Capt. E. R. Handcock : educated privately : entered the Bengal Army, 1858 : and the Indian Staff Corps, 1866 : became Maj-General, 1896 : served in the Bhutan expedition, 1865-6 : Afghan war, 1878-80, as A.A.G. : present at Ahmad Kheyl : Brevet-Lt-Colonel : A.A.G., Bengal, 1880-5 : C.B., 1893 : Lt-General.

HANKIN, ERNEST HANBURY (1865-)

Born Feb. 4, 1865 : son of Rev. D. B. Hankin : educated at Merchant Taylors', University College, London, St. Bartholomew's Hospital, and St. John's College, Cambridge : Scholar and Fellow : studied under Koch and Pasteur : Chemical Examiner and Bacteriologist, Agra, and Oudh, since 1892 : author of several papers on medical subjects, including Anthrax, Cholera, etc. : Fellow of Allahabad University.

HANNAY (? - ?)

Major : in the service of the E.I. Co. in the time of Warren Hastings : with permission, he left the Company's service for a time, and entered that of the Nawab of Oudh, 1778 : managed the district of Gorakhpur : disturbances in it were said to be owing to his oppression and misconduct. The Nawab dismissed him in 1781, and later would not hear of his return : he took part in the war against the Rohillas in 1774, and was afterwards examined with reference to alleged cruelties practised on that people.

HARDING, FRANCIS PYM (? - 1875)

Maj-General : entered the Army, 1838 : in the 22nd regt. at the defence of the residency at Hyderabad (Sind) on Feb. 15, 1843 : and at Miani on Feb. 17 : dangerously wounded : Persian interpreter to Sir C. Napier in the Afridi expedition, and the forcing of the Kohat Pass, 1850 : in the Crimea, at all the battles, 1854-5 : C.B. : Maj-General in 1868 : died Feb. 26, 1875.

HARDING, RIGHT REV. JOHN, D.D. (1805-1874)

Born Jan. 7, 1805 : son of William Harding : educated at Westminster and Worcester College, Oxford : ordained in 1827 : rector at Blackfriars, and Secretary of the Church Pastoral Aid Society : Bishop of Bombay, 1851-68 : D.D. in 1851 : his views were of a pronounced Evangelical type : died June 18, 1874.

HARDINGE, HON. SIR ARTHUR EDWARD (1828-1892)

Second son of Henry, first Viscount Hardinge (*q.v.*) : educated at Eton : joined the 41st foot in 1844 : to India as A.D.C. to his father, when Governor-General (1844-8) : was in the first Sikh war of 1845-6, at the battles of Mudki, Firozshahr and Sobraon : exchanged to the Coldstream Guards in 1849 : in the Q.M.G.'s Department in the Crimea, 1854-5, at all the battles : Brevet-Major and C.B., 1857 : Equerry to the Prince Consort and afterwards to Queen Victoria : Maj-General, 1871 : commanded a Division in Bengal, 1873-8 : C. in Ç. of the Bombay Army, 1881-5 : General, 1883 : K.C.B. and C.I.E. in 1886 : Governor of Gibraltar, 1886-90 : died July, 1892, from the effects of a carriage accident.

HARDINGE, CHARLES STEWART, SECOND VISCOUNT (1822-1894)

Eldest son of the first Viscount Hardinge (*q.v.*), the Governor-General: born Sep. 12, 1822: educated at Eton and Christ Church, Oxford: was Private Secretary to his father the whole time the latter was Governor-General, 1844-8: M.P. for Downpatrick, 1851-6: succeeded to the Peerage, 1856: Under Secretary for War, 1858-9: a good amateur artist: a volume, *Recollections of India*, published from his drawings: he wrote a life of his father for the "Rulers of India" series: he died July 28, 1894.

HARDINGE, HENRY, FIRST VISCOUNT, OF LAHORE (1785-1856)

Governor-General: Field Marshal: born March 30, 1785: son of Rev. Henry Hardinge: entered the Army in 1799: went through the Royal Military College at High Wycombe, 1806-7: through the Peninsular war, first as D.A.Q.M.G., afterwards with the Portuguese Army: present in a number of battles, several times wounded: K.C.B. in 1815: lost an arm at Quatre Bras: Commissioner with the Prussians in France, 1818: D.C.L. of Oxford: M.P. 1820-44, for Durham, Newport and Launceston: Secretary at War, 1818-30: and 1841-4: Irish Secretary in 1830, and 1834-5: Lt-General in 1841: G.C.B. in 1844: was Governor-General of India from July, 1844, to Jan. 1848: the first to go out overland. The Panjab being in a state of anarchy since Ranjit Singh's death in 1839, and the Sikh *khalsa* army dominant, Hardinge strengthened the Satlaj frontier with troops: when the Sikhs crossed the Satlaj, they were defeated at Mudki and Firozshahr in Dec. 1845, and in Feb. 1846, at Sobraon, Hardinge serving as second in command under Sir Hugh Gough, the C. in C. On peace being made, on terms dictated to the Sikhs, Hardinge received a Peerage, and pensions from Parliament and the E.I. Co. Kashmir was annexed and made over to the Raja of Jammu for a large sum: a British Resident (Sir H. Lawrence), at Lahore, was appointed. On retiring from India he claimed to have left it in complete peace. Hardinge also left his mark on the internal administration of India: he

established schools: prohibited Sunday work in Government offices: promoted railways and irrigation: determined important military questions, both in the native and the European armies. His equestrian statue was subsequently erected in Calcutta. He was made Master-General of the Ordnance in 1852, and was C. in C. of the Forces, 1852-6: Field Marshal in 1855: died Sep. 24, 1856.

HARDWICKE, ALBERT EDWARD PHILIP HENRY YORKE, SIXTH EARL OF (1867-1904)

Born March 14, 1867: son of the fifth Earl: educated at Eton: in the Diplomatic service, 1886-91: worked eight years as member of a firm of stockbrokers: part proprietor of the *Saturday Review*: Under Secretary of State for India, 1900-2: for War, 1902-3: and again for India, 1903-4: died suddenly Nov. 29, 1904.

HARDY, REV. ROBERT SPENCE (? -1868)

Missionary: in 1825, appointed to the Wesleyan Mission in Ceylon: from 1835 methodically studied the authentic sources of Buddhism: published *Eastern Monachism*, 1850, and *Manual of Buddhism*, 1852, on the condition of the Buddhist priesthood in Ceylon, the Buddhist system and legendary history of Gautama Buddha in the South: General Superintendent of the S. Ceylon mission, 1863-6: wrote on the *Sacred Books of the Buddhists, compared with History and Modern Science:* Honorary Member of the Royal Asiatic Society: died April 16, 1868.

HARE, DAVID (1775-1842)

An enthusiastic promoter of the English education of Indians: born in Scotland in 1775: brought up as a watchmaker: went out to Calcutta in 1800: in a few years acquired a competence, and before 1816 made over his business to a relative named Grey: in 1814 proposed to his friend, Raja Ram Mohan Roy, the establishment of an English school at Calcutta: with the help of Sir Edward East and Bengali friends, opened the Hindu College on Jan. 20, 1817: locating it on a piece of his land on the N. side of College Square: in Sep. 1818, founded the Calcutta

School Book Society for printing and publishing English and Bengali books : worked hard for the repeal of the Regulations against the Press : to secure trial by jury in civil cases in the Supreme Court : to prevent emigration of Indian labourers to Mauritius and Bourbon : in 1838 was appointed by Government a Judge of the Calcutta Court of Requests, in recognition of his services for the cause of native education : died June 1, 1842, of cholera : his full-sized marble statue was erected by public subscription, between Presidency College and the Hare School : the anniversary of his death is still observed by the Bengalis with great veneration, and a memorial tablet has been placed by the Government of India at his residence.

HARIDAS, NANABHAI (1832–1889)

Born Sep. 5, 1832, at Surat : a Gujarati Hindu : educated at the Bombay Elphinstone College : Assistant Translator in the Supreme Court, Bombay, 1832–63 : LL.D. at the Madras University, 1863 : Vakil of the Bombay *Sadr* Court, 1861, and of the High Court, 1862 : acted as Judge of the Bombay High Court several times after 1873, and was confirmed in the appointment : died June, 1889.

HARINGTON, SIR HENRY BYNG (1808–1871)

Son of Henry Hawes Harington, of Madras : born 1808 : entered the E.I. Co.'s Bengal Army in 1824 : served with the 37th Bengal N.I. : present at Bhartpur, 1826 : transferred by regular nomination to the Civil Service, about 1828 : returned to England, and passed the required tests : served in the N.W.P. : rose to be Judge of the *Sadr* Court at Agra, 1852 : shut up in the Fort at Agra in the mutiny : became the Member, representing the N.W.P., of the Governor-General's Legislative Council, 1858–62 : was twice a temporary Member of the Supreme Council, confirmed in 1862 : retired in March, 1865 : declined the Lieutenant-Governorship of the N.W.P. on the retirement of Sir G. F. Edmonstone (*q.v.*) : K.C.S.I. in 1866 : died Oct. 7, 1871.

HARINGTON, JOHN HERBERT (1764–1828)

Joined the E.I. Co.'s service at Calcutta in 1780 : held subordinate appointments in Bengal until he became Fourth Member of the Board of Revenue, 1799 : Puisne Judge of the *Sadr Diwani* and *Nizamat Adalat*, 1801 : Chief Judge, 1811 : Senior Member of the Board of Revenue for the Western Provinces, and Agent to the Governor-General at Delhi, 1823 : Member of the Supreme Council and President of the Board of Trade, 1822–3 : and again, 1825–7 : he was also Professor of the Laws and Regulations at the College of Fort William, and President of the Council of the College : edited *The Persian and Arabic Works of Sadi*, and published an *Analysis of the Laws and Regulations*, etc., 1805–17 : retired, 1828 : died in London, April 9, 1828.

HARISH CHANDRA (1859–1885)

The son of Gopal Chandra Sahu, of Benares (a prolific author, died 1859, aged 27) : educated at Queen's College, Benares, and early commenced to write : became the most celebrated of the native poets of modern times, and did more for the popularisation of vernacular literature than almost any Indian of the last century : wrote and excelled in many styles : his best known work is the *Sundari Tilak*, an anthology of poems from the works of 69 authors. Another, *Prasiddh Mahatma ka Jiban Charitra*, was a series of lives of great men, European and Indian. Another very popular work is the *Kabi Bachan Sudha*, a collection of poems dealing with the rainy season. His works numbered over a hundred, and include several plays. He also conducted for many years an excellent vernacular magazine, called the *Harishchandrika*. In 1880 he received the title of Bharatendu, or Moon of India, by the unanimous consent of all the editors of vernacular papers in the country : was certainly the best critic Northern India has yet produced : died, universally regretted, in 1885.

HARLAN, JOSIAH (? – ?)

Adventurer : of Philadelphia : son of a Quaker : studied for medical profession : went to India : sent by Lord Amherst as Assistant Surgeon with the Army to Burma : left it and tried to conquer part of the Panjab : captured by Ranjit Singh (*q.v.*), who employed him : twice envoy to Dost Muhammad, and secret agent of Shah Shuja : and agent of the former : made Governor of Jasrata, Nurpur and Gujarat till 1835 : sent on a mission to Dost Muhammad : won over Sultan Muhammad Khan, the Afghan Governor of Peshawar, and gained it for Ranjit : entered Dost Muhammad's service : 'sent on expedition against Kunduz : deputed by Dost Muhammad in 1839 to negotiate with Sir A. Burnes (*q.v.*) : returned to India and America, and was heard of no more.

HARNESS, SIR HENRY DRURY (1804–1883)

Son of John Harness, M.D. : born 1804 : entered the Royal Engineers, 1827 : Colonel, 1862 : in the mutiny as Lt-Colonel R.E. : in the operations at Cawnpur, against the Gwalior contingent : at the siege and capture of Lucknow : in Rohilkund : in Oudh : C.B. : K.C.B., 1873 : Colonel Commandant R.E. and Colonel in the Army : retired as Maj-General, 1877 : died Feb. 10, 1883.

HARPER (? – ?)

Captain : in the E.I. Co.'s service prominent in the Oudh charges against Hastings : Resident at the Court of the Nawab of Oudh : sent by Sir Robert Barker to negotiate with the Rohillas in 1772 : recalled from the Nawab's Court, 1773.

HARRIS, GEORGE, FIRST BARON, OF SERINGAPATAM AND MYSORE (1746–1829)

Son of the Rev. George Harris : born March 18, 1746 : educated at the Royal Military Academy, Woolwich : Cadet in the Royal Artillery, 1759 : was with the 5th Foot in America : engaged at Bunker's Hill in 1775, severely wounded : served in the W. Indies : went out to India with General Sir William Medows (*q.v.*), as A.D.C. and Private Secretary, while the latter was Governor and C. in C. at Bombay (1788–90), and at Madras (1790–2) : in the campaigns of 1790–1, against Tippoo, and in the attack on Seringapatam, 1792 : saved £40,000 for Medows : commanded at Fort William, Calcutta, in 1794 : Maj-General : commanded at Madras, 1796–1800, with a seat in Council, and acting Governor from Feb. to Aug. 1798 : in 1799 commanded 50,000 men against Tippoo : routed him

at Malavilli on March 27, and took Seringapatam on May 4, 1799 : Mysore was annexed : retired to England, 1800 : Lt-General, 1801 : General, 1812 : made a Peer, 1815 : G.C.B., 1820 : Governor of Dumbarton Castle : died May 19, 1829.

HARRIS, GEORGE FRANCIS ROBERT, THIRD BARON (1810–1872)

Governor : son of General William George, the second Baron, and grandson of the first Baron Harris (*q.v.*) : born Aug. 14, 1810 : educated at Eton, privately, at Merton and Christ Church, Oxford : B.A., 1832 : D.C.L., 1863 : Governor of Trinidad, 1846 : Governor of Madras from April, 1754, to March, 1859 : during the mutiny he allowed Madras to be denuded of troops for service in Upper India : the rebellion did not extend to Madras : in a minute on the newspapers he made some disparaging rewarks on the want of loyalty and principle on the part of the British Press throughout the country : he was made K.C.S.I. in 1861 : G.C.S.I. in 1866 : and Chamberlain to H.R.H. the (then) Princess of Wales on her marriage in 1863 : he died Nov. 23, 1872.

HARRIS, GEORGE ROBERT CANNING, FOURTH BARON (1851–)

Born Feb. 3, 1851 : educated at Eton and Christ Church, Oxford : Captain of the Eton Cricket Eleven, 1870 : three years in the Oxford Eleven : Under Secretary for India, 1885–6 : Under Secretary for War, 1888–9 : Governor of Bombay, 1890–5 : served in S. Africa, 1901 : a well-known cricketer, for England and Kent : G.C.S.I. : G.C.I.E. : D.L.

HARRIS, SIR WILLIAM CORNWALLIS (1807–1848)

Major : son of James Harris : born in 1807 : educated at a military college : joined the E.I. Co.'s Bombay Engineers in 1823 : on leave to the Cape, 1835–7, made an expedition to shoot big game in the interior of South Africa : field engineer to the Army in Sind, 1838 : Superintending Engineer in 1841 : negotiated a commercial treaty with Shoa in Abyssinia : knighted, 1844 : again Superintending Engineer in Bombay : died of fever, Oct. 9, 1848 : published accounts of the game animals of S. Africa : and scientific papers on zoology and certain trees.

HARRIS, WILLIAM GEORGE, SECOND BARON (1782-1845)

Son of the first Baron (q.v.) : born Jan. 19, 1782 : educated at Chelsea : joined the Army in 1795 : and the 74th Highlanders in Madras, 1797 : served in his father's Army against Tippoo, 1799 : in the storming party at Seringapatam : conveyed home the standards taken there to the King : at the battle of Copenhagen : in Canada : was a volunteer in Sir D. Baird's re-capture of the Cape, 1805 : served in N. Germany and in the Netherlands, 1813-4 : wounded at Waterloo, 1815 : held commands in Ireland and England : succeeded as Peer, 1829 : Lt-General, 1837 : C.B. : K.C.H. : died May 30, 1845.

HARRISON, SIR HENRY LELAND (1837-1892)

I.C.S. : son of Rev. James Harwood Harrison : educated at Westminster and Christ Church, Oxford : went to Bengal in the Civil Service, 1860 : Junior Secretary to Government of Bengal, 1867 : Secretary to Board of Revenue, 1878 : Commissioner of Police and Chairman of the Corporation of Calcutta, 1881-90 : knighted : Member of the Bengal Legislative Council : Member of the Board of Revenue, 1890 : died of cholera, at Chittagong, May 5, 1892.

HART, GEORGE VAUGHAN (1752-1832)

Born 1752 : entered the Army, 1775 : fought in the American war, 1775-8 : in the West Indies, 1778-9 : went to India : in the naval actions with Admiral Suffrein : was on Sir Edward Hughes's ship off Madras : was at the taking of Bangalore, 1791, and of the hill forts : at Malavilli and at the siege of Seringapatam : commanded in Canara, 1799 : Maj-General, 1805 : Lt-General, 1811 : commanded in Ireland : M.P. for Donegal, 1812--31 : died June 14, 1832.

HARTLEY, JAMES (1745-1799)

Born 1745 : entered the E.I. Co.'s military service at Bombay in 1764 : in the expeditions against the pirates on the Malabar coast, 1765 : A.D.C. to the Governor of Bombay, 1770 : in 1778 he was in the Army sent by the Bombay Government to the Konkan, which re-

treated before the Mahrattas in 1779 : by his skilful conduct of the rearguard, he saved the force from utter defeat. He was opposed to the Convention of Wargaum, Jan. 14, 1779 : captured Ahmadabad, Feb. 15, 1780 : was further engaged against the Mahrattas, 20,000 of whom he defeated at Doogaur, Dec. 9, 1780 : his promotion to Lt-Colonel was disallowed by the Court of Directors, but granted by the King in England : Q.M.G. of the Bombay Army, 1788 : in Dec. 1790, he defeated Tippoo's general, Husain Ali, at Calicut : co-operated against Seringapatam in 1791 : captured the French settlement of Mahé in 1793 : Maj-General in 1796 : made Supervisor of Malabar : second in command of the Bombay Army under General Stuart against Tippoo in 1799 : fought at Seedaseer on March 5, 1799 : at the storming of Seringapatam, May 4 : died at Cannanore, Oct. 4, 1799.

HARTMANN, RIGHT REV. DR. ANASTASIUS (1803-1866)

Born Feb. 25, 1803, in the Canton of Lucerne : studied at Soleure, and entered the Capuchin Order, Sep. 1822 : ordained Priest, 1826 : became master of novices at Fribourg : at Rome, 1841-3, as Professor of Controversy : sent to Agra, 1843, and, after six months, appointed Chaplain at Gwalior : Bishop of Derbe : in 1846 appointed Vicar Apostolic of Patna, and Bishop at Agra, also in 1846 : Vicar Apostolic of Bombay from 1849 : founded the *Catholic Examiner* : made Assistant Prelate to the Pontifical Throne and Count of the Roman Empire, also Procurator-General of the Capuchin Mission : again went to Patna as Vicar Apostolic, 1860 : laboured in the interests of his charge : published an Urdu version of the New Testament : secured the exemption of Catholic natives from the Bill for the marriage of native Christians : survived an attack of cholera in June, 1865, but succumbed to another attack, April 24, 1866.

HARVEY, SIR GEORGE FREDERIC (1809-1884)

I.C.S. : son of Sir John Harvey, K.C.B. : educated at Haileybury, 1825-7 : joined the Civil Service in the N.W.P., 1827 : Commissioner of Agra in the mutiny : with the Bhartpur troops tried to keep open the communications with Delhi, May to July, in the Mathura and Gurgaon districts, until the Contingent mutinied : retired, 1863 : K.C.S.I. : died Nov. 4, 1884.

HARVEY, ROBERT (1842–1901)

Maj-General : son of Alexander Harvey : educated at Aberdeen and Glasgow Universities : M.D. Aberdeen and LL.D. : entered the Bengal Medical Service, 1865 : Surg-Major, 1877 : in the Bhutan expedition, 1864–6 : in Lushai expedition, 1871–2 : Professor of Midwifery at the Medical College Hospital, Calcutta, 1880 : officiating Principal, 1882 : P.M.O. in both Miranzai expeditions : in the Hazara Field Force, 1891 : Isazai expedition, 1872 : Inspr-General of Civil Hospitals, Bengal, 1894 : P.M.O. to the Panjab forces, 1895 : Director-General, I.M.S., 1898 : Fellow of the Calcutta University : President of the first Indian Medical Congress : wrote constantly in medical Journals : C.B. : D.S.O. : died Dec. 1, 1901.

HASTINGS, FRANCIS RAWDON, FIRST MARQUIS OF (1754–1826)

Governor-General : born Dec. 9, 1754 : eldest son of first Earl of Moira : educated at Harrow and University College, Oxford : entered the Army, 1771, and the 5th foot, 1773 : to America : engaged at Bunker's Hill, 1775 : and in other battles till 1781 : Lt-Colonel, and Adjutant-General in America, 1778 : captured by the French on his voyage to England, 1781 : made Baron Rawdon, 1783 : opposed Fox's India Bill, 1783 : took the additional name of Hastings, 1790 : succeeded as Earl of Moira, 1793 : commanded reinforcements in Flanders : Lt-General, 1798 : C. in C. in Scotland : General in 1803 : Master of the Ordnance, 1806 : Constable of the Tower of London : K.G., 1812 : Governor-General of India, and C. in C., Oct. 4, 1813, to Jan. 9, 1823 : war against Nipal, 1814–6 : created Marquis of Hastings for his success : took command in the Pindari war of 1817–8 : made subsidiary treaties against them : deposed the Peshwa, and defeated the Mahrattas : thus making the British power supreme over all India : G.C.B. and G.C.H. : acquired Singapore and entered into communications with Siam : granted £60,000 by the E. I. Co. :

allowed the banking house of W. Palmer & Co., at Hyderabad, to lend 60 lakhs to the Nizam, an act which the Court of Directors disallowed : Hastings resigned in 1821 : but was not relieved until 1823 : Governor and C. in C. of Malta, 1824 : the Court of Proprietors of the E. I. Co. agreed to an amendment adverse to his action in the case of Palmer & Co. : died off Naples, on Nov. 28, 1826 : his statue by Chantrey was erected in Calcutta by the British residents there. He wrote, 1824, a summary of his Indian administration, which is remembered for its length, for his victorious wars, and extension of British territory, as well as for his personal ability, both in his civil and military capacities.

HASTINGS, WARREN (1732–1818)

Governor-General : born Dec. 6, 1732 : son of Pynaston Hastings : educated at Newington Butts and Westminster : first King's Scholar, 1747 : went to Calcutta in civil employ of the E. I. Co. 1750 : to Kasimbazar in 1753 : Member of Council there : imprisoned at Murshidabad, 1756, joined the British refugees from Calcutta at Falta : Resident at Murshidabad, 1757–60, corresponding with Clive, the Governor of Calcutta : had difficulties with Raja Nuncomar (q.v.) : Member of Council in Calcutta, 1761 : sent to Patna to negotiate about inland trade : was struck in Council by a colleague : to England, 1764–9 : sent to Madras as second in Council there, 1769, the Baron and Baroness von Imhoff being fellow-passengers on his ship : Governor of Bengal from April 13, 1772 : the whole revenue and judicial administration was revised, and the conduct of superior native officials investigated : Hastings sent troops, according to an existing treaty, to assist the Nawab of Oudh against the Rohillas, who were defeated : by the Regulating Act of 1773, Hastings was appointed Governor-General, with four colleagues : the new regime took effect from Oct. 20, 1774 : Francis, Clavering, Monson opposed him, Barwell siding with him : Nuncomar accused Hastings of corruption, Hastings charged Nuncomar and others with conspiracy : Nuncomar was himself arrested on a charge of forgery, tried, convicted and hanged on Aug. 5, 1775. Hastings sent George Boyle (q.v.) on a mission to the Teshu Lama of Tibet : and.

o

later, Samuel Turner (q.v.) to Tashilhunpo in Tibet : originated the acquisition of revenue by farming out the opium trade. Hastings' conditional resignation of his office, accepted by the Court of Direectors, but annulled by the Supreme Court : by the deaths of Monson and Clavering, he obtained predominance in Council : he married the divorcée, Baroness Imhoff, in Aug. 1877 : he frustrated the operations of the Mahrattas and of Hyder Ali : on Aug. 17, 1780, he fought a duel with Francis (q.v.) and wounded him. By a force under Sir Eyre Coote, he drove Hyder Ali out of the Carnatic and made the treaty of Salbai on May 17, 1782, with Sindia for the Mahrattas : his demand on Chait Singh, Raja of Benares, for a war contribution, being resisted, he went to Benares to levy it ; had to flee to Chunar, but eventually succeeded, and deposed Chait Singh : the Court of Proprietors approved his action : large sums of money were recovered by the Nawab of Oudh from "the Oudh Begams" to meet Hastings' demands, and he has been much blamed for his share in the occurrence. He established the Calcutta Madrasa and assisted in the foundation of the Asiatic Society of Bengal : he embarked for England Feb. 1, 1785 : wrote his *Review of the State of Bengal* at sea. His impeachment, for maladministration, began in Feb, 1788, Burke and others being the managers, with the assistance of Sir P. Francis : Hastings was acquitted on all the charges in April, 1795, after a trial lasting 145 days : the trial cost him £70,000: the E. I. Co. gave him a grant of money. He received no honours. When he attended the House of Commons, in 1813, the whole House rose and did him honour. He was made Privy Councillor and D.C.L. of Oxford. He repurchased the family estate of Daylesford. He died Aug. 22, 1818. His great public services are admitted : his character and the means he employed have been keenly criticised, and will probably be always discussed, but later writings have done much to remove the unfavourable impression which Mill and Macaulay created against him. His motto, "Mens aequa in arduis," represents the tranquil fortitude with which he met the difficulties of his troubled career. His statue is in Calcutta.

HATHAWAY, CHARLES (1817–1903)

Doctor : born 1817 : educated at King Edward's School at Sherborne : studied for his profession at St. Thomas's and Guy's hospitals : entered the E. I. Co.'s medical service in 1843 : in the Satlaj campaign,1845–6 : Civil Surgeon at Lahore: was, in 1852, appointed Inspr-General of Prisons in the Panjab, in which he effected many reforms, largely reducing the mortality : was made Sanitary Commissioner in 1862 : and appointed Private Secretary to Sir John Lawrence, then Governor-General of India, from 1864–6, when he retired : died Aug. 29, 1903.

HAUG, MARTIN H. (1827–1876)

Born Jan. 30, 1827, at Ostdorf in Würtemburg : son of a peasant : early showed an aptitude for languages : studied Oriental languages, at Stuttgart and Tübingen, where he graduated Phil.D. in 1851, and at Gottingen : was admitted "Privat-docent," 1854, at Bonn: studied at Zend under Lassen, for 6 years, under great privations : became temporarily Secretary to Baron Bunsen in Heidelberg. In 1859 he was appointed Professor of Sanskrit at Poona : stayed in India till 1866 : acquired great knowledge of Brahminism, and of the ancient Zoroastrian religion : collected in Gujarat, 1863–4, ancient MSS. Zend-Pahlavi and Vedic documents, which the State Library at Munich bought after his death : returned to Europe on account of ill-health : appointed Professor of Sanskrit and Comparative Philology at the University of Munich, retaining this post till his death : published *Die fünf Gathas*, 1858, 1860 ; *Essays on the Sacred Language, Writings and Religion of the Parsees*, 1862–78 ; an edition, with translation, of the *Aitareya Brahmana*, 1863, and a Zend-Pahlavi glossary, 1868. His Pahlavi - Pazand glossary, brought out in conjunction with a Parsi scholar, 1870, the *Book of Arda Viraf*, and other lesser works, mark a distinct epoch in the study of Pahlavi : translated part of the *Vendidad* and published other works on the Zendavesta : besides treatises on Brahma and the Brahmans, and on the nature and value of the Vedic accent in Sanskrit : died at Ragatz, June 3, 1876.

HAUGHTON, SIR GRAVES CHAMPNEY
(1788–1849)

Son of Dr. John Haughton : born 1788 : went to India in the E. I. Co.'s Bengal Army in 1808 : attained great proficiency in Oriental languages by study at Baraset and at the College of Fort William : in 1815 he returned to England from ill-health : was appointed Assistant Oriental Professor at Haileybury, and became Professor of Sanskrit and Bengali, 1819–27 : published Bengali works, and in 1825 an edition of the Sanskrit text of Manu : M.A. at Oxford : F.R.S. : was one of the originators of the Royal Asiatic Society : and its Honorary Secretary, 1831–2 : Member of foreign Asiatic Societies : made in 1833 a Knight of the Guelphic Order : in 1833 he brought out a Bengali and Sanskrit dictionary, explained in English. He latterly occupied himself with science and metaphysics : wrote, 1833, an *Inquiry into the Nature of Cholera and the Means of Cure* : died of cholera at St. Cloud on Aug. 28, 1849.

HAUGHTON, JOHN COLPOYS (1817–1887)

Born Nov, 25, 1817 : son of Richard Haughton, nephew of Sir G. C. Haughton (*q.v.*) : educated at Shrewsbury : volunteered for the sea, 1830 : was a Midshipman, 1832–5, then invalided : entered the E. I. Co.'s Bengal Native Infantry in 1837 : in the Afghan war of 1839–42 was Adjutant of the 4th Gurkhas in Shah Shuja's force : made a gallant defence, in command, of Charikar, a town 40 m. from Kabul, Nov. 5–14, 1841, when besieged by 20,000 Afghans : severely wounded, lost a hand : reached Kabul on Nov. 16 : in captivity in Afghanistan, Jan. to Sep. 1842 : served in native infantry at Moulmain, the Andamans, in Assam, in the Khasia-Jaintia expedition, 1862–3, in the Bhutan expedition, 1864–5 : in the Garo expedition, 1872–3 : Commissioner of Cooch-Behar and Manager of the State, 1865–73 : C.S.I., 1866 : left India, 1873 : Lt-General, 1882 : died Sep. 17, 1887 : wrote an account of the occurrences at Charikar.

HAVELOCK, SIR ARTHUR ELIBANK
(1844–)

Born 1844 : son of Lt-Colonel W. Havelock, K.H. : nephew of Sir H. Havelock (*q.v.*) : entered the Army, 1862, and retired as Captain in 1877 : held various Colonial appointments, including those of Governor of the West African Settlements, Governor of Trinidad, Governor of Natal : became Governor of Ceylon, 1890–5 : Governor of Madras, 1895–1900 : described as " a most vigilant and patriotic champion of Madras interests " : Governor of Tasmania, 1901–4 : G.C.M.G., 1895 : G.C.I.E., 1896 : G.C.S.I., 1901.

HAVELOCK, SIR HENRY (1795–1857)

Maj-General : born April 5, 1795 : educated at Swanscombe and the Charter-house : entered at the Middle Temple for the bar, but in 1815 went into the Army, studied military works diligently : to Calcutta in Jan. 1823, with the 13th Light Infantry : in 1824 he was nominated D.A.A.G. of the Burma expedition, and, with an interval of sick leave, served until the conclusion of the war : in 1827 he was made Adjutant of the Depôt at Chinsura : in 1828 published his *Campaigns in Ava*, and in 1829 married a daughter of Dr. Marshman, the Serampur Missionary, and joined the Baptist community. He was deeply religious all his life. Captain in 1838. In that year he was appointed to the Staff of Sir Willoughby Cotton in the Kabul expedition through Kandahar and Ghazni. After the capture of Kabul, he returned to Serampur to complete a narrative of the expedition. It attracted no attention. In 1841 he returned to Kabul as Persian Interpreter to General Elphinstone (*q.v.*), then in command. In Oct. 1841, he joined Sir R. Sale's brigade returning to Jalalabad, was in the " illu-trious garrison " during its seige and at the defeat of Akbar Khan in April, 1842 : at Maharajpur in 1843, and in the Satlaj campaign of 1845–6 under Sir Hugh Gough : in 1854, Quarter-Master-General, and, in 1855, Adjutant-General. He commanded a Division in the Persian war of 1856–7, and was present at Muhamra. On his way from Bombay to Calcutta he was wrecked off Ceylon. From Calcutta in June, 1857, he hurried to Allahabad, and in command of the movable column fought several actions, occupying Cawn-pur after defeating the Nana Sahib on July 16, 1857 : fought more engagements, and after three failures relieved Lucknow in Sep. 1857, Sir James Outram accompanying his force. Compelled to remain

inactive in Lucknow until Sir Colin Campbell arrived in Nov.: he fell ill and died at
the Dilkusha on Nov. 24, 1857, before his
Baronetcy and pension reached him.
They were both granted to his son, and an
annuity to his widow. His statue is in
Trafalgar Square.

HAVELOCK, WILLIAM (1793-1848)

Eldest son of William Havelock, and
brother of Sir Henry Havelock (q.v.):
born Jan. 23, 1793: educated at Charterhouse, and privately: joined the 43rd
regt. in 1810: served with it in the Peninsula, as A.D.C. to Count Alten, and at
Waterloo: showed gallantry in action at
the second combat of Vera in Oct. 1813:
called by the Spaniards 'the fair boy':
went to India with the 4th Dragoons:
A.D.C. to Sir C. Colville, when C. in C. at
Bombay: Military Secretary to Lord
Elphinstone, when Governor of Madras:
commanded the 14th Light Dragoons,
under Lord Gough: in the second Sikh
war: killed in a charge at Ramnagar on
Nov. 22, 1848.

HAVELOCK-ALLAN, SIR HENRY MARSHMAN, BARONET (1830-1897)

Eldest son of Sir H. Havelock (q.v.):
born at Chinsura, Aug. 6, 1830: educated
at St. John's Wood, London: joined the
39th regt. in 1846: went out to India,
1848: suffered from sunstroke and felt it
all his life: in the Persian war, 1857:
at Muhamra: was A.D.C. to his father when
commanding the relief column at Cawnpur:
in several actions: won the V.C. at Cawnpur:
July 16, 1857, leading the 64th regt.
against severe fire: D.A.A.G. to the force
from Cawnpur to the relief of Lucknow,
Sep. 1857: recommended by Outram for
the V.C.: wounded: received a Baronetcy
in Jan. 1858, for the services of his father
(died Nov. 24, 1857): D.A.A.G. to Brig-
General Franks (q.v.), at the siege of
Lucknow: further engaged against the
rebels, and in the Oudh campaign: Brevet-
Major and Lt-Colonel: in the Maori war
1863-4: C.B., 1866: A.Q.M.G. in Canada,
1867-9: M.P. for Sunderland, 1874-81,
and for a Division of Durham county,
1885-92, and in 1895: added the name
of Allan to his own, 1880: Lt-General,
1881: K.C.B., 1897: went to India to see
the frontier fighting and troops in Afghanistan in 1897: shot by the Khyberis near

Ali Masjid, Dec. 30, 1897: he wrote on
military subjects.

HAVILLAND, THOMAS FIOTT DE (1775-1866)

Colonel: son of Sir Peter de Havilland,
Kt.: born April 10, 1775: entered the
Madras Engineers, 1793: at the siege of
Pondicherry, 1793: the capture of Ceylon,
1795-6: served against Tippoo, 1799, and,
under Baird in Egypt, 1801: there surveyed Lake Mareotis, and the Cairo-Suez
desert for water: captured by the French
when returning to India, 1803: Superintending Engineer at Seringapatam, 1804:
Chief Engineer and Architect for Madras,
1814-25: built the Madras Cathedral
and Presbyterian Church: also, by 1822,
the sea-wall: carried out other important
works: after retirement, in 1825, became,
until 1855, a Jurat of the Royal Court of
Guernsey: died Feb. 23, 1866.

HAY, REV. JOHN, D.D. (1812-1891)

Born April 23, 1812: son of Patrick
Hay of near Aberdeen: educated at
Aberdeen University: M.A., 1833: in
1839 joined the Madras Mission of the
L.M.S.: and the staff of the British and
Foreign Bible Society about 1883: D.D.
of an American University about 1881:
Fellow, Madras University, 1888-9: made
benefactions to the native community,
Vizagapatam: wrote religious works and
articles in missionary periodicals: for
about 20 years took a leading part in the
revision of the Telugu translation of the
Bible.

HAYES, SIR JOHN (1767-1831)

Commodore, Indian Navy: constantly
engaged in active service as Midshipman
and Lieutenant in the Indian and Eastern
seas from 1782: attached to the land
forces in the war against Tippoo, 1790-1:
commanded two vessels on a voyage of
discovery in the Eastern Archipelago and
to Australia: in 1797 on a mission to the
Hakim of Somniana: fought an action
with pirates at the Gulf of Cutch, severely
wounded: in 1800 took Vengorla from
pirates: performed more varied service at
the Moluccas, at Ternate, in the Celebes,
at Sumatra became, 1807, Deputy, and,
1809, Master Attendant at Calcutta: in
the expedition to Java in 1811 as Commodore: commanded the armed flotilla

in the first Burmese war : died at the Cocos Island, July 3, 1831.

HAYES, CAPTAIN M. HORACE
(? -1904)

F.R.C.V.S : served in the R.A., Bengal Staff Corps and the Buffs : author of many books on Horses and Horsemanship, including *Indian Racing Reminiscences, Veterinary Notes for Horse-owners*, 1884 ; *Practical Horsemanship*, 1891 ; *A Guide to Training and Horse Management in India*, 1896 ; *Illustrated Horse-breaking*, 1896 ; *Riding and Hunting*, 1901 ; *Horses on Board Ship*, 1902 : died Aug. 1904.

HAYTHORNE, SIR EDMUND
(1818–1888)

Son of John Haythorne : born 1818 : educated at Sandhurst : entered the Army 1837 : served in the 98th in China, 1841–3 : A.D.C. to Sir Colin Campbell in the Panjab campaign, 1848–9, at all the battles : at the forcing of the Kohat Pass by Sir C. Napier, 1850 : in the Mohmand expedition, 1851 : in the Crimea : Chief of the Staff in China, 1859–60 : Adjutant-General in Bengal, 1860–5 : K.C.B., 1873 : General, 1879 : died Oct. 18, 1888.

HAYWARD, GEORGE W. (? –1870)

Traveller : envoy of the Geographical Society : went to Yasin in 1869, when the Yasin chief, Mir Wali, enlisted his support against the Maharaja of Kashmir : went again to Yasin, on his way to the Pamir steppe : Mir Wali had him killed, perhaps through anger, fear, or cupidity, the Governor of Chitral, Amin-ul-Mulk, being implicated, in July, 1870.

HEARSEY, HYDER YOUNG (1782-3 –1840)

Major : son of Captain Harry Thomas Hearsey by a Ját lady : born Dec. 1782 or 1783 : was sent to England for his education : entered Sindia's service under Perron, and afterwards served under George Thomas (*q.v.*), the adventurer, being with him when he surrendered Georgeghar to Bourguien, Sindia's general. In 1804 he joined Lord Lake and fought at Deeg. He explored the sources of the Jamna and Ganges and visited Chinese Tartary to the Mansarowar Lake. In 1815 he fought against the Gurkhas, was taken prisoner by the Nipalese, and

released at the treaty of Segowlie. He helped to quell an insurrection at Bareli in 1816, and was at the siege of Bhartpur : died at his house at Kareli, near Budaon, Aug. 5, 1840.

HEARSEY, SIR JOHN BENNET
(1793–1865)

Lt-General : son of Lt-Colonel Andrew Wilson Hearsey : born at Midnapur, 1793 : Cornet in the 6th Bengal Cavalry : served in Bundelkund, Rewa and the Pindari war : distinguished himself at Sitabaldi, Nagpur, and battles in the Mahratta war : at Bhartpur, Deeg, Chilianwala and Gujarat : suppressed mutiny in a native regiment at Wazirabad, 1849 : C.B : in 1857 was in command of the Division at Barrackpur, when the native troops showed disaffection, which he reported to Government : showed personal bravery on the occasion of the outbreak of Mangal-Pandi, March 29, 1857 : disbanded the 19th N.I. : and gained credit for his conduct throughout the mutiny : K.C.B : commanded the 6th Bengal Light Cavalry, and, later, the 21st Hussars : died at Boulogne, Oct. 23, 1865.

HEAVISIDE, REV. JAMES WILLIAM LUCAS (1808–1897)

Educated at Trinity and Sidney Sussex College, Cambridge : B.A., 1830 : 2nd Wrangler, Smith's Prizeman and Fellow : Professor of Mathematics at Haileybury, 1838–58 : Canon of Norwich, 1860 : died March 5, 1897.

HEBER, RIGHT REV. REGINALD
(1783–1826)

Bishop of Calcutta : born April 21, 1783 : son of Rev. Reginald Heber : educated at Whitchurch and privately : at Brasenose College, Oxford : wrote the Carmen Sæculare, 1800 : gained the English verse prize for his " Palestine " in 1803 : and the English Essay Prize in 1805 : Fellow of All Souls' College in 1805. After a tour of nearly two years in Europe, he was ordained, 1807 : held the living of Hodnet from that year : Prebendary of St. Asaph, 1812 : was appointed Bishop of Calcutta, 1822, which he accepted with much hesitation : completed Bishop's College, Calcutta : travelled continually, performing his episcopal duties, through the whole of India, and in Ceylon, as shown by his *Journey through India, from Calcutta to Bombay, with Notes upon Ceylon, and a Journey to Madras and the Southern Provinces* : he died in a swimming-bath at Trichinopoly on April 3, 1826, from the bursting of a blood-vessel. His hymns, 57 in all, were published in the *Christian Observer* from 1811 : his poetical works in 1812 : his *Bampton Lectures, Life of Jeremy Taylor*, and volumes of sermons were also published. A kneeling statue of Heber is in St. Paul's Cathedral, Calcutta : other monuments were erected to his memory in India.

HENCKELL, TILMAN (? – ?)

Notable as a great local administrator in India in the latter part of the 18th century : specially connected with the district of Jessore, in Bengal : was appointed Judge and Magistrate of Jessore in 1781, with Mr. Richard Roche as his assistant. A man of great ability, who made the real good of the natives of his district his chief aim, not, like most others, considering only the commercial interests of the Company : carried out many reforms in Jessore : remodelled the police force : defended the people against the oppression of subordinate officers : the first to develop the Sundarbans, and to originate the plan for reclaiming them by granting plots of land to persons undertaking to bring them under cultivation. About 1782 or 1783 he established three " ganjes " in places where clearings had been made in the jungle : one was named after him—Henckellganj : made Collector of Jessore in 1786 : helped to bring about the " Permanent Settlement " of Bengal by the information he was able to give to Cornwallis when making inquiry into the land revenue of the Presidency : when the Settlement was made, 1789, Henckell had left Jessore to become Collector, Judge, and Magistrate of Rajshahi : was succeeded by Richard Roche : the rule of these two men covers the period 1781–93, when Lord Cornwallis' reforms were completed.

HENDERSON, JOHN (1780–1867)

Born 1780 : son of Robert Henderson : was a drysalter in Glasgow and an East India merchant in London. For many years he spent about £30,000 annually on religious and charitable purposes :

one of his principal aims was the promotion of mission work in India : he died May 1, 1867.

HENDERSON, PHILIP DURHAM (1840–   )

Maj-General : born Aug. 19, 1840 : son of General R. Henderson, R.E. : educated privately : joined Madras Cavalry, 1857 : Under Secretary to the Foreign Department of the Government of India, 1872 : on special duty in Kashmir, 1874 : Superintendent of operations for suppression of Thagi and Dakaiti, 1878 : Resident in Mysore, 1892 : left India, 1895 : C.S.I., 1876, for his services in attendance on H.R.H. the Prince of Wales on his visit to India, 1875–6.

HENDLEY, THOMAS HOLBEIN (1847 –   )

Educated privately and at St. Bartholomew's Hospital : joined the Indian Medical Service : was employed for 27 years under the Foreign Department in India, as Residency Surgeon in the Jaipur States : Inspr-General of Hospitals, Bengal, 1898–1903 : retired, 1903 : Chairman Executive Committee, Jaipur Exhibition, 1883 : C.I.E., 1891. Author of several works on Indian Art, *Rulers of India and Chiefs of Rajputana*, 1897 ; *Medico-Topographical Histories of Jaipur and Rajputana*, etc.

HENLEY, SAMUEL (1740–1815)

A clergyman and professor in America before the Independence : came to England : was a teacher at Harrow School, then a curate : Rector of Rendlesham in Suffolk : in 1805 was made the first Principal of the East India College at Hertford, and at Hertford Heath, and D.D. : resigned his appointment, Jan. 1815 : wrote poems : paid much attention to literary matters : was author of theological, classical and archæological treatises : F.S.A. : died Dec. 29, 1815.

HENNESSY, SIR GEORGE ROBERTSON (1837–1905)

Born April 22, 1837 : son of Maj-General John Hennessy, Bengal Army : entered the 34th Bengal N.I. 1854 : served with 93rd Highlanders in the Indian mutiny : present at Maharajganj, Alambagh and the relief of Lucknow by Sir

C. Campbell : with 75th regt. under Outram at the Alambagh : joined the Bengal Staff Corps, 1861 : served with the 15th Sikhs, 1867–90 : in the Afghan war, 1878–80 : in the march from Kandahar to Kabul and battles of Ahmad Kheyl and Urzoo : in the march from Kabul to Kandahar and battle of Kandahar : commanded 15th Sikhs at Suakin, 1885 : in several engagements : C.B., 1885 : left India, 1890 : Maj-General, 1894 : on unemployed supernumerary list, 1891 : K.C.B., 1903 : Colonel of 15th Sikhs, May, 1904 : died July 26, 1905.

HENRY, EDWARD RICHARD
(1850–   )

I.C.S. : born July 26, 1850 : entered the Indian Civil Service in Lower Bengal in 1873 : Private Secretary to the Lieutenant-Governor of Bengal, the Hon. Sir A. Eden (*q.v.*): Inspr-General of Police,Bengal, 1891–1900 : C.S.I., 1898 : resigned, 1901 : Assistant Commissioner of the Metropolitan Police, London, 1901–3 : Commissioner thereof, since 1903 : adapted the system of taking the finger and thumb impressions of criminals for the purpose of establishing their identity and proving previous convictions.

HENRY, GEORGE (1846–   )

Born Aug. 23, 1846 : educated at Woolwich : entered the R.E., 1868 : and became Maj-General, 1901 : served in the Afghan war, 1878–80 : Burmese expedition, 1885 : Chin-Lushai expedition, 1889–90 : commanding R.E.: Brevet-Lt-Colonel : Q.M.G. India : C.B., 1903.

HERBERT, WILLIAM (1718–1795)

Born Nov. 29, 1718 : educated at Hitchin : in 1748 went out to India as a purser's clerk : made a long journey in the country there : drew plans of settlements for the E. I. Co : published, in 1758, *A New Directory for the East Indies*, dedicated to the E. I. Co, styling himself hydrographer. From being a chart-engraver, he became a dealer in books, and brought out *Typographical Antiquities* : died March 18, 1795.

HERKLOTS, G.A. (? –after 1832)

Surgeon on the Madras Establishment : the *Qanoon-e-Islam*, or the customs of the Muhammadans of India, comprising a full and exact account of the various rites and ceremonies, from the moment of birth till the hour of death, by Jaffur Shurreef, (a Native of the Dekkan), was composed under the direction of Herklots and translated by him : published in 1832 : a second edition issued at Madras, 1863.

HERTZ, HENRY FELIX (1863–   )

Born May 14, 1863 : son of A. W. T. Hertz : educated at St. Xavier's College, Calcutta : passed the Higher Standard in Burmese, Shan and Kachin languages : took active part in the operations round Mandalay, 1886–7, and Shan States, 1887–90, and in operations in Kachin Hills, 1890–1900 : author of *A Practical Hand-book of the Kachin Language* : C.I.E., 1900.

HESSING, JOHN (1740–1803)

Colonel : born in Holland, 1740 : went to India, 1764 : after employment at other Native Courts, entered the service of De Boigne (*q.v.*), and was engaged in his battles, but left him after a quarrel : accompanied Madhava Sindia (*q.v.*) to Poona, 1792 : was made Commandant of the Agra Fort, 1800, where (Lord) Metcalfe (*q.v.*) met him : a brave and intrepid officer : died July 21, 1803 : his mausoleum is at Agra.

HEWETT, SIR GEORGE, BARONET
(1750–1840)

Born June 11, 1750 : son of Major Schuckburgh Hewett : educated at Wimborne and the R.M.A., Woolwich : entered the 70th regt., 1762 : served in the W. Indies ten years, and in N. America, at Charleston, again in the W. Indies : Adjutant-General in Ireland to 1799 : head of the Recruiting Department : Inspr-General of the Army of Reserve : was C. in C. in India, Oct. 1807, to Dec. 1811 : had to deal with the case of the Madras officers and the expeditions to Mauritius and Java : commanded in Ireland, 1813–16 : Baronet, 1818 : G.C.B. : General : 40 years Colonel of the 61st regt. : died March 21, 1840.

HEWETT, JOHN PRESCOTT
(1854–   )

I.C.S. : born Aug. 25, 1854 : son of Rev. John Hewett : educated at Winchester and Balliol College, Oxford : entered the Bengal Civil Service, 1877 : served in N.W.P. and Oudh, 1877–86, then in the Government Secretariat : acted as Private Secretary to the Viceroy, 1888, 1890, and was Secretary to the Government of India, Home Department, 1894–1902 : Chief Commissioner of the Central Provinces, 1902 : C.I.E., 1891 : C.S.I., 1899 : acting Member of the Supreme Council, 1904 : Member of it for Commerce, 1905.

HEWETT, SIR WILLIAM NATHAN WRIGHTE (1834–1888)

Born Aug. 12, 1834 : son of Dr. W. Hewett : entered the Navy, 1847 : saw service in the Burmese war, 1851 : in the Crimea, where he won his V.C., and was promoted to be Lieutenant : in China, and on the W. coast of Africa, during the Ashanti war, 1873–4 : K.C.B. : Naval C. in C. in the E. Indies, 1882 : commanded the naval forces engaged in the Egyptian war, 1882 : at Suakin, 1884 : sent on a mission to Abyssinia : K.C.S.I. : Vice-Admiral, 1884 : commanded the Channel Fleet, 1886–8 : died May 13, 1888.

HEXT, SIR JOHN (1842–   )

Born Oct. 14, 1842 : son of Rev. J. H. Hext : entered the R.N., 1857 : served in Ashanti war, 1878 ; Egyptian war, 1882 : and Burma : Capt., 1882 : Director of Royal Indian Marine, 1883–98 : C.I.E., 1889 : K.C.I.E., 1897 : Rear-Admiral, 1887.

HICKEY, THOMAS (1740 ?–1822)

Portrait-painter : exhibited at the Royal Academy, 1772–92 : went out to India, and said to have written *The History of Painting and Sculpture from the Earliest Accounts*, published at Calcutta, 1788 : went also to China, with Lord Macartney's embassy, 1792–4 : painted historical pictures at Seringapatam, 1799 : between 1800 and 1822 at Madras and Calcutta, where many of his pictures are in Government House : given a pension by the Madras Government.

HICKSON, SAMUEL ARTHUR EINEM (1858–   )

Born Sep. 6, 1858 : son of James Hickson : educated at Highgate : joined

the R.E., 1879 : served in the Afghan war, 1879–80 : relief of Kandahar : Suakin campaign, 1885 : Gordon relief expedition : Burma campaign, 1885–7 : capture of Mandalay : D.S.O., 1887 : commanded R.E. at Shorncliffe : Lt-Colonel.

HICKY, JAMES AUGUSTUS (? – ?)

Engaged in trade : experienced very heavy losses by sea, 1775–6, for which he was delivered to his creditors and sent to jail at Calcutta, Oct. 1776 : on coming out he established *Hicky's Bengal Gazette*, 1780 : at first dull and vulgar, it became full of personalities and scurrilous attacks, often directed at Warren Hastings and Sir E. Impey : it never attacked Sir P. Francis : its circulation through the General Post Office was stopped in Nov. 1780 : in June, 1781, Hicky was arrested and imprisoned under Impey's order at the suit of Hastings and fined : the paper continued, and Hicky was again fined : and in 1782, after his imprisonment for 19 months, the types were seized and the paper ceased : he is described as " a worthless man, but as the pioneer of the Indian Press " in Busteed's *Echoes from Old Calcutta*.

HIDAYAT ALI, KHAN BAHADUR (? –1882)

Attached at first to Rattray's Sikhs (45th N.I.) : was at the sieges of Multan, 1848–9, and at Ramnagar and Gujarat : in 1856, in Rattray's Police Battalion : in the mutiny at Dinapur assisted the civil authorities to arrest rebels : gained the first class of the Order of British India, made Sirdar Bahadur : at several engagements defeated the Shahabad rebels in 1858 : gained the first class Order of Merit : in the Sikhim expedition, 1861 : and helped with Rattray's police force to suppress disturbances at Sambalpur : with the police in 1862, helped to put down the rebellion in the Khasia and Jaintia hills : assistant to the Political Officer in the Bhutan expedition : Commandant of the Cooch Behar troops : in charge of the Coolie Corps in the Lushai expedition, 1871–2 : Khan Bahadur : A.D.C. to the C. in C. : C.I.E. : died at Dinapur, July 3, 1882 : Lt-Colonel : an officer of great soldierly qualities and capacity.

HIGHAM, SIR THOMAS (1847-   )

Born Dec. 18, 1847: son of Samuel Higham: entered the Indian P.W.D., 1867: served in the Irrigation Department: Chief Engineer and Secretary to Government, Panjab Irrigation branch, 1894: Inspr-General of Irrigation, India, 1896: Secretary to Government of India, P.W.D., 1897: retired, 1902: C.I.E., 1896: K.C.I.E., 1902.

HILL, HEADON (1857-   )

(Nom de plume of F. Grainger): son of Rev. J. Grainger: educated at Eton: after serving in the Army a few years in India and Egypt, he became a Journalist in London: began to write fiction, 1890: author of *Zamba the Detective,* 1894 ; *The Raja's Second Wife,* 1894 ; *Diversions of Kala Persad,* 1895, and many other novels.

HILL, MARY (1790-1847)

Born March 9, 1790: went to Calcutta with her husband, the Rev. Micaiah Hill, of the London Missionary Society's Mission, 1821-32: removed to Berhampur, 1824, doing mission work there for 25 years, till 1847: the oldest female missionary in the country at the time of her death: on a visit to England she originated the Walthamstow Institution for the Education of Missionaries' daughters: died Sep. 7, 1847.

HILL, SIR WILLIAM (1805-1886)

Son of the Hon. Daniel Hill, of Antigua: born 1805: joined the Madras Army, 1821: served in the first Burma expedition, 1824-5: at Rangoon, Kemendine, Donabew, etc.: and in the second Burmese war, 1852-3, at Pegu: was offered the command of the Gwalior Contingent: became Brig-General of the Hyderabad contingent, 1856: commanded the Nizam's contingent in the mutiny: engaged against Tantia Topi: Maj-General, 1861: retired, 1861: K.C.S.I., 1867: died Aug. 20, 1886.

HILL, WILLIAM (1846-1903)

Entered the Indian Army in 1866: in the Lushai expedition of 1871-2: in the Afghan war, with the 2nd Gurkhas: was at Ali Masjid and Charasia: in the march from Kabul to Kandahar, and at the battle of Kandahar: in the Manipur expedition, 1891: commanded the Kuram movable column in the Tirah campaign, 1897-8: was appointed Inspr-General of Volunteers in India, August, 1901: Maj-General: he laboured with zeal and enthusiasm to improve the utility of the Volunteer force: died in London, Sep. 7, 1903.

HILLS, SIR JOHN (1834-1902)

Maj-General: son of James Hills of Nischindipur, Bengal: born 1834: educated at Edinburgh Academy and University: entered the Bombay Engineers, 1854: in the Persian war,1856-7: at the capture of Muhamra, in Abyssinia, 1867-8: in Afghan war, 1879-80: at the defence of Kandahar: C.B.: in the Burma war commanded R.E. at headquarters: retired, 1890: K.C.B., 1900: died June 18, 1902: F.R.S., Edinburgh.

HILLS-JOHNES, SIR JAMES (1833-   )

Born Aug. 20, 1833: son of James Hills, indigo planter, of Nischindipur, in Bengal: educated at Edinburgh Academy and Military College, and Addiscombe: entered Bengal Artillery, 1853: served throughout the Indian mutiny: siege and storming of Delhi: gained the V.C. on July 9: at capture of Lucknow: dangerously wounded: Brevet-Major: A.D.C. to Lord Canning, 1859-62: Assistant-Resident, Nipal, 1862-3: served in the Abyssinian campaign, 1867-8, at the capture of Magdala: Brevet-Lt-Colonel: Lushai campaign, 1871-2: C.B.: A.A.G. Kandahar Field Force, 1878-80: accompanied Sir F. Roberts to Kabul in 1879: battle of Charasia: Military Governor of Kabul: commanded a Division N. Afghanistan Field Force, 1880: K.C.B., 1881: took the additional name of Johnes, 1883: G.C.B., 1893: General.

HIPPISLEY, SIR JOHN COXE, BARONET (1748-1825)

Born 1748: son of William Hippisley: educated at Hertford College, Oxford: called to the bar from the Inner Temple, 1771: D.C.L., 1776: employed by the British Government in Italy: the Directors of the E.I. Co., on the recommendation of Lord North, appointed him paymaster of Tanjore in 1786, but he returned home in 1789, and did_not revisit India: was

M.P. for Sudbury for 23 years, and engaged in various matters of politics and public affairs: Baronet in 1796: died May 3, 1825.

HIRST, REV. WILLIAM (? – 1769 ?)

Son of William Hirst, D.D.: educated at Peterhouse, Cambridge: F.R.S., 1755: was appointed a Navy chaplain: present at the sieges of Pondicherry and Vellore: in June, 1761, observed the transit of Venus at Madras: was Chaplain at Calcutta, 1762–4: observed an earthquake and two eclipses: reported on transit of Venus of June, 1769: went out to India, 1769, as Chaplain to Vansittart and other Commissioners of the E. I. Co.: all drowned at sea after passing the Cape outwards in Dec. 1769.

HIRST, W. A. (1870–   )

Born 1870: son of Alfred Hirst: educated at Clifton and Worcester College, Oxford: joined the Indian Educational Department, 1894: Professor of History, Lahore College, 1895–6: First Professor, Meerut College, 1896–1902: Principal of Gujarat College, Ahmedabad, 1902: author of *Survey of Ethics*, 1902.

HISLOP, STEPHEN (1817–1863)

Born Sep. 8, 1817: son of Stephen Hislop, a mason: educated at Duns, Edinburgh University, Glasgow, and in divinity under Chalmers at Edinburgh: joined the Free Church of Scotland, 1843: went out to India in 1844 as a missionary of the Free Church to Bombay: stationed at Sitabaldi, near Nagpur, in the Central Provinces: and opened a school at Nagpur: through a warning from a native friend, he was able to save the lives of the Europeans there in the mutiny of 1857. He was drowned in trying to cross a swollen river, while on tour with the Chief Commissioner, Sir R. Temple, Sep 4, 1863: he had much ability, not only for his own work, but also in languages, philology, antiquarian research, geology, natural history, botany, zoology, entomology, and conchology. Sir R. Temple edited his *Papers relating to the Aboriginal Tribes of the Central Provinces,* —the Gonds, and others.

HISLOP, SIR THOMAS, BARONET (1764–1843)

Born July 5, 1764: son of Lt-Colonel William Hislop, R.A.: educated at the R.M.A., Woolwich: entered the 39th regt. in 1778: in the siege of Gibraltar, 1779–83: served in Corsica: commanded his regt. in the W. Indies, 1796: commanded the captured Dutch colonies for six years: Lt-Governor of Trinidad, 1803–11: at the capture of Guadeloupe, 1810: appointed C. in C., Bombay, 1812: but was captured by an American ship and returned home: C. in C. at Madras, 1814–20: Baronet: K.C.B., 1814: commanded the Army of the Dekkan in the Mahratta war, 1817–8: defeated the Mahrattas under Holkar at Mahidpur, Dec. 21, 1817: was blamed for his severity in executing the Mahratta Governor of the fort at Talner: the booty acquired by the Dekkan Army was, after litigation, shared by the Army of Upper India: G.C.B., 1818: died May 3, 1843.

HOBART, VERE HENRY, BARON (1818–1875)

Governor: son of the Hon. and Rev. Augustus Edward Hobart, sixth Earl of Buckinghamshire: born Dec. 8, 1818: educated at Cheam, Surrey; Trinity College, Oxford (Scholar): was a clerk in the Board of Trade, 1840–61: went to Brazil as Secretary to a diplomatic mission: Private Secretary to the Secretary of State for the Colonies, and at the Home Office: sent to investigate the condition of the Turkish finances, and became Director-General of the Ottoman Bank: was Governor of Madras from May, 1872, until his death from typhoid at Madras on April 27, 1875. He promoted education, and the demand for a harbour and better drainage: he wrote on political questions: a collection of his *Essays and Miscellaneous Writings* was brought out by his widow.

HOBHOUSE, ARTHUR, FIRST BARON (1819–1904)

Born Nov. 10, 1819: son of Right Hon. Henry Hobhouse: educated at Eton and Balliol College, Oxford: 1st class Classics, 1840: called to the bar at Lincoln's Inn, 1845: Q.C., 1862: Charity Commissioner, 1866: Endowed Schools Commissioner, 1869: Legal Member of the

Supreme Council in India, 1872-7 : K.C.S.I., 1877 : Member of Judicial Committee of Privy Council, 1881-1901 : Member of the London School Board, 1882-4 : Alderman of the London County Council, 1889-92 : made a Peer, 1885 : C.I.E'. : died Dec. 6, 1904 : some of his addresses have been printed under the title of *The Dead Hand*.

HOCKLEY, WILLIAM BROWNE
'(1792-1860)

Born Nov. 9, 1792 : went to Haileybury, Jan. 1812 : to Bombay, May, 1813 : dismissed from his judgeship, Sep. 1821 : tried in Bombay, 1823, and acquitted : finally dismissed with a pension of £150 a year, 1824 : disappeared from view, and died Aug. 22, 1860 : wrote *Pandurang Hari* (to which Sir Bartle Frere wrote an introduction) : also the *Tales of a Zenana*, published in 1827, with a new edition, 1874, with an introductory Preface by Lord Stanley of Alderley : described as a " writer of genius."

HODGES, WILLIAM (1744-1797)

Born in 1744 : son of a smith : learnt to draw : exhibited at the Society of Artists : became a draughtsman on Captain Cook's second expedition, 1772-5 : exhibited at the Royal Academy : went to India, 1778-84, under the patronage of Warren Hastings : in 1785 he published in London, *A Comparative View of the Ancient Monuments in India :* and in 1793 his *Travels in India during the years* 1780-83, illustrated from his own pictures : he had become R.A. in 1789 : paid a visit to St. Petersburg in 1790 : retired from his profession of painting before 1795 : 21 of his pictures, the property of A. Cleveland (*q.v.*), sold in Calcutta in 1794 : he died March 6, 1797.

HODGSON, BRIAN HOUGHTON
(1800-1894)

I.C.S. : born Feb. 1, 1800 : son of Brian Hodgson, a banker : educated at Macclesfield, Richmond, and Haileybury : went to India, 1818 : after passing through the College of Fort William, Calcutta, he was Assistant Commissioner in Kumaon for 2 years, 1818-20 : Assistant Resident at Katmandu, in Nipal, 1820-9, acting Resident, 1829-31, Resident, 1833-44.

He kept Nipal quiet during the first Afghan war, but Lord Ellenborough hastily removed him from Nipal, whereupon he resigned the service. While in Nipal, Hodgson studied its literature, religion and language, discovering the literature of Northern Buddhism, collecting original MSS., Tibetan and Sanskrit, which he distributed to libraries : gathering together encyclopædic information on Nipal : he also worked at ethnology, zoology, geography. He returned to India in 1844-5 and lived at Darjeeling, to continue his researches in ethnology, and his collections : also advocated some useful practical measures, such as the enlistment of Gurkhas, hill stations for Europeans, normal colleges : finally left India in 1858 : became F.R.S. in 1877 : D.C.L. in 1889 : an honorary member of many learned Societies : received many honours by his literary attainments : universally praised by competent judges : died in London, May 23, 1894. He wrote a number of works and papers : among them *Illustrations of the Literature and Religion of the Buddhists, Essays on the Languages, Literature, and Religion of Nipal and Tibet,* etc. : *Aborigines of India: Miscellaneous Essays relating to Indian Subjects :* described by Burnouf (*q.v.*) as the founder of the true study of Buddhism.

HODGSON, JOHN STUDHOLME
(1805-1870)

Son of John Hodgson : born May, 1805 : educated at the R.M.A., Woolwich : entered the Bengal N.I. in 1822 : in the first Sikh war, 1845-6, was at Sobraon : raised the first Sikh regt. enrolled in the British service : commanded it in the second Sikh war, 1848-9 : took Ukrot : organized the Panjab Irregular Force : commanded the Derajat frontier, and in operations against the hill tribes : held the command at Peshawar after Sir Colin Campbell : Maj-General, 1861 : died in 1870.

HODSON, WILLIAM STEPHEN RAIKES (1821-1858)

Son of the Rev. George Hodson : born March 19, 1821 : educated at Rugby and Trinity College, Cambridge : B.A., 1844 : entered the E. I. Co.'s service, 1845 : was, in the second Grenadiers, present at the battles of Mudki, Firozshahr, Sobraon : Adjutant of the Guides in 1847 : Assistant

Commissioner in the Panjab after its annexation in 1849 : commanded the Guides Corps, 1852 : was removed from his appointment on charges of dishonesty, etc., from which he was exonerated on second inquiry : in the mutiny he was given a commission to raise the irregular cavalry named " Hodson's Horse " : was at the siege of Delhi : after its capture, he seized the King of Delhi at Humayun's tomb : and, on Sep. 22, arrested the princes, whom he shot when their rescue by the native mob appeared imminent : was further engaged near Cawnpur : was killed at the siege and capture of Lucknow, March 12, 1858. His character and actions have been the subject of controversy. The testimony to his brilliant qualities of bravery, energy, coolness, is universal. Lord Napier of Magdala, who, as a contemporary and present, must have known all the circumstances, was always fully convinced of his honour and integrity.

HOERNLE, AUGUSTUS RUDOLF FREDERIC (1841–)

Born Oct. 19, 1841 : son of Rev. T. C. Hoernle, C.M.S. : educated at Stuttgart and Universities of Basel and Tubingen : joined the C.M.S., 1865 : Professor in Jay Narain's College, Benares, 1870 : Principal of the Cathedral Mission College, Calcutta, 1877 : joined the Indian Educational Service, 1881 : Principal of the Calcutta Madrasa, 1881–99 : C.I.E., 1897 : author of *Comparative Grammar of the N. Indian Languages :* editor of *Chanda's Prakrit Grammar, Report on the British Collection of Central Asian Antiquities,* and numerous contributions to the *Journal of the Asiatic Society of Bengal,* the *Indian Antiquary.* etc. : editor of the Bower manuscript : studied archæology, epigraphy, and palæography.

HOGG, ADAM GEORGE FORBES (1836–)

Born June 18, 1836 : son of Colonel Charles Robert Hogg : educated at Leamington College and Wimbledon : joined the Bombay Army, 1854 : became Maj-General, 1890 : Lt-General, 1893 : served in the Persian campaign, 1857 : the Indian mutiny, 1858–9 : China war, 1860 : Abyssinian war, 1867–8 : Brevet-Major : Afghan war, 1878–9 : Brevet-Colonel : Q.M.G. of the Bombay Army, 1880–5 : Political Resident at Aden, and had command of a 2nd Class District, 1885–90 : C.B., 1886.

HOGG, SIR FREDERICK RUSSELL (1836–)

I.C.S. : born 1836 : son of Sir James Weir Hogg, *Bart.* : educated at Eton and Haileybury : entered the Indian Civil Service, 1857, and retired, 1889 : Postmaster-General, Panjab, 1863 ; Bombay, 1867 ; Bengal, 1868 : Director-General of the Post Office of India, 1880 : C.S.I., 1888 : K.C.I.E., 1888.

HOGG, SIR JAMES WEIR, BARONET (1790–1876)

Son of William Hogg : born Sep. 7, 1790 : educated at Belfast and Trinity College, Dublin (Scholar) : entered at Gray's Inn, London : said to have been called to the Irish bar : practised at the Calcutta bar, 1814–22 : Registrar of the Supreme Court, Calcutta, 1822–33, when he left India with a large fortune : M.P. for Beverley, 1835–47 ; for Honiton, 1847–57 : Director of the E.I. Co., 1839 : Chairman in 1846 and 1852, representing, practically, the E.I. Co., in Parliament : made a Baronet, 1846 : refused the Governorship of Bombay in 1853 : nominated, by the E.I. Co., one of the original members of the Council of India in Sep. 1858 : retired in 1872 : Privy Councillor : died May 27, 1876.

HOGG, SIR STUART SAUNDERS (1833–)

I.C.S. : born at Calcutta, 1833 : son of Sir James Weir Hogg, *Bart.* : educated at Eton : entered the Indian Civil Service, 1853 : served in Political Department, N.W.P., and in the Panjab during the mutiny : attached to General John Nicholson's flying column : transferred to Oudh, and then to Bengal : Commissioner of Police and Chairman of the Calcutta Municipality, 1863–77 : knighted in 1875 on the occasion of the visit of H.R.H. the Prince of Wales to Calcutta.

HOLDERNESS, THOMAS WILLIAM (1849–)

I.C.S. : born June 11, 1849 : educated at Cheltenham and University College, Oxford : entered the Indian Civil Service, 1872 : Secretary to Government of India in the Department of Revenue and

Agriculture, 1898–1901 : C.S.I., 1898 : Secretary at the India Office in the Department of Revenue, Statistics and Commerce, 1901.

HOLDICH, SIR EDWARD ALAN (1822–)

General : son of Rev. Thomas Holdich : educated privately : entered the Army, 1841 : served in Satlaj campaign, 1845–6 : at the battles of Mudki, Firozshahr, Aliwal and Sobraon.: Boer war, 1848, Bronplatz : Kafir war, 1852 : Burmese war, 1853 : at Donabew : Indian mutiny, 1857–8 : commanded Cork and Dublin districts, 1871–6 : K.C.B., 1875 : retired.

HOLDICH, SIR THOMAS HUNGERFORD (1843–)

Born Feb. 13, 1843 : son of Rev. Thomas Peach Holdich : educated at Godolphin Grammar School and Woolwich : joined the Royal Engineers, 1862, and became Brevet-Colonel, 1891 : served in the Bhutan expedition, 1865 : Abyssinian war, 1867 : Afghan war, 1878–80 : and Tirah expedition, 1897–8 : on special duty with the Afghan Boundary Commission, 1884–6 : Superintendent of Frontier Surveys, India, 1892–8 : Pamir Commission, 1895 : Perso-Beluch Commission, 1896 : Argentine-Chili Boundary, 1902–3 : C.B. and C.I.E., 1894 : K.C.I.E., 1897 : K.C.M.G., 1902 : Gold Medallist, Royal Geographical Society, 1887 : author of *The Indian Borderland*, 1901, and various papers on military surveying and geographical subjects.

HOLLAND, TREVENEN JAMES (1836–)

Born 1836 : son of Col. J. Holland : educated at Cheltenham and St. John's College, Oxford : entered the Army, 1852 : served in the Crimea : A.Q.M.G. in Sir Henry Havelock's force in the Persian campaign and in the Indian mutiny and China, 1857–60 : D.Q.M.G. in Abyssinian campaign, 1867–8 : C.B. and Brevet-Major and Lt-Colonel.

HOLLOWAY, WILLIAM (1828–1893)

I.C.S. : son of William Holloway : born 1828 : educated at Haileybury, 1846–7 : one of the most distinguished pupils of Empson (*q.v.*): went to Madras in 1848 : took great interest in Education ;

in 1853 wrote a masterly pamphlet, *Notes on Madras Judicial Administration :* was Secretary to the Commission of Inquiry into the system of judicature in the Madras Presidency : Judge of Tellicherry, 1861 : in 1863 made a High Court Judge, Madras : retired, 1877 : died Aug. 11, 1893 : translated the first volume of *Savigny's System of Modern Roman Law :* C.S.I., 1875.

HOLMES, SIR GEORGE (1764–1816)

Ensign in the Bombay European Regt., 1780 : transferred to the 10th N.I. : in the Mahratta war, 1780–1 : besieged at Tellicherry, 1781–2, by Hyder Ali's troops : at the capture of Cannanore, 1783 : in the Mysore war, 1791–2, and in Malabar : at Seringapatam, 1799 : commanded at the reduction of forts in Canara, and the relief of Montana : in Egypt under Baird, 1801–2 : at the siege of Baroda, 1802 : in the Mahratta war, 1803–5 : commanded a subsidiary force in Gujarat some years to 1815 : retired as Maj-General : K.C.B., 1815 : for nearly 36 years a regimental officer : died Oct. 29, 1816.

HOLMES, JOHN (1808–1878)

Maj-General : entered the Army in 1825 : in the Kolapur campaign, 1827 : in Upper Sind and Afghanistan, 1842 : with England's force in the return from Kandahar, actions in the Pishin Valley, Kojak pass, and retreat to the Indus : volunteered for service in the Crimea : in the mutiny, in the Central India campaign, capture of Awa, assault of Kotah, and pursuit of Tantia Topi : C.B. : Maj-General, 1862 : died Nov. 19, 1878.

HOLWELL, JOHN ZEPHANIAH (1711–1798)

Governor : son of Zephaniah Holwell, timber merchant : born Sep. 17, 1711 : educated at Richmond, and Iselmond, near Rotterdam : studied surgery at Guy's Hospital : to Calcutta in 1732 as surgeon's mate on an Indiaman : employed as surgeon in the . Company's ships to the Patna factory : at the Dacca factory : at Calcutta, 1736–48 : alderman : principal surgeon : twice Mayor : perpetual *zamindar* of the 24 *Parganas* in 1751 : Seventh in the Council : when the fort at Calcutta was attacked by the Nawab Suraj-ud-daula on June 18, 1756, and the Governor Drake and others retreated down the river on 19th, Holwell was called on to take charge of the defence. He was one of the 23 survivors of the 146 persons in the Black Hole on the night of June 20–1 : was sent to Murshidabad and kept in irons there : set at liberty, July 17 : joined the ships at Fulta : went to England in Feb. 1757 : returned to Bengal : in the Council : succeeded Clive as temporary Governor of Bengal from Jan. 28, 1760, until Vansittart assumed office on July 27, 1760. In 1761 he and others were dismissed by the Court of Directors for signing a despatch remonstrating against Vansittart's appointment, but he had retired in Sep. 1760 : in retirement, he wrote on historical, philosophical and social science subjects : also his *Narrative of the Black Hole, Interesting Historical Events relative to the Province of Bengal and the Empire of Hindustan, 1765–71 ; Indian Tracts,* 1758, 1774, and other works, showing his knowledge of the religion and customs of the Hindus. He erected, at the N.E. corner of Dalhousie Square, Calcutta, a monument to those who died in the Black Hole : this monument was removed in 1819 : re-erected in 1902 : Holwell died at Pinner, Nov. 5, 1798.

HOME, SIR ANTHONY DICKSON
(1823–   )

Born 1823 : entered the Army Medical Department, 1848, and retired, 1886 : served in the Crimea, 1854–5 : Indian mutiny, 1857–8 : gained the V.C. on Sep. 26, 1857, at the first relief of Lucknow : China, 1860 : New Zealand, 1863–5 : Ashanti, 1873–4 : P.M.O. : Cyprus, 1878–9 : P.M.O. : Surgeon-General to the Forces in India, 1881–5 : K.C.B., 1874.

HOME, DUNCAN CHARLES
(1828–1857)

Son of Maj-General Richard Home, Bengal Army : born 1828 : educated at Elizabeth College, Guernsey, at Wimbledon and Addiscombe, 1845–6 : after the course at Chatham, went to Bengal, 1848 : at the siege of Multan, and at Gujarat : employed on the Ganges Canal construction, and at Madhupur in charge of a division of the Bari Doab Canal : commanded several companies of Muzbi Sikhs at the siege of Delhi : had charge of

a breaching battery : ordered to blow in the Kashmir gate on Sep. 14, 1857 : escaped being wounded : gained the V.C. : blew in the gate of the Palace : was field engineer to Greathed's column : was at Bulandshahr : killed by accident at the blowing up of the Malaghar fort, Oct. 1, 1857.

HOME, FREDERIC JERVIS
(1839–   )

Born Oct. 22, 1839 : son of Maj-General Richard Home, Bengal Army : educated at Kensington Grammar School and Addiscombe : joined the Bengal Engineers, 1858, and landed in India, 1860 : in the Irrigation Branch of P.W.D., 1861–94 : Inspr-General of Irrigation and Deputy Secretary, P.W.D., India, 1890–4 : C.S.I., 1892 : Colonel.

HOME, ROBERT (1764 ?–1834)

Artist : son of Robert Boyne Home : from 1770 exhibited portraits at the Royal Academy and at Dublin : went to Madras in 1790 : with Lord Cornwallis' Army before Seringapatam, 1791–2 : went to Calcutta, 1792 : at Lucknow he was chief painter to the King of Oudh for some years, and made a large fortune : he returned to Calcutta in 1797 and died there about 1834 : was Secretary to the Asiatic Society of Bengal, 1802, and painted for it. Indian pictures by Home were exhibited at the Academy : he published *Select Views in Mysore, the Country of Tippoo Sultan,* and *A Description of Seringapatam, the Capital of Tippoo Sultan,* illustrated : he painted in India pictures of Marquis Wellesley and Colonel Arthur Wellesley, Bishop Heber and Dr. Carey.

HONNER, SIR ROBERT WILLIAM
(1800 ?–1869 ?)

Son of a military officer : born about 1800 : entered the Army, 1821 : nearly 20 years a subaltern, 17 years Adjutant of his regt. : as Brevet-Major commanded the 4th Bombay N.I. at 27 years' service : served in Mahi Kanta against the Bhils, 1823 : with the Field Force in 1824 in the Meena Hills, and against various predatory tribes : with the Bombay column in the Panjab campaign, 1848–9 : at the capture of Multan : Brevet-Lt-Colonel : Brigadier in the Persian war, 1856-7 : commanded the advance Division at the capture of Reshire and surrender of Bushire : at Khushab : C.B. : commanded at the island of Karrak for some months : commanded the Nasirabad Brigade in the mutiny, in the pursuit of Tantia Topi and other chief rebels : Maj-General, 1861 : Resident at Aden, 1862-3 : General of the Sind Division from 1863 : K.C.B. : left India, 1866, after about 45 years' continuous service there : died about 1869.

HOOKER, SIR JOSEPH DALTON
(1817-   )

Born June 30, 1817 : son of Sir William Jackson Hooker : educated at High School and University of Glasgow : joined R.N. Medical Department : served as Surgeon and Naturalist in H.M.S. *Erebus* in Antarctic expedition under Sir James Ross, 1839-43 : brought out a series of volumes on the botany of the Antarctic regions : visited the Himalayas on the North of Sikhim, and was badly treated, being kept a prisoner, by the Sikhim authorities : also visited the Khasia hills as naturalist, 1847-51 : made botanical collections of great value : visited Syria and Palestine, 1860 : Morocco, 1871 : the Rocky Mountains, 1877 : served as Assistant Director and Director of Kew Gardens, 1855-85 : C.B., 1869 : K.C.S.I., 1877 : G.C.S.I., 1897 : author of *Himalayan Journals, The Rhododendrons of the Sikhim Himalaya, The Flora of British India*, and many other scientific works.

HOOLE, ELIJAH (1798-1872)

Son of Holland Hoole, a shoemaker : born 1798 : educated at Manchester : went to India as a Wesleyan Methodist missionary, 1820 : made a Member of the Committee for revising the Tamil version of the Bible : published a number of Tamil translations, including portions of the Bible : left India, 1828 : became Superintendent of Schools in Ireland, and a general Secretary of the Wesleyan Missionary Society : wrote *A Personal Narrative of a Mission to the South of India*, 1820-8, and missionary works : and contributed to literary journals : died June 17, 1872.

HOPE, SIR THEODORE CRACROFT
(1831-   )

I.C.S : born 1831: son of James Hope, M.D. : educated at Rugby and Haileybury : entered the Bombay Civil Service, 1853 : Educational Inspector, 1855-8 : called to the bar from Lincoln's Inn, 1866 : Member of the Governor-General's Legislative Council, 1875-80 : Provisional Member of Council, Bombay, 1880 : Secretary to the Government of India in the Finance and Commerce Department, 1881-2 : Officiating Finance Minister, 1882 : Member of the Supreme Council, in charge of Public Works, 1882-7 : author of *Church and State in India*, 1892, and various educational and architectural works : C.I.E., 1882 : K.C.S.I., 1886.

HOPE, SIR WILLIAM, BARONET
(1819-1898)

Born Jan. 12, 1819 : son of Sir John Hope, *Bart* : entered the Army, 1835 : with 71st Highlanders in the Crimea : Lt-Colonel, 1857 : served in Central India, 1858 : C.B., 1859 : Colonel, 1862 : commanded the 71st regt. in the frontier operations under Sir N. Chamberlain, 1863 : Maj-General, 1868 : commanded at Stirling, 1873 : retired as General, 1881 : K.C.B. : succeeded his brother as Baronet, 1892 : died Sep. 5, 1898.

HOPKINS, EDWARD WASHBURN
(1857-   )

Born Sep. 8, 1857 : son of Lewis S. Hopkins, M.D. : educated at Columbia University, New York : at Leipzig and Berlin Universities, 1878-81 : engaged in tuition in Columbia, 1881-5 : Professor of Sanskrit, first at Bryn Mawr College, 1885-95 : and later at Yale, 1895, in succession to Professor Whitney (*q.v.*) : A.B., 1878 : A.M. and Ph.D. of Leipzig, 1881 : LL.D., Columbia, 1902 : Member of the German Oriental Society : Secretary of the American Oriental Society since 1897 : has written *The Four Castes*, 1881 : *Manu*, in Trübner's Oriental Series, 1884 : *Religions of India*, 1895 : *The Great Epic of India*, 1900 : *India, Old and New*, 1901 : engaged in University teaching since 1881 : spent a year in India, 1896-7.

HOPKINSON, HENRY (1820–1899)

Son of B. Hopkinson : entered the Indian Army, 1837 : Political Officer in 1847–8 in the expedition against the Koladyne hill tribes : in the Panjab campaign, 1848–9, at Chilianwala and Gujarat : in the Burmese war, 1852–3, at the capture of Martaban : Commissioner in British Burma : in Bhutan expedition, 1864–6 : at capture of Dewangiri : Commissioner of Assam and A.G.G. on the N.E. frontier : C.S.I., 1874 : General in 1889 : died Dec. 22, 1899.

HORSBURGH, JAMES (1762–1836)

Captain : born Sep. 23, 1762, of humble parents : went to sea at 16 : went to Calcutta after 1780 : served as mate in ships trading thence from 1784 : wrecked, through error in a chart : while engaged on voyages to China, and from Bombay, he collected information and studied navigation : made several charts of Eastern waters : in command of a ship, 1798, made voyages between England, India and China, and kept barometrical observations : published more charts and his *Directions for Sailing to and from the East Indies*, etc., 1809–11, a work noted for its accuracy and utility, still the basis of the *East India Directory* : F.R.S. in 1806 : hydrographer to the E.I. Co. in 1810 : his works were regarded as invaluable safeguards to life and property in the Eastern regions : contributed scientific writings to Magazines : died May 14, 1836.

HORSFORD, SIR ALFRED HASTINGS (1818–1885)

Son of General George Horsford : born 1818 : educated at the R.M.C., Sandhurst : joined the Rifle Brigade, 1833, and rose to be General, 1877 : served in the Kafir wars, 1847–8, 1852–3 : in the Crimea, in all the battles : C.B. : to India in the mutiny : commanded the 3rd Battalion at Cawnpur, and the advance to Lucknow, a Brigade at the siege of Lucknow, in the operations in Oudh, and on the Nipal frontier, 1858 : held staff appointments in England and at Malta : commanded the S.E. District, 1872 : Military Secretary at the Horse Guards, 1874–80 : represented Great Britain at the Brussels Conference on the usages of war, 1874 : K.C.B., 1860 : G.C.B., 1875 : died Sep. 13, 1885.

HORSFORD, SIR JOHN (1751–1817)

Born May 13, 1751 : son of John Horsford : educated at Merchant Taylors' and St. John's College, Oxford : Fellow, 1768–71 : enlisted under the name of " John Rover " in the E.I. Co.'s Artillery, 1772 : his identity was discovered in 1778, and he received a Commission as Lieutenant Fireworker : rose to be Maj-General, 1811 : served in the Bengal Artillery under Cornwallis in the Mysore war, 1790–1, at Bangalore, Arikera and Seringapatam : commanded the Artillery under Lord Lake, 1803–5, at Alighar, Delhi, Agra, Deeg, Bhartpur : at the siege of Komanur, 1807 : commanded the Bengal Artillery, 1808–17 : and at the siege of Hatras, 1817 : K.C.B., 1817 : died at Cawnpur, April 20, 1817, a few days after his return from Hatras : never had a day's leave in his 45 years' service.

HOUSTOUN, SIR ROBERT (1780–1862)

Entered the Indian Army at an early age : to Bengal in 1795 : served for 25 years, taking part in all Lord Lake's actions, including 12 battles and 9 sieges : General, 1854 : was 10 years Governor of the Military College, Addiscombe : on retirement, received a present of plate worth £500 from the E.I. Co. : General and K.C.B. : died April 5, 1862.

HOWARD, SIR CHARLES (? –   )

Son of A. Howard : educated privately : served with Rattray's Sikhs in the Indian mutiny, and in various posts in the Civil and Military Police, Bengal : thanked by Government for arresting and obtaining conviction of the chief of the Wahabi sect, 1858 : Assistant Commissioner of Police, London, 1890–1902 : C.B., 1894 : K.C.B., 1902.

HOWARD, JOHN ELIOT (1807–1883)

Son of Luke Howard : born Dec. 11, 1807 : connected, all his life, with his father's chemical manufactory : and with cinchona and quinine in every aspect : in 1869 he published *The Quinology of the East Indian Plantations*, which was officially acknowledged : F.R.S. in 1874 : died Nov. 22, 1883.

HOWDEN, JOHN FRANCIS CARADOC, FIRST BARON (1762–1839)

Born Aug. 12, 1762 : son of the Right Rev. John Cradock, Archbishop of Dublin : entered the Cavalry : 1777, Lt-Colonel of the 13th regt., 1789 : served in the W. Indies, 1790 and 1793–5 : Maj-General, 1798 : was Q.M.G. in Ireland under Lord Cornwallis during the rebellion of 1798 : was M.P. in the Irish Parliament, 1785–1900 : on the Staff of Sir Ralph Abercromby in the Mediterranean and Egypt : Knight of the Bath, 1803 : C. in C. at Madras, 1804–7, and Lt-General : during his tenure of office the mutiny at Vellore occurred, 1806 : which he attributed to efforts to restore the Muhammadan cause, while it was also ascribed to orders issued about uniform : recalled in 1807 : commanded the forces in Portugal, 1808 : Governor of Gibraltar, 1809 : C. in C. at the Cape, 1811–14 : General, 1812 : made Lord Howden in the Irish Peerage, 1819 : changed his name to Caradoc, 1820 : made an English Peer, 1831 : died July 6, 1839.

HOWELL, MORTIMER SLOPER (1841–)

I.C.S. : born Feb. 3, 1841 : son of John Warren Howell : educated at Christ's Hospital and Corpus Christi College, Oxford : Fellow of the Universities of Calcutta and Allahabad : LL.D., Edinburgh : entered the Indian Civil Service, 1862, and retired in 1896, as Judicial Commissioner of Oudh : author of *Grammar of the Classical Arabic Languages* : C.I.E., 1886.

HOWLETT, SIR ARTHUR (1819–1904)

General : entered the Indian Army in 1838 : joined the 27th Madras N.I. in 1839 : saw much service in the Indian mutiny at Cawnpur, Lucknow, Tulsipur, Bansi, in Bundelkund, in the Sagar Field Division : Madras Staff Corps, 1861 : C.B., 1873 : Maj-General, 1881 : General, 1889 : K.C.B., 1896 : died at Upper Norwood, July 31, 1904.

HUDLESTON, WILLIAM (? –1894)

I.C.S. : educated at Haileybury, 1843–44 : went out to Madras, 1845 : became Secretary to Government, Madras, in the Revenue Department, 1870 : and Chief Secretary, 1875 : Member of Council, temporary, in 1873, and from June, 1877, to June, 1882 : acted as Governor of Madras, May 24, to Nov. 5, 1881 : died Oct. 25, 1894.

HUDSON, SIR JOHN (1833–1893)

Born June 30, 1833 : son of Captain John Hudson, R.N. : educated at the Royal Naval School, New Cross : entered the 64th regt. in 1853 : Adjutant in the Persian war, 1856–7 : present in all the engagements : in the mutiny was Adjutant with his regt. in Havelock's force, and in his actions from Fatehpur, July 12, to Bithur, Aug. 16 : in the advance to Lucknow, the defence of Cawnpur, the defeat of the Gwalior contingent : and in subsequent engagements : in the Abyssinian campaign, 1867–8 : commanded the 28th Panjab N.I. in the Afghan war of 1878–80 : was in Sir F. Roberts' advance on Kabul, 1879 : in the operations round Kabul, defended the Lataband post : commanded in the Khyber in 1881 : C.B. : commanded the Indian Contingent in the Soudan, 1885 : K.C.B. : Maj-General, 1887 : commanded a Division, 1888–92 : Lt-General : C. in C., Bombay in 1893 : died at Poona, June 9, 1893, instantaneously, from a fall from his horse.

HUDSON, SIR WILLIAM BRERETON (1843–)

An indigo planter in Bihar : commanded the Bihar Light Horse : Member of the Indian Public Service Commission, 1886–7 : K.C.I.E., 1893.

HUGHES, CHARLES FREDERICK (1844–)

Born 1844 : son of W. S. P. Hughes : educated at Cheltenham and Addiscombe : entered the Bombay Army, 1861, and became Colonel, 1889 : served against Fudhli Arabs, 1865–6 : in the Afghan war, 1878–80 : present at Ahmad Kheyl, Brevet-Major : Burmese war, 1886–7 : Commissary-General of Bombay, Madras and Bengal Armies in succession, 1890–5 : C.B., 1897.

HUGHES, SIR EDWARD (1720 ?–1794)

Born about 1720 : entered the Navy, 1734–5 ; was at Porto Bello, 1739 : Cartagena, 1741 : Toulon, 1743–4 : America and the W. Indies : Captain, 1747–8 : at Louisburg, 1758 : Quebec, 1759 : Naval

P

C. in C. in the E. Indies, 1773–7 : Rear Admiral and K.C.B., 1778 : again held the command in the E. Indies, 1779–83 : destroyed Hyder Ali's ships at Mangalore, 1780 : helped to take Negapatam, 1781 : took Trincomalee, Jan. 1782 : between that month and June, 1783, Hughes was engaged five times between Madras and Trincomalee with the French fleet under Admiral M. de Suffrein, without any decisive results : Hughes returned to England and had no further command : Admiral of the Blue in 1793 : made a large fortune in India : died Feb. 17, 1794.

HUGHES, THOMAS ELLIOTT
(1830–1886)

Maj-General : born 1830 : educated near Exeter : entered the Royal Artillery, 1849 : in frontier warfare under Sir Colin Campbell, 1852 : against the Bozdars, 1857 : in the Mahsud-Waziri expedition, 1860 : commanded a mountain battery in the N.W. frontier expedition, 1863, at the storming of Laloo and capture of Umbeyla : Brevet-Major : in the Black Mountain expedition under Wilde, 1868 : Lt-Colonel, 1875 : Maj-General, 1885 : for four years A.A.G. at headquarters in England : D.A.G. for R.A. in India, 1882 : Director-General of Ordnance in India, 1884 : Military Member of the Supreme Council, Jan. to May, 1886 : died May 24, 1886, at Simla : C.B.

HUGHES, SIR ROBERT JOHN
(1821–1904)

Born May 5, 1822 : son of Lt. Robert Hughes : entered the Army, 1841 : served in the Crimea : Colonel in 1878 : in the Afghan war, 1878–80 : commanded a Brigade of the Kandahar column : in the Ghazni Field Force, under Sir Donald Stewart in the Kandahar to Kabul march : at Shabjui, Ahmad Kheyl, and Urzoo, near Ghazni : C.B. : commanded the Presidency District, Calcutta, 1880–3 : retired in 1883, as Maj-General : K.C.B., 1894 : died April 19, 1904.

HUGHES, SIR WILLIAM TEMPLER
(1822–1897)

Born April 2, 1822 : son of Rev. Henry Arkwright Hughes : entered the Bengal Army, 1842 : in the Satlaj and Panjab campaigns and in the battles, 1845–6 and 1848–9 : in the Peshawar frontier expeditions, 1851–2 : commanded the 1st Panjab Cavalry on the Yusufzai frontier, 1852, and through the mutiny, 1857–8 : at Multan, in Rohilkund, Oudh campaign, in the Trans-Gogra column, etc. : died April 4, 1897 : C.B., 1869 : General, 1884 : K.C.B., 1891.

HULTZSCH, EUGEN (1857–   )

Born March 29, 1857, at Dresden : studied classical and Oriental philology, especially Sanskrit, at Bonn and Leipzig : Ph.D. : Privat-docent for Oriental studies at the University of Vienna : was introduced by G. Bühler to the study of Indian |epigraphy : travelled for six months in N. India and Kashmir, 1884–5, and collected valuable MSS. and inscriptions : appointed, 1887, Epigraphist of the Archæological Survey for the Presidency of Madras : and examiner in Sanskrit at Madras University. In 1903, resigned his post as Epigraphist, and has since been Professor of Sanskrit at the University of Halle : is Secretary to the Deutsche Morgenländische Gesellschaft : Corresponding Member of the Batavian Society of Arts and Sciences, of the Royal Society of Science at Gottingen, etc. : has written : *Prolegomena zu Vasantaraja Sakuna*, 1879 : an edition of Baudhajanas' *Lawbook*, 1884 : *South-Indian Inscriptions* (Tamil and Sanskrit) : Reports on Sanskrit MSS. in South India, 1893, etc. : many of his treatises on Indian epigraphy have appeared in the *Indian Antiquary*.

HUMBERSTON, THOMAS FREDERIC MACKENZIE (1753 ?–1783)

Son of Major William Mackenzie : born about 1753 : entered the 1st Dragoon Guards in 1771 : took his mother's name of Humberston : Captain, 1778 : at the repulse of a French attack on Jersey, 1779 : commanded the 100th regt. in 1781 under General Medows at the Cape, and sailed for Madras : landed at Calicut in Feb. 1782, captured forts of Hyder Ali, and made a treaty with Travancore : retreated before Tippoo, but repulsed him at Paniane in Nov. 1782 : commanded the 78th : joined the Army under General Matthews in Malabar : went to Bombay to complain against the General : on his way back, his ship was captured by the

Mahratta fleet, and he died of his wounds at Gheria, April 30, 1783.

HUME, ALLAN OCTAVIAN (1829–)

I.C.S.: born 1829: son of Joseph Hume, M.P. (*q.v.*): educated at Haileybury: entered the Bengal Civil Service, 1849: served in the N.W.P.: Commissioner of Inland Customs: Secretary to Government of India in the Revenue and Agriculture Department: Member of Board of Revenue, N.W.P., 1879: in the mutiny was Magistrate of Etawah, N.W.P.: rendered good service against the mutineers, with whom he was several times engaged: C.B., 1860: retired in 1882: took a prominent part in organizing and supporting the National Congress, and in criticizing the actions of the Government of India, for years: author of several works on ornithology.

HUME, JOSEPH (1777–1855)

The Radical politician: born Jan. 22, 1777: son of a shipmaster: educated at Montrose: studied medicine at Aberdeen, Edinburgh, London: M.C.S., Edinburgh, 1796: in 1797 entered the marine medical service of the E. I. Co.: in 1799 joined the land service: studied the native languages: employed in political work, as army surgeon, as interpreter, postmaster and paymaster in the Mahratta war under Lord Lake: left India in 1807 and the service, with £40,000: was M.P. for various constituencies, 1812–55: attended to Indian affairs, but failed in his efforts to become a Director of the E. I. Co.: advocated freedom of trade with India: became a leader of the Radical party for 30 years: his parliamentary career forms part of English politics: Vice-President, Society of Arts: F.R.S.: and Fellow of the Royal Asiatic Society: died Feb. 20, 1855.

HUME, SIR ROBERT (1828–)

Born 1828: entered the Army, 1847, and became Lt-General, 1883: served in the Crimea, 1854–5: twice severely wounded: Bhutan expedition, 1865: commanded Sagar District, 1874–7: Allahabad Division, 1879–80: S. Afghanistan Field Force, 1880–1: Quetta Division, 1881: and Lahore Division, 1881–4: K.C.B., 1887: G.C.B., 1902.

HUNTER, ROBERT (1823–1897)

Born Sep. 3, 1823: son of John M. Hunter: educated at Aberdeen University: was licensed as Precentor of the Free Church of Scotland: in 1846 joined Stephen Hislop (*q.v.*) at the Free Church mission at Nagpur: performed educational and missionary work for nine years: returned home in 1855: made discoveries in geology: devoted himself to literary and evangelistic work: edited Lloyd's *Encyclopædic Dictionary*, 1889: LL.D.: Fellow of learned Societies: published a *History of India*, 1863: and *History of the Missions of the Free Church of Scotland in India and Africa*, 1873: died Feb. 25, 1897.

HUNTER, WILLIAM (1755–1812)

Born 1755: educated at the Marischal College, and the University, Aberdeen: went to India, 1781, in the E. I. Co.'s medical service: in 1782, driven to Burma by a storm, he wrote an *Account of Pegu*, 1785: Surgeon at the Agra Residency: on the Resident's expedition from Agra to Ujain, 1792–3: Surgeon to the marines, 1794–1806: Secretary to the Asiatic Society of Bengal for 11 years, between 1798 and 1811: examiner in Persian and Hindustani at the College of Fort William: Secretary of the College: M.D.: Superintendent Surgeon of Java, 1811–2: contributed scientific articles to *Asiatic Researches*: published a Hindustani-English Dictionary, 1808: and a Collection of Proverbs in Persian and Hindustani: revised the Hindustani New Testament: wrote on medical subjects: died in Java, Dec. 1812.

HUNTER, SIR WILLIAM GUYER (1828–1902)

Educated at King's College, London, and Aberdeen University: entered the Bombay Medical Department, 1850: was in the second Burmese war: and in the mutiny: Principal and Professor of Medicine of the Grant Medical College, Bombay: Surgeon-General: Vice-Chancellor of the Bombay University: M.P. for Central Hackney, 1885–92: K.C.M.G.: died March 14, 1902.

HUNTER, SIR WILLIAM WILSON (1840–1900)

I.C.S.: born July 15, 1840: son of Andrew Galloway Hunter: educated at

Glasgow Academy and University : studied at Paris and Bonn : went out to Lower Bengal in 1862 : published the *Annals of Rural Bengal,* 1868 ; *A Comparative Dictionary of the Non-Aryan Languages of India and High Asia,* 1868 ; *Orissa,* 1872 : was chosen by Lord Mayo to organize a statistical survey of the Indian Empire, in 1869 : made Director-General of Statistics in 1871 : wrote the *Life of Lord Mayo,* 1875 : published *The Statistical Account of Bengal,* 20 volumes, 1875–7 : and, in all, 128 volumes of local Gazetteers : from which he prepared *The Imperial Gazetteer of India,* 9 volumes, in 1881 ; 14 in 1885–7 : wrote a *Brief History of the Indian Peoples,* 1883 : his article on "India" was re-issued in 1895 as *The Indian Empire, its Peoples, History and Products :* for 6 years Additional Member of the Governor-General's Legislative Council, 1881–7 : President of the Education Commission, 1882–3 : Member of the Indian Finance Commission, 1886 : Vice-Chancellor of the Calcutta University, 1886 : retired in 1887 : settled near Oxford : wrote weekly articles in *The Times* on Indian affairs : brought out a number of biographies in the "Rulers of India" series : himself writing those of Lords Dalhousie and Mayo : wrote also *Bombay,* 1885–90, the Life of Brian H. Hodgson (*q.v.*) : an introduction to *Bengal MS. Records,* 1894 ; *The Old Missionary ; The Thackerays in India :* he had projected a comprehensive work on the History of India, but reduced it to a work on the growth of British dominion : the first volume was published in 1899, the second after his death : C.I.E., 1878 : C.S.I., 1884 : K.C.S.I., 1887 : LL.D. of Glasgow and Cambridge : M.A. of Oxford, by decree of Convocation : Vice-President of the Royal Asiatic Society, and member of learned Societies : he adopted the system of transliteration of vernacular names and words called after him : through his writings, and his picturesque style, India has been made better known to England : died Feb. 7, 1900.

HUTCHINS, SIR PHILIP PERCIVAL
(1838–   )

Born Jan. 28, 1838 : son of William Hutchins : educated at Merchant Taylors' and Haileybury : entered the Madras Civil Service, 1857 : called to the bar from the Inner Temple, 1875 : held several judicial appointments, and was Judge of the High Court, Madras, 1883–6 : Member of Council, Madras, 1886–8 : Member of the Supreme Council, 1888–93 : Judicial Secretary, at the India Office, 1893 : Member of the Council of India, 1898 : C.S.I., 1888 : K.C.S.I., 1891.

HUTCHINSON, HENRY DOVETON
(1847–   )

Born Sep. 13, 1847 : son of T. Cayley Hutchinson, M.D. : joined the Indian Army : served in the Sikhim campaign, 1887–8 : relief of Chitral, 1895 : Tirah campaign, 1897–8 : commanded troops in Chitral after the British occupation : Director of Military Education in India, 1896–1901 : Assistant Military Secretary for Indian affairs, 1902 : author of *Military Sketching made Easy, Field Fortifications, The Story of Waterloo, The Story of 1812, The Story of Corunna, The Campaign in Tirah :* C.S.I., 1902.

HUTHWAITE, SIR EDWARD
(1794–1873)

Born 1794 : son of William Huthwaite, a draper, Alderman and Mayor : educated at the R.M.A., Woolwich : joined the E. I. Co.'s Bengal Artillery, 1810 : became Lt-General, 1868 : was in the Nipal war, 1815–16 : in Oudh, 1817 : in the Mahratta war, 1817–18 : in Cachar in 1824, to repel the Burmese invasion : at the capture of Bhartpur, 1825–6 : Brig-Major of Artillery, 1834 : held various important artillery commands : in the first Sikh war of 1845–6, at Firozshahr and Sobraon : C.B. : in the Panjab campaign, 1848–9 : at the Chenab, Chilianwala, and Gujarat, the surrender of the Sikhs, and pursuit of the Afghans to the Khyber : commanded a Brigade at Ludiana, and at Meerut : retired, 1854 : in 1860 transferred to the Royal Artillery : K.C.B. in 1869 : died at Naini Tal, April 4, 1873.

HUTT, SIR GEORGE (1809–1889)

Son of Richard Hutt : born 1809 : entered the Artillery in Bombay, 1826 : served in Sind and Afghanistan, 1839–44 : at Miani and Hyderabad : C.B. : commanded the Artillery in the Persian war, 1857 : did good service in Sind in the mutiny, anticipated and stopped a rising of rebels at Karachi : retired, 1858 : became Registrar and Secretary to the Commissioners of Chelsea Hospital, 1865–87: K.C.B., 1886: died Oct. 27, 1889.

HUTTON, JAMES (1818–1893)

Entered the E. I. Co.'s military service: left the Army after a few years: edited newspapers in India—the *Delhi Gazetteer*, the *Bengal Harkaru*, the *Englishman*, the *Madras Times*: returned to England: became joint, and, later, sole editor of the *Leader* newspaper: wrote *The Aryan and the Cossack*, *A Hundred Years Ago*, and other works: as a journalist and author he advocated the strengthening of the defences on the N.W. frontier: died March, 1893.

HUYSHE, ALFRED (1811–1880)

General: educated at Addiscombe: joined the Bengal Artillery in 1827: served in the Gwalior campaign of 1843: in the Panjab campaign of 1848–9: commanded a battery at Sadulapur, Chilianwala and Gujarat: Brevet-Major: after the annexation of the Panjab, was in several expeditions on the Peshawar frontier: Inspr-General of Artillery in Bengal for some years: retired as General in 1877: C.B.: died March 3, 1880.

HYDE, JOHN (1737?–1796)

Called to the bar from Lincoln's Inn: appointed a Puisne Judge of the Supreme Court, Calcutta, on its establishment, 1774: was one of the magistrates who, on May 6, 1775, committed Nuncomar (*q.v.*) to trial for forgery: was one of the Judges who tried Nuncomar. After more than 21 years' uninterrupted service as Judge, he died July 8, 1796, and was buried in Calcutta: a Government notification and lengthy epitaph testified to his virtues and the esteem in which he was held.

HYDERABAD, SIR ASAF JAH, NIZAM-UL-MULK OF (1866–)

Born Aug. 18, 1866: succeeded his father in 1869, when a Regency was established: he was invested with full power by Lord Ripon, when Viceroy and Governor-General, and assumed charge of his Government, Feb. 5, 1884: has more than once offered to the Government of India the services of his troops, and in 1887 offered a present of 60 lakhs for

frontier defence: he is the Premier Prince of the Indian Empire: G.C.S.I., 1884: G.C.B., 1903.

HYDERABAD, NIZAM ALI, NIZAM OF (? –1803)

Son of Kamaruddin, the first Nizam-ul-Mulk: dethroned and imprisoned his brother, the Nizam Salabat Jang, 1761, and became Nizam: devastated the Carnatic, 1765, but was driven back: the Madras Government made a treaty at Hyderabad, Nov. 12, 1766, through Brig-General Caillaud with Nizam Ali for mutual assistance, and the grant of territory for a subsidiary force. Nizam Ali treacherously deserted the English, and with Hyder Ali invaded the Carnatic, but, by another treaty of Feb. 26, 1768, renounced Hyder and regained the English alliance on certain terms: in 1788 he made over the Guntur Sircar to the English on certain payments: in the war with Tippoo, Nizam Ali made a treaty of offensive and defensive alliance with Cornwallis, 1790, and gained territory at the end of the war, 1792: the Mahrattas revived a claim against the Nizam for arrears of *chout*, and war resulted in the defeat of the Nizam and his army at Kurdla in March, 1795: he had to cede territory and pay three crores of rupees: his eldest son, Ali Jah, rebelled, but was captured by the Nizam's French troops: another treaty of Sep. 1, 1798, was made between the British and the Nizam: Nazim Ali agreed to disband his French battalions: in the second war with Tippoo, 1799, the Nizam's army co-operated with the British troops, and the Nizam received territories by the partition treaty of Mysore: these territories were ceded to the British for the payment of the British subsidiary force at Hyderabad: Nizam Ali died, 1803.

HYDER ALI (1717 or 1722–1782)

Son of Fatah Muhammad, a military commander, and *jagirdar* of Budikota in Mysore: born in 1717 or 1722: first known as Naik: employed by the Mysore Raja as a volunteer in the siege of Devanhalli in 1749: next against Arcot, and in the subsequent struggle for the Nizamat: by 1755 he was military governor of Dindigul, then a Mysore stronghold: by 1759 he commanded the Mysore Raja's Army, and received the title of Fatah

Bahadur. He gradually obtained the control of affairs and assumed the sovereign power, deposing the Hindu Raja, Chikka Krishnaraj Wodiar, captured Bednore and conquered Malabar in 1766. Allied with the Nizam, he invaded the Carnatic in 1767, and, on the Nizam's retirement, prosecuted the war alone : in 1769 he was within five miles of Madras, when the Madras Governor concluded an offensive and defensive treaty with him, and the Bombay Government made another treaty with him in 1770. He was more than once reduced to great straits by the Mahrattas, who several times invaded the Mysore dominions, but the English declined to assist him. When the French and English declared war in 1778, and the English took Mahé, Hyder, who had become the most formidable power in the Peninsula, received the missionary, Schwartz, as an envoy from the Governor of Madras, but, negotiations failing, invaded the Madras territory in 1780, defeated Colonel Baillie at Perambakam, took Arcot and other places : he was defeated at Porto Novo on July 1, 1781, by Sir Eyre Coote, who relieved Vellore, and met him in the indecisive action at Arni on June 2, 1782 : he died near Chitore, Dec. 7, 1782. Hyder was a born soldier, a first-rate horseman, heedless of danger, full of energy and resource, severe, cruel, cold, indifferent to religion, shrewd in business — though quite uneducated—with a retentive memory : he inspired great terror : with better support from the French, he might have driven the English out of Southern India.

IBBETSON, SIR DENZIL CHARLES JELF (1847–   )

I.C.S. : born Aug. 30, 1847 : son of Rev. Denzil John Holt Ibbetson : educated at St. Peter's College, Adelaide, South Australia, and St. John's College, Cambridge : entered the Indian Civil Service, 1870 : posted to the Panjab : after serving in various posts, including Superintendent of Census, Director of Public Instruction and Financial Commissioner, was appointed Secretary to the Government of India in the Revenue and Agriculture Department : Chief Commissioner of the Central Provinces : Member of the Supreme Council since 1902 : author of

Handbook of Panjab Ethnography, Gazetteer of the Panjab, etc., etc. : K.C.S.I., 1903 : Officiating Lieutenant-Governor of the Panjab 1905.

IDAR, SIR PRATAPSINGHJI, MAHARAJA OF (1845–   )

Son of Maharaja Takhtsinghji, of the Ahmadnagar branch of the Idar family (Maharaja of Jodhpur, 1841–73) : born at Jodhpur, 1845 : brought up, 1866–78, under his brother-in-law, H.H. the Maharaja Ramsinghji of Jaipur : Prime Minister of Jodhpur, 1878–95 : on the death of his elder brother H.H. the Maharaja Jaswantsinghji of Jodhpur, he was appointed Regent and continued so until, in 1898, the present Chief of Jodhpur was installed : was early in 1902 selected by right and merit to succeed to the vacant *gadi* of Idar : installed Feb. 12, 1902 : appointed, in 1878, Member of the Indian Government's Mission to Kabul : made C.S.I : in 1885, K.C.S.I : in 1887, attended Queen Victoria's Jubilee : A.D.C. to H.R.H. the Prince of Wales (now H.M. the King-Emperor Edward VII) : Hon. Lt-Colonel in the British Army : helped, in 1889, to found the Imperial Service Troops : formed the Jodhpur Lancers : in 1897, attended Queen Victoria's Diamond Jubilee : made G.C.S.I : decorated by Her Majesty in person : LL.D. of Cambridge : in 1897–8, joined the Mohmand expedition, with an escort of the Jodhpur Lancers for General Elles, and the Tirah campaign as A.D.C. to Gen. Sir W. Lockhart : wounded in the latter campaign : C.B. and Colonel : joined the China expedition in 1900–01 with the Jodhpur Lancers : in 1902 attended the Coronation of H.M. the King-Emperor : commanded the Indian Imperial Service Force contingent : K.C.B. for China service : Maj-General and A.D.C. to H.M. : Hon. Commandant of the Indian Imperial Cadet Corps.

IDDESLEIGH, STAFFORD HENRY NORTHCOTE, FIRST EARL OF (1818–1887)

Born Oct. 27, 1818 : son of Henry Stafford Northcote : educated at Brighton, Eton, Balliol College, Oxford : Scholar : called to the bar in 1847 from the Inner Temple : was Private Secretary to Mr. Gladstone : Legal Secretary to the Board of Trade : succeeded as Baronet in 1851 :

was Commissioner to inquire into the civil establishments of the Crown, 1853-4 : became M.P. for Dudley, 1855 ; for Stamford, 1858-66 ; for N. Devon, 1866-85, when he was made a Peer. From 1855 his life was devoted to English politics on the Conservative side. He was connected with India, as Secretary of State, from March 9, 1867, to Dec. 10, 1868 : he had to deal with the questions of the Abyssinian expedition, the Orissa famine, Afghanistan, Mysore and financial decentralizatioñ : in later years, 1878-9, he spoke in favour of the later portion of the second Afghan war : died Jan. 11, 1887.

IKBAL-UD-DAULA MUHSIN ALI KHAN, NAWAB (1808-1887)

Grandson of Nawab Saadat Ali Khan of Oudh : born March 15, 1808 : went to England, 1838, to claim the throne of Oudh. Failing to obtain any satisfaction of his claim, he retired to Bagdad, to pass his life in sanctity. He was much liked and respected by the English in England, Constantinople and Bagdad : was made G.C.S.I. in 1882 : died at Bagdad, Dec. 21, 1887.

ILBERT, SIR COURTENAY PEREGRINE (1841-   )

Born June 12,1841: son of Rev. Peregrine Arthur Ilbert : educated at Marlborough and Balliol College, Oxford : Scholar : Hertford, Ireland, Craven and Eldon Scholar : called to the bar from Lincoln's Inn, 1869 : Legal Member of the Supreme Council, 1882-6 : in that capacity had charge, on behalf of the Government of India, of the " Ilbert Bill," which raised so much opposition : Vice-Chancellor of Calcutta University, 1885-6 : Parliamentary Assistant Counsel and Counsel to the Treasury, 1886-1901 : Clerk to the House of Commons, 1901 : author of *The Government of India*, 1898 ; *Legislative Methods and Forms*, 1901, etc : C.I.E., 1882 : C.S.I. 1885 : K.C.S.I. 1895.

IMADUDDIN, REV. D.D. (1830 ?-1900)

Son of Maulvi Sirazuddin, a Muhammadan theologian : descended from the Persian royal house and the Muhammadan Saint Kutb Jamal : born about 1830, at Panipat, near which town his family had large estates : educated at Agra Government College : became a Sufi or Muham-

madan mystic : travelled about, all over India, preaching Islam : was present on behalf of Islam against Christianity in the " Agra Controversy " : subsequently became a teacher in the Government Normal School, Lahore : baptized at Umritsar, April 29, 1866 : ordained Deacon, 1868 ; Priest, 1872, by the Bishop of Calcutta : made D.D. by the Archbishop of Canterbury, 1884 : invited to attend the "World's Parliament on Religions" in Chicago, to which he sent a paper : wrote a. number of Hindustani books, the principal being a *Life of Christ*, Lectures on Christian evidence, commentaries in Urdu on St. Matthew's Gospel and the Acts of the Apostles : died at Umritsar, Aug. 28, 1900.

IMPEY, SIR ELIJAH (1732-1809)

Son of Elijah Impey, merchant : born June 13, 1732 : educated at Westminster (with Warren Hastings) : King's Scholar : and at Trinity College, Cambridge: Scholar: Fellow : called to the bar from Lincoln's Inn, 1756 : in 1772, counsel for the E. I. Co. before the House of Commons : under the Regulating Act of 1773 was appointed the first Chief Justice of the new Supreme Court at Calcutta, i.e. Chief Justice of Bengal : knighted : to India in 1774 : presided in 1775 at the trial of Nuncomar (*q.v.*) for forgery, and, after the jury's verdict of guilty, passed sentence of death : and Nuncomer was hanged, Aug.5 : Impey's conduct on the trial has been impugned as having been actuated in behalf of Warren Hastings : there is no proof of collusion, and Impey has been pronounced by high authority to have behaved with absolute fairness : in 1777, he decided in favour of Hastings on the question of his alleged resignation of the Governor-General-ship : he sentenced (Sir) P. Francis (*q.v.*) to pay Rs. 50,000 damages in the Grand case : he was in 1780 made President of the new *Sadr Diwani Adalat* : there is no proof that he received extra salary for the office : at the instigation of Francis, through Burke in England, he was recalled in 1783, to answer six charges of illegality, which Sir Gilbert Elliot, afterwards Lord Minto (*q.v.*), brought forward in 1787 : Impey defended himself at the bar of the House of Commons and the impeachment was abandoned : M.P. for New Romney, 1790-6 : died Oct. 1, 1809. Owing to Burke (prompted by Francis) and to

Mill's history (followed by Thornton and Macaulay,) Impey was long regarded as " one of the ogres of Indian history, a traditional monster of iniquity." His Life, by his son, E. B. Impey, 1846, did something to rehabilitate his name, and, later, high authorities have done more : the fact that the virulent attempts to impeach him failed is most significant.

IMPEY, EUGENE CLUTTERBUCK
(1830–1904) ·

Colonel : born 1830 : son of Edward Impey, B.C.S., and grandson of Sir Elijah Impey : educated privately and at Wadham College, Oxford : joined the 5th Bengal N.I., 1851 : A.A.G.G. Rajputana, 1856 : served through the mutiny : at the siege of Kotah, 1858 : Political Agent at Ulwar, 1858 : Military Secretary to the Viceroy, Lord Lawrence, 1863–4 : Political Agent, Jodhpur, Oodeypur, and Gwalior : Resident in Nipal : retired, 1878 : C.I.E., 1879 : died Nov. 1904.

INDORE, JASWANT RAO HOLKAR MAHARAJA OF (1775 ?–1811)

An illegitimate son of Maharaja Tukaji Rao : on the murder of his half-brother, Kashi Rao, he asserted himself, raised a large army and fought with Sindia, defeating both him and the Peshwa, Baji Rao, in 1802 at Poona, which he took : he declined to join the other Mahratta chiefs against the British, but took his own line, as a freebooter, in Rajputana, and, after compelling Colonel Monson to make a disastrous retreat in July, 1804, was defeated by Lord Lake in 1804–5, and compelled to make peace and surrender territory. He became insane in 1806, and his wife, Tulsi Bai, became regent. He died Oct. 20, 1811.

INDORE, MALHAR RAO HOLKAR, MARAHAJA OF (? –1766)

The first and greatest Prince of the Holkar family : came to notice first as an officer in the service of the Peshwa, Baji Rao, about 1724 : was an early Mahratta adventurer in Northern India, and obtained the Indore district in *jagir* about 1733 : was most active after Baji Rao's death in 1740, until his own death, May 19, 1766.

INDORE, MALHAR RAO HOLKAR, MAHARAJA OF (1805–1833)

Son of Jaswant Rao Holkar (*q.v.*) : succeeded as an infant : adopted by Jaswant's widow, Tulsi Bai, who became regent : the Army became predominant in the State, and in 1817 took up arms against the British : Tulsi Bai, on being suspected of British proclivities, was murdered : the army was routed by Malcolm at Mahidpur, Dec. 21, 1817 : terms were made, Malhar Rao being treated as an independent prince : he died in 1833.

INDORE, TAKOJI RAO HOLKAR I, MAHARAJA OF (? –1797)

Was made Commander in Chief of Holkar's force in 1767 by Ahlia Bai (*q.v.*), the daughter-in-law of the late Maharaja Malhar Rao Holkar I, and served her with devoted fidelity till her death in 1795. He was defeated by De Boigne (*q.v.*), Sindia's general, 1794, and ruled from 1795 until he died Aug. 15, 1797.

INDORE, SIR TAKOJI RAO HOLKAR II, MAHARAJA OF (1832–1886)

Was nominated successor by the Regent mother of the late Maharaja and recognized in 1843 by the British Government: invested with authority, 1852 : the thoroughness of his loyalty during the mutiny of 1857 was doubted, but, after the defeat of his army, which attacked the British Residency at Indore, his prudent and circumspect behaviour was held to entitle him to confidence : and he was made a G.C.S.I. in 1861. He developed the resources of his State, which he administered with skill and attention to business : giving much time to military and police matters : he received the Prince of Wales with great ceremony when H.R.H. visited India in 1875–6 : was made a General in 1877 : he died June 17, 1886.

INGLIS, SIR JOHN EARDLEY WILMOT (1814–1862)

Born Nov. 15, 1814 : son of the Very Rev. John Inglis, D.D., Bishop of Nova Scotia : joined the 32nd regt. in 1833, in Canada, 1837 : in the second Sikh war of 1848–9 was at the sieges and capture of Multan, at Cheniote and Gujarat : at Lucknow in the mutiny, was second in command at Chinhut, June 30, 1857 :

and, on Sir Henry Lawrence being mortally wounded on July 2, succeeded to the command of the garrison until the relief by Sir Henry Havelock on Sep. 25 : was Maj-General and K.C.B. " for his enduring fortitude and persevering gallantry in the defence of the Residency of Lucknow for 87 days against an overwhelming force ʹof the enemy " : in the subsequent action against Tantia Topi in Dec. 1857 : commanded the troops in the Ionian Islands, 1860 : died at Homburg, Sep. 27, 1862.

INGLIS, HON. JULIA SELINA, LADY
(1833–1904)

Daughter of the first Lord Chelmsford : married to Sir John E. W. Inglis, K.C.B. (*q.v.*), who defended the Residency at Lucknow in the mutiny : in recognition of his services she received a pension. She herself went through the siege of 87 days and published *The Siege of Lucknow, a Diary*, 1892 : she was shipwrecked off Ceylon on her way home : died on Feb. 3, 1904.

INNES, JAMES JOHN MACLEOD
(1830–)

Lt- General : born Feb. 5, 1830 : son of Surgeon James Innes, H.E.I.C.S. : educated at Edinburgh University and Addiscombe : joined Bengal Engineers, 1848 : P.W.D. 1851 : served through the mutiny : in the defence of Lucknow Residency, 1857 : at siege of Lucknow, 1858, and actions of Chanda, Amirpur and Sultanpur : severely wounded : gained the V.C. for gallantry in capturing, and holding singlehanded, a gun which was being trained on an advancing column : Brevet-Major : Panjab Irrigation works : Accountant-General, P.W.D. India, 1870-80 : Inspr-General of Military Works, India : retired as General, 1886 : author of *Lucknow and Oudh in the Mutiny*, *The Sepoy Revolt*, 1897 ; *Sir Henry Lawrence* (Rulers of India series), 1898 ; *Life of Sir James Browne, K.C.S.I., R.E.*

INNES, SIR JOHN HARRY KER]
(1820–)

Born 1820 : educated at University College, London : entered the Army Medical Department, 1842, and became Surgeon General, 1872 : served in the Crimea, 1855 : Indian mutiny, 1857 : Oudh, 1858–9 : British Sanitary Com-

missioner during Franco-Prussian war, 1870–1 : P.M.O., India, 1876–80 : K.C.B., 1887 : F.R.S., 1887.

IRVINE, WILLIAM (1840–)

I.C.S. : born July 5, 1840 : son of William Irvine : educated privately and at King's College, London : went out to the N.W.P., India, 1864 : rose to be Magistrate-Collector : retired, 1888 : wrote the *Rent Digest* (1868) on agricultural tenures and rent law procedure : has also written articles on the Bangash Nawabs of Farrukhabad, 1878 : since 1888, has had in preparation a History of the Moguls in the 18th century (portions published in the *J.A.S.B.*) : has written on " India in the 18th Century " in the *Indian Antiquary*, the *Asiatic Quarterly Review*, and the *Indian Magazine* : also the chapters on Muhammadan India (1000–1750. A.D.) in the new edition of the *Imperial Gazetteer* : is engaged ,for the Government of India, on a translation, with notes, etc., of the *Memoirs of Niccolo Manucci, Venetian* (1656 *to* 1717 *A.D.*), 4 vols. in the Indian Text series : since 1896, Member of the Council of the Royal Asiatic Society.

IVES, EDWARD (? – ?)

Surgeon on Admiral Watson's ship, the *Kent*, which was sent out to the relief of the British Settlements in India against Dupleix, 1754 : wrote an account of the voyage from England to India, and of the subsequent naval and military operations, 1755–7. In this book, published in 1773, he describes the people of India, their customs, etc., and the vegetation of the country : calls himself " Surgeon of His Majesty's Hospital in the East Indies."

ITISAM-UD-DIN (? – ?)

Native of Nadia district, Bengal : son of Shekh Tajuddin : in the service of Mir Jafar, Nawab of Bengal : on the accession of Mir Kasim attached himself to Major Yorke, whom he accompanied on a campaign against Asad Zaman Khan, Raja of Birbhum : fought for the English against Mir Kasim : employed by the English in negotiations with the Mahratta Government : entered the service of General Carnac, 1765–6 : soon changed to that of Shah Alam : about 1765–7 accompanied Capt. Swinton to Europe as *munshi*, on a mission to deliver Shah Alam's letter to King George III : he was the first educated native of Bengal to visit England and describe his journey : returned after nearly three years' absence to India : wrote the *Shigurf-nama*, or "wonder-book," about 1784, describing his travels : a popular work in India : he was careful and painstaking in his observations.

IYENGAR, S. SRINIVASA RAGHAVA, DIWAN BAHADUR (? -1903)

Inspr-General of Registration, Madras : one of the ablest Hindu officials in the Presidency : wrote *Forty Years of Progress in Madras*, 1893, as a reply to assertions that British rule had impoverished the country : Diwan of Baroda, 1896–9, when he rejoined his appointment under the Madras Government : represented Madras on the Police Commission : an authority on revenue matters and economic questions in S. India : died Dec. 11, 1903.

JACK, ALEXANDER (1805–1857)

Son of the Rev. William Jack : born Oct. 10, 1805 : educated at King's College, Aberdeen : joined the 30th Bengal N.I., 1824 : in the Satlaj campaign was at Aliwal, and was Brigadier of the force sent against Kangra : commanded his battalion at Chilianwala and Gujarat : C.B. : Colonel, 1854 : Brig-General at Cawnpur, in 1857, under Sir Hugh Wheeler : when the entrenchment was evacuated, by arrangement with the Nana Sahib, Jack was, with many others, shot in the boats at the *ghat* : died June 27, 1857.

JACKSON, ABRAHAM VALENTINE WILLIAMS (1862–   )

Born Feb. 9, 1862, in New York City U.S.A. : son of David S. Jackson, merchant : educated at New York : studied at Columbia University, N.Y., and at Halle in Germany : L.H.D. : Ph.D. : and LL.D. : Professor of Indo-Iranian languages at Columbia University : his special field of research as a scholar is the sarced literature of the Zoroastrian religion : visited India and Ceylon in 1901 : travelled in Persia and Central Asia in 1903 for purposes of archæological research, especially of Zoroastrianism : collated part of the Persian inscription of King Darius on the Behistun rock : Director of the American

Oriental Society : Hon. Member of the Society for making Researches into Zoroastrian Religion, Bombay, (1899) : twice delegated by the U.S. Government to International Congresses of Orientalists : his chief works are *A Hymn of Zoroaster*, 1888 ; *Avesta Grammar in Comparison with Sanskrit*, 1892 ; *Avesta Reader*, 1893 ; *Zoroaster*, 1898 ; *Die iranische Religion*, 1900 ; *Persia, Past and Present* ; *Transcaspian and Turkistan*, 1905 ; besides articles contributed to Journals and Encyclopædias.

JACKSON, SIR CHARLES ROBERT MITCHELL (? - ?)

Barrister-at-law : Temporary Member of the Supreme Council from Sep. 19, 1851 : Puisne Judge of the Supreme Court, Calcutta, 1855–62 : and of the High Court, Calcutta, 1862–63 : officiated as Chief Justice of the Supreme Court, 1859 : also was Member of the Governor-General's Legislative Council : retired, April, 1863.

JACKSON, SIR LOUIS STEUART (1824–1890)

I.C.S. : son of Lt-Colonel Henry George Jackson, R.A. : educated at Royal School, Enniskillen and Trinity College, Dublin, and Haileybury : went to Bengal in the Civil Service, 1843 : employed under the Government in the Straits Settlements, 1847–50 : Judge of Rajshahi : Judge of the *Sadr* Court, 1862 : and Puisne Judge of the High Court, 1862–80 : officiated as Chief Justice, 1878 : Fellow of the Calcutta University : C.I.E., 1878 : knighted : died April 9, 1890 : F.R.G.S : F.Z.S.

JACOB, SIR GEORGE LE GRAND (1805–1881)

Son of John Jacob : born April 24, 1805 : educated at Elizabeth College, Guersey, and in France privately : joined the 2nd Bombay N.I. in 1821 : on the Staff at Addiscombe, 1831–4 : was in political charge in Kattiawar, 1839–43 : at the assault on Munsantosh in the S. Mahratta country : Political Agent in Sawantwari, 1845–51 : in Cutch, 1851 : commanded the native light battalion in the Persian war, 1856–7 : in the mutiny was sent to Kolapur, and disarmed the mutinous 27th Bombay N.I. : and behaved with great vigour : appointed special Political Commissioner of the South Mahratta country, 1858, and to Goa : C.B., 1859 : retired as Maj-General, 1861 : K.C.S.I., 1869 : he transcribed the Asoka inscriptions at Girnar, Kattiawar, and wrote many papers on the history, etc., of Western India : published in 1871, *Western India before and during the Mutiny*: died Jan. 27, 1881.

JACOB, JOHN (1812–1858)

Son of the Rev. Stephen Long Jacob : born Jan. 11, 1812 : cousin of Sir George Le Grand Jacob (*q.v.*) : educated at Addiscombe : entered the E. I. Co.'s Bombay Artillery, 1828 : in the first Afghan war, 1838, was in Sind with Sir John Keane's Army of the Indus, and in 1839 commanded Artillery in the Cutchi expedition : in 1841 was chosen by Outram (*q.v.*), for command of the Sind Irregular Horse, and political charge of E. Cutchi : led his regt. at Miani, Feb. 17, 1843, Shahdadpur, Oomercote, with great gallantry : Political Superintendent of Upper Sind, 1847 : C.B., 1850 : constantly engaged with the hill tribes : Jacobabad called after him, in 1851 : negotiated a treaty, in 1854, with the Khan of Kelat : officiating Commissioner in Sind, 1856 : Colonel and A.D.C. to Queen Victoria, 1857 : commanded the cavalry in the Persian war, 1857 : was left as Brig-General, in command of the whole force towards the end : raised " Jacob's Rifles," two regiments of infantry, armed according to his own inventions : died of brain fever on Dec. 5, 1858 : besides his great soldierly qualities, and able views on military matters, he was an advanced and active administrator, full of energy and ideas, imprinting his name and character strongly on Sind, its officers and inhabitants : he wrote largely on Sind and military questions, and in defence of Outram.

JACOB, SIR SAMUEL SWINTON (1841–)

Born Jan. 14, 1841 : son of Col. W. Jacob, Bombay Artillery : educated at Cheam and Addiscombe : entered the Bombay Artillery, 1858, and Indian Staff Corps, 1862 : Colonel, 1888 : served in P.W.D., Rajputana, and in Aden with Field Force against Arabs, 1865–6 : services lent to the Jaipur State, 1867 :

Chief Engineer, Jaipur State : C.I.E., 1890 : K.C.I.E., 1902 : author of *Jaipur Portfolios of Architectural Details, Jaipur Enamels* (with Surgeon-Colonel Hendley) : M.R.I.B.A : A.I.C.E.

JACOB, WILLIAM STEPHEN (1813–1862)

Son of the Rev. Stephen Long Jacob, and brother of John Jacob (*q.v.*) : born Nov. 19, 1813 : educated at Addiscombe and Chatham : joined the Bombay Engineers, 1831 : established a private observatory at Poona, 1842 : left the service as Captain in 1845, to devote himself to science : was Director of the Madras Observatory, 1848–59 : and for three years at Poona Observatory, of which he procured the establishment : he was F.R.A.S., 1849 : made a number of scientific astronomical observations, and wrote papers on meteorology and astronomy : died at Poona, Aug. 16, 1862.

JACOBI, HERMANN GEORG (1850–)

Born Feb. 11, 1850, at Cologne : son of a merchant : educated at Cologne, Berlin and Bonn : visited India, 1873–4 : Professor of Sanskrit at the Universities of Münster, 1876 ; Kiel, 1885 ; Bonn, 1889 : has written the following works :—
Kalpasutra, 1879 ; *Ayaranga Sutta*, 1882 ; *Jaina Sutras*, " Sacred Books of the East," Vols. xxii, xlv ; *Ausgewählte Erzählungen in Maharastri* ; *Das Ramayana* : *Mahabharata* (statement of contents) ; *The Computation of Hindu Dates* ; *Dhvanyaloka* (translation) ; and the following (in the Press), *Upamitibhava prapandra Katha* ; *Samaraichcha Kaha*, and *Samaraditya Samksepa* : contributed to the *Zeitschrift der Deutschen Morgenländischen Gesellschaft, Indian Antiquary*, etc.

JACQUEMONT, VICTOR (1801–1832)

A distinguished French botanist : born at Paris, Aug. 8, 1801 : son of a writer on psychological speculations : toured in Hayti and the United States, and, having early evinced a strong attachment to natural history, was, on his return, appointed to a post in the Royal Museum of Natural History at Paris. By Baron Cuvier's influence he was selected for a scientific mission for 7 years to the East, as its travelling naturalist, to investigate the Natural History of India in all its branches, and collect materials for the museum : went to London, 1828 : reached Pondicherry in April, 1829 : then to Calcutta : through Upper India to Simla in 1830 : Ladak : the frontiers of Ladak and Chinese Tartary : Kashmir : down to Poona : saw Ranj'it Singh, Shah Shuja, the Begam Samru, travelling for 3½ years ; encountered difficulties and privations in his arduous labours, the fruits of which have greatly enriched the science of Natural History : fell ill at Tanna, in Salsette : died at Bombay, Dec. 7, 1832, after a month's agony. His collections were transmitted to Paris, described by Decaisne, and the result published in 6 quarto volumes. His letters, written in India to his family, give a most vivid account of the botany of the N.W. Himalayas and particularly of the social condition of India in those days. His remains were exhumed from the Sonapur cemetery at Bombay on Feb. 26, 1881, and taken to France in the *Laclocheterie* man-of-war : a wreath on his coffin bore the legend " Voici le fleur que Victor Jaçquemont a introduisit dans Bombay de la Cachemire, et qui porte son nom Jacquemontia."

JAIPUR, MAHARAJA SAWAI SIR MADHO SINGH BAHADUR, OF (1861–   )

Born 1861 : head of the Kuchhwaha clan of Rajputs : succeeded to the Raj, 1880 : organized a Transport Corps, 1890 : a wise and capable administrator of his State and takes an interest in affairs of the British Empire : a liberal contributor to the Famine Fund for India, Transvaal War Fund, King Edward Hospital Fund : guest of the nation at the Coronation of H.M. King Edward VII, 1902 : G.C.S.I. : G.C.I.E. : G.C.V.O.

JAIPUR, MAHARAJA DHIRAJ SAWAI SIR RAM SING, OF (1833–1880)

A Rajput of the solar line, claiming descent from Rama : son of the Maharaja Jai Sing, on whose death he succeeded, in 1835 : during his minority a Council of Regency of five nobles, under the superintendence of the Political Agent, administered the State : Ram Sing did good service during the mutiny, placing his whole force at the disposal of the British Government : received a grant of the *pargana* of Kot-Kassim : also showed liberality in the Rajputana famine of 1868 : G.C.S.I., 1866 : Member of the Governor-General's Legislative Council, 1869–75 : Member of the mixed Commission which tried Malhar Rao, the Gaekwar of Baroda, in 1875 : made enlightened efforts to promote the welfare of his subjects, supporting schools and medical charities : died Sep. 18, 1880.

JAMES, SIR HENRY EVAN MURCHISON (1846–   )

I.C.S. : born 1846 : son of William Edward James : educated at Durham school : entered the Bombay Civil Service, 1865 : retired in 1900 : Postmaster-General, Bombay, 1875, and Bengal, 1880 : Director-General of the Post Office of India, 1886 : Commissioner in Sind, 1891–1900 : C.S.I., 1898 : K.C.I.E., 1901 : author of *The Long White Mountain ; or Travels in Manchuria*, 1889.

JAMES, RIGHT REV. JOHN THOMAS (1786–1828)

Bishop of Calcutta : son of Dr. Thomas James, Headmaster of Rugby : born Jan. 23, 1786 : educated at Rugby, Charterhouse, Christ Church, Oxford : Student and Tutor : made a long tour through Europe : studied painting in Italy : ordained, and, Vicar in Bedfordshire, 1816 : was made Bishop of Calcutta in 1827 : D.D. : reached Calcutta in Jan. 1828 : was taken ill in June, and died, Aug. 22, 1828, on a voyage to China for his health.

JAMES, LIONEL (1871–   )

Born 1871 : son of Lt-Colonel L.H.S. James, R.A : educated at Cranleigh : Reuter's Special Correspondent, in the Chitral campaign, 1894–5 ; Mohmand, Malakand and Tirah campaigns, 1897–8 ; Soudan, 1898 : *Times* Special Correspondent in S. Africa, 1899–1901 : author of *With the Chitral Relief Force*, 1895 ; *Indian Frontier War*, 1897–8.

JAMES, SIR WILLIAM, BARONET (1721–1783)

Born of poor parents in 1721, and went early to sea : to the E. Indies, 1747 : entered the naval service of the E. I. Co., and distinguished himself against the pirate Angria : made Commander of the Co.'s marine force, 1751 : captured Savandrug, the pirates' stronghold, 1753 : and Gheria, on Feb. 13, 1756, with Admiral

Watson and Colonel Clive : took to Bengal the news of the French declaration of war, and helped Clive, enabling him to take Chandernagore, March, 1757 : returned to England in 1759, enriched with prize money : joined the Board of Directors of the E. I. Co. : Deputy-Chairman in 1778 and 1781 . Chairman in 1779: Baronet, 1778 : was also M.P. for West Looe, and for 15 years Deputy-Master of the Trinity House : died Dec. 16, 1783 : his widow erected a tower on Shooter's Hill to his memory.

JAMESON, SIR G. J. (? -1871)

Of the Bombay Infantry, which he entered, 1820 : Lt-General, 1871 : entered the Bombay Audit Department, and, in 1848, became Deputy Military Auditor-General, and Military Auditor-General at Bombay, 1853 : in 1859, was President of the Military Finance Commission at Calcutta : retired, 1860 : Auditor at the India Office, 1861–71, and Parliamentary Auditor of Indian accounts : K.C.S.I. : died Oct. 24, 1871.

JAMESON, WILLIAM (1815–1882)

Born 1815 : educated at Edinburgh High School and University : went into the Bengal medical service : Curator of the museum of the Asiatic Society of Bengal : Superintendent in 1842 of the Saharanpur garden : he vigorously promoted the cultivation of tea in India, obtained plants and distributed them, thus originating the commencement of the present tea-planting industry : retired in 1875 : died March 18, 1882.

JANG BAHADUR, KOONWAR RANA-JI, MAHARAJA SIR (1816–1877)

Prime Minister of Nipal : nephew of Mataber Sing, who was a high functionary in Bengal : he acquiesced in the murder of his uncle at the instigation of the Queen-Regent in 1834, and was made by her C. in C. in the Nipalese Army. When the new Prime Minister was murdered by his enemies, Jang Bahadur seized and put the ringleaders to death, and made himself Prime Minister, 1846 : he then turned out the Queen and the imbecile King, raised the heir-apparent to the throne, and thus established himself without a rival. Having waded to power through

bloodshed and cruelty, Jang Bahadur developed into an enlightened ruler : it was his policy to keep on good terms with the English : he visited England, arriving in May, 1850, was the "lion of the London season": was knighted and made G.C.B. : he brought a force of Gurkhas to our aid, rendering valuable assistance in Oudh, in the mutiny of 1857 : G.C.S.I., 1873 : died at Purthur-ghatta on Feb. 25, 1877.

JARDINE, SIR JOHN (1844–)

I.C.S. : born 1844 : son of William Jardine : educated at Christ's College, Cambridge : Chancellor's Gold Medal for English verse : entered the Bombay Civil Service, 1864 : Political Officer in Kattiawar, 1871 : Secretary for the trial of the Gaekwar of Baroda, 1875 : Judicial Commissioner of Burma, 1878 : Chief Secretary to Bombay Government, 1885 : Fellow of Bombay University, 1872, and Vice-Chancellor, 1895 : President of the Asiatic Society, Bombay : Judge of Bombay High Court, 1885 : acted as Chief Justice, 1895 : retired, 1897.

JARRETT, HANSON CHAMBERS TAYLOR (1836–1891)

Lt-Colonel : in the Bengal Staff corps : gained the V.C. in the mutiny, for daring bravery at the village of Baroun Oct. 14, 1858, when with four men he charged, under heavy fire, up a narrow street, to a building occupied by about seventy sepoys : Deputy Conservator of Forests in the Central Provinces : died at Sagar on April 11, 1891.

JARRETT, HENRY SULLIVAN (1839–)

Colonel : born June 17, 1839 : son of Thomas Jarrett : educated at Prior Park, Bath : joined the Indian Army, 1856 : served in the mutiny, 1857–8 ; in the Mahsud-Waziri expedition, 1860 ; the second Yusufzai expedition, as A.D.C. to Sir Neville Chamberlain : Secretary and Member, Board of Examiners, Fort William, Calcutta, and Assistant Secretary in the Legislative department of the Government of India, 1870–94 : C.I.E., 1895 : author of *History of the Caliphs*, *Institutes of the Emperor Akbar*, etc.

JÄSCHKE, HEINRICH AUGUST
(1817-1883)

Moravian missionary : born at Herrnhut, May 17, 1817 : trained at the Moravian College at Niesky, in Silesia, 1842-56 : superintended the mission at Kyelang, in Lahoul, in the W. Himalayas, 1856-68 : translated the New Testament into Tibetan and collected materials for a Tibetan Dictionary : wrote a Tibetan grammar and other works : greatly assisted by Dr. A. C. Burnell (*q.v.*), brought out his Tibetan-German dictionary, 1873, and a revised edition of it for the India Office, which greatly advanced the knowledge of Tibetan : died Sep. 29, 1883.

JEE, JOSEPH (1821-1899)

Deputy Surgeon-General : son of Christopher Preston Jee : educated at London and Edinburgh Universities, and Paris : Assistant Surgeon in the 1st Dragoons, 1842 : in the Persian war, 1857 : with Havelock in the mutiny : gained his V.C. at the final capture of Lucknow : was in the Rohilkund campaign : C.B. : died March 17, 1899.

JEFFREYS, JULIUS (1801-1877)

Son of the Rev. R. Jeffreys : born 1801 : studied medicine at Edinburgh and London : entered the E. I. Co.'s medical establishment in 1822 : and, after meteorological observations, recommended that hill stations should be formed as health resorts, and suggested Simla as one, there being then only a single house there : he had an inventive turn of mind, proposed various chemical manufactures, invented a respirator, and obtained patents for a number of inventions connected with ships : F.R.S. and other learned Societies : died May 13, 1877.

JENKINS, SIR FRANCIS HOWELL
(1832-   )

Born 1832 : son of Rev. David Jenkins : educated at Marlborough : entered the Bengal Army, 1851 : Colonel, 1879 : and retired in 1885 : served in the mutiny of 1857, at the siege of Delhi : Umbeyla expedition, 1863 : Afghan war, 1878-80 : K.C.B., 1897.

JENKINS, SIR LAWRENCE HUGH
(1858-   )

Born Dec. 22, 1858 : son of Richard David Jenkins : called to the bar, 1883 :

Puisne Judge of the Calcutta High Court, 1896-9 : Chief Justice of the Bombay High Court since 1899 : K.C.I.E., 1903.

JENKINS, SIR RICHARD (1785-1853)

I.C.S. : son of Richard Jenkins : born Feb. 18, 1785 : went out to Bombay in the E. I. Co.'s service in 1800 : was an Assistant in the office of the Governor-General, and, in 1804-5, Assistant Political at Poona and Assistant Resident at Sindia's Court : and acting Resident : officiating Resident at Nagpur in 1807, and permanently there from 1810 to 1827 : he proposed to the Governor-General the suppression of the Pindaris : in 1817, the troops of Appa Sahib, the Raja of Berar, attacked the British Residency troops at Sitabaldi, Nov. 26-7 : Appa was dethroned, 1818, and, during the minority of his successor, Jenkins governed Nagpur : retired in 1828 : was M.P. for Shrewsbury, 1830-1 and 1837-41 : D.C.L. Oxford, 1834 : G.C.B. in 1838 : Chairman of the E. I. Co.'s Directors, 1839 : died Dec. 30, 1853.

JENNINGS, ROBERT MELVILLE
(1841-   )

Born 1841 : entered Bengal Cavalry, 1859, and became Maj-General, 1895, and Lt-General, 1900 : served on the N.W. Frontier, 1863-4 : Egyptian war, 1882 (Brevet-Colonel), and Hazara campaign, 1888 : C.B., 1896.

JERDON, THOMAS CLAVERHILL
(1811-1872)

Born 1811 : son of Archibald Jerdon : joined the medical service in Madras, 1835 : retired, 1864, and died June 12, 1872 : he is best known as a zoologist, by his *Illustrations of Indian Ornithology*, 1844 ; *Birds of India*, 1862-4 ; *Mammals of India*, 1867, which are standard works of reference to this day.

JEREMIE, VERY REV. JAMES AMIRAUX (1802-1872)

Son of James Jeremie, merchant : born April 12, 1802 : educated at Elizabeth College, Guernsey ; Blundell's School, Tiverton ; Trinity College, Cambridge : distinguished himself : Fellow : ordained, 1830 : Professor of Classical and General Literature at the E. I. Co.'s College at Haileybury, 1830-50 : Christian Advocate in the University, Cambridge, 1833-50

Dean at Haileybury, 1838 : Regius Professor of Divinity at Cambridge, 1850–70 : Dean of Lincoln, 1864–72 : D.D. in 1850 : D.C.L. in 1862 : as Dean he presided over the discipline of the College : though much liked, his sensitive and nervous temperament rendered him unsuccessful as a disciplinarian : he was excellent as a classical lecturer and preacher : of fastidious and refined taste. It was written of him that his " labour at Haileybury contributed in no slight measure to the formation of that high and firm tone of character in the East Indian Civil Service, which was signally displayed when the mutiny of 1857 broke out " : died June 11, 1872.

JEROME, HENRY EDWARD (1829–1901)

Educated at Sandhurst : entered the 86th regt., 1848 : in the mutiny, at Kalpi, part of his head was torn away : at the captures of Chandairi and Jhansi, and action of Koonch : gained the V.C. for gallantry at Jhansi, April 3, 1858, for saving a wounded officer under heavy fire, and for bravery on various occasions : in the Hazara expedition, 1868 : on the Staff, 1876–84 : retired as Maj-General, 1885 : died Feb. 25, 1901.

JIJIBHAI, BYRAMJI (1821–1890)

Son of Jijibhai Dadabhai : born June 16, 1821 : educated privately : at 17 became a member of Jijibhai Dadabhai, Sons & Co. : later became a broker to several firms : established the Royal Spinning and Weaving Company : Member of the Board of Direction of several joint-stock Companies : established, in 1870, a Fire Insurance Company : kept aloof from the speculation mania of 1864 : Additional Member of the Bombay Legislative Council, 1868 – 72 : founded a Charity Fund, endowed Medical Schools at Poona, Ahmadabad and Thana, called by his name : promoted the Madrasa at Nowsari : founded a Parsi girls' school : contributed funds for the amelioration of the Parsis in Persia : C.S.I. in 1875 : died Sep. 1890.

JIJIBHAI, SIR JAMSETJI, BARONET (1783–1859)

Born July 15, 1783, of poor but respectable parents, at Nowsari in Baroda, the birthplace of the Parsi religion in India : lived with his father-in-law in Bombay. Realizing that large profits in trade could only be made by dealings with foreign countries, he visited China at the age of 16. He was twice taken prisoner by the French, but released. In 1807, after three voyages to China, he set up business in Bombay, and in twenty years amassed a large fortune. He gave away his wealth liberally, founding hospitals, schools, refuges, and in other works of benevolence. In 1842 he was knighted. In 1855 he was presented with the freedom of the City of London. In 1856 a statue was erected to him in the Town Hall of Bombay. It was owing principally to his munificence that the Causeway connecting Bombay with Salsette was erected. In 1858 he was made a Baronet, the highest honour ever conferred on a native of India : he died April 14, 1859.

JOHNSON, SIR ALLEN BAYARD (1829–)

Born May 2, 1829 : son of Sir H. A. Johnson, *Bart.* : educated at Winchester : entered the Bengal Army, 1846, and became General, 1892 : Indian Staff Corps : served in the second Burmese war, 1853, and Indian mutiny, 1857–8 : in the Jaunpur Field Force, at the capture of Lucknow, and with the Oudh Field Force : for many years in the Military Secretariat of the Government of India : Military Secretary at the India Office, 1877–89 : C.B., 1881 : K.C.B., 1889.

JOHNSON, SIR CHARLES COOPER (1827–)

Born Dec. 20, 1827 : General : son of Sir Henry Allen Johnson, *Bart.* : educated at Addiscombe : joined the Indian Army, 1844 : served in the Satlaj campaign, 1846 : at Sobraon : in the Indian mutiny, 1857–58 : at the siege of Lucknow : in the Hazara campaign as Q.M.G., 1868 : Brevet-Colonel and C.B. : Q.M.G. of the Army in India during the Afghan war, 1878–80 : K.C.B., 1881 : G.C.B., 1900.

JOHNSON, RIGHT REV. EDWARD RALPH, D.D. (? –)

Son of William Ponsonby Johnson : educated at Rugby and Wadham College, Oxford : ordained 1851 : Minor Canon of Chester, 1861–6 : Rector of

Northenden, 1866–76 : Archdeacon of Chester, 1871–6 : D.D., Oxford and Durham : Bishop of Calcutta and Metropolitan in India, 1876–98 : during this time the Episcopate in India was extended from four to ten sees : he had a great capacity for administration, and devoted his attention largely to the organization of the Church in India, establishing Provincial Episcopal Synods, Diocesan Conferences and Councils, etc.

JOHNSON, SIR EDWIN BEAUMONT
(1825-1893)

Son of Sir Henry Allen Johnson, *Bart.* : born July 4, 1825 : educated at Addiscombe : went to India in the Bengal Artillery in 1842 : rose to be Lt-General, and General, 1877 : Colonel Commandant, R.A., 1890 : was in the Satlaj campaign, in the Artillery, at Firozshahr and Sobraon : in the Panjab campaign at Ramnagar, Chilianwala, and Gujarat, and in the pursuit of the Sikhs and Afghans : Brevet-Major : was A.D.C. to the C. in C. in 1855, and A.A.G. of Artillery in Oudh : in the mutiny was with Archdale Wilson at the actions on the Hindun and at Badli-ka-Sarai, and at the siege and assault of Delhi : at the siege and capture of Lucknow : Brevet-Lt-Colonel : C.B. : Assistant Military Secretary for Indian affairs at the Horse Guards, 1865 : Q.M.G., in India, 1873 : Member of the Council of India, 1874 : K.C.B., 1875 : Military Member of the Supreme Council in India, 1877–80 : C.I.E., 1878 : Director-General of Military Education at the War Office, 1884–6 : G.C.B., 1887 : died June 18, 1893.

JOHNSON, FRANCES (1725-1812)

Born April 10, 1725 : daughter of Edward Crook, Governor of Fort St. David : married, (1st) in 1738, Parry Purple Templer (d. 1743) : (2nd) James Altham, B.C.S. who died of smallpox, 12 days after the marriage : (3rd) William Watts, Senior Member of Council, and appointed Governor of Calcutta : when he was Chief of Murshidabad, in 1756, they were both placed in custody, but protected by the Nawab's mother, who sent Mrs. Watts to Chandernagore and afterwards procured Watts' release. Their eldest daughter, Amelia, married (1769) Charles Jenkinson, first Earl of Liverpool, father of the Prime

Minister, the second Earl. Watts died in England. Mrs. Watts returned to Bengal, 1769, and married (4th) June 1, 1774, the Rev. William Johnson, a Chaplain of the Presidency of Fort William : he finally left India in Feb. 1788. She remained in Calcutta till her death, Feb. 3, 1812 : "the oldest British resident in Bengal, universally beloved, respected and revered." The Governor-General and high officials attended her funeral. The Duke of Wellington talked of having known her. She "abounded in anecdote," "had a strong understanding " : was known as "the old Begam," dispensing a dignified hospitality, her mansion being one of the most popular rendezvous.

JOHNSON, FRANCIS (1795-1876)

Born 1795 : learnt Arabic and Sanskrit at Rome : Assistant Oriental Professor at Haileybury, 1824, and Professor from 1823, teaching Sanskrit, Bengali and Telugu : brought out the third edition of Richardson's Persian-Arabic dictionary, 1829, and a new edition, greatly revised and enlarged, in his own name, in 1852 : which he continued to revise : was strongest in Arabic : edited the *Gulistan* in 1863 : in Sanskrit he published the *Hitopadesa*, selections from the *Mahabharata*, and the *Meghaduta*, and assisted H. H. Wilson (*q.v.*) in completing his Sanskrit grammar : resigned his Professorship in 1855 : died at Hertford, Jan. 29, 1876.

JOHNSTONE, CHARLES (1719 ?-1800 ?)

Born in Limerick county about 1719 : educated at Dublin University : called to the bar : took to literature : wrote 1760–5, a novel, *Chrysal : or, the Adventures of a Guinea*, which made a sensation : went to India in 1782, shipwrecked on the way : at Calcutta acquired a fortune : became joint proprietor of a newspaper in Bengal, and contributed regularly to the periodical press under the *nom de plume* of Oneiropolos : wrote other novels : died in 1800 in Calcutta, though the place of his death has been disputed.

JOHNSTONE, SIR JAMES (1841-1895)

Born Feb. 9, 1841 : son of Dr. James Johnstone, F.R.C.P. : educated at the Birmingham Grammar School and Gosport : entered the Bengal Army, 1858 : Maj-General, 1894: in the Trans-Gogra force in the mutiny, 1858–9 : in the Bhutan campaign, 1864–6 : in charge of elephant Kheddas in Orissa, 1868–74 : Political Agent at Keonjhur during the rebellion, and in charge of the State for 3 years : Political Agent at Manipur, 1877 : at the head of the Manipur Army relieved Kohima, 1878, where 545 British subjects were besieged by 6,000 Nagas : at assault and capture of Khonoma : Commissioner in 1881 for settling disputes on Burmese frontier : made a great march in 1886 from Manipur and saved lives of Europeans employed in Upper Burma : K.C.S.I., in 1887 : wrote at length to the newspapers in 1891, after the outbreak and troubles at Manipur : died from a fall from his horse on June 13, 1895, after his retirement : was a claimant to the dormant Marquessate of Annandale.

JOHNSTONE, JAMES HENRY
(1787–1851)

Entered the Navy in 1803 : was at Trafalgar and variously employed : on half-pay in 1815 : went to Calcutta in 1817 : obtained a ship and made voyages to England : was nominated to certain appointments which he never took up : his proposals, in 1823, for establishing steam communication with India *via* the Mediterranean and Red Sea, not accepted : took the *Enterprise*, a private steam-vessel, from England round the Cape to India, 1825 : his scheme for establishing steam navigation on the Ganges, in iron vessels, accepted : controller of the Co.'s steamers, 1833–50 : died on his voyage home to retire, May 5, 1851.

JOHNSTONE, JAMES WILLIAM DOUGLAS (1855–)

Born Aug. 30, 1855 : son of Maj-General Henry Campbell Johnstone : educated at Edinburgh Academy and University : appointed to Panjab Education Department, 1877 : transferred to Foreign Department, Government of India, on appointment as Headmaster, Mayo College, Ajmir : Principal of the Daly College, Indore, 1885 : Tutor of Maharaja Sindia, 1890 : Inspr-General of Education in Gwalior State, 1894 : Fellow of Allahabad University.

JOLLY, JULIUS E. (1849–)

Born Dec. 28, 1849, at Heidelberg : son of Philipp von Jolly, Professor of Physics

at the University of Munich : studied at Munich, Berlin and Leipzig : his principal subjects were Comparative Philology, Oriental Languages and Jurisprudence : Ph.D. : became Privat-docent at the University of Würzburg, Bavaria, 1872 ; Professor Extraordinary, 1877 ; Professor Ordinary (Sanskrit and Comparative Philology), 1886 : has visited England frequently, to study Sanskrit MSS. in London : to India, 1882–3 : was Tagore Law Professor at the University, Calcutta : had made the ancient legal literature of India his special study, and is recognized as the leading authority on native Indian law : his chief works as a Sanskritist are : *The Institutes of Narada* (translated from the Sanskrit), 1876 ; *The Institutes of Vishnu* (in the " Sacred Books of the East "), 1880 ; *Vishnusmriti*, 1881 ; *History of the Hindu Law*, 1885 (Tagore Law Lectures) ; *Naradasmriti*, 1885–6 ; *Manutikasaingraha*, 1885–90 ; *Manava Dharma-Sastra*, 1887 ; *Minor Law-Books*, 1889 ; *Recht und Sitte* (in Bühler's Encyclopædia of Indo-Aryan Research), 1896 ; *Medicin* (ibid), 1901 : has written numerous articles on Indian Philology in English and German periodicals, besides other philological works : assisted Sir R. West in the preparation of a new edition of West and Bühler's *Digest of the Hindu Law*, still to be published : belongs to several learned Societies : is Corresponding Member of the R. Bavarian Academy of Science, 1886, and of the R. Society of Science at Gottingen, 1904 : Honorary Member of the R. Asiatic Society, 1904, etc.

JONES, HENRY RICHMOND
(1808–1880)

General : son of the Rev. Inigo Jones : born 1808 : entered the Army in 1825 : commanded the 6th Dragoon Guards in the Crimea : in the mutiny commanded a column in action, and a Brigade of cavalry at Bareli : C.B. : also under Sir Colin Campbell at Dunderkera, and in the Trans-Gogra campaign, including several actions and the pursuit of the rebels to the Rapti : became a General in 1877 : died Oct. 7, 1880.

JONES, JOHN (? – ?)

Captain : when the Bhutanese in 1772 invaded and took possession of a large portion of Cooch Behar, and carried off the Raja, the Cooch Behar family solicited the aid of the Government of India, which was accorded : Captain Jones was despatched with four companies of sepoys and two guns to drive back the Bhutanese. He not only drove them back, but followed them into Bhutan and carried the three forts of Dalimkote (April, 1773), Chichacottah and Passakha, pressing the Bhutanese so hard that they were compelled to invoke the aid of the Tibetan General at Lhasa : Jones soon after fell a sacrifice to the unwholesome climate of Cooch Behar.

JONES, SIR JOHN (1811–1878)

Born 1811 : entered the 5th foot regt. in 1828, but exchanged into the 60th Rifles : Lt-Colonel, 1854 : at Meerut in the mutiny of 1857 : commanded his battalion at the Hindun, Badli-ka-sarai, and the siege of Delhi : led the left attack : Brigadier of the Rurki Field Force, in the Rohilkund campaign, and at Bareli : his success gained for him the name of " Avenger " : in the subsequent campaign in Oudh : C.B. : Brevet-Lt-Colonel : K.C.B. : Maj-General, 1868 : Lt-General, 1877 : died Feb. 21, 1878.

JONES, JOHN FELIX (? –1878)

Captain in the Indian Navy : made charts of the Red Sea : in the survey of Ceylon and Mesopotamia : from 1843 was on the survey of the Tigris and Euphrates : discovered the ancient Opis in 1850 : mapped and wrote on Nineveh and surrounding country and Bagdad, 1852–3 : Political Agent at Bagdad, 1854 : in the Persian Gulf, 1855 : served in the Persian war and the mutiny : then retired : made a map of Western Asia : F.R.G.S. : died Sep. 3, 1878.

JONES, REV. RICHARD (1790–1855)

Born 1790 : son of a solicitor at Tunbridge Wells : educated at Caius College, Cambridge : ordained, 1819 : performed ministerial duties for some years in Kent and Sussex : appointed, in 1833, Professor of Political Economy and History at King's College, London, and in 1835 at Haileybury : co-operated in forming the scheme of comparison for the commutation of tithes, and became Tithes Com-missioner, and later a Charity Commissioner : published *Jones on Rent :* died at Haileybury, Jan. 26, 1855.

JONES, SIR WILLIAM (1746–1794)

Youngest son of William Jones the mathematician : born Sep. 28, 1746 : educated at Harrow, for more than ten years : Scholar of University College, Oxford, 1764 : there began his studies in Oriental and other languages : became tutor to young Lord Althorp : Fellow of his College, 1766 : M.A. in 1773 : translated a life of Nadir Shah from Persian into French, 1770 : wrote a Persian grammar, 1771 : translations of Poems, and six books of commentaries on Asiatic Poetry : F.R.S. in 1772, and Member of the Literary Club, 1773 : called to the bar from the Middle Temple in 1774 : was a Commissioner of bankrupts, 1776 : published an Essay on the Law of Bailments, 1881 : unsuccessful candidate for the Arabic Professorship at Oxford : published a translation of the Arabic *Moallakat :* appointed a Judge of the Supreme Court at Calcutta, 1783 : knighted : founded the Asiatic Society of Bengal in 1784 and was its President till his death : contributed 29 papers to the first four volumes of the Asiatic Researches, translated the ordinances of the Hind : lawgiver, Manu : the *Sakuntala* of Kalidasu the *Gitagobinda* of Jagadeva, the *Hitopadesa* of Pilpai, and some works on Muhammadan law : he was the first English scholar to know Sanskrit : he studied every department of Oriental learning and literature, and advanced them all : he aimed at making Eastern learning known to the West. He was intimate with Warren Hastings and his successors, and had their support. His judicial work was also well performed : he commenced a digest of Hindu and Muhammadan law : but is best known by the results of his literary labours. He overtaxed his strength, and died, April 27, 1794. A monument was erected to him in St. Paul's Cathedral. His scholarship was of world-wide renown, " and his memory is dearly cherished by all Oriental scholars."

JONES, SIR WILLIAM (1808–1890)

Born 1808 : son of William Jones : educated at Sandhurst : entered the 60th regt. in 1825 : and became a General in 1877 : was with his regt. in the Panjab campaign of 1848–9 : at the Chenab, Sadulapur, Chilianwala, Gujarat and the pursuit to the Khyber : C.B. : commanded a Brigade at the siege of Delhi, and led a storming party on Sep. 24, 1857 : was in charge, after Nicholson's death, during the street fighting : K.C.B., 1869 : G.C.B., 1886 : died April 8, 1890.

JONES, WILLIAM BRITTAIN (1834–)

I.C.S. : son of Rev. W. Jones : educated at 'University College, London : called to the bar from the Inner Temple : entered the Bengal Civil Service, 1856 : Resident at Hyderabad, 1882–3 : Chief Commissioner of Central Provinces, 1883–4 : retired, 1885 : C.S.I., 1883.

JONES-VAUGHAN, HUGH THOMAS (1841–)

Born 1841 : son of Canon Jones : educated at Sandhurst : passed Staff College, 1871 : served in the Indian mutiny, 1857–8, actions of Chanda, Amirpur and Sultanpur, final siege and capture of Lucknow : Afghan war, 1878–80, as Brig-Major of 1st Division of Peshawar Field Force : capture of Ali Masjid : Brig-Major in the Zaimusht expedition : Brevet-Lt-Colonel : A.A.G., Western District, 1887–92 : Maj-General, 1899 : General Officer commanding troops Straits Settlements : C.B.

JOSHI, ANANDIBAI (1865–1887)

Born March, 1865 : daughter of Ganpatrao Amritaswar Joshi of Kalyan : given the name "Jamuna" : learnt Sanskrit : married, 1874, to Gopal Vinayek Joshi, in the Postal Department : took to the study of medicine : left her husband in Calcutta and went in 1883 to England and America, to Mrs. Carpenter in N. Jersey : instructed at the Women's Medical College in Philadelphia : gained a scholarship : took her degree as Doctor of Medicine there, 1886 : appointed Resident Physician to the female ward of the Albert Edward Hospital, Kolapur : her health failed, and she died of consumption at Poona, Feb. 27, 1887 : her body was burnt, and the ashes sent to America to be buried there.

JOYNER, ROBERT BATSON (1844–

Born March 1, 1844 : son of H. St. John Joyner : educated privately : entered the Bombay P.W.D. 1868 : employed in Irrigation Works in Belgaum, Dharwar and S. Mahratta country : Superintending Engineer of Sind, 1891 : Superintending Engineer South, and Central, Division, Bombay, 1893 and 1896 : C.I.E., 1898, for Famine Relief Work, 1896–8 : author of Reports on Indian Irrigation and Indian Famines.

JUDSON, REV. ADONIRAM, D.D. (1788–1850)

Missionary : born at Malden, Massachusetts, Aug. 9, 1788 : son of a Congregational minister : educated at the Brown University and Andover Theological Seminary : attracted, by reading a sermon of Dr. Claudius Buchanan (q.v.), to missionary work in India : sent by the American Board of Commissioners for Foreign Missions to India, 1812 : ordered by the Bengal Government to leave Calcutta, went viâ Mauritius to Madras and Rangoon in July, 1813 : preached to the Burmese : went up to Ava, established schools : taken prisoner on outbreak of first Burmese war : imprisoned at Oungpenla for 19 months, cruelly treated, released on the conclusion of peace in 1826 : published a Burmese-English dictionary in 1826 : and a Burmese grammar : translated the Bible into Burmese, 1835, revised, 1840 : went to Amherst and Moulmain : visited America in 1845, enthusiastically received : returned to Moulmain : unable to complete his larger Burmese dictionary : died at sea on April 12, 1850, on a voyage to the Isle of Bourbon for his health : thrice married : the first Mrs. Judson wrote A History of the Burman Mission : Colonel Sir H. M. Durand wrote an article on Judson as "The Apostle of Burma," in vol. xiv, number 28, of the Calcutta Review.

JUDSON, ANN HASSELTINE (1789–1826).

Missionary : born Dec. 22, 1789, at Bradford, Massachusetts : daughter of John and Rebecca Hasseltine : educated at Bradford : joined the Congregational Church there, 1806, and taught a school in several places : married Adoniram

Judson (q.v.) Feb. 5. 1812 : went with him and other Missionaries to work, arriving at Calcutta, June, 1812 : resided at Serampur with Dr. W. Carey (q.v.) : summoned by the Government to Calcutta, and peremptorily ordered to leave India : they went to the Isle of France, thence to Rangoon, July, 1813 : Mrs. Judson went to England and the United States, 1822 ; at Washington, her advice was taken by the Baptists respecting the Burmese Mission : she published her *History of the Burmese Mission :* returned to Rangoon, 1823, and joined her husband at Ava : where he and other Missionaries were taken prisoners : in the first Burmese war she underwent terrible sufferings, " but by her eloquent and forcible appeals" procured their release : still she persevered with the Mission to the Burmese : she died of violent fever, Oct. 24, 1826.

KABRAJI, KAIKHUSRU NAOROJI
(1842-1904)

Born Aug. 21, 1842, at Bombay : descended from a Surat family : son of Naoroji Kabraji : educated in the Jamsetji Jijibhai school : took to journalism, 1858 : became editor of the *Parsi Mitra* : joined the *Rast Goftar*, as sub-editor, and editor, 1863–1902 : making the paper an instrument for social reform in the whole native community : was Fellow of the Bombay University, 1882 : Secretary of the Guzarati Society for the Diffusion of Knowledge, 1880, lecturing for it : Secretary of the Sir Dinshaw Petit Gymnastic Institution, 1867–75 : supported female education, founding girls' schools : an active member of the Bombay Municipal Corporation, 1882–1904 : a warm champion of British rule in India, and a moderate critic : to England in 1900, and was made a member of the British Institute of Journalists : on the fiftieth anniversary of his paper, Nov. 1901, was specially congratulated on his editorship : retired from it 1902 : died April, 1904 : raised the tone of the vernacular Press in W. India : also wrote a number of novels dealing mostly with Parsi social life.

KAMRAN SHAH, ABDALI or DURANI
(? -1842)

Son of Mahmud Shah, grandson of Timur Shah, and great-grandson of Ahmad Shah Abdali, ruler of Afghanistan: he seized Fateh Khan, the Barakzai wazir of Afghanistan, blinded him and then killed him : he succeeded his father, when murdered in 1829, as ruler of Herat. He was cruel and dissipated, and would have given up Herat to the Persians : but his wazir and the presence of Eldred Pottinger during the siege of Herat, from Nov. 1837, to Sep. 1838, prevented him. A treaty, dated Aug. 13, 1839, was negotiated on behalf of the Governor-General by Major E. D'Arcy Todd, envoy to Herat, with Kamran Shah, who opened treacherous correspondence with Persia : Todd's subsequent action was disapproved by Lord Auckland. Kamran was strangled in 1842 by his minister Yar Mahomed Khan Alakozai.

KAPUR, RAJA BAN BIHARI (1853-   )

Born Nov.11,1853 : adopted as a son by the third brother of Maharaja Mahtab Chand Bahadur (q.v.) of Burdwan on Aug. 31, 1856 : appointed Vice-President of the Burdwan Raj Council, 1879 : Member of the Bengal Legislative Council, Jan. 1885 : in the same year joint Manager of the Burdwan Raj : and sole Manager in 1891 : given the title of Raja as a personal distinction, Jan. 1893 : C.S.I., Jan. 1903 : again Member of the Bengal Legislative Council, Jan. 1905 : the late Maharaja Aftab Chand Bahadur married his sister, and she adopted Raja Ban Bihari's son, Bijoy, the present Maharaja Bahadur.

KAPURTHALA, KUNWAR SIR HARNAM SINGH, OF (1851-   )

Born Nov. 15, 1851 : son of Raja Sir Randhir Singh Bahadur of Kapurthala, G.C.S.I : educated at Kapurthala : managed the Kapurthala estates for 18 years : Hon. Life Secretary of the B.I. Association of Talukdars of Oudh : Fellow of the Panjab University : Member of the Panjab Legislative Council, 1900–2 : K.C.I.E., 1899 : and Member of the Governor-General's Legislative Council : resigned all claims to the succession to the State by becoming a Christian : guest of the nation at the Coronation, 1902.

KAPURTHALA, RAJA SIR JAGATJIT SINGH, BAHADUR, OF (1872-   )

Succeeded his father, Raja Kharak Singh, Sep. 5, 1877 : K.C.S.I. in 1897 : has visited England.

KAPURTHALA, RAJA SIR RANDHIR SINGH, OF (1831-1870)

Born March, 1831: succeeded his father, Nihal Singh, Sep. 13, 1852. In the mutiny he volunteered his assistance, first at Jalandhar, and, later, marched to Oudh at the head of a mixed force: he was engaged there for 10 months, was in several actions against the rebels near Cawnpur and Lucknow, showing great bravery. In 1864 he was made K.C.S.I. was rewarded with estates confiscated from rebels, and received the right of adoption. He died near Aden on April 2, 1870, on a visit to Europe: his body was taken back to India.

KARAKA, DOSABHAI FRAMJI (1829-1902)

Born May 8, 1829, educated at the Elphinstone Institution: edited the *Jam-i-Jamshid*, Gujarati newspaper, for 5 years and became manager of the *Bombay Times* under Dr. Buist: was made Censor of the Native Press at Bombay during the mutiny: wrote *The Company's Raj contrasted with its Predecessors*: went to England 1858-9, wrote there *The Parsis: their History, Manners, Customs, and Religion*: republished, 1884: in 1859 was Assessor to the Bombay Municipality: Income Tax Assessor for 4 years: Presidency Magistrate in Bombay: Licence Tax Officer and Income Tax Collector in 1869: again Presidency Magistrate: Sheriff of Bombay, 1872: a Chief Presidency Magistrate, 1874: J.P.: in 1875 Chairman of the Bombay Corporation: C.S.I., 1877: in the Bombay Legislative Council: acted as Collector of Bombay: Fellow of the Bombay University: resigned the service, 1887: died March 17, 1902.

KARAMAT ALI, SYAD (1796-1876)

Born at Jaunpur, N.W.P: of a family descended from the Prophet: left home at 18, in quest of knowledge, spent 2 years at Lucknow. 10 in Persia: travelled widely in Persia and Turkistan: accompanied A. Conolly on his journey to India through Afghanistan and saved his life in that country: chiefly on Conolly's recommendation, was appointed representative of the Indian Government at the Court of Dost Muhammad Khan (the Sirdar, afterwards Amir) at Kabul: went up there *viâ* Ludiana: maintained friendship with C. M. Wade (*q.v.*), the A.G.G. at Ludiana: much esteemed at Dost Muhammad's Court: reported to the Indian Government the intrigues of the Russians and French at Kabul, and advised a definite understanding with the Sirdar, who was then anxious to unite himself to England. Karamat Ali was recalled from Kabul in 1835: and in 1837, appointed Superintendent (*mutawali*) of the Hughli Imambara: where he remained till his death in 1876: had great influence with the Muhammadans: much respected by the highest European officers. His predictions of the conduct of Russia toward Persia, the Khanates and Afghanistan, have proved remarkably accurate. A longer account of his career has been given in Syad Ameer Ali's article on "England and Russia in Afghanistan" in the *Nineteenth Century* for May, 1905.

KARKARIA, RUSTOMJI PESTONJI (1869-)

Born at Bombay, May 16, 1869: educated at St. Xavier's School and College: B.A., 1888: Senior Fellow: Asst. Professor of English and History, 1891: Examiner to the Bombay University in History, Geography, Logic, Moral Philosophy, Political Economy: helped to found, 1896, the Collegiate Institution: became its Principal and Professor of English Literature: his action in obtaining the recognition of private colleges led partly to the Universities Act of 1904: Fellow of the Royal Historical Society, 1898: M.R.A.S. Bombay, 1888: M.R.A.S. Great Britain 1900: Member of the American Oriental Society, 1897: has contributed papers to many Journals of Societies, also to the Anglo-Indian and English newspapers on Indian subjects: discovered and published Carlyle's Lectures on European Literature, with notes; author of works on Indian History and Politics, Sivaji, Akbar, Essays on English History, India under Victoria, on the Native Press, translated the Parsi Sacred Book, the Dinkard: served on Committees of the Parsi community to consider questions of Religious Education, of Social Amelioration, of admitting proselytes, and other subjects on which he has written largely.

KASHMIR, MAHARAJA GOLAB SINGH OF (? -1857)

A horseman in a cavalry troop of Ranjit Singh (*q.v.*): obtained an independent command, and for good service received from Ranjit the principality of Jammu: resided there and extended his authority into Ladak: was elected minister of the Sikh Khalsa: after Sobraon used his influence in favour of friendly relations with the British, who sold Kashmir to him, after the treaty of Lahore, 1846, and made a separate treaty with him: he maintained very amicable relations with the British Government, and had just arranged to furnish a strong auxiliary force for the suppression of the mutiny in the N.W.P., when he died of fever, Aug. 2, 1857.

KASHMIR, MAHARAJA PARTAB SINGH SADAR MAHINDAR BAHADUR (1850–)

Son of Maharaja Ranbir Singh (*q.v.*), and grandson of Maharaja Golab Singh (*q.v.*): born, 1850: succeeded his father, Sep. 12, 1885, as Maharaja of Kashmir and Jammu: G.C.S.I., 1892: Maj-General in the Army and Honry. Colonel, 37th Dogras.

KASHMIR, MAHARAJA RANBIR SINGH, OF (1832?–1885)

Succeeded his father, the Maharaja Golab Singh, in 1857 and supplied a contingent of troops to co-operate with the British forces against Delhi: was given an adoption *sanad* in 1862: K.C.S.I., 1861: G.C.S.I., 1866: made a Commercial Treaty with the Viceroy and Governor-General for the purpose of developing trade with Eastern Turkistan, in May, 1870: he reduced all transit duties through his territories: his maladministration, especially in connexion with the famine in his country in 1879, attracted the attention of the Government of India: died, Sep. 12, 1885.

KAVANAGH, THOMAS HENRY (? –1883)

A clerk in one of the civil offices in Lucknow, who, volunteering in disguise, " on the night of Nov. 9, 1857," as is recorded in the memorial to him in the church at Lucknow, " with the devotion of an ancient Roman hero, taking his life in his hand,

went forth from the beleaguered Residency, and passing through a city thronged with merciless enemies, triumphantly guided Sir Colin Campbell on his way to the relief of the garrison " : he conveyed information from Sir J. Outram, of the greatest value to Sir Colin Campbell: he wrote *How I Won the Victoria Cross*, which he was awarded for his bravery: he was given an appointment in the Oudh Commission and rose to be Deputy Commissioner: he died about 1883.

KAY, REV. WILLIAM (1820–1886)

Son of Thomas Kay: born April 8, 1820: educated at Giggleswick and Lincoln College, Oxford: Scholar, Fellow and Tutor: Pusey and Ellerton Hebrew Scholar: ordained 1843: B.D., 1849: D.D., 1855: Principal of Bishop's College, Calcutta, 1849–65, where he exerted much influence: received a College living at Great Leigh's. Essex: Hon. Canon of St. Albans: was one of the revisers of the Old Testament in 1870, and devoted his life to his parish and to critical and learned works on the Scriptures: he died Jan. 16, 1886.

KAYE, SIR JOHN WILLIAM (1814–1876)

Born 1814: son of Charles Kaye, solicitor to the Bank of England: educated at Eton and Addiscombe: went out to India in the Bengal Artillery, 1832–3: retired from the Army, 1841, to adopt a literary career: established the *Calcutta Review* in 1844: edited the first 5 numbers, and wrote 47 articles in the first 50 numbers: returned to England, 1845: in 1856 entered the Home Civil Service of the E. I. Co.: and in 1858 succeeded J. S. Mill as Secretary in the Political and Secret Department at the India Office: K.C.S.I., 1871: retired, 1874: was F.R.S.: died July 24, 1876. He wrote his *History of the War in Afghanistan*, 1851; the *Administration of the East India Company*, 1853; the *Life and Correspondence of Lord Metcalfe*, 1854; of *Henry St. George Tucker*, 1854; also of *Sir John Malcolm*, 1856; *Christianity in India*, 1859; *The History of the Sepoy War in India*, 1857-8, 1864– 76: *Lives of Indian Officers*, 1867: besides editing Buckle's *Memoirs of the Services of the Bengal Artillery*, 1852; *Tucker's Memorials of Indian Government*, 1853, and Taylor's *People of India*, 1868.: also contributed largely to periodical literature, such as " Writings of an Optimist " etc.

KEANE, JOHN, FIRST BARON
(1781–1844)

Born Feb. 6, 1781 : second son of Sir John Keane, *Bart.* : in the 44th regt. in 1799 : A.D.C. to Lord Cavan in Egypt : commanded the 13th regt. at the capture of Martinique, 1809 : was in the Peninsula in several engagements from 1813 : Maj-General, 1814 : K.C.B., 1815 : in the landing and attack of New Orleans, 1814–5 : commanded the troops in Jamaica, 1823–30 : C. in C. at Bombay from July 2, 1834, to Feb, 14, 1840 : in 1838 commanded the Bombay Division of the Army of the Indus under Sir H. Fane (*q.v.*) : ordered to Sind : given the command of both the Bengal and Bombay columns advancing into Afghanistan *via* Quetta and Kandahar : took Ghazni, July 23, 1839 : occupied Kabul, Aug. 7, 1839 : in Oct. 1839, the Army of the Indus being dispersed, Keane returned to England *via* Lahore : G.C.B. : made Baron Keane of Ghazni in Dec. 1839 : died Aug. 26, 1844.

KEARY, HENRY D'URBAN (1857–   )

Born April 28, 1857 : Lt-Colonel : son of Hall William Keary : educated at Marlborough : joined the Indian Staff Corps, 1876 : served in Afghan war, 1879–80 : Burmese campaign, 1885–6 : commanded a Military Police Battalion in Burma, 1887–92 : Northern Chin Hills, 1892–;, China, 1901 : Lt-Colonel, 1903 : D.S.O., 1900.

KEATINGE, RICHARD HARTE
(1825–1904)

General : born June 17, 1825 : son of Right Hon. Richard Keatinge, Judge of the Court of Probate, Ireland : educated privately : entered the Bombay Artillery, 1842 : Maj-General, 1884 : General, 1894 : Assistant Superintendent, Nimar, 1847 : served through the Indian mutiny : disarmed the Asirghar garrison : Political Officer with the Mhow force and the 1st Brigade, Central India Field Force : at the siege of Dhar, and battle of Mandiswar : with the Bombay Artillery at the siege of Chandairi : gained the V.C., March 17, 1858 : he voluntarily led the column

through the breach, under heavy cross fire, and led into the fort : twice severely wounded : success mainly due to him : commanded irregular troops in Satpura hills, 1858–9, against insurgents : joined Brig. Parke's Brigade in the pursuit of Tantia Topi : Political Agent in Malwa, 1857 : in Nimar, 1860 : at Gwalior, 1862–3 : and Kattiawar, 1863–7 : took the field against rebel Wagheers in Kattiawar, 1865–6 : Governor-General's Agent in Rajputana, 1867–70 : acting Chief Commissioner, Central Provinces, 1870–2 : the first Chief Commissioner of Assam, 1874–8 : C.S.I., 1866 : died May 25, 1904.

KEEN, SIR F. J. (1843–1902)

Colonel : joined the 35th Bengal N.I., 1854 : in the mutiny, at the siege and capture of Delhi, relief of Lucknow ; showed great gallantry at the storming of the Sikandrabagh, at the battle of Cawnpur, capture of Lucknow : at Bareli and other actions : retired, 1892 : K.C.B., 1900 : died June 25, 1902.

KEENE, REV. HENRY GEORGE
(1781–1864)

I.C.S. : son of Thomas Keene : born Sep. 30, 1781 : educated privately : went out to the Indian Army, 1798 : was in the siege of Seringapatam, May 4, 1799 : transferred to Madras Civil Service, by influence of his uncle, Lord Harris (*q.v.*) : passed through the College of Fort William, Calcutta : served in Madras, but resigned his appointment in 1811 : graduated at Sidney Sussex College, Cambridge, in 1815 : resigned the Indian Civil Service and was ordained in 1817 : became Professor of Arabic and Persian at Haileybury in 1824, and Registrar : resigned his Professorship in 1834 : edited some Persian works : died Jan. 29, 1864.

KEENE, HENRY, GEORGE (1827–   )

I.C.S. : Son of Rev. Professor Keene : educated at Rugby, Oxford, and Haileybury : entered the Indian Civil Service, 1847 : served in N.W. Provinces and retired in 1882 : Fellow of Calcutta University : C.I.E. 1882 : author of *Fall of the Mogul Empire*, 1876 ; *Madhava Rao Sindia*, 1892 ; *History of India*, 1898 ; *A Servant of John Company* : edited *Oriental Biographical Dictionary* : contributed articles to *Dictionary of National Biography*.

KEIGHLEY, CHARLES MARSH
(1847–   )

Born 1847 : entered the Army, 1867, and became Lt-Colonel, 1897 : served in the Afghan war, 1878–9 : Mahsud- Waziri expedition,1881 : Hazara expedition, 1888 : D.S.O.. 1889 : N.W. Frontier, 1897–8 : C.B., 1898.

KEITH-FALCONER, HON. ION GRANT NEVILLE (1856–1887)

Born July 5, 1856, third son of the Earl of Kintore : educated at Cheam, Harrow, and Trinity College, Cambridge : studied Hebrew, Syriac and Arabic: gained the Tyrwhitt University Hebrew Scholarship and a first-class in the Semitic Languages tripos : came under the influence of General C. G. Gordon (*q.v.*) R.E. in 1880–1 : studied Arabic . at Assiout on the Nile, 1881–2 : was University Examiner in 1883–4 : determined to go to Aden as Missionary to the Arabs : went out for 6 months to Aden experimentally, 1885–6 : was formally appointed on May 26, 1886, by the General Assembly of 'the Free Church of Scotland to found and carry on a Mission to the Arab Muhammadans : he was appointed Lord Almoner's Professor of Arabic at Cambridge in 1886 : went to Aden again, Dec. 1886 : lived in a temporary abode at Sheikh Othman, nine miles inland from Aden, to learn Somali : he soon suffered from fever and yielded to successive attacks, dying on May 11, 1887. The Keith-Falconer Mission has since continued there. He translated the Syriac version of the *Fables of Bidpai* 1885. He was also a great cyclist : and performed a number of feats, breaking previous records of time and distance : he was President of the London Bicycle Club, 1877–86.

KELLNER, SIR GEORGE WELSH
(1825–1886)

Educated at the Parental Academy, now the Doveton College, Calcutta : entered the service of the Indian Government, 1841: was Inspr-General of Accounts, 1866–70 : Military Accountant-General, 1871–77 : Financial Commissioner and Member of Council, Cyprus, 1878–83 : Assistant Paymaster-General in the Court of Chancery, 1884 : K.C.M.G. 1879: C.S.I. : died June 10, 1886.

KELLOGG, SAMUEL H. (1839–1899)

Born in Westhampton, N.Y., Sep. 6, 1839 : graduated from Princeton Seminary, 1864 : to India as a Missionary, 1864, sent by the American Presbyterian Board : became Instructor in the Theological Training School at Allahabad, 1872 : a corresponding member of the American Oriental Society : returned home, 1876 : D.D. at Princeton, 1877 : Pastor of a Presbyterian Church at Pittsburg, 1877, and at Toronto, 1886–92 : lectured, 1879, on Comparative Religion in the Western Theological Seminary : returned to India, 1892, on behalf of the North India and British and Foreign Bible Societies, to join a committee for translating the Old Testament into Hindi : died May 3, 1899 : wrote :—*Grammar of the Hindi Language,* 1876 ; *The Light of Asia,* and *The Light of the World,* 1885.

KELLY, JAMES GRAVES (1843–   )

Born 1843 : entered the Army, 1863, and became Colonel, 1895 : served in Hazara expedition, 1891 : Miranzai expedition, 1891: Chitral expedition, 1895 : Brevet-Colonel and C.B.

KELLY, SIR RICHARD DENIS
(1815–1897)

Entered the Army, 1834 : son of Colonel Kelly : served in the Crimea : taken prisoner when wounded : in the mutiny commanded the 34th regt. in the actions at Cawnpur, capture of Lucknow and relief of Azimghar : commanded a column in Oudh in 1858–9, and a Field Force in 1859, and on the Nipal frontier : C.B., 1858 : K.C.B., 1860 : retired, 1864 : Maj-General, 1868 : General, 1880 : died July 2, 1897.

KEMBALL, SIR ARNOLD BURROWES
(1820–   )

Born Nov. 18, 1820 : son of T. Kemball : Political Officer : educated at Addiscombe : joined the Bombay Artillery, 1837 : served in the first Afghan war, 1838–9 : at Ghazni and Kabul : Assistant Resident at Bushire, 1842 : Political Resident, Persian Gulf, 1852 : Consul-General, Bagdad, and Political Agent, Turkish Arabia, 1855–73 : in the Persian war, 1857, at Ahwaz and Muhamra : C.B. : and Brevet-Major : on the Turko-Persian

Boundary Commission, 1873 : Military Attaché with the Turkish Army in the Russo-Turkish war, 1876–77 : K.C.S.I., 1866 : K.C.B., 1878 : General, 1880.

KEMBALL, GEORGE VERE (1859–   )

Born Oct. 1859 : son of Maj-General J. S. Kemball : educated at Harrow : joined R.A., 1878 : and became Lt-Colonel, 1901 : served in Afghan war, 1879–80 : Chitral Relief Force, 1895 : Brevet-Major : N.W. Frontier, 1897–8 : West Africa, 1901 : commanded Kano-Sakoto expedition, 1903 : C.B.: D.S.O., 1902 : Brig-General, West African Field Force.

KENNAWAY, SIR JOHN, BARONET (1758–1836)

Political : son of William Kennaway : born March 6, 1858 : educated at Exeter Grammar School : entered the E. I. Co.'s military service in 1772 : wrecked at the mouth of the Ganges : in 1781 he was Persian Secretary to Col. T. D. Pearse, commanding the force sent from Bengal to the Carnatic : Captain in 1781 : served under Sir Eyre Coote against Hyder in the Carnatic : in subsequent campaigns up to 1786 : then became A.D.C. to Lord Cornwallis, who sent him in 1788 to insist on the cession of the Guntur Sircar, as agreed upon, and to make a treaty of July, 1790, with the Nizam : Baronet, in 1791 : he also made the treaty of Seringapatam, of March 1792, with Tippoo : he was the first Resident at Hyderabad from April 28, 1788 : retired to England in 1794 : died Jan. 1, 1836.

KENNEDY, JAMES (1842–   )

I.C.S. : born 1842 : son of Rev. J. Kennedy, M.A., missionary in Benares and Kumaon, and minister of Portobello, Scotland : educated at Edinburgh High School and University : went out to India, 1863 : retired, 1890 : Magistrate and Collector of several districts in the United Provinces : Honorary Treasurer of the Royal Asiatic Society and Member of the Bishop of London's Diocesan Conference : has written, " Early Commerce of Babylon and India," " Buddhist Gnosticism," " The System of Basilides " and other articles in the *J.R.A.S* : the " Mediæval History of India," in the *Imperial Gazetteer* : *History of the N.W.P.* in the

British Empire series (India), "Anglo-Indian Novelists and Hinduism," the "Tendencies of Hinduism," and other articles on Indian Religions and Indian Education in *The East and the West*, the *Asiatic Quarterly Review*, etc. : lectures on India at University College, London.

KENNEDY, JOHN PITT (1796–1879)

Son of John Pitt Kennedy : born May 8, 1796 : educated at Foyle College, Londonderry, and the R.M.A., Woolwich, entering the R.E. in 1815 : became Secretary and Director of Public Works in Cephalonia, 1822–8, under Sir Charles Napier : devoted himself to Irish agriculture and education : Secretary to the Devon Commission and the Famine Relief Committee : was Military Secretary to Sir Charles Napier when C. in C. in India, 1849–50 : at the forcing of the Kohat Pass, 1850 : made the Kennedy Road from Simla towards Tibet : Consulting Engineer to Government for Railways : retired in 1852 : Lt-Colonel : managing Director of the Bombay, Baroda and Central India Railway, surveying the line, 1853–4 : died June 28, 1879 : wrote extensively on Irish and Indian subjects.

KENNEDY, SIR MICHAEL KAVANAGH (1824–1898)

General : born April 28, 1824 : son of G. M. Kennedy : educated at Addiscombe : entered the E. I. Co.'s service in the Engineers in Bombay, 1841 : Lt-Colonel, 1861 : Secretary to the Government of Bombay in the P.W.D., 1863 : K.C.S.I. for services during the famine, 1876–8, in Bombay and Madras : Director-General of transport during the Afghan war of 1879–80 : in the operations round Kabul in Dec. 1879 : retired at end of 1880 after the campaign : Colonel Commandant R.E., 1891 : died Feb. 1, 1898.

KENNEDY, VANS (1784–1846)

Son of Robert Kennedy : born 1784 : educated at Edinburgh, Berkhamsted, Monmouth : went to Bombay in the E. I. Co.'s military service in 1800 : studied languages, and became Persian interpreter to the Peshwa's subsidiary force at Sirur, 1807 : Judge-Advocate-General to the Bombay Army, 1817–35 : Oriental Translator to the Bombay Government, 1835–46 : became a Maj-General : was a great student : published a Mahratti dictionary : wrote on questions connected with languages and mythology, and on military law, e.g. the *Ancient Chronology and History of Persia* ; *Researches into the Origin and Affinity of the Principal Languages of Asia and Europe* ; also on *Ancient and Hindu Mythology*, 1831 ; on the *Vedanta Philosophy of the Hindus*, and on Muhammadan Law : an active member of the Bombay Literary Society : for some time its President : died at Bombay, Dec. 29, 1846.

KER, ROBERT (1776 ?–1819)

Son of Ker of Kersfield in Peebles : to India in the B.C.S., 1791 : Collector of Chittagong about 1798 : Judge-Collector of Cuttack : Judge of Bareli : and of the *Sadr Adalat* in 1814 : restored order in Cuttack in 1818, after the insurrection there : died off Sagar Island, Dec. 3, 1819, on his way from Cuttack to Bengal.

KERN, JOHN HENRY CASPAR (1833–)

Born April 6, 1833, in Java : son of a Major in the Dutch Indian Army : to Holland, when seven years old : educated at Utrecht and Leiden : studied Sanskrit and Classical Philology : Litter. Doct., 1855 : studied Sanskrit under A. Weber at Berlin : appointed Professor of Greek in the Athenæum at Maestricht, 1858 : studied in London from 1862 : Sanskrit Professor at Queen's College, Benares, 1863–65 : held the same position at Leiden University, 1865–1903 : great linguist and scholar : noted for his researches into the ancient civilization of India, and of the East Indian archipelago : his chief works on Indian subjects are— his Dutch translation of Kalidas' drama *Sakuntala*, 1862 : text of *Brhat-Samhita by Varaha-Mihira*, 1865, followed by English translation, 1870 ; *History of Indian Buddhism* in Dutch, 1881, translated into German by Jacobi : English translation of the *Saddharma-Pundarika* (Sacred Books of the East, vol. xxi), 1884 : *Manual of Indian Buddhism*, 1896, etc. : collaborated in the great Sanskrit Dictionary with Böhtlingk and Roth : Hon. M.R.A.S. : Member of the Royal Academy of Sciences, Amsterdam ; and of many other learned Societies of different countries.

KERR, FREDERIC WALTER (1867–)

Born May 20, 1867 : son of Admiral Lord Frederic H. Kerr : educated at Charterhouse : joined the Army, 1886 : served as Adjutant Gordon Highlanders in Chitral Relief expedition, 1895 : D.S.O.: Tirah campaign : Dargai, etc., 1897–8 : South African war as Brig-Major, 1900–1901 : Brevet-Major.

KERR, LORD MARK (1817–1900)

Entered the Army at 18 : served in the Crimea : in the Indian mutiny he commanded the 13th Light Infantry, and relieved Azimghar in April, 1858 : in the pursuit of Kooer Singh : wounded at Jagdishpur : in the Trans-Gogra campaign : C.B. : Brig-General at Delhi : commanded the Poona Division, 1874–7 : Maj-General, 1868 : General, 1878 : G.C.B., 1893 : died May 17, 1900.

KERSHAW, SIR LOUIS ADDIN (1845–1899)

Son of Matthew Kershaw : educated at Bradford and at Pembroke College, Oxford : called to the bar at the Inner Temple, 1872 : Q.C., 1895 : Revising Barrister in Yorkshire : Chief Justice of the High Court at Allahabad, 1898 : knighted : subsequently Chief Justice of the High Court, Bombay, 1898 : died Feb. 17, 1899.

KETTLE, TILLY (1740–1786)

Artist : born 1740 : son of a house-painter : exhibited portraits at the Free Society of Artists, 1761, and the Society of Artists, 1765 : was in India from 1770 to 1777, and made a fortune, painting portraits, historical and fancy scenes, some of which he sent to be exhibited in England : exhibited at the Royal Academy, 1777–83 : in 1781, a historical piece, "The Mogul of Hindustan reviewing the E. I. Co.'s troops" : became bankrupt : started again for India in 1786, overland : died at Aleppo. His picture of Warren Hastings is in the National Portrait Gallery : F.S.A.

KETTLEWELL, THOMAS (1831–1903)

Colonel : his family connected with India from early days of the 18th century, when the firm of Kettlewell and Bullen was founded in India: entered the E. I. Co.'s service in 1852: joined the Bombay Staff Corps later: was in the Persian expedition, at the landing in Hallilah Bay, at the storming and capture of Reshire, and at the surrender of Bushire: Captain, 1864: Colonel, 1882: died April, 1903.

KEYES, SIR CHARLES PATTON
(1823-1896)

Son of Thomas Keyes: born 1823: entered the 30th Madras N.I., 1843: served in all the principal Panjab border campaigns, 1849–70: with Sir C. Napier at the Kohat Pass, 1850: against the Waziris, 1860: in the Umbeyla campaign, 1863: Brevet-Lt-Colonel: C.B.: commanded an expedition against the Waziris in 1869: Brevet-Colonel: commanded the Dour Valley expedition, 1870: served against the Jowaki Afridis, 1877–8, as Brig-General commanded the Panjab Frontier Force and the Kohat column: K.C.B.: commanded the Hyderabad Subsidiary Force, 1881: retired, 1884: Maj-General, 1887: General, 1889: died Feb. 5, 1896.

KHAIRUDDIN MUHAMMAD, FAKIR
(1751-1827 ?)

Of Allahabad: in the service of the British Government, and earned a pension for the assistance rendered to Mr. Anderson in his negotiations with the Mahrattas: left Anderson, and took employment under one of the Imperial Princes: obtained some favour from Nawab Saadat Ali at Lucknow: lived latterly, and died, at Jaunpur, about 1827: wrote the Ibratnama, a history up to 1790 A.D. of the reigns of Alamgir II and Shah Alam (q.v.), including the atrocities and death of Ghulam Kadir: wrote also the history of Jaunpur: and Balwant-nama, or history of the Benares Rajas, including Balwant Singh, Chait Singh, Mahipat Narain, and Udit Narain Singh.

KHOTE, RAGHANATH NARAYAN
(1821-1891)

Born Sep. 21, 1821: a Shenvi or Gond Brahmin: educated at the Elphinstone Fort School: and at the College, as a Scholar, 1840: engaged in mercantile pursuits, 1841–78: J.P.: Member of the Municipal Corporation, Town Council, etc.: Sheriff of Bombay, 1883: C.I.E.: Chairman of the Bombay Corporation, 1883: took an active share in public movements: Joint Secretary of the Famine Relief Committee, 1876–7: a warm advocate of Life Assurance among the native community: Director of Oriental Life Association: died April 25, 1891.

KHURSHID JAH BAHADUR, NAWAB
SIR (? -1902)

Shams-ul-Umra, Amir-i-Kabir: representative of the great Shams-ul-Umra family: premier noble of Hyderabad, holding the high hereditary position of Commander of the Nizam's household troops: Member of the Council of Regency, 1882: Member of the Council of the State on the accession of the Regency, 1884: died July 17, 1902.

KHWAJA ABDUL GHANI MIA,
NAWAB SIR (? -1896)

He was descended from a family which came, some generations ago, from Kashmir. An ancestor held an appointment at the Mogul Court at Delhi, and on its overthrow moved to Sylhet, embarking on business there: a later ancestor removed to Dacca, and established the family as wealthy zamindars in Eastern Bengal. Nawab Abdul Ghani improved its position and, by his personal energy and character, acquired great influence. During the mutiny, his loyalty to Government, and his firmness in remaining at Dacca helped to save Eastern Bengal: in 1869 he prevented serious disturbances between the Shias and Sunnis: in the Lushai and Naga expeditions, and in famine relief he materially aided Government. His public and private charity was munificent, his donations amounting to lakhs of rupees: he gave Dacca a pure water-supply at great expense: he was highly esteemed by Government and all classes, for his wealth, position and loyalty. He was an Honorary Magistrate: Member of the Bengal Legislative Council (1866), and of the Governor-General's Legislative Council (1867): C.S.I. (1871): K.C.S.I. (1886), and was granted the personal title of Nawab in 1875, which was made hereditary on Jan. 1, 1877. He was presented with a medal by H.R.H.

the Prince of Wales in Calcutta in 1875 :
died at Dacca in 1896 at an advanced
age.

KHWAJA AHSANULLA, NAWAB BAHADUR, SIR (1846-1901)

Son of ' Nawab Sir Khwaja Abdul
Ghani Mia (q.v.) : born in 1846 : succeeded
to the management of the family estates
in 1868, and after his father's death
worthily upheld all the best traditions of
his house as a landowner, an open-handed
dispenser of charity and hospitality, an
enlightened and loyal supporter of Government : for years a Municipal Commissioner
and Honorary Magistrate of Dacca : made
Khan Bahadur (1871): Nawab (1875):
C.I.E. (1891): Nawab Bahadur (1892):
K.C.I.E. (1897) : Member of the Governor-
General's Legislative Council in 1890,
and again in 1899. He died suddenly
at Dacca, Dec. 16, 1901.

KHWAJA SALIMULLA, NAWAB (? –)

Succeeded his father, Khwaja Ahsanulla
(q.v.), as head of the family of the Dacca
Nawabs in Dec. 1901 : was a Deputy
Magistrate for some years : a nominated
Member of the Bengal Legislative Council
in 1903.

KIELHORN, FRANZ (1840–   )

Born 1840 : Hon. LL.D. Edinburgh
and Glasgow : Professor of Oriental
languages at the Dekkan College, Poona :
Hon. D. Litt., Oxford : Professor of Sanskrit, Gottingen : C.I.E., 1886 : author
of several publications on Indian grammar,
epigraphy and chronology.

KIERNANDER, REV. JOHN ZACHA-RIAH (1711-1799)

Danish missionary : born in Sweden,
Nov. 21, 1711 : educated at Lindkoping
and Upsal : at Halle, 1735–9 : sent out
in 1739–40 by the S.P.C.K. as a missionary
to Cuddalore : on its capture by Lally in
1758, Kiernander went to Tranquebar,
and, after a few months, to Calcutta, also
in 1758 : established a Mission there
with the consent of the Government :
a Mission school opened Dec. 1, 1758 : he
built the Mission Church, founded May,
1767, consecrated Dec. 1770 : called Beth
Tephilla (the House of Prayer): about

1786 he signed bonds to raise money
required for his son's building speculations,
which failed : in 1878 the Sheriff of
Calcutta attached his church : Charles
Grant (q.v.) paid 10,000 rupees to release
it, when it was transferred to trustees :
Kiernander retired, 1788, to Chinsura, and
became Chaplain to the Dutch there. He
was taken prisoner when the English took
Chinsura in 1795, went to Calcutta, and
lived there in poverty till he died in 1799,
after a continuous residence in India
from 1740 : great success attended his
labours among the Portuguese and native
congregations at Cuddalore and Calcutta.

KILPATRICK, JOHN (? –1787)

Major : after the tragedy of the Black
Hole at Calcutta in June, 1756, he was
sent up with 230 soldiers from Madras :
this was the first relieving force to reach
Calcutta : it is said that he was one of
those who voted in Clive's council of
war at Plassy against an advance : a
decision to which Clive did not adhere :
died 1787.

KIMBERLEY, JOHN WODEHOUSE, FIRST EARL OF (1826-1902)

Born Jan. 7, 1826 : son of Hon. Henry
Wodehouse : succeeded his grandfather
as third Baron, 1846 : created first Earl
of Kimberley, 1866 : educated at Eton
and Christ Church, Oxford : first class
honours, 1847 : Under Secretary of State
for Foreign Affairs, 1852 : for India,
April–Nov. 1864 : Lord Lieutenant of
Ireland, Lord Privy Seal, Secretary for
the Colonies, etc.: Secretary of State for
India, Dec. 16, 1882, to June 24, 1885 :
again Feb. 7, to Aug. 4, 1886 : and
again Aug. 19, 1892, to March 10, 1894 :
Lord President of the Council, and Foreign
Secretary, 1894–5 : K.G., 1885 : died
April 8, 1902.

KING, SIR GEORGE (1840–   )

Born April 12, 1840 : Lt-Colonel :
educated at Aberdeen Grammar School
and University : M.B. : Superintendent
of the Calcutta Royal Botanic Garden,
1870–98 : author of several monographs
on Indian Orders, *Materials for a Flora
of the Malay Peninsula* : K.C.I.E., 1898 :
F.R.S. : LL.D. : Member of several
foreign Botanical Societies.

KING, SIR HENRY SEYMOUR
(1852-   )

Son of Henry Samuel King : educated at Charterhouse and Balliol College, Oxford : Head of the firm of H. S. King & Co., London (with branches at Bombay and Calcutta), bankers : founder of the *Overland Mail* : K.C.I.E., 1892 : M.P. for Hull (Central) since 1885 : Mayor of Kensington, 1901, and 1902 : M.A. : J.P. : F.R.G.S.

KING, JAMES STEWART (1848-   )

Son of Rev. Robert Belsham King : born May 15, 1848 : educated at Fairfield, Wexford, Dublin University and R.M.C., Sandhurst : joined the 107th regt., 1868 : the Bombay Staff Corps, 1874 : Major, 1888 : retired, 1892 : Superintendent, Army Schools, Bombay, 1877-8 : on duty to collect and translate Persian historical MSS. relating to the minor Muhammadan dynasties, to help Professor Dowson (*q.v.*), 1879-80 : Assistant Political at Sawantwari, Aden, Kolapur, and Agent at Zaila : wrote a full account of the Island of Perim, 1877 : led an expedition, 1884, against the rebellious Kotaibi Hill Arabs, 75 m. N. of Aden : subdued them and made peace between them and their Amir, of Dhtali : sent on political missions to S. coast of Arabia, Sokotra, the Somali coast : took over the W. Somali country, 1884, when the Egyptians left it : successfully counteracted French schemes on the W. Somali coast, 1885-7 : explored into the interior, 1885-6 : wrote for the *Indian Antiquary*, 1887-98, on *Somali as a Written Language, The Fate of St. Mark, The Aborigines of Sokotra, The Siege of Ahmadnagar* : published, 1900, *The History of the Bahmani Dynasty :* contributed also to *J.R.A.S.* : M.R.A.S. in 1892.

KING, LUCAS WHITE (1856-   )

I.C.S. : born 1856 : son of Deputy-Surgeon-General Henry King : educated at Ennis College, and Dublin University : entered the Indian Civil Service, 1878 : Assistant Resident at Mysore, 1887 : Deputy Commissioner, Dera Ismail Khan, 1890-95 : Political Officer Zhob Valley Field Force, 1890 : Waziristan Field Force, 1894 : Boundary Officer Indo-Afghan demarcation, 1895 : Deputy

Commissioner, Peshawar, 1895, and Kohat, 1897-1900 : Political Officer, Tirah expedition, 1897-8 : C.S.I. : Commissioner of Lahore : Commissioner of Salt Revenue, N. India : Commissioner of Multan : author of *Monographs on Oriental Numismatics and the Orakzai Country and Clans.*

KING, SIR RICHARD, BARONET
(1730-1806)

Son of Curtis King, master in the Navy : born Aug. 10, 1730 : entered the Navy in 1738 : served in the E. Indies : Lieutenant in 1746 : again in the E. Indies, was in the flagship of Admiral C. Watson (*q.v.*), in 1754 : in Jan. 1757, commanded the landing-party at the capture of Calcutta and Hughli : went to the W. Indies : in 1762 he took General Draper (*q.v.*) out to India : in 1779 again in India with Sir E. Hughes (*q.v.*) : in Hughes' action with Suffrein off Sadras in Feb. 1782, his ship, the *Exeter*, was nearly sunk : in four other actions between the same Admirals he distinguished himself : first knighted : made a Baronet in 1792 : M.P. for Rochester : Admiral, 1795 : died Nov. 7, 1806.

KINLOCH, ALEXANDER ANGUS AIRLIE (1838-   )

Born Dec. 27, 1838 : son of Colonel John Grant Kinloch : educated at Woolwich : entered the Army, 1855 : D.A.A.G. for Musketry, India, 1870-7 : D.A.Q.M.G. in Afghan war, 1878-80 : Brevet-Major and Lt-Colonel : commanded 2nd and 4th Battalions K.R.R. : commanded three 2nd class Districts in India, and 1st Brigade Chitral Relief Force, 1895 : retired as Maj-General, 1895 : author of *Large Game Shooting in Tibet, the Himalayas, Northern and Central India :* C.B., 1893.

KINNEIR, SIR JOHN MACDONALD
(1782-1830)

Political : son of John Macdonald : born Feb. 3, 1782 : joined the 24th Madras, N.I. in 1807 : attached to Sir J. Malcolm's mission to Persia, 1808-9 : travelled to England across Europe, and in 1813 from Constantinople through Armenia, Kurdistan, to Bagdad and Bombay : wrote his account of it : took his mother's name of Kinneir : published a Gazetteer of Persia : Town-Major of

Madras, and Resident with the Nawab of the Carnatic : Envoy to Persia, 1824–30 : was in the hostilities with Russia, and mediated, before the treaty of Turkaman-chai of Feb. 23, 1828 : died at Tabriz, June 11, 1830.

KIPLING, JOHN LOCKWOOD
(1837–   )

Born 1837 : son of Rev. Joseph Kipling : educated at Woodhouse Grove : Architectural Sculptor, Bombay School of Art, 1865–75 : Principal, Mayo School of Art : Curator Central Museum, Lahore, 1875–93 : author of *Beast and Man in India* : retired from the Indian Education Department, 1893 : C.I.E., 1886.

KIPLING, RUDYARD (1865–   )

Born Dec. 30, 1865 : son of J. Lockwood Kipling (*q.v.*) : educated at Westward Ho : Assistant Editor of the *Civil and Military Gazette*, Lahore, and the *Pioneer*, Allahabad, 1882–9 : author of *Departmental Ditties*, 1886, *Plain Tales from the Hills*, 1887 ; *Soldiers Three, Wee Willie Winkie*, etc., 1888–9 ; *The ' Light that Failed*, 1891 ; *Barrack Room Ballads*, 1892 ; *The Jungle Book*, (1) 1894, (2) 1895 ; *Kim*, 1901, etc., etc.

KIRKPATRICK, JAMES ACHILLES
(1764–1805)

Lt-Colonel : son of Colonel James Kirkpatrick, and brother of William Kirkpatrick (*q.v.*) : born Aug. 1764 : educated in France and at Eton : joined the E. I. Co.'s Madras Army in 1779–80 : in the Mysore war, 1791–2 : in charge of garrison at Vizianagram, 1793 : Assistant to his brother William, Resident at Hyderabad, in 1795 : succeeded him in 1797 : negotiated the several treaties of 1798, 1799, 1800, 1802, 1803, 1804 on behalf of the Governor-General with the Nizam of Hyderabad, for various objects, the suppression of French influence, etc., gaining the full confidence of the Marquess Wellesley : brought the Nizam's contingent of 60,000 men into the field against Tippoo, 1799 : died, while Resident at Hyderabad, on a visit to Calcutta, on Oct. 15, 1805.

KIRKPATRICK, WILLIAM (1754–1812)

Born 1754 : son of Colonel James Kirkpatrick of the Madras cavalry :

joined the Bengal Infantry in 1773 : became Maj-General in 1811 : was Persian Interpreter to General Stibbert, C. in C. in Bengal, for periods between 1777 and 1785 : was Resident at Gwalior, and Persian Interpreter with Lord Cornwallis in the Mysore war, 1791–2 : mediated in Nipal, until then unvisited by any Englishman, between the Nipalese and Chinese in 1793 : Resident at Hyderabad in 1795 : met Lord Mornington at the Cape in 1798 and became his Military Secretary in 1798, and Private Secretary in 1799 : after Seringapatam in 1799, was made a Commissioner for the partition of Mysore : Resident at Poona in 1801 : left India in 1801 : he was well versed in Oriental languages and Indian lore : translated Tippoo's diary and letters from Persian, and wrote an account of his mission to Nipal : he died Aug. 22, 1812.

KITCHENER OF KHARTOUM, HORATIO HERBERT, FIRST VISCOUNT (1850–   )

Born June 24, 1850 : son of Lt-Colonel H. H. Kitchener : educated at Woolwich : entered R.E., 1871, and became Maj-General, 1896 : employed in Palestine Survey, 1874–8, and Cyprus Survey, 1878–82 : commanded Egyptian Cavalry, 1882–4 : Nile expedition, 1884–5 : Brevet-Lt-Colonel : Governor of Suakim, 1886–8 : Soudan Frontier, 1889 : engagement at Toski : C.B. : Sirdar of Egyptian Army, 1890 : commanded Dongola expeditionary force, 1896 : Maj-General : K.C.B. : commanded Khartoum expedition, 1898 : raised to Peerage with grant of £30,000 and G.C.B. : Chief of Staff of Forces in South Africa, 1899–1900, C. in C., S. Africa, 1900–2 : Lt-General and General : received Viscountcy and grant of £50,000 : C. in C., India, since 1902.

KITSON, GERALD CHARLES
(1856–   )

Born Oct. 6, 1856 : son of Rev. J. B. Kitson : educated at Winchester : entered the Army, 1875, and became Lt-Colonel, 1896 : D.A.A.G. at Meerut, 1890–2 : A.A.G., Umbala, 1892–4 : served at Manipur, 1891 : at the Staff College, 1885–6 : Commandant of Military College, Kingston, Canada : Military Attaché of British Embassy, Washington : Commandant of R.M.C., Sandhurst, 1902 : C.M.G., 1901.

KNOX, SIR ALEXANDER (? -1834)

Went out to Bengal in 1780 in the Army : rose to be Maj-General, 1830 : in the campaign against Chait Singh, at the capture of Benares in 1781 : in Baghelkund and Bundelkund, 1782–4 : at the siege of Bangalore, 1791 : at Savandrug, Dec. 1791 : in Cornwallis' campaign, 1792 : fought against the Rohillas under Abercromby : in Lord Lake's actions in 1803 : at Deeg, 1804 : Bhartpur, 1805 : took Ajmir, 1818 : in Rajputana, 1823 : commanded the Dinapur Division : K.C.B. 1831 : died at Barrackpur after 54 years' service, Sep. 1, 1834.

KNOX, SIR WILLIAM GEORGE (1847–)

Born Oct. 20, 1847 : son of General T. E. Knox, C.B. : educated at Woolwich : joined the R.A., 1867 : served in the Abyssinian campaign, 1867–8 : Ashanti campaign, 1874 : Afghan campaign, 1878–9 : at Ali Masjid : Zulu and Transvaal campaign, 1879 : commanded a Brigade in S. African war : siege of Ladysmith : K.C.B., 1900 : Maj-General commanding R.A., 3rd Army Corps, since 1902.

KŒNIG, JOHANN GERARD (1728–1785)

Doctor : born in 1728 : of Courland in Lithuania : pupil of Linnæus : visited India in search of natural curiosities : became a friend of Sir Thomas Munro (*q.v.*) : travelled widely over India from the Ganges to the Indus, from Delhi to Cape Comorin : was in 1778 in the service of the E. I. Co., who sent him to Siam and the Straits of Malacca, in search of plants and minerals : while travelling along the coast from Ceylon to Calcutta, died June 26, 1785.

KOSEGARTEN, JOHANN GOTTFRIED LUDWIG (1792–1862)

Born Sep. 10, 1792, at Altenkirchen in Rügen : son of a pastor : studied theology at Griefswald in Prussia, 1808–12, and Oriental languages in Paris, 1812–14 : went to the University of Jena, 1817 : appointed to Professorship of Theology, Oriental Languages and Literature, hold-

ing it till his death. Besides his labours in Arabic, Persian, and Turkish, was known as a Sanskrit scholar : published a translation of *Nala and Damayanti* from the Mahabharata, 1820 : and the *Pantchatantra* collection of fables : died. at Griefswald, 1862.

KRUPABAI, (1862–1894)

Daughter of Haripunt, a Mahratta Brahman, Christian convert and missionary at Ahmadnagar : born Feb. 14, 1862 : educated at a missionary school, Bombay, and the Madras Medical College, which she was the first Indian lady to join : she married Samuel Sathianadhan, M.A., LL.B. (Cantab), F.S.S., Assistant D.P.I., Madras, and Professor of Logic and Moral Philosophy at the Madras Presidency College : author of *History of Education in the Madras Presidency*, etc. She founded a school for Muhammadan girls at Ootacamund, and was prominent in several schemes for the education of women in S. India : wrote *Saguna*, a novel of Indian Christian life, and *Kamala*, a novel of Hindu life : died at Madras, Aug. 8, 1894.

KURZ, W. SULPIZ (1833 ?–1878)

Native of Augsburg in Bavaria : botanist : joined the Army of Netherlands, India, in order that he might see something of the rich botany of the Malayan Archipelago : was Assistant Curator of the Herbarium at Buitenburg in Java : in 1864, Dr. T. Anderson obtained his services as Curator of the Herbarium in the Botanic Garden near Calcutta : he explored Burma and Pegu and the Andaman Islands in the interests of botany : wrote the *Forest Flora of British Burma*, 1877 : and many botanical papers in the Journals of various learned Societies : died at Pulo-Penang, Jan. 15, 1878.

KYD, JAMES (1786–1836)

Shipbuilder : son of Lt-General Alexander Kyd, who was related to and heir of Colonel Robert Kyd (*q.v.*) : born in India, 1786 : went home with his brother Robert to England, as boys, to be brought up to shipbuilding : returned to Calcutta in 1800, and were apprenticed to Waddell. the E. I. Co.'s master-builder. On his retirement, in 1807, they purchased the Kidderpur dockyard, near Calcutta, and James Kyd became Master Shipbuilder to the E.I. Co. In 1814 he visited England in the *General Kyd*, 1,279 tons, which he had constructed, and received, in 1815, testimonials from the Admiralty and Court of Directors for the repairs executed by him to H.M.S. *Semiramis* at St. Helena. Twenty-five vessels were built at his dockyard, including the *Hastings* man-of-war, 1,732 tons, 74 guns, in 1818, said to have been the only line-of-battle ship ever built in Calcutta, and the *Diana* steamer, 89 tons, in 1823, the first steamer built on the Hughli. He was universally recognized as the head of the East Indian class to which he belonged. He died Oct. 26, 1836, when the Kidderpur dockyard was purchased by Government : the brother Robert Kyd died in 1825.

KYD, ROBERT (1746–1793)

Colonel : of an old Forfarshire family : Cadet and Ensign Bengal Engineers, 1764 : Lt-Colonel, 1782 : Military Secretary to Government, when, in 1786, he proposed to the acting Governor-General, Sir John Macpherson, the formation of a Botanic Garden at Calcutta for the growth of teak timber for ship-building, the cultivation of spices, e.g. cinnamon, the introduction of cotton, tobacco, coffee, tea and other commercial products. The Governor-General supported the scheme, which, in 1787, received the most hearty approbation of the Court of Directors. Kyd's country house and garden were at Sibpur, Howrah, near Shalimar Point. For the Botanic Garden he selected 300 acres contiguous to his property : was Honorary Superintendent of the garden until his death. The area was reduced to 270 acres, in 1820, when teak-growing had been found impossible, and the area devoted to it was given up for the Bishop's College. Colonel Robert Kyd died May 26, 1793, bequeathing the bulk of his property to Major (afterwards Lt-General, died Nov. 25, 1826) Alexander Kyd, son of Capt. James Kyd, R.N., and father of James (*q.v.*), Robert, and Alexander Kyd. A beautiful marble urn, by Banks the sculptor, was erected in 1795 to the memory of Col. Robert Kyd, in the Botanic Garden, on a site selected by Dr. Roxburgh, his successor.

LA BOURDONNAIS, BERTRAND FRANCIS MAHE DE (1699–1753)

Went to India at 10, and on other voyages in 1713 and 1722 : led the attack on Mahé, when captured by the French in 1725 : traded in the Arabian seas : served under the Governor of Goa for 2 years : returned to France, 1733, and was Governor of the Isle of France, and Bourbon, 1735–40 : from France in 1741, he took out ships and troops to the Isle of France : resumed his Governorship, and, when ordered to send back his squadron, collected more ships, and, in 1746, took them to the Coromandel coast and fought some actions with indecisive results off Ceylon and Negapatam against the English squadron under Peyton, who retired : went to Pondicherry : reinforced there, he, under pressure from the Governor, Dupleix (*q.v.*) appeared with his fleet before Madras, landed his forces on Sep. 15, 1746, and besieged it by sea and land until the English surrendered on Sep. 21, the question of ransom of the town being left for future adjustment. This condition Dupleix refused to ratify and superseded La Bourdonnais. While they were disputing, a severe monsoon shattered the French fleet on Oct. 13, 1746. La Bourdonnais signed a treaty with the English authorities at Madras : it is stated that he was induced, by a personal bribe, to consent to the ransom of Madras. He made his way to the Isle of France, and, proceeding homewards, was captured in a Dutch vessel by the English, but released. On his return to France, he was confined in the Bastille for 3 years, and soon after his realease, on being acquitted by the Privy Council of the charges against him, he died on Sep. 9, 1753.

LACROIX, REV. ALPHONSE FRANCOIS (1799–1859)

Swiss Missionary, born May 10, 1799 : at first a tutor : became agent of the Netherlands Missionary Society at Chinsura, where he arrived, March 21, 1821 : when Chinsura became British, in 1825, he removed to Calcutta : became a British subject, and a member of the London Missionary Society : initiated religious Missions in the delta of the Ganges, in the Sundarbans, in Sagar island : a scholar in Bengali : founded the Bhawanipur Missionary Institution, 1851 : revised the Bengali version of the Scriptures and trained native preachers : died July 3, 1859.

LAESSOE, ALBERT F. DE P.
(1848–1903)

Son of Rev. C. de F. Laessoe : educated. at Copenhagen : obtained a Commission in the Danish Army, 1866 : joined the French Army, 1870 : resigned Danish service, 1878 : appointed to the Indian Foreign Office, 1881 : served with the Commission for delimitation of northern boundary of Afghanistan, 1884–7 : Assistant Commissioner Merwara, 1889 : Ajmir, 1892 : Political Agent, Bhopawar, 1893–9 : Political Agent in charge for years in India of Ayub Khan of Afghanistan : C.M.G. and C.I.E., 1887 : died from a pistol accident at Copenhagen, May 18. 1903.

LAFONT, REV. EUGENE, S.J.
(1837–)

Born March 26, 1837 : son of Pierre Lafont : educated at College of S. Barbara, Ghent : entered the Order of the Jesuits, 1854 : sent to Calcutta, 1865 : tutor at S. Xavier's College, Calcutta : lecturer in Experimental Science and Rector of S. Xavier's since 1871 : C.I.E. 1880 : a leading authority on Science in Bengal.

LAHA, MAHARAJA DURGA CHARAN
(1882–1904)

Merchant and landowner : son of Pran Kissen Laha, of the Subarnabanik (gold merchant) caste : the family was engaged in trade. Durga Charan was educated at the old Hindu College, and became head of the firm called by his father's name, in 1853 : Fellow of the Calcutta University : first native Port Commissioner of Calcutta : Member of the Bengal Legislative Council, 1874 : of the Governor-General's Legislative Council. 1882 and 1888 : President of the British Indian Association in 1885, 1895 : Sheriff. 1882 : C.I.E., 1884 : Raja. 1887 : Maharaja, 1891 : an able man of business, both in his own trade and in his landed estates, and attained great wealth : was consulted by Government on public. especially financial, questions : was a Commissioner for the reduction of public debt in 1882 : died March 20, 1904.

LAHIRI, RAMTANU (1813–1898)

Born at Krishnagar, 1813 : educated from 1826 at the Hare School : in 1828 joined the Hindu College : in 1834 was appointed a teacher there, and continued his work at Krishnagar, Burdwan, Bally, Barasat, Rasapagla for the education of the descendants of Tippoo Sultan : to Barisal and again to Krishnagar, whence he retired on pension, 1865 : he gave up the Brahmanical thread in 1851 and became a Brahmo : he lived an exemplary life and enjoyed great respect as a teacher he died in Aug. 1898.

LAING, SAMUEL (1812–1897)

Born Dec. 12, 1812 : son of Samuel Laing educated at Houghton-le-Spring, privately, and at St. John's College, Cambridge : second wrangler in 1831 : Fellow called to the bar at Lincoln's Inn, in 1837 : Secretary to the Railway Department of the Board of Trade. 1842–6 : Member of Lord Dalhousie's Railway Commission of 1845 : Chairman and Managing Director of the L.B. and S.C. Ry., 1848–55 and 1867–94 : Financial Secretary to the Treasury, 1859–60 : Finance Member of the Supreme Council in India from Jan. 1861, to July, 1862 : M.P., 1852–7, 1859, 1865–8, and 1868–85. He wrote *Modern Science and Modern Thought*, 1885 : *Problems of the Future*, 1889 ; *Human Origins*, 1892 : also *India and China : England's Mission in the East*, 1863 : he died, Aug. 6, 1897.

LAKE, EDWARD JOHN (1823–1877)

Son of Edward Lake, Major in the Madras Engineers : who served with distinction in the Mahratta war and was author of *Sieges of the Madras Army* : born June 19, 1823 : educated at Wimbledon and Addiscombe : went to India in the Royal Engineers, 1841–2 : joined the Sappers and Miners at Delhi : suppressed an outbreak near Kythul : was in the Satlaj campaign of 1845–6, at Mudki and Aliwal : served under John Lawrence at Kangra and Jalandhar in 1846 : commanded the Bahawalpur troops in the operations about Multan, 1848 : in the battle of Gujarat, the pursuit of the Sikhs and Afghans. 1849 : Brevet - Major : Commissioner of Jalandhar. 1855 : held fort of Kangra throughout the mutiny : Lt-Colonel. 1861 : Financial Commissioner

R

of the Punjab, 1865 : C.S.I., 1866 : retired as Maj-General, 1870 : became Honorary Secretary of East London Mission Relief Fund in 1868: and Honorary Lay Secretary of the Church Missionary Society, 1869 to 1876 : edited the *Church Missionary Record*, 1871–4 : died June 7, 1877.

LAKE, GERARD, FIRST VISCOUNT
(1744–1808)

Son of Launcelot Charles Lake : born July 27, 1744 : entered the first Foot Guards in 1758 : rose to be General in 1802 : served in N. Carolina under Cornwallis, 1781 : M.P. for Aylesbury, 1790–1802 : was in the war with France, 1793–4 : commanded in Ulster, 1796, and in Ireland, 1798, seeing active service there during the rebellion : was C. in C. in India and Member of Council from July, 1801, to July, 1805 : introduced some improvements : in 1802 took Sasni, Bijghar, Catchoura : in 1803 in two months he engaged the Mahrattas at Coel : stormed Alighar, Sep.4: took Delhi,Sep. 13: defeated Sindia's forces under Perron : took Agra, Oct. 18: won at Laswari, Nov 1, thus conquering Sindia : made a Peer in Sep. 1804 : defeated Holkar at Farrukhabad, Nov. 17, 1804 : took Deeg, Dec. 1804 : made four attempts to storm Bhartpur early in 1805 without success, but the Raja gave in and made peace. Lord Cornwallis was C. in C. from July to Oct. 1805 : on his death, Lake again commanded till Oct. 1807 : Holkar surrendered to Lake at Umritsar in Dec. 1805 : he returned to England and was made Viscount : died Feb. 20, 1808 : very popular as a commander with all ranks, and a great General in the field.

LAKSHMI CHAND, RAO BAHADUR
(1810–1866)

A member of the famous family of Seths of Mathura, celebrated as the leading bankers in N. India, and for their charity and beneficence : eldest son of Mani Ram (died 1836), founder of the firm, under whom the business flourished greatly, and the wealth and influence of the family rapidly increased. During the mutiny, Lakshmi Chand and his brothers, Radha Krishan and Gobind Das, displayed conspicuous loyalty. They warned the Collector of the impending outbreak, and sent information to Agra, which enabled the authorities there to disarm the native troops. When the station of Mathura was burnt, the Seths sheltered the European residents and conveyed them by boat to Agra : took charge of the treasure, maintained public order : made large advances of money to Govermennt, when none was procurable elsewhere, and throughout the mutiny maintained communication between Agra and Delhi at their own expense. For these services, Lakshmi Chand was made Rao Bahadur and presented with confiscated estates assessed at over Rs. 16,000, on favourable terms. Many of the religious and other buildings in Mathura were erected by the Seths, whose liberality was proverbial. Lakshmi Chand remained a Jain, but his brothers were converted to Vaishnavism : he left an only son, Raghunath Das.

LALLY, THOMAS ARTHUR, COUNT DE—AND BARON DE TOLLENDAL (1700–1766)

French General : born 1700 : son of Sir Gerard O'Lally, an Irish exile, inheriting an implacable hatred of England : distinguished himself in the French-Austrian war of 1734 at Philipsburg, and later at Fontenoy, Laffelat, Bergen-op-Zoom : to England in 1745, possibly as a spy : on the declaration of war between France and England in May, 1756, Lally was appointed, as one of the most promising French officers, to be Governor-General and C. in C., to command the French expedition to India, to expel the British thence : he, with Count d'Achè, reached Pondicherry in April-May, 1758, at once took Cuddalore, Fort St. David and Devikota : unsuccessfully attacked Tanjore : captured Arcot in Oct. 1758 : was joined by Bussy : besieged Madras for two months from Dec. 12, 1758, but retired on the appearance, in Feb. 1759, of an English fleet, under Admiral Pocock. Lally took the field in 1759, and met Colonel Eyre Coote at Wandiwash, was defeated there on Jan. 22, 1760, and lost other towns. Lally was then besieged from May, 1760, in Pondicherry by Coote, and forced to capitulate on Jan. 14, 1761, the French power in India thus collapsing, chiefly through want of proper support from France. Lally was sent to Madras, and to England as a prisoner of war : on his return to France, he was thrown into the Bastille, kept under trial for 2½ years, accused of having betrayed the interests of the King; condemned on May 9, 1766, and executed the same day. In 1783 the sentence was annulled, and Lally's estates were restored to his son.

LAMB, CHARLES (1775–1834)

Born Feb. 10, 1775: son of John Lamb: educated at Christ's Hospital: became a clerk in the accountant's office in the India House, 1792, and retired in 1825 on a pension of three-fourths of his salary: died Dec. 27, 1834: he corresponded with Thomas Manning (*q.v.*): apart from this his connexion with India appears to have been limited to his official duties: his literary work requires no mention here.

LAMBERT, SIR JOHN (1838–   )

Entered the Bengal Police Department, 1863: Deputy Commissioner of Police, Calcutta, 1874–89: officiating Superintendent for the suppression of Thagi and Dakaiti, 1882–4: Chief Commissioner of Police in Calcutta, 1889–97: Member of the Bengal Legislative Council, 1892: K.C.I.E., 1893.

LAMBTON, WILLIAM (1756–1823)

Born 1756: educated at Northallerton Grammar School and Newcastle-on-Tyne: entered the Army in 1781: went with the 33rd regt. under Arthur Wellesley to the Cape in 1796, to Bengal and Madras in 1798: was Brig-Major to Baird at the siege of Seringapatam (May, 1799), engaged in Mysore: was appointed Superintendent of the survey connecting the Malabar and Coromandel coasts, proposed by him: Superintendent of the Great Trigonometrical Survey: the survey necessitated the measurement of base lines, scientific observations and other operations connected with geodesy, which occupied him apparently the rest of his life: F.R.S., and Fellow of the Asiatic Society: Lt-Colonel: died at Hinganghat, Jan. 26 1823.

LAMINGTON, CHARLES WALLACE ALEXANDER NAPIER COCHRANE BAILLIE, SECOND BARON (1860–   )

Born July 29, 1860: son of first Baron: educated at Eton and Christ Church, Oxford: M.P. for N. St. Pancras, 1886–90:

Governor of Queensland, 1895–1901: Governor of Bombay since 1903: G.C.M.G, 1900: G.C.I.E., 1903.

LANE, CHARLES EDWARD WILLIAM (1786–1872)

Son of John Lane: born Oct. 23, 1786: joined a Bengal N.I. regt. in 1807: became General in 1870: was in the first Burmese war, 1825: commissariat officer at Dinapur, in 1832: commanded a regt. in Afghanistan under Nott in 1842: when in temporary command of Kandahar, he repulsed an attack of Afghans: C.B., 1842: died Feb. 18, 1872.

LANG, JOHN (1817–1864)

Went to India as a barrister: established and edited the *Mofussilite* on the ruins of the *Meerut Observer* in 1845–6 at Meerut: wrote with great ability and vigour: several novels by him first appeared in the *Mofussilite*: for a short time in Calcutta, he issued the *Optimist*: he died at Mussoorie, Aug. 20, 1864.

LANGLÉS, LOUIS MATHIEU (1764–1824)

Born near Montdidier, 1764: son of a military officer: educated at Paris: studied Oriental languages, Persian, Arabic and Chinese: translated the Institutes of Tamerlane from Persian into French: and *Contes, Fables et Sentences* from Arabian and Persian authors, 1877: first made known, to France and the Continent, the existence of the Asiatic Society of Bengal: wrote a Mahratta History: addressed the National Assembly, 1790, on "The importance of Oriental languages for the extension of commerce and the progress of the arts and sciences": published *Fables et Contes Indiens*, with an essay on the Hindus: and part of the *Hitopadesa*: was keeper of the Oriental MSS. of the Royal Library: suggested the formation of a special school for Oriental living languages, which he was charged to organize, and became its Principal and Persian Professor: on the formation of the French Institute was chosen a member of the literary committee: contributed articles on Oriental subjects, and wrote the *Ancient and Modern Monuments of Hindostan*, 1824: at a meeting of the Institute read a memoir demonstrating "the possibility of opening a passage to

India through Egypt, and thereby striking a death-blow at British supremacy in the East " : Napoleon, who was present, thereupon planned the conquest of Egypt : Langlès' library was the richest private Oriental collection then in existence, containing the only exact and complete autograph copy of the Ain-i-Abkari : was a leading member of several Societies and Academies : died Jan. 28, 1824.

LANMAN, CHARLES ROCKWELL
(1850–   )

Born July 8, 1850, at Norwich, Connecticut : son of Peter Lanman : graduated at the Norwich Free Academy, 1867 : at Yale, 1871 : studied Sanskrit and linguistic science under Whitney till 1873 : Ph. D : to Germany, and studied at Berlin, Tübingen, and Leipzig : called to the John Hopkins University at Baltimore when it opened, 1876 : and to Harvard University, Cambridge, Massachusetts, in 1880, as Professor of Sanskrit : Secretary of the American Philological Association, 1879–84 : President, 1889–90 : Corresponding Secretary of the American Oriental Society, 1884–94 : Vice-President, 1894–1905 : joint-editor of its Journal : travelled in India, 1888–9 : collected valuable books and MSS., Sanskrit and Prakrit, for Harvard University : Hony. Member, 1896, of the A.S.B : and, 1902, of the Royal Asiatic Society : Foreign Member, 1897, of the Royal Bohemian Society of Sciences : lectured at the J. Hopkins University, 1897, on the Poetry of India, and in 1898 at Boston, on Indian Literature : LL.D. at Yale, 1902 : is editing, with the help of other scholars the Harvard Oriental Series, published by Harvard University, which has reached 20 volumes of important Sanskrit works such as the *Jataka Mala, Buddhism, Karpura Manjani, Bhrad-Devata, Atharva-Veda*, a Vedic Concordance, *Visuddhi-Magga, Panchatantra, Sakuntala, Brahmanas*, and other works.

LANSDOWNE, HENRY CHARLES KEITH PETTY - FITZMAURICE, FIFTH MARQUESS OF (1845–   )

Born Jan. 14, 1845 : succeeded his father, 1866 : Under Secretary for War, 1872–4 : for India, 1880 : Governor-General of Canada, 1883–8 : Viceroy and Governor-General of India, 1888–94 :

his Viceroyalty was a period of peace, solid progress and internal development without ambitious projects : the Legislative Councils were reconstituted and its members were given the rights of financial discussion and of interpellation : an Act was passed to protect young girls up to 12 : also a revised Factory Act : and the law for preventing cruelty to animals was improved : the police were reorganized : an Imperial Library and Record Office were founded : the Presidential Army system was abolished : the Indian mints were closed to the free coinage of silver : the misrule in Manipur was dealt with, and punishment inflicted for the murder of British officers there : the policy of a " sphere of influence " on the frontiers was carried out : by a mission to Kabul, arrangements were made for the demarcation of the Afghan-British frontier : railways and irrigation works were greatly extended : Secretary for War, 1895–1900 : Foreign Secretary since 1900. K.G : P.C. : G.C.S.I. : G.C.I.E. : G.C.M.G. : D.C.L. Oxford : LL.D.

LASSEN, CHRISTIAN L (1800–1876)

A Norwegian : born at Bergen, Oct. 22, 1800 : son of Nicolai C. V. Lassen : educated at Bergen, Christiania, Heidelberg, 1822, and Bonn : with a Government pension went to London and Paris : with Burnouf, published at Paris, his *Essai sur le Pali*, 1826 : wrote on the Panjab, or Pentapotamia Indica, 1827 : edited the *Hitopadesa*, with Schlegel, 1829 : they founded the critical and historical school of Sanskrit philology in Germany : Lassen was appointed Professor of Sanskrit at Bonn : founded and edited, 1837–50, the periodical *Zeitschrift für die Kunde des Morgenlandes* : published in it his " Beitrage zur Kunde des Indischen Alterthums aus dem Mahabharata," which began the critical study of Indian epic poetry : known for his work on Prakrit Grammar and the decipherment of the Persian cuneiform inscriptions, 1836, and 1845 : published, 1847–61, the *Indische Alterthumskunde*, 4 vols., a laborious and learned classical work on Indian antiquities : he edited an Indian drama, a textbook of Sankhya philosophy, the *Gitagovinda* and *Anthologia Sanskritica*, 1838 : one of the greatest Sanskrit scholars : his work afforded solid foundations for future researches in the ancient literature of India : a foreign Member of the French Institute : died at Bonn, May 8, 1876.

LA TOUCHE, SIR JAMES JOHN DIGGES (1844–   )

I.C.S. : born Dec. 16, 1844 : son of William Digges La Touche : educated at Trinity College, Dublin : joined the Civil Service in the N.W.P., 1867 : Settlement Officer, Ajmir : and at Gorakhpur : Commissioner, in Burma, 1886 : and of Allahabad, 1901 : Member of the Legislative Council, N.W.P., 1891 : Chief Secretary, 1893 : Additional Member of the Governor-General's Legislative Council : officiating Lieutenant-Governor, U. P. 1898 : Lieutenant-Governor of Agra and Oudh since 1901 : K.C.S.I., 1901.

LAW, SIR EDWARD FITZGERALD (1846–   )

Born Nov. 2, 1846 : son of Michael Law : educated privately and at Woolwich : entered the Royal Artillery, 1868, and became Major, 1886 : served at Suakin, 1885 : entered the Diplomatic Service as Financial and Commercial Secretary, 1887 : British Delegate for commercial treaty with Turkey, Bulgaria, and, at Athens, Minister Resident, 1898 : British Delegate on the Council of the Ottoman Public Debt, 1898 : Financial Member of the Supreme Council, 1900–5 : K.C.M.G., 1898 : C.S.I., 1903.

LAW, JACQUES FRANÇOIS (1724–1767)

Son of William Law of Lauriston, and brother of Jean Law, Governor of Pondicherry : born 1724 : like his brother, went to India as an officer in the French service : rose to the rank of Colonel, and saw much active warfare in South India, during the struggle for supremacy between England and France. At the time of the siege of Trichinopoly, he was fighting on the side of Chanda Sahib, but his " vacillation " has been blamed for the failure of the latter : afterwards he was appointed C. in C. of the troops of the French E. I. Co. : died 1767, at the Isle of France, on his way out to Pondicherry.

LAW, JEAN (1720– ?)

English by birth : son of William Law, who settled in France : was Chief of the French factory at Saidabad, Kasimbazar,

when Suraj-ud-daula became Nawab Nazim of Bengal in 1756, and took the English factory at Kasimbazar : protected by the Nawab : declined to give up his factory to Watts, the English Agent : withdrew himself from Kasimbazar in April, 1757, to Patna : was returning to the Nawab's assistance after Plassy, but Suraj-ud-daula was killed : Law continued his flight to Ghazipur and Lucknow, to Shuja-ud-daula (q.v.), Nawab of Oudh : went to Delhi, Agra, Bundelkund : accompanied the Shahzada's unsuccessful invasion of Bengal, 1759 : again attacked Patna with him (now become Shah Alam), in 1760 : they fought against the English and Mir Kasim at Suan, near Bihar, Jan. 15, 1761 : Law surrendered to Major Carnac : sent to Calcutta : left India, 1762 : arriving at France, was made a Chevalier and Colonel, Commissary of the King, Commandant in the E. Indies, Governor of Pondicherry.

LAWRENCE, SIR ALEXANDER, BARONET (1838–1864)

I.C.S. : son of Sir Henry Lawrence, Bart. : born Sep. 6, 1838 : was Assistant Commissioner at Simla : he fell with his horse through a bridge which gave way on the Hindustan-Tibet road, and was killed instantaneously, Aug. 27, 1864.

LAWRENCE, ALEXANDER WILLIAM (1763 ? – 1835)

Father of the Lawrences (Sir G. St. P. Sir H. M : and the first Lord L.) : went out to India as a volunteer, but was disappointed of a Commission, which he purchased later in the 77th regt. : led the forlorn hope of the left column at Seringapatam, May 4, 1799 : for his gallantry made a Captain in the 19th regt. : returned to England in 1808 as Major : Lt-Colonel of the garrison in Guernsey : in 1815, during the Walcheren campaign, commanded the Veteran Battalion, and was Governor of Ostend : Governor of Upnor Castle, 1816 or 1817 : died, while in that post, May, 7, 1835.

LAWRENCE, SIR GEORGE ST. PATRICK (1804–1884)

Elder brother of Sir Henry M., and of Lord Lawrence : third son of Lt-Colonel Alexander Lawrence : born at Trincomalee, March 17, 1804 : educated at Foyle College, Londonderry, and Addiscombe : in 1822 joined the 2nd Bengal light cavalry : Adjutant, 1825–34 : in the first Afghan war, 1838–42 : at Ghazni, and in the pursuit of the Amir, Dost Muhammad : Political Assistant and Military Secretary to Sir W.H. Macnaghten (q.v.), from Sep. 1839 : in charge of Dost Muhammad : in the outbreak in Nov. 1841, narrowly escaped, and again when Macnaghten was murdered on Dec. 23 : had charge of the ladies and children in the retreat from Kabul : was one of the hostages made over to Akbar Khan in Jan. 1842, and imprisoned until the captives were all recovered in Sep. 1842 : Assistant Political Agent in Peshawar, 1846 : made prisoner by the Sikhs in the Panjab campaign, Oct. 1848 : thrice released on parole : released after Gujarat : Deputy Commissioner of Peshawar : at the forcing of the Kohat Pass under Sir C. Napier, 1850 : Political Agent in Mewar, 1850–7 : A.G.G. for Rajputana, 1857–64 : kept the States quiet in the Mutiny : C.B., 1860 : Maj-General, 1861 : resigned, 1864 : K.C.S.I., 1866 : Lt-General, 1867 : died Nov. 16, 1884 : wrote *Forty-three Years in India*, 1874.

LAWRENCE, SIR HENRY MONT-GOMERY (1806–1857)

Brother of Sir George (q.v.) and of Lord Lawrence (q.v.) and fourth son of Colonel Alexander Lawrence : born in Ceylon, June 28, 1806 : educated at Foyle College, Derry, Bristol and Addiscombe : joined the Bengal Artillery, Feb. 1823 : in the first Burma war, 1826 : invalided home : joined the trigonometrical survey in Ireland : in the revenue survey, N.W.P., 1833–8 : nearly fought a duel : in the first Afghan war, was under G. R. Clerk (q.v.), in charge of Firozpur, Assistant to the A.G.G., 1840 : went with Pollock's Army of Retribution up to Kabul in Sep.-Oct.1842 : Brevet-Major : settled Kythul : Resident in Nipal, 1843–6 : wrote for the *Calcutta Review* and advocated asylums in the hills for children of European soldiers : in the first Sikh war, as A.G.G. for the Panjab : was at Sobraon : opposed to annexation : appointed Resident at Lahore, Jan. 1847 : compelled the surrender of Kashmir to Golab Singh : K.C.B., 1848 : at the siege of Multan, Jan. 1849, and at Chilianwala : appointed President of the

Board of Administration of the Panjab, and A.G.G. in April, 1849, after its annexation : the Board broke up in 1853 and Lawrence was transferred to Rajputana as A.G.G : A.D.C. to Queen Victoria, 1854 : Chief Commissioner and A.G.G. in Oudh from March 21, 1857 : prepared, with great skill and foresight, for the defence of Lucknow in the mutiny, from May, 1857, after the engagement at Chinhut, on June 30, limited the defence to the Residency : wounded during the siege on July 2 : died on July 4 : wrote for his own epitaph " Here lies Henry Lawrence, who tried to do his duty." He had been meanwhile, in England, appointed provisional Governor-General of India : his eldest son was created a Baronet in recognition of his services : his statue was erected in St. Paul's Cathedral. He wrote essays and books on Indian subjects, and had considerable literary merits. But he is best remembered for his administrative ability, his energy, his sympathies with the native aristocracy, his high character, and his tragic death. He established the Lawrence Asylums in the hills, for the children of European soldiers.

LAWRENCE, JOHN LAIRD MAIR, FIRST BARON (1811–1879)

I.C.S. : Governor-General : sixth son of Lt-Colonel Alexander Lawrence : brother of Sir George (q.v.) and Sir Henry (q.v.) : born March 4, 1811 : educated at Bristol, Foyle College, Londonderry. Wraxall Hall, Haileybury : reached Calcutta in the Civil Service in Feb. 1830 : to Delhi and its neighbourhood as Assistant and as District Officer for 8 years, and again, 1843–6 : noticed by Lord Hardinge at end of 1845 : provided efficient transport before Sobraon : in 1846 made Commissioner of the Trans-Satlaj Jalandhar Doab : acted as Resident at Lahore : suppressed the Kangra rebellion : after the Panjab campaign, and the annexation of the Panjab in 1849, became a Member of the Board of Administration, with his brother Henry and Mr. C. G. Mansel : selected in 1853 by Lord Dalhousie to be Chief Commissioner of the Panjab, the Board being broken up : his differences of opinion from his brother, on public questions, were radical and serious : negotiated a treaty with the Amir of Afghanistan in 1855 : K.C.B., 1856 made another agreement with Dost Muhammad in 1857 : in the mutiny he saved the Panjab, and, by sending the movable column and all available forces down to Delhi for its siege and capture, worked for the eventual suppression of the mutiny : at one time contemplated the abandonment of Peshawar : first Lieutenant-Governor of the Panjab from Jan. 1, 1859 : G.C.B. : Baronet : P.C. : K.C.S.I. : appointed by the Crown, in Sep. 1858, an original member of the new Council of India : D.C.L. : LL.D. : refused the Governorship of Bombay : Governor-General and Viceroy of India, Jan. 12, 1864, to Jan. 12, 1869 : he had to deal with the Bhutan war, and the Orissa famine : was strong in his policy of non-interference with Afghan politics : his policy was described as " masterly inactivity " : he recognized Shir Ali as *de facto* Amir : paid much attention to sanitation, railways, irrigation : enforced strict economy : settled the Oudh land question : was the first Governor-General to take the whole Government to Simla : he was vigorous and prompt in action, cautious, masterful, laborious, sincerely religious : after retirement, he was made Baron Lawrence of the Panjab and of Grateley : was, 1870–3, Chairman of the London School Board, and Chairman of the Committee formed to oppose the policy of the Afghan war of 1878–9 : died June 27, 1879 : buried in Westminster Abbey : statues erected to him in Calcutta and London.

LAWRENCE, RICHARD C. (1818–1896)

General : brother of Lord Lawrence (*q.v.*) : entered the Indian Army, 1834 : served with Bengal N.I. in the Satlaj campaign, 1845–6 : at Sobraon : with the Kashmir Contingent at the siege and assault of Delhi, 1857 : C.B. : served under his brother in the Panjab : commanded the military police : advocated the disarmament of native troops in Lahore : Military Secretary to Sir John Lawrence in part of the mutiny : Deputy Commissioner of the Simla Hill states : Resident in Nipal : died Jan. 24, 1896.

LAWRENCE, STRINGER (1697–1775)

Born March ,6, 1697 : son of John Lawrence of Hereford : entered the Army in 1727 : saw service in Spain, Flanders, and the Highlands in 1745 : sent out by the Court of Directors in 1747 to be Major of the Garrison at Fort St. George : arrived at Fort St. David and commanded the troops in 1748 : taken prisoner by the French in his attack on Ariancopang near Pondicherry : released in 1749 when Madras was restored to the English : took Devikota in Tanjore in 1749 : was appointed by the Directors to be C. in C. in the E. Indies in 1852 : relieved Trichinopoly, with Clive's help, defeating the French and captured Seringham : again defeated them at Bahur, Aug. 26, 1752 : engaged till 1754 with the French and their native allies about Trichinopoly : generally victorious, so that Dupleix was recalled in 1754. Lawrence was superseded in the command when the 39th regt., the first King's troops, arrived in 1754 : was too ill to go to Bengal in 1756, when Clive was sent up. Lawrence commanded the defence of Madras, during its siege by Lally, Dec. 1758–Feb. 1759 : the siege raised on Admiral Pocock's fleet appearing. Lawrence went home, for health, in 1759, but came out again in 1761 as C. in C., Member of Council and Maj-General : retired in April, 1766 : died in London, Jan. 10, 1775. He was called " The Father of the Indian Army." His monument in Westminster Abbey bears the inscription : " Discipline established. Fortresses protected. Settlements extended. French and Indian Armies defeated, and Peace concluded in the Carnatic." He recognized the merits of Clive.

LAWRENCE, SIR WALTER ROPER (1857–   )

I,C.S. : born Feb. 9, 1857 : son of George Lawrence : educated at Cheltenham and Balliol College, Oxford : joined the Civil Service in the Panjab, 1879, passing first : Under Secretary to Panjab Government, and in the Revenue Department of the Government of India : Commissioner in Kashmir, 1889–95 : retired in 1898, without pension : went out to India again as Private Secretary to Lord Curzon, while Viceroy, 1898–1903 : K.C.I.E., 1903 : author of *The Valley of Kashmir* : designate to be Chief of the Staff of H.R.H. the Prince of Wales on his tour in India, 1905–6.

LAWSON, SIR CHARLES ALLEN
(1838–   )

Son of Jonathan Wise Lawson : born May 17, 1838 : Secretary of the Madras Chamber of Commerce, 1862–92 : Editor *Madras Daily News*, 1863 : *Madras Times*, 1864–68 : founded and edited *Madras Mail*, 1868–92 : author of *At Home on Furlough*, 1868 and 1874 : *The Private Life of Warren Hastings*, 1895 : knighted, 1887.

LEACH, ESTHER (1809–1843)

Actress : daughter of a soldier, and wife of Serg-Major John Leach, Fort William : educated at Berhampur by the regimental schoolmaster : selected when a girl to take part in the regimental performances : attracted the notice of the officers, and presented with a copy of Shakespeare : for 20 years the favourite actress at the Calcutta and Chowringhi Theatres : visited England, and, after her return, joined the new Sans Souci Theatre in Park Street (now St. Xavier's College), Calcutta. On Nov. 2, 1843, while playing a part in the *Handsome Husband*, her dress caught fire on the stage : she was severely burnt, and died a few days later : entirely self-taught, but a very versatile actress : styled the " Indian Siddons," also good in comedy : described as " for talent and personal attractions, without a rival, even in England."

LE BAS, REV. CHARLES WEBB
(1779–1861)

Born April 26, 1779 : son of Charles Le Bas, a shopkeeper in Bond Street : educated at Hyde Abbey School, Winchester, and Trinity College, Cambridge : Scholar, 4th Wrangler and Craven Scholar : Fellow : B.A., 1800 : called to the bar from Lincoln's Inn, but not ordained in 1809 : Prebendary of Lincoln, 1812 : Mathematical Professor and Dean at the E.I. College, Haileybury, in 1813, and Principal, 1837–43 : retired : died Jan. 25, 1861 : wrote about 80 articles in the *British Critic* and in the *British Magazine* : author of geographical works, and several biographies (among them that of Bishop Middleton, the first Bishop of Calcutta) and tracts and sermons : he was equally vigorous and copious as a preacher.

LEBEDEFF, HERASIM (1749–1815 ?)

A Russian : said to be a Ukraine peasant : took part in a Russian Embassy to Naples, 1775 : visited Paris and London : left England, 1785, apparently as a bandmaster, for Madras : stayed there 2 years : to Calcutta in Aug. 1787 : there met with a Pandit who taught him Sanskrit, Bengali, Hindustani (the mixed Indian dialect, as he called it) : built, with Government permission, an Indian theatre at Calcutta, 1795 : translated two English plays (*The Disguise* and *Love is the Best Doctor*) into Bengali : the former was publicly performed in Nov. 1795, and March, 1796, with great applause (according to its author) : he then became theatrical manager to the Great Mogul and finally returned to England, 1801, after more than 20 years in the East. In London he published his Hindustani grammar (*Grammar of the Pure and Mixed East Indian Dialects, arranged according to the Brahmenian System of the Shamscrit Language*), 1801, and made the acquaintance of Woronzow, the Russian Ambassador, who sent him to Russia. He was employed in the Russian Foreign Office and given a large subvention towards founding at St. Petersburg the " Imprimerie Indienne," a Sanskrit Press : died after 1815.

LE COUTEUR, JOHN (1761–1835)

Of a Jersey family : entered the 95th regt. in 1780 : went to India in 1781 : led two forlorn hopes against Hyder Ali : was under General Mathews in Malabar, and with him besieged at Bednore by the French and Tippoo, and taken prisoner in 1783 : cruelly treated as a prisoner at Chitaldrug : released in 1784 : served in Jersey as inspecting officer of militia : in Jamaica : Lieutenant-Governor of Curaçoa in 1813 : Lt-General, 1821 : died April 23, 1835 : wrote *Letters from India*, 1790.

LEEKE, SIR HENRY JOHN
(1790 ?–1870)

Son of Samuel Leeke : entered the Navy in 1803 : served in the Mediterranean, on the coast of Africa : knighted in 1835 : and K.H. : Superintendent and C. in C. of the Indian Navy, 1852 : in the Persian war, 1856–7, he commanded the squadron which conveyed the troops : bombarded

Bushire on Nov. 10, 1856, and in 4 hours took it : K.C.B. in 1858 : Admiral in 1864 : died in Feb. 1870.

LEES, WILLIAM NASSAU (1825–1889)

Son of Sir Harcourt Lees, *Bart.* : born Feb. 26, 1825 : educated at Nut Grove and Trinity College, Dublin : joined the 42nd Bengal N.I. in 1846 : Maj-General, 1885 : was for some years Principal and Professor of the Calcutta Madrasa, Secretary to the Board of Examiners at Fort William, and Translator to the Government of India : was an eminent Oriental scholar : edited a number of works in Arabic and Persian and Hindustani, and wrote many papers for the *Journals* of the Royal Asiatic Society and the Asiatic Society of Bengal : wrote also for the Daily Press in India, and was part proprietor of the *Times of India* : LL.D. of Dublin, 1857 : and Doctor of Philosophy of Berlin : died March 9, 1889.

LEE-WARNER, SIR WILLIAM
(1846–   )

I.C.S. : born April 18, 1846 : son of Canon James Lee-Warner : educated at Rugby and St. John's College, Cambridge : Scholar : joined the Indian Civil Service, in Bombay, 1869 : was Secretary to the Government of Bombay in the Political-Judicial Departments : Additional Member of the Governor-General's Legislative Council : Chief Commissioner of Coorg, and Resident of Mysore, Feb.–Sep. 1895 : retired, 1895 : Secretary in the Political Department, at the India Office, 1895–1902 : Member of the Council of India, since 1902 : author of *The Protected Princes of India*, *The Citizen of India*, *The Marquis of Dalhousie*, 1904 : C.S.I., 1892 : K.C.S.I., 1898.

LEIGHTON, SIR DAVID (1774–1860)

Son of Thomas Leighton : born 1774 : was a banker's clerk in Montrose : obtained a military cadetship in the E.I. Co.'s service, 1795 : went to Bombay : Ensign and Lieutenant in Jan. 1797 : with the 5th N.I. in the Mysore campaign, 1799 : at the siege of Seringapatam and the capture of Jalalabad : under Colonel A. Wellesley in the operations against Dhoondia Waugh, and the capture of several hill forts : served with the 4th N.I. in suppressing the Malabar rebellion : Lt-Colonel in 9th N.I. in Dec. 1808 :

Brigadier in the Dekkan Field Force, 1815 : Adjutant-General of Bombay Army, 1817, and member of the Military Board for 9 years : second in command of the expedition to Arabia, 1820, at the defeat of the Joasmi Arabs and capture, 1821, of Beni-Boo-Ali : Colonel, 7th N.I. from 1824 until his death : in 1826 commanded the Surat Division and the Presidency Division for 3 years : President of the Military Board for 4 years : retired, 1831 : Maj-General, 1837 and K.C.B. : Lt-General, 1848 : General, 1854 : died June 1, 1860, at his small estate near Cheltenham.

LEITH, JAMES (1826–1869)

Son of General Sir Alexander Leith, K.C.B. : with the 14th Hussars in the Persian war, 1857 : in the mutiny at Aurangabad : with the Malwa Field Force at Dhar, and with the Central India Field Force up to Kalpi : gained the V.C. at Betwa, April 1, 1858, charged alone and rescued an officer of his regt. when surrounded by a large number of rebel infantry : Major, 1858 : was a member of the Honble. Corps of Gentlemen-at-Arms, 1863 : died May 12, 1869.

LEITH, JOHN FARLEY (1809–1887)

Called to the bar : Q.C. : practised as a barrister at Calcutta, 1832–46 : Professor of Law at Haileybury, 1853–7 : M.P. for Aberdeen, 1872–80 : died 1887.

LEITNER, GOTTLIEB WILHELM
(1840–1899)

Born in Budapest, 1840 : son of a physician : to Turkey, 1847 : educated at Malta Protestant College : at 15 was appointed Chief Interpreter to H.M.'s Commissariat in the Crimean war, with rank of Colonel : attended the Muhammadan Theological School at Constantinople : entered at King's College, London, 1858 : appointed there, 1861, Professor of Arabic and Muhammadan Law : M.R.A.S., 1861 : M.A. and Ph.D., Freiburg, 1862 : Principal of the Government College, Lahore, 1864 : founded the Anjuman-i-Panjab : worked for the foundation of the Panjab University : organized many schools, free libraries, literary Societies and Journals in India : Registrar of the Lahore University College : explored among, studied, and wrote on, the wild tribes of the N.W. frontier, Dards,

Hanzas, etc.: established the Journal *Indian Public Opinion* : collected information on the origins of Indian art, and specimens of Græco-Buddhistic art : claimed to be the originator of the title Kaisar-i-Hind : retired, 1887 : acquired the Royal Dramatic College at Woking, and adapted it to an Oriental Institute there : published *Languages and Races of Dardistan, The Language and People of Hanza,* and many works on education, philology, trade, dialects, etc. : spoke, read, and wrote 25 languages : edited the *Asiatic Quarterly Review,* from Jan. 1890 : died at Bonn, March 22, 1899 : Ph.D. : LL.D. : D.O.L., 1882.

LELY, SIR FREDERICK STYLES PHILPIN (1846–)

I.C.S. : born Dec. 16, 1846 : educated at Pembroke College, Oxford : went to Bombay in the Indian Civil Service, 1869 : Member of the Dekkan Agriculturists Relief Act Commission, 1891–2 : Commissioner, N. Division, Bombay : Member of the Legislative Council, Bombay, 1899 : of the Governor-General's Legislative Council, 1903–4 : officiating Chief Commissioner, Central Provinces, 1904–5 : retired, 1905 : C.S.I., 1901 : K.C.I.E., 1905.

LE MARCHANT, SIR JOHN GASPARD (1803–1874)

Son of Maj-General John Gaspard Le Marchant : born 1803 : educated at the R.M.C., Sandhurst : joined the 10th foot, 1820 : served at the Cape, 1832 : under Sir De Lacy Evans, in the Carlist war in Spain, 1835–7 : Knight Bachelor, 1838 : Lieutenant-Governor of Newfoundland, 1847–52 : of Nova Scotia, 1852–7 : Governor of Malta, 1859–64 : C. in C. at Madras, 1865–8 : G.C.M.G., 1860 : K.C.B., 1865 : Lt-General : died Feb. 6, 1874.

LENNOX, SIR WILBRAHAM OATES (1830–1897)

Son of Lord John George Lennox, and grandson of the fourth Duke of Richmond : born May 4, 1830 : privately educated and at the R.M.A., Woolwich : entered the R.E. in 1848 : General in 1893 : served in the Crimea, 1854–6 : won the Victoria Cross : on the way out to China, in 1857, was sent up to India,

and up to Cawnpur : temporarily Chief Engineer under Sir Colin Campbell at his relief of Lucknow, in Nov. 1857 : was at the siege and capture in March, 1858 : was in a number of actions : in Rohilkund : commanding Engineer in the Oudh campaign and in the Trans-Gogra campaign : two Brevets : left India in 1859 : C.B., 1867 : served at Chatham : attached to the German armies in France in the Franco-German war : Military Attaché at Constantinople, 1876 : with the Turkish Armies in 1877 : commanded the garrison of Alexandria, 1884–7, and in Ceylon, 1887–8 : K.C.B., 1891 : Director of Military Education, 1893–5 : died Feb. 7, 1897.

LESLIE, SIR BRADFORD (1831–)

Born 1831 : son of Charles R. Leslie, R.A. : Civil Engineer : designed and built the first bridge over the Hughli between Howrah and Calcutta, 1874, and the Jubilee Bridge over the Hughli at Naihati, 1887 : Fellow of the Calcutta University : K.C.I.E., 1887.

LESTER, FREDERICK PARKINSON (1795–1858)

Son of John Lester : born Feb. 3, 1795 : educated at Camberwell and Addiscombe : joined the Bombay Artillery, 1811 : rose to be Maj-General, 1854 : in 1857 commanded the Southern Division of the Bombay Army : his excellent precautionary measures prevented the mutiny from spreading to Western India : died at Belgaum, July 3, 1858.

LETHBRIDGE, SIR ALFRED SWAINE (1844–)

Born Sep. 30, 1844 : son of W. F. Lethbridge : educated at King's College, London, and Aberdeen : M.D. : entered the Bengal Medical Service, 1867, and became Lt-Colonel, 1887 : served in Burma and Bengal : Inspr-General of Jails in Bengal, 1878–92 : general superintendent for the suppression of Thagi and Dakaiti, 1892 : Additional Member of the Governor-General's Legislative Council, 1895–7 : retired, 1898 : K.C.S.I., 1896.

LETHBRIDGE, SIR ROPER (1840–)

Born Dec. 23, 1840 : son of E. Lethbridge : educated at Plymouth, Mannamead College and Exeter College Oxford : Scholar : called to the bar at the Inner Temple, 1880 : served in the Bengal Educational Department, 1868-76 : joined the Political Department and appointed Press Commissioner with the Government of India, 1877-80 : M.P. for North Kensington, 1885 and 1886 : retired, 1892 : author of a *History of India* and several educational works for use in India : *The Golden Book of India :* edited the *Calcutta Review*, 1871-8 : Fellow of the Calcutta University : C.I.E., 1878 : K.B., 1885 : K.C.I.E., 1890 : D.L. : J.P.

LEUMANN, ERNST (1859-   )

Born April 11, 1859 : son of Konrad Leumann, a Swiss country clergyman : educated at Frauenfeld, Switzerland : at Leipzig and Berlin, 1878-82 : Phil.D. at Leipzig, 1881, with the edition of a text belonging to the Jain canon : assisted Monier-Williams (*q.v.*), 1882-4 and 1886-9, in preparing the new edition of his Sanskrit-English dictionary, 1899 : Sanskrit Professor at Strasburg since 1884 : has devoted himself chiefly to researches concerning the Jain religion and the history of Sanskrit : has written books and papers on that religion, and on linguistic questions concerning Sanskrit : has procured, for the Strasburg Library, a good collection of Jain manuscripts.

LEVI, SYLVAIN (1863-   )

Born March 28, 1863, at Paris : son of Louis Levi, merchant : studied at Paris : Doctor of Letters, 1890 : appointed Professor of Sanskrit at the "Ecole des Hautes Études," 1886, and at the Collège de France, 1894 : among his chief works are *Le Théâtre Indien*, 1890 : *La Doctrine du Sacrifice dans les Brahmanas*, 1898 : *Le Népal*, 1905, besides numerous articles in the *Journal Asiatique*, etc. : he went on a scientific mission to India and Japan, 1897-8 : co-operated in the *Revue Critique*, and in *La Grande Encyclopédie* : wrote the article on "India" in this latter work.

LEYDEN, JOHN (1775-1811)

Son of John Leyden : born Sep. 8, 1775, educated at Kirktown and Edinburgh University : studied languages and contributed to literary periodicals and produced independent works, besides colla-

borating with Sir Walter Scott : licensed as a preacher, 1798 : studied medicine, and became M.D. at St. Andrew's : went to Madras in 1803 : Assistant Surgeon : surveyed in, and reported on, Mysore : travelled to Penang : to Calcutta in 1806 : wrote on Oriental languages, became Professor of Hindustani at the College of Fort William, and Judge of the 24 *Parganas*, near Calcutta, and in 1809 Commissioner of the Court of Requests in Calcutta : Assay Master of the Mint, 1810 : to Java in 1811 with Lord Minto, as Malay interpreter : died of fever at Cornelis, Aug. 28, 1811 : he translated *Malay Annals* into English, and the *Commentaries of Baber* : his early death was deplored by leading literati as a loss to Oriental learning and literature.

LIGHT, FRANCIS (1740-1794)

Born at Dallingho, Suffolk, Dec. 1740 : educated at Woodbridge Grammar School : entered the R.N. : becoming afterwards a trader at Junk, Ceylon : he later founded the settlement of Pulo Penang in the Straits Settlements, and was first Superintendent there, his Commission being dated March 2, 1786. He took possession of the settlement as " Prince of Wales' Island," Aug. 11, 1786 : and administered it till his death in 1791. He destroyed a pirate fleet sent against the settlement by the Raja of Keddah : died, much regretted, at Penang, Oct. 21, 1794.

LILLY, WILLIAM SAMUEL (1840-   )

I.C.S. : born July 10, 1840 : son of William Lilly : educated at Peterhouse, Cambridge : entered the Madras Civil Service, 1862 : Under Secretary to Madras Government, 1869 : retired, Oct. 1872 : has published many works connected with philosophy, politics and Catholicism, including *India and its Problems*, 1902 ; *Christianity and Modern Civilization*, 1903.

LINDSAY, SIR ALEXANDER (1785-1872)

Son of James Smyth Lindsay : born 1785 : Ensign in the 104th regt. at the age of 9 : educated at the R.M.A., Woolwich : joined the Bengal Artillery, 1804 : at the siege of Gohud, 1806 : in Bundelkund, 1807-8 : in the Nipal campaign, 1814-16, severely wounded at Hariharpur :

at the siege of Hatras, 1817 : in the Pindari war, 1817–18 : commanded the Artillery in Arakan in the first Burmese war, 1824–5 : C.B., 1831 : General in 1859 : K.C.B., 1862 : died Jan. 22, 1872.

LINDSAY, HON. CHARLES ROBERT
(1784–1835)

I.C.S. : born Aug. 20, 1784 : son of the sixth Earl of Balcarres : arrived in Calcutta as a writer, 1803 : assistant to the Magistrate of Sylhet, 1806–10 : nearly the whole time engaged against the incursions of Kullian Sing, a native chief of marauders : employed at Dacca and the 24 *Parganas* : Agent in charge of the Salt Monopoly, 1811–34 : on a voyage for health to Singapore, died there July 4, 1835.

LINDSAY, CHARLES ROBERT
(1826–1895)

Born Jan. 18, 1826 : son of Colin Lindsay, of the Balcarres family : educated at Haileybury, 1842–4 : went out to India, 1845 : employed in the N.W.P. : in Rohilkund, as Magistrate-Collector and Judge of Fatehghar, Judge and Commissioner of Gorakhpur : Judge, of the *Sadr* Court at Agra : Judge of Moradabad : Judge of the Chief Court of the Panjab, 1870–80 : retired, 1880 : died Feb. 23, 1895.

LINTON, SIR WILLIAM (1801–1880)

Son of Jabez Linton : born 1801 : educated at Edinburgh University : joined the Army Medical Department, 1826 : M.D. of Glasgow : Staff Surgeon, 1848 : served in Canada, W. Indies, etc., in the Crimea as D.I.G. of hospitals : C.B. : in the Indian mutiny was Inspr-General of Hospitals, and P.M.O. of the European Army : retired, 1863 : K.C.B., 1865 : died Oct. 9, 1880.

LITTLE, SIR ARCHIBALD (1810–1891)

Son of Archibald Little : born 1810 : educated at Charterhouse : entered the Army, 1831 : with the 9th Lancers in the Satlaj campaign, 1846 : at Sobraon : Brig-General of Cavalry at the relief of Lucknow : at the Dilkusha and at Cawnpur on Dec. 6, 1857 : at the actions of Serajghat and Khudaganj : Colonel of 11th Hussars, 1873–5, and of 9th Lancers after 1875 : K.C.B., 1870 : General, 1880 : G.C.B. : died June 10, 1891.

LITTLER, SIR JOHN HUNTER
(1783–1856)

Son of Thomas Littler : born Jan. 6, 1783 : educated at Acton, near Nantwich : joined the 10th Bengal N.I. in 1800 : captured by a French privateer on his outward voyage : served in Lord Lake's campaigns of 1804–5 : in Java, 1811–16 : Assistant Commissary General, 1816–42 : Maj-General in 1841 : commanded the Agra Division, 1843, and a Division at Maharajpur, 1843 : K.C.B. : in 1845 commanded the Firozpur Division : offered battle, which they avoided, to the Sikhs, when they crossed the Satlaj in Dec. 1845 : commanded a Division at Firozshahr : G.C.B., 1849 : Member of the Supreme Council in India, Feb. 1848, to Dec. 1852 : Deputy-Governor of Bengal, March, 1849, to Jan. 1852 : retired as Lt-General : Colonel of the 36th N.I. : died Feb. 18, 1856.

LOCKHART, SIR GRÆME ALEXANDER SINCLAIR, BARONET
(1820–)

Born Jan. 23, 1820 : son of Robert Lockhart : succeeded his cousin in the Baronetcy, 1899 : educated privately : entered the Army, 1837 : served in the Persian war, 1857, and in the Indian mutiny, 1857–8 : entered Lucknow with Havelock's force : commanded his regiment at Lucknow : C.B.

LOCKHART, SIR WILLIAM STEPHEN ALEXANDER (1841–1900)

Son of the Rev. Lawrence Lockhart : born Sep. 2, 1841 : joined the 44th Bengal N.I. in 1858 : became General in 1896 : served in the mutiny, with the 5th Fusiliers, in 1858–9 : in Bhutan, in 1864–6 as Adjutant : in the Abyssinian campaign of 1867–8 : D.A.Q.M.G. in the Hazara expedition, 1868 : served in Achin with the Dutch, 1875–7 : in the Q.M.G.'s department in Afghanistan, 1878–80 : at Kabul and in the Khyber : D.Q.M.G., Intelligence Branch, 1880–5 : sent to Chitral : Brigadier in the Burma war, 1886–7 : K.C.B. : C.S.I. : Assistant Military Secretary for Indian affairs at the Horse Guards, 1889–90 : commanded the Panjab Frontier Force, 1890–5 : in the Miranzai, Isazai, Waziristan expeditions, in command : K.C.S.I. : commanded 40,000 men in the Tirah expedition, 1897 :

G.C.B. : and appointed C. in C. in India in 1898 : died at Calcutta, March 18, 1900.

LOCKWOOD, SIR GEORGE H.
(? -1884)

Joined the 3rd Light Dragoons, 1825 : ' commanded them in Afghanistan in 1842 under General Pollock : at the forcing of the Khyber, Jagdalak, Tezin, Haft-Kotal, Kabul and Istalif : C.B. : in the Panjab campaign of 1848–9 : commanded a Brigade at Gujarat : K.C.B. : Lt-General, 1862 : General, 1870 : retired, 1877 : died April 15, 1884.

LOGAN, JAMES RICHARDSON
(? -1869)

Educated for the law : went (1830–40) to Penang in the Straits Settlements, where he acquired a leading position, and worked for the good of the settlement : wrote scientific papers for the Asiatic Society of Bengal's journal, on the Geology of Singapore, and edited the *Journal of the Indian Archipelago and Eastern Asia*, 1847, dealing with the languages and ethnology of the Indian Archipelago : he also initiated and edited the *Penang Gazette* : was Notary Public of the Supreme Court, and member of learned Societies of England : died at Penang, Oct. 20, 1869.

LOGIN, SIR JOHN SPENCER
(1809–1863)

Educated at the University of Edinburgh : became an Assistant Surgeon in the E. I. Co.'s service, 1832 : was appointed to the Bengal Horse Artillery : served with the Nizam's Army : in 1836, on Sir C. Metcalfe's Staff, when Lieutenant-Governor of the N.W.P. : in the Afghan war, in medical charge of the Horse Artillery, and of the British Mission to Herat, also in a political capacity : on the C. in C.'s staff, 1840 : Surgeon to the British Residency at Lucknow, and Superintendent of Hospitals to the King of Oudh : in the Panjab campaign, 1848–9 : on the annexation of the Panjab became Guardian and Superintendent of the Maharaja Dulip Singh : knighted, 1854 : retired, 1858 : died Oct. 18, 1863.

LONG, REV. JAMES (1814–1887)

Born in 1814 : passed some time in Russia : ordained in 1839 : went to India in 1846 as a Missionary of the Church Missionary Society : stationed near Calcutta : in 1861 he wrote a preface to, and superintended the translation of, the *Nil Darpan*, a Bengali play, directed against the indigo planters. "Padre" Long, as he was called, was indicted for libel, and sentenced to Rs. 1,000 fine and a month's imprisonment. He wrote a number of works, chiefly connected with Bengal, its people, language and literature, Calcutta and its history, but also on wider questions of Indian politics. He was F.R.G.S. and member of the Asiatic Society of Bengal : returned to England in 1872 : wrote *Eastern Proverbs and Emblems, illustrating Old Truths*, for Trübner's Oriental series : died March 23, 1887.

LONGDEN, SIR HENRY ERRINGTON
(1819–1890)

General : born Jan. 1829 : son of Thomas Hayter Longden : educated at Eton and Sandhurst : joined the 10th regt. in 1836 : was in the Sikh wars of 1845–6 and 1848–9, at Sobraon, the sieges of Multan, Cheniote, Gujarat. In the mutiny of 1857, he was under Sir Colin Campbell, and engaged in the Azimghar and Jaunpur districts, in the advance on Lucknow, its siege and capture, at the reliefs of Azimghar in 1858, and in the Jagdishpur jungles : Adjutant-General in India, 1866–9 : K.C.B. and C.S.I. : died Jan. 29, 1890.

LOPES, DAVID MELLO (1867-   )

Born April, 1867 : son of José Amaro Lopes : educated at Lisbon (Curso Superior de Letras), and at L'Ecole des Langues Orientales in Paris : appointed, in 1895, Professor of the French Language at the Lyceum Central : in 1901, Professor of French Language and Literature to the Curso Superior de Letras at Lisbon : has written *Chronica dos Reis de Bisnaga*, 1897 ; *Historia dos Portugueses in Malabar*, 1898.

LORD, PERCIVAL BARTON (1808–1840)

Son of the Rev. John Lord : born 1808 : educated at Dublin University : M.D., 1832 : studied for the medical profession at Edinburgh : assistant surgeon in the E. I. Co.'s service at Bombay, 1834 : medical officer with Sir A. Burnes on his mission to Kabul : into Tartary in 1837, to Kunduz : Political Assistant to (Sir)

W. H. Macnaghten (*q.v.*) in 1838, in the
fighting in the Khyber, 1839 : sent to
obtain information, in 1839–40, of the
Amir Dost Muhammad after his flight :
during the winter at Bameean : killed,
when Dost Muhammad defeated the
British force, at Parwandarra, Nov. 2,
1840.

LORIMER, JOHN GORDON
(? –)

I.C.S. : educated at Edinburgh University and Christ Church, Oxford : joined
the Indian Civil Service in the Panjab,
and became a Deputy Commissioner,
1902 : Political Officer, North Waziristan,
1898–9, and in the Khyber, 1899 :
Assistant Secretary in the Foreign Department of the Government of India, 1899–
1900 : author of *Customary Law of the
Peshawar District*, Grammar and Vocabulary of Waziri-Pashtu : C.I.E., 1902.

LOW, CHARLES RATHBONE
(1837–   )

Born Oct. 30, 1837 : son of Major J. H.
Low : educated at Douglas College, Isle
of Man : joined the Indian Navy, 1853 :
served in Indian and China seas, the
Persian Gulf, Red Sea, and East Coast of
Africa : Assistant Secretary and Librarian,
Royal United Service Institute, 1865–8 :
author of many books, including *History
of the British Navy*, 1872 ; *Life of Sir G.
Pollock*, 1873 ; *History of the Indian
Navy*, 1877 ; *The First Afghan War*,
1879 ; *Life of Lord Roberts*, 1883.

LOW, SIR JOHN (1788–1880)

Son of Captain Robert Low : born Dec.
13, 1788 : educated at St. Andrew's ·
University : entered the 1st Madras N.I.,
in 1805 : became Brig-General, 1854 :
General, 1867 : in the Java expedition,
1811 : against the Guntur rebels, 1816 :
A.D.C. to Sir J. Malcolm at Mahidpur,
1817 : in the Chindwarra district, 1818 :
Resident with Baji Rao (*q.v.*), the Ex-
Peshwa, at Cawnpur, 1819–25 : Political
Agent at Jaipur, 1825 : at Gwalior, 1830 :
Resident at Lucknow, 1831–42 : C.B.,
1838 : Agent to the Governor-General for
Rajputana, 1848–52 : Resident at Hydera-
bad, 1852–3 : negotiated the treaty of
May 21, 1853, with the Nizam : Military
Member of the Supreme Council, Sep.
1853 : resigned in April, 1858 : advocated

interference in Oudh in 1855 : K.C.B.,
1862 : G.C.S.I., 1873 : died Jan. 10, 1880.

LOW, SIR ROBERT CUNLIFFE
(1838–   )

General : born 1838 : son of General
Sir John Low, K.C.B. : entered the Bengal
Cavalry, 1854 : served in the Indian
mutiny, 1857–8 : Afghan war, 1879–
80 : Burmah war, 1886–8 : commanded
the Chitral expedition, 1895 : commanded
the forces in Bombay, 1898–1903 : G.C.B.,
1896.

LOWE, EDWARD WILLIAM HOWE
DE LANCY (1820–1880)

Son of Sir Hudson Lowe : born Feb. 8,
1820 : educated at Sandhurst : entered
the 32nd regt., 1837 : served in the Panjab
campaign of 1848–9, at Multan and
Gujarat : at Lucknow, in command of
the 32nd, throughout the defence, and in
the subsequent operations : in the Oudh
campaign, 1858–9 : C.B. : retired, 1872 :
Maj-General, 1877 : died Oct. 21, 1880.

LOWIS, JOHN (1801–1871)

I.C.S. : son of Capt. Ninian Lowis of
the E. I. Co.'s Navy : born Jan. 19, 1801 ;
educated at the High School, Edinburgh,
and at Haileybury, 1817–19 : served in
Lower Bengal, Magte-Collr of Rajshahi,
1823 : Commissioner of Dacca, 1836 :
Member of the Board of Revenue, 1842,
Member of the Supreme Council of the
Governor-General, Dec. 1, 1848, to Dec. 1,
1853 : died Jan. 1, 1871.

LUCAS, SIR ALFRED WILLIAM
(1822–1896)

General : son of Charles Lucas : entered
the Bombay Army, 1838 : served in the
S. Mahratta campaign, 1844–5 : in the
Persian war, 1856–7 : at Muhamra : in
the mutiny, 1857–9 : in the Rajputana
Field Force, at the taking of Kotah, in the
pursuit of Tantia Topi : Brevet-Major :
Head of the Commissariat Department in
the Abyssinian expedition, 1867–8 : Brevet-
Colonel : C.B. : Deputy Commissary
General, Bombay, 1863–77 : General,
1889 : K.C.B., 1893 : died Feb. 19, 1896.

LUCK, SIR GEORGE (1840–   )

Born Oct. 24, 1840 : educated privately :
joined the Army, 1858 : Lt-Colonel, 15th

Hussars, 1879 : Brig-General, commanding Sind District, 1884 : Inspr-General of Cavalry in India, 1887–93 : commanded Quetta District, 1893 : Lt-General in command of Bengal Army, 1898–1903 : K.C.B., 1897.

LUDLOW, JOHN MALCOLM
(1821–   )

Born at Nimach, March 8, 1821 : son of Colonel John Ludlow, C.B., H.E.I.C.S. : educated at College Bourbon, Paris : called to the bar from Lincoln's Inn, 1843, and practised as Conveyancer till 1874 : Secretary to the Royal Commission on Friendly and Benefit Societies, 1870–4 : Registrar of Friendly Societies in England, 1874 : Chief Registrar of Friendly Societies, 1874–91 : C.B., 1887 : author of several books, including *British India, its Races and its History*, 1858 ; *The War in Oudh*, 1858 ; *Thoughts on the Policy of the Crown towards India*, 1859 : has contributed to various Journals and Magazines : Member of the " British India Society " and of the " India Reform Society," and on the Council of the original " Imperial Federation League."

LUGARD, SIR EDWARD (1810–1898)

Born 1810 : son of Capt. John Lugard : educated at the R.M.A., Sandhurst : entered the Army, 1828 : in the Afghan war, 1842, as Brig-Major : A.A.G. in the Satlaj campaign, 1845–6 : Adjutant-General of the Queen's troops in the Panjab campaign, 1848–9 : C.B. : A.D.C. to Queen Victoria : Chief of the Staff in the Persian expedition, 1856–7 : Adjt-Genl. in India : Brig-General at capture of Lucknow : Maj-General and K.C.B. : Secretary for military correspondence in the War Department, 1859–61 : Permanent Under Secretary, 1861–71 : Privy Councillor, 1871 : Commissioner for the Abolition of Army Purchase : retired, 1880 : General, 1872 : G.C.B. : died Nov. 1, 1898.

LUMLEY, SIR JAMES R. (? –1846)

Maj-General : joined the Army, 1796 : commanded his regt. at Bhartpur, 1805 : was present at the capture of the Isle of France : in the Nipal war, 1814–6 : in the Pindari war, 1817–8 : at Maharajpur and Gwalior, 1843 : Colonel of the 9th N.I. : Adjutant-General of the Army, 1833–46 : K.C.B. : was 50 years in India : died at Firozpur, March 2, 1846.

LUMSDEN, SIR HARRY BURNETT
(1821–1896)

Born Nov. 12, 1821 : son of Colonel Thomas Lumsden, C.B., of the Bengal Artillery : educated at Aberdeen and Bromley : joined the 59th Bengal N.I. in 1838 : with the 33rd N.I. in the forcing of the Khyber, 1842 : in the Satlaj campaign of 1845–6, wounded at Sobraon : Assistant to Sir H. M. Lawrence at Lahore in 1846 : with a force through the Hazara country : formed the corps of Guides, horse and foot, and originated the *khaki* uniform for the Indian Army : with the Guides at Multan, 1848–9 : at Gujarat : in affairs with the frontier tribes : in 1857–8 sent on a mission to Kandahar with (Sir) P. S. Lumsden and Dr. H. W. Bellew, to ensure the proper application of the subsidy to the Amir : C.B. in 1859 : in the Waziri expedition, 1860 : attacked by a fanatic : commanded the Hyderabad Contingent, 1862–9 : Maj-General, 1868 : left India in 1869 : K.C.S.I., 1873 : Lt-General, 1875 : died Aug. 12, 1896.

LUMSDEN, MATTHEW (1777–1835)

Son of John Lumsden : born 1777 : educated at King's College, Old Aberdeen : to India in 1794 in the E. I. Co.'s employ : studied Persian and Arabic : appointed in 1803 Assistant Professor of Arabic and Persian at the College of Fort William : Professor in 1808 : Secretary to the Calcutta Madrasa in 1812 : in charge of the Company's Press at Calcutta, 1814–7 : Secretary to the Stationery Committee, 1818 : made a journey through Persia, Georgia and Russia to England, 1820 : again in India, as Professor, 1822–5 : retired, 1826 : died in England, March 31, 1835 : wrote Persian and Arabic grammars, and edited the *Shahnama* : LL.D. of Old Aberdeen.

LUMSDEN, SIR PETER STARK
(1829–   )

General : born Nov. 9, 1829 : son of Colonel T. Lumsden, C.B. : educated at Addiscombe : entered the Indian Army, 1847 : served in N.W. Frontier campaign, 1851–4 : on the special mission to Kandahar, 1857 : in the China war, 1860, at the capture of Taku Forts and Pekin : with Bhutan Field Force, 1865 : D.Q.M.G., 1864–8 : Q.M.G., 1868–73 : acting Resident at Hyderabad, 1873 : Adjutant-General,

1874–9 : Chief of the Staff in India, 1879 : A.D.C. to Queen Victoria, 1870–81 : Member of the Council of India, 1883–93 : British Commissioner for the demarcation of the N.W. boundary of Afghanistan, 1884–5 : C.S.I., 1870 : K.C.B., 1879 : G.C.B., 1885 : D.L. : J.P. : author of *Lumsden of the Guides*, 1899.

LUNDGREN, EGRON⸲SELLIF (1815–1875)

A Swedish artist : born Dec. 18, 1815 : studied art at Stockholm and Paris : in the Indian mutiny he accompanied Sir Colin Campbell in his Oudh campaign : made 500 sketches and many portraits, which were exhibited in England, and sold : he published *Letters from India :* died at Stockholm, Dec. 12, 1875.

LUSHINGTON, CHARLES (1785–1866)

I.C.S. : son of Sir Stephen Lushington, *Bart.* : born 1785 : arrived in India, 1801 : Assistant in the Governor-General's office, 1804 : Deputy Secretary in the Secret, Political and Foreign Departments in 1809 : Secretary in the Public Department, officiating in the S.P. and F. Depts. : Private Secretary to the Governor-General (Mr. John Adam) in 1823 : Chief Secretary to the Government of India, 1825 : Acting Superintendent of the Botanical Garden, 1826 : member of a number of Committees : retired in 1827 : was M.P. for Ashburton, 1833–41, and for Westminster, 1847–52 : died Sep. 23, 1866 : published a *History of Calcutta's Religious Institutions*, 1824 : his first wife wrote a narrative of her *Journey from Calcutta to Europe, by Way of Egypt in* ˙1827–8, 1829.

LUSHINGTON, EDWARD HARBORD (1822–1904)

I.C.S. : son of the Right Hon. Stephen Lushington : entered the Bengal Civil Service, 1841 : Magte.-Collr. : Secretary to the Board of Revenue : Commissioner, during the mutiny, of Burdwan, with Manbhum and Singhbhum attached : present in engagements with mutineers, and wounded : Commissioner of the Nadia Division : Secretary to the Government of Bengal, 1861: Secretary to the Government of India in the Financial Department, 1863, until he left India in

1869 : retired, 1871 : Treasurer of Guy's Hospital for many years : died Oct. 29, 1904.

LUSHINGTON, SIR JAMES LAW (1779–1859)

Son of Rev. James Stephen Lushington, and brother of Stephen Rumbold Lushington : entered the Madras Army in 1797, and rose to be a full General, 1854 : was a Director of the E. I. Co., 1827, and Chairman of the Court in 1838, 1842, 1848 : M.P. for many years : died May 29, 1859 : G.C.B.

LUSHINGTON, STEPHEN RUMBOLD (1776–1868)

I.C.S. : son of Rev. James Stephen Lushington : born May, 1776 : educated at Rugby : went to Madras, 1790 : Secretary and Persian Translator to the Board of Revenue in 1798 : Private Secretary to General (Lord) Harris when C. in C. at Madras and Acting Governor : left the E. I. Co.'s service in 1807 : M.P. for Rye, 1807–12 : and for Canterbury, 1812–30 : Chairman of Committees in the House of Commons : Joint Secretary of the Treasury, 1824–7 : Privy Councillor, 1827 : Governor of Madras, Oct. 1827–Oct. 1832 : again M.P. for Canterbury, 1835–7 : D.C.L. : died Aug. 5, 1868 : wrote a life of his father-in-law, Lord Harris, 1840.

LYALL, SIR ALFRED COMYN (1835–   )

I.C.S. : son of Rev. Alfred Lyall : born 1835 : educated at Eton and Haileybury : entered the Bengal Civil Service, 1855 : in the Indian mutiny saw service in the Bulandshahr District, at Meerut, and with the Khaki Risala of volunteers : Commissioner in Berar, 1867 : Secretary to the Government of India in the Home, 1873–4, and Foreign, 1878–82, Departments : A.G.G. for Rajputana, 1874–8 : Lieutenant-Governor of N.W.P., 1882–7 : Chancellor of the Allahabad University : Member of the Council of India, 1888–1903 : author of *Verses written in India, British Dominion in India, Asiatic Studies, Life of Warren Hastings* (English Men of Action series). K.C.B., 1881 : G.C.I.E.: 1896 : D.C.L., Oxford : LL.D., Cambridge, P.C., 1902.

LYALL, SIR CHARLES JAMES
(1845-   )

I.C.S.: born March 9, 1845: son of Charles Lyall: educated at King's College School and College, and at Balliol College, Oxford: went to the N.W.P. in the Bengal Civil Service, 1867: Assistant Under Secretary in the Foreign Department of the Government of India, 1872: Under Secretary in the Revenue, Agriculture and Commerce Department, 1873-80: Secretary to Chief Commissioner, Assam, 1880-3: Judge and Commissioner, Assam, 1883-4: Secretary to Government of India in the Department of Revenue and Agriculture, 1886: returned to Assam, 1887-9: Secretary to the Government of India, Home Department, 1889-94: Chief Commissioner, Central Provinces, 1895-8: Secretary at the India Office in the Judicial and Public Department, 1898: C.I.E., 1880: K.C.S.I., 1897: author of *Translations in Arabic Poetry*, 1885; *Ten Arabic Poems*, 1894; and contributed to the *Encyclopædia Britannica*.

LYALL, DAVID ROBERT (1841-   )

I.C.S.: born Nov. 24, 1841: son of David Lyall: educated at Edinburgh Academy: went to Lower Bengal in the Civil Service, 1861: Inspr-General of Police, L.P., 1883-7: Commissioner of Chittagong, 1887-91: Commissioner of Patna, 1891-2: Member of Board of Revenue, 1892-6: retired, 1896: Political Officer with the Chin-Lushai expedition, 1888: C.S.I.: Superintendent of the Cooch Behar State, 1896-9.

LYALL, SIR JAMES BROADWOOD
(1838-   )

I.C.S.: born March 6, 1838: son of Rev. Alfred Lyall: educated at Eton and Haileybury: went to the Panjab in the Bengal Civil Service, 1858-9: Financial Commissioner in the Panjab: Resident in Mysore, 1883-7: Lieutenant-Governor of the Panjab, 1887-92: Member of the Royal Opium Commission, 1893-4: President of the Indian Famine Commission, 1898 : K.C.S.I., 1888: G.C.I.E., 1892.

LYALL, JOHN EDWARDES (1811-1845)

Son of George Lyall, M.P.: educated at Eton, Haileybury, Balliol College, Oxford: called to the bar at the Inner Temple, 1837: appointed by the Court of Directors in 1842 to be Advocate-General, Bengal: applied himself to education of the Hindus: Member of the Council of Education: highly esteemed by the natives, for whose welfare and happiness he exerted himself: the law students of the Hindu College erected there a tablet to him as "the zealous friend of the native, and the first gratuitous lecturer on jurisprudence in this Hall": died of cholera at Government House, Barrackpur, March 9, 1845.

LYNCH, HENRY BLOSSE (1807-1873)

Captain: son of Major Henry Blosse Lynch: born Nov. 24, 1807: joined the Indian Navy, 1823: employed in the Survey of the Persian Gulf, acting as interpreter in Persian and Arabic to the Squadron, 1829-32: commanded the *Enterprise*, 1830-2, and examined S. Persia: shipwrecked in the Red Sea: served in command of the expedition under Col. F. R. Chesney to explore the Euphrates route to India, 1834: in command of it, 1837: ascended the Tigris, and completed the map of it, 1839: extended, by his explorations, the geographical knowledge of Mesopotamia: had charge of the postal service across Syria till 1842: commanded a flotilla to co-operate with Sir C. Napier in Sind, 1843: held various naval shore appointments in Bombay, 1844-51: in the second Burmese war commanded a squadron in the naval operations: C.B., 1853: retired to Paris, 1856: after the Persian war, of 1856-7, conducted at Paris the negotiations with the Persian Ambassador which led to the Treaty of Paris, March 4, 1857: made Knight Grand Cross of the Order of the Lion and Sun: died April 14, 1873.

LYON, ISIDORE BERNADOTTE
(1839-   )

Born May 28, 1839: educated at Edinburgh High School, and University College, London: joined the Indian Medical Service, 1865: Professor of Anatomy, Grant Medical College, Bombay, 1866, and of Chemistry, 1867, and subsequently of Medical Jurisprudence: retired, 1892: C.I.E., 1889: author of *Food Tables for India*, 1877; *Text Book of Medical Jurisprudence for India*, 1889, 1890: Brig-Surgeon: Lt-Colonel: M.R.C.S.: F.C.S.: F.I.C.

LYSTER, HARRY HAMMON (1830–)

Born 1830 : son of A. Lyster : served in the Indian mutiny, in Central India, 1857–8 : V.C. : Afghan war, 1878–9 ; Commanded 3rd Gurkha regt., 1879–87 : C.B., 1881.

LYTTELTON, HON. SIR NEVILLE GERALD (1845–   )

Born Oct. 28, 1845 : son of 4th Baron Lyttelton : educated at Eton : entered the Army, 1865, and became Lt-Colonel, 1892 : was A.D.C. to Earl Spencer as Viceroy of Ireland, 1868–73 : Military Secretary to Sir John Adye, as Governor of Gibraltar, 1883–5, and to Lord Reay as Governor of Bombay, 1885–90 : was in the Jowaki expedition, 1877 : Egyptian campaign, 1882, at Tel-el-Kebir : brevet-Lt-Colonel : in Nile expedition, 1898, in command of a Brigade, at Khartum : Maj-General : A.A.G., at the War Office, 1895 : Assistant Military Secretary, War Office, 1897–8 : in command of a Brigade at Aldershot, 1899–1900, and of a Brigade in S. Africa, 1899–1900 : commanded in Natal, 1901–2 : K.C.B. and Lt-General : commanded the Forces in South Africa, 1903–4 : Chief of the Staff in the Army Council, 1904.

LYTTON, EDWARD ROBERT BUL-WER, FIRST EARL OF (1831–1891)

Viceroy and Governor-General : son of the first Baron Lytton : born Nov. 8, 1831 : educated at Harrow and Bonn : was Private Secretary to his uncle, Lord Dalling, at Washington and Florence : paid Attaché at the Hague, St. Petersburg, Constantinople and Vienna : wrote, under the name of Owen Meredith, *Clytemnestra, the Earl's Return, and other Poems, The Wanderer, Lucile, Tannhauser, The Ring of Amasis :* held diplomatic appointments at Belgrade, Vienna, Copenhagen, Athens, Lisbon, Madrid, again at Vienna, Paris, and was Minister at Lisbon, 1872–6, when he was, after declining the Governorship of Madras, chosen by Lord Beaconsfield to be Viceroy and Governor-General of India : wrote *Chronicles and Characters, Orval, or the Fool of Time, Fables in Song,* etc. He succeeded his father in the Peerage, 1873, and held the Viceroyalty from April 12, 1876, to June 8, 1880 : it was an eventful and important time.

Negotiations with the Amir of Afghanistan were resumed, but fruitless : the reception of a Russian envoy at Kabul, and the rejection of a British mission, led to the Afghan war, 1879–80, which is a matter of history : Lytton's policy, denounced at the time, can appeal to its results. He conducted the Imperial Assemblage at Delhi on Jan. 1, 1877, for the proclamation of H.M. Queen Victoria's assumption of the title of Empress of India : he had to deal with the famines in Bombay, Madras, Mysore, and visited these Provinces in Aug.–Sept. 1877 : the Famine Commission sat, and the system of " famine insurance " was established : the finances were further decentralized : internal customs were abolished : the cotton duties repealed : the Vernacular Press Act was passed : provision was made for the admission of more natives of India to civilians' appointments : his speeches, minutes, and despatches have never been surpassed : his disregard of convention gave opportunity to hostile critics, who gave little credit to his genius and great qualities. He was made an Earl in 1880 on his resignation with Lord Beaconsfield's Ministry. After leaving India, he was Ambassador to France, 1887–91 : and wrote his father's Life, *Glenaveril, After Paradise, King Poppy :* died at Paris, Nov. 24, 1891.

LYVEDEN, ROBERT VERNON SMITH, FIRST BARON (1800–1873)

Born Feb. 23, 1800 : son of Robert Percy Smith, " Bobus," (*q.v.*), and nephew of Sydney Smith : educated at Eton and Christ Church, Oxford : M.P. for Truro, 1829–30 : for Northampton, 1831–59 : Junior Lord of the Treasury, 1830–4 : Joint Secretary to the Board of Control for the affairs of India, 1835–9 : Secretary for War and the Colonies, 1839–41 : President of the Board of Control, Feb. 1855, to Feb. 1858, during the Indian mutiny : made a Peer, 1859 : G.C.B., 1872 : died Nov. 10, 1873.

MACARTNEY, GEORGE, FIRST EARL (1737–1806)

Governor : son of George Macartney : born May 14, 1737 : educated at Trinity College, Dublin : Envoy Extraordinary to St. Petersburg, 1764–7 : knighted : Chief Secretary for Ireland, 1767–72 :

K.B. : Captain-General and Governor of the Caribbee islands, 1775–9 : made an Irish Peer, 1776 : defended Grenada and made prisoner of war, but released : appointed Governor of Madras and held the office from June 22, 1781, to June 8, 1785 : reduced the Dutch settlements in S. India : conducted war against Hyder Ali and Tippoo : resented control from the Bengal Government : sent home Coote's successor, Major-General James Stuart : made treaty of Mangalore with Tippoo, 1783 : resigned because his policy in S. India was not upheld : declined the Governor-Generalship, Feb. 1785 : granted a pension by the E. I. Co. : severely wounded by Stuart in duel in Hyde Park, 1786 : made an Irish Earl in 1792 : sent as Plenipotentiary on an embassy to Pekin, 1792–4 : deputed on a mission to Louis XVIII of France at Vevrai, 1795 : made an English Baron, 1796 : Governor of Cape of Good Hope, 1796–8 : declined the Presidency of the Board of Control : died May 31, 1806 : wrote accounts of his Embassies.

MACAULAY, COLMAN PATRICK LOUIS (1848–1890)

I.C.S.: son of Patrick Macaulay : born Sep. 1848 : educated at Liege and Queen's University, Ireland : went to Bengal in the Civil Service, 1870 : Financial Secretary to the Government of Bengal and Member of the Bengal Legislative Council : went to Pekin, 1885 : obtained Chinese Government passports, and was organizing a mixed political and scientific mission to Lhasa, to open up trade, when it was suddenly stopped, in 1886, in deference to Chinese susceptibilities : Acting Chief Secretary to the Bengal Government : died May 2, 1890 : C.I.E.

MACAULAY, THOMAS BABINGTON, FIRST BARON (1800–1859)

Born Oct. 25, 1800 : son of Zachary Macaulay : educated at private schools and at Trinity College, Cambridge : Fellow, 1824 : gained the Chancellor's English verse prizes on *Pompeii* and *Evening* : Commissioner in Bankruptcy, 1828 : M.P. for Calne, 1830 ; for Leeds, 1831 : Commissioner of the Board of Control, 1832 : Secretary, 1833 : helped to carry the Bill of 1833 for renew-ing the charter of the E. I. Co. : made a

great speech on the second reading : appointed Legal Member of the Supreme Council in India : went out in 1834 : landed at Madras in June : was at Ootaca-mund with Lord W. Bentinck, the Gover-nor-General, until he went on to Calcutta in September. As Legal Member, he was head of the Law Commission and largely responsible for the preparation of the Penal Code and the Code of Criminal Procedure. He also wrote a great minute on Education in India, and obtained a decision in preference of English studies rather than of Oriental languages and literature. His sister married (Sir) Charles Trevelyan, and Macaulay lived with them in Calcutta, in the house in Chowringhi now occupied by the Bengal Club. He resigned his appointment on Jan. 17, 1838. He wrote his essay on Clive in Jan. 1840, and on Warren Hastings in Oct. 1841 : M.P. for Edinburgh, 1839–47, and 1852–6 : Secretary at War, and in the Cabinet, 1839–41 : in 1853 he supported the India Bill for the renewal of the E. I. Co.'s Charter : in 1854 he was Chairman of the Committee appointed to arrange for the examination of candidates for the Indian Civil Service by open competition, and wrote the report. He died Dec. 28, 1859. His parliamentary career, his *History of England* and literary productions had, except in respect of the matters above mentioned, no special connexion with India.

MACBEAN, FORBES (1857–)

Born Jan. 3, 1857 : son of Colonel Forbes Macbean : educated at Upping-ham : entered the Army, 1876, and became Lt-Colonel, 1898 : was in the Afghan war, 1879–80 : in engagements at Kabul and march from Kabul to Kandahar : Transvaal campaign, 1881 : Tirah, 1897–8, severely wounded : Brevet Lt-Colonel : South African war, 1899–1902. C.B. and Brevet-Colonel.

MAC CULLOCH, WILLIAM (? –1843)

Assistant Examiner of Indian corre-spondence at the India House, and Chief Examiner, 1818–30, when he retired : died March 17, 1843 : had a high reputa-tion as an administrator, his despatches being accounted perfect models, and even superior to James Mill's, who succeeded him.

MACDONALD, SIR HECTOR (1853–1903)

Born in Ross-shire, March 4, 1853 : son of a crofter and stonemason : while a draper's assistant, joined Volunteers : in June, 1870, enlisted in thé 92nd Gordon Highlanders : went to India and became a colour-sergeant in 3 years : in the Kabul force under Sir F. Roberts in 1879 : distinguished for his bravery in the Hazardarakht defile, and for conspicuous courage at Charasia : at Sherpur and the fighting about Kabul : in the Kabul-Kandahar march, and at battle of Kandahar : given a Commission : at Majuba Hill, taken prisoner and released : served in Egypt, in the constabulary, in the Nile expedition, in the Egyptian Army : at Suakin, at Toski : D.S.O. : Major, Royal Fusiliers, 1891 : Brig-General at Atbara, 1898 : at Omdurman : A.D.C. to Queen Victoria : LL.D., Glasgow: commanded the Sirhind Division, 1899 : and the Highland Brigade in S. Africa, 1899–1900 : K.C.B. : commanded the Belgaum District, 1901 : and the forces in Ceylon, 1902 : died at Paris, March 25, 1903 : Maj-General.

MACDONALD, SIR JAMES RONALD LESLIE (1862–)

Born 1862 : son of Surgeon-Major James Macdonald : educated at Aberdeen University and Woolwich : entered the Royal Engineers, 1882 : served in the Hazara expedition, 1888 : in the Uganda Railway Survey, 1891–2 : acting Commissioner of the Uganda Protectorate, 1893 : commanded the operations there, 1897–8 : in charge of the British operations at Fashoda, 1896 : commanded the Juba expedition, 1898–9 : Brevet-Lt-Colonel : C.B. : in the China expedition, 1901 : commanded the forces in the Tibet expedition, 1903–4 : K.C.I.E.

MACDONALD, JOHN (1759–1831)

Son of Allan and the famous Flora Macdonald : born Oct. 30, 1759 : educated at Portree and Edinburgh : went out to the Bombay Infantry in 1780 : transferred to the Bengal Engineers in 1782 : sent to Bencoolen, Sumatra : surveyed the Dutch Settlements there : remained at Sumatra as Military and Civil Engineer until 1796 : made many maps and charts : retired in 1800 : F.R.S. : an original member of the Asiatic Society : wrote scientific and military papers, and a work in favour of the civilization and education of the natives of India : died Aug. 16, 1831.

MACDONALD, KENNETH SOMERLED, REV. DR. (1832–1903)

Born 1832 at Glen Urquhart, Inverness : joined the United Free Church Mission in Calcutta in 1861, and was engaged there in Missionary work for 41 years, a prominent figure in religious and missionary life. While he constantly conducted Evangelical services, he laboured chiefly as an educational Missionary, and was an indefatigable writer, editing Periodicals, Journals, such as the *Indian Evangelical Review*, publishing studies of the Hindu sacred books, etc. He was a prominent Fellow of the Calcutta University : died July 30, 1903.

MACDONALD, SIR REGINALD JOHN (1820–1899)

Son of Reginald George Macdonald, Chief of the Clan Ranald : joined the Navy, 1833 : Captain, 1854 : commanded the Channel Squadron, 1872–3 : Naval C. in C. in the East Indies, 1875–7 : K.C.S.I., 1877 : Vice-Admiral, 1877 : commanded at the Nore, 1879–82 : retired, 1884 : K.C.B., 1887 : died Dec. 15, 1899.

MACDONELL, ARTHUR ANTHONY (1854–)

Son of Charles Alexander Macdonell, of the Indian Army : born May 11, 1854, at Muzaffarpur : educated at the Public School, Gottingen, 1870–5 : Gottingen University, 1875–6 : Corpus College, Oxford, 1876–80 : B.A., 1880 : M.A., 1883 : Ph.D., Leipzig, 1884 : Taylorian Teacher of German, Oxford University, 1880–99 : Deputy-Professor of Sanskrit, 1888–99 : Boden Professor of Sanskrit, since 1899 : Fellow of Balliol College, 1899 : Keeper of the Indian Institute, Oxford : representative of Great Britian in Sanskrit at the International Congress of Arts and Science at St. Louis, Sep. 1904 : has written the *Sarvamikramani* of the Rigveda (Anecdota Oxoniensia), 1886 ; a Sanskrit-English dictionary, 1892 ; *Vedic Mythology*, 1897 ; a History of Sanskrit Literature, 1900 ; a Sanskrit grammar, 1901 ; the *Bhraddevata*, 1904.

MACDONNELL, SIR ANTONY PATRICK (1844–   )

I.C.S. : educated at Queen's College, Galway : joined the Indian Civil Service in Lower Bengal, 1865, and retired, 1901 : Revenue Secretary to the Government of Bengal : Secretary to the Government of India, Home Department : Acting Chief Commissioner of Burma, 1889 : Chief Commissioner of the Central Provinces, 1891 : Acting Lieutenant - Governor of Bengal, 1893 : Member of the Supreme Council, 1893–5 : Lieutenant - Governor of N.W.P., 1895–1901 : Member of the Council of India, 1902 : his services lent, to be Under Secretary to Lord Lieutenant of Ireland, 1902 : K.C.S.I., 1893 : G.C.S.I., 1897 : P.C., 1902 and P.C. Ireland, 1903 : K.C.V.O., 1903.

MACDOWALL, SIR ANDREW (? –1835)

Lt-General : entered the E. I. Co.'s Madras Establishment, 1783 : at the siege and capture of Palicaudcherry, 1783, and the reduction of many of Tippoo's forts : in the defence of the Raja of Travancore's lines, 1789 : in the force under Corn-wallis and Medows at Seringapatam, 1791–2 : at Malavilli and the capture of Ser-ingapatam, 1799 : in the settlement of the ceded country, 1801–3 : commanded a Brigade under Sir T. Hislop, C. in C., Madras, at Mahidpur, 1817 : commanded a detachmment in Khandesh and took many forts, 1818 : C.B. : K.C.B., 1831 : died May 15, 1835.

MACGREGOR, SIR CHARLES MET-CALFE (1840–1887)

Born Aug. 12, 1840 : son of Major Robert Guthrie Macgregor : educated at Marlborough : entered the Indian Army, 1856 : in the mutiny, at Firozpur : at the siege of Delhi, afterwards in several hand-to-hand combats : at the siege and capture of Lucknow : in Oudh, constantly engaged, 1858–9, under Hope Grant, Horsford, Holdich : in Fane's horse in China : Brig-Major in the Bhutan cam-paign, 1864 : severely wounded : D.A.Q.-M.G : in Abyssinian expedition : compiled the *Gazetteer of Central Asia*, 1868–73 : Director-General of Transport in the Bihar famine, 1874, for which he received the C.S.I. : on expeditions on the Af-ghan and Beluchistan frontiers in

1875 : wrote accounts thereof : pre-vented from entering Herat : in the Afghan war, 1878–9, on the Khyber line : C.I.E. and C.B. : Chief of the Staff to Sir F. Roberts and other Generals : at Charasia, Kabul, Sherpur : commanded a Brigade in the Kabul-Kandahar march, and at the battle of Kandahar : com-manded the Marri expedition : K.C.B., 1881 : Q.M.G. in India : given the com-mand of the Panjab Frontier Force, 1885 : Maj-General : died at Cairo, Feb. 5, 1887 : compiled also the History of the second Afghan war, and wrote *The Defence of India* : *Our Native Cavalry* : and *Mountain Warfare* : a great soldier, full of knowledge, keenness, courage, and determination.

MACGREGOR, SIR GEORGE HALL (1810–1883)

Son of General John Alexander Paul Macgregor : born May 1, 1801 : educated at Addiscombe : entered the Bengal Artillery, 1826 : A.D.C. to Lord Auckland, 1836 : Political Agent at Jalalabad, 1838 : Political Assistant and Military Secretary to Sir W. H. Macnaghten, (*q.v.*), 1838 : served in Afghanistan, at Ghazni, in actions from Kabul to Jalalabad, and the defence of the last place : A.D.C. to General Pollock, 1842 : present in the actions up to capture of Kabul : C.B. : Principal Assistant to the Resident at Lahore, 1846 : Political Resident at Benares : Deputy Commissioner of Lahore : A.G.G. at Murshidabad : Military Com-missioner and A.G.G. with the Gurkha auxiliary force under Sir Jang Bahadur in the mutiny : Brig-General at the cap-ture of Lucknow : K.C.B., 1861 : retired as Maj-General, 1859 : died Jan. 3, 1883.

MACGREGOR, SIR JOHN (1791–1866)

Son of Duncan Macandrew : assumed the name of Macgregor, 1863 : educated at Edinburgh University : entered the medical service, 1809 : in the Walcheren expedition, 1809, the Peninsula, 1811–3 : served in the Presidencies of Madras, Bombay, twice in Bengal, in Ceylon : present at the capture of Fort Manora and Karachi : at the investment of Kandahar, 1841–2 : at Kabul and Ghazni, and with Nott's Army, 1841–2 : at Maharajpur, 1843 : at the rebellion in Ceylon, 1848 : P.M.O. at Hongkong for 2 years : Deputy Inspr-General at Madras : Hony. Physician to Queen Victoria, 1859 : K.C.B., 1859 : died June, 13 1866.

MACINTYRE, DONALD (1832–1903)

Born 1832 : educated at Addiscombe : entered the Army, 1850 : with the 66th Gurkhas, in the Peshawar frontier expeditions, 1852, 1853, 1856, 1864 : in 1857–8 protected the hill passes on the Kale-Kumaon frontier from the Rohilkund rebels : with the 2nd Gurkhas in the Lushai expedition,1871–2 : gained the V.C. : climbed over a stockade 8 to 9 feet high under heavy fire : Brevet-Lt-Colonel : in the Afghan war, 1878–9, commanded 2nd Gurkhas in the Khyber, and in the Bazar valley : retired as Maj-General, 1880 : F.R.G.S. : wrote *Wanderings and Wild Sport on and beyond the Himalaya* : died April 15, 1903.

MACK, REV. JOHN (1797–1845)

Born March 12, 1797 : a native of Edinburgh : his father was a Writer to the Signet : educated at Edinburgh University and distinguished himself at the Baptist College at Bristol : was selected by the Rev. W. Ward (*q.v.*) on his visit to England, in 1821, to be a Professor at the Serampur College : arrived there, Nov. 1821 : worked as Professor for 14 years : ordained in June, 1832, as co-pastor of the Serampur Church : succeeded Dr. Marshman (*q.v.*) in charge of the Serampur College, and raised it to be the first private establishment of education in India : highly proficient in classics, mathematics and natural science : gave the first chemical lectures ever delivered in Calcutta : translated into Bengali an elementary treatise on Chemistry : was deeply attached to the Missionary cause : made his mark as a public writer : shared in the editorial management of the *Friend of India* at Serampur, from the commencement of its publication in 1835 : died of cholera, April 30, 1845.

MACKAY, SIR JAMES LYLE (1852–   )

Born Sep. 11, 1852 : educated at Arbroath and Elgin : went to India to Mackinnon, Mackenzie & Co., 1874 : President of the Bengal Chamber of Commerce, 1890–93 : Member of the Governor-General's Legislative Council, 1891–3 : Director of the British India Steam Navigation Co. : Member of the

Council of India since 1897 : Special Commissioner and Plenipotentiary to negotiate a commercial treaty with China. 1901–2 : K.C.I.E., 1894 : G.C.M.G., 1902.

MACKENZIE, SIR ALEXANDER (1842–1902)

I.C.S. : born Jan. 28, 1842 : educated at King Edward VI's Grammar School, Birmingham, and Trinity College, Cambridge : arrived in India in Dec. 1862 : was early taken into the Bengal Secretariat, and served only a short time away from the headquarters of Government : wrote a history of the relations of Government with the tribes on the N.E. frontier of Bengal : Financial Secretary to the Government of Bengal in 1877 : Member of the Bengal Legislative Council in 1877 and 1879 : Home Secretary to the Government of India, 1882 : Chief Commissioner of the Central Provinces, 1887 : Chief Commissioner of Burma, 1890 : K.C.S.I., 1891 : Member of the Supreme Council, 1895 : Lieutenant-Governor of Bengal from Dec. 1895, to April, 1898. During this time he was absent for 6 months for his health, and for the same reason resigned his office. He successfully, and with economical results, directed the relief policy in the famine of 1896–7 : he was thorough in his regard for economy in principle and in practice. When plague appeared in Bengal and Calcutta, he made effective arrangements to combat it. He attended to the commercial interests of Calcutta. He attempted to improve the sanitary condition of Calcutta and initiated legislation to reform its municipal administration. This made him unpopular with certain classes in Bengal, though his ability, industry, and honesty of purpose were recognized. After his retirement he became Chairman of the India Development Company : died Nov. 10, 1902.

MACKENZIE, COLIN (1753 ? –1821)

Born about 1753 : went to India in 1782 and joined the Madras Engineers: rose to be Colonel in 1819 : stayed with friends at Madura, 1783, and formed plans of collecting materials for Indian history : was in the war of 1790–2 against Tippoo : after Seringapatam sent by Cornwallis to examine the geography of the ceded territory, including the Dekkan : at the siege of Pondicherry, 1793 : Commanding

Engineer at the taking of Ceylon, 1796 : at the siege of Seringapatam, May, 1799 : surveyed Mysore, until 1810 : Surveyor-General of Madras, 1810 : commanded the Engineers in Java, 1811–15 : Surveyor-General of India, 1816 : died near Calcutta, May'8, 1821 : from 1783 he made extensive and valuable collections of Indian MSS., plans, tracts, drawings, antiquities, coins, statues, etc. : initiated detailed topographical surveys : wrote in the *Oriental Annual Register* and in *Asiatic Researches* : on the Life of Hyder Ali, the Bijyanagar and Unaganda Rajas, on the Bhats, or Indian bards : on buildings and sculptures, and on survey matters : his collections purchased from his widow for the E. I. Co. for £10,000 : a large portion of them sent to England : the S. India books and tracts made over to the Madras College Library, and later to the Madras Literary Society.

MACKENZIE, COLIN (1806–1881)

Lt-General : born March 25, 1806 : son of Kenneth Francis Mackenzie : educated at Dublin and at Oswestry : joined the 48th Madras N.I., 1825 : in the Coorg campaign, 1834, at the taking of Merkara : in the Straits of Molucca, 1836 : in 1840, Assistant Political Agent at Peshawar : went to Kabul : led Sale's returning force as far as Gandamak, and returned to Kabul : present at the conference at which Macnaghten was killed : escaped : was selected as one of the hostages to Akbar Khan : he was called " the Moollah " on account of his religious character : sent down on dangerous missions from Kabul to Jalalabad and back : after release, he joined in the attack on Istalif, Sep. 29, 1842 : raised and commanded a Sikh regt. on the frontier during 1848–9 : slighted by Lord Ellenborough, he was highly regarded by Lord Dalhousie : C.B. : made Brig-General in Hyderabad contingent : in a mutiny in 1855 at Bolarum against his orders, he was dangerously wounded : Government blamed his action : made A.G.G. at Murshidabad : Superintendent of Army Clothing : left India, 1873 : died Oct. 22, 1881.

MACKENZIE, HOLT (1787–1876)

I.C.S. : son of Henry Mackenzie, the wit, essayist, and man of letters : born 1787 : educated at Haileybury, 1806–7 :

arrived in India in 1808, in the E. I. Co.'s Civil Service : was, in 1817, Secretary to Government in the Territorial Department : Member, 1820 ; President, 1825, of the Council of the College of Fort William: is best remembered for his work as a settlement officer, and for his connexion with the great Settlement Regulation, VII of 1822, which embodied his views and was said to have " immortalized the name of its framer " : in 1826 he was Secretary to the Governor-General on tour to the Upper Provinces : he returned to England in 1831, and was made a Privy Councillor and Commissioner of the Board of Control, 1832–4 : Vice-President of the Royal Asiatic Society, 1847 : died March 31, 1876.

MACKENZIE, KENNETH DOUGLAS (1811–1873)

Born Feb. 1, 1811 : son of Donald Mackenzie : entered the 92nd Gordon Highlanders in 1831 : served in the Mediterranean and West Indies : in the Irish rebellion of 1848, on the arrest of W. S. O'Brien, he stopped a railway train by threatening to shoot the engine-driver : his conduct was highly approved : he served on the staff in the Crimea, in the battles : gained Brevets : to India in 1858 : on the staff in Bengal : in June, 1859, sent to quell a mutiny of the 5th Bengal Europeans at Berhampur : D.Q.M.G., in China, 1860 : C.B., 1861 : Brevet-Colonel, 1869 : A.Q.M.G. : died of syncope, after being upset crossing a swollen river, Aug. 24, 1873.

MACKENZIE, SIR WILLIAM (1811–1895)

Born 1811 : educated at King's College, Aberdeen : M.R.C.S., London, 1832 : M.D. : appointed to the Madras medical service, 1835 : served in the Rohilla wars, 1841 and 1851 : M.D., 1856 : in the mutiny, as Staff Surgeon to Brigade under Sir Hugh Rose, in many actions in the Central India Field Force, 1857–8 : in the Berar Field Force, 1858–9 : C.B., 1859 : C.S.I., 1867 : Inspr-General of the Madras Medical Department, 1861–71 : author of various medical and other works : K.C.B., 1887 : died Oct. 29, 1895.

MACKESON, FREDERICK (1807–1853)

Son of William Mackeson : born Sep. 28, 1807 : educated at Canterbury and in France : entered the Indian Army in Bengal, in 1825 : in the 14th N.I. : stationed as Assistant Political Agent at Ludiana : accompanied Sir A. Burnes (*q.v.*) to Cabul in 1837 : distinguished as a Frontier and Political Officer in the first Afghan war,in the Khyber and at Peshawar: C.B., 1842 : in the battle of Aliwal : in 1846, Superintendent of Cis-Satlaj territory: was in the Panjab campaign of 1848–9 : Political Officer with the Army : after Chilianwala he swam the Jhelum in full flood : local Lt-Colonel, 1849 : Commissioner of Peshawar in 1851 : he was, while engaged in official work in his verandah, assassinated by a religious fanatic from Koner, Sep. 10, 1853 : he died on Sep. 14. Lord Dalhousie wrote his epitaph, which included the following words—" He was the beau ideal of a soldier—cool to conceive, brave to dare, and strong to do. . . . The loss of Col. Mackeson's life would have dimmed a victory : to lose him thus, by the hand of a foul assassin, is a misfortune of the heaviest gloom for the Government, which counted him among its bravest and its best."

MACKINNON, SIR WILLIAM, BARONE (1823–1893)

Son of Duncan Mackinnon : born March 31, 1823 : educated at Campbeltown : after mercantile work at Glasgow, went to India in 1847, and, with Robert Mackenzie, who was engaged in the coasting trade, established the firm of Mackinnon, Mackenzie, and, in Sep. 1856, the Calcutta and Burma Steam Navigation Co., renamed the British India Steam Navigation Co., in 1862, which has increased and opened out trade from India in all directions, and round its coast : obtained in 1878 from the Sultan of Zanzibar a lease of the territory now called German East Africa, but the British Government refused to sanction it : was Chairman, 1888–93, of the Imperial British East Africa Co., whose territory Government took over in 1895 : he promoted Stanley's expedition for the relief of Emin Pasha, 1886 : founded the East African Scottish Mission, 1891 : C.I.E. in 1882 : Baronet, 1889 : died June 22, 1893.

MACKINTOSH, SIR JAMES (1765–1832)

Born Oct. 24, 1765 : son of Captain John Mackintosh : educated at Fortrose, and Aberdeen University : studied medicine at Edinburgh : obtained his diploma, 1787 : went to London in 1788 and paid much attention to politics, literature, society, somewhat neglected his profession of medicine : called to the bar from Lincoln's Inn in 1795 : gave lectures on the Law of Nature and Nations : acquired a considerable practice : failed to obtain the appointment of Advocate-General of Bengal, but was knighted and made Recorder of Bombay, and held the appointment from Feb. 1804 to Nov. 1811 : founded the Literary Society of Bombay in 1805 and became its President : was out of his element in Bombay : became M.P. for Nairn, 1813, and for Knaresborough, 1819 : Professor of Law and General Politics at Haileybury, 1818–24 : wrote on Philosophy for the *Edinburgh Review* and the *Encyclopædia Britannica* : and the *History of England* : was made a Privy Councillor and a Commissioner of the Board of Control, 1830 : joined in the inquiry into East Indian affairs preparatory to the renewal, in 1833, of the Co.'s Charter : died May 30, 1832.

MACLEAN, CHARLES (*circa* 1768–1824)

Studied medicine, and entered the E.I. Co's service : made several voyages to India in East Indiamen : was in medical practice at Calcutta in 1792 : wrote on fevers in 1796 : in 1798 he was ordered by the Governor-General to leave India for making an insinuation in a newspaper against a magistrate : left the service of Government : in 1806 he bitterly attacked the Governor-General, Marquis Wellesley : became a lecturer on the diseases of hot climates to the E. I. Co., and opposed the Government project of opening the trade to India : he attacked the quarantine laws, and wrote on medical subjects : died about 1824.

MACLEAN, CHARLES SMITH (1836–)

Born 1836 : entered the Army, 1853, and became Maj-General, 1893 : served in Indian mutiny, 1857, severely wounded : China war, 1860; Afghan war, 1878–80 : Brevet-Lt-Colonel and C.B. : Mahsud-

Waziri expedition, 1881 : Consul-General for Khorasan and Seistan : C.I.E., 1888.

MACLEAN, SIR FRANCIS WILLIAM (1844–)

Son of Alexander Maclean : born Dec. 13, 1844 : educated at Westminister and Trinity College, Cambridge : called to the bar at the Inner Temple, 1868 : Q.C., 1886 : M.P. for Mid-Oxfordshire, 1885–91 : Master in Lunacy, 1891 : Chief Justice of Bengal since 1896 : knighted : Chairman of Indian Famine Relief Committees, 1897 and 1900 : Vice-Chancellor of Calcutta University, 1898–9 : K.C.I.E., 1898.

MACLEAN, FREDERICK GURR (?–)

Appointed to the Telegraph Department, 1868 : was Superintendent of the Field Telegraph in the Afghan war, 1878–80 : Director-General of Indian Telegraphs, 1900 : C.I.E., 1903 : retired.

MACLEAN, SIR HECTOR (1756–1848),

Son of Hugh Maclean : in the E. I. Co.'s service : in an expedition to Arcot, a siege of Pondicherry, and the reduction of Pulicat : commanded Cuddalore and its defences, 1786 : under Cornwallis at Bangalore, and at Seringapatam, 1792 : commanded a native corps in Ceylon, 1798 : and the 9th N.I. in 1800, under Colonel Arthur Wellesley : Brigadier, 1800-3 : at Asirghar, Gawilghar, and Argaum : commanded the forces near Hyderabad, 1805 : K.C.B., 1815 : Lt.-General, 1821 : General, 1838 : died Dec. 11, 1848.

MACLEAN, JAMES MACKENZIE (1835–)

Born Aug. 13, 1835 : son of Alexander Maclean : editor of the *Newcastle Chronicle*, 1855–58 : on the staff of the *Manchester Guardian*, 1858–9 : editor and proprietor of the *Bombay Gazette*, 1859–79 : M.P. for Oldham, 1885–92 : M.P. for Cardiff, 1895–1900 : author of *Maclean's Guide to Bombay, Recollections of Westminster and India* : President of the Institute of Journalists, 1897–8.

MACLEOD, SIR ALEXANDER (1767–1831)

Entered the Artillery, 1784, and served in India for 47 years without interruption :

was at Cornwallis' siege of Seringapatam : under Lord Lake in the Mahratta war : at the siege of Kamona, Gunnouri, and Bhawani : commanded Ochterlony's Artillery in the Nipal war, 1814 : at the siege of Hatras, 1817 : commanded the Artillery of a Division in the Mahratta-Pindari war, 1818 : commanded the Artillery in the field, 1819–20, and the Regiment of Artillery, 1823 : in command at capture of Bhartpur, 1825–6 : Brig-General, K.C.B.: died at Dum Dum, Aug. 20, 1831.

MACLEOD, SIR JOHN MACPHERSON (1792–1881)

I.C.S. : born 1792 : son of Donald Macleod : educated at Edinburgh University and at Haileybury : went out to Madras, 1811 : was Financial and General Secretary to the Madras Government, 1824 : Persian translator to Government, 1826: Revenue and Judicial Secretary, 1827: Member of the Board of Revenue, 1829 : Commissioner in Mysore, 1832–3 : Member of the Indian Law Commission with Macaulay (*q.v.*), 1835 : Member of the Commission for Revising the System of Prison Discipline, 1836: returned to England, 1838 : retired, 1841 : K.C.S.I. in 1866 : Privy Council, 1871 : died March 4, 1881.

MACLEOD, NORMAN (1754–1801)

General : born at Brodie House, Nairnshire, March 4, 1754 : educated under Professor George Stuart at Edinburgh : succeeded his grandfather in 1772, as Chief of the Clan : took up his residence at Dunvegan : entertained Dr. Johnson there in 1773 : entered the Army, 1774, as Captain of the 71st regt. : went out to America with his bride, Mary Mackenzie : both were taken prisoners, but were kindly treated by Washington : at Madras, in 1782, as Lt-Colonel of the 2nd Battalion of the 42nd Highlanders, raised by himself : fought against Tippoo in several brilliant engagements : in 1783 took the fortress of Bednore : promoted, 1783, to Brig-General : appointed C. in C. of the Malabar Army in place of General Matthews : returned to England in 1789 : died at Guernsey, Aug. 1801.

MACMILLAN, MICHAEL (1853–)

Born Jan. 23, 1853 : son of John Macmillan : educated at Rugby, Marlborough, and Brazenose College, Oxford : Scholar : 1st Class Moderations, 2nd Class Final Classical School : B.A., 1876 : joined the Bombay Education Department, 1878 : Professor at Elphinstone College, Bombay : Principal, since 1900 : author of several educational works—*Promotion of General Happiness, Globe-Trotter in India Two Hundred Years Ago, Tales of Indian Chivalry*, etc.

MACNABB, SIR DONALD CAMPBELL (1832–   )

I.C.S. : born 1832 : educated at Haileybury, 1851–3 : entered the Indian Civil Service in the Panjab, 1853, and retired, 1881 : in the Indian mutiny helped, at Shahpur in the Panjab, to raise a considerable body of Irregular Horse, sent to Delhi : Commissioner of Rawal Pindi, and of Peshawar, 1875–81 : C.S.I. : K.C.I.E., 1887.

MACNAGHTEN, CHESTER (1843–1896)

Son of Elliot Macnaghten (*q.v.*) : educated at Bonchurch, and Trinity College, Cambridge : went to India, 1866, as tutor to the Maharaja of Darbhanga (*q.v.*) : held the post, 1866–70 : transferred to Bombay as first Principal of the Rajkumar or Chiefs' College at Rajkot in Kattiawar, 1870–96 : died there, Feb. 10, 1896 : worked with the greatest zeal and devotion and marked success : his character attracted the warm affection of his Indian pupils : his constant intercourse with them, in games and studies, had an excellent effect on the pupils, who justified, by their careers, the pains bestowed on them. He wrote on " Rajkumar Colleges " in the *Calcutta Review*, 1879 : his addresses to the students at his college were published as *Common Thoughts on Serious Subjects*, both in India and in London, 1896.

MACNAGHTEN, ELLIOT (1807–1888)

Son of the first Sir Francis Workman Macnaghten (some time Judge of the Supreme Court at Madras, and at Calcutta), and brother of Sir W. H. Macnaghten (*q.v.*) : educated at Rugby : went to India, and held legal appointments in the Supreme Court at Calcutta : one of the last survivors of the old body of E. I. Co.'s Directors : for many years a Director : Chairman, 1855 : after the transfer of India to the Crown, was chosen

by the E. I. Co. one of the original Members of Council, Sep. 21, 1858 : Vice-President, 1866 : died Dec. 24, 1888.

MACNAGHTEN, SIR FRANCIS WORKMAN, BARONET (1763–1843)

Son of Edmond Macnaghten : appointed Puisne Judge of the Supreme Court, Madras, 1809 : knighted : transferred to Calcutta, 1815 : retired, 1825 : Baronet, 1836 : assumed the additional name of Workman, 1823 : greatly affected by the death of his second son, Sir W. H. M. (*q.v.*), at Kabul in 1841 : died Nov. 22, 1843.

MACNAGHTEN, SIR WILLIAM HAY, BARONET (1793–1841)

I.C.S. : second son of Sir Francis Workman Macnaghten, |*Bart.*, Judge of the Supreme Courts of Madras and Calcutta : born in Aug. 1793 : educated at Charterhouse : went to Madras in the Army, 1809 : was in the Governor's bodyguard : gained prizes in languages : served at Hyderabad and in Mysore : appointed to the Bengal Civil Service, 1814 : gained great distinction in languages at Fort William : became Registrar of the *Sadr Diwani Adalat*, 1822–30 : published his works on Hindu and Muhammadan Law, and reports of cases : on tour to Upper India, 1830–3, with Lord W. Bentinck at his meeting with Ranjit Singh at Roopar : Secretary in the Secret and Political Departments, 1833–7 : accompanied Lord Auckland on tour, 1837, to the N.W.P. : made the treaty with Ranjit Singh and Shah Shuja in June, 1838 : signed Auckland's manifesto of Oct. 1, 1838 : appointed Envoy and Minister at the Afghan Court of Shah Shuja : accompanied the Army of the Indus *viâ* Kandahar and Ghazni to Kabul : the whole policy accepted by Macnaghten : had difficulties with the military authorities : Shah Shuja reinstated in Aug. 1839 : Macnaghten made a Baronet in Jan. 1840 : had great troubles in Afghanistan with Shah Shuja and the tribes, and in re-organizing the government of the country : Dost Muhammad surrendered on Nov. 3, 1840 : and was sent to India : Macnaghten nominated Governor of Bombay in Sep. 1841 : on the reduction of their stipends the Afghan chiefs rebelled : Burnes was murdered on Nov. 2, 1841 : the military authorities failed, and the Army remained inactive : Macnaghten accepted the terms of the rebel chiefs on Dec. 11 : the terms were not adhered to by the Afghans : Macnaghten negotiated further with Akbar Khan, son of Dost Muhammad, and at an interview on Dec. 23, 1841, was treacherously killed by Akbar himself. His character and capacity for his task have been much discussed. The whole policy was surrounded by the greatest difficulties, and the inefficiency of the military commanders added to them : Macnaghten's optimism and confidence prevented him from realizing the situation correctly : his high character and courage were conspicuous throughout : a monument was erected to him at Calcutta.

MACNAMARA, N. CHARLES (? -)

Joined the Indian Medical Service : was in the Sonthal rebellion and Indian mutiny : Fellow of Calcutta University : Professor of Ophthalmic Medicine, Calcutta Medical College : founder of the Mayo Hospital, Calcutta : Vice-President of Royal College of Surgeons and of B.M. Association : author of several works, including *Diseases of the Eye, History of Asiatic Cholera, Diseases of Bones, Hunterian Oration*, 1901 : F.R.C.S.

MACNEILL, JAMES GRAHAM ROBERT DOUGLAS (1842–)

Born Feb. 11, 1842 : son of Capt. Thomas MacNeill : educated privately : joined the Madras Army, 1859, and became Maj-General, 1898 : served on the Staff, in the Intelligence Department, 1880–2 : D.A.Q.M.G., 1882–5 : D.A.G. and Q.M.G. Burmese expedition, 1885–6 : severely wounded : C.B. : commanded 14th regt. M.I., 1887–9 : A.A.G., Mandalay, 1889–90 : commanded 14th regt. M.I., 1887–9 and 1890–4 : retired, 1898.

MACPHERSON, SIR ARTHUR GEORGE (1828–)

Born Sep. 26, 1828 : son of Hugh Macpherson, M.D. : educated at Aberdeen and Edinburgh : called to the bar, Inner Temple, 1852 : practised before the Supreme Court, Calcutta, 1852 : Legislative Secretary to the Government of Bengal, 1862–4, and to the Government of India, 1864 : Puisne Judge of Calcutta

High Court, 1864–77 : officiating Chief Justice, 1875 : Legal Adviser to Secretary of State for India, 1879–82 : Judicial Secretary, India Office, 1882–93 : K.C.I.E. 1889.

MACPHERSON, DUNCAN (? –1867)

Joined the Army Medical Service in Madras in 1836 : was in China in 1840–2, and wrote an account of his time there : in the Russian war, 1855, head of the medical staff of the Turkish contingent : wrote his *Antiquities of Kertch and Researches in the Cimmerian Bosphorus*, 1857 : Inspr-General of the medical service, Madras, 1857 : was an active and advanced sanitary officer : Hon. physician and surgeon to Queen Victoyia : died at Merkara, Coorg, June 8, 1867.

MACPHERSON, SIR HERBERT TAYLOR (1827–1886)

Son of Lt-Colonel Duncan Macpherson : born Feb. 27, 1827 : joined the 78th Highlanders, 1845 : Adjutant in the Persian war, 1856–7 : under Havelock at the relief of Lucknow, Sep. 25, 1857, when he gained the Victoria Cross, " setting an example of heroic gallantry to the men of the regiment at the period of the action in which they captured 2 brass 9-pounders at the point of the bayonet," under heavy fire : under Outram at the defence of the Alambagh : at the capture of Lucknow, severely wounded : joined the Bengal Staff Corps as Major in 1865 : in the Hazara Black Mountain campaign, 1868 : in the Lushai expedition, 1871–2 : in the Jowaki campaign, 1877 : commanded a Brigade in the Khyber in the Afghan war, 1878 : in Sir F. Roberts' march on Kabul, 1879 : in the fighting round Kabul : in the march to Kandahar and the battle there, Sep. 1880 : K.C.B. : Maj-General in command of Indian troops in Egypt, 1882, at Tel-el-Kebir : K.C.S.I. : C. in C. of Madras, 1886 : Lt-General : went to Burma to complete the pacification of the country : on his way down from Prome to Rangoon, he died of fever on board the steamer, Oct. 20, 1886.

MACPHERSON, SIR JAMES DUNCAN (1811–1874)

Son of Lt-Colonel Duncan Macpherson of the 78th Highlanders : born 1811, educated at King's College, Aberdeen: joined the 22nd Bengal N.I. 1828: transferred to the 6th Europeans in Bengal: was Brig-Major in the Panjab campaign, 1848–9; at Chilianwala and Gujarat: Brevet-Major: Military Secretary to the Panjab Government, 1852–8, that is, during the mutiny, the siege of Delhi, etc.: was Q.M.G. in Bengal, 1858–9: commanded Brigades at Dinapur and Agra: Commissary-General of the Bengal Army, 1864–8: Maj-General, 1868: C.B., 1858: K.C.B., 1873: died May 29, 1874.

MACPHERSON, SIR JOHN, BARONET
(1745–1821)

Governor-General: son of Rev. John Macpherson: born 1745: educated at King's College, Aberdeen, and Edinburgh University: went to India, 1767, as the purser of a ship: sent to England on a secret mission by Muhammad Ali, Nawab of the Carnatic: went to Madras, as a "writer," in 1770: dismissed the service by Lord Pigot, Governor of Madras, in 1777: M.P. for Cricklade, 1779–82: reinstated by the Court of Directors: Member of the Supreme Council in India, 1781–5 and 1786–7: Governor-General from Feb. 1785, to Sep. 1786: had to restore the finances, which were in a state of deficit: made a Baronet, 1786: M.P. for Horsham, 1796–1802: died Jan. 12, 1821.

MACPHERSON, JOHN (1817–1890)

Brother of S. C. Macpherson (q.v.), and son of Dr. Hugh Macpherson: born 1817: educated at Aberdeen: studied medicine in London, and on the Continent: M.R.C.S.: to Calcutta in the E. I. Co.'s medical service, 1839: retired, 1864, as Inspr-General of Hospitals: published several medical works in India: died March 17, 1890.

MACPHERSON, JOHN MOLESWORTH
(1853–   )

Born Aug. 8, 1853: son of John Macpherson: educated at Westminster: called to the bar, Inner Temple, 1876: Advocate of the Calcutta High Court: Deputy Secretary to Government of India in the Legislative Department, 1877: Secretary to it since 1896. C.S.I., 1897: author of Lists of British Enactments in Force in Native States, 6 vols.; Law of Mortgages in British India.

MACPHERSON, SAMUEL CHARTERS
(1806–1860)

Major: brother of John (q.v.) and of William (q.v.), and son of Dr. Hugh Macpherson: educated at Edinburgh and Trinity College, Cambridge: entered the Madras Army, 1827: in the operations against the Raja of Gumsur in Orissa, 1835: inquired and reported on the wild tribe of Khonds in Gumsur, and the measures required for the suppression of the Meriah, or human, sacrifices among them, 1837–9: as Principal Assistant to the Collector of Ganjam, he reformed the Khonds, 1842–4: appointed Agent to the Governor-General in 1845 to suppress human sacrifice, and female infanticide, in the hill tracts of Orissa: his conduct investigated and charges against him found untenable: Political Officer at Benares, Bhopal and Gwalior. where. with Dinkar Rao, he kept Sindia loyal in the mutiny of 1857: died at Calcutta, April 15, 1860.

MACPHERSON, WILLIAM (1812–1893)

Brother of John and S. C., and son of Dr. Hugh Macpherson: educated at Charterhouse and Trinity College, Cambridge: called to the bar at the Inner Temple, 1837: went out to practise at the Calcutta bar, 1846: Master of Equity in the Supreme Court there, 1848–59: published the Procedure of the Civil Courts of India: editor of the Quarterly Review, 1860–7: Secretary to the Indian Law Commission, 1861–70: practised before the Privy Council: Legal Adviser to the India Office, 1874–9: Secretary in the Judicial Department, 1879: retired in 1882: died April 20, 1893.

MACPHERSON, SIR WILLIAM
(1835–   )

I.C.S.: educated at Haileybury, 1854–6: entered the Bengal Civil Service, 1856: Puisne Judge of the Calcutta High Court, 1885–1900: retired: knighted.

MACRABIE. ALEXANDER (? –1776)

Brother-in-law to Sir Philip Francis (q.v.) and his Private Secretary: was Sheriff of Calcutta at the time of Nuncomar's execution, Aug. 1775: died at Ganjam, 1776.

MADDOCK, SIR THOMAS HERBERT
(1790–1870)

I.C.S.: son of Rev. Thomas Maddock : born 1790 : educated at Manchester Free Grammar School and at Haileybury, 1812–3 : went out to India, 1814 : served in the Sagar and Nerbudda territories : Political Agent at Bhopal : Political Resident at Lucknow, 1829–31 : Political Officer in Nipal, 1831 : Secretary to the Government of India in the Legal, Judicial and Revenue Departments, 1838–43 : Member of the Supreme Council, 1843–9, Deputy-Governor of Bengal in 1845 and 1848 : knighted and C.B. : retired, 1849 : M.P. for Rochester, 1852–7 : died Jan. 15, 1870.

MADEC, RENÉ (1736–1784)

Born at Quimper in Brittany, Feb. 7, 1736, of poor parents : began life as a sailor : in 1748 went out to India as a recruit in the service of the French E.I. Co. : soon wearied of this : deserted, and joined the French troops at Pondicherry : taken prisoner by the English at Jinji, on the Coromandel coast : consented, with many of his companions, to serve in the English Army in Bengal : after several years a mutiny among the troops afforded them a chance of escape : Madec was chosen captain by his comrades ; gradually collected a body of troops, both Frenchmen and Sepoys, and from 1765 to 1777 pursued a brilliant career as a guerilla leader and adventurer : served thus under various native princes, but always under the French flag, and never losing sight of the interests of his country in India : was in the service of Shuja-ud-daula, Nawab of Oudh, till his defeat by the English at Baxar, when he passed over to the Jats : took service in 1772 under the Mogul Emperor : performed many brave deeds and was granted many honours : made a Nawab of the first class. After the siege of Delhi by the united forces of the Mahrattas and the Jats, and the defeat of the Emperor, Madec rejoined his countrymen at Pondicherry, and took part in its defence against the English : after its capitulation he left India (1778),· returned to France, where he died, worn out by all his many hardships, in 1784.

MAHMUDABAD, RAJA SIR MUHAMMAD AMIR HASAN KHAN. KHAN BAHADUR. KHANZADA OF (1849–1902)

A Siddiki Sheikh of a famous old Oudh family : son of Nawab Ali Khan,· a younger brother of Ibad Ali Khan, Raja of Paintipur : adopted son of Musahib Ali Khan of Mahmudabad : the father, Nawab Ali Khan, died in 1858, while the son was a minor : educated at the Sitapur *talukdars'* school, afterwards at the Benares and Canning (Lucknow) Colleges : at Lord Lawrence's *darbar* at Lucknow, he was presented with a sword : elected, 1871, Vice-President of the British Indian Association in Oudh, an Hon. Magistrate and Hony. Munsif and a member of the Legislative Council, N.W.P. In 1877 he obtained recognition of the hereditary title of Raja : made, in 1883, Khan Bahadur : this title was made hereditary in 1884 : his other honorific titles were granted in 1871, in recognition of his public services : K.C.I.E.

MAINE, SIR HENRY JAMES SUMNER
(1822–1888)

Son of Dr. James Maine : born Aug. 15, 1822 : educated at Christ's Hospital, London, and Pembroke College, Cambridge : Exhibitioner and Scholar : Craven Scholar : Chancellor's English verse, 1842 : Senior Classic in 1844 : Tutor at Trinity Hall, 1845–7 : Regius Professor of Civil Law, 1847–54, called to the bar from Lincoln's Inn and the Middle Temple, 1850 : Reader in Roman Law and Jurisprudence at the Inns of Court, 1852 : one of the principal writers in the *Saturday Review* from 1855 : published his *Ancient Law* in 1861 : became Legal Member of the Supreme Council in India from Nov. 12, 1862, to Oct. 9, 1869 : Vice-Chancellor of the Calcutta University for 4 years : Corpus Professor of Jurisprudence, 1871–78 : published *Village Communities*, 1871 : K.C.S.I., 1871 : and Member of the Council of India,1871–88: published *EarlyHistory of Institutions*, 1875 : Master of Trinity Hall, Cambridge, 1877–88 : published *Dissertations on Early Law and Custom*, 1883,· and *Popular Government* in 1885 : and wrote for the *St. James's Gazette* : also on " India " in *The Reign of Queen Victoria* : became Whewell Professor of International Law at Cambridge, 1887 : died at

Cannes Feb. 3, 1888. He had declined the Chief Justiceship of Bengal, the Permanent Under Secretaryship of State for the Home Department, the Chief Clerkship of the House of Commons, and other appointments: was F.R.S., and had many honorary distinctions: one of the first to apply the historical method to the study of the philosophy of institutions: wrote other articles on legal and Indian subjects.

MAITLAND, SIR FREDERICK LEWIS
(1777–1839)

Born Sep. 7, 1777 : son of Capt. Frederick Lewis Maitland, R.N. : served at sea, in European waters, in Egypt, 1801, and on American and West Indian stations, 1813–14 : when commanding the *Bellerephon*, conveyed Napoleon in July, 1815, to England : C.B., 1815 : K.C.B. and Rear-Admiral, 1830 : Naval C. in C. in the E. Indies and China in 1832 : in 1837 in the Afghan war, took Karachi and protected the landing of the troops : in the disturbances at Bushire brought away the Resident and Staff : died on his ship at sea, near Bombay, Nov. 30, 1839 : a monument was erected to him in Bombay cathedral.

MAITLAND, SIR PEREGRINE (1777–1854)

Son of Thomas Maitland : born 1777 : joined the Guards, 1792 : served in Flanders, Spain, at Walcheren : Maj-General : C.B., 1815 : commanded a Brigade at Waterloo : K.C.B. : Lieutenant-Governor of Upper Canada, 1818–28, and of Nova Scotia, 1828–34 : Lt-General, 1830 : C. in C. of the Madras Army, Oct. 1836, to Dec. 1838 : C. in C. at the Cape, 1844–7 : General, 1846 : G.C.B., 1852 : Colonel of the 17th regt. : died May 30, 1854.

MAITLAND, RICHARD (1714 ?–1763)

Born about 1714 : enlisted in the Royal Artillery, 1732 : obtained a Commission : Captain in 1755 : to India in 1755 : fought under Clive at the capture of Gheria, the pirate Angria's stronghold, 1756: was in command of the expedition sent with Watson's ships, to the capture of Surat, effected in March, 1759 : Major, 1762 : died at Bombay, Feb. 21, 1763.

MALABARI, BEHRAMJI MERWANJI
(1853–   )

A Parsi by birth : educated at Surat : taught in the Parsi Proprietary School : after a hard struggle in early life, he became a journalist : author of poems, in 1875, and social reformer : in 1880 he purchased the *Indian Spectator* and was editor for more than 20 years : it is now merged in *The Voice of India* : he was mainly instrumental in procuring the passing of " The Age of Consent Act " and removing restrictions against the remarriage of widows : author of a translation of Max Müller's *Origin and Growth of Religion*, 1882 ; *Gujarat and the Gujaratis*, 1884 ; *The Indian Eye on English Life*, 1893 ; *The Indian Problem*, 1894 : has edited *East and West* since Nov. 1901.

MALAN, REV. CESAR JEAN SALOMON (1812–1894)

Born April 12, 1812 : son of Dr. Cesar Henri Abraham Malan : educated at Vandœuvres : took early to the study of languages : was at St. Edmund's Hall, Oxford, 1833–7 : Boden Sanskrit Scholar, 1834 : Pusey and Ellerton Scholar, 1837 : in 1838 became classical lecturer at Bishop's College, Calcutta : ordained, 1838 : Secretary to the Asiatic Society of Bengal : studied Indian languages : left India, 1840 : became member of Balliol College, Oxford, 1843 : was Rector of Broadwindsor, 1845–85 : travelled in Asia Minor, Mesopotamia, Armenia, 1849–50, going to Nineveh with Sir A. H. Layard, and in 1872 to the Crimea, Georgia, Armenia : D.D. of Edinburgh, 1880 : gave many of his books to the Indian Institute at Oxford : was a great Oriental scholar, and a voluminous writer on linguistic subjects ; an accomplished artist, and an ardent lover of Natural History : nearly all his publications dealt with the Scriptures and ecclesiastical subjects, e.g. *Original Notes on the Book of Proverbs* : he knew about 40 languages : he died Nov. 25, 1894.

MALCOLM, SIR GEORGE (1818–1897)

Born at Bombay, Sep. 10, 1818 : son of David Malcolm, and nephew of Sir John (*q.v.*) : entered the E. I. Co.'s Bombay Native Army, 1836 : in the Bombay Division of the Army of the Indus in the Afghan war, 1838–9 : at Ghazni and

Kabul : in the Sind Irregular Horse in Beluchistan, 1840–1, and in E. Cutchi, 1844–5 : with the Sind Horse in the Panjab campaign, 1848–9, at Multan, Gujarat the occupation of Peshawar : in the Persian war, 1857, commanding S. Mahratta Horse : and against Shorapur, 1858 : commanded in the operations against the Chief of Nargoond, 1858 : C.B. : commanded a Division in Abyssinia, 1867–8 : K.C.B. : General, 1877, and G.C.B., 1886 : died April 6, 1897.

MALCOLM, SIR JOHN (1769–1833)

Son of George Malcolm : born May 2, 1769 : educated at Westerkirk : to India in the E. I. Co.'s military service, 1782 : reached Madras, 1783 : in 1792 was at the siege of Seringapatam, under Cornwallis, and appointed Persian Interpreter to the Nizam's troops : Secretary to Sir Alured Clarke (q.v.), who was C. in C., Madras, 1795–7 : at the taking of the Cape : Secretary to Lord Harris (q.v.), 1797–8 : Assistant Resident at Hyderabad, 1798 : present with the Nizam's troops at the capture of Seringapatam, May 4, 1799 : Secretary, jointly with Munro, to the Commission for the Settlement of Mysore : selected by Lord Wellesley to be an Envoy to Persia, 1799–1801 : negotiated two treaties, commercial and political : on his return appointed Private Secretary to the Governor-General, Lord Wellesley, 1801–3 : sent on special mission to Bombay in 1802 : nominated Resident in Mysore, Feb. 1803 : Political Officer with General Arthur Wellesley on the outbreak of the Mahratta war, 1803 : drew up the treaties of Sirji-Anjengaum of Dec. 30, 1803, and of Burhanpur of Feb. 27, 1804 : Resident at Sindia's court, 1804, and in Mysore, 1805 : served with Lord Lake, 1805 : made the treaty of Nov. 22, 1805, with Daulat Rao Sindia, and of Dec. 24, 1805, with Jeswant Rao Holkar : sent by Lord Minto on a mission to Persia, 1808, which was foiled by French influence : deputed to deal with the mutinous Madras officers at Masulipatam : again sent to Persia, 1810 : overshadowed there by Sir Harford Jones : wrote his Political History of India, 1811 : and History of Persia, 1815 : knighted and K.C.B. in 1815 : D.C.L. at Oxford, 1816 : Political Agent to the Governor-General, and Brig-General with the Army of the Dekkan in

the Pindari-Mahratta war, 1817–8 : won the battle of Mahidpur, Dec. 21, 1817 : made the treaty of Mandiswar of Jan. 6, 1818, with Malhar Rao Holkar : made Baji Rao, the Peshwa, abdicate : took Asirghar, April 9, 1819 : administered Central India, including Malwa : disappointed of being Governor of Bombay, or Madras, he returned to England, 1822 : made Governor of Bombay, 1827 : had disputes with the Supreme Court of Bombay, the Government declining to execute the process of the Court, which Sir J. P. Grant (q.v.), then sole Judge, thereupon closed : new Judges were appointed, and Grant resigned : left India in Dec. 1830 : M.P. for Launceston, 1831–2 : began the Life of Lord Clive : wrote on the Government of India : died July 30, 1833 : his statue, by Chantrey, placed in Westminster Abbey : wrote also on Central India and Sketch of the Sikhs : he had great diplomatic experience and skill, and was very successful and influential with all classes.

MALET, ARTHUR (1806–1888)

I.C.S. : son of Sir C. W. Malet (q.v.) : born 1806 : educated at Winchester, Addiscombe and Haileybury : went out to Bombay in the Civil Service in 1826 : Political Agent in Cutch and Kattiawar, 1842–3 : Secretary to the Bombay Government in the Secret and Political Department, 1846 : Chief Secretary, 1847 : Member of the Legislative Council of the Governor-General, 1854 : Member of Council, Bombay, 1855, also Chief Judge of the Sadr Court, 1857 : retired, 1860 : died Sep. 13, 1888.

MALET, SIR CHARLES WARRE, BARONET (1752–1815)

I.C.S. : son of Rev. Alexander Malet : born 1752 : went out to Bombay in the E. I. Co.'s Civil Service : became Resident at Poona, 1785 : negotiated at Poona, on June 1, 1790, an offensive and defensive alliance with the Peshwa and the Nizam against Tippoo : Baronet, 1791 : Member of Council, Bombay, April, 1797 : retired, 1798 : F.R.S. : F.S.A. : died Jan. 24, 1815.

MALET, GEORGE GRENVILLE (1804–1856)

Son of Sir C. W. Malet (q.v.) : born 1804 : entered the 3rd Bombay Light

Cavalry, 1822 : Lt-Colonel, 1854 : served in Gujarat, Kattiawar, Mahi Kanta, Rajputana : in the Afghan war, 1842 : wounded : at Hyderabad, Sind, under Sir C. Napier : Political Officer at Khairpur, Sind : in an expedition against the Beluchis : Superintendent of the Gaekwar's Horse, 1850 : killed in the Persian war at the capture of Bushire, Dec. 9, 1856 : wrote *A History of Sind.*

MALKIN, SIR BENJAMIN HEATH
(1797-1837)

Son of Benjamin Malkin, the miscellaneous writer : born Sep. 29, 1797 : educated at Bury St. Edmunds, and Trinity College, Cambridge : 3rd Wrangler, 1818 : Fellow : called to the bar at Lincoln's Inn, Feb. 11, 1823 : Recorder of Penang, 1832 : Judge of the Supreme Court at Calcutta : knighted : died there, Oct. 21, 1837 : a friend of Macaulay, who wrote his epitaph, " A man eminently distinguished for his literary and scientific attainments, by his professional learning and ability, by the clearness and accuracy of his intellect, by diligence, by patience, by firmness, by love of truth, by public spirit, ardent and disinterested, yet always under the guidance of discretion, by rigid uprightness, by unostentatious piety, by the serenity of his temper, and by the benevolence of his heart." Macaulay had previously written—" Malkin is a man of singular temper, judgment, and firmness of nerve. Danger and responsibility, instead of agitating and confusing him, always bring out whatever there is in him."

MALLESON, GEORGE BRUCE
(1825-1898)

Born May 8, 1825 : son of John Malleson : educated at Wimbledon and Winchester : joined the Bengal N.I. in 1844 : in the second Burmese war of 1852–3 : in the Commissariat Department till 1856 : wrote *The Mutiny of the Bengal Army*, called " the red pamphlet," in 1857 : Sanitary Commissioner in Bengal, 1866–8 : Controller of the Military Finance Department, 1868–9 : Guardian of the young Maharaja of Mysore, 1869–77 : C.S.I., 1872 : Colonel, 1873 : retired, 1877 : died March 1, 1898 : wrote constantly in the *Calcutta Review*, and works on Indian subjects : among them *Essays and Lectures on*

Indian Historical Subjects, 1866 ; *History of the French in India*, 1868 ; *Recreations of an Indian Official*, 1872 ; *Historical Sketch of the Native States of India*, 1875 ; *Final French Struggles in India and on the Indian Seas*, 1878 ; *History of the Indian Mutiny*, 1878–80 ; *History of Afghanistan*, 1879 ; *Herat*, 1880 ; *The Founders of the Indian Empire, Lord Clive*, 1882 ; *The Decisive Battles of India*, 1883 ; *The Russo-Afghan Question and the Invasion of India*, 1885 ; *Wellesley* ; *Akbar* ; *Dupleix* ; *Warren Hastings*.

MALLET, SIR LOUIS (1823-1890)

Son of John Lewis Mallet : born March 14, 1823 : became a clerk in the Audit Office in 1839 : Private Secretary to the President of the Board of Trade, 1848–52 : and 1855–7: Assistant Commissioner for carrying out commercial treaties with several nations, 1860–5, and with Austria, 1865–7 : C.B., 1866 : K.C.B., 1868 : Member of the Council of India, 1872–4 : Permanent Under Secretary of State for India, 1874–83 : visited India, 1875–6 : Privy Councillor, 1883 : represented the India Office at the Monetary Conference at Paris : was a Member of the Royal Commission on Gold and Silver, and on several other Royal Commissions : was a great authority on commercial policy, and an official exponent of free trade views : advocated bimetallism : his writings published in *Free Exchange*, 1891 : died Feb. 16, 1890.

MALTHUS, REV. THOMAS ROBERT
(1766-1834)

Son of Daniel Malthus : born Feb. 17, 1766 : educated at Warrington, privately, and at Jesus College Cambridge : ninth Wrangler in 1788 : Fellow : ordained in 1798 : published his *Essay on the Principle of Population*, in 1798, the precursor of the greater work which appeared in 1803 : after travelling widely in Europe, he became, in 1805, Professor of History and Political Economy at the E. I. Co.'s College, Haileybury, a post which he occupied during the remainder of his life. He wrote also on the *Principles of Political Economy*, and on the *Nature and Progress of Rent*. He was F.R.S : member of the National Institute of France, Fellow of the Statistical Society. The tradition of his great amiability and charm of character lingered among the students at the East

Indian College to the end of Haileybury. His character is fully described in the *Gentleman's Magazine* of June, 1835, where it is said that " his appearance, no less than his conduct, was that of a perfect gentleman " : died Dec. 29, 1834. He wrote other works on subjects connected with his Professorship.

MANDLIK, VISVANATH NARAYAN RAO SAHIB (1833–1889)

Born March 8, 1833, in the Ratnagiri District in the Konkan : educated at the Elphinstone High School : distinguished himself there : began life as Personal Assistant to Colonel Jacob in Sind, and afterwards held several Government appointments : resigned them in 1862, and joined the Bombay bar, soon obtaining lucrative practice as Pleader : appointed Government Pleader in 1884 : as Justice of the Peace, Municipal Commissioner, Fellow of the Bombay University, Member of the Legislative Council, Journalist, and Author, he won universal respect : in 1874 was made a Member of the Bombay Legislative Council (retaining the position for 8 years), and in 1884 a Member of the Legislative Council of the Governor-General. He translated into Gujarati *Elphinstone's History of India*, and published *A Manual of Hindu Law*, etc. : C.S.I., 1877 : he advocated political and educational advancement, but opposed any State intervention in social reforms : died May 9, 1889.

MANGLES, ROSS DONNELLY (1801–1877)

I.C.S. : son of James Mangles : born 1801 : educated at Eton and Haileybury : went to India in 1820 : after some minor appointments, he became, in the Burmese war of 1825, Secretary to the Commissioner of Pegu and Ava, and, in 1826, Deputy Secretary in the Judicial and Territorial Departments : in 1832, Deputy Secretary in the General Department : held charge of several districts : Secretary to the Government of Bengal in the Judicial and Revenue Departments, 1835–9 : in 1838, also temporary Member of the Board of Revenue : retired in 1839 : was M.P. for Guildford, 1841–58 : Director of the E. I. Co. : Chairman in 1857 : one of the original members of the new Council of India in Sep. 1858 till 1866 : died Aug. 16,

1877 : wrote articles on India in the *Edinburgh Review*.

MANGLES, ROSS LOWIS (1833–1905)

I.C.S. : born April, 14, 1833 : son of Ross D. Mangles, M.P. (*q.v.*) : educated at Bath Grammar School and Haileybury : joined the Bengal Civil Service in 1853. In the mutiny he served as a volunteer in the expedition for the relief of the Arrah garrison : the force fell into an ambush, and had to retreat : he, at great personal risk, carried and supported, for five miles, a wounded soldier, who otherwise must have been left to die. Mangles received the V.C. He was Judicial Commissioner of Mysore : Secretary to the Bengal Government : Member of the Board of Revenue in Bengal : retired, 1883 : died Feb 28, 1905.

MANI BEGAM (? –1802)

Wife of Mir Jafar, Nawab Nazim of Bengal : born at Balkunda near Sikandra : a dancing girl at Delhi, went to Murshidabad and there met Mir Jafar : became mother of Nawab Nazim Najm-ud-daula and his brother Saif-ud-daula : after their deaths her stepson Mubarak-ud-daula became Nawab Nazim, and she was appointed in 1772 by Warren Hastings and his Council as his Guardian : it was alleged by Nuncomar in 1775 that Hastings had been bribed to make this appointment : the charge, based on a letter which the Begam admitted to be forged, was not proved. She was removed from her Guardianship by the Council, and allowed a lakh of rupees as pension : died in 1802, and was buried at the Jafarganj cemetery at Murshidabad.

MANNING, ELIZABETH ADELAIDE (1828–1905)

Daughter of James Manning, Serjeant-at-Law, Recorder of Oxford : on the death, in 1877, of Miss Mary Carpenter (*q.v.*), who had formed the National Indian Association at Bristol in 1870, its centre was transferred to London : Miss Manning became its Honorary Secretary, and began then to edit the *Indian Magazine and Review*, carrying on these works until her death : she twice visited India in connexion with the Branches of the Association, and to inquire into education, especially of women and girls : she often lectured and wrote papers on India

T

and education : was connected, as pupil and one of the Governing Body, with Girton College from its foundation : and was on the Council of various Societies for promoting education and the progress of women : she received the Kaisar-i-Hind medal in June, 1904 : her stepmother, Mrs. Manning, who died April 1, 1871, wrote *Life in Ancient India*, and *Ancient and Mediæval India* : died Aug. 10, 1905.

MANNING, THOMAS (1772–1840)

Born Nov. 8, 1772 : son of the Rev. William Manning : educated at Caius College, Cambridge : Scholar, 1790–95 : private tutor : studied mathematics : friend of Porson and Charles Lamb : studied Chinese at Paris, 1800–3 : attended the Westminster Hospital : went out to Canton as a doctor in 1807–10 : was unable to enter China : went to Calcutta, 1810 : went in 1811 to Lhasa in Tibet, with only a single Chinese servant, *viâ* Rangpur, Bhutan, Parijong : stayed there for some months : had interviews with the Dalai Lama : under orders from Pekin, left Lhasa in April, 1812 : the first Englishman to enter Lhasa : returned to Canton : in 1816 accompanied Lord Amherst's embassy to Pekin as interpreter : returned to England a disappointed man, 1817 : led an eccentric life : regarded as the first Chinese scholar in Europe : died at Bath, May 2, 1840 : the notes of his journey to Lhasa were published in Sir C. R. Markham's *Narratives of Bogle's Mission to Tibet and Manning's Journey to Lhasa*, 1876.

MANSEL, CHARLES GRENVILLE (1806–1886)

I.C.S. : born 1806 : joined the E. I. Co.'s Civil Service in 1826 : served in the N.W.P. : in several appointments at Agra, up to Magistrate-Collector, 1835, and Settlement Officer, 1838–41 : in the Financial Department : Member of the Board of Administration of the Panjab with the Lawrences, 1849–50 : Resident at Nagpur, 1852–4 : retired : died Nov. 19, 1886.

MANSFIELD, SAMUEL (1815–1893)

I.C.S. : brother of Sir W. Mansfield, (Lord Sandhurst)(*q.v.*): educated at Hailey-bury, 1832–3 : entered the Bombay Civil Service, 1833 : in the mutiny, in charge of Khandesh District, did good service

in maintaining order when the Bhils rose in rebellion : Revenue Commissioner, N. Division, 1860 : Commissioner in Sind, 1863, and Member of Council, Bombay, May, 1867, to May, 1872 : a patron and supporter of the Western Indian Turf : died Dec. 12, 1893 : C.S.I.

MAN SINGH, MAHARAJA SIR—BAHADUR, KAIM JANG (1820–1870)

Youngest son of Raja Darshan Bahadur Singh Bahadur of Mahdauna, Faizabad, of a notable family of Sakaldipi Brahmans. Darshan Singh (died 1844), was brother of Raja Bakhtawar Singh, who accompanied Sleeman and was the King's Quarter-master-General and premier Raja in Oudh. In 1845 Man Singh was appointed Nizam of Daryabad, Rudauli and Sultanpur : made Raja Bahadur and acquired a vast estate : in 1855 became heir to his uncle, Bakhtawar Singh. At the annexation of Oudh, he was deprived of much of his property and soon after imprisoned at Faizabad as a revenue defaulter. When the mutiny broke out he was released by Col. Goldney, the Commissioner, and agreed to protect the European women and children : received 29 fugitives into his fort at Shahganj and escorted them in safety to Gorakhpur : in August, 1857, he went to Lucknow with a large contingent and a battery : but the rebels knew of his constant communication with the British, and after the fall of the capital besieged him at Shahganj, where he was relieved by Sir Hope Grant. He then rendered great assistance to the British and assisted in the restoration of order in Faizabad and elsewhere. In reward he regained all his old estates and those of the rebel Raja of Gonda, besides the remission of all outstanding balances : the foremost man among the Oudh *talukdars*, he acted as their mouthpiece in all the great controversies with regard to rights in land : Hony. Magistrate in 1860 : K.C.S.I., 1869 : died Oct. 11, 1870 : his daughter's son is the present Maharaja of Ajodhya.

MARGARY, HENRY JOSHUA (1811–1876)

Maj-General : born 1811 : educated at Addiscombe : entered the Bombay Engineers in 1830 : served in the Mahratta campaign, 1844 : Commanding Engineer at the siege of Samnieghar : Field Engineer of the Sind reserve in the Afghan war of 1838–9 : at the capture of Boodurghar : carried out important engineering works at Aden, Poona and other stations : retired as Maj-General in 1863 : died Jan. 21, 1876 : the father of Augustus Raymond Margary, who was murdered by the Chinese at Manwein, on the Chinese frontier, Feb. 21, 1875.

MARKBY, SIR WILLIAM (1829–   )

Born 1829 : son of Rev. William Henry Markby : éducated at King Edward's School, Bury St. Edmunds, and Merton College, Oxford : Scholar : 1st Class in Mathematics : Fellow of All Souls' College, and Fellow of Balliol College : called to the bar, 1856 : Recorder of Buckingham, 1865–6 : Puisne Judge of the Calcutta High Court, 1866–78 : Vice-Chancellor of Calcutta University : Reader in Indian Law, University of Oxford, 1878–1900 : author of *Lectures on Indian Law, Elements of Law*, 1896 : D.C.L., 1879 : K.C.I.E., 1889 : Commissioner 1892, to inquire into the administration of justice in Trinidad and Tobago.

MARKHAM, SIR CLEMENTS ROBERT (1830–   )

Born July 20, 1830 : son of Rev. David F. Markham : educated at Cheam and Westminster : entered the Navy in 1844 : served in the Arctic expedition, 1850–1 : retired from the Navy, 1852 : travelled in Peru, 1852–4 : introduced cinchona trees from Peru into British India, 1859–62 : Geographer to the Abyssinian expedition : Secretary to the Roy. Geog. Society, 1863–8 : Secretary to the Hakluyt Society, 1858–87 : Assistant Secretary in the India Office, 1867–77 : President of Roy. Geog. Society, 1894–1900, and of the Hakluyt Society : K.C.B. 1896 : author of many works, including *Memoirs of the Indian Surveys, History of Persia, History of the Abyssinian Expedition, Missions to Tibet, Travels in Peru and India*.

MARKHAM, FREDERICK (1805–1855)

Son of Admiral John Markham : born Aug. 16, 1805 : educated at Westminster : joined the 32nd regt. in 1824 : imprisoned for a year for being a second in a fatal duel, 1830 : commanded a Brigade at the siege of Multan, 1848–9, and the Division at Surajkund: at Gujarat : C.B. and A.D.C. to Queen Victoria : Adjutant-General in India, 1854 : Lt-General in the Crimea : commanded a Division at the Redan, 1855 : died in London, Dec. 21, 1855 : wrote *Shooting in the Himalayas : a Journal of Sporting Adventures in Ladak, Tibet, and Kashmir*, 1854.

MARRIOTT, WILLIAM FREDERICK (? –1879)

General : went out to India as a cadet in 1838 : went up at once to the campaign in Sind and Afghanistan : took a prominent part in the storm and capture of Ghazni, 1839 : afterwards served in the engineer corps of the Bombay Army, and in the Secretariat : joined the Bombay Staff Corps : from 1865, to the time of his leaving the service, about 1876, he was Secretary to the Bombay Government in the Military, Marine and Ecclesiastical Departments : during this period he was constantly consulted in confidential matters by Sir Bartle Frere and succeeding Governors : was Member of the Legislative Council, Bombay. After his retirement, General Marriott took service under the Egyptian Government, and was engaged in several engineering works of importance in Egypt : was C.S.I. : died Dec. 17, 1879.

MARSDEN, WILLIAM (1754–1836)

Son of John Marsden : born Nov. 16, 1754 : educated at Dublin schools : went out as a writer in the E. I. Co.'s service to Bencoolen in Sumatra, 1771 : stayed eight years : became Principal Secretary to the Government : devoted his time to literature and science : established an E.I. agency business in London, 1785 : became Second Secretary, 1795, and in 1804 First Secretary to the Admiralty till 1807 : F.R.S., Treasurer and Vice-president : Member of Asiatic and several other learned Societies : D.C.L. of Oxford, 1786 : died Oct. 6, 1836 : wrote the *History of Sumatra*, 1783 ; *Dictionary and Grammar of the Malayan Language*, 1812 ; *The Travels of Marco Polo*, 1818 ; *Numismata Orientalia illustrata*, 1823–5 : and other works : presented his whole collection of coins to the British Museum in 1834, and his library and Oriental MSS. to King's College : voluntarily resigned a pension of £1,500.

MARSHMAN, HANNAH (1767–1847)

Daughter of J. Shepherd : born 1767 : married, in 1791, to the Rev. Joshua Marshman (*q.v.*), and accompanied him to India, reaching Serampur, Oct. 1799 : she superintended the "Mission Family at Serampur," of Carey, Ward, and Marshman : herself established in 1800 a "Ladies' School," chiefly for Eurasian girls, many of whom took to missionary work and education. She opened a Native school in 1807. By 1819–24, her Serampur Native Female Education Society managed, in its vicinity, 14 girls' schools, 260 pupils : with a total of 27 schools, 554 pupils. Of her twelve children, six survived. She was the "first woman missionary to women" : died at Serampur, March 1, 1847.

MARSHMAN, JOHN CLARK (1794–1877)

Born Aug. 18, 1794 : son of Dr. Joshua Marshman (*q.v.*) : went out with his father in Oct. 1799 to Serampur in Bengal, where he received his education at the mission establishment of Carey (*q.v.*), Marshman (*q.v.*), and Ward (*q.v.*) : formally joined the brotherhood in 1819 and became an active director of its affairs, working, as a layman, for 20 years "as a sort of secular and unpaid bishop" : he set up the first paper-mill in India : issued the first monthly Bengali magazine, the *Dig-Darsan*, in April, 1818 : and, in the next month, issued the first weekly, the *Samachar Darpan* : the *Friend of India* was issued by him and his father, as a monthly, and later a quarterly Magazine, becoming a weekly paper from Jan. 1, 1835 : he was also for years the official Bengali Translator to Government. He also published *Guide to the Civil Law of the Presidency of Fort William*, 1845–6, a "Darogah" Manual, 1850, and other law books : wrote constantly in the *Calcutta Review* : and other historical works. He was one of the founders of the Serampur College, at a cost of £30,000. He left India in 1852 : and was examined by Parliament before the renewal of the Charter in 1853, and influenced the Education despatch of 1854 : he also advocated the promotion of forestry, telegraphs and railways in India : and had an influential position in the E. I. Railway Company in London. He wrote *The Life and Times of Carey, Marshman and Ward*, 1859 ; *Memoirs of*

Maj-General Sir Henry Havelock, K.C.B., 1860 (his brother-in-law) : his *History of India*, 1863, 1867. He failed to obtain a seat in the new Council of India : was made C.S.I. in 1868 : died July 8, 1877.

MARSHMAN, REV. JOSHUA, D.D. (1768–1837)

Son of John Marshman, a weaver : born April 20, 1768 : educated at the village school of Westbury Leigh : apprenticed to a bookseller and read unceasingly : was master of a Baptist school, 1794–9, when, with his son and others, he went out to Serampur in Bengal, as a Missionary of the Baptist Missionary Society, not being allowed to remain in British territory : the Serampur Church was opened in 1805 : he and his wife opened a boarding school : he studied Chinese : established the Loll Bazar Chapel and the Benevolent Institution at Calcutta, and devoted much time to native schools. The Mission translated the Scriptures into many Oriental languages. Marshman was made D.D. of Brown University, U.S., in 1811 : he and his son issued the *Friend of India* as a monthly and, later, a quarterly Magazine : in 1818 they issued the first Bengali weekly newspaper, the *Samachar Darpan*, and built the Serampur College at a cost of £30,000 : in 1826–9 he visited England and Denmark to urge on the cause of missions. In 1827 he became involved in controversy with the Baptist Missionary Society, and their connexion was severed. Besides Chinese, he worked at Sanskrit and the local vernaculars : he died at Serampur on Dec. 5, 1837.

MARTIN, ALFRED ROBERT (1853–)

Born March 30, 1853 : son of Colonel D. W. Martin : educated at Harrow : entered the Army, 1874, and became Colonel in 1899 : served against the Jowaki-Afridis, 1877 : in the Afghan war, 1878–80 : Hazara expedition, 1888 : in the Miranzai expedition in command of 5th Gurkhas : Brevet-Major :in Waziristan, 1894–5 : Tirah, 1897–8 : Assistant Military Secretary for Indian Affairs at the Horse Guards : D.A.G., Bengal, with rank of Brig-General : C.B., 1902.

MARTIN, CLAUDE (1735–1800)

General : a French soldier of fortune : born Jan. 5, 1735 : son of a silk manufacturer at Lyons : enlisted in French Army : went out as a trooper in Lally's bodyguard to India, 1758 : to avoid Lally's severity, he deserted with the bodyguard at Pondicherry, 1761, to the British, for whom he raised a French company of cavalry : sent up to Bengal : Captain : employed in survey in N.E. Bengal, and in Oudh : joined, with permission, the service of the Nawab Wazir of Oudh as Superintendent of his artillery and arsenal : gained great influence and accumulated large wealth : still an officer in the E.I. Co.'s service, he rose to be Maj-General in 1796 : built at Lucknow a very large castellated residence for himself, which he called Constantia : he directed in his will that it should never be sold, but should serve as a college for educating children in the English religion and language : in this building, now called "La Martiniere," he was himself buried, as he directed : he left 33 lakhs of rupees, and bequeathed large sums, the interest thereof to be distributed to the poor of Lucknow, Calcutta, Chandernagore and Lyons : and largely endowed the Martiniere College at Calcutta, which was constructed, 1833-5, from his legacy for the purpose : he died at Lucknow, Sep. 13, 1800.

MARTIN, CUNLIFFE (1834–   )

Colonel : son of Sir James Ranald Martin, C.B. (q.v.) : educated at Cheltenham : entered the Indian Army, 1852 : served in the suppression of the Sonthal rebellion, 1855 : in the Indian mutiny, 1857–8 : severely wounded in Abyssinia as A.D.C. to Sir Donald Stewart (q.v.), 1868 : in Afghan war, 1880, commanded the Central India Horse : in the march from Kabul to Kandahar and battle of Kandahar : C.B., 1881 : retired.

MARTIN, SIR JAMES RANALD (1793–1874)

Son of Rev. Donald Martin : born 1793 : educated at the Royal Academy of Inverness, and St. George's Hospital : joined the Medical Department of the E. I. Co.'s Bengal Army, 1818 : served in the first Burmese war : Presidency Surgeon, 1830 : Surgeon to the Calcutta General Hospital : wrote *Notes on the Medical Topography of Calcutta, on the Draining of the Salt-water Lake* : F.R.C.S., 1843 : F.R.S., 1845 : Inspr-General of Army Hospitals : collaborated in a work *On the Influence of Tropical*

Climates on European Constitutions and *A Brief Topographical and Historical Notice of Calcutta* : C.B., in 1860 : knighted, 1860 : he was appointed President of the India Office Medical Board, 1859 : died Nov. 27, 1874.

MARTIN, ROBERT MONTGOMERY (1803 ?–1868)

Born about 1803 : went to Ceylon, 1820 : travelled as assistant surgeon, botanist, and naturalist, and was in India, 1828–30 : published *The History of the British Colonies*, 1834 : the *History of the Antiquities of Eastern India*, 1838 : Member of the Court of Directors of the E. I. Co. : witness before a Commission on the East Indian trade, 1840 : Treasurer of Hong-kong, 1844–5 : resigned : on a mission to Jamaica, 1851 : was one of the first members of the East India Association, 1866 : died Sep. 6, 1868 : brought out *The Marquis of Wellesley's Despatches*, 1836 ; *The Monetary System of British India*, 1841 ; *The Indian Empire*, 1857 ; *The Rise and Progress of the Indian Mutiny*, 1859 : and other works on the Colonies and commercial questions.

MARTINDALE, SIR ARTHUR HENRY TEMPLE (1854–   )

I.C.S. : born March 13, 1854 : son of Colonel Benjamin Martindale, C.B. : educated at Cheltenham : joined the Indian Civil Service in Madras, 1875 : served in the Foreign Department of the Government of India, and held various political appointments : has been A.G.G. for Rajputana since 1898 : C.S.I., 1900 : K.C.S.I., 1904.

MARTINDELL, SIR GABRIEL (1756 ?–1831)

Born about 1756 : Cadet in " the Select Picket " corps, 1772 : Ensign in the Bengal N.I., 1776 : in the Mahratta war of 1804–5 : commanded the troops in Bundelkund, 1809, 1812 : captured the fort of Kalinjar, 1812 : Maj-General, 1813 : commanded a Division in the Nipal war, 1814–5 : K.C.B., 1815 : held a command in the Pindari war : and in Cuttack, 1818 : Lt-General : commanded a Division at Cawnpur, 1820 : died at Baxar, Jan. 2, 1831.

MARTYN, REV. HENRY (1781–1812)

Son of John Martyn, a miner : born near Truro and educated at the grammar school there, and at St. John's College, Cambridge : was Senior Wrangler in 1801 and first Smith's Prizeman : Fellow of St. John's College, 1802 : ordained in 1803 and became a curate to the Rev. C. Simeon, at Cambridge : in 1805 he went out to India on the Bengal Establishment as a Military Chaplain,and worked at Serampur, Dinapur, and Cawnpur. In 1811 he obtained leave to visit Persia. Leaving Shiraz in 1812 on his way *viâ* Tabriz to England, he died of fever at Tokat, in Asia Minor, Oct. 16, 1812. He had great zeal as a Missionary and laboured greatly, in spite of ill-health. He translated the New Testament into Persian and Hindustani. Macaulay wrote an epitaph on him.

MARZBAN, FARDUNJI (1787–1847)

Born at Surat, 1787 : grandson of Dastur Kawoos (1717–79), a founder of the Kadmi sect of the Parsis : went to Bombay, 1805 : settled under Mulla Firoz (*q.v.*) as librarian, and became proficient in Oriental languages : was a book-binder, 1808, and opened a printing-press, 1812, publishing, 1815, an edition of the *Avesta*, in 1815 a translation of the *Dabistan*, in 1818 of the *Avesta* into Gujarati ; published also translations of the *Shahnameh*, 1833 ; the *Gulistan*, 1838 ; the *Bostan* (published posthumously, 1849) : and composed original poetry : with Mulla Firoz's help he brought out, on July 1, 1822, the first number of the *Bombay Samachar*, which still exists, and conducted it till Aug. 1832, when he failed in business, losing a ship, and in his journalistic enterprize : he had to leave Bombay and go to the Portuguese settlement at Damaun, 1832 : he published a Persian dictionary, 1832 : knew the principles of Oriental medicine, which he practised at Damaun : a social refomer among the Parsis : died at Damaun, March 23, 1847.

MASON, REV. FRANCIS, D.D. (1799–1874)

Born at York, 1799 : where his grandfather had founded a Baptist Society : in 1818 joined an uncle in the United States and went thence as a Missionary to India, to Burma : for years laboured among the Karens : translated the Bible into Karen : author of a Pali grammar, and a Karen grammar of both dialects : *The Story of a Working Man's Life*,

Burma, 1860 ; *Fauna, Flora and Minerals of Burma* : Profesor of Pali in the Government High School, Rangoon : died after a journey to Bhamo in 1874.

MASON, GEORGE HENRY MONCK (1825–1857)

Born 1825 : son of Captain Thomas Monck Mason, R.N. : joined the 74th Bengal N.I., 1842 : Assistant A.G.G. in Rajputana, 1847 : Political Agent at Karauli : Resident at Jodhpur, 1857 : when the Jodhpur troops mutinied he arranged for the safety of the Europeans, and, on his way to join Sir George Lawrence (*q.v.*), was shot dead by mutineers, Sep. 18, 1857.

MASON, JOHN CHARLES (1798–1881)

Born March, 1798 : son of Alexander Way Mason : educated at Hackney and Warminster : appointed in the Secretary's office at the East India House, 1817 : employed in confidential work, 1817–37 : Secretary in the Marine branch : made a number of improvements : in the mutiny, arranged for transport of 50,000 troops : Secretary at the India Office in the Marine and Transport Department, 1859 : represented the Government of India in the Committee on the Transport Service, which led, in 1867, to the construction of troopships : died Dec. 12, 1881.

MASSY, HENRY STANLEY (? –)

Entered the Bengal Army, 1874, and became Lt-Colonel, 1900 : served against Jowaki-Afridis, 1877–8 : in the Afghan war, 1878–80 : Burma war, 1886–8 : second Miranzai expedition, 1891 : Tirah campaign, 1897–8 : C.B., 1903 : Commandant, 19th Bengal Lancers.

MASSEY, WILLIAM NATHANIEL (1809–1881)

Son of William Massey : born 1809 : called to the bar from the Inner Temple,. 1844 : Recorder of Portsmouth and Plymouth : M.P. for Newport and Salford,. 1855–65 : Under Secretary in the Home Department : Chairman of Committees in the House of Commons : succeeded Sir C. E. Trevelyan (*q.v.*), as Financial Member of the Supreme Council, April 10, 1865, to April 25, 1868 : Privy Councillor :. M.P. for Tiverton, 1872–81 : wrote a History of part of George III's reign,. and *Common Sense versus Common Law* : died Oct. 25, 1881.

MASTER, CHARLES GILBERT
(1833–1903)

I.C.S. : son of an Archdeacon of Manchester : educated at Haileybury, 1852–3 : went to India, 1854 : was Commissioner of Income Tax, 1860–5 : Revenue Secretary to Government, Madras, 1877 : Chief Secretary, 1882, and Member of the Legislative Council : Member of Council, Madras, 1884–9 : C.S.I., 1887 : died March 9, 1903.

MASTER, WILLIAM CHARLES CHESTER (1821–)

Born Nov. 6, 1821 : son of Colonel W. Chester Master : educated privately : entered the Army, 1839, and became Colonel, 1863 : in the Indian mutiny, 1857–8, was at the relief of Lucknow, commandant of Fort Alambagh, promoted Lt-Colonel for service in the field : in the Oudh campaign, 1858–9 : C.B.

MATCHAM, GEORGE (1753–1833)

I.C.S. : son of Simon Matcham, who was Member of Council, Bombay : born 1753 : educated at Charterhouse : joined the E.I. Co.'s Civil Service : Resident at Broach : retired in 1783 : travelled to England through Persia, Arabia, Egypt, Asia Minor, Turkey, Greece, Hungary, etc. : died Feb. 3, 1833.

MATHER, REV. ROBERT COTTON
(1808–1877)

Missionary : son of James Mather : born Nov. 8, 1808 : educated at Edinburgh and Glasgow Universities and Homerton College : ordained, 1833 : went to India for the London Missionary Society : after Benares, settled at Mirzapur, founding a mission : built schools and churches : revised and edited the Bible in Hindustani : LL.D., Glasgow : wrote in Hindi and Urdu : wrote on *Christian Missions in India :* and a commentary on the New Testament in Hindustani : and began one on the Old Testament : died April 21, 1877.

MATTHEW, RIGHT REV. HENRY JAMES, D.D. (1837–1898)

Educated at Trinity College, Cambridge : ordained, 1861 : Chaplain on the Bengal Establishment from 1866 : Archdeacon of Lahore, 1878 : Bishop of Lahore, 1888 : D.D. : died Dec. 2, 1898.

MAUDE, FRANCIS CORNWALLIS
(1828–1900)

Son of Capt. Hon. Francis Maude, R.N. : born Oct. 28, 1828 : commanded the Royal Artillery with Havelock's column : with Outram's force at the Alambagh : at the capture of Lucknow, 1858 : Brevets, Major and Lt-Colonel : V.C. and C.B. : Consul-General at Warsaw, 1876–88 : Military Knight of Windsor, 1895 : died Oct. 19, 1900.

MAUDE, SIR FREDERICK FRANCIS
(1821–1897)

Born Dec. 20, 1821 : son of the Rev. Hon. J. C. Maude : joined the Buffs, 1840 : served in the Gwalior campaign, 1843–4 : at Punniar : through the Crimea : gained the V.C. there for conspicuous and devoted bravery at the assault of the Redan : Colonel, 1861 : Maj-General, 1868 : commanded a Division in India, 1875–80 : and the 2nd Division of the Peshawar Field Force in the Afghan war, 1878–9 : K.C.B. : General : retired, 1885 : G.C.B., 1886 : died June 20, 1897.

MAUNSELL, SIR FREDERICK RICHARD (1828–)

Born Sep. 4, 1828 : educated at King Edward's School, Birmingham, Grosvenor College, Bath and Addiscombe : joined the Royal Engineers, 1846, and became General, 1887 : was in the Panjab campaign, 1848–9, at siege of Multan, and at Gujarat : in the Indian mutiny, 1857–8 : at Delhi and Lucknow : in the Oudh campaign, 1858 : Afghan campaign, 1878 : C.B., 1873 : K.C.B., 1897 : Colonel Commandant R.E., 1886.

MAUNSELL, THOMAS (1822–)

Maj-General : born Sep. 10, 1822 : son of George Meares Maunsell : educated at Clifton, Bristol and Trinity College, Dublin : entered the Army : was in the Panjab campaign : at the siege of Multan, and at Gujarat, 1848–9 : in the Crimean war, 1854–5 : Indian mutiny, 1858 : C.B., 1875 : retired.

MAURICE, REV. THOMAS (1784–1824)

Son of Thomas Maurice : born 1754 : educated at Christ's Hospital, Ealing and Bath, and at St. John's and University Colleges, Oxford, 1774–8 : ordained :

held several curacies and a vicarage,
1798 : assistant-keeper of MSS. in the
British Museum, where he died March 30,
1824 : one of the first to make the history
and religions of India generally known :
also wrote poems : published *The History
of Hindustan*, 1795 ; *A Dissertation on
the Oriental Trinities*, 1800 ; *Indian
Antiquities*, 1806 ; *Modern History of
Hindustan*, 1802–10.

MAYNE, GEORGE NISBET (? –)

Entered the Army, 1874, and became
Lt-Colonel, 1902 : served in Afghan
war, 1878–80 : Burmese expedition, 1886–
8 : Chitral Relief Force, 1895 : Tirah
campaign, 1897–8 : at Dargai : in the
South African war, 1900–2 : C.B., 1902.

MAYNE, JOHN DAWSON (1828–   )

Born Dec. 31, 1828 : son of John
Mayne, Barrister-at-law, Dublin : educated at Trinity College, Dublin : called
to the bar, 1854 : practised at the English
bar, 1854–6 : at the Madras bar, 1857–72,
and at the Privy Council, 1873–1903 :
Professor of Law at Presidency College,
Madras : Clerk of the Crown, High
Court, Madras : Acting Advocate-General
of Madras : Professor of Common Law to
the Inns of Court, 1880–5 : author of
Treatise on Damages, *Commentaries on
the Indian Penal Code*, *Hindu Law and
Usage*, *Criminal Law of India*, etc.

MAYNE, RICHARD CHARLES GRAHAM (1852–   )

Born Aug. 27, 1852 : son of Major
Robert Graham Mayne : educated at
Wellington : entered the Army, 1872,
and became Brevet-Colonel, 1900, in the
Indian Staff Corps : in the Afghan war,
1878–80, in the Kabul-Kandahar march,
and battle of Kandahar : Egypt, 1882,
at Tel-el-Kebir : Zhob expedition, 1890 :
in command of Mekran expedition,
1898 : C.B. : China expedition, 1900.

MAYNE, WILLIAM (1818–1855)

Born Oct. 28, 1818 : son of the Rev.
Robert Mayne : educated at Addiscombe :
joined the 4th Bengal N.I. in 1837 : in
the Afghan war, 1838–40 : under Sir
Robert Sale : at Julgar, Oct. 3, 1840 : at
the defence of Jalalabad : at Istalif,
Sep. 29, 1842 : Adjutant of the bodyguard
to Lord Ellenborough : Commandant

under Lord Dalhousie : at Maharajpur,
1843 : in command of the Hyderabad
contingent, quieted the Dekkan, 1851–4 :
Brevet-Colonel : A.D.C. to Queen Victoria :
died at Cairo, Dec. 23, 1855.

MAYO, RICHARD SOUTHWELL BOURKE, SIXTH EARL OF (1822–1872)

Viceroy and Governor-General : son of
the fifth Earl : born Feb. 21, 1822 : took
his degree at Trinity College, Dublin :
LL.D. : travelled in Russia, 1845 : wrote
St. Petersburg and Moscow : M.P. 1847–
67 successively for Kildare, Coleraine
and Cockermouth : Chief Secretary for
Ireland in three administrations, from 1852,
1858, and 1866 : K.P. : he became
Viceroy of India on Jan. 12, 1869 : was
assassinated at Port Blair, Andaman
Islands, Feb. 8, 1872. His administration
was very successful, and concerned with
matters of great importance. He met
Shir Ali, the Amir of Afghanistan, in
darbar at Umbala in March, 1869, and
established satisfactory relations. He advocated the acquisition of influence over
neighbouring States. He was opposed to
any expansion of Persia. The Mayo
College at Ajmir was founded for the
education of young native chiefs. He
initiated, with the help of his advisers,
the policy of decentralization of the
finances : paid much attention to Public
Works, Railways, Irrigation, Forests, Port
defences : while Education and Land
Revenue measures were advanced, and a
Department for Agriculture, Revenue and
Commerce was opened. The Lushai expedition took place in 1871–2, but otherwise India was at peace. H.R.H. the
late Duke of Edinburgh visited India in
1869–70. Lord Mayo's personality, his
great presence, his genial and dignified
bearing, impressed all who came into
contact with him. He travelled widely.
His loss was greatly regretted by all
classes in India. His body was conveyed
to Ireland, after a funeral service at Calcutta.

McBEAN, WILLIAM (? –1878)

Maj-General : rose from being a drum-
mer boy in the 93rd foot (the Sutherland
Highlanders) to be Lt-Colonel in command
of the regt., in which he served 45 years.
He obtained his Commission in 1854 in

the Crimea : Lt-Colonel, 1872 : served all through the Crimea : in the mutiny was at Sir Colin Campbell's relief of Lucknow, at Cawnpur, Kalinadi, siege and capture of Lucknow, Alaganj, Bareli and other actions, gaining the Victoria Cross for distinguished bravery : died in the hospital at Woolwich, that he might " die among the soldiers," on June 16, 1878.

McCABE, ROBERT BLAIR (? –1897)

I.C.S. : educated at Victoria School, Jersey : sent out to India, 1876 : served in Assam : in charge of the Naga Hills : a distinguished frontier officer : did much to civilize the Angami Nagas : in the difficulties with the Lushais showed great bravery and judgment : in Feb. 1897, released captives in their hands : Inspr-General of Police, Assam : killed in the earthquake at Shillong, June, 1897 : wrote an outline grammar of the Angami Naga language.

McCASKILL, SIR JOHN (? –1845)

Entered the Army in the 53rd regt., 1797 : served at Porto Rico and St. Lucia, 1797 : in the Mahratta war under Sir T. Munro and Brig-General Pritzler : present at the siege and capture of Satara, Singhar, etc. : and at the taking of Sholapur : at the defeat of 5,000 of the Peshwa's troops, 1818 : in the first Afghan war, commanded a Brigade in Pollock's force : at the forcing of the Khyber and at Tezin : defeated the Afghans at Istalif : K.C.B. : and Maj-General : Lt-Colonel of the 9th foot : General of Division at Mudki, where he was killed, Dec. 18, 1845.

McCLEVERTY, WILLIAM ANSON (1806–1897)

Lt-General : son of Maj-General Sir Robert McCleverty : joined the 48th regt., 1824 : became General, 1876 : commanded against the Raja of Coorg, 1834 : in N. Zealand, 1847 : commanded the Madras District as Maj-General, 1860–5 : C. in C., Madras, 1867–71 : died Oct. 6, 1897.

McCLUER (? –1794 ?)

Commander in the Bombay Marine, and hydrographer : surveyed the Persian Gulf, 1785 : the bank of soundings off Bombay, 1787, and performed other similar work in the Eastern seas : settled in the Peter Islands in 1793 : sailed for China, reached Macao, returned to the islands and sailed to Calcutta : left Calcutta and disappeared altogether.

McCRINDLE, JOHN WATSON (1825–)

Son of John McCrindle : born Feb. 16, 1825, near Maybole, Ayrshire : educated at Maybole, and Edinburgh University : Stratton Gold Medal, 1853 : B.A., 1854 : M.A., 1855 : was Classical Master in 3 Edinburgh schools, 1854–9 : to India, 1859, as Principal of the Doveton College, Calcutta : entered Government service, 1866 : Professor, Patna College : Professor of Logic and Philosophy at Krishnagar College : first Principal of the Patna College, 1867 till 1880, when he retired : Fellow, Calcutta University, 1860 : Examiner in History, Logic and Political Economy at the University : LL.D. at Edinburgh, 1898. At Patna, with his wife's help, founded a school for native girls : his contributions to the knowledge of Indian history comprise the following works : *Ancient India as described by Megasthenes and Arrian*, 1877 ; *The Commerce and Navigation of the Erythraean Sea*, 1879 : *Ancient India as described by Ktesias the Knidian*, 1822 ; *Ancient India as described by Ptolemy*, 1885 ; *Invasion of India by Alexander the Great*, 1893, and 1896 : *Ancient India as described in Classical Literature*, 1901 : these six books give a nearly complete collection of all works and incidental notices relating to India contained in Greek and Roman literature : another of his works, *The Christian Topography of Cosmas, an Egyptian Monk*, which he translated and edited for the Hakluyt Society in 1897, contains some valuable notices of Sokotra, Ceylon and India : Member of Council of the R.A.S., 1801 : also of R. Scot. G.S. : and contributed largely to its Journal.

McCULLOCH, WILLIAM (1816–1885)

Lt-Colonel : son of John Ramsay McCulloch : born Feb. 28, 1816 : educated at Addiscombe : went to Calcutta in the Army, 1835 : joined the N.I. : Assistant to the Political Agent at Manipur, 1840 : Political Agent there, 1845–63, and 1864–7 :. retired as Lt-Colonel from the Army in 1867 : died in 1885 : wrote an *Account of the Valley of Manipur and the Hill Tribes*, 1859.

McDONELL, WILLIAM FRASER
(1829-1894)

I.C.S. : son of Æneas Ranald McDonell, of the Madras Civil Service : born Dec. 17, 1829 : educated at Cheltenham and Haileybury : went out to Lower Bengal in 1850, and served chiefly in the Judicial line, as Judge of Krishnagar, and Patna : Judge of the High Court from 1874 to 1886, when he retired. He was a keen sportsman, and for years a Steward of the Calcutta Turf Club. A memorial was erected in his honour, near the High Court. In the mutiny, he accompanied, as a volunteer, the expedition sent by General Lloyd under Captain Dunbar to the relief of the Arrah garrison : the party fell into an ambush and had to retreat : the survivors reached a stream which had to be crossed in boats, but these were fastened to the bank, and the party was subjected to a heavy fire from the rebels. McDonell, at the imminent risk of his life, exposed himself to free one of the boats full of men, and, amidst a perfect storm of bullets, managed to unfasten it, and it quickly drifted down the stream and out of range. For this gallant act he received the Victoria Cross. He subsequently was engaged in the operations against Kooer Singh in Bihar. He died at Cheltenham on July 31, 1894.

McGRIGOR, JAMES (1819-1863)

Son of Lt-Colonel Charles McGrigor : born 1819 : educated at Addiscombe : joined the 21st Bombay N.I. in 1835 : served under Sir C. Napier in the Sind campaigns : in the mutiny commanded his regt. at Karachi : he was warned just in time of their intention to mutiny and massacre Europeans on Sep. 16, and with the greatest promptitude disarmed them : Lt-Colonel, 1862 : drowned accidentally at Aden, June 28, 1863.

McINROY, CHARLES (1838-   )

Born March 3, 1838 : son of J. P. McInroy : educated at Wimbledon : entered the Army, 1855, and became Colonel, 1885 : served in the Indian mutiny, 1857-9 : at the surrender of Kirwi, and in Central India : Abyssinian campaign, 1868 : Egyptian war, 1882, Kassassin and Tel-el-Kebir : Burma expedition, 1885-6 : Unemployed Supernumerary List since 1895 : C.B., 1894.

McLEOD, SIR DONALD FRIELL
(1810-1872)

Lieutenant-Governor : son of Lt-General Duncan McLeod : born May 6, 1810, at Fort William, Calcutta : educated at Edinburgh High School, Dulwich, Putney, and Haileybury : arrived in Bengal in 1828, commencing his career ⁎ in ⁎ that province : in the Sagar and Nerbudda territories and Benares, 1831-49 : Commissioner of Jalandhar, 1849 : Judicial Commissioner of the Panjab, 1854 : was at Lahore during the mutiny of 1857 : C.B. : Lieutenant-Governor of the Panjab, 1865-70 : K.C.S.I. in 1866 : Chairman of the Sind, Panjab and Delhi Railway : he had pronounced religious opinions, and was a philanthropist : established the Panjab University, and had warm sympathy with the people : he advocated a greater encouragement of Oriental studies, and the promotion of the acquisition of Western knowledge through the vernacular. Sir John Lawrence called him " cunctator " : he died from the effects of an accident on the London Underground Railway, Nov. 28, 1872.

McLEOD, DONALD JAMES SIM
(1845-   )

Born Feb. 22, 1845 : son of Lt-General W. C. McLeod : educated at Kensington School : joined the Madras Army, 1861 : served on the Army Staff, India, 1877-88 : D.Q.M.G. on service in Burma 1886-7 : D.S.O. : Commanding 3rd Madras Lancers, 1890-3 : C.B., 1898 : Lt-General commanding troops in Burma.

McLEOD, SIR JOHN CHETHAM
(1831-   )

Born Jan. 23, 1831 : son of Lt-Colonel Alexander McLeod : educated at St. Andrew's and Perth Academy : served for 32 years in 42nd Royal Highlanders : in Crimea, 1854-5 : Indian mutiny, 1857-8 : Cawnpur, siege and capture of Lucknow, Aliganj, etc. : Brevet-Lt-Colonel and C.B. : Ashanti war, 1873-4 : K.C.B., 1874 : Lt-General : retired : G.C.B., 1891.

McMAHON, ARTHUR HENRY
(1862-   )

Major : born Nov. 28, 1862 : son of Lt-General C. A. McMahon : educated at

Haileybury and Sandhurst : joined the Army, 1883, and Indian Staff Corps, 1885 : entered the Panjab Commission, 1887, and the Indian Political Department, 1890 : Political Agent at Zhob, 1891, and 1893 : accompanied Durand Mission to Kabul, 1893 : C.I.E. : British Commissioner for demarcating boundary between Beluchistan and Afghanistan, 1894–6 : C.S.I. : Political Agent, Gilgit, 1897–8 : Political Agent, Dir, Swat, and Chitral, 1899–1901 : Revenue and Judicial Commissioner, Beluchistan, 1901 : Commissioner to settle the Perso-Afghan boundary, 1903 : Agent to the Governor-General in Beluchistan, 1905 : F.S.A. : F.L.S.

McMAHON, CHARLES ALEXANDER
(1830–1894)

Son of Capt. Alexander McMahon of the E. I. Co.'s service : born 1830 : reached India in 1847 : was eight years in the Madras N.I. : joined the Panjab Commission in 1856 : rose to be Commissioner and officiating Financial Commissioner : Maj-General : retired in 1885. He acted with vigour when the troops at Sealkot mutinied in 1857. He studied geology, petrology and mineralogy, publishing papers on the geology of the Himalayas in the records of the Geological Survey of India. He was a Fellow of the Royal and Geological Societies, and President of the Geological Association in 1894–5 : died Feb. 21, 1904.

McMAHON, SIR THOMAS, BARONET
(1779–1860)

General : son of John McMahon : entered the Army before 1800 : saw active service in almost every quarter of the globe : served in the Portuguese Army in the Peninsula : Adjutant-General in India : C. in C., Bombay, Feb. 1840, to April, 1847 : succeeded to the Baronetcy, 1817 : G.C.B. : Colonel of the 10th foot : died April 10, 1860.

McMURDO, SIR WILLIAM MOGUNTA SCOTT (1819–1894)

Son of Lt-Colonel Archibald McMurdo : born May 30, 1819 : educated at Sandhurst : joined the 8th foot in 1837 : went out to Karachi, 1841 : head of the Q.M.G. department in Sind, 1842–7 : in Sir C. Napier's force in 1842 : at Miani, 1843 :

and Hyderabad, 1843 : was A.D.C. to Napier when C. in C., 1849–50 : in the Afridi operations, and in the forcing of the Kohat Pass, 1850 : Director-General of the land transport corps in the Crimea : A.D.C. to Queen Victoria : Brevet-Colonel : C.B. : Colonel Commandant of the military train, 1857 : Inspr-General of Volunteers, 1860–5 : commanded a District in Bengal, 1870–3 : Maj-General, 1868 : General, 1878 : K.C.B., 1881 : died March 2, 1894.

McNALTY, GEORGE WILLIAM
(1837–   )

Born 1837 : son of G. W. McNalty : educated at Dublin, Wiesbaden and London : joined the Army Medical Staff, 1863, and retired, 1892 : served in the British Ambulance in Franco-German war, 1871 : Ashanti war, 1873–4 : Russo-Turkish war : Afghan war, 1878–80, in the march from Kabul to Kandahar : Egyptian war, 1882 : Tel-el-Kebir : Hony. Surgeon to Viceroy of India : C.B.

McQUEEN, SIR JOHN WITHERS
(1836–   )

Born July 20, 1836 : son of Rev. John McQueen, Chaplain E. I. Co. : educated at Edinburgh Academy, and Trinity College, Glenalmond : entered Indian Army, 1854 : became Lt-General, 1895 : served in the Indian mutiny : in 4th Panjab Infantry at the siege of Delhi, relief of Lucknow, severely wounded (recommended for V.C.) : at the battles of Agra, Cawnpur, Bareli and other engagements : served against the Kabul Kheyl Waziris, 1859 : Mahsud Waziris, 1860, and 1881 : Bizotis, 1869 : Jowaki-Afridis, 1877–8 : commanded the Queen's Own Corps of Guides, 1871–3 : commanded 5th Panjab Infantry in Afghan war, 1878–80, at Peiwar Kotal, Sherpur, etc. : Brevet-Lt-Colonel and C.B. : A.D.C. to Queen Victoria and Brevet-Colonel, 1881–93 : commanded the Hazara expedition, 1888 : K.C.B., 1889 : Military Secretary to Panjab Government, 1883–5 : commanded the Hyderabad Contingent, 1885–6 : and Panjab Frontier Force, 1886–90 : appointed Colonel 57th Wilde's Rifles (late 4th Panjab Infantry, Panjab Frontier Force), 1904 : Unemployed Supernumerary List, 1897. .

McRAE, HENRY NAPIER (1851–   )

Born Jan. 27, 1851 : son of Surgeon-Major James McRae : educated privately : entered the Army, 1871, and the Indian Staff Corps, 1874 : served in Afghanistan, 1878–80 : Bazar Valley expedition, etc. : in the Zhob Valley, 1884 : Hazara expedition, 1888, Brevet-Major : N.W. Frontier, 1897–98 : the relief of Malakand, Buner, etc. : C.B. : Waziristan expedition, 1901–2 : Officiating in Command of the Assam District : A.D.C. to H.M. the King.

McSWINEY, EDWARD FREDERICK HENRY (1858–   )

Born 1858 : son of the Rev. J. H. McSwiney : educated at Oxford Military College and Sandhurst : entered the Army, 1879, and Indian Staff Corps, 1882 : served in the Burma campaign, 1886–8 : D.S.O. : Intelligence Department Headquarters, India, 1892–7 : Waziristan Field Force, 1894–5 : Pamir Boundary Commission, 1895, Brevet-Major : Kuram-Kohat Force as D.A.A.G., 1897 : Tirah campaign, 1897–8, Brevet-Lt-Colonel : War Office Intelligence Department, 1898–9 : China expedition, 1900–1 : Commandant 1st Lancers, Hyderabad Contingent, since 1899 : C.B., 1903.

MEADE, SIR RICHARD JOHN (1821–1894)

Son of Captain John Meade, R.N. : educated at the Royal Naval School : entered the Bengal Army, 1838 : Lt-General, 1883 : General, 1889 : in the mutiny of 1857–9, while in charge of a column, captured Tantia Topi (q.v.) : Political Agent at Gwalior : A.G.G., Central India, 1861 : C.C., Mysore, 1870 : A.G.G. and Special Commissioner at Baroda, 1875 : Member of the Court for the trial of Malhar Rao, Gaekwar of Baroda, 1875 : Resident at Hyderabad, 1876–81 : died March 20, 1894.

MEDLICOTT, HENRY BENEDICT (1829–1905)

Born Aug. 8, 1829 : son of Rev. Samuel Medlicott : educated at Trinity College, Dublin : appointed to Geological Survey of Ireland, 1851 ; England, 1853 ; and India, 1854 : Professor of Geology,

Thomason College, Rurki, 1854 : Volunteer in Bundelkund in the mutiny, 1857–8 : Director of the Geological Survey of India, 1878 : Fellow of the Calcutta University : author of *A Manual of the Geology of India*, 1878 : retired 1887 : F.G.S. and F.R.S. : died April 6, 1905.

MEDOWS, SIR WILLIAM (1738–1813)

Governor : son of Philip Medows : born Dec. 31, 1838 : joined the 50th regt., 1756 : served in Germany, America, at Brandywine, 1776 ; at St. Lucia ; at the Cape of Good Hope, 1781 : to India, 1782, co-operated with Sir E. Hughes in dispersing the French fleet under Suffrein : Governor and C. in C., Bombay, from Sep. 1788, to Jan. 1790 : held similar appointments at Madras from Feb. 1790, to Aug. 1792 : took the field, 1790, against Tippoo : took some places, but the campaign was generally unsuccessful : Cornwallis took command in person in 1791–2 : Medows captured Nandidrug, Oct. 19, 1791 : led a column in the attack on Seringapatam, Feb. 1792 : to England in 1792 : K.C.B. : General, 1798 : Governor of the Isle of Wight : C. in C. in Ireland 1801 : died Nov. 14, 1813.

MEHTA, SIR PHIROZSHAH MERWANJI (1845–   )

Born Aug. 1845 : B.A. in 1864 : called to the bar, 1868 : Municipal Commissioner of the Bombay Corporation, 1873 : its Chairman, 1884–5 : Additional Member of the Legislative Council of the Governor of Bombay : elected representative of the non-official members of the Bombay Legislative Council to the Governor-General's Legislative Council : C.I.E., 1895 : K.C.I.E., 1904 : presided over the sixth session of the Indian National Congress held at Calcutta, Dec. 1890.

MEHTA, RUSTUMJI DHUNJIBHOY (1849–   )

Born at Bombay, July 26, 1849 : son of Dhunjibhoy Byramji Mehta : educated at the Bombay Branch School and at the Bengal Academy from 1860, when his father settled in Calcutta : joined his father's business, Messrs. D. B. Mehta and Co. : in 1870 went to Hongkong to manage a branch of the business there and visited Japan : went to England in 1877 to purchase machinery for the " Empress of India Cotton Mills," and again in 1891 for the education of his sons : Sheriff of Calcutta, 1893 : Consul for Persia at Calcutta, 1899 : Member of the Bengal Asiatic Society, Port Commissioner, Calcutta : and Chairman of the Alipur Local Board : C.I.E.

MEIKLEJOHN, SIR WILLIAM HOPE (1845-)

Born 1845 : entered the Bengal Army, 1861 : was in the Black Mountain campaign, 1868 : Jowaki expedition, 1877–8 : Afghan war, 1878–80, at Ali-Masjid : in the Mahsud-Waziri expedition, 1881 : Egyptian expedition, 1882, at Tel-el-Kebir : in the Waziristan expedition, 1894–5 : C.B. in the Malakand Field Force, 1897 : commanded Chakdara relief column : K.C.B., 1898 : Buner Field Force ; Afghan Boundary Commission, 1884–6 : C.M.G., 1887 : commanded Oudh District : retired.

MELLISS, SIR HOWARD (1847- ·)

Colonel : born April 2, 1847 : son of George Melliss : educated privately and at Sandhurst : entered the Army : in the Abyssinian campaign, 1868, was at the capture of Magdala : in the Intelligence Branch, Q.M.G.'s Department, Simla : A.Q.M.G. of Indian contingent in Egypt, 1882 : A.Q.M.G. Bombay Army : Military Attaché in Burma, 1885 : organized the Imperial Service Corps and became Inspr-General of Imperial Service troops of India : K.C.S.I., 1897.

MELVILL, REV. HENRY (1798–1871)

Son of Capt. Philip Melvill of the 73rd regt. : born Sep. 14, 1798 : Sizar of St. John's College, and of Peterhouse, Cambridge : second Wrangler and Smith's prizeman, 1821 : Fellow and Tutor : B.D., 1836 : incumbent at Camberwell, 1829–43 : Chaplain of the Tower of London, 1840 : Principal of the E. I. College, Haileybury, from 1843 till the closing of the College in 1857 : Chaplain to Queen Victoria : Canon of St. Paul's from 1856, and Rector of Barnes from 1863. His tenure of the Principalship of Haileybury is estimated to have been successful : of his success as a preacher there can be no doubt : he was noted for his eloquence, earnestness, and skilful management of

his voice : published numerous sermons and lectures : died Feb. 9. 1871.

MELVILL, SIR. JAMES COSMO (1792–1861)

Born 1792 : son of Captain Philip Melvill : was in the E. I. Co.'s home service from 1808 : auditor of Indian accounts, 1824 : Financial Secretary, 1834 : Chief Secretary, 1836, until 1858, when the Government of India was assumed by the Crown : Government Director of Indian railways, 1858 : F.R.S., 1841 : K.C.B., 1853 : died July 23, 1861.

MELVILL, SIR MAXWELL (1834–1887)

I.C.S. : educated at Haileybury, 1853–5: went out to Bombay, 1855 : was Judicial Commissioner in Sind : Puisne Judge of the High Court Bombay, 1869–84 : Member of Council, Bombay, from April 8, 1884 : C.S.I., 1886 : and K.C.I.E., 1887 : died at Poona Aug. 5, 1887.

MELVILL, SIR PETER MELVILL (1803–1895)

Entered the E. I. Co.'s military service in Bombay, 1819 : was in the Revenue Survey in Gujarat, 1822–7 : A.D.C. to the Governor of Bombay, 1828 : Assistant to the Bombay Members of the Financial Commission, 1829 : First Assistant to the Resident in Cutch and Sind, 1836 : Political Agent in Cutch, 1838 : Secretary to the Bombay Government in the Military and Marine Departments, 1840–59: K.C.B.: retired as Maj-General, 1861 : Member of Lord Hotham's Committee on the Amalgamation of the Indian with the British Army, 1860 : died Nov. 4, 1895.

MELVILL, PHILIP SANDYS (1827-   )

I.C.S. : born Nov. 29, 1827 : son of Philip Melvill : educated at Rugby and Haileybury : entered the Bengal Civil Serivce, 1846 : served in the Panjab Commission up to the appointment of Judge of the Chief Court, Panjab, 1849–75 : Member of the Commission for the trial of the Gaekwar of Baroda, 1875 : Resident at Baroda 1875–81 : C.S.I.

MELVILLE, HENRY DUNDAS, FIRST VISCOUNT (1742–1811)

Son of Robert Dundas : born April 28, 1742 : educated at Edinburgh High School and University : Advocate, 1763 :

Solicitor-General for Scotland, 1766 : M.P. for Midlothian and Newtown from 1774–90 : Lord Advocate, 1775–83 : Chairman in 1781 of a Committee of Inquiry into the Carnatic war, and the state of the British possessions in S. India : in May, 1782, carried Resolutions for the removal of Warren Hastings from the Governor-Generalship : an order to this effect was made, but cancelled : in 1783 he brought in a Bill to regulate the Government of India, which was given up for a Government measure with the same object. When Pitt's East India Bill was passed in 1784, Dundas became a Member of the Board of Control, and henceforth always had a potential voice in Indian affairs : he defended Warren Hastings in 1786, when Burke attacked his conduct in connexion with the war against the Rohillas : he called Hastings the " Saviour of India " : he was Home Secretary, 1791 : President of the Board of Control, June 22, 1793, to April 25, 1801 : in 1793 his speech in defence of the Government of India and in favour of the renewal of the East India Company's monopoly was highly applauded by Pitt : Secretary for War, 1794–1801 : Keeper of the Privy Seal of Scotland, 1800 : created Viscount Melville in 1802 : First Lord of the Admiralty, 1804–5 : was impeached for malversation of public moneys, 1806, and acquitted, and restored in 1807 to the Privy Council, from which his name had been removed : he refused an Earldom : died May 28, 1811. His influence over Indian affairs was great during his connexion, either as Member, or as President, with the Board of Control, though Mr. James Mill contests the value of his advice.

MELVILLE, HENRY DUNDAS, THIRD VISCOUNT (1801–1876)

General : born Feb. 25, 1801 : son of the second Viscount and grandson of the first Viscount Melville (*q.v.*) : entered the Army, 1819 : commanded the 83rd regt. in Canada, 1837–8 : and the Bombay column of the Panjab Army, at the siege of Multan and at Gujarat, 1848–9 : C.B. and thanks of Parliament and the E. I. Co. : succeeded as Peer, 1851 : commanded in Scotland, 1856 : Governor of Edinburgh Castle, 1860 : G.C.B. 1865 : A.D.C.

to King William IV and Queen Victoria : died Feb. 1, 1876.

MENPES, MORTIMER (? –)

Eminent painter : has travelled round the world : author of many illustrated books, including *World Pictures*, 1902 : *The Darbar*, 1903 : R.I. : R.E. : F.R.G.S.

MEREWETHER, SIR WILLIAM LOCKYER (1825–1880)

Son of Serjeant Henry Alworth Merewether : born Feb. 6, 1825 : educated at Westminster : joined the Bombay Army in 1841 : served with the 21st N.I. in the Sind campaign of 1842–3 : present at the battle of Hyderabad : in the S. Mahratta campaign : in the Sind Irregular Horse on the Upper Sind frontier from 1847 : defeated a large body of Bugtis : at the siege and capture of Multan, in 1848–9 : at Gujarat and the pursuit and surrender of the Sikhs : in charge of the Sind frontier in 1856, crushed tribal rebellions and insubordination of his troops : C.B., 1860 : Military Secretary to the Bombay Government, 1861 : Resident at Aden in 1865 : conducted active operations against the Fudhli tribes : and the negotiations with King Theodore of Abyssinia, 1866–7 : commanded the pioneer force in Abyssinia, 1867 : K.C.S.I., 1868, and Chief Commissioner in Sind 1868–77 : Member of the Council of India from Nov. 1877 : died Oct. 4, 1880. He is well remembered in Sind and in Bombay as a keen soldier of the school of John Jacob ; a skilful Political Officer, his administration was popular and based upon full knowledge of the country.

MERIVALE, HERMAN (1806–1874)

Born Nov. 8, 1806 : son of John Herman Merivale : educated at Harrow, and Trinity College, Oxford (Scholar) : Ireland Scholar, 1825 : Fellow of Balliol College, 1828 : called to the bar at the Inner Temple, 1832 : Professor of Political Economy at Oxford, 1837, and lectured on " Colonization and Colonies " : Assistant Under Secretary for the Colonies, 1847 : permanent Under Secretary, 1848 : transferred in 1859 to the permanent Under-Secretaryship for India : C.B. : D.C.L. Oxford, 1870 : died Feb. 8, 1874 : he devoted himself to literature as opportunities offered : completed Parkes'

Life of Sir Philip Francis : wrote the second volume, Sir Herbert Edwardes writing the first, of the *Life of Sir Henry Lawrence* : " *Historical Studies* " : for the *Edinburgh Review* for forty years : also in the *Quarterly Review* and *Pall Mall Gazette*.

METCALFE, CHARLES THEOPHILUS, BARON (1785–1846)

Governor-General (provisional) : I.C.S. : born Jan. 30, 1785, at Calcutta : son of Major Thomas Theophilus Metcalfe, afterwards Director of the E.I.Co. and Baronet: educated at Bromley and Eton : to Calcutta as a " writer " in the E. I. Co.'s service in Jan. 1801 : the first Student of the College of Fort William : Assistant Resident at Daulat Rao Sindia's Court : in the Governor-General's office, 1803 : Political Officer with Lake, in the Mahratta war, 1804 : at the storming of Deeg, Dec. 24 : Assistant to Resident at Delhi, 1806 : on a special mission to Ranjit Singh at Lahore, 1808, leading up to the treaty of 1809 : Deputy Secretary with Lord Minto, 1809–10 : Resident at Gwalior, 1810 : Resident at Delhi, 1811–19 : Secretary in the Secret and Political Department and Private Secretary to the Governor-General, Marquess of Hastings, Jan. 1819–Sep. 1820 : Resident at Hyderabad, 1820 : had to deal with the case of the banking firm of Palmer & Co.: succeeded to the Baronetcy, 1822 : in 1825, Resident at Delhi and A.G.G., Rajputana : Member of the Supreme Council, Aug. 1827–Nov. 1834 : Governor of Agra, Nov. 1834 : acting Governor-General, March, 1835–March, 1836 : liberated the Press : G.C.B., 1836 : Lieutenant-Governor of the N. W. P., June, 1836, to June, 1838 : disappointed of the Governorship of Madras : resigned : Privy Councillor : appointed Governor of Jamaica, 1839–42 : Governor-General of Canada, 1843–5 : suffered from cancer in the cheek : lost sight of an eye : created a Peer, 1845 : died Sep. 5, 1846 : his bust is at the Metcalfe Hall, Calcutta. His epitaph was written by Macaulay, including the words, " A statesman tried in many high posts and difficult conjunctures and found equal to all. The three greatest dependencies of the British Crown were successively entrusted to his care. In India, his fortitude, his wisdom, his probity and his

moderation are held in honourable remembrance by men of many races, languages and religions," etc., etc.

METCALFE, JAMES (1817–1888)

Born 1817 : natural son of Lord Metcalfe (*q.v.*): educated at Addiscombe : joined the 3rd Bengal N.I., 1836 : inherited £50,000 from his father : A.D.C. to Lord Dalhousie, 1848–53 : as interpreter to C. in C. in India, with Sir Colin Campbell, 1857–60 : C.B. : Brevet Lt-Colonel : retired, 1861 : died March 8, 1888.

METCALFE, SIR THEOPHILUS JOHN, BARONET (1828–1883)

I.C.S. : son of Sir Thomas Theophilus Metcalfe, fourth Baronet, and nephew of Lord Metcalfe : born at Delhi, Nov. 28, 1828 : educated at Addiscombe and Haileybury : joined the E. I. Co.'s service in 1848 : became Baronet, 1853 : Magistrate at Delhi at the outbreak of the mutiny, May, 1857 : gave information to the magazine officers at Delhi : with the Army before Delhi : foremost in the work of retribution : Assistant to the Agent at Delhi : C.B., 1864 : retired, 1866 : died Nov. 10, 1883.

MEURIN, RIGHT REV. LEO, D.D. (1825–1895)

Vicar Apostolic of Bombay (Catholic) : of French extraction : born in Berlin, June 23, 1825 : entered the Society of Jesus (German Province), April 8, 1853 : arrived in India, Oct. 1858 : was Military Chaplain at Poona, parochial priest at Candolim and Bombay Cathedral : Superior of the Diocesan Seminary, 1860 : nominated, 1867, Bishop of Arcalon *in partibus*, and Vicar Apostolic over the Vicariate of Bombay and Western India : also, in 1867, Superior of the Jesuit Mission : consecrated, Feb. 2, 1868, henceforward residing at the Fort Chapel, Bombay : attended the Vatican Council at Rome, 1869–70 : acted, 1876–7, as Visitor Apostolic to the community of the Syrian rite on the Malabar coast : recalled to Rome, July, 1886, and made Archbishop of Mauritius : died June 1, 1895 ; buried in the Cathedral there. In Bombay he showed himself a ruler of vast enterprise in founding schools, colleges and missions, as well as delivering public lectures on religious subjects, chiefly of interest to Hindus and Parsis : through a newspaper controversy, he converted Luke Rivington, a prominent Anglican clergyman in Bombay, to the Catholic faith. A volume of his *Select Works* was edited after his death, chiefly pamphlets and Pastorals : he founded the *Pastoral Gazette* and the *Indian Messenger* : his zeal and talents did much for the prestige of his Church in Western India. He played an important part in the establishment of St. Xavier's High School and College, Bombay (now about 1,400 pupils and 300 University students) ; St. Mary's College, Bombay (now about 250 boarders and 500 day scholars) ; St. Vincent's High School, Poona (now about 400 day scholars); an Orphanage at Bandora (now about 500); a College at Mangalore, and other educational and charitable institutions.

MEYRICK, JAMES JOSEPH (1834–   )

Born Sep. 6, 1834 : son of Theobald Meyrick : educated at City of London School and Royal Veterinary College, London : served in the R.A., in Canada and Egypt : superintendent of horse-breeding operations in the Panjab, 1878–80 : Egyptian campaign, 1882, C.B. : author of *Stable Management and Prevention of Disease among Horses in India* : *Veterinary Manual for use of Native Horseowners in India*, translated into Hindustani.

MICHEL, SIR JOHN (1804–1886)

Field Marshal : son of General John Michel : born Sep. 1, 1804 : educated at Eton : joined the 57th foot in 1823 : at the R.M.C., Sandhurst, 1832–3 : A.D.C. to his uncle, Sir H. Fane (*q.v.*), when C. in C. in India, 1835–9 : commanded Brigades in the Kafir wars of 1846–7 and 1852–3 : C.B. : Chief of the Staff of the Turkish contingent in the Crimean war : to Bombay in 1858 : commanded the Malwa Field Force : in several engagements defeated Tantia Topi, who was eventually captured and hanged : K.C.B. : commanded a Division in China, 1860 : at the occupation of Pekin : burned the Summer Palace : G.C.B., 1871 : Lt-General, 1866 : General, 1874 : commanded the forces in Ireland, 1875–80 : Field Marshal, 1885 : died May 23, 1886.

MIDDLETON, NATHANIEL (? – ?)

In the service of the E. I. Co : appointed Resident at the Court of Shuja-ud-daula, Nawab of Oudh, by Warren Hastings, 1774 : recalled from Lucknow in the same year, after the Rohilla war, by the majority in Council, but reinstated in 1776 : seems to have incurred the displeasure of Hastings by his slowness in pressing Asaf-ud-daula, the new Nawab, for the treasure of the Begams of Oudh : later, Middleton was called as a witness at the trial of W. Hastings, 1788–94.

MIDDLETON, RIGHT REV. THOMAS FANSHAW, D.D. (1769–1822)

Son of Rev. Thomas Middleton : born Jan. 26, 1769 : educated at Christ's Hospital, and Pembroke College, Cambridge : ordained in 1792 : curate of Gainsborough : brought out weekly *The Country Spectator*, 1792–3 : Rector of Tansor, 1795 ; of Bytham, 1802 : published *The Doctrine of the Greek Article applied to the Criticism and the Illustration of the New Testament*, 1808 : D.D., 1808 : Prebendary of Lincoln, 1809 : Vicar of St. Pancras, 1811 : Archdeacon of Huntingdon, 1812 : edited the *British Critic*, 1811 : appointed the first Bishop of Calcutta : consecrated, May, 1814 : reached Calcutta Nov. 1814 : established schools and committees : made long visitation tours in S. India, Bombay, Madras : founded Bishop's College at Howrah, opposite to Calcutta, 1820 : died of fever at Calcutta, July 8, 1822 : his monument is in St. Paul's Cathedral, London : F.R.S. and Vice-President of the Asiatic Society of Bengal.

MILES, WILLIAM (? –1860)

Joined the Bombay N.I., 1800 : served at Baroda : made a treaty in 1820 with the Raja of Rodanpur : commanded a regt. in the first Burmese war : took Mergui : made a treaty with the Suigam chiefs, in Gujarat, in 1826 : Political Officer at Palanpur, 1829 : retired, 1834 : Maj-General : died May 21, 1860 : translated works on the *History of Hyder Naik*, 1842 : and *History of the Reign of Tipu Sultan*, 1844.

MILL, JAMES (1773–1836)

Philosopher and historian : born in 1773 : son of a shoemaker : educated at Montrose Academy and Edinburgh University: studied philosophy: was licensed as a preacher in 1798, and became a tutor: went to London in 1802, for a literary career. In 1806 he began his History of British India, which he completed in 1818, writing, besides, largely for Periodicals, Reviews, the *Encyclopædia Britannica*, etc., etc.: he was the friend of Bentham, Ricardo, Joseph Hume, Lord Brougham, George Grote, etc., and held pronounced views on political economy, utilitarianism, etc.: has been called the founder of Philosophic Radicalism. He was appointed to the India Office in 1819 as an Assistant Examiner of Correspondence, and by 1830 was at the head of the office, and had great influence with his official superiors. Before the renewal of the E. I. Co's charter in 1833 he was examined for days before the House of Commons Committee, and did not advocate the application of his advanced views to India: he was the father of John Stuart Mill (*q.v.*): died June 23, 1836. A new edition of his History was brought out, with notes by H. H. Wilson (*q.v.*).

MILL, JOHN STUART (1806-1873)

The philosopher: son of James Mill (*q.v.*): born May 20, 1806: educated privately: he was never in India, but was connected with it by joining the India House as a junior clerk in 1823: he was third in the office, on £1,200 a year, when his father died in 1836: chief of the office in 1856, on £2,000 a year: he prepared, in 1858, the document in which the E. I. Co. stated their case against their threatened termination: when the statute of 1858 was passed and the government of the E. I. Co. came to an end, Mill retired on a pension of £1,500 a year. It is said that, for 23 years, he wrote all the political despatches from the India House: he wrote no single special work on India: died May 8, 1873.

MILL, REV. WILLIAM HODGE, D.D. (1792?-1853)

Born about 1792: educated by Dr. Belsham, the Unitarian preacher: went to Cambridge: sixth Wrangler in 1813: Fellow of Trinity College, 1814: for 5 years studied Oriental languages: appointed Principal of Bishop's College, Calcutta, 1820, then recently established:

learnt Sanskrit and the vernacular languages: published an Arabic version of the Book of Common Prayer and the Psalms: and the *Christa Sangita*, the Life of Christ, rendered into 5,000 stanzas of Sanskrit, his own compilation: gave much attention to education: was Vice-President of the Asiatic Society of Bengal: deciphered the inscriptions on the Allahabad column, and wrote on the inscriptions on pillars and on the ancient history of India: returned to England, 1837: failed as a candidate for the Sanskrit Professorship at Oxford: became Chaplain to the Archbishop of Canterbury, 1839: and Christian Advocate at Cambridge, 1840: also Regius Professor of Hebrew there, 1848, and a Canon of Ely: F.R.A.S.: a profound Oriental scholar: D.D.: died Dec. 25, 1853.

MILLER, SIR ALEXANDER EDWARD (1828-1903)

Born Aug. 28, 1828: educated at Rugby and had a distinguished career at Trinity College, Dublin, 1851: was called to the bar from Lincoln's Inn, 1854: Q.C. and Bencher in 1872. From 1877-88 he was a Member of the Railway Commission: Knight Bachelor in 1889: a Master in Lunacy from 1889 to 91: Legal Member of the Governor-General's Supreme Council, 1891-6, when he retired: Honorary LL.D. in 1875, and C.S.I. in 189: died at Ballycastle, County Antrim, Sep. 13, 1903.

MILLER, JOHN ONTARIO (1857-)

I.C.S.: born Aug. 7, 1857: educated at King's College, Aberdeen: joined, in 1879, the Civil Service in the N.W.P.: Private Secretary to the Lieutenant-Governor: rose to be Chief Secretary to the Government, N.W.P. and Oudh, 1898-1902: Secretary to the Government of India in the Revenue Department, 1902-5: Private Secretary to Lord Curzon and Lord Ampthill, Viceroys of India, 1903-4: C.S.I., 1901: Chief Commissioner of the Central Provinces, 1905.

MILLER, REV. WILLIAM (1838-

Born Jan. 13, 1838: educated at Marischal College, Aberdeen, and New College, Edinburgh: Principal of the Madras Christian College since 1863

U

Member of the Legislative Council, Madras, 1893–7 : Moderator, Free Church of Scotland, 1896–7 : Vice-Chancellor of the University of Madras, 1902–3 : author of several educational and religious works.

MILLER, WILLIAM HENRY (1805–1873)

Maj-General : born May 1, 1805 : son of Major W. Miller : educated at Addiscombe : entered the Madras Artillery, 1823 : present in several actions against insurgents in Mysore, 1831 : commanded the Artillery Brigade with the Sagar Field Force : under Sir G. C. Whitlock, in Bundelkund, 1858 : again in several actions : lost his right arm at Banda, April 19, 1858 : A.D.C. to the Queen : Maj-General and C.B. : retired, 1860 : President of the Prize Committee in the Banda and Kirwi prize case : a great *shikari* and authority on all sport : died May 15, 1873.

MILLETT, FREDERICK (? –1856)

I.C.S. : was in the Civil Service, 1816–48 : Member of the Indian Law Commission : Member of the Supreme Council from 1845 until he retired : died 1856.

MILLS, SIR CHARLES, BARONET (1792–1872)

Born 1792 : son of William Mills : Director of the E. I. Co., 1822 : was M.P. for Northallerton : Member of the Council of India, 1858–68 : made Baronet in 1868 for his public services as Member of Council : died Oct. 4, 1872.

MILLS, JOHN (1722–1811)

Captain : was in the Black Hole at Calcutta, June, 1756, and there gave up his place at the window to J. Z. Holwell (*q.v.*) : his pocket-book supplied Orme (*q.v.*) with his account of the siege of Calcutta, 1756 : he survived 55 years, dying in 1811.

MILMAN,˙RIGHT REV. ROBERT, D.D. (1816–1876)

Third son of Sir William George Milman, *Bart.* : born Jan. 25, 1816 : educated at Westminster and Exeter College, Oxford : Scholar : B.A., 1838 : D.D., 1867 : ordained, 1839 : Vicar of Chaddleworth, 1840 : of Lambourn, 1851 : held the living of Great Marlow from 1862 until he went to Calcutta as Bishop in March, 1867 : was energetic in touring round his extensive diocese : and in his visitations as Metropolitan : he belonged to the High Church party : desired to increase the number of the Bishops in India, pressing specially for the erection of a Bishopric in Lahore : as a good linguist he mastered several native languages, so as to be able to preach in them : he was much loved and respected by all classes, including the natives : died at Rawal Pindi on March 15, 1876 : the Government erected a memorial to him in the Cathedral at Calcutta : the Notification issued by the Government testified to Dr. Milman's indefatigable energy, his charity and munificence, his zeal in promoting all good works, especially the education of the poorer classes of Europeans in India, and his broad and benevolent sympathies with all classes of the community.

MILLS, LAWRENCE HEYWORTH (1837–)

Born 1837 : son of P. L. Mills : educated at New York University : came to Oxford, 1887, on the invitation of Prof. Max Müller, and has resided there since : Professor of Zend Philology at Oxford since 1898 : succeeded Professor Darmesteter at his request, on " Sacred Books of the East " : author of translations of Gathas with Zend, Pahlavi, Sanskrit and Persian texts.

MINCHIN, JAMES INNES (1825–1903)

I.C.S. : born 1825 : educated at Haileybury, 1842–3 : went out to Madras, 1844 : rose to be Collector of Kurnool for 6 years, Collector and Political Agent, Vizagapatam : Chief Secretary to the Madras Government : Additional Member of the Governor-General's Legislative Council, 1868 : Acting Resident of Travancore and Cochin : left Madras, 1871 : a great proficient at the game of chess : Honorary Secretary of the St. George's Chess Club : a classical scholar, contributing to the *Academy* and other journals : wrote Sonnets *Ex Oriente*, and translated Dante's *Divina Comedia*, 1885 : a keen sportsman : died Jan. 18, 1903.

MINOCHER-HOMJI, MANECKJI BARJORJI (1840-1898)

Indian journalist and novelist : born July 30, 1840 : educated at the Elphinstone Institution, Bombay : served in the Military Board office : editor of the *Dost-i-Hind*, 1861 : and the *Suryodaya*, 1864-6 : editor and part-proprietor of the *Bombay Samachar*, 1866, with which he was connected intimately till his death, raising it to a leading position among native papers in W. India : its sole proprietor from 1871 : brought out the *Loke-mitra*, or " People's Friend," 1868 : a great humorist, he conducted a comic weekly the *Daterdoo* (the Scythe) 1874-90, in which he published his novel of Parsi social life, 1878-87, until he closed this paper. He wrote much on the foreign policy and relations of England and India, and the European position of the rulers of India : published 12 vols., 1879, of the ancient Persian legends of Iran, which he called *Burjornama* : cultivated Indian music scientifically, and published a collection of Indian odes : was a member of the Indian Philharmonic Society : made a great reputation among Indian journalists : his editorship of the *Samachar* being formally acknowledged by Government : made J.P. in 1885 : died 1898.

MINTO, SIR GILBERT ELLIOT, FIRST EARL OF (1751-1814)

Governor-General : son of Sir Gilbert Elliot, *Bart.* : born April 23, 1751 : educated privately, at the Pension Militaire, Fontainebleau ; Edinburgh, and at Christ Church, Oxford : called to the bar at Lincoln's Inn, 1774 : M.P. for Morpeth, 1776-84 : for Berwick, 1786-90 : schoolfollow of Mirabeau and friend of Burke : in 1787-8 he at first carried a motion in Parliament, condemning the conduct of Sir Elijah Impey at Calcutta, chiefly about the trial of Nuncomar (*q.v.*) : but the motion was afterwards lost : he tried, but failed, to become the Speaker of the House of Commons : M.P. for Helston, 1790 : D.C.L. Oxford, 1793 : in 1794-6 he was Governor of the Protectorate of Corsica : returned to England in 1798, and was made Baron Minto : Envoy and Minister-Plenipotentiary at Vienna, 1799 : F.R.S. London and Edinburgh, 1803 : President of the Board of Control, 1806, and Governor-General of India, July, 1807, to Oct. 1813 : reformed the finances of India, despatched Missions to Kabul, Lahore and Persia, to make alliances, with the object of defence against French invasion : made a treaty with Sind : he annexed Amboyna, 1810 ; the Molucca Islands, the Isle of Bourbon, the Mauritius, and went himself on the expedition under the military command of Sir S. Auchmuty to Java in 1811. He endeavoured to introduce reforms into the native government of Oudh, and paid much attention to the internal administration of India generally, in respect of the press, religious toleration, education, the suppression of local disturbances : he was created Earl of Minto and Viscount Melgund, 1813 : he embarked for England in Dec. 1813 : arrived there in May 1814 : died June 21, 1814, and was buried in Westminster Abbey.

MINTO, GILBERT JOHN MURRAY KYNYNMOND ELLIOT, FOURTH EARL OF (1845-)

Viceroy and Governor-General : born July 9, 1845 : son of third Earl : educated at Eton and Trinity College Cambridge ; B.A : in the Scots Guards, 1867-70 : was in Paris during the Communist outbreak, 1871 : correspondent, three years later, for the *Morning Post*, with the Carlist Army in Biscay and Navarre : served with the Turkish Army in the Russo-Turkish war, 1877 : at the bombardment of Nikopolis, and the crossing of the Danube : with Lord Roberts in the Afghan war, 1878-9 : was nearly accompanying Cavagnari (*q.v.*) to Kabul, 1879 : Private Secretary to Lord Roberts on his mission to the Cape, 1881 : was a volunteer, as Captain in the Mounted Infantry in Egypt, 1882 : wounded, and rejoined : Military Secretary to the Marquis of Lansdowne, when Governor-General of Canada, 1883-5 : Chief of the Staff to General Middleton in quelling the Riel rebellion in N.W. Canada, 1885 : candidate for Hexham, 1886 : succeeded to the title, 1891 : Governor-General of Canada, 1898-1904 : received there T.R.H. the Prince and Princess of Wales : appointed Viceroy and Governor-General of India, August, 1905 : G.C.M.G., 1898 : P.C., J.P. : Hony. LL.D. Toronto.

292   DICTIONARY OF INDIAN BIOGRAPHY

MIR IZZET ULLAH (? - ?)

A servant of the traveller Moorcroft (*q.v.*) : despatched on a preparatory tour to the countries which Moorcroft proposed to visit : Izzet Ullah travelled from Delhi to Kashmir, Tibet, Yarkand, Kashgar, Khokand, Samarkand, Bokhara, Balkh, Khulm, Kabul and Hindustan : he kept a journal of his stages and collected much information, which was translated and published as "Travels beyond the Himalaya" in the *Calcutta Oriental Quarterly Magazine*, 1825, and republished in the *J.R.A.S.*, 1843.

MIR JAFAR, (1691–1765)

Jafar Ali Khan : early brought up in the family of Aliverdi Khan, the usurper of the Government of Bengal : appointed C. in C. by Aliverdi for his successful expedition against the Mahratta raids in Bengal : after the death of Aliverdi, entered into conspiracy against Suraj-ud-daula, the new Nawab : though present at the battle of Plassy in 1757, he held aloof from both sides : after the murder of Suraj-ud-daula by Miran, son of Jafar, the latter was made Nawab Nazim of Bengal, Bihar and Orissa, in June, 1757 : in 1759 he intrigued with the Dutch to expel the English, and was deposed by the English in 1760, his son-in-law, Mir Kasim, being substituted as Nawab : in 1763 Mir Jafar was restored as Nawab, and Mir Kasim deposed : reigned quietly until he died in Jan. 1765 from an attack of leprosy : buried at Murshidabad.

MIR KASIM (? –1777)

Mir Kasim Ali Khan : son-in-law of Mir Jafar : appointed Nawab Nazim of Bengal, Bihar and Orissa by the English in place of Mir Jafar, on Sep. 27, 1760 : but serious disputes soon arose between him and the English, regarding commerce and the conduct of the servants of the E. I. Co., which led to war : fortified Monghyr for his defence against the English : the English defeated his troops at Katwa on July 19, at Gheria on Aug. 1, 1763, and again at Udwanala : he left Monghyr, and at Patna ordered the massacre of the English prisoners there, 50 gentlemen and 100 others, on Oct. 5, 1763 : fled to Oudh to Shuja-ud-daula, the Wazir of Oudh, who refused to deliver him to the English : he then escaped to Rohilkund

and took shelter with the Rana of Gohud : after staying there some years, he went to Jodhpur, and thence to Delhi to serve the Emperor Shah Alam, in 1774, but was disappointed : died at Kotwal, near Delhi, in 1777.

MIRZA MUHAMMAD ALI BEG KHAN, NAWAB BAHADUR (? –)

Son of Mirza Wilayat Ali Beg : Rasaldar, 3rd Lancers, Hyderabad Contingent : served in the Hyderabad Contingent, Afghan war, 1879–80 : Black Mountain expedition, 1888 : China expedition, 1900 : raised and first commanded the 1st and 2nd Lancers, Hyderabad Imperial Service troops : Commandant of H.H. the Nizam's Regular Forces since 1897.

MITCHELL, REV. DR. J. MURRAY (1814–1904)

Missionary : ordained in 1838 and went to Bombay that year : taught in the Free General Assembly's Institution and College in Bombay, and afterwards at Poona, 1834–66 : was the first Indian Missionary to receive the degree of LL.D. : an accurate scholar, well versed in Mahratti : was for a time Minister of the English Free Church of Scotland in Calcutta : after leaving India he was Presbyterian Minister at Nice for some years : wrote *Letters to Indian Youths*, recommending Christianity to educated Hindus : *The Great Religions of India :* and a *Biography of the Rev. Robert Nesbitt, Missionary :* was Duff Missionary Lecturer, 1895–1903 : died Nov. 1904.

MITRA, RAJA DIGAMBAR (1817–1879)

Born in 1817 : educated at the Hare School and Hindu College : appointed Assistant Secretary to the British Indian Association, 1851 ; Vice-President, 1869, and, later, President : was a Member of the Epidemic Fever Commission, 1864, after which he held the theory that obstructed drainage is the chief cause of fever : was thrice Member of the Bengal Legislative Council : Sheriff of Calcutta, 1874 : C.S.I., 1876 : Raja, 1877. As a manager of large estates in early life, and as a landowner, he had a great knowledge of *zamindari* affairs, which was most useful in his public life : he died April 20, 1879.

MITRA, DINA BANDHU, RAI BAHADUR (1829–1873)

Born in 1829 : educated at the Hare School and the Hindu College : while a student began to write in Bengali and contribute to the *Sambad Pravakar*, edited by Iswar Chanda Gupta : in 1855 went to Patna as Postmaster : within two years became Inspector of Post Offices in Orissa, and subsequently at Nadia and Dacca : in 1858, while at Dacca, published the celebrated Bengali novel, *Nil Darpan*, or the Mirror of Indigo, which was translated into English in 1860, under the superintendence of the Rev. James Long (*q.v.*), of the Church Missionary Society : in 1870 became Supernumerary Inspecting Postmaster of Calcutta : in 1871 accompanied the Lushai expedition as Superintendent of Postal Intelligence : in 1872 made a Rai Bahadur : died Nov. 1, 1873 : wrote many Bengali books in prose and verse, and is generally regarded as the greatest humorist of the Bengali language.

MITRA, DWARKANATH (1833–1874)

Son of a Law Agent practising in the Hughli Courts : educated in the Hughli and Presidency Colleges, where he had a distinguished career : joined the Calcutta bar as a Pleader in 1856, and in 1862, when the High Court was established, was the leader of the Native bar : distinguished himself in arguing the case of the *raiyats* in the famous Rent case of 1865 before a full bench of 15 judges : became Government Pleader, and was promoted to the High Court Bench in 1867. He studied Comte in the original French, and corresponded with some eminent Positivists : was a Fellow of the Calcutta University : was a "most learned, upright, able and independent judge," remarkable for his intellectual qualities, his keen discrimination, his retentive memory and his wonderful command of the English language : was a great reader : died Feb. 25, 1874.

MITRA, KISORI CHAND (1822–1873)

Brother of Piari Chand Mitra (*q.v.*) : born May, 1822 : educated at the Hare School and Hindu College : appointed, in 1844, Assistant Secretary to the Asiatic Society : his writings attracted such favourable notice that he was appointed a Deputy Magistrate in 1846 : for some years Junior Magistrate in Calcutta, but lost his appointment : then devoted himself to literature and politics ; conducted a newspaper until his health failed, and wrote constantly in the *Calcutta Review*, and a life of Dwarka Nath Tagore : he set on foot a Social Reform Association : died Aug. 6, 1873.

MITRA, PIARI CHAND (1814–1883)

One of the zealous social reformers inspired by Derozio at the old Hindu College : adopted a commercial career, but literature was the real work of his life : contributed largely to the local Journals, and to spiritualistic Journals out of India : helped to found the British Indian Association, and worked hard for a number of societies. In 1868, as Member of the Bengal Legislative Council, he helped to pass the Act for the Prevention of Cruelty to Animals, and was Secretary to the Society formed for that purpose : was a J.P. : Fellow of the Calcutta University : Hony. Magte. : Member of the Calcutta Corporation. In later life he became a spiritualist and Theosophist, aiding in the foundation of the Theosophic Society of Calcutta. His life was one of literary activity and public usefulness : he wrote a life of David Hare (*q.v.*) : died Nov. 1883.

MITRA, RAJA RAJENDRA LAL (1824–1891)

Scholar and antiquarian : belonged to a respectable Sudra family : born Feb. 15, 1824 : son of Janamejaya Mitra : educated in Calcutta at English schools, and later at the Calcutta Medical College : turned his attention to Law, but only for a short period : next studied Sanskrit, Greek, Latin, French and German. At the age of 22 he was appointed Assistant Secretary and Librarian of the Bengal Asiatic Society : in 1856 he was appointed Director of the Wards' Institution : when it was closed, in 1880, he retired on a pension. He contributed 114 articles to the *Journal of the Asiatic Society :* several of his essays were collected and republished in two volumes under the title of *Indo-Aryans :* also wrote *Antiquities of Orissa* and *Buddha Gaya :* and on *The Sanskrit Buddhist Literature of Nipal,* 1882 : his 128 volumes of writings showed his research, scholarship and erudition : wrote largely for the *Hindu Patriot*, often inspiring its policy. In 1885 he was elected President of the Asiatic Society of Bengal, and in 1886 took a prominent part in the Second National Indian Congress : was Member of the Calcutta Corporation : D.L. of the Calcutta University, 1875 : Vice-President and President of the British Indian Association : Raj Bahadur, 1877 : C.I.E., 1878 : and Raja, 1888. The most learned Hindu of his time : he received a special pension in recognition of his services to Literature and Archæology : his name is well known to antiquarians and savants in every part of the world : died July 26, 1891.

MITRA, TRAILOKYA NATH (1844–1895)

Born May 2, 1844 : son of Joy Gopal Mitra : educated at Uttarpara : M.A., 1864 : B.L., 1865 : Doctor in Law, 1877, of Calcutta University : Lecturer in Mathematics at the Presidency College : Law Lecturer and Acting Professor of Philosophy at Hughli College : joined the bar : practised at Hughli and in the Calcutta High Court, 1875 : Fellow of the Calcutta University, 1879 : and Tagore Law Lecturer, 1879, on " Hindu Widows " : President of the Faculty of Law : M.R.A.S. : died of fever, April 18, 1895.

MITTER, SIR ROMESH CHUNDER (1840–1899)

Born 1840 : son of the Head Clerk of the *Sadr Adalat* at Calcutta : educated in the Hare School and the Presidency College there : passed his B.L., and became a Pleader when he was 21 : rose to the front rank of his profession, and was a Judge of the High Court, 1874–1890 : on two occasions acted as Chief Justice : was a Fellow, and President of the Faculty of Law, of the University. For the remainder of his life he rendered many services to his countrymen : was a Member of the Governor-General's Legislative Council and of the Public Service Commission : joined the National Congress : and was Vice-President of the Indian Science Association. He was first knighted, and afterwards K.C.I.E. : died July 13, 1899.

MITTER, SARADA CHARAN (1848–   )

Born Dec. 17, 1848 : took his B.A. degree in 1870, and, later, M.A. at the Calcutta University : was Premchand Roychand Scholar in 1871 : B.L., 1873 : practised in the Calcutta High Court from 1874 : officiating High Court Judge, 1903 : confirmed, 1904 : has written a law book on the Land Laws of Bengal.

MOHAN LAL (? –1870)

Munshi : son of Pandit Budh Singh of Delhi : educated at the English College at Delhi : when still quite a youth, he accompanied Lieutenant Alexander Burnes and Dr. J. G. Gerard on their journey to Persia in 1832 in the capacity of Persian munshi. The expedition was undertaken by order of the Government of India, with the object of gaining a knowledge of the general condition of the countries west of the Indus. Mohan Lal assisted Burnes in his Persian correspondence. The latter, in his book, *Travels into Bokhara*, speaks highly of Mohan Lal's trustworthiness and interest in the expedition, as well as of the detailed journal which Mohan Lal kept at the request of Burnes. This diary was published in 1834, under the title of *Journal of a Tour through the Panjab, Afghanistan, Turkistan, Khorasan, and Part of Persia*. During the first Afghan war he was employed as Attaché to the British Agency : but the greater part of his life was spent at Delhi, where he died about 1870.

MOHL, JULIUS (1800–1876)

Born Oct. 25, 1800, at Stuttgart : son of a high civil official in Wurtemburg : went to Tübingen to study theology : attracted by Eastern studies, he went to Paris, 1823, to the School of Oriental Learning in the Collège de France : attended lectures on Arabic, Persian and Chinese : made Professor of Oriental Languages at Tübingen, 1826 (which he resigned in 1831), but allowed to continue his studies at Paris : in England, 1830–1 : at Paris, selected by the French Government to translate Firdusi's *Shah Nameh* : 6 volumes appeared, 1838–68 : the seventh and last unfinished at his death : Member of the French Institute, 1844 : Professor of Persian at the Collège de France : Inspector of the Oriental Department at the Imperial Press, 1852 : Assistant Secretary, then Secretary, and eventually President of the Société Asiatique : through this Society he greatly advanced Oriental scholarship : his Annual Reports, delivered from 1840 to 1867, contained reviews of the whole addition to the stock of Oriental learning in Europe for each year, i.e. the progress of Oriental research in the principal Indian languages and other branches of Indian literature. They have been collected and published in 2 volumes. He was indefatigable in promoting discoveries in Mesopotamia, by excavations, explorations, the acquisition, publication and decipherment of newly found inscriptions in the Persian, Median and Babylonian languages : announcing yearly the results attained. He retained his position in Paris throughout the Franco-German war, generally respected for his devotion to science : died in Paris, Jan. 4–5, 1876.

MOLESWORTH, SIR GUILDFORD LINDSEY (1828–)

Born May 3, 1828 : son of Rev. J. E. N. Molesworth : educated at King's School, Canterbury, and College of Civil Engineers, Putney : Engineer in England, and on Ceylon railways : Consulting Engineer to the Government of India, 1871–89 : acting Director-General of Railways and Deputy Secretary to Government, 1880 : British delegate to the International Monetary Conference, Brussels, 1892 : author of several works on Railway Engineering and Currency questions, Iron manufacture in India, Masonry Dams, Engineer Volunteer Corps for India, Imperialism for India, Text-book of Bimetallism, 1886, etc.

MOLLOY, EDWARD (1842–1905)

Son of Robert Molloy : educated at Radley and Addiscombe : entered the Army at 18 : served in Assam, in the Khasia and Jaintia Hills rebellion, 1862–3 ; Bhutan campaign, 1865 ; N.W. Frontier Hazara campaign, 1868 ; Afghan war, 1878–80 : in the Kabul-Kandahar march and battle of Kandahar : Brevet-Major : Achakzai and Marri expeditions : Lt.-Colonel : commanded the 2nd Gurkhas, Hazara Campaign, 1891 : Isazai expedition, 1892 : C.B., 1900 : Unemployed Supernumerary List, 1899 : died Feb. 1, 1905.

MONEY, SIR ALONZO (1723–1900)

I.C.S. : son of George Money, Master of the Supreme Court, Calcutta : educated at Haileybury : went out to Lower Bengal, 1843 : in the mutiny, as Magistrate-Collector of Gaya, returned to the station when ordered away, saved the treasure at great personal risk, escorted it to Calcutta : constantly engaged with the rebels in Bihar : C.B., 1860 : Commissioner of Bhagalpur, 1863 : Member of the Board of Revenue, 1869, and of the Bengal Legislative Council : left India, 1877 : English Commissioner of the Public Debt of Egypt from 1880 : K.C.M.G., 1898 : died at Cairo, April 7, 1900.

MONEY, ELLIOT ALEXANDER (1843–)

Born Aug. 16, 1843 : son of W. Money, B.C.S. : entered the Indian Army, 1860, and the Indian Staff Corps, 1869 : served in the Panjab Cavalry, and Corps of Guides, 1869–87 : A.A.G., Panjab, 1887–90 : commanded the 3rd Bengal Cavalry, 1891–4 : D.A.G., India, 1894–97 : officiated in command of Allahabad, Assam and Agra Districts, 1897–9 : C.B. 1897.

MONEY, WILLIAM JAMES (1832–)

I.C.S. : educated at Haileybury, 1850–2 : went out to Bengal in the Civil Service, 1853 : Civil Officer with the troops in the Sonthal rebellion, 1855 : Private Secretary to Sir James Outram (*q.v.*) during the mutiny : at the relief of Lucknow and Alambagh : Magistrate and Collector of Cuttack, 1861–6 : District and Sessions Judge, 1873 : retired, 1879 : C.S.I., 1869.

MONIER-WILLIAMS, SIR MONIER (1819–1899)

Son of Colonel Monier-Williams, R.E., Surveyor-General, Bombay : born at Bombay, 1819 : educated at Chelsea, Brighton, King's College, London ; Balliol College, Oxford : went to Haileybury, 1840 : but gave up his idea of going to India : went to University College, Oxford : gained the Boden Sanskrit scholarship, 1843 : Professor of Sanskrit, Persian and Hindustani at Haileybury, 1844–58 : Boden Professor of Sanskrit at Oxford, 1860 : founded, in 1883, the Indian Institute at Oxford, as a centre of

Indian learning and interests: making three journeys to India to obtain native sympathy and help: was Fellow of Balliol, 1882–6: Hon. Fellow of University College, 1892: Curator of the Indian Institute: D.C.L., 1875: LL.D., Calcutta: Ph.D. Göttingen: K.C.I.E., 1887: wrote a Sanskrit grammar, English-Sanskrit and Sanskrit-English dictionaries; *Indian Epic Poetry,* 1863; *Indian Wisdom,* 1875; devoted himself to the practical study of Sanskrit and later rather than the oldest Sanskrit literature; some Hindustani works, *Hinduism,* 1877; *Modern India and the Indians,* 1878; *Religious Life and Thought in India,* 1883; *Buddhism,* 1889: *Brahmanism,* 1891: co-editor of *Memorials of Old Haileybury*: he supported Missionary enterprise in India, and aimed at increasing the knowledge of Indian religions in England: he died April 11, 1899.

MONRO, JAMES (1838–   )

I.C.S.: born Nov. 25, 1838: son of George Monro, S.S.C. Edinburgh: educated at the Edinburgh High School, Edinburgh and Berlin Universities: went out to Lower Bengal, 1858: was Civil and Sessions Judge, 1874: Inspr-General of Police, Bengal, 1877: Commissioner of a Division, 1881: strongly opposed Lord Ripon's policy of Local Self Government: retired, 1883: became Assistant-Commissioner, Metropolitan Police, London, 1884: Commissioner of Police of the Metropolis, 1888–90: C.B., 1888: as Commissioner of Police, London, Monro stopped the dynamite outrages, and controlled the great strikes of the dock labourers and South London gasworkers: got justice done to the men of the Metropolitan Police in the matter of their pensions: went to India again about 1892: organized and superintended the Ranaghat Medical Mission till 1905.

MONRO, SEYMOUR CHARLES HALL (? – ?)

Entered the Army, 1877, and became Colonel, 1900: in the Afghan war, 1878–80: was in the Kabul-Kandahar march and battle of Kandahar: severely wounded: Egypt, 1882: Tel - el - Kebir: South Africa, 1884, Brevet - Major: Hazara campaign, 1891: Chitral Relief Force, 1891: Brevet-Lt-Colonel: N.W. Frontier

1897–8: South Africa, 1899–02, Brevet-Colonel: C.B., 1903.

MONSON, HON. GEORGE (1730–1776)

Son of John, first Lord Monson: born April 18, 1730: educated at Westminster: entered the footguards in 1750: M.P. for Lincoln, 1754–68: went out to Bombay 1758; Madras, 1759: second in command at the siege of Pondicherry, 1760: superseded Eyre Coote, but was wounded and had to yield his position: at Manilla under Colonel Draper in 1762: Brig-General, 1763: A.D.C. to George III, 1769: appointed, under the Regulating Act of 1774, Member of the Supreme Council in India: assumed office Oct. 20, 1774: with Francis and Clavering opposed Warren Hastings, who regarded him as a dangerous opponent: resigned in Sep. 1776: but died on 25th of that month at Hughli.

MONSON, HON. WILLIAM (1760–1807)

Son of John, second Baron Monson: born Dec. 15, 1760: to India with the 52nd regt. in 1780: in the attack on Seringapatam under Cornwallis in 1792: Lt-Colonel, 1797: in the Mahratta war, 1803, commanded a Brigade under Lake: led the storming party at Alighar, Sep. 4, 1803: severely wounded: sent in 1804 as Brig-General, with a detachment, to remain during the rainy season about the Jaipur frontier and watch Jaswant Rao Holkar, whom he followed along the river Chambal: Holkar's force was so great that Monson desisted from attacking him, and retreated from July 8 to Aug. 30, 1804, before him, Holkar pursuing: Monson lost all his guns and baggage before he reached Agra: again employed by Lake against Holkar: at battle of Deeg, Nov. 14, 1804: led the last of the four assaults on Bhartpur, 1805: returned to England, 1806: M.P. for Lincoln: died Dec. 1807.

MONTAGU, EDWARD (1755–1799)

Son of Admiral John Montagu: born 1755: educated at the R.M.A., Woolwich: went out to Bengal, 1770: joined the Bengal Artillery, 1772: was under General Goddard in the Mahratta campaign, 1781: in Bundelkund: and in the Carnatic against Hyder Ali and the French, 1782–3: with Cornwallis in the invasion of Mysore

1791 : commanded the Artillery at Nandidrug and Savandrug : Lt-Colonel, 1794 : commanded the Bengal Artillery at Seringapatam, 1799 : shot, and died of his wounds, May 8, 1799.

MONTEATH, SIR JAMES (1847-)

I.C.S. : born Sep. 7, 1847 : son of Thomas Monteath : educated at Royal Academical Institution and Queen's College, Belfast : entered the Bombay Civil Service, 1870 : held a succession of appointments in the Secretariat : was Private Secretary to the Governor, 1886 : and finally became Chief Secretary to the Bombay Government : C.S.I., 1897 : Member of Council, Bombay, 1900 : K.C.S.I., 1903.

MONTEITH, WILLIAM (1790-1864)

Son of William Monteith : born June 22, 1790 : became a Lieutenant in the Madras Engineers, 1809 : with Sir J. Malcolm's Embassy to Persia, 1810 : saw service, with the Persians, against the Russians, 1810-3 : with the Persians in the war against Turkey : and settled the Persia-Turkey boundary in 1821 : in the Perso-Russian operations, 1826-8 : and at the settlement of the Russo-Persian boundary, 1829, when he left Persia : Chief Engineer at Madras, 1832-4, and 1836-42 : Maj-General, 1842 : Lt-General, 1854 : died April 16, 1864 : F.R.S. and F.R.G.S : wrote on geography, and an account of the campaign of 1826-8.

MONTGOMERIE, SIR PATRICK (1793-1872)

General : son of Robert Montgomerie : educated at the Ayr Academy and Woolwich : joined the Madras Artillery, 1810 : served in the Mahratta war, 1817-8 : at the battle of Nagpur Dec. 16, 1817, and siege of Chanda : in the Burmese war óf 1824-5 : commanded the Artillery in China, 1840-2 : A.D.C. to Queen Victoria : Lt-General in 1859 : General in 1868 : Colonel Commandant of the Royal Artillery : C.B., 1847 : K.C.B., 1865 : died Oct. 5, 1872.

MONTGOMERIE, THOMAS GEORGE (1830-1878)

Born April 23, 1830 : son of Colonel W. E. Montgomerie : educated at Addiscombe : went to India in the Bengal Engineers, 1851 : joined the Trigonometrical Survey in 1582 : took 'a leading part in the measurement of the base lines of Chach and Karachi : had charge of the topographical survey of Jammu and Kashmir, 1855-64, for which he received the Royal Geographical Society's medal : surveyed 77,000 sq. m. in 9 years : in charge of the Kumaon and Garhwal survey, 1867 : he trained intelligent natives to survey and map, and sent them, disguised as merchants or otherwise, across the frontier, thus acquiring information of great value of the geography and routes to Yarkand, from Nipal to Lhasa, of the upper valley and source of the Brahmaputra, in Badakshan, Kafiristan, etc., for 4,500 miles of route survey : himself working out the results of their observations : officiated as Superintendent of the G. T. Survey, 1870-2 : F.R.S., 1872 : British Commissioner at the Paris Geographical Congress, 1875 : retired as Colonel, 1876 : contributed many papers on geography, surveys and glaciers, to scientific Journals : died Jan. 31, 1878.

MONTGOMERY, SIR HENRY CONYNGHAM, BARONET (1803-1878)

I.C.S. : eldest son of Sir H. C. Montgomery, *Bart.* : educated at Eton and Haileybury : was Assistant Private Secretary to Lord Wellesley when Lord Lieutenant of Ireland, 1822-4 : finally left Haileybury, 1824 : out to Madras, 1825, in the Civil Service : succeeded to the Baronetcy, 1830 : sent on a special commission to the Rajamundry (Godavery) district, which led to the irrigation of that district from the Godavery : Secretary to the Madras Government in the Revenue and Public Works Department, 1845-50 : Chief Secretary, 1850-5 : Member of Council 1855-7, when he retired : one of the original members of the new Council of India, chosen by the Crown, in Sep. 1858 : retired, 1876 : Privy Councillor : died June 24, 1878.

MONTGOMERY, SIR ROBERT (1809-1887)

I.C.S. : son of the Rev. Samuel Law Montgomery : born 1809 : educated at Foyle College, Londonderry ; Wraxall Hall and Addiscombe, 1823-5 : entered the Bengal Civil Service, 1828 : served in the N.W.P. : Magistrate-Collector of

Allahabad, 1839 : transferred to the Panjab : Commissioner of Lahore, 1849 : succeeded Mr. C. G. Mansel (*q.v.*) as Member of the Panjab Board of Administration, 1851 : Judicial Commissioner, 1853 : disarmed several native regiments at Lahore and Mian Mir on May 13, 1857, on his own responsibility, and sent warning to Multan, Firozpur and Kangra : appointed Chief Commissioner of Oudh, April, 1858 : Lieutenant-Governor of the Panjab, Feb. 1859, to Jan. 1865 : K.C.B., 1859 : G.C.S.I., 1866 : Member of the Council of India, 1868, till his death on Dec. 28, 1887 : the Montgomery Hall at Lahore erected as a memorial to him.

MONTRIOU (? –1857)

Captain, of the Indian Navy : served in the first Burmese war : in charge of the E. I. Co.'s maritime surveys in Bengal : commanded the *Hastings* at Bombay from 1839 : in charge of the Observatory, 1847–51 : senior naval officer at Aden : distinguished himself in boat attacks on the Arabs : commanded other vessels at Bombay : Master Attendant and Captain of the Port, 1855 : died of cholera at Colaba, Bombay, after 32 years' service, April 29, 1857.

MOOKERJI, ASUTOSH (1865–   )

Born 1865 : educated at the Presidency College, Calcutta : graduated M.A. in Mathematics, 1855 : Premchand Roychand Scholar, 1886 : practised on the Appellate Side of the Calcutta High Court, from August, 1888 : Fellow of the Calcutta University, 1889 : D.L. in 1894 : elected representative of the Calcutta University to the Bengal Legislative Council, 1899 and 1901 : of the Calcutta Corporation, 1903 : elected, in 1903, representative to the Governor-General's Legislative Council of the non-official members of the Bengal Legislative Council : Tagore Law-Lecturer on Perpetuities in British India, 1898 : Acting Judge of the Calcutta High Court, 1904 : wrote, in 1892, a work on *Conic Sections* : F.R.A.S. and F.R.S.E.

MOOR, EDWARD (1771–1848)

Major : born 1771 : went out to India in 1782 : reached Madras, 1783 : served with the Mahratta Army against Tippoo, 1790–1, at Dharwar, Doridrug, Gadjnur :

wrote, 1794, an account of the operations : officiated as Q.M.G : garrison storekeeper, i.e. Commissary-General, at Bombay, 1799–1805 : retired in 1805 : compiled the military orders and regulations : Member of the Asiatic Society of Bengal, 1796 : F.R.S., 1806 : F.S.A., 1818 : original member of the Royal Asiatic Society, which he helped to found : member of other learned societies : published his *Hindu Pantheon*, 1810 : wrote *Hindu Infanticide*, 1811 ; *Oriental Fragments*, 1834 : and on India in a Cyclopædia : died Feb. 26, 1848.

MOORCROFT, WILLIAM (1765 ?–1825)

Born about 1765 : educated at 'Liverpool as a surgeon : studied veterinary science in France : made a fortune by his veterinary practice in London, but lost it over patents : appointed, in 1808, veterinary surgeon to the Bengal Army and Inspector of military studs : in 1811–2 crossed the Himalaya and traced the sources of the Satlaj and Indus : in 1819 went to Lahore, Ladak, residing at Leh, to Kashmir, *viâ* Attock and Peshawar to Kabul, to Bokhara, disposing of his merchandise : commenced his return journey, Aug. 1825 : soon after died at Andkhui, and was buried at Balkh : wrote on veterinary subjects and on the countries which he visited : his *Travels in the Himalayan Provinces of Hindustan and the Panjab*, etc., edited by H. H. Wilson, 1841.

MOORE, SIR HENRY (1829–   )

Entered the Bombay Army, 1850, and became Lt-General, 1892 : was in the Persian war 1857 : Indian mutiny, 1858 : Abyssinian war, 1867–8 : Lushai expedition, 1871-2 : was Persian Interpreter to the C. in C. in India, Lord Napier of Magdala : in the Afghan war, 1878–9 : Egypt, 1882 : C.I.E., 1878 : C.B., 1879 : K.C.B., 1897.

MOORE, SIR WILLIAM JAMES (1828–1896)

Son of Edward Moore : entered the Bombay Medical Service, 1852 : served in the Persian war, 1856–7 : Residency Surgeon at various places in Rajputana from 1862 : Deputy-Surgeon-General, Bombay, 1877 : Surgeon-General, 1885 : retired, 1888 : K.C.I.E., 1888 : Hony. Physician to Queen Victoria : died Sep. 9, 1896.

MOORSOM, WILLIAM ROBERT
(1834-1858)

Son of Captain William Scarth Moorsom: joined the 52nd Light Infantry, 1852: when the mutiny broke out he returned from Ceylon : was A.D.C. and D.A.Q.M.G. to Havelock at the relief of Lucknow : his skilful plans greatly helped the advance of the Generals and their forces : killed at Lucknow on March 24, 1858.

MORADABAD, RAJA JAI KISHAN DAS, BAHADUR OF (1832-1905)

He belonged to a family of Chaube Brahmans : his brother, Ghanshiam Das, had been a *tahsildar* at Hatras, but retired before the mutiny, being blind and paralysed : in spite of his infirmities, he rendered valuable assistance to Government in 1857, but was surprised and slain by the rebels at Khasganj. He had been loyally supported by his brothers, Jai Kishan Das and Mohan Lal : Jai Kishan was made Raja in 1860, given a *khilat* and lands assessed on favourable terms : he served for several years as a Deputy Collector : Fellow of the Allahabad University : C.S.I. in 1870 : active supporter of the Countess of Dufferin's Fund : died 1905.

MOREHEAD, CHARLES (1807-1882)

Son of Rev. Robert Morehead D.D.: brother of W. A. Morehead (*q.v.*) : born in 1807 : M.D. of Cambridge : entered the Bombay Medical Service in 1829 : was on the Staff of Sir Robert Grant, Governor of Bombay, 1835-8 : was President of the Medical and Physical Society, Bombay, 1835-59 : Surgeon of the General Hospital, 1838 : in 1845 the Grant Medical College was erected at his instance, and he was the first Principal and Professor of Medicine : he also initiated native medical education in the Bombay Presidency, as Secretary to the Board of Native Education, 1840-5 : and was the first physician of the Jamsetji Jijibhai Hospital, till 1859 : Hony. Surgeon to Queen Victoria : retired in 1862 : F.R.S. of Edinburgh : C.I.E., 1881 : author of various medical works relating to India : died Aug. 24, 1882.

MOREHEAD, WILLIAM AMBROSE
(1805-1863)

Of the I.C.S. : son of Rev. R. Morehead, D.D. : and brother of Dr. C. More-head (*q.v.*) : born 1805 : arrived at Madras, 1825 : dealt well and strongly with a native outbreak connected with the murder of Macdonald of the Civil Service at Cuddapah in 1832 : was made a Judge of the *Sadr* Court in 1846, and in 1850 was deputed to hold an inquiry in Ceylon relating to Lord Torrington's administration : while Member of Council, Madras, from 1857 to 1862, he acted twice as Governor, for a month in 1860 on Sir C. E. Trevelyan's recall, and for 6 months in 1860-61 after Sir H. G. Ward's death. He was Vice-Chancellor of the Madras University. But for ill-health he might have been a Member of the Governor-General's Supreme Council in 1862 : retired in Oct. 1862 : died at Edinburgh, his native city, Dec. 1, 1863.

MORE-MOLYNEUX, GEORGE HAND
(1851-1903)

Born May 6, 1851 : son of Lt-Colonel A. More-Molyneux : educated at Bedford : joined the Army, 1870, and became Colonel, 1894 : passed the Staff College, 1884 : in the Afghan war 1878-80, commanded the Jezailchi Corps—now the Khyber Rifles : Soudan expedition, 1885, as D.A.Q.M.G.: Burma expedition, 1885-9, as D.A.A.G., Brevet-Lt-Colonel : Tirah campaign, 1897-8, as A.Q.M.G. : D.S.O. : Military Attaché, Russia, 1890-2 : commanded 1st Bengal Infantry, 1892-93 : A.Q.M.G., India, 1893-8 : Brig-General commanding Bundelkund, 1898-01, and Rohilkund District since 1901 : C.B., 1900 : died Nov. 21, 1903 : Maj-General.

MORGAN, SIR WALTER (1821-   )

Son of W. Morgan : educated at King's College, London : called to the bar at the Middle Temple, 1844 : an advocate of the Supreme Court, Calcutta, 1851 : Clerk to the Legislative Council of India, 1854-9 : Master in Equity of the Supreme Court, Calcutta, 1859-62 : Puisne Judge, Calcutta High Court, 1862-6 : Chief Justice of the High Court, N.W.P., 1866-71 : knighted : Chief Justice, Madras, 1871-9.

MORLAND, SIR HENRY (1837-1891)

Born April 9, 1837 : son of John Morland : educated at Haversham and Bromsgrove, and privately : joined the Indian Navy, 1852 : served on the coasts of Africa, Arabia, at Perim, Jeddah, off

Kattiawar : transferred to the Indian Marine, 1863 : Captain, 1877 : Transport Officer at Bombay, 1865–79 : despatched the Abyssinian expedition, 1867 : Conservator of the Port, and temporarily Secretary of the Port Trust : concerned with the Commissariat and Transport of the Afghan war, 1878–80 : Chairman of the Bombay Corporation in 1886–7 : took to England the Jubilee address, 1887 : knighted : died at Bombay, July 28, 1891 : an ardent freemason : from 1874 Grandmaster of all Scottish freemasonry in India : fellow of the University, and of learned Societies at Bombay.

MORLEY, WILLIAM HOOK
(1815–1860)

Born about 1815 : son of George Morley, of the Inner Temple : educated for the legal profession : called to the bar in 1840 : a notable Oriental scholar, well versed in Arabic and Persian literature : member of the Royal Asiatic Society from 1847 : Librarian to the Society from 1859 : wrote on Indian Law : on the *Muhammadan Law prevalent fn India*, and other important works : author of *Coins of the Atabak Princes of Syria and Asia Minor* : compiler of the Catalogue of Arabic and Persian MSS. in the Library of the Royal Asiatic Society : died May 21, 1860.

MORRIS, HENRY (1829–   )

I.C.S. : born April 22, 1829 : son of John Carnac Morris, M.C.S. (*q.v.*) : educated at Rugby and Haileybury, 1846–8 : in India, 1848–75, in the Madras C.S. : rose to be Judge of Godavery : was for a year Inspector of Schools : wrote a History of India, 1856, and a History of England, 1858 ; *History of the Godavery District*, 1878 ; a simplified Telugu grammar, 1890 ; *Anglo-Indian Worthies*, 1891 ; *Brief Lives of Governors-General of India*, 1894 and 1896 ; *Founders of the Bible Society*, 1895 ; *Life of Charles Grant*, 1904.

MORRIS, JOHN CARNAC (1798–1858)

I.C.S. : son of John Morris, Bombay Civil Service : born Oct. 16, 1798 : Midshipman R.N., 1813–5 : was at Haileybury, 1815–7 : to India in the Madras Civil Service, 1818 : had paralysis in 1823 : Telugu Translator, 1832 : Accountant-General, 1839 : established the Madras Government Bank, 1834, and was Super-

intendent, 1835 : compiled Telugu dictionaries, selections and other works : edited the Madras *Journal of Literature and Science* : F.R.S. : a keen freemason : retired in 1846 : embarked in commercial enterprise : Chairman of a Bank which was wound up in 1858 : he died in Jersey on Aug. 2, 1858.

MORRIS, SIR JOHN HENRY (1828–   )

I.C.S. : born April 9, 1828 : son of Henry Morris, M.C.S. : educated at Haileybury : entered the Bengal Civil Service, 1848 : served in the Panjab, 1849–59 : N.W.P., 1861–3 : Central Provinces, 1863–8 : Chief Commissioner of the Central Provinces, 1867–83 : Officially described in 1883 as " an administrator of the first rank " : C.S.I., 1877 : K.C.S.I., 1883, when he retired.

MORRISON, JOHN (? – ?)

Soldier and adventurer in the second half of the 18th century : at first in the E. I. Co.'s service : arrived in Bengal, 1768, as a Major in the Company's forces. In 1769 the idea came to him of re-establishing Shah Alam on his throne : about two years after resigned his post under the Company, 1771 : about 1772 he entered Shah Alam's service, and received from him the titles of " General and C. in C. of the Great Mogul's forces," and " Ambassador Extraordinary and Plenipotentiary " to George III : went to England, empowered by the Great Mogul to lay before Government his proposal to invest the King of England with the absolute sovereignty of the Kingdom of Bengal, and the provinces of Bihar and Orissa, in exchange for a body of British troops to defend his throne at Delhi : to press home this scheme, Morrison wrote his Tract on *The Advantages of an Alliance with the Great Mogul*, published in 1774.

MORSE, NICHOLAS (1700–1772)

Governor of Fort St. George, Madras, at the time of its capture by La Bourdonnais in 1746 : was a descendant of Oliver Cromwell, through the Protector's daughter Bridget, who married Ireton : he befriended Clive on the latter's arrival at Madras and allowed him to use his library : died 1772.

MORTON, SIR GERALD DE COURCY
(1845-)

Born Feb. 7, 1845 : Maj-General : son of T. C. Morton : educated at Eton and Sandhurst : entered the Army, 1863 : A.D.C. and Private Secretary to Lieutenant-Governor of the Panjab, 1871-77 : in the Afghan war, 1878-80, as Brigade Major in the Kabul Field Force, and in the Kabul-Kandahar march and battle of Kandahar : A.A.G., Oudh and India, 1883-9 : commanded 1st Batt. Munster Fusiliers, 1889-91 : Brig-General in Bundelkund, 1891-5 : Adjutant-General, India, 1895-8 : commanded Lahore District, 1898-02 : commanding Dublin District since 1902 : C.B., 1893 : K.C.I.E., 1899 : C.V.O., 1903.

MOUAT, FREDERIC JOHN (1816-1897)

Son of Surgeon James Mouat : born 1816 : educated at University College, London, Paris, and Edinburgh University: M.D., 1839 : LL.D., 1886 : F.R.C.S., 1844 : served in India as Local Government Inspector and Deputy Inspr-General, Bengal Army : Inspr-General of Prisons in Bengal for many years : Professor of Chemistry and Materia Medica : Chemical Examiner to Government : Professor of Medicine and Medical Jurisprudence : first Physician of the Medical College, Calcutta : Secretary of the Council of Education, Bengal : Fellow, Calcutta University : J.P. : President Royal Statistical Society, 1890-2 : F.R.G.S. : Fellow of the Society of Arts : wrote a number of medical works with Hindustani versions of some : papers in scientific Journals, on prisons and questions connected therewith, hospitals, medical statistics, the *Origin and Progress of Universities in India*, 1888 : died Jan. 12, 1897.

MOUNTAIN, ARMINE SIMCOE HENRY
(1797-1854)

Born Feb. 4, 1797 : son of the Right Rev. Jacob Mountain, Bishop of Quebec : joined the 96th regt. in 1815 : served in Nova Scotia : went to India in 1829 in the 26th Cameronians : to Madras : Military Secretary to Sir Colin Halkett, C. in C. at Bombay, 1832-4 : A.D.C. to Lord W. Bentinck, when Governor-General : D.A.G. to the Indian forces in the China war, 1840-2 : in all the chief engagements : wounded at Chefoo : C.B. : A.D.C. to Queen Victoria : Military Secretary to Lord Dalhousie, when Governor-General, Jan. to Oct. 1848 : Brig-General in the Panjab campaign : commanded a Brigade at Chilianwala and Gujarat, and the Bengal Division in the pursuit of the Sikhs : Adjutant-General, 1849, under Sir C. Napier and Sir W. Gomm : died at Fatehghar, Feb. 8, 1854 : there is a tablet to his memory in the church at Simla.

MOZUMDAR, PRATAP CHANDRA
(1840-1905)

Born Oct. 1840 : educated at the Hare School and the Hughli and Hindu and Presidency Colleges : became a Brahmo by signing the covenant in 1859 : served for a time in a bank : became Assistant Secretary of the Brahmo Samaj, and editor of the *Tatwa Bodhini Patrika*, the Brahmo paper : some time in 1869 edited the *Indian Mirror* ; made missionary journeys throughout India, from 1870 : in 1874 went to England : in 1883 revisited it and extended his journey to America : in 1899 was present as a representative of the Indian Brahmo Samaj at the Parliament of Religions held at Chicago : wrote *The Faith and Progress of the Brahmo Samaj*, *Life and Teachings of Keshab Chandra Sen*, *The Oriental Christ*, *The Spirit of God* and *Heart-beats* : was, after Keshab Chandra's death, the principal leader and exponent of the Brahmo Samaj until his death, May 27, 1905.

MUDALIAR, PANDI RUNGANADA
(1847-1893)

Son of Subbaraya Mudaliar, who held the appointments of Manager of the Irrigation Department and Head Accountant of the Madras Railway, and was a fair English scholar : was educated at home until 1860, when he went to Pachaiyappa's school. In 1862 he joined the Presidency College. In mathematics, in English, in philosophy and in Tamil he surpassed all the other pupils. After passing his B.A. degree he was appointed Assistant Master in the Presidency College, and remained a Teacher or Professor till the end of his life. In 1872 he was appointed Fellow of the University. As Tamil Translator to Government, as Sheriff of Madras, and as a member of the Madras

Municipality he did good and useful work. He died Dec. 10, 1893. He was a particularly outspoken man, and never scrupled to point out his countrymen's defects.

MUDALIAR, RAMASAWMY (1852-1892)

Son of a landowner in the Salem district (Madras): educated at the Madras High School and Pachaiyappa's, afterwards at the newly formed Presidency College: B.A. in 1871, M.A. in 1873, and B.L. in 1875: became a Vakil of the High Court in 1876, and practised at Salem: became a District Munsif, but resigned in 1882, and practised in the High Court: editor of the *Law Journal*, which he established: Examiner for the B.L. and M.L. degrees, and a Fellow of the Madras University: visited England as delegate for the redress of the people's grievances in 1885: a prominent member of the National Congress and a member of the Public Service Commission in 1886.

MUHAMMAD AKBAR SHAH II.
(1760-1837)

King of Delhi: son of Shah Alam (*q.v.*): born April 23, 1760: succeeded his father as King, Nov. 19, 1806: received an increase to his allowance from the British: only a titular King without power: died Sep. 28, 1837.

MUHAMMAD ASLAM KHAN (? –)

Served in the Indian mutiny: appointed to command the Jezailchis, 1881: assisted in forming the Khyber Rifles and appointed to command them, 1897: Political Officer in the Tirah expedition, 1897-8: retired on pension with title of Nawab and Sirdar Bahadur after 41 years' service, 1898: C.I.E., 1887: guest of the nation at the Coronation, 1902: A.D.C. to H.M. the King, 1902.

MUHAMMAD AZIMULLA KHAN
(? – ?)

He was found with his mother during the famine of 1837-38, and sustained by charity: educated in the Cawnpur Free School, receiving a subsistence allowance, and there, after ten years' study, became a teacher: two years later he was made a clerk to Brig-General Scott and afterwards to Brig-General Ashburnham: subsequently he attached himself to Nana Sahib (*q.v.*) and was sent in 1853 to

England to plead the cause of his master before the Court of Directors. He resided in England for two years, made many acquaintances and gathered information on European affairs: went to the Crimea and visited the camp before Sebastopol. In the mutiny, in June, 1857, Azimulla advised the Nana, then marching on Delhi, to return to Cawnpur: he arranged the capitulation of the defenders of Cawnpur: instigated, and was present at the massacre of June 27, at the Ghat: fled with Nana Sahib to Nipal on the approach of the English troops, and was not seen again.

MUHAMMAD BAHADUR SHAH
(? –1862)

King of Delhi: Abu Zaffar: son of the Emperor Akbar Shah: assumed the title of Bahadur Shah, on succeeding as Emperor at Delhi, on Sep. 28, 1837, at the age of about 60: Lord Dalhousie proposed to remove him from the Palace at Delhi and received permission of the Home Government to do so, but deferred action. At the beginning of the mutiny he was old and helpless: surrendered to Captain Hodson (*q.v.*) on Sep. 21, 1857, after the capture of Delhi by the English: was brought to trial, Jan. 29 to March 9, 1858, on four main charges, including mutiny, rebellion, abetment of murder, and sentenced to transportation for life: was sent to Rangoon, and died there, 1862.

MUHAMMAD HAYAT KHAN, NAWAB
(? –1901)

Joined the Panjab Commission, 1862: accompanied Sir Frederick Roberts in the Afghan war, 1879-80, as Political Officer: Member of Council in Kashmir: and of the Panjab Legislative Council: Divisional Judge at Multan: retired 2 or 3 years before his death in June, 1901: C.S.I.: wrote a *History of Afghanistan*, 1867.

MUHAMMAD MAHMUD, SYAD
(1850-1903)

Born at Delhi, 1850: son of Sir Syad Ahmad (*q.v.*): educated at Delhi, Queen's College, Benares, and Christ's College, Cambridge: studied a number of languages, Oriental, European, classical: called to the bar at Lincoln's Inn, 1872: practised in the High Court, Allahabad: made a District Judge at Rai Bareli in

Oudh, 1879 : member of the Education Commission, 1882 : acted as a Puisne Judge of the High Court, N.W.P., 1882, '84, '86, '87 : confirmed May 9, 1887 : retired, Nov. 1893 : helped his father at the M.A.O. College, Alighar : from 1898, successively, Hon. Secy., President, and Visitor of the College : author of *Law of Evidence in British India*, in Hindustani : and edited Muhammadan law books in Arabic : published a History of Education in India : began a History of Islam : gave much attention to philosophy, theology, law and education : died May 8, 1903.

MUHAMMAD REZA KHAN
(? –1785 ?)

Son-in-law of Rabia Begam : when Mir Jafar was Nawab Nazim of Bengal for the second time, he was Governor of Dacca, but Nuncomar's influence with the Nawab led to his dismissal from the Governorship of Dacca, and he was brought as a prisoner to Murshidabad. On the downfall of Nuncomar, Clive appointed Reza Khan to be Deputy to Nawab Najm-ud-daula : next he was sent by Clive to Azimabad (Patna) as Governor to recover sums due to Government : he was then made Deputy Nazim by the English when they obtained the *Diwani* of Bengal, Bihar and Orissa : in 1772 he was charged by Warren Hastings with misappropriation of revenue and brought to Calcutta for trial, but was acquitted : then joined the party of General Clavering, who procured for him the post of Deputy to Nawab Mubarak-ud-daula, and the Faujdari of Murshidabad, but, soon after General Clavering's death, he lost power and was dismissed : in 1780 he was in power for the third time as " General Faujdar " : died about 1785 at Murshidabad.

MUIR, CHARLES WEMYSS (1850–   )

Born 1850 : son of Sir W. Muir (*q.v.*) : educated at Rugby and Sandhurst : entered the Army, 1869, and the Staff Corps and became Lt-Colonel, 1895 : was A.D.C. to the Viceroy for some years : served in the Afghan war, 1880 : Soudan, 1885 : Burma war, 1885–7 : Tirah expedition, 1897–8 : C.I.E., 1887 : C.B., 1902.

MUIR, JOHN (1810–1882)

I.C.S. : son of William Muir of Glasgow : born Feb. 5, 1810 : educated at Irvine, Glasgow University, and Haileybury : went to India in 1829 : served in the N.W.P. : Collector of Azimghar : in 1844 was Principal of the Victoria or Queen's College at Benares : Judge of Fatehpur : retired in 1854 : was made D.C.L. of Oxford in 1855 ; LL.D. of Edinburgh in 1861 ; C.I.E. in 1878 : Doctor of Philosophy of Bonn : and member of learned Foreign Societies. He commenced the study of Sanskrit early in his Indian career : founded, in 1862, a professorship of Sanskrit and Comparative Philology at Edinburgh University. He wrote, both in India and England, a number of Sanskrit works, on Indian history, biography and religious subjects, and *Original Sanskrit Texts on the Origin and History of the People of India*, 5 vols. : he specially studied the Vedas, and contributed articles on India to the *Indian Antiquary*, the Bengal Asiatic Society's and Royal Asiatic Society's Journals : died March 7, 1882.

MUIR, SIR JOHN, BARONET
(1828–1903)

Merchant : born Dec. 8, 1828 : head of the firm of Finlay Muir & Co., Bombay, Karachi and Calcutta : and of James Finlay & Co., E.I. merchants : practically controlled the largest area under tea of any Company : Lord Provost of Glasgow, 1890–2 : made a Baronet, 1892 : died Aug. 6, 1903.

MUIR, SIR WILLIAM (1819–1905)

I.C.S. : born April 27, 1819 : son of William Muir : educated at Kilmarnock, Edinburgh, and Glasgow Universities, and Haileybury : entered the Bengal Civil Service, 1837 : Secy. to the N.W.P. Government, 1852 : Member of the Board of Revenue, N.W.P., 1856 : during the mutiny was in charge of the Intelligence Department, Agra : Member of the Governor-General's Legislative Council, 1864 : Secretary to the Government of India, in the Foreign Department, 1865 : Member of the Supreme Council, 1868 : Lieutenant-Governor, N.W.P., 1868–74 : Finance Minister in the Supreme Council, 1874–6 : Member of the Council of India, 1876–85 : Principal and Vice-Chancellor,

Edinburgh University, 1885–02: Author of *Life of Mahomet, Annals of the early Caliphate, The Mameluke Dynasty, The Koran, etc.. The Muhammadan Controversy*: K.C.S.I., 1867: D.C.L., Oxford: LL.D. of Glasgow and Edinburgh: Ph.D. of Bologna: died July 11, 1905.

MUIR, SIR WILLIAM MURE
(1817–1885)

Educated at the University, Edinburgh. and St. George's Hospital, London: M.D., Edinburgh, 1840: Assistant Surgeon, 1842: Surgeon-General, 1873: served in the Mediterranean, Turkey, Crimea, Mauritius, India, China, N. America: in the mutiny, in 1857–8: P.M.O. in China, and of British troops in Bengal: head of Sanitary Branch of A.M.D.: Director-General of the A.M.D., 1874: introduced, in the face of opposition, many beneficial changes in the position and duties of Army Surgeons: obtained the Warrant of 1879, changing the old system of attaching medical officers to regiments: K.C.B.: died June 2, 1885.

MUKERJI, ANUKUL CHANDRA
1829–1871)

Born 1829: educated at the Hindu College: Senior Scholar: Nazir under the Magistrate of Howrah: passed the Law Examination, 1855, and became Pleader of the *Sadr* Court: Fellow of the Calcutta University, and Junior Government Pleader, 1868: Senior in 1870: and Member of the Bengal Legislative Council: Puisne Judge of the High Court, Calcutta, 1870: died Aug. 17, 1871. He is best remembered by the Memoir, dated June 1, 1873, of his life written by Mohindranath Mukerji, and dedicated to the Chief Justice of the day. It was a revelation of the capabilities of a half-educated Bengali author. Its first few lines will give some idea of the style :—
" Let me hold my *Penna* after a few months, to write the memoir of the individual above named : but *quid agis* ? if any one put me such a query, I will be utterly thrown into a great jeopardy and hurley-burley, and say—a fool of myself ! "

MUKERJI, BHUDEB (1825–1894)

Son of Pandit Bisva Nath Tarkabhusan : born March 25, 1825, in a family distin-

guished for generations for its Sanskrit culture and strict Brahmanical tenets : educated at the Sanskrit and Hindu Colleges : after holding some minor scholastic appointments, became Assistant Inspector in the higher educational service : C.I.E. in 1877 : appointed in 1882 to the Bengal Legislative Council, and a Member of the Education Commission : had a great reputation as an educationist, was proprietor of the *Education Gazette*, and made a valuable endowment for the promotion of Sanskrit learning : he retired in July, 1883 : he wrote extensively on a great variety of subjects : an orthodox Hindu, he had read widely and held liberal views on many social matters : he died May 16, 1894.

MUKERJI, RAJA DAKHINARANJAN
(1814–1878)

Born Oct. 1814 : son of Jagamohan Mukerji : grandson of Babu Surji Kumar Tagore, of Calcutta : educated at the Hindu College : was a linguist : practised as a Vakil in the *Sadr* Court : joined in establishing the *Bengal Spectator*, an Anglo-Indian Periodical : was a member of the British Indian Association and a *zamindar* of the Jessore District : was Tax Collector of the Calcutta Municipality, and Diwan of the Nawab Nazim of Murshidabad : received, in 1859, the forfeited estate of Sankarpur in Rai Bareli, in Oudh, from Lord Canning, for mutiny services : the first Secretary of the Oudh Talukdars' Association : helped to establish the Canning College at Lucknow : made a Raja, 1871, for his philanthropy and patriotism : established a vernacular newspaper and purchased the *Luknow Times* as the organ of the Oudh Talukdars : gave some of the land and laboured zealously for the Bethune Female School : died July 11, 1878.

MUKERJI, HARISH CHANDRA (1824–1861)

Son of a high-caste Kulin Brahmin in poor circumstances, by the youngest of his seven wives : at 14 had to earn his livelihood by writing petitions, etc. : in 1848 obtained a post in the Military Auditor-General's office by competition, and gradually became Assistant Military Auditor : a great reader, he acquired a good knowledge of English, and took to literature : in 1855 became sole editor of the *Hindu Patriot* : in 1857 he upheld Lord Canning's "clemency" policy in a series of articles, which attracted the Viceroy's notice : he espoused, in 1860, the cause of the raiyats against the indigo planters, and so incensed the latter that they instituted civil and criminal proceedings against him, and after his death sold up his property : he was the first native journalist of any note in India : the British Indian Association built a library in his memory : died June 14, 1861.

MUKERJI, JOY KISHEN (1808–1888)

Born in 1808 : his father was "banian" to H.M.'s 14th regt. : he was educated in the regimental school, and, as a clerk, accompanied the regiment to the siege of Bhartpur, 1825–6, and shared in the prize-money : became (1830) record keeper in the Hughli collectorate : acquired large landed estates : established a College at his native town, Uttapara, and a Public Library : helped to found the British Indian Association. He was convicted and sentenced for forgery on March 31, 1862 : the Privy Council on his appeal were unable to interfere, but expressed such a strong opinion of his innocence that he was at once released by order of Government. At the age of 70 he lost his eyesight, but retained his interest in public affairs and his position as a leading *zamindar* in Bengal. He was father of Raja Piari Mohan Mukerji, C.S.I. (*q.v.*). He died in July, 1888.

MUKERJI, RAO BAHADUR KANTI CHANDRA (1835–1901)

Educated at the Free Church Institution, Chinsura : taught in his village in the 24 *Parganas*, and at Jonai, Hughli : appointed Principal of the College at Jaipur, Rajputana : attended the Maharaja's *darbar* and appointed Member of his Council : became the foremost man in Jaipur, and Prime Minister to successive Maharajas : received a *jagir* and became a noble of the State : organized the Jaipur Transport Corps for Imperial Service : helped the Maharaja to initiate the Famine Trust Fund : the Jaipur State greatly prospered under his management : made Rao Bahadur and C.I.E. for

his services : member of the Famine Commission, 1899 : died at Nagpur, 1901.

MUKERJI, RAJA PIARI MOHAN
(1840–   )

Son of Joy Kishen Mukerji (*q.v.*) : born Sep. 17, 1840 : took his degree of M.A. at the Calcutta University, 1864, and B.L., 1865 : Member of the Bengal Legislative Council, 1879, and of the Governor-General's Legislative Council in 1884 and 1886, and took a prominent part, showing great ability, in the discussions on the Bengal Tenancy Bill. He was Honorary Secretary of the British Indian Association and President subsequently. He was made C.S.I. and Raja on Feb. 16, 1877, in recognition of his own, and his father's, distinguished public services.

MUKERJI, SAMBHU CHANDRA
(1839–1894)

Born May 8, 1839 : son of Mathur Mohan Mukerji : educated at the Oriental Seminary and the Hindu Metropolitan College : became sub-editor of the *Hindu Patriot* in 1858, and during the ill-health of its editor, Harish Chandra Mukerji, who died, 1861, was virtually the editor, and for a time was sole editor : M.D. of an American University : in 1862 was appointed editor of the *Samachar Hindustani* and Assistant Secretary to the Talukdars' Association at Lucknow : in 1864, Diwan to the Nawab Nizam at Murshidabad : in 1868 became Secretary to Maharaj Seoraj Singh of Kashipur : in 1869 was at Rampur a short time as the Nawab's Secretary : from 1872 he conducted *Mukerji's Magazine* up to 1876 : in 1877, was Minister to the Maharaja of Tippera : in 1882 founded the Calcutta journal, *Reis and Rayyet :* wrote well and clearly and carried weight in public discussions : in 1888 became well known to Lord Dufferin, then Viceroy : in 1890 was made a Fellow of the Calcutta University, in recognition of his journalistic work : died Feb. 7, 1894. In 1857 he wrote *On the Causes of the Mutiny :* in 1860, *Mr. Wilson, Lord Canning and the Income Tax ;* in 1869, *The Career of an Indian Princess ;* in 1872, *The Prince in India and to India ;* in 1875, *The Empire is Peace* and *the Baroda Coup d'Etat ;* in 1887 a book of Travels in Bengal.

x

MULJI, DAMODAR THACKERSI
(1847–1893)

A member of the Bhatia caste : born at Verawal in Kattiawar. His father migrated to Bombay. At the age of 14 he joined his father in business and, in 1864, was placed in sole charge during his father's absence from Bombay. He studied English in his leisure hours, and went on an extensive tour through India. He built a piece-goods market and several cotton mills in Bombay, representing a capital of £400,000 and giving employment to 5,000 hands. He agitated effectively for the passing of the Merchandise Marks Act. He was a zealous Member of the Municipal Corporation from 1884 to the time of his death, a steady supporter of the Indian National Congress, and played a conspicuous part in all public movements. He gave away large sums to charities. He died in Oct. 1893.

MULJI, KURSENDAS (1832–1875)

Born July 25, 1832 : member of the Bhatia caste of traders : educated at the Elphinstone Institution, but offended his aunt, with whom he lived, by writing an essay in favour of the re-marriage of Hindu widows, and was turned out of the house when 21 years of age : became Headmaster of the Gokuldas Tejpal Seminary : started a weekly paper called the *Satya Prakash* : wrote against the high priests of the Vallabhacharya, and exposed the immoralities of the Maharajas, or priests, of the Bhatias and Banias : he was sued, in 1862, for libel, but the verdict was in his favour. At the time of the cotton mania, Kursendas joined a commercial firm and visited England to do business, but returned in 1874, having been unsuccessful : published a volume of his travels. He was appointed Administrator of a Native State, but only lived there for a year : died in Aug. 1875.

MULL, MATHIAS (? –1886)

Printer : went out to Bombay about 1850–5, to take charge as manager of the Bombay Education Society's (official) Press : became manager (with his relative, Craig) of the local *Standard and Telegraph* newspaper, and afterwards of the *Bombay Gazette* ; subsequently of the *Times of India*, as part proprietor with the late Robert Knight, holding this position until 1873 : returned home 1879 : after his retirement, Mull, who was a thoroughly skilled typographer and a Milton enthusiast, published a revised edition of *Paradise Lost*, correcting, according to his view, the punctuation throughout, also some few readings of the existing text : he afterwards essayed the more formidable task of revising the punctuation, besides criticizing and readjusting the many doubtful passages, in *Macbeth* and some other Shakespearian dramas : he had a good knowledge of musical science and the construction of organs : he died at home in or about 1886.

MULLER, FRIEDRICH MAX
(1823–1900)

Son of Wilhelm Müller : born Dec. 6, 1823, at Dessau : educated at Leipzig from 1841 : Ph.D., 1843 : translated the *Hitopadesa*, 1843 : studied under Bopp and Schelling at Berlin, and under Burnouf at Paris : came to England, 1846 : commissioned by the Directors of the E. I. Co. to edit the Sanskrit classic, the Rigveda, with Sayana's commentary : lived at Oxford from 1848 : Deputy, and, in 1854, substantive Taylorian Professor of European Languages : Curator of the Bodleian, 1856 : Fellow of All Souls', 1858 : wrote *History of Ancient Sanskrit Literature*, 1859 : failed to obtain the Sanskrit Professorship at Oxford, 1860 : wrote *The Science of Languages* and other works on languages : first Professor of Comparative Philology from 1868 : made researches in comparative mythology and the comparative study of religions : wrote on the *Science of Religion :* his Hibbert lectures on *The Origin and Growth of Religion*, 1878 : edited, from 1875, the series of " Sacred Books of the East," 51 volumes of translations of Oriental religious works : wrote *India, what can it teach us ?* 1883 : brought out Sanskrit works and lectures, and helped Sanskrit scholars : literary adviser to Oxford University on Indian subjects, 1877–98 : wrote *Chips from a German Workshop* and *Auld Lang Syne :* also on philosophy : Privy Councillor, and received many honours from Governments, Universities ; and learned bodies : a leading member in Oriental congresses, and President of the International Congress of Orientalists, 1892 : distinguished also for his great literary and social qualities : his works have been classified under several heads of the languages, and sciences, etc., with which he dealt: he died at Oxford, Oct. 28, 1900: a fund was raised to perpetuate his memory at Oxford by providing for the promotion of Oriental learning and research.

MUNK, SALOMON (1802–1867)

Born at Gross-Glogau, in Prussian Silesia, May 2, 1802 : of Jewish parentage, the son of a poor servant of the Synagogue : educated at the Rabbinical School of his town, afterwards at Berlin : in spite of great poverty, made his way at the latter University : went on to study Oriental languages at Bonn under Schlegel, Lassen, etc. : being, as a Jew, debarred from lecturing in a Prussian University, he removed to Paris in 1828, where he worked at Sanskrit, etc. : attached to the Bibliothèque Impériale from 1838 : in 1840, travelled in Egypt : engaged in cataloguing Oriental MSS. for the Library until attacked by blindness in 1847 : bore the affliction bravely, even continuing to write, and accepting the appointment of Professor of Hebrew at the Collège de France : died in Paris, Feb. 6, 1867. Though chiefly known as a Hebrew and Arabic scholar, he also wrote on Indian subjects, as : " Fragments de littérature Sanskrite," in the *Temps*, 1836 : *Mahabharata*, 1838 : a member of the Académie des Inscriptions.

MUNRO, SIR HECTOR (1726–1805)

Born 1726 : son of Hugh Munro : was Ensign in the 48th regt. in 1749 : commanded the 89th regt. out to Bombay in 1761 : suppressed a mutiny of sepoys at Patna in 1764 : won the decisive battle of Baxar, Oct. 23, 1764, defeating the Nawab Wazir of Oudh, Shuja-ud-daula, and Mir Kasim : Lt-Colonel, 1765 : M.P. for the Inverness burghs, 1768–1801 : commanded the Madras Army, 1778 : took Pondicherry from the French, 1778 : K.B., 1779 : engaged in the field against Hyder Ali, 1780–1 : commanded a Division in Sir Eyre Coote's victory at Porto Novo, July 1, 1781 : captured Negapatam, Nov. 1781 : returned to England : Maj-General, 1782 : General, 1798 : died at Novar, Dec. 27, 1805.

MUNRO, SIR THOMAS, BARONET (1761–1827)

Maj-General and Governor : son of

Alexander Munro, of Glasgow : born May 27, 1761 : educated at Glasgow : entered the mercantile profession, but left it and joined the E. I. Co.'s Madras Army in 1780 : was in the Mysore war of 1780–3 under Sir Hector Munro and Sir Eyre Coote : in 1788 in the Intelligence Department : in the actions under Lord Cornwallis : after 1792 served in the Baramahal under Capt. Read in the civil line : rejoined the Army in 1799, and after Seringapatam was appointed, with Capt. Malcolm, Joint Secretary to the Commissioners for the Settlement of Mysore : he next administered Canara on the Malabar coast and suppressed disorder : from 1800 to 1807 he ruled the ceded districts S. of the Tungabhadra, and elaborated the *ryotwar* system of land tenure : was in England, 1807–13 : was examined by the House of Commons regarding the renewal of the Company's charter, and on important questions connected with the civil and military administration in India : Colonel in 1813 : employed on a Commission for improving the judicial and police Departments. He returned to military service as Brig-General in the war of 1816–8 against the Pindaris and Mahrattas : made K.C.B. : he was appointed Governor of Madras in June, 1820, and assisted in the first Burmese war of 1824 : made a Baronet : his government of Madras was very successful, based as it was on his thorough knowledge of the country and languages, his ability and principles, power of work and firmness. His death was universally deplored : died of cholera while on tour at Puttaconda in the ceded districts, on July 6, 1827. His equestrian statue by Chantrey was erected at Madras.

MUNRO, WILLIAM (1818–1880)

Son of William Munro : born 1818 : entered the 39th foot, 1834 : with his regt. in India for many years : at Maharajpur, Dec. 29, 1843, severely wounded : in the Crimea, Canada, Bermuda : General, 1878 : died Jan. 29, 1880 : a learned botanist, was an authority on grasses : wrote papers in Journals of learned Societies, on bamboos, antidotes to snake-bites, timber trees of Bengal, grasses, etc.

MUNSTER, GEORGE AUGUSTUS FREDERICK FITZCLARENCE, FIRST EARL OF (1794–1842)

Eldest son of the Duke of Clarence, afterwards William IV, by Mrs. Jordan : born in 1794 : educated at Sunbury and Marlow : entered the Army in 1807 : was in the Peninsula, 1808–14 : went to India in 1815 in the 24th Light Dragoons : was A.D.C. to Lord Hastings when Governor-General, in the Mahratta war of 1816–7 : was sent home overland, from Bombay, up the Red Sea, and through Egypt, with the duplicate despatches, announcing peace : was at the defeat of the Pindaris at Jabalpur : left Bombay on Feb. 7, and reached England *viâ* Egypt on June 16, 1818 : wrote a narrative of his journey, 1819 : made a Peer in 1830 : Lieutenant of the Tower and Maj-General, 1841 : he steadily supported Oriental studies : was, in 1841, President of the Royal Asiatic Society, and of the Society for the Publication of Oriental texts, and Vice-President of the Oriental Translation Fund : and contemplated a *History of the Art of War among Eastern Nations*, for which he collected a large mass of materials : he died March 20, 1842.

MURDOCH, JOHN (1819–1904)

Educationist and philanthropist : born in 1819 : educated at the High School, Glasgow, and on the Continent : went to Ceylon in 1844 as Principal of the Government Normal School, Kandy, resigning it in 1849 : established the Singhalese Tract Society and became a " Literary Evangelist." After visiting Scotland in 1852 to obtain funds, he went to Madras as an agent of the United Presbyterian Church of Scotland : joined the Christian Vernacular Education Society, now the Christian Literature Society of India, on its formation in 1858, and for 46 years toiled for the good of the natives, travelling annually from Ceylon to Peshawar, reporting on their literary and educational needs, organizing supplies of vernacular and English literature for them, himself writing largely on moral and religious subjects. The Government frequently consulted him regarding vernacular literature. He was LL.D. of Glasgow, 1878 : a Fellow of the Madras University : in 1896 he received the silver, and in

1904 the gold, Kaisar-i-Hind medal. He also visited China, helping to found the Christian Literature Society there. He died at Madras, Aug. 10, 1904, universally esteemed.

MURPHY, ROBERT XAVIER (1803–1857)

Sir G. Birdwood, in a letter to the *Times*, states, of Murphy, that he went out to Bombay as a master under the Bombay Native Education Society : a classical scholar and· quick at acquiring Oriental languages : edited the *Bombay Gazette*, 1834 : acted, 1839, as Secretary to the Bombay Chamber of Commerce, and as Editor of the *Bombay Times* before Dr. G. Buist (*q.v.*): Oriental Translator to Government, 1852 : wrote largely on Oriental subjects, philological, literary, antiquarian, sociological, ethnographical, and the folk-lore of Bombay ; had a map of Bombay, town and island, prepared : wrote in the Journal of the Geographical Society, Bombay, and in the *Dublin University Magazine* : was the first to invent and apply the expression " Towers of Silence " to the places where the Parsis expose their dead : his health failed, and he was sent home, 1855 : died at Kingstown, Dublin, Feb. 26, 1857.

MURPHY, WILLIAM REED (1849–

Born Oct. 23, 1849 : educated at Kildare and Trinity College, Dublin : entered the Indian Medical Service, 1872 : was with the Indian contingent at Malta, and Cyprus, 1878 : in the Afghan war, 1878–80 : Hazara campaign, 1888 : Lushai expedition, 1888–9 : Chin-Lushai Field Force, 1889–90, as P.M.O.: D.S.O.: Chitral relief force, 1895 : Kuram-Kohat Force, 1897, as P.M.O.: Tirah Field Force, 1897–8 : Lt-Colonel.

MURRAY, SIR JOHN IRVINE (? –1902)

General : entered the Army, 1842 : in the Panjab campaign, 1848–9 : in the mutiny raised " Murray's Jat Horse," known as the 14th Bengal Lancers : served with it in numerous actions : kept the Alighar and Etah districts quiet : held the Rohilkund rebels in check : in the second Oudh campaign, and the operations on the Nipal frontier : in the Bhutan campaign, 1864–6 : C.B.: commanded the Lahore Division : K.C.B., 1895 : died May 20, 1902.

MURRAY, ROBERT HUNTER
(1847–)

Born Aug. 12, 1847 : son of John Murray : educated at Edinburgh University : entered the Army, 1867, and became Colonel, 1892 : in the Afghan war, 1878– 80 : in the march from Kabul to Kandahar, and battle of Kandahar : severely wounded : Egypt, 1882, as Brig-Major of Indian Contingent : Brevet-Lt-Colonel : Soudan campaign, 1885, and again 1898, severely wounded at Atbara : commanded Infantry Brigade, Aldershot, 1900–2 : commanding troops at Alexandria since 1902 : C.B., 1896.

MURSHIDABAD, SIR SYAD HASSAN ALI KHAN, NAWAB BAHADUR, OF (1846–)

Eldest son of the last titular Nawab Nazim, Nawab Syad Mansur Ali Khan Bahadur (*q.v.*) : born Aug. 25, 1846, and succeeded to the *masnad* on March 27, 1883 : he traces his descent from the Prophet and also from Ali, the Prophet's son-in-law. Educated under private tutors : in 1865 he was sent to England for some years for education. His father having resigned his position and titles on Nov. 1, 1880, the hereditary title of Nawab Bahadur was conferred on Syad Hassan Ali Khan on Feb. 17, 1882 : made K.C.I.E. and Amir-ul-Umra in 1887 and G.C.I.E. in 1890. By a legal document, he confirmed his father's act of resignation, and in return received a fixed hereditary position with a settled income, landed estates, the rank and dignity of Premier Noble in Bengal and the hereditary title of Amir-ul-Umra. He has always been most loyal to Government, liberal, hospitable, and widely charitable. Some years ago he was crippled by ill-health, and, in the earthquake of June 12, 1897, nearly lost his life.

MURSHIDABAD, MANSUR ALI FARIDUN JAH, NAWAB NAZIM OF (1829–1884)

The last Nawab Nazim of Bengal : born Oct. 1829 : succeeded his father, Humayun Jah, Dec. 19, 1888 : educated in English by General Showers and in the Oriental languages by Moulvi Abul Kasim : he

lost the honours and emoluments previously attached to the Murshidabad Nizamat : his salute of nineteen guns and his exemption from appearance in civil courts were taken away and his pension was greatly reduced : in Feb. 1869 he went to England to represent his grievances to the House of Commons, who rejected his appeal by a majority of 57 on July 4, 1871 : while he resided for some years in England, his affairs became greatly involved : a Commission was appointed to arrange with his creditors : on Nov. 1, 1880, he abdicated his position as Nawab Nazim of Bengal, Bihar and Orissa, by executing an indenture with Her Majesty's Secretary of State for India : his eldest son, Hassan Ali Mirza (*q.v.*), the present Nawab Bahadur of Murshidabad, inherited all his property : after staying in England twelve years, the ex-Nawab Nazim, Mansur Ali, returned to India in 1881, and died of cholera, Nov. 4, 1884.

MURTAZA HUSAIN BILGRAMI
(1720–1795–?)

Known as Shekh Allahyar Usmani, or Sani : employed, about 1729 to 1773, under various nobles of India, and shared in their engagements : introduced, about 1776, to Captain Jonathan Scott (*q.v.*), Persian Secretary to Warren Hastings : appointed one of his munshis : wrote the *Hadikat-ul-Akalim*, an admirable work, geographical and historical, exceedingly valuable for events of the writer's own period : died about 1795 : described by Sir H. M. Elliot (*q.v.*) as " the accurate Murtaza Husain."

MYLNE, RIGHT REV. LOUIS GEORGE, D.D. (1843–)

Born April 20, 1843 : son of Major Charles David Mylne, E. I. Co.'s Service : educated at Merchiston Castle School, Edinburgh, St. Andrew's University and Corpus Christi College, Oxford : Assistant Curate of North Moreton, Berks, 1867–70 : Tutor of Keble College, Oxford, 1870–6 : D.D., Oxford, 1876 : Bishop of Bombay, 1876–97 : Canon of Woodford and Wilsford in Salisbury Cathedral, 1900–5 : Rural Dean of Marlborough, 1897–05 : Rector of Alvechurch, Worcestershire, 1905 : author of *Sermons Preached in Bombay*, various *Charges and Sermons ;* articles in *Church Quarterly Review*, etc., etc.

MYSORE, MAHARAJA SIR CHAMA RAJENDRA WODYAR, OF (1863–1894)

Born in a branch of the ruling family of Mysore : his adoption by Maharaja Kristna Raj Wodyar (deposed 1831) in June, 1865, was eventually recognized by Government : and, on Kristna Raj's death on March 27, 1868, Chama Rajendra succeeded, was installed Sep. 23, 1868, and was invested with power at the age of 18 : he was carefully educated under a British officer as guardian and became an enlightened ruler, during whose reign the resources of the State were greatly developed : G.C.S.I. : died of diphtheria during his visit to Calcutta, Dec. 27, 1894.

MYSORE, KRISTNA RAJ WADIAR, MAHARAJA OF (1896–1868)

A descendant of the old Hindu reigning family of Mysore, who was restored to the throne when a child, after the death of Tippoo at the fall of Seringapatam, May 4, 1799 : in 1811 he dismissed his Diwan, the famous Purnia (q.v.), and assumed charge of the Government, which continually grew worse, until the people rebelled in 1830 and the British Government interposed and took over the administration on Oct. 3, 1831. The Maharaja's applications to be reinstated were never accepted : after adopting an heir, he died in 1868.

NABA KISHEN, MAHARAJA BAHADUR (1732 ?–1797)

Son of a Kayasth, Ram Charan : born about 1732 in the village of Gobindpur : while he was still young his father died : at 18 he was Persian munshi to Warren Hastings : he early entered the service of Lucki Kanta (alias Naku Dhur), banian of Lord Clive : subsequently became a munshi to Clive : in 1765 Clive procured from Shah Alam the title of Raja Bahadur for him, besides appointing him Political Diwan to the Company : in 1766 he was made Maharaja Bahadur and began to preside over Caste Tribunals : his appointments were continued under Warren Hastings, who, in 1780, appointed him manager of the Burdwan zamindari : died Nov. 22, 1797.

NABHA, RAJA SIR HIRA SINGH, MALWINDAR BAHADUR OF (1843–   )

Succeeded his father, 1871 : served in Afghan war, 1878–80 : Hon. Colonel in British Army : G.C.I.E., 1903 : G.C.S.I.

NAIRNE, SIR CHARLES EDWARD (1836–1899)

Born June 30, 1836 : son of Capt. Alexander Nairne : educated at Addiscombe : entered the Bengal Artillery, 1855 : was in the Indian mutiny : in the Yusafzai expedition, 1863 : commanded a battery in the Afghan war : in the Peshawar Field Force, 1879–80 : in Egypt in 1882, commanded the Horse Artillery at Kassassin and Tel-el-Kebir : C.B., 1882 : Commandant at Shoeburyness, 1884 : Inspr-General of Ordnance in India, 1887–92, and effected a remarkable improvement in Artillery shooting : Maj-General, 1890 : C. in C., Bombay, 1893 : Lt-General, 1895 : K.C.B., 1899 : acted as C. in C. in India, March to Nov. 1898 : died Feb. 19, 1899.

NANA, FARNAVIS (1741–1800)

The famous Mahratta Brahman minister: his real name was Balaji Janadhan : he was present at, and fled from, the battle of Panipat, 1761. When Madho Rao I became Peshwa in 1761, his uncle, the Regent, Raghunath Rao, gave Nana Farnavis the office of Fardnavisi (record-writing). He became the intimate friend of his sovereign, Madho Rao, who died in 1772, and was succeeded by his brother, Narayan Rao. Nana Farnavis became head of the Civil Department, and chief director of all Poona political movements until Madho Rao II died. Narayan Rao was murdered in 1773 by his uncle Raghunath, who usurped the Peshwaship, until Narayan's widow, Gunga Bai, had a child named Madho Rao Narayan. A Regency, consisting of Nana Farnavis, Sakaram Bapu, and the widow, ruled the State until Nana Farnavis became virtually supreme ruler of Poona. In March, 1776, the treaty of Purandhar was concluded between the Mahrattas and the English : this treaty Nana Farnavis obstructed, and he was believed to have made a secret engagement with the French. He and Sakaram quarrelled : the latter, striving for the restoration of

Raghunath, sought help from the Bombay Government : Nana Farnavis, being the paramour of Gunga Bai, supported Madho Rao the Peshwa : further hostilities occurred,{the English supporting Raghunath : the Convention of Wargaum, made in 1779,,was disavowed : eventually peace was restored by the treaty of Salbai of May 17, 1782, which Nana Farnavis ratified. Raghunath's cause failed, and he soon died. Sakaram was made over to Nana Farnavis by Sindia, confined in a fort, and died there. Madho Rao's title as Peshwa and Nana Furnavis' Regency were recognized. The latter was then the real head of affairs at Poona. Lord Cornwallis received from him a contingent of Mahrattas against Tippoo in 1791. Antagonism arose between Nana Farnavis and'Madhava Rao Sindia (q.v), each having claims against the other. Sindia died in 1794, leaving Nana Farnavis without a rival among the Mahrattas. They made great demands on the Nizam and defeated his army at Kurdla in March, 1795. Nana Farnavis was then at the height of his prosperity as minister, when the Peshwa, Madho Rao, committed suicide. Raghunath's son, Baji Rao, became Peshwa. Nana fled, was seized at Poona and imprisoned : became reconciled to Baji Rao : they evaded alliance with the British Government : Nana Farnavis died on March 13, 1800.

NANA SAHIB (1820 ?–1859 ?)

The chief rebel leader in the mutiny, whose barbarous cruelty and treachery have never been forgotten : his real name was Dundupant, of Bithur, near Cawnpur : the adopted son of Baji Rao (q.v.), the ex-Peshwa, who died in Dec. 1852. His claim to the continuation of Baji Rao's annual pension of 8 lakhs was fully considered and rejected, but he maintained friendly relations with, and showed hospitality to, the English residents at Cawnpur. He was allowed a retinue of all arms. He aimed at restoring the Mahratta Empire and proclaimed himself Peshwa. In the mutiny he attacked Sir Hugh Wheeler's entrenchments at Cawnpur, and, on the latter's surrender, treacherously ordered the massacre of Europeans, men, women and children, on the Ganges, on June 27, and again on July 15. He was defeated at Bithur by Havelock on July 16, 1857, when he fled. He was in action again later, and continued to instigate hostilities : until Sir Colin Campbell drove him into Nipal at the end of 1858. Government offered a reward of a lakh of rupees for his capture, but he escaped, probably in the Nipal jungles, and was never caught. He is supposed to have died about 1859.

NAOROJI, DADABHAI (1825–)

Born Sep. 4, 1825 : son of a Parsi priest : educated at Elphinstone School and College, Bombay : Professor there of Mathematics and Natural Philosophy, 1854 : took part in the public movements of the time, and in the associations for the amelioration of the natives : established the *Rast Goftar* newspaper : came to England as partner in the Parsi firm of Cama & Co. in London, 1855 : Professor of Gujarati, University College, London : worked for the East India Association : advocated admission of Indians to the Civil Service, 1870 : Prime Minister, Baroda, 1874 ; Member of the Bombay Corporation and Town Council, 1875–6 : and of the Legislative Council, Bombay, 1885 : M.P. for Central Finsbury, 1892–5 : President, Indian National Congress, 1886 and 1893 : Member of Royal Commission on Indian Expenditure, 1895 : author of numerous papers and books on Indian grievances, including *Poverty and un-British Rule in India*, 1901 ; *England's Duties to India, Financial Administration of India*, etc., etc. : J.P.

NAOROJI, REV. DHANJIBHAI (1822–)

A Parsi : born near Broach in Gujarat, 1822 : educated at the Rev. Dr. J. Wilson's school, 1835 : converted May, 1, 1839 : was the subject of a writ of Habeas Corpus issued to Dr. Wilson : accompanied him to England in 1843, travelling on the way in Egypt, Syria and the Continent : after 3 years' theological study at Edinburgh, was ordained in 1846 by the Free Presbytery of Edinburgh : returned to India, 1847 : Missionary at Surat for 9 years, at Bombay from 1856, at Poona, 1873–7, labouring in the native churches, schools and the Press till after 1899.

NAPIER, SIR CHARLES JAMES (1782–1853)

Born Aug. 10, 1782 : son of Col. the Hon. George Napier : entered the 33rd regt., 1794 : educated at Celbridge : A.D.C. to Sir James Duff, 1799 : and to General H. E. Fox, 1803, both in Ireland : commanded the 50th under Moore in Spain, 1808 : taken prisoner at Corunna in the Peninsula : engaged against the United States, 1813 : against Napoleon. 1815 : C.B. : studied at the Military College. Farnham, 1815–7 : resident of Cephalonia, 1822–30 : friend of Byron : declined to be Commander of the Greeks : Maj-General, 1837 : K.C.B., 1838 : commanded the N. district, 1839 : kept Chartism under : to India in 1841 : advised Ellenborough on the military policy, 1842 : took command in Sind in 1842 : offered the Amirs a fresh treaty : occupied their fortress of Imamghar in Dec. 1842 : fought and won the battle of Miani on Feb. 17, 1843, with 2,200 men against 22,000 : and beat Shir Muhammad, the Lion of Mirpur, at Dubba, near Hyderabad, March 24, 1843, finally at Shahdulpur, on June 14, routing him to the hills : controversy arose between Napier and (Sir James) Outram (q.v.) about the necessity for the conquest of Sind and the question of the treatment of the Amirs : Napier organized the new government of the province, and received the submission of the Chiefs in 1844 : G.C.B., 1843 : defeated the hill tribes on the N. frontier of Sind, 1844–5 : assembled an Army at Rohri, 1846, but was not engaged in the Satlaj campaign of 1845–6 : Lt-General, 1846 : resigned the government of Sind, 1847 : named by Wellington for the military command in India after Chilianwala : the Court of Directors objected, but yielded to the public demand for Napier : he arrived in India after the conclusion of the Panjab campaign, 1849 : C. in C. in India, May 7, 1849, to Dec. 6, 1850 : suppressed a mutiny in a native regiment : he suspended, on his own responsibility, a Government Regulation on the subject of compensation allowance to the Native Army : the Governor-General, Lord Dalhousie, expressing his disapprobation, Napier resigned and went home : died Aug. 29, 1853 : on his statue in St. Paul's Cathedral are the words " A prescient general, a beneficent governor, a just man " : another statue is in Trafalgar Square, London : wrote on the *Defects, Civil and Military, of the Indian Government,* and various papers on military subjects, the colonies and miscellaneous literature : his despatches and civil work

attracted as high praise as his military achievements : he had heroic qualities, and was both loved and detested.

NAPIER OF MERCHISTOUN, FRANCIS, NINTH BARON, FIRST BARON ETTRICK OF ETTRICK (1819–1898)

Governor : born 1819 : son of eighth Baron : succeeded as Peer in 1834 : educated privately, at Saxe Meiningen, and Trinity College, Cambridge : entered the diplomatic service, 1840 : served as Attaché and Secretary at several places : Ambassador at St. Petersburg, 1860–4 ; Berlin, 1864–6 : Governor of Madras, March, 1866, to Feb. 1872 : specially concerned himself with questions affecting the public health, and public works, including irrigation, and such schemes as the Periyar project : on Lord Mayo's assassination, he, as the Senior Governor in India, officiated as Viceroy and Governor-General from Feb. 23 to May 3, 1872 : created Baron Ettrick, 1872 : worked for some years, presiding and speaking at meetings and congresses, and on the London School Board : presided over the Royal Commission on the Scottish Crofters, 1883 : LL.D. of Edinburgh, Glasgow, Harvard : died Dec. 19, 1898.

NAPIER OF MAGDALA AND CARYNG-TON, ROBERT CORNELIS, FIRST BARON (1810–1890)

Field Marshal : son of Major Charles Frederick Napier, R.A. : born in Ceylon, Dec. 6, 1810 : educated at Addiscombe : joined the Bengal Engineers at Calcutta, 1828 : employed on the E. Jumna Canal irrigation works, 1831 : in Europe studied engineering and railway works 1836–9 : laid out the settlement of Darjeeling and made the road thither, 1839–42 : laid out the cantonment at Umbala, 1842 : in the Satlaj campaign of 1845–6 : at Mudki and Firozshahr : severely wounded : at Sobraon : Major : took the hill fort of Kangra, 1846 : Engineer to the Resident at Lahore : directed the siege of Multan in the Panjab campaign, 1848 : at its capture : at Surajkund, Cheniote, the pursuit of the Sikhs and Afghans : Brevet-Lt-Colonel : Civil Engineer to the Panjab Board of Administration, 1849 : executed great public works, roads, canals, and buildings, bridges, frontier defences : served in frontier expeditions, 1852–3 :

Chief Engineer to the Chief Commissioner of the Panjab till 1856 : Lt-Colonel, 1856 : in 1857 was Chief of the Staff to Outram (*q.v.*), at the relief of Lucknow, Sep. 25, and the actions before and after : severely wounded at the second relief by Sir Colin Campbell : Brig-General at the capture of Lucknow in March, 1858 : C.B. : second in command to Sir Hugh Rose at Gwalior : defeated Tantia Topi at Jaora Alipur : routed Firozshah in Dec. 1858 : destroyed the Parone forts, and suppressed the mutiny in Central India : K.C.B. : commanded a Division in China, 1860 : Maj-General, 1861 : Military Member of the Supreme Council, Feb. 1861, to March, 1865 : acted as Viceroy and Governor-General, Nov. 21-Dec. 2, 1863 : C. in C. at Bombay, 1865-9, during which time he commanded the Abyssinian expedition, 1867-8 : made a Peer : G.C.B : G.C.S.I., 1868 : D.C.L. of Oxford : F.R.S., 1869 : C. in C. in India, April 1870 – April 1876 : Governor of Gibraltar, 1876-83 : Field Marshal, 1883 : Constable of the Tower, 1886 : he died Jan. 14, 1890 : buried at St. Paul's Cathedral : statues of him are in Calcutta and London : besides his distinction as an engineer and a soldier, he was highly cultured, with a knowledge of art and poetry : and was remarkable for his attractive personal qualities.

NARAIN, PANDIT SARUP (? -1903)

Political : entered service in 1850 as Superintendent of one of the first educational institutions in Central India : was, later, head of the Gwalior office : Diwan of the Bundelkund office : promoted to the graded list of the Political Department and C.I.E., in 1880 : was in 1883 an Assistant to the Agent to the Governor-General at Indore, and Political Agent in Bhopawar : retired in 1884, and received a special pension : died in 1903.

NATHAN, ROBERT (? -)

I.C.S. : educated at St. Peter's College, Cambridge : called to the bar : went to Bengal in the Civil Service, 1888 : served as Under Secretary to the Government of India in the Financial Department, 1895 : U. Secy. in the Home Department, 1897 : Deputy Secretary, 1904 : Secretary to India Universities Commission, 1902 :

C.I.E. : Private Secretary to H.E. the Viceroy, 1904-5 : author of *Official History of Plague in India*, and of *Progress of Education in India*, 1897-8 and 1901-2.

NATHUBHOY, SIR MANGALDAS
(1832-1890)

Born in Oct. 1832 : a member of the Gujarati section of the Kapol Banian caste : son of Seth Nathubhoy Ramdas : his grandfather amassed a fortune, which he inherited at the age of 11. He devoted himself to social reforms, more especially the suppression of the orgies at the Holi festival, and the immoral practices of the Vallabhacharya Maharajas : also took a great interest in the education of girls and boys, and assisted in founding the Hindu Boys' School in Bombay : endowed a travelling scholarship for Hindu graduates : founded a Dispensary at the cost of Rs. 70,000 : and established a charitable fund for his own caste. In 1859 he was appointed a Commissioner of the Income Tax. In politics, he revived the Bombay Association, and was, for some periods, a non-official member of the Legislative Council : was a member of the Royal Asiatic and Geographical Societies : C.S.I. in 1872 : knighted in 1875 : bequeathed, by will, a large sum of money to charitable uses : died March 9, 1890.

NATION, SIR JOHN LOUIS (1825-)

Son of Colonel Stephen Nation, C.B, : educated privately : entered the Bengal Army, 1841: became Colonel, 1872 : General, 1982 : in the Indian mutiny, 1857-8 : commanded Naga Hills expedition and Eastern Frontier Brigade, 1879-82 : C.B., 1881 : K.C.B., 1900.

NATORE, RANI BHAWANI OF
(1716 ?-1795)

Born about 1716 : married about 1727 to Maharaja Ram Kant Rai of Natore : in 1748 became a widow and succeeded to the Natore estate : adopted Maharaja Ram Krishna as son and managed the extensive property during his minority : in Benares alone she built 380 . temples, besides religious edifices in other parts of the country : she annually paid 70 lakhs of *sicca* rupees to Government, as revenue, her gross income being about one crore and a half of rupees : in her old age she lived principally at Barnagore in Murshidabad: died there in 1795: her extensive *zamindari* was spread over several districts: she was devoted to piety, and her name is still a household word in Bengal.

NEILL, JAMES GEORGE SMITH (1810–1857)

Son of Colonel Neill: born May 27, 1810: educated at Ayr, and Glasgow University: joined the E. I. Co.'s Madras first European regt. in 1827 : D.A.A.G. in 1841 : wrote the *Historical Record* of his regt, : in the Burmese war in 1852 : in the Crimean war, appointed second in command of the Turkish contingent, which he organized and reformed : in the mutiny of 1857, sent off with his regt. to Upper India : at the mutiny at Benares, June 4, defeated the rebels : Brig-General : reinforced Allahabad and the fort : A.D.C. to Queen Victoria : superseded by Havelock in the advance to Cawnpur, but appointed his second in command : when commanding at Cawnpur, he punished, with great severity the mutineers caught : had to keep open communications with Havelock on the latter's advance to Lucknow : Neill showed for a time a want of loyal subordination to Havelock : went with him as Brig-General to the relief of Lucknow in Sep. 1857 : was shot dead in the street fighting on the day of the attack, Sep. 25 : on his monument at Ayr, the inscription runs : "A brave, resolute, self-reliant soldier, universally acknowledged as the first who stemmed the torrent of rebellion in Bengal. He fell gloriously at the relief of Lucknow." He would have been K.C.B. had he lived.

NELSON, SIR ALEXANDER ABERCROMBY (1816–1893)

Born 1816 : educated at Sandhurst : joined the 40th regt., 1835 : commissariat officer in sole charge of the Bombay force with Nott to Kandahar and in Afghanistan 1841–2 : at Ghazni and Kabul, and the engagements in the Khyber on the return to India: with Sir C. Napier in Sind : at Hyderabad, March 24, 1843: at Maharajpur, Dec. 29, 1843, as A.D.C. to Sir Thomas Valiant : served no more in India : Brig-General at the suppression of the insurrection in Jamaica, 1865 : Lieutenant-Governor of Guernsey, 1870–83: C.B., 1875: Lt-General, 1883 : K.C.B., 1891 : died Sep. 28, 1893.

NELSON, HORATIO, VISCOUNT AND DUKE OF BRONTE (1758–1805)

Admiral : born Sep. 29, 1758 : Midshipman in his 12th year : after sailing to the W. Indies and on an expedition to the N. Pole, he went to the E. Indies in 1773 in the *Seahorse* frigate, under Captain George Farmer. He was there for 2 years, visiting " every port in India from Bengal to Bussora," when his health broke down, and the Commodore, Sir Edward Hughes, ordered him to England in the *Dolphin*. There is evidence that he was transferred from the *Seahorse* to the *Dolphin* at Bombay on March 15, 1776. His service on the E. I. station was uneventful, but he appears to have felt the effects of the climate, probably from that of the Persian Gulf, about Bussora and Muscat. It is not recorded that he was in India again. After the battle of the Nile he wrote Aug. 9, 1798, to the Governor of Bombay, to tell him of the destruction of the French Fleet, and the consequent preservation of India from any attempt against it by the French. The extraordinary expenses which would have been incurred for the defence of Bombay—which Nelson knew would have been their first object—were thus prevented. His autograph letter of July 3, 1799, is extant, thanking the E. I. Co. for their present of £10,000 on the occasion of his victory at Aboukir Bay. Nelson was killed at Trafalgar on Oct. 21, 1805.

NEPEAN, SIR EVAN, BARONET (1751–1822)

Governor : born 1751 : son of Nicholas Nepean : entered the Navy as a clerk : Secretary to Lord Shuldham, 1782: Under Secretary of State in the Shelburne Ministry : in 1794, Under Secretary for War : Secretary of the Admiralty, 1795–1804 : Baronet, 1802 : Chief Secretary for Ireland, 1804 : Governor of Bombay, 1812–9 : died Oct. 2, 1822.

NEWAL KISHOR (1836–1895)

Known as Munshi : born at Bastoi : son of Munshi Jamna Parshad, a Bhargava land owner in the Alighar district : educated at Agra College : became the most eminent of the vernacular publishers in India : was first editor and manager of the *Koh-i-Nur*, the oldest paper in the Panjab : to Luck-now in 1858, and, under official patronage, founded a press there, which rose to be the largest printing concern in India, employing nearly 1,000 hands : opened branches at Cawnpur and Lahore, and agencies throughout and beyond India : aimed at educating the people : for this purpose he maintained an Urdu daily news-paper, the *Oudh Akhbar*, and translated into Urdu numerous standard works in Arabic, Persian, Sanskrit and English : published more than 4,000 different works. The *Oudh Akhbar* was originally a weekly, but in 1878 became a daily publication, and is still one of the leading vernacular organs in N. India. Newal Kishor attained to great wealth, and was very liberal, especially in the cause of education : helped to establish the Jubilee High School at Lucknow, and the Lyall Library at Alighar : gave large collections of books, numerous scholarships and medals, to other institutions : did much for the Dufferin Fund and his own community, building and endowing a boarding-house for Bhargava students at Agra : supported all public movements in the United Provinces, was always ready to help charit-able institutions and schemes of all creeds : founded the Lucknow Paper Mills, one of the chief concerns in the United Pro-vinces under Indian ownership and management : Hony. Magte. : Municipal Commissioner : Fellow of the Allahabad University : C.I.E., 1888 : died Feb. 19, 1895.

NEWBOLD, THOMAS JOHN (1807-1850)

Son of Dr. Francis Newbold : born Feb. 8, 1807 : joined the E. I. Co.'s 23rd Madras light infantry in 1828 : served in Malacca, 1832-5 : wrote a book on the British settlements in the Straits and a History of the Malayan States : studied the geology of Southern India : travelled largely in Arabia, Asia Minor, on the Continent : F.R.S. : Member of the Asiatic Society, 1841, for which he wrote scientific papers : chiefly on geology and literary subjects : Oriental scholar : Captain, 1842 : assistant at Kurnoul, 1842-5 : travelled in Syria and Egypt : Assistant Resident at Hyderabad, 1846 : travelled to Shiraz, Nineveh, Bagdad, 1849 : died at Mahableshwar, May 29, 1850.

NEWMARCH, SIR OLIVER RICHARD-SON (1834-)

Born Oct. 31, 1834 : son of Dr. Henry Newmarch M.D. : educated at Charter-house and Merton College, Oxford : entered Bengal Army, 1855 : served in Indian mutiny, 1857-8 : Military Secre-tary to Government of India, 1884 : Accountant General, Military Department, 1878 : Military Secretary, India Office, 1889-99 : Maj-General : retired, 1887 : C.S.I., 1888 : K.C.S.I., 1894.

NICHOLSON, SIR FREDERICK AUGUSTUS (? -)

I.C.S. : went out to Madras, 1869 : Member of Board of Revenue, Madras, 1899 : of the Governor-General's Legisla-tive Council, 1897-9, and 1900-2 : reported on the establishment of Agricul-tural Banks in India : Member of the Famine Commission, 1901 : C.I.E., 1899 : K.C.I.E., 1903 : retired.

NICHOLSON, JOHN (1821-1857)

Son of Dr. Alexander Nicholson : born Dec. 11, 1821 : his mother's brother, (Sir) James Weir Hogg (*q.v.*), obtained for him an appointment in the Bengal Infantry : reached Calcutta, 1839 : went to Afghanistan with the 27th N.I. in 1840, to Jalalabad, Kabul, Ghazni, where he was, with Colonel Palmer's force, besieged in Dec. 1841 : made prisoner in April, 1842 : sent to Kabul in Aug. and released in Sep. : in the Satlaj campaign, in the commissariat at Firoz-shahr : sent to instruct the troops of the Maharaja of Kashmir : Assistant to Sir Henry Lawrence at Lahore : in the Panjab campaign of 1848-9, seized Attock and the Margalla Pass : at Chilianwala and Gujarat, and in the pursuit of the Sikhs : Deputy Commissioner under the Panjab Board of Administration : at Bannu, 1851-6 : he was " a tower of strength," Lord Dalhousie said : the natives re-garded him as a demigod and worshipped him as " Nikkul Seyn " : Brevet-Lt-Colonel, 1854 : Deputy Commissioner of Peshawar in 1857 : succeeded (Sir) N. B. Chamberlain (*q.v.*), in command, as Brig-General of the Panjab movable column, to Delhi : disarmed suspected native regiments : cut off rebels at Trimmu Ghat and on the Ravi river : reached Delhi, Aug. 14, 1857 : commanded in the action of Najafghar, Aug. 25 : at the storming of Delhi, Sep. 14, he commanded the main storming party : shot through the chest, in the street fights : mortally wounded : lingered till Sep. 23 : buried near the Kashmir gate of Delhi : his death deplored as a public misfortune : opinions are unanimous of his qualities for command : his great physique, his fearlessness, decision, judgment, forethought, energy : trusted and followed anywhere by his men : noble, tender and kind, but stern to evil : would have been K.C.B. had he lived.

NICHOLSON, SIR LOTHIAN (1827–1893)

Son of George Thomas Nicholson : born Jan. 19, 1827 : educated at Brighton and Woolwich : joined the R.E. in 1846 : served in N. America : and through the Crimea : Brevet-Major, 1855 : in the mutiny, joined Sir Colin Campbell's Staff : present at the Alambagh and at the capture of Lucknow, March, 1858 : in the operations in Oudh and in 'the Tarai : C.B., 1859 : Maj-General, 1877 : Lieutenant-Governor of Jersey, 1878–83 : Lt-General, 1881 : Inspr-General of Fortifications, 1886 : K.C.B., 1887 : Governor of Gibraltar, 1891 : died there, June 27, 1893 : wrote papers on military engineering subjects.

NICHOLSON, SIR WILLIAM GUSTAVUS (1845–   )

Born March 2, 1845 : son of William Nicholson : entered the Royal Engineers 1865, and became Colonel, 1891 : served in the Afghan war, 1878–80 : in the march from Kabul to Kandahar, and at the battle of Kandahar : Brevet-Major : Egyptian war, 1882, Tel-el-Kebir : Burmese expedition, 1886–7, as A.A.G. : Brevet-Lt-Colonel : Tirah expedition, 1897–8, as Chief of the Staff : K.C.B. : Adjutant-General in India, 1898–9 : South African war, 1899–1900, as Military Secretary to C. in C. and Director of Transport at Headquarters : Maj-General : Director-General of Mobilisation and Military Intelligence, War Office, 1901–4 : attached to the Japanese army, 1904–5 : appointed Governor of Gibraltar, 1905 : resigned the appointment.

NICOLLS, SIR JASPER (1778–1849)

Born July 15, 1778 : son of Col. Nicolls : educated at Dublin University : joined the Army, 1793 : went to India, 1802, as Military Secretary to his uncle when C. in C., Bombay : at Argaum and Gawilghar : Major, 1804 : distinguished himself at Buenos Ayres, 1807 : at Corunna : at Walcheren : Q.M.G. in India, 1812 : C.B. : in the Nipal war, 1814–6, conquered Kumaon : commanded a Brigade in the Pindari-Mahratta war, 1817–8 : Maj-General, 1821 : commanded a Division in Madras, 1825–9, and at Bhartpur, 1826, commanded one of the attacking columns : K.C.B. : Lt-General, 1837 : C. in C., Madras, 1838 : C. in C., in'India, 1839–43 : opposed the continued occupation of Kabul : Colonel of the 5th foot : died May 4, 1849.

NIGHTINGALL, SIR MILES (1768–1829)

Born Dec. 25, 1768 : joined the Army at Madras, 1787 : served at Dindigul and Palicaudcherry, 1790 : Brig-Major under Cornwallis at Bangalore and Seringapatam, 1792 : at the capture of Pondicherry, 1793 : Captain, 1794 : in the W. Indies and America : on Cornwallis' Staff in Ireland and France : Q.M.G. in Bengal, 1803 : at Agra and Laswari under Lake : Military Secretary to Cornwallis when Governor-General, 1805 : in Portugal and the Peninsula : C. in C. in Java, 1813–5 : Lt-General, 1814 : K.C.B., 1815 : C. in C., Bombay, 1816–9 : M.P. for Eye, 1820 and 1826 : died Sep. 12, 1829.

NIXON, JOHN ECCLES (1857–   )

Maj-General : born Aug. 16, 1857 : son of Maj-General J. P. Nixon : educated at Wellington : served in the Afghan war, 1879–80 : Mahsud-Wuziri expedition, 1881 : Chitral Relief Force as D.A.Q.M.G. : Brevet-Lt-Colonel : Tirah expedition, 1897–8, as Chief Staff Officer : Tochi Field Force : commanded a Brigade in S. Africa, 1901–2 : commanding Bangalore District since 1903 : author of *Military Notes on Tactics, Law, and Staff Officers on Field Service*.

NOBLE, REV. ROBERT TURLINGTON (1809–1865)

Son of Rev. John Noble : born Jan. or Feb. 1809 : educated (Scholar) at Oakham,

Sidney Sussex (Scholar) and Christ's Colleges, Cambridge: tutor to Sir T. Blomefield, 1833–8: curate of Old Dalby, 1839–41: ordained, 1839: went out, as a Missionary of the Church Missionary Society, in 1841, to the Telugu Mission at Masulipatam, and worked there continuously for 24 years, preaching and teaching: took up Ellore, 1854, and Bezwada, 1858, as Missionary stations: refused a Chaplaincy: succumbed to exposure to the cyclone of Nov. 1, 1864, and illness: died Oct. 17, 1865.

NOER, PRINCE FREDERIC CHRISTIAN CHARLES AUGUSTUS SCHLESWIG - HOLSTEIN - SONDERBURG - AUGUSTENBURG COUNT VON (1830–1881)

Born Nov. 16, 1830, at Schleswig: son of Friedrich Emile August of Noer: served under his father in the insurrectionary Army of Schleswig-Holstein, 1848–9: travelled through Egypt, Australia, India, and Asia Minor, 1849–50: entered, as a Fellow-Commoner, at Trinity College, Cambridge, 1852: stayed there 18 months: studied at Heidelburg, and Paris, languages and historic documents: published *Altes und Neues aus den Lindern des Ostens*, 1859, under the name of Onomander: read Sanskrit with Goldstucker (*q.v.*) in London: to S. India in 1865: returned to Noer, near Kiel: again visited India, June, 1867–April, 1869, travelled in Mysore, to Calcutta, and Upper India: became enthusiastic about Akbar: published the first volume of a Life of Akbar, 1880–1, and, after his death, the second volume was issued, 1885: left to Cambridge University the bulk of his valuable Oriental, principally Indian, literature, including some very rare works: resided many years in England and France: attained considerable literary eminence: his widow published his memoirs, 1886: died Dec. 25, 1881.

NORMAN, SIR FRANCIS BOOTH (1830–1901)

Son of James Norman: brother of Sir H. W. Norman (*q.v.*): born April 25, 1830: educated at Addiscombe: joined the 14th Bengal N.I., 1848: in the Umbeyla campaign, 1863: A.Q.M.G. in the Bhutan campaign, 1864–6, at the recapture of Dewangiri: Major, 1865: in the Black Mountain expedition, 1868: commanded the 24th Panjab N.I. in Afghan war, 1879–80: in the Bazar Valley expedition and defence of Jagdalak: in the Kabul-Kandahar march, Aug. 1880, and battle of Kandahar: C.B.: commanded a Brigade in Burma, 1885–6: K.C.B.: Maj-General, 1889: Lt-General, 1892: died June 25, 1901.

NORMAN, SIR HENRY RADFORD (1818–1899)

General: son of Rev. J. H. Norman: entered the 10th foot in 1838: served in the Satlaj campaign, 1845–6, at Sobraon: in the Panjab campaign, 1848–9: at Multan, Surajkund, Gujarat: in the mutiny at the capture of Lucknow and other actions: C.B.: retired, 1885: K.C.B., 1899: died Dec. 16, 1899.

NORMAN, SIR HENRY WYLIE (1826–1904)

Field Marshal: born Dec. 2, 1826: son of James Norman, of Calcutta: educated privately and at Addiscombe: joined the E.I. Co.'s 31st Bengal N.I. in 1844: Adjutant: in the Panjab campaign of 1848–9: present at the passage of the Chenab, Sadulapur, Chilianwala, Gujarat, pursuit of the Sikhs: in 1850, Brig-Major at the fighting in the Kohat Pass: D.A.A.G.: constantly in frontier expeditions: in the campaign of the Sonthal rebelion, 1855: in the mutiny of 1857 was A.A.G. under Sir H. Barnard: at Badli-ka-sarai: D.A.G. through the siege of Delhi, June 8–Sep. 20: at the reliefs of Lucknow and Cawnpur, and the operations, Nov. 28–Dec. 6, against the Gwalior Contingent: at Khudaganj, at the capture of Lucknow, at Fatehghar, in Rohilkund, at Bareli, in the Oudh campaign: Brevets, Major and Lt-Colonel: C.B., 1859: acted as Adjutant-General, April–Nov. 1859: Assistant Military Secretary for Indian affairs at the Horse Guards: his proposals for the Indian Staff Corps accepted with modifications: in 1862, Secretary to the Government of India, Miltary Department: A.D.C. to Queen Victoria: Military Member of the Supreme Council in India, 1868, and 1870–7: Lt-General, 1877: Member of the Council of India, 1878–82: General, 1882: Captain-General and Governor in Chief of Jamaica, 1882–7: Governor of Queensland, 1889–95: refused the ap-

pointment of the Viceroyalty of India
,(between Lords Lansdowne and Elgin):
Agent for Queensland in London, 1896 :
in April, 1901, Governor of Chelsea
Hospital : Field Marshal, ^lJune 26, 1902 :
was on the Royal Commission to investi-
gate the conduct of the S. African campaign : K.C.B., 1873 : G.C.B., 1887 :
G.C.M.G., 1887 : C.I.E., 1878 : died
Oct. 26, 1904.

NORMAN, JOHN PAXTON (1819-1871)

Son of John Norman, a Somersetshire
banker : born Oct. 21, 1819 : educated
at Exeter Grammar School, and Exeter
College, Oxford : practised as a special
pleader : called to the bar at the Inner
Temple, 1862 : was a Puisne Judge of
the Calcutta Supreme Court, 1862–71,
officiating as Chief Justice in 1864–5, and
again in 1870–1 : he was attacked and
mortally wounded by an assassin as he
was ascending the steps of the Town
Hall, Calcutta, on his way to his Court
(which was temporarily being held
there), and died of his wounds early the
next morning, Sep. 21, 1871. The mur-
derer, Abdulla, a Panjabi, gave no intelli-
gible account of his motives. Norman
was the most popular of men, always
accessible to natives, and very kindly
disposed towards them, and intended to
retire soon : he was a sound lawyer : the
author, in England, of many legal treatises
and papers, and the editor of law reports.
He took an active part in the Calcutta
University as President of the Faculty of
Law. A monument was erected to him
by the Government in St. Paul's Cathedral,
Calcutta.

NORTHBROOK, THOMAS GEORGE BARING, FIRST EARL OF (1826-1904)

Governor-General and Viceroy : born
Jan. 22, 1826 : son of the first Baron
Northbrook : educated at Christ Church,
Oxford : was Private Secretary succes-
sively to Mr. Labouchere (Lord Taunton)
at the Board of Trade, Sir George Grey at
the Home Office, Sir C. Wood (Lord
Halifax) at the India Office and Admiralty :
M.P. for Falmouth and Penryn, 1857–66 :
Junior Lord of the Admiralty, 1857–8 :
Under Secretary for India, 1859–61 and
1861–4 : Under Secretary for the Home
Department, 1864–6, and for War, 1868–
72 : Viceroy and Governor-General of

India, May, 1872 to April, 1876 : made an
Earl : First Lord of the Admiralty,
1880–5 : during this time he was sent on
a special mission to Cairo : G.C.S.I. :
G.C.I.E. : P.C. : D.C.L. : LL.D. : F.R.S. :
Lord Lieutenant, and Chairman of the
County Council of Hampshire. His Viceroyalty was comparatively uneventful.
The Amir of Afghanistan sent an Envoy,
Nur Muhammad Shah, to make requests
for assistance and protection, which Lord
Northbrook was not authorized to con-
cede. The Bengal famine occurred in
1874, which he controlled with vigour and
success, not going up to Simla during the
whole year : he refused to prohibit the
exportation of grain from India, but
imported enormous quantities of rice to
feed the famine-stricken : he sanctioned
the Sone canal and N. Bengal railway as
relief works. He had the Gaekwar of
Baroda tried for an attempt on the life of
the Resident, and deposed for misgovernment : he entertained H.R.H. the
Prince of Wales on his visit to Calcutta,
Dec. 1875 : he abolished the Income
Tax : and disagreed with the Secretary
of State about the cotton duties, and
resigned. He paid special attention to
Finance. He was greatly respected and
esteemed by all classes, and his memory
is held in high regard to this day. The
business of the Government was never
better performed than in his time. His
statue is in Calcutta. He founded and
presided over the Northbrook Indian
Club in London. He died Nov. 15, 1904.

NORTHCOTE, HENRY STAFFORD, FIRST BARON (1846-   )

Born Nov. 18, 1846 : second son of
Sir Stafford Northcote, afterwards Earl of
Iddesleigh : educated at Eton and Merton
College, Oxford : Private Secretary to
Lord Salisbury, on his embassy to Constantinople 1876–7 : Financial Secretary
to War Office, 1885–6 : Surveyor-General
of the Ordnance, 1886–7 : Charity Commissioner, 1891–2 : M.P. for Exeter,
1880–99 : Governor of Bombay, 1899–
1903 : Governor-General of Common-
wealth of Australia, 1903 : C.B. : G.C.I.E.

NORTON, JOHN BRUCE (1815-1883)

Son of Sir John David Norton, Puisne
Judge of the Madras Supreme Court :
born July 8, 1815 : educated at Harrow,
and Merton College, Oxford : Scholar :

played in the Harrow cricket Eleven in 1832-3 : called to the bar at Lincoln's Inn, 1841 : to India, 1842 : Sheriff of Madras, 1843-5 : Clerk of the Crown, 1845-62 : Government Pleader : Advocate-General, 1863-71 : Member of the Legislative Council, Madras : Fellow and Law Lecturer of the Madras University : was an ardent advocate and supporter of native interests and education : Patron of Pachaiyappa's school at Madras : appointed, in 1873, the first lecturer on Law to Indian students at the Temple, London : died July 13, 1883 : wrote on *The Law of Evidence*, etc., 1858 : and chiefly on legal subjects : also *The Rebellion in India : how to prevent another* 1857 ; *Topics for Indian Statesmen*, 1858 : *Nemesis, a Poem*, and other books of verse.

NORTON, SIR JOHN DAVID (1787-1843)

Entered Royal Artillery, but changed to the law : became Private Secretary to Sir Edward Sugden (Lord St. Leonards, Lord Chancellor) : Puisne Judge of the Supreme Court, Madras, 1841 : knighted, 1842 : died, 1843, on a sea voyage to Malacca : his monument in the Cathedral, Madras : father of John Bruce Norton (*q.v.*).

NOTT, SIR WILLIAM (1782-1845)

Maj-General : son of Charles Nott : born Jan. 20, 1782 : educated at Neath and Cowbridge : in 1800 joined the Bengal European regt. at Berhampur : served in Sumatra : commanded the 20th N.I. at Barrackpur, 1825 : Colonel, 1829 : in 1838, Brig-General of the Brigade in the first Division of the Army of the Indus : commanded the Division to Quetta : in command at Kandahar, 1839 : defeated the Ghilzais : caused the enemy to evacuate Kelat : in military and political command in Lower Afghanistan and Sind in Jan. 1842 : repulsed all attacks on Kandahar : after Macnaghten's death, declined to retire to India without express orders : in July, 1842, ordered to withdraw from Afghanistan, but allowed choice of route : sent General England back to Quetta, and himself marched *via* Ghazni towards Kabul : successful engagements on Aug. 30 at Karabagh, near Ghazni, and en route to Kabul, which he reached Sep. 17, 1842, meeting Pollock

there : returned to India *via* Jalalabad : appointed Resident at Lucknow with the King of Oudh : made G.C.B., 1843 : to England in 1844 : died Jan 1, 1845 : his statue erected at Carmarthen.

NUGENT, SIR GEORGE, BARONET (1757-1849)

Field Marshal : born June 10, 1757 : son of Lt-General Honble. E. C. Nugent : educated at Charterhouse and R.M.A., Woolwich : entered the Army, 1773 : served in several Royal regiments during the American war : in the campaign in Flanders, 1793 : Adjt-General in Ireland, 1798-1801 : raised a corps of 600 in Buckinghamshire : M.P. for Buckingham, 1790-1800 and 1819-32, and for Aylesbury, 1806-7 : Maj-General, 1796 : Lieutenant-Governor and C. in C., Jamaica, 1801-6 : Baronet, 1806 : C. in C. in India, 1811-3 : General, 1813 : G.C.B., 1815 : D.C.L. : Colonel of the 6th regt. : Field Marshal, 1846 : died March 10, 1849.

NUGENT, JOHN (? -1900)

I.C.S. : educated at the Royal Institute School, Liverpool, and Trinity College, Dublin : entered the Bombay Civil Service, 1864 : Secretary to the Bombay Government : Additional Member of the Governor-General's Legislative Council : Member of Council, Bombay, 1896 : died of cholera, Aug. 5, 1900.

NUNCOMAR RAI, MAHARAJA (? -1775)

(Also spelt Nanda Kumar) : born early in the 18th century in the Murshidabad district : early appointed *Amin* or revenue collector of *Parganas* Hijli and Moisadal : accompanied Clive to Patna as Vakil : and, in 1756, was Governor of Hughli : attended Mir Jafar in the war against Mir Kasim : made, about 1764, Maharaja by the Emperor Shah Alam : appointed by the E. I. Co. to be Collector of Burdwan, Nadia and Hughli, in place of W.Hastings : in 1765 was Naib Subah of Bengal, deposed, and Muhammad Reza Khan appointed : in 1772, when Warren Hastings became Governor-General, Nuncomar made complaints against the Revenue Administration of Muhammad Reza Khan, Naib Subah, and helped Warren Hastings in prosecuting Reza Khan, who was then deposed : obtained the appointment of

his son, Raja Goordas, as assistant to
Mani Begam, Superintendent of the
Nawab's Household: in March, 1775,
brought before the Council some grave
charges against Warren Hastings: in
April, 1775, was prosecuted, along with
Joseph Fowke, by Barwell, for conspiracy: while this case was pending, a
charge of forgery of a bond in connexion
with a civil case in progress against him
was brought against him on May 6, 1775,
before Justices Lemaistre and Hyde,
sitting as committing magistrates. He
was tried at the Sessions, June 8–16,
before Sir E. Impey, C.J., and Justices
Chambers, Lemaistre and Hyde: was
convicted of the forgery, sentenced to
death, and hanged on Aug. 5, 1775.

NUNN, JOSHUA ARTHUR (1853–   )

Born May 10, 1853: son of Edward W.
Nunn: educated at Wimbledon and
Royal Vet. College, London: called to
the bar at Lincoln's Inn: Veterinary
Surgeon, R.A., 1877: served in Afghan
war, 1878–80: Vet. Surgeon to Panjab
Government, 1880–5: on special duty
in Natal and Cape Colony investigating
horse-sickness, 1885–8: served in Chin-
Lushai expedition as P.V.O., 1889–90:
D.S.O.: Principal, Lahore Veterinary
College, 1890–6: C.I.E.: Deputy Direc-
tor-General A.V.D., 1901: author of
Stable Management in India and other
veterinary works.

NUTTALL, SIR JAMES MANSFIELD
(1823–1897)

Born June 8, 1823: served in the
Satlaj campaign, 1845–6: in the mutiny
engaged around Allahabad: in the
Lushai campaign, 1871–2, under Bourchier: commanded in the Naga Hills
expedition, 1875: in the Naga campaign,
1879–80: at the capture of Kohima:
C.B., 1872: K.C.B., 1894: Bengal Staff
Corps: Maj-General: died Oct. 12, 1897.

NUTTALL, THOMAS (1828–1890)

Son of George R. Nuttall, M.D.: born
Oct. 7, 1828: educated at Aberdeen:
joined the Bombay N.I. in 1845: in the
Persian war, 1857: engaged against Bhil
rebels, 1857–61: joined the Bombay Staff
Corps, 1865: D.S. of Police, 1860–5: in
the Abyssinian expedition, 1867–8: Commandant of the Sind Frontier Force,
1877: in the Afghan war, 1878–80, com-

manded a Brigade: at the occupation of
Kandahar: commanded the Cavalry at
Girishk on the Helmund, July 14, 1880:
at Maiwand, July 27: at the defence of
Kandahar and the battle on Sep. 1, 1880:
Maj-General, 1885: Lt-General, 1887:
died Aug. 30, 1890.

OAKELEY, SIR CHARLES, BARONET
(1751–1826)

I.C.S.: Governor: son of the Rev.
William Oakeley: born Feb. 27, 1751:
went out to Madras in the E. I. Co.'s service, 1767: was a Secretary in 1773: and
1777–80, also Judge Advocate-General
and Translator: President in 1781–4 of
the Committee of the Assigned Revenue of
the Nabob of Arcot: President of the
Board of Revenue, Madras, 1786–8: made
Baronet in 1790: named Governor, but
had to remain as Second in Council until
Medows retired in Aug. 1792: the charge
of the civil government was very onerous
in supplying the wants of Cornwallis'
Army in the field: made possible by
reforms and good administration: he
converted the floating debt, and arranged
for siege of Pondicherry, 1793: retired,
Sep. 7, 1794: declined to be Governor-
General of India: died Sep. 7, 1826.

OAKES, SIR HENRY, BARONET
(1756–1827)

Son of Lt-Col. Hildebrand Oakes:
born July 11, 1756: entered the Bombay
Army, 1775: served in Gujarat, at Poona,
in Mysore, 1775–81: made prisoner by
Tippoo at Bednore, 1783–4: served at
Seringapatam, 1790, and in Malabar:
Adjutant-General of the Army, 1796:
Military Auditor-General, 1807: Maj-
General, 1810: Lt-General, 1814: suc-
ceeded his brother as Baronet, 1822:
committed suicide, Nov. 1, 1827.

**O'CALLAGHAN, SIR FRANCIS
LANGFORD** (1839–   )

Born July 22, 1839: son of James
O'Callaghan: educated at Cork College
and Queen's University, Ireland: joined
the Indian P. W. Department, 1862, and
rose through various grades to that of
Chief Enigineer, 1st class: Consulting
Engineer to Government of India for
State Railways, 1889: Secretary to
Government of India, Public Works

Department, 1892 : retired, 1894 : constructed the Attock bridge over the Indus : constructed the railway through the Bolan Pass to Quetta : constructed Uganda railway : C.I.E., 1883 : C.S.I., 1887 : K.C.M.G., 1902.

O'CALLAGHAN, HON. SIR ROBERT WILLIAM (1777-1840)

Second son of Baron Lismore : born Oct. 1777 : joined the 128th regt., 1794 : served in Sicily, the Peninsula, several battles : K.C.B., 1815 : Lt-General, 1830 : C. in C., Madras, from May 11, 1831, to Oct. 11, 1836 : acted as C. in C. in India between Lord W. Bentinck's departure in March, 1835, to Sir H. Fane's assumption of office, Sep. 1835 : G.C.B., 1838 : died June 9, 1840.

OCHTERLONY, SIR DAVID, BARONET (1758-1825)

Born Feb. 12, 1758 : son of David Ochterlony : joined the E. I. Co.'s Bengal Army, 1777 : served in Col. T. D. Pearse's force under Coote, 1781-3 : taken prisoner at the siege of Cuddalore, 1783, and released, 1784 : commanded a regt. under Lake in 1803 in the Doab : D.A.G. at Koel, Alighar, Delhi : appointed Resident at Delhi, 1803 : defended it against Holkar, 1804 : commanded at Allahabad, 1806 : and on the Satlaj against Ranjit Singh, 1808 : Maj-General, 1814 : commanded one of the four columns in the Nipal war, 1814-5 : the only one successful : took Fort Nalagur, 1814 : defeated Amar Singh, took Malown, 1815 : K.C.B. and Baronet : defeated the Gurkhas within 20 miles of Katmandu, and obtained the signature of a treaty, 1816 : G.C.B. : in the Pindari-Mahratta war of 1817-8 : commanded a column and made a treaty and settlement with Amir Khan, 1818 : appointed Resident in Rajputana, 1818 : Resident at Delhi : Resident in Malwa and Rajputana, 1822 : when Durjan Lal revolted in 1825 against Balwant Singh, the Raja of Bhartpur, aged 6, Ochterlony supported the Raja by proclamation and force : on Amherst's disapproving his action and deciding to investigate the question, Ochterlony resigned and died, heartbroken at his treatment, July 15, 1825. The Ochterlony column at Calcutta perpetuates his name and memory.

O'CONNOR, LUKE (1832-   )

Enlisted in Royal Welsh Fusiliers, 1849, and became Maj-General, 1887 : served in the Crimea : gained the V.C. and a Commission : Indian mutiny, 1857-8 : at the relief of Lucknow : in Ashanti expedition, 1873, Brevet-Lt-Colonel : retired.

O'CONNOR, PATRICK FENELON (1850-   )

Son of Patrick O'Connor : educated at Belvedere and Carlow Colleges, and at the Catholic University, Ireland : joined the Indian Medical Service, 1875, and became Surgeon-Major, 1895 : served in Afghan war, 1878-80 : Egypt, 1882 : Burma, 1886-7 : Chitral, 1895 : Tirah expedition, 1897-8 : China, 1900-2 : C.B., 1902.

ODLING, CHARLES WILLIAM (1847-   )

Son of William Odling : born 1847 : educated at Queen's College, Galway, and Queen's University, Ireland : entered the Indian P.W.D., 1865 : Chief Engineer and Secretary for Irrigation to Bengal Government, 1892, and to N.W.P. Government, 1895, and Member of Legislative Council, N.W.P. : Secretary to Government of India in the P.W.D., 1901 : Fellow of Calcutta University : retired, 1902 : C.S.I., 1898.

O'HALLORAN, SIR JOSEPH (1763-1843)

Son of Sylvester O'Halloran : born Aug. 13, 1763 : joined the Bengal Army, 1782 : Adjutant, and in the P.W.D. at Midnapur, 1796-1802 : served in 1803-4 in Bundelkund against the Bundelas, at the attacks on Rogouli and Adjighar, 1809 : in the Nipal war, 1815-6, and in Cuttack : C.B. : commanded a regt. in the Straits Settlements, 1818 : Brigadier at Sagar, 1828 : retired, 1833, never having taken any leave to Europe : knighted, 1835 : K.C.B., 1837 : G.C.B., 1841 : Maj-General, 1837 : died Nov. 3, 1843.

O'KINEALY, JAMES (1837-1903)

I.C.S. : educated at Queen's College, Galway : went out to India in 1861 : served in the judicial branch of the Civil Service in Lower Bengal : Legal Remem-

Y

brancer and District Judge : Member of the Rent Commission, and of the Bengal Legislative Council : acting Secretary to the Government of India, Home Department : Puisne Judge of the Calcutta High Court, 1883–99 : President of the Board of Examiners : a good Arabic scholar : edited law books : died Jan. 14, 1903.

OLDHAM, THOMAS (1816–1878)

Born May 4, 1816 : son of Thomas Oldham : educated privately and at Trinity College, Dublin : studied, 1837–8, at the Engineering School, Edinburgh : became assistant in the Geological Department in Ireland in 1839 : Professor of Geology at Trinity College, Dublin, 1845 : President of the Dublin Geological Society, 1846 ; and Director of the Geological Survey of Ireland. Went to India in 1851 as Superintendent of the Geological Survey of India, having to organize the Department : besides his annual reports, *Palæontologica Indica*, and other publications of the Indian Geological Survey, he wrote a number of papers in the *Journal of the Geological Society of London :* retired in 1876. He was four times President of the Asiatic Society of Bengal : member of the Royal Irish Academy : F.G.S., F.R.S. : and medallist : member of the Royal Irish Academy : LL.D. of Dublin : died July 17, 1878.

OLDHAM, WILLIAM BENJAMIN (1845–   )

I.C.S. : born April 16, 1845 : son of Thomas Wilson Oldham : educated at Kingstown School and Trinity College, Dublin : went to Bengal in the Civil Service, 1865 : was employed in Famine service in Orissa, Bihar, Madras and Bengal, and on frontier service in the Lushai Hills, 1892 : C.I.E. : Member of Board of Revenue, 1900 : commanded Calcutta Vol. Rifles : author of *Some Ethnical and Historical Aspects of Burdwan District.*

OLIPHANT, JAMES (? –1881?)

Lt-Colonel, Madras Engineers : Director of the E.I. Co., 1844–56 : Chairman of the Court, 1854 : died 1881.

OLIVER, WILLIAM (? –1846)

Joined the E. I. Co.'s Civil Service in Madras, 1801 : distinguished in Arabic and Persian : Persian Translator to Government : became a Judge of the *Sadr* Court, and Member of Council, Madras, 1831–6 : retired, 1836 : died 1845–6.

OLLIVANT, SIR EDWARD CHARLES KAYLL (1846–   )

I.C.S. : born Feb. 7, 1846 : educated at Marlborough : went to Bombay in the Civil Service, 1868 : Municipal Commissioner, Bombay, 1881–90 : Political Agent, Kattiawar, 1890–5 : Officiating Commissioner in Sind, 1895 : Officiating Chief Secretary to Government, 1896 : Member of Council, Bombay, 1897–1902 : retired : K.C.I.E., 1892.

OLPHERTS, SIR WILLIAM (1822–1902)

General : son of William Olpherts : born March 8, 1822 : educated at Addiscombe : entered the Bengal Artillery, 1839 : Maj-General, 1875 : General, 1885 : saw active service in Burma, 1841 : in the Sagar territory, 1842 : in the Gwalior campaign, 1843 : in Sind, 1844–5 : commanded Artillery against Kot Kangra, 1846 : at Peshawar, 1852 : in the Crimea and Asia Minor, 1854–6 : under General Neill suppressed the Benares mutiny, June 4, 1857 : with Havelock's force at Bithur, to the Alambagh : at the first relief of Lucknow, gained the V.C., which he deserved on many occasions : known throughout the Army as " Hell-fire Jack " : was in the defence of the Residency, Sep. to Nov. 1857 : at the final capture of Lucknow, 1858 : in the Oudh campaign, 1858 : against the Waziris, 1859–60 : commanded Artillery at Peshawar and Rawal Pindi, 1861–8 : Brigadier of Artillery in Gwalior and Rohilkund districts and in the Oudh Division, 1870–5 : K.C.B., 1886 : Colonel Commandant, R.A., 1888 : G.C.B., 1900 : died April 30, 1902.

OMICHAND (? –1758)

Amirchand : a Panjabi by birth and a Nanak-panthi, i.e. a disciple of Guru Govind Nanak : joined in Bengal the trading business of Boistab Chand Sett and his brother, Manick Chand Sett of Burra Bazar, Calcutta : while working under the Setts, amassed considerable wealth and set up business on his own account : made an immense fortune as Principal Contractor of the E. I. Company :

most of the best houses in Calcutta were owned by him. In the beginning of 1757, when the English were arranging with Mir Jafar and others to dethrone Suraj-ud-daula, Omichand, being cognisant of the conspiracy, asked for thirty lakhs as the price of silence : Clive designed to make him believe that the English intended to reward his services by inserting an article in the treaty drawn between them and Mir Jafar. Two treaties were drawn up, one fictitious, the other genuine. Omichand was shown the fictitious treaty, which provided for his reward. Admiral Watson had refused to sign this treaty, and his signature was written by another hand. After the battle of Plassy, Omichand was made aware of the genuine treaty, in which no mention was made of him. It is said that, on perceiving that he was cheated, he fainted away and lost his reason. The accuracy of this statement has been questioned. He died suddenly at Malda, Dec. 5, 1758.

OMMANEY, EDWARD LACON
(1834-   )
Born Aug. 24, 1834 : son of Maj-General Edward Lacon Ommaney, R.E. : educated at Bedford and Owen's College, Manchester : joined the Indian Army, 1855, and the Staff Corps, 1861 : became Colonel, 1885 : served in the Indian mutiny, 1857-8 : at the siege of Delhi : appointed to the Panjab Commission, 1858, in charge of State prisoners : continued in civil employ, on the N. W. Frontier : Commissioner of Multan, the Derajat, and Peshawar Divisions : served as Political Officer, 2nd Black Mountain expedition, 1888 : C.S.I. : retired, 1891.

OPPERT, GUSTAV (1836-   )
Born July 30, 1836 : brother of Julius Oppert : studied at Leipzig, Halle, and Berlin, 1858-60, especially history and Oriental languages : attached, for some time, to the Libraries of Oxford and Windsor : in 1872 made Professor of Sanskrit at the Presidency College, Madras, and Curator of the Government Oriental MS. Library : Fellow of Madras University, 1873 : Telugu Translator to Government, 1878 : returned to Europe, in 1893 : appointed Professor of Sanskrit at Berlin University, 1894 : published *List of Sanskrit MSS. in Southern India*, 1880, etc. : text and translation of the

Sukranitisara, 1882-90 : *Nitipra Karika*, 1882 : *On the Aborigines of India*, 1894 : Ph. D.

ORME, ROBERT (1728-1801)
Born at Anjengo, Dec. 25, 1728 : son of Surgeon Alexander Orme : educated at Harrow : went to Calcutta, 1742 : joined a mercantile house : became a writer in the E. I. Co.'s service, 1743 : returned to England in 1753 with Clive and became intimate with him : appointed by the Court of Directors to be a Member of Council at Madras, 1754-8, and was Commissary and Accountant-General : on his advice and nomination, Clive was sent up in command to Calcutta in 1756 : Orme was captured by the French on his way home and taken to the Mauritius, 1759 : reached London, 1760 : published *A History of the Military Transactions of the British Nation in Indostan from the year 1745*, in 1763 and 1778 : Historiographer to the E. I. Co., 1769-1801 : F.S.A., 1770 : published *Historical Fragments of the Mogul Empire, of the Morattoes, and of the English Concerns in Indostan from the year 1659*, in 1782 : died at Great Ealing, Jan. 13, 1801 : friend of Dr. Johnson : all books, printed tracts, manuscripts as left by him, presented to the E. I. Co. are now in the India Office Library.

ORR, JOHN (1760 ?-1835)
Born about 1760 : joined the Madras N.I. in 1777 : was at the siege of Pondicherry, 1778 : commanded a flying column to assist Coote's Army, 1780-4, and subsequently the Governor's body-guard : was in the Mysore war, 1790-2, at Seringapatam : Maj-General, 1809 : Lt-General, 1814 : died Nov. 26, 1835.

OSBORN, ROBERT DURIE (1835-1889)
Born Aug. 6, 1835 : son of Lt-Colonel Henry Roche Osborn : educated at Walthamstow : joined the 26th Bengal N.I., 1854 : in the Indian mutiny of 1857, at Bulandshahr and Alighar, in Oudh, Sagar, Bundelkund : Tutor to the Paikpara wards, 1872 : in the Afghan war, 1878 : retired as Lt-Colonel, 1879 : wrote *Islam under the Arabs*, 1876, and *Islam under the Khalifs of Bagdad*, 1877 : assisted in editing the London *Statesman*, 1879-80, and engaged in journalism and literature, to oppose Lord Beacons-

field's and Lord Lytton's policy in India : died April 19, 1889.

OSBORNE, JOHN WILLIAM WILLOUGHBY (1833–1881)

Born 1833 : son of Maj-General Willoughby Osborne : entered the Madras Army, 1850 : Lt-Colonel, 1871 : served through the Indian mutiny : wounded in action : C.B. : Honorary A.D.C. to the Viceroy, 1860 : Political Resident at Gwalior, 1880 : died Oct. 8, 1881.

O'SHAUGHNESSY, SIR WILLIAM BROOKE (1809–1889)

Son of David O'Shaughnessy : born at Limerick in 1809 : educated at Edinburgh University : M.D., 1830 : went to Bengal in the E. I. Co.'s Medical Service, 1833 : Surgeon-Major, 1861 : Professor of Chemistry at the Medical College, Calcutta : appointed Director-General of Telegraphs in India, 1853 : rapidly laid down lines to Agra, Bombay, Madras, Peshawar : in the mutiny, Sir John Lawrence said : "The telegraph saved India" : knighted in 1856 : retired, 1860 : Lord Canning, in a minute on his departure, referred to his ability and energy in extending and maintaining the gigantic work of the Indian telegraphs, with which his name is associated, and recorded a high appreciation of his services : F.R.S., 1843 : assumed the name of Brooke : wrote books on chemistry and medicine : died Jan. 10, 1889.

O'SULLIVAN, J. W. (? –1877 ?)

Said to have gone to India as a private in the Royal Artillery, and to have fought in the engagements of the second Sikh war, 1848–9 : kept a private day-school in Calcutta : was a journalist in Calcutta from about 1862 : wrote for the *Mofussilite* and other up-country journals : was special correspondent to the *Times of India* : acquired a facility in dealing with some of the more intricate questions of Indian policy : said to have secured the confidence of the Governor-General and other high officers of the time : edited the *Weekly Indian Statesman* at Bombay about 1874–6 : died about 1877.

OSWELL, WILLIAM COTTON (1818–1893)

I.C.S. : born April 27, 1818 : son of William Oswell : educated at Rugby and

Haileybury : went in 1837 to Madras, where, during his 10 years, he made a name as a linguist and an expert catcher of elephants : spent some years in S. Africa in sport and exploration, partly with Livingstone, in the discovery of Lake Ngami, 1849, and the Zambesi, 1851 : did service in the Crimea as a volunteer : wrote on "South Africa Fifty Years ago," in *Big Game Shooting* : died May 1, 1893.

OTTLEY, SIR JOHN WALTER (1841–)

Born July 22, 1841 : son of Major Thomas Henry Ottley : educated at Lancaster, privately, and at Woolwich : entered R.E., 1864, and became Colonel, 1895 : Inspr-General of Irrigation in India : served as Engineer-in-Chief in Tirah expedition, 1897–8 : President Royal Indian Engineering College, Cooper's Hill, since 1899 : C.I.E., 1892 : K.C.I.E., 1904.

OUDH, SHUJA-UD-DAULA, NAWAB WAZIR OF (1731–1775)

Born 1731 : son of the Nawab-Wazir, Safdar Jang, whom he succeeded in 1753 : was present at the battle of Panipat, 1761, in which the Afghan invader, Ahmed Shah Abdali, and the Rohillas defeated the Mahrattas : was made Wazir to the Emperor Shah Alam : he was defeated at Baxar, Oct. 23, 1764, by the English under Major Hector Munro : fled to Delhi : was defeated again and surrendered to the English : Clive restored Oudh to him, 1765, and made him an ally. Warren Hastings made the treaty of Benares with him, 1773 : sending English troops, paid for by the Nawab, against the Rohillas, and ceding districts to the Nawab, on payment : he died at Faizabad, Jan. 29, 1775.

OUSELEY, SIR GORE, BARONET (1770–1844)

Son of Capt. Ralph Ouseley : born June 24, 1770 : went out to India in 1788, in commerce : entered the service of Saadat Ali, the Nawab Wazir of Oudh : became his A.D.C. : returned to England in 1805 : Baronet in 1808 : Ambassador Extraordinary to Persia, 1810 : made the Perso-English treaty of 1812 : mediated between Russia and Persia, 1813 : Privy Councillor, 1820 : G.C.H., 1831 : died

Nov. 16, 1844 : was a good Oriental scholar : helped to establish the Royal Asiatic Society : was Chairman of the Oriental Translation Committee : President of the Society for the Publication of Oriental Texts : F.R.S. : and Fellow of the Antiquarian Society : his *Biographical Notices of Persian Poets* published after his death.

OUSELEY, JOSEPH W. J. (1800–1889)

Colonel : born June 21, 1800 : educated at Limerick : went to Madras in 1819, joining the 98th Bengal N. I. : passed honour examinations in Arabic and Persian and became, in 1825, Professor of Sanskrit, Mahratti, Bengali, at the College of Fort William : and Secretary to the College : Superintendent of the Mysore Princes, 1838–44 : was Professor of Arabic and Persian at Haileybury, 1844–59 : edited the *Anwar-i-Suhaili* : Examiner in Oriental Languages to the Civil Service Commission, 1862–83 : in 1857 was employed as Persian interpreter to the British Plenipotentiary, when negotiating with Persia the Treaty of Paris in 1857 : one of the Council of King's College : died Nov. 1889.

OUTRAM, SIR JAMES, BARONET (1803–1863)

Lt-General : born on Jan. 29, 1803 : educated at the Marischal College, Aberdeen : entered the Indian Army at 16 : acting Adjutant of a Bombay regt. in 1820 : was a keen sportsman, from 1822 : in 1823-4 took 74 " first spears " out of 123 : and between 1825 and 1834 was at the deaths of 191 tigers, besides many other large animals : was employed in Khandesh for some years, disciplining the Bhils by his Bhil corps and politic measures, and in Guzarat, 1835–8, reducing turbulent chiefs : Political Agent in Mahi Kanta : he was attached, in 1838, to Sir John (Lord) Keane's staff, when commanding the Bombay Army through Kandahar and Ghazni to Kabul. Outram, from Kabul, led the pursuit of Amir Dost Muhammad across the Hindu Kush, in 1839, and took a prominent part in the operations in South Afghanistan. In 1839 he was Political Agent at Hyderabad in Sind, and in 1841 in Upper Sind, and cultivated friendship with the Amirs. Outram, differing in his views from his superior, Sir Charles Napier, and Lord

Ellenborough, regarding the annexation of Sind, a prolonged controversy ensued : he advocated the cause of the Amirs in England as strongly as in India. He heroically defended the Hyderabad Residency on Feb. 15, 1843, against 8,000 Beluchis : Lt-Colonel : and C.B. : he was Resident at Satara in 1845, and in 1847 at Baroda, where he exposed corruption in high places. The Bombay Government removed him, but Lord Dalhousie reinstated him, and made him Resident at Lucknow in Dec. 1854, and, later, when Oudh was annexed in 1856 on Outram's recommendation, the first Chief Commissioner, and K.C.B. Outram was given the command of the Persian war in 1856-7, and made G.C.B. on its conclusion. In the mutiny he commanded two Divisions of the Bengal Army, and accompanied the relief column to Lucknow, as a volunteer, in Sep. 1857, magnanimously yielding the command to Sir Henry Havelock, subsequently assuming his superior military rank, besides his position as Chief Commissioner. On the second relief, in Nov. Outram retired to the Alambagh, and held it against 120,000 rebels until the final capture of Lucknow in March, 1858. He was Military Member of the Supreme Council from 1858 to 1860, when he retired. He was made K.C.S.I. in 1861, and D.C.L. He died on March 11, 1863, and was buried in Westminster Abbey. He was made a Baronet after the mutiny. In 1842, at a public dinner, Sir Charles Napier described him as the " Bayard of India," and the name has clung to him. His exploits and his great character—brave, high-minded, ambitious, warm-tempered, humble, modest, chivalrous, kind-hearted—have made Outram conspicuous among the heroes of Indian history. Statues of him have been erected in London and Calcutta.

OWEN, SIR EDWARD CAMPBELL RICH (1771–1849)

Son of Captain William Owen : born 1771 : entered the Navy in 1786 : served on a number of stations and actively against France, 1802-5 : in the Walcheren expedition, 1809 : K.C.B., 1815 : C. in C., West Indies, 1822-3 : Surveyor-General of Ordnance, 1825 : Naval C. in C. in the East Indies, 1828-32 : G.C.H., 1832 : C. in C. in the Mediterranean, 1841-5 :

G.C.B., 1845 : Admiral, 1846 : died Oct. 8, 1849.

OZANNE, EDWARD CHARLES
(1850–1905)

I.C.S. : son of Rev. T. D. Ozanne : educated at Elizabeth College, Guernsey , entered the Bombay Civil Service, 1872, and retired in 1897 : gained the diploma of the M.R.A.C. at the Royal Agricultural College, Cirencester : Director of Agriculture, Bombay, 1883–91 :. Survey and Settlement Commissioner, Bombay : C.S.I., 1902, for services as Delegate for India on International Sugar Bounty Conference in Brussels, 1898 : for 8 years Jurat of the Royal Court of Guernsey : President of the States Education and Finance Committees, and States Supervisor : died at Guernsey, Jan. 28, 1905.

PAGET, HON. SIR EDWARD
(1775–1849)

Fourth son of the Earl of Uxbridge, and brother of the first Marquis of Anglesey : born Nov. 3, 1775 : entered the 1st Lifeguards in 1792 : served in Flanders, the W. Indies, at Cape St. Vincent, in Egypt, Sicily, the Peninsula : commanded the reserve at Corunna, Jan. 16, 1809 : in the advance to Oporto lost an arm : Lt-General, 1811, second in command to Sir A. Wellesley : made prisoner : G.C.B., 1812 : Governor of Ceylon, 1821–3 : C. in C. in India, Jan. 1823 to Oct. 1825 : the Burmese war of 1824–5 took place during his command : the mutiny of three sepoy regiments at Barrackpur occurred in 1824 : his stern measures for its repression were censured in some quarters and nearly led to his recall : retired in 1825 :. General, 1825 : died May 13, 1849.

PAHASU, MUHAMMAD FAIYAZ ALI KHAN, NAWAB OF (1851–)

Born Nov. 4, 1851 : son of Nawab Bahadur, Sir Muhammad Faiz Ali Khan : hereditary head of Lalkhani family of Rajputs : Honorary Magistrate : Member of the Legislative Council of the United Provinces, 1898–1902 : and the Governor General's Legislative Council, 1898–1900 : guest of the nation at H.M the King's Coronation, 1902, as representative of the United Provinces : Foreign Minister of Jaipur State Council, 1901 : C.S.I., 1903 : devoted a large estate to charitable purposes, 1899 : founded an Anglo-vernacular school, 1899 : has made large donations to public and charitable objects.

PAHASU, SIR MUHAMMAD PAIZ ALI KHAN, NAWAB BAHADUR OF
(1821–1894)

Born Aug. 26, 1821 : of the great Lalkani family of Muhammadan Rajputs, of the Bargujar clan : son of Murad Ali Khan (died 1858) : educated privately : in his father's lifetime became Paymaster and C. in C. of the Jaipur forces : during the mutiny, both his father and he behaved well : he marched with a force to aid the British at Delhi, but the force proved disloyal : he rescued the Customs officers and their families in Gurgaon. Faiz Ali Khan rendered good service in guarding the ferries over the Ganges and keeping the jail at Bulandshahr : rewarded with a large grant of land on favourable terms, and title of Khan Bahadur : was given a *jagir* by Jaipur : Prime Minister of Jaipur, 1863 : received, in 1869, titles, made hereditary in 1881 : C.S.I., 1870 : K.C.S.I., in 1876 : Member of the Baroda Commission, 1874 : Superintendent of the Kotah State : Attaché to the Foreign Office, 1877 : Fellow of the Allahabad University : Member of the Provincial Legislative Council, and, 1877, representative of the Muhammadans in the Governor-General's Legislative Council : died Aug. 5, 1894.

PAIKPARA, PRATAP CHANDRA SINGH, RAJA BAHADUR OF
(? –1868)

The adopted son of Sri Narayan Singh, who was descended from Ganga Gobind Singh, Diwan to the E. I. Co. in the time of Warren Hastings. He was a Vice-President of the British Indian Association : Raja Bahadur, and C.S.I. in recognition of his liberality and public spirit. He died in 1868.

PAL, KRISTO DAS (1838–1884)

Educated at the Oriental Seminary and the Metropolitan College, Calcutta : appointed Assistant Secretary to the British Indian Association, Calcutta, in Dec. 1858, and Secretary in 1879 : made editor in Nov. 1861, and subsequently manager of the *Hindu Patriot*, then the leading native paper : in 1863, appointed a Justice of the Peace for Calcutta, and took a prominent position in municipal affairs : nominated a Member of the Bengal Legislative Council in 1872, and an Additional Member of the Governor-General's Legislative Council in Feb. 1883, as the representative of the Bengal zamindars in the discussions on the Bengal Tenancy Bill : his services were highly valued by Government : his natural eloquence was developed by constant practice,' while his force of character, combined with industry and independence, gave him a leading position in public affairs : in advocating the cause of the natives of India his moderation conduced greatly to his success. Sir C. P. Ilbert said of him : "A great orator and a great journalist, who would have made his mark in any country and at any time ": Rai Bahadur in 1877, and a C.I.E. in 1878 : after his death, on July 24, 1884, a statue was erected in his honour at Calcutta.

PALK, SIR ROBERT, BARONET
(1717-1798)

Governor : son of Walter Palk : born Dec. 1717 : went out to Madras as an E. I. Co.'s Chaplain : gave up his orders and entered the Civil Service : became Member of Council, 1753 : Envoy to the Raja of Tanjore, 1753-4 : and conducted negotiations with the French : he installed the Nawab of the Carnatic,1755 : was Governor of Madras, Nov. 1763, to Jan. 1767 : protected the Raja of Tanjore against the Nawab : made a treaty, which has been generally condemned, with the Nizam of Hyderabad, in Nov. 1766 : returned to England, 1767 : M.P. for Ashburton, 1767-8, and 1774-87 : made Baronet, 1772 : a strong supporter of Warren Hastings : died May, 1798.

PALLISER, SIR CHARLES HENRY
(1830-1895)

Son of Maj-General Henry Palliser, R.A. : educated at Addiscombe : entered the Army, 1847 : severely wounded on the Derajat frontier, 1853 : in the Indian mutiny, with Renaud's force from Allahabad to Cawnpur, and with Havelock's force : commanded Irregular Cavalry at Fatehpur, at the Alambagh, and the first relief of Lucknow : in defence of the Residency until the second relief by Sir Colin Campbell : at the Alambagh under Outram, Nov. 1857, to March, 1858 : at capture of Lucknow : and with Hodson's

Horse : commanded 10th Bengal Cavalry in Abyssinia : in Afghan war, 1879-80, with Sir D. Stewart's force to Kandahar : commanded the Cavalry Brigade at Ahmad Kheyl and Urzoo : K.C.B. : Lt-General : G.C.B. : died Nov. 22, 1895.

PALMER, SIR ARTHUR POWER
(1840-1904)

Commander-in-Chief in India : son of Capt. Nicholas Power Palmer, who was killed during the retreat from Kabul, 1842 : born June 25, 1840 : educated at Cheltenham : entered the Indian Army in 1857, and in the mutiny was in Hodson's Horse, and in the Oudh campaign and at Nawabganj : joined the Bengal Staff Corps, 1861 : was in the N.W. frontier campaign of 1863-4 against the Mohmands: in Abyssinia in 1868 : A.D.C. to General Stafford in the Dafla expedition, 1874-5 : served with the Dutch in their war in Achin, 1876-7 : in the Afghan war of 1878-9 : was A.A. and Q.M.G. of the Kuram Field Force, at Peiwar Kotal and in the Khost Valley : in the Soudan expedition of 1885, commanded the 9th Bengal Cavalry at Suakin : C.B. : Maj-General, 1893 : commanded in the N. Chin Hills in Burma, 1892-3 : K.C.B., 1893 : in the Tirah expedition, 1897-8, commanded the communications and the Second Division : was at Chagra Kotal : commanded the Panjab Army : General, 1899 : C. in C. in India, March 19, 1900, till the autumn of 1902, when he left India : was G.C.I.E., 1901 : G.C.B., 1903. As C. in C. he introduced many practical improvements, suggested by the experience of recent campaigns. He died Feb. 28, 1904.

PALMER, EDWARD HENRY
(1840-1882)

Born Aug. 7, 1840 : son of William Henry Palmer : educated at the Perse Grammar School, Cambridge : learnt Romany as a boy : three years in business in London : learnt Italian, French, Persian, Arabic, and Hindustani at Cambridge : Sizar of St. John's College, 1863 : Scholar : B.A., 1867 : continued his studies in Oriental languages, composing and writing in them : wrote Oriental Mysticism : Fellow of St. John's College, 1867 : in 1869 travelled for the Palestine Exploration Fund in the survey of Sinai, and, again, from Sinai to Jerusalem and Damascus : wrote *The Desert of the Exodus*, 1871 : a history of Jerusalem etc., etc. : became Lord Almoner's Professor of Arabic, 1871 : lectured on Oriental languages at Cambridge : wrote an Arabic grammar, and manual, and a Persian dictionary : also translated the Koran, and Arabic poetry : wrote a life of the Caliph Haroun Alrashid : revised Henry Martyn's New Testament in Persian : wrote for the *Encyclopædia Britannica* : called to the bar from the Middle Temple, 1874 : wrote from 1881 for daily and weekly journals in London : sent in June, 1882, on a secret mission to the Bedouins in the desert *viâ* Jaffa : at first successful, but later was treacherously led into an ambush, and, on Aug. 11, 1882, was shot with his two companions, Gill and Charrington : their remains were buried in St. Paul's Cathedral in April, 1883.

PALMER, JOHN (1767–1836)

Born Oct. 8, 1767 : son of Lt-General W. Palmer, Military Secretary to Warren Hastings : was intended for the Navy, and took part in the naval actions on the Coromandel coast against Admiral Suffrein (*q.v.*) : left the Navy in 1783 and joined the firm of Burgh, Barber & Co. : became sole manager, as Palmer & Co. : and was styled the " Prince of British merchants " : he had great public spirit, and gave his support to J. S. Buckingham (*q.v.*) : he had intended to leave India in 1801–2, but losses compelled him to return : his firm failed in 1830 : he died, universally respected and regretted, Jan. 21, 1836 : his marble bust was erected by subscription in the Town Hall at Calcutta : " The friend of the poor " being inscribed on his tomb.

PALMER, WILLIAM (? –1814)

Lt-General : entered the Bengal Army from the King's service in 1766, joining the 3rd N.I. in 1767 : was Military Secretary to Warren Hastings for several years before 1782, when he became Resident at Lucknow : at Sindia's Court, 1794–8 : and at Poona, 1798–01 : afterwards he commanded at Monghyr : died at Berhampur, May 20, 1814.

PALMER, WILLIAM (1780–1867)

Born 1780 : son of General William Palmer, Military Secretary to Warren

Hastings : brother of John Palmer (*q.v.*) : founded, 1814, the great banking-house of Palmer & Co. at Hyderabad, in which the Rumbolds were partners : his heavy financial transactions with the Nizam ended in his ruin, and in the censure of the Governor-General : died 1867.

PARKE, SIR WILLIAM (1822–1897)

Son of Charles Parke : educated at Eton : entered the Army, 1840 : served in the Crimea : Lt-Colonel, 1855 : in the mutiny, as Brigadier, commanded a Brigade of the Rajputana Field Force, 1858–9 : commanded the assault at Kotah : in the Central India operations, in the pursuit of Tantia Topi : A.D.C. to the Queen : C.B. : General, 1882 : held commands in England : K.C.B., 1887 : died March 29, 1897.

PARKER, SIR GEORGE, BARONET (? –1857)

Second son of Vice-Admiral Sir William George Parker, *Bart* : educated at Addiscombe : went out to India in the Army, 1833 : became Baronet, 1852, on his brother's death : was Magistrate at Cawnpur in 1856–7 : did not abandon his house during the siege : died of sunstroke, July 6, 1857 : Major.

PARKER, SIR GEORGE ARTHUR (1843–1900)

I.C.S. : son of Rev. Richard Parker : born Feb. 28, 1843 : educated at Uppingham and Trinity Hall, Cambridge : went out to Madras, 1863 : District Judge of Tanjore : Puisne Judge of the High Court, Madras 1885–96 : knighted : died June 5, 1900.

[PARKER, HENRY MEREDITH (1796 ?–1868)

Said in his youth to have been a violinist at Covent Garden Theatre : through Lord Moira's influence, obtained a clerkship in the Commissariat in the Peninsula : entered the Bengal Civil Service, and rose to be a Member of the Calcutta Board of Customs, Salt, and Opium (merged in the Board of Revenue) : retired in 1842 : entertained at a farewell dinner at the Sans Souci Theatre in Park Street, Calcutta : wrote verses under the *nom de plume* of " Bernard Wycliffe," and published, under his own name, *The Draught of Immortality and other Poems*, and two volumes of prose and verse, entitled *Bole Ponjis* (The Punch-Bowl) : an accomplished musician, clever draughtsman, fluent speaker, a versatile writer, capital actor, adept in modern languages : died 1868.

PARKES, FANNY (? – ?)

Daughter of Major Edward C. Archer, A.D.C. to Lord Combermere : she went with her husband to India, 1822 : to Calcutta, Allahabad, Cawnpur, Lucknow, Agra, Meerut, Delhi, Landour, Mussorrie and other up-country stations : to England in 1839, to the Cape in 1843, again to India, 1844 : left Calcutta finally, Aug. 29, 1845, homewards by the Cape, to England, Jan. 1846. She wrote, in 2 vols., a journal of her 23–24 years in India, one of the best accounts of Indian life and events of that time.

PARLBY, BROOK BRIDGES
(1783–1873)

General : son of Rev. S. Parlby : born 1783 : educated at Rugby : joined the Madras Army : in the 7th N.I. of the Hyderabad Subsidiary Force, was at Argaum, 1803 : wounded at Sassouigarm, Oct. 8, 1804, and at Gawilghar, Dec. 15, 1805 : in the first Burmese war, 1824–5, commanded a Brigade in the attacks on Rangoon and Maloun, and other actions : C.B. : General, 1857 : died March 7, 1873.

PARSAD, MAHARAJA SIR PESHKAR KISHEN (? –)

Prime Minister of the Nizam of Hyderabad since 1901 : descended from the great Hyderabad Statesman, Chandu Lal : K.C.I.E., 1903 : decorated for services connected with the Berars Agreement.

PARSONS, ABRAHAM (? –1785)

Son of a merchant Captain : became a merchant at Bristol : consul for the Turkey Company at Scanderoon : travelled to Aleppo Bagdad, Bussora, Bombay, along the coast to Goa, returning by the Red Sea and Cairo : died 1785 : his *Account of Travels in Asia and Africa* published in 1808 from his MS.

PATCHEAPPA, CONJEVERAM MUDALIAR (1754–1794)

(Also spelt Pachaiyappa) : posthumous son of Vienanda Mudaliar : born 1754 : became a broker : and a *dubash* (interpreter) to a merchant travelling in S. India : became a contractor, and acquired great wealth by his commercial transactions with the E. I. Co. and others : made large gifts to charities and religious endowments : died March 31, 1794 : some of his wealth was, after litigation, devoted to the erection at Madras, in 1843, of the Hall called after him, for the improvement of charitable education.

PATERSON, WILLIAM SENOULT
(1819–1892)

I.C.S. : son of William Paterson of the 30th regt. N.I : born March, 1819, at Sagar : educated at Harrow, and Haileybury, 1838–9 : served in India, 1840–72 : in the N.W.P. : Magistrate of Gorakhpur in 1857 : stopped by the mutiny from going on sick leave : the troops there, Native Infantry and Irregular Cavalry, mutinied : order was maintained in the district until the mutineers from Segowlie approached Gorakhpur, when the civil officers retired with a Gurkha force to Azimghar, in Aug. 1857 : Paterson saved the lives of a number of Europeans : Judge at Agra, 1862, and of the High Court, 1867 : retired 1872 : died June 8, 1892.

PATIALA, MAHARAJA SIR NARIN-DAR SINGH OF (1823–1862)

Of the Phulkian family of Sikhs : succeeded his father, Karam Singh, in Dec., 1845, assisted Government in the Sikh wars, and was rewarded with lands and privileges and assurance of protection. During the mutiny of 1857 he again showed his unswerving and conspicuous loyalty to Government, by sending an auxiliary force to Delhi (in spite of temptation from the King of Delhi), Gwalior and Dholpur, and keeping open communications on the Grand Trunk road. Lord Canning said that he had surpassed the former achievements of his race by the constancy and courage he evinced during the mutiny. His services were acknowledged by a grant of territory and by additional titles and powers, and an adoption *sanad* : K.C.S.I. in 1861 : Member of the Governor-

General's Legislative Council in 1862 :
died Nov. 13, 1862.

PATIALA, MAHARAJA BAHADUR SIR RAJENDRA SINGH MAHENDRA, OF (1872-1900)

Born May 25, 1872 : as a minor succeeded his father, the Maharaja Mahindra Singh, April 14, 1876 : a Council of Regency was established until he came to the *gàdi* : for his active services with his Imperial Service troops in the Mohmand campaign of 1897 he was made G.C.S.I., in 1898 : he offered his services in the Transvaal : was devoted to sport of all kinds, including racing, polo, cricket : died of fever, Nov. 8, 1900.

PATIALA, SIR RANBIR SINGH OF (? –)

Kunwar Sahib of Patiala : uncle of the Maharaja of Patiala : presented his residence and estates at Kasauli for the use of the Indian Pasteur Institute : K.C.S.I., 1903.

PATON, JOHN STAFFORD (1821-1889)

Son of Capt. John Forbes Paton : born 1821 : educated at Addiscombe : Bengal infantry cadet in 1837 : was at Maharajpur, 1843 : in the Sikh war, 1845-6, at Firozshahr, Sobraon, and Kot-Kangra : D.A.Q.M.G. in the Panjab campaign, 1848-9, at Ramnagar, the Chenab, Sadulapur, Chilianwala : under C. J. Napier against the Afridis and at the Kohat Pass, 1850 : commanded the force sent to suppress the Gogaira insurrection, 1857 : joined the Staff corps, 1861 : Q.M.G. in Bengal, 1863-8 : commanded a Division, 1870 : C.B., 1873 : General, 1877 : died Nov. 28, 1889.

PAUL, SIR GREGORY CHARLES (1831-1900)

Son of Peter J. Paul, of Calcutta : born 1831 : educated at King's College, London, and Trinity College, Cambridge : called to the bar at the Inner Temple, 1855 : enrolled as an Advocate by the Calcutta High Court, 1862 : officiated as a Puisne Judge of the Court, 1871-2 : Advocate-General from 1872 : C.I.E., 1878 : K.C.I.E. 1888 : Additional Member of the Governor-General's Legislative Council, 1878-82 : Member of the Bengal Legislative Council while Advocate-General : died Jan. 1,

1900, at Calcutta, having resigned his appointment the previous day.

PAUL, JOHN LISTON (1827–)

Born Feb. 12, 1827 : son of John Paul, M.D. (Edin.) : educated at Elgin Academy and Aberdeen and Edinburgh Universities : entered the Madras Medical Service, 1850, and rose to be Deputy Surgeon-General : retired, 1874, and was appointed member of the Medical Board at the India Office, 1875.

PAYN, SIR WILLIAM (1823-1893)

Son of William Payn : born 1823 : entered the Army, 1842 : served in the Satlaj, Panjab, and other Indian campaigns, 1845-52 : in the Crimea manded a regiment of the Turkish Contingent : in the mutiny was at the battle of Cawnpur, the siege of Lucknow and other engagements : C.B. : Brevet-Lt-Colonel : commanded the Mysore Division of the Madras Army, 1879-83 : K.C.B., 1886 : General, 1887 : died June 14, 1893.

PAYNE, ARTHUR JAMES (1826–)

Born Oct. 21, 1826 : son of Captain John Payne : educated at King's College, London : graduated in London, A.B., M.D. : went out to India in the I.M.S., 1849 : after early service with troops, held Civil appointments in the N.W.P., and went to Bengal, 1856, where for 28 years he rendered " public services of the most exceptional and distinguished character " : nearly every Department of the Administration in which medical officers are employed having the advantage of his sound judgment and rare capacity for organization and control : as Superintendent of Lunatic Asylums, 1860-82, he introduced reforms making for economy and efficiency : for 10 years superintended the Lock Hospitals of Calcutta : twice officiated as Inspr-General of Jails : acted as Sanitary Commissioner, Bengal, 1871 : organized a system of State Emigration : as Health Officer of Calcutta, from 1876, was the first to propose and take real steps towards the improvement of the sanitary condition of the town : was a member of every important Medical Committee at Calcutta for 20 years : Surgeon-General of Bengal, 1879-84 : acting Surgeon-General with the Government of India, 1883 : retired,

1885, the Bengal Government recording their recognition of his vigorous administration and hostility to inefficiency and extravagance : in 1888 he rendered great assistance to the Secretary of State for India in connexion with a scheme of Army Nursing proposed by the Government of India.

PEACOCK, SIR BARNES (1810-1890)

Son of Lewis H. Peacock : born 1810 : practised as a special pleader : called to the bar, at the Inner Temple, 1836 : made his reputation by obtaining the acquittal of Daniel O'Connell on appeal to the House of Lords, 1843 : Q.C., 1850 : and Bencher of his Inn : Legal Member of the Supreme Council, April, 1852, to June, 1859 : in charge of the Indian Penal Code when it became law : Chief Justice of the Supreme Court at Calcutta, 1859-62, and of the High Court, 1862-70 : knighted 1859 : for some time Vice-President of the Legislative Council : retired, 1870 : Member of the Judicial Committee of the Privy Council, 1872 : died Dec. 3, 1890.

PEACOCK, FREDERICK BARNES (1836-1894)

I.C.S. : born 1836 : son of Sir Barnes Peacock (*q.v.*) : educated at Eton and Haileybury : joined the Bengal Civil Service, 1857 : Registrar of the High Court, 1864 : Commissioner of Dacca, 1878, and of the Presidency Division, 1881 : Chief Secretary of the Government of Bengal, 1883-7 : Member of the Bengal Legislative Council, 1889, and of the Board of Revenue, 1887 : retired, 1890 : C.S.I., died April 14, 1894, on P. and O. S.S. *Britannia,* off Sicily.

PEACOCK, THOMAS LOVE (1785-1866)

Born Oct. 18, 1785 : son of Samuel Peacock : educated at Englefield Green : published poetry and novels, and was intimate with Shelley, until, in 1819, he received an appointment in the India House. He still continued literary work, but his official duties necessarily occupied his time : he appeared on behalf of the E. I. Co. before Parliamentary Committees : was Chief Examiner from 1837-56, between James Mill (*q.v.*) and John Stuart Mill (*q.v.*): died Jan. 23, 1866 : is best known for his novels.

PEARS, SIR THOMAS TOWNSEND (1809-1892)

Born May 9, 1809 : son of the Rev. Dr. James Pears : educated at Addiscombe : went to Madras in the E. I. Co.'s Engineers, 1826 : Superintending Engineer, 1828 : Chief Engineer with the Kurnool Force, 1839 : Commanding Engineer in the China war, 1840-2, under Sir Hugh Gough : Brevet-Major and C.B., 1842 : Consulting Engineer for railways at Madras, 1851-7 : Chief Engineer, P.W.D., in Mysore, 1860 : retired, 1861, as Maj-General : Secretary in the Military Department at the India Office, 1861-77 : K.C.B., 1871 : died Oct. 7. 1892.

PEARSE, THOMAS DEANE (1738 ?-1789)

Born about 1738: educated at the R.M.A., Woolwich : entered the Royal Artillery, 1757, and was at the siege of Guadeloupe, the Havannah, and Bellisle : joined the Bengal Artillery as Major, 1768 : Colonel in 1779 : was Warren Hastings' second in the latter's duel with (Sir) Philip Francis on Aug. 17, 1780 : was sent in 1781 in command of a force of five regts., despatched through Orissa and the Northern Sircars, to the aid of the Madras Presidency : engaged under Sir Eyre Coote, 1781-3, against Hyder and the French : returned to Bengal, 1785 : was given a sword of honour for his services in the Carnatic : died on the Hughli above Calcutta, June, 15, 1789 : for the last 3 years of his life was senior officer of the Bengal Army.

PEARSON, THOMAS HOOKE (1806-1892)

Born June, 1806 : son of John Pearson, Advocate-General in Bengal : educated at Eton : joined the 11th Light Dragoons, 1825 : at Bhartpur, 1825-6 : A.D.C. to Lord Amherst on his visit to Ranjit Singh : with the 16th Lancers at Maharajpur : in the Satlaj campaign : at Aliwal : commanded his regt. at Sobraon : C.B., 1869 : Lt-General, 1877 : and General : died April 29, 1892.

PEDLER, ALEXANDER (1849-)

Born May 21, 1849 : arrived in India, 1873 : joined the Bengal Education Department : Professor of Chemistry at the Presidency College : Meteorological

Reporter to Government of Bengal in addition to his duties as Professor, 1889 : Principal of the Presidency College, 1896 : D.P.I. Bengal, 1899 : C.I.E., 1901 : Member of the Governor-General's Legislative Council, 1903 : Vice-Chancellor, Calcutta University, 1904.

PEEL, SIR LAWRENCE (1799–1884)

Son of Joseph Peel, and nephew of Sir Robert Peel, first Baronet, and first cousin of the second Baronet, the Prime Minister : born Aug. 10, 1799 : educated at Rugby and St. John's College, Cambridge : called to the bar at the Middle Temple, 1824 : Treasurer, 1866 : Commissioner of the Board of Control, 1828 : Advocate-General at Calcutta, 1840–2 : Chief Justice of Bengal in 1842 : knighted : Vice-President of the Governor-General's Legislative Council, 1854–5 : retired, 1855 : Member of the Judicial Committee of the Privy Council, 1856 : Director of the E. I. Co. from 1857 : D.C.L. Oxford, 1858 : died July 22, 1884.

PEEL, SIR WILLIAM (1824–1858)

Born Nov. 2, 1824 : third son of Sir Robert Peel, the Prime Minister : entered the Royal Navy in 1838 : saw service in the Mediterranean station, China, in the Pacific, N. America, W. Indies : Captain, 1849 : travelled, and wrote *A Ride through the Nubian Desert*, 1852 : with the Naval Brigade at Sebastopol : gained his V.C. and C.B : in the Indian mutiny, commanded the *Shannon* up to Calcutta, and formed and led the Naval Brigade up country, comprising ten 8-inch guns : in a number of actions : K.C.B. 1858 : at the relief of Lucknow,March 1858, severely wounded : died of smallpox at Cawnpur, April 27, 1858 : conspicuous by his bravery and personal example : a statue was erected to him at Calcutta.

PEILE, SIR JAMES BRAITHWAITE (1833–)

I.C.S. : born April 27, 1833 : son of Rev. T. W. Peile : educated at Repton and Oriel College, Oxford : Scholar : first class Moderations : first class, Final School : went to Bombay in the Civil Service, 1856 : Under Secretary to the Bombay Government : Director of Public Instruction, 1869–72 : acting Municipal Commissioner of Bombay : Political

Agent in Kattiawar, 1873–8 : acting Commissioner in Sind, 1878 : Member of Famine Commission, 1878–80 : Secretary and Acting Chief Secretary, Bombay, 1879–82 : Member of Council, Bombay 1883–6 : Vice-Chancellor of Bombay University, 1884–6 : Member of Supreme Council, Oct. 1886 to Oct. 1887, and of the Council of India, 1887–1902 : C.S.I., 1879 : K.C.S.I. 1888.

PEILE, SOLOMON CHARLES FREDERICK (1855–)

Son of General Peile, R.E. : educated at Rugby : entered the Indian Army : served in Afghan war, 1878–9 : Burma, 1885–93 : commanded Kachin operations : Brevet-Lt-Colonel : C.I.E., 1901 : Inspr-General of Police, Burma.

PELLEW, SIR FLEETWOOD BROUGH-TON REYNOLDS (1789–1861)

Son of first Lord Exmouth : born Dec. 13, 1789 : entered the Navy, 1799 : serving under his father in the East Indies : in actions against the Dutch, and the Malay pirates : Captain, 1808 : at the taking of the Mauritius, 1810 : Java, 1811 : C.B., 1815 : K.C.H., 1836 : C. in C. of the East India and China stations, 1852 : in the Burma war : recalled from his command for his severity : Admiral, 1858 : died July, 28, 1861.

PELLY, SIR LEWIS (1825–1892)

Born Nov. 14, 1825 : son of John Hinde Pelly : educated at Rugby : joined the E. I. Co.'s Bombay army, 1841 : Lt-General, 1887 : Assistant Resident at Baroda, 1851–2 : A.D.C. to John Jacob in the Persian war, 1857 : Secretary of Legation at Teheran and Chargé d'Affaires, 1859 : rode from Persia to India through Herat and Kandahar, without escort : on a special Mission to the Comoro Islands, 1861 : Political Agent at Zanzibar, 1861–2 : Political Resident in the Persian Gulf, 1862–71 : active in suppressing the slave trade : visited Riyadh, the capital of Nejd, Central Arabia, 1865 : C.S.I., 1868 : with Sir Bartle Frere's (*q.v.*) Mission to Zanzibar, 1872–3 : A.G.G., Rajputana, 1874 : K.C.S.I. : was Special Commissioner to Baroda in 1874 to inquire into the Gaekwar's maladmistration, whom he arrested in Jan. 1875, preparatory to his trial :

conducted negotiations at Peshawar-with the Amir's Envoy, Nur Muhammad Shah, Jan. 1877: K.C.B., 1877, and retired: M.P. for N. Hackney, 1885–92: died April 22, 1892: wrote *The Views and Opinions of Brig-General John Jacob, C.B.*, 1858: *The Miracle Play of Husan and Husain*, 1879: on the *North-West Frontier of India*, 1858; and papers for the Royal Geographical Society.

PELLY, SAVILLE MARRIOTT
(1819–1895)

Son of John Hinde Pelly, and brother of Sir Lewis Pelly (*q.v.*): educated at Winchester and Guy's Hospital: in the Indian Medical Service: in the Sind Irregular Horse under Sir C. Napier, 1844–7: and on the Sind frontier under Jacob: in the mutiny at Rajputana, in pursuit of Tantia Topi: P.M.O. of the I.M. Department in Abyssinia, 1867–8: C.B.: I.G. Hospitals, Bombay: retired, 1870: died April 3, 1895.

PEMBERTON, ROBERT BOILEAU
(1798–1840)

Born June 21, 1798: son of John Butler Pemberton, Barrister, and, later, Rector of a parish in the W. Indies: entered the Indian Army, 1817, joining the 44th N.I.: saw active service in Manipur, and employed there in survey and exploration work, and on similiar duties on the N.E. frontier: Capt. in July, 1835: was sent as a special Envoy to Bhutan, 1838: his reports on this State and on the N.E. frontier were, for a long time, the best information available to Government: appointed Governor-General's Agent at Murshidabad, and died there, June 26, 1840: was married to a sister of Sir D. F. McLeod (*q.v.*): and a daughter married Sir G. Yule (*q.v.*).

PEMBERTON, ROBERT CHARLES BOILEAU (1834–)

Born Nov. 15, 1834: son of Capt. Robert Boileau Pemberton: late 44th Bengal N.I.: educated privately and at Addiscombe: entered the Bengal Engineers, 1853: became Colonel, 1882: Maj-General, 1892, when he retired: served in the Indian mutiny, at the siege of Delhi (slightly wounded): in charge of the Engineer Park at the final capture of Lucknow by Sir Colin Campbell:

mentioned in despatches: held various appointments in the P.W.D., 1857–91, including Director-General of Railways, and Secretary to the Government of India: Member of the Supreme Council from Feb. 1891, to April, 1892: C.S.I., 1894.

PENNELL, HENRY SINGLETON
(1874–)

Captain: son of Edwin Pennell: educated at Eastbourne College: joined the Army, 1893: served in Tirah expedition, 1897–8: gained the V.C.: South African war, 1899–1900 (relief of Ladysmith).

PENNINGTON, CHARLES RICHARD
(1838–)

Entered the Army 1857: became Lt-General, 1899: served in the Indian mutiny, 1857–8: Umbeyla campaign, 1863: Afghan war, 1878–80: Brevet-Lt-Colonel: Egypt, 1882: C.B., 1887.

PENNY, EDMUND (1852–)

Born April 23, 1852: son of Alfred Penny: educated at Cheltenham and Cooper's Hill: entered the P.W.D., India, 1874: planned and carried out Nagpur Waterworks, 1890: Superintending Engineer and Secretary to Chief Commissioner of the Central Provinces, 1899: C.I.E., 1900.

PENNY, NICHOLAS (1790–1858)

Son of Robert Penny: born Nov. 1790: entered the Bengal N.I., 1807: Maj-General, 1854: at the siege of Bhartpur, 1825–6: in the Satlaj campaign, 1845–6, commanded a Brigade: was at Aliwal and Sobraon: in the Panjab campaign, was at Chilianwala and Gujarat: A.D.C. to Queen Victoria: commanded the Sirhind Division, 1852; the Cawnpur Division, 1855; the Meerut Division, June, 1857: commanded the Delhi Field Force after the taking of Delhi: killed by the rebels near Budaon, May 4, 1858.

PENNYCUICK, JOHN (? –1849)

Joined the 78th Highlanders, 1807: was in the Java expedition, 1811: in the Burmese war, 1825–6: in the Afghan war, 1839, at Ghazni, at Kelat: C.B.: Brevet-Lt-Colonel: at Aden, 1841: commanded the 24th regt. and a Brigade in the Panjab campaign: at the Chenab, and Chilianwala, where he was killed, Jan. 13, 1849.

PENNYCUICK, JOHN (1841–   )

Born Jan. 15, 1841 : son of Brig-General Pennycuick, C.B., who was killed at Chilianwala : educated at Cheltenham and Addiscombe : entered the R.E., 1858, and became Colonel, 1887 : served in the Abyssinian campaign, 1867, and for 34 years in the P.W.D., Madras : carried out the Periyar Reservoir project in the Madura hills : Chief Engineer and Secretary to Government, P.W.D., Madras : Fellow of the Madras University : Member of the Legislative Council, Madras : President of Cooper's Hill College : retired, 1899 : Adviser to Queensland Government, 1899.

PERCY, HENRY ALGERNON GEORGE, EARL (1871–   )

Born Jan. 21, 1871 : eldest son of seventh Duke of Northumberland : educated at Eton and Christ Church, Oxford : first class Honours, and English Verse Prize : M.P. for Kensington, 1895–1904 : Under Secretary of State for India, 1902–3 : Under Secretary of State for Foreign Affairs from 1903 : Lt-Colonel, Northumberland Fusiliers Militia.

PERKINS, SIR ÆNEAS (1834–1901)

General : born 1834 : son of Charles Perkins : entered the Bengal Engineers, 1851 : in the mutiny was at Badli-ka-sarai and the siege of Delhi : in the Bhutan war, 1864–5, commanding the Engineers : in the Afghan, war, 1879–80 : Chief Engineer to Sir F. Roberts in the Kuram Field Force, 1878–9 : at the Peiwar Kotal : C.B. : commanded the Engineers in the Kabul Field Force, 1879 : at Charasia : at capture of Kabul, and arranged the defence of Sherpur : commanded the Royal Engineers with Sir F. Roberts in his Kabul-Kandahar March, in Aug. 1880 : at the battle of Kandahar : C.B. and A.D.C. to Queen Victoria : Maj-General, 1887 : held high engineering and P.W.D. appointments in the Central Provinces and Panjab : commanded a first-class district, 1890–2 : Colonel Commandant, Royal Engineers, 1895 : K.C.B. : died Dec. 22, 1901.

PERRON, (1755–1834)

General : his proper name was Pierre Cuillier : a Frenchman : went out to India as a petty officer, in 1780 : deserted his ship, and entered the service of the Rana of Gohud about 1781 : afterwards of Bhartpur : and in 1790 was taken by De Boigne (*q.v.*) into Madhoji Sindia's Army : was at the battles of Patan and Merta, the siege of Kanaund, where he lost a hand: won the battle of Kurdla for Daulat Rao Sindia against the Nizam : on De Boigne's retirement, in 1796, Perron succeeded him as General, in command of Sindia's Army : subdued Rajputana : gained a victory at Sounda, 1801 : carried on fighting with George Thomas of Georgeghar and Hansi, who was defeated : said to have instigated Bonaparte's designs on India : offered his resignation to Sindia in 1803, but withdrew it : and was with his forces, under Sindia, during the second Mahratta war of 1803, and in possession of Shah Alam, the Mogul Emperor : dismissed all British officers from Sindia's service : after the capture of Alighar by Lake, on Sep. 4, 1803, from Sindia's troops, and defeat at Koil, Perron was superseded by Ambaji Inglia, and deposed from the command by Bourguien, and his life threatened : he fled to Lake : his troops were defeated at Delhi, Agra and Laswari : Perron went to Lucknow, losing most of his immense accumulated fortune : he then went to Calcutta and Chandernagore : reached Europe in 1805, and lived in retirement in France till his death in 1834.

PERRY, SIR THOMAS ERSKINE (1806–1882)

Son of James Perry of the *Morning Chronicle* : born July 20, 1806 : educated at Charterhouse and Trinity College, Cambridge : B.A., 1829 : was at the University of Munich, 1829–31 : took part in the Reform agitation : became Secretary to the National Political Union of London : called to the bar by the Inner Temple, 1834 : became law reporter : in 1841, on losing his fortune, he applied for and obtained a Judgeship in the Bombay Supreme Court : was knighted 1841 : became Chief Justice in 1847 : President of the Board of Education for 10 years : promoted higher education and educational institutions : retired from India, 1852 : a Professorship of Law was founded at Bombay in his memory. He was M.P. for Devonport, 1854–9, attacked Lord Dalhousie's administration, and spoke constantly on Indian subjects : Member of the Council of India, 1859–82 : Privy Councillor, 1882 : died April 22, 1882. He wrote on Indian Law and other subjects : *Cases illustrative of Oriental Life, A Bird's eye View of India.*

PETERSON, PETER (1847–1899)

Son of John Peterson : born Jan. 12, 1847 : educated at Edinburgh University, Lincoln and Balliol Colleges, Oxford : Boden Sanskrit scholar, 1870 : went to Bombay in the Education Department, 1873 : Professor of Sanskrit at Elphinstone College : Registrar of the University : found many valuable Sanskrit MSS. : edited Sanskrit works, and studied Jain literature : D.Sc. of Edinburgh, 1883 : Secretary and President of the R.A.S., Bombay, 1895 : contributed to its Journals and to the *J.R.A.S.* on Sanskrit subjects : wrote for the *Times of India* : died at Bombay, Aug. 28, 1899.

PETHERAM, SIR WILLIAM COMER (1835–)

Born 1835 : son of William Petheram : called to the bar at the Middle Temple, 1869 : Q.C., 1880 : Chief Justice of N.W.P., 1884 : Chief Justice of Bengal, 1886–96 : Vice-Chancellor of the Calcutta University for two years : wrote law books.

PETIT, SIR DINSHAW MANACKJI, BARONET (1823–1901)

Born June 30, 1823 : son of Manackj Nasserwanji Petit : educated at Sykes' School, Bombay : adopted, like his father, a commercial career, and became broker to European firms : during the period of speculation in Bombay in 1864, etc., he acquired great wealth : erected the Manackji Petit Spinning and Weaving Mill, and became the chief shareholder, agent and Director in five other mills, also a Director of the Bank of Bombay and of various Companies : a member of Parsi Societies, of the Bombay Royal Asiatic Society : J.P. : and Member of Bombay Municipal Corporation : in his philanthropy he spent large sums on public and private charities and charitable institutions, including Towers of Silence and Fire Temples for his co-religionists, a Hospital for animals, a College for Females, the Petit Hospital, gifts of land to Government, etc., etc. : Sheriff of Bombay,

1886 : C.S.I., and knighted in 1887 : Baronet, 1890 : Member of the Governor-General's Legislative Council, 1886 : died Feb. 1901.

PETIT, SIR DINSHAW MANACKJI, BARONET (1873–)

Born June 7, 1873 : son of Framji Dinshaw Petit : succeeded his grandfather, the first Baronet, 1901 : Delegate of the Parsi Chief Matrimonial Court : Chairman and Member of managing committees of all the principal Parsi charitable institutions of Bombay : a cotton mill-owner and merchant.

PETRIE, WILLIAM (? –1816)

Appointed a writer, 1765 : Factor, 1771 : Junior Merchant, 1874 : Senior Merchant, 1778 : to England, 1778 Member of Council, Madras, (the dates of his appointments being variously given), about 1790–1800 : also President of the Board of Revenue : acted for three months as Governor of Madras, 1807 : Governor of Prince of Wales' Island, 1809, where he died, 1816.

PEYTON, FRANCIS (1823–1905)

Born May 27, 1823 : son of Rev. Algernon Peyton : educated at Eton : entered the Army, 1841 : served in China war, 1842 : Panjab campaign, 1848 : at the forcing of the Kohat Pass, 1850 : in the Peshawar expeditionary force under Sir Sydney Cotton on the Yusafzai frontier, and at Sitana, 1858 : in the mutiny in the Peshawar Division : commanded Lichfield District, 1878 : Shorncliffe Camp, 1877 : 2nd and 3rd Brigades at Aldershot, 1877–81 : Lt-General : C.B. : died Feb. 1905.

PHAYRE, SIR ARTHUR PURVES (1812–1885)

Born May 7, 1812 : son of Richard Phayre : educated at Shrewsbury : entered the Bengal Army, 1828 : served in the administration of Burma, 1834–48 : in the Panjab, 1848–9 : Commissioner of Arakan, 1849, and of Pegu, 1852 : read the Proclamation announcing the annexation of the new territory : Interpreter to the King of Burma's mission to the Governor-General, 1854, to whom Dalhousie said : " As long as the sun shines in the heavens, the British flag shall wave over those possessions " : led a mission to the Burmese Court at Amarapura, 1855 : Lt-Colonel, 1859 : joined the Bengal Staff Corps, 1861 : the first Chief Commissioner of British Burma, 1862–7 : C.B., 1863 : went on two other missions : in 1862 and 1866, to Mandalay, then in Upper Burma : K.C.S.I., 1867 : Lt-General, 1877 : Governor of the Mauritius, 1874–8 : G.C.M.G., 1878 : wrote his *History of Burma*, 1883, a work on Burmese coins, and papers for the Asiatic and Royal Geographical Societies : died Dec. 14, 1885,

PHAYRE, SIR ROBERT (1820–1897)

Born Jan. 22, 1820 : son of Richard Phayre, and brother of Sir Arthur P. Phayre (*q.v.*): educated at Shrewsbury : entered the E. I. Co.'s service, 1839, in Bombay : in the first Afghan war : in Beluchistan : in the Sind campaign, 1843 : at Miani : in the Persian war, 1857 : Q.M.G. of the Bombay Army, in the mutiny, 1857–68 : Major, Bombay Staff Corps, 1861 : Q.M.G. in Abyssinia : C.B. : A.D.C. to Queen Victoria : commanded the Sind frontier force, 1868–72 : Resident at Baroda, 1873 : charged the Gaekwar with maladministration : Phayre's life attempted by poison, Nov. 9, 1874 : the Gaekwar was tried and deposed, 1875 : Phayre returned to military employ : commanded the Reserve Division in the Afghan war, 1879–80 : K.C.B., 1881 : commanded a Division of the Bombay Army, 1881–6 : retired, 1886 : General, 1889 : G.C.B., 1894 : died Jan. 28, 1897.

PHEAR, SIR JOHN BUDD (1825–1905)

Born Feb. 9, 1825 : son of Rev. J. Phear : educated privately and at Pembroke College, Cambridge : 6th Wrangler, 1847 : Fellow and Lecturer, Clare College, Cambridge : Senior Moderator, 1856 : called to the bar at the Inner Temple, 1854 : wrote law books : Puisne Judge of the High Court, Calcutta, 1864–76 : Chief Justice of Ceylon, 1877–9 : knighted : unsuccessful candidate for Parliament : author of *The Aryan Village in India and Ceylon, International Trade*, etc. : D.L. and J.P. : died April 7, 1905.

PIDDINGTON, HENRY (1797–1858)

Son of James Piddington : born 1797 : was a Commander in the mercantile marine : left the sea about 1830, and became Curator of the Museum of Economic Geology, and Assistant Secretary of the Asiatic Society, at Calcutta : wrote papers on meteorology and the storms in the Indian seas, and collected a quantity of information on storms : wrote *The Sailor's Horn-book for the Law of Storms*, 1848 : suggested the term "cyclone" for rotatory storms : was President of the Marine Court of Enquiry at Calcutta, and Coroner : died at Calcutta, April 7, 1858.

PIERSON, WILLIAM HENRY (1839–1881)

Son of Charles Pierson : born Nov. 23, 1839 : educated at Southampton, Cheltenham, Addiscombe : gained great distinction : to India in the Engineers, 1860 : saw service in Sikhim, 1861 : was in the Indo-European telegraph, 1863–73 : designed and constructed the residence of the British Legation at Teheran : Secretary to the Indian Defence Committee, 1877, for the defences of Indian Ports : Military Secretary in Aug. 1880 to the Marquis of Ripon, when Viceroy and Governor-General : Major, 1881 : commanded the R.E. in the Mahsud-Waziri expedition : died at Bannu, June 2, 1881 : he had a reputation for versatile talents as an artist, engineer and architect.

PIGOT, GEORGE, BARON (1719–1777)

I.C.S. : Governor : born March 4, 1719 : son of Richard Pigot : went to Madras in the E. I. Co.'s Civil Service, 1737 : was factor, junior merchant, senior merchant : in Council, and rose to be Governor of Madras, Jan. 14, 1755, to Nov. 14, 1763 : defended Madras against the French, 1758–9 : resigned, and returned to England, 1765 : made a Baronet in 1764 : M.P. for Wallingford and Bridgnorth : made an Irish Peer, 1766 : LL.D., Cambridge, 1769 : again became Governor and C. in C., Madras, Dec. 11, 1775 : and set himself to repress malpractices : reinstated the Raja of Tanjore, in April, 1776 : disputes arose between Pigot and his council regarding the claims of Paul Benfield on the Tanjore revenues, and the restoration of the Raja : Pigot suspended two Members of Council, and ordered the arrest of the Commandant, Sir Robert Fletcher : the Council retaliated, and on Aug. 24, 1776, had Pigot arrested, taken to St. Thomas' Mount and kept in confinement, where he died May 11, 1777. The Court of Proprietors of the E. I. Co. in London voted in Pigot's favour, and eventually, with the concurrence of the Court of Directors, Pigot was ordered to be restored to his Governorship, with instructions to resign directly. But he had meanwhile died. Four Members of Council were tried in England for his arrest and fined £1,000 each.

PISCHEL, KARL RICHARD
(1849–   )

Born Jan. 18, 1849 : son of Ernst Pischel : educated at Breslau and Berlin : studied in London and Oxford, 1872–3 : Professor of Sanskrit at the University of Kiel, 1875–85 : at Halle, 1885–1902 : has held the same position at the University of Berlin since 1902 : in 1901 obtained the Volney Prize from the French Academy : became Privy Councillor in 1904. His chief works are : Kalidasa's *Sakuntala, the Bengali Recension edited,* 1877 ; Hemacandra's *Grammatik der Prakritsprachen,* 1877, 1880 ; *The Desinamamala of Hemacandra,* 1880 ; *The Theri-Gatha,* 1883 : Rudrata's *Sringaratilaka,* 1886 ; *Vedische Studien,* (published together with Geldner), 1889–1901 ; and a Prakrit grammar, 1900 : is a member of several learned Societies, including the Royal Asiatic Society, the American Oriental Society, the Royal Academy of Sciences at Berlin, etc., and corresponding member of others.

PITMAN, CHARLES EDWARD
(1845–   )

Born May 14, 1845 : son of Capt. J. C. Pitman, R.N. : educated at Royal Naval School : joined Indian Telegraph Department, 1868 : served in Lushai expedition, 1871–2 : Afghan war, 1878–80 : Tirah expedition, 1897–8 : Director-General, Indian Telegraph Department, 1899 : retired, 1900 : C.I.E., 1880.

PITT, WILLIAM (1759–1806)

Second son of first Earl of Chatham : born May 28, 1759 : educated privately and at Pembroke College, Cambridge : called to the bar at Lincoln's Inn, 1780 : M.P. for Appleby, 1781 : for Cambridge, 1784 : Chancellor of the Exchequer, 1782 : Prime Minister, 1783–1801, and 1804–6. His influence on Indian affairs was exerted on several occasions. His first India Bill was rejected by 8 votes on Jan. 23, 1784 : his second Bill, passed May 18, 1784, as the Statute 24 Geo. III, c. 25, established the Board of Control, commonly called the India Board, to consist of Commissioners for the affairs of India, with very extensive powers. The Home Government of India nominally passed from the E. I. Co. to the Crown : but the Statute left large powers to the Court of Directors. The complex system of Government thus created endured until 1858. When the Opposition attacked Warren Hastings in 1786, Pitt voted silently against the Rohilla charge, June 2, but spoke and voted, June 13, for the Benares charge : again, for the charge relating to the Begams of Oudh : this vote, as Lord Rosebery has pointed out, made the impeachment of W. Hastings inevitable, and it was carried out. He passed also the Act of 1786, which gave the Governor-General power to over-ride his Council, and he passed the Declaratory Act of 1788, which required the Board of Control to maintain a permanent body of troops out of the funds of the E.I. Co. : died Jan. 23, 1806.

PLATTS, JOHN THOMPSON
(1830–1904)

Inspector of Schools in the Central Provinces during the mutiny : Head Master of the Benares College : returned to England, from ill-health : Teacher of Persian at Oxford, 1880 : examined in Hindustani at the Indian Civil Service examinations : published an Urdu-English dictionary, and part of a Persian grammar : translated many Persian works : died Sep. 1904 : buried at Oxford, Sep. 26.

PLAYFAIR, SIR HUGH LYON
(1786–1861)

Son of Dr. James Playfair : born Nov. 17, 1786 : educated at Dundee, St. Andrews, Edinburgh, Woolwich : entered the E. I. Co.'s Bengal Artillery, 1804 : to India, 1805 : saw general service in India, up country : in the Nipal war, 1814–5, in the bombardment and capture of Kalunga : Captain, 1818 : Superintendent of the great military road and postal department from Calcutta to Benares : commanded the Artillery at Dumdum : retired, 1834 : Provost of St. Andrew's, 1842–61 : revived and established the Golf Club : LL.D. and knighted, 1856 : died Jan. 12, 1861.

PLAYFAIR, SIR PATRICK (1852–   )

Son of Patrick Playfair : educated at Loretto, and Glasgow University : partner in firm of Barry & Co., merchants, Calcutta : has been President and Vice-President of the Bengal Chamber of Commerce, and Member of the Bengal Legislative Council : Additional Member of the Governor-General's Legislative Council, 1893–7 : Sheriff of Calcutta, 1896 : K.B., 1897.

PLAYFAIR, SIR ROBERT LAMBERT (1828–1899)

Born 1828 : son of George Playfair, Inspr-General of Hospitals in Bengal : joined the Madras Artillery, 1846 : and the Staff Corps, 1861 : Lt-Colonel, 1867 : Executive Engineer and Assistant Political Resident at Aden, 1852–62 : assisted in suppressing the slave trade, and in the occupation of Perim, 1857 : wrote the *History of ·Arabia Felix or Yemen from the Commencement of the Christian Era to the Present Time*, 1859 : F.R.G.S., 1860 : Political Agent at Zanzibar, 1862 : Consul-General in Algeria, 1867 : wrote works on Algeria, Tripoli, Cyrenaica, Morocco, Tunisia, and books of travel : *The Story of the Occupation of Persia*: 1886: K.C.M.G., 1886 : LL.D. St. Andrew's, 1899 : died Feb. 18, 1899.

PLOWDEN, SIR HENRY MEREDYTH (1840–   )]

Born 1840 : son of George Augustus Chichele Plowden : educated at Harrow, and Trinity College, Cambridge : in the Harrow XI, 1858 : Cambridge Cricket XI, 1860–3 : Captain, 1862–3 : called to the bar from Lincoln's Inn, 1866 : Government Advocate at Lahore, 1876–7 : Senior Judge of Chief Court, Panjab, 1880–94 : K.B., 1887.

PLOWDEN, SIR TREVOR JOHN CHICHELE (1846–1905)

I.C.S. : born 1846 : son of Trevor Chichele Plowden : educated at Winchester : went out to Bengal, 1868 :

Under Secretary to the Government of India, Home Department, 1872 : and in the Foreign Department, 1877 : Resident, Turkish Arabia, 1880 : Consul-General, Bagdad, 1880 : Commissioner of Ajmir, 1885 : Resident in Mewar, 1885 : in Kashmir, 1886 : Commissioner of Hyderabad Assigned Districts, 1888–91 : Resident at Hyderabad, 1891–1900 : retired : C.S.I., 1893 : K.C.S.I., 1898 : died Nov. 5, 1905.

PLOWDEN, SIR WILLIAM CHICHELE (1832–   )

I.C.S. : son of William Chichele Plowden, F.R.S. : educated at Harrow and Haileybury : went to the Upper Provinces in the Civil Service, 1852 : in the mutiny, 1857, was at Umbala, and in political charge of cavalry about Umbala, Meerut, Jalandhar, Saharanpur : Secretary, Board of Revenue, N.W.P. : Census Commissioner for India, 1881 : Member of Governor-General's Legislative Council : retired, 1885 : M.P. for Wolverhampton, 1886–92 : K.C.S.I., 1886.

POCOCK, SIR GEORGE (1706–1792)

Son of Rev. Thomas Pocock, F.R.S. : born March 6, 1706 : entered the Navy, 1718, under his uncle, the first Lord Torrington : served in a number of ships : in the West Indies : in command of the Leeward Islands station, 1747–8 : went out to India in 1754 : Rear Admiral, 1755, second in command to Admiral C. Watson (*q.v.*), whom he succeeded in 1757, and held the command until 1759 : fought two naval actions in 1758–9 with the French, off the Coromandel coast, without definite results : returned to England, 1760 : K.B. and Admiral, 1761 : took Havana, 1762 : retired, 1766 : died April 3, 1792.

POGSON, ·N. R. (1828 ?–1891)

Government Astronomer at Madras Observatory : held the post from 1861 : made important contributions to astronomical knowledge and literature, as gained from observations at the Madras Observatory : discovered 8 minor planets and 20 new variable stars, and acquired much additional information regarding the fixed stars : died at Madras, June 23, 1891 : C.I.E.

POLE-CAREW, SIR REGINALD
(1849-)

Born May 1, 1849 : son of W. H. Pole-Carew : educated at Eton and Christ Church, Oxford : served in the Coldstream Guards, 1869–90 : was Private Secretary to Sir Hercules Robinson in N. S. Wales, 1876–7 : A.D.C. to Lord Lytton, Viceroy of India, 1878–9 : A.D.C. to Sir F. Roberts in the Afghan war, 1879–80 : A.D.C. to H.R.H. the Duke of Connaught in Egypt, 1882 : Military Secretary to Sir F. Roberts when C. in C., Madras, 1884–5, and C. in C., India, 1885–90 : commanded the Coldstream Guards, 1895–9 : commanded the Guards Brigade in South Africa, 1900 : promoted to Maj-General : K.C.B. in 1900.

POLEHAMPTON, REV. HENRY STEDMAN (1824–1857)

Son of the Rev. Edward Polehampton : born Feb. 1, 1824 : educated at Eton, and Pembroke College, Oxford : Fellow : ordained, 1848 : Rector of St. Aldate's, Oxford : Chaplain in the E. I. Co. service, 1855 : went out to Calcutta, 1856 : Chaplain at Lucknow : in the Residency during the siege in 1857 : wounded : died from cholera, July 20, 1857 : his letters and diary were published in 1859.

POLIER, ANTOINE LOUIS HENRI (1741–1795)

Born at Lausanne, Feb. 1741 : son of Jacques H. E. Polier : of French extraction : naturalized in Switzerland : went out to India, 1757 : entered the service of the English E. I. Co. : was Assistant Engineer at Calcutta, and in 1762 Chief Engineer, as Captain : his post was given to an English officer, but restored to him after an interval, during which he saw active service under Clive. Further promotion being refused to him, on account of his nationality, he resigned, 1776, and by Hastings' help entered the service of the Nawabs of Oudh, Shuja and Asaf-ud-daula as architect and engineer : was driven thence by the enmity of the Council : served the Mogul Emperor at Delhi in a military command : Hastings appointed him Lt-Colonel, with leave to reside at Lucknow : where he wrote historical memoirs, and studied Hindu mythology and poetry : returned to

Europe, 1788 : to Avignon, 1792 : through his Oriental display of wealth he was attacked by robbers, and murdered, Feb. 9, 1795 : collected MSS. : the first European who succeeded in obtaining a complete copy of the Vedas : the Pote collection at Eton College was mainly made by him.

POLLOCK, SIR DAVID (1780–1847)

Son of David Pollock : brother of Sir George (q.v.), and Sir J. F. : born Sep. 2, 1780 : educated at St. Paul's School, and at Edinburgh University : called to the bar from the Middle Temple, 1803 : Recorder of Maidstone, 1808 : K.C., 1833: Chief Justice of the Supreme Court, Bombay, 1846, and knighted : died there May 22, 1847.

POLLOCK, SIR FREDERICK RICHARD (1827–1899)

Son of Sir J. F. Pollock, *Bart.*, Lord Chief Baron : educated at King's College School : entered the 49th Bengal N.I., 1844 : present as Political Officer at the sieges of Multan in the Panjab campaign, 1848–9 : in several frontier expeditions : Commissioner of Peshawar : on the Seistan Boundary Commission, 1872, as Maj-General : K.C.S.I., 1873 : retired, 1879 : died Dec. 24, 1899.

POLLOCK, SIR GEORGE, BARONET (1786–1872)

Field Marshal : son of David Pollock of Charing Cross, saddler to Geo. III : born June 4, 1786 : educated at Vauxhall and the R.M.A., Woolwich : joined the E. I. Co.'s Bengal Artillery in 1803 : in Lord Lake's Army against Holkar, in 1804 : was at the siege and occupation of Deeg, Dec. 25, 1804 : at the siege of Bhartpur, 1805 : commanded the Artillery in the Nipal war, 1814–5, in one of the Divisions : Brig-Major of the Bengal Artillery : Brevet-Major, 1819 : in the Burmese war of 1824–6, commanding Artillery, at Prome, Maloun, and Yandaboo : C.B. : Brig-General at Dinapur, 1838 : commanded Agra District : Maj-General, 1838 : at Peshawar in Feb. 1842, in command of the expedition to relieve Sale at Jalalabad, forced the Khyber with his Army of Retribution, and relieved Sale on April 16 : when ordered by Lord Ellenborough to withdraw from

Afghanistan, he remonstrated, and was allowed to advance at his own discretion, and with Nott to retire to India " by way of Kabul " : he defeated the Afghans at Mamu Kheyl, Jagdalak, Tezin : entered Kabul on Sep. 16, where Nott joined him directly : the British captives, officers, women and children, in the hands of Akbar Khan, came from Bamian into Pollock's camp on Sep. 22 : finally defeated the Afghans at Istalif on Sep. 29 : destroyed the Kabul bazar, leaving the city, Oct. ? :, to return to India : Lord Ellenborough received the victorious army at Firozpur on Dec. 19 : Pollock was made G.C.B. and given the command of a Division : acting Resident at Lucknow, 1843 : Military Member of the Supreme Council, from Sep. 20, 1844, to March 31, 1847, when he resigned : the E. I. Co. gave him a pension of £1,000 a year : Lt-General, 1851 : Government Director of the E. I. Co., 1854 : General, 1859 : K.C.S.I., 1861 : G.C.S.I., 1866 : Field Marshal, 1870 : Constable of the Tower of London, 1871 : Baronet ,“ of the Khyber Pass " in 1872 : died Oct. 6, 1872 : buried in Westminster Abbey.

POLLOCK, JOHN ARCHIBALD HENRY (? –)

Entered the Indian Army, 1874, and became Lt-Colonel, 1900 : served in Jowaki-Afridi expedition, 1877–8 : Afghan war, 1878–9 : Mahsud-Waziri expedition, 1881 : Tirah expedition, 1897–8 : China expedition, 1900 : Brevet-Colonel : C.B., 1903.

PONTIFEX, SIR CHARLES (1831–   )

Born June 5, 1831 : son of John Pontifex : educated at Trinity College, Cambridge : Captain of the Cambridge University Cricket XI, 1853 : called to the bar at the Inner Temple, 1854 : Puisne Judge of the High Court, Calcutta, 1872–82 : Legal Adviser to Secretary of State for India, 1882–92 : K.C.I.E., 1892.

POPE, REV. DR. G. U. (1820–   )

Born April 24, 1820 : son of John Pope : educated at Bury and Hoxton : worked in South Indian Missions : at Tinnevelly, 1839–49 : in England, 1849–51 : Tanjore, 1852–60 : Ootacamund, as Principal of Grammar School, 1860–70 :

Bangalore, as Warden of Bishop Cotton Schools, 1870–80 : Manchester, 1880–3 : Diocesan Secretary S.P.G., Oxford, 1883 : University Lecturer in Tamil and Telugu, Oxford : author and editor of a large number of Tamil books, including *The Poets of the Tamil Lands*.

POPHAM, SIR HOME RIGGS
(1762–1820)

Born Oct. 12, 1762 : son of Stephen Popham : educated at Westminster and Cambridge : entered the Navy, 1778 : served at Cape St. Vincent, in the W. Indies, Kafraria : in 1787 sailed from Ostend, commanding a merchant ship, to India : surveyed New Harbour in the Hughli for a dockyard : from Calcutta sailed to Pulo Penang, and took the Company's fleet to China : his ship was seized at Ostend for trading contrary to the E. I. Co.'s charter : served in Flanders : conveyed troops from the Cape and India to Egypt : further employed in India : charges against him of wasteful expenditure were disproved : Naval Commander of an expedition to the Cape in 1806 : severely reprimanded by court martial for leaving the Cape : Captain of the Fleet at Copenhagen, 1807 : Rear Admiral, 1814 : K.C.B., 1815 : C. in C. on the Jamaica station, 1817–20 : F.R.S., 1799 : died Sep. 20, 1820.

POPHAM, WILLIAM (1740–1821)

Brother of Admiral Sir Home R. Popham (*q.v.*) : in the 84th regt. : under Draper at the capture of Manilla : joined the Bengal Army as Captain, 1768 : sent with a force, in 1779, to assist the Rana of Gohud against the Mahrattas : took from Sindia the fort of Gwalior by surprise and escalade, Aug. 3, 1780 : on the rebellion of Chait Singh, Popham took the hill fort of Bijaighar : Lt-Colonel, 1782 : Maj-General, 1795 : at the sieges of Seringapatam under Cornwallis, 1791–2, and General Harris, 1799 : Lt-General, 1802 : died Feb. 20, 1821.

PORTER, RIGHT REV. GEORGE, D.D. (1825–1889)

First Catholic Archbishop of Bombay : of Scotch extraction : born Aug. 27, 1825: entered the Society of Jesus, Sep. 7, 1841 : nominated Archbishop of Bombay : the first to fill that post in the newly constituted Catholic hierarchy in India, Dec. 21, 1886 : arrived in India, Feb. 14, and consecrated at Allahabad, Feb. 27, 1887 : being sent to a tropical climate at so advanced an age (61), he soon succumbed to the climate and died, Sep. 28, 1889 : buried in the cemetery at Sewree : his remains were translated to the Bombay Cathedral : a collection of his private letters written from India was published in England.

PORTER, WILLIAM ARCHER
(1824–1890)

Son of Rev. James Porter, of the Presbyterian Church in Ireland : educated at Glasgow and Cambridge Universities : third Wrangler : Fellow and Tutor of Peterhouse, Cambridge : Barrister-at-law : Principal of Kombakonam College, Madras, 1863–78 : Tutor and Secretary to the Maharaja of Mysore, 1878–85 : died 1890.

POTTINGER, ELDRED (1811–1843)

Major : born Aug. 12, 1811 : son of Thomas Pottinger : educated at Addiscombe : went to Bombay in the Artillery, 1827 : became Assistant to his uncle, Sir H. Pottinger (*q.v.*), then Resident in Sind : sent in 1837 to explore and obtain information in Central Asia : he arrived at Kabul disguised as a horse-dealer, later assumed a religious garb : reached Herat in 1837. The Shah of Persia unsuccessfully besieged Herat, from Nov. 23, 1837 to Sep. 9, 1838 : during this time Pottinger openly assisted the Afghans. His skill, vigour, and personal courage in its defence saved the city. He was afterwards appointed Political Agent at Herat : made C.B. He was in the Kohistan above Kabul in 1841 when the Afghans rose : he escaped to Charikar and Kabul. When the capitulation to the Afghans was made, against his advice, he was one of the three hostages left with Akbar Khan, and was in captivity for 9 months, until the relief by General Pollock in Sep. 1842. He was brought before a Court of Inquiry in 1842–3, for drawing Bills for 19 lakhs in favour of the Afghans, and for signing a treaty, but was completely exonerated. On a visit to his uncle in China, he died from fever at Hongkong, Nov. 15, 1843 : C.B.

POTTINGER, SIR HENRY (1789–1856)

Lt-General and Political : born Oct. 3, 1789 : son of Eldred Curwen Pottinger : educated at Belfast : went to sea and to India to join the marine service, but entered the Army in Bombay in 1806 : was sent on a Mission to Sind in 1808, and in 1810 went in disguise through Sind to Kelat, Nushki, Shiraz, Ispahan, returning *viâ* Bagdad and Bussora to Bombay : served at Poona and Cutch : Lt-Colonel, 1829 : again sent on a Mission to Sind, 1831, and Political Agent there, 1836–40 : made Baronet on April 27, 1840, for services in the first Afghan war : became Maj-General. In 1841 he was sent to China as Envoy, and made the Nanking treaty of peace, 1842 : was made G.C.B. : Governor of Hongkong, 1843–4 : Privy Councillor, 1844 : Governor of the Cape of Good Hope, 1846–7, and Governor of Madras, 1848–54 : died March 18, 1856 : wrote *Travels in Beluchistan and Sind.*

POWELL, EYRE BURTON (1819–1904)

Born 1819 : son of E. B. Powell : educated at Pembroke College, Cambridge : Senior Wrangler : went to Madras, 1848, to take charge of the new High School : was made Principal of the Presidency College : Director of Public Instruction, Madras, 1862–75 : retired : C.S.I., 1866 : died Nov. 10, 1904 : his statue erected at the Presidency College.

POWIS, EDWARD, SECOND LORD CLIVE, and FIRST EARL OF
(1754– 1839)

Governor : born March 7, 1754 : son of the first Lord Clive : succeeded his father, 1774 : M.P. for Ludlow : English Peer, 1794 : Governor of Madras, as Lord Clive, Sep. 1799 to Aug. 1803 : thanked by Parliament, 1804, for his services in the Mahratta war : P.C. and created Earl of Powis and Viscount Clive, 1804 : nominated Lord Lieutenant of Ireland, but did not take up the appointment : remarkable for his physical vigour : died May 16, 1839.

PRAIN, DAVID (1857–   )

Educated at Fettercairn, Aberdeen, and Universities of Aberdeen and Edinburgh : entered the Indian Medical Service, 1884 : Curator of Calcutta

Herbarium, 1887: Professor of Botany, Calcutta, 1895: Director of Botanical Survey of India: Superintendent of Royal Botanic Garden, Calcutta: author of numerous monographs on botanical and other scientific subjects.

PRATT, HENRY MARSH (1838–)

Born Oct. 24, 1838: Colonel: son of Rev. William Pratt: educated at Marlborough: joined the Indian Army, 1856: served in China campaign, 1860: Taku Forts and Pekin: Afghan war, 1878–80, in the march from Kabul to Kandahar, and battle of Kandahar: Brevet - Lt-Colonel: commanded column in Black Mountain expedition, 1888: C.B., 1889: retired.

PRATT, VENBLE. JOHN HENRY
(? –1871)

Educated at Caius College, Cambridge: B.A., 1833: third Wrangler: in 1838 appointed Chaplain on the E. I. Co.'s establishment: Archdeacon of Calcutta, 1850: author of *Mathematical Principles of Mechanical Philosophy* and *Scripture and Science not at Variance*: died at Ghazipur, Dec. 28, 1871: described as " a quiet, earnest worker, solitary in his habits, incessant in his labours, a wise counsellor in times of difficulty, a gifted mathematician, and an ardent though undemonstrative controversialist."

PRENDERGAST, SIR HARRY NORTH DALYRMPLE (1834–)

Born Oct. 15, 1834: son of Thomas Prendergast, M.C.S.: educated at Cheltenham and Addiscombe: entered the Indian Engineers in Madras, 1854: became General, 1887: served in the Persian war, 1857: in the Indian mutiny, 1857–8: in the Central India Field Force: severely wounded: gained the V.C. on Nov. 21, 1857, at Mandiswar, saving the life of Lt. Dew, 14th Light Dragoons, at the risk of his own, by attempting to cut down a rebel: also for gallantry in actions, when A.D.C. to Sir Hugh Rose, at Ratghar and Betwa: severely wounded: Brevet-Major: in Abyssinian war, 1867–8: Brevet - Colonel: commanded Sappers in Indian expedition to Malta, 1878: acted as Military Secretary to Government of Madras: commanded Western District, 1880: Ceded Districts, 1881: as

Q.M.G., commanded the British Burma Division, 1883: Hyderabad Subsidiary Force, 1884: Burma expedition, 1885–6: Officiating Resident in Travancore and Cochin, 1887: Officiating Resident in Mysore, 1887: Governor-General's Agent in Baroda, 1889: Officiating Governor-General's Agent in Beluchistan, 1889: Officiating Resident in Mysore, 1891–2: K.C.B., 1885: G.C.B., 1902.

PRENDERGAST, SIR JEFFERY
(1769–1856)

Son of Thomas Prendergast: born 1769: given an appointment in S. Domingo at the age of 15, he was captured *en route,* taken to France, but escaped to England: became a cadet in the E. I. Co.'s Military Service: went to Madras: joined the Madras Fusiliers in Mysore and at Seringapatam, 1779: was on the guard placed over Tippoo's body: A.D.C. to General (Lord) Harris at Madras: stationed at Fort St. George, rose to be Military Auditor-General: absent from Europe for 40 years: knighted: died at Brighton, July, 1856.

PRENDERGAST, THOMAS (1806–1886)

I.C.S.: son of Sir Jeffery Prendergast: born 1806: educated at Haileybury, 1825–6: entered the E. I. Co.'s Madras Civil Service, 1826: Magistrate and Collector of Ganjam: retired, 1859: became blind: published *The Mastery System of Languages, or the Art of speaking Foreign Languages idiomatically,* and manuals for several languages on his system, which he had applied to the Madras vernaculars: died Nov. 14, 1886.

PRETYMAN, SIR GEORGE TINDAL
(1845–)

Born March 1, 1845: son of Rev. J. R. Pretyman: educated at Wimbledon and Woolwich: joined the R.A., 1865: served in Canada during Fenian raids, 1866 and 1870: A.D.C. to General Roberts during Afghan war, 1878–80: in the Kabul-Kandahar march: Brevet-Major and Lt-Colonel: Military Secretary to Sir F. Roberts as C. in C. Madras, 1881–4: A.A.G. for R.A. in India, 1887–9: commanded second class District, Bengal, 1889–94: Maj-General, 1897: Commandant, Headquarters, S. Africa, 1899–1900: commanded Kimberley District

1901 : commanding first-class District, India : C.B., 1896 : K.C.M.G., 1900.

PRICE, DAVID (1762–1835)

Major : born 1762 : educated at Brecknock, and Jesus College, Cambridge : Sizar : enlisted in the E. I. Co.'s service : went to India, 1781 : served under Sir Hector Munro in Madras and against Tippoo up to 1783 : at the siege of Dharwar, Feb. 1791, lost a leg : Judge Advocate of the Bombay Army, 1795 : served in Poona, Surat, Seringapatam, and Malabar in 1797–8 : studied Persian : collected MSS. at Surat : Persian Translator to General James Stuart (*q.v.*) in the Mysore war : left India, 1805 : wrote works on Indian, Persian and Arabian History, including *A Chronological Retrospect of Muhammadan History*, 1811–21 ; *Autobiography of the Emperor Jehangir*, 1829 ; *Autobiographical Memoirs*, published 1839 : gold medallist of the Oriental Translation Committee: M.R.A.S.: M.R.S.L. : died Dec. 16, 1835.

PRICE, SIR JOHN FREDERICK (1839–   )

I.C.S. : son of John Price : born Oct. 3, 1839: educated at Melbourne University: went to Madras in the Civil Service, 1862 : retired, 1897 : Chief Secretary to Government of Madras, 1888 : Member of Legislative Council, Madras : C.S.I., 1893 : K.C.S.I., 1898 : translated from Tamil *The Private Diary of Ananda Ranga Pillai, 1736–1761*, the confidential agent of Dupleix.

PRIDEAUX, WILLIAM FRANCIS (1840–   )

Born April 30, 1840 : son of F. W. Prideaux, Revenue Secretary, India Office : educated at Aldenham : served in India Office, 1859 : joined the Bombay Army, 1860, and Staff Corps, 1865 : served with Mr. Rassam's Mission to King Theodore of Abyssinia, 1864 : imprisoned at Magdala, July, 1866, to April, 1868 : employed under the Foreign Office in India : Acting Consul-General at Zanzibar, 1873–5 : in the Persian Gulf, 1876–7 : Resident in Jaipur, Oodeypur, and Kashmir : Colonel, 1890 : C.S.I., 1895 : has published *The Lay of the Himyariks*, many papers on archæology and numismatics, besides bibliographical works.

PRIMROSE, SIR HENRY WILLIAM (1846–   )

Born Aug. 22, 1846 : son of Hon. B. F. Primrose : educated at Glenalmond and Balliol College, Oxford : entered the Treasury, 1869 : Private Secretary to Lord Ripon, Viceroy of India, 1880–4 : C.S.I. : Private Secretary to Mr. Gladstone, 1886 : Chairman, Board of Customs, 1895–9 : Chairman, Board of Inland Revenue, since 1899 : K.C.B., 1899.

PRIMROSE, JAMES MAURICE (1819–1892)

General : educated at Sandhurst : joined the Army, 1837 : with the 43rd regt. in the Kafir war, 1851–3 : in the mutiny, at Kirwi and other engagements, 1857–8 : held a command at Aldershot : in the Afghan war, 1879–80 : commanded the first Division of the Kandahar Field Force, 1879, and the whole force in succession to Sir D. M. Stewart (*q.v.*) in 1880 : besieged at Kandahar by Ayub Khan after Maiwand, 1880 : died Nov. 25, 1892: C.S.I.

PRINGLE, A. T. (about 1852–1904)

Assistant Secretary to the Madras Government, and a writer of note, whose labours and research have earned the gratitude of many better known workers : he edited *Hand List of Old Madras Records* : compiled a *Catalogue of Books and Serial Articles relating to Language in the Imperial Library, Calcutta*, 1899 : edited the *Diary and Consultation Book of the Agent (President) Governor and Council of Fort St. George*, 1682, 1894 : died Jan. 1, 1904, at Madras.

PRINGLE, ROBERT KEITH (1802–1897)

I.C.S. : son of Alexander Pringle : educated at the old High School, Edinburgh, and at Haileybury : joined the Bombay C.S., 1820 : was Chief Secretary to the Government of Bombay: Master of the Mint : acting Member of Council : succeeded Sir C. Napier in the Government of Sind, 1847 : retired, 1854 : died Jan. 12, 1897.

PRINSEP, CHARLES ROBERT (1790–1864)

Second son of John Prinsep, brother of Henry Thoby Prinsep (*q.v.*) and James

Prinsep (*q.v.*) : born March 28, 1790 : educated at Tunbridge and St. John's College, Cambridge : called to the bar from the Inner Temple, 1817 : practised at the Calcutta bar from 1824 : LL.D. : became Standing Counsel : officiated as Advocate-General of Bengal, 1846, and 1849, and held the post from 1852–5, when he retired : died June 8, 1864.

PRINSEP, HENRY THOBY (1792–1878)

I.C.S. : son of John Prinsep, M.P. : (*q.v.*) : born July 15, 1792, at Thoby Priory, in Essex : educated privately, at Tunbridge and at the E. I. Co.'s College at Hertford Castle : arrived in Bengal in 1809 : became Assistant Secretary to the Governor-General, the Marquis of Hastings, in 1814, whom he accompanied on his tour through Oudh, the N.W.P. and in the Nipal, Pindari and Mahratta wars : published *A History of the Political and Military Transactions in India during the Administration of the Marquis of Hastings*, 1823 : was the first Superintendent and Remembrancer of legal affairs : inquired into *Patni* tenures, and, on his report, the famous *Patni* Regulation of 1819 was passed : Persian Secretary to Government, 1820 : Secretary, in the Territorial Department, 1826 : Chief Secretary, 1834 : Member of the Supreme Council, temporarily, in 1835, substantively, 1840–3 : retired, 1843 : was unsuccessful in attempts to enter Parliament for the Kilmarnock Burghs, Dartmouth and Dover : M.P. for Harwich, 1850, but unseated for defective property qualification, and unsuccessful at the fresh election : became a Director of the E.I. Co., 1850 : was one of the original members chosen by the E. I. Co. for the new Council of India in 1858, retaining the post till 1874 : translated the *Memoirs of a Pathan Soldier of Fortune, the Nawab Muhammad Amir Khan*, 1832 : wrote on *The Origin of the Sikh Power in the Panjab* : on *Tibet, Tartary and Mongolia*, 1851 ; on the *India Question* in 1853, *A History of the Life of Ranjit Singh, Historical Results from Discoveries in Afghanistan*, and published the *Register of the Bengal Civil Servants*, 1790–1842 : was the chief founder of the Bengal Civil Fund : on his actuarial calculations (approved by professional actuaries in London) the fund was started : also wrote poetry : died Feb. 11, 1878.

PRINSEP, SIR HENRY THOBY
(1836–   )

Born 1836 : son of Henry Thoby Prinsep (*q.v.*) : educated at Harrow and Haileybury : arrived in India on Dec. 7, 1855 : Assistant Magistrate at Midnapur during the mutiny, and as Civil Officer accompanied a Naval Brigade with light guns sent from Midnapur to join troops, to subdue a rising among the Kols : became Registrar of the *Sadr* Court in Jan. 1862, and of the High Court on its establishment on July 1 of the same year : held several temporary appointments before becoming a District Judge in 1867 : Judicial Commissioner in Mysore, 1875–6, officiating Judge of the Calcutta High Court, 1877, confirmed in 1878 : he acted as Chief Justice in 1902 : presided, in 1893–4, over the Jury Commission, and, in 1896–8, joined the Governor-General's Legislative Council to assist in revising the Codes of Criminal and Civil Procedure : knighted in 1894, and made K.C.I.E. on retirement in March, 1904. For 26 years he was District Grand Master of the Freemasons in Bengal, and was the last of the members of the Indian Civil Service educated at Haileybury employed in India.

PRINSEP, JAMES (1799–1840)

Seventh son of John Prinsep and brother of Charles Robert and Henry Thoby Prinsep (*q.v.*) : born Aug. 20, 1799 : went to India in 1819 as Assistant Assay-master to the Calcutta Mint : Assay-master at the Benares Mint, 1820–30 : Deputy in 1830, and Assay-master, 1832–8, at the Calcutta Mint : died April 22, 1840, from softening of the brain caused by overwork. At Benares, he constructed a new Mint, and Church : built a bridge over the Karamnassa : was Member and Secretary of the Benares Committee for public improvements : established a Literary Institution : published *Views and Illustrations of Benares*, 1825 : at Calcutta : contributed to and edited the *Gleamings of Science*, which was developed into the *Journal of the Asiatic Society of Bengal*, of which he was Secretary, 1832–8 : also, at Calcutta, finished the canal, linking the river Hughli with the Sundarbans, which had been commenced by his brother, Captain Thomas Prinsep, Bengal Engineers, who had died suddenly through an accident. He devoted himself to literary and scientific pursuits of many kinds—chemistry, mineralogy, meteorology, Indian inscriptions, numismatics and antiquities; deciphered the Asoka edicts on pillars and rocks, initiated projects, which were accepted, for reforming weights and measures, and for introducing a uniform coinage of the Company's rupees of 1835. His essays on Indian subjects were collected and published in two volumes. He was F.R.S., and corresponding Member of foreign learned institutions. "Prinsep's Ghat," south of Fort William, at Calcutta, was erected by the citizens of Calcutta in his memory.

PRINSEP, JOHN (1746-1830)

Born April 23, 1746 : son of Rev. John Prinsep, Vicar of Bicester : went out to India as a Cadet in 1771 : never joined the Army : resigned his Commission in 1772 : was employed in several commercial offices connected with the cotton investment of the E. I. Co., for his knowledge and experience of cotton fabrics acquired in mercantile houses in London : introduced the cultivation and manufacture of indigo into Bengal at a factory at Nilganj, near Baraset, 1779 : opened a copper mint at Pulta, under authority of Government, 1780 : left India, 1788 : was one of the founders of the Westminster Life Insurance Society : M.P. for Queensborough, 1802-6 : Alderman of the City of London, 1804-9 : and High Bailiff of Southwark, 1817-24 : died in London, Nov. 30, 1830.

PRITCHARD, SIR CHARLES BRADLEY (1837-1903)

Son of the Rev. Dr. C. Pritchard, Savilian Professor of Astronomy at Oxford : born in 1837 : educated at Rugby, Sherbourne, and Haileybury : joined the Bombay Civil Service in 1857. After holding various minor appointments, he was President of the Salt Commission in Madras in 1876, and in 1877-8 proposed a scheme for the working of the Abkari system in Bombay. He became Commissioner of Customs, 1881: Commissioner of Salt Revenue, 1882 : Commissioner in Sind, 1887 : Member of Council, Bombay, 1889 : Member of the Supreme Council (in charge of Public Works), from Nov. 1892, to March, 1896 : he was strongly opposed to the Cotton Duties : C.S.I. in

1886, and K.C.I.E. in 1891. He supported the Turf for many years in Western India. He died in London, Nov. 23, 1903.

PRITCHARD, GORDON DOUGLAS (1835-)

Born April 22, 1835 : son of William Waugh Pritchard : educated at King's College, London, and Woolwich : joined the R.E., 1855 : served in the Indian mutiny, 1857-8 : at the relief, siege, and capture of Lucknow : China war, 1860 : capture of Pekin : Abyssinian campaign, 1867-8 : led the assault at the capture of Magdala : wounded : C.B., 1886 : F.R.G.S. : F.R.C.I.

PRITCHARD, HURLOCK GALLOWAY (1836-)

Born Sep. 23, 1836 : son of William Waugh Pritchard : educated at City of London School : joined Madras Artillery, 1857 : R.A., 1860, and Staff Corps, 1871 : became Colonel, 1887 : served in part of Indian mutiny : Military Secretary to Lord Hobart, Governor of Madras, 1873-4 : Accountant-General to the Government of India, in the Military Department, 1886-93 : C.S.I., 1893.

PRITZLER, SIR THEOPHILUS (?-1839)

Entered the Army, 1793 : served in Holland and Germany, 1794-5 : Brevet-Colonel, 1814 : went to India, 1814 : Brig-General in the Mahratta war, 1817-8 : in pursuit of the Peshwa : took Singhar and Wasota, 1818, and co-operated in the siege of Sholapur in May, 1818, defeating the Mahrattas on the river Sena : made K.C.B., 1822 : died April 12, 1839.

PROBYN, SIR DIGHTON MAC-NAGHTEN (1833-)

Born Jan. 21, 1833 : son of Capt. G. Probyn : entered the Army, 1849, and became General, 1888 : served on the Trans-Indus Frontier, 1852-7 : in the 2nd Panjab Cavalry in the Indian mutiny, 1857-8 : distinguished for gallantry and daring throughout the campaign, especially at the battle of Agra : the despatch mentioned " only a few of the gallant deeds of this brave young officer " for which he gained the V.C. : China, 1860 : Umbeyla campaign, 1863 : Comptroller and Treasurer of the Household of H.M.

the King, when Prince of Wales, whom he accompanied on his Indian tour, 1875-6 : C.B., 1858 : K.C.S.I., 1876 : K.C.B., 1887 : G.C.B., 1902 : G.C.V.O., 1896 : Keeper of the Privy Purse to H.M. the King since 1901 : P.C.

PROTHEROE, MONTAGUE (1841–1905)

Born 1841 : son of Evan Protheroe, of Blackheath : entered Madras N.I., 1858 : became Colonel, 1886 : Maj-General, 1897 : served in Abyssinian expedition, 1867-8 : in Afghan war, as A.D.C. to Sir Donald Stewart, 1878-80 : in the march from Kandahar to Kabul : Burma war, 1885-7 : Chin-Lushai expedition, 1889-90 : D.A.G. and Q.M.G., Madras Army : commanded Hyderabad Contingent, 1890-5 : A.D.C. to Queen Victoria, 1894-7 : Assistant Military Secretary for India at Headquarters, 1897-8 : commanded Burma District, 1899-1903 : Maj-General, 1897 : Unemployed Supernumerary List, 1903 : C.S.I., 1881 : C.B., 1887 : died July 2, 1905.

PROUT, WALTER ROBERT (1821 or 2–1857)

Major : son of William Prout, M.D., F.R.S. : educated at Westminster and at the University and Military Academy, Edinburgh : obtained a cadetship in the 56th N.I. : Interpreter and Adjutant : distinguished himself at Maharajpur, 1843 : his principal services were in the Derajat with the Panjab Irregular Force, now the Panjab Frontier Force, of which he was selected to be the first Brigade Major by the Brigadier Commanding: Major, 1856 : a very promising officer : died of sunstroke while on outpost duty at Cawnpur, 1857.

PULFORD, RICHARD RUSSELL (1845–)

Born 1845 : entered the R.E., 1866, and became Colonel, 1895 : joined Indian Establishment, 1870 : served in the Afghan war, 1878-80 : Superintending Engineer, 1892 : officiating Chief Engineer, N.W.P., and Oudh, 1894 : Rajputana and Central India, 1896 : Chief Engineer, P.W.D., India, 1899-1901 : retired : C.I.E., 1897.

PULLER, SIR CHRISTOPHER (1774–1824)

Son of Christopher Puller : born 1774 : educated at Eton and Christ Church,

Oxford : Fellow of Queen's College : called to the bar from the Inner Temple, 1800 : Bencher of Lincoln's Inn : Law Reporter : K.C. : Chief Justice of the Supreme Court of Calcutta : knighted, 1823 : died at Calcutta, May 26, 1824, after a very brief tenure of his office.

PURNIA (? –1812)

A Brahman of the Madual sect : was a Treasury Officer in the employ of Hyder Ali in Mysore, and on Hyder's death kept the Army in order until Tippoo arrived from Malabar : was Diwan, or finance minister, to Tippoo for years : and on his death in 1799 was retained in the post under an English Resident, when the Hindu dynasty was restored by Kristna Raj Wadiar, a child of three, being made Maharaja. He was greatly trusted by the Residents, and during his administration of Mysore the country was greatly benefited by the improvements which he introduced, while he accumulated large sums in the Treasury: he received a *jagir*. Kristna Raj, at the age of 66, was permitted to assume the government in Dec. 1811 : Purnia, exasperated at the loss of power, but unable to resist, retired to Seringapatam on pension, and died March 29, 1812.

PURNIA NARASINGHARAO KRISHNA MURTI, SIR (1849–)

Born Aug. 12, 1849 : fourth in direct descent from Purnia (*q.v.*), the great Mysore statesman : educated at Bangalore : B.L. of the Madras University : Assistant Superintendent in Mysore, in 1870 : after the rendition of the State to the Maharaja in 1881, he remained in the State service, rising to be a Judge of the highest Court of the Province : Member of the Council of Regency, and Diwan, or Prime Minister, of Mysore in 1901 : C.I.E. in 1897, K.C.I.E. in 1903, in recognition of his eminent services : enlightened and liberal, he has introduced many improvements into the administration.

PYCROFT, SIR THOMAS (1807–1892)

I.C.S. : son of Thomas Pycroft : born 1807 : educated at Bath, privately, and Trinity College, Oxford: Exhibitioner : gained at Oxford, by open competition, in 1829, the "writership" offered to the University by the President of the Board of Control : went out to Madras, 1829 :

rose to be Secretary to the Board of Revenue : Revenue Secretary to Government, 1850 : Chief Secretary. 1855 : Member of Council, Madras, 1862–7 : K.C.S.I., 1866 : died Jan. 29, 1892.

PYNE, SIR THOMAS SALTER (1860–)

Born 1860 : son of John Pyne : educated privately : in the service of a mercantile firm in India, 1883–5 : from 1885 was for some years Chief Engineer to the Amir of Afghanistan ; Ambassador for the Amir to the Viceroy of India in 1893 : K.B., 1894 : C.S.I., 1894.

QUINTON, JAMES WALLACE (1834–1891)

I.C.S. : born 1834 : educated at Trinity College, Dublin : after open competition, joined the Civil Service in the N.W.P. in 1856 : acted as Judicial Commissioner in Burma, 1875–7 : Commissioner of a Division in the N.W.P. and Oudh : Additional Member of the Governor General's Legislative Council, 1883–4, and again : Member of the Board of Revenue, N.W.P., 1885, and of the Public Service Commissioner, 1886 : C.S.I., 1887 : Chief Commissioner of Assam, Oct. 1889 : sent to Manipur in March, 1891, to put down rebellion and restore order : the Manipuris attacked the British Residency, and, when Quinton visited the fort to negotiate with them, he and his escort were seized treacherously and all put to death, March 24, 1891.

RAFFLES, SIR THOMAS STAMFORD (1781–1826)

Son of Captain Benjamin Raffles : born July 5, 1781 : educated at Hammersmith : appointed at 14 a clerk in the India House : sent to Pulo Penang in 1805 as Assistant Secretary in the E. I. Co.'s service : Secretary, 1807 : on his suggestion, Lord Minto embarked on the Java expedition, 1811 : at its close he was made Lieutenant-Governor of Java : reformed the administration with energy : appointed also Resident at Bencoolen in Sumatra, 1813 : charges made against him by Gillespie (*q.v.*) held to be groundless : Raffles recalled in 1815 and Java restored to the Dutch : he wrote the *History of Java*, 1817 : knighted, 1817 : Governor of Bencoolen, 1818 : proposed the occupation of Singapore, which was permitted, 1819 : he greatly developed it, and founded a

College there : went home in 1824, but lost, his ship taking fire, all his valuable scientific collections, the result of his industry in zoology, philology, natural history, anthropology, etc. : was the founder of the Zoological Society of London, in 1825–6, and its first President : was F.R.S. : LL.D : and belonged to learned Societies : died July 5, 1826 : his statue is in Westminster Abbey.

RAGOZIN, ZENAIDE ALEXEIEVENA (? –)

Born in Russia : traveller : naturalized in United States, 1894 : author of *Story of Chaldea, Story of Assyria, Story of Media, Babylon and Persia; Story of Vedic India, History of the World*, etc., etc. : translator of *The Empire of the Czars and the Russians*.

RAI, PRATAP CHANDRA (? –1895)

Rose from the humble rank of a compositor to reputation as a scholar : was a bookseller : translated the *Mahabharata* from Sanskrit into Bengali, and later into English : the work was printed at the cost of Government : he was made C.I.E. : died Jan. 11, 1895.

RAI, RAJA SHITAB (? –1773)

Born at Delhi : a Kayastha : early served the Emperor Muhammad Shah : defender of Patna, when the town was attacked by the Shahzada in 1760 : also gallantly assisted Captain Knox in the subsequent fighting : was appointed Naib Diwan of Bihar, about 1763 : under charges of embezzlement and oppression, he was suspended by Warren Hastings in April, 1772, and detained in Calcutta under inquiry and trial before Hastings in 1773 : in July, 1773, he was acquitted and restored to his office at Patna as Roy-royan and Naib Nazim : he died there in Sep. 1773 : his son Kalian Singh succeeded and was made a Maharaja.

RAIKES, CHARLES (1812–1885)

I.C.S. : born 1812 : son of Job Matthew Raikes : educated at Haileybury, 1829 –30 : went out to the N.W.P., 1831 : was Commissioner of Lahore : Judge of the *Sadr* Court at Agra : in the mutiny was in the fort at Agra : was a volunteer and saw active service as Civil Commissioner : C.S.I., 1866 : died Feb. 16, 1885 : wrote *Notes on the N.W.P. of India*, 1858 ;

Notes on the Revolt of the N.W.P. of India, 1858 ; *The Englishman in India,* 1867.

RAINES, SIR JULIUS AUGUSTUS ROBERT (1827–   )

Born March 9, 1827 : son of Col. Joseph Robert Raines : educated at Brunswick Ecole Militaire and Sandhurst : joined the Army, 1842 : served for thirty years continuously in the 95th regt. : in the Crimea, 1854–6 : in the Indian mutiny, 1857–8 : twice wounded : held several Staff appointments, including a Bombay command : General, 1892 : K.C.B., 1893 : author of *The 95th Regiment in Central India*

RAINIER, PETER (1742–1808)

Born 1742 : son of Peter Rainier : of a French refugee family, originally Regnier : entered the Navy, 1756 : went to India : in the naval actions of 1758–9 against the French : at the siege of Pondicherry, 1760 : and of Manilla : commanded a ship from 1779 in the actions in the E. Indies, 1779–83, under Sir E. Hughes, and between him and Admiral Suffrein : friend of the explorer Vancouver, who, in 1792, called a mountain in the U.S. after him : was Naval C. in C. in the E. Indies, 1794–05 : at the taking of Trincomalee, Amboyna and Banda-Neira, 1795–6 : captured many prizes from the French and Dutch : detained the French squadron at Pondicherry : made £250,000 in prize money, and left much of it for the reduction of the National debt : Admiral, 1805 : M.P. for Sandwich : died April 7, 1808.

RAJANAIKAN (?–1772)

An inferior officer, a Surweicare of the Raja of Tanjore's Army : his parents belonging to the Roman Catholic Church, he was baptized as an infant, but did not learn to read until he was twenty-two : left the Army, and devoted himself to religion : joined the Protestant Church, and appointed to the charge of the Tanjore congregations : much persecuted for his change of faith, but he remained firm and converted others : after fourty-four years of labour and suffering for his faith, he died in 1772.

RALEIGH, SIR THOMAS (1850–   )

Born Dec. 2, 1850 : son of Samuel Raleigh : educated at Edinburgh and Tubingen and Balliol College, Oxford D.C.L : Fellow of All Souls' College : called to the bar, 1877 : Reader in English Law, Oxford : Registrar of the Privy Council, 1896–9 : Legal Member of the Supreme Council in India, 1899–1904 : author of *Elementary Politics, Outline of the Law of Property* : C.S.I., 1902 : K.C.S.I., 1904.

RAMIYENGAR, VEMBAUKUM (1826–1887)

Youngest son of the Record Keeper of the Revenue Board Office in Fort St. George during the last years of Sir Thomas Munro : was one of the first students to enter the High School in Madras established by Lord Elphinstone in 1841 : there acquired a taste for physical science, and astronomy in particular : his first appointment in the Government service was that of Mahratta Translator in the Board of Revenue : afterwards he served in the Nellore and Tanjore Districts, and in 1859 was appointed an Assistant to the Inam Commissioner. He was highly regarded by Sir Charles Trevelyan, then Governor of Madras. After again serving in Tanjore, Salem, and Trichinopoly, he was, in 1867, appointed Superintendent of Stamps in Madras : C.S.I., 1871 : in 1875, became Inspr-General of Registration, and was a member of various Commissions on public matters : retired, 1880, from the Government service, and became Diwan to his old friend the Maharaja of Travancore : remained there for seven years, introducing many useful reforms : retired, 1887, from Travancore, intending to settle down in Madras, but died almost immediately afterwards.

RAM NARAIN, RAJA (? –1763)

A native of Bihar : Aliverdi Khan, Nawab of Bengal, appointed him Deputy-Governor of Bihar : he retained his appointment in the time of Suraj-ud-daula, Aliverdi's successor : after the battle of Plassy and the deposition of Suraj-ud-daula, Clive sent Major Coote to wrest the government of Bihar from Ram-Narain in 1757 : Ram Narain satisfied Clive that he was not treasonable and was allowed to remain as Deputy Governor. Mir Jafir desired to remove Ram Narain from the Deputy Governorship of Bihar, but an accommodation was effected. In Dec. 1759, the Shahzada Ali Gohar (afterwards the Emperor Shah Alam) of Delhi marched against the Nawab of Bengal : Ram Narain gave him battle at Patna, and was defeated, but timely aid, in 1760, from the English, put the Imperial Army to flight. Later, in 1760, Mir Kasim became Nawab of Bengal, deprived Ram Narain of all power, and proceeded to call Ram Narain to account for the receipts of his Government. Vansittart, the Governor of Bengal, sided with Mir Kasim ; the local officers, Coote and Carnac, with Ram Narain : the latter was seized, imprisoned, and plundered, by Mir Kasim. In July, 1763, the English took arms against Mir Kasim : as they advanced to Patna, Ram Narain was drowned in the Ganges in Aug. 1763, by the order of Mir Kasim.

RAMPUR, SIR KALB ALI KHAN, NAWAB BAHADUR, OF (1834–1887)

Son of Nawab Muhammad Yusuf Ali Khan, whom he succeeded in 1865 : an able administrator : greatly developed his State : suffered constantly from ill-health : Member of Governor-General's Legislative Council : in 1872 he went on a pilgrimage, leaving Rampur in charge of his Minister, Usman Khan, who was assassinated at the Jami Masjid. In 1875 he received the G.C.S.I. from H.R.H. the Prince of Wales, at Agra. In 1877 his salute was raised to 15 guns, as a personal distinction : made a C.I.E. in 1878, for his services during the famine : died March 23, 1887 : 100 persons daily attend his tomb to recite passages from the Koran : he was a man of great culture a Persian and Arabic scholar of repute, an active patron of literature and learning, and actively promoted education in Rampur : unlike his predecessors, he was a strict Sunni.

RAMPUR, SIR MUHAMMAD YUSUF ALI KHAN, NAWAB BAHADUR OF (1815–1865)

Succeeded his father, Nawab Muhammad Saiyid Khan, as Nawab of Rampur, in 1855, inheriting his administrative capacity and excelling him as a statesman : a man of firmness, great mental vigour, and considerable literary attainments. His rule in Rampur, for little more than 10 years, was eventful. During the mutiny he rendered signal assistance to the British Government, although his people detested his policy in addition to Rampur, he

took charge of the Moradabad district after the British officers fled : rescued 32 Christian women and children, and conveyed them safely to Meerut : was active in forwarding supplies and money to Naini Tal : as an influential Muhammadan he stood alone, and successfully maintained his very difficult position in Rohilkund : was liberally rewarded with a large tract of land : at Fatehghar, in 1859, Lord Canning publicly acknowledged his services : his salute was raised to 13 guns : made K.C.S.I., and Member of the Governor-General's Legislative Council : succeeded by his son, Kalb Ali Khan (*q.v.*).

RAMSAY, HON. SIR HENRY (1816–1893)

Born 1816 : brother of the twelfth Earl of Dalhousie : educated at the Edinburgh Academy : went out to Bengal in the E. I. Co.'s military service, 1834 : was in the Panjab campaign, 1848–9 : was Commissioner of the districts of Kumaon and Garhwal from 1856 to 1884, 44 years there in all, and was called the "King of Kumaon" : he governed in the old paternal style, almost as an autocrat : trusted equally by his employers and the people, who called him "Ramjee Sahib" : his commanding influence kept Kumaon, and the dependent submontane tract, quiet and loyal during the mutiny. After retirement from office he remained there till 1892 : his patriarchal system was well adapted to the non-regulation districts, which flourished under his administration : he was earnestly pious : was asked to preside at a great Missionary Conference at Calcutta, 1884 : C.B. : K.C.S.I., 1875 : Lt-General, 1880 : died Dec. 16, 1893.

RANADE, MAHADEO GOVIND (1842–1901)

Son of a Mahratta Brahman employed in the Kolapur State : born Jan. 20, 1842 : educated at the Elphinstone College, where he distinguished himself : in 1866 entered the British service in the Education Department : in 1868 appointed Acting Professor of English in the Elphinstone College : remained there till 1871, when he was appointed Subordinate Judge of Poona : Judge of the S.C. Court there, 1884 : the rest of his life was spent in the Judicial Department. In 1886 he was a Member of the Indian Finance

Committee : C.I.E. in 1887 : he was several times a Member of the Bombay Legislative Council : was made a Judge of the High Court in 1893, and filled that office with conspicuous ability and profound learning till his death, on Jan. 17, 1901 : he was a Brahmo of the Parthana Samaj, and took much interest in social reform.

RANJITSINHJI, KUMAR SRI
(1872–   )

Born in Kattiawar, India, Sep. 10, 1872 : descended from a line of the Jams, or rulers, of Jamnagar : adopted in 1880 as his son and heir by the Jam Vibhaji, who, on the birth of a son, induced the Government to set aside the adoption of Ranjitsinhji : an allowance was given to the latter : he was educated at the Rajkumar College, Rajkote, India, and Trinity College, Cambridge : attained great prowess in the cricket field as a batsman : played for Cambridge against Oxford in 1893, and a number of years for the County of Sussex, and for the Gentlemen against the Players : went to Australia with the All-England Eleven : has several times, as a batsman, obtained the highest average score for the year : wrote the *Jubilee Book of Cricket*.

RAO, BAJI (1775–1852)

The last Peshwa, son of Raghunath Rao : was invested as Peshwa in 1795, Nana Farnavis being his Minister, against and with whom and Daulat Rao Sindia he treacherously intrigued : in Oct. 1802, he was defeated at Poona by Jaswant Rao Holkar : fled to Bassein, where, on Dec. 31, 1802, he made a treaty with the British, thereby becoming a feudatory : though thus restored to power at Poona, he intrigued against the British and connived at the murder of Gangadhur Sastri, the Minister of the Gaekwar of Baroda : disregarded the Bassein treaty and the treaty of Poona of June, 1817 : deceived Sir John Malcolm : burnt the Residency at Poona, and, on Nov. 5, 1817, was defeated at the battle of Kirki : he fled from Poona : he was again defeated at Korygaum and Ashti, and surrendered to Malcolm in June, 1818 : was allowed to live at Bithur, near Cawnpur, on a pension of 8 lakhs a year : he died Dec. 1852 : the Nana Sahib (*q.v.*) was his adopted son.

RAO, RAJA SIR DINKAR (1819–1896)

A Mahratta Brahman : born Dec. 20 1819, in the district of Ratnagiri : frequently resided at Agra and Cawnpur : his ancestors held a *Subah* in Gwalior territory : educated in Sanskrit and Persian, he did not learn English till he was nearly 40. He began life as an accountant in the Native State of Gwalior : succeeded his father as *Subadar* of a Division : in 1851 became Chief Minister of the State. He introduced numerous fiscal reforms, improved roads and public works, and published a Code of Regulations for the guidance of all subordinate officers. He rendered valuable services in the mutiny of 1857, loyally and sagaciously keeping the Maharaja Sindia of Gwalior to his allegiance to the British Government. For his services, Dinkar Rao obtained the grant of an estate in the Benares district. He resigned in Dec. 1859, his appointment at Gwalior, and later became Superintendent of the Dholpur State. In 1861 he became a Member of the Governor-General's Legislative Council : K.C.S.I. in 1866 : was member of the tribunal which tried the Gaekwar of Baroda, 1875. In 1877 the title of Raja was conferred on him and made hereditary in 1884 : he died Jan. 9, 1896.

RAO, MAHARAJA SIR GAJPATI
(1828–   )

Born Dec. 2, 1828 : educated at the Hindu College, Calcutta : a large landed proprietor in the Vizagapatam District, Madras Presidency, who has always interested himself in educational and social affairs : Member of the Madras Legislative Council, 1868–84 : Fellow of the Madras University : C.I.E., 1892 : K.C.I.E., 1903.

RAO HINDU (? –1855)

A Mahratta : brother of Bija, or Baiza Bai, the wife of Maharaja Daulat Rao Sindia. He had a claim to the Gwalior State, but failed to obtain it : was sent to Delhi, and lived there on a yearly pension of a lakh of rupees : was very hospitable to Europeans : he died in 1855 : his house, on the Ridge outside Delhi, was the main piquet of the British force during the siege of Delhi in 1857.

RAO, RAJA SIR MADHAVA (1828–1891)

A Mahratta Brahman : son of one and nephew of another Diwan of Travancore :

educated at the High School of the Madras University : chiefly excelled in mathematics and science : took his Proficient's Degree in 1846. After serving in some minor offices, he was soon transferred to Travancore as tutor to Rama Varma (*q.v.*); after serving the State in various capacities he became Diwan, at the early age of 30, and introduced important fiscal reforms : K.C.S.I. in 1865, and Fellow of the Madras University, but, in 1872, in consequence of misunderstandings with the Maharaja, he resigned the post of Diwan and retired on a handsome pension : was offered a seat in the Governor-General's Legislative Council, which he declined. In 1873 he was appointed as Diwan to Maharaja Holkar of Indore, where he did good work until, in 1875, he was appointed Diwan-Regent of Baroda, after the deposition of the Maharaja : he re-modelled the whole administration, and adopted many useful changes : was at Baroda when H.R.H. the Prince of Wales visited India. In 1877 he attended the Delhi *darbar* with his ward, and was made a Raja : resigned his position in the Baroda State in 1882, receiving a handsome honorarium in lieu of pension. Until his death, he lived in retirement in Madras, but continued to take great interest in political and social questions : in 1888 he was again offered a seat in the Governor-General's Legislative Council, but declined on the score of old age and ill-health : in 1889 he published a pamphlet entitled *Hints on the Training of Native Children* : died April 4, 1891.

RAO, RAGHOBA, OR RAGHUNATH (circa 1772)

Peshwa, son of Baji Rao I. Peshwa, and father of Baji Rao II (*q.v.*), the last Peshwa : was Commander of the Mahratta Army and fought with the Afghans near Delhi, but was defeated. On the death of his nephew, Madho Rao, the Peshwa, in 1772, Raghoba was implicated in the murder of Narayan Rao, brother of Mahdo, and became sixth Peshwa at Poona : by a revolution, he lost his capital and applied to Bombay for help. In 1775 the Bombay Government made a treaty at Surat with him, under which he ceded Bassein and Salsette. Intrigues ensued among the Mahratta chiefs for his restoration at Poona, but fell through : eventually Raghoba's claim

to be Peshwa was set aside by the treaty of Salbai, and the recognition of Narayan's infant son as Peshwa : and he was pensioned.

RAO, TANDALAM GOPAL (1832–1886)

A Mahratta Brahman of Tanjore District : received a good education from his father in Mahratti and Sanskrit, but in English was self-taught. After serving in the Tanjore District, he became, in 1854, First Assistant in the Provincial School at Kombakonam : B.A. at Madras in 1859. The rest of his life was spent in the Education Department, and for the greater portion of it he was connected with the Kombakonam College under Mr. Porter : chiefly in the teaching of mathematics and English. In 1870–2 he acted as Inspector of Schools : was Fellow of the Madras University. From 1872 to 1874 he was in sole charge of Kombakonam College. In 1878 he was Professor of History and Political Economy in the Presidency College, and was made Rai Bahadur. In 1883 he had a severe illness, never really recovering, though he continued his work as Professor for two years : died May 11, 1886.

RATTIGAN, SIR WILLIAM HENRY (1842–1904)

Born Sep. 4, 1842, at Delhi : educated at the High School, Agra, and King's College, London : LL.D. of Gottingen, and Hony. LL.D. of Glasgow and Panjab Universities : was in Govt. service as an Extra Assistant Commissioner : called to the English bar from Lincoln's Inn, 1873 : practised at Lahore : four times acted as Judge of the Panjab Chief Court : was in the Governor-General's Legislative Council 1892–3 : in the Panjab Legislative Council, 1898–9, Vice-Chancellor of the Panjab University : promoted the foundation of the Khalsa College of the Sikhs : left India in 1900 : M.P. for East Lanarkshire, 1901–4 : knighted in 1895 : Q.C. in 1897 : wrote many law books : was killed in a motor-car accident, July 4, 1904.

RATTRAY, THOMAS (1820–1880)

Colonel : entered the Army in 1839 : served under General Pollock in the Khyber in 1842, and was severely wounded : under Sir C. Napier in Sind against the hill tribes : in 1856 he raised and organized a body of Sikhs, included in the Army as the 45th Bengal N.I., and known as Rattray's Sikhs: commanded them througn the mutiny: Brevet-Major: Assistant-Adjutant General, 1878: died Oct. 21, 1880: C.B.: C.S.I.

RAVENSCROFT, EDWARD WILLIAM
(1831-   )

I.C.S.: educated at Ottery St. Mary, and Haileybury, 1848-50: entered the Bombay Civil Service, 1851, and retired in 1884 : served as President of the Municipality, Bombay : Collector-Magistrate : Chief Secretary to Government, Bombay : Member of the Commission for investigating charge against the Gaekwar of Baroda : C.S.I.: Member of the Bombay Council 1879-84.

RAVENSHAW, JOHN GOLDSBOROUGH
(1777-1840)

I.C.S.: born Nov. 14, 1777: son of John Goldsborough Ravenshaw, writer in the E.I. Co.'s service, 1796 : Collector in S. Canara districts, 1800 : Collector of S. Arcot, 1805 : in charge of revenue of Cuddalore and Pondicherry, 1809: to home, 1813 : out of the service, 1818 : Director of the E. I. Co., 1819 : Chairman of the Court, 1832 : devoted much attention to Haileybury College, and to the settlement of the E. I. Co.'s charter of 1833 : died June 6, 1840.

RAVERTY, HENRY GEORGE (1825-   )

Born May 31, 1825 : son of Peter Raverty, of Tyrone co., Surgeon, R.N.: his grandfather was O'Raverty : educated at Falmouth and Penzance : entered the E. I. Co.'s 3rd Bombay Infantry, 1843 : Major, 1863 : retired, 1864 : at the siege of Multan, 1848 : in the Panjab campaign, 1849-50 : at Gujarat : in the first frontier expedition, 1850, against tribes on the Swat border : wrote, and illustrated, an account of the District of Peshawar, 1849-50 : Assistant Commissioner in the Panjab, 1852-9 : highly proficient in Oriental languages : wrote a Pushto grammar 1855 : a thesaurus of Hindustani-English technical terms, 1859 : Pushto prose and poetical selections : Pushto-English dictionary : Afghan poetry, 16th to 19th century, with English translation : Æsop's Fables in Pushto : Translation of the Tabakat-i-Nasiri, i.e. a general history of Muhammadan dynasties in Asia, 810-

1260, A.D. : Notes on Afghanistan and Beluchistan, 1888 : numerous articles on geography, history, and ethnology in the J.A.S.B., 1854-1905 : engaged on a History of Herat and its Dependencies and Annals of Khurasan from its Conquest by the Muhammadans, and three other works on Eastern History.

RAWLINSON, SIR CHRISTOPHER
(1806-1888)

Son of John Rawlinson : born July 10, 1806 : educated at Charterhouse and Trinity College, Cambridge : called to the bar at the Middle Temple, 1831 : Recorder of Portsmouth : and in 1847 of Prince of Wales' Island, Singapore, and Malacca : knighted, 1847 : Chief Justice of the Supreme Court, Madras. 1849-59 : died March 28, 1888.

RAWLINSON, SIR HENRY CRESWICKE, BARONET (1810-1895)

Born April 11, 1801, son of Abram Tyzack Rawlinson : educated at Wrington and Ealing : went to Bombay in the E. I. Co.'s military service, 1827, Sir John Malcolm (q.v.) being a fellow-passenger : learnt Persian and the vernaculars : served in Persia, to discipline the Persian troops, 1833-9 : Political Assistant to Sir W. Macnaghten at Kabul : Political Agent at Kandahar : at the battle there, May 29, 1842 : with Nott retired to India viâ Kabul : C.B. : Political Agent in Turkish Arabia, 1843 : Consul-General at Bagdad, 1844 : deciphered the Persian cuneiform inscription of Darius Hystaspes at Behistun, 1846 : made great explorations and excavations in Babylonia and adjacent countries : returned to England, 1855 : K.C.B., 1856 : Lt-Colonel : Director of the E. I. Co. : M.P. for Reigate, 1858 : Member of the Council of India. 1858-9 : Minister to Persia, 1859-60 : M.P. for Frome, 1865-8 : Member, again, of the Council of India from 1868 for the rest of his life : G.C.B., 1889 : Baronet, 1891 : President of the Royal Asiatic Society, 1878-81, and its Director, 1862-95 : President of the Geographical Society, 1871-2, and 1874-5 : and of the Oriental Congress in London, 1874 : D.C.L. : LL.D. of Cambridge and Edinburgh, and a Member of several Foreign Academies : Trustee of the British Museum : died March 5, 1895 : wrote constantly in the

Royal Asiatic Society's Journal and for the Geographical Society, on Assyria and Babylonia, Persia, Turkistan, Central Asia : also in the periodical reviews : and published *England and Russia in the East,* 1875, expressing his pronounced views on Russian policy and action in Central Asia.

RAYMOND (? -1791)

Haji Mustapha was his other name, after his pilgrimage, in 1770, to Mecca : born in Constantinople: a native of Turkey: called himself a Turk : went to France, 1741 : educated at Paris : went to India, 1751 : employed as a writer in the French service on the coast till 1756 : joined the English service in Bengal, as interpreter or linguist to Clive (*q.v.*) : dismissed by him, 1758 : was stopped on his journey to Pondicherry at Masulipatam : sent with his papers to Bengal to be tried as a spy : imprisoned for some months, released in March, 1761 : went to Manilla, 1761 : returned to Bengal : employed by Vansittart in inland trade : translated the *Sair,* or *Siyar - ul - muta'akhkhirin* of Ghulam Hussein Khan (*q.v.*), and published it at Calcutta, 1789, the translation being dedicated to Warren Hastings : the whole edition of the translation lost on the voyage to England, except a few copies circulated in Calcutta : he died, 1791 : probate was refused to his will, as containing evidence that he was a Muhammadan : the translation reprinted, 1902.

RAYMOND, MICHEL JOACHIM MIRIE (1755-1798)

Born Sep. 20, 1755 : son of a merchant in France : went out to Pondicherry in 1775, in trade : took service under Hyder and Tippoo, and fought against the English : Bussy, on reaching India in 1783, made him his A.D.C. : after Bussy's death, in 1785, he entered the employ of Nizam Ali Khan, Subadar of the Dekkan : by 1795 he had organized 15,000 native troops under European officers, and was with them at the defeat of the Nizam's Army by the Mahrattas at Kurdla, March 12, 1795 : he suppressed the revolt of the Nizam's eldest son Alijah : he died suddenly, March 25, 1798 : much loved and admired by the natives.

RAYNAL, GUILLAUME THOMAS FRANÇOIS (1713-1796)

Abbé : born 1713 : educated by the Jesuits : became an historical and political writer, one of the writers of the Encyclopædia : the principal of his works published at Paris was the *Philosophical History of the Settlements in the East and West Indies,* anonymously, in 1770 : an enlarged edition was published in 1781 and burnt by the common hangman. He wrote in defence of the rights of property, greatly irritating the revolutionists : his property was taken from him, and he died in great poverty at Passy in 1796.

READ, KATHERINE (1723-1778)

Daughter of Alexander Read of Forfarshire : born Feb. 3, 1723 : studied painting in Paris : in 1751 took to painting portraits for money : settled at Rome,' 1751-3, studying under a French painter, painting portraits and figures : in London painted most of the notabilities, including Queen Charlotte : Paintress to the (then) Queen : visited by Fanny Burney : went to India, 1775, to her brother William at Madras : remained there, always occupied' in painting, though constantly invited to Bengal : died at sea on her voyage home, Dec. 15, 1778.

READE, EDWARD ANDERTON (1807-1886)

I.C.S. : born March 15, 1807 : son of John Reade : educated at Chichester and Haileybury, 1823-5 : went out to India, 1826 : served in the N.W.P. : Commissioner of Benares : Member of Board of Revenue, Agra, 1853 : on special duty in the Sagar and Nerbudda territories : in the mutiny was in the fort at Agra : and very active in taking defensive measures : saved the revenue records : on Mr. Colvin's death he, as the senior civil officer, temporarily carried on the administration : exerted himself to prevent indiscriminate vengeance : retired, 1880 : C.B. : died Feb. 11, 1886,

READE, SIR JOHN BY COLE (1832-

Born July 7, 1832 : son of George Hume Reade : educated privately and at Edinburgh University : entered Army Medical Department, 1854 : Surgeon-General, 1888 : retired, 1893 : served in the Crimea, 1854-5 : Indian mutiny, 1857-8 : Afghan

A A

war,░1879–80 : Assistant to Director-General, Army Medical Department, War Office, 1888–93 : C.B., 1886 : K.C.B., 1903.

READYMONEY, SIR COWASJI JEHANGIR (1812–1878)

Born May 24, 1812 : son of Jehangir Readymoney, of a Parsi family, who removed from Nowsari to Bombay : educated at an English school in Bombay : entered English offices as a clerk at 15 : broker to two European firms in 1837 : an independent merchant, about 1846 : had almost uninterrupted prosperity for 25 years : J.P., 1846 : Commissioner of Income Tax, 1860 : C.S.I., 1871 : knighted, 1872 : his statue by Woolner was erected by public subscription at the University Hall, Bombay : rheumatic gout for 14 years prevented him from sharing in public affairs : his philanthropic charity gained for him the title of " the Peabody of the East " : contributed largely to the Civil Hospital at Surat, 1863 : to the Ophthalmic Hospital at Byculla, Bombay : the Civil Engineering College, Poona : a Strangers' Home at Bombay : two lakhs of rupees to the Elphinstone College : one lakh for a Hall for the Bombay University : besides handsome donations for numerous minor purposes, including a drinking fountain in Regent's Park, London : founded a Lunatic Asylum at Hyderabad, Sind : his public charities amounted, it was said, to a total of eighteen lakhs, and his private gifts to four lakhs : universally respected : died July, 1878.

REAY, DONALD JAMES MACKAY, ELEVENTH BARON (1839–   )

Born 1839 : son of Baron Mackay Oppemert : educated at Leyden University : D.C.L., 1861 : member of the Second Chamber of the States General, Netherlands, 1871–5 : naturalized in England by Act of Parliament, 1877 : made a Peer of the United Kingdom, 1881 : Rector of St. Andrew's, 1884 : Governor of Bombay, 1885–90 : G.C.I.E., 1887 : G.C.S.I., 1890 : LL.D. Edinburgh D.Litt. : D.L. : J.P.: Under Secretary of State for India, 1894–5 : Chairman of the London School Board since 1897 : President of the Royal Asiatic Society.

REED, SIR THOMAS (1796–1883)

Son of Thomas Reed : born 1796 : educated at Sandhurst : joined the 12th Light Dragoons, 1813 : present at Waterloo : Brevet Colonel, 1841 : A.D.C. to Queen Victoria, 1841–54 : C.B. : commanded a Brigade at Firozshahr in the Satlaj campaign, 1845–6 : commanded in Ceylon, 1855 : a Division in Madras, 1856 : and was commanding in the Panjab when the mutiny of 1857 occurred : made the military disposition of the troops : through ill-health yielded the command at the siege of Delhi to Sir H. Barnard, but on his death, on July 5, assumed it, relinquishing it on July 17, appointing Archdale Wilson as his successor : K.C.B., 1865 : General, 1868 : G.C.B., 1875 : retired, 1877 : died July 24, 1883.

REES, JOHN DAVID (1854–   )

I.C.S. : born Dec. 16, 1854: son of Lodwich William Rees : educated at Cheltenham : entered the Madras Civil Service, 1875 : Private Secretary to three successive Governors—Sir M. E. Grant Duff, Lord Connemara and Lord Wenlock : Government Translator in Tamil, Telugu, Persian and Hindustani : British Resident in Travancore and Cochin : Additional Member of Governor-General's Council, 1895–1900 ; retired, 1901 : C.I.E. : author of *The Muhammdans*, etc.

REHATSEK, EDWARD (1819–1891)

Born in Hungary, July 3, 1819 : educated at Buda Pesth : toured in Europe and America : went out to Bombay in 1847 and stayed there : was Professor of Latin and Mathematics at Wilson's College : examined, in Persian and Arabic, for 12 years, for the University, of which he was a Fellow : retired from his Professorship in 1871 : translated the *Rauzat-ussafa* for the Oriental Translation Fund, and other works : contributed a number of articles to the *Calcutta Review* and *Indian Antiquary*, and papers to the Bombay Asiatic Society : distinguished as a linguist, but lived, as a hermit, in extraordinary fashion, in great squalor and uncleanliness, buying the simplest food for himself in the bazar, and keeping aloof from all but native society : accumulated some money : wrote a *Historical Sketch of Portuguese India, Life of Jesus according to the Muham-*

madans, The Relations of Islam to Christianity, and Christianity to Civilization, Bombay 115 *years ago,* and other valuable works : translated *Mirkhund's History of the World* from Persian into English : wrote for the Anglovernacular journal *Native Opinion* : knew 12 languages : died Dec. 11, 1891 : the first European cremated in Bombay.

REID, SIR ALEXANDER JOHN FORSYTH (1846–   )

Born Aug. 21, 1846 : son of Rev. William Reid : educated at Aberdeen University : joined the Indian Army, 1867, and the Staff Corps, 1871 : served in the Afghan war, 1878–80 : dangerously wounded, Brevet-Major : Hazara expedition, 1888 : Brevet-Lt-Colonel : 1st and 2nd Miranzai expeditions, 1891 : Chitral expedition, 1895 : relief of Chitral : N.W. Frontier expedition, 1897–8 : commanded Malakand relief column, Uthman Khel column : C.B. : and Brigade in China expedition, 1900–1 : K.C.B., 1901.

REID, SIR CHARLES (1819–1901)

General : son of George Reid : entered the E. I. Co.'s service in 1835 : served in Upper Sind under Sir C. Napier, 1843 : in the Satlaj campaign was at Badiwal, Aliwal, Sobraon : in the Burma war, 1852–3 : in the mutiny commanded the Sirmur battalion of Gurkhas, at Badli-ka-sarai and siege of Delhi, commanding the advanced posts on right of the Ridge : repulsed 26 separate attacks : commanded the fourth column at the assault on Sep. 14, 1857 : severely wounded : Brevet-Lt-Colonel : in the Oudh campaign, 1858–9 : Colonel : A.D.C. to Queen Victoria : Maj-General, 1867 : General, 1877 : K.C.B., 1871 : G.C.B., 1886 : died Aug. 23, 1901.

RENAULT, PIERRE (?–?)

Was Chief of the French Settlement of Chandernagore, in Bengal, when it was besieged by land by Clive, and by river by Admiral Watson : the Nawab, Suraj-ud-daula, his ally, sent him 2,000 men : and the French, after assault and bombardment, had to capitulate on March 23, 1757 : Renault was taken to Calcutta and not released until after

Plassy : he afterwards commanded at Karikal in S. India, and surrendered, April 5, 1760, to the British : court-martialled and cashiered.

RENDEL, SIR ALEXANDER MEADOWS (1829–   )

Born 1829 : son of John Meadows Rendel : educated at King's School, Canterbury, and Trinity College, Cambridge : Consulting Enginneer to the India Office : K.C.I.E., 1887.

RENNELL, JAMES (1742–1830)

Son of John Rennell, Captain R.A. : born in 1742 : first entered the Naval service, and in 1760 served in India, but left the Navy, entered the E. I. Co.'s marine service, and was appointed Surveyor-General of Bengal in 1764. He surveyed Bengal, was made Major of the Bengal Engineers in 1776, retired in 1777 : his *Bengal Atlas* was published in 1779 : F.R.S. in 1781 ; corresponded largely with men of learning, and was visited by travellers. He published his *Memoir and Map of Hindostan,* 1783 : *Observations on the Topography of the Plain of Troy* : memoirs on the *Geography of Africa,* the *Geographical System of Herodotus explained, The Marks of the British Army in the Peninsula of India.* He was "the father of Indian geography" : for years the chief of British geographers, and constantly consulted : was gold medallist of the Royal Society of Literature, 1825 : died March 29, 1830, and was buried in Westminster Abbey.

RENNIE, JAMES (1814–1903)

Joined the Indian Navy, 1829, and retired as Commander, 1858 : served in China, 1841–2 : Burma, 1852–8 : received a sword of honour from the E. I. Co.'s Directors : Persian Gulf, 1857 : Indian mutiny, 1857–8 : Superintendent of Indian Marine, 1858–63 : C.B., 1858 : died Nov. 30, 1903.

RENNY, GEORGE ALEXANDER (1825–1887)

Born 1825 : son of Alexander Renny : educated at Montrose and Addiscombe : joined the Bengal Artillery in 1844 : was in the Satlaj campaign, at Sobraon : in the mutiny, commanded a troop of Horse Artillery and a battery : at the

siege of Delhi, where he gained his V.C. :
served also with Artillery in Rohilkund
and other engagements, 1858–9 : in
the Hazara Black Mountain campaign,
1868 : retired, 1878 : Maj-General :
Colonel Commandant : died Jan. 5, 1887.

REWAH, MAHARAJA VENKAT RAMAN SINGH OF (1876–   )

Born July 23, 1876 : son of Maharaja
Raghuraj Singh Bahadur, G.C.S.I. : was
invested in 1895, with full powers of a
Ruling Chief : arranged for the relief
of the sufferers in the famine of 1896–7,
which severely strained the resources
of the State : G.C.S.I.

REYNOLDS, HERBERT JOHN (1832–   )

I.C.S : born 1832 : educated at Eton
and King's College, Cambridge : twice
won the Chancellor's medal for English
verse : went to Bengal in the Civil
Service, 1856, and retired in 1889 :
Revenue Secretary to Government of
Bengal, and Member of the Bengal Legislative Council : President of the Opium
Commission, 1883 : Member of the Board
of Revenue, Bengal, and of the Governor-
General's Legislative Council for some
years : President of the Asiatic Society of
Bengal, and presided at the Special Centenary Meeting, Jan. 15, 1884 : C.S.I., distinguished as a scholar and writer.

RICE, BENJAMIN LEWIS (1837–   )

Son of Rev. T. Rice : educated privately : appointed Principal of the High
School (now Central College), Bangalore,
1860–5 : Inspector of Schools, Mysore
and Coorg, 1865–8, 1870–3 : Director
of Public Instruction in Mysore and
Coorg, 1868–9, 1873–83 : Secretary to
the Mysore Government, Education Department, 1883–90 : Director of Archæological Researches in Mysore, 1890–1905 :
introduced the Hobli school system of
primary education in Mysore, 1868 :
was Secretary to the Education Commission (Sir W. W. Hunter's), 1882–3 :
C.I.E. : author of Gazetteers of Mysore
and Coorg : *Mysore Inscriptions* : *Epigraphia Carnatica*, 12 vols : *Bibliotheca
Carnatica.*

RICHARDS, SIR WILLIAM (1778–1861)

Maj-General : was a cadet in the
Army in 1794 : at the siege of Seringapatam : in the Mahratta war : served
in the Nipal war, in Arakan and other
parts of India : lived in India nearly 70
years without visiting England : K.C.B. :
died at Naini Tal Nov. 1, 1861.

RICHARDSON, DAVID LESTER (1801–1865)

Born 1801 : son of Lt-Colonel David
Thomas Richardson of the E. I. Co.'s
Bengal Army ; joined the 2nd Bengal
N. I. in 1819 : began in 1820 to contribute poetry to the *Calcutta Journal* :
in 1822 published his miscellaneous
poems : in 1824, returned for his health
to England, published his *Sonnets and
other Poems*, in 1825, and started *The
Weekly Review* in 1827 : on its collapse,
he returned to military service in Bengal
in 1829 : Captain in Oct. 1832, and, on
July 19, 1833, was invalided and retired
as a Major. He was A.D.C. to Lord W.
Bentinck, 1835. His life was afterwards
devoted to education and literature.
He undertook the editorship of the *Calcutta Literary Gazette*, the *Calcutta Magazine*, and the *Bengal Annual.* Later,
he brought out his *Literary Leaves*, his
Selections from the British Poets, *Anglo-
Indian Passage, Literary Chit-chat, Literary Recreations, Flowers and Flower
Gardens, History of the Black Hole of
Calcutta.* On (Lord) Macaulay's recommendation, the Trustees of the reconstituted Hindu College at Calcutta appointed
him Professor of English Literature
from Jan. 1836, and Principal in 1839.
He was subsequently Principal of the
new Krishnagar College (in 1845), of
the Hughli College, and again of the
Hindu College (1848–50), when he resigned
his post and became tutor of (Maharaja
Bahadur, Sir) Jotindra Mohan Tagore,
and editor of the Bengal *Hurkara.* In
1859 he was appointed Principal of the
Presidency College, Calcutta, but the
Secretary of State disallowed the appointment. He retired to England, Feb.
4, 1861 : assisted in the editing of *Allen's
Overland Mail,* and *Homeward Mail,*
and edited the *Court Circular* : died Nov.
17, 1865.

RICHARDSON, GEORGE LLOYD REILLY (1847-)

Maj-General : entered the Army, 1866, and became Lt-Colonel, 1896 : served in Afghan war, 1878–80, Brevet-Major : Egyptian war, 1882, Tel-el-Kebir, severely wounded : in the Zhob Field Force as C.O., 18th Bengal Lancers, 1890 : N.W. Frontier campaign, 1897–8 : China expedition, commanding Cavalry Brigade, 1900 : commanding second-class District, India : C.B. : C.I.E. : C.S.I.

RICHARDSON, JOHN (1741–1811 ?)

Son of George Richardson : born 1741 : educated at Wadham College, Oxford : joined the Middle Temple : his principal work was his *Dictionary of Persian, Arabic and English,* 1777, which was based on Meninski's Oriental Thesaurus, printed at Vienna in 1680, and has been several times re-edited and re-issued. He wrote also an Arabic grammar, and edited Persian poetry : was F.S.A. : died about 1811.

RICHEY, SIR JAMES BELLETT (1834–1902)

I.C.S. : son of Rev. James Richey : educated at Exeter College, Oxford : entered the Bombay Civil Service, 1856 : became Chief Secretary to Government, Bombay, 1885 : Member of Council, Bombay, 1886–90 : C.S.I., 1878 : K.C.I.E., 1890 : died June 27, 1902.

RICKETTS, GEORGE HENRY MILDMAY (1827-)

I.C.S. : son of Sir H. Ricketts, K.C.S.I. (*q.v.*): born June 20, 1827 : educated at Winchester and Haileybury : began his service in Bengal in 1847 : went to the Panjab in 1853 : in the mutiny was Deputy Commissioner of Ludiana, and with 2 guns and a small force of the 4th Sikhs, in June, 1857, fought a body of mutineers from Jalandhar at the crossing of the Satlaj near Philour : this was one of the first occasions on which the mutineers were met successfully. C.B. for his mutiny services : Member of the Board of Revenue, N.W.P. : retired, 1879.

RICKETTS, SIR HENRY (1802–1886)

I.C.S. : son of George William Ricketts : born March 25, 1802 : educated at Win-chester and Haileybury : went out to Bengal in the Civil Service, 1821 : served in Orissa between 1827–38 : conducted the resettlement of the Division, which suffered from two cyclones in 1831 and 1832 : Commissioner in 1836: quelled disturbances in the Tributary States : co-operated in suppressing the Khonds in Gumsur, and stopping human sacrifices : resettled the Chittagong Division, 1841 –8 : Member of the Board of Revenue, 1849–56 : Provisional Member of Council, 1854, but in 1857 he urged the appointment of Outram : was Member of Supreme Council, 1858–60 : declined the Chief Commissionership of Central Provinces and Lieutenant-Governorship of the N.W.P. : was Commissioner for the revision of Civil Salaries and Establishments in India, 1856–58 : retired, 1860 : K.C.S.I., 1866 : died Feb. 25, 1886.

RICKETTS, JOHN WILLIAM (1791–1835)

Son of Ensign John Ricketts, of the Bengal Engineers (killed at Seringapatam, 1792) ; educated at the Military Orphanage at Kidderpur. Calcutta ; went to Bencoolen in the E. I. Co.'s service ; afterwards employed in a Government office in Calcutta. In 1823 he founded the Doveton College, in Calcutta, for the education of East Indians. In 1829–30 he was deputed to England, on behalf of the East Indians, to petition Parliament for the redress of their grievances : was examined before Select Committees of both Houses on Indian affairs. He was finally Sub-Judge of Gaya, and died there, July 28, 1835. For his labours for the community, he was called the "East Indian Patriot."

RICKMERS, CHRISTIAN MABEL (1866-)

Daughter of William Pirie Duff, merchant in Calcutta, and granddaughter of Dr. Alexander Duff (*q.v.*): born Dec. 7, 1866 : educated at London and Berlin : travelled in Bokhara, 1898, and the Caucasus, 1900: translated Deussen's *Elemente der Metaphysik* into English, 1894 : wrote *The Chronology of India,* 1899.

RIDGEWAY, SIR JOSEPH WEST
(1844–   )

Born 1844 : son of Rev. Joseph Ridgeway : entered the Army, 1860 : and became Lt-Colonel, and Colonel, 1887 : served as Political Officer in Afghan war, 1879–80 : Under Secretary in Foreign Department of the Government of India, 1880–4 : commanded the Indian Contingent of the Afghan Frontier Commission from 1884, and became the Chief Commissioner, 1885 : on special duty to St. Petersburg, 1886–7 : Under Secretary for Ireland, 1887 : Envoy to Sultan of Morocco, 1892–3 : Governor of Isle of Man, 1893–5 : Governor and C. in C. of Ceylon, 1896–1903 : P.C. : K.C.B., 1891 : G.C.M.G., 1900 : K.C.S.I., 1885 : LL.D. Cambridge and Edinburgh.

RIDGEWAY, RICHARD KIRBY
(1848–   )

Born Aug. 18, 1848 : son of R. Ridgeway : educated privately and at Sandhurst : entered the Army, 1868, and Indian Staff Corps, 1872 : ٠Adjutant 44th Gurkhas, 1874–80 : Staff College, 1883 : D.A.Q.M.G., 1884 : A.Q.M.G. in India, 1889–90 : A.A.G., Peshawar, 1893–1900 : served in Naga Hills, 1875 and 1879–80 : Manipur, 1891 : A.A.G., second Division, Tirah, 1897 : V.C. for gallantry at Konoma in Assam, Nov. 22, 1879.

RIEU, CHARLES (1820–1902)

Born at Geneva, 1820 : educated at the Academy there and at Bonn, 1840–3 : took a Doctor's degree : read Arabic with Freytag and Gildemeister, Sanskrit with Lassen : Member of the French Société Asiatique, 1844 : worked with von Bohtlingk and published the St. Petersburg Sanskrit Dictionary, 1847 : joined the British Museum, 1847 : was Curator of Oriental MSS. from 1867 : completed Catalogues of Arabic, Persian, Turkish MSS : became Adams Professor of Arabic, Cambridge, 1894 : died March 19, 1902.

RINGELTAUBE, REV. WILLIAM TOBIAS (1770– ?)

Missionary : son of Gottlieb Ringeltaube, Vicar, near Brieg in Silesia : born, there, Aug. 8, 1770 : educated at Halle, from 1789 : ordained by the S.P.C.K. as Missionary to Calcutta, where he

arrived, Oct. 1797 : returned to England, 1799 : went out, *via* Copenhagen in 1804, for the London Missionary Society to the Mission at Tranquebar, in Travancore : became a pioneer of Mission work : took charge of the Tinnevelly Mission, and removed, 1806, to Palamcotta ; visited Tuticorin, Cochin, and scattered congregations in the South of India : toured also and preached to the converts at Madura, Trichinopoly, Ramnad, etc. : left the S.P.C.K., Tinnevelly, and returned to Travancore, 1807 : during the Tranvacore war of 1808–9 his life was in danger : built the first Protestant church at Mylandy, 1809, and churches in six other places : toured constantly : fell ill in 1815 : left Quilon in Feb. 1816, making over the Travancore Protestant Mission to his Catechist, Vedanayickam : from Madras he went to Ceylon and Malacca, and was never seen again.

RIPON, GEORGE FREDERICK SAMUEL, FIRST MARQUESS OF
(1827–   )

Viceroy and Governor-General : born Oct. 24, 1827 : son of first Earl : succeeded his father, 1859 : M.P. for Hull, 1852–3 : Huddersfield, 1853–7 : Yorkshire, W. Riding, 1857–9 : Under Secretary for War, 1859–61 : for India, 1861–3 : Secretary of State for War, 1863–6 : for India, 1866 : Lord President of the Council, 1868–73 : made a Marquess, 1871 : Governor-General of India, 1880–4 : the Afghan war was concluded, and Kandahar given up : he repealed the Vernacular Press Act : extended Local Self Government : appointed an Education Commission : the " Ilbert Bill " aroused the strongest opposition and was passed with a compromise : later, he became First Lord of the Admiralty, 1886 : Secretary for Colonies, 1892–5 : K.G. : P.C. : G.C.S.I. : G.C.I.E. : D.C.L. : F.R.S.

RISLEY, HERBERT HOPE (1851–   )

I.C.S. : educated at Winchester and New College, Oxford : went to Bengal in the Civil Service, 1873 : Secretary to the Government of Bengal, 1891 : Member of the Bengal Legislative Council, 1892–3 and again : acting Financial Secretary, Government of India, 1898 : Director of Ethnography for India, 1901 : Census

Commissioner, 1899–1902 : Home Secretary to the Government of India, 1902 : C.I.E., 1892 : C.S.I., 1904 : author of *Primitive Marriage in Bengal, Widow and Infant Marriage, Tribes and Castes of Bengal, Anthropometric India*, etc. : wrote the Preface to the *Sikhim Gazetteer*, 1892.

RITCHIE, RICHMOND THACKERAY WILLOUGHBY (1854–   )

Son of William Ritchie (*q.v.*) : Advocate-General of Bengal : educated at Eton and Trinity College, Cambridge : Scholar : entered the India Office, 1877 : Private Secretary to Under Secretaries of State, 1883–94, and to Lord George Hamilton, Secretary of State, 1895–1902 : Secretary, Political Department, India Office, 1902 : C.B., 1898.

RITCHIE, WILLIAM (1816–1862)

Born 1816 : son of John Ritchie, whose wife was a daughter of William Makepeace Thackeray, the grandfather of the novelist : educated at Eton and Trinity College, Cambridge : called to the bar by the Inner Temple : joined the bar in Calcutta about 1840 : Advocate-General of Bengal : Vice-Chancellor of the Calcutta University : Member of the Supreme Council of the Governor-General from Sep. 14, 1861, to his death on March 22, 1862. A marble monument, by J. H. Foley, was erected to his memory in St. Paul's Cathedral, Calcutta. The following is an extract from the inscription (written by Thackeray): " To a clear intellect and sweet and generous temper, England had added her highest education and God His grace. Public-spirited, wise and beloved, his career was one of rare success, breeding no envy. His death was felt to be a calamity, alike public and private."

RIVAZ, SIR CHARLES MONT-GOMERY (1845–   )

I.C.S. : son of John Theophilus Rivaz, B.C.S. : educated at Blackheath School : went to the Panjab in 1864 : served as Superintendent of the Kapurthala State : Deputy Commissioner of Kangra : Commissioner of Lahore : Financial Commissioner of the Panjab : Member of the Supreme Council, 1898–1902 : Lieutenant-Governor of the Panjab since 1902 : K.C.S.I., 1901.

RIVAZ, VINCENT (? –   )

Entered the Indian Army, 1860, and became Colonel, 1890 : served in Hazara campaign, 1868 : Dour Valley expedition, 1872 : Afghan war, 1878–9 : Mahsud-Waziri expedition, 1881 : Hazara expedition, 1891 : C.B., 1900.

RIVETT-CARNAC, SIR JAMES, BARONET (1785–1846)

Son of James Rivett, Member of the Bombay Council, who assumed the name of Carnac : Cadet, 1799 : entered the R.M.A. Woolwich, 1800 : entered the E. I. Co.'s Madras Native infantry, 1801 : transferred to Bombay : was A.D.C. to Jonathan Duncan, Governor of Bombay : served against the Mahrattas, 1802 : in 1802, first Assistant at Baroda, in the Political service and Secretary to the Resident : Resident at Baroda, 1807–19 : retired as a Major in 1822 : Director of the E. I. Co., 1827 : Chairman of the Directors, 1830 : Baronet, 1836 : M.P., 1837 : Governor of Bombay, May, 1839 to April, 1841. A scholarship called after him was founded in his honour, and his bust placed in the Town Hall. He died Jan. 28, 1846.

RIVETT-CARNAC, JOHN HENRY (1839–   )

I.C.S. : son of Admiral Rivett-Carnac : educated in Germany and at Haileybury : served in Bengal Civil Service, 1858–94 : Commissioner of Cotton and Commerce : Special Commissioner for Transport in Bengal famine of 1874 : raised and commanded the Ghazipur volunteer regiment : author of *Report on Indian Cotton Supply* : *Indian Railway Traffic, Indian Antiquities, Archaic Rock Markings in India and Europe* : C.I.E.

RIVINGTON, REV. LUKE, D.D. (1838–1899)

Son of Francis Rivington : educated at Magdalen College, Oxford : B.A., 1861 : an eloquent preacher : for many years attended the Cowley House, Oxford : visited India, preaching : joined the Church of Rome 1887 : frequently delivered Lenten courses in the Church for English Roman Catholics in Rome : the Pope made him a Doctor of Divinity : died May 30, 1899.

ROBERTS, SIR ABRAHAM (1784–1873)

General : born April 11, 1784 : son of the Rev. John Roberts, and father of Earl Roberts (*q.v.*) : entered the Army in 1803, and joined the E. I. Co.'s service, 1804 : served under Lord Lake, 1805 : in Bundelkund against the Pindaris, at the sieges of Komona and Gunnouri, 1806–7 : in the Nipal war, 1814–5 : at the storming of Kahorga : Lt-Colonel, 1832 : Brig-General in the first Afghan war,. 1838–9 : at Ghazni : C.B. : commanded Shah Shuja's force in 1840, but resigned and returned to India : anticipated the danger in Kabul, but his advice was disregarded : commanded the Lahore Division, and the Peshawar Division, 1852–4, when he retired : K.C.B., 1865 : G.C.B., 1873 : died Dec. 28. 1873.

ROBERTS, ARTHUR AUSTIN (1818–1868)

I.C.S. : son of Brown Roberts of the Indian Army : born May 12, 1818 : educated at Haileybury, 1836–7 : to India, 837 : succeeded John (Lord) Lawrence as Magte-Collr. of Dehli : Judge of the Sagar and Nerbudda territories, 1854 : formed a new code of law for them : Commissioner of Lahore, 1856 : C.B. for services during the mutiny : commanded the Lahore Volunteer Corps : Judicial Commissioner of the Panjab : Member of the Governor-General's Legislative Council : acting Judge of the Calcutta High Court : Judge of the Lahore Chief Court, 1866 : C.S.I. : Resident at Hyderabad, March 20, 1868 : died May 10, 1868.

ROBERTS, EMMA (1794 ?–1840)

Daughter of Captain William Roberts : went to India in 1828 with a married sister, Mrs. R. A. McNaghten, on whose death, in 1831, she went to Calcutta and wrote for the *Oriental Observer* : went to India again in 1839 : settled in Bombay and edited *The Bombay United Service Gazette*, and planned a book on the Bombay Presidency : died at Poona, Sep. 16, 1840. She wrote several works on India, including *The East India Voyager*, and an account of her overland voyage outwards.

ROBERTS, OF KANDAHAR, PRETORIA, AND WATERFORD, FREDERICK SLEIGH, FIRST EARL (1832–   )

Field Marshal : son of General Sir Abraham Roberts, G.C.B. (*q.v.*) : born at Cawnpur, Sep. 30, 1832 : educated at Eton, Sandhurst, Addiscombe : joined the Bengal Artillery, in April, 1852 : A.D.C. to his father, 1852 : D.A.Q.M.G. Peshawar, 1856 : in the mutiny he was Staff Officer to Sir N. Chamberlain and John Nicholson, successively commanding the movable column to Delhi : where, during the siege, he, as D.A.Q.M.G. rejoined the Artillery. After its fall, he was in the actions at Bulandshahr, Alighar, Agra, at Sir Colin Campbell's relief of Lucknow, the recapture of Cawnpur, the destruction of Bithur, in the fight near Khudaganj, where he won the V.C. for personal bravery in recovering a standard : in the capture of Lucknow by Sir Colin Campbell, in March, 1858 : served in the Umbeyla campaign, 1863 : in the Abyssinian campaign, 1867–8, was A.Q.M.G. : carried home Lord Napier's final despatches : was senior Staff Officer on the Lushai expedition, 1871–2 : C.B. : Q.M.G. in 1874 : commanded the Panjab Frontier Force, 1878. When the 2nd Afghan war broke out, he commanded the Kuram Field Force, fought the Peiwar Kotal action on Dec. 2, 1878 : halted at Alikheyl : was a member of Sir A. Eden's Army Commission, 1879 : K.C.B., 1879. After Sir L. Cavagnari's death at Kabul, on Sep. 3, 1879, he commanded the Kabul Field Force, fought the action at Charasia on Oct. 6, reached Kabul on Oct. 9. He received Yakub Khan's abdication and despatched him to India : was engaged in the operations in and around Sherpur in Dec.1879. After the defeat of General Burrows at Maiwand, on July 27, 1880, Roberts marched from Kabul to Kandahar, Aug. 9 to 31, over 313 miles in 22 days, and defeated Ayub Khan at Kandahar on Sep. 1 : Baronet : G.C.B. After Majuba Hill, in 1881, he was sent to South Africa as Commander of the Forces and Governor of Natal, but peace had been concluded before he arrived. He was C. in C. Madras, 1881–5 : C. in C. India, 1885–93 : commanded in Burma in 1886 : General in 1890 : Baron in 1892 : C. in C. Ireland, 1895–9 : Field Marshal, 1895 : C. in C. South Africa, 1899–1901 : Commander-in-Chief,

1901–4, Earl, 1901, and K.G. : he was also made G.C.S.I., G.C.I.E., K.P., P.C., D.C.L. Oxford, LL.D. of Dublin, Cambridge and Edinburgh : received the freedom of several cities : wrote *Rise of Wellington*, and *Forty-one Years in India.*

ROBERTS, SIR HENRY GEE
(1800–1860)

Maj-General : born July 18, 1800 : son of William Roberts M.B. of Gloucester, and grandson of W. Roberts : President of Magdalen College, Cambridge; entered the E. I. Co.'s Bombay military service, 1818 : Captain, 1824 : commanded Cutch Irregular Horse, 1825 : and employed politically as Assistant to the Resident : commanded a regiment of Irregular Cavalry in Gujarat, till 1841 : Lt-Colonel in the Sind campaign, 1843, commanding at Sukkur : denuded himself of troops there, in order to reinforce Sir C. Napier for Miani, which the latter fully acknowledged as contributing greatly to his success : Resident in Cutch : described in 1851, by Sir C. Napier, as the best officer in the Bombay Army, and perhaps in India, of his rank : and, later, as " capable of commanding any Army in the field " : in the mutiny, commanded the N. Division of the Bombay Army and in 1858 the Rajputana Field Force : took Kotah by assault, March, 1858, and 75 guns : defeated Tantia Topi on several occasions, at Sanganir, at Kankrauli, on the Banas, etc. : commanded in Gujarat ∙ Maj-General : K.C.B., 1859 : retired, 1859 : died Oct. 6, 1860.

ROBERTS, JOHN BLESSINGTON
(1819–1880)

Born July 17, 1819 : went to India as a private soldier in 1840 : joined the Bengal Sappers and Miners : and the Police as a Deputy Superintendent in 1849 : rose to be Deputy Commissioner of Police in Calcutta, 1856–63 : J.P. : Presidency Magistrate, 1862–71 : Coroner of Calcutta : Superintendent of Stamps and Stationery, 1871–80 : for many years, as Member of the Corporation of Calcutta, took an independent line : on behalf of the public interests, gaining the title of " Tribune of the people " : died May 5, 1880.

ROBERTSON, ARCHIBALD
(? –1847)

Entered the Bombay N.I., 1801 : commanded a local corps in Gujarat, 1803 : in the operations in Kattiawar in 1807–9 : Collr-Magte. of Khandesh, 1823–6 : Resident at Satara, 1827 : Colonel, 1829 : retired, 1831 : Maj-General, 1837 : Director of the E. I. Co. : died June 9, 1847.

ROBERTSON, CHARLES
(1833–1898)

I.C.S : born at Aberdeen, Sep. 18, 1833 : son of Charles Robertson, ironmonger there : educated at the Grammar School, Marischal College and University, Aberdeen : M.A. with special honours, 1853 : taught in England : passed fifth in the first open competition for the I.C.S : went to the N.W.P. in 1856: became Junior Secretary to the N.W.P. Government, 1867, and Secretary to that Government and Oudh, 1877–82 : retired 1883–4, on account of his wife's health : served in Edinburgh : resumed his classical studies : became a leading spirit of the Hellenic Society under Blackie : founded, with £8,000, a Fellowship in Classics, Mental Science and Philosophy at Aberdeen University, in memory of his brother Professor George Croom Robertson, editor of *Mind*—a Fellowship designed to stimulate the higher study of the subjects named : died March 24, 1898.

ROBERTSON, SIR DONALD (1847–   )

Born June 24, 1847 : Lt-Colonel : son of Col. J. S. Robertson   educated at Cheltenham, Bonn and Radley : entered the Army, 1865, and civil employment in Madras, 869 : served as Political Officer in Central India, Rajputana, Hyderabad, Rewah, Gwalior : Resident in Mysore, 1896–1903 : C.S.I., 1899 : K.C.S.I., 1903.

ROBERTSON, SIR GEORGE SCOTT
(1852–   )

Born Oct. 22, 1852 : son of Thomas J. Robertson : educated at Westminster Hospital : entered the Indian medical service, 1878 : served in Afghan campaign, 1879–80 : employed under the Indian Foreign Office from June, 1888 : British Agent at Gilgit : travelled in Kafiristan, 1890–1 : Chief Political Officer of the Hunza-Nagar expedition, 1891–2 : Political Mission to Chitral, 1893 : besieged and severely wounded at Chitral, 1895 : Administrator of Chitral, 1895 : C.S.I., 1892 : K.C.S.I., 1895 : author of *The Kafirs of the Hindu Kush, Chitral*, etc.

ROBERTSON, THOMAS CAMPBELL
(1789–1863)

I.C.S. : born Nov. 9, 1789 : son of Captain George Robertson, R.N : educated at Edinburgh and Glasgow : went out to Bengal in the Civil Service, 1805 : while at Chittagong, from 1823, was in the Burmese war of 1825, and went to Ava as Commissioner, helping to make the treaty : Commissioner at Bareli : A.G.G. on the N.E. frontier and Commissioner of Assam, 1831 : Commissioner of Cuttack, 1834 : Judge of the *Sadr* Court, 1835 : Member of the Supreme Council, Nov. 1835 to Jan. 1840 : Lieutenant-Governor of the N.W.P., Feb. 1840, to Dec. 1842 : Provisional Governor-General : retired 1843 : died July 6, 1863 : wrote on the first Burmese war and other Indian political subjects.

ROBINSON, SIR GEORGE ABER-CROMBY, BARONET (? –1832)

Military Auditor-General in Bengal : Director of the E. I. Co., 1808–29 : Chairman, 1826 : M.P. for Honiton : made a Baronet in 1823 : died 1832.

ROBINSON, PHILIP STEWART
(1849–)

Born 1849 : son of Rev. Julian Robinson, Editor of the *Pioneer* : educated at Marlborough : Assistant Editor of the *Pioneer*: Special Correspondent of the *Daily* · *Telegraph* in Afghan and Egyptian wars : and afterwards of the *Pall Mall Gazette* in Cuba : author of *In my Indian Garden*, 1878 ; *Under the Punkah*, 1881 : *Tigers at Large*, 1885, etc. etc.

ROBINSON, VINCENT JOSEPH
(1829–)

Son of Vincent Robinson : merchant : educated at King's College, London : formerly in East India trade : C.I.E. for service in connexion with spread of Indian art to Europe : author of *Ancient Furniture and other Works of Art, Eastern Carpets* and papers on *Eastern Fabrics*.

ROBINSON, SIR WILLIAM ROSE
(1822–1886)

I.C.S. : born 1822 : son of William Rose Robinson : educated at Bonn and Haileybury, 1840–1 : went out to Madras, 1842 : was Inspr-General of Police, 1865 : C.S.I., 1866 : Member of the Board of Revenue, 1870 : Additional Member of the Governor-General's Legislative Council : Member of Council, Madras, 1873–8 : acted as Governor of Madras, April 29, to Nov. 23, 1875 : K.C.S.I., 1876 : died April 27, 1886.

ROBSON, REV. JOHN (? –)

One of the founders of the Rajputana Mission, 1860 : retired from India on account of ill-health, 1872 : Senior Member of S. Nicholas U.F.C. Aberdeen, 1876–98 : Moderator of the Synod of the U.P. Church of Scotland, 1899–1900 : author of *Hinduism and Christianity*, etc. etc.

RODDY, PATRICK (1830–1895)

Entered the Bengal Army in 1848 : served with Havelock and Outram in the mutiny, 1858–9 : in the first relief of Lucknow : at the defence of the Alambagh, capture of Lucknow, and later engagements : obtained his Commission as Ensign, and V.C. for gallantry, 1858 : in Abyssinia, 1867–8 : and in Afghanistan, 1879–80 : retired as Colonel, Feb. 1887 : died Nov. 21, 1895.

RODGERS, CHARLES] JAMES
(1838–1898)

Born 1838 : educated at Shardlow and Milford in Derbyshire, and Borough Road College, London : while master of a National School near Cambridge, attended lectures on Oriental subjects at the University : to India, 1863, for the Christian Vernacular Education Society, to conduct a Training College for Native Teachers at Umritsar : its Principal for 22 years : Urdu and Persian scholar : made a special study of Indian numismatics : appointed Archæological Surveyor of the Panjab, 1886 : after 5 years his appointment was abolished : was a high authority on numismatics, and Honorary Numismatist to the Government of India : Secretary to the Religious Book Society at Lahore, 1898 : died at Lahore, Nov. 20, 1898 : wrote largely on

Coins and Coinages in the *J.A.S.B.* : and catalogued coin collections at Lahore and Calcutta.

ROE, SIR CHARLES (1841-)

I.C.S. : son of John D. Roe : educated at Merton College, Oxford : joined the Civil Service in the Panjab, 1863, and retired, 1898 : was Chief Judge of the Panjab Chief Court and Vice-Chancellor of the Panjab University : author of *Tribal Law in the Panjab* : K.B., 1897 : LL.D., Pennsylvania.

ROSE, HENRY METCALFE (1848-)

Born July 30, 1848 : son of General Hugh Rose : educated at Sandhurst : joined the Army, 1867, and Indian Staff Corps, 1869 : served in Afghan campaign, 1879-80 : N.W. Frontier, Hazara, 1891 : second Miranzai expedition, 1891 : Burma campaign, 1886-7 : Southern Shan column : D.S.O : Commandant of Malakand Force : Brig-General.

ROSE, SIR JOHN (? -1852)

Entered the E. I. Co.'s service, 1795 : was at Malavilli and Seringapatam : in Baird's expedition to Egypt : in the Bombay Army, in Gujarat, 1801-2 : in the Mahratta war under Lake, at Agra, Gwalior, Delhi, in the pursuit of Holkar, 1805 : in the Nipal war, 1815 : Pindari war, 1818 : retired, 1823 : K.C.B., 1838 : Lt-General, 1846 : died Sep. 9, 1852.

ROSS, ALEXANDER (1777- ?)

I.C.S. : went to India, at 18, in 1795-6 : Judge of the Provincial Court at Bareli, 1811 : was Resident at Delhi, 1820-3 : Puisne Judge of the *Sadr* Court, 1825 : First Judge, 1831 : Member of the Supreme Council, Jan. 1833 : permanently in Oct. 1833 : Governor of Agra, Dec. 1835, to June, 1836 : abolished transit duties : President in Council and Deputy-Governor of Bengal, Oct. 20, 1837, to Oct. 15, 1838, when he retired.

ROSS, ALEXANDER GEORGE (1840-)

Born Jan. 9, 1840: son of Alexander Ross, I.C.S. : educated at Edinburgh Academy and University : joined the Indian Army, 1857, and Indian Staff Corps, 1897: became Lt-General, 1897 : served in Indian mutiny, 1858-9 : raised mule transport

for Abyssinian campaign and commanded it, 1868 : at the capture of Magdala : in the N.W. Frontier, Jowaki expedition, 1877-8 : Afghan war, 1878-9 : at Ali-Masjid : Brevet-Lt-Colonel: N.W. Frontier, Mahsud-Waziri, 1881 : Zhob Valley, 1890 : commanded Panjab Frontier Force column : C.B., 1887.

ROSS, SIR CAMPBELL CLAYE GRANT (1844-1892)

Educated at the Edinburgh Academy : entered the Army, 1841 : became Lt-General, 1886 : General, 1890 : served in N.W. frontier operations, 1852-3 : in the mutiny: in the defence of the Kumaon hills, the action of Charpoora, and other engagements : in the Umbeyla campaign, 1863 : in action at the Craig picket : Brevet-Lt-Colonel : in Jowaki-Afridi campaign, 1878 : K.C.B. : died June 20, 1892.

ROSS, DANIEL (1780-1849 ?)

Born 1780 : a distinguished hydrographer : the first Surveyor of his age : Marine Surveyor-General for India : Master Attendant at Bombay till 1849, when he retired on account of old age : President of the Bombay Geographical Society : his service of fifty years was of the utmost value in the cause of science, especially of geography and navigation : his charts were always trustworthy.

ROSS, SIR EDWARD CHARLES (1836-)

Born Sep. 23, 1836 : son of D. R. Ross, M.P. : educated at Edinburgh Academy : entered the Indian military service, 1855 : served with Central India Field Force in the mutiny, 1857-8 : joined the Political Service, 1863 : Resident in Persian Gulf, 1872-91 : C.S.I., 1882 : K.B., 1892.

ROSS, EDWARD DENISON (1871-)

Born June 6, 1871 : son of Rev. Alexander J. Ross, D.D. : educated at Marlborough and University College, London : studied Oriental languages in Paris and Strasburg : Professor of Persian in University College, London, 1896-1901 : Principal of the Calcutta Madrasa, since 1901 : author of *The Early Years of Shah Ismail*, *The Tarikh-i-Rashidi* : a *History of the Moguls of Central India*, *The Heart of Asia* (with F. H. B. Skrine), *Life and Times of Omar Khayyam*, *Introduction to Beckford's Vathek*, etc. : Ph.D.

ROSS, SIR JOHN (1829-1905)

Born March 18, 1829 : son of F. M. Sir Hew Dalrymple Ross, G.C.B. : joined the Rifle Brigade, 1846 : served in the Crimea, at Alma, Inkerman and Sebastopol, 1854-5 : in Indian mutiny, at the battle of Cawnpur and capture of Lucknow : at Kalpi, and in the Central India campaign, 1857-8 : Brevet-Lt-Col. and C.B. : N.W. Frontier, 1863-4 : Brig-General, Bengal 1874, and 1875-80 : commanded Perak expedition in the Malay Peninsula, 1875-6, and the Indian forces sent to Malta, 1878 : in the Afghan war, 1878-80, commanded 2nd Division Kabul Field Force : and in the Kabul-Kandahar march commanded the Infantry Division, and was second in command under Sir F. Roberts : K.C.B. : commanded the Poona Division of Bombay Army, 1881-6 : C. in C. Canada, 1888-93 : General and G.C.B., 1891 : Colonel Commandant of the Rifle Brigade, 1903 : died Jan. 5, 1905.

ROSS, PATRICK (1740 ?-1804)

Born about 1740 : joined the Engineers, 1758 : served in the W. Indies : Chief Engineer and Lt-Colonel at Madras, 1770 : Member of Council : Chief Engineer in operations against Tanjore, 1771-5 : renovated the defences of Fort St. George at Madras, 1778 : served at the Cape against the Dutch and under Stuart against Tippoo, 1783 : at the siege of Cuddalore, 1783 : under Cornwallis in 1791 against Tippoo : took Savandrug, Dec. 1791: at siege of Seringapatam, 1792 : Maj-General, 1797 : superintended operations of 1798-9 : went home in 1802 : M.P. for Horsham, 1802 : died Aug. 24, 1804.

ROSS, RONALD (1857-   )

Major : son of General Sir C. C. G. Ross, (q.v.)K.C.B.: educated at St. Bartholomew's Hospital, London : entered Indian Medical Service, 1881 : commenced special study of malaria, 1892 : discovered life history of malaria parasites in mosquitoes, 1897-8 : visited West Africa, 1899 : retired, 1899 : author of scientific works : C.B., 1902 : F.R.S., 1901 : F.R.C.S., 1901 : Professor of Tropical Medicine, Liverpool.

ROSS-KEPPEL, GEORGE (? -   )

Major : joined the Royal Scots Fusiliers. 1886, and Indian Staff Corps, 1900 : served in the Burmese expedition, 1886-7 : Commandant Kuram Militia, 1894-7 : Political Officer with Kuram column, Tirah expedition, 1897-8 : N.W. Frontier. 1898-9 : C.I.E. and Brevet-Major, Political Officer in charge of Khyber Pass, 1899 : author of A *Manual of Pushtu*, etc. : F.R.G.S.

ROST, REINHOLD (1822-1896)

Born Feb. 2, 1822, at Eisenberg in Saxe-Altenburg : son of Charles Rost : educated at Jena University, Ph.D : came to England, 1847, and, 1851-96, was Oriental Lecturer at St. Augustine's Missionary College, Canterbury : became Secretary to the Royal Asiatic Society, 1863, and Librarian at the India Office, 1869 : retired 1839 : LL.D., Edinburgh, 1877 : C.I.E., 1888 : knew 20 to 30 Oriental languages, including Sanskrit, Pali, Tamil, Telugu, Burmese, Malay, Malagasy, Swahili, besides Arabic, Urdu, and dialects of Africa, China, etc., some completely, some sufficiently to teach : he edited H. H. Wilson's *Essays on Sanskrit Literature and the Religion of the Hindus* : Brian Hodgson's *Essays on Indian Subjects* : Trubner's *Oriental Record* : and published papers on Indo-China : among his works were articles in the *Encyclopædia Britannica*, and the *Athenæum*, on Oriental philology : a *Treatise on the Indian Sources of the Ancient Burmese Laws*, etc. etc. : one of the greaetst linguists of the age : honoured by learned Societies and decorated by foreign countries : died Feb. 7, 1896.

ROTH, RUDOLPH VON (1821-1895)

Born April 3, 1821, at Stuttgart : educated at Tübingen, under Heinrich Ewald : took the degree of Ph. D. : studied at Paris under Burnouf : and in England, working at Vedic and Zend MSS. at the India House and the Bodleian : at Tübingen, 1846, published treatises on the Literature and History of the Vedas : in 1848 Extraordinary, and in 1856 Ordinary Professor, and Chief of the University Library : collaborating with Bohtlingk (q.v.) he dealt with the Vedic period in the Sanskrit Dictionary of the Imperial Academy of St. Petersburg, 1855-75 : he was the real founder of Vedic philology : edited the *Atharva Veda* : catalogued the Indian MSS. in the University Library of Tübingen, 1865 : contributed largely to scientific Journals, chiefly articles on the Vedas : wrote also on Indian medicine, and on the Avesta, and lectured on the history of religions : ennobled by the King of Wurtemburg for his Oriental scholarship : died at Tübingen, June 23, 1895.

ROTHNEY OCTAVIUS EDWARD
(1824–1881)

Colonel : entered the Army, 1841 : in the Satlaj campaign, 1845–6 : in Colonel Mackeson's force against the Hasanzais, 1852–3 : in Pegu, 1854 : at Ludiana in 1857, held it with the 4th Sikh N.I : with the regt. at the siege and taking of Delhi, 1857, and many subscquent engagements : joined the Bengal Staff Corps : commanded the Lahore Division : Lt-Colonel, 1867 : C.S.I., 1868 : and C.B. : died Jan. 1, 1881.

ROTTLER, DR. JOHN PETER
(1749–1836)

Danish Missionary and botanist : born June, 1749 : educated at the Gymnasium and University, Strasburg : ordained at Copenhagen, 1775 : reached Tranquebar, 1776 : studied Tamil, and Indian Botany : made Doctor of Philosophy by the University of Erlangen, 1795 : supplied botanical specimens of S. Indian flora to Europe : toured in Ceylon, 1796 : many of his plants and the catalogue sent to Kew : to Madras, 1803 : Secretary and Chaplain of the Female Orphan Asylum from 1808 : Chaplain at Pulicat, 1814–8 : left the Danish Mission, and succeeded Paezold in the Vepery Mission, Madras, 1817, under the S.P.C.K. : died Jan. 24, 1836 : made a Tamil dictionary, and translated the Prayer Book into Tamil.

ROUSE, WILLIAM HENRY DENHAM
(1863–)

Born May 30, 1863 : son of Rev. G. H. Rouse : educated at Doveton College, Calcutta, and Christ's College, Cambridge : Scholar and Fellow : Master at Bedford Grammar School, 1886–8 : Cheltenham College, 1890–5 : Rugby School, 1896–1901 : Headmaster Perse Grammar School, Cambridge, since 1901 : editor of *The Jataka, or Stories of the Buddha's former Births*, translated from the Pali by various hands, *The Giant Crab, and other Tales of Old India*, *The Talking Thrush and other Indian Stories*, several of the Temple Classics and other school books : Litt. D. :

F.R.G.S. : M.R.A.S. : Univ. Teacher of Sanskrit, 1903.

ROUTLEDGE, JAMES (1829–1898)

Journalist : began his career in the N. of England : went to Calcutta, 1869 : edited the *Friend of India*, and was correspondent for India to the *Times* : left India in 1872 : became Editor of the *Oudh Advertiser*, and the *Western Daily Mercury* : died April 25, 1898 : wrote *English Rule and Native Opinion in India*, 1878.

ROWLANDS, SIR HUGH (1829–)

Entered the Army, 1849, and became General, 1894 : served in the Crimea, 1854–5 : V.C. and Brevet-Major : Kafir war, 1877–9 : commanded Bangalore District of the Madras Army, 1884–9 : commanded Scottish District, 1895–6 : K.C.B., 1898.

ROXBURGH, WILLIAM (1751–1815)

Born June 3, 1751 : educated at Edinburgh : became a Surgeon's Mate in the E. I. Co.'s marine : M.D. : and Assistant Surgeon in the Madras medical service in 1776 : in charge of the Botanic Garden at Samulcotta, near Coconada, 1781–93 : studied the flora of the Northern Sircars : the E. I. Co.'s Botanist in the Carnatic : *Plants of the Coast of Coromandel* published from his drawings : appointed first Superintendent of the Botanic Gardenn, ear Calcutta, and Chief Botanist of the E. I. Co. in 1793 : held the offices, until he retired in 1813 : died at Edinburgh, Feb. 18, 1815 : F.R.A.S. : F.L.S. : F.S. Arts, and F.R.S., Edinburgh : wrote the *Hortus Bengalensis*, and *Flora Indica*, which was not published complete until 1832, " an admirable production : the descriptions are accurate and graphic, and its authorship justly entitles Roxburgh to his title of the ' Father of Indian Botany ' " : wrote *A Botanical Description of a New Species of Swietenia, a Mahogany*, besides papers for the Linnæan Society, the Society of Arts, in Asiatic Researches, etc. etc. : a most ardent and enthusiastic botanist, and a good gardener : the first botanist who attempted to draw up a systematic account of the plants of India : he paid much attention also to economic botany. His monument, with a Latin inscription by Bishop Heber, is in the Royal Botanic Garden, near Calcutta.

ROYDS, SIR JOHN (1752-1817)

Puisne Judge of the Supreme Court, Calcutta, for more than 20 years, " during which period he conscientiously discharged his important duties with honour to himself and with advantage to the public, while he benefited and adorned the society in which he lived by the benevolence of his disposition and the accomplishments of a scholar and gentleman " : Vice-President of the Asiatic Society of Bengal, 1815 : died Sep. 24, 1817.

ROYLE, JOHN FORBES (1799-1858)

Son of Capt. William Henry Royle : born at Cawnpur, 1799 : educated at Edinburgh and Addiscombe, but became an Assistant Surgeon in Bengal, 1819 : M.D. : Superintendent of the Botanic Garden at Saharanpur, 1823-31 : cultivated useful vegetable products : retired : Doctor of Medicine, Munich : wrote *Illustrations of the Botany and Natural History of the Himalaya Mountains*, 1839 : advocated the introduction of cinchona into India : Professor of Materia Medica and Therapeutics at King's College, London, 1837-56 : had charge of a museum, at the India House, of vegetable productions of India : was F.R.S., F.L.S., Fellow and Secretary of the Geological, Linnæan, Royal Asiatic, and Royal Horticultural Societies : wrote a manual on Materia Medica, 1847 : a book on the fibrous plants of India, and works on cotton and other products, and the Natural History of India : distinguished for his practical application of botanic science : a Commissioner of the great Exhibition of 1851, and in charge of the Indian Department : also at the Paris Exhibition, 1855 : died Jan. 2, 1858.

ROYLE, JOSEPH RALPH EDWARD JOHN (1844-   )

Born Dec. 3, 1844 : son of Dr. John Forbes Royle (*q.v.*): educated at King's College School, London, and Addiscombe : joined the Army, 1862, and retired through ill-health, 1867 : Superintendent, Indian Museum, 1874-9 : Statistical Department, India Office, 1879-91 : C.I.E., 1886.

ROY, RAMA PRASAD (? -1862)

Youngest son of Raja Ram Mohan Roy (*q.v.*) : practised in the *Sadr* Court, Calcutta :

the first Government Pleader : Member of the Bengal Legislative Council on its formation, 1862 : would have been a Puisne Judge of the High Court, but for his death, 1862 : his family had been outcasted for his father's visit to England, but he had purchased re-admission to caste : left a very large fortune, made at the bar.

ROY, RAJA RAMMOHAN (1772-1833)

Son of Ramkanta Roy, who was manager of some estates of the Maharaja of Burdwan : studied Persian and Arabic at Patna : and Sanskrit at Benares : was particularly well versed in Sanskrit literature. At the age of 15 he published his famous work on *Idolatry* in Bengali, in which he contended that the popular religion of the Hindus was contrary to the practice of their ancestors and the doctrine of the ancient authorities. For this he incurred his father's displeasure and was turned out of the house : he wandered for 4 years, even to Tibet. He was readmitted by his mother on his father's death. At the age of 21 he commenced the study of English, in which he became proficient : he also studied French, Latin, Greek, and Hebrew. Employed in the Collectorate at Rangpur, he rose to be *Sarishtadar*, but retired from Government service in 1813. He then commenced a crusade against the popular religion. Going to Calcutta, he translated into Bengali the *Vedanta* and the *Vedantasara* and the *Upanishads* : the latter he also translated into English. He studied the Koran in Arabic, the Old Testament in Hebrew, and the New Testament in Greek. In 1820 he published, in Sanskrit and Bengali, *Precepts of Jesus, the Guide to Peace and Happiness*, in which he denied the Divinity of Christ. This brought him into controversy with the Serampur Missionaries, and on their refusal to print his *Final Appeal*, he established a press of his own. Dr. Marshman answered him, and the publications attracted considerable attention, both in England and America. Rammohan soon after founded a Periodical, called *The Brahmanical Magazine*, with the object of defending the religious books of the Hindus. He formed a religious association, called the Atmya Sabha, and in 1828 founded the Brahmo Samaj " for the worship and adoration of the Eternal, Unsearchable, Immutable Being, who is

the Author and Preserver of the Universe."
The objects of the new Church were
described in the trust-deed of 1830. This
new Theism aimed at " the calm worship
of the Deity, the practice of virtue and
charity, reverence for all that is sincere
and helpful in every faith, and active
participation in every movement for the
bettering of mankind." He claimed to
have established a pure monotheistic form
of worship for the benefit of Hindus,
Muhamadans, and Christians. As a
social reformer he preached against Sati,
Polygamy and Kulinism, and advocated
the remarriage of widows. In 1830 he
received the title of Raja from the ex-
Emperor of Delhi, and was deputed by
him to visit England, to advocate certain
claims. There, as a republican in his
politics, he was well received by the reforming liberals and advanced thinkers. In
1831 he visited France : returned to
England, he was present at the passing of
the India Bill in 1833. Max Müller,
Monier Williams, the poet Campbell,
Brougham and Bentham befriended him.
In 1833, on the invitation of Dr. Carpenter,
he went to live at Bristol and, while
meditating a voyage to America, died of
fever, at Stapleton Grove, on Sep. 27,
1833. He was one of the founders of the
Hindu College in Calcutta in 1817, and in
1823 addressed a letter to Lord Amherst
on the comparative merits of English and
Sanskrit education.

RUMBOLD, SIR THOMAS, BARONET
(1736-1791)

Governor : son of William Rumbold :
born June 15, 1736 : went out as a writer
in the E.I. Co.'s Civil Service, 1752, but
changed to the Army : served under Stringer Lawrence, 1754, under Clive at Calcutta,
1756-7, and was his A.D.C. at Plassy :
" Chief " at Patna, 1763 : Member of
Council in Bengal, 1766-9 : retired : M.P.
for Shoreham, 1770 : was Governor of
Madras, Feb. 1778, to April, 1780 : had
difficulties in connexion with the Northern
Sircars, readjusting the system previously
in force : took Pondicherry, Oct. 17, 1778 :
made a Baronet : in anticipation of Hyder
Ali's threatened invasion of the Carnatic,
made arrangements to depose him : retired
from ill-health : treated in England as
responsible for Hyder's invasion and
dismissed the service by the Court of
Directors : on inquiry by Parliament, the

charges, including those of corruption and
oppression, against him were defeated and
he was acquitted, but his case was unfairly
represented for a long time : was M.P. for
Yarmouth, 1781, and Weymouth, 1784-90 :
he died Nov. 11, 1791.

RUNDALL, FRANCIS HORNBLOW
(1823-   )

Born Dec. 22, 1823 : son of Col, Charles
Rundall : educated at Kensington and
Addiscombe : joined the Indian Engineers
at Madras, 1843 : served in the P.W.D.
under Sir Arthur Cotton, in the Godavery
District, till 1851 : held various irrigation
charges : Chief Engineer for E. I. Irrigation
Company's Bihar and Orissa Irrigation
works, 1861 : Chief Engineer to Government of Bengal for Irrigation, 1866 :
Inspr-General of Irrigation with the
Government of India, 1871-4 : retired,
1874 : C.S.I., 1875 : General, 1885.

RUNDALL, FRANK MONTAGU
(1851-   )

Born May 18, 1851 : son of General
F. H. Rundall (q.v.), R.E. : educated at
Marlborough : joined the Berkshire regt.,
and Indian Staff Corps : served in Upper
Burma on Staff of General Lockhart,
1886-7 : Chin-Lushai expedition, 1889-
90 : commanded in the Chin Hills and
conducted operations against Kanhow
Chins, 1891 : D.S.O. : Manipur expedition,
1891 : Waziristan campaign, 1895-6 :
China expedition, 1900-1 : Lt-Colonel :
author of Manual of Chin Language.

RUNGA CHARLU, CETTIPANIAM
VIRAVALLI (1831-1883)

Born 1831 : son of a clerk in the Chingle-
put District (Madras) : educated at
Pachaiyappa's School and the High
School, Madras : served in the Chingleput,
Salem and Nellore Districts : in 1859 was
appointed Special Assistant to the Inam
Commission, and, when that work came
to an end, was entrusted with the special
duty of reporting on the working of Indian
Railways : became Treasury Deputy
Collector at Calicut (1864), and in 1868
was appointed Comptroller of the Mysore
Palace : in 1874 he published a pamphlet
on The British Administration of Mysore :
became Revenue Secretary to the Chief
Commissioner of Mysore : C.I.E. in 1880 :
in 1881 was appointed Diwan of Mysore.

The reorganization of the Judicial and Forest Departments, the introduction of Railways, the reduction of the State debt, and the organization of the Representative Assembly of notables occupied his attention, but he did not live long enough to see his reforms completed, He died in 1883.

RUSSELL, SIR DAVID (1809–1884)

Son of Col. James Russell : born 1809 : educated at Edinburgh and Dresden : entered the Army, 1828 : commanded the 5th Brigade at the relief of Lucknow by Sir Colin Campbell : and a Brigade at the assaults on the Alambagh, and at the capture of Lucknow : C.B. : K.C.B. in 1871 : Lt-General, 1871 : General, 1877 : commanded the S.E. District, 1868–72 : died Jan. 16, 1884.

RUSSELL, SIR EDWARD LECHMERE (1818–1904)

Son of Maj-General L. C. S. Russell, C.B. : born in 1818 : educated at Trinity College, Cambridge : joined the 12th Bombay N.I. in 1837, and served in the Afghan and Sind campaigns of 1842–3 : was Adjutant of the Sind Irregular Horse at Miani, Hyderabad, Oomercote : Military Secretary in 1856 to Lord Elphinstone, Governor of Bombay : in command at the base in the Abyssinian expedition of 1868, and was made a K.C.S.I. for his services : Political Resident and Commandant at Aden, 1868–71 : commanded the Northern Division of the Bombay Army, 1872–6, and then retired : General, 1877 : died at Bath, Jan. 1904.

RUSSELL, GEORGE EDWARD (1787–1863)

I.C.S. : son of Claud Russell, M.C.S. : educated at Eton : went out to Madras in the Civil Service, 1802 : Member of the Board of Revenue, Madras, 1822 : First Member, 1824 : acting Resident at Mysore, 1832 : Special Commissioner, 1832, to inquire into the causes of disturbances in Ganjam and Vizagapatam : restored tranquillity in 1834 : on the occurrence of disturbances in Gumsur, 1835, Russell was sent on a special mission and quelled the insurrection there and among the Khonds : Member of Council, Madras, Sep. 1834, to Jan. 1838 : retired : died Oct. 20, 1863.

RUSSELL, GEORGE WILLIAM ERSKINE (1853–)

Born Feb. 3, 1853 : son of Lord Charles Russell : educated at Harrow and University College, Oxford : Scholar : M.P. for Aylesbury, 1880–5, and for N. Bedfordshire, 1892–5 : Parliamentary Secretary to the Local Government Board, 1883–5 : Under Secretary for India, 1892–4 : and for the Home Department, 1894–5 : on the London County Council, 1889–95 : wrote a life of W. E. Gladstone, and of Sydney Smith : *Collections and Recollections*, and edited Matthew Arnold's letters.

RUSSELL, SIR HENRY, BARONET (1751–1836)

Son of Michael Russell : born Aug. 8, 1751 : educated at Charterhouse and Queen's College, Cambridge : called to the bar at Lincoln's Inn, 1783 : Commissioner in Bankruptcy, 1775 : Puisne Judge of the Supreme Court, Calcutta, 1708 : knighted : made Chief Justice, 1807 : Baronet, 1812 : retired, 1813 : Privy Councillor, 1816 : died Jan. 18, 1836.

RUSSELL, SIR HENRY, BARONET (1783–1852)

Born May 27, 1783 : son of Sir Henry Russell, *Bart. (q.v.)*, Chief Justice of Bengal, 1807–13 : went to Calcutta with his father, May, 1798 : appointed a writer, Nov. 1798 : Assistant Secretary to the Resident at Hyderabad, 1800 : Secretary, 1802 : Third Member of the Commission appointed to investigate the claims of the Nawab of the Carnatic, 1807 : officiating Resident at Poona, 1809 : Resident at Hyderabad, 1811–20, during the Mahratta-Pindari war, in which the Nizam's Army proved of much service, Lord Wellesley spoke of Russell, when Resident, as the most promising young man he knew : proceeded to Europe, Dec. 27, 1820 : was out of service in 1826, having exceeded 5 years' absence from India : he wrote (1842–9) letters to the *Times*, signed " Civis," which were reprinted : died April 19, 1852.

RUSSELL, SIR JAMES (1781–1859)

Son of Col. William Russell : born at Madras, 1781 : entered the E. I. Co.'s military service, Madras, 1795 : engaged in the principal military affairs in India, 1799–1825 : Colonel of the 2nd Madras Cavalry, 1824 : General, 1854 : commanded a Brigade of Cavalry at Mahidpur, and distinguished himself : C.B., 1818 : K.C.B., 1837 : died May 16, 1859.

RUSSELL, PATRICK (1727–1805)

Son of John Russell : born Feb. 6, 1727 : M.D. Edinburgh : doctor at Aleppo, 1750 –71 : returned to London : F.R.S., 1777 : went to India, 1781, to Vizagapatam : became botanist in the Carnatic to the E. I. Co. 1785–9 : wrote on *The Poisonous Snakes of the Coromandel Coast*, a *Treatise on the Plague*, 1791 : edited the *Natural History of Aleppo*, and wrote a preface to Roxburgh's *Plants of the Coromandel Coast*, 1795 : also on Fishes · died July 2, 1805.

RUSSELL, SIR WILLIAM, BARONET (1822–1892)

Born April 5, 1822 : son of Sir William Russell, M.D., *Bart.* : succeeded to the Baronetcy, 1839 : entered the 7th Hussars, 1841 : M.P. for Dover, 1857–9 : in the Indian mutiny with his regt. at siege of Lucknow, March, 1858, and afterwards under Hope Grant at Nawabganj, and Sultanpur : in Horsford's Field Force : drove the rebels into Nipal, Feb. 1859 : Lt-Colonel, 1858 : C.B., 1859 : M.P. for Norwich, 1860–74 : Lt-General, 1881 : died March 19, 1892.

RUSSELL, SIR WILLIAM HOWARD (1820–)

Born March 28, 1820 : son of John Russell : educated at Trinity College, Dublin : journalist and war correspondent for the *Times*, in Schleswig-Holstein, 1850 : Crimea, 1854–6 : Indian mutiny, 1857–8 : Italian campaign, 1859 : Civil war in U.S.A., 1861–4 : Danish war, 1864 : Prussian-Austrian war, 1866 : Franco-German war, 1870 : South African war, 1879–80 : 1883–4 : accompanied H.R.H. the Prince of Wales on his Indian Tour, 1875–6 : editor, *Army and Navy Gazette* : author of several books, including *Diary of India*, etc.: K.B. 1895 : F.I.I.: F.R.G.S. : F.Z.S.

RUSSELL, SIR WILLIAM OLDNALL (1785–1833)

Son of Samuel Oldnall : born 1785 : took the name of his maternal grandfather, Russell, in 1816 : educated at Christ Church, Oxford : called to the bar from Lincoln's Inn, 1809 : was serjeant-at-law,

1827 : Chief Justice of Bengal in 1832 : knighted : died Jan. 22, 1833 : wrote *Treatise on Crimes and Misdemeanours*, declared to be the best general treatise on criminal law ; and on other legal subjects.

RUSTOMJI, HEERJIBHOY MANACKJI (1845–1904)

Born May 12, 1845 : son of Manackji Rustomji (*q.v.*), Sheriff of Calcutta : educated at St. Paul's School, Calcutta, 1854–61, and Calcutta University : became Deputy Accountant of the National Bank at Bombay : returned to Calcutta, 1866, and went into business : Member of the Corporation of Calcutta since 1882 : elected, 1892, Head of the Parsis on his father's death: Consul for Persia in Calcutta, and Fellow of Calcutta University : Vice-President of the Bengal National Chamber of Commerce : Sheriff of Calcutta, 1901–2 : a distinguished Freemason : Justice of the Peace : Hony. Magistrate : held a number of lesser offices : C.I.E., 1903 : died May 8, 1904.

RUSTOMJI, MANACKJI (1815–1891)

Born in Bombay, Sep. 26, 1815 : son of Rustomji Cowasji, a " merchant prince " in his day : head of the firm of Rustomji Cowasji & Co., Calcutta : educated at the Elphinstone School, Bombay : after establishing a branch firm in Canton, joined the firm in Calcutta, 1837, which owned the " opium clippers " to China : suffered in the Union Bank failure of 1849 : succeeded his father as head of the firm, 1852 : the first native gentleman appointed Sheriff of Calcutta, 1874 : was J.P. : Presidency Magistrate : Member of the Calcutta Corporation . head of the Parsi community in Calcutta : ` Consul for Persia from 1870 : Director of several companies : died at Calcutta, Dec. 22, 1891 : his picture is in the Town Hall, Calcutta, and a scholarship was founded at the University in his memory.

RYAN, SIR EDWARD (1793–1875)

Born Aug. 28, 1793 : son of William Ryan : educated at Trinity College, Cambridge : called to the bar at Lincoln's Inn, 1817 : appointed, in 1826, a Puisne Judge of the Supreme Court at Calcutta : knighted, and became Chief Justice of Bengal, 1833, until he retired in 1843 : President of the Asiatic Society of Bengal,

1832 : became a Privy Councillor, and Member of the Judicial Committee of the Privy Council, 1843 : Railway Commissioner, 1846 : Member of the Board of Trade, 1848 : Assistant Controller of the Exchequer, 1851–62 : Civil Service Commissioner, 1855, and President of the Commission in 1862 : and its guiding spirit : Vice-Chancellor of the University of London, 1871–4 : Vice-President of the Royal Asiatic Society, 1847–75 : F.G.S., and F.R.S. : died Aug. 22, 1875 : author of some legal works.

SACHAU, CARL EDUARD (1845–   )

Phil. Dr.: born July 20, 1845, at Neumünster, Schleswig-Holstein : son of Claus Jacob Sachau : studied at Rendsburg, Kiel, Leipzig and Berlin : catalogued the Persian MSS. in the Bodleian Library, 1869 : Professor of Semitic Languages at Vienna, 1869–76 : Professor of Oriental Languages at the Royal University, Berlin, from 1876 till now : since 1887 Director of the Seminar for living Oriental Languages at Berlin : has travelled much in different parts of Asia, and is well known as a Semitic scholar : his great work in relation to India is his Arabic edition of *Alberuni's India*, an account of the civilization of India about A.D. 1030 (published 1887, followed by an English edition of the same (1888) : has also published *Indo-Arabische Studien*, dealing with the same period : since 1887, a member of the Royal Academy of Sciences at Berlin : Doctor of Letters, *honoris causâ* at Oxford : Member of the Academies of Vienna and St. Petersburg : Hony. M.R.A.S.: of the American Oriental Society : of the London Society for Biblical Archæology.

SAHAI, JWALA (1838–   )

Born 1838, of the Kayastha Mathur caste : son of Lala Kripa Krishna, employé in the Ulwar State : educated at Ulwar and at the Government College, Delhi : Tutor and Private Secretary to the Raja of Khetri, and Civil and Criminal Judge there, 1859–70 : in the Bhartpur State, 1870–9, as Superintendent, P.W.D.: Civil and Criminal Judge, and Private Secretary to the Maharaja : in the Oodeypur State, 1879–80, as Boundary Commissioner : in the Jaipur State, 1880–8 : as Mir Munshi of the State Council, Census Superintendent of the State, 1881, Nazim (Collr-Magte)

in the Malpura Nizamat : in the Jhalawar State, 1889–95 as Census Superintendent 1891, and as Accountant and Comptroller : and again in Bhartpur, 1895–1905, as Nazim and District Magistrate and President of the Municipal Board : translated Aitchison's Treaties in Urdu : wrote the *Annals of Rajputana* in Urdu : and in English the *History of Bhartpur : Deeg, its History and Palaces, The Loyal Rajputana,* a record of the services of the Rajputana chiefs to the British Government during the mutiny ; and has in the press a History of Rajputana from the time of the advent of the British into Rajputana : was for some time President of the Jaipur Theosophical Society : constantly employed on inter-State disputes : retired from service on Aug. 3, 1905.

SALAR JANG, NAWAB SIR
(1829–1883)

Statesman : his real name was Mir Turab Ali Khan : born Jan. 1829, son of Mir Muhammad Ali Khan : a scion of a noble family settled in Hyderabad : his grandfather and great-grandfather had been in the service of the Nizam as Ministers of State : educated privately, and took service under the State : in May, 1853, on the death of his uncle, Suraj-ul-mulk, Prime Minister of Hyderabad, he was called on to administer its affairs as Prime Minister. He disbanded large bands of Arab troops, subdued robber chieftains, and put down lawlessness : refilled the Treasury, which was almost empty : during the mutiny of 1857 he rendered invaluable services to the Indian Government, and, through his influence, Central India and the Dekkan and Hyderabad remained loyal : he sent timely warning to the Residency, when it was threatened with attack. From 1859 to 1869 intrigues were on foot to depose him, and on two occasions his life was attempted. During the lifetime of the Nizam Afzal-ud-daula, he was hardly a free agent. In 1869, on the death of the Nizam, he was made a co-Regent of the State, during the minority of the successor. In 1876 he visited England, in the hope of obtaining the restitution of the Berars, which was the ambition of his life. On his return to India he continued to administer the affairs of the State till his death from cholera, on Feb. 8, 1883. His sudden death was attributed to poison, but there was no evidence. He was a remarkable man, a gentleman in every sense of the word, of great ability, and ever loyal to the Nizam, though he was always an object of suspicion to his jealous master. He was G.C.S.I., and a D.C.L. of Oxford.

SALAR JANG BAHADUR II, NAWAB SIR (1862–1889)

Son of Sir Salar Jung (*q.v.*), Prime Minister of Hyderabad : born 1862 : his birth name was Mir Laik Ali Khan : on his father's death, in 1883, he was appointed Secretary to the Council of Regency, and was made Prime Minister in 1884. The course of his administration not running smooth with the Nizam, he resigned his office in April, 1887, and in the same year visited England, where he was made K.C.I.E. : died July, 1889.

SALE, FLORENTIA, LADY (1790?–1853)

Daughter of George Wynch, of the Civil Service, grand-daughter of Alexander Wynch, Governor (1775–6) of Madras : married (Sir) Robert Henry Sale, 1809 : was with him in Kabul, 1840–1, and was in the disastrous retreat from Kabul, in Jan. 1842 : she and other women and children were carried off as captives by Akbar Khan as far as Bameean, until, in Sep. 1842, they bribed the Afghan officers in charge of them to release them, and were recovered by Sir Richmond Shakespear on Sep. 17. Lady Sale kept a diary throughout, published as her *Journal of the Disasters in Afghanistan*, 1843 : was given a pension of £500 a year : she remained in the hills in India, after Sale's death of his wound at Mudki in 1845 : died at the Cape, July 6, 1853.

SALE, SIR ROBERT HENRY (1782–1845)

Son of Colonel Sale : born Sep. 19, 1782 : educated at Ealing : entered the Army, 1795 : went to Madras, 1798 : was in the Mysore war of 1798–9, at Mallavilli and Seringapatam : against Tippoo and Dhoondia Waugh and Paichi Raja : against Travancore, 1809 : in the Mauritius expedition, 1810–3, and Bourbon, to 1815 : Major, 1813 : in the first Burmese war, 1824–6, at Kemendine and Kamarut took Bassein : at Prome and Maloun : C.B. : in the Afghan war, 1838, commanded advanced Brigade : to Kandahar, April, 1839 : at Girishk, Ghazni, Kabul : Maj-

General, K.C.B. : wintered at Jalalabad : in the fighting in the Kohistan : defeated Dost Muhammad at Parwandarra, Nov. 2, 1840 : on the rising of the hill tribes in Oct. 1841, Sale forced the Khurd Kabul and reached Jalalabad, Nov. 12, 1841 : being unable to return to Kabul, as ordered by Elphinstone (*q.v.*), was besieged with his force, "the illustrious garrison," in Jalalabad by Afghans until April 7, 1842, when he defeated Akbar Khan : made G.C.B. : relieved by Pollock's Army of Retribution : accompanied him to Kabul, Sep. 1842 : met the recovered captives on Sep. 18, and returned to India : Q.M.G. in India, 1844 : was with the C. in C. at Mudki, and was mortally wounded there : died Dec. 21, 1845.

SALE-HILL, SIR ROWLEY SALE (1839–)

Born Nov. 6, 1839 : son of Captain Rowley John Hill : educated at King William's College, Isle of Man : entered the Bengal Army, 1876, and became Maj-General, 1885 : Lt-General, 1890, and General, 1896 : served in the Indian mutiny, 1857–8 : Bhutan campaign, 1865–6 : Hazara campaign, 1868 : Malay Peninsula expedition, 1875–6 : Afghan campaigns, 1878–80 : C.B. : in command of Akka expedition, N.E. frontier, 1883–4 : commanded Rawal Pindi Brigade, 1882 : Eastern Frontier District, 1882–6 : K.C.B., 1902.

SALISBURY, ROBERT ARTHUR TALBOT GASCOIGNE CECIL, THIRD MARQUIS OF (1830–1903)

Born Feb. 3, 1830 : son of the second Marquis : educated at Eton and Christ Church, Oxford : Fellow of All Souls' College : M.P. for Stamford, 1853–68 : Marquis, 1868 : Secretary of State for India as Lord Cranborne, July 6, 1866, to March 9, 1867 : and again as Marquis of Salisbury, Feb. 22, 1874, to March 30, 1878 : Chancellor of the University of Oxford, 1869 : wrote for the *Quarterly Review* and other Periodicals : his career as Ambassador, etc., Foreign Secretary, and thrice Prime Minister, belongs to English and European politics and history : died Aug. 22, 1903 : K.G. : D.C.L. : LL.D.

SALKELD, PHILIP (? –1857)

Joined the Bengal Engineers, 1848, in Bengal : on the outbreak of the mutiny was Executive Engineer, P.W.D., at Delhi: escaped to Meerut from the massacre at Delhi, May 12, 1857: was at the battles of the Hindun and Badli-ka-sarai: through the siege of Delhi from June 8 to Sep. 14, 1857: "Salkeld's battery" was near Hindu Rao's house: was told off to blow up the Kashmir gate of Delhi, at the assault on Sep. 14: was wounded in endeavouring to fire the charge: lingered, and died Oct. 11, 1857: was awarded the V.C.

SALMONE, HABIB ANTHONY
(1860–1904)

Born at Beyrout, Sep. 1, 1860: son of a naturalized British subject and distinguished scholar: member of the R.A.S., 1884: wrote *On the Importance to Great Britain of the Study of Arabic*: Lecturer on Arabic at University College, London: published, 1890, an Arabic-English lexicon, Honorary Professor of Arabic at King's College: travelled through Turkey, Egypt, Mesopotamia, Syria, Persia, India, 1891–2: founded in 1892 the *Eastern and Western Review*, in Arabic and English, of Oriental and Imperial affairs, but it came to an end in 2 years: engaged in journalism: brought out *The Imperial Souvenir*, a metrical translation of part of the National Anthem into 50 of the languages spoken in the British Empire: died Oct. 1904.

SAMBHUNATH PANDIT (1820–1867)

A Kashmir Brahman, whose family had settled in Oudh, and a branch had been settled in Bengal for some generations: son of Sadasib Pandit: born in Calcutta, 1820: educated at Lucknow, Benares, and the Oriental Seminary: beginning as an assistant to the *Sadr* Court Record-keeper on Rs. 20 a month, he rose, from being a Pleader, to be Junior Government Pleader, 18 3: Senior, 1861: Law Professor at the Presidency College, 1855: and the first Native Judge of the High Court, Calcutta, 1863–7: died June 6, 1867: an authority on Hindu law, and questions of land tenure.

SAMRU (1720–1778)

Walter Reinhard was his proper name: born 1720: said variously to have been son of a butcher at Salzburg, or an Alsatian born at Strasburg: went to India as a sailor on a French ship: deserted at Pondicherry: enlisted in French Army as Sum-ner, or Somers, which the soldiers changed into Sombre and the natives pronounced Samru: enlisted in the E. I. Co.'s service in Bengal: was at Dacca: deserted in 18 days to Chandernagore, to M. Law: then to Nawab Safdar Jang in Oudh: then joined Suraj-ad-daula's service: as servant to an Armenian, Gregory, served under Mir Kasim, and commanded two battalions: treacherously captured and massacred 51 English gentlemen and 100 others at Patna, Oct. 1763: fled to the Nawab Wazir of Oudh at Lucknow: served under Bhartpur, and Jaipur, and Najaf Khan, the Wazir of the Emperor of Delhi: received a valuable estate at Sardhana, where he made a fort and settled, living with the Begam Samru (*q.v.*): an uneducated man of low, cruel character, of no military capacity, commanding a disreputable force: died at Agra, May 4, 1778.

SAMRU BEGAM (? –1836)

Named Zebulnissa, by birth a Kashmiri: by family Georgian: lived with Samru (*q.v.*) at Sardhana, and succeeded him in command of the estate and of a dissolute force of Europeans, over 200, which was at one time under the control of George Thomas (*q.v.*): she became a Roman Catholic after Samru's death in 1778, and married a French adventurer named Levassoult, who commanded her force: escaping from a mutiny of her soldiers, he killed himself: she was kept captive, but was re-established in power by George Thomas, after reconciliation: her forces were greatly increased by her commandant, Col. Saleur: they were defeated at Assaye in 1803: and submitted to General Lake: she lived afterwards on friendly terms with the English, disbanding her troops. She became very rich, and gave large sums in charity to Christian religions, including Rs. 50,000 to the Bishop of Calcutta, and built Christian churches at Meerut: there she entertained the highest officials in India. She died Jan. 27, 1836, over 80 years of age: leaving 70 to 80 lakhs, partly in charities, the remainder to Dyce Sombre, her step-grandson, well known by the great Dyce-Sombre lawsuit.

SANDEMAN, SIR ROBERT GROVES
(1835–1892)

Colonel: born Feb. 25, 1835: son of General Robert Turnbull Sandeman:

educated at Perth and St. Andrew's University: joined the 33rd Bengal Infantry, 1856: and, later, Probyn's Horse, the 11th Bengal Lancers: in the mutiny, was at the capture of Lucknow: was appointed to the Panjab Commission by John Lawrence: in charge of Dera Ghazi Khan district, 1866: negotiated the treaty with the Khan of Kelat, 1876: C.S.I., 1877: Agent to Governor-General for Beluchistan, 1877–92: K.C.S.I., 1879: he had immense influence with the Khan of Kelat and the Beluchi tribes, and initiated a new frontier policy of influence rather than of non-interference: he was described as the " kind of man who made empires ": died Jan. 29, 1892.

SANDFORD, JOHN DOUGLAS
(1833–1892)

I.C.S.: son of Venerable Archdeacon Sandford: educated at Rugby and at Trinity College, Oxford: Scholar: first class Moderations and in the Final Classical school: to India in 1856: served in the N.W.P.: Judicial Commissioner of Burma and of Mysore: left India, 1882: retired, 1884: died June, 1892.

SANDHURST, WILLIAM MANSFIELD, SECOND BARON (1855–)

Born Aug. 21, 1855: son of first Baron Sandhurst (*q.v.*): educated at Rugby: entered the Army, 1873, and retired shortly after: Under Secretary for War, 1886, 1892–4: Governor of Bombay, 1895–9: G.C.I.E.: G.C.S.I.

SANDHURST, WILLIAM ROSE MANS-FIELD, FIRST BARON (1819–1876)

Born June 21, 1819: son of John Mansfield and grandson of Sir James Mansfield: educated at the R.M.C., Sandhurst: joined the 53rd regt., 1835, with which he went to England: in the Satlaj campaign, at Badiwal, Aliwal, and at Sobraon was A.D.C. to Sir Hugh Gough: commanded his regt. in the Panjab campaign, 1848–9: was at Gujarat: Lt-Colonel, 1851: saw service on the Peshawar frontier, 1851–2: was military adviser to the British Ambassador at Constantinople, 1855: Consul-General at Warsaw, 1856: in the mutiny of 1857 was Chief of the Staff to Sir Colin Campbell: Maj-General in the relief and siege of Lucknow, at Cawnpur, in the campaign of Rohilkund

and Oudh in 1858, at Bareli, and other actions: K.C.B.: refused the command in China, 1860: C. in C., Bombay, 1860–5: Lt-General, 1864: C. in C. in India, 1865 –70: during which time a court martial was held on Jervis, a member of the personal Staff: K.C.S.I., 1866: G.C.S.I., 1866: G.C.B., 1870: commanded in Ireland, 1870–5: made Lord Sandhurst, 1871: General, 1872: D.C.L., 1870: took a prominent part in the debates on the organizing and reconstruction of the military system. He wrote *On the Introduction of a Gold Currency in India*, and had considerable talent in financial matters, whereas his right to be regarded as a great soldier has been questioned: died June 23, 1876.

SANKEY, SIR RICHARD HIERAM
(1829–)

Born March 12, 1829: son of Mathew Sankey: educated at Addiscombe: entered Madras Engineers, 1846, and became Lt-General, 1884: Superintendent of the East Coast Canal, 1856–7: in the mutiny on special duty at Allahabad: Field Engineer at Cawnpur: Senior Engineer Officer with the Gurkha Force under Jang Bahadur: recommended for the V.C.: at the capture of Lucknow: Chief Engineer in Mysore, 1864–77: deputed to Victoria to report on waterworks, 1871: Deputy Secretary to the Government of India, 1877. Commanding Engineer in S. Afghanistan under Sir D. Stewart, 1878–9: Chief Engineer and Secretary P.W.D., Madras, 1879, and Member of Legislative Council, Madras: Fellow, Madras University, 1881: resigned P.W.D., 1883: retired from Army, 1884: Chairman of Board of Works, Ireland, 1884–96: K.C.B., 1892.

SARASVATI, DAYANANDA (1827–1883)

Of a Brahman family in Morvi in Kattiawar: of the Siva sect: studied Sanskrit and the Vedas: left his family, went to Benares, and the banks of the Nerbudda river: became a Sanyasi and acquired his name (as above): studied Yoga ascetic philosophy at various places: went to Abu, Hardwar, Srinagar, to the Northern Himalayas, in search of the sages, called Mahatmas: was at Meerut in 1880: held public disputations all over India: at first he had regarded the Vedas as divine revelations: these views he modified, limiting the divine inspiration to the Mantras, or hymns only : became a teacher and lecturer and published Sanskrit texts : was the founder and leader of the sect of the Arya-Samaj : also, to some extent, a reformer, opposed to post-Vedic abuses : died at Ajmir, Oct. 30, 1883 : left an autobiographical sketch.

SARASVATI, PANDITA RAMABAI
(1858–   )

Born 1858 : daughter of Ananta Sastri, a Brahman of Mangalore district, who taught her Sanskrit and modern Indian languages : after her parents' death, when she was 16, she travelled with her brother, advocating female education : examined by the Pandits at Calcutta, received the title of Sarasvati : married Bipin Bihari Madhavi, a Bengali, who died : she became a lecturer : founded, 1881, the Arya Mahila Samaj at Poona : went to England, 1883, to the Sisters' Home at Wantage : was baptized there, Sep. 1883 : became Professor of Sanskrit at the Ladies' College, Cheltenham, 1884–6 : went to America, and became, 1886, a pupil in the training school of Kindergarten teachers : founded at Boston, Dec. 1887, the " Ramabai Association," to further the cause of Hindu child-widows : she wrote *The High-Caste Hindu Woman* : left America : went to Bombay, Feb. 1889 : opened a home, afterwards removed to Poona, for widows.

SARBADHIKARI, DR. SURJYA KUMAR (1832–1904)

Born 1832, educated at the Hindu College : the Dacca College, 1849, and the Calcutta Medical College, 1851 : passed the Senior Diploma examination, 1856, and joined the Government medical service : was a valued coadjutor of Dr. (Sir) Joseph Fayrer : in the siege of Lucknow in the mutiny : after it, resigned Government service and settled down to private practice in Calcutta : Fellow of the Calcutta University, 1879 : President of the Faculty of Medicine in the Syndicate, 1898 : made Rai Bahadur, 1898 : died Dec. 1904.

SARDHANA, MUHAMMAD JAN-FISHAN KHAN, NAWAB BAHA-DUR OF (1801–1864)

Of a family of Muzwi Syads, who resided at Paghman, near Kabul : for his services

rendered to Sir Alexander Burnes in his Kabul Mission, and subsequently to the English during their retreat in 1842 from Kabul, he was banished from Afghanistan, and took refuge with his family in British territory, residing at Sardhana near Meerut : granted the title of Khan Sahib and a pension : during the mutiny, he behaved with conspicuous loyalty : with a body of horse, he accompanied Sir Archdale Wilson to Delhi : in both actions on the Hindun : after the capture of Delhi, employed in maintaining order there : made Nawab Bahadur, and given a grant of land with a continuation of his former pension in perpetuity : died 1864.

SARGENT, SIR CHARLES (1821–1900)

Son of William Sargent : born 1821 : educated at King's College, London, and Trinity College, Cambridge : 5th Wrangler, 1843 : Fellow of Trinity, 1845 : called to the bar at Lincoln's Inn, 1848 : Member of the Supreme Council of Justice of the Ionian Islands, 1858–60, and Chief Justice, 1860–6 : knighted, 1860 : Puisne Judge of the Bombay High Court, 1866 : Chief Justice, 1882–95 : died June 21, 1900.

SARGENT, RIGHT REV. DR.
(1807–1889)

Educated at the Church Missionary College, Islington : ordained, 1841 : appointed a Church Missionary Society Missionary at Madras, 1842 : and filled the position till 1877, when he was consecrated Bishop Coadjutor to the Bishop of Madras, and made D.D. : Fellow of the Madras University, 1879 : author of works on the Scriptures and of translations into Tamil : died Oct. 13, 1889.

SARTORIUS, EUSTON HENRY
(1844–   )

Son of Admiral Sir G. R. Sartorius : educated at Woolwich and Sandhurst : joined the Army, 1862 : passed the Staff College : served in Afghan campaigns, 1878–9 : Brevet-Major and V.C. : Egyptian campaign, as D.A.A.G.: Brevet Lt-Colonel : Military Attaché, Japan : C.B. : Maj-General.

SARTORIUS, GEORGE (1840–   )

Born April 2, 1840 : son of Admiral Sir G. R. Sartorius : educated at Woolwich : entered the Royal Artillery, 1857, and

Indian Staff Corps, 1864 : served in the Afghan campaign, 1878–9 : Soudan, 1884 : Burma, 1886–9 : C.B. : A.Q.M.G., Bombay, 1876 : Colonel.

SARTORIUS, REGINALD WILLIAM
(1841–)

Son of Admiral Sir G. R. Sartorius : entered the Bengal Cavalry : served in the Indian mutiny, 1857–8 : Bhutan campaign, 1865–6 : Ashanti war, 1873–4 : on Staff of H. R. H. the Prince of Wales on his tour in India, 1875–6 : Afghan campaigns, 1879–80 : Maj-General, 1895 : V.C.

SASSOON, SIR ALBERT ABDULLAH DAVID, BARONET (1818–1896)

Son of David Sassoon, State Treasurer at Bagdad : born there, July 25, 1818 : educated in India, his father having removed first to Bushire and afterwards to Bombay, and established a banking and mercantile house : head of the firm in 1864: contributed largely to charitable institutions and made many handsome donations to Bombay, including the Sassoon wet dock at Colaba, 1872–5 : C.S.I., 1867 : Member of the Bombay Legislative Council, 1868–72 : K.B., 1872 : given the freedom of the City of London for his munificent charities, etc. etc. : settled in England : Vice-President of the Anglo-Jewish Association : made a Baronet, 1890 : died Oct. 24, 1896.

SASTRI, SIR AMARAVATI SESHIAH
(1828–1903)

Entered the public service in the Board of Revenue, Madras, 1848 : became its *Sarishtadar* : became Diwan of Travancore and Diwan of the Raja of Pudukota : Member of the Legislative Council, Madras, 1883 : public-spirited, capable and honest, he enjoyed for many years the high regard and confidence of Governors of Madras : was made K.C.S.I. : died Oct. 29, 1903.

SASTRI, CALAMUR VIRAVALLI RUNGANADA. (1819–1881)

Son of a poor Brahman in the Chitore District, Madras, who had a great reputation as a Sanskrit scholar. When his father fell into difficulties and was put into the Civil jail, he offered himself to the Collector of the District as his substitute and the Collector (Mr. Casamajor) had him educated in English : showed a great aptitude for mathematics : sent in 1836 to Bishop Corrie's school in Madras under Mr. Kerr : on the latter's transfer to Calcutta in 1839, Sastri became Teacher of Mathematics in the High School. In 1842 he took the Proficient's degree : returned to Chitore to be near his father and became Head Clerk in the Subordinate Judge's Court : studied several Oriental languages, in all of which he became proficient, and qualified to be Interpreter in the Supreme Court. Whilst employed in that post he mastered French and Latin, and in 1857 was made a Fellow of the Madras University. In 1859 he was made a Judge of the Small Cause Court and began to study Arabic. In 1880 he retired on pension : a tall, handsome man, his complexion differing but little from that of a European bronzed by a tropical sun : devoted to exercise, particularly to riding. At the time of his death he was master of 13 languages, Tamil, Telugu, Malayalam, Canarese, Mahratti, Hindustani, Persian, Arabic, Sanskrit, Latin, Greek, French, and German, and had begun to study Hebrew. As a social reformer he occupied a very high place and was a great believer in female education : died July 5, 1881.

SASTRI, PANDIT S. M. NATESA
(? –)

Bookseller and publisher : novelist and writer on Indian Folk-lore : noted for his translations from the Tamil :—*Folk-Lore in Southern India*, 1884, etc. ; *Dravidian Nights' Entertainments* ; a translation of the *Madanakamarajankadai*, 1886 ; *The King and his Four Ministers*, 1889 ; *Tales of Tennalirama*, 1900 : has also translated from Sanskrit and English into Tamil (Shakespeare's plays, etc.) : has brought out the text with translation of *Atmavidyavilasa* : also translated Tamil and Sanskrit inscriptions : is a member of the Folk-Lore Society, and writes in the *Indian Antiquary*.

SAUNDERS, JOHN O'BRIEN
(1852–1905)

Born 1852 : son of John O'Brien Saunders, whom he succeeded about 1878 in the proprietorship and management of the Calcutta *Englishman* : for his conduct of his newspaper he was given the C.I.E. on the occasion of the Delhi *darbar*, 1903 :

died at Posilippo, near Naples, Feb. 9, 1905.

SAUNDERS, THOMAS (? – ?)

Writer at Fort St. George, Madras, 1732 : Factor and Sub-accountant, 1737 : Second in Council at Vizagapatam, 1740 : Senior Merchant and Resident at Ingeram, 1743 : Fifth in Council at Fort St. David, 1748-9, and Chief at Vizagapatam, 1749 : Governor of Madras at Fort St. David, Sep. 19, 1750 : President in Council : his Government re-established at Fort St. George, April 5, 1752 : made a treaty with M. Godeheu, 1754 : he resigned the Governorship and service, Jan. 14, 1755.

SAUSSE, SIR MATTHEW RICHARD
(1809-1867)

Born 1809 : called to the Irish bar, 1829 : Q.C., 1849 : Puisne Judge of the Bombay Supreme Court, 1856-9 : Chief Justice, 1859-62 : and of the High Court, Bombay, 1862-6 : died Nov. 5, 1867.

SAWARD, MICHAEL HENRY
(1840–)

Born Dec. 22, 1840 : son of M. Saward : educated at Merchant Taylors' and Addiscombe : entered the Bengal Artillery 1859, and became Maj-General, 1896 : A.D.C. to General Sir H. Tombs and General Sir C. T. Chamberlain : A.Q.M.G., 1874 : A.A.G., Artillery in India, 1889-94 : Colonel on Staff, 1895-6 : Lieutenant: Governor of Guernsey and Alderney, 1899-1903.

SAYANI, RAHMATULLA MUHAMMAD
(1847-1902)

A leading Muhammadan in Bombay : Honorary Magistrate : President of the Municipal Corporation : Member of the Legislative Councils of Bombay and the Governor General : presided over the twelfth National Congress : died June 6, 1902.

SCALLON, ROBERT IRVIN
(1857–)

Born April 3, 1857 : son of T. N. Scallon : educated at University College, and King's College Schools, London : entered the Army, 1876, and Bombay Staff Corps, 1877 : Officiating C.O. of 23rd Bombay L.I., 1893-4 : Acting Inspr-General, Imperial Service troops,

1897 : served in Afghan campaigns, 1878-9, in the Kabul-Kandahar march, Burma expedition, 1886-8, D.S.O. : Tirah expedition, 1897-8 : Mahsud-Waziri expedition, 1900-2 : commanded Aden column in the Aden Hinterland, 1903 : D.S.O. : C.I.E. : C.B. : Colonel.

SCHALCH, VERNON HUGH
(1825-1877)

I.C.S. : educated at Haileybury, 1840-1 : went out to Lower Bengal, 1842 : was Commissioner of Orissa, 1867 : acted as Chairman of the Calcutta Corporation and Commissioner of Police : Member of the Board of Revenue, 1869-77 : and Member of the Bengal Legislative Council : an authority on revenue matters in Bengal : C.S.I. : retired, 1877 : died Dec. 3, 1877.

SCHARLIEB, MARY DACOMB
(1845–)

Born 1845 : wife of a practising barrister in Madras : took her M.B. and B.S. degrees in London, 1882 : went to India, 1883, and was appointed Lecturer in Midwifery at Madras Medical College, and Examiner to the Madras University : took M.D. degree in 1888 : M.S. in 1896 : practises in London : author of *A Woman's Words to Women.*

SCHIEFNER, FRANZ ANTON VON
(1817-1879)

A prominent Russian Orientalist : born July, 1817 : educated at Reval and the University, St. Petersburg : studied Philology under Prof. Græfe : also at Berlin, 1840-2, under Bopp and others : Professor of the Classics at St. Petersburg, 1843 : devoted himself to the study of Tibetan in the libraries of St. Petersburg : Librarian, 1848, and Member, 1852, of the Imperial Academy of Sciences, being specially charged with the study of Tibetan, particularly the investigation of Buddhist Legends of Indian and Occidental origin : wrote articles on the language and literature of Tibet in the Academy Memoirs : and prepared for a work on the Bonpo, or pre-Buddhistic, religion of Tibet : also studied the Caucasian languages : was Councillor of State : died at St. Petersburg, Nov. 16, 1879.

SCHLAGINTWEIT, EMIL (1835-1904)

Born 1835 : a member of the Bavarian Civil Service : made a special study of Buddhism, especially as regards the history and language of Tibet and Indian lore. His three brothers were great explorers and provided him with materials, which he edited. In 1863 he published *Buddhism in Tibet*, in English : with the support of the Munich Academy of Sciences, he published three German works: *The Kings in Tibet from the Rise of the Royal Power in Yarburg to its Extinction in Ladak : Die Gottesurtheile der Inder :* and a book on a work of 1591 A.D., on Buddhistic chronology. He also published an illustrated work on India : arranged his brother's Himalayan collections, and gave them to German museums : died Oct. 20, 1904.

SCHLEGEL, AUGUST WILHELM VON

(1767-1845)

Born Sep. 8, 1767, at Hanover : son of Johann Adolf Schlegel, poet and noted preacher : studied at Hanover and Gottingen : devoted himself to the study of language and literature : Professor at the University, Jena, 1798-1800 : resident for some years in Berlin : lectured on literature and art : in 1804, became tutor to Madame de Staël's children : lived for many years in her family, and accompanied her on her travels in different countries during her exile : in Sweden was, for a time, secretary to Bernadotte, 1813 : assumed the title " von Schlegel " from 1814 : up to Madame de Staël's death, 1817, Schlegel was known as an authority on the literature of Germany and other lands, as poet, critic, translator, but not as an Orientalist. In 1816-7, while in Paris, and at the age of 50, he threw himself eagerly into the study of Eastern languages, and soon became famous as a Sanskrit scholar : settled at Bonn, 1818 : appointed there Professor of Literature and the History of Art at the University : died May 12, 1845. Among other works, he published the *Indische Bibliothek*, 1820-30 ; critical editions of *Bhagavad-Gita*, 1823 ; *Ramayana* and *Hitopadesa* in 1829 ; and *Reflexions sur l'étude des langues asiatiques*, 1832.

SCHLICH, WILLIAM (1840-   )

Born 1840 : son of Kirchenrath Schlich of Hesse-Darmstadt : educated at Darmstadt, University of Giessen : entered Indian Forest Department, 1866 : Conservator of Forests, 1871 : Inspr-General of Forests, India, 1881 : Professor of Forestry, Cooper's Hill, since 1889 : C.I.E., 1891 : author of *A Manual of Forestry*, 5 vols. ; *The Outlook of the World's Timber Supply*, etc. : Ph. D., 1867 : F.R.S., 1901.

SCHNEIDER, SIR JOHN WILLIAM
(1822-1903)

Commanded the Contingent of the Raja of Satara in the S. Mahratta campaign, 1844-5 : at the capture of some forts : at the suppression of mutiny at Kolapur, and its recapture in Dec. 1857 : in Abyssinia, 1867-8, as Brig-General : led the advance on Magdala : at the battle of Arogee and the assault of Magdala : C.B. : Political Resident at Aden : K.C.B., 1889 : died May 27, 1903 : General.

SCHROEDER, LEOPOLD VON
(1851 -   )

Born Dec. 24, 1851, at Dorpat, in Livonia : son of Julius von Schroeder, Director of Government schools at Dorpat : studied at the Universities of Dorpat, Jena, and Tübingen : in 1882, Docent at Dorpat University : and, in 1894, Professor at that of Innsbrück : in 1899 appointed Professor of Old Indian Philology and Archæology at the University of Vienna : member of the Imperial Academy of Sciences, Vienna, 1900. Among his chief works are : *Maitrayani Samhita*, 1881-6 : *Pythagoras und die Inder*, 1884 ; *Indiens Litteratur und Cultur in historischer Entwicklung*, 1887 ; *Buddhismus und Christenthum*, 1893 ; *Mangoblüthen*, translations from the Sanskrit, 1892 : has brought out Indian tragedies, 1887, 1891, and plays adapted for the German stage.

SCHULZE, BENJAMIN (?-1760)

Danish by birth : born at Sonnenburg : graduate of Halle : went as a Lutheran Missionary to Tranquebar, 1719, and in 1726 to Cuddalore, Pulicat, and Madras : founded the S.P.C.K. Mission at Vepery, Madras, 1828 : returned home in 1743, and died in 1760 at Halle. He translated a part of the Bible into the native languages of India : wrote, in collaboration with J. F. Fritsch, the *Maitre des Langues, occidentales et orientales* (in German), containing 100 alphabets, the Lord's Prayer in 200 languages or dialects, etc., 1738 : a Hindustani grammar, 1745 : a *Conspectus litteraturæ Telugiæ : vulgo Warugicae*, 1747.

SCHUTZ, C. (1805-1892)

Doctor : one of the first of Sanskrit scholars : and the first, or one of the first, to discover the usefulness of Sanskrit Commentaries : in 1837 he published a translation of the *Five Songs of the Bhatti Kavya* : and of other Sanskrit works, in 1843 and 1845 : he was a painstaking and conscientious scholar : blindness attacked him in 1858 and stopped his writing : died Oct. 1892, at Bielefeld.

SCHWARTZ, REV. CHRISTIAN FRIEDRICH (1726-1798)

Danish Missionary : born Oct. 22, 1726, in Prussia : son of George Schwartz : educated at Sonnenburg, Kustrin, Halle University : assisted Schultz, the Danish Missionary, to edit the Tamil Bible : ordained at Copenhagen, 1749 : went out as a Missionary from the Government of Denmark to Cuddalore and to the Danish settlement at Tranquebar, 1750 : learnt to speak several Indian languages : placed in charge of the country S. of the Cavery : went to Ceylon and Trichinopoly : at the siege of Madura, 1764 : built a church there, 1766, Mission house and schools : worked as a Missionary under the S.P.C.K. : settled as Chaplain to the troops at Trichinopoly, 1868-78 : went to live at Tanjore, 1778 : built a church there : went on behalf of the Madras Government on a secret Mission to Hyder Ali at Seringapatam : Hyder gave him free passage, but Tippoo refused to see him : Schwartz initiated Government schools, including teaching of Christianity therein : founded the Tinnevelly church : appointed interpreter at Tanjore : guardian of Serfoji, the young Raja there : died there, Feb. 13, 1798 : monuments erected to him at Madras and Tanjore : said to have made 6,000 converts : was most devout, zealous and high principled.

SCOBLE, SIR ANDREW RICHARD (1831-   )

Born Sep. 25, 1831 : son of John Scoble : educated at City of London School : called to the bar at Lincoln's Inn, 1856 : Advocate-General and Member of Legislative Council, Bombay, 1872-7 : Q.C., 1876 : Legal Member of the Supreme Council, 1886-91 : M.P. for Hackney, 1892-1900 : Member of Judicial Committee of Privy Council,1901: translator of Mignet's *History of Mary, Queen of Scots*, Guizot's *History of the English Revolution* : K.C.S.I., 1890 : P.C.

SCOTLAND, SIR COLLEY HARMAN (1818-1903)

Son of Thomas Scotland, Registrar of Antigua : called to the bar at the Middle Temple, 1843 : appointed, in 1861. Chief Justice of the Supreme Court, Madras : knighted : C.J. of the High Court, 1862-71 : Vice-Chancellor of the Madras University, 1862-71 : died Jan. 20, 1903.

SCOTT, SIR BUCHANAN (1850-   )

Entered the R.E., 1871, and became Colonel, 1900 : served in the Afghan war, 1878-9 : Engineer-in-chief, Zhob -Valley survey, 1888 : Mint Master, Calcutta : C.I.E., 1888 : K.C.I.E., 1904 : retired. 1904.

SCOTT, CHARLES HENRY (1848-   )

Born June 15, 1848 : son of Edward John Scott : educated privately and at Woolwich : entered the Royal Artillery, 1868, and became Colonel, 1892 : served in the Tirah expedition, 1897-8 : Superintendent, Gunpowder Factory, Bengal, 1881-92 : Ordnance Consulting Officer for India, 1892-5 : Inspr-General of Ordnance, 1895-1900 : Director-General of Ordnance, India, since 1902 : C,B.. 1898 : Maj-General.

SCOTT, DAVID (1786-1831)

Son of Archibald Scott : born Aug. 1786 : served at Gorakhpur : Judge and Magistrate of Purnea, 1812-3 and of Rangpur : Commissioner, in 1823, of Rangpur : then A.G.G. on the N.E. frontier of Bengal and Commissioner of Revenue and Circuit in the districts of Assam, N.E. Rangpur, Shirpur and

Sylhet: he settled the Provinces of Upper and Lower Assam when conquered in the first Burmese war: laboured to advance the country: encouraged the Missionaries: carried out a survey: subdued the Garos, opening a school for them: made a treaty at Nunklow with the Khasias, who afterwards, April 4–5, 1831, murdered two British officers, Bedingfield and Burlton, Scott fortunately escaping: he had to suppress disturbances, in pacifying the Khasias: he was remarkable for the diversity of his knowledge and pursuits: a keen sportsman: recommended the Sanitarium established at Cherrapunji, where he died, Aug, 20, 1831, and the Supreme Government erected a monument to him: described as " indeed a second Cleveland " (q.v.).

SCOTT, SIR JAMES GEORGE (1851–)

Born Dec. 25, 1851: son of Rev· George Scott: educated abroad and at King's College School, London, and Edinburgh University and Lincoln College, Oxford: War Correspondent in Perak, 1875–6: Burma, 1879: Tonking, 1883–5: joined the Burma Commission, 1886: employed on Anglo-Siamese Boundary Commission, 1889–90: Superintendent N. Shan States, 1891: British Commissioner, Mekong Commission, 1894 –6, and Burma-China Boundary Commission, 1898–1900: C.I.E., 1892: Superintendent, S. Shan States, 1902: author of *The Burman, His Life and Notions: France and Tonking: Burma as it was, as it is, and as it will be: The Upper Burma Gazetteer,* 5 vols.: K.C.I.E.

SCOTT, JOHN (1747–1819)

Son of Jonathan Scott: born 1747: entered the E.I. Co.'s military service in Bombay, about 1766, went to Bengal, 1768: and became later a Major: was A.D.C. to Warren Hastings: commanded a native regt. at Chunar, 1780: was employed by Warren Hastings as his agent in England, 1781: Scott advocated his cause with more energy than discretion: published works on behalf of Hastings, 1782–4: M.P. for West Looe, 1784–90: for Stockbridge, 1790: his officious and over-zealous assertion of Hastings' praises and ill-treatment was practically the cause of the impeachment: he inherited the estates and took the additional name of a cousin,

Waring: died May 5, 1819: wrote *Observations,* on other Indian subjects,

SCOTT, SIR JOHN (1797–1873)

General: born 1797, son of J.F. Scott: educated at Chiswick and Westminster: entered the Army, 1815: was at Paris, and the siege of Antwerp, 1832: in 1838–9 commanded the Cavalry of the Division of the Army of the Indus: at Ghazni: in 1839 commanded a detached column in Upper Sind: was at Maharajpur, 1843, commanding a Brigade of Cavalry, and at Sobraon, 1846: C.B., and A.D.C. to Queen Victoria: K.C.B., 1865: Maj-General, 1854: General, 1868: died, while riding in Rotten Row, Jan. 18, 1873.

SCOTT, SIR JOHN (1841–1904)

Born 1841: educated at Bruce Castle, near Birmingham, and Tottenham, and Pembroke College, Oxford: played in the Cricket Eleven for Oxford against Cambridge in 1863: called to the bar from the Inner Temple in 1865: from 1872 he practised and held judicial appointments at Alexandria, as British Representative in the Court of Appeal, and as Vice-President: Judge of the High Court, Bombay, 1882 to 1892: Judicial Adviser to the Khedive, 1892– 8: Deputy Judge-Advocate-General to Her Majesty's Forces, 1898: K.C.M.G. in Feb. 1894, and D.C.L. of Oxford: died at Norwood, March 1, 1894: known in Egypt as " Scott the Just."

SCOTT, JONATHAN (1754–1829)

Born 1754: son of Jonathan Scott: brother of John Scott (q.v.): educated at Shrewsbury: to India, in the 29th N.I., in 1772: Captain, 1778: Persian Secretary to Warren Hastings: helped to found the Asiatic Society of Bengal, 1784: returned to England, 1785: published translations of various Oriental works, including *A Translation of Ferishta's History of the Dekkan, with a History of Bengal from the Accession of Aliverdi Khan to the year* 1780, and an edition, with introduction and additions, of the *Arabian Nights,* from the French of M. Galland, 1811: Professor of Oriental Languages at the R.M. College, 1802–5: and the first to hold a similar appointment at Haileybury: D.C.L., 1805: died Feb. 11, 1829,

SCOTT, LOTHIAN KERR (1841–   )

Born May 24, 1841 : son of George Scott : educated at Winchester and Woolwich : entered the Royal Engineers, 1862 : volunteered for service in India, and was employed in public works, railways and irrigation : Musketry Inspector at Chatham : Instructor in Fortifications, Sandhurst : Professor of Artillery and Fortifications, 1882–9 : inventor of telescopic and automatic sights : retired : C.B., 1897.

SCOTT, WILLIAM WALTER HOPTON (1843–   )

Born Dec. 5, 1843 : son of Maj-General W. S. Scott, Bengal Artillery : educated at Marlborough and Addiscombe : entered the Indian Army, 1861 : served in Abyssinian expedition, 1867–8, at the capture of Magdala : A.D.C. to Lord Napier of Magdala when C. in C. in India : Chitral Relief, 1895, as C.O. of 11th Bengal Lancers : C.B. : Maj-General : retired.

SCOTT-MONCRIEFF, SIR COLIN CAMPBELL (1836–   )

Born Aug. 3, 1836 : son of Robert Scott-Moncrieff : educated at Edinburgh Academy and Addiscombe : entered the Bengal Engineers, 1856, and retired with rank of Colonel, 1883 : served in the mutiny, 1857–8 : in Irrigation Department, N.W.P.: in Burma as Chief Engineer: Under Secretary of State, Public Works, Cairo. 1883–92 : President of Indian Irrigation Commission, 1902–3 : Under Secretary for Scotland, 1892–1902 : C.S.I., 1878 : K.C.S.I., 1903 : K.C.M.G., 1887 : LL.D., Edinburgh.

SCOTT-MONCRIEFF, GEORGE KENNETH (1855–   )

Born Oct. 3, 1855 : son of Major A.P. Scott : educated at Edinburgh Academy and Woolwich : entered the Royal Engineers : served in Afghan campaigns, 1878–80 : Waziristan, 1901 : Instructor. School of Military Engineering, 1893–8 : commanded R.E., China expedition, 1900–1 : C.I.E., 1900.

SCRAFTON, LUKE (?– 1769)

In the service of the E. I. Co. : was Third at Dacca in 1756, and was made prisoner by the Nawab of Bengal : in 1757 was employed by Clive in the negotiations which resulted in Mir Jafar's being made Nawab Nazim : Scrafton was made Resident at Murshidabad : it devolved on him, under Clive's order, to tell Omichund that the duplicate treaty given to him was a trick. When Clive was made Governor of Bengal, 1857, Scrafton succeeded him in the Calcutta Council, Warren Hastings succeeding Scrafton at Murshidabad. He was appointed in 1769, with Vansittart and Colonel Francis Forde, to be a Commission of Inquiry into Bengal affairs : they were all lost at sea in the *Aurora*.

SCUDAMORE, ARTHUR (1816–1880)

Entered the Army in 1835 : in the 4th Light Dragoons in the Afghan war, 1838–9, at Ghazni : in the Panjab campaign of 1848–9, in the principal engagements : seriously wounded at Gujarat : commanded his regt. under Sir Hugh Rose in Central India during the mutiny : at Jhansi, Koonch, Kalpi, Morar, Gwalior : in command of a flying column in the Gwalior and Jhansi territory : C.B. : Brevet - Lt-Colonel : Maj-General, 1875 : died Jan. 11, 1880,

SCUDDER, REV. HENRY MARTYN, D.D. (1822–1895).

Born 1822 : the eldest and probably the most distinguished of Dr. John Scudder's sons : one of the most gifted men that have laboured in India : probably no Missionary in South India has used the spoken Tamil with greater power, and but a few have attained a greater mastery over the classical dialect. His books, notably *Spiritual Teaching, The Bazaar Book*, and *Jewel Mine of Salvation*, have proved invaluable aids to Missionaries and native preachers : they are still used in the Arcot districts : also he made an excellent translation of the liturgy. Arriving in America, he became pastor of a prominent church in San Francisco, and afterwards built up strong churches in Brooklyn and Chicago : thus he worked with distinguished success on two continents : died 1895 : M.D, and D.D.

SCUDDER, DR. JOHN (1793– ?   )

Born Sept. 3, 1793, at Freehold, New Jersey, son of Joseph Scudder and grandson of Dr. Nathaniel Scudder (killed in the revolutionary war, 1781) : his ancestor,

Thomas Scudder, settled in America from England about 1635 : a pioneer Missionary of the Reformed Church in India. Having chosen the medical profession, Dr. Scudder settled in New York City : while there engaged in his profession, the claims of the heathen were brought vividly before his mind in a peculiar manner : in professional attendance on a lady, while in the ante-room, he took up a tract with the title, " The Conversion of the World ; or, the Claims of Six Hundred Millions ; and the Ability and Duty of the Churches respecting them." The words of the tract pierced his heart, and he had no rest until he had offered his services to the Foreign Mission Board. At 26 he abandoned home and friends, and with his young family sailed for India : arrived in Ceylon, Feb., 1820 : entered upon his work with the earnestness and devotion which characterized his whole life. After labouring with great success as a medical Missionary in Ceylon for 16 years, he removed in 1836 to Madras, where a new Mission was opened : there his eldest son, Henry Martyn, joined him as a Missionary in 1844. In 1853 the father and son decided to open a Mission in the Arcot District, 80 miles W. of Madras. The Arcot Mission has ever been associated with the name of Scudder, no fewer than 9 children of Dr. John Scudder and 9 grandchildren having been connected with it.

SCUDDER, REV. LEWIS R.
(1861-   ).

Grandson of Dr. John Scudder (*q.v.*) : he graduated from Princeton University, U.S.A., in 1882, and M.D. from New York Medical College in 1888, and has worked 17 years in India : has considerably enlarged the medical institution at Arcot, having opened Branch Dispensaries and special accommodation for high caste people : he has maintained his family's name by his earnest and successful work at the Arcot Mission.

SCUDDER, REV. SILAS D. (1833-1877).

℗ Seventh son of Dr. John Scudder (*q.v.*) : was a medical Missionary in the Arcot Mission : he established the Hospital and Dispensary there, and was one of the first

to introduce western medical science among the natives of the district : the Madras Governemnt gave over to him a fine building and ample ground for the hospital and contributed its expenses. Lord Napier of Ettrick (*q.v.*), Governor of Madras, conducted Mr. W. H. Seward, U.S. Sec. of State, when visiting India, to this hospital and dispensary as one of the chief objects of interest in his Presidency. Many thousands of Hindus sought the benefits of the treatment granted gratuitously. Dr. Scudder worked with untiring industry, with great spirit and vigour : attending also to a large out-door practice. High-caste ladies placed themselves under his treatment. A class of medical students was also taught : some of them are now successful practitioners. He was in India nearly 13 years. When his health was broken he went home to die : he never recovered from the injuries received from overwork, from a tropical sun and malarious climate : died 1877.

SEAL, MATI LAL (1791-1854)

Son of a petty tradesman : educated at a primary village school : at 17 went on pilgrimage, and travelled in Upper India : became a clerk, and storekeeper at Fort William, Calcutta : and established a business, first as a dealer in empty bottles and corks, then as a ship's banian : became, by 1823, Director of 3 mercantile firms, and was connected with many firms and houses in Calcutta : greatly respected for his integrity, and the good use he made of his wealth : he became a large owner of land and houses : founded, in 1842, a higher-class English school in Calcutta and liberally endowed it : gave land for the erection of the Calcutta Medical College : " Seal's Free School " is still one of the best of its kind in Calcutta : the poor-house which he established in 1848 at Belgharia still exists : died May 20, 1854.

SEATON, SIR THOMAS (1806-1876)

Born 1806 : son of John Fox Seaton : joined the E. I. Co.'s 10th N.I. in 1823 : at the siege of Bhartpur, 1826 : with the 35th regt. in Kabul in 1839 : returned to India with Sale's Brigade, fighting their way to Jalalabad : was in its defence : at the re-occupation of Kabul : C.B., and Major : Brig-Major at Agra : in the mutiny, his regt., the 60th N.I., mutinied : he was at the siege of Delhi : Lt-Colonel of the 1st European Fusiliers : held Fatehghar, and was engaged in 1858 at Kankar, Bunhaganj : K.C.B., 1858 : retired as Maj-General, 1859 : wrote his autobiography, *From Cadet to Colonel*, 1866 : died Sep. 11, 1876.

SECCOMBE, SIR THOMAS LAWRENCE (1812–1902)

Born July, 29, 1812 : entered the East India House in 1829, in the Financial Department : appointed Assistant Financial Secretary in it, 1858 : Financial Secretary, 1859 : Director of Military Funds, 1866 : C.B., 1869 : Assistant Under Secretary of State, 1872 : Accountant General, 1872 : K.C.S.I., 1877 : representative of India at Paris Conference on Bimetallism, 1878 : resigned the Financial Secretaryship, 1879 : Assistant Under Secretary of State till 1881 :' on Lord Northbrook's Commission to determine the contribution payable by India towards Army effective charges, 1881–92 : G.C.I.E., 1892 : died April 9, 1902.

SEDDON, FELIX JOHN VAUGHAN (1798–1865)

Son of William Seddon : born 1798 : educated at Manchester : went to India, 1815 : accompanied the Army in the Burmese war, 1824–5, as translator : translated into Manipuri, and made an Assamese grammar and dictionary : translated the Bible : Professor of Oriental Languages at King's College, 1833 : after 1837, when he returned to India, became tutor to the Nawab Nazim, and lived at Murshidabad till his death there, Nov. 25, 1865.

SELL, REV. CANON EDWARD, D.D. (1839–   )

Born 1839 : son of William John Sell : educated at a private school and the C.M.S. College, London : Head Master of the Harris High School for Muhammadans, Madras, 1865–80 : Secretary of the Church Missionary Society, Madras, 1880–1905 : Fellow, Madras University,

1874 : D.D. of Edinburgh University 1902 : Hon. Canon, St George's Cathedral, Madras, 1901 : Examining Chaplain to the Bishop of Madras, 1900 : Chairman of the Arabic, Persian and Hindustani Board of Studies : Member of the Syndicate and also Examiner in the University of Madras : author of the *Faith of Islam*, 1896 ; *Essays on Islam*, 1901 : *Historical Development of the Koran*, 1905 : M.R.A.S.

SEN, KESHAB CHANDRA (1838–1884)

Born Nov. 19, 1838 : a kinsman of the Sena Rajas : grandson of Ram Kamal Sen, who was Diwan of the Calcutta 'Mint, and a Secretary of the Asiatic Society of Bengal : and son of Piari Mohan Sen, who survived his father only three years, and died in 1848 : educated at the Hindu, Metropolitan, and Presidency Colleges, Calcutta : was thrown much into the society of the Christian Missionaries : in 1857 he joined the Brahmo Samaj, the reformed Theistic Society founded by Raja Rammohan Roy (*q.v.*) and extended by Debendranath Tagore (*q.v.*) : served as a clerk in the Bank of Bengal, 1859–61, but resigned his appointment : the rest of his life was spent as a Brahmo Missionary. In 1862 he established a central association at Calcutta, and was appointed Minister of the Brahmo Samaj by Debendranath Tagore : he visited Bombay and Madras on a Missionary tour and established branches of the Samaj. Differences arose between him and Debendranath Tagore as to the abandonment of old national customs, the advocacy of the re-marriage of widows and the removal of the Brahmanical thread : in 1866 he retired from the Brahmo Samaj and established what is known as the Brahmo Samaj of India as opposed to the Adi, i.e. the original Brahmo Samaj : in 1866 he lectured on "Jesus Christ, Europe and Asia," and his conversion to Christianity seemed probable until the publication of *Great Men*, in which he contended that other men also were "above ordinary humanity." He opened his own Brahmo Mandir on Aug. 22, 1869, and then went on a Missionary tour to the North-West Provinces and Bombay. He visited the Viceroy (Lord Lawrence) at Simla and induced him to introduce a Bill for legalizing Brahmo marriages. In 1870 he visited England and was well received, visiting the chief towns of England and Scotland, and speaking at more than 70 public meetings and chapels. On his return to India he established the Indian Reform Association : the Bharat Asram, or Indian Hermitage, was opened in 1872 : in 1872 he saw the Brahmo Marriage Act passed. From 1875 to 1878 he was employed in improving the organization of the Brahmo Samaj, but his popularity among his countrymen decreased, chiefly on account of his marrying his daughter to the young Maharaja of Cooch Behar, both of them being under the ages fixed by the Brahmo Marriage Act. His appeal to Adesa, or the voice of his conscience, in this and other matters, failed to satisfy his followers. This created a schism, and a new Samaj, called the Sadharan or Catholic Brahmo Samaj, was founded on May 15. From 1880 he preached a new dispensation, in which simple Theism was replaced by mystical doctrines, claiming special divine inspiration. For the rest of his life he suffered from nervous depression. In person Keshab Chandra Sen was a handsome, powerfully built man, 6 feet high. He was simple and pure in character, almost austere in his habits, singularly modest, and thoroughly independent : died Jan. 8, 1884.

SEN, NARENDRA NATH (1843–   )

Born Feb. 23, 1843 : educated at the Hindu College and privately : joined the staff of the *Indian Field*, then edited by Kisori Chand Mitra : in 1861 became a contributor to the *Indian Mirror* and edited it in 1863, when Manmohan Ghose (*q.v.*) went to England : admitted an Attorney of the Calcutta High Court, Dec. 1866 : became in 1879 sole proprietor and editor of the *Indian Mirror*, then a daily paper : a Municipal Commissioner and Honorary Magistrate, 1880 : joined the Indian National Congress at Bombay, 1885 : represented the Calcutta Municipality in the Bengal Legislative Council, 1897–9.

SEN, RAM DAS (1845–1887)

Born Dec. 10, 1845 : son of Lal Mohan Sen, who was nephew of Krisna Kanta

Sen, of Berhampur, Musshibabad, Diwan to the Salt Board of the E·I. Co. in the eighteenth century : wrote both poetry and prose : contributed to vernacular journals : entered upon antiquarian and philosophical researches, for which he visited Europe in 1885 : was called " the literary *zamindar* " : wrote the *Aitihasik Rahazza* and numerous Bengali books : M.R.A.S. : M.R.A.S.B : member of the British Indian Association of Bengal : of the Sanskrit Text Society of London : of the Asiatic Society of Italy, and the Oriental Academy of Florence, from which he received the title of Doctor : he died Aug. 19, 1887 : on his bust, placed at Berhampur, he was described as an eminent Oriental scholar, a learned antiquarian, and a staunch friend of education.

SEN, RAM KOMAL (1783–1844)

Born March 15, 1783 : commenced his English studies in Calcutta about 1801 : held appointments at a Hindustani Press and a hospital before he served at the Fort William College in 1812 : clerk of the Asiatic Society of Bengal in 1818, afterwards its Native Secretary, and rose to a membership of its Council : member of the managing Committee of the Hindu College, on its opening in 1817 : on the first Committee of the Calcutta School Book Society, 1818 : completed his English-Bengali dictionary of 700 pages in 1830 : appointed Diwan, or Head, of the Native Establishment of the Calcutta Mint by Dr. H. H. Wilson, 1831 : Treasurer of the Bank of Bengal, 1833 : member of the Council of Education, 1839 : a manager of the Parental Academy: jointfounder (with Dr. W. Carey), Native Secretary, 1829, and one of the Vice-Presidents, of the Agricultural and Horticultural Society, 1844 : member of the Medical Education Committee : wrote on the sanitation of Calcutta : died Aug. 2, 1844.

SENART, EMILE CHARLES MARIE (1847–   )

Oriental scholar : born at Rheims. March 26, 1847 : son of J. Senart, a magistrate : educated at the Lycée at Rheims, at the Universities of Munich and Gottingen (studying Sanskrit under Benfey) : of independent means : devoted himself to Indian studies : made voyages to India, to obtain information on Indian history and literature : member of the Academy : published works on *Kaccyana et la littèrature grammaticale du Pali*, 1871 ; *The Inscriptions of Piyadasi*, 1881–6 ; *Essay on the Legend of Buddha*, 1875 ; *The Mahavastu*, 1882 ; *Notes on Indian Epigraphy ; Les Castes dans l'Inde*, 1896 : numerous publications in the *Journal Asiatique* : has been a member of the Institute since 1882 : corresponding member of the Berlin Academy, 1900, and of the Academy of St. Petersburg, 1901 : Vice-President of the Société Asiatique : has taken an active part in political life : conseiller-général of la Sarthe since 1883 : elected member of the Chamber of Deputies, 1902.

SETON, SIR HENRY WILMOT
(?–1848)

Educated at Westminster and Trinity College, Cambridge : B.A., 1807 : called to the bar at Lincoln's Inn, 1809 : Puisne Judge of the Supreme Court, Calcutta : knighted : Vice-President of the Asiatic Society, Bengal, 1840–7 : died on his voyage to England, July 26, 1848.

SETON-KARR, WALTER SCOTT
(?–   )

I.C.S. : educated at Rugby and Haileybury, 1840–2 : went to Bengal in the Civil Service, 1842 : Under Secretary to the Government of Bengal, 1847–53 : President of the Indigo Commission, 1860 : Secretary to the Government of Bengal, 1860–1 : Member of the Legislative Council of the Governor-General, 1861 : and of the Bengal Legislative Council, 1862 : Judge of the *Sadr* Court, 1862 : Puisne Judge of the High Court, 1862–8 : Secretary to the Government of India in the Foreign Department, 1868 : Vice-Chancellor of the Calcutta University, 1868–9: wrote in the *Calcutta Review* ; President of the Records Commission, and edited *Selections from the Calcutta Gazette* : retired, 1870 : wrote *The Marquess Cornwallis* (Rulers of India series) : and *Grant of Rothiemurchus*, 1899.

SEWELL, ROBERT (1845–   )

I.C.S. : born June 4, 1845 : son of Robert Burleigh Sewell : educated at

Radley : in the Madras Civil Service, 1868–94 : Judge and then Collector of Bellary : Fellow of Madras University : introduced the Archæological Survey of S. India, 1881–3 : M.R.A.S. since 1876, and on the Council : M.A.S.B. : F.R.G.S. : F.S.A. : has written an *Analytical History of India*, 1870 ; *The Amravati Tope and Excavations on its Site in* 1877; *Chronological Tables for S. India, from the Sixth Century A.D.* : *Antiquarian Remains in Presidency of Madras*, 1882; *A Sketch of the Dynasties of S. India*, 1883 ; *Sir W. Elliot's Coins of S. India* ; *Mrs. Hawtey's India and the West in Old Days* ; *South Indian Chronological Tables*, 1889 ; *Sir Walter Elliot* ; *The Indian Calendar* (with Pandit S. B. Dikshit), 1896 : *Eclipses of the Moon in India*, 1898 ; *A Forgotten Empire*, 1900 ; and a number of articles on Buddhistic and antiquarian subjects in the *J.R.A.S.* and on coins, etc. in the *Indian Antiquary*.

SEYMOUR, HENRY DANBY
(1820–1877)

Son of Henry Seymour, M.P. : born 1820 : educated at Eton and Christ Church, Oxford : M.P. for Poole, 1850–68 : Joint Secretary to the Board of Control, 1855–8 : died Aug. 3, 1877.

SHAHABUDDIN KAZI, KHAN BAHADUR (1832–1900)

Born 1832 : son of Kazi Ibrahim : educated at the Poona College and Engineering School : became Secretary to the Council of Regency at Bhuj Cutch : and a Deputy Collector : Minister at Cutch : resigned the service : sent to England in 1869 on behalf of the Rao of Cutch : Hony. Secretary, in London, for 3 years, of the East India Association, and Professor of Oriental Languages at University College : Attaché to Sir B. Frere's Mission to Zanzibar, 1873 : Diwan of Cutch : resigned in 1874 : Head of the Revenue Department at Baroda for 13 years : Khan Bahadur, 1877 : C.I.E., 1880 : Minister at Baroda, 1883–6, when he retired : Member of the Bombay Legislative Council, 1886, and of the Public Service Commission : Fellow of the Bombay University : J.P. : died March 6, 1900.

SHAH ALAM (1728-1806)

Son of the Emperor, Alamgir II. : born June 15, 1728 : known as the Shahzada Ali Gohar : proclaimed a rebel by his father, and escaped from Delhi to Shuja-ud-daula (*q.v.*), Wazir of Oudh : after the death of Suraj-ud-daula (*q.v.*) and election of Mir Jafar (*q.v.*), he claimed Bengal, and advanced into Bihar, supported by Shuja-ud-daula : compelled to retreat from Patna : re-appeared on the then N.W. frontier, 1759, and assumed the name of Shah Alam on his father's death, 1759 ; defeated Ram Narain (*q.v.*) near Patna, but was routed, Jan. 1760, by Caillaud (*q.v.*) and Miran, son of Mir Jafar : marched towards Murshidabad : compelled again to retreat : besieged Patna, but was beaten off by Capt. Knox's force : was taken prisoner by Major Carnac, 1761, in Bihar : and allowed to retire to Oudh, Mir Kasim agreeing to pay him 26 lakhs a year from Bengal : after the battle of Baxar, in which Shuja-ud-daula was defeated, Shah Alam sought British protection and made a treaty : in 1765, at Allahabad, he granted the *diwani* (the superintendence of the revenue) to Lord Clive for the E. I. Co. on payment of a tribute of 26 lakhs a year : in 1771 he found himself under Mahdaji Sindia, the Mahratta, who installed him as Emperor of Delhi : he lost the English tribute : the Rohilla chief Ghulam Kadir seized Delhi and put out Shah Alam's eyes, 1788 : the Mahrattas restored him to the throne : he was taken under British protection after the Mahratta war of 1803 : died Nov. 10, 1806.

SHAH SHUJA (1780?-1842)

Amir of Afghanistan : son of Timur Shah of the Abdali or Durani tribe : made Governor of Peshawar by his brother, Zaman Shah, and in 1803 was invited to the throne of Kabul : met Mountstuart Elphinstone in 1809 at Peshawar, to negotiate an alliance, but was himself driven out of Afghanistan by his half-brother, Mahmud Shah, being routed at Nimla : fled to British territory and became a pensioner at Ludiana. A restless adventurer, he never ceased to plot to recover the throne. He was defeated by Dost Muhammad in 1833, when making an attempt at Kandahar. The British Government, distrusting Dost Muhummad, replaced Shah Shuja on the throne at Kabul, on Aug. 7, 1839, in the first Afghan war. The British force continued their occupation of Kabul, to support Shah Shuja, but he was not accepted by the people, and failed to establish himself as ruler. After the death of Macnaghten, and the destruction of the British force, he shut himself up in the Bala Hissar, at Kabul. When he left it, on April 5, 1842, to place himself at the head of the army, he was killed at Akbar Khan's instance by an ambushed body of the Barakzais.

SHAHNAWAZ KHAN (1700-1758)

His real name was Abdur-razzak : Persian by origin : an ancestor came to Akbar's court at Agra : born at Lahore, March 10, 1700, his father, aged 19, dying shortly before his birth : taken by his grandfather to Aurangabud : entered service early : was *Diwan* of the Berars in 1732 : attracted by his smartness the attention of the Nizam Asaf Jah : dismissed, for siding with the heir apparent against Asaf Jah : while out of employ for six years, he wrote the *Maasir-al-umra*, said to be the most important historical book produced in India in the eighteenth century, a biographical work on the officers of the Timur dynasty : late in his life Asaf Jah restored Shahnawaz to office, and his successor, Salabat Jang, favoured him more, raising him to the command of 7,000, with the title of Samsam-ud-daula. Shahnawaz was opposed to Europeans, especially the French of Pondicherry. Bussy (*q.v.*) had him arrested and kept in a tent : while being conveyed to Bussy's camp, he was, in the confusion connected with another assassination, put to death with others of his family, May 12, 1758. The *Maasir* was completed, with a life of Shahnawaz, by Abdul Hai, the author's son : it is said to contain 730 biographical notices : it was published by the Asiatic Society of Bengal, and contains much information on Indian history of the sixteenth-eighteenth centuries.

SHAKESPEAR, JOHN (1774-1858)

Born Aug, 1774 : son of a small farmer : educated at the parish school, and privately : learnt Arabic with a view to an appointment in N. Africa, but joined the Commissariat, 1792-6 : Professor of Oriental Languages at the Royal Military

cc

College, Marlow, 1805 : Hindustani Professor at Addiscombe, 1807–30 : wrote a Hindustani grammar, 1812; *Selections*, an *Introduction to Hindustani*, and a dictionary, 1816 : also philological papers for the *Journal of the R.A.S.*, of which he was Honorary Librarian : left above £250,000 : died June 10, 1858.

SHAKESPEAR, JOHN (1861–   )

Born Sep. 1, 1861 : son of Colonel Sir R. C. Shakespear, C.B.: educated at Wellington College and Sandhurst : entered the Army, 1881, and became Major, 1895 : Intelligence Officer, Lushai and Chin-Lushai expeditions, 1888–9 ; D.S.O.: Superintendent, South Lushai Hills, 1891–6 : C.I.E. 1896 : joined the Indian Staff Corps, 1896 : Deputy Commissioner, Assam : author of *The Lushais and the Land they live in*.

SHAKESPEAR, SIR RICHMOND CAMPBELL (1812–1861)

Colonel : son of John Talbot Shakespear, B.C.S.: born May 11, 1812 : educated at Charterhouse and Addiscombe : went to India in the Bengal Artillery, 1829 : in the Afghan war of 1838–9, went to Kandahar, and to Girishk with Sale : Political Assistant to D'Arcy Todd in the mission to Herat : sent by Todd to Khiva to induce the Khan to surrender Russian captives : collected many and took them all to Russia : knighted, 1841 : wrote *A Journey from Herat to Orenburg* : went, as Military Secretary, with Pollock to Kabul, 1842 : from there he proceeded to Bameean to liberate the British captives, met them after their release, and bought them back to Kabul, Sep. 1842 : returned with Pollock to India : Political Assistant at Gwalior : A.D.C. to Gough at Maharajpur, 1843 : in political charge of Gwalior, 1844–8, and 1849–51 : in the Panjab Campaign, at Ramnagar, Sadulapur, Chilianwala, Gujarat, in command of a battery : Political Agent at Jodhpur, 1851 : Resident at Baroda, 1857 : and Brig-General of Bombay Army, N. Division : A.G.G. for Central India, 1859 : C.B., 1860 : died at Indore, Oct. 29, 1861.

SHAW, ROBERT BARKLEY (1839–1879)

Son of Robert Grant Shaw : born July 12, 1839 : educated at Marlborough and Trinity College, Cambridge : became a tea-planter in Kangra : travelled in 1868 as a merchant to Eastern Turkestan, reaching Yarkand and Kashgar, Jan. 1869 : well treated by Yakub Beg : went again with Sir T. D. Forsyth (*q.v.*) to Yarkand in 1870 : received the Royal Geographical Society's medal in 1872 : British Joint Commissioner in Ladak : again at Yarkand, in 1875, with Forsyth's treaty of 1874 : came to England in charge of the Yarkand Envoy : Resident at Mandalay, then in Upper Burma, in 1878 : died there, June 15 1879 : he wrote *A Visit to High Tartary, Yarkand and Kashgar*, 1871 : and works on Asiatic languages,

SHEARER, JOHNSTON (1852–   )

Born Oct. 22, 1852 : son of J. Shearer : educated at Aberdeen Grammar School and University : M.B. (Honours), 1877 : joined the Indian Medical Service, 1880 : served in Egyptian expedition, 1882 : Burmese expedition, 1887–8 : Hazara and Miranzai expeditions, 1891 : Waziristan expedition, 1894–5 : Tirah expedition, 1897–8 : D.S.O. : Secretary to P.M.O. Indian Forces.

SHEIL, SIR JUSTIN (1803–1871)

Political : son of Edward Sheil : born Dec. 2, 1803 : educated at Stonyhurst : joined the 3rd Bengal Infantry in 1820 : present at Bhartpur, 1826 : went to Persia in 1833 : as second in command of officers and sergeants sent, under Pasmore, to discipline the Shah's Army : Secretary to the British Legation in Persia, 1836–44 : British Envoy and Minister in Persia, 1844–54 : C.B., 1841 : K.C.B., 1855 : Maj-General, 1859 : died April 18, 1871.

SHELTON, JOHN (? –1845)

Entered the 9th foot, 1805 : served in Portugal, 1808 ; Walcheren, 1809 ; the Peninsula, 1812–3, losing an arm : to India in 1822 : in the first Burmese war : commanded the 44th in India, 1827–40, and a Brigade in Afghanistan, 1841 : in the defence of the cantonments, after the Afghans had risen : on the retreat from Kabul in Jan. 1842 he was detained as a hostage and kept among the British prisoners by the Afghans till Sep. 1842 : tried by court-martial in 1843 and honourably acquitted : Colonel,

1841 : died May 10, 1845, from a fall from his horse at Delhi.

SHEPHARD, HORATIO HALE
(1842–   )

Born 1842 : son of John Shepherd of Doctors' Commons : educated at Eton, and Balliol College, Oxford : called to the bar at Inner Temple, 1867 : practised in Madras, 1872–89 : Professor of Law at the Presidency College : Fellow of Madras University : Member of the Legislative Council, Madras : Advocate-General, Madras : Judge of High Court, Madras, 1889–1901 : author of Commentaries on *The Indian Contract Act, The Transfer of Property Act, Limitation :* Legal Adviser to Secretary of State for India since 1902.

SHEPHERD, JOHN (1792–1859)

Captain : son of a Minister of the Church of Scotland : born 1792 : served in the Indian Marine : fourth officer in 1813–4 : commanded the *Duke of York,* 1,326 tons, 1821–2 : retired, 1826 : became E. I. Co.'s Director, 1835 : Chairman, 1844, 1850, and 1851 : Deputy Master of the Trinity House : Member, for " Shipping Interests," of the Council of India, established Sep. 1858 : resigned at the end of the year : died Jan. 12, 1859.

SHERER, JOHN WALTER (1823–   )

I.C.S : born 1823 : son of J. W. Sherer, B.C.S : educated at Rugby and Haileybury : entered the Bengal Civil Service, 1846 : in the mutiny was Magistrate of Fatehpur : reached Cawnpur with Havelock, and remained as Magistrate : had to manage the district, besides providing supplies and information for the relief and recapture of Lucknow : Judge of Mirzapur : Fellow of the Calcutta University : author of *Daily Life during the Indian Mutiny,* and (in conjunction with Colonel Maude, C.B., V.C.) *Memoirs of the Mutiny* ; C.S.I. for services during the mutiny.

SHERIDAN, RICHARD BRINSLEY
(1751–1816)

Son of Thomas Sheridan : born Oct. 30, 1751 : educated at Harrow, 1762–8, and privately : took to literature and wrote his famous comedies : M.P. for Stafford, 1780 ; for Westminster, 1806–7 ;

for Ilchester, 1807–12 : Under Secretary for Foreign Affairs, 1782 : Secretary to the Treasury, 1783 : brought forward, in Parliament, on Feb. 7, 1787, the charge against Warren Hastings, touching the spoliation of the Begams of Oudh, spoke for nearly 6 hours and carried it by 175 to 68 votes : during the trial, he conducted the case on the above charge on June 3, 1788 : and replied, on May 14, 1794, to the defence on the same charge : always in most eloquent speeches : died July 7, 1816.

SHERRING, REV. MATTHEW ATMORE (1826–1880)

Born Sep. 26, 1826 : educated at Coward College, and University College, London : became a Missionary of the London Missionary Society : ordained, 1852 : to Benares, 1852, in charge of the mission, and to Mirzapur : died of cholera at Benares, Aug, 10, 1880 : wrote *The Indian Church during the Rebellion,* 1859 ; *The Sacred City of the Hindus, an Account of Benares,* 1868 ; *Hindu Tribes and Castes,* 1872–81 ; *History of Protestant Misions in India,* 1875.

SHERWOOD, MARY MARTHA
(1775–1851)

Born May 6, 1775 : daughter of George Brett, D.D. : educated at the Abbey School at Reading : married her cousin, Capt. Henry Sherwood, of the 53rd regt., 1803 : went to India, 1804–5 : paid much attention to charity and orphans' homes : wrote *The Indian Pilgrim, Little Henry and his Bearer*—her child Henry died at Berhampur, July 22, 1807, aged 1½ years— and other works : returned to England : studied Hebrew and wrote many stories, including *The History of the Fairchild Family :* died Sep. 22, 1851.

SHIPP, JOHN (1784–1834)

Son of Thomas Shipp, a marine : born March, 1784 : enlisted in the 22nd foot, 1797 : to India : served at capture of Deeg, Dec. 1804, and at Bhartpur, 1805 : given a Commission for bravery : sold out to pay his debts, 1808 : re-enlisted : again to India in the 24th Light Dragoons, and again won a Commission in 1815 : in the Gurkha war, 1815, and in the Mahratta-Pindari war, 1817–8 : discharged from the service by a court-martial, 1823 : pensioned by the E. I. Co., 1825 : wrote *Memories of the Extraordinary Military Career of John Shipp*, 1819 : and *Flogging and its Substitute*, 1831 : became Master of the Workhouse at Liverpool : died Feb. 17, 1834.

SHIR ALI (1842 ?–1872)

Son of Wulli : a Khyberi, of the Kuki-Kheyl clan, a resident of Pakhi, in Afghanistan : was a mounted orderly of the Commissioner of Peshawar before 1862 : accompanied Reynell Taylor (*q.v.*) in the Umbeyla campaign, 1863 : inherited a serious blood feud with a rival branch of his own family : violating the recognized sanctuary of British territory, he killed his hereditary enemy in the suburbs of Peshawar : was tried, found guilty of murder, by the Commissioner of Peshawar, on April 2, 1867, and sentenced to death, but eventually transported for life, in May, 1869, to the Andaman Islands. He was doing duty, as barber, at Hopetown, when Lord Mayo visited Mount Harriet on Feb. 8, 1872. As the Viceroy was on the pier, to return to his steamer, about 7.15 p.m., Shir Ali inflicted on him two fatal stabs. Shir Ail was duly tried by the Superintendent of the Andamans settlement, General (Sir Donald) Stewart (*q.v.*), and hanged on March 11. No trace of any political plot could be discovered.

SHIRT, REV. GEORGE (1843–1887)

Missionary : born 1843 : educated at the C.M.S. College, London, and at Cambridge : took honours in the Oriental Tripos, 1864 : to India, 1866, shipwrecked : was Missionary of the Church Missionary Society at Karachi, Hyderabad, Sukkur in Sind, 1866–86 : translated the Bible into Sindi, besides other works in that language : travelled through Persia, 1885 : opened a new Mission at Quetta, 1886 : learnt Persian, Arabic and Brahui : died June 16, 1887 : Fellow of the Bombay University : M.R.A.S.

SHONE, WILLIAM TERENCE (1850–)

Entered the Royal Engineers, 1871, and became Lt-General, 1903 : served in Afghan war, 1878–80 : Mahsud-Waziri expedition, 1881 : Burma expedition, 1885–7 : D.S.O. : Miranzai expeditions, 1891, as C.O. of Royal Engineers : Brevet-Lt-Colonel : Chitral Relief Force, 1895 : C.B. : Colonel on the Staff R.E., China expedition, 1900–1 : Director-General of Military Works, India, 1901-03 : Inspr.-General of Fortifications since 1903.

SHUJAAT ALI, REV. (1791–1865)

Eldest son of the chief Physician at the Oudh Court, a very wealthy man : educated there in Arabic and Persian : appointed, when young, Prime Minister of one of the smaller States in the N.P. : gave it up, at his father's death, to manage the estates. Travelling for pleasure to Calcutta in 1822, he came under the influence of the Rev. Eustace Carey (*q.v.*) : baptized by Dr. Yates, 1824 : all his property confiscated : ordained a Baptist Minister : his life was attempted by some Muhammadans : appointed to a Baptist native church in Calcutta, and to supervise a number of smaller churches in and about Calcutta : was the means of effecting many conversions : died 1865.

SHUJA-UD-DAULA (1731–1775)

Son of Safdar Jang. Nawab Wazir of Oudh : born 1731 : his real name was Jalal-ud-din Haidar : succeeded his father as Nawab Wazir, 1753 : was present at Panipat, 1761, when the Afghans defeated the Mahrattas : supported Shah Alam's attempt on Bengal : received the fugitive Mir Kasim, 1763 : attacked the English in Bengal, 1764 : defeated at Patna by Carnac, in May, 1764, and retired to Baxar, where he was again defeated by Hector Munro, Oct. 23, 1764 : sued for peace, and fled to the Rohillas and then to the Mahrattas : negotiated : defeated in further fighting by the English : threw himself on the clemency of the British Government, surrendering to Carnac, 1765 : Clive restored Oudh to him, and made him an ally, 1765 : he demanded payment of his claims on the Rohillas : engaged with Warren Hastings for an English Brigade to defeat them : made a treaty with the Rohillas : died at Faizabad, Jan. 29, 1775.

SIBLEY, GEORGE (1824–1891)

Born Aug. 12, 1824 : son of Robert Sibley : educated at University College, London : was on the Bristol and Exeter Railway under Brunel, 1845 : was a Civil Engineer on the East Indian Railway,

1851–75, rising in 1868 to be Chief Engineer of the line and a member of the Board of Agency. He completed the Allahabad bridge and constructed that at Delhi, both over the Jamna river, besides other railway works at Delhi: left India, 1875 : C.I.E : died Oct. 25, 1891 : founded Engineering Scholarships at the Calcutta University: M.I.C.E.: F.R.G.S.

SIBTHORPE, CHARLES (1847–   )

Born Feb. 13, 1874 : son of Charles Sibthorpe : educated privately, Dublin : Fellow of the Royal College of Physicians, Ireland, and of Madras University : entered the Indian Medical Service, 1870 : served in the Afghan campaign, 1878–9 : Burma expedition, 1885–6 : Brigade Surgeon : C.B., 1897 : author of *Clinical Manual for India* : retired, Surgeon-General.

SIM, JAMES DUNCAN (1823–1888)

I.C.S. : born 1823 : son of General Duncan Sim, R.E. : educated at Haileybury, 1840–1 : went out to Madras in the Civil Service, 1842 : became Secretary to the Board of Revenue : Revenue Secretary to Government, Madras : Member of the Board of Revenue, 1868 : Member of Council, March, 1870, to March, 1875 : retired 1875 : C.S.I., 1868 : died Jan. 4, 1888.

SIMPSON, SIR BENJAMIN (1831–   )

Born 1831 : educated at Dublin University : M.D. : joined the Indian Medical Department, 1853 : in medical charge of Sir A. Eden's Bhutan Mission, 1863–4 : P.M.O., Quetta, 1881 : Surgeon-General, Panjab, 1883–4 : Bengal, 1884–5 : Surgeon-General and Sanitary Commissioner with the Government of India, 1885–90 : K.C.I.E., 1887 : retired 1890.

SIMPSON, THOMAS THOMSON (?–   )

Entered the Army, 1857, and became Colonel, 1884 : served in the Indian mutiny, 1858 : Waziri expedition, 1860 : Zhob Valley Field Force, 1884 : C.B., 1893 : retired.

SIMPSON, WILLIAM JOHN RITCHIE (1855–   )

Born 1855 : educated at Aberdeen University : M.D., 1880 : Health Officer of Calcutta, 1886–97 : Member of Government Commission to inquire into dysentery and enteric in S. Africa, 1900–1, and plague at Hong Kong, 1902 : Professor of Hygiene, King's College, London, since 1898 : editor of *Journal of Tropical Medicine* : F.R.C.P., 1899.

SINCLAIR, ALFRED LAW (1853–   )

Born April 30, 1853 : educated at Kingstown and Wimbledon schools : Lieutenant in Militia, 1872–4 : joined the Army, 1874, and the Bombay Staff Corps, 1877 : became Lt-Colonel, 1900 : commanded 29th Beluch Infantry, 1896–1903 : served in Burmese expedition, 1886–8 : D.S.O.

SINCLAIR, DAVID (1847–   )

Born Jan. 26, 1847 : Surgeon-General : son of William Sinclair : educated at Aberdeen Grammar School and University: joined the Indian Medical Service : M.B. : served in Burmese expedition, 1886–7 : C.S.I. : Surgeon-General with Government of Madras.

SINGH, RAJA SIR DEO NARAYAN (1820–1870)

Son of Babu Har Narayan Singh or Saiyidpur Bhitari, Ghazipur, a Bhuinhaf of the same family as the Maharaja of Benares : succeeded his father in 1846 : the *jagir* of Saiyidpur Bhitari had been resumed in 1828, but in its place a perpetual pension of over Rs. 36,000 p.a. was allowed to the former owner and his heirs. Deo Narayan Singh was made Rao Bahadur for his services in the disturbances of 1853 : in the mutiny he rendered invaluable assistance to the civil authorities : rescued the fugitive Missionaries, and was largely responsible for the maintenance of order : made a Raja, given a *khilat*, and a further annual grant of Rs. 25,000 from the revenues of Saiyid Bhitari : Member of the Governor-General's Legislative Council : K.C.S.I. in 1866 : died suddenly at Benares in Aug. 1870.

SINGH, MAHARAJA BAHADUR, SIR DULIP (1837–1893)

Born Feb. 1837 : son of Maharaja Ranjit Singh (*q.v.*) of the Panjab : was placed on the throne in 1843 : during his minority the Sikh wars of 1845–6 and 1848–9 occurred : a Council of Regency and a British Resident at Lahore were appointed. On the annexation of the Panjab, the Maharaja, by a Treaty, dated March 29, 1849, made over his dominions to the E. I. Co., receiving an annuity. Dr. Sir John Login was his Superintendent: he lived at Fatehghar, 1850–4, where he became a Christian in 1853 : he went to England in 1854, was made a K.C.S.I., 1861; G.C.S.I., 1866 : lived at various places like an English gentleman. finally at Elvedon in Suffolk, which cost £283,000. His extravagance necessitated an inquiry into his debts in 1880. After this he turned against the British Government, wrote letters to the *Times*, etc. In 1886 he was allowed to revisit India, but, on his issuing a political proclamation to the Sikhs, claiming the Panjab, was stopped at Aden, in April, 1886 : stayed there till June : abjured Christianity and re-embraced Sikhism : returned to England, a dissatisfied political refugee : Queen Victoria forgave his misconduct : he died in Paris Oct. 22, 1893.

SINGH, PANDIT NAIN (1826?–1882)

A hillman, of the Kshatriya caste: was serving under Schlagintweit, the traveller, while the latter was murdered in Kashgar : became, in 1863, a trained explorer of the Indian Survey Dept. in the Trans-Himalayan regions under Montgomerie (*q.v.*) : was the first to fix the position of Lhasa, which he reached in Jan. 1866, by way of Mansarowar Lake and the Sanpo river : he reached it again in 1874 by the Ladak-Tegrinor route : in 1867 visited the gold mines of Thok Talong, crossing Tibet from W. to E. : in 1877, he was awarded a Gold Medal by the Royal Geographical Society : for his services he received a special pension and grant of land : died Jan. 1882.

SINGH, MAHARAJA SIR PARTAB NARAYAN (1855–   )

Born July 13, 1855 : grandson of Sir Man Singh, K.C.S.I. : belongs to Sankildeep sect of Brahmans : one of the largest landowners in Oudh : Member of Legislative Council, U.P. and Oudh : K.C.I.E., 1895 : Life President of the British Indian Association : M.R.A.S.

SINGH, MAHARAJA RANJIT (1780–1839)

Maharaja : ruler of the Panjab : born Nov. 2, 1780 : son of Sirdar Mahan Singh,

whom he succeeded, in 1792, as head of the Sukarchakia branch of the Sikh confederacy : early in life he lost an eye from smallpox : at 17 he seized the government, and poisoned his mother : he allied with Shah Zaman, the Afghan ruler, when the latter invaded the Panjab : was given Lahore, 1799 : in 1802 he attacked and annexed Umritsar. When Jaswant Rao Holkar took refuge with Ranjit in 1805, the latter made a treaty with the E.I. Co. to exclude Holkar from the Panjab : Ranjit seized Ludiana, and other States : (Sir C.) Metcalfe was sent on a Mission to negotiate with Ranjit in 1808, to frustrate his extending his dominions across the Satlaj, when the latter was making further annexations : a treaty was concluded at Umritsar on April 25, 1809, by which the E. I. Co. and Ranjit recognized the Satlaj as the boundary of his territories : he marched against Multan from 1806 until 1810, when he levied a ransom, and made it eventually a dependency : in 1810 he subdued the Nakkai and Kanheya Sikh confederacies : in 1812, having established his authority, he proclaimed himself Raja of the Panjab, and Maharaja in 1819 : annexed Kashmir in 1819 : by 1820 his power was consolidated between the Satlaj and the Indus : he made the city and province of Peshawar tributary in 1823. He received Shah Shuja when a fugitive from Afghanistan, and obtained the Kohinur diamond from him, as well as the Derajat and Peshawar in 1833 : in 1835 the Amir Dost Muhammad attacked the Sikhs at Peshawar, but was compelled to retire. Ranjit employed European officers to train his troops : he kept at peace with the British Government and met Lord W. Bentinck at Roopur on Oct. 26, 1831. In 1838 he made a tripartite treaty with Shah Shuja and the British Government and helped Sir W. H. Macnaghten and the British force on their way to Afghanistan : he visited Lord Auckland, the Governor-General at Lahore, in 1838 : he died June 27, 1839, of paralysis. Though uneducated, selfish and sensual, he, by natural ability and indefatigable labour, by his genius for military affairs and civil administration, built up the kingdom of the Panjab and created a large and trained army of Sikhs : he never failed in his alliance with the British Government.

SINNETT, ALFRED PERCY (1840–   )

Born Jan. 18. 1840 : son of E. W. P. Sinnett : educated at London University school, London : journalist : editor of *Hong-Kong Daily Press*, 1865–8 : editor of the *Pioneer*, India, 1872 : devoted much attention to the Theosophical movement, 1879 : author of *The Occult World, Esoteric Buddhism, Karma and United, The Growth of the Soul* : President of the London branch of the Theosophical Society : editor of *Broad Views Review*, 1904.

SIRCAR, DR. MAHENDRA LAL
(1833–1904)

Scientist : born Nov. 2, 1833 : educated at the Hare school, the Hindu, Presidency, and Calcutta Medical, Colleges : M.D. in 1863. Before the Bengal Branch of the British Medical Assiocation. of which he was Secretary and Vice-President, he early denounced Homœopathy, but in 1867 declared his faith in it, and started the *Calcutta Journal of Medicine*, to advance his views. In 1876, with the support of Sir R. Temple, he founded the Indian Association for the Cultivation of Science, and devoted his life to the cause of science for the benefit of his fellow-countrymen : physical science, astronomy, literature and general research fully occupied his time. He was a Fellow of the Calcutta University, 1870 : Honorary Magistrate, 1877–1902 : Sheriff of Calcutta, (1887), Member of the Bengal Legislative Council, 1887–93 : Doctor of Law, 1898 : Member of the Council of the Asiatic Society : Trustee of the Indian Museum : Commissioner of the Calcutta Corporation for years : made C.P.E. in 1883, in recognition of his services to science. He was an advanced Liberal, but never virulently attacked Government measures : his speeches were often very eloquent : died at Calcutta, Feb. 23, 1904.

SIRCAR, PIARI CHARAN (1823–1875)

Educated at the Hindu College : entered the Education Department : for several years Head Master of the Hare school, Calcutta : one of the first Bengali officers of the Education Service : became an Assistant Professor of English Literature at the Calcutta Presidency College : was an advocate of female education and of widow-marriage : the Chief promoter

of the Bengal Temperance movement : his death was deeply lamented for his literary attainments, his educational labours and his sterling moral worth : died Sep. 30, 1875.

SITWELL, WILLIAM HENRY
(1860–   )

Born Nov. 20, 1860 : son of Major Francis Henry M. Sitwell : educated at Harrow and Sandhurst : entered the Army, 1880 : served in the Afghan campaign, 1880 : Bechuanaland Police, 1891–3 : Ashanti expedition, 1895–6 : Nile expeditions, 1897–8–9 : Atbara, Khartoum, and Omdurman : Brevet-Lt-Colonel : S. African war, 1900–2 : D.S.O., 1900 : A.A.G., 1900 : F.R.G.S. : Colonel.

SIVA PRASAD, RAJA (1823–1895)

An Oswal Vaisya by caste : related to the Seths of Murshidabad, whence his ancestors fled from the Nawab to Benares : son of Babu Gopi Chand : born 1823 : owned land in Benares and Gorakhpur : educated at Benares College : became in 1839 a vakil of the Maharaja of Bhartpur, to attend the Court of Colonel Sutherland, the A.G.G. at Ajmir : attended Lord Ellenborough's *darbar* at Delhi : left the Bhartpur service : joined William Edwards, then Under Secretary in the Foreign Department, and was appointed, 1840, Naib Mir Munshi in that Department : was, 1848, Mir Munshi of the Simla Agency when Mr. Edwards became Superintendent of the protected Hill States : became, 1852, Mir Munshi of the Benares Agency under H. C. Tucker : was Joint-Inspector in the Department of Public Instruction and Inspector of Schools, about 1860, under Sir W. Muir : C.S.I., May, 1870 : Raja, March, 1874 : the same title declared hereditary, Feb. 1887 : was in 1883 a Member of the Governor-General's Legislative Council and Fellow of Allahabad University : died at Benares, May 23, 1895 : succeeded by his son Raja Sachit Prasad : his literary work was chiefly devoted to the popularization of Hindustani as the colloquial tongue midway between the Persianised Urdu and the Hindi of the Pandits. His works numbered 32, 18 in Hindi, the rest in Urdu : many are schoolbooks, such as a translation of *Sandford and Merton* ; others were historical or philological.

SKINNER, JAMES (1778–1841)

Son of Lt-Colonel Hercules Skinner, a Scotchman, and a Rajput lady : born in 1778 : joined the Mahratta Army under Count De Boigne in 1796, and remained in it, performing active service under Perron, until 1803. He fought against the adventurer, George Thomas. Being obliged to resign Sindia's service on the outbreak of the Mahratta war, James Skinner was employed by Lord Lake to raise " Skinner's Horse," with which " Irregnlar Horse " he distinguished himself, rendering great assistance to General Monson on his retreat before Holkar and in subsequent engagements : his regiment, the " Yellow Boys," was at the siege of Bhartpur, 1825–6. He was granted, in 1818, a *jagir* yielding Rs. 20,000 a year, and appointed to be a Lt·Colonel in his Majesty's service and made C.B. He was highly regarded by successive Governors-General, Commanders-in-Chief, and high officials. He died Dec. 4, 1841, at Hansi, and was eventually buried, on Jan, 17, 1842, in the church which he had himself built at Delhi at a cost of £20,000.

SKINNER, THOMAS (1800?–1843)

Son of Lt-General John Skinner : born about 1800 : joined the 16th foot, 1816 : wrote *Excursions in India*, about his travels in the Himalayas : took the overland route to India, 1833, *viâ* Egypt, Palestine, Syria, Euphrates and the Persian Gulf, and wrote an account of his adventures, 1836 : commanded the 31st regt. with Pollock's Army of Retribution to Kabul, 1842 : at Tezin, Sep. 13, 1842 : C.B. : Brevet-Lt-Colonel : died May 6, 1843.

SKRINE, FRANCIS HENRY BENNETT (1847–   )

I.C.S. : born Dec. 23, 1847 : son of Captain Clarmont Skrine : educated at Blackheath School : entered the Indian Civil Service, 1868 : Collector of Customs, Calcutta, 1895 : Commissioner of Chittagong Division, 1896 : retired 1897 : author of *Laborious Days*, 1892 ; *An Indian Journalist, The Heart of Asia, The Life of Sir W. W. Hunter, K.C.S.I.* ; *The Expansion of Russia*, etc.

SLADE, JOHN RAMSAY (1843–   )

Born March 16, 1843 : Maj-General : son of General Sir Marcus Slade : educated

at Woolwich : entered the Royal Artillery, 1861 : served in Bazar Valley expedition, 1878 : Afghan campaign, 1879–80 : commanded a battery at battle of Maiwand, and battle of Kandahar : C.B. 1881 : Transvaal campaign, 1881–2 : Military Attaché at Rome, 1887–95 : in Abyssinia with Italian troops : A.D.C. to Queen Victoria : commanded R.A. in N.E. District : has commanded British troops in Egypt since 1903.

SLADEN, SIR EDWARD BOSC (1827–1890)

Colonel : born Nov. 20, 1827 : son of Dr. Ramsey Sladen : educated at Oswestry : went to India in 1849 : joined the 1st Madras Fusiliers : was in the Burmese war of 1852–3 and in the operations against rebels in 1856–7 : at the taking of Lucknow in March, 1858, and in the Oudh campaign : joined the Staff Corps, and returned to Burma : on special duty to Mandalay, 1866, saved the lives of Christians there : negotiated a treaty at Mandalay, 1867 : led a political Mission to Chinese frontier, 1868 : Commissioner of Arakan, 1876–85 : Chief Political officer in the Burmese, war, 1885–6 : knighted, 1886 : retired, 1887 : died Jan. 4, 1890 : wrote an account of the *Expedition to China viâ Bhamo*, 1869.

SLEEMAN, SIR WILLIAM HENRY (1788–1856)

Born Aug. 18, 1788 : son of Philip Sleeman : joined the Bengal Army in 1809 : was in the Nipal war, 1814–6 : Assistant A.G.G. for the Sagar and Nerbudda territories, from 1820 : General Superintendent of the Operations for the suppression of Thagi, 1835 : and of Dakaiti also, from 1839 : was Resident at Gwalior, 1843–9 : and at Lucknow 1849–56 : advised against the annexation of Oudh : his assassination attempted, 1851 : died at sea off Ceylon, Feb. 10, 1856 : wrote *Rambles and Recollections of an Indian Official*, 1844 ; *A Journey through the Kingdom of Oudh in* 1849–50, 1858 ; a vocabulary of the peculiar language used by the Thags, 1836, and other works on Indian subjects : Maj-General.

SLIGO, HENRY ULICK BROWNE, FIFTH MARQUIS OF (1831–   )

I.C.S. : son of second Marquis : born March 14, 1831 : educated at ·Rugby and Haileybury: went, then ·Lord H. U. Browne, to India, 1851: Private Secretary to the President in ·Council, 1858 : Under Secretary to the Bengal Government, 1859 : to the Government of India in the Home and Financial Departments, 1860: Registrar of the *Sadr* Court, 1861 : Magte-Collector, 1866 : ·Commissioner,1869: acting Chairman of the Calcutta Corporation, 1872 : Commissioner ·of the Chittagong and Presidency Divisions : and of the Rajshahi Division. 1875–86 : acting Member, Board of Revenue, 1878 : retired, 1886 : succeeded as Marquis, Dec. 1903.

SMEATON, DONALD MACKENZIE
(1846–)

I.C.S. : born Sep. 9, 1846 : educated at the Abbey Park Institution, St. Andrew's, and at St. Andrew's University : M.A. : arrived in India 1867, held minor appointments in the N.W.P. : went to Burma in 1879 : Chief Secretary, 1887 : officiated as Chief Commissioner in 1892 and 1896 : Member of the Governor-General's Legislative Council in 1898 and 1901 : C.S.I. in 1895 : retired in Nov. 1902 : published an edition of the *N.W.P. Revenue Act, The Currency of India, The Karens of Burma,*

SMITH, SIR CHARLES BEAN EUAN
(1842–)

Entered the Indian Army, 1859, and became Colonel, 1885 : served in the Abyssinian war, 1867–8, at capture of Magdala : Secretary to Sir F. Goldsmid's Mission to Persia, 1870–2 : P.S. to Sir B. Frere on his Mission to Zanzibar and Muscat, 1872–3 : in the Indian Political Department : in the Afghan war, 1879–80 : in the Kabul-Kandahar march : Consul-General, Zanzibar, 1888 : K.C.B., 1890 : Minister at Tangier, 1891–2 : D.C.I., 1893 : C.S.I., 1872 : retired,

SMITH, GEORGE (1833–)

Born April 28, 1833 : son of Adam Smith : educated at the Royal High School and University of Edinburgh : LL.D., 1868 : Professor, 1854, and Principal, 1855–8, of the Doveton College, Calcutta : Editor of the *Friend of India,* Serampur, 1859–75 : of the *Calcutta Review,* 1857–64 : of the *Annals of Indian Administration,* 1859–75˙: the *Times'* India

Correspondent, 1859–75 : ·Hony Magistrate and J.P. in Bengal : Fellow of Calcutta University, 1856–75 : C.I.E. in 1878, for services, educational and literary, to the people of India. Since leaving India in 1879 Smith has been Foreign Secretary of the Free Church of Scotland : F.R.G.S. and F.S.S. London : Member of Council of Royal Scottish Geographical Society : has written *Students' Geography of British India ; Short History of Christian Missions; Twelve Indian Statesmen ; Twelve Pioneer Missionaries : Life of William Carey, D.D.; Henry Martyn, Saint and Scholar; Life of John Wilson, D.D., F.R.S.: Bishop Heber: Life of Alexander Duff, D.D.: Stephen Hislop ; The Conversion of India,* besides many articles in the *Encyclopædia Britannica, Quarterly Review, Good Words, Chambers's Journal,* the *Times,* the *Scotsman,* etc., and pamphlets on India and Missions.

SMITH, SIR HARRY GEORGE WAKE-
LYN, BARONET (1787–1860)

Born June 28, 1787 : son of John Smith, surgeon, of Whittlesey : baptized as Henry, but called Harry : entered the 95th Rifles in 1805 : served in S. America, at Monte Video and Buenos Ayres, 1806–7 : throughout the Peninsular war, 1808–14 : again in America, at Bladensburg and New Orleans, 1814–5 : was at Waterloo : C.B. Brevet-Lt-Colonel : at Halifax, Nova Scotia, and D.Q.M.G. in Jamaica, 1826, and at the Cape, 1828 : commanded a Division in the Kafir war of 1834–6 : D.Q.M.G. : Brevet-Colonel, 1837 : Adjt-General in India, 1839 : at Maharajpur, Dec. 1843 : K.C.B. : commanded a Division in the Satlaj campaign : at Mudki and Firozshahr, and Sobraon : commanded the Force and led the final charge at Aliwal, Jan. 28, 1846 : Maj-General : made Baronet of Aliwal : and G.C.B. : LL.D., Cambridge : made Governor of the Cape, 1847 : Lt-General (local rank) : defeated the Boers under Pretorius at Boom Plaatz : resisted successfully the landing of convicts at the Cape : carried on a harassing war against the Kafirs, 1850–1, but was recalled in 1852 : held District commands in England, 1853–59 : Lt-General, 1854 : several towns in S. Africa called after him and his (Spanish) wife : Col. Commandant of 2nd and subsequently of 1st Battalion of the Rifle Brigade :

authoi of an *Autobiography*, published in 1901 : died in London, Oct. 12, 1860.

SMITH, HENRY BABINGTON
(1863–   )

Born Jan. 29, 1863 : son of Archibald Smith, LL.D., F.R.S : educated at Eton and Trinity College, Cambridge (1st Class Classical Tripos and Chancellor's Medal) : Principal Private Secretary to Chancellor of the Exchequer, 1891–2 : clerk in the Treasury, 1892 : Secretary to the British Delegates at the Brussels monetary conference, 1892 : Private Secretary to Lord Elgin, when Viceroy of India, 1894–9 : C.S.I., 1897 : Secretary to the Post Office since 1903.

SMITH, JOHN MANNERS (1864–   )

Major : born Aug. 30, 1864 : son of Surgeon-General Charles Manners Smith : educated at Norwich and Sandhurst : entered the Army, 1883, and Indian Staff Corps, 1885 : joined the Political Department, India, 1887 : went with Sir M. Durand to Sikhim, 1888, and Kabul, 1893 : served in N.W. Frontier expeditions : at the capture of Nilt position : V.C. in Hunza-Nagar, 1891 : Isazai, 1892 : Tirah, 1897–8 : C.I.E., 1894 : Political Agent.

SMITH, JOHN RICHARD BULLEN
(?–1887)

Son of the Rev. J. Smith : for many years a prominent merchant : head of the firm of Messrs. Jardine, Skinner & Co., Calcutta : thrice President of the Bengal Chamber of Commerce : Sheriff of Calcutta for 2 years : Member of the Legislative Councils of Bengal and the Governor-General : C.S.I. : Member of the Council of India, 1885–7 : died Jan. 5, 1887.

SMITH, JOHN THOMAS (1805–1882)

Son of George Smith : born April 16, 1805 : educated at Repton, Edinburgh High School, Addiscombe : entered the Madras Engineers in 1824 : reached Madras, 1825 : served in the P.W.D., and worked for the improvement of lighthouses in that Presidency : F.R.S. in 1837 : constructed the Madras lighthouse : Superintending Engineer at Madras, 1839 : Mint-master there, 1840, and at Calcutta, 1855, effecting many improvements : he retired as Colonel,

1857. Fellow of Society of Actuaries : Consulting Engineer of Madras Irrigation Co. : F.S.S. : he studied deeply the question of the currency of India, advocating a gold standard for India, and attended the International Monetary Congress at Paris in 1865, and wrote constantly on this and similar scientific subjects : member of several scientific Societies : from 1866 to 1880, he was on the consulting committee, Military Fund Department, at the India Office : died May 14, 1882.

SMITH, JOSEPH (1733?–1790)

Born about 1733 : served under Clive in the Carnatic in 1752 : taken prisoner by the French, 1753 : commanded the Trichinopoly garrison, 1757–8 : at the taking of Karikal and siege of Pondicherry. 1760–1 : Colonel, 1766 : in command of the forces which defeated Hyder and the Nizam at Trinomalai, Sep. 26, 1767 : made treaty with the Nizam, 1768 : Maj-General : took Tanjore, 1773 : retired : died Sep. 1, 1790.

SMITH, SIR LIONEL, BARONET
(1778–1842)

Born Oct. 9, 1778 : son of Benjamin Smith of Liss, West India merchant : entered the Army in 1795 : served in various regiments in America, Africa and the West Indies : rapidly promoted : in 1807 at Bombay : Colonel, 1813 : noted for his share in the Mahratta war of 1817–18 : he commanded the 4th Division of the Dekkan Army under Sir Thomas Hislop : in 1817 captured Poona : pursued the Peshwa, finally overtaking and defeating him at Ashti : left India : was made Governor of Barbadoes, 1833, and later C. in C. at Jamaica ; in both islands he was unpopular with the planters on account of his sympathy with the coloured inhabitants : Lt-General, 1837 : made a Baronet at the Coronation of Queen Victoria : in 1840 appointed Governor of the Mauritius, where he died in 1842.

SMITH, MICHAEL WILLIAM
(1809–1891)

Son of Sir Michael Smith, *Bart.* : born April 27, 1809 : joined the 82nd foot in 1830 : served in India : in the Crimea, commanded Turkish Irregular Cavalry :

in the mutiny commanded a Brigade in Rajputana, against Tantia Topi : at the capture of Gwalior, etc.: C.B., 1859 : commanded the Poona Division : General, 1877: died April 18, 1891 : wrote on military subjects

SMITH, REGINALD BOSWORTH
(1839-   )

Born June 28, 1839 : son of Canon Reginald Southwell Smith : educated at Marlborough and Corpus Christi College, Oxford (1st Class in Mods. and Final Classical School): Fellow of Trinity College, Oxford : Assistant Master, Harrow School : author of *Muhammad and Muhammadanism, The Life of Lord Lawrence,* etc. etc.

SMITH, RICHARD BAIRD
(1818-1861)

Born Dec. 31, 1818 : son of Richard Smith, Surgeon R.N. : educated at Lasswade, Dunse Academy, and Addiscombe : joined the Madras Engineers at Madras in 1838, Adjutant, 1839 : appointed Assistant to Sir Proby Cautley, Superintendent of the Doab canal, in 1840 : was in charge of the Jamna canal in 1843 : in the first Sikh war was with Sir Harry Smith at Badiwal and Aliwal, also at Sobraon : after the war resumed his canal work : in the Panjab campaign of 1848-9, was at Ramnagar, Sadulapur, Chilianwala, and Gujarat : on furlough was deputed to examine the irrigation canals of Piedmont and Lombardy, 1850-2 : reported on the irrigation works of the Madras Presidency : in 1854 succeeded Cautley as Superintendent of Canals, N.W.P. : in the mutiny he put Rurki into a state of defence, then went to Delhi as Chief Engineer, He advised an immediate assault of the city, which could not be carried out : but, on his persistence, the siege was continued, the siege train arrived, and Archdale Wilson, the General commanding, yielded to Smith's judgment as to the necessity of assaulting Delhi : breaches were effected by bombardment, and Delhi was taken by assault on Sep. 14, 1857 : Baird Smith, though painfully wounded, carried the operations through, bearing great responsibility, and deserving full credit for their success : " his indomitable courage and determined

perseverance " are mentioned (by Lord Roberts) : " We must hold on," he said to Wilson : he was ably supported by Capt. Alexander Taylor, R.E. : C.B., and Lt-Colonel :   Mint-master of   Calcutta in Sep. 1858 : Member of the Calcutta University : A.D.C. to Queen Victoria : Secretary to the Govt, of India in the P.W.D. : did excellent service in connection with the famine of 1861 : on his way home, died off Madras, Dec. 13, 1861. A monument was erected to his memory in St, Paul's Cathedral, Calcutta.

SMITH, SIR ROBERT MURDOCH
(1835-1900)

Born Aug. 18, 1835 : son of Hugh Smith : educated at Kilmarnock, and Glasgow University : entered the Royal Engineers, 1855 : on the archæological expedition to Asia Minor which discovered the mausoleum at Halicarnassus. 1856-9 : explored the Cyrenaica, in N. Africa, 1860-1 : employed on the Persian portion of the telegraph line to India, 1863 : became Director of the Persian telegraph at Teheran, 1865-85 : Director of the Edinburgh Museum of Science and Art, 1885 : Director in Chief of the Indo-European Telegraph Department, 1887 : on special Mission to Persia, 1887 : K.C.M.G., 1888 :   Maj-General :   wrote on Persian art, and subjects connected with Persia ; died July 3, 1900.

SMITH, ROBERT PERCY (1770-1845)

Known as " Bobus " Smith : son of Robert Smith, and brother of Sydney Smith, and father of Lord Lyveden (*q.v.*) : born 1770 : educated at Eton and King's College, Cambridge : called to the bar from Lincoln's Inn, 1797 : appointed Advocate-General of Bengal, 1803 : Sir James Mackintosh wrote of him—" I hear frequently of Bobus. His fame among the natives is greater than that of any pandit since the days of Manu" : Smith returned to England in seven years with a fortune : M.P. 1812, and 1818-26 : had a great reputation for his wit and conversation, and Latin verse : died March 10, 1845.

SMITH, SAMUEL (1836-   )

Born at Kirkcudbright, 1836 : son of James Smith, merchant, Liverpool : educated at Borgue Academy : M.P. for

Liverpool, 1882-5 : 'for Flintshire, since 1886 : President of the Liverpool Chamber of Commerce, 1876 : has devoted much time and attention to Indian affairs in Parliament : is opposed to the opium trade : has toured in India, and advocated various measures of reform for that country : is a bimetallist.

SMITH, REV. THOMAS, D.D.
(1817-)

Born at Lymington, July 8, 1817 : educated at Edinburgh University : went out to Calcutta, Aug. 1839, as a Missionary of the Church of Scotland Mission : joined the Free Church : also acted as Presbyterian Chaplain of the 42nd regt. and accompanied it in the field, until recalled by the Home Government : in 1840 devised the plan of the Zenana Mission : left India, 1858, for ministerial duty in Edinburgh : also edited the *Calcutta Review*, Nos, 35-49, and wrote 32 articles in it : was a keen mathematician and wrote on the Astronomy of the Hindus and various subjects : succeeded Dr. Alexander Duff (*q.v.*) as Professor of Evangelistic Theology in the Free Church of Scotland : was Moderator of the General Assembly of the Free Church in 1891 : wrote also *Mediæval Missions*, 1880 ; *Alexander Duff*, 1883 ; *Modern Missions and Culture*, and *History of Protestant Misions* (both translated from the German), 1884 : edited a series of *The Protestant Divines*.

SMITH, VINCENT ARTHUR
(1848-)

I.C.S. : born June 3, 1848 : son of Aquilla Smith, M.D. of Dublin : educated at Trinity College, Dublin : M.A. : Fellow of the Allahabad University : arrived in India, 1871 : served in the N.W.P. and Oudh : in the settlement department and subordinate posts, until he became Magistrate-Collector, 1889 : District Judge, 1895 : Chief Secretary, 1898 : Commissioner, 1898 : retired, 1900 : Reader in Indian History and Hindustani in the University of Dublin, 1902-3 : author of *The Settlement Officer's Manual for the N.W.P.*, 1881 ; *General Index to Cunningham's Archæological Survey Reports*, 1887 ; *The Remains near Kasia*, 1896 ; *The Jain Stupa and other Antiquities of Mathura*, 1901 ; *Asoka, the Budd-*

hist Emperor of India, 1901 ; *The Early History of India*, 1904 ; *Catalogue of the non-Muhammadan Coins in the Indian Museum* (in the press), and of numerous papers on history, antiquities, and numismatics in the *J.A.S.B., J.R.A.S., Z.D.M. G., Calcutta Review, Quarterly Review*, and *Indian Antiquary :* Editor of Sleeman's *Rambles and Recollections*, 1893.

SMITH-DORRIEN, HORACE LOCK-WOOD (1858-)

Maj-General : educated at Harrow : entered the Army, 1876, and became Lt-Colonel, 1899 : served in Zulu war, 1879 : Egyptian war, 1882 : Soudan campaign, 1885 : Soudan Frontier Field Force, 1885-6 : D.S.O. : D.A.A.G., Bengal, 1893-4 : A.A.G., Panjab, 1894-6 : Tirah campaign, 1897-8 : Brevet-Lt-Colonel : Nile expedition, 1898 : Brevet-Colonel : Maj-General commanding 19th Brigade, S. Africa, 1900 : commanding First Class District, India, since 1903 : C.B., 1904 : F.R.G.S.

SMYTH, ETWALL WALTER (1843-)

Son of Rev. George Watson Smyth : educated at Cheltenham and Addiscombe : entered the Indian Army, in Bengal, 1861 : served on the N.E. Frontier, 1865-6 : in the Malta and Cyprus expedition, 1878 : Afghan campaign, 1879 : Isazai expedition, 1892 : Chitral expedition, 1895 : C.B., 1896 : Colonel.

SMYTH, OWEN STUART (1853-)

Entered the Royal Artillery, 1873, and became Lt-Colonel, 1898 : served in the Afghan war, 1878-80 at Kandahar : in the Burma war, 1885-6 : Wuntho expedition, 1891 : Manipur : Colonel commanding mountain batteries, Jutogh : D.S.O., 1886 : Colonel.

SMYTH, SIR ROWLAND (? -1873)

Entered the Army, 1821 : served with the 26th Lancers at Bhartpur, 1825-6 : at Maharajpur, 1843, and Aliwal : C.B. : Maj-General, 1860 : Lt-General, 1870 : commanded the Central Division of the Madras Army : K.C.B. : died 1873.

SOLLY-FLOOD, FREDERICK RICHARD (? -)

Entered the Indian Army, 1849, and became Maj-General, 1885 : served in

N.W. Frontier, 1851–2; Indian mutiny, 1857–9: Brevet-Major: C.B., 1877: Maj-General.

SOLVYNS, FRANÇOIS BALTHAZAR (1760–1824)

Artist : born at Antwerp, 1760 : showed genius at 12 : drew sea-pieces : patronized by the Arch-duchess Maria Christina till her death : accompanied Sir Home Popham in a voyage to the East : made charts of the coasts of the Red Sea : visited India and thoroughly studied the country : present at the siege of Seringapatam : after 15 years of labour, in which he was assisted by Sir W. Jones, he returned home and brought out, " to delineate the people of Hindustan in all their customs and usages, both of their public and their private life," his great work *Les Hindous*, 1807–12, dedicated to the French Institute : Captain of the Port of Antwerp till his death there, Oct. 10, 1824.

SOMERSET, SIR HENRY (1794–1862)

Born Dec. 30, 1794 : son of Lord Charles Somerset and grandson of fifth Duke of Beaufort : entered the Army, 1811 : in the Peninsula, 1813–4 : in the Netherlands in 1815, in the 18th Hussars : at Walcheren : A.D.C. to his uncle, Lord R. E. Somerset : saw service at the Cape of Good Hope in the Kafir war with his regt., the Cape Mounted Rifles : K.C.H. and C.B. in 1834 : Maj-General in the Kafir war of 1853, and K.C.B. after it : C. in C. in Bombay, 1855–60 : Lt-General : Colonel of the 25th regt. : died Feb. 15, 1862.

SORABJI, CORNELIA (1866–   )

Fifth daughter of Rev. Sorabji Kharsedji, a Missionary of the Church Missionary Society at Poona, who married a Hindu convert to Christianity : born at Nasik, 1866 : highly educated : taught in the Victoria High School, Poona, opened by her mother : matriculated in the Bombay University : entered, as a student, the Dekkan College at Poona : was head student of the College in the B.A. degree examination of the Bombay University, 1887 : gained, 1888, a Fellowship in the Gujarat College at Ahmadabad : lectured on English Literature and Languages : acted as Professor of English in the College : resigned : went

to England : resided, as a Scholar, at Somerville Hall, Oxford, 1888 : studied law.

SORENSEN, SOREN (1848–1902)

Born 1848 at Danstrup in Denmark : at the University his principal study was Philology, with Sanskrit as a help towards it : after taking his degree, became a schoolmaster, but resigned this work for the sake of his Oriental studies : Doctor of Philology, 1833 : gained the gold medal of the Danish Academy of Sciences by his paper on The Position of Sanskrit in the General Development of Languages in India : published *The Position of the Mahabharata in Indian Literature* : appointed Lecturer at the University of Copenhagen, 1899 : elected Member of the Academy of Sciences, 1900 : May, 1902, appointed Professor of Indian Philology at Copenhagen, but died Dec. 1902. The study of the Mahābhārata was the chief work of his life : he lived to complete his *Index to the Names in the Mahabharata* written in English, though not to see it published. Part I appeared in 1904. It is a work of the highest importance, not only as an aid towards the publication of a final critical text of the Mahabharata, but also for any student of Indian antiquity. Sörensen concentrated all his energies on one great work, and is therefore less known than he deserves to be.

SOUTER, SIR FRANK H. (? –1888)

Son of Captain Souter of the 44th regt., who was a prisoner in Afghanistan, 1842 : served as a volunteer against the rebels in the Nizam's dominions, 1850 : appointed Superintendent of Police at Dharwar, 1854 : in the mutiny of 1857, captured the Nurgoond Mahratta Chief, for which he received a sword of honour : suppressed Bhil brigands in the N, Dekkan, 1859 : killed Bhagoji Naik, the notorious Bhil outlaw : recommended for the Victoria Cross : Commissioner of Police in Bombay, 1864–88 : C.S.I. in 1868 : knighted by H.R.H. the Prince of Wales at Bombay, 1875 : C.I.E. in 1886 : Member of the Bombay Municipal Corporation from 1872 and of the Town Council : died at the Nilgiris, June 5, 1888 : a Souter Memorial Fund was raised.

SPEECHLY, RIGHT REV. JOHN MARTINDALE (1836–1898)

Son of Thomas Kelfall Speechly : educated at St. John's College, Cambridge : ordained, 1860 : devoted himself to foreign Mission work, 1862 : was made Bishop of Travancore and Cochin, 1879 : resigned, 1889 : Vicar of Hernhill, Faversham, 1892 : died Jan. 20, 1898.

SPEKE, PETER (1745–1811)

Of the Civil Service, on the Bengal Establishment : Member, from Sep. 17, 1789, to Oct. 2, 1801, of the Supreme Council, where his was "long a ruling voice." At the time of his death, on Nov. 30, 1811, he was acting President of the Board of Trade, and President of the Marine Board : buried in Calcutta.

SPENCER, HON. SIR AUGUSTUS ALMERIC (1807–1893)

Third son of first Lord Churchill : born March 25, 1807 : educated privately : entered the Army, 1825 : served in Portugal, Canada : throughout the Crimea, in all the battles : commanding the 44th regt., and as Brigadier : Maj-General : commanded the Bangalore Division, 1860 : C. in C. Bombay, Aug. 1869, to Oct. 1874 : General : died Aug. 28, 1893 : G.C.B.

SPENCER, RIGHT REV. GEORGE TREVOR (1799–1866)

Son of William Robert Spencer, and great-grandson of the third Duke of Marlborough : educated at Charterhouse and University College, Oxford : incumbent of Buxton, 1824–9 : rector of Leaden Roding, Essex, 1829–37 : Bishop of Madras, 1837–49 : D.D., 1837 : Coadjutor Bishop in the Diocese of Bath and Wells : Chancellor of St. Paul's : rector, 1861, of Walton in the Wolds : died July 16, 1866.

SPENCER, LIONEL DIXON (1842–

Born June 16, 1842 : son of William Spencer : educated at Newcastle and St. Andrew's University : M.D. : entered Indian Medical Service, 1865, and retired, 1902 : served in Waziristan expedition, 1894–5, as P.M.O. : C.B., 1895 : Principal Medical Officer, Panjab command : Surgeon-General.

SPRENGER, ALOYS (1813–1893)

Son of Christopher Sprenger : born in the Tyrol, Sep. 3, 1813 : educated at Innsbruck, Vienna, Paris : studied Medicine and Oriental languages : naturalized in England, 1838 : M.D. at Leyden University, 1841 : went to India in the E. I. Co.'s Medical Service, 1843 : Principal of the Muhammadan College at Delhi, 1844 : Assistant Resident at Lucknow, 1847–50 : Principal of the Calcutta Madrasa, of the Muhammadan College at Hughli, and Persian Translator to Government, 1851–4 : Secretary to the Asiatic Society of Bengal, 1851–4 : retired, 1857 : Professor of Oriental Languages at Berne : settled at Heidelberg : died there, Dec. 19, 1893 : wrote an English-Hindustani grammar, *Selections from Arabic Authors*, *The History of Mahmud of Ghazni*, an edition of the *Gulistan*, the *Life of Muhammad* from original sources : on *Old Arabian Geography* : compiled a Catalogue of the MSS. in the library of the King of Oudh : knew 25 languages and Oriental literature thoroughly : printed in Hindustani, at Delhi, the first vernacular paper printed in India, a weekly Periodical.

SPRY, HENRY HARPER (1804–1842)

Of the Bengal Medical Staff : travelled greatly in India : wrote *Modern India* : Secretary to the Agri-Horticultural Society of India, whose Journal he established : F.R.S. : M.R.A.S : Member of the Asiatic Society of Bengal : Member of the Statistical Society of London : died in Calcutta, Sep. 4, 1842.

SPURGIN, SIR JOHN BLICK (1821–1903)

Lt-General : entered the Army in 1842 : served with the Royal Dublin Fusiliers till 1872 : Colonel of that regt. in 1895 : served with distinction through the mutiny : Brig-Major to General Neill at Cawnpur, and at the entry and defence of Lucknow : assisted Sir D. Russell at the capture of the Kaisarbagh and the final siege of Lucknow. His later service was in Ireland and England. He was made C.S.I. in 1869 : C.B. in 1871 : K.C.B. in 1893. He died in London, Nov. 27, 1903.

STABLES, JOHN (? – ?)

"A young officer of great ability," went to Bengal from Madras as an Ensign, volunteering, with Col. Caillaud,. Nov. 1759 : commanded a detachment at Monghyr, Dec. 1760 : was reinforced : attacked and defeated the Raja of Kurrakpur : his action and conduct highly approved by the Council (in India) and Court of Directors : supported by Col. Caillaud : commanded a battalion at the battle of Baxar, Oct. 23, 1764 : retired, 1769 : Member of the Supreme Council, Nov. 1782, to Jan. 1787 : where he was opposed to W. Hastings.

STACK, SIR MAURICE (1796–1880)

Son of Rev. John Stack : born 1796 : entered the Army, 1815 : served with the 1st European Fusiliers in Kattiawar and Cutch : against marauders in Gujarat in 1818 : commanded a Brigade in Sind, 1843, under Sir C. Napier : at the battle of Hyderabad : C.B. 1843 : K.C.B., 1867 : Lt-General, 1868 : General, 1873 : died July 20, 1880.

STANHOPE, HON. EDWARD (1840–1893)

Son of the fifth Earl Stanhope : born Sep. 24, 1840 : educated at Brighton, Harrow, Christ Church, Oxford : Fellow of All Souls' College : called to the bar at the Inner Temple, 1865 : M.P. for Mid-Lincolnshire and the Horncastle Division, 1874–93 : Parliamentary Secretary to the Board of Trade, 1857 : was Under Secretary of State for India from April 6, 1878, to April 29, 1880, during the important time of the Afghan war and part of Lord Lytton's Viceroyalty : and had to deal with great financial measures and political questions : was subsequently Vice-President of the Committee of Council of Education : President of the Board of Trade : Secretary of State for the Colonies, and for War, 1887–92 : died Dec. 21, 1893.

STANLEY, SIR EDMOND (1760–1843)

Son of James Stanley : Scholar of Trinity College Dublin : called to the Irish bar, 1782 : K.C. in Ireland, 1789 : M.P. in Ireland, 1790–1800 : King's Prime Serjeant, 1800 : Recorder of Prince of Wales' Island, 1807 : knighted : Puisne Judge of the Supreme Court, Madras, 1815 : Chief Justice 1820 : retired, 1825 : died April 28, 1843.

STANLEY, SIR JOHN (1846–   )

Born Nov. 22, 1846 : son of John Stanley : educated at Armagh and Trinity College, Dublin : called to the Irish bar, 1872 : Q.C., 1892 : Judge of Calcutta High Court, 1898–1901 : Chief Justice of High Court, of the United Provinces, since 1901 : LL.B : K.B., 1901.

STANNUS, SIR EPHRAIM GERRISH (1784–1850)

Son of Ephraim Stannus : born 1784 : went to India in the Bombay Army, 1799–1800 : in Kattiawar, 1807 : in the Pindari-Mahratta war, 1817–8 : at the capture of Bhuj, in Cutch, 1819 : at Dwarka, 1820 : Major : Private Secretary to Mountstuart Elphinstone, whilst Governor of Bombay : Lt-Colonel, 1822 : C.B., 1823 : the first British Resident in the Persian Gulf, 1824–6 : Lieutenant-Governor of the East India College, Addiscombe, 1834–50 : knighted, 1837 : Maj-General : died Oct. 21, 1850.

STANSFELD, SIR JAMES (1820–1898)

Born, 1820 : son of James Stansfeld : educated at University College, London : called to the bar from the Middle Temple : M.P. for Halifax, 1859–95 : his only connexion with India was his brief tenure of the office of Under Secretary of State for India in Lord John Russell's Government, from Feb. 17 to July 6, 1866 : was twice President of the Local Government Board and a prominent Liberal in politics: G.C.B., 1895 : died Feb. 17, 1898.

STAUNTON, FRANCIS FRENCH (1779 ?– 1825)

Born about 1779 : joined the Cheshire Fencible Infantry, 1795, and the Bombay N.I., Sep. 1798 : in the Mysore war, at Seringapatam, 1799 : in Egypt, 1801 : in the Mahratta war, 1815–8 : at Kirki : commanded a small detachment which defeated the Peshwa's army of 20,000 men at Korigaum, Jan. 1, 1818 : " one of the most heroic actions which has ever been fought and gained by a handful of men over a large army " : C.B. : Lt-Colonel, 1823 : died at sea, June 25, 1825.

STAUNTON, SIR GEORGE LEONARD, BARONET (1737–1801)

Born April 19, 1737 : son of George Staunton : educated in France : M.D. at

Montpellier, 1758 : went to the W. Indies, 1762 : Attorney-General for Grenada, made a fortune : went to India in 1781, as Secretary to Lord Macartney, when appointed Governor of Madras : sent on a Mission to Warren Hastings at Calcutta, 1782 : negotiated wtth Bussy and Suffrein, 1783 : arrested General James Stuart 1783 : negotiated a treaty with Tippoo, 1784 : to England, 1784 : pensioned by the Court of Directors, and made a Baronet, 1785 : F.R.S., 1787 : D.C.L., Oxford, 1790 : Secretary to Lord Macartney's Embassy to China, 1792, and wrote an account of it, 1797 : died Jan. 14, 1801 : buried in Westminster Abbey.

STAVELEY, SIR CHARLES WILLIAM DUNBAR (1817-1896)

Son of Lt-General William Staveley : born Dec. 18, 1817 : educated at the Scottish Military Academy, Edinburgh : entered the 87th regt., 1835 : A.D.C. to Governor of Mauritius, 1840-3, and in N. America, 1846-7 : served at Hong-Kong : in the Crimea : Lt-Colonel, 1854 : C.B. : served in Madras, 1857 : in the Pekin expedition, 1860 : commanded British Force in China, 1862 : named C. G. Gordon, R.E., to the Chinese to command their forces in the Taiping rebellion : K.C.B., 1865 : commanded a Division in Bombay : and the first Division in Abyssinia : C. in C., Bombay, Oct. 1874, to Oct. 1878 : General, 1877 : G.C.B., 1884 : died Nov. 23, 1896.

STAVELEY, WILLIAM (1784-1854)

Born July 29, 1784 : entered the Royal Staff Corps, 1804 : served in the Peninsula, 1809-14 : D.A.Q.M.G. at Waterloo : C.B. : in the Mauritius, 1821-47 : D.Q.M.G. and Commandant of Port St. Louis, 1825 : acted as Governor, 1842 : Maj-General, 1846 : commanded at Hong-Kong : and a Division of the Bombay Army : C. in C., Madras, Oct. 1853, to April 4, 1854, when he died en route to the Nilgiris : Colonel of the 94th regt.

ST. CLAIR, HON. LOCKHART MATTHEW (1855-)

Born July 25, 1855 : son of Baron Sinclair : educated at Wellington and Cooper's Hill : joined the Indian P.W.D., 1876 : Engineer to the Nipal State, 1899 : Superintending Engineer and Secretary,

P.W.D., Central Provinces, 1900 : C.I.E., 1902.

STEDMAN, SIR EDWARD (1842-)

Born July 27, 1842 : entered Royal Artillery, 1860, and became Colonel, 1885 : served in Hazara campaign, 1868 : Afghan war, 1878-80 : Inspr-General of Police, in Burma, 1887-91 : Q.M.G., India, 1892-5 : Chitral Relief Force, 1895 : commanded 1st Class District, India, 1895-9 : Military Secretary at the India Office since 1899 : C.B., 1887 : K.C.I.E., 1897 : K.C.B., 1902.

STEEL, FLORA ANNIE (1847-)

Born April 2, 1847 : daughter of George Webster : married a [Bengal civilian, 1867 : lived in India till 1889 : author of many novels, dealing with India, *From the Five Rivers*, *The Potter's Thumb*, *Tales from the Panjab*, *On the Face of the Waters*, *In the Permanent Way*, etc., etc.

STEEL, SIR SCUDAMORE WINDE (1789-1865)

Entered the Madras Army of the E. I. Co., in 1805 : served in Berar, in the Pindari war, 1808-9 : in the Mahratta war, 1817-8 : in the Burmese war, 1826 : Secretary in the Military Department at Madras, 1832-45 : in the taking of Coorg, 1834 : Lt-Colonel : C.B., 1838 : Military Auditor-General, 1845 : commanded the Madras Division in the Burmese war, 1852-3 : K.C.B., 1853 : retired, 1856 : Lt-General, 1861 : died March 11, 1865.

STEEVENS, CHARLES (1705-1761)

Lieutenant in the Navy, 1729 : at the attack on Cartagena, 1741 : took reinforcements to India in 1757 : second in command under Sir G. Pocock (*q.v.*), at Madras, in naval actions, 1758-9 : Rear Admiral : as Naval C. in C. at Madras co-operated with Coote in the capture of Pondicherry, 1760-1 : died May 17, 1761.

STEIN, MARK AUREL (1862-

Born Nov. 26, 1862 : son of M. N. Stein, merchant, of Zombor and E idapest, Hungary : educated at Budapest and Dresden : studied, 1879-84, the classical languages and antiquities of India and Iran at the Universities of Vienna, Leipzig and Tübingen : Phil.D. in 1883 :

DICTIONARY OF INDIAN BIOGRAPHY 401

carried on, 1885-7, research work at Oxford and London bearing on old Persian philology and early Indian history : went to India for the same purpose : appointed, 1888, both Principal of the Oriental College and Registrar of the Panjab University at Lahore, which he held up to 1899 : utilized his .leisure for philolgical and antiquarian labours, chiefly concerning the ancient history and geography of Kashmir and the Indian N.W. Frontier : he critically edited, 1892, Kalhana's *Chronicle of Kashmir*, the only truly historical text of Sanskrit literature : after protracted archæological researches in Kashmir, published a full commentated translation, 1900 : in a separate publication he reconstructed the historical geography of Kashmir : by repeated archæological tours along the Frontier he identified important old sites, especially in 1898 by penetrating with General Blood's Field Force into Buner, a tribal territory previously unsurveyed : also catalogued over 5,000 Sanskrit MSS. of the Raghunath Temple Library, at Jammu, In 1899 he entered the Indian Educational service as Principal of the Calcutta Madrasa : proceeded, 1900-1, on a year's journey of archæological and geographical exploration in Chinese Turkestan : excavated a series of ancient sites buried under the sands of the Taklamakān Desert, in the region of Khotan : his discoveries, including hundreds of documents and MSS. in Indian scripts, Chinese and Tibetan, amongst them the oldest extant written specimens of these languages, have thrown new light on the Indian civilization which, together with Buddhism, flourished in E. Turkestan from the commencement of our era. The International Orientalist Congress of 1902 recognized the important archæological results of his expedition : for his geographical explorations in the Eastern Pamirs and the Kuen-luen Range he was awarded the Back Grant by the R. Geographical Society : employed as Inspector of Schools in the Panjab, 1901-2 : deputed to England, 1902, to elaborate the scientific results of his journey : the personal narrative of the latter appeared in 1903 : returned to India, 1904, as Inspr-General of Education and Archæological Surveyor-of the N.W. Frontier Provinces and Baluchistan : towards the end of 1904 explored the historically important and previously inac-

cessible hill tract of Mahaban, across the Peshawar border : among his publications are : *Zoroastrian Deities on Indo-Scythian Coins*, 1887 ; *Kalhana's Rajatarangini, a Chronicle of the Kings of Kashmir*, Sanskrit text, 1892 : commentated translation with numerous appendices, 1900 : *Catalogue of the Sanskrit MSS. in the Raghunatha Temple Library*, 1894 ; *Memoir on the Ancient Geography of Kashmir*, 1899 ; *Sandburied ruins of Khotan*, 1903 : and numerous papers in the Journals of learned Societies.

STEINGASS, FRANCIS JOSEPH
(1825–1903)

Born at Frankfort-on-Maine, March 16, 1825 : educated at Munich : Ph.D. : to England about 1870 : Professor of Modern Languages at Birmingham : Professor of the same, and Resident Lecturer on Arabic Languages, Literature, and Law at the Oriental Institute, Woking : acquainted with 14 languages, especially Arabic, Persian, Sanskrit : published dictionaries, English-Arabic, Arabic-English, Persian-English : and other Arabic works : assisted in Hughes' *Dictionary of Islam* : died Jan. 1903.

STEINS, RIGHT REV. WALTER. D.D.
(1810–1867)

Vicar Apostolic of Bombay, May 3, 1861, to Jan 11, 1867 : born at Amsterdam, July 1, 1810 : entered Society of Jesus, Dec. 6, 1832 (Dutch Province) : arrived in India, Jan. 5, 1853 : left Bombay in 1867, when he became Vicar Apostolic of Western Bengal : died March 31, 1867.

STENZLER, ADOLF FRIEDRICH
(1807–1887)

Born July 9, 1807, at Wolgast, in Swedish Pomerania : where, in his early education, he showed his inclination for Oriental languages : educated also at Friedland in Mecklenburg till 1826, and at Greifswald University, at Berlin and at Bonn, where he studied under Schlegel, Freytag, and Lassen in Sanskrit : at Paris, 1829, studied under De Lacy and Burnouf : left Paris, in the disturbances of 1830, for London : associated with Orientalists : translated Kalidas's *Raghuvansa* : Professor of Oriental Languages at Breslau, 1832-3, and first Professor of

D D

402   DICTIONARY OF INDIAN BIOGRAPHY

Sanskrit : Custos of the Library : edited Kalidas's *Kumarasambhava*, 1838 : ordinary Professor, 1847 : wrote on the principles of Sanskrit lexicography : edited the *Mrcchakatika*, and Yajnavalkya's Laws, 1849 : wrote on Gautama, and on Indian medicine, customs and folklore : also on Manu, and a commentary on the *Grhyasutra*, on the *Paraskara*, *Gobhila* and *Sankhayana* : published an elementary work on Sanskrit : edited Kalidas's *Meghaduta*, 1874 : was one of the foremost Sanskritists of the day, an enthusiastic, thorough, and kindly scholar : left much material unpublished : died Feb. 27, 1887.

STEPHEN, SIR JAMES FITZJAMES, BARONET (1829–1894)

Born March 3, 1829 : son of Sir James Stephen : educated at Brighton, Eton, King's College, London; Trinity College, Cambridge : called to the bar at the Inner Temple : wrote for the *Saturday Review* : Secretary to the Education Commission, 1858–61 : Recorder of Newark, 1859–69 : wrote for *Fraser*, the *Cornhill Magazine*, the *Pall Mall Gazette* : Q.C., 1868 : Legal Member of the Supreme Council, Dec. 14, 1869, to April 12, 1872 : left his mark on Indian legislation : passed the Evidence Act, a revised Code of Criminal Procedure, and continued the work of codification : wrote *Liberty, Equality, Fraternity* : applied himself to attempts at codification in England : was a Judge of the High Court, 1879–91 : wrote letters to the *Times* in defence of Lord Lytton's policy as Viceroy : Member and Chairman of various legal Commissions : K.C.S.I., 1877 : D.C.L., Oxford, 1878 : LL.D., Edinburgh, 1884 : Hon. Fellow of Trinity College, Cambridge: Baronet, 1891 : wrote *A History of the Criminal Law of England*, 1883 ; *The Story of Nuncomar, and Sir Elijah Impey*, 1885 ; *Horæ Sabbaticæ*, 1892 : died March 11, 1894 : his life was written by his brother, Sir Leslie Stephen.

STEPHENSON, J. D. (? – ?)

Officer in the Madras Cavalry : saw active service as Captain of one of the Nawab's regiments under Maj-General Stuart, during the war with Hyder Ali (1780–4) : his regiment transferred to the E. I. Co. in 1784 : fought in the wars against Tippoo, 1790 and 1799 : served under Cornwallis and Wellesley : became Colonel : commanded in Malabar, 1800 :

won his chief renown in the Mahratta war of 1803 : took the city of Burhanpur, Oct. 16, and Asirghar, Oct, 21, 1803 : present at Argaum : praised by Wellesley for his services at the siege of Gawilghar : obliged by illness to give up his command returned home, 1804.

STEVENS, SIR CHARLES CECIL (1840–)

I.C.S. : born July 5, 1840 : son of C. G. Stevens of Melbourne : educated at Edgbaston and Melbourne University : entered the Indian Civil Service, 1862 : Commissioner of Chota Nagpur, Bhagalpur and Patna Divisions successively : Officiating Chief Secretary, Bengal, 1890 : Member of the Board of Revenue, Bengal, 1891–8 : Additional Member of Governor-General's Legislative Council, 1893 : Officiating Lieutenant-Governor of Bengal, 1897 : retired, 1898 : C.S.I., 1895 : K.C.S.I., 1899.

STEVENS, HENRY BORLASE (1824–1904)

General : son of John Borlase Stevens : born Dec. 3, 1824 : educated at Addiscombe : entered the Army, 1841 : in the Satlaj campaign, 1845–6 : at Firozshahr and Sobraon : commanded the Sylhet Light Infantry at Hailakandi in Cachar, Jan. 1858 : destroyed the mutineers : in Bhutan, 1864–6 : at the taking of stockades in the Durrunga Pass, at the retaking of Dewangiri : commanded at Delhi in 1875 : General : died Sep. 5, 1904.

STEVENS, SIR JOHN FOSTER (? –)

I.C.S. : educated at Birmingham Grammar School, at Versailles and at King's College, London : went out to Bengal, 1864 : District Judge : Judicial Commissioner of the Central Provinces, 1891–3 and 1894 : Puisne Judge of the High Court, Calcutta, 1897–1904, when he retired : knighted 1905.

STEVENSON, REV. JOHN, D.D. (1798–1858)

Born Nov. 3, 1798, son of William Sevenson, of Alton Campsie, Stirlingshire : educated at Glasgow and Edinburgh Universities : M.A. Glasgow : ordained Aug. 1823 : sent out by the Scottish Missionary Society, 1823, to their Bombay

Mission, which was the first Scottish Mission established in India, 1822 : Missionary at Hurnee and Poona until appointed, 1834, a Chaplain of the E.I.C. in Bombay : Senior Chaplain 1841, and Minister of St. Andrew's : resigned 1854 : Parish Minister of Ladykirk, Berwickshire, 1855–8 : a zealous Missionary and distinguished Sanskrit scholar, one of the pioneer editors and translators of Vedic literature : a founder of the *Bombay Gazette* and joint editor for its first 3 years : intimately acquainted with native thought and native dialects : was President of R.A.S., Bombay, and of the Government Committee for examination of officers in native languages : Hony. D.D. of St. Andrew's University : a "Stevenson scholarship" founded by the General Assembly's Institution on his departure : he published the *Sanhita of the Rig-veda*, with translation, 1833 : *Principles of Mahratti Grammar*, 1833 : *Sanhita of the Sama-veda*, 1842 : *Sama-veda*, edited from MSS., 1843 : *Kalpa Sutra* and *Nava Tatva*, illustrative of the Jain religion and philosophy, 1848 ; wrote, for the R.A.S., Bombay, papers on the Kanheri, Nasik and Sahyadri inscriptions of the Bombay Presidency, which he was most successful in deciphering, and on the comparative vocabulary of the non-Sanskrit vocables of the Indian vernacular languages : his Mahratti grammar was long a standard work : he died Aug. 11, 1858.

STEVENSON, ROBERT CHARLES
(1851–1905)

Of the Burmese Commission, 1870–1902 rose from being a police officer to be a Deputy-Commissioner in Burma : in 1885, was Chief Interpreter to Sir H. Prendergast, V.C., commanding the Forces operating against Upper Burma : up to his retirement, the only officer who had gained the Degree of Honour for knowledge of Burmese : prepared in 9 years and published the present standard Burmese-English dictionary : his linguistic attainments, and knowledge of Burma and its people, were of special value during the military operations of 1886–7 : died at Oxford, May 8, 1905.

STEWART, CHARLES (1764–1837)

Born 1764 : son of Captain Poyntz Stewart : joined the E. I. Co's Army in Bengal, 1782 : retired as Major, 1808 : saw service in Upper India and Rohilkund :

second in command of Col. Symes' Embassy to Amarapura, 1802–3 : Assistant Professor of Persian at Fort William College, Calcutta, 1800–6 : Professor of Arabic, Persian and Hindustani at Haileybury, 1807–27 : died April 19, 1837 : published an introduction to the Anwar-i-Suhaili : made a catalogue of Tippoo's Library, with memoirs of Hyder and Tippoo : wrote *The History of Bengal from the First Muhammadan Invasion until 1757*, 1813 ; *Original Persian Letters, etc. with Translations*, 1825, and other works on Oriental subjects.

STEWART, CHARLES EDWARD
(1836–1904)

Son of Algernon Stewart, grandson of the seventh Earl of Galloway : educated at Marlborough : entered the Indian Army, 1854 : in the mutiny, in several engagements in Oudh : served in the 11th Bengal Lancers and the 5th Panjab Infantry : in the Umbeyla campaign, 1863 : in the Jowaki-Afridi expedition, 1877-8 : Brevet-Lt-Colonel : Lt-Colonel, 1879 : Colonel, 1883 : in political employ in Persia, 1880–5, and Assistant Commissioner in the Perso-Afghan boundary demarcation, 1885 : C.I.E. and C.M.G., 1884 : C.B., 1886 : Consul at Resht, and at Tabriz, 1889–92 : and Consul-General at Odessa, 1892–9 : died Dec. 1904.

STEWART, SIR DONALD MARTIN, BARONET (1824–1900)

Field Marshal : son of Robert Stewart : born March 1, 1824 : educated at King's College, Aberdeen : gazetted Ensign, Bengal Army, Oct. 12, 1840 : Adjutant of the 9th Bengal N.I., 1845 : Interpreter and Quartermaster, 1852. In 1854–5 he was actively employed on the Peshawar frontier against the hill tribes : served throughout the mutiny, rode with despatches from Agra to Delhi through the enemy's lines : was Deputy Assistant Adjt-General of the Delhi Field Force during the siege : at the relief of Lucknow, and engaged in the operations in Rohilkund : joined the Staff Corps and served in the Adjt-General's Department till 1867 : commanded a Brigade in the Abyssinian expedition, 1867–8, was made C.B. : and commanded the Peshawar District in July, 1869. He was Chief Commissioner of the Andaman Islands, 1871–75, when the Earl of Mayo was assassinated there on Feb. 8, 1872. He next commanded the Lahore Division : in the Afghan war led the Southern Army to Kandahar : was made K.C.B. : and, after fighting the actions of Ahmad-Kheyl and Urzoo, assumed,on May 5, 1880, the supreme military and political command at Kabul. It was under his orders that Lord Roberts made his famous march from Kabul to Kandahar in Aug. 1880 : Stewart and the rest of the troops returned to India *viâ* the Khyber : made G.C.B. and Baronet. He was Military Member of the Supreme Council, 1880–1, and Commander-in-Chief in India from 1881 to 1885 : on his return to England, Stewart was appointed to the Council of India, and in March, 1895, made Governor of the Royal Hospital, Chelsea. He died at Algiers on March 26, 1900. He was also G.C.S.I., 1885 : C.I.E., 1881 : D.C.L. of Oxford, 1889: LL.D. of Aberdeen. Memorials were erected to him at the Royal Hospital, and at King's College, Aberdeen University. The inscription on the latter runs as follows :—" Strong, brave, genial, eminently wise and just, forgetful of self and modest, Donald Stewart did with his might whatever his hand found to do."

STEWART, GEORGE (1839–   )

Born July 20, 1839 : son of Major W. Murray Stewart : educated at St. Andrew's and London : entered the Bengal Army, 1856, and became Maj-General, 1887 : retired : served in Indian mutiny, 1857–9 : relief of Cawnpur and Lucknow : China war, 1860 : Umbeyla campaign and Jowaki expedition, 1878 : Afghan war, 1878–80 : Ali-Masjid, Kabul and Sherpur : C.B., 1887.

STEWART, JAMES CALDER (1840–   )

Born June 20, 1840 : son of Dr. Duncan Stewart : educated at Clapham Grammar School : entered the Bengal Army, 1857, and became Colonel, 1887, and Maj-General, 1895 : served in the Indian mutiny, 1857–9 : in the relief of Lucknow and Oudh : Jowaki campaign, 1878 : Afghan war, 1878–80 : at Kabul, Charasia, and Sherpur : C.B., 1891.

STEWART, JOHN (1749–1822)

Born 1749 : a Scotchman : at school at Harrow and Charterhouse : went out to Madras as a writer, 1763 : resigned his appointment, in a letter of " juvenile insolence and audacity," 1765 : served

under Hyder Ali, from Interpreter to General : was wounded, and escaped : became Prime Minister to the Nawab of Arcot : left him and took to traʋelling on foot in Persia, Ethiopia, Abyssinia, across Arabia, through France and Spain, to England, from Calais to Vienna, 1784 : visited N. America : friend of De Quincey : obtained £10,000 from the E. I. Co. for his claims against the Nawab of Arcot, 1813 : died Feb. 20, 1822 : a doctrinaire : wrote curious works, such as *Travels to Discover the Source of Moral Motion* : *Opus Maximum*, etc, : called " Walking Stewart."

STEWART, JOHN (1833–   )

Born March 24, 1833 : son of Major W. M. Stewart : educated at St. Andrew's and Addiscombe : entered the Bengal Artillery, 1851, and Ordnance Department, Bengal, 1857 : served in the Indian mutiny, 1857–8 : established the Government harness and saddlery factory at Cawnpur, and had charge of it till 1888 : C.I.E., 1887 : retired, 1888, as Colonel.

STEWART, PATRICK (1832–1865)

Son of James Stewart : born Jan. 28, 1832 : educated at Sunderland, Sydenham, Addiscombe : joined the Bengal Engineers, 1850 : went to Calcutta, 1852 : employed on telegraph construction and twice officiated as head of the Telegraph Department : in the mutiny fortified Raj Ghat at Benares : at Sir Colin Campbell's relief of Lucknow, Nov. 1857 : and at its capture, 1858 : as Deputy Superintendent of Telegraphs did excellent service in active warfare : Brevet-Major : served on a Cholera Commission, 1861–2 : on telegraph service in Persia : Director-General of the Government Indo-European Telegraph, 1863 : C.B., 1864 : died at Constantinople, Jan. 16, 1865 : Lt-Colonel.

STEWART, SIR RICHARD CAMPBELL (1836–1904)

Born 1836 : son of Lt-General Thomas Stewart : joined the Madras Cavalry, 1853 : in the mutiny served with the Mysore Siladar Horse : at the attack on Shorapur, Feb. 1858 : dangerously wounded : with the Hyderabad Contingent under Brig-General Hill, in the Tapti Valley, in Berar, and the Dekkan, Nov. 1858, to March, 1859 : Military Secretary to Governor of Madras : Major, 1871 : Q.M.G., Madras 1881–3 : in the Burmese expedition, 1886-7, commanded a Brigade sent to the Ruby Mines : C.B. : Brig-General of the Hyderabad Contingent : commanded in Burma, 1890-5 : in operations in the Chin-Lushai hills, 1892-3 : K.C.B. : Lt-General, 1895 : General, 1900 : died Dec. 14, 1904.

STIBBERT, GILES (? - ?)

Raised a battalion of N.I. at Bankipur, 1761 : at the siege of Patna, 1763, and battle of Baxar, Oct. 23, 1764 : captured Chunar, 1765 : officiating C. in C. of the Bengal Army in 1777 and 1783 : framed the reform of that Army, 1780 : Maj-General, 1783 : Lt-General, 1796 : died after several years' residence in England.

STIFFE, ARTHUR WILLIAM
(1831-)

Born Aug. 12, 1831 : son of William Stiffe : educated at Stuttgart Polytechnic : served in the Indian Navy from 1849 to 1862 : was present at capture of Bushire and Muhamra in Persian war, 1857 : employed in hydrographic surveys : Engineer in Chief and Electrician for the Indian Government Telegraph in Persian Gulf, 1864-79 : Port Officer and Master Attendant, Calcutta : retired, 1888 : author of *Charts and Sailing Directions for Persian Gulf and Makran Coast*, and of papers in scientific Journals : F.R.A.S. : F.R.G.S. : F.G.S.

STIRLING, ANDREW (1793 ?-1830)

I.C.S. : born about 1793 : son of Admiral Stirling : educated at Haileybury, 1811-12 : to India in 1813 : Persian Secretary to Government and Deputy Secretary in the Political Department : Private Secretary to W. B. Bayley (*q.v.*) while Acting as Governor-General, 1828 : he was the author of a valuable work on Orissa : distinguished by great talents throughout his career : died at Calcutta, May 23, 1830.

STIRLING, SIR WILLIAM (1835-)

Lt-General : born Aug. 4, 1835 : son of Charles Stirling : educated at Edinburgh Academy and R.M.A., Woolwich : with the R.A. in the Crimea, the Mutiny, and in China, 1860 : in the Afghan campaign, 1878-9 : made C.B. 1880 and K.C.B., 1893 : Lt-General : Colonel Commandant R.A. : Lieutenant of the Tower of London since 1900.

ST. JOHN, SIR OLIVER BEAUCHAMP COVENTRY (1837-1891)

Son of Capt. Oliver St. John : born March 21, 1837 : educated at Norwich and Addiscombe : went to India in the Bengal Engineers in 1859 : in the P.W.D. in the N.W.P. : employed under Patrick Stewart (*q.v.*) in constructing the telegraph line through Persia, 1863-7 : in the Abyssinian expedition, 1867-8, as Director of the Field Telegraph and Army Signalling : Brevet-Major : returned to Persia : Boundary Commissioner of the Persian-Kelat frontier, 1871 : and wrote an account of it : Principal of the Mayo College, Ajmir, 1875-8 : Chief Political Officer with Sir D. Stewart's Kandahar Field Force, 1878 : C.S.I., 1879 : Political Agent for S. Afghanistan, 1880 : in the pursuit to the Helmund of the troops of the Wali of Kandahar, and at the battle of Maiwand, July 27, 1880, against Ayub Khan : at the battle of Kandahar, Sep. 1, 1880 : officiated as A.G.G. for Beluchistan, 1882, 1886, 1891 : K.C.S.I., 1882 : in Kashmir, 1883-4 : acting Resident at Hyderabad, 1884 : acting Resident at Baroda, 1887 : Chief Commissioner of Mysore, 1889-1891 : died at Quetta, June 3, 1891 : contributed to scientific Journals on geography and natural history : Lt-Colonel.

STISTED, SIR HENRY WILLIAM
(1817-1875)

Son of Lt-Colonel Charles Stisted : born 1817 : educated at Sandhurst : joined the 2nd regt., 1835 : served in Afghanistan, at Ghazni, the capture of Kelat, the occupation of Kabul : was in the Persian war of 1856-7, at Khushab and Muhamra : in command of Havelock's advance guard at the relief of Lucknow, Sep. 25, 1857, commanded a Brigade after Neill's death : with Outram at the Alambagh : at the capture of Lucknow : in Rohilkund, at Bareli : C.B. : served on the N.W. frontier, 1863 : commanded a Division in Canada, 1867 : Lieutenant-Governor of Ontario : K.C.B., 1871 : Lt-General, 1873 : died Dec. 10, 1875.

STOCQUELER, JOACHIM HAYWARD
(1800-1885)

Son of Joachim Christian Stocqueler : born 1800 : was in Calcutta from 1821 for 20 years, as a journalist : bought the

John Bull and changed it into the *Englishman* : edited *Bengal Monthly Sporting Magazine, East Indian United Service Journal, Indian Racing Calendar, Fifteen Months' Pilgrimage through Khuzistan and Persia,* 1832 ; *Memorials of Afghanistan,* 1843 : lectured in England on Indian subjects : established an East Indian Institute : was a correspondent in the American war : died, 1885 : wrote *A Handbook of India,* 1844 ; *India, its History, Character etc. etc.* 1853 ; *Memoirs, etc. of Maj-General Sir William Nott,* 1854 : and other works.

STODDART, CHARLES (1806–1842)

I.S.C. : born July 23, 1806 : son of Major Stephen Stoddart : entered the Royal Staff Corps, 1823 : Captain 1834 : Secretary to the Royal United Service Institution, 1833–5, and to the Institute of Civil Engineers : went to Persia as Military Secretary to the British Envoy, 1835 : with the Persian Force at the siege of Herat, 1837–8 : through him the siege was raised : Lt-Colonel : sent to Bokhara to treat for relief of Russian captives there, and to make treaty with the Amir, 1838 : imprisoned : released in 1839 : again imprisoned, 1839–40 : served the Amir, who desired to make alliance with England : Stoddart and Arthur Conolly imprisoned in Dec. 1841, by Amir's order : both publicly beheaded on June 17, 1842 : no evidence of their having become Muhammadans.

STOKES, SIR HENRY EDWARD (1841–   )

I.C.S. : born July 23, 1841 : son of Henry Stokes, County Surveyor of Kerry : educated at Trinity College, Dublin : entered Madras Civil Service, 1858 : Chief Secretary to Government, Madras, 1883–8 : Member of Council, Madras, 1888–93 : K.C.S.I., 1892.

STOKES, WHITLEY (1830–   )

Son of Dr. William Stokes of Dublin : educated at Dublin and Edinburgh Universities : ' called to the bar at the Inner Temple, 1855 : went to India, 1862 : Acting Administrator General, 1863–4 : Secretary to Legislative Council of Governor-General, and later to Legislative Department of the Government, 1865–77 : Legal Member of the Supreme Council,

India, 1877–82 : drafted the greater portion of the Codes of Civil and Criminal Procedure, Transfer of Property, Trusts, Easements, Specific Relief, and Limitation Acts : author of *The Anglo-Indian Codes,* 1887–8, 1889 *and* 1891 : has devoted himself to philological studies and edited many Irish texts : the greatest living Celtic scholar, equally versed in the Irish, Breton and Cornish languages : C.S.I., 1877 : C.I.E., 1879 : Honorary Doctor of Law, Edinburgh.

STOLICZKA, FERDINAND (? –1874)

Had a reputation as a naturalist and geologist in connexion with the Imperial Geological Survey of Austria before he joined the Geological Survey of India, 1862 : Palæontologist to the Indian Survey : wrote on the Cretaceous Fauna of S. India : was a laboratory-zoologist : in 1869 commenced to study, systematically, the anatomy, physiology and morphology of the mollusca and other invertebrata : an accomplished naturalist : accompanied, as the scientific member, Sir T. D. Forsyth's Mission to Kashgar, 1873 : wrote papers on the geology of the route to Kashgar : died from exposure at Boolak-i-Moorghai, 12 marches from Leh, June 9, 1874.

STONE, VEN. ARTHURE EDWARD (? –   )

Educated at St. Peter's, York, and Trinity College, Dublin : Chaplain on the Bengal establishment, 1877–1902 : served with Upper Burma Field Force, 1886–8 : Archdeacon of Calcutta, 1898–1902 : Fellow of Calcutta University : Rector of Islip, Oxford, since 1902.

STRACHEY, SIR ARTHUR (1858–1901)

Born Dec. 5, 1858 : son of Sir John Strachey *(q.v.)* : educated at Charterhouse and Trinity Hall, Cambridge : LL.D : called to the bar from the Inner Temple, 1883 : practised in the Allahabad High Court : in 1892, Public Prosecutor and Standing Counsel to Government, N.W.P. : Puisne Judge, Bombay High Court, 1895 : Chief Justice of the High Court, Allahabad, 1899 : knighted : died at Simla, May 14, 1901.

STRACHEY, SIR HENRY, BARONET
(1736–1810)

Son of Henry Strachey: born May 23, 1736: was Private and Political Secretary to Lord Clive in India, 1764 : M.P. for several places between 1768 and 1807 : Secretary to the Commissioners for restoring peace to North America, 1776 : introduced indigo into America : Storekeeper of the Ordnance, 1780–2, and again in 1783 : Joint Secretary of the Treasury and Joint Under Secretary for the Home Department, 1782 : assisted the King's Commissioners in negotiating the peace with North America in Paris, 1782. John Adams, one of the American Peace Commissioners, writing from Paris, described Henry Strachey thus : " Strachey is as artful and insinuating a man as they could send : he pushes and presses every point as far as it can possibly go ; he has a most eager, earnest, pointed spirit." Master of the King's household, 1794 : Baronet, 1801 : F.S.A. : died Jan. 1, 1810.

STRACHEY, SIR JOHN (1823–)

I.C.S. : son of Edward Strachey, B.C.S. : born June 5, 1823, educated at Hailey-bury : went out to India in 1842 : served in the N.W.P. in important appointments : presided over a Commission to inquire into the cholera epidemic of 1861 : was Judicial Commissioner in the Central Provinces in 1862 : President of the Sanitary Commission, 1864 : Officiating Chief Commissioner of Oudh, 1866–7 : Member of the Governor-General's Supreme Council from March, 1868, to Nov. 1872 : during which time he acted as Viceroy and Governor-General from Feb. 9, 1872, on the death of the Earl of Mayo, to Lord Napier of Merchistoun's arrival on Feb. 23 : Lieutenant-Governor of the N.W.P. from April, 1874, to Dec. 1876 : Financial Member of the Supreme Council from Dec. 1876, to Dec. 1880, when he left India : Member of the Council of India from 1885–95 :. he published *Hastings and the Rohilla War*, 1892 : and *India, its Administration and Progress*, 1903 : and, with Lt-General Sir R. Strachey (*q.v.*), *The Finance and Public Works of India*, 1869–81, in 1882 : K.C.S.I. 1873 : G.C.S.I., 1878.

STRACHEY, SIR RICHARD
(1817–)

Son of E. Strachey, of the Bengal Civil Service : born July 24, 1817 : educated privately and at Addiscombe : entered the Bombay Engineers in 1836 : was transferred to Bengal and employed in the Irrigation Department : was in the battles of Badiwal, Aliwal, and Sobraon in 1845–6, Brevet-Major : in 1857 was Under Secretary, P.W.D. : in the mutiny was Secretary to Sir J. P. Grant (*q.v.*), in the temporary Lieutenant-Governorship of "the Central Provinces": Consulting Engineer, Railway Department, 1858 : Secretary P.W.D., 1862 : Inspr-General of Irrigation, 1866 : in the Governor-General's Legislative Council, 1869 : originated the schemes for decentralizing the finances, and for carrying out Railway and Irrigation works on borrowed capital : in 1871, Inspr-General of railway material and stores, India Office : in 1875, Lieutenant-General and Member of the Council of India : in 1878–9, presided over the Indian Famine Commission : acted as Finance Member, and as Military Member of the Supreme Council, 1878–9 : again Member of the Council of India, 1879–89 : became Chairman of the East Indian Railway Co., 1889 : in 1892 he represented the Indian Government at the Brussels Monetary Conference and, later, was a Member of Lord Herschell's Currency Committee : F.R.S., 1854 : Royal Medallist of the Royal Society, 1897 : Chairman of the Meteorological Council : President of the Royal Geographical Society, 1887–9 : LL.D. Cambridge, 1892 : C.S.I. in 1861 : G.C.S.I., 1897 : wrote *Lectures on Geography*, and, with his brother, Sir John Strachey (*q.v.*), *The Finances and Public Works of India*, 1869–81, 1882.

STRAIGHT, SIR DOUGLAS
(1844–)

Born Oct. 22, 1844 : son of Robert Marshall Straight : educated at East Sheen and Harrow : engaged in journalism till 1865 : called to the bar, 1865. and had a large practice in criminal cases : M.P. for Shrewsbury, 1870–4 : Puisne Judge of the Allahabad High Court, 1879–92 : retired, 1892 : Editor of the *Pall Mall Gazette* since 1896 : Knighted, 1892 : LL.D.

STRANGE, ALEXANDER (1818–1876)

Son of Sir Thomas Andrew Lumsden Strange : born April 27, 1818 : educated at Harrow : joined the 7th Madras Cavalry in 1834 : was an assistant in the Great Trigonometrical Survey of India in 1847, and did much valuable triangulation work until 1859, when, as Major, he left the survey : retired in 1861 as Lt-Colonel : was a distinguished man of science : made Inspector, in 1862, of scientific instruments for use in India : and himself designed standard instruments : F.R.G.S.: F.R.A.S. : F.R.S. : he had great natural ability for mechanical science and invention : he initiated, in 1868, the movement for the appointment of a Royal Commission on Scientific Instruction and the Advancement of Science, by which many of his proposals were favourably received : he died March 9, 1876.

STRANGE, SIR THOMAS ANDREW LUMISDEN (1756–1841)

Son of Sir Robert Strange, the eminent engraver : born Aug. 30, 1756 : educated at Westminster and Christ Church, Oxford : called to the bar from Lincoln's Inn, 1785 : Chief Justice of Nova Scotia, 1789 : Recorder of Madras, 1798 : and President of the Court of Mayor and Aldermen : knighted : Chief Justice of the Supreme Court, Madras, 1800 : Commanded a battalion of volunteers : his judicial action effected the collapse of the mutiny of Company's officers, 1809 : returned to England, 1817 : D.C.L. Oxford, 1818 : published *Elements of Hindu Law*, 1825 : and *Reports of Cases adjudged in the Madras Supreme Court* : died July 16, 1841.

STRANGE, THOMAS LUMISDEN (1808–1884)

I.C.S. : born Jan. 4, 1808 : son of Sir T. A. L. Strange (*q.v.*) : educated at Westminster and Haileybury, 1824–6 : joined the Madras Civil Service, 1826 : was a Commissioner to inquire into the Moplah disturbances in Malabar, 1852 : Judge of the *Sadr* Court, and of the High Court, Madras, 1862 : wrote a *Manual of Hindu Law*, 1856 : retired, 1863 : died Sep. 4, 1884 : wrote largely on religious subjects.

STRATHNAIRN, HUGH HENRY ROSE, BARON (1801–1885)

Field-Marshal : son of Sir George Henry Rose : born April 6, 1801 : educated at Berlin : joined the 19th foot in 1820 : Lt-Colonel, 1839 : employed, 1840, on special duty in Syria on the side of the Turks against the Egyptians : and succeeded to the command : Consul-General for Syria, 1841–8 : C.B., 1842 : Secretary to the Embassy at Constantinople, 1851 : Chargé d'Affaires, 1852 : in the Crimean war was Queen's Commissioner at the headquarters of the French Army : Brig-General : in the Crimean battles : K.C.B.: recommended for the V.C. : General of the Poona Division, 1857 : commanded the Central India Field Force : took Ratghar, and Garhakota : relieved Sagar : took Maltun and Madanpur : defeated Tantia Topi on April 1, 1858, and took Jhansi on the 3rd : again defeated Tantia Topi at Kunch and occupied Kalpi : again defeated him and the Rani of Jhansi at Morar, and recovered Gwalior for Sindia, June, 1857 : resumed the Poona command : G.C.B. : Lt-General : C. in C., Bombay, 1860 : and C. in C. in India, 1860–5 : General : amalgamated the Armies of the Queen and the E. I. Co. : K.C.S.I., 1861 : G.C.S.I., 1866 : D.C.L. Oxford : C. in C. in Ireland, 1865–70 : made Baron Strathnairn of Strathnairn and Jhansi, 1866 : General, 1867 : LL.D. of Dublin : Field-Marshal, 1877 : died Oct. 16, 1885 : his equestrian statue was erected in London, 1895.

STRATTON, GEORGE (? – ?)

Writer at Fort St. George, 1751 : Factor, 1756 : Junior Merchant, 1759 : Senior Merchant, 1762, and Second in Council at Vizagapatam : Eleventh in Council at Fort St. George, 1764 : rose to be Second in Council, 1775 : Governor of Madras, Aug. 1776, after he and other members of the Madras Council had arrested the Governor, Lord Pigot, Aug. 24, 1776 : himself suspended from the service, Aug. 1777 : tried in the King's Bench in Dec. 1779 for arresting Lord Pigot, and fined £1,000.

STRATTON, JOHN PROUDFOOT (1830–1895)

Son of David Stratton : born July 2, 1830 : passed the Royal College of Surgeons, Edinburgh, and M.D. of Aberdeen, 1852 : entered the Indian Medical Service in Bombay, 1852 : acted as Resident of Baroda, 1858 : was Political Agent in Bundelkund : Resident in Mewar : in the W. states of Rajputana : and Jaipur : retired, 1885, as Brigade Surgeon : died Aug. 8, 1895.

STUART, SIR CHARLES SHEPHERD (1804–1879)

Son of William Stuart : entered the E. I. Co.'s military service in Bombay, 1820 : Colonel in 1854 : Commander of the Malwa Field Force, 1857, and a Brigade in the Central India Field Force under Sir H. Rose : took Chandairi, March 17, 1858 : defeated Tantia Topi before Jhansi, April 1, 1858 : showed great bravery at Kalpi, May 22, 1858 : at the capture of Gwalior, June 19, 1858 : Extra K.C.B., 1859 : commanded a Brigade at Bombay : G.C.B., 1875 : General 1877 : died April 2, 1879.

STUART, JAMES (? – 1793)

Brother of Andrew Stuart : Captain in 1755 : served in Nova Scotia, the W. Indies, etc. : entered the E. I. Co.'s military service in Madras, 1775 : C. in C. as Brig-General there : arrested the Governor of Madras, 1776 : himself suspended : acquitted by court-martial,1780 : commanded at Madras, 1781 : served under Coote (q.v.) at Porto Novo : lost a leg at Polilore, Aug. 1781 : Maj-General : at siege of Cuddalore, was suspended by Madras Government and sent to England : fought a duel with Lord Macartney, 1786 : died Feb. 2, 1793.

STUART, JAMES (1741–1815)

Son of John Stuart : born March 2, 1741 : educated at Culross, Dumfermline, Edinburgh : entered the Army : in American War of Independence : to India as Brevet-Lt-Colonel, 78th regt. in 1781 : Lt-Colonel : under Coote against Hyder : at Cuddalore, 1788 : under Medows, 1790; and Cornwallis, 1791–2, against Tippoo : Maj-General : commanded the expedition against the Dutch in Ceylon, 1795 : commanded the Forces at Madras, 1796 : and the Bombay Force at Seringapatam, 1799 : C. in C., Madras, 1801 : Lt-General, 1802 : in the Mahratta war, 1803 : retired, 1805 : General, 1812 : died April 29, 1815.

STUART, SIR ROBERT (1816–1896)

Son of Robert Stuart : educated at the University of Edinburgh : Member of the Faculty of Advocates, Edinburgh : called to the bar from Lincoln's Inn, 1856 : Q.C., 1868 : Treasurer, 1889 : Chief Justice of the High Court, N.W.P., 1871–84 : knighted : died Aug. 26, 1896.

STURT, ROBERT RAMSAY NAPIER (1852–)

Son of Colonel William M. N. Sturt : educated at Repton : entered the Army, 1872, and Indian Staff Corps, 1875 : served in the Afghan war, 1878–9 : Mahsud-Waziri expedition, 1881 : Zhob Valley expedition, 1890 : Miranzai expedition, 1891 : Waziristan expedition, 1894 : N.W. Frontier, Tirah expedition, 1897–8 : C.B. 1902.

SUFFREIN SAINT TROPEZ, PIERRE ANDRE DE (1726–1788)

French Admiral : born July 13, 1726, in Provence, of a noble family : third son of the Marquis Suffrein St. Tropez : went to sea, 1743 : served at Martinique ; taken prisoner in 1748 to England : served in the Mediterranean ; again captured off Lagos : Captain of a frigate, 1767 : of a ship in 1772 : on the American station, 1778 : was selected by the French Government in 1781 to command a squadron to the E. Indies : engaged the English in the Bay of Praya : went, viâ the Cape, to the Isle of France, joining the fleet of Count d'Orves, whom he succeeded in the command : failed in surprising Madras, sailed to Pondicherry and Porto Novo in 1782 : fought an indecisive action with Hughes (q.v.) off Sadras : treated with Hyder Ali ; reduced Cuddalore : fought the English again off Providien and Negapatam, and took Trincomalee Aug. 31, 1782 : his four actions with Hughes all indecisive : he went to Sumatra and returned to Cuddalore : the Peace of Versailles, 1783, closed the war : Suffrein went home to Toulon, 1784 ; received by the States of Provence with great honour : a medal struck with the inscription : " The Cape protected : Trincomalee taken, Cuddalore delivered : India defended : six glorious combats : 1784 " : was made Chevalier, Vice-Admiral and " Bailli " : selected again in 1787 for the naval command against the English, but he was killed in a duel in which, in spite of his obesity and age, he engaged Dec. 8, 1788.

SULLIVAN, JOHN (? – ?)

In the E. I. Co.'s Service in Madras : in 1785 represented the Madras Government at the Court of the Raja of Tanjore : he originated the scheme for the founding of English schools for natives, that is, for their instruction in the English language, with a view to the breaking down of prejudice against British rule : his scheme received the support of the Company, and several such schools were founded.

SUNKERSETT, JAGANNATH
(1802–1865)

Head of the Indian community at Bombay for many years : Member of the Legislative Council, Bombay : took active interest in municipal affairs : President of the Bombay Association, of the Agri-Horticultural Society, and of the Board of Trustees of the Elphinstone funds : original member of the Board of Education : a founder of the Elphinstone College : promoted education generally : was voted a statue at a public meeting : died July 31, 1865.

SURAJ-UD-DAULA (1731 ? or 1736– ? 1757)

His name was Mirza Muhammad : eldest son of Zain-un-din Ahmad, called Haibat Jang, the nephew and son-in-law of Aliverdi Khan, Governor of Bengal : adopted by Aliverdi as his heir : succeeded Aliverdi as Nawab on April 9, 1756 : was offended with the English for giving protection at Calcutta to Kishen Das, who escaped with treasure from Dacca : actuated by rapacity, he attacked Calcutta and took it, June 20, 1756 : was finally responsible for the tragedy of the Black Hole, and callous to the sufferings of the survivors : European and native historians have dilated on his cruel and profligate character. Clive and Watson retook Calcutta on Jan. 2, 1757 : the treaty made between them and the Nawab proved only temporary : a confederacy was made against him by Clive, who marched on Murshidabad : Suraj-ud-daula was defeated at the battle of Plassy, June 23, 1757 : he fled to Rajmahal, where he was captured, and put to death at Murshidabad by order of Miran, son of Mir Jafar (q.v.), on July 4, 1757.

SURAJ MAL, JAT (? –1763)

Also called Sujan Singh : son of Badan Singh Jat (died 1755), founder and Raja of Bhartpur. Badan Singh, having become blind, lived in retirement at Deeg, and Suraj Mal governed. He took part in Wazir Safdar Jang's campaign against Farrukhabad in 1750, sided with the Mahrattas in their subsequent encroachments, 1750–60, and lost his life in a skirmish near Ghaziuddinnagar, near Delhi, Dec. 30, 1763 : he took possession of Agra Fort, June, 1761, and the Jats held it for nearly 20 years : succeeded by his son, Jawahir Singh. Suraj Mal is the hero of a Hindi poem by Sudan, in 7 cantos, entitled Sujan Charitr, 1850, and 1902.

SUTHERLAND, JAMES (1794– ?)

Went to sea at 14 for 7 years : in 1816 to India, to Madras, Calcutta : entered the Indian Marine service at Bombay and Calcutta : commanded several vessels : joined J. S. Buckingham (q.v.) in 1828 in editing the Calcutta Journal : was for some years partly at sea, partly engaged in journalism and in a mercantile house : concerned with various papers, the Bengal Chronicle, which became the Bengal Harkaru; the Calcutta Chronicle, which was suppressed by the Government; the Bengal Herald : resigned editorship : and became Professor of English Literature at the Hughli College, 1837.

SUTHERLAND, SIR THOMAS
(1834–   )

Born Aug. 6, 1834 : son of Robert Sutherland : educated at Aberdeen Grammar School and University : entered the service of the P. and O. Company : was at Hong-Kong for many years : M.P. for Greenock, 1884–1900 : Chairman of the P. and O. Company and of the London Board of Suez Canal Company : K.C.M.G., 1891 : G.C.M.G., 1897 : LL.D.

SVARNAMAYI, MAHARANI
(1827–1897)

At 11 she was married to Kumar, afterwards Raja, Krishna Nath of Kasimbazar, who died in 1845. She contested the validity of her husband's will, under which the E. I. Co had taken possession of his estates, and it was declared null and void. She spent the greater part of her large income munificently on charities and public purposes. The Government of India recognized her liberality (which became a proverb) and public spirit, made her Rani, and Maharani (1871), and in 1878 a Member of the Imperial Order of the Crown of India. She died in Aug. 1897.

SWINLEY, GEORGE (1842–   )

Entered the Bengal Artillery, 1860, and became Maj-General, 1895 : served in Bhutan expedition, 1865–6 : Black Mountain expedition, 1868 : Jowaki-Afridi expedition, 1877–8 : Afghan war, 1878–80, Brevet-Major and Lt-Colonel : C.B., 1893.

SYDENHAM, THOMAS (1780–1816)

Entered the Madras Army : was Assistant Private Secretary to Lord Mornington (Marquis Wellesley) in 1799 : Resident at Hyderabad, 1806–10 : Chargé d'Affaires at Lisbon, 1811 : appointed Minister Plenipotentiary at Lisbon, 1815 : died at Geneva, 1816.

SYDENHAM, WILLIAM (1752–1801)

In the E.I. Co.'s service : joined the Madras Artillery, as Lieutenant, in 1768 : at the time of the war with Tippoo, the Artillery was divided into two battalions, and Major Sydenham was promoted to the command of the 1st battalion : became Maj-General : died June 13, 1801.

SYKES, PERCY MOLESWORTH (1867–   )

Educated at Rugby and Sandhurst : a great athlete : entered the Army, 1888 : travelled constantly in India, Kashmir, Ladak, Persia, Beluchistan, etc. : founded the Consulate of Kerman and Persian Beluchistan : served in South Africa in command of Welsh Imperial Yeomanry : inventor of Sykes' patent tent and sleeping valise : C.M.G. for services in Persia, 1902 : author of *Ten Thousand Miles in Persia,* 1902, and of many papers for learned Societies.

SYKES, WILLIAM AINLEY (1859–   )

Entered the Indian Medical Service, 1882, and became Lt-Colonel, 1902 :

served at Suakin, 1885:in Burma campaign, 1886–8 : Zhob Valley expedition, 1890 : Waziri expedition, 1894 : Malakand, 1897 : Buner expedition, 1897 : China expedition, 1900 : Administrative Medical Officer, N.W. Frontier Province : D.S.O., 1887.

SYKES, WILLIAM HENRY (1790–1872)

Colonel : son of Samuel Sykes : born Jan, 25, 1790 : entered the E. I. Co.'s Bombay Army in 1804 : was present at Bhartpur under Lord Lake, 1805 : served in the Dekkan, 1817–20 : and commanded native troops at the battles of Kirki and Poona : was employed by the Bombay Government as Statistical Reporter from 1824 until he left India in 1831 : wrote a number of reports, statistical, on Natural History, etc. : retired as a Colonel in 1833 : was a Royal Commissioner in Lunacy, 1835–45 : became Director of the E. I. Co. in 1840 : Chairman in 1856 : in 1854 he was Lord Rector of the Aberdeen University : M.P. for Aberdeen, 1857–72 : F.R.S. : Member of the Royal Asiatic Society. President of it in 1858 : as also, in 1863, of the Statistical Society, and of the Society of Arts. In Bombay he advocated education for the natives, and, in Parliament, urged the rights and privileges of the Indian Army : he was the author of numerous works on scientific and literary questions, and contributed largely to the transactions of learned Societies on the ancient history, antiquities, statistics, geology, natural history and meteorology of India : died June 16, 1872.

SYM, JOHN MUNRO (1839–   )

Born Feb. 15, 1839 : son of Rev. John Sym of the Free Church : educated at Edinburgh High School and University : entered the Bengal Army, 1858, and became Maj-General, 1896 : served on N.W. Frontier : at Umbeyla, 1863 : Hazara, 1868 : in Afghan war, 1878–80 : Brevet-Lt-Colonel : Hazara, 1888, in command of 1st Brigade : C.B. : Miranzai, 1896, in command of 1st Brigade.

SYMES, SIR EDWARD SPENCE (1852–1901)

I.C.S. : son of E. S. Symes, M.D. : educated at University College School and University College, London : went out to

N.W.P., 1875 : transferred to Burma, 1876 : Junior Secretary to Government, 1880 : Settlement Secretary and Secretary to the Chief Commissioner, 1882, 1886 : and Chief Secretary from 1897 : Member of the Legislative Council, Burma : C.I.E., 1886 : K.C.I.E., 1900 : died at Rangoon, Jan. 8, 1901.

SYMONS, SIR WILLIAM PENN
(1843–1899)

Maj-General : born July 17, 1843 : son of William Symons : educated privately : joined the 24th regt., 1863 : served in the Kafir and Zulu wars, 1878–9 : to India, 1880 : A.A.G. for Musketry, Madras, 1882 : D.A.Q.M.G. in the Burmese expedition, 1885–6 : commanded mounted infantry : Brig-General in the Chin Field Force : commanded the Burma column in Chin-Lushai expedition, 1889 : C.B., 1890 : A.A.G. for musketry, Bengal, 1893 : commanded as Brigadier in the Panjab, 1895 : a Brigade in Waziristan, 1894–5 : Tochi, 1898 : and a'Division in Tirah, 1897–8 : K.C.B., 1898 : commanded the Forces in Natal, 1899 : died Oct. 23, 1899, of his wounds at assault of Talana Hill.

TAGORE, MAHARSHI DEBENDRA, NATH (1818–1905)

Eldest son of Dwarka Nath Tagore (*q.v.*) : born 1818 : educated at the Hindu College : in early manhood he took a strong religious turn, and founded, in 1839, a Society for the Knowledge of Truth, with a Journal : was a leader in the Hindu Deistic movement : joined the Brahmo Samaj in 1842, and introduced the Brahmic Covenant in 1843 : his impassioned eloquence conduced greatly to his success as a reviver of religion : he was the spiritual father of Keshab Chandra Sen (*q.v.*) : suffered great losses of property at one time, but, later, recovered his principal landed estates : during his prolonged life, he maintained his interest in spiritual subjects, and, though he was not an orthodox Hindu in faith and practice, was immensely revered as a great religious guide (*rishi*), living for the last few years of his saintly life in religious retirement : died Jan. 19, 1905.

TAGORE, DWARKA NATH
(1795, ? –1846)

Second son of Ram Mani Tagore : educated at Sherbourne's School, Calcutta, and by a private tutor : entered and left Government service : established, 1834, the firm of Carr, Tagore & Co. : helped to found the Union Bank and the Landholders' Society : used his ample means in active philanthropy and the advancement of his countrymen : agitated for the abolition of Suttee, the freedom of the Press, the repeal of the " Black Act " : he showed profuse hospitality, and was constantly consulted by the Governor-General : he was the first native J.P. He left for Europe in Jan. 1841 : travelled on the Continent : was entertained in England by Queen Victoria, and the Court of Directors, who gave him a medal in recognition of his services to his country. On his return to India, in 1842, he refused to perform the expiatory ceremony of *Prayaschittra*. He again visited England in 1845 : was received as previously : died in London on Aug. 1, 1846, and was buried at Kensal Green. The *Times* and other newspapers dwelt on his unbounded philanthropy : at a public meeting held at Calcutta in his honour, an endowment fund, called after him, was established to give native youths of India the benefit of European education.

TAGORE, SIR JOTINDRA MOHAN MAHARAJA BAHADUR (1831–)

Eldest son of Huro Coomar Tagore : born in 1831 : studied at the Hindu College, and under Capt. D. L. Richardson (*q.v.*), as private tutor : early in life he composed Bengali dramas : was for some years Hony. Secretary of the British Indian Association, and its President in 1879 and 1891 : Member of the Bengal Legislative Council, 1870 and 1872, of the Governor-General's Legislative Council, 1877, 1879, 1881 ; of the Education Commission, 1882, and the Jury Commission, 1893 : was made Raja Bahadur, 1871 ; Maharaja, 1877 ; C.S.I., 1879 ; K.C.S.I., 1882 ; Maharaja Bahadur, 1890, and in Jan. 1891 the title of Maharaja was made hereditary in his family. He was for years J.P. for Calcutta, Hony. Magistrate, Member of the Calcutta Corporation, Fellow of the Calcutta University, Trustee of the Indian Museum, Governor of the Mayo Hospital. He inherited extensive landed property in several districts, and by a decree of the Privy Council holds a life interest in the estates of his uncle, Prasanna Kumar Tagore (*q.v.*). He has made munificent endowments and donations for religious, charitable and educational purposes, and has for years held a leading position in Bengal, being universally respected. A strictly orthodox Hindu, devoted to religious observances, he has, with advancing age, sought retirement from public affairs, but is often consulted by Government.

TAGORE, PRASANNA KUMAR
(1801–1868)

Son of Gopi Mohan Tagore : educated partly at home, partly at Sherbourne's School, Calcutta, in English, and at the old Hindu College : though possessing considerable landed property, he joined the legal profession, became the Government Pleader, made a very large income, and wrote on legal subjects. Lord Dalhousie appointed him in 1854 clerk assistant to the Legislative Council of the Governor-General, where he showed conspicuous ability and, later, was made a Member of the same Council. He gained a high reputation for his public spirit, liberality, and prominence in public affairs. In 1831 he started a native newspaper, *The Reformer*, to advocate the interests of natives. He was a Governor of the Hindu College : Member of the Council of Education, of the Bengal Legislative Council, and of the Calcutta Municipal Corporation : a founder of the British Indian Association in 1851, and in 1867 its President : Fellow of the Calcutta University : Governor of the Mayo Hospital : he possessed a very fine library : C.S.I. in 1866 : died in 1868, disinheriting his son Gayendra Mohan Tagore, on the latter's conversion to Christianity : his marble statue is in the vestibule of the Senate House at Calcutta.

TAGORE, MAHARAJ KUMAR PRODYOT COOMAR (1873–)

Born Oct. 21, 1873 : son of Raja Sir Sourindro Mohan Tagore, Kt.: C.I.E. : adopted son of Maharaja Bahadur Sir Jotindra Mohan Tagore, K.C.S.I. : educated at the Hindu School, Calcutta, and privately by Mr. F. Peacock, Barrister-at-law : holds a number of honorary appointments : is Hony. Presidency Magistrate : a Municipal Commissioner for Calcutta : Trustee of the Indian Museum and of the Victoria Memorial Hall : Hony. Secy. of the British India Association : represented the city of Calcutta at the Coronation of H.M. the King-Emperor, 1902.

TAGORE, MAHARAJA RAMA NATH
(1800–1877)

Brother of Dwarka Nath Tagore (*q.v.*) educated at Sherbourne's School : was Treasurer, 1829, of the Union Bank until its failure. He adopted the theistic views of Raja Ram Mohan Roy, and took a prominent part in the affairs of the Brahma Sabha. He was early interested in politics and political economy, helped to found a newspaper, the *Indian Reformer*, and the British Indian Association, of which he was President for about 10 years : was a Member of the Bengal Legislative Council, 1866, and of the Governor-General's Legislative Council, 1873 : was made Raja, 1873 : C.S.I. 1874, and Maharaja on Jan. 1, 1877 : was also a Member of the Calcutta Corporation : Fellow of the Calcutta University and Governor of the College : died June 1, 1877.

TAGORE, RAJA SIR SOURINDRO MOHAN (1840–)

Younger brother of Maharaja Bahadur Sir Jotindra Mohan Tagore (*q.v.*) : born in 1840 : educated at the Hindu College. At 16 he began the study of music, both English and Bengali : established, 1871, the Bengal Music School, and founded, 1881, the Bengal Academy of Music : collected books, and published works, on music and musical instruments, encouraging the science in every way : Doctor in Music of Oxford in 1896, and of the Universities of Philadelphia and Utrecht : received titles of honour, with knighthood, from most of the sovereigns of Europe, and the title of Nawab Shahzada from the Shah of Persia : Knight Bachelor of the United Kingdom : Fellow of the Calcutta University : Honorary Magistrate, and J.P. : has also studied Sanskrit, and published translations.

TALBOT, SIR ADELBERT CECIL
(1845–)

Born June 3, 1845 : son of Hon. and Rev. W. W. C. Talbot : educated at Eton and Woolwich : entered the Royal Artillery : Lt-Colonel in Indian Staff Corps : in the Political Department in India : Consul-General, Bushire : Deputy Secretary to the Government of India in the Foreign Department : Resident in Kashmir : accompanied the second son of the Amir of Afghanistan to England, 1895 : C.I.E., 1885 : K.C.I.E., 1895.

TALBOT, HON. GERALD CHETWYND (1819–1885)

Born Oct. 3, 1819 : son of second Earl Talbot : originally in the Ceylon Civil Service : Private Secretary from Aug. 1856, to April, 1858, to Lord Canning, when Governor-General : Private Secretary, 1858, to Lord Stanley, when Secretary of State for India : Director-General of the Military Store Department at the India Office, 1860–79 : died Feb. 13, 1885.

TALEYARKHAN, PESTONJI JEHANGIR, KHAN BAHADUR (1833–)

Born 1833 : of an old and historical Parsi family : educated at the Elphinstone Institute and College : joined the Education Department as Assistant Professor : edited the *Rast Goftar* : became Alienation Settlement Officer : President, in the Baroda State, of the " Sirdars' Commission," to inquire into their grievances : and Military, Settlement, and Political Officer in Baroda, 1875 : made Khan Bahadur in 1879 : C.I.E. in 1882 : resigned the Baroda service, 1883 : appointed *Talukdari* Settlement Officer in Gujarat, etc.

TALEYARKHAN, SORABJI JEHANGIR (1836–1900)

A scholar of the Elphinstone Institution, Bombay : in Government service as Assistant Settlement Officer : joined the Baroda State Service and rose to be a Judge : introduced the Abkari system into the State : wrote the *Representative Men of India* : died Oct. 19, 1900.

TANNER, SIR ORIEL VIVEASH (1832–)

Entered the Bombay Army, 1851, and became Lt-General, 1892 : served in the Indian mutiny, 1858 : Afghan war, 1878–80 : commanded Quetta Division, 1883–8 : K.C.B., 1882.

TANTIA TOPI (1819 ? –1859)

A rebel leader in the mutiny : a Mahratta Brahman of Poona, in the service of Nana Sahib : he instigated the Cawnpur massacre of June 27, 1857 : commanded at the battle of Bithur on Aug. 16, won by Havelock after the re-occupation of Cawnpur : with the Gwalior Contingent,he made General Windham (*q.v.*) retreat from Cawnpur, but was defeated by Sir Colin Campbell : with the Rani of Jhansi he was besieged by Sir Hugh Rose at Jhansi, but escaped and collected a force of 20,000 men, which Sir Hugh utterly routed : he intrigued against Sindia and seized the fortress of Gwalior, but Sir Hugh Rose retook it : he escaped into Central India, was defeated by Brigadier Robert Napier : evading pursuit for 10 months in Central India, Rajputana and Bundelkund, he was caught by Major Meade (*q.v.*) in the jungles on April 7, 1859, tried, convicted and executed on the 18th. He has been described as cruel and crafty and the only rebel leader who showed a real genius for war.

TARANATH TARKAVACHASPATI (1812–1885)

Born 1812 : educated at the Sanskrit College, Calcutta : went to Benares to study Vedanta philosophy : taught Sanskrit at his native village Kalna, Burdwan : made Professor of Grammar at the Sanskrit College : gained a reputation in Europe and India by his publication of ancient Sanskrit manuscripts : his Sanskrit dictionary occupied him for 12 years, and cost about Rs. 80,000 : a monumental work, highly esteemed by European and Indian scholars : known as a great grammarian : died 1885.

TARKABARGIS, PREM CHAND (1806–1867)

Received his early education privately : studied the higher branches of literature in the Sanskrit College, Calcutta, under H. H. Wilson (*q.v.*) : was a favourite pupil, winning his esteem by proficiency in grammar, and translating Bengali passages into Sanskrit verse : was for 32 years Professor of Rhetoric in the Sanskrit College, discharging his duties with such zeal, assiduity and success as to gain the highest approbation of the Government, and public regard : he helped James Prinsep (*q.v.*) in bringing to light the pur-port of many old records of great historical value,and deciphering ancient inscriptions : he left commentaries on difficult poems and dramas : died 1867.

TARKAPANCHANAN JAGANNATH
(1695 ? ? –1806 ?)

A very distinguished member of the race of Pandits, who flourished in Bengal in the early days of British rule : son of Rudradeva Bhattacharji, a poor Brahmin of Tribeni, Hughli : the date of his birth is based on tradition. He had a wonderful memory, and became a remarkable logician and unrivalled in his knowledge of Hindu law : was consulted by Sir W, Jones (*q.v.*) and Harrington (*q.v.*) : held in great respect by the highest Hindu nobles and the Hindu community : had a free college for students : left a great reputation as a scholar : died at a very great age in 1806.

TATA, JAMSETJI NASARWANJI
(1839–1904)

Born in 1839 at Nowsari in Gujarat : educated at the Elphinstone College : a successful and philanthropic merchant of Bombay: founder of the firm of Tata & Co. at Bombay, with branches in the Far East, Europe and America. After losing one fortune, he acquired a second. He was a pioneer of the cotton manufacturing industry in Western India : made the Alexandra mills at Bombay : built the Empress mills at Nagpur and the Swadeshi mill : aimed at developing other Indian industries, such as silk culture in Mysore, the working of iron and copper ore in the Central Provinces, and built the Taj Mahal Palace Hotel at Bombay : he travelled widely, knew England well, and sought no honour : his ambition was to create an Institute of Research, with a view to provide new careers for promising youths and to promote the development of the resources of India : until this Institute could be started, on a financial basis of £14,000 a year, he intended to endow a Trust for sending Indian students to London, to complete their education, and offered to the Government of India properties producing a large annual income for an Institute of Scientific Research in India : which it is proposed to establish at Bangalore. He died at Nauheim, May 19, 1904.

TAWNEY, CHARLES HENRY
(1837–)

Son of Rev. RichardTawney : educated at Rugby and Trinity College, Cambridge : Scholar : Senior Classic, 1860 : Fellow of Trinity College, 1860 : for many years Professor and President of the Presidency College, Calcutta, and Registrar of the Calcutta University : officiated thrice as Director of Public Instruction, Bengal : author of several translations from the Sanskrit : C.I.E. : Librarian of the India Office : retired, 1903.

TAW SEIN KO (1864–)

Son of Taw Kheng Sun. merchant : born Dec. 7, 1864 : educated at Rangoon College, Christ's College, Cambridge : studied law at the Inner Temple : appointed Government Translator, Burma, 1888 : Assistant Secretary to the Government of Burma, 1889 : Government Archæologist and Adviser on Chinese affairs, 1899 : was instrumental in keeping the Burma-Chinese frontier quiet during the Boxer rebellion of 1900, and in the election and installation of the Buddhist Archbishop of Upper Burma, 1903 : has written the following works : *Mahajanaka Jataka : Kalyani Inscriptions, Handbook of the Burmese Language, suggested Reforms for China.*

TAYLER, WILLIAM (1808–1892)

I.C.S. : born April 8, 1808 : son of Archdale Wilson Tayler : educated at Charterhouse, and Christ Church, Oxford : went to Bengal in the E.I. Co.s Civil Service 1829 : Postmaster-General, Bengal : Commissioner of Patna, 1855 : in the mutiny his measures were so regarded by the highest authorities as so injudicious and improper that he was suspended from his appointment, and given another appointment of lower rank : after issuing violent pamphlets and failing on appeal to obtain redress, he resigned the service, 1859 : he appealed many times subsequently to Secretaries of State : he found supporters, but obtained no official revision of his case : retired to England, 1867 : died March 8, 1892 : wrote pamphlets on his case, *Thirty-eight Years in India*, 1878–81, *Justice in Excelsis*, 1870, etc.

TAYLOR, SIR ALEXANDER
(1826-   )

General, R.E : born 1826 : son of William Taylor : educated at Hofuzl, Switzerland, and Addiscombe : entered the Bengal Engineers in 1843 : served through the Satlaj campaign of 1845-6, and the Panjab campaign of 1848-9, being present at the siege of Multan, and at Gujarat : in the Public Works Department in 1849 : in the mutiny he was present throughout the siege and capture of Delhi, as Assistant Engineer to Baird Smith (*q.v.*) : he commanded the Engineers at the siege and capture of Lucknow : severely wounded : C.B. in 1858 : commanded the Engineers in the Umbeyla campaign, 1863 : Secretary to the Panjab Government, in the P.W.D. between 1865 and 1872 : President of the Defence Committee of India, 1876-8 : Lt-General, and K.C.B., in 1877 : General in 1878 : President of the Royal Engineering College, Cooper's Hill, 1880-96 : G.C.B. in 1889.

TAYLOR, GEORGE NOBLE
(1820-1903)

I.C.S. : born 1820 : son of General Sir Henry G. A. Taylor : educated at Haileybury : went to Madras in 1840 : held subordinate appointments before, until in 1863 he was made special Commissioner for Railways at Calcutta, to report upon affairs of the E. I. Railway, and held a similar post at Bombay : was Member of the Supreme Council, 1865-70 : died March 4, 1903.

TAYLOR, SIR HENRY GEORGE ANDREW (1784-1876)

General : born in 1784 : entered the Madras Army in 1798 : in 1803 was at Assaye and Argaum, and at Gawilghar, Dec. 15, 1805 : in 1809, under Sir Barry Close : served many years in the Commissariat up to 1822 : under Sir J. Doveton against the Pindaris : was Town Major at Madras, as Lt-Colonel, 1825 : Brigadier at Vellore, 1828 : commanded the Northern Division of the Army in India, 1832-7 : suppressed rebellions in the Vizagapatam and Ganjam districts : retired, 1838 : C.B., 1839 : General in 1857 : K.C.B., 1862 : G.C.B., 1873 : died Feb. 9, 1876,

TAYLOR, JOHN HENRY
(1822-1887)

Son of George Ledwell Taylor, Architect to the Admiralty : educated at Blackheath School : entered the Merchant Service, 1839 : was well known as Captain of the *Renown* and *Trafalgar*, two of Green's Liners between London and Calcutta : R.N.R. : Master Attendant, Madras, 1874-87 : Sheriff of Madras, 1885 -86 : Trustee of the Harbour Board Trust, 1886 : author of *The Law of Storms* : died 1887.

TAYLOR, JOSEPH (1793 ?-1835)

Arrived in India, 1808, in the Engineers : Garrison Engineer at Agra : Executive Engineer at Dinapur : Civil Architect at Fort William : Acting Chief Engineer : Superintending Engineer N.W.P., 1830 : reduced many small forts near Agra occupied by refractory *zamindars* : repaired the Taj at Agra, and Akbar's tomb at Sikandra, besides constructing other works of beauty and utility : was a volunteer at Hatras, 1817 : at Bhartpur, 1825-6 : Brevet-Major : Lt-Colonel, 1831 : died April 20, 1835.

TAYLOR, PHILIP MEADOWS
(1808-1876)

Colonel : born Sep. 25, 1808 : son of Philip Meadows Taylor, merchant : went to Bombay, at 15, to a commercial house. but left it and entered the Nizam's military service, 1824, to which he reverted after a period in the civil branches. He was the *Times'* correspondent in India, 1840-53. In 1841 the Nizam's Government appointed him to administer, during a long minority, the principality of the young Raja of Shorapur. He raised this state to a very prosperous condition until 1853. when the dissipated Raja acceded, Taylor was given charge of a district, and in the mutiny kept the Booldana District in N. Berar quiet, without troops : Commissioner of Shorapur in 1858 : retired in 1860 : C.S.I. in 1869 : died May 13, 1876 : wrote several books showing great knowledge of Indian life and character : the *Confessions of a Thug*, 1839 ; *Tara, a Mahratta Tale*, 1863 ; *Ralph Darnell*, 1865 ; *Tippoo Sultan, a Tale of the Mysore War*, 1840 ; *A Noble Queen*, 1878 : a *Manual of the History of India* : *Seeta*, and other books, besides addresses and lectures on

Indian subjects : his autobiography, *The Story of my Life*, was published by his daughter after his death.

TAYLOR, REYNELL GEORGE
(1822–1886)

Son of Thomas William Taylor, Lieutenant-Governor of Sandhurst : born Jan. 25, 1822 : educated privately and at Sandhurst : entered the Indian cavalry in 1840 : was in the Gwalior campaign, 1843, at Punniar : Adjutant of the Body Guard : at Mudki in the first Sikh war. 1845 : Assistant to the Superintendent at Ajmir : in 1847 was under Sir H, Lawrence at Lahore, and in charge of Peshawar and Sikh troops: occupied Bannu in 1847–8 with a Sikh force : in 1848 was at the siege of Multan, besieged Lukkee and took it, Jan. 11, 1849 : promoted Captain and Major : in charge of Dera Ismail Khan : commanded the Guide Corps in 1855 : in charge of Kangra in the mutiny : Commissioner of the Derajat, 1859 : in the Waziri expedition, 1860 : Commissioner of Peshawar, 1862 : in political charge in the Umbeyla campaign, 1863 : C.B. : Commissioner of Umbala, 1865 : of Umritsar, 1870 : C.S.I., 1866 : retired, 1877, as Maj.-General : General, 1880 : died Feb. 28, 1886. He was called the " Bayard of the Panjab," and greatly beloved by the natives, who regarded him as their " good angel " : established a Mission of the Church Missionary Society at Dera Ismail Khan, and was deeply religious throughout his career : he wrote papers on military and political subjects.

TAYLOR, SIR WILLIAM (1843_   )

Born April 5, 1843 : educated at Glasgow University : entered Army Medical Department, 1864 : served in Canada, 1865–9 ; in India, 1870–80, and 1892–3 : Jowaki expedition, Burma campaign. 1886–7 : Attaché to the Japanese Army in China-Japan war : P.M.O. in Ashanti expedition and Khartoum expedition, at Omdurman : P.M.O. of the Forces in India, 1898–1901 : Director-General, Army Medical Service, since 1901 : C.B., 1898 : K.C.B., 1902,

TEIGNMOUTH, JOHN SHORE, FIRST BARON (1751–1834)

I.C.S. : Governor-General : born Oct. 8, 1751 : son of Thomas Shore : educated at Harrow : reached Calcutta in 1769 as a writer in the E. I. Co.'s Civil Service : became Member of the Revenue Council, Calcutta, 1775–80 : Member of the Committee of Revenue : Revenue Commissioner in Dacca and Bihar : Member of the Supreme Council, 1787–9 : wrote copiously on Bengal revenue affairs, in favour of a *zamindari* system, but opposed to the permanency of the revenue settlement, which Cornwallis introduced : assisted Cornwallis in many reforms : returned to England, 1790 : created Baronet, 1792 : Governor-General of India, Oct. 28, 1793, to March 12, 1798 : adopted a policy of non-interference, as ordered from England : but deposed Wazir Ali (*q.v.*) and substituted Saadat Ali, as Nawab of Oudh : met a mutiny of the officers of the Indian Army, 1795–6, with concessions : President of the Asiatic Society of Bengal, 1794 : F.S.A. : made Baron Teignmouth, 1798 : appointed Member of the Board of Control, 1807–28, and Privy Councillor : gave evidence before Parliamentary Committees on Indian affairs : joined " the Clapham Sect " : was President of the British and Foreign Bible Society, 1804–34 : died Feb. 14, 1834 : wrote in *Asiatic Researches*, the *Christian Observer* : published *Memoirs, etc. of Sir William Jones*, 1804 : and edited his works.

TEJPAL, GOKULDAS (1822–1867)

His father began life at an early age as a hawker in Bombay, with his brother, who was 5 years older, and amassed a small fortune, which he left to Gokuldas at his death in 1833. His uncle, too, left him his fortune. He prospered as a merchant in Bombay. He was chiefly known for his charities, which included a Hospital named after him. At his death he left large sums of money in charity for various institutions, including a boarding school and several other schools. He died in 1867.

TELANG, KASHINATH TRIMBACK
(1850–1893)

Born Aug. 30, 1850 : a Sarasvat Gond Brahman of good family in Thana, in the Bombay Presidency : son of Bapu Telang : adopted by his father's elder brother : educated at the Elphinstone High School : Fellow of the Elphinstone College under

E E

Mr. K. M. Chatfield : a teacher in the Elphinstone College, 1867-72, until he joined the bar as an Advocate : M.A. in 1868, and LL.B. in 1871 : studied English literature, philosophy and political economy, and became an accomplished public speaker and writer. He was also highly proficient in Sanskrit, and translated the *Bhagavad Gita* into English verse for Max Müller's " Sacred Books of the East " : was very successful at the bar, and was frequently consulted by the Judges on points of Hindu Law. In politics he was generally on the side of the Opposition, and criticised the Salt Bill, the Revenue Jurisdiction Bill, the License Tax and the Cotton Duties : appointed a Law Professor, and a Fellow of the Bombay University, of which he ultimately became Vice-Chancellor. In 1882 he was a Member of the Education Commission : made a C.I.E. : in 1884 he became a member of the Bombay Legislative Council, and in 1889 a Judge of the High Court, Bombay. He helped to organize the Indian National Congress in 1885. In 1892 he was elected President of the Bombay branch of the Royal Asiatic Society : contributed to the *Indian Antiquary* : as lawyer, politician, scholar and social reformer he deserved well of his country : he died Sep. 1, 1893 : he wrote *Gleanings from Mahratta Chronicles*.

TEMPLE, SIR RICHARD, BARONET
(1826–1902)

I.C.S : eldest son of Richard Temple, of the Nash, Kempsey, Worcestershire : born March 8, 1826 : educated at Rugby and Haileybury : arrived in India, Jan. 1847 : he was soon transferred to the Panjab and chosen to be Secretary to the Panjab Government. In 1860 he became Chief Assistant to the Financial Members of Council, Mr. James Wilson (*q.v.*) and Mr. Samuel Laing (*q.v.*), Member of the Bengal Indigo Commission and other Commissions : in 1862 he was appointed Chief Commissioner of the Central Provinces, where he " initiated good government " : Resident at Hyderabad, 1867 : Foreign Secretary to the Government of India, 1868 : Financial Member of Council, 1868–74, taking a leading part in advocating a legal tender gold currency for India. In Jan. 1874 he was appointed by Lord Northbrook to superintend the relief operations in the

famine districts of Bengal, and was Lieutenant-Governor of Bengal, April, 1874, to Jan. 1877. This was the first occasion on which complete measures were taken by Government to combat famine. The expenditure was very large, but success was fully attained. In Jan. 1877 Temple was deputed by the Government of India to Madras and Bombay, to advise on the famine-relief operations required in those Presidencies. He entered on the Governorship of Bombay on May 1, 1877 : despatched thence the Indian troops to Malta in 1878, and afforded great assistance in the movements connected with the Afghan war. His statue was erected in Bombay by public subscription. He retired to England in March, 1880, to contest East Worcestershire as a Conservative, but was unsuccessful. He subsequently sat in Parliament for the Evesham Division of Worcestershire, 1885-92, and the Kingston Division of Surrey, 1892-5. For some years he was Vice-Chairman and Chairman of the Finance Committee of the London School Board. He travelled largely, and presided over and addressed many scientific and religious Societies and Associations connected with India. Among his literary works were : *India in 1880* : *Men and Events of my Time in India*, 1882 ; *Oriental Experiences*, 1883 ; *Cosmopolitan Essays*, 1886 ; *Journals kept in Hyderabad, Sikhim and Kashmir* ; *The Story of my Life*, 1896 ; *A Bird's-eye View of Picturesque India*, 1898 ; *John Lawrence* ; *James Thomason*. He was made a C.S.I., 1866 ; K.C.S.I., 1867 ; a Baronet, 1876, for his famine services, and G.C.S.I., Jan. 1878 : also D.C.L. of Oxford, LL.D. of Cambridge, and F.R.S. On Jan. 8, 1896, he was sworn a member of the Privy Council, and retired from Parliament. He died at Heath Brow, Hampstead, on March 15, 1902. His activity and energy of mind and body, and the enormous capacity for work which had distinguished him in India were maintained to the last. His kindness of heart, geniality and moderation made him generally popular throughout his career.

TEMPLE, SIR RICHARD CARNAC,
BARONET (1850-)

Born Oct. 15, 1850 : son of Sir Richard Temple, *Bart.* (*q.v.*), whom he succeeded in 1902 : educated at Harrow and Trinity Hall, Cambridge : entered the Army,

1871, and Indian Staff Corps, 1877 : Lt-Colonel, 1897 : served in Afghan campaign, 1878-9 : Burma war, 1887-9 : President, Rangoon Municipality, 1891 : Chief Commissioner, Andaman Islands, 1894-1904 : author (with E. H. Man) of *Andamanese Language* (with Mrs. Steel), of *Wide-awake Stories, Legends of the Panjab*, 2 vols,; Editor of *Fallon's Hindustani Proverbs, Burnell's Devil Worship of the Tuluvas* : Editor and Proprietor of *The Indian Antiquary* : C.I.E., 1894.

TENDOOK PULGER, RAJA
(? -1902)

A Lepcha by birth : early became manager of Chibu Lama's estate in Darjeeling District : in 1875-6 accompanied Sir R. Temple on his travels in Sikhim : was made Revenue Collector of Kalimpong estate about 1879 : Honorary Magistrate of Darjeeling District in 1885 : during the Sikhim expedition of 1888, he rendered the greatest service to the Intelligence Department, and otherwise throughout the campaign : was made Raja in Jan. 1889 : his loyalty on the N.E. frontier and services to Government were rewarded, on his retirement, with pension and a grant of land : died in 1902.

TENNANT, SIR JAMES (1789-1854)

Son of William Tennant : born April 21, 1789 : educated at Great Marlow military school : to India as a cadet, 1805 : at the capture of the Cape, 1806 : joined the Bengal Artillery, 1806 : at Kalinjar, 1812 : in the Nipal war, 1814-5 : in the Pindari-Mahratta war, 1817-9 : Adjutant-General of Artillery, 1824 : at siege of Bhartpur, 1825-6 : in charge of gunpowder factory at Ishapur, 1835 : on the Special Committee of Artillery Officers, 1836 : Lt-Colonel, 1837 : commanded Cawnpur Division of Artillery, 1842 : as Brig-General, commanded the Artillery 'in the Panjab Campaign, 1848-9, at Chilianwala and Gujarat : C.B., 1849 : commanded Jhelum Division, 1852 : K.C.B. : died at Mian Mir, March 6, 1854.

THACKERAY, SIR EDWARD TALBOT (1836-)

Born Oct. 19, 1836 : son of Rev. Francis Thackeray : educated at Marlborough and Addiscombe : entered the Royal Engineers, 1854, and became Colonel, 1884 : retired, 1888 : served in the Indian mutiny, 1857-8 : at the siege of Delhi, where he gained the V.C. for his daring in extinguishing a fire in the Delhi magazine enclosure, while under fire : at capture of Lucknow, 1858 : in the Rohilkund Field Force, 1858 : Afghan war, 1879-80 : severely wounded : held appointments in P.W.D. : commanded Bengal Sappers : C.B., 1886 : K.C.B., 1897 : F.R.G.S. : wrote *Two Indian Campaigns, Biographies of Officers of the Bengal Engineers*.

THACKERAY, WILLIAM (1778-1823)

Born 1778 : son of William Makepeace Thackeray, Collector of Sylhet, a noted elephant-hunter : uncle of the novelist : went out to India, 1796, as a writer in the Company's Civil Service at Madras : rose rapidly, partly through his mastery of the Telugu language : Translator to Government : Assistant in 1800 to Sir Thomas Munro in the settlement of the ceded territories : won his regard, and, under his training became one of the most notable administrators of his time : appointed, 1803, Collector to a southern district which included Tinnivelly : soon after made a Judge at Masulipatam : employed by Lord William Bentinck to inquire into the rural conditions of Southern India, later as sole Commissioner on the western coast : Member of the Board of Revenue, 1806 : by his part in the land settlement of India, has a claim to be considered as one of the builders of our Indian Empire : again engaged, 1818, in inquiry as to administration of the N. frontier of Madras : became Judge in the High Court of the Province : Provisional Member of Council, 1828 : President of the Board of Revenue : suffered from the climate for some time : died on a voyage to the Cape, Jan. 11, 1823.

THACKERAY, WILLIAM MAKEPEACE (1811-1863)

The novelist : was born in Calcutta on July 18, 1811 : son of Richmond Thackeray, of the E. I. Co,'s Civil Service, who was then Secretary to the Board of Revenue, Bengal, and died Sep. 13, 1815, while Collector of the 24 *Parganas* : he was sent to England as a child in 1817 : died Dec 23/4, 1863.

THACKWELL, COLQUHOUN GRANT ROCHE (1857-   )

Entered the Indian Army, 1878, and became Major, 1898 : served in the Afghan war, 1878–80 : Mahsud-Waziri expedition, 1881 ; Egypt, 1882 : Chitral, 1895 ; N.W. Frontier, 1897 : D.S.O., 1898 : Chief Supply and Transport Officer, Rawal Pindi District.

THACKWELL, SIR EDWARD JOSEPH (1781–1859)

Born Feb. 1, 1781 : son of John Thackwell : entered the Army, 1798 : with the 15th Light Dragoons in the Peninsula : in several battles : at Waterloo : lost his left arm : Brevet Lt-Colonel, 1817 : commanded the 15th Hussars, 1820–32 : K.H., 1834 : commanded the Cavalry in the Afghan war, 1838–9 : at Ghazni : returned from Kabul, 1839 : C.B., 1838 : K.C.B., 1839 : commanded the Cavalry in the Gwalior campaign, 1843 : and at Sobraon, 1846 : Maj-General, 1846 : commanded the Cavalry at Chilianwala and Gujarat, 1849 : G.C.B., 1849 : Inspr-General of Cavalry, 1854 : Lt-General, 1854 : died April 8, 1859 : wrote *Narrative of the Second Sikh War in 1848–49, 1851.*

THANAWALA, KHAN BAHADUR CURSETJI RUSTAMJI (? –1903)

Began as translator of the Supreme Court : became a Subordinate Judge, and interpreter at the trial of the Gaekwar, Malhar Rao, 1875 : Chief Judge at Baroda : Member of Council of the Baroda Administration, during the Gaekwar's absence in Europe : Diwan of the Rutlam State : Khan Bahadur : C.I.E. : died April 24, 1903.

THIBAUT, GEORGE FREDERICK WILLIAM (1848-   )

Born at Heidelberg, 1848 : son of Karl Thibaut, Librarian to the University, and himself son of the celebrated jurist, A. F. J. Thibaut : educated at the Gymnasium, Heidelberg, and the Universities of Heidelberg and Berlin : went to England, 1871 : worked several years as assistant to Max Müller (*q.v.*) : appointed, 1875, Anglo-Sanskrit Professor in the Benares Sanskrit College : Principal of the College, 1879–88 : Professor, Muir Central College, Allahabad, 1888–95 ; Principal there since

1895 : his literary work has been done chiefly in the departments of Indian Philosophy, Astronomy, and Mathematics : his more important publications are, *On the Sulva-sutras,* 1875 : *The Sulva-sutra of Bandhayana,* with translation, 1875 : *The Arthasangraha,* a treatise on Purva Mimamsa, with translation, 1882 : *The Panchasiddhantika,* the astronomical work of Varaha Mihira, with translation (in collaboration with Pandit Sudhakara Dvivedi), 1889 : the *Vedanta sutras,* with Sankara's Commentary, translated (Sacred Books of the East, vols. 34, 38) : Indian Astronomy, Astrology and Mathematics in Bühler's *Encyclopædia of Indian Research,* 1899 : *The Vedanta sutras,* with Ramanuja's Commentary, translated (Sacred Books, etc., vol. 48), 1904 : has edited (with R. Griffith), the "Benares Sanskrit Series," of which more than 100 fasciculi have appeared.

THOMAS, EDWARD (1813–1886)

I.C.S. : numismatist and Indian antiquary : born Dec. 31, 1813 : son of Honoratus Leigh Thomas : educated at Haileybury : went to India, 1832 : was Judge of Sagar : suffered greatly from ill-health : refused the Foreign Secretaryship offered to him in 1852 : retired, 1857 : devoted himself to literary and scientific pursuits : wrote many papers on branches of Indian and old Persian archæology, including Bactrian, Sassanian and Indo-Scythic coins, Indian weights and measures, Sassanian gems and inscriptions, in the Journals of the Royal Asiatic Society and Asiatic Society of Bengal, the *Numismatic Chronicle,* and the *Indian Antiquary* : many of them were collected in his *Chronicles of the Pathan Kings of Delhi,* 1847 : he edited James Prinsep's *Essays on Indian Antiquities* and the *International Numismata Orientalia* : his was a "name recognized over Europe as a prince in Oriental numismatics." He was 25 years treasurer of the Royal Asiatic Society : more than any one, he encouraged the study of Oriental antiquities in England, and rendered great services to archæology : F.R.S. : corresponding member of the French Institute and of the Academy of St. Petersburg : C.I.E. : died Feb. 10, 1886.

THOMAS, FREDERICK WILLIAM
(1867–   )

Born March 21, 1867 : educated at King Edward's School, Birmingham, and Trinity College, Cambridge : Fellow : Assistant Librarian to the India Office, 1898–1903 : Librarian, 1903 : author of *Translation of the Sanskrit Harsa-Carita of Bana* (with Professor Cowell); *British Education in India, Mutual Influence of Muhammadans and Hindus in India*, etc. ett. : Member of Council of the Royal Asiatic Society.

THOMAS, GEORGE (1756 ?–1802)

Born in Ireland about 1756 : a sailor in the Navy : deserted his ship off Madras, 1781 : took native service, and went to Delhi, 1787 : commanded the Army of Begam Samru of Sardhana : left her and commanded forces of Appa Rao : built Georgeghar near Hariana, and established Hansi fort : reconciled to Begam Samru : proclaimed his independence and, from Hansi, ruled over Hissar, Hansi, Sirsa, Rohtak, 1797–9 : became a military power : and had ambitious projects : but the Sikhs and Sindia's General, Perron, attacked him at Georgeghar in force : he fled to Hansi, and had to surrender, 1802 : deposed : *en route* to Calcutta, he died of fever, on board his pinnace at Berhampur, Aug. 22, 1802 : left his widow about £6,000 a year : his military genius, gallantry, and capacity have been acknowledged.

THOMAS, HENRY SULLIVAN (? –   )

I.C.S. : educated at Haileybury, 1853–4 : joined the Madras Civil Service, 1855) Collr-Magte. in several districts : acting Member of the Board of Revenue, 1878 : Revenue Secretary to Government, 1878–9 : second Member, 1881, first Member, of Board, 1884 : Member of Governor-General's Legislative Council, 1882–3–5 : on special duty connected with the Pearl Fisheries, Tuticorin, and Ceylon, 1884 : Fellow, Madras University : retired, 1889 : wrote *The Rod in India*, 1873 ; *Tank Angling in India*, 1887.

THOMAS, JOHN (1757–1801)

Was the first Baptist Missionary in Bengal : born May 16, 1757, at Fairford, Gloucestershire : son of the deacon of the Baptist Chapel there : educated for the medical profession, and obtained an appointment in the Navy as Assistant Surgeon : poverty and debt caused him gladly to accept the post of Surgeon on the *Earl of Oxford*, a ship belonging to the E. I. Co. : sailed for Madras and Calcutta, 1783 : made a second voyage in the same ship, 1786, when he decided to remain in India and become a Missionary to the Bengalis. His friend and patron was Charles Grant (*q.v.*) : he first studied Bengali at Malda, residing there with Mr. Udny, commercial resident at the E. I. Co.'s factory there. After a visit to England, 1792–3, he returned to Bengal with Mr. Carey (*q.v.*) to work under the newly formed Baptist Missionary Society. His career was a sad one : though earnest in his Mission work, he wanted balance, and brought discredit on himself and his work by frequent misunderstandings with his friends and constant money difficulties. He and Carey were employed for a time as indigo factors by Udny : later Thomas was engaged in the sugar trade : but none of his undertakings prospered. Under the strain his mind gave way : though he recovered and resumed indigo cultivation, he was again unfortunate : died of fever at Dinajpur, 1801.

THOMAS, JOHN FRYER (1797–1877)

I.C.S. : born 1797 : educated at Haileybury, 1814–5 : went to Madras, 1816 : became Secretary to Government, Madras, 1844, and Chief Secretary, 1845 : Chief Judge of the *Sadr* Court, Madras : Member of Council, Madras, 1850–55 : held strong views on native education, and supported the Missionaries : died April 7, 1877.

THOMASON, JAMES (1804–1853)

I.C.S. : born May 3, 1804 : son of Rev˙ Thomas Truebody Thomason, Indian Chaplain : educated at Stansted, and Haileybury, 1820–2 : to India, 1822 : Registrar of the *Sadr* Court : Secretary to Government, 1830–2 : Magistrate-Collector of Azimghar, 1832–7 : Secretary to the Agra Government, 1837–41 : Member of the Board of Revenue, 1841 : Foreign Secretary to the Government of India, 1842–3 : Lieutenant-Governor of the N.W.P., Dec. 1843, to Sep. 1853 : died at Bareli, Sep. 29, 1853 : appointed Governor of Madras on the day of h s death : was a very successful administrator in every branch, and greatly advanced the N.W.P.

THOMPSON, SIR AUGUSTUS RIVERS (1829-1890)

I.C.S.: son of J. Powney Thompson, B.C.S.: and great grandson of George Nisbet Thompson, Private Secretary to Warren Hastings in June, 1783 : he was educated at Eton (where he both rowed in the Eight and played in the Cricket Eleven), and at Haileybury : went to India in 1850 : was Secretary to the Bengal Government, 1869–75 : Chief Commissioner of British Burma, 1875–8 : Member of the Supreme Council, 1878–82 : Lieutenant-Governor of Bengal, 1882–7 : K.C.S.I., 1885. He was strongly opposed to the " Ilbert Bill," as it was called—a project of law, emanating from the Government of India, for removing the bar which then existed upon the investment of native magistrates in the interior with powers over European British subjects : and his opposition conduced to the modification of the proposed measure, which was producing great excitement and race-feeling. He suffered greatly from ill-health, and died at Gibraltar on Nov. 27, 1890.

THOMPSON, GEORGE (1804-1878)

Son of Henry Thompson : born June 18, 1804 : best known as a public agitator against slavery in the British Colonies, for which cause he lectured in large towns in Great Britain and visited America in 1834 and 1851, and in the civil war of 1860–4 : also joined the Anti-Corn League. He visited India in 1842 and worked with the Bengal Landholders' Society, regarding what he called the Hill Cooly system of slavery, the oppressive land-tax, the opium and salt monopolies : was a prominent member of the British India Society of London, which was formed in 1840 : lectured on Indian topics in England, with a view to advance the claims of the Indian people to better government, and formed a Branch of this Society in Calcutta in 1843. In India he took up the case of the ex-Raja of Satara, then at Benares, and was appointed Ambassador of the Emperor of Delhi : again visited India in 1855, but left it in the mutiny. He was also

a member of the National Parliamentary Reform Association : was M.P. for the Tower Hamlets, 1847–52 : died Oct. 7, 1878 : was an eloquent speaker and said to have been brilliant in conversation.

THOMSON, GEORGE (1799-1886)

Son of George Thomson : born Sep. 19, 1799 : educated at Addiscombe : went to Calcutta in the Engineers, 1818 : joined the Bengal Sappers and Miners, 1820 : in the Burmese war, 1824–6, took Arakan, 1825 : did various important works in India as Executive Engineer P.W.D. : in 1838 was Chief Engineer of the Army of the Indus marching on Afghanistan ; bridged the Indus at Rohri-Sukkur in 11 days : under Keane to Kandahar : proposed the storming of Ghazni : to Kabul, Aug. 1839 : returned to India, in Nov. 1839 : C.B. : Brevet-Major : retired from the service, 1841 : Recruiting Officer at Cork, 1844–61, and Pension Paymaster, 1844–77 : Brevet-Lt-Colonel, 1854 : died Feb. 10, 1886 : wrote *The Storming of Ghazni*, 1840.

THOMSON, SIR GEORGE (1843-1903)

Surgeon Colonel: son of James Thomson: born May 14, 1843 : graduated in medicine at Aberdeen University : entered the Indian Medical Service in 1865 and served in India during the Afghan war : P.M.O, in the Chitral Relief Force and in the Tirah expedition : C.B., 1896 : was Principal Medical Officer of the Lahore District : returned to England, 1898 : K.C.B. in 1898 : died Dec. 23, 1903.

THOMSON, HENRY (1851-)

Maj-General : son of Major James Thomson, R.A. : entered Army Vet. Department, 1871, and, after serving in Egypt for many years, became Inspecting Vet. Surgeon, 1900 : Principal Vet. Officer in India, 1897–1902 : Director-General, Army Vet. Department since 1902 : C.B., 1900.

THOMSON, SIR JAMES (1848-)

I.C.S.: born July 6, 1848 : son of John Thomson : educated at Grammar School and University of Aberdeen : entered the Madras Civil Service, 1871 : Resident in Travancore and Cochin, 1895 : Member of Board of Revenue, 1897 : Member of Madras Council since 1901 : Officiating Governor of Madras, April to Dec. 1904 : K.C.S.I., 1904.

THOMSON, SAMUEL JOHN (1853–)

Born Jan. 7, 1853 : son of J. B. Thomson : educated at Hurstpierpoint and St. Mary's Hospital, London : entered the Indian Medical Service, 1877 : served in Afghan war, 1880, and then devoted himself to sanitary science and epidemiological inquiries : Surg-Major, 1889 : C.I.E., for services connected with plague and famine : Lt-Colonel, 1897 : Sanitary Commissioner, N.W.P., since 1896.

THOMSON, THOMAS (1817–1878)

Born Dec. 4, 1817 : son of Thomas Thomson : educated at Glasgow : studied botany : M.D. : went to Calcutta in the medical service of the E. I. Co., 1840 : curator of the museum of the Asiatic Society : sent to Kabul, 1841 : besieged and taken prisoner at Ghazni, March, 1842 : escaped by bribing : through the Satlaj campaign, 1845–6 : on the Boundary Commission between Kashmir and Chinese Tibet : travelled with Sir J. D. Hooker (*q.v.*) in Sikhim, Assam, etc., on botanical research : they brought out the *Flora Indica*, 1855 : Superintendent of the Botanic Garden, Calcutta, 1854–61 : Professor of Botany, Calcutta : F.L.S. : F.R.G.S. : F.R.S. : wrote *Western Himalaya and Tibet*, 1852, and other works, also for scientific Journals : died April 18, 1878.

THORBURN, SEPTIMUS SMET (1844–)

I.C.S. : born Aug. 12, 1844 : son of D. Thorburn : educated at Cheltenham : entered the Bengal Civil Service, 1865, and retired, 1899 : conducted the Peasant Indebtedness Inquiry, 1895–6 : President, Indian Transport Committee, 1897 : Financial Commissioner, Panjab : author of *Bannu, or our Indian Frontier*; *David Leslie, a Story of the Afghan Frontier*; *Musalmans and Money-lenders*; *The Panjab in Peace and War*, etc. : F.R.G.S. : F.R.A.S.

THORN, SIR WILLIAM (1781–1843)

Born 1781 : joined the 29th Light Dragoons in India, 1799 : served in the Mahratta war under Lord Lake, 1803 : at Laswari, Nov. 1, 1803 : at Delhi, and Deeg, 1804 : Bhartpur, 1805 : in the capture of Mauritius, 1810, and of Java, 1811, and of Palembang in Sumatra, 1812 : returned to England, 1814 : wrote *Memoirs of the Conquest of Java*, etc., 1815, and *A Memoir of the Late War in India*, 1803 to 1806, 1818 : Brevet-Lt-Colonel : knight of the Royal Hanoverian Guelphic Order, 1832 : died Nov. 29, 1843.

THORNHILL, CUDBERT (1723–1809)

Was resident in India some time before 1756 : present during the greater part of the siege of Calcutta : sought shelter with other fugitives at Fulta, thus escaping the Black Hole. Captain Thornhill had traded to almost every part of India, and to Jeddah in the Red Sea : was " an eighteenth-century Sindbad, honourably mentioned by Bruce, the Abyssinian traveller " : was Master Attendant at Calcutta, 1785–1808 : died at Calcutta, Sep. 21, 1809.

THORNHILL, CUDBERT BENSLEY (? –1868)

I.C.S. : educated at Haileybury, 1836–7 : went out to India, 1838 : appointed Inspector of Prisons, N.W. Province, 1853 : in the mutiny, he served throughout the siege of Agra : took part with the Volunteers, and acted as Secretary to the Government : Commissioner of Allahabad, 1861 : Member of the Board of Revenue, N.W.P., 1867 : died at sea, July 1, 1868.

THORNTON, EDWARD (1799–1875)

On the staff of the East India House from 1814 to 1857 : head of the Statistical Department there, 1846–57, and of the Marine Department from 1847 : the pioneer in the systematic collection and publication of Indian statistics : wrote *India, its State and Products*, 1835 ; *Chapters of the Modern History of British India*, 1840 : *History of the British Empire in India*, 1841 to 1858 ; *A Gazetteer of the Countries adjacent to India on the North-West*, 1844 ; *Gazetteer of the Territories under the Government of the E. I. Co.*, 1854 : died 1875.

THORNTON, EDWARD PARRY (1811–1893)

I.C.S.: born Oct. 7, 1811 : son of John Thornton : educated at Charterhouse and

Haileybury, 1828-9 : went to India, 1830, to the N.W.P. : transferred to the Panjab, 1849 : Commissioner of Jhelum : wounded in arresting Nadir Khan of Mandla : suppressed revolt in Hazara, 1857 : Judicial Commissioner of the Panjab, 1888 : C.B., 1860 : retired, 1862 : died Dec. 10, 1893.

THORNTON, SIR JAMES HOWARD
(1834-   )

Son of Major John Thornton : educated at King's College, London, and University of London : M.B. : M.A.C.S., 1855 : entered the Indian Medical Service, 1856, and retired as Surg-General, 1891 : served in the Indian mutiny, 1857-9 : China war, 1880 : Khasia and Jantia Hills, 1862-3 : wounded, in the Bhutan war : Egyptian expedition, 1882 : Suakin expedition as P.M.O., 1885 : Hazara expedition, 1888 : C.B. : author of *Memories of Seven Campaigns* : K.C.B., 1904.

THORNTON, THOMAS HENRY
(1832-   )

I.C.S. : born Oct. 31, 1832 : son of Thomas Thornton : educated at Merchant Taylors' and St. John's College, Oxford : Fellow of St. John's College, 1855-62 : entered the Bengal Civil Service, 1856 : served in the mutiny : Secretary to Panjab Government, 1864-76 : Officiating Foreign Secretary to the Government of India, 1876-7 : Judge of Chief Court, Panjab, 1878-81 : Member of Governor-General's Legislative Council, 1878-81 : Fellow of Calcutta University : C.S.I. : author of *Life and Work of Colonel Sir Robert Sandeman. General Sir Richard Meade, Account of the City of Lahore*, etc.

¡THORNTON, WILLIAM THOMAS
(1813-1880)

Born Feb. 14, 1813, son of Thomas Thornton : educated at Ockbrook : be came a clerk in the E. I. House, 1836, and first Public Works Secretary there, 1858 : C.B., 1873 : wrote largely on economical questions : friend of John Stuart Mill : also published *Indian Public Works and Cognate Indian Topics*, 1875 : and a paper on *Irrigation regarded as a Preventive of Indian Famines* : died June 17, 1880.

THUILLIER, SIR HENRY EDWARD LANDOR (1813-   )

Born July 10, 1813 : son of John Pierre Thuillier : educated at Addiscombe : entered the Bengal Artillery : appointed to the Survey of India, 1836 : Superintendent of Revenue and Topographical Surveys of India, 1847-78 : Surveyor-General of India, 1861-78, when he retired : C.S.I., 1872 : K.B., 1879 : General : F.R.S.

THUILLIER, SIR HENRY RAVEN-SHAW (1838-   )

Born March 26, 1838 : son of General Sir H. E. L. Thuillier (*q.v.*) : educated at Wimbledon and Addiscombe : entered Bengal Engineers, 1857, and retired as Colonel, 1895 : joined the Survey of India Department, 1859 : Surveyor-General of India, 1886-95 : K.C.I.E., 1895.

TILLARD, JOHN ARTHUR (1837-   )

Born Sep. 13, 1837 : son of Philip Tillard : educated at Brighton College and Trinity College, Cambridge : entered the Bengal Artillery, 1857, and became Maj-General, 1891 : served in the Afghan war, 1878-80, at Ahmad Kheyl, in the march from Kabul to Kandahar, and battle of Kandahar : Brevet-Lt-Colonel : Burma expedition, 1886-7 : C.B. : retired, 1895.

TIPPOO, SULTAN (1753-1799)

Born 1753 : commanded a part of his father Hyder Ali's Army in the second Mysore war with the English : the death of his father was kept concealed until Tippoo could, from Malabar, rejoin the Army : he defeated General Matthews at Bednore and put him and others to death : he besieged and took Mangalore, and made a treaty with the English in March, 1784, regaining Canara and Malabar : he attacked Coorg, 1785 : in 1786 he called himself " Padshah," a king : he fought against the Nizam and the Mahrattas, and made peace with them in 1787 : he sent envoys to Turkey and France, with little success : in Dec. 1789 he attacked Travancore ; was repulsed at first, but afterwards inflicted great damage : Cornwallis allied with the Mahrattas and the Nizam against Tippoo, who held his own against General Medows, but lost Malabar :

Cornwallis in person, in 1791, besieged and took Bangalore on March 21 : attacked Seringapatam, but failed and had to retire : he took the Nandidrug and Savandrug forts, and again besieged Seringapatam in Feb. 1792, where, finding resistance hopeless, Tippoo yielded, and made great cessions of money and territory, but kept his throne and capital : Tippoo sought the aid of Zaman Shah, the Afghan ruler, and of the French in the Mauritius, against the English, but obtained little help. Lord Mornington, arriving in India in May, 1798, regarded Tippoo's conduct as openly hostile, and, failing to obtain any satisfaction from correspondence with him, declared war early in 1799. Tippoo's forces were defeated by the English under Generals Harris, Stuart, Baird, and Colonel Arthur Wellesley ; and at the capture of Seringapatam, on May 4, 1799, by the English, Tippoo was killed : his sons were made prisoners and sent to Vellore : the greater part of his territory divided between the E. I. Co. and the Nizam : a portion being made over to the Hindu titular Raja of Mysore. His energy and ability as a ruler were overshadowed by his ferocity, cruelty and vindictiveness, and by the bigotry, fanaticism and duplicity which attach to his memory.

TITCOMB, RIGHT REV. JONATHAN HOLT, D.D. (1819–1887)

Born July 29, 1829 : educated at King's College, and St. Peter's College, Cambridge : Scholar : ordained 1842 : D.D., 1877 : was Secretary of the Christian Vernacular Education Society of India for 3 years : held various charges in the Church in England before he was appointed the first Bishop of Rangoon in 1877 : held the see from 1878 to 1882 : injured by an accident : appointed a Bishop for Northern and Central Europe, 1884–6 : died April 2, 1887 : wrote *Personal Recollections of British Burma, and its Church Mission Work in 1878–9,* on Buddhism, and two works on Religion.

TOD, JAMES (1782–1835)

Son of James Tod : born March 20, 1782 : went to Bengal in 1799 in the E. I. Co.'s service : joined the 2nd European regt. : with the embassy to Sindia, 1805 : while attached to the Resident at Gwalior, 1812–7, he collected much information

of the country : surveyed and mapped Rajputana : in charge of Intelligence Department in the Pindari campaign, 1817 : appointed in 1818 Political Agent in W. Rajput States : retired, 1822–3 : wrote the *Annals and Antiquities of Rajasthan, or the Central and Western Rajput States of India,* 1829–32 ; *Travels in Western India,* published in 1839 : was Librarian to the Royal Asiatic Society, and wrote in the Society's Transactions : Lt-Colonel : died Nov. 17, 1835.

TODD, ELLIOTT D'ARCY
(1808–1845)

Major : son of Fryer Todd : born Jan. 28, 1808 : educated at Ware, London and Addiscombe : joined the Bengal Artillery at Calcutta, 1824 : at the capture of Bhartpur, Jan. 1826 : studied Persian : sent to Persia as Artillery Instructor of the Persian troops, 1833 : Military Secretary to Sir H. L. Bethune, 1836 : went as Secretary of the Legation with Sir John McNeill to the Persian camp at Herat, 1838 : travelled from Herat *viâ* Kandahar, Kabul, and Peshawar with despatches to Simla in 60 days : Military Secretary in 1838 to (Sir W. H.) Macnaghten : sent to make a treaty with Shah Kamran at Herat : became Political Agent at Herat, 1839–41 : in consequence of Kamran's duplicity, withdrew in Feb. 1841, to Kandahar : Lord Auckland, annoyed at this independent action, removed Todd from political employ, and he rejoined the Artillery : in the Satlaj campaign : was at Mudki, and was killed at Firozshahr, Dec. 21, 1845.

TOKER, ALLISTER CHAMPION
(1843–   )

Born Dec. 10, 1843 : son of Philip Champion Toker : educated at Victoria College, Jersey : entered the Bengal Army, 1860, and became Maj-General, 1897 : served in Bhutan expedition, 1864–5 : Egyptian expedition, 1882, as D.A.A.G., Indian Contingent : Brevet-Lt-Colonel : Burma war, 1886–7, in command of 18th Bengal Infantry : C.B. : Deputy Secretary to Government of India, Military Department, 1887–92 : Superintendent of Army Clothing, Bengal, 1892–7 : passed high examinations in Oriental languages : author of translations of several military text books into the Urdu, Hindi and Gurmukhi languages.

TOLFREY, SAMUEL (? – ?)

An attorney of the Supreme Court, Calcutta, while Sir E. Impey (q.v.) was Chief Justice : acted for Sir P. Francis (q.v.) in the crim. con. case brought against him by G. F. Grand (q.v.) : sailed for England (according to Hicky's *Bengal Gazette*) about Dec. 1780, with three lakhs of rupees, Madame Grand (q.v.) being a passenger on the same ship.

TOLFREY, WILLIAM (1778 ?–1817)

Born about 1778 : to India, 1794 : joined the 76th regt. : served in Mysore under General Harris and in the Mahratta war, 1803–4 : at Assaye : left the Army, and joined the Ceylon Civil Service, 1806 : died there Jan. 4, 1817 : translated the New Testament into Pali.

TOLLY, WILLIAM (? –1784)

Colonel : made " Tolly's nullah " between Calcutta and Alipur, in 1775 : purchased Belvedere from Warren Hastings in Feb. 1780 : died 1784.

TOMBS, SIR HENRY (1824–1874)

Maj-General : son of Maj-General Tombs of the Bengal Cavalry : born Nov. 10, 1824 : educated at Sandhurst and Addiscombe : joined the Bengal Artillery, 1841 : was in the Gwalior campaign, at Punniar, Dec. 29, 1843 : in the Satlaj campaign of 1845–6 : at Mudki, Firozshahr, Badiwal, and Aliwal : A.D.C. to Sir Harry G. W. Smith : in the Panjab campaign of 1848–9 : D.A.Q.M.G. of Artillery, at Ramnagar, Chilianwala, and Gujarat : in the mutiny was at Meerut, at the Hindun, and Badli-ka-sarai : at the siege of Delhi, won the Victoria Cross on July 9, when he saved the life of Lt. James Hills, V.C. : commanded the Horse Artillery at the assault of Delhi, on Sep. 14 : wounded : C.B. : at the siege and capture of Lucknow, March, 1858 : in Rohilkund, at Aliganj, and Bareli, on May 5, 1858 : Brevet-Colonel : highly praised in Parliament : commanded the force in the Bhutan campaign, 1864–5, and recovered Dewangiri on April 2, 1865 : K.C.B., 1868 : Maj-General, 1868 : commanded the Bundelkund and the Oudh Divisions in 1871 : died Aug. 2, 1874. Lord Roberts wrote of Tombs as " an unusually handsome man, and a thorough soldier " : " as a cool, bold leader of men, Tombs was unsurpassed."

TONK, SAHIBZADA SIR OBEIDULLA KHAN, OF (? –1900)

Uncle of the Nawab, and for many years Minister of the State of Tonk : a man of fine presence and liberal ideas, sympathizing with progress and advancement in every direction : effected many improvements in the State : C.S.I., 1879 : K.C.I.E. : died Oct. 1900.

TORRENS, HENRY WHITELOCK (1806–1852)

I.C.S. : son of Maj-General Henry Torrens : born May 20, 1806 : educated at Brook Green, the Charterhouse, and Christ Church, Oxford : B.A. in 1825, and entered at the Inner Temple. After a short service under the Foreign Office, he obtained a writership from the Court of Directors of the E.I. Co. Arriving in India in Nov. 1828, he held various appointments at Meerut : in 1835 joined the Secretariat, in which he served in several Departments under the Government of India, accompanying Lord Auckland to the N.W.P. in Oct. 1837, as Deputy Secretary under Sir W. Macnaghten. In Dec. 1846 he was appointed Agent to the Governor-General at Murshidabad, where, in his endeavours to improve the *Nizamat* administration, his relations with the Nawab Nizam and his officials became greatly strained : died of dysentery at Calcutta, while on a visit to the Governor-General, Aug. 16, 1852 : buried in the Lower Circular Road Cemetery. In 1839 he assisted in the editing of the *Calcutta Star*, a weekly paper, which became a daily paper, called the *Eastern Star* : was Secretary, 1840 to 1846, to the Bengal Asiatic Society and a Vice-President in 1843–5 : founded the *Meerut Observer* at Meerut, and made an incomplete translation of the *Arabian Nights*, besides editing Professor Lassen's *History of the Greek and Indo-Scythian Kings* ; and writing a novel, *Madame de Malquet*, and a series of articles on the " Uses of Military Literature and History."

TORRIANO, JOHN SAMUEL (? – ?)

Educated at the Royal Academy, Woolwich : arrived at Bombay, 1768, in the E. I. Co.'s Artillery : served at Surat and Cambay on behalf of the Peshwa, Raghunath Rao, against his subjects : at the battle of Arras : commanded European

Artillery under General Goddard at the capture of Bassein : in 1782 commanded the Bombay Artillery under General Matthews against Hyder : commanded at the capture of Onore, Jan. 6, 1783 : refused to abandon the fortress : sustained a siege by Tippoo's troops from May 14 to Aug. 25, 1783, when a cessation of arms took place : after a blockade of 7 months, Torriano received orders and surrendered it on March 28, 1784, on the ratification of the treaty of peace, to Tippoo : made a Brevet-Major : after retirement he commanded the Kensington Volunteer Corps during the European war.

TOWNSEND, MEREDITH
(1831–   )

Journalist : studied with the Orientalist, Professor E. B. Cowell; at Ipswich Grammar School : in 1848 joined the *Friend of India* at Serampur, first as Sub-Editor under J. C. Marshman, C.S.I., afterwards as Editor for some years : was also Assistant Translator to Government and Indian Correspondent of the *Times* : he retired to England in 1860 and purchased and edited the *Spectator*, giving up the editorship about 1898 : wrote *Asia and Europe*. While in India, he was much consulted on public questions.

TOWNSHEND, CHARLES VERE
FERRERS (1861–   )

Cousin and heir of sixth Marquis Townshend : entered the Militia, 1881, and Indian Staff Corps, 1886 : became Lt-Colonel, 1896 : served in the Soudan expedition, 1884–5, Hunza-Nagar expedition, 1891–2 : commanded garrison of Chitral Fort during siege : Brevet-Major and C.B. : Dongola expedition : Brevet-Lt-Colonel : Omdurman, 1898 : D.S.O. : South Africa, 1899–1900.

TRAVANCORE, SIR RAMA VARMA
MAHARAJA, OF (1837–1884)

Born May 19, 1837: a member of the Royal family of Travancore, the succession to which is in the female line. At 12 years old he was placed under the tuition of (afterwards Sir) T. Madhava Row (*q.v.*), for a period of four years : an accomplished Sanskrit scholar : subsequently he educated himself and learnt English thoroughly. Among his earliest contributions to literature were *The Horrors of War and the*

Benefits of Peace, written at the time of the Crimean War, followed by "A Political Sketch of Travancore," which appeared in the Madras *Athenæum*. As an ardent student of the experimental sciences he also acquired fame. In 1857 Sir T. Madhava Row was appointed Diwan of Travancore. Rama Varma was at this time a constant contributor to the *Indian Statesman*, edited by Mr. J. B. Norton. In 1861 he visited Madras and was made a Fellow of the University. He travelled widely in India. In 1880 he succeeded to the throne of Travancore, by the death of his brother, and, with the assistance of his friend of 21 years' standing, Vembaukum Ramiyengar, whom he made Diwan, introduced valuable reforms in the administration : steadily set his face against bribery and corruption and recognized merit wherever found : took a special interest in education : made G.C.S.I. in 1882 : died Aug. 5, 1884.

TRAVERS, JAMES (1820–1884)

Son of Maj-General Sir Robert Travers, C.B. : K.C.M.G. : born Oct. 10, 1820 : educated at Addiscombe : joined the Bengal Infantry, 1838 : was in the Afghan war, 1841, in several engagements : and under Nott near Kandahar in 1842 : at Ghazni : at Kabul : Brevet-Major, 1846 : in the Satlaj campaign, commanded Gurkhas at Sobraon : commanded the Bhopal Contingent : commanded, and in the retreat from Indore in the mutiny, defended the Residency, July, 1857 : saved the Europeans : gained the V.C. for bravery, charging the enemy's guns with only 5 men to support him, and drove off the gunners : Brevet-Lt-Colonel and Colonel : commanded the Central India Horse, 1860 : and the Meerut Division, 1869–73 : Lt-General, 1873 : C.B., 1874 : retired, 1874 : General, 1877 : died April 1, 1884 : wrote *The Evacuation of Indore*, 1876.

TREGEAR, VINCENT WILLIAM
(1842–   )

Born June 25, 1842 : son of Vincent Tregear, of the Indian Education Department : educated privately : entered Bengal Army, 1859 : commanded the 9th Bengal Infantry : Colonel on the Staff at Multan and in the Panjab, 1895–7 : served in the Afghan war, 1879–80 : Lushai expedition, 1889, in command of the

Force : Chin-Lushai expedition, 1889–90, in command of Chittagong column : C.B., 1890 : retired : Maj General.

TREVELYAN, SIR CHARLES EDWARD, BARONET (1807–1886)

I.C.S. : Governor : son of George Trevelyan : born April 2, 1807 : educated at Taunton, Charterhouse and Hailey-bury, 1824–5 : went out to India in the E. I. Co.'s. Civil Service in 1826 : Assistant Commissioner at Delhi : Under Secretary in the Foreign Department of the Government of India, 1831 : took a prominent part with Macaulay (whose sister he married), in favour of education through the medium of English against the Orientalists, and wrote on the subject of Education : Secretary to the Board of Revenue, 1836–8, when he retired : was Assistant Secretary to the Treasury, 1840–59 : did good service in the Irish famine : K.C.B., 1848 : reported in favcur of reforms in the Civil Service, which were generally adopted : was Governor of Madras, March, 1859, to June, 1860, when he was recalled for having published his opposition to the financial proposals of the Government of India : nevertheless he was appointed Financial Member of the Supreme Council, Jan. 1863, to April, 1865 : was always liberal in his views : wrote on Army questions : Baronet in 1874 : died June 19, 1886 : wrote on *The Application of the Roman Alphabet to all the Oriental Languages*, letters to the *Times* under the signature of " Indophilus," etc. etc.

TREVELYAN, SIR GEORGE OTTO, BARONET (1838–   )

Born July 20, 1838 : son of Sir Charles Trevelyan (*q.v.*), and Hannah More, sister of Lord Macaulay : succeeded his father, 1886 : educated at Harrow and Trinity College, Cambridge : Scholar : 2nd Classic, 1861 : Hony Fellow : M.P., 1865–97 : held several subordinate posts in the Government, and was Secretary for Ireland, 1882, and Secretary for Scotland, 1886 and 1892 : author of *The Competition Wallah*, 1864; *Cawnpore*, 1865; *The Life and Letters of Lord Macaulay*, 1876; *Selections from the Writings of Lord Macaulay*, 1876 : P.C. : LL.D. : D.C.L.

TREVELYAN, HENRY WILLOUGHBY (1803–1876)

Maj-Generai : son of George Trevelyan and brother of Sir C. E. Trevelyan (*q.v.*) : born in 1803 : educated at Addiscombe : entered the Army, 1820 : became Maj-General, 1867 : served in the Persian war, 1856–7 : was at Hallilah Bay : commanded the Artillery Brigade at Reshire, also at Bushire, Khushab and Chagadak : C.B., 1858 : died Aug. 31, 1876.

TREVOR, SIR ARTHUR CHARLES (1841–   )

I.C.S. : born at Jalalabad, Afghanistan, April, 1841 : son of Capt. R. S. Trevor, Bengal Cavalry, killed at Kabul, 1841 : educated at St. John's School and Trinity and Lincoln Colleges, Oxford : went to Bombay in the Civil Service, 1861 : Collector of Customs, Bombay, 1879 : Collector of Salt Revenue, 1885 : Commissioner of Customs, Salt, Opium, and Abkari, 1881 : Commissioner in Sind, 1890 : Member of Council, Bombay, 1892 : Member of the Supreme Council, 1895–1901 : C.S.I., 1895 : K.C.S.I., 1898.

TREVOR, GEORGE HERBERT (1840–   )

Colonel : born Jan. 29, 1840 : son of Rev. George Trevor, D.D. : educated at Marlborough : entered the Royal Artillery, 1858, and Indian Staff Corps, 1862 : held various appointments in the Political Department, 1867–95 : retiring, as Agent to the Governor-General for Rajputana and Chief Commissioner of Ajmir : C.S.I., 1891.

TREVOR, WILLIAM SPOTTISWOODE (1831–   )

Maj-General : born Oct. 9, 1831 : son of Capt. R. S. Trevor, murdered at Kabul, 1841 : was a prisoner in Afghanistan in 1842 : educated at Addiscombe : entered Bengal Engineers, 1849 : served in Burma war, 1852–3 : severely wounded : Bhutan war, 1865, received five wounds ; with Lt. Dundas, R.E., gained the V.C. : at the attack on the blockhouse at Dewangiri in Bhutan, April 30, 1865 : " they had to climb up a wall which was 14 ft. high, and then to enter a house occupied by some 200 desperate men, head-foremost through an opening not·more than 2 ft. wide between the top of the wall and the roof of the blockhouse " : Brevet-Major : employed in P.W.D. in Burma and Bengal and in Military Works Department : Chief Engineer, in Bengal Famine, 1874 ; Chief Engineer, Central India and Burma : Director-General of Railways and Secretary to the Government of India : retired, 1887 : C.S.I.

TRIMBAKJI DANGLIA (? – ?)

Mahratta Brahman : minister and favourite of the Peshwa, Baji Rao (*q.v.*), on whose behalf intrigues were carried on, 1815–7, at Poona with Sindia and Holkar, with a view to restore the Peshwa to the headship of the Mahratta empire, and to combine the native powers against the British Government : when Gangadhur Sastri was sent by the Gaekwar of Baroda, under the guarantee of the British Government, to Poona to settle the pecuniary differences between the Peshwa and the Gaekwar, Trimbakji contrived his murder at Pundarpur on the night of Sep. 19, 1815 : the British Government demanded his surrender ; he was imprisoned at Tanna, but, by means of a Mahratta horsekeeper, he escaped, and fled to the Bhils : he assembled a number of rebels : in 1818 he was captured, and imprisoned at Chunar till his death.

TROTTER, ARCHIBALD
(1789-1868)

B.C.S. : born Dec. 23, 1789 : brother of John Trotter (*q.v.*): appointed a writer in July, 1807, and arrived in Bengal, Nov. 1807: related to the Governor-General, Lord Minto : held Secretariat appointments in the Public Department and Board of Revenue : Superintendent of Government Lotteries, 1812 : was in 1816 in charge of measures for the relief of inhabitants of the Isle of France : Senior Merchant, 1818 : Collector of Bihar, 1824 : Secretary to the Board of Revenue, 1826 : employed at Bihar, and was Commercial Resident and Opium Agent, Patna, 1835–40 : served with Mr. Stockwell, in 1837, on a Commission to reform the Department of the Post-master-General in Bengal : an accomplished scholar and an able man of business : Commissioner of Supply, J.P. for Midlothian, and Director of the Bank of Scotland : died at the Bush, May 7, 1868.

TROTTER, HENRY (1841–)

Born Aug. 30, 1841 : son of Alexander Trotter : educated at Cheltenham and Addiscombe : entered the Bengal Engineers, 1860, and retired as Lt-Colonel, 1890 : served in the Trigonometrical Survey of India, 1863–75 ; with Sir Douglas Forsyth's mission to Yarkand and Kashgar, 1873–4 : on special service in China, 1876 : Military Attaché at Constantinople during Turko-Russian war, 1877–8 : Consul for Kurdistan, 1878–82 : Military Attaché, Constantinople, 1882–8 : Consul General in Syria, 1890–4 : C. B., 1880.

TROTTER, JOHN (1788-1852)

B.C.S. : son of Robert Trotter of Bush, Midlothian : born July 10, 1788 : appointed a writer, April, 1808 : arrived in Bengal, Oct. 1808 : became a Senior Merchant, 1820 : was Naval Storekeeper and Mint-master at Calcutta, 1821–2 : Secretary at the Board of Customs and Marine Board, 1826 : Opium Agent at Benares, 1833 : was also Senior Member of the above Boards when he retired in 1842 : he and his brother are both referred to in Miss Eden's *Up the Country* : was Deputy Lieutenant and J.P. of Midlothian : took an active part in County business up to his death at the Bush, Nov. 15, 1852 : married a daughter of Sir F. W. Macnaghten (*q.v.*).

TROTTER, LIONEL JAMES (1827–)

Captain : son of Edward Trotter, of Calcutta : educated at Charterhouse and Merton College, Oxford : entered Indian Army, 1847 : served in Panjab campaign, 1848–9, at Chilianwala and Gujarat ; Burma war, 1853 : commanded at Sabathu during the mutiny : retired, 1862 : author of many books on India, including *History of India*, 1874 ; *Warren Hastings*, a biography, 1879 ; *Warren Hastings and Lord Auckland*, in the " Rulers of India " series ; *John Nicholson*, 1897 ; *A Leader of Light Horse*, 1901.

TROUPE, COLIN (? –1876)

Entered the Army, 1820 : served against the Bhils, 1827 : in the Afghan war, 1839–42 : at Ghazni : was taken prisoner in the retreat from Kabul in Jan. 1842 : commanded the 48th regt. at Aliwal in the Satlaj campaign, 1845–6 : Brevet-Major : C.B., Lt-General, 1872 : died at Meerut, April 9, 1876.

TRUBNER, NICHOLAS (1817–1884)

Born at Heidelberg, June 17, 1817: son of a goldsmith : joined a bookseller in 1832, and publishing houses at Gottingen, Hamburg and Frankfurt to 1843 ; was connected with the firm of Longman & Co., in 1843–51 : established himself with Nutt, in Paternoster Row and Ludgate Hill, as a publishing firm, dealing with Oriental languages : became the foremost of Oriental publishers and Orientalists, studying Sanskrit under Goldstucker (*q.v.*) : brought out Marsden's *Numismata Orientalia* and from 1878 the " Oriental Series " of numerous volumes, besides his *American and Oriental Literary Record*, from 1865 : did much to advance and popularize Oriental and Linguistic knowledge : received many honours and decorations : died March 30, 1884.

TRUMPP, ERNEST (1828–1885)

Born March 13, 1828, in Wurtemburg : educated at Heilbronn and Tübingen University : Ph.D. : took Lutheran Orders : visited England : went, in the service of the Church Missionary Society, to Karachi in 1854, for linguistic research : ordained Deacon by the Bishop of Bombay, 1856 : invalided : went again to India, three times : studied the Afghan language at Peshawar : in India for two years, from 1870, to translate from the original Gurmukhi the *Adi Granth*, the Sacred Code of the Sikhs, for the Secretary of State for India : lectured at Tübingen on Oriental Languages : Professor of Oriental Languages and Literature at Munich : became totally blind in 1883 : published also a grammar and works in Sindi, a Pushto grammar, 1873, and many papers on languages, Persian, Ethiopic, Arabic, the N. Indian vernaculars of the Kafirs, Brahuis, Dards : died April 10, 1885.

TUCKER, CHARLOTTE MARIA (1821–1893)

Daughter of Henry St. George Tucker *q.v.*) : born May 8, 1821 : known as A.L.O.E. : " a lady of England " : after her father's death, in 1851, she took to writing, and giving the proceeds to charity: learnt Hindustani in 1875 and went out to India, 1875, as member of the Church of England Zenana Society : resided at Batala, N.E. of Lahore, for her Missionary work : visited zenanas and wrote stories for translation, published by the religious societies : died at Umritsar, Dec. 2, 1893 : published 142 books between 1854 and 1893.

TUCKER, HENRY CARRE (1812–1875)

I.C.S. : son of Henry St. George Tucker, (*q.v.*), Chairman of the E. I. Co. born 1812 educated at Haileybury : went to India, 1831 : from 1853 to 1858 was Commissioner and Agent to the Governor-General at Benares, during the crisis of the mutiny, culminating with the disarmament of the 37th N.I. on June 4. Tucker's conduct and policy have been the subject of discussion, Kaye and Malleson taking opposite sides : a later writer adopting the view that Tucker was strongly opposed to the idea of retiring from that station to the fort at Chunar : he was energetic in despatching up-country the reinforcements from Calcutta intended for Cawnpur and Lucknow : was made C.B. for his mutiny services : retired in 1861 : took great interest in education, and published numerous works and pamphlets on the subject in India and England : was active also in philanthropic movements : died Nov. 9, 1875.

TUCKER, HENRY PENDOCK ST. GEORGE (1823–1905)

I.C.S. : educated at Haileybury, 1840–2 : went to India, 1843, to the Bombay Presidency : was Deputy Registrar of the *Sadr* Court, Bombay : after the mutiny, was in the Account Department : and a Judge in the Konkan : officiated as Judge of the High Court, 1863 : Member of Council, Bombay, April, 1869, to April, 1874 : retired, 1876 : died April 20, 1905.

TUCKER, HENRY ST. GEORGE (1771–1851)

Born Feb. 15, 1771 : son of Henry Tucker : educated at Hampstead : went to Calcutta as a Midshipman in 1786 : obtained clerical work : Secretary to Sir W. Jones, 1790 : obtained a " writership " in 1792 : was Captain of the Volunteer Cavalry corps : Military Secretary to Lord Wellesley in 1799 : Secretary in the Rev. Judl. Department to the Government of India, 1799 : Accountant-General, 1801 : joined Cockerell, Traill, Palmer & Co., 1804 : again Accountant General, 1805 : made large economies : Member of the Board of Revenue, 1808 : Secretary to Government, 1812 ; Chief Secretary, 1814 : left India, 1815 ; became a Director of the E. I. Co., 1826 : Chairman of the Court, 1834, 1847 : died June 14, 1851 : wrote on Indian Finance, and *The Sphinx.*

TUCKER, HENRY TOD (1808–1896)

Son of Colonel G. P. Tucker : entered the Bengal Infantry, 1824 : on the head-quarters staff under Sir Hugh Gough in the Satlaj campaign, 1845–6, at Sobraon : Deputy Adjutant-General in the Panjab campaign, 1848–9, at Chilianwala and Gujarat : Brevet-Lt-Colonel and C.B. : Adjutant-General, 1850–54 ; A.D.C. to Queen Victoria : retired, 1856: Maj-General: died Aug. 6, 1896.

TULLOCH, SIR ALEXANDER MURRAY (1803–1864)

Son of John Tulloch : born 1803 : educated at Edinburgh : joined the 45th regt. in Burma in 1827 : paid much attention to Army reform and brought to light many abuses in respect of the soldiers' food, pay, liquor, pensions, health : passed through the R.M.C., Sandhurst : Colonel, 1854 : on the Commission of Inquiry into the Commissariat in the Crimea, the subject of much controversy : K.C.B., 1857 : Maj-General, 1859 : died May 16, 1864.

TULLOCH, HECTOR (1835–)

Major: born April 16, 1835: son of General John Tulloch : educated at Kensington Grammar School and Addiscombe : entered the Indian Engineers, 1855 : served in P.W.D. till 1868 : Municipal Engineer of Bombay, 1868 to 1873 ; Engineering Inspector to Local Government Board, Whitehall, 1873–97 : retired, 1897 : C.B., 1898.

TULSI BAI (? –1817)

Wife of Jaswant Rao Holkar, Maharaja of Indore : on his becoming insane in 1808, she assumed the regency of the State, adopting an infant, Malhar Rao : she was of profligate habits, cruel and vindictive : administered justice from behind the curtain : she put down rebellion by help of Amir Khan (*q.v.*) : killed her Prime Minister, Balaram Set : fled in 1817 from her capital, and meditated a peaceful arrangement with the British force entering on the Mahratta war of 1817–8. But the faction in Indore, bent on war with the

British, seized her and decapitated her shortly before the battle of Mahidpur on Dec. 21, 1817.

TUPP, ALFRED COTTERELL (? – ?)

I.C.S. : educated at University College, London : entered the Bengal Civil Service, 1862 : Accountant-General, Madras, 1878–81 : Bombay, 1882 : Calcutta, 1883 : Allahabad, 1883–9 : retired, 1889 : formed the Bimetallic League, 1881 : co-operated in establishing the Central Asian Society, 1901 : lectured for East Indian Association on various Indian topics : author of *The Indian Civil Service and the Competitive System,* 1875 ; *Gazetteer of the N.W.P., India,* 1877 ; *The Indian Civil Service List,* 1880 ; *The Competitive Civil Service of India,* 1882 : F.S.S.

TURNER, AUGUSTUS HENRY (1842–)

Entered the Indian Army, 1861, and became Colonel, 1891 : served in the Hazara campaign, 1868 : Afghan war, 1878–80: Mahsud-Waziri expedition, 1881 : Zhob Field Force, 1890 : Miranzai expedition, 1891 : Brevet-Colonel : Waziristan expedition, 1894–5 : C.B., 1897 : Colonel on the Staff at Faizabad, Oudh.

TURNER, SIR CHARLES ARTHUR (1833–)

Born March 6, 1833 : son of Rev. John Fisher Turner : educated at Exeter Grammar school and Exeter College, Oxford : called to the bar, 1858 : appointed Puisne Judge of the High Court at Allahabad, 1866 : Chief Justice of the High Court, Madras, 1879–85 : Member of the Council of India, 1888–98 : K.C.I.E., 1879.

TURNER, SIR FRANK (1813–1890)

General : entered the Royal Artillery, 1830 : commanded a battery of Artillery during the mutiny : rendered important service at Delhi, Lucknow, Cawnpur : Colonel, 1858 : Inspr-General of Ordnance in Bengal, 1864–74 : General, 1877 : Colonel Commandant R.A., 1882 : K.C.B., 1886 : died Dec. 19, 1890.

TURNER, RIGHT REV. JOHN MATHIAS (1786–1831)

Educated at Christ Church, Oxford : First Class, 1804 : Rector of Wilmslow :

D.D., 1829 : went out to Calcutta as Bishop, 1829 : formed the District Charitable Society : extended Church accommodation : supported Missionary work : took measures to improve the education of the Christian community, including the High School, now St. Paul's School : his health gave way on his tour to Madras, Bombay, Ceylon, 1830–1   died at Calcutta, July 7, 1831.

TURNER, SIR MONTAGU CHARLES
(? –   ) .

Son of Rev. John Fisher Turner : educated at Winchester : joined the firm of Mackinnon, Mackenzie & Co., Calcutta, 1877, and subsequently became a partner : President of Bengal Chamber of Commerce, 1898, 1901 and 1902 : Member of the Governor-General's Legislative Council, 1901–2 : K.B., 1903.

TURNER, SAMUEL (1749 ? or 1759–1802)

Traveller and diplomatist : born about 1749 or 1759 : connected with Warren Hastings : entered the military service of the E. I. Co., 1780, and was Captain in 1799 : was sent by Warren Hastings on an embassy to Tibet, from Jan. 1783, to March, 1784 : he travelled through Tassisudon, Bhutan, to Tashilhunpo, near Shigatze, Terpaling, and back to Punakha in Bhutan. The object of the Mission was to offer congratulations on the incarnation of the young Teshu Lama and to continue friendly relations with the Tibet Government. Turner was subsequently at Cornwallis' siege of Seringapatam in 1792, and was afterwards deputed as Ambassador to Mysore: for his conduct, he was rewarded by the E. I. Co.: on his return to England, he published his *Account of an Embassy to the Court of the Teshoo Lama in Tibet*, 1800 : was F.R.S. : died Jan. 2, 1802.

TURNOUR, HON. GEORGE (1799–1843)

Born 1799 : son of Earl of Waterton : entered the Ceylon Civil Service, 1818 : was a famous Pali scholar : devoting himself to this language, to acquaint himself with the native records of the island : the first to publish authentic facts as to the origin and progress of the Buddhist religion in Ceylon : these were first contributed to the *Ceylon Almanack*,

and were derived chiefly from the *Mahawanso* a Singhalese work, in Pali, containing a dynastic history of Ceylon from B.C. 543 to 1758, A.D.: published later, under the title of : *Epitome of the History of Ceylon, compiled from Native Annals*, 1836, and followed by *The Mahawanso*, with translation, 1837. : M.R.A.S. : contributed frequently to the *J.A.S.B.* on Buddhist History and Indian Chronology : on the inscriptions on the columns at Delhi, Allahabad, Bettia, *The Tooth Relic of Ceylon* : rose to be a Member of the Supreme Council in Ceylon : impaired health necessitated his return to England, 1841–2 : to Italy for his health : died at Naples, April 10, 1843.

TURTON, SIR THOMAS EDWARD MICHELL, BARONET (1789–1854)

Registrar of the Supreme Court at Calcutta : succeeded his brother as Baronet,'1844 : died at the Mauritius on his way to England for health, April 13, 1854.

TWEEDDALE, GEORGE HAY, EIGHTH MARQUIS OF (1787–1876)

Governor : born Feb. 1, 1787 : son of George, seventh Marquis : entered the Army and succeeded to the title, 1804 : served in Sicily, the Peninsula, America : C.B., 1815 : K.T. in 1820 : Governor and C. in C. of Madras, Sep. 1842—Feb. 1848 : Lt-General, 1846 : K.C.B., 1862 : G.C.B., 1867 : Field Marshal, 1875 : a representative peer for Scotland : devoted much time and attention to improvements in agriculture and the application of machinery : died Oct. 10, 1876.

TWEEDIE, WILLIAM (1836–   )

Born Oct. 31, 1836 : son,of Rev. W. K. Tweedie, D.D. : educated at Edinburgh University : entered the Indian Army, 1857 : served in the Indian mutiny, 1857–8 : in the action at Benares, June 4, 1857 : at Havelock's relief, and the capture, of Lucknow : Political Secretary to C. in C., Abyssinian expedition : Political Officer in the Afghan war, 1879–80 : held several appointments in the Political Department, including that of Political Resident in Turkish Arabia and Consul-General of Bagdad : C.S.I. : author of *The Arabian Horse, his Country and People*.

TYTLER, JOHN ADAMS
(? -1880)

General : entered the Indian Army, 1844 : in the 66th N.I. under Sir Colin Campbell in 1851, on the Peshawar frontier : in the mutiny, was in the Kumaon Hills : in Feb. 1858, at Chorpura, his men being staggered by the enemy's fire, he dashed forward and engaged the gunners in hand-to-hand fight : gained the V.C. : commanded the 4th Gurkhas in the Umbeyla campaign, 1863 : in the Hazara expedition under Sir Alfred Wilde : in the Lushai expedition, 1871–2 : C.B. : in the Afghan war, 1878–9, commanded a Brigade on the Khyber line : resigned after the treaty of Gandamak for ill-health : after the rising of Kabul on Sep. 3, 1879, he returned to duty, commanded against the Zaimushts : died of pneumonia at Thal, Feb. 14, 1880.

TYLER, SIR JOHN WILLIAM
(1839–)

Educated at the Parental Academy, now the Doveton College, and the Medical College, Calcutta : M.D. St. Andrew's : F.R.C.S., Edinburgh : L.R.C.P. : L.M. : L.S.A. : joined the Indian Medical Department, 1863 : Superintendent of Central and District jails at Meerut and Agra : C.I.E., 1886 : accompanied the Maharaja of Bhartpur to England for Queen Victoria's Jubilee, 1887 : K.B., 1888 : Inspr-General of Prisons, N.W.P. and Oudh,1884, and from 1890 till he retired : knighted.

TYLER, TREVOR BRUCE (1841–)

Born Jan. 7, 1841 : son of Rev. Roper Trevor Tyler : educated at Woolwich : entered the Royal Artillery, 1859, and became Maj-General, 1900 : Colonel on the Staff, Poona, 1893–5 : Brig-General, R.A., Panjab, 1895–7 : Inspr-General of Artillery, India, since 1897 : C.S.I., 1903.

UDNY, SIR RICHARD (1847–)

I.C.S. : son of George Udny, B.C.S. : educated at Aberdeen University : entered the Bengal Civil Service, 1869, and retired, 1899 : served as Political Officer in the following expeditions : Jowaki, 1877–8 : Mahsud-Waziri, 1881 : Miranzai, 1891 : Isazai, Black Mountain, 1892 :

Tirah, 1897–8 : Commissioner of Peshawar Division, 1891 : Boundary Commissioner of the Indo-Afghan frontier, 1894–7 : K.C.S.I., 1897.

UNWIN, HENRY (1810–1870)

I.C.S. : son of John Unwin of the Treasury : educated at Charterhouse, 1816–26, and Haileybury, 1826–8 : to Calcutta, 1829 : served at Balasore, 1830 : nearly died from his exertions in a famine in that district : served in the Customs in Calcutta : Magte-Collector of Mainpuri, N.W.P. : in the famine of 1838 there : Commissioner, Agra Division : Judge of the *Sadr* Court at Agra, throughout the mutiny of 1857 : wrecked in the P. and O. *Ava* off Trincomalee, on his voyage home : returned to India, 1859 : retired, as Senior Judge of the Agra *Sadr* Court, 1860 : died 1870.

UNWIN, ROBERT (1821–1903)

Maj-General : entered the Indian Army in 1840 : served in 1842 with the force under Sir W. Nott from Kandahar to Kabul : in the Gwalior campaign and at Maharajpur in 1843 : at the battles of the Satlaj campaign, 1845–6 : and in the Panjab Campaign, 1848–9 : through the Indian mutiny : at the relief of Lucknow and its final capture in March, 1858 : Cantonment Magistrate, 1858–74, when he retired and became Maj-General : died Oct. 12, 1903.

UPCOTT, FREDERICK ROBERT
(1847–)

Born Aug. 28, 1847 : son of J. S. Upcott : educated at Sherborne and King's College, London : entered the P.W.D., India, 1868, and was employed in construction of Indian railways : Consulting Engineer for Railways, Madras, 1892 : Director-General of Railways, India, 1896 : Secretary in the P.W.D. of the Government of India, 1898–1901 : Government Director of Indian Railways, England, 1901–4 : President of the new Railway Board, India, 1905.

VALENTIA, GEORGE ANNESLEY, LORD (1770–1844)

Born Dec. 7. 1770 : educated at Stanford, Rugby, and B.N.C., Oxford : joined

F F

the Army, but only till 1790 : started, 1802, on his voyage to India : attended by Henry Salt, his draughtsman and secretary : returned to England, 1806 : published *Voyages and Travels in India, the Red Sea, Abyssinia and Egypt*, 1802-6, in 1809-11 : was M.P., 1808-12 : succeeded to the Irish peerage as second Earl of Mountnorres, on his father's death, 1816 : died July 23, 1844.

VALIANT, SIR THOMAS (1784-1845)

Born 1784 : entered the Army, 1804: Maj-General, 1844 : in the campaign of 1805-6 in Gujarat : and against Ranjit Singh of Lahore, 1809 : while in the Afghan war, in command of the reserve of the Army of the Indus, Feb. 1839, he, in concert with Rear Admiral Sir F. Maitland, the Naval C. in C., took the fort of Manora, at the mouth of Karachi harbour : the town and fortress of Karachi surrendered the following day : served in Upper and Lower Sind : and at Quetta : commanded a Brigade at Maharajpur, 1843 : severely wounded : C.B. and K.C.B., 1844 : died April 22, 1845, while commanding the garrison at Fort William, Calcutta.

VAMBÉRY, ARMINIUS (1832-   )

Educated at Pressburg and Constantinople : Professor of Oriental Languages, Pesth University : has travelled much in Central Asia and has defended British interests in his writings : author of *Travels in Central Asia*, 1864 ; *Sketches of Central Asia*, 1867 ; *History of Bokhara*, 1873 ; *Central Asian Question*, 1874 ; *The Coming Struggle for India*, 1885 : C.V.O., and many foreign Orders.

VAN CORTLANDT, HENRY CHARLES (1815-1888)

General : son of Lt-Colonel Henry Clinton Van Cortlandt : born 1815 : educated in England : was employed in the military service of the Sikh Government, under the Maharaja Ranjit Singh, from 1832 : present at the assault and capture of Fort Chumaille in Hazara and occupation of other strongholds : in action against Amir Dost Muhammad at Peshawar, and the battle of Jamrud, 1832 : co-operated with British troops in the Khyber Pass : in the Satlaj campaign, acted as Political Officer in the British service at Firozshahr and Sobraon :

rejoined the Sikhs, and assisted Edwardes at Multan in 1848 : at Kineyri and Sadusain : at the capture of Multan : on the annexation of the Panjab took civil employ : served in the mutiny : raised the Hariana Field Force : in several actions : brought the districts N.W. of Delhi into order, after the siege: C.B. : Commissioner of Multan : retired, 1868 : died in London, March 15, 1888.

VANDELEUR, SIR JOHN ORMSBY (1763-1849)

Born 1763 : son of Captain Richard Vandeleur : joined the 5th foot in 1781 : Major in the Light Dragoons, 1794 : served in Flanders and at the Cape : Lt-Colonel, 1798 : to India, 1802 : commanded a Brigade of Cavalry under Lake in the Mahratta war, 1803-5 : at Laswari, Nov. 1, 1803, took 2,000 prisoners : at the defeat of Holkar at Fatehghar : and of Amir Khan at Afzalghar, 1805 : returned to England, 1806 : in the Peninsula : commanded the British Cavalry at Waterloo, and afterwards : K.C.B : G.C.B., 1833 : Lt-General, 1838 : died Nov. 1, 1849.

VANSITTART, HENRY (1732-1770)

Governor : born June 3, 1732 : son of Arthur Vansittart : educated at Reading and Winchester : went out as a writer of the E. I. Co. to the Madras service, 1745 : to Fort St. David, 1746 : Factor at Fort St. George, 1752 : became a friend of Clive : deputed to negotiate with the French E. I. Co., 1754-5 : became Member of Council, 1759 : in the defence of Madras, 1759 : appointed Governor of Bengal, Nov. 23, 1759 : assumed office, July 27, 1760 : removed Mir Jafar, the Subadar of Bengal, from his position and substituted Mir Kasim, his son-in-law : had differences with his Council and the officials, regarding private trade : and hostilities with Mir Kasim, reinstating Mir Jafar : returned to England, 1764 : wrote *Original Papers Relative to the Disturbances in Bengal*, 1764, and *A Narrative of the Transactions in Bengal from 1760 to 1764*, 1766 : M.P. for Reading, 1768 : Director of the E. I. Co., 1769 : deputed with Scrafton and Forde to enquire and report on Bengal : touched at Cape Town, Dec. 1769, and perished at sea, in the *Aurora*, (Falconer, the poet, and Pitcairn, the discoverer of Pitcairn island, being among the lost).

VAN STRAUBENZEE, SIR CHARLES THOMAS (1812–1892)

Son of Major Thomas Van Straubenzee: R.A.: born Feb. 17, 1812: went to Ceylon in the Ceylon rifles, 1829: to Mysore, 1833, in the 39th regt.: in the Coorg expedition, 1834: in the battle of Maharajpur, 1843: Brevet-Lt-Colonel, 1844: in the Crimea as Brig-General, 1855–6: wounded at the Redan: C.B.: commanded a Brigade and, later, the Land Forces in China, 1857–60: K.C.B., 1858: commanded a Division in Bombay, 1862–6, and the Bombay Army temporarily from March to Nov. 1865: Governor of Malta, 1872–8: General and G.C.B., 1875: retired, 1881: died Aug. 10, 1892.

VAN STRAUBENZEE, TURNER (1838–   )

Son of Colonel Henry Van Straubenzee: educated at Woolwich: entered the Royal Artillery, 1855, and became Lt-Colonel, 1882: A.D.C. to the Governor of Bombay, 1869–72: Instructor in Gunnery, Shoeburyness, 1874–9: commanded R.A., Indian Contingent in Egypt, 1882: C.B.: commanded Madras District as Brig-General, 1891–5: retired, 1895, as Maj-General.

VARMA, RAVI (1848–   )

An artist: born 1848: connected by marriage with the Maharaja of Travancore: chiefly taught himself to paint, but also received help from British artists in S. India: has taken prizes at many exhibitions in India, London, and America, and painted portraits of high officials and native Princes in India.

VAUGHAN, HUGH THOMAS JONES (1841–   )

Entered the Army, 1857, and became Colonel, 1887: served in the Indian mutiny, 1857–8: Afghan war, 1878–80: Zaimusht expedition: Brevet-Lt-Colonel: Lt-Colonel commanding the troops in Straits Settlement, 1894–1901: C.B., 1894.

VAUGHAN, SIR JOHN LUTHER (1820–   )

Maj-General: son of Rev. E.T.Vaughan: educated at Rugby: entered the Indian

Army, 1840: served as A.D.C. to Sir John Littler at Maharajpur: in the Crimea, 1855: commanded a Field Force in the Yusafzai expedition, 1857: in the mutiny commanded the 5th Panjab N.I. in Oudh, after the capture of Lucknow: Brevet-Lt-Colonel: commanded a Column on the Rapti, 1859: in the Umbeyla campaign, 1863: commanded a Brigade in the Black Mountain expedition, 1868: author of *A Grammar and Vocabulary of the Pashtu Language: My Service in the Indian Army and After:* K.C.B., 1887.

VETCH, GEORGE ANDERSON (1786–1873)

Lt-Colonel: joined in India the E. I. Co.'s 54th N.I. in 1807: severely wounded in the storming of Kumaon: in the Nipal war, 1815–16, distinguished himself by great personal bravery: retired in 1836, wrote his Eastern reminiscences in *Gregory's Gong* and *Dara, or the Minstrel Prince,* works of literary merit: died Oct. 10, 1873.

VENABLES, EDWARD FREDERICK (1818–1858)

Born May 5, 1815: son of Lazarus Jones Venables, barrister: was an indigo planter near Azimghar, N.W.P.: in the mutiny of 1857, he raised a force of volunteer cavalry and police, re-occupied Azimghar, released Europeans from confinement: commanded the mixed body of Cavalry at Mandori: and did good service in Oudh under Franks and Lugard: wounded and died in pursuit of Kooer Singh, April 19, 1858.

VENTURA (? –1858)

General: one of the first of the foreign Generals who trained the army of Ranjit Singh on the European model: said to have been an Italian by birth: an Infantry Colonel in Napoleon's army: also (doubtfully) said to have been a Jew, named Reuben-Ben-Toora: employed in Persia: reached Lahore, March, 1822: commanded a Brigade: with Allard (*q.v.*) helped to defeat the Afghans in 1823: received high pay (often in arrear) and grants of land from Ranjit Singh: constantly engaged in his campaigns and expeditions, sometimes, to stop the Sikhs' jealousy, sharing the command with a member of Ranjit's family: in 1831–3, on service to Multan: made *Kazi* and Governor

of Lahore : retired in 1843 : died near
Toulouse, April 3, 1858 : a man of honour
and high character, greatly respected.

VERELST, HENRY (? –1785)

Governor : grandson of Cornelius Verelst : went to Bengal in the service of
the E. I. Co., about 1750 : was taken
prisoner by the Nawab's force, 1757 :
released after Plassy : Member of the
Bengal Council : was in charge of Chittagong, 1761–5 : Member of the Select
Committee in Bengal : in charge of Burdwan and Midnapur, 1765–6 : succeeded
Clive as Governor of Bengal, Jan. 1767,
to Dec. 1769 : friend of Clive : opposed
to extension of sovereignty : after retirement, was impoverished by litigation
resulting from his action in Bengal against
mutinous and illegal conduct : mulcted
in heavy damages : died at Boulogne,
Oct. 24, 1785 : wrote, in reply to Bolts,
*A View of the Rise, Progress and Present
State of the English Government in Bengal,*
1772.

VIDYASAGAR, ISVAR CHANDRA (1820–1891)

Educationist, reformer, philanthropist :
of a Kulin Brahmin family in reduced
circumstances : educated at the Sanskrit
College, Calcutta, where he distinguished
himself : studied Hindu philosophy and
law and obtained the title of Vidyasagar
in 1839 : Head Pandit of the College of
Fort William, and Professor, 1850 : Principal, 1851, of the Sanskrit College :
during this period he mastered the English
language. His first literary work was
Betal Panchabinsati, 1846, remarkable for
purity of style. In 1851, on the death of
Drinkwater Bethune, the Bethune school
was placed under his care, and he was
associated with it for twenty years. In
1855 he was appointed, in addition, Inspector of Schools and established several girls'
schools in Hughli and Burdwan. In 1858,
in consequence of a difference of opinion
with the Director of Public Instruction,
he resigned his appointment : from 1864
he managed the Metropolitan Institution,
Calcutta : Fellow of the Calcutta University in 1857. After leaving the public
service, he continued to interest himself
in educational questions, especially in
female education. He laboured to break
down, by legislation, the system of polygamy, but without success : he started

the widow-marriage movement. Though
persecuted for his reforming zeal, he never
lost heart in his educational, social, and
philanthropic efforts. He published numerous works, chiefly in Bengali, on education : his name will long be remembered
by his countrymen. A carriage accident
in 1865 gravely affected his health. He
was made C.I.E. on Jan. 1, 1890. Honesty and independence were the chief
features of his character. His advice was
constantly sought by Government. He
died July 29, 1891.

VIGNE, GODFREY THOMAS (1801–1863)

Son of Thomas Vigne : born 1801 : educated at Harrow : called to the bar at
Lincoln's Inn, 1824 : travelled in America.
1831 : went to India, 1832, through
Persia : visited Kashmir, Ladak, Afghanistan, saw the Amir, and wrote *A Personal
Narrative of a Visit to Ghazni, Kabul and
Afghanistan,*1840 ; and *Travels in Kashmir,*
1842 : travelled in the W. Indies, Mexico
and Nicaragua : died July 12, 1863,

VIVEKANANDA, SWAMI (1863–1902)

Born in Calcutta, 1863 : his original
name was Narendra Nath Dutt : educated
at the General Assembly's Institution :
B.A. in 1884 : early became attached
to Ramkrishna Paramhansa, a religious
devotee : in 1890 went to Madras : in
1893 was sent by the Raja of Ramnad as
Representative of Hinduism to the Parliament of Religions at Chicago, and made
a great impression : in 1896 went to
England and lectured on Vedantism :
in 1897 returned to India, and made a tour
through Almora, Kashmir, Lahore,Madras,
discoursing on religion : in 1899 again
went to England and the United States :
founded in San Francisco a Vedanta Society : in 1900 returned to India, with
broken health : died July 4, 1902, at
Belur near Calcutta.

VIVIAN, HON. SIR ROBERT JOHN, HUSSEY (1802–1887) ·

Born 1802 : son of the first Lord Vivian :
educated at Gosport : entered the E. I.
Co.'s Madras Army, 1819 : in the Burma
war of 1824–6 : at the engagements at
Rangoon, Kemendine, Maloun, etc., : took
Fort Nipani in Feb. 1841 : Adjt-General of
the Madras Army, 1849–54 : was a Direc-

tor of the E. I. Co.: Maj-General: had command of the Turkish contingent of 20,000 men in the Crimea : K.C.B., 1857 : was chosen by the Crown to be a Member of the new Council of India, Sep. 1858– 75 : Lt-General, 1862 : General, 1870 : G.C.B., 1871 : died May 3, 1887.

VIZIANAGRAM, MAHARAJA SIR MIRZA GAJAPATI VIZIARAM RAJ BAHADUR OF (? -1878)

The leading Maharaja in the Madras Presidency: Member of the Governor-General's Legislative Council : introduced into Council the Bill on the subject of Majority, which was passed : was granted a salute, 1876 : died, 1878.

VIZIANAGRAM, MAHARAJA ² SIR PASUPATI ANANDA GAJA PATI RAJ OF (1850-1897)

Chief of the Maharajas of the Madras Presidency : of high lineage: a generous philanthropist, and a wealthy landowner : succeeded his father, 1878 : K.C.I.E., 1887 : G.C.I.E., 1892 : Maharaja, 1881 : for many years a member of the Legislative Council, in Madras : and rendered good service as intermediary between Government and the people : died May 23, 1897.

VOUSDEN, WILLIAM JOHN (1845-1902)

Born 1845 : son of Captain Vousden : educated at King's School, Canterbury, and R.M.C., Sandhurst : joined 35th regt., 1864 : joined the Indian Staff Corps : transferred to the 5th Panjab Cavalry : in the Jowaki-Afridi expedition, 1877–8 : and the Afghan war, 1879–80 : in the operations round Kabul : gained the V.C. for gallantry, Dec. 14, 1879, on the Koh Asmai heights, near Kabul : charged with a small party several times through and through the retreating Kohistanis : in two Miranzai expeditions, 1891 : Colonel, 1894 : in the Tirah expedition, 1897, as base Commandant : C.B., 1900 : Maj-General,acting as Inspr-General of Cavalry: died Nov. 12, 1902.

WACE, RICHARD (1842–)

Son of Rev. R. H. Wace : educated at Marlborough : joined the Royal Artillery, 1864 : ʃserved in the Afghan war, 1878–80 :

Brevet-Major : Director-General of Ordnance in India, 1897–1902 : Ordnance Consulting Officer for India, 1902–4 : C.B., 1897 : Maj-General : retired 1904.

WACHA, DINSHAW EDULJI (1844–)

Born Aug. 2, 1844 : educated at Elphinstone College, Bombay : joint Hony. General Secretary of Indian National Congress : President of the 17th National Congress meeting, held at Calcutta, Dec. 1901 : President of the Bombay Municipal Corporation, 1901–2 : Editor of English columns of the *Kaisar-i-Hind :* constant writer in Indian newspapers and journals.

WADDELL, LAWRENCE AUSTINE (1854–)

Born May 29, 1854 : Lt-Colonel : son of Rev. J. C. Waddell, D.D. : educated at Glasgow University : entered Indian Medical Service, 1880 : Professor of Chemistry and Pathology, Medical College, Calcutta, for six years : served in Burma campaign, 1886–7: Chitral Relief Force, 1895 : China expedition, 1900: C.I.E. : Mahsud-Waziri expedition, 1901–2 : in the Tibet Mission, 1903–4: author of *The Buddhism of Tibet, Among the Himalayas, The Birds of Sikhim, Discovery of the Birthplace of Buddha, Tribes of the Brahmaputra Valley, Palibothra, Lhasa,* 1905 : and papers on archæology and anthropology, etc.

WADDINGTON, CHARLES (1796– ?)

Born Oct. 22, 1796 : entered the Army, 1813 : in the Bombay Engineers : commanded the Engineer Corps, 1830 : Commanding Engineer in Sind, 1840, and Beluchistan : at Imamghar against the Amirs of Sind, Jan. 1843 : showed great bravery in lighting the mines at the destruction of the fort : at Miani on Feb. 17, 1843 : Lt-Colonel and C.B. : Commanding Engineer at Aden, 1848 : Chief Engineer at Bombay, 1851 : retired, 1853.

WADE, SIR CLAUDE MARTIN (1794-1861)

Son of Lt-Colonel Joseph Wade: born in Bengal, April 3, 1794 : called after Claude Martin (*q.v.*) to Bengal in the E. I. Co.'s military service, 1809 : served in Bundelkund, 1812 : in the operations against Sindia and Holkar, 1815 : in the

Pindari war, 1816–9 : at the taking of Chanda : did good service in the Surveyor-General's office, 1822 : as Diplomatic Agent at Ludiana had charge of Shah Shuja, 1823 : negotiated with Ranjit Singh, keeping him quiet during the Burmese war, 1824–6, and was the medium of intercourse with him and the Trans-Indus states from 1827 till Ranjit's death in 1839 : knighted for those services : in the Afghan war, 1838–40, was sent on a special mission to Peshawar to lead a mixed force into Afghanistan : the Sikhs failed to appear : as Lt-Colonel in command, forced the Khyber Pass, July 23, 1839 ; captured Ali Masjid ; entered Kabul at the head of his Force : after the fall of Kabul, returned to India : Resident at Indore, and Political Agent in Malwa, 1840 : retired, 1844 : Colonel, 1854 : C.B. : died Oct. 21, 1861.

WADESON, RICHARD (1826–1885)

Born July 31, 1826 : enlisted in the 75th regt., 1843 : went to India, 1849 : sergeant-major, 1854 : given a Commission, 1857 : with his regt. at Badli-ka-sarai and at the siege and assault of Delhi : gained the Victoria Cross for conspicuous bravery on July 18, 1857, at the Sabzi Mundi in saving separately the lives of two soldiers, when attacked by horsemen, both of whom he killed : appointed Adjutant : served with the regt. all over the world : commanded it, 1875–80 : Lt-Colonel, 1877 : Colonel, 1880 : Lieutenant-Governor of the Chelsea Royal Hospital : died Jan. 24, 1885.

WAGHORN, THOMAS (1800–1850)

Born Jan. 20, 1800 : son of a Rochester tradesman : was in the Navy, 1812–7 : to Calcutta as a third mate : was in the Bengal Marine, 1819–24 : commanded a vessel in the Burmese war, 1824–6 : urged, in 1827, the establishment of steam communication between India and England : met with great opposition : in 1829, showed its feasibility by performing the voyage out and back by the Red Sea : systematized the transit of mails and passengers across the desert, *viâ* Cairo to Suez, the Bombay Marine supplying the steamers for the Red Sea until the P. and O. Co. commenced in 1840 : organized a shipping business with Wheatley, as Waghorn & Co : left Egypt, 1841 : made a Lieutenant R.N., 1842 : died

Jan. 7, 1850 : statues to him erected at Chatham and at the Suez end of the Suez Canal : published pamphlets on the Overland Journey, 1831, and Mails, 1843, and on Egypt, 1837.

WAHAB, ROBERT ALEXANDER
(? –)

Entered the Indian Army, 1873, and became Colonel, 1899 : served in Afghan war, 1878–80 : Mahsud-Waziri expedition, 1881 : Zhob Valley expedition, 1884 : Hazara expedition, 1888 : Isazai Field Force, 1892 : Waziristan, 1894–5 : Brevet-Lt-Colonel : Anglo-Russian Boundary Commission, 1895 : Tirah expedition, 1897–8 : C.I.E., 1897 : Colonel.

WAKE, HEREWALD CRAUFURD
(1832–1901)

I.C.S. : fourth son of Sir Charles Wake, *Bart.* : educated at Haileybury : served in the Bengal Civil Service, 1851–68 : in the mutiny, was magistrate at Shahabad : he was, with a small party of Europeans and subordinates and about 50 men of Rattray's Sikh Police, besieged at Arrah in a small bungalow, which was put into a state of defence, being attacked by thousands of mutineers from Dinapur and by Kooer Singh and his force. The siege lasted from July 27 to Aug. 3, when the heroic garrison was relieved by Major Vincent Eyre, R.E. (*q.v.*). Wake commanded the Sikh Police in the subsequent defeat of Kooer Singh at Jagdishpur on Aug. 12 : he retired early from ill-health : received the freedom of the borough of Northampton in recognition of his galtry : C.B., 1860 : died Dec. 9, 1901.

WALCOTT, EDMUND SCOPOLI
(? –)

Colonel : son of John Minchin Walcott : educated privately and abroad : entered the Bombay Army, 1860, and became Brevet-Colonel, 1885 : served 'in the China war, 1860–3 : Afghan war, 1879–80 : Soudan expedition, 1885 : C.B., 1885 : retired.

WALCOTT, EDWARD (? –1756)

Ensign : survived the Black Hole : was sent with J. Z. Holwell (*q.v.*) to Murshidabad : when released, went to Chandernagore : served subsequently under Kilpatrick (*q.v.*) but died, apparently at Fulta, from the hardships which he had undergone.

WALES, JAMES (1747-1795)

Educated at the Marischal College, Aberdeen : took to art and exhibited portraits at the Royal Academy, 1783-91, when he went to India : painted portraits of native Princes and others : worked with the Daniells (*q.v.*) in India, at Ellore, and drew the sculptures at Elephanta, near Bombay : said to have died at Tanna, Nov. 13, 1795,

WALKER, ALEXANDER (1764-1831)

Born May 12, 1764 : son of William Walker : went out to Bombay in the E. I. Co.'s Army, 1780 : in the Malabar campaign against Hyder : at the siege of Mangalore : commanded an expedition, 1785-7, sent by the Bombay Government to N. America, which failed : served in Travancore, 1790 : against Tippoo, 1791-2 : Military Secretary to the officer commanding in Malabar : and to General James Stuart, while C. in C., Bombay : Q.M.G., Bombay : at Seringapatam, 1799 : served in Cochin, Malabar, and the Wynaad : Resident at the Court of the Gaekwar of Barado, 1802-7 : quieted Kattiawar, 1807 (suppressing infanticide), and Gujarat, 1809 : retired, 1812 : Brig-General : Governor of St. Helena, 1822-30 : died March 5, 1831 : his Oriental MSS. presented to the Bodleian Library.

WALKER, SIR GEORGE TOWNSHEND, BARONET (1764-1842)

Son of Major Nathaniel Walker : born May 25, 1764 : joined the 95th regt., 1782 : served in Southern India in 1784-7 : in Flanders, Portugal, at Copenhagen, at Walcheren, in the Peninsula : commanded a Division : K.C.B., 1815 : G.C.B., 1817 : Lt-General, 1821 : C. in C., Madras, March, 1826, to May, 1831 : Baronet, 1831 : Lieutenant-Governor of Chelsea Hospital, 1837 : General, 1838 : died Nov. 14, 1842.

WALKER, SIR JAMES LEWIS (1845-)

Son of John Walker, Panjab Police : established the Alliance Bank, of which he was first General Manager and then Director (1874-91) : commanded 2nd Panjab Volunteers, 1884-91 : one of the Proprietors of *The Pioneer* and *Civil and Military Gazette :* partner of two Brewery firms : C.I.E., 1888 : K.B., 1903.

WALKER, JAMES THOMAS (1826-1896)

Son of John Walker, Madras : C.S. : born Dec. 1, 1826 : educated privately and at Addiscombe : went to Bombay in the Bombay Engineers, 1846 : in the Panjab campaign, 1848-9, at Gujarat, and in the pursuit of the Sikhs and Afghans : made a military survey of the frontier from Peshawar to Dera Ismail Khan : in frontier expeditions, 1849-53 : appointed to the Great Trigonometrical Survey of India, 1853 : at the siege of Delhi, 1857, as a Field Engineer : Brevet-Major : in the Mahsud-Waziri expedition, 1860 : Superintendent of the Great Trigonometrical Survey, 1861-1883 : Lt-Colonel, 1864 : published from 1871 the *Account of the Operations of the Great Trigonometrical Survey of India*, bringing out 9 of the 20 volumes : did much work as a geographer, and in promoting tidal observations : C.B., 1877 : Surveyor-General of India, 1878-83 : General, 1884 : Member of Council of the Royal Geographical Society, 1885 : F.R.S., 1865 : LL.D., Cambridge, 1883 : member also of foreign Societies, and wrote for the *Encyclopædia Britannica*, and scientific Journals : died Feb. 16, 1896.

WALKER, SIR WILLIAM HARRISON (1800-1872)

Son of Benjamin Walker : entered the E. I. Co.'s naval service at 15 : retired in 1839, on the expiration of the Company's charter, but afterwards commanded several ships trading between England and Calcutta : F.R.G.S. : Senior Professional Member of the Marine and Harbour Departments of the Board of Trade : knighted in 1871, in recognition of his services under the Company and the Crown : died Sep. 1872.

WALLACE, SIR DONALD MACKENZIE (1841-)

Born Nov. 11, 1841 : son of Robert Wallace : educated at Edinburgh, Berlin, Heidelberg, and Paris : Private Secretary to Marquess of Dufferin and Marquess of Lansdowne, as Viceroys of India, 1884-9 : attached to the Czarewitch as Political Officer during his tour

440   DICTIONARY OF INDIAN BIOGRAPHY

in India, 1890–1 : author of *Russia*, 1877 ; *Egypt and the Egyptian Question*, 1883 ; *The Web of Empire*, 1902 : K.C.I.E., 1887 : K.C.V.O., 1901.

WALLACE, JAMES ROBERT
(1856 ?–1903)

M.D. : born Jan. 20, 1856 (?) educated at the Lawrence Military School, Sanawar, and Medical College, Calcutta : went to England in 1879 : on his return, entered Government service, but resigned it in 1883. In 1892 he joined the Directors of the Eurasian and Anglo-Indian Association, and in 1897 and 1902 was delegated to represent the grievances of the community to the Secretary of State and the Members of Parliament. In 1901 he was elected President of the Imperial Anglo-Indian Association, and laboured hard for the domiciled Anglo-Indian community. He died in 1903.

WALLICH, NATHANIEL (1786–1854)

A Dane : born Jan. 28, 1786 : M.D. of Copenhagen : entered the Danish Medical Service, and went to Serampur : joined E. I. Co.'s service, 1813 : Superintendent of the Botanic Garden, Calcutta, 1817–46 : "an able and most energetic botanist," organized collecting expeditions into the remote and then little known regions of Kumaon, Nipal, Sylhet, Tennaserim, Penang, Singapur : took, and sent home, enormous collections (8,000 specimens) of dried plants, distributing them to the leading botanical institutions in Europe : helped W. Carey (*q.v.*) to publish Roxburgh's *Flora Indica :* published his *Plantæ Asiaticae Rariores*, 3 vols., 1830–2 : explored Nipal and Assam for the wild tea plant : returned to England, 1847 : F.R.S., 1829 : F.R.A.S.: Fellow and Vice-President of the Linnæan Society : wrote botanical papers in the various scientific Journals : died in London, April 28, 1854.

WALPOLE, SIR HORATIO GEORGE
(1843–   )

Born Sept. 9, 1843 : son of Rt. Hon. Spencer Walpole, Q.C. : for some time Home Secretary : educated at Eton : entered the India Office : has been Assistant Under-Secretary of State for India since 1883 : Clerk to the Council : Secy. to Royal Commission on Civil Establishments, 1886–90 : C.B., 1880 : K.C.B., 1892 : J.P.

WALPOLE, SIR ROBERT
(1808–1876)

Son of Thos. Walpole, StagburyPark : born Dec. 1, 1808 : educated at Ealing and Eton : entered the Army in 1825 : served in Nova Scotia : D.A.Q.M.G.: at Corfu, 1847–56, and went to India with the Rifle Brigade in 1857 : commanded a Brigade at Cawnpur under Windham, and under Sir Colin Campbell on Dec. 6 : commanded a Division at the siege and capture of Lucknow in March, 1858 : in Rohilkund, 1858–9, was over-matched and defeated at Fort Ruiya on April 15, 1858 : was continued in his command : victorious at Allahganj, Bareli, Malerghat : commanded the Lucknow Division, 1861 : at Gibraltar and Chatham : C.B. and K.C.B., 1859 : Lt-General, 1871 : died July 12, 1876.

WALSH, JOHN (1725 ?–1795)

Son of Joseph Walsh : born about 1725 : joined the E. I. Co.'s military service : Private Secretary to Clive (*q.v.*), 1757, and with him in Bengal : laid Clive's plans for government of Bengal before Pitt, 1759 : M.P. for Worcester, 1761–80 : F.R.S., 1770 : F.S.A., 1771 : investigated the properties of the torpedo fish : died March 9, 1795.

WARBURTON, SIR ROBERT
(1842–1899)

Son of Lt-Colonel Robert Warburton, R.A., and an Afghan lady, niece of the Amir Dost Muhammad (*q.v.*): born in Afghanistan, July 11, 1842 : educated at Mussoorie, Kensington, Addiscombe, Woolwich : to India in the Royal Artillery, 1862 : served in the 21st Panjab Infantry in the Abyssinian campaign, 1868 : appointed to the Panjab Commission, 1870 ; Political Officer in the Khyber, 1879–97 : under Sir R. O. Bright (*q.v.*), 1879–80 : raised the Khyber Rifles : had great influence with the frontier Afghans : C.S.I., 1890 : Brevet-Colonel, 1893 : resigned, 1897 : served in the Tirah expedition, 1897–8 : K.C.I.E., 1898 : died April 22, 1899 : wrote *Eighteen years in the Khyber*, published in 1900.

WARD, FRANCIS SWAIN
(1750 ?–1794)

Artist and soldier : born in London about 1750 : gained some reputation a a landscape painter: entered. the Madras establishment of the E. I. Co.'s military service: Captain, 1773: Lt-Colonel, 1786: several of his pictures of India are at the India Office: died 1794.

WARD, SIR HENRY GEORGE
(1797-1860)

Governor: son of Robert Plumer Ward: born Feb. 29, 1797: educated at Harrow: in the diplomatic service at Stockholm, the Hague, Madrid, Mexico, to 1827: M.P., 1832-49: Secretary to the Admiralty, 1846: founded and edited the *Weekly Chronicle*: Lord High Commissioner of the Ionian Islands, 1849-55: G.C.M.G., 1849: Governor of Ceylon, 1855-60: denuded Ceylon of English troops to send them to India in the mutiny, 1857: Governor of Madras, July 5, 1860: died of cholera at Madras, Aug. 2, 1860: his statue erected at Kandy in Ceylon.

WARD, REV. WILLIAM
(1769-1823)

Born Oct. 20, 1769: son of John Ward, carpenter and builder: apprenticed to a printer: edited the *Derby Mercury*, the *Stafford Advertiser* and the *Hull Advertiser*: baptized at Hull, 1796: studied at the Rev. Dr. Fawcett's training establishment at Ewold Hall: sent to India in 1799, with Joshua Marshman (*q.v.*) by the Baptist Missionary Committee: reached Serampur, the Danish settlement, Oct. 13, 1799: joined there by W. Carey (*q.v.*) and established the Serampur Mission: Ward, besides preaching, superintended the printing press and set the type of the Bengali translation of the New Testament, and printed translations of the Scriptures in more than 20 languages: the press was burnt in 1812 but re-established: Ward travelled widely in Europe and America, 1819-21, collecting money for the Mission College at Serampur: died there of cholera, March 7, 1823: wrote on the *History, Literature, and Mythology of the Hindus*, 1811: and a *Memoir of Krishna-Pal, the first Hindu Convert in Bengal*, 1823.

WARD, SIR WILLIAM ERSKINE
(1838-)

I.C.S.: son of Hon. John Petty Ward, brother of Viscount Bangor: educated at Trinity College, Cambridge: went to Bengal in the Civil Service, 1861: Judicial Commissioner of Lower Burma, 1888-91: Chief Commissioner of Assam, officiating 1883 and 1885, and substantively 1891-6: K.C.S.I., 1896.

WARRE, SIR HENRY (1819-1898)

General: son of Lt-General Sir William Warre: born 1819: educated at Sandhurst: entered the Army, 1837: General, 1881: served in Canada and the Crimea: in the mutiny commanded the 57th regt. on the line of the Tapti river: in New Zealand, 1861-6: C. in C., Bombay, 1878-81, and Member of Council Bombay: K.C.B., 1886: retired, 1886: died April 3, 1898.

WARREN, SIR CHARLES
(1798-1866)

Son of John Warren: born Oct. 27, 1798: joined the 30th foot, 1815: served at Madras, 1816-9: at the Cape, 1822-5: again in India, 1830-8: at Madras: and in the expedition against the Raja of Coorg, 1834, led an assault and was at the capture of stockades: Major, 1830: was in China, 1841-4: commanded the 55th regt. in the Crimea and a Brigade: in the battles: at Malta, 1856-61: Maj-General, 1858: K.C.B., 1865: died Oct. 27, 1866.

WARREN, HENRY CLARKE
(1854-1899)

Born in Boston, Nov, 18, 1854: son of Samuel Dennis Warren: educated at Harvard College: B.A., 1879: continued the study of Sanskrit under Professors Lanman and Bloomfield at Johns Hopkins University: returned to Boston, 1884: suffered throughout life from the effects of an accident in childhood: studied Oriental Philosophy: devoted himself to Pali literature of Southern Buddhism: published *Buddhism in Translations*, in the Harvard Oriental series, 1896 drawing his material from original sources in Buddhaghosa's *Visuddhimagga* (way of purity): he left his edition of this work, as a whole, unfinished: Treasurer of the American Oriental Society for years, and one of its Directors: died early in Jan. 1899.

WASOODEW, JANARDAN (1804?-1894)

Was senior Principal Sadr Amin at Dhoolia, in the Bombay Presidency, when he was chosen, in 1864, to be the first native Judge of the Bombay High Court : retired many years before his death : died July 18, 1894.

WATERFIELD, SIR HENRY
(1837-   )

Born June 30, 1837 : son of Thomas Nelson Waterfield, Senior Clerk of the India Board : educated at Westminster : served at the India Board and Office, 1853-1902 : Secretary in the Financial Department, 1879-1902 : C.B., 1885 : K.C.S.I., 1893 : G.C.I.E., 1902.

WATSON, CHARLES (1714-1757)

Son of the Rev. Dr. John Watson : born 1714 : joined the Navy, 1728 : Rear Admiral, 1748 : C. in C. in East Indies, 1754-7 : defeated the pirate Angria of Gheria at sea, Feb, 13, 1756, while Clive co-operated by land : went up with Clive to Calcutta in 1756 (after the Black Hole tragedy): retook Calcutta and Hughli, and took Chandernagore : his name, not written by Watson, was appended, with Clive's knowledge, as a fraud to a fictitious engagement with Omichund, the intermediary between Clive and Mir Jafar : his Force assisted Clive at Plassy : he died, from the climate, on Aug. 16, 1757 : his monument erected at Westminster Abbey.

WATSON, HENRY (1737-1786)

Born 1737 : joined the 52nd foot, 1755 : educated at Woolwich : became an engineer, 1759 : served at Belleisle, 1761, and Havana, 1762 : joined E. I. Co.'s service at Calcutta, 1764 : Field Engineer, and commanded the troops : Chief Engineer, 1765 : commenced docks at Calcutta, and was engaged on the defences of Fort William and works at Budge Budge and Melancholy Point : built vessels and commenced docks at Kidderpur, near Calcutta : was again in India, 1780-6 : resigned : died Sep. 17, 1786.

WATSON, SIR JAMES (1772-1862)

Son of Major Watson : served under the Duke of York in 1793-4 : also in the W. Indies : commanded the 14th regt. at the capture of the Isle of France and of Java : in the Pindari and Mahratta wars : General Officer on the Staff in

India, 1830 : to England in 1837 : Colonel of the 14th regt.: died Aug. 12, 1862.

WATSON, JOHN (? - 1774)

Commodore : as a volunteer at Surat, 1748, drove off an attack of the natives : and in 1751 brought the E. I. Company's cruisers up the Surat river to assist the factory, when again besieged : by swimming a river he gave information to the garrison : commanded a squadron in 1761, against Surat, and assisted at the conquest of Pondicherry : destroyed the fortresses of pirates, 1765 : Superintendent of Naval Department and Member of Council, Bombay, 1767 : commanded the ships at the capture of Mangalore, 1768, and of Broach, 1772 : mortally wounded at the siege of Tanna, and died at Bombay, 1774.

WATSON, SIR JOHN (1829-   )

Born 1829 : entered the Bombay Army, 1848 : served in the Panjab campaign, 1848-9 : Bozdar expedition, 1857 : in the 1st Panjab Cavalry in the mutiny, 1857-9 : gained the V.C. during Sir Colin Campbell's relief of Lucknow, Nov. 14, 1857, for his gallant attack on a number of the enemy's cavalry, and for gallantry on many other occasions : Umbeyla campaign, 1863, commanded the Central India Horse, 1871 : Resident at Gwalior, 1877 : Officiating A.G.G. for Central India : commanded the Cavalry despatched from Bombay to Malta, 1878 : commanded the Panjab Chiefs' Contingent in the Afghan war, 1879-80 : Agent to the Governor-General at Baroda, 1882-6 : K.C.B., 1886 : General 1891 : G.C.B., 1902.

WATSON, JOHN FORBES
(1827-1892)

Born 1827 : educated at Aberdeen University : M.D., 1847 : and at Guy's Hospital, and Paris : was in the Bombay Medical service, 1850-3 : in England investigated, for the Court of Directors, the nutritive values of the food grains of India : appointed Reporter on the Products of India and Director of the Indian Museum, 1858-79 : proposed, in 1874, an Indian Museum, Library, and Institute, which conduced to the establishment of the Imperial Institute : represented India at International Exhibitions, 1862–73, and at S. Kensington Exhibitions, 1870–4 : retired, 1880 : died July 29, 1892 : F.L.S., 1889 : published works on *The Textile Manufactures and Costumes of People of India*, 1866 ; *Index to the Native and Scientific Names of Indian and other Eastern Economic Plants and Products*, 1868 : and edited *People of India*, 1868–72.

WATT, SIR GEORGE (1851–)

Born April 24, 1851 : son of John Watt : educated at Marischal College, Aberdeen, and Glasgow University : Professor of Botany, Calcutta University, 1873 : Medical and Scientific Officer in Burma-Manipur Boundary Commission, 1882 : scientific Assistant-Secretary to the Government of India, 1884 : Reporter on Economic Products to Government of India since 1887 : Director, Indian Art Exhibition, Delhi, 1903 : author of *Dictionary of the Economic Products of India*, 9 vols.; Reports on *Pests and Blights of the Tea Plant* ; *Rhea and China Grass, Lac Industries* ; *Indian Art*, etc.: C.I.E. : K.B., 1903 : M.B. : C.M. : F.L.S.

WATTS, WILLIAM (? – ?)

In the E. I. Co.'s service : Second in Council at Fort William, Calcutta, and Chief at Kasimbazar in 1756, where he was taken prisoner by the Nawabs' orders : appointed President at Fort William, 1758, in supersession of Roger Drake (*q.v.*), but almost at once handed over charge to Clive : was the third husband of Frances Johnson (*q.v.*) : his daughter Amelia was mother of Robert Banks Jenkinson, second Earl of Liverpool (1770–1828), who was Prime Minister, 1812–27.

WAUGH, SIR ANDREW SCOTT (1810–1878)

Son of General Gilbert Waugh : born Feb. 3, 1810 : educated at Edinburgh, Addiscombe and Chatham : joined the Bengal Engineers, 1827 : to India, 1829 : attached to the Great Trigonometrical Survey, 1832 : engaged in the scientific operations connected with this survey, conducting the triangulation, 1832–43 : became Surveyor-General of India, 1843, as a Subaltern : Captain, 1844 : determined the heights, etc., of numerous Himalayan peaks, and gave its name to the highest, Mount Everest, 29,002 ft. high : continued

the survey work to the W. and N.W. of India, and to Kashmir : Gold Medallist of the R.G.S., 1857 : F.R.S., 1858 : retired as Maj-General, 1861 : and was knighted : Vice-President of the R.G.S. : died Feb. 21 1878.

WAZIR ALI (1781–1817)

Nawab of Oudh : putative, or adopted, son of Asaf-ud-daula, the Nawab of Oudh, on whose death, in Sep. 1797, he became Nawab. His wedding at Lucknow in 1795 cost about £300,000. Doubts being thrown on the legitimacy of his birth, Sir John Shore, after personal inquiry, deposed him in Jan. 1798, and deported him to Calcutta on a pension of two lakhs of rupees, *vid* Benares. There Wazir Ali murdered Mr. Cherry, the Agent to the Governor-General, Jan. 14, 1799, and unsuccessfully attacked the Judge, Samuel Davis (*q.v.*). Wazir Ali fled, but was captured and taken to Calcutta, where he was imprisoned in a bomb-proof building in Fort William for years, being subsequently transferred to Vellore. There, after a total incarceration of more than seventeen years, he died in May, 1817.

WEBBE, JOSIAH (1768–1804)

I.C.S. : appointed a writer at Fort St. George, Madras, 1783 : Secretary to the Board of Revenue, 1790 : Secretary to Government, 1797 : the First Chief Secretary, 1800 : wrote an able Minute deprecating resumption of hostilities against Tippoo, which greatly displeased Lord Mornington and the Directors of the Company : appointed Resident in Mysore, 1804, and was shortly transferred in the same capacity to Gwalior : on his journey thither died on the banks of the Nerbudda : a monument was erected to him in the Fort Church, Madras : Col. Wellesley (Duke of Wellington) included him among his friends and took home an engraving from his portrait, which occupied a prominent place at Strathfieldsaye. The Duke is reported to have said of Webbe : " He was one of the ablest men I ever knew, and, what is more, one of the most honest.".

WEBBER, CHARLES EDMUND (1838–1904)

Born Sep. 5, 1838 : son of Rev. T. Webber : educated at Woolwich : entered the Royal Engineers, 1855 : served in the

Indian mutiny, 1857–8 : at Chandairi, Jhansi, Kalpi, Gwalior, in the Central India campaign against leading mutineers : in Transport Department,Abyssinia : in charge of R.E. postal telegraphs ; A.A. and Q.M.G. in South Africa, 1879 : in the Zulu campaign and the Transvaal : in the Egyptian expedition, 1882 : at Tel-el-Kebir : C.B. : in the Soudan expedition, 1884–5 : retired, 1885 : joint founder of the Institution of Electrical Engineers : President of it : author of various papers on military subjects, telegraphy, telephony, and electrical engineering : died Sep. 23, 1904 : General.

WEBER, ALBRECHT FRIEDRICH (1825–1901)

Born at Breslau, Feb. 17, 1825 : studied at Bonn and Berlin : settled as Privatdocent at Berlin, 1848 : Member of the Berlin Academy of Sciences, 1857 : Professor, 1867 : edited the *White Yajur-Veda*, 1849–59, and other Sanskrit works : made a valuable catalogue of the Sanskrit MSS. in the Royal Library at Berlin, 1853–92 : wrote many essays on all branches of Indian research : himself wrote the greater part of the *Indische Studien*. 17 vols., published 1850–85 : one of the greatest Orientalists of the time, a great teacher as well as an enthusiastic worker : and one of the first to promote actively the scientific study of Sanskrit : the first real pioneer in the study of Prakrit : edited texts, especially of the Jain religion : lectured on Indian literature ; and wrote the *History* of it, 1882 : his sight failed : died Nov. 30, 1901.

WEDDERBURN, HENRY (1722–1777)

Captain : son of Charles Wedderburn, of Gosford : baptized, July 19, 1722 : bred to the sea : settled in Bengal as a free mariner soon after 1740 : in 1757 made Captain of the Grenadier Company of Militia, and, for his services, Master Attendant of Marine, 1758 : commanded forts, and in the engagement with the Dutch at Chandernagore : joined the Army as volunteer : became a Captain in the Merchant Service : examined the harbour of Mauritius : assisted Admiral Cornish, July, 1762 : saved vessels from the French cruisers : in the war with Mir Kasim : on service at and about Patna, as Captain, 1763–5 : again Master Attendant of Marine,

1769, until his death at Calcutta, Nov. 17, 1777.

WEDDERBURN, SIR JOHN, SECOND BARONET (1789–1862)

Of Balindran : I.C.S. : born May 1, 1789 : son of (Sir) John Wedderburn (sixth *Baronet*) of Blackman (1729–1806) : went to Bombay in the Civil Service, 1807 : rose to be Accountant-General and Military, Commercial and Revenue Accountant, Jan.1830 : retired May, 1837 : presented on his departure with a service of plate as a testimonial from his European and Native friends in Bombay, 1836 : succeeded his half brother, Sir David, as Baronet, 1858 : died July 2, 1862.

WEDDERBURN, JOHN (1825–1857)

I.C.S. : eldest son of Sir John Wedderburn (*q.v.*), second *Baronet* : born May 9, 1825 : educated at Loretto, Edinburgh Academy, and Haileybury : entered the Bengal Civil Service, 1844 : served in Bihar: transferred to the Panjab, 1849 : Deputy Commissioner of Lahore : in the mutiny was Magte-Coll. of Hissar : raised Irregular Cavalry, who proved traitors and murdered him, his wife and child, at Hissar. May 29, 1857.

WEDDERBURN, SIR WILLIAM, FOURTH BARONET (1838–   )

I.C.S. : born March 25, 1838 : fourth son of second *Baronet*, Sir John, succeeding his brother, Sir David, in the title, 1882 : educated at Hofwyl, Worksop, Loretto, and Edinburgh University : entered the Bombay Civil Service, 1860, and retired in 1887 : served as District Judge and Judicial Commissioner in Sind : acted as Secretary to the Bombay Government in the Judicial-Political Departments, and as Judge of Bombay High Court, 1885 : Officiating Chief Secretary to Bombay Government : retired, 1887 : M.P. for Banffshire, 1893–1900 : Chairman of Indian Parliamentary Committee : Member of the Royal Commission, 1895, on Indian Expenditure : has shown great sympathy with the Indian National Congress ; of the fifth meeting he was President, 1889 : Chairman of its British Committee : author of pamphlets, papers and schemes on Arbitration Courts, Agricultural Banks, Village Panchayats and subjects relating to the condition of the Indian people.

WEGUELIN, THOMAS MATTHIAS
(? -1828)

Son of John Christopher Weguelin : went to Calcutta in the E. I. Co's military service, 1782 : served against Tippoo, 1790-2. : at Seringapatam, 1791-2 : in the Mahratta war of 1803, at sieges of Gwalior and Bhartpur ; commanded expedition to defend the Portuguese at Macao against the French : in the Mauritius expedition, 1810-2 : Commissary-General there : and of Bengal, 1812 : in the Nipal war, 1814-6, and in the Pindari war, 1816-8 : resigned, 1820 : Colonel Commandant, 1823 : died May 23, 1828.

WELLDON, RIGHT REV. JAMES EDWARD COWELL, D.D. (1854-   )

Son of Rev. Edward Welldon, Master at Tonbridge : educated at Eton (Newcastle Scholarship, 1873) and King's College, Cambridge (Senior Classic and Senior Chancellor's Medallist, 1877) : Master of Dulwich College, 1885 : Headmaster of Harrow, 1885-98 : Bishop of Calcutta and Metropolitan of India, 1898-1902 : Canon of Westminster since 1901 : author of *Translation of Aristotle's Politics, Rhetoric and Ethics* ; *Sermons*, etc.

WELLESLEY, RICHARD COLLEY, MARQUESS (1760-1842)

Governor-General : born June 20, 1760 : eldest son of first Earl of Mornington : educated at Trim, Harrow, Eton, Christ Church, Oxford : Student : Latin Verse Prize, 1780 : became Earl Mornington, 1781 : M.P., 1787-96 : Knight of St. Patrick, 1783 : Lord of the Treasury, 1786 : Member of the Board of Control, 1793 : Privy Councillor, 1793 : made Baron Wellesley, 1797 ; accepted Governorship of Madras, 1797 : became Governor-General of India, May 18, 1798, to July 30, 1805 : met high Indian officers at the Cape, on his voyage outwards : reversed his predecessor's policy of non-interference : induced the Nizam to remove his French officers, and made the Mahrattas neutral : opposed French intrigues : found Tippoo seeking help from the French at Mauritius : when negotiations failed, declared war on Tippoo : went to Madras : Tippoo defeated and killed at Seringapatam, May 4, 1799 : Hindu dynasty restored in Mysore : some Mysore territory annexed : the Nizam

ceded districts for support of troops and became an ally and a protected ruler : Wellesley created a Marquess, Dec. 1799 : assumed the administration of Tanjore, maintaining the Raja : annexed the Carnatic, pensioning the Nawab with a fifth of its revenues : made treaty with Saadat Ali, Nawab of Oudh, for cession of territory and for reforms : sent Malcolm (*q.v.*) to Persia to make treaty against Afghanistan : sent Baird's expedition to Egypt against the French : refused to restore, as ordered, the French possessions in India : resigned his appointment, but requested to remain : made Commander-in-Chief : made treaty of Bassein, Dec. 1802, with the Peshwa : compelled to make war against Mahratta Chiefs, Sindia, Bhonsla, Holkar : defeated them at Assaye, Argaum, Delhi, Laswari, but, in consequence of Monson's disastrous retreat before Holkar, Wellesley was recalled, 1805. He established, in 1800, the College of Fort William for education of civilians : it was only allowed by Court of Directors, on a reduced scale, for native languages : ordered the observance in India of Sunday as a day of rest : after retirement, was unsuccessfully attacked in Parliament by Paull and others, for his policy in Oudh : sent to Spain as Ambassador Extraordinary in 1809, in furtherance of Peninsular war : became Foreign Secretary, 1809-12 : K.G., 1812 : failed to form a coalition ministry, 1812 : differed in opinion on important subjects from the Duke of Wellington : Lord Lieutenant of Ireland, 1821-8 and 1833-4, advocated Catholic emancipation, suppressed disturbances, combated famine : Lord Steward of the Household, 1832-3 : Lord Chamberlain, 1835 : retired, 1835 : granted £20,000 by the E. I. Co. : his Despatches, Minutes, etc. printed, 1836-7 : his statues erected in London and Calcutta : died Sep. 26, 1842 : he maintained his classical scholarship and studies to the end : he, also, was called " The great Proconsul."

WELLINGTON, ARTHUR WELLESLEY, FIRST DUKE OF (1769-1852)

Commander-in-Chief and Prime Minister : fourth son of the first Earl of Mornington : born May 1, 1769 : educated at Chelsea, Eton, and Angers in France : gazetted Ensign in March, 1787, and, passing through several regiments, became Major and Lt-Colonel in the 33rd regt. in 1793. After some campaigning in the Netherlands, 1794-5, and starting for the W. Indies, he landed with his regiment at Calcutta on Feb. 17, 1797. His brother, the Earl of Mornington, assumed office as Governor-General at Calcutta, on May 18, 1798. Wellesley commanded, as far as Penang, the Bengal Division of an expedition to Manilla, but was recalled on account of Tippoo, who had been intriguing with the French and native courts to turn the English out of India. After negotiations, the war with Tippoo of Mysore broke out early in 1799 : Wellesley commanded the Nizam's troops, invading Mysore : Tippoo's troops were routed at Malavilli, in March, 1799, by a Force under him : Tippoo was then besieged in Seringapatam by General Harris, Wellesley commanding the reserve during the attack, May 4, 1799. On its capture and the death of Tippoo, Wellesley was placed in command of Seringapatam, stopped the plundering, and restored order. He subsequently administered the lately conquered territory as Governor, with great ability : and hunted down " the freebooter of Mysore," Dhoondia Waugh, in Sep. 1800. In 1802-3, the Mahratta powers, Sindia, Holkar and the Raja of Berar, formed a confederacy against the English. General Wellesley, with the Madras Army, reached Poona in time to save it from destruction by Holkar. He was made Chief Political and Military Officer in the Dekkan and S. Mahratta country : after taking Admednagar on Aug. 12, he attacked, on Sep. 23, 1803, with about 8,000 men, including only about 1,500 Europeans, and defeated the whole Mahratta force of 50,000 men, near the village of Assaye. He was equally victorious in the battle of Argaum on Nov. 29, 1803, in which the Mahratta power was broken : he took Gawilghar on Dec. 15, 1803, and made peace by treaties which secured great cessions of territory to the E. I. Co. In 1804 he disbanded the Army of the Dekkan. At Bombay he was presented with a sword of honour, and before he left Madras for England, in March, 1805, was made K.C.B. : declined the Commander-in-Chiefship of Bombay. The remainder of his career is included in English and European history. He died at Walmer, Sep. 14, 1852.

WELLS, HENRY LAKE (1850-1898)

Son of Rev. Thomas Bury Wells : born March 8, 1850 : educated at Woolwich : entered R.A., 1871 : became Lt-Colonel, 1896 : went to India, 1875 : in the Afghan war, 1878-9 : made a road across the Kojak : P.W.D. Engineer at Quetta : served also on the Khyber line : surveyed for telegraph lines in Kashmir and Gilgit, 1879-80 : Assistant Director, 1880, and Director, 1891, of the Indo-European telegraph in Persia : surveyed routes in Persia, and contributed scientific papers to learned Societies : C.I.E., 1897 : died Aug. 31, 1898 : Lt-Colonel.

WELLS, SIR MORDAUNT (1817-1885)

Born 1817 : called to the bar at the Middle Temple, 1841 : Recorder of Bedford : Puisne Judge of the Supreme Court, Calcutta, 1859-62, and of the High Court, 1862-3 : Member of the Governor-General's Legislative Council, 1860 : died, Nov. 26, 1885 : he provoked the Calcutta native public by denouncing the wholesale forgeries of Bengali litigants, so that a petition was presented for his recall, which the Secretary of State rejected : when he resigned, a testimonial was presented to him.

WELSH, JAMES (1775-1861)

Son of John Welsh, W.S., Edinburgh : born March 12, 1775 : went to Madras in the E. I. Co.'s European Army, 1791 : took part in the siege of Pondicherry, 1793 : and the capture of Ceylon, 1796 : under Arthur Wellesley (*q.v.*) in the Mahratta war, 1803-4 : at Poona, Ahmadnagar, Argaum, Gawilghar, Mankarsir. He discovered a plot to murder Europeans at Palamcotta, Nov. 1805 : led the assault at Arambooly, Travancore, 1809, and held several military commands in Madras : checked a rising at Kolapur, 1824 : Maj-General 1837 : commanded the N. Division, Madras, 1837 : retired, 1847 : General 1854 : died at Bath, Jan. 24, 1861 : wrote *Military Reminiscences of Nearly Forty Years' Active Service in the E. Indies.*

WENGER, REV. DR. JOHN (1811-1880)

Born near Berne, 1811 : showed great aptitude for languages : sent out to India as a Missionary by the Baptist Missionary Society, 1839 : translated, with Yates, the

Scriptures into Bengali : and part òf the Old and New Testaments into Sanskrit, and the poetical portions, including the Book of Job, from the Hebrew into Sanskrit verse : also many tracts and hymns into Bengali or Sanskrit : died at Calcutta, Aug. 20, 1880.

WENLOCK, BEILBY LAWLEY, SECOND BARON, (1849–)

Born May 12, 1849 : educated at Eton and Trinity College, Cambridge : succeeded his father, 1880 : M.P. for Chester, 1880 : Governor of Madras, 1891–6 : paid speeial attention to great public works and famine-relief : K.C.B. : G.C.S.I., G.C.I.E. : P.C. : Lord of the Bedchamber to H.R.H. the Prince of Wales since 1901.

WEST, SIR EDWARD (1782–1828)

Son of Balchen West : born 1782 : educated at University College, Oxford : Fellow : called to the bar from the Inner Temple, 1814 : Recorder of Bombay : knighted, 1822 : Chief Justice of the Supreme Court, Bombay, 1823 : died at Bombay, Aug. 1828 : wrote treatises on Political Economy.

WEST, E. W. (1824–1905)

Civil Engineer in the Bombay Presidency, 1844–66 : interested in the inscriptions on Buddhist Cave Temples, he studied Pali : made a glossary of the words in the Maha Vamsa of Ceylon in Pali : published, in the Bombay *R.A.S. Journal*, facsimiles of certain inscriptions : studied at Munich with Professor Haug, 1866–9, the records of the Zoroastrian religion in the Avesta and Pahlavi dialects of Persia : published old Persian texts : and translated, 1880–7, five Pahlavi books for the series of Sacred Books of the East : became the most eminent of Pahlavi scholars, and the greatest living authority on Pahlavi literature—on which he published a book, and many articles in the *R.A.S. Journals*—and the history of the Zoroastrian faith : began a catalogue of the Zend and Pahlavi MSS. at the India Office : Gold Medallist of the R.A.S., July, 1900 : Hon. D.Phil. of Munich, and member of American and Bavarian learned Societies : died Jan, 1905,

WEST, SIR RAYMOND (1832–)

I.C.S. : son of Frederick West : educated at Queen's University, Galway :

went out to Bombay, 1856 : in the mutiny in the S. Mahratta country : Under Secretary to Bombay Government, 1862 : Registrar of the High Court, 1863 : Judge of Canara, 1866 : Judicial Commissioner in Sind, 1868, and 1872 : called to the Irish bar, 1871 : Judge of the High Court, Bombay, 1873–87 : Member of the Indian Law Commission, 1879 : on special duty in Egypt, to reform the judicial administration, 1885 : Vice-Chancellor of the Bombay University, 1886 : Member of Council, Bombay, Nov. 1887 to April, 1892 : K.C.I.E., 1888 : LL.D., Edinburgh : President of the Bombay Branch of the Royal Asiatic Society : Vice-President of the R.A.S. : edited the *Bombay Regulations and Acts*, and wrote on *Hindu Law* : Reader in Indian Law, Cambridge.

WESTCOTT, FOSS (? – ?)

In the E. I. Co.'s Service on the Madras establishment, 1741–56 : Ninth in Council : Storekeeker and Scavenger at Fort St. George, Madras, 1748 : one of the three Commissioners appointed in 1749 to receive back the Fort from the French, the other two being Stringer Lawrence (*q.v.*), Mayor of Fort St. David, and Alexander Wynch (*q.v.*), afterwards Governor of Madras.

WESTERGAARD, NIEL LUDWIG (1815–1878)

Danish Oriental scholar : published, 1841, his *Radices Linguæ Sanskritæ*, a work of great research : studied Sayana's Commentary on the Rigveda and other Vedic works : wrote the *Verbal Dictionary* : travelled from 1841 for 3 years in the East, in Persia and India, to search for Zend MSS. and copy the cuneiform inscriptions at Persepolis, etc. : published the results in the *Journal of the Northern Society of Antiquaries at Copenhagen* : also his *Zendavesta*, 1852 : elected, 1848, Deputy to the Constituent Assembly in Denmark, and appointed its Secretary.

WESTLAND, SIR JAMES (1842–1903)

I.C.S. : born Nov. 14, 1842 : son of James Westland : educated at Marischal College, Aberdeen, and Wimbledon : arrived in Bengal, 1862 : was in 1870 Under Secretary to the Government of India in the Financial Department, and filled a succession of offices in the financial branch of the administration : was Accountant-General, in the Central Provinces, and Bengal, 1873–80 : Comptroller-General, 1881 : Member of the Finance Committee, 1886 : Secretary to Government in the Department of Finance and Commerce : Chief Commissioner of Assam in 1889 for a few months : resigned and went to New Zealand : Finance Member of the Supreme Council, 1893–9 : K.C.S.I., 1895 : Member of the Council of India, 1899 : died May 9, 1903.

WESTMACOTT, SIR RICHARD
(1841–   )

Son of Rev. Horatio Westmacott : educated at Rossall : entered the Bombay Army, 1859, and became Maj-General, 1899 : served in the Indian mutiny, 1857–8 : Afghan war, 1879–80 : Soudan expedition, 1885 : commanded advance column, Chin-Lushai expedition, 1889–90 : D.S.O. : commanded 28th Bombay Pioneers, 1887–94 : A.A.G., Poona, 1894–5 : Colonel on the staff, 1895–6 : commanded Nagpur District, 1896–9 : commanded 1st Brigade Mohmand Field Force, 1897 : and 4th Brigade, Tirah expedition, 1897–8 : K.C.B. : commanding 1st Class District, Mhow, 1900–3.

WESTON, CHARLES (1731–1809)

Son of the Recorder of the Mayor's Court : born in Calcutta, 1731 : apprenticed to J. Z. Holwell (*q.v.*), but applied himself to book-keeping : in the local militia at Calcutta, 1756 : fortunately absent on duty at the time of the Black Hole : received pecuniary help from Holwell when the latter left India : made a fortune by agency business : retired in 1782 : very benevolent and charitable : helped Holwell in his old age : had many pensioners and dependants : left a lakh of rupees to the poor : died Dec. 25, 1809.

WESTROPP, SIR MICHAEL ROBERTS
(1817–1890)

Born 1817 : son of Captain Henry B. Westropp, 7th Dragoon Guards : educated at Trinity College, Dublin : called to the Irish bar, 1840 : to the Bombay bar, 1854 : Advocate General at Bombay, 1856–7, and 1861–2 : Remembrancer of Legal Affairs, 1860–3 : Puisne Judge of the High Court, Bombay, 1863–70 : knighted as Chief Justice, 1870–82 : retired, 1882 : died Jan .4, 1890,

WETHERALL, SIR EDWARD ROBERT (? –1869)

Son of Sir George Augustus Wetherall : educated at the Naval and Military Academy, Edinburgh, and at Sandhurst : joined the 1st Royals, 1834 : served in Canada, 1837–9, in the Crimea as A.Q.M.G. : C.B. : D.Q.M.G. in China, 1857 : Chief of the Staff of the Central India Field Force to Sir Hugh Rose (Lord Strathnairn) (*q.v.*) in the mutiny : in his engagements up to Kalpi : commanded a Brigade in Oudh, 1858 : A.D.C. to Queen Victoria and Colonel, 1855 : Chief of the Staff in N. America : K.C.S.I., 1867 : Under Secretary in Ireland, 1868 : Maj-General, 1869 : died May 11, 1869.

WHEELER, SIR HUGH MASSY
(1789–1857)

Son of Capt. Hugh Wheeler, E.I.C.S. : born June 30, 1789 : educated at Richmond and Bath : joined the 24th Bengal N.I., 1804 : at Delhi, 1804 : in the Afghan war, 1838–9 : commanded the 48th N.I. at Ghazni and Kabul, 1839 : C.B. : escorted Dost Muhammad to India, 1840 : in the Satlaj campaign, commanded a Brigade at Mudki and Aliwal : and in the Panjab campaign commanded the Jalandhar Field Force and the Panjab Division : K.C.B. : Maj-Gen. : in the mutiny, in command of the Cawnpur Division : entrenched his force there, and sent help to Lucknow : his weak entrenchments were besieged by the mutineers, and heroically defended from 6th to 26th June, 1857, when he surrendered to the Nana Sahib (*q.v.*), on terms : as he and the other survivors were embarking on the 27th in boats on the river for Allahabad, they were treacherously attacked, by the Nana's orders, and most of them massacred at the Sati Chaora Ghat : some women and children being murdered later.

WHEELER, JAMES TALBOYS
(1824–1897)

Son of James Luff Wheeler : born Dec. 22, 1824 : began as a publisher and bookseller : War Office extra clerk : went to Madras to edit the *Madras Spectator*, 1858 : became a Professor in the Madras Presidency College : employed to examine the old Madras records and wrote *Madras in the Olden Times*, 1639–1748, 1860–2 : Assistant Secretary to the Government of

India, Foreign Department, 1862-70 : Secretary to the Chief Commissioner of British Burma, 1870-3 : reported on the Government Records : retired, 1891 : died Jan. 13, 1897 : wrote articles in the Calcutta, and *Asiatic Quarterly, Reviews* : wrote *History of India*, 1867-81 ; *Summary of Foreign Affairs (India)*, 1864-9 ; *Early Records of British India*, 1877 ; *History of the Imperial Assemblage at Delhi*. 1877 ; *India under British Rule*, 1886 ; and other works on Indian history.

WHELER, EDWARD (1733-1784)

Member of the Supreme Council at Calcutta from 1777,in succession to Colonel Monson (*q.v.*), who died in 1776 : at one time much opposed to Warren Hastings : but later supported him steadily in Council: laid the foundation-stone of St. John's Church the old Cathedral, Calcutta, in Hastings' absence, in April, 1784 : died in Oct. 1784.

WHELER, SIR FRANCIS, BARONET (1801-1878)

Born 1801 : entered the Indian Army in 1818 : served in Bundelkund, 1821-2 : in the Afghan war of 1839-40, at Ghazni and in the pursuit of Dost Muhammad : in the Panjab campaign of 1848-9, at the siege and capture of Multan and subsequent operations at Surajkund : in the mutiny was Brig-General of the Sagar district : C.B. : Maj-General, 1861 : commanded the Meerut Division : Lt-General, 1870 : died April 4, 1878.

WHISH, SIR WILLIAM SAMPSON (1787-1853)

Son of Rev. Richard Whish : born Feb. 27, 1787 : went to India in the Bengal Artillery in 1804 : in the Pindari war, 1817-8, under Marquis of Hastings : Major, 1821 : at siege of Bhartpur, 1825 -6 : Lt-Colonel : C.B., 1838 : Member of Military Board : commanded Artillery at Dumdum, 1839 : and the Lahore Division, 1848 : commanded the Multan Field Force, 1848 : besieged Mulraj at Multan from Sep. 7: with reinforcements made him surrender, Jan. 1849 : in the Panjab campaign, captured Cheniote : commanded a Division at Gujarat : K.C.B., 1849 : commanded the Bengal Division, 1849 : Lt-General, 1851 : died Feb. 25, 1853.

WHITE, ADAM (1790-1839)

Colonel : son of Adam White of Fens, merchant, Provost of Leith : born 1790 : Political Agent in Upper Assam: Commander of Assam Light Infantry, at time of death, and Lt-Colonel in 59th Bengal N.I. : killed at Sadiya, Upper Assam, in repelling an attack by Kampti tribes : a monument to his memory erected there : died Jan. 28, 1839 : wrote *Considerations on the State of British India*, 1822.

WHITE, DAVID EMMANUEL STARK-ENBURGH (1832-1889)

Son of an apothecary on the Madras establishment : educated at St. Andrew's Parochial School : became Assistant to the Director of Public Instruction, Madras, and thrice officiated as Registrar of Assurances : was a member of the Public Service Commission in Dec. 1886 : was best known as Life-President of the Eurasian and Anglo-Indian Association of Southern India : founded Whitefield Colony near Bangalore, and various benevolent funds for Eurasians, in whose interests he laboured long and assiduously : a capable leader of men, gifted with a remarkable power of organization, and a patriot : died at Nungumbarkum and buried at St. Andrew's cemetery, Madras, 1889.

WHITE, SIR GEORGE STUART (1835-   )

Field Marshal: born July 6, 1835 : son of J. R. White : educated at Sandhurst, entered the Army, 1853, and became Colonel, 1885, and Lt-General, 1895 : served in the Indian mutiny, 1857-8, Afghan war, 1878-80, with the Gordon Highlanders : at Charasia, where he gained the V.C. : at Kabul, Sherpur, in the march from Kabul to Kandahar, Brevet-Lt-Colonel : C.B. : Military Secretary to the Marquis'of Ripon, when Viceroy, 1880: commanded Gordon Highlanders, 1881: Nile expedition, 1884-5 : commanded Brigade in Burma, 1885-6 : Maj-General :[1] conducted Zhob Valley expedition : C. in C. in India, 1893-8 : Q.M.G. at War Office, 1898-9 : General on the Staff, commanding Natal in S. Africa war, 1899-1900 : defended Ladysmith from Nov. 2, 1899, to March 1, 1900 : G.C.I.E. : G.C.B. : G.C.S.I. : G.C.M.G. : G.C.V.O. : D.C.L. : LL.D. : J.P. : D.L : Governor of Gibraltar, 1900-5 : Governor of Chelsea Hospital, 1905.

WHITE, SIR HENRY
(1742–1822)

Cadet on the Bengal Establishment, 1772 : served against the Mahrattas, 1773, and 1780–2, against the Rohillas, 1774 : at Cutra : in the Carnatic, 1782 : at Cuddalore, 1783 : against Tippoo, 1790 : at Bangalore, Seringapatam and Savandrug, 1791 : under Cornwallis at Seringapatam, 1792 : Major in 1798 : suggested the formation of battalions of 2,000 marine sepoys : joined Lord Lake's Army against the Mahrattas, 1803 : greatly contributed to the capture of Agra, Oct. 18 : wounded at Laswari, Nov. 1 : at the capture of Gwalior, Feb. 4, 1804 : Maj-General, 1813 : K.C.B., 1815 : died Nov. 7, 1822.

WHITE, SIR HERBERT THIRKELL
(1855–   )

I.C.S. : son of Richard White : educated at Dulwich and Brasenose College, Oxford : Scholar : went out to Burma in the Civil Service, 1877 : Chief Judge of Chief Court, Lower Burma : Commissioner, Burma-China Boundary Commission, 1897–8 : K.C.I.E., 1903 : Lieutenant-Governor of Burma, 1905.

WHITE, SIR MICHAEL
(1791–1868)

Son of Major Robert White : educated at Westminster : entered the 24th Light Dragoons, 1804 : in the field, on the Satlaj, 1809 : at the capture of Hatras, 1817 : in the Mahratta campaign, 1817–8 : at Bhartpur, 1826 : commanded Cavalry in Afghanistan : in the Khyber, to the occupation of Kabul : in the Satlaj campaign, 1845–6 : in Cavalry commands at the battles : as also in the battles of the Panjab campaign : C.B., 1843 : K.C.B., 1862 : died Jan. 29, 1868 : Lt-General.

WHITEHEAD, RIGHT REV. HENRY
(1853–   )

Educated at Trinity College, Oxford, of which he became a Fellow : Principal of Bishop's College, and Superior of the Oxford Mission, Calcutta : Bishop of Madras since 1899.

WHITEHILL, THOMAS (? – ?)

Governor of Madras, 1777–8, and again in 1780 at the time of Hyder Ali's inva-sion of the Carnatic : removed by Warren Hastings from his post, according to one account, for refusing to restore the Guntur Sircar to Basalat Jung, brother to the Nizam, and according to another account, for his connexion with the Nuzveed zamin-dari scandal which led, in 1783, to the introduction against him in Parliament of a Bill of pains and penalties.

WHITLEY, RIGHT REV. JABEZ CORNELIUS (1837–1904)

Born in 1837 : son of the Rev. E. Whit-ley : educated at the Mercers' School, Holborn, and Queen's College, Cam-bridge : ordained in 1860 : went to India in 1862 as a Missionary of the Society for the Propagation of the Gospel : worked at Delhi, 1862–9 : at Ranchi in Chota Nagpur with a colony of Native Christians of the Church of England, 1869–90 : consecrated, in 1890, Bishop of Chota Nagpur, his district remaining part of the Calcutta diocese, the new Bishop promising canonical obedience to the Metropolitan of Calcutta : he wrote a *Primer of the Mundari Language*, on *Hindu Catechisms*, and on the works of St. Ignatius : died at Darjeeling, Oct. 18, 1904.

WHITLOCK, SIR GEORGE CORNISH
(1798–1868)

Born Dec. 3, 1798 : son of George Whit-lock : entered the E. I. Co.'s service in Madras, 1818 : in the Mahratta cam-paign, 1819 : the Burmese war, 1826 : in the Coorg campaign, 1834 : Brig-General in command of the Kurnool movable column, 1857, which became the Sagar Field Force : in April, 1858, captured the fort and palace of Banda, and Kirwi in June : gained a victory at Kirwi, Dec. 1858 : K.C.B., 1859 : Colonel of the 108th regt., 1862 : commanded the N. Division of the Madras Army, 1860–3 : retired, 1863 : Lt-General, 1864 : died Jan. 30, 1868.

WHITNEY, WILLIAM DWIGHT
(1827–1894)

Born Feb. 9, 1827, in Northampton, Massachusetts : son of Josiah Dwight Whitney : graduated at Williams College, 1845 : clerk at the Northampton bank : an assistant in the U.S. Geological Survey : studied Sanskrit at Yale, 1849–50 : to

Europe, 1850 : attended lectures of Weber at Berlin, and Roth at Tübingen : Professor of Sanskrit at Yale, 1854 : also of Comparative Philology from 1870 : Librarian, 1855-73, Secretary, 1857-84, President from 1884, of the American Oriental Society : published Sanskrit works and translations : was head of the school of Vedic Studies in the U.S. : edited the *Atharva Veda* : wrote on *Language and the Study of Language, Oriental and Linguistic Studies :* wrote on numerous Oriental subjects : contributed to Roth's and Bohtlingk's Sanskrit Dictionary : published his Sanskrit Grammar, 1879, a standard work : wrote in the American *Journal of Philology* and other Periodicals : was editor in chief of the *Century Dictionary* : received many honorary degrees, and was correspondent of foreign Academies : first President, in 1869, of the American Philological Association : was opposed to the native system of Sanskrit grammar : died June 7, 1894.

WHITTINGHAM, SIR SAMUEL FORD
(1772-1841)

Son of William Whittingham : born Jan. 29, 1772 : joined a commercial house at Bristol : joined the Army, 1803 : studied at the Military College at High Wycombe : sent by Pitt on a secret mission to the Peninsula, 1804 : served at Buenos Ayres : D.A.Q.M.G. under Wellesley in Spain, in the Spanish Army : commanded Spanish Cavalry : severely wounded at Talavera : C.B. : and knighted, 1815 : Lieutenant-Governor of Dominica, 1820-1 : K.C.H. : Q.M.G. in India, 1821-5 : dealt with the Burmese war and the Barrackpur mutiny : at the siege of Bhartpur, 1825-6 : K.C.B. : commanded the Cawnpur and Meerut Divisions : Military Secretary to Lord W. Bentinck, 1833-5 : commanded in the Windward and Leeward Islands, 1836-9 : Lt-General, 1838 : C. in C. at Madras, Aug. 1, 1840 : died Jan. 19, 1841.

WILAYAT ALI, NAWAB SYAD, KHAN BAHADUR (1815-1899)

Born 1815, at Patna : trained by his grandfather, Mir Abdulla, in his banking business and, at 15-16, was sent to Muzaffarpur to learn business under his uncle : became acquainted with many Government officers : in the mutiny, helped William Tayler, then Commissioner of Patna, to check the spread of the rebellion in Bihar : received H.R.H. the Prince of Wales' personal thanks for his good services to the empire : made C.I.E., Jan. 1878 : and Nawab in April, 1882 : died June 3, 1899.

WILDE, SIR ALFRED THOMAS
(1819-1878)

Son of Edward Archer Wilde : born Nov. 1, 1819 : educated at Winchester : entered the E. I. Co.'s Madras N.I. in 1839 : served in the disturbances of 1843, on the Malabar coast : engaged on the Panjab frontier, in a Panjab regiment, against the Waziris in 1853-4 ; against the Bozdar Beluchis in 1857 : in the mutiny was at the sieges of Delhi and Lucknow, leading storming parties at both, and was in other engagements : C.B. : commanded the 4th Panjab N.I. in the Mahsud-Waziri expedition of 1860 : in command of the Guides in the Umbeyla campaign, 1863 : A.D.C. to Queen Victoria : commanded the Panjab Frontier Force : C.S.I., 1866, : in 1868 commanded the Hazara Field Force in the Black Mountain expedition : K.C.B. : and Maj-General in 1869 : Military Secretary to the Government of Madras, 1869-70 : retired in 1871 : Member of the Council of India, 1877 : Lt-General : died Feb. 7, 1878.

WILKINS, SIR CHARLES
(1749 or 1750-1836)

I.C.S. : Orientalist : born in 1749 or 1750 : son of Walter Wilkins : to Bengal as a writer in the E. I. Co.'s service in 1770 : the first Englishman to acquire a thorough knowledge of Sanskrit : published a grammar of it in 1779 : translated the *Bhagavadgita*, under Warren Hastings' patronage, in 1785 : deciphered Sanskrit inscriptions : himself prepared the first Bengali and Persian types : set up a printing-press for Oriental languages : helped Sir W. Jones to found the Asiatic Society of Bengal, 1784 : established the Asiatic Researches : returned to England in 1786 : published translations of the *Hitopadesa, or Fables of Pilpai,* and of *Sakuntala :* in 1800 was made Custodian of the Oriental MSS. received from Seringapatam, and first Librarian of the India House Library : was, in 1806, appointed visitor of Haileybury and Addiscombe in the Oriental Department. In 1808 he produced another Sanskrit grammar :

452   DICTIONARY OF INDIAN BIOGRAPHY

edited, in 1806, *Richardson's Persian and Arabic Dictionary*, and wrote many valuable papers upon Indian subjects. Oxford made him a D.C.L.: the Royal Society of Literature gave him their medal as "Princeps Literaturæ Sanskriticæ": he became an Associate of the French Institute: King George IV knighted him, 1833, and gave him the badge of the Guelphic Order: he was also LL.D. and F.R.S.: died May 13, 1836.

WILKINS, HENRY ST. CLAIR
(1828–1896)

Son of Ven. George Wilkins: born Dec. 3, 1828: educated at Addiscombe: joined the Bombay Engineers, 1847: Lt-General, 1878: General, 1882: commanded the R.E. in the Abyssinian campaign, 1868: A.D.C. to Queen Victoria: in the P.W.D. in the Bombay Presidency: architect of many important works: e.g. the waterworks at Aden, the Secretariat buildings at Bombay, the Dekkan College and Sassoon buildings at Poona, the palace atBhuj, the restoration of the ancient buildings at Bijapur: died Dec. 15. 1896: author of *Reconnoitring in Abyssinia*.

WILKINS, WILLIAM J. (1843–1902)

Born at Sutton Coldfield, 1843: studied at Hackney College and Highgate: became a Congregationalist Minister: in 1867 went to India as a Missionary: for four years pastor of Union Chapel, Calcutta, but later devoted himself to Bengali evangelistic work: his experiences in India, and intercourse with educated natives, resulted in the writing of his *Hindu Mythology, Vedic and Puranic*, 1882, 1901; *Modern Hinduism*, 1881, 1901, and other works: in 1884 returned to England: died suddenly in 1902.

WILKINSON, SIR HENRY CLEMENT (1837–   )

Entered the Army, 1856, and became Lt-General, 1894: served in the Indian mutiny, 1857–8: Inspr-General of Auxiliary Cavalry, 1877–9: Military Secretary to C. in C., India, 1880: commanded Cavalry Brigade, Afghanistan, 1880–81, and in Egyptian campaign, 1882: commanded Brigades at Sealkot, Quetta, Sagar and Calcutta: and Divisions at Meerut, Rawul Pindi and Allahabad, 1880–7: C.B., 1882: K.C.B., 1897.

WILKINSON, OSBORN (1822–   )

Born Oct. 8, 1822: educated at Eton and Christ's College, Cambridge: served with Jalandhar Field Force against the Sikh insurgents, 1848–9: against Mohmand tribes, 1854, in Indian mutiny, 1858: at the siege of Lucknow: in Oudh campaign: under Sir J. Douglas in Bihar: Brevet-Major: Adjutant of 10th Bengal Cavalry: commanded 2nd Bengal Cavalry for ten years: commanded frontier post of Kohat in Afghan war, 1878–9, and was with Sir F. Roberts in the Kuram valley: C.B.: joint author of *The Gemini Generals*.

WILKS, MARK (1760 ?–1831)

Born about 1760: went to Madras in the E. I. Co.'s military service, 1782: Deputy Secretary to the Military Board, 1786: Secretary to Sir B. Close's Mission to Mysore, 1787: A.D.C. to the Governor, Madras, 1789: A.D.C. and Military Secretary to Colonel James Stuart in the War against Tippoo, 1790–5: Military and Private Secretary to the Governor, Lord Clive, and Town-Major of Fort St. George, 1798–1803: Military Secretary to the C. in C., General James Stuart, 1803: Resident in Mysore, 1803–8: Lt-Colonel, 1808: left India, 1808: Governor of St. Helena, 1813–6: Brevet-Colonel, 1814: retired from the service, 1818: died Sep. 19, 1831: wrote *Historical Sketches of the South of India in an Attempt to trace the History of Mysore*, 1810–4: also *A Report on Government of Mysore*, 1805: and an analysis of the *Akhlak-i-Nasiri*, a metaphysical treatise: F.R.S.: and Vice-President of the Asiatic Society.

WILLCOCKS, SIR JAMES (1857–   )

Brig-General: son of Captain W. Willcocks: educated privately: entered the Indian Army, 1878: served in Afghan war, 1879–80: Waziri expedition, 1881: Soudan campaign, 1885: Burma war, 1886–9: D.S.O.: Chin-Lushai expedition, 1889–90: Manipur expedition, 1891: A.A.G. to Tochi Field Force, 1897: Brevet-Lt-Colonel: second in command, W. African Field Force, 1898: commanded W. African Frontier Force, 1899–1900: at relief of Kumassi: Brevet-Colonel: K.C.M.G., 1900: wrote *From Kabul to Kumassi*.

WILLIAMS, CLEMENT (1834-1879)

Doctor : Assistant Surgeon in 68th regt. in 1858 : chiefly served in Burma : in 1860 went on leave to Mandalay, and acquired, by his operations for cataract, singular influence at the Court there : the first Political Agent in Upper Burma : in 1863 travelled to Bhamo, to open up trade to N. China : recalled by the King when insurrection broke out at Mandalay : he wrote in the *Asiatic Society's Journal* of the practicability of a trade route : resigned the British service in 1866, and became a Minister of the State at Mandalay : directed the King's attention to the vast mineral wealth of Burma : he was, at the time of the massacres at King Thebaw's accession, the medium of communication with the British Government, and saved some lives : had great knowledge of the Burmese : caught typhoid at Naples and died at Florence, June 26, 1879.

WILLIAMS, SIR EDWARD CHARLES SPARSHOTT (1831-)

Born March 27, 1831 : educated at the Royal Naval School, New Cross, and at Addiscombe : joined the Bengal Engineers, 1848 : in the Burmese war, 1852-3, at the taking of Martaban, Rangoon, Prome : Principal, Civil Engineering College, Calcutta, 1856-60 : Under Secretary, Government of India, P.W.D., 1863-9 : Deputy Secretary, Railway branch, 1869-74 and 1877-8 : Director of State Railways, 1874-7 : Deputy Government Director of Indian Railway Companies, India Office, 1880 : Government Director, 1892-7 : General, 1895 : C.I.E. : 1878 : K.C.I.E., 1893.

WILLIAMS, SIR WILLIAM JOHN (1828-1903)

Entered the Army in 1848, in the Royal Artillery : served through the Crimea : commanded the Artillery in the Jowaki-Afridi expedition, 1877-8 : in the Afghan war, 1878-9 : at the capture of Ali Masjid : Lt-General, 1891 : K.C.B., 1891 : retired, 1895 : Colonel-Commandant R.A., 1898 : died April 22, 1903.

WILLOCK, SIR HENRY (1790-1858)

Went to India in the Madras Cavalry, 1804 : learnt Persian and became Interpreter and Commander of the Escort of Sir Harford Jones-Brydges, the Envoy to Persia : Persian Secretary to Sir Gore Ouseley : in charge of the British Mission at Teheran,1815-26 : received the decoration of the Lion and Sun : knighted in 1827 : resigned the service, 1834 : Director of the E. I. Co., 1835 : Chairman, 1846-7 : made collections of coins of ancient and modern Persian dynasties, which he presented to the India House : died Aug. 17, 1858.

WILLOCK, HENRY DUNDAS (1830-1903)

I.C.S. : son of Sir Henry Willock : born in Persia, Dec. 25, 1830 : educated at Haileybury : went to India to the N.W.P., in 1852 : was joint Magistrate at Allahabad in the mutiny : commanded the volunteers there : helped to disarm mutineers : served under General Neill in the storming and capture of Kydganj : with Major Renaud's force to Cawnpur : with Havelock, on his advance to Cawnpur and Lucknow and at Bithur : constantly in action : in the Lucknow garrison until the relief by Sir Colin Campbell : Political Officer with Berkley's column, at the capture of several forts in Oudh : and with Maxwell's column till the capture of Kalpi by Sir Hugh Rose's Central India Force in May, 1858 : with the Field Force watching the south borders of Oudh : Judge of Azimghar : retired, 1884 : died April 26, 1903.

WILLOUGHBY, SIR JOHN POLLARD, BARONET (1798-1866)

I.C.S. : third son of Sir Christopher Willoughby, first *Baronet* : entered the Bombay Civil Service, 1817 : became Chief Secretary to the Bombay Government, 1835 : Member of Council, Bombay, April, 1846, to April, 1851 : Director of the E. I. Co., 1854 : Member of the Council of India, 1858-66 : succeeded his brother, Sir Henry, as Baronet, in March, 1865 : died Sep. 15, 1866.

WILLSHIRE, SIR THOMAS, BARONET (1789-1862)

Born Aug. 24, 1789 : son of Capt. John Willshire : joined the 38th regt. : educated at King's Lynn and Kensington : served in S. America, Portugal, Walcheren, the Peninsula, the Netherlands, at the Cape : Commandant of

British Kafraria, 1819 : went out to India, 1822 : Brigadier at the capture of Kittur, 1824 : Lt-Colonel, 1827 : commanded the Bombay Division in the Afghan war, 1839 : at Ghazni and Kabul : returning to India, took Kelat, Nov. 13, 1839 : C.B., 1838 : K.C.B., 1839 : Baronet, for Kelat, 1848 : commanded at Chatham, 1841-6 : General and G.C.B., 1861 : Colonel of the 51st (K.O.) L.I. : died May 31, 1862.

WILMOT, SIR HENRY, BARONET (1831-1901)

Son of Sir Henry Wilmot, *Bart.* : born Feb. 3, 1831: educated at Rugby : entered the Army, 1849 : in the mutiny in the Rifle Brigade and on the Staff of Sir Hope Grant (*q.v.*) : at the capture of Lucknow, on March 11, 1858, near the Iron Bridge, under severe fire, rescued a wounded soldier, and gained the V.C. : Brevet-Major : Deputy Judge Advocate : with the Oudh Field Force, 1857 : Judge Advocate-General, 1860-1, in China : M.P., 1869-85 for S. Derbyshire : succeeded his father, 1872 : Captain of English shooting eight at Wimbledon meetings : K.C.B., 1897 : D.L. : J.P. : died April 7, 1901.

WILSON, SIR ALEXANDER (1843-)

Born May 2, 1843 : son of the Very Rev. Dean Wilson, Aberdeen : educated at Glenalmond : in India, 1865-91 : partner in the firm of Jardine, Skinner & Co., Calcutta : President of the Bengal Chamber of Commerce and of the Bank of Bengal : Member of the Governor-General's Legislative Council : Sheriff of Calcutta, 1887 : knighted : commanded the Calcutta Light Horse : Chairman of the Mercantile Bank of India, London.

WILSON, ANDREW (1831-1881)

Son of the Rev. Dr. J. Wilson (*q.v.*) : born 1831 : educated at Edinburgh and Tübingen Universities : went to India, and took charge of the *Bombay Times* : in England, edited a Journal at Berwick, and wrote for *Blackwood's Magazine* : in 1860-3, edited the *China Mail* and accompanied the expedition to Tientsin : wrote *England's Policy in China* : travelled in the S. of China and wrote *The Ever-Victorious Army, a History of the Chinese Campaigns under Lt-Colonel C. G. Gordon, C.B., R.E., and of the Suppression*

of the Taiping Rebellion, 1878 : edited, 1873, the *Bombay Gazette* : and the *Star of India* : travelled on the borders of Chinese Tibet and in the W. Himalayas, 1874-5, and wrote *The Abode of Snow* ; *Observations on a Journey from Chinese Tibet to the Indian Caucasus through the Upper Valleys of the Himalaya :* died June 9, 1881.

WILSON, SIR ARCHDALE, OF DELHI, BARONET (1803-1874)

Son of Rev. George Wilson : born Aug. 3, 1803 : educated at the R.M.C., Addiscombe : entered the E. I. Co.'s Bengal Artillery in 1819 : at Bhartpur, Jan. 18, 1826 : commanded the Artillery at Lucknow, 1839 : Superintendent of the gun-foundary at Cossipur, 1841-5 : in the Panjab campaign, 1848-9 : commanded the Artillery at Dumdum, 1854 : was commanding at Meerut in 1857 : was at Ghaziuddinnagar on May 30 : at Badli-ka-sarai, and at Delhi commanded the Artillery : on Barnard's death and Reed's resignation was selected to command at the siege of Delhi from July 17 : after the arrival of the siege train on Sep. 4, he yielded to the judgment of the Chief Engineer, Baird-Smith (*q.v.*), assaulted Delhi on Sep. 14 : its capture completed by Sep. 20 : Wilson, not a strong character, luckily relied on strong advisers, Baird-Smith, Nicholson (*q.v.*) and others : K.C.B., Nov. 17 : Baronet, Jan. 1858 : commanded the Artillery at Sir Colin Campbell's capture of Lucknow, March, 1858 : left India, 1858 : G.C.B., 1867 : Lt-General, 1868 : died May 9, 1874.

WILSON, SIR ARTHUR (1837-)

Born 1837 : called to the bar at the Inner Temple, 1862 : Puisne Judge of the High Court, Calcutta, 1878 : Vice-Chancellor of the Calcutta University, 1880-3 : Legal Adviser at the India Office, 1892-02 : Privy Councillor : Member of the Judicial Committee from 1902.

WILSON, CHARLES ROBERT (1863-1904)

Born 1863 : educated at City of London School and Wadham College, Oxford : entered the Bengal Education Department, 1887 : was Principal of the Patna College : also Assistant Secretary to the Government of India, and in charge of the Records : he brought out two volumes of the *Early Annals of the English in Bengal*, which furnish much hitherto unknown information on the beginnings of the English connection with India : and edited the *Inscriptions on Tombs and Monuments in Bengal :* he was a zealous and painstaking student of Indian historical records : and laboured at clearing up all the details of the tragedy of the Black Hole of Calcutta, its site, the survivors, etc. : he died in England, July 24, 1904.

WILSON, RIGHT REV. DANIEL
(1778–1858)

Son of Stephen Wilson, a rich silk manufacturer : born July 2, 1778 : educated at St. Edmund Hall, Oxford : D.D., 1832 : Tutor of his College, 1804–11 : Assistant and Incumbent of St. John's Chapel, Bedford Row, London, 1809–23 : Vicar of Islington, 1824–32 : appointed Bishop of Calcutta and Metropolitan of India, 1832 : held the see till his death on Jan. 2, 1858 : made long visitation tours through India and Ceylon, and to Burma, the Straits, Singapur and Malacca : he built St. Paul's Cathedral at Calcutta between Oct. 8, 1839, and Oct. 8, 1847 : he insisted on the absolute abandonment of the caste system among native Christains in S. India : he infused energy into all Church matters, and was described as the Champion of Evangelicalism, strongly opposed to Tractarianism. Lord Dalhousie spoke of him to Lord Canning as " the best man of business he had to do with in India " : his liberality was princely : traditions of his style of preaching and eccentricities survive to this day : he was buried in the Cathedral at Calcutta : volumes of his sermons and writings were published. His life was written by his son-in-law, the Rev. Josiah Bateman, 1860.

WILSON, HORACE HAYMAN
(1786–1860)

Born Sep. 26, 1786 : educated in Soho Square, London, and at St. Thomas's Hospital : arrived in Calcutta in 1808, in the medical service of the E. I. Co.*: was at once attached to the Mint at Calcutta, for his knowledge of chemistry and assay : was Secretary to the Asiatic Society of Bengal, 1811–33, with short intervals. He studied Sanskrit steadily and translated the *Meghaduta* of Kalidasa

in 1813. In 1816 he was appointed Assay-master of the Calcutta mint, and held the appointment until he left India in 1832. He published the *Theatre of the Hindus* and Sanskrit-English dictionary (two editions), besides contributing to Asiatic Researches, the Journals of the Asiatic, Medical, and Physical Societies, and other Oriental Literature. He wrote an *Historical Account of the Burmese War* : catalogued Col. Colin Mackenzie's MSS. : was Secretary to the Committee of Public Instruction, introducing the study of European Science and English Literature into native education : and was visitor to the Sanskrit College. He became Boden Professor of Sanskrit at Oxford in 1833, Hon. M.A. at Exeter College : Librarian of the India House in 1836, Examiner at Haileybury, and Director of the Royal Asiatic Society from 1837 till his death : F.R.S., 1834. He continued his labours on Indian subjects, publishing the *Vishnu Purana* ; *Lectures on the Religious and Philosophical Systems of the Hindus*, 1840 ; a Sanskrit grammar ; the *Ariana Antiqua* ; a new edition of Mill's *History of British India* ; a translation of the *Rig-Veda* ; a *Glossary of Indian Terms*, and an edition of Macnaghten's *Hindu Law* : the greatest Sanskrit scholar of his time, conbining a variety of attainments as general linguist, historian, chemist, accountant, numismatist, actor and musician : died May 8, 1860.

WILSON, JAMES (1760–1814)

Captain : son of a Captain in the mercantile navy : in the American war, at Bunker's Hill and Long Island : mate on an East Indiaman, joined the local Indian mercantile, or transport, service : to convey supplies to Sir Eyre Coote and Admiral Hughes in Madras, he ran the blockade established by Admiral Suffrein : was captured, and sold with others as prisoners to Hyder Ali : made a bold attempt to escape, was recaptured, and taken to Seringapatam : imprisoned in irons for twenty-three months : on release, he shipped to Java and nearly died at Batavia : made a fortune by trading, and retired. In 1796 he took strong religious views, bought a ship and on behalf of the London Missionary Society conducted a voyage of thirty Missionaries to the Islands of the S. Pacific Ocean : returned in 1798, and, for sixteen years, was a Director of the Society, until he died in 1814.

WILSON, JAMES (1805–1860)

Born at Hawick, June 3, 1805 : third son of William Wilson, a woollen manufacturer : educated at Quaker schools at Ackworth and Earl's Colne : apprenticed to a hat manufacturer at Hawick, 1821 : removed to London, 1824 : was partner of Wilson, Irwin & Wilson, till 1831 : then was alone, and, with the exception of an unfortunate speculation in indigo, was prosperous and successful in business until he retired, in 1844. Three works published before his retirement from business brought him to the front as a financial authority : he wrote, like a practical political economist, *Influences of the Corn Laws*, 1839 ; *Fluctuations of Currency*, 1840, and *The Revenue*, 1841 : also, about the same time, he wrote the City articles in the *Morning Chronicle*, and contributed political articles to the *Examiner* and *Manchester Guardian*, for several years : after consultation with Cobden and other leaders of the Anti-Corn-Law League, he established, in 1843, the *Economist*, which forthwith gained the authority it has always retained as a newspaper devoted to special monetary and political subjects : he wrote, as a "bullionist," on "Capital, Currency, Banking," 1847 : also on the railway mania, the famine in Ireland, and the crisis of 1847 : was M.P. for Westbury, 1847–57, and for Devonport, 1857–9 : made a reputation in Parliament on financial questions, and was appointed Joint Secretary to the Board of Control, 1848–52 : Financial Secretary to the Treasury, 1853–8 : and in 1859 was Vice-President of the Board of Trade and Paymaster-General, and was made Privy Councillor, 1859 ; specially selected to be the first Finance Member of the Supreme Council of India to reorganize the Indian finances and meet the deficit of revenue and great increase of the public debt caused by the mutiny : held the post from Nov. 29, 1859, to his death : he imposed an Income Tax, created a Government paper currency, and remodelled the whole system of Indian finance and accounts : he had other projects in hand when his health gave way in the rains, and his Indian career was cut short after 9 months' work : he died at Calcutta,

Aug. 11, 1860, to the deep regret of Lord Canning and the Government : his statue was erected in the Dalhousie Institute, Calcutta : his bust was placed in the National Gallery of Edinburgh, and his portrait hangs in the Town Hall of Hawick. He was a very hard worker, and had great gifts, a wonderful memory, a well-balanced judgment, a robust constitution : he gave the impression of massive power and firm determination : he was practical, tolerant, active-minded, and clear in his views and language.

WILSON, JAMES (1825–1902)

Educated at the People's College, Sheffield, and for a time a teacher : trained for business in the cutlery firm of Rodgers & Sons of Sheffield : went to Calcutta to establish a direct trade in Sheffield manufactures, but this failed : wrote, for the *Delhi Gazette*, about the Calcutta Agricultural Exhibition of Jan. 1864 : was Editor and joint proprietor of the *Indian Daily News*, 1863–80 : was one of the first to draw attention to the impending famine in Orissa, 1866, by placing his information before the Secretary of State, which led to the appointment of Sir George Campbell's Orissa Famine Commission : his Journal for some time had influence with the highest officers in India : he was an active member of the Calcutta Corporation for some years : died Oct. 1902.

WILSON, REV, JOHN, D.D. (1804–1875)

Born Dec. 11, 1804 : son of Andrew Wilson : educated at Edinburgh University : studied surgery and medicine : ordained Missionary of the Scottish Missionary Society, 1828 : to Bombay, 1829 : founded the *Oriental Christian Spectator*, 1830 : the first to establish schools for native girls, and a native church on Presbyterian principles : specially attended to vernacular education : his College, under various names, eventually became "Wilson's College" : he was transferred to the Church of Scotland, but left that Church at its disruption in 1843 : was Superintendent of the Free Church of Scotland's Indian Mission at Bombay : travelled extensively in the Bombay Presidency and adjacent provinces, collecting MSS., and acquiring Oriental knowledge : President of the Bombay Literary Society, 1835 : M.R.A.S., 1836 : the first to decipher Asoka inscriptions at Girnar : wrote on *The Parsi Religion*, 1843 : F.R.S., 1845 : President of the " Cave Temple Commission," 1848–61, to examine the antiquities connected with the cave temples, and wrote about them and the Commission's work : in the mutiny he deciphered the rebels' cryptic correspondence : original Fellow, 1857, and Vice-Chancellor of the Bombay University, 1868 : in 1870, Moderator cf the General Assembly of the Free Church of Scotland : died Dec. 1, 1875, near Bombay : greatly esteemed by the highest officers, the natives and visitors. He travelled in Palestine, 1843, and wrote *The Lands of the Bible* : wrote also a *History of the Suppression of Infanticide in W. India*, 1855 : *India Three Thousand Years Ago*, 1858 ; on the Hindu religion ; on Caste, and on the Evangelization of India.

WILSON, SIR JOHN CRACROFT
(1808–1881)

I.C.S. : born 1808 : son of Alexander Wilson, M.C.S. and F.R.S. : educated at Brasenose College, Oxford, and Hailey-bury : was in the Bengal Civil Service, 1827–59 : in the mutiny was Judge of Moradabad : led an attack, May 21, 1857, against Muhammadan fanatics from Rampur and routed them : the sepoys threatened to shoot him : he escaped to Meerut and searched through the country for fugitive Christians : helped to save 64. Lord Canning mentioned him first of civil officers, as having " saved more Christian lives than any man in India " : was in action with Seaton's column at Gangari : rendered important services, after the mutiny. as Special Commissioner for the trial of rebels and mutineers : retired, 1859 : C.B., 1860, for his services : in New Zealand, was Member of the House of Representatives in three Parliaments : K.C.S.I., 1872 : died there March 2, 1881.

WILSON, THOMAS FOURNESS
(1820 ?–1886)

Lt-General : born about 1820 : entered the Army, 1838 : in the mutiny was Captain : A.A.G. to Sir H. Lawrence at Lucknow : was at the action at Chinhut : spiked 2 guns : in the room at the Residency, Lucknow, when Lawrence was

mortally wounded : was General Inglis' right-hand man : his " splendid conduct " recorded : A.D.C. to Queen Victoria : C.B. : Secretary in the Military Department at the India Office : was Military Member of the Supreme Council from May 2, 1881 : died, while Member, Feb. 28, 1886.

WINDHAM, SIR CHARLES ASH
(1810–1870)

Born Oct. 8, 1810 : son of Admiral William Windham : educated at Sand-hurst : joined the Coldstream Guards at 16 : served in Canada in 1838–42 : Colonel, 1854 : A.Q.M.G. of a Division in the Crimea : engaged at Alma and Balaclava, and commanded a Division at Inkerman : C.B. in 1855 : commanded a Brigade : led the storming party at the assault of the Redan, Sept. 1855 : showed heroic bravery : " seemed to bear a charmed life " : Major-General : Chief of the Staff to Sir W. J. Codrington : M.P. for East Norfolk, 1857 : volunteered for India in the mutiny of 1857 : placed in command at Cawnpur : on Nov. 26, 1857, he defeated Gwalior troops under Tantia Topi, but later, through the failure of a sub-ordinate officer, was unable to hold Cawn-pur against the attack of a larger Gwalior force : was transferred to the command of the Lahore Division : returned to England in 1861 : Lt-General, 1863 : K.C.B., 1865 : commanded the Forces in Canada, 1867–70 : died Feb. 4, 1870.

WINGATE, SIR ANDREW (1846–   )

I.C.S. : son of Rev. William Wingate : educated at Elizabeth College, Guernsey ; at Kensington, and Universities of London and Heidelberg : went to Bombay in the Civil Service, 1869 : Commissioner in Sind : Member of the Governor-General's Legislative Council, 1897 : Secretary to Bombay Government in the Plague Department, 1898 : Commissioner, Central Division, Bombay, 1900–02 : C.I.E., 1879 : K.C.I.E., 1899.

WINGATE, SIR GEORGE (1812–1879)

Son of Andrew Wingate : educated at Addiscombe : served in the Bombay Engineers from 1829 : retired as Major : was Revenue Survey Commissioner in Bombay : K.C.S.I., 1866 : died Feb, 7, 1879.

WINGFIELD, SIR CHARLES JOHN
(1820–1892)

I.C.S.: son of W. Wingfield-Baker: educated at Westminster and Haileybury, 1837–9: to the N.W.P. in the Civil Service, 1839: Commissioner of the Baraich Division in Oudh in the mutiny: retired to Gonda, Balrampur and Gorakhpur: C.B., 1860: Chief Commissioner of Oudh, 1859–65: retired, 1866: K.C.S.I., 1866: M.P. for Gravesend, 1868–74: died Jan. 27, 1892.

WINTERBOTHAM, SIR HENRY MARTIN (1847–)

I.C.S.: born Jan. 13, 1847: son of John Brend Winterbotham: entered the Madras Civil Service, 1869: Commissioner of Revenue Settlement, Board of Revenue, 1895: Member of Council, 1898–1903: retired: C.S.I., 1900: K.C.S.I., 1903.

WODEHOUSE, JOSCELINE HENEAGE (1852–)

Born July 17, 1852: son of Admiral George Wodehouse: educated at Woolwich: entered the Royal Artillery, 1872: served in the Zulu war, 1879: Afghan war, 1880: Soudan, 1883–94: commanded 3rd Brigade, Malakand Field Force, 1898: severely wounded: Egyptian campaign, 1898–1900: commanded Presidency District, Bengal, 1898–9. Sikandarabad, 1900–1: Lahore, 1902,: C.B., 1889: C.M.G., 1890.

WODEHOUSE, SIR PHILIP EDMOND
(1811–1887)

Governor: son of Edmond Wodehouse: born Feb. 26, 1811: entered the Ceylon Civil Service, 1828: became Government Agent for the Western province, 1843: was Superintendent of British Honduras, 1851: Governor of British Guiana, 1854–61: C.B., 1860: Governor of the Cape and High Commissioner in South Africa, 1862–70: K.C.B., 1862: was Governor of Bombay, May 6, 1872, to April 30, 1877: G.C.S.I., 1877: his successor, Sir R. Temple, refers to his strong sense, steady judgment and practical ability: died Oct. 25, 1887.

WOLFF, REV. JOSEPH (1795–1862)

Born of Jewish parents, 1795: educated at Stuttgart and Bamberg: converted to Christianity near Prague, 1812:
studied Arabic, Syriac, Chaldæan: attended theological lectures at Vienna: also studied, at Tübingen, Arabic, Persian, religious subjects: went to Rome, 1816, but was expelled in 1818 from the Propaganda and the city: joined the Church of England, 1819, and studied Oriental languages at Cambridge: as a Missionary, chiefly to the Jews, visited, 1821–6, Malta, Alexandria, Sinai, Jerusalem, Cyprus, Bagdad, Ispahan, Tiflis, the Crimea, Turkey: in search of the lost tribes, he travelled, from 1828, to Alexandria, Asia Minor, Persia, Bokhara, Balkh, Kabul, Calcutta, Kashmir, Madras, Pondicherry, Goa, Bombay, Egypt, Malta: in 1836 he went to Abyssinia, Jeddah, Yemen, Bombay, and the United States, where he became D.D. and was ordained, 1837: given a living in Yorkshire, 1838: in 1843 he again went to Bokhara to ascertain the fate of Stoddart and Conolly, who had been killed: himself escaped narrowly: published a *Narrative of the Mission to Bokhara*, 1845: he died at his Somerset Vicarage, May 2, 1862. He called himself "The Protestant Xavier": he wrote his *Travels and Adventures*, 1860–2, and several series of journals of his missionary labours.

WOLLASTON, ARTHUR NAYLOR
(1842–)

Born Oct. 14, 1842: son of Henry Francis Wollaston: educated at Stockwell Grammar School: joined the India Office, 1859: became a senior clerk, 1873: Assistant Secretary, 1884, in charge of the Revenue and Statistics Department, 1886–8: Registrar and Superintendent of Records since 1898: Examiner in Persian at the Staff College, 1880: superintended the translation of Oriental inscriptions in the S. Kensington Museum, 1881: translated the *Anwar-i-Suhaili*, 1877: edited Sir L. Pelly's miracle play of *Hasan and Husain*, 1879: published English-Persian dictionaries, 1882 and 1889: *Half-hours with Muhammad*, 1886; and (with Sir Roper Lethbridge) a *Gazetteer of the Territories under the Government of India*: C.I.E., 1886, for his Oriental scholarship.

WOLSELEY, GARNET JOSEPH, FIRST VISCOUNT (1833–)

Born June 4, 1833: son of Major Garnet Joseph Wolseley: entered the

Army, 1852, and became Colonel, 1865 : served in Burmese war, 1852–3 : Crimean war, 1855–6 : Indian mutiny, 1857–8, at Lucknow and the Alambagh : China, 1860 : commanded Red River expedition, 1870 : Brevet-Lt-Colonel : commanded the Forces in Ashanti war, 1872 : Maj-General : K.C.B. : G.C.M.G. : Governor of Natal, 1879 : Q.M.G. at War Office, 1880 : A.G. at War Office, 1882–5 : C. in C., in Egyptian campaign, 1882, and of Gordon relief expedition, 1884–5 : A.G. at War Office, 1885–90 : C. in C., Ireland, 1890–5 : Field Marshal, 1894 : C. in C. of the Army, 1895–1900 : K.P. : P.C. : G.C.B. : G.C.M.G. : D.C.L. : LL.D. : author of *The Soldier's Pocket Book, Life of the Duke of Marlborough, Decline and Fall of Napoleon, The Story of a Soldier's Life.*

WOLSELEY, SIR GEORGE B.
(1839–   )

Born July 11, 1839 : son of Major Garnet J. Wolseley, and brother of Viscount Wolseley : educated privately : entered the Army, 1857, and became Maj-General, 1892 : served in the Indian mutiny, 1857–8 ; Afghan campaign, 1878–80 : Brevet-Lt-Colonel : Egyptian campaign, 1882 : Tel-el-Kebir : in the Nile campaign, 1884–5 : C.B. : Burmese war, 1886–8, as Brig-General : K.C.B. : Lt-General in command of the Forces, Panjab, 1897–8, and Madras, 1898–1904.

WOOD, SIR DAVID EDWARD
(1812–1894)

Son of Colonel Thomas Wood, M.P. : born Jan. 6, 1812 : educated at the R.M.A., Woolwich : joined the Royal Artillery, 1829 : became Maj-General, 1867 : General, 1877 : served at the Cape, 1842–3 : in the Crimea, at the battles, and commanded R.H.A. : C.B. : in the mutiny, commanded Artillery under Sir Colin Campbell : as Brig-General at the capture of Lucknow, and in subsequent operations, 1857–9 : K.C.B. : commanded the R.A. at Aldershot, 1864–5, and Woolwich Garrison, 1869–74 : Colonel Commandant, R.H.A. : G.C.B., 1877 : died Oct. 16, 1894.

WOOD, SIR HENRY EVELYN
(1838–   )

Field Marshal : born Feb. 9, 1838 : son of Rev. Sir John Page Wood, *Bart.* : edu-

cated at Marlborough : entered the Navy, 1852 : was in the Naval Brigade in the Crimea, 1854–5 : severely wounded at the Redan, June 18, 1855, when A.D.C. to Sir W. Peel (*q.v.*) : joined the 13th Light Dragoons, 1855 : in the 17th Lancers in the Indian Mutiny : gained the V.C. : called to the bar from the Middle Temple, 1874 : passed the Staff College : served in the Ashanti, Kafir, Zulu and Transvaal campaigns : commanded a Brigade in the Egyptian Expedition, 1882 : raised the Egyptian Army, 1883 : was in the Nile Expedition, 1894–5 : at different times, commanded at Chatham, the Eastern District, and the Aldershot Division : Q.M.G. of the Army, 1893–7 : Adjt-Gen., 1897–1901 : has commanded the 2nd Army Corps since 1901 : has written on military subjects : C.B., 1874 : K.C.B., 1879 : G.C.M.G., 1882 : G.C.B., 1891 : D.L. and Field-Marshal.

WOOD, SIR HENRY HASTINGS AFFLECK (1826–1904)

Son of General John S. Wood, Lieutenant of the Tower of London : born in 1826 : entered the Indian Army in 1843 : joined the 4th Bombay N.I. in 1844 : served under Sir C. Napier in 1845–6 : in the Panjab campaign, 1848–9 : in Persia, 1856–7 : in the Indian mutiny, throughout the Central India campaign under Sir Hugh Rose : frequently mentioned in despatches : entered the Bombay Staff Corps in 1861 : in the Abyssinian expedition, 1867–8 : C.B. : Brig-General in Bombay, 1875–80 : in the Afghan campaign, 1879–80 : General in 1889 : K.C.B. in 1894 : in May, 1904, gazetted Colonel of the 104th (" Wellesley's ") Rifles in the Indian Army : died at Boulogne, Aug. 5, 1904.

WOOD, HERBERT WILLIAM
(1837–1879)

Son of Lt-Colonel Herbert William Wood, Madras N.I. : born July 17, 1837 : educated at Cheltenham and Addiscombe, Chatham : to Madras in the Engineers, 1857 : in the mutiny in the Sagar Field Division under Whitlock, at Banda and Kirwi and other engagements in 1858 : Field Engineer in Abyssinia, 1868 : Major : while on furlough went in the Grand Duke Constantine's expedition to investigate the Amu Darya : wrote *The Shores of Lake Aral,* 1876 : died in India, Oct.

8, 1879 : F.R.G.S. and Member of Russian Geographical Societies.

WOOD, JOHN (? – ?)

During the war of 1767 with Hyder Ali, Col. John Wood saw much active service, distinguishing himself in the campaign : in 1769, at the instance of a Major Fitzgerald, he was tried by court-martial for misappropriation of public moneys, but acquitted : the Madras Government did not concur in the verdict, and dismissed him : the Court of Directors reversed this decision, 1771, and reinstated him.

WOOD, JOHN (1811–1871)

Born 1811 : joined the E. I. Co.'s naval service, 1826 : commanded the first vessel, the *Indus*, in the navigation of the Indus river, 1835–6 : Assistant to Burnes (*q.v.*) in his commercial mission to Afghanistan, 1836 : reported on the Kabul Valley : discovered the source of the Oxus river : in 1858, Manager of the Oriental Steam Navigation Co. in Sind : Superintendent of the Indus steam flotilla from 1861 : died in Sind, Nov. 13, 1871 : wrote *A Personal Narrative of a Journey to the Source of the Oxus*, 1841.

WOOD, SIR MARK, BARONET
(1747–1829)

Son of Alexander Wood : born 1747 : joined the E. I. Co.'s military service, in the Bengal Engineers, 1772 : Colonel, 1795 : Surveyor-General, 1787 : Chief Engineer in Bengal, 1790 : returned to England, 1793 : was elected M.P. in 1794, 1796 and 1802, retiring in 1818 : made a Baronet, 1808 : died Feb. 6, 1829 : wrote on *The Late War with Tippoo, Sultan*, 1800 ; *A Journey from England to India through Egypt in* 1779, 1803 : he surveyed Calcutta and the country on the banks of the Hughli river to the sea, 1780–5.

WOOD, WILLIAM MARTIN
(1828–)

Born Nov. 23, 1828 : son of William Wood, schoolmaster : educated at Scarborough, Sheffield People's College, and University College, Gower Street : leader writer on the *Lancaster Guardian*, 1862, and its London Correspondent to end of 1864 : Editor of the *Times of India*, holding that post, with brief intervals, until

March, 1874 : wrote for other Indian journals all over India, also for *Vanity Fair* : was the *Times*' correspondent for the Baroda State Trial, 1875 : sent weekly notes to London journals : Proprietor and Editor of the *Bombay Review* and *Indian Advertiser*, 1878–80 : Fellow of the Bombay University, 1876 : Examiner for several years in Political Economy, History, Literature : wrote *Things of India made plain*, and several pamphlets, 1865–80.

WOODBURN, SIR JOHN
(1843–1902)

I.C.S. : born at Barrackpur, July 13, 1843 : son of David Woodburn, M.D., of the E. I. Co.'s service : educated at Ayr Academy, Glasgow and Edinburgh Universities : arrived in India in Dec. 1863 : served in the N.W.P. and Oudh in minor appointments until he became first Revenue, and afterwards Chief Secretary to the Local Government in 1888 : was a Member of the Governor-General's Legislative Council in 1891 and 1893 : Chief Commissioner of the Central Provinces, 1893–5 : Member of the Supreme Council, 1895–7 : Lieutenant-Governor of Bengal from April, 1898, till his death. He was made C.S.I. in 1892 and K.C.S.I. in 1897. He had great influence in, and affection for, Oudh : in Bengal he had everything to learn. His Lieutenant-Governorship was comparatively uneventful. It devolved on him to pass the Calcutta Municipal Act of 1899, and to combat the plague. His policy was to inculcate the necessity of cleanliness and disinfection, but to avoid irritating the people by compulsory segregation and evacuation of buildings. The relaxation of the plague regulations endeared him to the native public. His geniality, tact, courtesy, and kindness of heart rendered him generally popular among all classes. He was generous and delighted in hospitality. He fell ill on tour in Aug. 1902 : died Nov. 21, 1902, and was buried in the Circular Road Cemetery, Calcutta.

WOODROFFE, JAMES TISDALL
(1838–)

Born March 16, 1838 : son of Very Rev. John Canon Woodroffe : educated at Trinity College, Dublin : called to the bar at the Inner Temple, 1860 : practised before the Calcutta Supreme and High Courts from 1860 : Advocate-General of Bengal, 1899–1904 : Member of the Governor-General's Legislative Council, 1899–1900 : of the Bengal Legislative Council, 1899–1904 : decorated by H,H. Pope Leo XIII for services rendered to the Catholic Church in India.

WOODROW, HENRY (1823–1876)

Born July 31, 1823 : son of Henry Woodrow : educated at Rugby and Caius College, Cambridge : Scholar, and Fellow : went to Calcutta, 1848, as Principal of the Martinière College : became Secretary to the Council of Education, 1854 : on the formation of the Education Department in Bengal, became Inspector of Schools, 1855–72 : he devoted much attention to primary education, and to physical science in education : Director of Public Instruction, 1875 : died at Darjeeling, Oct. 11, 1876.

WORKMAN, WILLIAM HUNTER (? – ?)

Of English-American parentage : educated at Yale and Harvard Universities : practised in America for 13 years : has since been a great traveller in out-of-the-way parts of Europe, North Africa and Asia : has explored the higher Himalayas : author of *In the Ice World of Himalaya.*

WORSLEY, SIR HENRY (1768–1841)

Born Jan. 20, 1768 : son of Rev. Francis Worsley : joined the E. I. Co.'s mllitary service in Madras, 1781 : in the siege thereof, 1781 : to Sumatra, 1789 : in the Mysore war, 1791: at Seringapatam, 1792 : in Mahratta war, 1803 : at Alighar, Delhi, Agra, Laswari, Mathura : Adjutant-General and Lt-Colonel, 1806 : Private Secretary to the Marquis of Hastings, 1813 : Secretary to Government in the Military Department, 1818 : resigned, 1819 : C.B., 1815 : K.C.B., 1821 : Maj. General, 1830 : G.C.B., 1838 : died Jan. 19, 1841.

WRIGHT, WILLIAM (1830–1889)

Born in India, 1830 : son of Capt. Alexander Wright, of the E. I. Co.'s service : educated at St. Andrew's, and at Halle University : studied under Rödiger, the Orientalist, the Semītic languages, especially Arabic, but also Sanskrit, Persian, Turkish and other Oriental languages : went to Leyden : edited the travels of Ibn Jubair in Arabic : and Syriac and Arabic texts : 1855–61, Professor of Arabic, in University College London : at Dublin, 1856–61 : Assistant and Assistant-keeper in the Oriental Branch of the MS. Department of the British Museum, 1861–70 : distinguished in epigraphy and palæography : Professor of Arabic and Fellow of Queen's College at Cambridge, 1870 : Head of the Semitic school : wrote an Arabic reading book, 1870, and a grammar : greatly stimulated the study of the Semitic languages : obtained Indian MSS. for the Cambridge University Library : received many foreign distinctions and honours : member of the Old Testament Revision Committee : died May 22, 1889.

WYLIE, HENRY (1844–)

Entered the Indian Army, 1861, and became Maj-General, 1899 : served in N.W. Frontier, 1863: Bhutan, 1865: Abyssinian expedition, 1868 : Hazara expedition, 1868 : on special duty in Beluchistan, 1877: Afghan campaign,. 1878–80 : Assistant to Resident in Mysore, 1882 : Political Agent at Bahawalpur,. Jhalawar and Bhopal : Resident in Nipal, 1898–1900 : retired : C.S.I., 1881.

WYLLIE, JOHN WILLIAM SHAW (1835–1870)

I.C.S. : son of General Sir W. Wyllie, K.C.B. : born at Poona, Oct. 6, 1835 : educated at the Edinburgh Academy and Cheltenham : resigned a scholarship won at Lincoln College and gained one at Trinity College, Oxford : after open competition for the Indian Civil Service, went to Bombay in 1856. He joined the Political Department in Kattiawar, 1858–60 : transferred to Oudh, and was made Assistant Secretary to Sir George Yule, the Chief Commissioner. In 1862 he joined the Government of India Secretariat in the Foreign Department, and, with short periods spent in other Departments, remained there till 1867, acting once for three months as Foreign Secretary. While on furlough in 1868, he gave up, on the advice of his uncle,Sir W. Hutt, his Indian career and stood as a Liberal for the city of Hereford. He was elected, but was unseated for technical bribery by his agent..

He was made C.S.I. in 1869 and died in Paris, March 15, 1870. He was a brilliant writer, and much esteemed for his personal qualities. His essays on the *External Policy of India* were edited by Sir W. W. Hunter (*q.v.*). The best known are those on "The Foreign Policy of Lord Lawrence," "Masterly Inactivity," and "Mischievous Activity," from the *Edinburgh* and *Fortnightly* Reviews : he wrote also in other Journals on political questions.

WYLLIE, SIR WILLIAM (1802–1891)

Son of John Wyllie : born Aug. 13, 1802 : educated at Kilmarnock : joined the E. I. Co.'s Bombay N.I., 1819 : General in 1871 : served in the Dekkan, Konkan, Gujarat, and Cutch in 1825–6 : in 1838–9 he was Brig-Major with the Bombay column of the " Army of the Indus " under Sir John Keane : was at Ghazni and at the capture of Kabul, Aug. 7, 1839 :. was, under Sir T. Willshire (*q.v.*), at Quetta, and the capture of Kelat, Nov. 3, 1839 : was again Brig-Major in the Sind force under Sir R. England (*q.v.*), 1840–2, reaching Kandahar, May, 1842 : was Assistant Adjutant-General under Sir C. Napier in Sind and at Miani on Feb. 17, 1843 : C.B. : commanded against the rebels in the S. Mahratta country, 1844–5 : was D.A.G. Bombay, 1849 : commanded at Bombay and Ahmadnagar : retired from India in 1858 : K.C.B. in 1866 : G.C.B., 1877 : General : died May 26, 1891.

WYLLIE, SIR WILLIAM HUTT CURZON (1848–   )

Born Oct. 5, 1848 : son of General Sir William Wyllie, G.C.B : entered the Army, 1866, and the Indian Staff Corps, 1868, joined the Oudh Commission, 1870 : the Indian Political Department, 1879 : served in Beluchistan under Sir Robert Sandeman during the Afghan war, 1879–80 : Military Secretary to William Patrick Adam (*q.v.*), Governor of Madras, 1881 : Resident in Nipal : Governor-General's Agent in Central India and in Rajputana : retired : Political A.D.C. at India Office : C.I.E., 1881 : K.C.I.E., 1902.

WYMER, SIR GEORGE PETRE (1788–1868)

Born Aug. 19, 1788 : educated at N. Walsham : entered the E. I. Co.'s military

service, 18 >4 : in the campaign of 1805 : and the Nipal war, 1815–6 : under Nott at Kandahar, 1840 : relieved Kelat-i-Ghilzai : C.B. : commanded the First Brigade of the Kandahar Force : present at many engagements, including Ghazni : A.D.C. to Queen Victoria, 1842 : K.C.B., 1857, for his services in India : Colonel of the 107th Bengal Infantry, 1862 : died Aug. 12, 1868 : General.

WYNCH, ALEXANDER (1720– ?)

Born 1720 : writer at Fort St. George, 1740 : at Fort St. David, 1741 : Sixth in Council at Fort St. David, 1744 : Factor, 1745 : Ninth in Council at Fort St. George, 1752 : Second in Council, 1772, and Chief at Masulipatam : Governor of Madras, Feb. 2, 1773 : resigned, Dec. 11, 1776.

WYNN, CHARLES WATKIN WILLIAMS (1775–1850)

Born Oct. 9, 1775 : son of Sir Watkin W. Wynn : educated at Westminster, and Christ Church, Oxford : called to the bar from Lincoln's Inn, 1798 : M.P. for Old Sarum, 1797, and for Montgomeryshire, 1797–1850 : Under Secretary in the Home Department, 1806–7 : D.C.L., 1810 : President of the Board of Control, 1822–8, and P.C. : impracticable and unbusinesslike : Secretary at War, 1830–1 : Chancellor of the Duchy of Lancaster, 1834–5 : said to have declined, three times, the offer of the Governor-Generalship of India : the first President of the Royal Asiatic Society, 1823–41 : F.S.A. : died Sep. 2, 1850.

YAKUB KHAN (1849–   )

Amir of Afghanistan : third son of Shir Ali (*q.v.*) : at Herat, in 1863, recognized Vambéry as a European : in 1868–9 defeated his uncle Muhammad Azam and his cousin Abdur Rahman at Tinak Khan, near Ghazni : filled high posts as Governor of Kabul, Kandahar and Herat : in 1870 rebelled against his father, because he made Abdalla Jan his heir : he fled to Kandahar and Persia and took Herat : was reconciled with his father, and made Governor, but was treacherously imprisoned, 1874–8. When Shir Ali left Kabul, in 1878–9, Yakub became Amir : as Amir he made the Treaty of Gandamak of May 26, 1879, with Sir Louis Cavagnari on behalf of the Governor-General, and accepted a British Resident at Kabul: He made no effort to protect or rescue the British Resident, Sir Louis Cavagnari (*q.v.*) and party, when they were attacked and killed on Sep. 3, 1879 : he surrendered to Sir F. Roberts, and, being held responsible for their deaths, abdicated, after a weak reign of 9 months : was sent down to India on Dec. 1, 1879, and kept there as a State prisoner.

YARDLEY, SIR WILLIAM (1810–1878)

Son of Edward Yardley : born 1810 : educated at Shrewsbury : called to the bar from the Middle Temple : appointed to be a Puisne Judge of the Bombay Supreme Court, 1847 : knighted : Chief Justice, 1852–8 : was an unsuccessful candidate for Parliament : died Dec. 15, 1878.

YATE, ARTHUR CAMPBELL (1853–)

Born Feb. 28, 1853 : son of Rev. Charles Yate : educated at Shrewsbury and St. John's College, Cambridge : entered the Army, 1875, and became Lt-Colonel, 1982 : Bombay Staff Corps, 1879 : served in Afghan war, 1879–81 : Afghan Boundary Commission, 1884–5 : Burmese war, 1886–8 : author of *Lt-Colonel John Haughton, a Hero of Tirah* ; *The Army and the Press in* 1901.

YATE, CHARLES EDWARD (1849–)

Educated at Shrewsbury : entered the Army, 1867, and became Colonel, 1901 : served in Afghan war, 1880–1 : Afghan Frontier Commission, 1884–8 : British Commissioner, Russian-Afghan Frontier, 1887 and 1892 : Consul-General, for Khorasan and Seistan at Mashad, Persia, 1893–8 : Resident, Western Rajputana, 1898 : Chief Commissioner of Beluchistan, 1900–5 : C.S.I., 1887 : C.M.G., 1888.

YATES, REV. WILLIAM, D.D. (1792–1845)

Born Dec. 15, 1792 : son of a shoemaker at Loughborough : was a schoolmaster : studied at Baptist College at Bristol : ordained Aug. 31, 1814 : to India in 1815 under the Baptist Missionary Society : joined W. Carey (*q.v.*) at Serampur : left him in 1817, and established the Calcutta Missionary Union : preached and toured : and wrote a number of educational works,

in Bengali, Hindustani, Hindi, Sanskrit. and Arabic : was Pastor of the English Church, Circular Road, Calcutta, 1829–39 : translated the Bible into Bengali : portions of it into Sanskrit, the Psalms into Bengali and into Sanskrit metre : also studied the Classics, Hebrew, Chinese : D.D. of Brown University, 1839 : died at sea, July 3, 1845 : published also Sanskrit and Hindustani dictionaries : and an edition of the Sanskrit Nalodaya : *Essays in Reply to Rammohan Roy*.

YEATMAN-BIGGS, ARTHUR GODOLPHIN (1843–1898)

Maj-General : son of Harry Farr Yeatman : took the additional name of Biggs : intended for the bar : entered the Royal Artillery, 1860 : in the China war, 1861–2 : in India on the Staff : in S. Africa, 1879 : in Egypt, 1882 : A.A.G. in India, 1894 : commanded the Presidency District, 1895 : in the Tirah campaign, 1897, commanded a Division which captured the Dargai heights : died Jan. 4, 1898 : C.B.

YOUNG, ROBERT (1822–1888)

Son of George Young : born Sep. 10, 1822 : educated at private schools : became printer and bookseller, 1847 : studied Hebrew and Oriental languages : was at Surat, 1856–61, as literary Missionary and Superintendent of the Mission press there : learnt Gujarati and other Oriental languages : published the *Analytical Concordance of the Bible* : died Oct. 14, 1888.

YOUNG, SIR WILLIAM, BARONET (1773–1848)

Entered the E. I. Co.'s service in Bombay : served at Seringapatam, in Malabar, at capture of Colombo, in the Cingalese war : organized an efficient plan for recruiting the Army, adopted by Government : in the Dekkan war forwarded supplies to the Army under Sir A. Wellesley : Baronet, 1821 : Director of the E. I. Co. : died March 10, 1848.

YOUNG, SIR WILLIAM MACKWORTH (1840–)

I.C.S. : son of Captain Sir George Young, R.N. : educated at Eton and King's College, Cambridge : Fellow : entered the Bengal Civil Service, 1863 : Financial Commissioner of Panjab, 1889–95 : Member of the Governor-General's Legislative

Council, 1893: Resident in Mysore, 1895-7: Lieutenant Governor of the Panjab, 1897-1902 : C S.I., 1890 : K.C.S.I., 1897.

YOUNGHUSBAND, SIR FRANCIS EDWARD (1863-   )

Colonel : son of Maj-General John William Younghusband : born 1863 : joined the 1st Dragoon Guards, 1882 : and Indian Staff Corps, 1889 : in 1886 travelled through Manchuria, *viâ* the Long White Mountain, and Chinese Turkistan : in 1889-91, travelled in the Pamirs : Political Agent at Hunza, 1892 : and at Chitral, 1893-4 : Special Correspondent of the *Times* in the Chitral expedition, 1895, and in S. Africa, 1903 : Political Agent at Haraoti and Tonk, 1898 : Resident at Indore : British Commissioner to Tibet, 1903-4 : negotiated a treaty at Lhasa, Sep. 1904 : C.I.E. : K.C.I.E.

YOUNGHUSBAND, JOHN WILLIAM (1823-   )

Born Jan. 1823 : son of Maj-General Charles Younghusband, R.A.: entered Bombay Army, 1840, and became Maj-General, 1878 : served in Afghan campaign, 1842 : Sind campaign, 1843 : at the battle of Hyderabad, Sind : in the Beluch Hills campaign,1845,against the Mandranis, 1847 : in several expeditions on the Panjab Frontier, 1851-7 : Indian mutiny, 1857 : Inspr-General of Police, Berar and Panjab : C.S.I., 1866.

YOUNGHUSBAND, ROBERT ROMER (1819-   )

Entered the Army, 1837, and became General, 1877 : served in Sind and Beluchistan, 1840-2 : Brig-Major at Miani and Hyderabad : Brig-Major, Hyderabad, 1843-8, and of Rajputana Field Force, 1852-4 : A.A.G., Sind, 1854-6 : D.A.G., Persian expedition, 1856-7 : at Reshire, Bushire, Barazjan, Khushab : C.B.: Brig-General at Nasirabad, 1862-6.

YULE, SIR GEORGE UDNY (1813-1886)

I.C.S. : brother of Sir Henry Yule (*q.v.*) : born 1813 : educated at Haileybury, 1829-31 : went to Lower Bengal, 1832, gaining a "reputation as a mighty hunter, alike with hog-spear and double barrel." After the Sonthal rebellion of 1855, he was speci-

ally selected to be Commissioner of Bhagalpur, to pacify the country. In the mutiny, 1857, he maintained order until July : when the mutineers threatened his Division, he raised volunteers and took most active measures, defeating and driving the rebels across the Nipal frontier and averting the danger by his personal energy and promptness. He officiated as Chief Commissioner of Oudh, 1861-3 : was Resident at Hyderabad, 1863-7 : Member of the Supreme Council from May, 1867, until he retired in Jan. 1868 : he proposed a private expedition to rescue the Abyssinian captives from King Theodore : and helped greatly to establish the celebration of "Primrose Day" : K.C.S.I. in 1866 : was also C.B. : died Jan. 13, 1886.

YULE, SIR HENRY (1820-1889)

Colonel : son of Major William Yule of the E. I. Co.'s service : born May 1, 1820 : educated at the High School, Edinburgh ; Addiscombe and Chatham : joined the Bengal Engineers, 1840 : served in the Khasia hills in Assam. and on the W. Jamna canals : in both the Sikh wars : was at Chilianwala : on the Ganges canal : wrote on Fortification : was Deputy Consulting Engineer for Railways : and Under Secretary P.W.D. : Secretary to Colonel Arthur Phayre's mission to Ava in 1855 : wrote his *Narrative of the Mission to the Court of Ava*, 1858 : in the mutiny he was at Allahabad : later, resumed work in the Secretariat of the Government of India as Secretary P.W.D : retired in 1862 : C.B. in 1863 : published *Mirabilia descripta* of Friar Jordanus, 1863 ; *Cathay and the Way Thither*, 1866 ; the *Book of Ser Marco Polo*, 1871, 1875 : gained the medals of the Royal Geographical Society : and of the Geographical Society of Italy : edited Capt. Wood's *Journey to the Source of the Oxus*, 1873 : brought out, with Dr. A. C. Burnell (*q.v.*) the *Glossary of Anglo-Indian Words, or Hobson-Jobson*, 1886 : and in 1887 the *Diary of Sir William Hedges* : wrote many papers and articles in the Asiatic Journals, and on geography, and in the *Encyclopædia Britannica* : greatly advanced the knowledge of, and the public interest in, the mediæval history and geography of Central Asia : Member of the Council of India, 1875-89 : LL.D. Edinburgh, 1883 : K.C.S.I., 1889 : corresponding member of the Institute of France : President of the Hakluyt Society, 1877 : and of the Royal Asiatic Society, 1885 : died Dec. 30, 1889.

ZAMAN SHAH ABDALI (before 1793–after 1800)

Grandson of Ahmad Shah Abdali, or Durani, ruler of Afghanistan, who died 1773 : and son of Timur Shah, who died 1793. He reigned oppressively at Kabul, and reduced to poverty Payinda Khan, the Barakzai chief. to whom he owed his throne. He marched on Lahore, 1796, reduced the Sikhs, threatened to invade Hindustan, and invited Lord Wellesley to join with him in conquering the Mahrattas. The fear of an Afghan invasion was seriously regarded by Lord Wellesley, but came to nothing. Zaman Shah returned to Afghanistan, to establish his authority at Kandahar, and had the leading Barakzais massacred. He was dethroned by his brother Mahmud Mirza of Herat, assisted by Fateh Khan Barakzai, about 1800, and was blinded : Zaman Shah

fled to Ludiana, and became a pensioner of the E. I. Co.

ZOFFANY, JOHN or JOHANN (1733–1810)

Artist : born in 1733, of a Bohemian family, at Ratisbon : after long residence in Italy came to England in 1758 : fell into great difficulties : worked as a clock-painter and assistant : came into notice as a portrait-painter, and painted dramatic scenes : Member of the Society of Artists, and of the Royal Academy, 1769 : spent some years in Italy and Vienna : member of Foreign Academies : went to India, 1783–90 : was at Calcutta and Lucknow : painted subjects combining incident and portraiture, " dramatic scenes and conversation pieces," such as " Colonel Mordaunt's Cock-match." " Tiger Hunt in the E. Indies. " : " Embassy of Hyder Beck (sic) to Calcutta " : some of which were engraved by Richard Earlom, the celebrated mezzotinto engraver (1743–1822) : he also painted Sir Elijah Impey (q.v.), and " The Last Supper " for an altar-piece in St. John's Church in Calcutta (opened for service in June, 1787). He died in England, Nov. 11, 1810.

H H

ADDENDA

ANDERSON, REV. PHILIP (1816–1857)

Son of Captain Anderson, of the E. I. Co's service: educated at St. Paul's school, from 1824 : Pauline Exhibitioner, C.C. College, Cambridge, 1834 : B.A., 1838 : M.A., 1849 : ordained : Chaplain at Colaba, Bombay, 1849–57 : he began *The Bombay Quarterly Magazine*, 1850 : edited *The Bombay Quarterly Review* from Jan. 1850 : died at Malabar Hill, Bombay, Dec. 13, 1857 : he published *The English in Western India*, 1854 and 1856, an interesting account of the early factories of the Bombay coast and the life therein, believed to be the first attempt to popularize this information : his sermons are in the British Museum : was Vice-President of the Bombay R.A.S. : a memorial window and tablet were erected to him in Colaba Church.

ATKINSON, GEORGE FRANCKLIN
(? –1861 ?)

Joined the Bengal Engineers : Captain in 1859 : he wrote and illustrated numerous occasional papers in the periodicals of the sixties, especially *The Leisure Hour*, familiarizing English readers with the civil and military life of Europeans in India : he published *Pictures from the North, in pen and pencil, sketched during a summer ramble*, 1848 : *The Campaign in India*, 1857–8, *from drawings made during the eventful period of the Great Mutiny* : dedicated to H.M. Queen Victoria, 1859 : this was his most finished work : *Curry and Rice, on 40 Plates, or the Ingredients of Social Life at our Station in India* : second edition, 1859 : an unrivalled series of pictures of life in the old cantonments in pre-mutiny days, dedicated to W. M. Thackeray, a book still in demand : he wrote also *Indian Spices for English Tables*, 120 *humorous sketches*, 1860 : died about 1861.

COLVIN, SIR WALTER MYTTON
(1847–)

Born 1847 : youngest son of J. R. Colvin, I.C.S. (*q.v.*) : educated at Rugby and Trinity Hall, Cambridge : LL.B. : called to the Bar from the Middle Temple, 1871 : practised at Allahabad : was Member of

the Indian Police Commission, 1902–3 : knighted 1904.

CONNON, JOHN (? –1874)

Educated at Aberdeen : M.A. : went out to Bombay about 1859, and then became Editor, and soon after Proprietor, of the *Bombay Gazette*, the oldest local journal, which Connon conducted with much vigour, generally in opposition to the Government of the day. He always took an active part in the public affairs of the City : was a racy conversationalist : returned to England about 1863 : kept his law terms, and was called to the bar : went back to Bombay and resumed charge of the *Bombay Gazette* (edited in his absence by J. M. Maclean (*q.v.*). Though Connon had little or no practice in the Courts, his status as a barrister qualified him as Chief Police Magistrate for the Town and Island of Bombay, which post was given him and occupied efficiently until his health broke down : he died at Suez on his way home in 1874 : he had been prominent as a member of the Bench of Justices, the Corporation of that day, of which, in its later form, Connon became Chairman : his memorial bust stands now in the Municipal Hall, Bombay.

FINLAY, JAMES FAIRBAIRN
(1852–)

I.C.S. : son of William Finlay, F.R.C.P., Edinburgh : educated at Edinburgh Academy and University : went to India in 1875 : to the Panjab : served chiefly in the Finance Department : Under Secretary to the Government of India in that Department : Accountant General, Bengal : also in the N.W.P. and Oudh : Deputy Secretary to the Government of India, 1889 : and Secretary in that Department, 1891–1903 : officiating Member of the Supreme Council, 1902 : Member of the Council of India, 1903 : C.S.I., 1896.

HALL, REV. GORDON (1781–1826)

Born April 8, 1781, at Granville, Hampden County, Massachusetts : son of Nathan Hall of Ellington, Connecticut : early showed a taste for books and writing : educated at Williams College : graduated,

1808 : tutor there, 1809 : studied theology : licensed to preach, 1809 : was a student of the Theological Seminary at Andover, 1811 : attended medical lectures at Philadelphia, 1811 : ordained as a Missionary at Salem, Massachusetts, Feb. 1812 : went to Calcutta : met with difficulties there : went to Bombay : overcame similar obstacles and remained there : actively engaged in Mission work until his death of cholera at Doulee Dhapoor, Mar. 20, 1826 : one of the first and most distinguished Missionaries of the American Board of Commissioners for Foreign Missions : took an important part in translating the Scriptures into Mahratti.

KERR, REV. DR. RICHARD HALL, D.D. (1769–1808)

Born in Dublin, Feb. 3, 1769 : son of Rev. Lewis Kerr : educated at Trinity College, Dublin : B.A., 1788 : studied at Hospitals in London and Dublin : visited Virginia, 1788–9 : ordained, 1789 : went to Bombay, 1790 : made Superintendent of the Portuguese College in Bombay : went to Madras, 1792 : established a seminary in Black Town, Madras : appointed an E. I. Co.'s Chaplain, 1793 : ministered to European troops at Ellore, and had a church erected : Superintendent of the Military Male Orphan Asylum at Egmore, Madras, 1796 : Junior Chaplain at Madras, 1796, Senior, 1801 and 1804 : D.D. of Dublin, 1803 : published religious writings : reported on the early establishment of Christianity and the native Christians on the Malabar ʿCoast : died April 15, 1808.

LAWSON, REV. JOHN (1787–1825).

Born at Trowbridge, July 24, 1787 : became a wood-engraver in London, and a punch-cutter : joined the Baptist Missionary Society : went to the United States in 1810, and on from Philadelphia to Calcutta, 1812 : resided at the Mission House, Serampur : assisted in improving Chinese types : ordered to leave Calcutta and return to England : imprisoned for refusing : released by Government and allowed to remain for his Chinese type-work : taught the natives how to produce Bengali and Chinese types : ordained, 1816, Co-pastor with Rev. E. Carey of the first Baptist Church at Calcutta : was afterwards pastor of the second : preached in the Fort : laboured in education, scientific pursuits

and music : had considerable knowledge of chronology, mineralogy and botany : made researches in cryptogamous plants : published *Orient Harping* and other ƴorks, besides a volume of poems : died Oct. 22, 1825.

LUDLOW, JOHN, (1801–1882)

Maj-General : eldest son of Edmund Ludlow : born in Monmouthshire, May 16, 1801 : educated at Merchant Taylors' School : became, in 1819, an Ensign in the E. I. Co.'s 3rd Regt. N.I. : served in the first Burmese and Bhil wars : appointed to the Political Department in 1832 : Assistant A.G.G. in Rajputana, 1835 : Political Agent at Jodhpur, 1839–44 : and at Jaipur, 1844–7 : while there he carried out a system of uniform and fixed ceremonial presents at weddings throughout Rajputana : this went far to check the infanticide which was common in anticipation of the pecuniary burdens associated with the rearing of female children. By pointing out that the most ancient Hindu scriptures forbade, and did not inculcate, Suttee, he persuaded the Head Priest at Jaipur to advocate its abolition and brought the Council of Regency to discourage and forbid the practice in 1846. Thereupon many of the Rajput and other states prohibited it : the A.G.G. for Rajputana attributed their prohibition almost exclusively to Ludlow's influence : and Lord Hardinge thanked him. He became Lieut-Colonel, 1850 : Colonel, 1853 : and Maj-General, 1856, after his return to England : married and lived for many years at Yotes Court in Kent, and died there Nov. 30, 1882 : he had great muscular strength : was fond of literature and quotation : he always spoke with admiration and regard for the Rajputs.

MACPHERSON, REV. DUNCAN (1837–1881)

Born at Fort St. George, 1837 : went out to Bombay as Chaplain of the Church of Scotland, arriving Mar. 1860 : stationed at Poona, Belgaum, Karachi, 1862 : was Chaplain of St. Andrew's, Bombay, until his death : besides his pastoral work, he laboured indefatigably on behalf of Scottish and other British Railway Engineers, and others in Bombay : founded, with others, the Bombay Scottish Education Society : was Fellow of the Bombay University and Member of the

Senate: for several years Examiner, chiefly in Literature and Mental Science: was greatly esteemed for his public services and high character: his *Last Words*, with a memoir by the Rev. Robert Geoffrey, Minister of the Free Scottish Church, 1882, form a memorial of him: he died Aug. 1881.

PRICE, REV. JONATHAN D. (?-1828)

Received a medical education: was elected May,' 1821, at Philadelphia, as a Medical Missionary to Burma: sailed from Salem to Calcutta, 1821: joined Judson (*q.v.*) at Rangoon: ordered by the King of Burma to his capital: reached Ava, Sep. 1822: well received and a house built for him: on the outbreak of the first Burmese war he and other Missionaries were, on June 8, 1824, seized, fettered and put in the death prison, and fastened to a pole. On the approach of the English troops, the Missionaries were daily taken to the palace, consulted about the terms, and sent to the English camp to negotiate. On peace being made, Price was given employment by the Burmese King at Ava: much valued for his medical skill: he taught a number of Burmese boys religion and science: died of consumption, near Ava, Feb. 14, 1828.

RAO, VISHWANATH PATANKER MADHAVA (1850-)

Mahratta Brahman: born 1850: educated at the Kumbakonam College, under Mr. W. A. Porter: B.A., 1869: entered the Mysore service, under the British Government, as Head Master of the Royal School: was made Public Prosecutor: served in the Judicial and Revenue Departments: made Major-Genl. of Police in Mysore: also Plague Commissioner in Mysore: given the C.I.E., and a Kaisar-i-Hind medal: became Member of the Council of Regency, Mysore, 1898, and Revenue Commissioner: in 1904 was appointed Diwan of Travancore: has already introduced various reforms in the administration in Travancore.

RHENIUS, REV. CHARLES THEO-PHILUS EWALD (1790-1838)

Born Nov. 5, 1790, at Grandens in W. Prussia: son of Otto Rhenius, Officer in the Prussian Army: educated in the Cathedral School at Marienwerder: employed in an office under Government, near Königsberg: while residing near Memel, in 1807, commenced the study of Divinity: entered a Missionary Seminary at Berlin, 1810: ordained there Aug. 1812, as a Minister of the Lutheran Church and Missionary to the heathen: resided eighteen months in England under the Church Missionary Society: embarked in 1814, with the permission of the Court of Directors, as a Missionary to Madras: formed a congregation and founded a Church in Black Town, Madras, 1819: removed to Palamcotta, 1820: laboured there and at Tinnevelly, converting and baptizing: wrote *The Essence, or the True Vedam*: translated the Scriptures into Tamil, and appointed E. I. Co.'s Chaplain at Palamcotta, 1825: in consequence of some writings his connexion with the Home Mission Society was severed: he left Tinnevelly: founded a new Mission at Arcot, 1835, but was invited back to Tinnevelly by the Catechists and Christians, among whom he was very successful: he died June 5, 1838.

ROSS, JOHN TYRELL CARTER (1823-1897).

Born 1823: son of John Tyrell Ross, of Ringwood, Hants, Private Secretary to Lord Malmesbury: educated at St. George's Hospital: M.R.C.S., 1845: Fellow, 1857: entered the Medical Establishment of the Bengal Army, 1845: served in the Satlaj campaign, 1846: in the Panjab campaign, 1848-9: in the first Miranzai expedition, 1851: under Sir Colin Campbell in the Ranazai Valley, 1852: at Kohat Kotal, 1853: highly praised by Sir J. Lawrence for his benevolent exertions: in the mutiny, at Khudaganj, in medical charge of the Cavalry Brigade under Sir J. Hope Grant, by whose order he led a squadron: at the reoccupation of Fatehghar: medical officer on the Staff of Sir W. Mansfield (Lord Sandhurst) (*q.v.*) while C. in C. in India: P.M.O. in the Dafla Expedition, 1874-5: Sanitary Officer of the Imperial Assemblage, 1876-7: Deputy-Surgeon-General, Central Provinces,for five years: C.I.E., and retired, 1878: Surgeon-General: was Chief Commissioner of the Stafford House Committee in S. Africa during the Zulu war, 1879: Commissioner of H.R.H. the Princess of Wales' Branch of the National Aid Society for Home Service, 1885: died April 27, 1897.

SCHROTER, REV. FREDERIC CHRISTIAN GOTTHELF (? –1820–)

A native of Saxony : prepared for missionary labours under the Rev. John Jaenické of Berlin : ordained there Aug. 28, 1813 : went to England : chosen by the Church Missionary Society to go to India : left England, May 1815, for Ceylon : went *viâ* Colombo to Calcutta, 1816 : sent to Titalya, in the plains near Darjeeling, to learn Tibetan, with a view to Missionary work in Tibet, but he died in July, 1820 : he left MSS. of (1) a Tibetan-English dictionary (based on an Italian-Tibetan one, composed by Roman-Catholic Missionaries at Lhasa), (2) a Supplement to the above, (3) the commencement of an English-Tibetan dictionary, (4) a Treatise on the Tibet alphabet, (5) heads of a Tibetan grammar, (6) a Tibet MS. and a part translation.

SHEPHERD, JAMES (? – ?)

Colonel : served under Ambaji Inglia, 1799, and assisted very materially in the overthrow of Lakwa Dada at Sounda in 1801. On the breaking out of war with the English, Shepherd and his party passed over to the Company's service, and he distinguished himself in Bundelkund in 1804, when he gave the celebrated freebooter Amir Khan, a sound beating at Maltaon Ghat, and on June 24 completed his discomfiture by entirely defeating and dispersing his force near Koonch. Shepherd's Corps at this time consisted of 3,180 men and was highly praised for its efficiency when Gen. Lake reviewed it in 1805.

SHEPHERD, W. J. (? –1891)

Son of Colonel James Shepherd (*q.v.*) : on the outbreak of the Mutiny in 1857 he took a conspicuous part in the defence of Wheeler's entrenchment at Cawnpur, eventually leaving the entrenchment to glean information of the enemy's movements, by whom he was captured and sentenced by the Nana Sahib to hard labour. He was one of the few survivors of Wheeler's entrenchment, and was congratulated by the late Lord Dufferin : died at Lucknow, 1891.

STRANGE, JAMES CHARLES STUART (1753–1840)

Born 1753 : eldest son of the Scotch engraver, Sir Robert Strange : educated at the college of Navarre, Paris : obtained a writership in the E. I. Co.'s service : reached Madras, July, 1773 : held lucrative posts until invalided home, 1780 : returned to India, 1785 : compiled a scheme (based on Capt. Cook's voyage of 1778) for the establishment of a trade in furs by the E. I. Co. between the N.W. coast of America and the ports of China. The Bombay Government placed at his disposal two experienced officers from their Marine and a small party of picked soldiers : a Bombay merchant, David Scott, provided funds for the purchase and equipment of the two small vessels. Strange had entire control of the expedition, embarking the whole of his private fortune in it, and sailed from Bombay, Dec. 1785 : financially the voyage proved a failure : Strange found himself forestalled by other adventurers, one from Calcutta reaching Nootka Sound just before him in 1786 : but his journals and chart forwarded to the Court of Directors contained valuable additions to the geographical knowledge of N.W. America : he forwarded to the Court on his return to India, 1788, a detailed scheme for a permanent trading station at Nootka Sound, where he had left his surgeon, Mackay, (who was kidnapped and carried off to Macao by a rival trader). Strange was Collector and Paymaster of Tanjore, until he retired in 1795 : he was M.P. for East Grinstead, 1797–1802 : he lost his considerable fortune as partner in a bank which failed, and was allowed by the Court of Directors, in consideration of the special circumstances, to return to the Madras service, 1803–4 : there he was Magte.-Collr. at Pondicherry, 1806, Judge of Court of Appeal, Southern Division, 1807 : Postmaster-General and Senior Member of the Board of Trade, 1813–5 : retiring Jan. 1, 1816 : he died in 1840.

SUBBYAR, S. SHUNGRA (1836–1904)

Born April, 1836, of respectable parentage : educated in a Travancore State Seminary : served as a schoolmaster : Assistant to the Diwan in the Police, Educational and other Departments : as Diwan Peshkar and District Officer in several districts : was Special Commissioner in boundary disputes with the Cochin State : in the Revenue Settlement for nine years : Diwan in 1892 : retired, 1898 : effected administrative improvements, his services being highly appreciated : C.I.E., 1897 : Member of the Madras Legislative Council, 1898 : died Sept. 1904.

BIBLIOGRAPHY

Arranged, 1st, under the name of the person whose "life" is treated; 2nd, under the name of the author or the subject of the book, whichever supplies the more prominent word.

ABBOTT, COL. SIR JAMES, by Major Broadfoot : 1893.
—————— **Narrative of a Journey from Herat to Khiva, Moscow, and St. Petersburg :** 1843.
ABDUL LATIF, A Short Account of my Public Life : 1885.
ABDUR RAHMAN, THE AMIR, by Stephen Wheeler : 1895.
—————— **The Life of, G.C.B., G.C.S.I.,** edited by Mir Munshi Sultan Mahomed Khan : 1900.
ABERIGH-MACKAY, G., Twenty-one Days in India, being the Tour of Sir Ali Baba : 1880.
—————— **The Chiefs of Central India :** 1879.
—————— **The Native Chiefs and their States in 1877 :** 1878.
ADAMS, A. L., Wanderings of a Naturalist in India, the W. Himalayas, and Kashmir : 1867.
ADAMS, W. H. D., Episodes of Anglo-Indian History.
—————— **India, Pictorial and Descriptive :** 1888.
—————— **The Makers of British India :** 1902.
ADYE, GEN. SIR J. M., G.C.B., Defence of Cawnpur by the Troops under the Orders of Maj.-Gen. C. A. Windham, Nov. 1857 : 1858.
—————— **Indian Frontier Policy : an Historical Sketch :** 1897.
—————— **Recollections of a Military Life :** 1895.
—————— **Sitana, a Mountain Campaign on the Borders of Afghanistan in 1863 :** 1867.
AFGHANISTAN and its Inhabitants, by Muhammad Hayat Khan : 1874.
—————— **and the Afghans,** by Surgeon-General H. W. Bellew, C.S.I. : 1879.
—————— **A Short Account,** by P. F. Walker : 1881.
—————— **Expedition into,** by J. Atkinson : 1842.
—————— **History of, from the Earliest Period to 1878,** by Col. G. B. Malleson, C.S.I. : 1878.
—————— **History of War in, from its Commencement to its Close,** edited by C. Nash : 1843.
—————— **Memorials of, 1838-42,** by J. H. Stocqueler : 1853.
AFGHAN POLICY, OUR, and the Occupation of Kandahar, by D. Boulger : 1880.
AFGHAN WAR, 1838-42, THE, by C. R. Low : 1879.
—————— **THE FIRST, AND ITS CAUSES,** by Sir H. M. Durand · 1879.
AFGHANS, THE, by Rev. T. P. Hughes : 1874.
AFLALO, F. G., The Sportsman's Book for India : 1904.
AHMED KHAN, (SIR) SAIYAD, K.C.S.I., The Life and Work of, by Lt.-Col. G. F. I. Graham : 1885.
AGA KHAN, A Brief History of the, with an Account of his Predecessors, by Naoroji M. Dumasia : 1903.
AITKEN. E. H., Behind the Bungalow : 1880.
—————— **The Tribes on my Frontier :** 1881-92.

471

472   *BIBLIOGRAPHY*

ALEXANDER, MAJ.-GEN. SIR J. E., Travels from India to England, 1825-6 : 1827.
ALLEN, REV. J. M., Diary of a March through Sind and Afghanistan : 1843.
AMEER KHAN, the Pathan Soldier of Fortune, by Basawan Lal and H. T. Prinsep : 1832.
AMHERST, EARL, by A. Thackeray Ritchie and R. Evans : 1894.
ANDAMAN ISLANDERS, THE, Adventures and Researches among, by Dr. F. I. Monatt : 1863.
——————ISLANDS, THE, On the Aboriginal Inhabitants of, by E. H. Man : 1883.
ANDERSON, PHILIP, The English in Western India : 1854.
ANDREW, SIR W. P., India and her Neighbours : 1878.
—————— Indian Railways : 1884.
—————— Our Scientific Frontier : 1880.
ARGYLL, THE DUKE OF, India under Dalhousie and Canning : 1865.
ARNOLD, SIR EDWIN, India Revisited : 1886.
—————— The Light of Asia (a poem) : 1900.
—————— East and West : 1896.
ARRAH, Siege, Defence, and Victory of, in July, 1857, by One of the Garrison : 1897.
ATLAS OF INDIA (HAND), Constable : 1893.
——————(JOHNSTON'S), with an Introduction by Sir W. W. Hunter : 1894.
—————— by T. W. Saunders : 1889.
—————— (STATISTICAL), by T. W. Saunders : 1888.
AUBER, PETER, Rise and Progress of the British Power in India : 1837.
AUCKLAND, EARL OF, by Capt. L. J. Trotter : 1893.
AYNSLEY. MRS. MURRAY, Our Visit to Hindustan, Kashmir, and Ladak : 1879.

BADEN-POWELL, B.H., C.I.E., The Land System of British India : 1892.
—————— The Origin and Growth of Village Communities in India : 1899.
BAIRD, SIR DAVID, G.C.B., Bart., by Theodore Hook : 1832.
BAKER, GENL. SIR W. ERSKINE, K.C.B., : by Two Old Friends : 1882.
BALL, V., Jungle Life in India : or the Journeys and Journals of an Indian Geologist : 1880.
BANESS, J. F., Index Geographicus Indicus : 1881.
BANERJEE, REV. K. M., by Ram Chandra Ghosa : 1893.
BARRAS, COL. JULIUS, India and Tiger-Hunting : 1883.
—————— The New Shikari at our Indian Stations : 1885.
BATEMAN CHAMPAIN, SIR JOHN, Career of, by Col. R. Murdoch Smith . 1887.
BAYLEY, SIR E. C., The History of India as told by its own Historians : The Local Muhammadan Dynasties, Gujarat : 1886.
BEATSON, LT.-COL. A., War with Tippoo Sultan in 1799 : 1800.
BEATSON, SURG.-GENL. W. B., Indian Medical Service, Past and Present : 1902-3.
BELL, ANDREW, by R. Southey and his Son.
BELL, MAJOR EVANS, Our Great Vassal Empire : 1870.
BELL, J. H., British Folks and British India, 50 years ago : 1891.
BELLEW, SURG.-GENL. H. W., C.S.I., An Enquiry into the Ethnography of Afghanistan : 1891.   ◌
—————— From the Indus to the Tigris in 1872 : 1874.
—————— Journal of a Political Mission to Afghanistan in 1857 : 1862.
—————— Kashmir and Kashgar : 1875.
BENDALL, CECIL, A Journey of Literary and Archæological Research in Nipal and N. India, during the Winter of 1884-5 : 1886.
BENGAL, Historical and Ecclesiastical Sketches in, from the Earliest Settlement until 1757 : 1829.
BENTINCK, LORD W., by Demetrius Boulger : 1892.
BEYNON, LT. W. G. L., With Kelly to Chitral : 1896.
BHOPAL, SIKANDAR BEGAM OF, by Sambhu Chunder Mookerjee.
BHUTAN WAR, Story of the, by Dr. Rennie.

BIDDULPH, MAJOR J., B.S.C., Political Officer at Gilgit, 1880, Tribes of the Hindu Kush : 1880
BIGNOLD, T. F., Leviora, being the Rhymes of a Successful Competitor : 1888.
BIRDWOOD, SIR G. C. M., The Industrial Arts of India : 1880.
BIJAPUR, by H. Cousens : 1863.
BLACK, C.E.D., A Memoir of Indian Surveys, 1875–90, by : 1891.
BLACKER, LT.-COL. V., Operations of the British Army in India during the Mahratta War of 1817-9 : 1821.
BLANFORD, H. F., An Elementary Geography of India, Burma, and Ceylon : 1890.
BLANFORD, W. T., The Fauna of British India : 1888, etc.
BLOCHMANN, H., Calcutta during Last Century.
————— Contributions to the Geography and History of Bengal : Muhammadan Period, A.D. 1203–1538 : 1873.
BOGLE, G., Narrative of the Mission of, to Tibet : edited by Sir C. R. Markham : 1879.
BOLTS, W., Considerations on India Affairs : 1772, 1775.
BOMBAY, An Historical Account of the Settlement and Possession of, by the English E. I. Co., by S. Pechel : 1781.
————— The Rise of, a Retrospect, by S. M. Edwardes : 1902.
BOULGER, D. C., India in the Nineteenth Century : 1901.
————— The Story of India : 1898.
BOURCHIER, COL. G., Eight Months' Campaign against the Bengal Sepoy Army during the Mutiny of 1857 : 1858.
BOWER, REV. H., An Essay on Hindu Caste : 1851.
BOWRING, L. B., C.S.I., Eastern Experiences, Mysore, and Coorg : 1872.
BOYD, HUGH, Miscellaneous Works of, by L. D. Campbell : 1800.
BRADDON, SIR E. N., Life in India : 1872.
————— Thirty Years of Shikar : 1895.
BRADLEY-BIRT, F. B., The Story of an Indian Upland : 1905.
BRANDIS, SIR D., Indian Forestry : 1897.
BREEKS, J. W., An Account of the Primitive Tribes and Monuments of the Nilgiris : 1873.
BREMNER, MRS. C. S., A Month in a Dandi : 1891.
BRIGGS, MAJ.-GENL. JOHN, Memoir of, by Major Evans Bell : 1885.
————— Translation (revised) of the Siyar-ul-Mutakherin : 1832.
BROADFOOT, MAJOR G., C.B., Career of, by W. Broadfoot : 1888.
BROOKE, SIR JAMES, Life of, by S. St. John : 1879.
————— Life of, by J. C. Templer : 1853.
BROUGHTON, MAJ. T. D., Letters written in a Mahratta Camp, during the year 1809 : 1809 : 1892.
BROWN, C. P., Some Account of my Literary Life : 1866.
BRUCE, JOHN, Annals of the Hon. E. I. Co. : 1810.
BRUCE, R. I., The Forward Policy and its Results : 1900.
BUCHANAN, REV. DR. CLAUDIUS, Christian Researches in Asia : 1812.
————— Memoirs of, by Rev. H. Pearson : 1817.
BUCHANAN-HAMILTON, F., Mysore, Canara, and Malabar : 1807.
————— An Account of the Kingdom of Nipal : 1819.
BUCKINGHAM, J. S., Autobiography of : 1855.
BUCKLAND, C. T., Sketches of Social Life in India : 1884.
BUHLER, G., by Julius Jolly : 1899.
BUIST, G., Notes on India : 1853.
————— The Second Panjab War.
BURGESS, J., The Ancient Monuments, Temples, and Sculptures of India, with Descriptive Notes : 1897.
————— Archæological Survey of W. India, by, and others : 1874, etc.
BURMA, by Sir J. G. Scott : 1886.
————— History of, by Lieut.-Gen. Sir A. P. Phayre, K.C.S.I. : 1883.

BURMA, Its People and Natural Productions, by Rev. F. Mason : 1860.
——————— **Under British Rule, and Before,** by J. Nisbet : 1901.
BURMESE WAR, Narrative of the, 1824–6, by Major J. J. Snodgrass : 1827.
——————— **The Second, a narrative of the Operations at Rangoon in 1852,** by W. F. B. Laurie : 1853.
——————— **Wars, Our, and Relations with Burma,** by Col. W. F. B. Laurie : 1882.
BURNELL, DR. A. C., C.I.E., Elements of South Indian Palæography : 1874.
——————— **AND SIR H. YULE,** Hobson-Jobson : 1886 : 1903.
BURNES, COL. SIR A., Kabul : being a Personal Narrative of a Journey to, and Residence in, that City in 1836–8 : 1842.
——————— **Travels into Bokhara :** 1834.
BURNES, SURG. J., A Narrative of a Visit to the Court of Sind : 1831.
——————— **A Sketch of the History of Cutch :** 1829.
BURTON, SIR R. F., Sind Revisited : 1877. Memorial edition, edited by his wife : 1893.
——————— **True Life of,** by G. M. Stisted : 1896.
BUSHBY, H. J., Widow-burning, a Narrative : 1855.

CAINE, W. S., Picturesque India, by, 1890.
CALDWELL, BISHOP, Reminiscences, by Rev. J. L. Wyatt : 1894.
——————— **Early History of the Tinnevelly Mission :** 1881.
——————— **A Political and General History of the District of Tinnevelly :** 1881.
CAMBRIDGE, R. O., The War in India, between the English and French, . . . 1750 to 1760, . . . : 1761.
CAMPBELL, CAPT. DONALD, Journey Overland to India : 1795.
CAMPBELL, SIR GEORGE, Memoirs of my Indian Career, edited by Sir C. E. Bernard : 1893.
——————— **Modern India :** 1852.
CAMPBELL, MAJ.–GEN. J., C.B., Personal Narrative of Thirteen Years' Service among the Wild Tribes of Khondistan for the Suppression of Human Sacrifice : 1864.
CANNING, Life of, by H. W. V. Temperley : 1905.
CANNING, CHARLOTTE COUNTESS OF, The Story of Two Noble Lives, being Memorials of, and . . ., by A. J. C. Hare : 1893.
CANNING, EARL, by Sir H. S. Cunningham : 1891.
CAREY, EUSTACE, Memoir, by Mrs. Eustace Carey : 1857.
CAREY, MARSHMAN, AND WARD, The Life and Times of, by J. C. Marshman : 1859.
CAREY, W., D.D., by his Nephew, Eustace Carey : 1836.
——————— by Dr. G. Smith, C.I.E. : 1885.
CAREY, W. H., The Good Old Days of Hon. John Company, 1600–1858 : 1882.
CARPENTER, E., From Adam's Peak to Elephanta : 1892.
CARPENTER, MARY, Life and Work of, by her Nephew. J. E. Carpenter : 1879.
——————— **Six Months in India :** 1868.
CARSTAIRS, R., British Work in India : 1893.
CAVAGNARI, MAJOR SIR LOUIS, K.C.B., C.S.I., Life and Career of, by K. P. Dey : 1881.
CAVENAGH, GEN. SIR ORFEUR, Reminiscences of an Indian Official : 1884.
CAWNPUR, A Personal Narrative of the Outbreak and Massacre at, 1857, by W. J. Shepherd, one of the survivors : 1879 : 1886.
——————— by Sir G. O. Trevelyan, Bart. : 1865.
——————— **The Story of,** by Capt. Mowbray Thomson : 1859.
CHAMBERLAIN, JOHN, A Missionary Biography, by Rev. C. B. Lewis : 1876.
CHANDRA, BHOLANATH, The Travels of a Hindu to Various Parts of Bengal and Upper India : 1869.
CHEEM, ALIPH, Lays of Ind. 1876
CHIN HILLS, THE, by B. S. Carey, C.I.E., and H. N. Tuck : 1896.
CHIN-LUSHAI LAND, by Surg.-Lieut.-Col. A. S. Reid : 1893.

BIBLIOGRAPHY 475

CHIROL, VALENTINE, The Middle Eastern Question or some Political Problems of Indian Defence : 1903.
CHITRAL CAMPAIGN, THE, by H. C. Thomson : 1895.
CHITRAL, THE RELIEF OF, by Maj. G. J. and Capt. F. E. Younghusband : 1895.
CHITRAL, The Story of a Minor Siege, by Sir G. S. Robertson : 1898.
CHOTA-NAGPUR, by F. B. Bradley-Birt : 1903.
CHRISTIANITY IN INDIA, by J. W. Kaye : 1859.
————— History of, with its Prospects : 1895.
————— Its Progress, etc., by Dr. G. Smith, C.I.E. : 1864.
————— The History of, by Rev. J. Hough : 1839–60.
CLARKE, SIR ANDREW, The Life of Lt.-Genl., G.C.M.G., C.B., C.I.E. : by Col. R. H. Vetch, R.E., C.B. : 1905
CLIVE, by Gen. Sir W. F. Butler, K.C.B.
————— by C. Caraccioli : 1775.
————— by Rev. G. R. Gleig : 1848.
————— by Sir John Malcolm : 1836.
CLIVE, LORD, by Sir A. J. Arbuthnot, K.C.S.I. : 1899.
————— by Col. G. B. Malleson, C.S.I. : 1893.
————— by Col. Sir C. W. Wilson, K.C.B. : 1890.
————— And the Establishment of the English in India, by Professor Seeley.
CLYDE, COLIN CAMPBELL, LORD, by Archibald Forbes.
————— by Lieut.-Gen. Shadwell, C.B. : 1881.
CLYDE AND STRATHNAIRN, by Maj.-Gen. Sir O. T. Burne, K.C.S.I. : 1891.
COLEBROOKE, H. T., by Sir T. E. Colebrooke : 1873.
————— Miscellaneous Essays on Hindu History, Literature, etc. : 1872.
COLLEY, SIR G. POMEROY, by Lieut.-Gen. Sir W. F. Butler, K.C.B. : 1899.
COLQUHOUN, A. R., Amongst the Shans : 1855.
————— Russia against India, the Struggle for Asia : 1900.
COLQUHOUN, MAJ. J. A. S., R.A., With the Kurram Field Force, 1878–9 : 1881.
COLVIN, JOHN RUSSELL, by Sir Auckland Colvin, K.C.S.I., K.C.M.G. : 1895.
COMBERMERE, FIELD-MARSHAL VISCOUNT, by Lady Combermere : 1866.
CONNELL, A. K., Discontent and Danger in India : 1880.
CONOLLY, LIEUT. ARTHUR, A Journey to the North of India, Overland from England : 1834.
CONWAY, SIR W. M., Climbing and Exploration in the Karakoram-Himalayas : 1894.
COOPER, T. T., The Mishmee Hills : 1873.
————— Travels of a Pioneer of Commerce in Pigtail and Petticoats : 1871.
CORNWALLIS, THE MARQUIS OF, by W. S. Seton-Karr : 1890.
————— Correspondence of, by C. Ross : 1859.
CORRIE, THE RIGHT REV. DANIEL, LL.D., First Bishop of Madras, by his Brothers : 1847.
COTTON, GENERAL SIR ARTHUR T., R.E., K.C.S.I., by Lady Hope : 1900.
————— by H. Morris : 1901.
COTTON, G. E. L. (The Right Rev.), Memoir of, by Mrs. Cotton : 1871.
COTTON, SIR HENRY J. S., New India, or India in Transition : 1885.
COTTON, LIEUT.-GENL. SIR SYDNEY, Nine Years on the N.W. Frontier of India, 1854–63 : 1868.
COWELL, E. B., by G. Cowell : 1904.
COX, REV. SIR G. W., BART., History of the Establishment of British Rule in India : 1881.
CRAWFURD, JOHN, History of the Indian Archipelago : 1820.
————— Journal of an Embassy to the Court of Ava, 1827 : 1829.
CROOKE, W., The North-Western Provinces of India : 1897
CSOMA DE KOROS, ALEXANDER, Life and Work of, by T. Duka : 1885.
CUMMING, C. F. GORDON, From the Hebrides to the Himalayas : 1876.
————— In the Himalayas and on the Indian Plains : 1884.

CUNNINGHAM, MAJ.-GEN. SIR ALEXANDER, The Ancient Geography of India :
    1871.
CURRY AND RICE, on forty plates : by Capt. G. F. Atkinson : 1858.
CUST, R. N., Linguistic and Oriental Essays : several series : 1840–1903.
——————— Memoirs of Past Years of a Septuagenarian : 1899.
——————— Pictures of Indian Life, 1852–81 : 1881.
CUTHELL, E., AND CAPT. W. S. BURRELL, Indian Memories : 1893.

DACOSTA, J., Essays on Indian Affairs : 1892–5.
DALHOUSIE, MARQUIS OF, by Sir W. W. Hunter, K.C.S.I. : 1890.
——————— by Sir W. Lee Warner, K.C.S.I. : 1904.
——————— by Capt. L. J. Trotter : 1895.
——————— Vindication of his Indian Administration, by Sir C. Jackson : 1865.
DALHOUSIE'S Administration of British India : by Sir E. Arnold, K.C.I.E., 1862,
    1865.
DALRYMPLE, ALEXANDER, Account of the Subversion of 'the Legal Govern-
    ment at Madras, by imprisoning the Governor, Lord Pigot, in August, 1776 :
——————— Oriental Repertory : 1791–4 : 1808.
DALTON, COL. E. T., Descriptive Ethnology of Bengal : 1872.
DALTON, CAPT. J., Memoir of, Defender of Trichinopoly, 1752–3, by Charles Dalton :
    1886.
DALY, GENERAL, SIR H. D., G.C.B., C.I.E., Memoir of, by Major H. Daly, C.S.I.,
    C.I.E. : 1905.
DANIELL, T. AND W., Oriental Scenery of Hindostan : 1816.
DANVERS, F. C., Bengal, its Chief Agents and Governors : 1888.
——————— India : 1877.
——————— The Portuguese in India : 1894.
DARMSTETER, J., Lettres sur l'Inde. A la frontière Afghane : 1888.
DAS, ABHAY CHARAN, The Indian Ryot, etc. . . . the Famine : 1881.
DAS, DEBENDRO NATH, Sketches of Hindu Life : 1887.
DAY, SURG.-MAJ., The Land of the Permauls, or Cochin, its Past and Present :
    1863.
DE, REV. LAL BIHARI, Convert, Pastor, etc., by G. Macpherson : 1900.
——————— Bengal Peasant Life, by : 1879 : 1898
DEAKIN, A., Irrigated India : 1893.
——————— Temple and Tomb in India : 1893.
DEKKAN, A History of the, by J. D. B. Gribble : 1896.
——————— An Historical and Political View of the : 1798.
DELHI, Past and Present, by H. C. Fanshawe, C.S.I. : 1902.
——————— Siege of, The Chaplain's Narrative of the, by Rev. J. E. W. Rotton :
    1858.
DELHI, 1857, The Siege, etc., by Col. Keith Young, C.B. : edited by Gen. Sir. H. W.
    Norman and Mrs. Keith Young : 1902.
DENISON, SIR W., Varieties of Vice-Regal Life : 1870.
DENNIE, COL. W. H., Personal Narrative of the Campaigns in Afghanistan, Sind,
    Beluchistan : 1843.
DEROZIO, HENRY, The Eurasian Poet, by T. Edwards : 1884.
DEY, RAM DULAL, by Girish Chandra Ghose : 1868.
DICKINSON, JOHN, India : its Government under a Bureaucracy : 1853.
DIGBY, W., "Prosperous" British India : 1901.
——————— The Famine Campaign in Southern India, 1876–8 : 1878.
DILKE, SIR C. W., Greater Britain : 1869.
DIROM, MAJOR A.. A Narrative of the Campaign in India in 1792 : 1793.
DOST MUHAMMAD KHAN, Life of the Amir, by Mohan Lal : 1846.
DOW, LIEUT.-COL. A., The History of Hindustan, translated by : 1768.
DOWNING, LIEUT. CLEMENT, A Compendious History of the Indian Wars : 1737.
DOWSON, JOHN, A Classical Dictionary of Hindu Mythology and Religion, etc. :
    1879.

DREW, F., The Jammu and Kashmir Territories : 1875.
——————— The Northern Barrier of India : 1877.
DRURY, COL. HEBER, Life and Sport in Southern India : 1890.
DUBOIS, J. A., Description of the Character, Manners, and Customs of the People of India, etc., translated and edited by H. K. Beauchamp : 1897.
DUFF, REV. A., D.D, India and India Missions : 1839.
——————— Recollections of, by Rev. Lal Bihari De : 1879.
DUFFERIN AND AVA, MARQUIS OF, by C. E. D. Black : 1903.
——————— by Sir A. C. Lyall, G.C.I.E., K.C.B. : 1905.
——————— Speeches delivered in India, by D. M. Wallace : 1890.
DUFFERIN AND AVA, MARCHIONESS OF, Our Vice-regal Life in India, : 1889.
DUPLEIX, J. F., by Col. G. B. Malleson, C.S.I. : 1890.
DURAND, COL. A. G. A., The Making of a Frontier : 1899.
DURAND, MAJ.-GEN. SIR H. M., K.C.S.I., C.B., R.E., by Sir H. Mortimer Durand 1883.
DUTT, ROMESH CHUNDER, C.I.E., Economic History of India, 1757-1837 : 1902.
——————— England and India, 1785-1885 : 1897.
——————— History of Civilization in Ancient India : 1889-90.
——————— India in the Victorian Age : 1904.
——————— Literature of Bengal : 1877 : 1895.
DUTTON, MAJ. THE HON. C., Life in India : 1882.

EAST INDIA COMPANY, Administration of, by Sir J. W. Kaye : 1853.
——————— History and Management of the, from its Origin in 1600, by J. Macpherson : 1799.
——————— Summary of the History of the, from their First Charter . . . to the Present Period, by E. Thornton : 1833.
EAST-INDIAN WORTHIES, being Memoirs of Distinguished Indo-Europeans, by H. A. Stark and E. W. Madge : 1892.
EASTWICK, E. B., The Kaisarnamah-i-Hind, or Lay of the Empress (a poem with appendices containing the histories of the Princes of India) : 1877-82.
EASTWICK, CAPT. R. W., by H. Compton : 1891.
EASTWICK, CAPT. W. J., Dry Leaves from young Egypt (Sind) : 1851.
EDEN, HON. SIR ASHLEY, Sketch of the Official Character of the, by K. P. Dey.
EDEN, C. H., India, Historical and Descriptive : 1876.
EDEN, HON. EMILY, Letters from India : 1872.
——————— Portraits of the Princes and People of India : 1844.
——————— Up the Country : 1866.
EDWARDES, MAJ.-GEN. SIR H. B., K.C.B., K.C.S.I., by Lady Edwardes : 1886.
——————— A Year on the Panjab Frontier in 1848-9 : 1851.
EDWARDS, W., Reminiscences of a Bengal Civilian : 1866.
ELGIN, EIGHTH EARL OF, Letters and Journals of James, by T. Walrond : 1872.
——————— by G. M. Wrong ; 1905.
ELLENBOROUGH, EARL OF, History of the Indian Administration of, by Lord Colchester : 1874.
ELLIOT, SIR H. M., History of India as told by its own Historians, The : 1867-77.
——————— Memoirs on the History, Folklore and Distribution of the Races of the N.W.P. of India, edited by J. Beames : 1869.
ELLIOT, RIGHT HON. HUGH, by the Countess of Minto : 1868.
ELLIOT, R. H., Experiences of a Planter in the Jungles of Mysore : 1871.
——————— Gold, Sport and Coffee Planting in Mysore : 1894.
ELPHINSTONE, MOUNTSTUART, Account of the Kingdom of Kabul, etc. : 1815.
——————— Life of, by Sir T. E. Colebrooke, Bart. : 1884.
——————— Rise of the British Power in the East, by, edited by Sir E. Colebrooke : 1887.
——————— Selections from the Minutes, etc., of, edited by G. W. Forrest : 1884.

ELWOOD, A. K. (MRS. COL.), Narrative of a Journey Overland from England
    . . . to India, including a residence there and voyage home, in the years
    1825-8 : 1830.
EPISODES in the Life of an INDIAN CHAPLAIN, by a retired Chaplain : 1882.
ESDAILE, DR. J., Mesmerism in India : 1902.
EWART, DR. (SIR) J., The Poisonous Snakes of India : 1878.
EXMOUTH, VISCOUNT, by E. Osler : 1835.
EYRE, MAJ.-GEN. SIR V., Military Operations at Kabul . . . 1842, with a Journal
    of Imprisonment in Afghanistan : 1843.

FALCONER, DR. HUGH, Palæontological Memoirs and Notes, with a biographical
    sketch of the author, edited by C. Murchison : 1868.
FANE, H. E., Five Years in India ; comprising a Narrative of Travels in the Presi-
    dency of Bengal, etc., : 1842.
FAWCETT, RIGHT HON. HENRY, by Leslie Stephen : 1885.
FAY, MRS. E., Original Letters from India : 1817.
FAYRER, SURG.-GENL. SIR J., BART., Recollections of My Life : 1900.
————————— The Thanatophidia of India, being a Description of the Venomous
    Snakes of the Indian Peninsula : 1872.
FENTON, MRS., The Journal of, a Narrative of Her Life in India, etc., 1826-30,
    with Preface by Sir H. Lawrence, Bart. : 1901.
FERGUSSON, DR. J., History of Indian and Eastern Architecture : 1876.
————————— Archæology in India, etc. : 1884.
————————— Tree and Serpent Worship : 1868.
FERRIER, ADJT.-GENL. J. P., Caravan Journeys and Wanderings: 1856 : 1857.
————————— History of the Afghans : 1858.
FERISHTA (MUHAMMAD KASIM), History of the Dekkan . . . and . . . of
    Bengal, to the year 1780, translated by Jonathan Scott : 1794.
FITZCLARENCE, GEORGE, EARL OF MUNSTER, Journal of a Route across
    India through Egypt to England, 1817-8 : 1819.
FORBES, ARCHIBALD, The Afghan Wars, 1839-42, and 1878-80 : 1892.
————————— The Soldiers I have Known.
FORBES, CAPT. C. J. F. S., British Burma and its People : 1878.
FORBES, DUNCAN, Sketch of the Early Life of, written by himself : 1859.
FORBES, GORDON S., Wild Life in Canara and Ganjam : 1885.
FORBES, JAMES, Oriental Memoirs, 1813 : 1834-5.
FORBES-MITCHELL, W., Reminiscences of the Great Mutiny, 1857-9 : 1893.
FORCHHAMMER, E., Notes on the Early History and Geography of British
    Burma : 1891.
FORJETT, C., Our Real Danger in India : 1877.
FORREST, G. W., Cities of India : 1903.
————————— Selections from the Letters, Despatches and other State Papers
    preserved in the Foreign Department of the Government of India, 1772-85 :
    1890.
————————— ditto, ditto, in Bombay Secretariat, Home Series, 2 vols. : 1887 ;
    Mahratta Series, vol. I. : 1885.
————————— ditto, ditto, in the Military Department . . ., 1857-8 : 1893.
FORSTER, G., A Journey from Bengal to England, through the Northern Part
    of India, etc., etc. : 1798.
FORSYTH, SIR DOUGLAS, C.B., K.C.S.I., Autobiography and Reminiscences of,
    edited by his Daughter : 1887.
FORSYTH, CAPT. J., The Highlands of Central India : 1872.
FOSTER, W., A Descriptive Catalogue of the Paintings, Statues, and Framed
    Prints in the India Office : 1902-3.
FRANCIS, SIR PHILIP, by J. Parks and H. Merivale : 1867.
————————— The —— Letters, by Sir Philip Francis and other Members of the
    Family, edited by B. F. and E. Keary : 1901.

FRANCKLIN, LT.-COL. W., History of the Reign of Shah-Alam : 1798.
——————— Observations made on a Tour from Bengal to Persia in 1786-7 : 1788.
FRASER, COL. HASTINGS, Our Faithful Ally, the Nizam : 1865.
FRASER, GENL. J. S., of the Madras Army, by Col. Hastings Fraser : 1885.
FRASER, LT.-COL. T. G., Records of Sport and Military Life in W. India : 1881.
FRAZER, R. W., A Literary History of India : 1898.
——————— British India : 1896.
FRENCH IN INDIA, History of the, by Col. G. B. Malleson, C.S.I., : 1893.
FRENCHMEN IN BENGAL, THREE, by S. C. Hill : 1903.
FRENCH STRUGGLES IN INDIA and on the Indian Seas, Final, by Col. G. B.
　　Malleson, C.S.I. : 1878.
FRENCH, THE RIGHT REV. T. V., Bishop of Lahore, by Rev. H. Birks : 1895.
FRERE, RIGHT HON. SIR H. BARTLE E., Bart., G.C.B., by J. Martineau : 1895.
——————— On the Impending Bengal Famine : 1874.
FRESHFIELD, D. W., Round Kangchenjunga, a Narrative of Mountain Travel
　　and Exploration : 1903.
FULLARTON, COL. W., A View of the English Interests in India, and an Account
　　of the military Operations in . . . 1782-4 : 1787.
FYTCHE, LT.-GENL. A., Burma, Past and Present, with Personal Reminiscences :
　　1878.

GARCIN DE TASSY, Les Auteurs Hindustanis et leurs Ouvrages : 1868.
——————— Histoire de la Litterature Hindoui et Hindoustani : 1839 : 1847.
GARDNER, COL. A. H., Colonel of Artillery in the Service of Ranjit Singh, edited
　　by Major H. Pearse : 1898.
GARRETT, J., A Classical Dictionary of India, illustrative of the Mythology, etc.,
　　of the Hindus : 1871-3.
GAUR, its Ruins and Inscriptions, by J. H. Ravenshaw, edited by his Widow : 1878.
GAWLER, COL. J. C., Sikhim, with Hints on Mountain and Jungle Warfare : 1873.
GEOLOGY OF INDIA, A Manual of the, by R. D. Oldham : 1893.
GERARD, CAPT. A., Account of an Attempt to Penetrate . . . to . . . the Lake
　　of Manasarowara : 1840.
GERARD, LT.-GENL. SIR M. G., K.C.B., K.C.S.I., Leaves from the Diary of a
　　Soldier and Sportsman during 20 years' Service in India in 1865-85 : 1903.
GHOSE, RAM GOPAL, Public Speeches, with a brief sketch of his life : 1871.
GHULAM HUSAIN KHAN, SAIYAD, the Siyar ul Mutakharin, by, translated by
　　Raymond, 1789 : revised by Maj.-Genl. J. Briggs, 1832 : 1902.
GILBERT'S (SIR W. R.), GENERAL, Raid to the Khyber, a Personal Narrative,
　　by R. W. Bingham : 1850.
GILL, CAPT. W., The River of Golden Sand, edited by Col. (Sir) H. Yule : 1883.
GILLESPIE, MAJ.-GENL. SIR R. R., K.C.B., A Memoir of, by Major W. Thorn :
　　1816.
GLADWIN, F., A Narrative of the Transactions of Bengal, translated by : 1788.
GOA, An Historical and Archæological Sketch of the City of, by J. N. Da Fonseca :
　　1878.
GOLDSMID, MAJ.-GENL. SIR F. J., Telegraph and Travel : 1874.
GOLDSTÜCKER, PROF. THEODOR, Literary Remains of the late : 1879.
GOMES, F. LUIZ, The Brahmans, translated from the Portuguese, by J. de Silva,
　　Bombay : 1889.
GOMM, FIELD-MARSHAL SIR W. M., G.C.B., by F. C. Carr-Gomm : 1881.
GORDON, MAJ.-GENL. C. G., by Archibald Forbes : 1884.
——————— by Lt.-Genl. W. F. Butler : 1891.
GORDON, J. D., Work and Play in India and Kashmir : 1893.
GORE, F. St. J., Lights and Shades of Hill Life in the Afghan and Hindu Highlands
　　of the Panjab : 1895.
GOUGH, HUGH, FIELD-MARSHAL, FIRST VISCOUNT, The Life and Campaigns
　　of, by R. S. Rait : 1903.

GOUGH, GENL. SIR HUGH, Old Memories : 1897.

GOURISHANKAR, UDAYASHANKAR, by Javerilal U. Yajnik : 1889.

GRAHAM, ALEXANDER, Genealogical and Chronological Tables, illustrative of Indian History : 1863.

GRAHAM, MARIA (LADY CALLCOTT), Journal of a Residence in India : 1812.

GRANDPRÈ, L. DE, A Voyage in the Indian Ocean and to Bengal in 1789-90, etc. : 1803.

GRANT, DR. A., Physician and Friend : his Autobiography, etc., edited by Dr. G. Smith, C.I.E. : 1902.

GRANT, C., by H. Morris : 1904.

GRANT, COLESWORTHY, Rural Life in Bengal, illustrative of Anglo-Indian Suburban Life : 1860.

GRANT, GENL. SIR JAMES HOPE, by Col. H. Knollys . 1894.

———— **Incidents in the Sepoy War, 1857-8, from the Private Journals of,** by H. Knollys : 1873.

GRANT, SIR JOHN PETER, OF ROTHIEMURCHUS, G.C.M.G., K.C.B., by W. S. Seton-Karr : 1899.

GRANT-DUFF, JAMES, A History of the Mahrattas : 1826 ; 1874.

GRANT-DUFF, RIGHT HON. SIR MOUNTSTUART E., Notes of an Indian Journey : 1876.

———— **Notes from a Diary, kept chiefly in Southern India, 1881-6 :** 1899.

GREENWOOD, LIEUT. J., Narrative of the late Victorious Campaign in Afghanistan under General Pollock : 1844.

GRIER, S. C., In furthest Ind, the Narrative of Mr. E. Carlyon of the Hon. E. I. Co.'s Service, edited by : 1894.

GRIERSON, G. A., Bihar Peasant Life, by : 1885.

GRIFFIN, SIR L. H., The Panjab Chiefs, historical and biographical notices : 1865.

GRIFFITH, MRS., India's Princes, short Life-sketches of Native Rulers : 1894.

GRIFFITH, DR. W., Journal of the Mission which visited Bhutan in 1837-8, under Capt. R. B. Pemberton : 1839 (?)

———— **Journals of Travels in Assam, Burma, Bhutan, Afghanistan, etc. :** 1847.

GRIMWOOD, ETHEL ST. C., My Three Years in Manipur, etc. : 1891.

GROSE, J. H., A Voyage to the E. Indies : containing authentic Accounts of the Mogul Government, . . . and of the Muhammadan, Gentoo, and Parsi Religions : 1772.

HAMILTON, CAPT. C., A Historical Relation of . . . the Government of the Rohilla Afghans in the Northern Provinces of Hindostan, etc. : 1787.

HAMILTON, W., The East India Gazetteer : 1815 : 1828.

HANNA, COL. H. B., The Second Afghan War, 1878-80 : 1899.

———— **The Defence of India's N. W. Frontier :** 1898.

HARDINGE, VISCOUNT, by his Son, Charles, Viscount Hardinge : 1891.

HARE, DAVID, by Piari Chand Mitra : 1881.

HARRIS, LORD, by Stephen Lushington : 1840.

HARTLEY, MRS. JAMES, Indian Life, a tale of the Carnatic : 1840 : 1845.

HARTMAN, RIGHT REV. DR. A., O.C., Vicar Apostolic of Patna, by Rev. Fathei Anthony Mady : 1868.

HASTINGS, MARQUESS OF, by Lt.-Col. J. Ross, of Bladensburg : 1893.

———— **History of the Political and Military Transactions in India during the Administration of, 1813-23,** by H. T. Prinsep : 1825.

———— **Private Journal of, Gov.-Gen. and C. in C. in India,** edited by the Marchioness of Bute : 1858.

———— **Summary of the Administration of the Indian Government,** by : 1824.

———— **Summary of the Mahratta and Pindari Campaign, 1817-9, under the direction of :** 1820.

HASTINGS, WARREN, by Rev. G. R. Gleig: 1841.
————— by Sir A. C. Lyall, G.C.I.E., K.C.B.: 1891.
————— by Col. G. B. Malleson, C.S.I.: 1894.
————— by Capt. L. J. Trotter: 1878: 1890.
————— Administration of, by H. Beveridge: 1889.
————— Administration of, 1772-85, by G. W. Forrest: 1892.
————— and the Rohilla War, by Sir J. Strachey, G.C.S.I.: 1892.
————— Articles of Charges of High Crimes and Misdemeanours against, presented to the House of Commons, April 12, 1786, by the Right Hon. Edmund Burke: 1786.
————— Defence of, at the bar of the House of Commons, . . . in the year 1786: 1786.
————— History of the Trial of, late Governor-General of Bengal: 1796.
————— Memoirs relative to the State of India, by: 1787.
————— Narrative of the Insurrection which happened in the Zamindari of Benares in the month of Aug.: 1853.
————— Private Life of, by Sir C. Lawson: 1895.
HAUG, Dr. M., by E. P. Evans: 1877.
HAUGHTON, COL. J. C., Charikar and Service there . . . in 1841: 1879.
HAUGHTON, LT.-COL. JOHN, Commander of the 36th Sikhs, by Major A. C. Yate: 1900.
HAVELOCK, MAJ.-GENL., SIR H., K.C.B., by Rev. W. Brock: 1858.
————— by Archibald Forbes: 1890.
————— by J. C. Marshman: 1860.
————— Memoir of the Three Campaigns of Maj.-Genl. Sir A. Campbell's Army in Ava: 1828.
————— Narrative of the War in Afghanistan in 1838-9: 1840.
————— by Rev. W. Owen: 1858.
HEADLAM, CECIL, Ten Thousand Miles through India and Burma: 1903.
HEBER, THE RIGHT REV. REGINALD, D.D., Bishop of Calcutta, Narrative of a Journey through the Upper Provinces of India, from Calcutta to Bombay. 1824-5, etc.: 1828.
————— Last Days of, by Rev. T. Robinson: 1830.
————— Life, by his widow: 1830.
————— Life, by Dr. G. Smith, C.I.E.: 1895.
————— Memoirs, by T. Taylor: 1835.
HENDLEY, SURG.-COL. T. H., The Rulers of India, and the Chiefs of Rajputana, 1550-1897: 1897.
HENSMAN, H., The Afghan War of 1879-80: 1881.
HERKLOTS, G. A., Qanoon-i-Islam, or the Customs of the Mussulmans of India, translated by: 1832: 1863.
HEWITT, J. F. K., The Ruling Races of Pre-historic Times in India, South-Western Asia, and Southern Europe: 1894-5.
HILL, S. C., List of Europeans and others in the English Factories in Bengal at the time of the Siege of Calcutta in 1756: 1902.
HIMALAYA, HOLY. The Religion, Traditions and Scenery of a Himalayan Province (Kumaón and Garhwál), by E. Shearman Oakley: 1905.
HINDUS, THE, including a General Description of India, etc., illustrated from drawings by W. Westlake: 1847.
————— AS THEY ARE, by Shib Chandra Bose: 1881.
HINDUSTAN, ETC., Illustrated, with descriptions by Emma Roberts: 1850.
HISLOP, REV. S., Papers relating to the Aboriginal Tribes of the Central Provinces: 1866.
————— Pioneer Missionary and Naturalist in Central India, by Dr. G. Smith. C.I.E.: 1888.
HISTORY OF THE BRITISH EMPIRE IN INDIA, by Rev. G. R. Gleig: 1835.
————— THE BRITISH SETTLEMENTS IN INDIA: 1855.
————— EUROPEAN COMMERCE WITH INDIA: 1812.
————— INDIA, CASSELL'S ILLUSTRATED, by James Grant: 1876-7.

HOBBES, R. G., Reminiscences of 70 years' Life, Travel and Adventure, by a Retired Officer of H.M.'s Civil Service, 1893, 5.

HOBHOUSE, A Memoir of the Right Hon. Arthur, Baron, P.C., K.C.S.I., by L. T. Hobhouse and J. L. Hammond : 1905.

HODGES, W., Travels in India, 1780-3 : 1793.

HODGSON, BRIAN H., by Sir W. W. Hunter, K.C.S.I. : 1896.

————— Essays on the Language, Literature, and Religion of Nipal and Tibet, etc. : 1874.

————— Miscellaneous Essays relating to Indian Subjects : 1880.

————— Papers on the Colonization, Commerce, Geography, etc., of the Himalayas and Nipal : 1857.

HODSON, MAJ. W. S. R., of "Hodson's Horse," by Capt. L. J. Trotter : 1901.

————— Twelve Years of a Soldier's Life in India : by Rev. G. H. Hodson, 1859 : 1889.

HOFFMEISTER, W., Travels in Ceylon and Continental India, including Nipal, etc. : 1848.

HOLDICH, SIR T. H., The Indian Borderland, 1880-1900 : 1901.

HOLCOMB, HELEN H., Men of Might in India : the Leaders and their Mission Epochs, 1706-1899 : 1901.

HOLMES, T. R. E., Four Famous Soldiers : 1889.

HOLWELL, J. Z., India Tracts, by, and friends : 1774.

————— Interesting Historical Events, relative to the Provinces of Bengal, and the Empire of Indostan : 1765-71.

HOME, ROBERT, Select views in Mysore, with historical descriptions : 1794.

HONIGBERGER, DR. J. M., Thirty-five Years in the East : 1852.

HOOKER, SIR J. D., Himalayan Journals : 1854.

HORSBURGH, J., India Directory, or Directions for sailing to and from the E. Indies, 1826 : 1841.

HOUGH, MAJOR W., A Narrative of the March and Operations of the Army of the Indus, in 1838-9 : 1840.

————— Political and Military Events in British India, 1756-1849 : 1853.

HUBNER, J. A. von, BARON, Through the British Empire : 1886.

HUGEL, CARL von, BARON, Travels in Kashmir and the Panjab, notes by Maj. T. B. Jervis : 1845.

HUME, CAPT. G. H., Outram and Havelock's Persian Campaign : 1858.

HUNTER, SIR W. W., K.C.S.I., by F. H. B. Skrine : 1901.

————— Annals of Rural Bengal : 1868.

————— Bombay, 1885-90 : 1892.

————— Brief History of the Indian Peoples : 1903.

————— England's Work in India : 1881 : 1889.

————— Famine Aspects of Bengal Districts : 1874.

————— Guide to the Orthography of Indian Proper Names : 1871.

————— India of the Queen, and other Essays by, edited by Lady Hunter : 1903.

————— Indian Musulmans, The : 1871 : 1876.

————— Orissa : 1872 : 1893.

————— The Old Missionary : 1895.

————— The Thackerays in India, and some Calcutta Graves : 1897.

HUTCHINSON, MAJ.-GENL. G., Narrative of the Mutinies in Oudh : 1859.

————— A Brief Memorial of, by H. Morris : 1900.

HUTCHINSON, COL. H. D., The Campaign in Tirah, 1897-8 : 1898.

HUTTON, J., A Hundred Years Ago : An Historical Sketch, 1775-6 : 1857.

————— The Thugs and Dacoits, the hereditary garotters and gang robbers of India : 1857.

HYDE, REV. H. B., The Parish of Bengal, 1678-1788 : 1899.

————— Parochial Annals of Bengal : 1901.

HYDER ALI AND TIPPOO SULTAN, by L. B. Bowring, C.S.I., : 1893.

—————   by Capt. Francis Robson : 1786.

HYDER NAIK, History of, translated by Col. W. Miles : 1842.

HYDER SHAH, History of, and his son Tippoo Sultan, by Prince Ghulam Muhammad : 1855.

IDDESLEIGH, EARL OF, by A. Lang : 1890.
ILBERT, SIR C., The Government of India : 1898.
IMPEY, SIR ELIJAH, by E. P. Impey : 1846.
INDIA, Ancient, its Language and Religions, by H. Oldenberg . 1898.
——————— **and its Problems,** by W. S. Lilly : 1902.
——————— by Col. Sir T. H. Holdich, K.C.M.G., K.C.I.E. : 1904.
——————— by Rev. Hobart Caunter : 1895.
——————— **from the Aryan Invasion to the Great Sepoy Mutiny,** by A. E. Knight : 1897.
——————— **Imperial,** by John Oliver Hobbes.
——————— **in 1983 :** 1888.
——————— **its Government under a Bureaucracy,** by John Dickinson : 1852.
——————— **Past and Present,** by J. Murdoch, LL.D. : 1903.
——————— **Past and Present,** by J. Samuelson : 1890.
——————— **The Land and People,** by Sir J. Caird : 1883.
——————— **The Story of,** by D. C. Boulger : 1898.
INDIAN ALPS, THE, and how we crossed them, by a Lady Pioneer : 1876.
INDIAN PROBLEM SOLVED, The : Undeveloped Wealth in India and State Reproductive Works : 1874.
INDIAN RECORDS, the Relations between the British Government and the Nawabs Nazim of Bengal, Bihar, and Orissa : 1870.
INDIA, THE PEOPLE OF, edited by J. F. Watson and J. W. Kaye : 1868–72.
INDIA, UNDER VICTORIA, 1836-86, by Capt. L. J. Trotter : 1886.
INDIKA, the Country and the People of India and Ceylon, by Dr. J. F. Hurst : 1891.
IND, THE LAND OF, or Glimpses of India, by James Kerr : 1873.
INGLIS, HON. JULIA, LADY, The Siege of Lucknow, a Diary : 1858 : 1892.
INNES, A. D., Britain and her Rivals in the 18th Century : 1895.
——————— **A Short History of the British in India :** 1902.
INNES, LIEUT.-GEN. J. J. McLEOD, Lucknow and Oudh in the Mutiny : 1896.
INNES, LIEUT.-COL. P. R., The History of the Bengal European Regiment, now the Royal Munster Fusiliers, and how it helped to win India : 1885.
INVASIONS OF INDIA from Central Asia : 1879.
IRVING'S BOOK OF EMINENT SCOTSMEN.
IRWIN, H. C., The Garden of India ; or Chapters on Oudh History and Affairs : 1880.
IVES, E., A Voyage from England to India in 1754, and an Historical Narrative . . . Watson and Col. Clive . . . Surajuddaula, etc. : 1773.

JACKSON, JOHN, F.S.A., Journey from India, towards England in 1797 : 1799.
JACOB, MAJ.-GEN. SIR G. LEGRAND, Western India before and during the Mutinies : 1871.
JACOB, GEN. JOHN, by A. Innes Shand : 1900.
——————— **The Views and Opinions of,** by Capt. (Sir) Lewis Pelly : 1858.
JACQUEMONT, VICTOR, Letters from India, during the years 1828-31, by : 1834.
JAMES, RIGHT REV. DR. J. T., Bishop of Calcutta, by Rev. E. James : 1830.
JAMES, LIONEL, The Indian Frontier War, 1897 : 1898.
——————— **With the Chitral Relief Force :** 1895.
JAMES, W., The Naval History of Great Britain, 1793-1827: 1886.
JAMES, RIGHT HON. SIR W. M., The British in India : 1882.
JIJIBHAI, SIR JAMSETJI, BART., Memorandum of the Life, etc., of : 1854.
JOHNSTON, REV. J., A Century of Christian Progress : 1888.
JOHNSTONE, MAJ.-GEN. SIR J., My Experiences in Manipur and the Naga Hills : 1896.
JONES, CAPT. O. J., Recollections of a Winter Campaign in India in 1857-8 : 1859.
JONES, SIR W., The Works of, with the life of the Author, by Lord Teignmouth : 1807.

JOURNAL OF THE MARCH of the Bombay Detachment across the Mahratta Country, from Kalpi to Surat in 1778, commanded by Lieut.-Col. Goddard : 1779.

JUDSON, REV. ADONIRAM, by Francis Wayland, D.D.: 1853.

KAFIRS OF THE HINDU KUSH, THE, by Sir G. S. Robertson : 1896.
KANDAHAR, in 1879, by Col. A. Le Messurier, R.E.: 1880.
——————, the Indian Empire and the Turkomans : 1881.
—————— The Mission to, by H. B. Lumsden : 1860.
KARACHI, Past, Present, and Future, by A. F. Baillie : 1890.
KASHMIR, its new Silk Industry, etc., by Sir Thomas Wardle : 1904.
—————— The Valley of, by W. R. Lawrence : 1895.
KAVANAGH, T. H., How I won the Victoria Cross : 1860.
KEENE, H. G., C.I.E., Fall of the Mogul Empire : 1876 . 1887.
—————— a Servant of John Company : 1897.
—————— Sketch of the History of Hindustan : 1885.
KEITH-FALCONER, HON. ION, by Rev. R. Sinkar : 1888.
KENNEDY, JAMES, Christianity and the Religions of India, Essays, by : 1874.
—————— Essays, Ethnological and Linguistic : 1861.
—————— Life and Work in Benares and Kumdon, 1839-77, by, : 1884.
KENNEDY, R. H., Narrative of the Campaign of the Army of the Indus, in Sind and Kabul, in 1838-9 : 1840.
KIERNANDER, THE REV. J. Z., founder of the Old or Mission Church : 1877.
KINDERSLEY, MRS., Letters from . . . and the E. Indies : 1777.
KING, MRS. R. MOSS, The Diary of a Civilian's Wife in India, 1877-82 : 1884.
KIPLING, RUDYARD, an Attempt at Appreciation, by G. F. Monkshood : 1899.
KIRKPATRICK, COL. W., Account of the Kingdom of Nipal, in 1793 : 1811.
KITTS, E. J., A Compendium of the Castes and Tribes found in India : 1885.
KNIGHT, E. F., Where Three Empires Meet : 1893.

LAIRVIX, REV. A. F., Brief Memories of, Missionary, by J. Mullens : 1862.
LAKE, E., Journals of the Sieges of the Madras Army, 1817-9 : 1825.
LAKE, GEN. LORD, Memoir of the War in India, conducted by, 1803-6, by Maj. W. Thorn : 1818.
LALLY TOLLENDAL, T. A. DE, COUNT, Memoirs of : 1766.
LANSDOWNE, MARQUIS OF, The Administration of, 1888-94, by G. W. Forrest : 1894.
LAWRENCE, LIEUT.-GEN. SIR G. ST. P., K.C.S.I., C.B., Reminiscences of 43 years in India : 1875.
LAWRENCE, SIR H. M., BART., K.C.B., by Maj.-Gen. Sir H. B. Edwardes, K.C.B., K.C.S.I., and H. Merivale, C.B. : 1872.
—————— Adventures of an Officer in the Service of Ranjit Singh : 1845.
—————— the Pacificator, by Lieut.-Gen. J. J. McLeod Innes, V.C.: 1898.
—————— Some Passages in the Life of an Adventurer in the Panjab : 1842.
LAWRENCE, JOHN LAIRD MUIR, by W. St. Clair.
—————— Saviour of India, by C. Bruce : 1893.
LAWRENCE, LORD, by Sir C. Aitchison, K.C.S.I. : 1893.
—————— by R. Bosworth Smith : 1883.
—————— by Sir R. Temple, Bart., G.C.S.I. : 1889.
—————— by Capt. L. J. Trotter : 1880.
LAWRENCE, MAJ.-GEN. STRINGER, by Col. J. Biddulph : 1901.
LAWRENCE-ARCHER, MAJOR J. H., Commentaries on the Panjab Campaign, 1848-9 : 1878.
LEE WARNER, SIR W., K.C.S.I., The Citizen of India : 1897.
—————— The Protected Princes of India : 1894.
LEITNER, DR. G. W., Dardistan in 1895 : 1896.
—————— Life and Labours of, by J. H. Stocqueler : 1875.
—————— The Languages and Races of Dardistan : 1877.

LEWIN, LIEUT.-COL. T. H., A Fly on the Wheel : 1885.
——————— **The Hill Tracts of Chittagong :** 1869.
——————— **Wild Races of South-Eastern India :** 1870.
LIFE IN THE MOFUSSIL, or the Civilian in Lower Bengal, by an Ex-Civilian (G. Graham) : 1878.
LIGHT, FRANCIS AND WILLIAM, the Founders of Penang and Adelaide, etc., etc., by A. Francis Steuart : 1901.
LLOYD, HELEN, Hindu Women : 1881.
LLOYD, MAJ. SIR W., Narrative of a Journey to the Boorendo Pass in the Himalaya Mountains, by, edited by G. Lloyd : 1840.
LOGIN, SIR JOHN, and Dulip Singh, by Lady Login : 1890.
LONG, REV. J., Calcutta and Bombay in their Social Aspects : 1870.
——————— **Handbook of Bengal Missions :** 1848.
LOVE, LIEUT.-COL. H. D., Descriptive List of Pictures in Government House, and the Banqueting Hall, Madras : 1903.
LOWE, T., Central India during the Rebellion of 1857-8 : 1860.
LUCKNOW, SIEGE OF, A Lady's Diary of the, by Mrs. J. Harris : 1858.
——————— **A Personal Journal of the,** by Col. R. P. Anderson : 1858.
——————— **A Personal Narrative of the,** by L. E. R. Rees : 1858.
——————— **Day by Day at the, a Journal of the Siege of,** by A. Case : 1858.
LUMSDEN OF THE GUIDES (Lieut.-Gen. Sir H. B.), by Gen. Sir P. S. Lumsden and G. R. Elsmie : 1899.
LYALL, RIGHT HON. SIR A. C., G.C.I.E., K.C.B., Asiatic Studies : 1882 : 1899.
——————— **The Rise and Expansion of the British Dominion in India :** 1894.
LYTTON'S, EARL OF, Indian Administration, 1876-80, The History of, by Lady Betty Balfour : 1899.

MACARTNEY, EARL OF, Account of the Public Life of, by J. Barrow : 1807.
MACAULAY, LORD, Essays on Lord Clive (1840) and Warren Hastings (1841).
——————— **Life and Letters of,** by G. O. Trevelyan, M.P. : 1876.
MACGREGOR, MAJ.-GEN. SIR C. M., Life and Opinions of, by Lady Macgregor : 1888.
——————— **Military Report on the Country of Bhutan :** 1873.
——————— **Narrative of a Journey through the Province of Khorasan and of the N.W. Frontier of Afghanistan in 1875 :** 1879.
——————— **Wanderings in Beluchistan :** 1882.
MACINTYRE, MAJ.-GEN. D., Hindu-Koh : 1891.
MACKENZIE, SIR A., K.C.S.I., History of the Relations of the Government with the Hill Tribes of the N. E. Frontier of Bengal : 1884.
——————— **Memorandum on the N. E. Frontier of Bengal :** 1869.
MACKENZIE, COLIN, Surveyor-General of India, The Mackenzie Collection, A descriptive Catalogue of, collected by : 1828 : 1882.
MACKENZIE, LIEUT.-GEN. COLIN, Storms and Sunshine of a Soldier's Life, 1825-81 : 1884.
MACKENZIE, MRS. COLIN, Six Years in India, A new edition of The Mission, the Camp, and the Zenana : 1857.
MACKINTOSH, RIGHT HON. SIR J., by R. J. Mackintosh : 1835.
MACNAGHTEN, CHESTER, Common Thoughts on Serious Subjects : 1896.
MACPHERSON, S. C., Memorials of Service in India, by W. Macpherson : 1865.
MADRAS ARMY, History of, from 1746 to 1826, by Lieut.-Col. W. J. Wilson : 1882-9.
——————— **ARTILLERY, History of the Services of the, with a Sketch of the Rise of the Power of the E. I. Co. in S. India,** by Maj. P. J. Begbie : 1852.
MADRAS, FORT.ST. GEORGE, by Mrs. F. Penny : 1900.
——————— **The Church in,** by Rev. F. Penny : 1904.
MAINE, SIR H. J. S., K.C.S.I., by Sir M. E. Grant Duff, G.C.S.I. : 1893.
——————— **European Views of India :** 1875.

MALABARI, BAHRAMJI M., by Dayaram Gidumal: 1891.
———— Gujarat and the Gujaratis : 1884.
———— India . . . being a Sketch of the Life of, by R. P. Karkaria : 1896.
MALABAR, NAYARS OF, by F. Fawcett : 1901.
MALAKAND FIELD FORCE, The Story of the, by W. L. Spencer Churchill : 1898.
———— Operations of the, and Buner Field Force, 1897-8 ; a Frontier Campaign, by Viscount Fincastle, V.C., and P. C. Eliott-Lockhart : 1898.
MALAN, S. C., D.D., by Rev. A. N. Malan : 1897.
MALCOLM, MAJ.-GEN. SIR J., by Sir J. W. Kaye, K.C.S.I. : 1856.
———— The Government of India : 1833.
———— Instructions by, to Officers acting under his Orders, 1821 : 1824.
———— Memoir of Central India : 1824.
———— Political History of India, 1784-1823 : 1826.
MALDIVE ISLANDS, THE, by H. C. P. Bell : 1882.
MALLESON, COL. G. B., C.S.I., Essays and Lectures on Indian Historical Subjects : 1876.
———— Founders of the Indian Empire.
———— Historical Sketch of the Native States of India, An : 1875.
———— Recreations of an Indian Official : 1872.
———— The Russo-Afghan Question, and the Invasion of India : 1885.
———— Seringapatam, Past and Present : 1876.
MALLET, SIR LOUIS, by Bernard Mallet : 1905.
MANDLIK, VISHVANATH NARAYAN, C.S.I., by N. V. Mandlik : 1896.
MANGALORE, Account of the Gallant Defence made at, by a British Officer : 1786.
MANIPUR, compiled from the columns of the *Pioneer* : 1891.
MANNING, T., Narrative of the Journey of, to Lhasa, edited by Sir C. R. Markham : 1879.
MARKEAM, SIR C. R., A Memoir on the Indian Surveys : 1871 : 1878.
MARSDEN, W., A Brief Memoir of the Life of . . ., written by himself : 1838.
———— Numismata Orientalia Illustrata : 1869.
MARSHALL, COL. W. E., A Phrenologist amongst the Todas, or the study of a primitive tribe in South India : 1873.
MARTIN, MAJ.-GEN. C., by S. C. Hill : 1901.
MARTIN, SIR J. RANALD, by Sir J. Fayrer, K.C.S.I. : 1897.
MARTIN, R. MONTGOMERY, History, Topography and Sketches of E. India : 1838.
———— History of the Possessions of the Hon. E. I. Co. : 1837.
———— The Indian Empire : 1858-61.
MARTINEAU, H., Eastern Life, Present and Past : 1848.
———— History of British Rule in India : 1857.
MARTYN, REV. H., Journals and Letters of, edited by Bishop S. Wilberforce : 1839.
———— Saint and Soldier, 1781-1812, by Dr. G. Smith, C.I.E. : 1892.
MASSON, C., Narrative of Various Journeys in Beluchistan, Afghanistan, and the Panjab, 1826-38 : 1842.
MAURICE, REV. T., History of Hindustan : 1795-8 : 1820.
MAYO, EARL OF, by Sir W. W. Hunter, K.C.S.I. : 1875 : 1891.
McCULLOCH, W., Account of the Valley of Manipur and the Hill Tribes : 1859.
MEADE, GENERAL SIR RICHARD, and the Feudatory States of Central and Southern India, by T. H. Thornton : 1898.
MEDLEY, MAJ.-GEN. J. G., A Year's Campaigning in India, 1857-8 : 1858.
MELVILL, SIR MAXWELL, K.C.I.E., C.S.I., by Phirozshah Dhanjibhai : 1887.
MEMOIRS OF THE WAR IN ASIA, 1780-4, by W. Thomson, LL.D. : 1788.
MEMPES, MORTIMER, The Darbar : 1903.
METCALFE, LORD, by Sir J. W. Kaye, K.C.S.I. : 1858.
MEURIN, MOST REV. DR. LEO, S.J., Select Writings, with a biographical sketch by P. A. Colaco : 1891.
MIDDLETON, THE RIGHT REV. T. F., Bishop of Calcutta, by the Rev. C. W. Le Bas : 1831.
MILL, JAMES, by A. Bain : 1882.

MILL, JOHN STUART, Autobiography : 1873.
———————— Memorandum of the Improvements in the Administration of India during the last thirty years, and the petition of the E. I. Co. to Parliament, [The petition drawn up by Mr. J. S. Mill] : 1858.
MILLS, A., India in 1858 : 1858.
MILMAN, RIGHT REV. ROBERT, D.D., Bishop of Calcutta, by his Sister, F. M. Milman : 1879.
MINTO, EARL OF, Lord Minto in India, by his Great-niece, the Countess of Minto : 1880.
MISSIONS, SHORT HISTORY OF CHRISTIAN, by Dr. George Smith, C.I.E. : 1904.
———————— The Conversion of India, by Dr. George Smith, C.I.E. : 1893.
MITCHELL, REV. J. MURRAY, LL.D., in Western India. Recollections of my Early Missionary Life : 1899.
MITFORD, MAJ.-GEN. R. C. W. R., To Kabul with the Cavalry Brigade : 1881.
MITRA, RAJA DIGAMBAR, C.S.I., by Bholanath Chandra : 1893.
MITRA, RAJA RAJENDRA LAL, C.I.E., Antiquities of Orissa, The : 1875 : 1880.
———————— Buddha Gaya, the hermitage of Sakya Muni : 1878.
MOHAN LAL, MUNSHI, Journal of a Tour through the Panjab, Afghanistan, etc., with Lieut. Burnes : 1834.
———————— Travels in the Panjab, Afghanistan, Turkistan, etc. : 1846.
MOHL, JULES, Vingt-Sept Ans d'Histoire des Etudes Orientales, 1840-62 : Paris, 1879-80.
MONIER-WILLIAMS, SIR M., by H. Morris : 1900.
———————— Indian Wisdom : 1876.
———————— Modern India and the Indians : 1878.
———————— Religious Thought and Life in India : 1883.
MOOKERJEE, HON. JUSTICE ONOCOOL CHUNDER, by Mohendra Nath Mukhopadhyaya : 1873 : 1889.
MOOR, LIEUT. E., Narrative of the Operations of Capt. Little's Detachment . . ., against the Nawab Tippoo Sultan : 1794.
MOORCROFT, W., AND G. TREBECK, Travels in the Himalayan Provinces of Hindustan and the Panjab . . . 1819-25 ; edited by H. H. Wilson : 1841.
MORISON, THEODORE, Imperial Rule in India : 1899.
MORRIS, H., Anglo-Indian Worthies : 1890.
———————— The Governor-Generals of India : 1894 : 1896.
MOUNTAIN, COL. A. S. H., Memoirs, etc., edited by Mrs. Mountain : 1857.
MUIR, SIR W., K.C.S.I., The Muhammadan Controversy : 1897.
MUKERJL, DR. SAMBHU CHANDRA, by F. H. B. Skrine : 1895.
MÜLLER, RIGHT HON. F. MAX, Life and Letters of, edited by his wife : 1902.
———————— Autobiography : 1901.
———————— Biographical Essays : 1884.
———————— History of Ancient Sanskrit Literature, A : 1859.
———————— India, what it can teach us : 1892.
———————— Indian Philosophy : 1899.
———————— Sacred Books of the East, The, edited by : 1879.
MULTAN, Siege of, by Maj. Siddons.
MUNRO, CAPT. I., A Narrative of the Military Operations on the Coromandel Coast . . . 1780-4, . . all the battles fought under Sir Eyre Coote . . . : 1789.
MUNRO, MAJ.-GEN. SIR T., BART., K.C.B., by Sir A. J. Arbuthnot, K.C.S.I. 1881.
———————— by J. Bradshaw : 1894.
———————— by Rev. G. R. Gleig : 1830.
MURDOCH, REV. JOHN, India : Past and Present : 1903.
———————— Twelve Years of Indian Progress, extracted from the Indian National Congress : 1898.
MURRAY, HUGH, History of British India : 1850.
MUTINIES IN RAJPUTANA, THE, by I. T. Prichard : 1860.

488 — BIBLIOGRAPHY

MUTINY, INDIAN, Daily Life during the, Personal Experiences of 1857 : by J. W. Sherer : 1898.
————— **With H.M. 9th Lancers during the,** by Brevet-Major O. H. L. G. Anson : 1896.
MUTINY MEMOIRS, by Col. A. R. D. Mackenzie : 1892.
MUTINY, MEMORIES OF THE, by Col. F. C. Maude, V.C., and J. W. Sherer. C.S.I. : 1894.
MYSORE AND COORG, by B. Lewis Rice : 1876-8.

NABA KISHEN, MAHARAJA BAHADUR, by Nagendra Nath Ghose : 1887 : 1901.
NANA FARNAVIS, by A. Macdonald : 1851.
NAPIER, GEN. SIR C. J., K.C.B., by Gen. Sir W. F. P. Napier : 1857.
————— by Lieut.-Gen. Sir W. F. Butler : 1890.
————— by W. N. Bruce : 1855.
NAPIER'S Administration of Sind, by Gen. Sir W. F. Napier : 1851.
NEILL, J. M. B., CAPT., Four Years' Service in the East, in Sind, and the Army under Maj.-Gen. Sir W. Nott : 1845.
NEILL, BRIGADIER, A Brief Review of his Military Career : 1859.
NEW INDIA, or India in Transition, by Sir H. Cotton, K.C.S.I. : 1885.
NICHOLSON, JOHN, by Capt. L. J. Trotter : 1898.
NILGIRI DISTRICT, THE, A Manual of, by H. B. Grigg : 1880.
NIPAL, Account of the Kingdom of, by Buchanan Hamilton : 1819.
————— **History of,** translated from the Parbatiya by Munshi Shew Shunker Singh and Pandit Shri Gunanand, edited by D. Wright : 1877.
————— **Sketches from,** by Dr. H. A. Oldfield : 1880.
NIZAM ALI KHAN, Soobah of the Dekkan, A History of, by W. Hollingberry : 1805.
NOBLE, REV. R. T., by Rev. J. Noble : 1868.
NORMAN, GEN. SIR H. W., A Narrative of the Campaign of the Delhi Army : 1858.
NORTH, MAJOR, C. J., Journal of an English Officer in India : 1858.
NORTH, MISS M., Autobiography, edited by Mrs. Symonds : 1892.
NORTON, J. B., The Rebellion in India : how to prevent another : 1857.
————— **Topics for Indian Statesmen :** 1858.
NOTT, MAJ.-GEN. SIR W., G.C.B., by J. H. Stocqueler : 1854.
NOTT'S BRIGADE, in Afghanistan, 1838-42, being the Private Diary of an Officer : 1880.
NUNCOMAR, The Story of, by Sir J. FitzJames Stephen, K.C.S.I. : 1885.
————— **The Trial of (Maharaja Nanda Kumar),** by H. Beveridge : 1886.

OAKLEY, SIR C., Some account of the Services of, in India, by H. Oakley : 1829.
OLIPHANT, L., A Journey to Katmandu, the Capital of Nipal, by : 1852.
OLIVER, E. E., Across the Border, or Pathan and British : 1890.
OMAN, J. C., Indian Life, Religious and Social : 1889.
————— **The Mystics, Ascetics and Saints of India :** 1903.
ORIENTAL ANNUAL, THE, or Scenes in India ; drawings by W. Daniell, 1834-6 : 1837-8.
ORISSA, etc., by Col. W. F. B. Laurie : 1850.
ORLICH, CAPT. LEOPOLD VON, Travels in India, including Sind and the Panjab ; translated : 1845.
ORME, R., Historical Fragments of the Mogul Empire, of the Morattoes, and the English Concerns in Indostan, from 1659 : 1782 : 1805.
OUTRAM, LIEUT.-GEN. SIR J., BART., G.C.B., the Bayard of India, by Capt. J. L. Trotter : 1903.
————— **a Biography,** by Maj.-Gen. Sir F. J. Goldsmid, K.C.S.I. : 1880.
————— **Campaign in India, 1857-8:** 1860.
————— **Conquest of Sind, by :** 1846.
————— **Persian Campaign in 1857 :** 1860.
————— **Rough Notes of the Campaign in Sind and Afghanistan, in 1838-9 :** 1840.

OUVRY, COL. H. A., Cavalry Experiences and Leaves from my Journal : 1892.

PAGET, LIEUT.-COL. W. H., and Lieut. A. H. MASON, R.E., A Record of the Expeditions . . . against the N. W. Frontier Tribes, 1874 : 1884.
PAL, KRISTO DAS, C.I.E., by Nagendra Nath Ghose : 1887.
———— by Ram Gopal Sanyal : 1886.
PALMER, E. H., by W. Besant : 1883.
PAMIRS, THE, by the Earl of Dunmore : 1894.
PANDURANG HARI, or Memoirs of a Hindu, by W. B. Hockley : 1826 : 1883.
PANJAB, CRISIS IN THE, from the 10th of May until the Fall of Delhi : 1858.
———— HISTORY OF THE, and of the Rise, Progress, etc., of the Sikhs : 1846.
———— HISTORY OF THE, from the remotest Antiquity, by Saiyid Muhammad Latif : 1891.
PARKES, FANNY, Wanderings of a Pilgrim in Search of the Picturesque, during Twenty-four years in the East, with Revelations of Life in the Zenana, by, 1850.
PARLBY, LIEUT.-COL. S., The British Indian Military Repository : 1822–7.
PARSIS, THE, their History, Manners, etc., by Dosabhai Framji (Karaka) : 1858.
PARSONS, A., Travels in Asia and Africa : 1808.
PATHAN REVOLT, THE, in N. W. India : by H. W. Mills : 1897.
PIGOT, GEORGE, LORD, Narrative of the late Revolution in the Government of Madras, 1776 : 1777.
PINCOTT, F., Analytical Index to Sir J. W. Kaye's History of the Sepoy War, and Col. G. B. Malleson's History of the Indian Mutiny : 1880.
POLEHAMPTON, REV. H. S., by Rev. E. and Rev. T. S. Polehampton : 1859.
POLLOCK, FIELD-MARSHAL SIR G., BART., by C. R. Low : 1873.
POLLOK, LIEUT.-COL. F. T., Fifty Years' Reminiscences of India : 1896.
POPE, REV. G. U., Text-Book of Indian History : 1871 : 1880.
POTTINGER, LIEUT. H., Travels in Beluchistan and Sind, by : 1816.
PRICE, MAJOR D., Chronological Retrospect, or Memoirs of Principal Events of Muhammadan History : 1811–21.
———— Memoirs of the Early Life and Services of a Field Officer of the Indian Army : 1839.
PRICHARD, I. T., The Administration of India, 1859–68 : 1869.
PRINSEP, JAMES, Essays on Indian Antiquities, Historic, Numismatic, and Palæographic : 1858.
PRINSEP, VAL C., Imperial India ; an Artist's Journals : 1878.

RAFFLES, SIR T. STAMFORD, by D. C. Boulger : 1897.
———— by H. E. Egerton : 1900.
———— by Lady Raffles : 1830.
RAIKES, C., The Englishman in India : 1867.
RAJPUTANA, Chiefs and Leading Families in : 1903.
RAMAKRISNA, Life in an Indian Village : 1891.
RAM RAJ, Essay on the Architecture of the Hindus : 1834.
RANADE, M. G., JUSTICE, by G. A. Mankar : 1902.
———— Rise of the Mahratta Power : 1900.
RAWLINSON, MAJ.-GEN. SIR H. C., BART., by Canon G. Rawlinson : 1898.
———— England and Russia in the East : 1875.
RAYMOND, i.e. HAJI MUSTAPHA, Translation of the Sair (or Siyar) ul-Mutakhirin: 1789.
RAYNAL, G. T. F. ABBÉ, A Philosophical and Political History of the Settlements and Trade of Europeans in the E. and W. Indies ; translated by J. Justamond : 1776.
READYMONEY, SIR COWASJI JEHANGIR, Kt., C.S.I., by J. Cowasji Jehangir : 1890.

REES, J. D., H.R.H. The Duke of Clarence and Avondale in S. India : 1891.
———————— Narratives of Tours in India made by H. E. Lord Connemara, Governor of Madras, 1886-90 : 1891.
REMINISCENCES of 70 Years' Life, Travel and Adventure : Military and Civil : Scientific and Literary, by a Retired Officer of H.M.'s Civil Service : 1893.
RENNELL, MAJ. J., A Bengal Atlas : 1781.
———————— Memoir of a Map of Hindustan ; or the Mogul Empire : 1788.
REVOLT, NOTES ON THE, in the N. W. P. of India, by C. Raikes : 1858.
RICE, REV. H., Native Life in S. India : 1887.
RICHARDSON, MAJ. D. L., History of the Fall of the Old Fort of Calcutta and the Calamity of the Black-hole : 1856.
ROBERTS, EARL, by C. R. Low : 1883.
———————— as a Soldier in Peace and War, by Capt. W. E. Cairnes : 1901.
ROBERTS, EMMA, Scenes and Characteristics of Hindustan, with Sketches of Anglo-Indian Society : 1835.
ROBERTSON, W., D.D., An Historical Disquisition concerning the Knowledge which the Ancients had of India : 1792.
ROBINSON, PHIL, In my Indian Garden : 1878.
———————— Under the Punkah : 1881.
RODRIGUEZ, E. A., Hindu Castes of the British Empire : 1846.
RONALDSHAY, THE EARL OF, F.R.G.S., Sport and Politics under an Eastern Sky : 1902.
ROST, ERNST REINHOLD, Memoir of : 1898.
ROST, REINHOLD, DR., Der Orientalist, sein Leben und sein Streben, by Prof. Dr. O. Weise : 1897.
ROUTLEDGE, J., English Rule and Native Opinion in India, 1870-4 : 1878.
ROXBURGH, WILLIAM, Brief Memoir of : 1895.
ROY, RAJA RAMMOHAN, by Kisori Chand Mitra : 1866.
———————— by Deena Nath Ganguli : 1884.
———————— The English Works of, by J. E. Ghose : 1901.
———————— The Last Days in England of, by Mary Carpenter : 1866.
———————— by S. D. Collet : 1900.
RUSSELL, SIR W. H., My Diary in India, 1858-9 : 1860.
———————— The Prince of Wales' Tour : a Diary in India : 1877.
RUSSIAN PROJECTS AGAINST INDIA, by H. Sutherland Edwards : 1885.

SAINT-JOHN, H., History of the British Conquests in India : 1852.
SALAR JANG, SIR, G.C.S.I., by Syed Hossain Bilgrami . 1883.
SALE (F.), LADY, A Journal of the Disasters in Afghanistan, 1841-2 : 1843.
SANDEMAN, COL. SIR R. G., by Dr. T. H. Thornton, C.S.I. : 1895.
SANDERSON, G. P., Thirteen Years among the Wild Beasts of India : 1878.
SARASVATI, MAHATMA DAYANANDA : 1898.
———————— by Durga Prasad : 1892.
SARASVATI, PANDITA RAMABAI, The High-caste Hindu Woman : 1901.
SASTRI, SIR A. SASHIAH, by B. V. Kameswara Aiyar : 1902.
SAVILE, REV. B. W., How India was won by England under Clive and Hastings: 1881.
SCHWARTZ, REV. C. F., by H. Pearson : 1834.
———————— Missionary at Travancore, 1750-98 : 1855.
SCOTT, DAVID, Memoir of, by Archibald Watson : 1832.
SCRAFTON, LUKE, Reflections on the Government of Hindustan . . . and an Account of the English Affairs to 1758 : 1763.
SEATON, MAJ.-GEN. SIR T., From Cadet to Colonel : 1866.
SEN, KESHAB CHANDRA, by P. C. Mozumdar : 1891.
SEN, RAM KOMUL, by Piari Chand Mitra : 1880.
SETH, MESROOB J., History of the Armenians in India : 1895.

SEWELL, R., Archæological Survey of Southern India : 1882-4.
———————— Chronological Tables for S. India from the Sixth Century A.D. : 1881.
———————— Forgotten Empire, A, (Vijyanagar) : 1900.
———————— Sketch of the Dynasties of S. India, A : 1883.
SHAW, R. B., Visits to High Tartary, Yarkand, and Kashgar : 1871.
SHERER, T. W., C.S.I., At Home and in India : 1883.
SHERRING, REV. M. A., Hindu Tribes and Castes : 1872-81.
———————— The History of Protestant Missions in India, 1706-1881 : 1875.
———————— The Indian Church during the Great Rebellion : 1859 : 1884.
———————— The Sacred City of the Hindus : an Account of Benares : 1868.
SHERWOOD, (MRS.) M. M., Life of, chiefly autobiographical, edited by Sophia Kelly : 1854.
SHIPP, JOHN, Memoirs of the Extraordinary Career of, late Lieut. in H.M.'s 87th Regt. : 1829.
SHORE, HON. F. J., Notes on Indian Affairs : 1837.
SIKHIM EXPEDITION OF 1888, the 2nd Battalion Derbyshire Regiment in the, by Capt. H. A. Iggulden : 1900.
SIKHS, A HISTORY OF THE, by Capt. J. D. Cunningham : 1849 : 1853.
———————— and the Sikh War, The, by Gen. Sir C. Gough and A. D. Innes : 1897.
———————— THE, by Gen. Sir John J. H. Gordon, K.C.B. ; 1904.
———————— THE HISTORY OF THE, by Dr. W. L. Macgregor : 1847.
SIKH WAR, Narrative of the Second, 1848-9, by E. J. Thackwell : 1851.
SIMPSON, W., India, Ancient and Modern : 1867.
SIMSON, F. B., Letters on Sport in Eastern Bengal : 1886.
SIND, Personal Observations on, etc., by Capt. T. Postans : 1843.
———— THE CONQUEST OF, by Maj.- Gen. Sir W. F. P. Napier : 1845.
SINDIA, MADHAVA RAO, by H. G. Keene, C.I.E. : 1893.
SINGH, DULIP, see Sir John Login.
———— MAHARAJA RANJIT, Political Life of, Origin of the Sikh Power, etc., by H. T. Prinsep : 1897.
———————— by Sir Lepel Griffin, K.C.S.I. :
SKINNER, LIEUT.-COL. J., C.B., Military Memoir of, by J. Baillie Fraser : 1851.
SLEEMAN, MAJ.-GEN. SIR W. H., K.C.B., A Journey through the Kingdom of Oudh, in 1849-50 : 1858.
———————— Rambles and Recollections of an Indian Official : 1844.
SMITH, LIEUT.-GEN. SIR HARRY, BART., G:C.B., of Aliwal, The Autobiography of, by G: C. Moore-Smith : 1901.
SMITH, MAJ. L. F., Sketch of the Rise . . . of the Regular Corps . . . in the service of the Native Princes—with details of the late Mahratta War : 1805.
SMITH, LIEUT.-COL. R. B., by Col. H. M. Vibart, R.E. : 1897.
SMITH, MAJ.-GEN. SIR ROBERT MURDOCH, K.C.M.G., R.E., by W. K. Dickson : 1901.
SMITH, SAMUEL, India and its Problems : 1905.
SPRY, H. H., Modern India : 1837.
STANHOPE, EARL OF, The Rise of Our Indian Empire . . . till . . . 1783 : 1858.
STAVORINUS, REAR-ADML. J. S., Voyages to the E. Indies ; translated from the original Dutch by S. W. Wilcocke : 1798.
STEEVENS, G. W., In India : 1899.
STEPHEN, SIR J. F., BART., K.C.S.I., by Sir Leslie Stephen : 1895.
STEWART, MAJ. C., The History of Bengal . . . until . . . A.D. 1757 : 1813.
STEWART, FIELD-MARSHAL SIR D. M., BART., G.C.B., etc., by G. R. Elsmie : 1903.
ST. GEORGE, FORT, Vicissitudes of, by D. Leighton : 1902.
STOCQUELER, J. H., Progress in India, from 1859-60-1872 : 1873.
STOLICZKA, DR. F., Diary of the late, Yarkand Mission, 1873-4, corrected by A. Hume, C.B. : 1875.
STRACHEY, SIR H., BART., Narrative of the Mutiny of the Officers of the Army in Bengal in 1766 : 1773.

STRACHEY, SIR J., G.C.S.I., and LIEUT.-GEN. SIR R., G.C.S.I., The Finances and Public Works of India, 1869-81 : 1882.
SUFFREIN, Histoire du Bailli de, by Canat : 1852.
————— Essai Historique sur la vie et les campagnes du Bailli de, by Hennequin : 1824.
SULLIVAN, SIR E. R., BART., The Conquerors, Warriors, and Statesmen of India : 1866.
————— The Princes of India : 1875.

TAGORE, DWARKANATH, by K. C. Mitra : 1870.
TAGORE FAMILY, THE, by J. W. Furrell : 1892.
TAGORE, PROSUNNO COOMAR, by Rev. K. M. Banerjea : 1870.
TAYLER, W., Thirty-eight Years in India : 1881-2.
TAYLOR, COL. MEADOWS, The Story of my Life, edited by his daughter : 1878.
TAYLOR, MAJ.-GEN. REYNELL, C.B., C.S.I., by E. Gambier Parry : 1898.
TEIGNMOUTH, LORD, Memoirs, etc. : 1843.
TEMPLE, SIR R., BART., A Bird's Eye View of Picturesque India : 1898.
————— Cosmopolitan Essays : 1886.
————— India in 1880 : 1880.
————— Oriental Experiences : 1883.
————— The Story of my Life : 1896.
————— and Col. R. C., Journals kept in Hyderabad, Kashmir, Sikhim, and Nipal : 1887.
THACKERAY, COL. SIR E. T., K.C.B., V.C., Biographical Notices of Officers of the Royal (Bengal) Engineers : 1900. ·
————— Two Indian Campaigns in 1857-8 : 1896.
THOMAS, GEORGE, Military Memoirs of, by Col. W. Francklin : 1803.
THOMAS, REV. JOHN, First Baptist Missionary to Bengal, by Rev. C. B. Lewis : 1873.
————— The Life of a Great Missionary, 1836-70, by Rev. A. H. Grey Edwards, M.A. : 1904.
THOMASON, JAMES, by Sir R. Temple, Bart. : 1893.
————— by Sir W. Muir : 1897.
THOMSON, DR. THOMAS, Journey in Western Himalaya and Tibet : 1852.
THORBURN, S. S., Asiatic Neighbours : 1894.
————— Bannu, or our Afghan Frontier : 1876.
————— The Panjab in Peace and War : 1904.
THORN, MAJ. W., Memoir of the Conquest of Java : 1815.
————— Memoir of the War in India, conducted by Lake and Wellesley, 1803-6 : 1818.
THORNHILL, MARK, The Personal Adventures and Experiences of a Magistrate, during the Indian Mutiny : 1884.
TIPPOO SULTAN, A Sketch of the War with, 1789-92, by Lieut. Roderick Mackenzie : 1793-4.
————— History of the Reign of, by Col. W. Miles : 1864.
————— Official Documents relative to the Negotiations carried on by, with the French Nation, etc. : 1799.
————— A Tale of the Mysore War, by Col. Meadows Taylor : 1890.
TIRAH, CAMPAIGN IN, 1897-8, The, by Col. H. D. Hutchinson : 1898.
————— by H. W. Mills : 1898.
————— LOCKHART'S ADVANCE THROUGH, by Capt. L. J. Shadwell : 1899.
TOD, LIEUT.-COL. JAMES, Annals and Antiquities of Rajasthan : 1829-32.
————— Travels in Western India : 1839.
TOM RAW, THE GRIFFIN, A Burlesque Poem, by a Civilian : 1828.
TORRENS, H. W., Selections from the Writings of, with a Biographical Memoir, by J. Hume : 1854.

TOWNSEND, MEREDITH, Annals of Indian Administration, edited by : 1856.
————— **Asia and Europe, Studies . . . of the relations between Asia and Europe :** 1903.
TRAVANCORE, CHURCH HISTORY OF, by C. M. Agur : 1903.
TREVELYAN, RIGHT HON. SIR G. O., BART., The Competition-wallah : 1866.
TROTTER, CAPT. L. J., History of India under Queen Victoria, 1836-80 : 1886.
TUCKER, H. ST. G., by Sir J. W. Kaye, K.C.S.I. : 1854.
TUPPER, SIR C. L., Our Indian Protectorate : 1893.
TURNER, CAPT. SAMUEL, Account of an Embassy to the Court of Tesho Lama in Tibet : 1800.
TWINING, THOMAS, Travels in India 100 Years ago of, by Rev. W. Twining : 1893.
TYACKE, LIEUT.-COL. R. H., The Sportsman's Manual in quest of Game in Kulu, Lahoul, Ladak . . . Spiti, Chamba, and Kashmir : 1893.
TYACKE, MRS. R. H., How I shot my Bears : 1893.

VADIVELU, A., Some Mysore Worthies : 1900.
————— **The Aristocracy of Southern India :** 1903.
VALENTIA, VISCOUNT, Voyages and Travels to India, etc., 1802-6 : 1809.
VAMBERY, ARMINIUS, The Coming Struggle for India : 1885.
VANSITTART, H., Narrative of the Transactions in Bengal from 1760-4, during the Government of : 1766.
VAUGHAN, GEN. SIR J. LUTHER, My Service in the Indian Army and after : 1904.
VERELST, H., View of the Rise, Progress and Present State of the English Government in Bengal : 1772.
VIBART, COL. H. M., Military History of the Madras Engineers : 1881–3.
VICTORIA CROSS, THE, Official Chronicle from the Institution of the Order, 1856-80, by R. W. O'Byrne : 1880.
VIDYASAGAR, ISVAR CHANDRA, by Subal Chandra Mitra : 1902.
VIGNE, G. T., Personal Narrative of a Visit to Ghazni, Kabul, and Afghanistan : 1843.
————— **Travels in Kashmir, etc. :** 1842.
VOLUNTEERING IN INDIA, by J. T. Nash : 1893.

WADDELL, LIEUT.-COL. A., C.B., Among the Himalayas : 1899.
WAKEFIELD, DR. W., The Happy Valley : Sketches of Kashmir and the Kashmiris : 1879.
————— **Our Life and Travels in India :** 1878.
WALLACE, R. G., Memoirs of India : 1824.
WARBURTON, COL. SIR R., Eighteen Years in the Khyber : 1900.
WARD, REV. W., History, Literature, and Religion of the Hindus : 1817–20–1.
————— **Memoirs of,** by S. Stennett : 1825.
WARING, E. SCOTT, History of the Mahrattas : 1810.
WATSON, DR. JOHN FORBES, Index to the Native and Scientific Names of Indian and other Eastern Economic Plants and Products : 1868.
————— **The Textile Manufactures and the Costumes of the People of India :** 1866.
WAZIR ALI KHAN, or the Massacre at Benares, by J. F. Davis : 1844.
WEBER, DR. A., History of Indian Literature ; translated : 1882.
WELLESLEY, THE MARQUESS, by the Rev. W. H. Hutton : 1893.
————— by Col. G. B. Malleson · 1889 : 1895.
————— by W. M. Torrens : 1880.
————— **Despatches of,** by Montgomery Martin : 1836-40.
————— **History of the Mahratta War :** 1804.
————— **Selections from the Despatches of,** by S. J. Owen : 1877.
————— **Memoirs and Correspondence of,** by R. R. Pearce : 1846.
————— **Notes Relative to the late Transactions in the Mahratta Empire,** by· Dec. 15, 1803 1804.

494 *BIBLIOGRAPHY*

WELLINGTON, FIELD-MARSHAL THE DUKE OF, Maxims and Opinions, with biographical Memoir by G. H. Fraser : 1845.
————— Military History of the, in India : 1852.
————— Selections from the Despatches of, relating to India, by S. J. Owen : 1881.
WEST, SIR ALGERNON, Sir C. Wood's Administration of Indian Affairs, 1859-66 : 1867.
WHEELER, J. TALBOYS, Madras in the Olden Time : 1861.
————— Tales from Indian History : 1881 : 1890.
WHEELER, STEPHEN, History of the Delhi Coronation Darbar, held on the 1st January, 1903 : 1904.
WHITE, MAJ. ADAM, Considerations on the State of British India . . . and Indian Army : 1822.
WHITE, COL. DEWÉ, Complete History of the Indian Mutiny.
WHITE, SIR GEORGE, V.C., by T. Coates, F.G. : 1900.
WHITTINGHAM, LIEUT.-GEN. SIR S. F., by Maj.-Gen. F. Whittingham : 1868.
WILKINS, W. J., Daily Life and Work in India : 1888.
————— Modern Hinduism : 1887.
WILLIAMS, C. R., The Defence of Kahun : 1886.
WILLIAMS, CAPT. JOHN, The Rise and Progress of the Bengal Native Infantry, 1757-96 : 1817.
WILLIAMSON, CAPT. THOMAS, Oriental Field Sports : 1807 : 1891.
WILSON, ANDREW, The Abode of Snow : 1875.
WILSON, RIGHT REV. DANIEL, by Rev. J. Bateman : 1860.
WILSON, H. H., Complete Works of : 1862-71.
————— Narrative of the Burmese War in 1824-6 : 1852.
————— Select Specimens of the Theatre of the Hindus : 1871.
WILSON, THE REV. DR. JOHN, by Dr. G. Smith, C.I.E. : 1878.
WINDHAM, REDAN, by Major Hugh Pearse.
WINDT, H. DE, A Ride to India across Persia and Beluchistan : 1891.
WOLFF, REV. JOSEPH, Travels and Adventures of the : 1860-1.
WOLSELEY, F. M., VISCOUNT, by C. R. Low : 1878.
————— The Story of a Soldier's Life : 1903.
WOOD, CAPT. JOHN, A Journey to the Source of the River Oxus : by Col. H. Yule : 1872.
WYLLIE, J. W. S., Essays on the External Policy of India, edited by Sir W. W. Hunter, K.C.S.I. : 1875.

YATE, A. C., The Afghan Boundary Commission : 1887.
YATE, LIEUT.-COL. C. E., Northern Afghanistan : 1888.
YATES, DR. W., of Calcutta, by Dr. J. Hoby : 1847.
YOUNGHUSBAND, CAPT. AND BREVET-MAJOR G. J., Indian Frontier Warfare, 1898.
————— Eighteen Hundred Miles on a Burmese Tat, through Burma, Siam, and the Eastern Shan States : 1888.
YULE, COL. SIR H., Narrative of Major Phayre's Mission to the Court of Ava : 1858.